CONNECTING WITH AUSTRALIAN TORT LAW

THIRD EDITION

Connecting with Australian Tort Law is a practical introduction to the principles and application of tort law. It guides students to expand their knowledge of tort law, improve their problem-solving and communication skills, and advance their professional development.

Now in its third edition, *Connecting with Australian Tort Law* maintains its clear two-part structure. Part 1 introduces students to the fundamentals of tort law, and provides them with the practical tools needed to succeed academically. Students will learn how to structure a legal argument and answer complex questions before arriving at Part 2. This part covers specific areas of tort law, including trespass to the person, trespass to land and personal property, nuisance, defamation and the complex tort of negligence. It examines the principles of tort law and uses case examples and legislation to demonstrate their application. Pedagogically rich, *Connecting with Australian Tort Law* includes problem-solving questions, tips and legislation alerts to keep students engaged and actively learning.

Connecting with Australian Tort Law is an essential resource for students new to studying tort law.

Marco Rizzi is Associate Professor and Co-Director of the Centre for Health Law and Policy at the UWA Law School.

Kate Offer is a Senior Lecturer at Curtin Law School and an Adjunct Associate Professor at the UWA Law School.

Jamie Walvisch is a Senior Lecturer at the UWA Law School.

Julia Davis is an Adjunct Associate Professor at Adelaide University and is now retired after many years teaching torts at the University of Tasmania and the University of South Australia.

Cambridge University Press acknowledges the Australian Aboriginal and Torres Strait Islander peoples of this nation. We acknowledge the traditional custodians of the lands on which our company is located and where we conduct our business. We pay our respects to ancestors and Elders, past and present. Cambridge University Press is committed to honouring Australian Aboriginal and Torres Strait Islander peoples' unique cultural and spiritual relationships to the land, waters and seas and their rich contribution to society.

CONNECTING WITH AUSTRALIAN TORT LAW

THIRD EDITION

Marco Rizzi

Kate Offer

Jamie Walvisch

Julia Davis

CAMBRIDGE UNIVERSITY PRESS

CAMBRIDGE
UNIVERSITY PRESS

Shaftesbury Road, Cambridge CB2 8EA, United Kingdom

One Liberty Plaza, 20th Floor, New York, NY 10006, USA

477 Williamstown Road, Port Melbourne, VIC 3207, Australia

314–321, 3rd Floor, Plot 3, Splendor Forum, Jasola District Centre,
New Delhi – 110025, India

Cambridge University Press is part of Cambridge University Press & Assessment,
a department of the University of Cambridge.

We share the University's mission to contribute to society through the pursuit of
education, learning and research at the highest international levels of excellence.

www.cambridge.org
Information on this title: www.cambridge.org/highereducation/isbn/9781009593267

First published 2012
Second edition 2020
Third edition 2026

Cover designed by Simon Rattray

Typeset by Lumina Datamatics Ltd

A catalogue record for this publication is available from the British Library

A catalogue record for this book is available from the National Library of Australia

ISBN 978-1-009-59326-7 Paperback

Additional resources for this publication at www.cambridge.org/highereducation/
isbn/9781009593267/resources.

*Please be aware that this publication may contain several variations of Aboriginal and Torres
Strait Islander terms and spellings; no disrespect is intended. Please note that the terms
'Indigenous Australians', 'Aboriginal and Torres Strait Islander peoples' and 'First Nations
peoples' may be used interchangeably in this publication.*

CONTENTS

FIGURES AND TABLES

FIGURES

TABLES

ABOUT THE AUTHORS

Marco Rizzi is Associate Professor and Co-Director of the Centre for Health Law and Policy at the UWA Law School, where he teaches in the areas of torts, health law and policy, and risk regulation. His scholarly work critically examines the interface between regulatory frameworks and private law remedies, with a particular focus on the regulation of risks and their implications for liability regimes concerning therapeutic goods, from medical devices to vaccines. He is a chief investigator on multiple national interdisciplinary projects dedicated to advancing understanding in complex areas of health and technology law, ethics, and governance.

Kate Offer is a Senior Lecturer at Curtin Law School and an Adjunct Associate Professor at the UWA Law School. She primarily teaches in the areas of torts and evidence. While at UWA, she created the innovative undergraduate unit 'Law for Everyday Lives', designed to equip students with practical legal knowledge for everyday decision-making. Kate is the co-author of Field and Offer, *Western Australian Evidence Law*, and her research focuses on legal education. From 2013 to 2023, Kate served as Chair of the Disciplinary Committee of the Teachers Registration Board of Western Australia, and was a board member from 2018 to 2023, contributing her legal expertise to the regulation and governance of the teaching profession. Kate's teaching has been recognised at the faculty, university and national levels, including receiving an Australian Award for University Teaching Citation for Outstanding Contributions to Student Learning.

Jamie Walvisch is a Senior Lecturer and a member of the Centre for Health Law and Policy at the UWA Law School, where he teaches torts, evidence and criminal law. Before joining UWA, he held academic appointments at Monash and Melbourne Law Schools, and previously worked as a research and policy officer at the Victorian Law Reform Commission, the Australian Institute of Criminology, and the Judicial College of Victoria. Jamie is a leading scholar on the intersection of mental health and criminal law. He is the co-editor of two major international collections: *The Future of Mental Health, Disability and Criminal Law* and *Feminist Legislation: Australia*. He has led numerous law reform projects and played a key role in developing the *Victorian Criminal Charge Book*, a widely used judicial resource. His teaching has been recognised with multiple awards, including an Australian Award for University Teaching Citation for Outstanding Contributions to Student Learning.

Julia Davis is an Adjunct Associate Professor at Adelaide University and is now retired after many years teaching torts at the University of Tasmania and the University of South Australia.

PREFACE

This book aims to help you to connect with the law of torts as it has evolved in Australia, and to inspire you to be successful and confident in your study. It will give you the advice and assistance that you need to improve your study skills so that you can do justice to yourself at every assessment opportunity and get the results that you deserve.

Part 1 is divided into four chapters, outlined as follows:

- The first two chapters provide you with an overview of the law of torts and its challenges. Once you know what the challenges are, you will be better prepared to master them.
- The third chapter tells you how to structure the legal arguments that you will be using in many of your assessment tasks and explains how to answer a problem question.
- The fourth chapter tells you how to study the law of torts so that you can start the term with a clear set of goals and arrive at the end of the term not only having completed your assessment tasks successfully, but also having put together a well-prepared summary of the law that will help you to succeed in your final exam.

In Part 2 we put the insights gained from Part 1 to work – its features are as follows:

- Part 2 contains chapters on each of the most important torts and builds from some of the oldest torts of trespass up to the most important and most complicated modern tort, the tort of negligence.
- These chapters identify the elements of each tort, provide a succinct summary of the law, and explain the underlying principles that justify the tort's existence and structure.
- As the law becomes more complicated, the book's coverage becomes more detailed. So, in the early chapters on the intentional torts, where the law is more straightforward, the coverage is relatively succinct. As the book moves towards the more complicated torts like nuisance, defamation and negligence, the coverage becomes more comprehensive. These chapters contain more examples from the cases to explain how the law has developed and to help you to understand how the law is applied.
- This book has been designed to mirror your learning needs, reflect your increasing understanding of the law, and encourage and support the development of your legal skills. So, as your skills develop and you become more confident, the learning features change, and you will notice that you will be asked to engage more deeply with the law and encouraged to take on more responsibility for your own study.
- Where appropriate, chapters contain 'Active Reading' tasks to help you focus on the law as you read the chapter and to reinforce your understanding of the way that the law is derived from the cases. You will also be prompted by a 'Legislation Alert' to note down any statutes in your jurisdiction that modify the common law.

- Handy 'look-up charts' that are designed to assist you in diagnosing problem questions are provided in Chapter 7. These exam aids contain all of the basic elements of each tort and the ingredients of each defence.
- Many chapters contain problem-solving tips and exercises that will assist you to build up your basic skills in:
  - recognising and clearly identifying both the defendant's conduct that gives rise to a complaint and its effects on the plaintiff;
  - working out the appropriate remedies;
  - identifying the issues;
  - stating the appropriate rules and principles; and
  - constructing arguments and counterarguments that apply the law to the facts to resolve the issues.

The philosophy of this book

The philosophy of *Connecting with Australian Tort Law* is that everyone learns best by doing – but it also recognises that when we start out to study something new, we often need a guide that can show us by example what to do and how to go about doing it. So, this book aims to inspire students to learn better (and faster) by showing them how to approach their learning and how to organise their study. It emphasises skills development and active learning – and helps modern law students to make the most of the new learning and teaching environment in which they must study. It also aims to support the development of the graduate attributes and qualities that every torts teacher is now expected to address in their courses. So, it guides and supports the development of each student's:

- knowledge of the law of torts;
- problem-solving skills;
- communication skills; and
- professional development.

This book is not a traditional practitioner's treatise on the law of torts; rather, it has been written to help students to understand and connect with their torts courses. It recognises not only that the learning environment in Australian universities is ever-changing, but also that the legal profession is continuously evolving. Therefore, it provides students with a guide to the content of the law of torts and an essential guide to success that explains how to study the law of torts. Crucially, these skills remain essential in the age of generative AI. To safely rely on ChatGPT or other bots, you need to be able to do the hard work yourself, and this book aims to help you with that task! Whether students are learning by the case method or by the lecture/tutorial method of instruction, this book will help them to understand the law, to organise their study and to prepare for their exams and assessment exercises. *Connecting with Australian Tort Law* is premised on the belief that while each law course in each state and territory is different, each student's development requires them to understand each of the torts, organise that knowledge and practise putting it to work so that they can connect with – and enjoy studying – the law of torts.

ACKNOWLEDGEMENTS

The authors would like to thank our colleagues at the UWA Law School, whose intellectual generosity and collegiality have been a continual source of encouragement. Special thanks also to the editorial and production teams at Cambridge University Press who supported this project from manuscript to publication with skill and care. We also thank our families and loved ones for their ongoing support and encouragement.

A special and most heartfelt thank you goes, of course, to Julia Davis. We're immensely grateful for Julia's vision in writing the first edition of *Connecting with Tort Law* and for bringing us on board to keep this wonderful book going. Her foundational work has been invaluable, and we extend our deepest appreciation as she steps down as an active author.

Julia Davis would like to extend her grateful thanks to Marco Rizzi, Kate Offer, Jamie Walvisch, and all the team at Cambridge University Press, not only for their enthusiasm and expertise in updating the book, but also for their commitment to keeping it available to Australian torts students and teachers. It is now almost twenty years since *Connecting with Australian Tort Law* had its beginnings in a discussion at a Law Teachers Conference and I am confident that the book and its approach to teaching and learning will flourish in the hands of its new custodians.

Cambridge University Press and the authors would like to acknowledge the feedback provided by peer reviewers of the draft manuscript, including Wendy Bonython, Gerard Everett and Prue Vines. Their feedback and comments were invaluable to the development of this textbook.

The authors and Cambridge University Press would like to thank the following for permission to reproduce material in this book.

Extracts from Privacy and Other Legislation Amendment Bill 2024 Explanatory Memorandum, Parliament of Australia website. Reproduced under CC BY-NC-ND 4.0 Deed. Attribution-NonCommercial-NoDerivs 4.0 International licence: <https://creativecommons.org/licenses/by-nc-nd/4.0/>.

Extracts from New South Wales legislation: sourced from the New South Wales Legislation website at June 2025. For the latest information on New South Wales Government legislation please go to <www.legislation.nsw.gov.au>. Reproduced under a CC BY 4.0 licence: <https://creativecommons.org/licenses/by/4.0/>.

Extracts from South Australian legislation: sourced from the South Australian Legislation website at June 2025. For the latest information on South Australian Government legislation, please go to <www.legislation.sa.gov.au/>. Reproduced under Creative Commons Attribution 4.0 International Licence (CC BY 4.0): <https://creativecommons.org/licenses/by/4.0/>.

Extracts from Western Australian legislation: sourced from the Western Australian legislation website at June 2025. For the latest information on Western Australian legislation, visit <www.legislation.wa.gov.au>. Reproduced under a CC BY 4.0 licence: <https://creativecommons.org/licenses/by/4.0/>.

Every effort has been made to trace and acknowledge copyright. The publisher apologises for any accidental infringement and welcomes information that would redress this situation.

1

THE NATURE OF TORT LAW, AND HOW TO STUDY IT

Developing your strategies to be successful

Your success in any torts course will usually depend on three factors, each of which is introduced in Part 1 of the book. These crucial factors are:

- your knowledge and understanding of the distinctive nature and content of the law of torts, which are introduced in Chapters 1 and 2;
- your mastery of the core legal skills and techniques of case analysis, legal argument and practical problem solving as they apply to the subject of torts, which are covered in Chapter 3; and
- your ability to understand yourself, identify your most effective learning strategies and master the particular study skills required for your torts course, which is covered in Chapter 4.

It takes time and effort to acquire this understanding and master these skills. This part of the book will help you to focus your efforts on the most profitable aspects of your study. The aim of Part 1 is to help you to jump the skills gap by outlining what you need to understand and what you need to do to become a successful torts student. Many torts courses have a strong skills-based component that is designed to help you to develop your foundational legal skills, and most torts teachers use problem-solving questions as one of the primary assessment tasks. Part 1 allows you to fast-track your skills development by identifying, explaining and illustrating the four essential skills you will need.

- *Study skills:* how to work effectively as a torts student.
- *Skills in argument:* how to argue like a torts lawyer.
- *Analytical skills:* how to analyse problem questions and torts cases.
- *Problem-solving skills:* how to identify issues and structure an answer to a torts problem.

This part of the book also aims to demystify the processes of legal argument and legal problem solving and give you a structure within which you can build your own understanding of the law of torts and develop confidence in your approach to the most common assessment tasks. However, a warning is needed. There is no magic bullet or special secret tip for success. No book can, of itself, guarantee success in skills acquisition. This is because skills are learned not through reading a book, but through practice. So, once you have familiarised yourself with the first four chapters of the book, it is important that you give yourself every opportunity to develop your skills by putting in the time and effort necessary to acquire and refine them. There is a certain degree of tension associated with acquiring new skills – especially in the competitive and sometimes daunting environment of a law school. However, if you apply yourself to the task and have faith in yourself and in your own determination, you will lay a solid foundation for success, not only in your current course but also in your future as a law graduate entering the workforce with a full set of professional skills.

How to use Part 1

This part of the book contains four chapters that will prepare you for success and encourage you to develop a strategy that is consciously focused on mastering the two equally important aspects of knowledge and skills acquisition. Many students feel quite comfortable with the law when they hear it being explained and discussed in classes – but they do not always understand what to do with that knowledge. The key to success is to realise that your study strategy should be based upon:

- organising your knowledge of the content by constructing effective, assessment-based tools (eg case notes, summaries of the law and problem-solving checklists); and then
- using those tools to gain the necessary legal skills by practising and preparing for common assessment tasks.

Chapters 1 and 2 together provide a concise introduction to the subject and identify several different perspectives from which you can gain a better understanding of the law of torts. These chapters explain the special nature and functions of the law of torts, outline its important role in resolving disputes and providing justice for those who have been wronged by the conduct of another, and describe the dynamic process by which the law of torts develops and changes over time. The first two chapters will prepare you for the more defined and specific content modules in Part 2. Once you have read them you will be able to explain to another person what a 'tort' is, and to tell them why the law of torts is an essential part of our civil justice system in Australia. You will also understand why your approach to studying torts is directly determined by the distinctive nature of tort law and its key functions in the community. You will see that because tort law is deeply concerned with justifying, defining and refining the rules governing fundamental aspects of interpersonal wrongdoing, you will need to master the arts of *legal argument* and *case analysis*. Finally, you will understand that because the law of torts plays a crucial part in the dispute resolution function of our civil justice system, you must develop your skills in *legal problem solving*.

Chapter 3 focuses on illuminating these two core *legal techniques*. It is unlikely that your previous studies will have equipped you with these skills, and you may well find that studying law is not like anything that you have studied before and that success in law exams does not come easily. There are three reasons for this distinctive, and rather unsettling, feature of studying torts. The first lies in the fact that torts is often among the first subjects that students take as part of their law degree – so the skills are new. The second is that the workload is high. Many courses use the case study method of instruction – and this means that you will be expected to read a large number of cases so that you can immerse yourself in the legal method and acquire it almost by osmosis, practice and discussion rather than by overt step-by-step instruction in lectures. The third reason is found in the primary assessment task – the practical problem-solving question – which requires you not only to *acquire* knowledge but to *apply* it to solve a problem that you have not encountered before. So, once you understand that tort law is not just a set of rules and principles about interpersonal wrongdoing that you have to know, but is a method of argument and counterargument about those rules and principles that you have to master, you will be on the path to success.

Chapter 3 will also help you to understand and analyse the arguments that you will find in the cases you have to read in your torts courses, and to discover how to construct the legal arguments – and anticipate the counterarguments – that you will need to use in essays, exams and problem-solving exercises. It will also guide you in the foundational art of torts problem solving. It provides an overview of the structure of a generic torts problem-solving answer, worked sample arguments, and a full range of hints and tips that will help you to understand the legal method, identify and cope with ambiguity and uncertainty in both the law and in the facts, and work with the rules, principles and policies that together make up the body of the law of torts. Once you have worked through Chapter 3, you should have a basic understanding of the two core legal techniques as they apply in the law of torts. You will learn how to:

- analyse, understand and argue critically about tort law;
- read and analyse torts cases; and
- apply the law to the facts in order to resolve torts problem questions.

By completing Chapter 3, you will have taken the first step towards learning how to argue like a torts lawyer. You will also be ready to develop, practise and improve these skills in argument and problem solving when you tackle the content chapters in Part 2, each of which identifies the current issues and challenges within the law of torts and offers guidance on how to deal with problem-solving exercises in that particular area.

Chapter 4 focuses on identifying the *study skills* needed for success as a torts student. It offers advice on time management and study habits, and explains how to put together a useful, comprehensive and assessment-focused summary of the law. This chapter also outlines basic strategies for managing your case reading load, writing a torts essay, preparing an oral presentation and achieving success in torts exams. Once you have read Chapter 4 you will understand how to develop and improve your mastery of the foundational skills that you will need not only to become a successful torts student, but to become a successful and valuable member of the workforce as well.

Our top tips

1. *Be organised and start studying in the first week of term.* It is very hard to catch up once you fall behind. Aim to complete each week's work in that week – this will allow you to spend study breaks preparing and practising some problem questions.
2. *Make a summary of the law.* Make *your own* summary, based on the advice given in this book and the advice given by your own torts teachers. Be wary of summaries that can be found on the internet – or that have been given to you by previous students or are AI-generated. They can be wrong, or out of date, or incomplete. If they are from another jurisdiction they will be based on different statutory provisions. We strongly recommend avoiding AI-generated summaries, as the law is often a matter of nuance and that nuance often gets lost in the operation of a large language model. Also, you learn by doing – so make a point of teaching yourself the law by making your own summary. This book will get you started.
3. *Read as many cases as you can.* This will help you to pick up the method, the style and the knowledge that you need. This book is designed to help you to connect with the law of torts, but you cannot fully connect with this subject without connecting with the primary sources, cases and statutes.
4. *Get involved.* Prepare for classes, get involved in the debates, participate in moots and start talking about the law with other people. Law is a community conversation – so make a point of connecting with that conversation as soon as you can.
5. *Look after yourself.* Stay fit and healthy. Remember that everyone needs help at times and that problems are better dealt with early. Make sure that you look after your physical and mental health by balancing your study with some exercise and recreation. If you get sick, see a doctor. If you feel anxious or depressed, see a doctor. If you feel overwhelmed, make an appointment with your university's counselling services; the counsellors are experienced in helping students and will be able to guide you. If you feel demotivated, connect with some friends and get motivated – go for a walk and talk about torts!

We wish you all the best for your study of torts – and we hope that you enjoy it as much as we do!

INTRODUCING TORT LAW AND ITS CHALLENGES

1

1.1 Introducing the law of torts

1.1.1 What is a tort?

A tort is a special kind of wrongdoing. 'Tort' is a legal term that describes a particular category of interpersonal wrongdoing dealt with by the civil justice system. The law of torts covers a wide range of different types of misconduct, including many torts with well-known names like 'assault', 'battery', 'trespass to land', 'defamation' and 'negligence'. The task of defining the word 'tort' is notoriously difficult, given that more than seventy torts are known to the common law world, each with a different focus and a distinctive set of elements to protect different personal interests.

Curiously, there does not appear to be any shared identifying characteristic nor any unified set of interests that the law of torts seeks to protect to the exclusion of any other area of the law. The search for a clear definition is further complicated by the constant state of development of the law of torts. Some torts are outdated and no longer recognised in Australia, while others that have existed in other common law jurisdictions for many years have not yet been widely accepted here.

Tort law tells us what our rights and obligations are. Each tort describes, forbids and provides a legal remedy for a particular kind of interpersonal wrongdoing.

Examples

- The tort of **battery** tells us that we must not interfere with or touch the body of another person without lawful justification.
- The tort of **false imprisonment** tells us that we must not restrain another person's liberty without lawful justification.

- The tort of **trespass to land** tells us that we must not interfere with another person's exclusive possession of land without lawful justification.
- The tort of **negligence** tells us that under certain conditions we must take reasonable care to avoid acts or omissions that we can reasonably foresee would be likely to injure another person.
- The tort of **private nuisance** tells us that we must not cause a substantial and unreasonable interference with another person's use and enjoyment of land.
- The tort of **defamation** tells us that we must not publish imputations about another person that may lower their reputation in the eyes of others without lawful justification.
- The tort of **deceit** tells us that we must not knowingly make false statements that induce another person to act to their detriment.

Each tort is further defined by a list of ingredients or elements that help us to identify (and avoid) the occasions where we might wrongfully harm others. The law of torts also provides defences that spell out the conditions that must be satisfied if we claim that our conduct was justified. Taken as a whole, the law of torts tells us how to plan our activities so that we can live up to our legal obligations.

Although many of the torts listed above are frequently encountered in the daily life of a community, you may not have heard the word 'tort' before you enrolled in your law degree. The word is a legal term that comes from the Latin word *tortus*, meaning twisted or crooked, and this image explains why the word is used to describe this particular – and rather elusive – category of the law. Tortious wrongdoing deviates from the right path; it is conduct that is twisted and crooked when it ought to be straight and true. However, not every type of wrongful conduct is dealt with by the law of torts. To be classified as a tort, the conduct must satisfy four conditions relating to the seriousness and effects of the conduct, the legal response to the conduct and the categorisation of the conduct.

First, the conduct must be regarded as a serious matter that justifies community action. It must be seen as so wrongful, so antisocial or so unwarranted that the community itself should make a rule against it and respond when that rule is broken. Second, the wrongdoing must be interpersonal and harmful. It must be the kind of conduct that can affect other people adversely, either by invading their personal rights or by causing them actual damage or harm. A simple act of moral wrongdoing will not be categorised as a tort unless the conduct also has the capacity to harm someone else. So, for example, privately thinking evil thoughts about another person and planning ways to hurt them may be morally wrong, but it is not a tort. Nor will harming another person be enough on its own; even if the harm was deliberately inflicted, the conduct itself must also be recognised as wrongful before it is classified as tortious.

A tort attracts a legal response, which is seen as doing justice between the parties. The response is an essential component of the law; without an enforceable remedy, the law's pronouncements are merely exhortations to do the right thing that carry no power and deliver no promises to victims whose rights are invaded. So, the third criterion distinguishing tortious wrongdoing from other forms of wrongdoing is that it is dealt with by the civil justice system and attracts particular legal remedies. In the usual case, a victim of the wrongdoing (or plaintiff) is entitled to seek a remedy from the wrongdoer (the defendant or 'tortfeasor'). That remedy is precise: it is normally an award of monetary damages that aims to restore the plaintiff to the position that they would have been in had the tort not occurred (the typical outcome of the tort of negligence); but occasionally, justice requires the courts to make an order known as an 'injunction' that requires a defendant to do something practical to ameliorate the effects of the conduct or to refrain from any further wrongdoing (as can happen with the tort of defamation).

The fourth criterion is an artificial one that derives from the history of the English legal system, which created a range of different common law and equitable causes of action to deal with different kinds of wrongs. Before any particular example of wrongdoing is classified as a tort, it must be accepted that it does not belong more appropriately to any other branch of private law such as the law of contract, trusts or restitution. In this sense, the law of torts is a catch-all category that deals with any interpersonal wrongs that do not seem to fit better elsewhere in the civil justice system. To add to the uncertainty, parts of the law of torts overlap with the category of criminal wrongdoing. Given that there are many different ways to wrong another person and many different ways in which a person can suffer harm as a result of the conduct of another, these criteria explain why there is such a large and apparently disparate family of individual torts and why it is difficult to find any unique identifying feature that unites that family and marks out any given example of wrongdoing as 'a tort'. The four crucial dimensions of a tort are set out below. Each of these matters gives rise to challenges that make the law of torts a fundamentally important subject of study. We examine these four aspects of the law in detail in this chapter and the next.

1.1.1.1 The four dimensions of a tort

1. The dimension of *wrongdoing:* A tort is a civil or interpersonal wrong that is committed by a person engaging in conduct that deviates from a standard that the community thinks is right.
2. The dimension of *harm:* The conduct must have the capacity to affect other persons adversely, either by invading their personal rights and interests, or by doing actual damage to them.
3. The dimension of *justice:* The conduct must attract certain legal consequences, including a duty imposed on the tortfeasor to do justice to the victim of that wrongdoing.
4. The *technical legal* dimension: A tort is a civil or interpersonal wrong that does not fit better into any other category of common law or equitable wrongdoing.

If we combine each of these four aspects, we can define a tort as an act of *civil wrongdoing* that has the capacity to *harm* another person, which in turn attracts a legal *remedy* that is seen as doing *justice* between the parties, and which does not fit better into any other *civil law category.* The two central tasks performed by the law of torts are to define this particular kind of wrongful conduct and to provide a system of justice aimed at righting those wrongs once they occur. The first task is the general one of laying down the law for the benefit and guidance of the community as a whole. The second is more specific, and requires the courts to apply the law to resolve disputes between the parties in individual cases. These two tasks explain why you need to master the foundational skills of legal argument, case analysis and practical problem solving. Because tort law is deeply concerned with justifying, defining and changing the rules governing fundamental aspects of interpersonal wrongdoing, you need to master the art of legal argument and case analysis; and because the law of torts plays a crucial part in resolving disputes, you must develop your legal problem-solving skills.

1.1.2 The moral and coercive power of the law of torts

The law is a powerful force in the community. It can force a person into bankruptcy and strip them of their assets, and for this reason alone it demands our respect. The law is also aspirational. We are supposed to obey the law not just out of fear but also because the law tells us what is considered acceptable or not acceptable in our community and society - or, more precisely, what dominant portions of our community and society consider acceptable or not acceptable at particular points in time (you should always keep this in mind whenever you encounter references to communal and societal values in this book, the case law, and your studies more generally). The law's rules set the standards by which we ought to live, and their force is both moral and coercive. The law of torts specifies the conditions that allow individuals and certain officers of the state (eg police) to interfere with the rights and liberties of other members of the community. Consequently, we have a double duty: to ensure that the rules made and enforced by our courts are grounded in our shared moral values and that they serve the greater good of the community. This means you need to be aware not only of the moral values underlying the law of torts but also of the social, economic and political values that may affect our critique of the law. As you will discover in Chapter 3, the law has its own set of values that affect the way that judges decide torts cases. You need to be aware of your own values so that you can recognise your blind spots. You need to be perceptive of the values of others so that you can construct arguments that will persuade them of your case. Finally, you need to understand that sometimes our moral, social, political and legal values compete - so there will be difficult cases where we must choose between competing values. It is relatively easy to decide a contest between a good thing and a bad thing - but it is quite a different matter to choose between two good things, or to decide upon the lesser of two evils, and what is understood to be good and bad may vary significantly from person to person.

1.1.3 Tort law's guiding principles

The rules laid down by the law of torts are based on principles as well as values. This follows from the definition of a tort as an act of wrongdoing. Many of these principles have played a crucial role in defining some of our basic personal rights and in protecting many of our most important interests. The principles found in the law of torts tell us in a general sense how to live a life in accordance with societal expectations and how to treat others properly, and they justify and support the more precise rules of conduct that are laid down in individual cases. These principles help us to better appreciate tort law's functions, its moral authority and its meaning. Some of these principles are presented in Table 1.1. You need to understand that the principles that underpin the law of torts are just as much a part of 'the law' as the rules themselves. Each of the content chapters in Part 2 will help you to identify the key principles that support, justify and shape each one of these different areas of the law.

Table 1.1 Tort law's guiding principles

The principles	The area of law
The principle of human dignity	underpins the trespass torts.
The principle of bodily inviolability	is the basis of the tort of battery.
The principles of self-determination and autonomy	support the rules on consent in the trespass torts and the duty to advise of risks in negligence.
The principle of individual liberty	underpins the tort of false imprisonment.
The principles of personal privacy and security of the home	underpin the tort of trespass to land.
The principle of humanity towards others	grounds the action on the case for the intentional infliction of personal injury.
The principle that human life is sacred	prevents a person who kills another in order to save their own life from claiming the defence of necessity.
The principle of illegality	underpins some of the defences to the trespass torts and negligence law.
The 'neighbour' principle	is the basis of the tort of negligence.
The coherence principle	ensures that tortious rules emerging from the common law do not clash with other legal duties.
The '*volenti*' or 'assumption of risk' principle	bars liability in negligence where a plaintiff has accepted the risk of a particular kind of harm occurring.
The principle of vicarious liability	imposes legal liability on a person on the basis of a defined legal relationship with the tortfeasor.
The principle of personal responsibility	supports some decisions about duty in negligence and the doctrine of contributory negligence.
The principle of honesty	is the basis of the tort of deceit.
The 'give and take' or 'live and let live' principle	underpins some of the rules of private nuisance.
The principle of freedom of speech and opinion	grounds some of the defences to defamation.
The compensation principle and the 'once and for all' principle	are the basis of the common law rules on awarding damages.

As we have seen, one of tort law's challenges lies in the fact that our values, and consequently the principles they support, may point in different directions. Another challenge lies in the fact that principles are necessarily vague. There is not always one single and obviously right answer to every legal problem. This is because competing answers to any question may be based on competing goods or evils – and deciding upon the relative ranking of those good or evil things is a matter upon which reasonable people often differ. One of the secrets to constructing successful legal arguments lies in learning how to overcome these difficulties. We return to this issue in much more detail in the following chapters.

1.1.4 The central concerns of the law of torts

Tort law seeks answers to these two essential questions:

- What standards of right and wrong should govern our conduct towards others?
- How should we do justice between the parties when these standards are breached?

The difficulties that the courts experience in carrying out these essential functions account for many of the features of the law of torts that frustrate and fascinate torts students, academics, lawyers and judges who must grapple with this complex and constantly evolving body of law. These challenges, which are discussed below, are:

- the problem of uncertainty, which lies at the heart of the law of torts;
- the difficulty of defining wrongdoing and setting precise standards of conduct;
- the conflict between the desires for stability and change in the law; and
- the need to limit the law.

To understand the special nature of the law of torts, you need to appreciate how these difficulties arise and master the methods the courts have developed to meet them. The first two chapters focus on developing that understanding. This chapter explores the sources of tort law's special challenges and identifies some of the solutions that have been found by the common law judges. Chapter 2 explains how the law of torts is shaped by judges and parliaments into a meaningful category of law that serves a distinctive role in the community. We conclude that chapter by reflecting upon how successful some of those solutions are, identifying some of the criticism that has been levelled at the law of torts, and considering the suggestion that the system does not deliver upon its promise of justice.

1.2 Exploring tort law's challenges

1.2.1 Tort law's heart of uncertainty

It is not possible to define a tort precisely. Most definitions in legal dictionaries and textbooks suffer from the same vagueness that affects the one given in section 1.1.1 (that a tort is a special kind of wrongdoing), and this suggests that the notion of 'a tort' is somewhat artificial. This ambiguity at the heart of the law of torts is both significant and pervasive. Any survey will reveal that many of the crucial standards and tests that determine whether a tort has been committed are subject to vagueness and uncertainty, and that, within the common law world, there are significant disagreements about the overall scope of the law as well as the definitions and elements of many of the torts. However, the temptation to conclude that torts is a meaningless body of law should be resisted, because its ambiguity does not prevent us from understanding it. It simply means that our understanding must be found by taking a different route.

The first step is to appreciate that the three highly contested and abstract aspects of wrongdoing, harm and justice, all of which are built into our concept of a tort, all give rise to difficulties when we try to give them practical form. A system that forbids wrongdoing must be able to define that wrongdoing clearly. A system that aims to do justice to the victims of wrongdoing and compensate them fairly for the harms done to them must be able to define and measure those harms and to justify and limit its responses to the wrongdoers who caused them. The law of torts cannot be reduced to a simple, certain and unchanging set of rules because of the inherent problems that we encounter when we try to shift from theory to practice and give precise legal form to moral matters.

The second step is to accept the ambiguity and recognise that human beings have found ways to manage the conflict between the desire for certainty and the fact of uncertainty. We live not only in a physical world where people get hurt, but also in a world of moral values and of desire – and inevitably there are times when our values conflict and our desires point us in different directions. We have learned how to balance our competing values and navigate a way between our contrasting goals. So, although we feel the need for defined rules so that we can live together as a community in some kind of harmony, the secret to coping with the uncertainty in the law of torts lies in understanding that 'law' is not just a set of rules and principles, but is also a culture of argument about those rules and principles. Our institutions of justice are built upon this knowledge and once you master the methods of argument that have been developed over hundreds of years by judges, lawyers and more recently parliaments who have shaped tort law's solutions to these problems, you will do well.

Uncertainty is not a barrier to understanding tort law. Rather, it is the source of that understanding. Success does not lie in memorising definitions and rules, but in exploring the full range of possibilities that open up as a result of this uncertainty. This means accepting that change is a permanent feature of the law of torts and supplementing your knowledge and skills in argument with imagination, ingenuity and creativity. Learning how to exploit tort law's inherent ambiguity is a necessary and exciting part of your legal education. The techniques for dealing with uncertainty are explored in greater depth in section 3.4.8 of Chapter 3.

1.2.2 Defining wrongdoing and managing disagreement

Tort law is about resolving conflicts about acceptable conduct in a given societal context. However, the everyday concept of wrongdoing, just like the legal concept of a tort, resists practical definition. Both words carry the same core meaning of misconduct or transgression against prevailing morality,[1] but the problem for law makers is that these definitions are legally empty. They do not give us any practical guidance or 'litmus test' that enables us to draw a clear line that neatly divides right from wrong, much less to do so in a particular context. This leads to another set of problems, because our characterisation of any given conduct as a tort depends, not upon the fact that we have detected a special mark of 'tortiousness' within the conduct itself, but upon the fact that we have agreed that it deviates from community standards of acceptable conduct and have decided that the law of torts should be used to deal with it. Wrongdoing is a concept that often creates disagreement and because the claim that something is wrong is a claim that must be justified, the issue of where to draw the line poses one of tort law's greatest challenges. We need rules – but not just any rules will do. To state the law clearly and precisely is an

1 The *Shorter Oxford English Dictionary* (*SOED*) provides an early use of the adjective 'wrong' as meaning 'twisted, bent' or having 'a crooked or curved form' (at 3732–3); see also section 1.1 above.

essential skill that takes time to develop, but learning how to justify the state of the law takes even more effort.

Central examples of wrongdoing are usually uncontroversial, but at the boundaries of the law of torts opinions will differ. In these controversial or 'hard' cases, competing values make the ruling difficult and even when the judges turn to moral theories or community standards for guidance, they may find only more reasons to disagree – as you will see. On some matters the community itself remains divided. However, disputes cannot be left undecided while we wait for consensus to emerge. So, we solve the problem by allowing designated representatives of the community to decide the matter by a vote based on informed debate, experience and conscience. In a legal case, the issues can ultimately be decided by the majority of the judges sitting on the case in the High Court of Australia. If Parliament decides that a court's decision is not in the best interests of the community, then it can change the law, again by a majority vote.[2]

The challenges posed by the concept of wrongdoing for lawyers and for law students are directly related to these inherent difficulties. Lawyers have the task of advising clients, predicting how a case may be resolved and, if necessary, arguing the case in court. In straightforward cases the matter may never need to go that far, but in contested cases, lawyers have to construct more complicated arguments to put before the courts. While judges have to make and justify the decisions in these difficult cases, lawyers from each side must present the arguments and the counterarguments that lead to those decisions. It should come as no surprise to learn that while you are at law school, you will focus far more on the difficult cases and the complicated arguments and spend much less time on the easy ones. So, how do you acquire the art of legal argument? The best way to learn how to construct your own persuasive and reasoned legal arguments is to start by deconstructing the arguments that have been made in earlier cases, and this is why so many torts teachers require you to discuss so many 'hard cases' as part of your legal training.

This focus on hard cases means that you have to be aware of the kinds of arguments that lawyers and judges use when they disagree about the proper state of the law. The key to solving these disagreements can be found in the nature of the concept of wrongdoing itself, which can be defined as conduct that deviates from a standard that is thought to be right. The negative concept of a wrong therefore implies the existence of a corresponding positive notion of something thought to be right or good. This is a useful insight, because when judges have to decide hard cases and set (or reset) the boundaries of the law of torts they will often justify their decisions by pointing to the positive objects that the proposed rules and standards of behaviour aim to protect. In this way, the judges use their perception of the community's *positive* needs and values to define and justify the community's *negative* laws that forbid certain kinds of interpersonal wrongdoing. We have already looked at some of the principles that animate the law of torts in Table 1.1. Chapter 2 considers some of tort law's other positive goals and associated policies that justify the decisions made by judges in hard cases. You will practise using all of these legal tools to help construct arguments (and counterarguments) in Part 2.

2 See Cane, 'Taking Disagreement Seriously: Courts, Legislatures and the Reform of Tort Law' (2005); Spigelman, 'Negligence: Is Recovery for Personal Injury Too Generous?' (2005).

1.2.3 Making rules and setting standards

Human life is complex and tort law mirrors that complexity.[3] So, even in cases where we agree, the law itself must inevitably reflect the fact that matters of right and wrong are not always simple, straightforward and absolute, but include many shades of grey. Plain, clear rules are always desirable, but they are not always possible. One method the courts have adopted to overcome this problem is to lay down a broad rule first and then modify that rule in subsequent cases, either by adding a series of exceptions or by allowing a number of defences so that the defendant can escape liability in deserving cases. This ensures that the rules can capture all of the complexity and nuances of interpersonal wrongdoing.

Example

In the tort of **battery**, the very broad rule forbidding any contact with the body of another is immediately qualified by an 'everyday contact' exception, which covers ordinary, innocent and unavoidable daily contact that may occur on social occasions or in crowded spaces. It is then limited even further by a range of defences such as consent, discipline, self-defence and necessity. In this way, the fundamental right that each person has to bodily integrity is announced and protected, but at the same time, the value that the community places on the other competing interests that it deems worthy of recognition can also be weighed in the balance.

A second method of dealing with the difficulty of setting standards that fully reflect the community's views and values is to incorporate express references to 'the ordinary reasonable person', 'right-thinking members of society' or 'ordinary people of fair average intelligence' within the rules and tests for liability. In fact, the fundamental concept of reasonableness appears throughout the law of torts – sometimes in the elements of the torts themselves, sometimes in the defences to the torts, and often at both stages of the process.

Examples

- In rights-based trespass torts like **battery** and **false imprisonment**, we can observe a pattern where strong, broad rules that draw very clear lines are counterbalanced by the 'fuzzy' reasonableness criteria that are embedded in many of the available defences.
- In the torts of **negligence** and **nuisance**, an assessment of reasonableness is carried out in the initial liability-imposing phase, where the elements of both torts contain express reference to the concept of reasonableness. While defences to the tort of nuisance are relatively few in number and do not include a reasonableness criterion, in the blurry tort of negligence the ubiquitous concept of reasonableness appears not only in the elements of the tort, but also in many of the defences.

3 See Cane, *The Anatomy of Tort Law* (1997) at 21–2.

The incorporation of a reasonable person standard into the law recognises that a set of rules cannot necessarily anticipate and describe every possible eventuality in advance. As the case law builds up, the courts provide further guidance on the application of these rules; lawyers are constantly being supplied with more examples to help them to advise their clients and predict their chances of success. This is why legal research skills are included in your torts studies and assessment tasks.

Questions about reasonableness are not always easy to answer. This is because the very concept of reasonableness, and what constitutes a reasonable person, is in and of itself contentious – if not an altogether artificial abstraction that bears little resemblance to reality. Also, even if we were to reach an agreement as to what that means objectively, reasonable people can disagree on moral and practical matters. This suggests that the price we pay for increasing the law's flexibility and responsiveness to community values is to make the law more complicated, more open to argument, and consequently, more uncertain. A rule that contains a meaningful but inherently fuzzy concept such as reasonableness cannot draw a clear, bright and easily discernible line between right conduct and wrongful conduct. So, if we want the law of torts to fully reflect the fine distinctions of human wrongdoing, the complexity of human lives and the standards of reasonable persons within the community, we must engage in a constant process of balancing and negotiating compromises between our conflicting desires and competing values. This process of weighing argument against counterargument is an eternal and familiar part of doing justice. This method of argument is explained and illustrated in Chapter 3. You will have many opportunities to develop this skill as you work through the later chapters of this book.

1.2.4 Forms of wrongdoing: Acts and omissions

Tort law focuses on wrongful conduct by one person that has the capacity to harm another. It is important to understand that in the law of torts, the term 'conduct' can include both overt actions and failures to act, which are known as omissions. We can wrong other people by what we actually *do to them* as well as by the things that we *fail to do for them*. This is implied by the idea of wrongdoing as a failure to live up to, or a deviation from, a proper standard of conduct. Logically, there is no necessary condition that the behaviour under consideration be limited only to positive actions. So, while the law of torts forbids positive acts, such as hitting another person without lawful justification, it also deals with certain kinds of omissions – for example, by declaring it to be wrong for doctors to fail to advise their patients of material risks inherent in their medical treatment. Courts have traditionally been slower to impose liability for omissions ('nonfeasance') than for positive acts of wrongdoing ('misfeasance'), and we explore this issue in greater depth in the chapters on negligence, where the history of legal liability for omissions is most significant.

1.2.5 Wrongdoing and the concept of fault

The notion of wrongdoing is closely associated with the idea of fault. Both concepts carry a common connotation of a poor fit or mismatch with a moral or normative standard.[4] We can wrong others not only by our external physical conduct towards them but also by our internal mental conduct or our attitudes towards them. As a community we are normally reluctant to impose legal liability on a person unless we are convinced not only that their conduct has fallen short of a proper standard but also that they were personally at fault for engaging in that conduct. A person is seen to be at fault if their conduct is motivated by societally unacceptable values or characterised by an attitude that fails to respect the value of other persons. Assessments of fault are based on a specific reading of an individual's responses to the situation they have found themselves in and, ultimately, a judgement of the values that have guided their choices. When courts consider fault, they take into account matters such as the person's state of mind, intentions and motives, attitudes to others, knowledge, capacity, and degree of control over events, all considered in the light of their surrounding circumstances. So, while our assessments of fault and wrongdoing are closely related, the issue of fault directs us towards a more particularised analysis of individuals, events and circumstances.

In the law of torts, fault is generally found in a defendant's state of mind. So, if a defendant has intended to harm another person or has been reckless or careless about harming other people, they will generally be held to be at fault. The dimension of wrongdoing, which is essential to our concept of a tort, has a double focus on these two linked aspects of fault and conduct (or mind and body).

Examples

- If a person deliberately intends or desires a particular harmful result, their conduct is described as **intentional**.
- If a person foresees that a particular result may occur, but goes ahead regardless, and knowingly accepts the risk of the harm occurring, their conduct is described as **reckless**.
- If a person's mind never turns towards the particular result and they do not realise that their conduct may risk harm to others, their conduct is described as **inadvertent**, **careless** or **negligent**.

Tort law tends to equate reckless conduct with intentional conduct because in both cases the defendant's mind has turned towards ('adverted to') the harmful consequences that may result. So, when you find the word 'intentional' in the definition of any tort, you need to remember that the term 'intentional' includes recklessness. You also need to remember that the word 'negligence' is used in two different ways in tort law. In the *intentional torts*, the word 'negligence' is used in its ordinary sense as a synonym for 'carelessness'. We use it when we want to distinguish negligent (or inadvertent) conduct from intentional (or advertent) conduct. When you encounter the *tort of negligence*, you need to remember that the word is being used as a special legal category or 'term of art' and carries the connotation of a breach of a legal duty to take reasonable care to avoid causing foreseeable harm to others.

4 The *SOED* defines a 'fault' as a 'deficiency, lack or want of'; a 'default, failing, neglect'; or a 'defect, imperfection, or blemish of character'. The verb to 'fault' is defined by the *SOED* as to 'be wanting'; to 'come short of an accepted standard, fail'; or to 'be deficient or lacking in' some quality.

An important feature of our deliberations about fault in the law of torts is the fact that we often base an inference of fault directly on our observations of a person's conduct. If we see someone wildly shooting a gun in a crowded street, we infer that they must have known the risks that they were undertaking, whatever they may say in the witness box. Lawyers, witnesses, judges and juries cannot read a person's mind; but in some cases, we judge a person to be blameworthy because we 'read' their conduct as conveying an attitude of disrespect or we interpret the conduct as being intrinsically faulty. Some conduct speaks for itself. However, in certain circumstances liability is imposed even in the absence of one of these recognised types of fault. This kind of liability is described as 'strict liability' to contrast it with the more common fault-based liability.

Different torts require different levels of fault. Some torts specify that certain conduct must be accompanied by a specific state of mind; some require a person to live up to an objective standard; some require a specific intention to cause a defined result; and others require only that a defined act be voluntary and intentional. There is a tendency to counterbalance the fault elements and the harm-based elements of any tort: so, if the conduct directly threatens harm to a particularly important interest or right, the fault element may often be correspondingly low, and vice versa.

Example

Specified degrees of fault

- In the tort of **battery**, the law does not require an intention to cause actual damage because our right to bodily integrity and control access to our own body is so important. The definition of this tort specifies that the defendant must directly cause physical contact or interference with the body of the plaintiff. The fault element requires only that the defendant should intend to make that physical contact (or be reckless or negligent as to contact occurring). It does not require any higher element of hostility or personal ill will towards the plaintiff.
- In the tort of **deceit**, the conduct element specifies that the defendant must have made a false representation to the plaintiff. The two fault-based elements require first, that the defendant made the statement with knowledge that it was false (or was reckless or careless as to whether it was false or not), and second, that the defendant intended the plaintiff to rely upon the false representation.[5]
- The tort of **negligence** requires either an act or, in some circumstances, an omission by the defendant that causes a recognised form of harm. The fault element in this tort specifies that the defendant must have failed to live up to an objective standard of reasonable care.

Fault is considered at two different stages. In most cases, it is considered at the initial liability-imposing phase, because most torts include a fault-based element in their definition, like intention, recklessness or negligence. However, the issue of fault can also be considered again at a later stage, when the defendant raises a defence. Some of these defences are *partial* and are based on the view that, while the defendant's conduct was faulty, the full cost of compensating for the damage that flowed from that wrongdoing

5 See *Magill v Magill* (2006) at [114].

should not be imposed on the defendant because the plaintiff was also at fault and should therefore bear part of the blame. Other defences provide a *total* justification.

Examples

Total and partial defences

- In cases of **contributory negligence**, a defendant will have to pay only a proportionate share of the damages bill. If liability is imposed on the basis of fault, then fairness and consistency require that it should also be limited by an assessment of relative fault. Other defences to negligence, such as *volenti non fit injuria*, provide a total justification.
- If a person has deliberately stabbed someone else, their conduct has fallen short of the rule of **battery** that says we should not apply force to the body of another person. Nevertheless, if they were acting reasonably in *self-defence* we do not judge them as being at fault for their conduct. Liability is completely excused when we decide that a person is not at fault, even if they have intentionally caused harm and their conduct would normally be seen as a breach of the law. Such people are absolved of blame because their response is seen to be fair and reasonable in the circumstances. The true blame for the events is cast upon the other person who was initially at fault by making the threat or attack.

Table 1.2 Wrongdoing: Conduct and fault

	The conduct aspect	**The aspect of fault**
Definition	Wrongful conduct is an act or an omission that deviates from a standard or norm of conduct that is thought by the community to be acceptable.	A person is at fault if their personal responses and attitudes to others are not as they should be in the circumstances – ie if they deviate from those that are thought by the community to be acceptable.
Focus	The body – or physical conduct. Externally observed conduct towards others.	The mind – or mental attitudes. Internal responses and attitudes to the value of others.
Location in the law	The conduct aspect is specified in the elements of the tort.	The aspect of fault is considered in the elements of the tort and/or in the defences to the tort.

The feature uniting these two concepts is the idea of a deviation from a moral or normative (value-based) standard. That deviation can be found in:

- actions – or what a defendant has done;
- omissions – or what a defendant has failed to do; and
- a defendant's state of mind – or their attitudes or responses to others (which are sometimes revealed in, or read from, their conduct).

The two concepts of wrongdoing and fault are compared and contrasted in Table 1.2. They both feature in the explanations of the elements of the various torts that are discussed in Part 2. For a person to be held liable for their wrongful conduct, they must normally be at fault, but as you will see when we discuss vicarious liability, this is not always the case: there are times when the law imposes liability on one person for the torts committed by another, regardless of fault.

1.2.6 The conflict between stability and change

The fundamental uncertainty that lies at the heart of the law of torts arises from the nature of its two primary tasks. Tort law must define the boundaries between acceptable and unacceptable conduct and do justice in individual cases by righting wrongs once they occur. The answers that we give to these questions will be determined by our values; and, because as a society we constantly debate and re-evaluate our conception of what it means to live a good and valuable life, our judges and legislators are constantly being asked to change the law of torts and redraw the boundaries of behaviour that will attract legal sanctions. This creates a conflict between the desire for stability and certainty in the law and the need to keep the law in line with changing community values.

The law of torts is dynamic and contingent. You need to understand that it could be different, depending on our choices and the balance that we strike between our competing interests, values and principles. More than any other area of private law, the law of torts has been shaped by visions of what the law *ought to be* rather than by the need for stability in the law. On the other hand, the law needs to be clear, predictable and certain so that people can plan their lives and their enterprises to comply with their legal obligations, avoid legal liability and protect themselves from claims. The law of torts is not set in stone, and much of the time in your torts classes will be spent in examining the arguments and reasons put forward by judges, academics and legislators to justify changing and improving the law. Many of the disputes about the law of torts arise from the different views that compete to fill the gaps created by tort law's inevitable uncertainty and from opposing views about the proper boundaries of the law. At times, judges, parliaments and members of the community feel that the pendulum has swung too far in one direction, and decide that the law needs to be rebalanced to achieve a more moderate position.[6] These characteristic features of the debates about tort law explain why you need to:

- be aware of what the law *could* and *should be*, rather than become fixated only on what it *currently is*; and
- supplement the art of critical analysis and the art of argument with an imaginative and creative approach to the law.

1.2.7 The need for limits

Tort law needs limits. The requirement for limits on the scope and reach of the law is a consistent theme in the law of torts, and our need to limit the law takes three forms, each of which is directly related to the three most important dimensions of a tort, namely, wrongdoing, harm, and doing justice in response. First, we need to set limits on what is

6 See Ipp, 'Themes in the Law of Torts' (2007); Spigelman, 'Negligence: Is Recovery for Personal Injury Too Generous?' (2005); and Cane, 'Taking Disagreement Seriously: Courts, Legislatures and the Reform of Tort Law' (2005).

to count as wrongdoing so that the law does not forbid conduct that we agree should be left unregulated. Second, we need limits on the kind of adverse effects that will be classified as harms and are therefore seen as worthy of the law's protection. Finally, we need limits on the extent of the remedies and responses that the law of torts can impose so that we do not go too far when we track the harmful results of a wrongdoer's conduct. Justice does not require wrongdoers to keep on paying forever for all the consequences of their wrongdoing – in fact, justice itself requires us to limit the legal responses to those that are fair. The need for limits is particularly acute in the ever-expanding tort of negligence, and we will examine the difficulties that the courts and parliaments have faced in justifying and imposing limits on the law in much more depth in Part 2.

Conclusion

This chapter has given you a definition of the elusive concept of a tort and introduced you to some of the challenges that inevitably arise from the nature of this important category of the civil law, which serves the community by setting standards of acceptable and unacceptable conduct, and doing justice in individual disputes. It has explained that the law of torts is inherently uncertain and ambiguous, and shown you how this ambiguity creates fertile opportunities for argument and openings for change.

You can understand tort law better once you understand that it is not just a set of rules backed up by legal remedies. This chapter has explained tort law as an evolving set of aspirational rules based on the shared principles and underlying values that together make up our community's conception of what is expected of individuals who are part of that community. Moreover, tort law is a culture of argument about those rules, principles and values, and, because people may disagree about the relative weight to be given to these competing goods, you need to understand that there is sometimes no obviously right answer to the problems posed by the law of torts.

The next two chapters will help you learn how to participate in this culture of argument by further explaining the law's solutions to the challenges posed by this particular category of legal wrongdoing. Chapter 2 extends your understanding of the law of torts by explaining its special conception of justice, identifying its two-part account of harm, and outlining its structure and functions. Chapter 3 shows you how to use this knowledge to deconstruct the arguments that you will find when you have to read torts cases and that you must use when you have to construct your own arguments in problem-solving questions, essays and other commonly encountered torts assessment tasks.

Test your understanding ...

... of the nature of tort law

1. Explain what a tort is by referring to its four key dimensions.
2. Explain why these four aspects of a tort result in the fact that the law of torts is inevitably uncertain and is in a constant state of development.
3. Explain how this uncertainty creates opportunities for legal arguments.

... of the nature of law

4. Identify two reasons why we should obey the law.
5. Explain this statement: 'The law is not just a set of rules backed up by remedies.'
6. Explain why there is sometimes no single right answer to a legal problem.

... of the nature of wrongdoing and its challenges

7. Explain why the concept of wrongdoing poses a challenge to law makers.
8. Identify and explain two ways that the law of torts deals with the problem of making rules and setting standards about right and wrong.
9. What is the difference between an act and an omission?
10. Explain how the concepts of wrongdoing and fault are linked, and give three examples of when a person's conduct is seen as 'faulty'.

REFERENCES

CASE

Magill v Magill (2006) 226 CLR 551

ARTICLES AND BOOKS

Cane, P, 'Taking Disagreement Seriously: Courts, Legislatures and the Reform of Tort Law' (2005) 25 *Oxford Journal of Legal Studies* 393.

Cane, P, *The Anatomy of Tort Law* (1997) Hart Publishing, Oxford.

Ipp, D, 'Themes in the Law of Torts' (2007) 81 *Australian Law Journal* 609.

Shorter Oxford English Dictionary, 6th ed (2007) Oxford University Press, Oxford.

Spigelman, J J, 'Negligence: Is Recovery for Personal Injury Too Generous?' (2005) 14 *Tort Law Review* 5.

UNDERSTANDING THE LAW OF TORTS

2

Introduction

There is no officially recognised 'Code of Tort Law'. The law of torts has to be distilled from two sources: case law and statutes. It has been formed primarily by the decisions of the common law judges who have developed the law case by case over hundreds of years. To an increasing extent, it has also been shaped by the acts of parliaments, which have responded to the perceived shortcomings of the common law. The role played by each of these two law-making institutions is different, and the range of choices open to them varies. This chapter will explain how these different roles allow different goals to be taken into account when the law is shaped into an integrated system that best serves the needs of the community – and again, remember that this is not an immutable objective standard, but rather one that is dictated by evolving relations of power and influence in our communities and societies.

One consequence of the fact that the law of torts is found in cases and statutes rather than a single code is that it becomes open to selection, interpretation and choice. One of the guiding tenets of our legal system is that the choices made by our courts should be made logically and in a consistent fashion. The consistent application of principle is aimed at doing justice by treating like cases alike and ensuring that tort law's body of rules forms a rational and coherent whole. There are critics who argue that the law of torts fails to deliver upon this goal, and their views will be introduced at the end of this chapter; however, many aspects of the law of torts do help us to understand its role in society, which suggests that it is a meaningful – even if somewhat elusive – category of the law. Part of this understanding can be found by looking at tort law's distinctive vision of justice, its special structure, and its wider functions, as well as the interests it protects from harm and the balance it constructs between our rights and the duties that we owe to each other.

2.1 Justice and the law of torts

2.1.1 Corrective justice and the law of torts

The law of torts is dominated by an ideal vision of justice. It requires a person who has wronged another to make amends by correcting the harmful consequences that flow from their conduct. Tort law is immediately concerned to respond justly to wrongdoers who have failed to comply with the community's standards, and at the same time to respond justly to the victims whose protected rights and interests have been invaded. A breach of the duties imposed by the law of torts is seen as creating an injustice or imbalance, which is then corrected by imposing a corresponding duty on the wrongdoer to remedy the breach. We can understand tort law's vision of corrective justice better if we contrast it with the vision of retributive justice that is found in the criminal law. The criminal law rights the wrong by imposing a burden of punishment directly on the wrongdoer, but it does little or nothing for the victim (if there is one). The two forms of justice both share a common vision of justice as balance: in the criminal law, the wrongdoer's negative act is counterbalanced by another negative act of state retribution; but in the law of torts, the negative act is counterbalanced by requiring the wrongdoer to perform a positive act. In one sense the law of torts seeks a more complete form of justice because the single act that publicly sanctions the wrongdoing both imposes a burden upon the wrongdoer and gives a compensating benefit to the victim.

Examples

- The defendant's initial breach of duty to the victim is counterbalanced by imposing a new duty on the defendant to remedy the consequences of the breach.
- The plaintiff's initial rights that were invaded are counterbalanced by the creation of a new right to have the consequences of the wrong repaired.

Ideally, justice requires wrongdoers themselves to pay the full cost of their torts, although in many cases insurance may cover the costs. Wrongdoers must 'take their victims as they find them', so full compensation must be paid, whether a tortfeasor has destroyed the career of a wealthy investment banker or harmed a casual worker.[1] However, there are limits on the remedies the law will enforce, and not every harmful consequence that flows from a tort is covered by tort law's remedies. Furthermore, tort law's ideal of corrective justice is not always attainable, because the availability of these remedies depends upon the wrongdoer's financial circumstances. If a wrongdoer has no

1 The common law imposes no caps or thresholds on liability, but recently parliaments have done so in their reforms to the law of negligence. See the chapters on negligence and the principles of damages in Part 2.

assets to comply with an order for compensation and no insurance to cover their liability, the state allows the plaintiff to force the wrongdoer into bankruptcy, but it will do nothing more to right the wrong or to redress the harm. This means that plaintiffs must also take their wrongdoers as they find them – and so, even though the complete form of corrective justice that tort law aims for is not always done, tort law's vision of justice is maintained, and its inherent uncertainty is revealed once again.

2.1.2 Distributive justice and the law of torts

The law of torts has been developed over a lengthy period. In Australia, the common law for the whole nation is ultimately determined by the High Court, with the result that there is a degree of uniformity across Australian states and territories. However, at the start of the 21st century the largely uniform common law of torts was changed by legislative intervention. In 2002 an important review of the law of negligence was carried out by a panel of nationally preeminent experts, appointed by the Commonwealth, state and territory governments and led by former Justice David Ipp. In October 2002 the panel delivered the *Review of the Law of Negligence: Final Report* – known as the Ipp Report.[2] After this report and the outcry over the insurance crisis that accompanied it (as further discussed in Chapter 10), parliaments throughout Australia enacted many changes to the law, which can be found in the following statutes:

- *Civil Law (Wrongs) Act 2002* (ACT);
- *Civil Liability Act 2002* (NSW);
- *Personal Injuries (Civil Claims) Act 2003* (NT), *Personal Injuries (Liabilities and Damages) Act 2003* (NT);
- *Civil Liability Act 2003* (Qld), *Personal Injuries Proceedings Act 2002* (Qld);
- *Civil Liability Act 1936* (SA);
- *Civil Liability Act 2002* (Tas);
- *Wrongs Act 1958* (Vic);
- *Civil Liability Act 2002* (WA), *Volunteers and Food and Other Donors (Protection from Liability) Act 2002* (WA).

Part 2 explains the current state of the common law, alerting you whenever you need to consult your study materials. These identify the legislation in your jurisdiction that may have modified the common law.

From the theoretical point of view, these legislative changes to the law of negligence reflect the different roles played by judges and legislators. As we have seen, judges are primarily and immediately concerned with doing corrective justice (determining specific cases in accordance with the principle of requiring tortfeasors themselves to fully compensate victims for the harm done by their wrongdoing). Legislators have a broader scope and a duty to govern for the health, welfare and security of the entire community. This wider duty allows them to take distributive justice into account. Distributive justice focuses on the general distribution of benefits and burdens, resources and opportunities between different members of the community. Legislators can therefore consider the financial consequences

2 The report can be found at <https://treasury.gov.au/review/review-of-the-law-of-negligence>.

of their decisions and are legitimately entitled to tailor the law to satisfy wider welfare aims and to follow policies that provide special benefits for certain groups of citizens, encourage insurance, or limit the overall costs to society of particular legal measures.

An argument can be made that judges can also take distributive justice into account;[3] however, legislators have a far greater ability to create unequal or limited distributions of benefits and burdens. By contrast with corrective justice, which aims at imposing full personal responsibility for harmful wrongdoing, distributive justice allows for collective responsibility, collective solutions and even limited or partial solutions to the problems posed by individual wrongdoing. Consequently, parliaments can draw on a wider range of justifications for their decisions and can provide more flexible solutions to perceived problems or shortcomings in the law.

Example

Limiting thresholds and caps on damages awards were laid down in many of the statutes passed by the state and territory legislatures after the Ipp Report. These were legislative measures that would have been beyond the power of a judge to introduce.

The fact that the law of torts is animated by these two conceptions of justice means that the law's rules and principles are also shaped by policy considerations. Chapter 3 returns to discuss the role played by rules, principles and policy matters in structuring legal arguments.

2.2 Tort law and the concept of harm

2.2.1 Tort law's distinctive vision of harm

All torts contain an aspect of harm. Harm has been defined as 'hurt, injury or damage',[4] and ordinarily, before we can describe someone as having been harmed, we must establish that they have been made worse off in some tangible or intangible way.

Example

Harm

- *Tangible harm* includes physical damage to the body, goods or land.
- Examples of *intangible harm* include the loss of future income, emotional distress or grief, damage done to reputation, and interferences that diminish a person's ability to make decisions about the direction and control of their life.

3 See *McFarlane v Tayside Health Board* (2000) from the United Kingdom and *Cattanach v Melchior* (2003) from Australia. Some theorists suggest that corrective justice is simply a subcategory of distributive justice, but this is a controversial and complex theoretical issue. See, for example, Peter Jaffey's book *Justice in Private Law* (2023).

4 *SOED* at 1191.

A tort consists of conduct by one person that has the capacity to affect another person adversely, and there are two different kinds of adverse effects that the law of torts recognises as relevantly harmful: those that set back our welfare interests, and those that set back our interests in autonomy by interfering with our entitlement or ability to make our own decisions and put them into effect. These two different aspects of the dimension of harm, which are noted in Table 2.1, help us to understand the function that the law of torts plays in constructing and protecting the rights and freedoms we enjoy within our community.

The law of torts can be seen not only as one of the ways through which a community responds to a defendant's wrongdoing but also as one of the ways that a community uses to protect a broader vision of how its individual members ought to behave in a collective setting. It does this by protecting the essential interests in welfare and autonomy shared by individuals. Welfare interests encompass all the aspects that are essential to an individual's human health and well-being, including their physical and mental health, their possessions, homes and wealth, their reputations and relationships, and their surrounding environment. Autonomy interests cover an individual's desire to control their own lives, bodies, possessions and activities. The law of torts protects both kinds of interests and in fact many torts protect both aspects of people's lives.

Example

Welfare interests

The tort of **battery**, which forbids conduct by the defendant that causes direct physical contact with the plaintiff's body, protects both our welfare interest in maintaining our physical bodily integrity as well as our autonomy interest in controlling access to our bodies.

Table 2.1 Adverse effects on our interests in welfare or autonomy that make us worse off

	Welfare	**Autonomy**
Definition	Welfare encompasses all those things, both internal and external to the person, that are important for human existence.	Autonomy is the exercise of control over one's own life by defining, choosing and pursuing the good life on one's own terms.
Focus	Passive states of well-being.	Active states of well-being.
Basis	Welfare interests are based on our human needs for: • physical and mental health and well-being; • possessions and income; • dignity, reputation and privacy; • social support and relationships; and • a safe and secure physical environment.	Our interests in autonomy are based on our human desires to: • define the good life for ourselves; and • choose when and how to pursue it. An autonomous life comprises both: • capacity; and • the factual opportunities for choice, decisions and action.

Some kinds of effects are not necessarily recognised by the law of torts as relevantly harmful, and these contentious effects of a defendant's wrongful conduct challenge our law makers. Examples of such effects include:

- death;
- unplanned pregnancy and the consequent birth of a child;
- a child being born with severe disabilities;
- unwanted attention or unwanted observation by others that invade our privacy;
- certain kinds of emotional distress and upset; and
- certain technological interferences (eg changing data stored on a computer).

Central examples of harm are usually unchallenged and uncontroversial, but at the boundaries of the law we encounter difficulty. In each case, law makers must recognise that a particular setback to a given interest should count as a 'harm' before they protect that interest or count it towards a damages award. A significant feature of the common law is its traditional refusal to recognise death itself as a harm that can ground a claim for compensation – a problem that has been solved by legislative action. More recent debates over the controversial issue of harm have arisen out of cases where doctors have failed in their duties to their patients and the courts have had to decide whether an unplanned and unwanted pregnancy itself can count as a harm and whether the subsequent birth of a child is a compensable harm.[5] Another example involves the difficulties of categorising the effects of climate change as harm in the context of tortious claims. These issues and other difficult questions about harm are discussed in Part 2.

2.2.2 Protected interests in the law of torts

The law of torts gives either direct or indirect protection to our individual welfare and autonomy interests, which include the following groupings:

- our physical bodily integrity and mental health;
- our dignity, reputation and privacy;
- our possession and enjoyment of land and goods;
- our assets and wealth;
- some of our business relationships and contractual interests;
- some of our civic and political interests; and
- some of our very intimate private relationships.

The web of human interests that tort law defends is protected in different ways by different torts – but not every protected interest maps onto a particular tort, and some interests are not directly protected at all. Some members of the family of torts, such as the rights-based trespass torts, do have a primary focus on a particular interest (like bodily integrity, freedom from confinement, possession of goods and land, etc) but they also offer secondary protection to other interests as well. Some other kinds of adverse effects (eg distress, pain and suffering) are not currently the primary subjects of tort

5 See *Cattanach v Melchior* (2003), *Harriton v Stephens* (2006) and the legislative response to those cases in the civil liability legislation in some jurisdictions.

law's protection, but if these effects occur as the result of the commission of some other recognised tort, the plaintiffs may receive compensation.

2.2.3 Balancing competing interests

Tort law's protection of our welfare and autonomy interests is not absolute. Furthermore, not all interests carry the same value, and, because there are often times when our interests collide, the law must decide which interest is to take precedence. Tort law's idea of justice as balance is reflected in the rules that it constructs to deal with this problem of competing interests. The compromises that tort law has to make are often seen in the balance that it maintains between setting the conditions of liability on the one hand and allowing defences to liability on the other. Some of tort law's rules weigh two private interests against each other, whereas others weigh private interests against communal interests.

Examples

- Under certain conditions, in a case of *necessity*, a starving person lost in the forest may enter another's land, break into their house and eat their food without being held liable to compensate the owner for the torts of **trespass to land, trespass to goods** or **conversion.**
- The tort of **nuisance** initially weighs the competing private rights of the two parties to use their land as they please to arrive at a prima facie finding of liability. Then it allows some, but not all, of the competing community interests to be taken into consideration at the point where the defences are added to the scales. So, if parliament has authorised the commission of the nuisance, the defence of *statutory authorisation* is allowed to outweigh the private interest of the plaintiff in living on their land free from unreasonable interference by others.
- In the tort of **defamation**, the law must strike a balance between the private interests of individual plaintiffs in the protection of their reputation and the wider public interest of the community as a whole in freedom of speech.

It is possible to analyse the law of torts by looking at the different interests that it protects and identifying the range of torts that offer this protection,[6] but the usual classification of a tort depends not only on the kind of harm that the conduct causes but also on the kind of wrongdoing that the tort describes. Once liability is imposed, however, a number of different kinds of harm to specified interests may be taken into account when the full claim for damages is assessed.

Example

Deceit

The tort of **deceit** imposes liability for knowingly making false statements that induce another to act to their detriment. Once the plaintiff proves the five elements of deceit, they can then claim

6 See Cane, *The Anatomy of Tort Law* (1997) at 66–95.

compensation for a range of different kinds of harm that may have flowed from that deceit, such as past and future economic losses and any pain, suffering or psychological harm.[7]

2.2.4 A classification based on harm

One of the organising schemes in the law of torts is a by-product of its common law history. The old English forms of action divided torts into two groups, depending on whether the legal proceedings were originated by a special 'writ of trespass' or by a writ that made out an 'action on the case' stated in the document. The writs of trespass were reserved for cases where nominated, recognised rights had been intentionally and directly invaded, whether they led to actual damage or not, and these torts became known as the 'intentional torts'. The actions 'on the case' were more flexible, and allowed plaintiffs to claim compensation for harm done indirectly or unintentionally. In recent times, the differences between these two kinds of torts have become very blurry (particularly in relation to the issue of intention),[8] but some of the essential differences between the two different kinds of torts are explained in the two subsections below. It classifies the torts into two important groups: those that protect our personal rights and dignity (ie the torts that are rights based), and those that require an aspect of actual damage before liability is imposed (ie the torts that are harm based).

Tort law protects a number of fundamental common law rights through the trespass torts (eg assault, battery, false imprisonment, trespass to land and trespass to goods), but by far the larger group of torts is found under the category of harm-based 'actions on the case'. Within this category, the blockbuster tort of negligence dominates the law courts. In these torts, damage is the gist of the action, but in some cases the damage can be somewhat intangible, and in other cases, like defamation, damage is presumed once it has been proved that some matter that has the capacity to lower the reputation of the plaintiff has been published to a third party.

2.2.4.1 The rights-based trespass torts

- The adverse effect
  - In the trespass torts, the adverse effect on the plaintiff is located in the invasion of the plaintiff's rights and the denial of their dignity, autonomy and control over their interests in their body, land and goods.
  - To mark the fundamental importance of the rights protected by these torts, the trespass torts are actionable per se – that is, without proof of actual damage.
- The immediacy of the effect
  - In the trespass torts, the interference must be a direct result of the defendant's conduct.
- Examples
  - Trespass to the person, including assault, battery, false imprisonment
  - Trespass to goods
  - Trespass to land

7 See *Magill v Magill* (2006).
8 See Howarth, 'Is There a Future for the Intentional Torts?' (1997).

2.2.4.2 The harm-based actions on the case

- The adverse effect
  - In the torts known as the 'actions on the case', the adverse effect on the plaintiff is located in the setback to the plaintiff's interests that makes them factually worse off.
  - These torts all include an element requiring actual damage; however, in some cases damage is presumed – for example, in the tort of defamation.
- The immediacy of the effect
  - In an action on the case, the effect may be the indirect or consequential result of the defendant's conduct.
- Examples
  - Negligence
  - Defamation
  - Nuisance
  - Deceit, passing off, injurious falsehood

The wide range of interests that tort law protects from harm explains why torts cases – particularly negligence cases – are some of the most common causes of action litigated in our courts. However, the immediate effects of the conduct on the plaintiff's interests do not always point directly to the relevant tort, and this is why the problem-solving skill of diagnosis is so important (and why it is essential to pay careful attention to all of the elements of the possible torts when you try to work out which of them may hold the solution to your client's problem). The difficulties that the courts have encountered in deciding upon which interests should be protected and what kinds of adverse effects should be recognised as harms explain why you must learn the art of legal argument and critical analysis, which will assist in gaining an understanding of some of the most important debates that have dominated the law of torts in recent years. Each of these skills is explained further in Chapter 3.

2.3 The structure and functions of tort law

2.3.1 The structure of tort law

Tort law is structured. In a very deep sense, the law of torts – like all law – is one way of imposing order and structure on a messy and uncontrolled world, which can be thrown out of balance by people who break the rules and cause harm to others. Tort law imposes a remedy that aims to put plaintiffs into the same position that they would have been in if the tort had not occurred. Given this ambitious aim of restructuring reality and attempting to impose order on a disordered set of circumstances, it is no coincidence that torts cases are analysed in an orderly and structured way. The substantive part of a torts case is traditionally divided into three separate stages. The first stage focuses on the elements of the tort, the second stage focuses on the defences and the third focuses on the remedies. As you will see in the next chapter, this three-part structure of the litigation process will help you to structure your answers to torts problem-solving questions. Each tort has its own list of ingredients – or elements – that the plaintiff must prove. Some of those elements relate to the defendant, some relate to the plaintiff, and others are related to the contextual or circumstantial aspects of the tort.

Examples

- The *defendant*-related elements define the nature of the wrongdoing by identifying the *conduct* and the *fault* aspects of the tort.
- The *plaintiff*-related elements define the kinds of adverse effects or *harm* that must result from the conduct.
- The *contextual* or *circumstantial* elements add more clarity to the conditions under which the rules apply – for example, by setting a threshold precondition or identifying the surrounding circumstances or context in which the events must occur.

Once the plaintiff has made out a prima facie case by proving on the balance of probabilities that each element has been satisfied, the onus of proof switches to the defendant to raise any relevant defences. These defences have their own set of ingredients that must be proved. Some elements and defences contain more than one of these aspects, and you should remember that not everyone agrees on the precise formulations of these elements and their defences. (For example, some texts state that the tort of negligence contains three elements, while others suggest there are four.) The elements of a tort set the conditions that establish a prima facie case of liability. The defences set the conditions for excusing or avoiding liability.

Examples

The elements of **defamation** to be proved by the plaintiff are as follows:

- The matter must contain a defamatory imputation.
- The defamatory imputation must be about the plaintiff.
- The defamatory matter must be published by the defendant to a third party.

The defences to **defamation** that may be raised by the defendant are as follows:

- triviality;
- truth or justification;
- absolute privilege;
- qualified privilege;
- protected reports and documents; and
- fair comment or honest opinion.

The law maintains a balance between the elements and the defences, and this balance reflects the relative weight or value that the courts have given to the competing interests at stake.

Example

The elements of **defamation** listed above set a very wide net that appears to offer broad protection to an individual's personal reputation. However, because of the importance of the countervailing community interests in freedom of speech, open and critical discussion of important political and public matters, and knowledge of the truth about these matters, the defences to defamation cut down the scope of that protection quite severely. Consequently, many defamatory imputations that will damage reputations can lawfully be published.

The next chapter explains how to use the elements of and the defences to the torts to structure your answers to torts problem-solving questions. Later chapters explain the elements and defences in more detail.

2.3.2 Tort law's 'bilateral' structure and community-based nature

The law of torts protects some of our most fundamental rights and basic freedoms. It balances the rights we have as individuals with the corresponding duties we owe to others to respect those rights. So, in the law of battery, our rights to bodily integrity are matched by our duties to avoid causing unwanted physical contact with others. This special feature has been described by Peter Cane in *The Anatomy of Tort Law* (1997) at 11–12 as 'bilateralness' or 'correlativity', which he explains as follows:

> What this means in simple terms is that civil law organises relationships between individuals on a one-to-one basis. In the law of obligations, one person's obligation corresponds to (is 'correlative') to another person's right. The rules of tort, contract and so on are couched in terms of bilateral relationships between individuals, and ... every cause of action in the law of obligations is two-sided.

Cane makes the point that all principles of tort liability and all causes of action in tort have elements concerned with the two interacting parties. However, while it is true that disputes in the law of torts are two-sided affairs between parties whose rights and duties correspond, the law of torts is not simply a matter between a plaintiff and a defendant. In every tortious case, there is a powerful and essential third presence, the community itself, which shapes the law and gives effect to its vision of justice. As we have seen, it is the community whose common interests, prevalent needs and dominant vision of acceptable conduct grounds the law and sets the standards. The essential role played by the community suggests that the law of torts should be viewed as not only serving the interests of the individual parties who are linked together by the tortious wrongdoing but also as serving the needs of the wider group. So, while it is important to realise that there are elements in every tort that link the defendant's conduct with the harm done to the plaintiff, it is equally important to understand that the rules and principles of tort law take their shape from their setting – and that setting is collective in nature.

2.3.3 The functions of the law of torts

The law of torts is meant to benefit the community. The positive effects of the tort system are intended to reach beyond its immediate tasks of providing direct benefits to the plaintiffs in individual cases and extend to provide more indirect benefits for the community as a whole. As we saw in the last chapter, some of tort law's immediate tasks are to protect our rights and interests, and resolve individual disputes in light of accepted standards of conduct. We have also seen that one of tort law's goals is to provide compensation to victims by holding wrongdoers liable to make amends for their wrongdoing. The law of torts therefore has a loss-shifting function and a deterrent function. Another function of the system is to enable individuals to plan their lives in order to avoid liability and take loss-spreading measures to protect themselves from the cost of failing to meet legal obligations.

Jules Coleman and Arthur Ripstein have suggested that the law of torts must answer the question about who owns life's misfortunes – and who must therefore bear the costs of those misfortunes.[9] These questions are not simply questions for lawyers; they are political and social questions that must be answered by the community as a whole. When misfortune strikes and causes harm, we have three options:

- we can do nothing, let the loss lie where it falls and leave the victims to cover their own costs;
- we can shift the loss from the victim by requiring the person who wrongfully caused the loss to bear the cost; or
- we can find a way to spread the cost across the wider community.

In fact, we do all of these things. At times we do nothing; at other times we adopt solutions designed to shift or spread the costs. The solution based on corrective justice suggests that if a person is at fault for a harmful act of wrongdoing, then it is only right that they should bear the cost. This feature of tort law will deter many members of the community from intentionally causing harm, but the problem is that human beings can inadvertently cause losses that are far beyond their capacity to pay. Just think of the damage that a single moment of inattention at the wheel of a car could cause. A lifetime's earnings would not be enough to cover such catastrophic damage. Even large, well-funded corporations can cause damage that their profits alone cannot always cover – consider the damage caused by oil spills, tobacco or asbestos, for example.

There are two ways of spreading the cost of these massive losses, and each relies on the fact that the community's resources are far greater than those of any individual person. The first way is to look to private enterprise and encourage potential defendants to take out insurance in the form of accident liability, professional liability or enterprise liability.[10] This is why the insurance industry has a strong interest in limiting the scope of the law of torts.

9 Coleman and Ripstein, 'Mischief and Misfortune' (1995).

10 Think about why it might not be a good idea to allow a person to insure themselves against intentionally harming another and you will be able to work out why insurance is not available in the case of the intentional trespass torts.

Examples

- If everyone who owns a car contributes a relatively small amount each year, we can collect enough money to cover the bills if an accident occurs.
- If every doctor contributes a sum each year, a fund can be created to cover the damage caused by medical negligence.
- If corporations that manufacture and distribute products are required to take out insurance against causing harm to consumers, then consumers as well as the enterprise are protected, and the cost can be factored into the price of the goods.

The second method looks to the 'deep pockets' of governments. It resolves the problem by going outside the tort system altogether and using the money collected from tax-paying members of the community to provide welfare services, health services, income support benefits and sometimes accident coverage that will help to fix the damage. These solutions do not rely on operating a system of corrective justice that imposes individual liability; instead, they create a welfare system based on communal responsibility and distributive justice. Rather than relying on a fault-based system of loss-shifting, we adopt a needs-based system of cost sharing. The following list lays out some of the functions of the law of torts, and the next section considers some of the other methods of dealing with life's misfortunes.

2.3.3.1 Objectives and outcomes

- In practice, the broad functions of the law of torts can be described by reference to specific material tasks and concrete objectives. Immediate tasks: to define our rights, make the law and apply it to individual cases.
  - Defining and vindicating our shared common law rights: The law of torts protects some of our most fundamental rights and freedoms and requires each person within the community to respect the rights of others.
  - General law-making role: Tort law defines the rules and sets the standards of interpersonal wrongdoing, and defines the rules that specify a just response to wrongdoing. It aims to set precise norms of conduct that govern our interpersonal relations.
  - Specific dispute resolution role: Tort law is used to resolve disputes in individual cases.
- Direct outcomes: to promote corrective justice between the individual parties.
  - Corrective justice provides the benefits of compensation to plaintiffs: Tort law provides a remedy (or benefit) to the victims, primarily in the form of compensatory damages that aim to put them back into the position that they would have been in, but for the commission of the tort.
  - Corrective justice imposes a burden of responsibility on wrongdoers: Tort law imposes a burden of personal responsibility upon tortfeasors to make amends for their wrongs, either by paying damages or by complying with an injunction.

- Indirect outcomes: to promote wider community benefits.
  - Deterring harmful interpersonal wrongdoing: By providing a system that imposes defined responses to defined conduct that wrongfully causes harm to others, the law of torts deters this unethical and harmful conduct.
  - Distributing (or sharing) costs and encouraging insurance: The existence of this system also encourages individuals to take out insurance and spread the losses caused by accidental tortious wrongdoing across the community.

One of the most important functions of the law of torts is to provide an appropriate remedy in cases of proved wrongdoing; these remedies are outlined in the list below.

2.3.3.2 Remedies in the law of torts

Damages are awarded to a plaintiff once the defendant is found liable.

- *Nominal damages* recognise the fact that the plaintiff's rights have been invaded. These damages are awarded even if no actual damage has been caused.
- *Compensatory damages* are based on different tests, depending on the tort.
  - In the *intentional torts* the plaintiff is compensated for all the harmful consequences directly caused by the defendant's conduct.
  - In the *torts of negligence and nuisance* the plaintiff is compensated only for the reasonably foreseeable consequences that are not too 'remote' a result of the defendant's conduct.
- *Aggravated damages* may be awarded to compensate for any extra distress, insult or humiliation suffered by the plaintiff when the harm done by a wrongful act was aggravated by the manner in which the act was done.
- *Contemptuous damages* of a trifling amount may be awarded when the court or a jury wants to mark the fact that it believes that the plaintiff's case was worthless or decides to mark its disapproval of the plaintiff's conduct. They are rarely awarded in modern times.
- *Exemplary or punitive damages* are awarded to punish the defendant in cases where there has been a 'contumelious and flagrant disregard'[11] of the plaintiff's rights. These damages go to the plaintiff, not to the state, and there are limits on the torts where this remedy is available.
- In some cases, a plaintiff may also be entitled to an *injunction.*
  - *Mandatory injunctions* order the defendants to do something positive.
  - *Prohibitive injunctions* are negative or restrictive and order the defendants to refrain from engaging in some defined conduct.
  - *Interlocutory injunctions* are interim orders, which may be replaced by a final order or a perpetual order once the case is actually decided.

The injunction may be in addition to, or in substitution for, an award of damages. An injunction is an equitable remedy and is awarded at the discretion of the court.

Different torts are linked with different kinds of remedies and the chapters in Part 2 identify the primary remedies that are available in each category of the law.

11 *Whitfeld v De Lauret & Co Ltd* (1920), Knox CJ at 77.

2.4 Tort law in context

2.4.1 Distinguishing the law of torts as a legal category

The law of torts can also be understood by comparing and contrasting it with other areas of the law. Both tort law and contract law are part of the civil justice system, and they both share a common conception of justice. Contract law deals with a specific kind of interpersonal wrong, namely, the breaking of promises that are thought to be justifiably binding on the parties that exchange them. Despite these similarities, there are some differences between the duties imposed by these two areas of the civil law.

Examples

- *Contractual obligations* are generally created by the specific parties themselves and involve specific duties owed only to specific individuals for specific purposes. For example, when one person buys goods from another for an agreed price, only the two parties to the contract are bound by the reciprocal obligations to deliver and to pay for the goods.
- *Tort law's obligations* are externally imposed and owed by all persons to all other persons simply because of their common status as human beings in a given community. So, we all owe a reciprocal duty to all others to respect the integrity of their bodies, their possessions and their land.

As we have seen, the law of torts can also be usefully compared and contrasted with the criminal law (see Table 2.2). Some acts are both crimes and torts – for example, hitting someone and taking their laptop not only constitutes the crimes of assault and robbery but can also give rise to civil claims in trespass to the person, trespass to goods and possibly conversion of goods. However, not all crimes are torts, and not all torts are crimes. Criminal law is the body of law that specifies the rules, principles and policies governing the state's right to bring offenders to justice for both interpersonal and communal wrongs, whereas tort law, like contract law, is the body of rules, principles and policies governing a victim's rights to claim a private remedy such as damages and/or an injunction from the wrongdoer for some selected interpersonal wrongs. While tort law is generally seen as a species of corrective justice and criminal law as a species of retributive justice, it is important to realise that some kinds of civil remedies do impose a form of punishment on wrongdoers; however, in the law of torts these punitive damages do not go to the state, but to the plaintiff.

Table 2.2 Legal action and outcome

Legal action	P	v	D	=	Legal outcome
Tort	Victim	v	Tortfeasor	=	damages/injunction
Crime	State	v	Offender	=	punishment
Contract	Promise receiver	v	Promise breaker	=	damages/injunction

2.4.2 Alternatives to tort law

Many torts courses also cover some of the statutory alternatives to the law of torts that offer compensation to some victims of misfortune. These include universal accident insurance schemes and no-fault compensation measures, such as motor accident insurance, workers compensation, fatal accidents and criminal injuries compensation schemes.

LEGISLATION ALERT!

Consult your study materials to see which statutory schemes are covered in your torts course.

The differences between fault-based laws and no-fault laws can be accounted for by the different priorities that each displays; fault-based systems such as tort law aim to hold wrongdoers responsible for correcting the consequences of their conduct, whereas no-fault schemes give a higher priority to looking after injured victims, regardless of how the injuries came about. In these no-fault schemes based on distributive justice, contributions or insurance premiums are paid to the government by all who participate in a given area of activity, and the costs are thereby shared across a wider group. The value of the benefits given to those who are injured in motor accidents or as a result of their employment is generally lower than the compensation provided by the law of torts. However, because the benefits are paid for by a wider group – and in some cases are guaranteed by governments – the certainty of receiving some (admittedly limited) compensation is higher than the (admittedly limited) chances of receiving full compensatory damages via the expensive and risky system of civil litigation.

2.4.3 The future of the law of torts: Critique and reform

The uncertainty of the justice that the law of torts offers has led some critics like Patrick Atiyah, and others who wish to abolish or limit the law of torts and replace it with welfare-based universal no-fault accident compensation schemes, to suggest that tort law's system of justice amounts to no more than a 'damages lottery' that cannot guarantee either to bring compensation to victims or to impose justice on wrongdoers.[12] Others argue that the vagueness and imprecision that characterise the law of torts, combined with its internal inconsistency, its inherited common law biases and sometimes illogical prejudice, racism and sexism, render it an incoherent, unfair, unbalanced and meaningless body of law that is in need of wholesale reform. Some critics attack the law of torts because of its cumbersome legalisms and time-wasting inefficiencies, claiming that it should be taken out of the hands of competitive lawyers who are so immersed

12 See Atiyah, *The Damages Lottery* (1997) and Conaghan and Mansell, *The Wrongs of Tort* (2006).

in the adversarial nature of their profession that they cannot communicate properly with their clients, much less understand and promote their best interests. (This is why mediation and other approaches to alternative dispute resolution are an increasingly important aspect of legal training.) Another impetus for change comes in the form of the insurance industry, which often foots the bill for many acts of negligence. As a consequence, this industry has a strong voice with which to lobby politicians, and a strong interest in urging changes to the law of torts. Later chapters explore these criticisms in more depth and highlight the areas where each area of tort liability is in need of further improvement and reform.

Conclusion

The law of torts is an important topic of study. Our first two chapters have provided you with an overview of its essential tasks and functions, offering a definition of the elusive concept of a tort and introducing you to some of the challenges of defining wrongdoing, compensating for harm, and doing justice. They have also introduced and explained some of the solutions to the inevitable difficulties associated with its goal of righting interpersonal wrongs that have emerged within the law of torts. We return to many of these themes in the content-based chapters in Part 2, where we look at the individual torts and examine the particular challenges that each one entails.

The most important lessons to be drawn from these two chapters are as follows:

1. Tort law is constantly evolving. Tort law's task of separating acceptable from not acceptable conduct makes it inherently uncertain and ambiguous, and this ambiguity creates opportunities for argument and openings for change.
2. Tort law's goal of doing justice and righting interpersonal wrongs creates an inevitable tension in the law, which requires us to engage in a constant process of balancing. To do justice we must learn how to balance competing goals and weigh competing interests at the system level, and how to decide between competing arguments in individual cases.

Tort law mirrors the community (or rather the dominant portions of it) that creates it. It reflects that community's aspirations and flaws. It is meant to preserve human dignity, and individual rights and freedoms, and thereby protect individuals from harm. It changes as the community to which it applies changes. It creates a system that aspires to do justice by correcting the harm caused by wrongs – justice to victims, to wrongdoers and to the community that contains them – and in this sense, it is arguably intrinsically doomed never to live up to its ambitions. However, while tort law remains an imperfect tool administered by imperfect beings, its vision of justice and its goal of discerning acceptable from unacceptable conduct will always offer inspiration to those who join the ongoing community conversation about this aspirational body of law. We pick up the threads of this conversation in the next chapter, where you will learn how to participate in the arguments that mark the law of torts out as one of the most significant and intriguing parts of your early legal education.

Test your understanding ...

... of the nature of justice

1. Explain the difference between corrective justice, retributive justice and distributive justice.
2. Identify the sources of tort law and explain why different law makers have different responsibilities and can make different choices about justice when they make the law.
3. Explain why the tort system may not always achieve perfect justice.

... of the nature of harm

4. Explain the difference between tangible and intangible harms, giving examples of each.
5. Identify two different kinds of interests that the law of torts protects.
6. Explain how the concept of harm creates opportunities for legal arguments.

... of the sources, structure and functions of tort law

7. Identify the two different sources of the law of torts and explain how different law makers have different roles and methods of justifying their choices about the shape of the law of torts.
8. Explain the three-part structure of a torts case.
9. Explain what the 'bilateral' structure of tort law is.
10. Identify the functions of the law of torts and explain how it serves the community.
11. Explain the similarities and differences between contract law, criminal law and the law of torts.

REFERENCES

CASES

Cattanach v Melchior (2003) 215 CLR 1
Harriton v Stephens (2006) 226 CLR 52
McFarlane v Tayside Health Board [2000] 2 AC 59
Magill v Magill (2006) 226 CLR 551
Whitfeld v De Lauret & Co Ltd (1920) 29 CLR 71

ARTICLES, BOOKS AND REPORT

Atiyah, P, *The Damages Lottery* (1997) Hart Publishing, Oxford.
Cane, P, *The Anatomy of Tort Law* (1997) Hart Publishing, Oxford.
Coleman, J L & Ripstein, A, 'Mischief and Misfortune' (1995) 41 *McGill Law Journal* 91.
Conaghan, J & Mansell, W, *The Wrongs of Tort*, 2nd ed (2006) Pluto Press, London.
Howarth, D, 'Is There a Future for the Intentional Torts?', in Birks, P (ed), *The Classification of Obligations* (1997) Oxford University Press, Oxford, 233.
Ipp, D, Cane, P, Sheldon, D & Macintosh, I, *Review of the Law of Negligence: Final Report* (2002) <https://treasury.gov.au/review/review-of-the-law-of-negligence>
Jaffey, P, *Justice in Private Law* (2023) Hart Publishing, London.

TORTS TECHNIQUES: LEGAL ARGUMENT AND PRACTICAL PROBLEM SOLVING

3

Introduction

The first two chapters explained that the law of torts is an evolving body of rules shaped by principles and policy considerations and animated by two different conceptions of justice. It is held in a constant state of tension by individuals' and communities' shifting allegiance between competing interests, goals and values. This means that the law of torts is more than just a set of rules, principles and policy; it is also an ongoing culture of argument that has been developed to manage this inbuilt tension. So, if you want to be successful as a torts student you need to supplement your knowledge of the law by mastering this culture of argument. The first two sections of this chapter will help you to understand how to use the basic building blocks of the law (rules, principles and policy) to construct effective legal arguments. The last two sections will show you how to structure your legal arguments and apply the law to solve practical legal problems.

3.1 Using rules, principles and policy

3.1.1 Defining rules, principles and policy

Before you can understand the arguments made about the law in cases and construct your own arguments in essays and problem-solving exercises, you need to understand the relationship between rules, principles and policy. They are defined below and illustrated in Figure 3.1.

Figure 3.1 Rules are supported by principles and policies

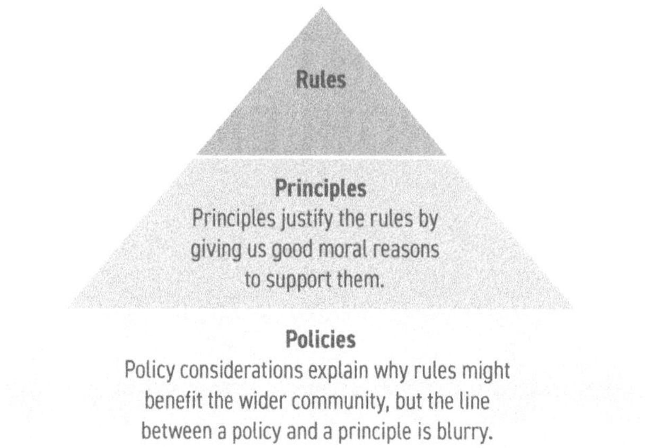

3.1.1.1 Rules, principles and policy

- **Rules** tell us what we should do. A rule is a categorical and precise precept specifying that a distinct legal effect or consequence must follow upon the existence of prescribed facts.
- **Principles** give us good moral reasons for following the rule. A principle is a broad formulation of reasons or generalisations, often moral in nature, that underlie and justify particular rules.
- **Policy justifications** explain why it might benefit the community to have a particular rule. Policy reasons provide an alternative justification for legal rules; however, 'policy' is one of the most difficult terms to define because judges and academics use the term in inconsistent ways to refer to different things. When judges refer to 'policy' they may be referring to any of three different things.
  - A 'policy' is sometimes based on a moral precept (and functions in the same way as a 'principle').
  - The term 'policy' is sometimes used as a shorthand term for a generally accepted approach to a particular issue that has long been established in previous legislative or judicially made rules (the 'policy of the law' or 'legal policy').
  - 'Policy' also describes goal-based arguments of a non-ethical kind that seek to justify a rule on the basis that it will achieve a socially or economically desirable consequence or state of affairs that will benefit society at large or specific portions of it. In this sense, it is usually known as 'public policy'. Policy looks to the social or economic effects of a decision and explains what good it would do to have such a rule.

3.1.2 What is a rule?

A rule is a categorical and precise precept which specifies that a distinct legal effect or consequence must follow upon the existence of certain prescribed facts or the drawing of a particular conclusion. So, a legal rule usually takes the following form: if X exists, then legal consequence Y follows. Remember that each time you cite a legal rule you must identify its source (or 'authority'), which will be either a case or a statute.

Examples

- If plaintiffs put their land to an abnormally sensitive use, they will not be entitled to relief solely because of that hypersensitivity: *Robinson v Kilvert* (1889).
- It is a defence to the publication of defamatory matter if the defendant proves that the circumstances of publication were such that the plaintiff was unlikely to sustain any harm: *Defamation Act 2005* (Tas) s 33.

Legal rules are usually formulated in general terms so they can be applied not just to the case at hand but also to other cases in the future. For example, the famous rule of liability laid down in *Donoghue v Stevenson* (1932) does not mention ginger beer, snails or bottles, but refers more widely to manufacturers of products and their ultimate consumers. Not all legal rules are the same; some are easy to state and apply, whereas others require more work. The list below defines and illustrates four different kinds of rules that you will encounter in your torts courses.

1. **Bright-line rules:** These rules draw a clear and unambiguous line. They are the easiest kind of rules to apply because any given case can only be in or out – there is no zone of uncertainty.

   Example: the rule from *Cole v Turner* (1704) that 'the least touching of another in anger is a battery'.
2. **Fuzzy rules:** Some rules have an inbuilt uncertainty that makes them more challenging and difficult to apply. They may include 'fuzzy' concepts like 'reasonableness' or 'abnormal' in them. Tort law contains many fuzzy rules, especially the torts of nuisance and negligence. The defences also contain many fuzzy terms.

   Example: the remoteness rule from *Overseas Tankship (UK) Ltd v Morts Dock & Engineering Co Ltd* (1961) (*'The Wagon Mound (No 1)'*), which specifies that only the reasonably foreseeable kinds of damage caused by a breach of duty will be compensable.
3. **Complicated rules – or rules with exceptions:** These rules look clear, but require some extra elaboration before you can go ahead and apply them – for example, a definition of a special term or the application of an exception.

   Example: the law of trespass, where you need to understand the legal meaning of 'land' before you can properly apply the rule that forbids trespass to land.
4. **Rules that have been criticised or are out of date:** When you are dealing with these rules, you may need to develop an argument based on the underlying principles, purposes or policies to justify a change or refinement in the rule.

   Example: the rule in *Rylands v Fletcher* (1868) that imposed strict liability on an occupier of land for damage caused by the escape of an inherently dangerous substance or thing brought onto the land in the course of a 'non-natural use' was abolished in *Burnie Port Authority v General Jones Pty Ltd* (1994) after it had been criticised for being out of date and no longer compatible with development of the modern law of negligence.

When you are dealing with a practical problem, the first step is to find out whether there is a well-recognised rule covering your case. If a rule exists then it should be applied to the facts and your argument should be fairly straightforward. If no relevant rule exists, or if one does exist but has been criticised or cast into doubt, you need to provide a more complicated argument that focuses directly on the proper state of the law itself – and only then can you turn to consider how it might apply to the facts.

Case example

Deceit

In the High Court of Australia ('High Court') case of *Magill v Magill* (2006), the judges had to consider first whether the well-recognised tort of deceit (which had been developed in a business setting) could be used in a purely domestic setting before they could then go ahead and apply the established rules of deceit to the facts of the case.

In the torts case of *Cattanach v Melchior* (2003), Justice Kirby explained that when the law is not clear, further guidance can be found in considerations of legal principle and legal policy.[1]

3.1.3 What is a principle?

A legal rule is only as good as the argument that justifies its existence – and the quality of the reasoning used in that argument. As we saw in Chapter 1, one of the most common ways of justifying the existence and content of a legal rule is to show how that rule is based on principle. A principle is a broad formulation of reasons or generalisations, often moral in nature, that underlie and justify particular rules. Many of the principles that you will use are listed in Table 1.2 in Chapter 1. Rules and their principles can be paired together.

Examples

- The principles of bodily integrity and autonomy justify the rule of battery, which states that no person may touch the body of another without lawful justification. They also justify the rule that consent is a defence to battery and the rule that doctors must respect a competent adult's refusal of medical treatment.
- The famous 'neighbour principle' in *Donoghue v Stevenson* (1932) gave rise to a rule about the liability of manufacturers:
    - the *principle* (at 580): 'You must take reasonable care to avoid acts or omissions that you can reasonably foresee would be likely to injure your neighbour.'

1 See *Cattanach v Melchior* (2003) at 42, where Kirby J identified three sources of argument: analogy, legal principle and legal policy.

- the *rule* (at 599): 'A manufacturer of products, which he sells in such form as to show that he intends them to reach their ultimate destination in the form in which they left him ... and with knowledge that the absence of reasonable care ... will result in an injury to the consumer's life or property, owes a duty to the consumer to take that reasonable care.'

The law must be based on principle, but principles on their own are not enough to determine the outcome of a legal dispute. There are two reasons why we need rules as well as principles. The first is that principles are pitched at a higher level of abstraction than a rule – they are necessarily vaguer. This contrast between the more detailed nature of rules and the broader nature of principles can be seen in the example from *Donoghue v Stevenson* (1932), above. The second and equally important reason is the fact that our ethical principles can often point us in different directions. When this occurs, we have to make a choice between them and settle upon a specific rule to guide our conduct in those tricky situations.

Case example

A clash between competing principles can be found in the case of *Magill v Magill* (2006), where the principle of honesty that underpinned the tort of deceit was counterbalanced by the 'welfare of the child' principle and the principle of privacy in reproductive and family matters.

Arguments at this level of debate are often more complicated than arguments about the application of rules to factual scenarios.[2] They are also more likely to lead to disagreement because, as James Boyle and Duncan Kennedy have explained, principles often come in contradicting pairs, so for each argument there is often a valid and equally compelling counterargument.[3]

Examples

- The 'no liability without fault' principle can conflict with the counterprinciple 'as between two innocents she who causes the harm must pay'.
- The principle of altruism requiring one person to avoid causing foreseeable harm to another may conflict with the principle that people should take personal responsibility to protect themselves from harm.

So, you need to understand that, while our system of tort law cannot allow one rule to contradict another rule without risking inconsistency, it does contain principles that can point in different directions and promote competing goods. This feature helps to explain why there is sometimes no obviously 'right answer' to a legal question.

2 There are exceptions to this claim: the judges in the case of *Chappel v Hart* (1998) generally agreed on the relevant law, but split 3:2 on how the law applied to the facts. See section 14.6 of Chapter 14.

3 Boyle, 'The Anatomy of a Torts Class' (1985) at 1052–3. As Boyle points out, arguments based on principle may appear to be very convincing – if the judge uses only one at a time. See also Kennedy, 'A Semiotics of Legal Argument' (1991), for a list of paired arguments and counterarguments.

Case example

- The High Court case of *Cattanach v Melchior* (2003) was closely decided by a 4:3 majority. When you read this case you should try to identify the competing goods that underpinned the arguments made by the minority and majority judges. The community's reaction to the decision was similarly divided.

Cases tend to form clusters of authority on any given issue. So, a case authority specifying a particular formulation of a rule can be described as contrary to principle if it does not fit with the reasoning or the principles found in the wider set of authoritative cases in that area. Furthermore, a new rule may be justified by analysing groups of previous cases and identifying the underlying principle that appears to explain and justify the pattern of past decisions.

Case examples

- Lord Atkin's famous judgment in *Donoghue v Stevenson* (1932) contains an outstanding instance of this method of legal reasoning, as Chapter 10 explains.
- In *Breen v Williams* (1996), Gaudron and McHugh JJ said at 115:

> Advances in the common law must begin from a baseline of accepted principle and proceed by conventional methods of legal reasoning. Judges have no authority to invent legal doctrine that distorts or does not extend or modify accepted legal rules and principles. Any changes in legal doctrine, brought about by judicial creativity, must 'fit' within the body of accepted rules and principles. The judges of Australia cannot, so to speak, 'make it up' as they go along. It is a serious constitutional mistake to think that the common law courts have authority to 'provide a solvent' for every social, political or economic problem. The role of the common law courts is a far more modest one.
>
> In a democratic society, changes in the law that cannot logically or analogically be related to existing common law rules and principles are the province of the legislature. From time to time it is necessary for the common law courts to re-formulate existing legal rules and principles to take account of changing social conditions. Less frequently, the courts may even reject the continuing operation of an established rule or principle. But such steps can be taken only when it can be seen that the 'new' rule or principle that has been created has been derived logically or analogically from other legal principles, rules and institutions. [References omitted.]

Justice requires that like cases should be treated alike. If one principle is favoured over another in one set of legal rules, then this pattern should also be followed in another situation unless it can be distinguished in some morally relevant way.

Case examples

In the negligence cases of *Sullivan v Moody* (2001) and *Tame v New South Wales* (2002), judges refused to impose a duty of care that would have been inconsistent with other duties, principles and remedies existing in another related area of the law, such as defamation.

The consistent application of principle is aimed at ensuring that our body of legal rules forms a rational and morally coherent whole. An awareness of the role played by principle and the need for a series of consistent choices between principles will strengthen your understanding of how the law develops and the way that legal arguments are constructed.

3.1.4 What is policy?

Policy-based arguments are generally contrasted with arguments based on principle. Judges and academics sometimes use the terms 'policy' and 'principle' interchangeably, and Sir Anthony Mason, a former Chief Justice of the High Court, has noted that 'policy' has 'become a hideously inexact word' in legal discourse and pointed out that judges 'have been reticent about the role of policy in judicial decision-making'.[4] Judges sometimes refer to the 'policy of the law' or 'legal policy' when they appear to be making an argument based on principled moral grounds. However, the label of 'public policy' is most often used to refer to arguments of the third kind identified in the rules, principles and policy list in section 3.1.1 above – those that are strictly *political* or *economic* in nature. Ronald Dworkin has suggested that policy-based arguments are used to promote collective economic, political or social goals, by contrast with arguments based on principle, which tend to explain how a rule secures an individual's rights (which are themselves 'based on justice, fairness or some other dimension of morality').[5] Neil MacCormick has suggested that policy arguments justify a legal decision on the grounds that the proposed rule would 'secure a desirable state of affairs' that benefits the community as a whole, rather than the individual parties concerned in the case.[6] As you saw at section 2.1.2 of Chapter 2, this type of policy argument is often (but not always) seen as properly belonging to the role of legislators rather than judges, whereas the first two kinds of 'policy' are more clearly relevant to the judicial role. The issue of policy will arise most frequently to complicate our discussion of the tort of negligence.

Examples

Policy-based arguments

- Justifying a decision on the basis that it is economically desirable to distribute liability for a particular kind of accident among a certain group or party.
- Justifying a decision on the basis that the proposed rule would reduce the number of motor vehicle accidents.
- Suggesting that a proposed rule might lead to too many cases coming before the courts, thereby creating delay and inefficiency (the 'floodgates' argument).

4 Mason, 'Policy Considerations' (2001).

5 Dworkin, *Taking Rights Seriously* (1977) at 22. See also MacAdam and Pyke, *Judicial Reasoning and the Doctrine of Precedent in Australia* (1998), ch 18.

6 See MacAdam and Pyke (1998) at 285, citing MacCormick's 1978 book, *Legal Reasoning and Legal Theory* (1994).

- Allowing barristers a special immunity from a suit in negligence because such suits might lead to endless and costly rounds of litigation.[7]
- Lord Atkin referred to public health as part of the justification for imposing a duty of care on manufacturers in *Donoghue v Stevenson* (1932) at 579.

You need to be aware that some academics refer generally to 'legal principles' as an umbrella term when they discuss the law, whereas others distinguish more precisely between rules and principles. Because of the difficulties associated with the use of the three terms 'rules', 'principles' and 'policy', lawyers, judges and commentators are sometimes tempted to avoid them altogether and use different terminology.[8] So, as well as these three terms mentioned in your reading, you may also find the following terms being used: 'legal concerns', 'legal standards', 'legal arguments', 'legal or moral norms', 'moral standards', 'moral values', 'common sense' and 'aims'. When you read cases you need to make some effort to classify what you find into the categories of rules, principles and policies, but if you become confused, remember that you are reading cases primarily to find the relevant law and to understand the steps in the reasoning used by the judge to construct a convincing legal argument, no matter how the law is classified.

3.1.5 Working with rules, principles and policy in a legal hierarchy

You also need to be familiar with the doctrine of precedent and the concepts of *ratio decidendi* and *stare decisis*. The term '*ratio decidendi*' is notoriously difficult to define, but *Osborn's Concise Law Dictionary* (1983) describes it at 278 as 'the reason or ground of a judicial decision that makes a decision a precedent'. It is often contrasted with the term '*obiter dictum*', which is 'a saying by the way' or an observation by a judge that does not form part of the binding precedent laid down in that case. In *Legal Technique* (2002), Christopher Enright explains (at 235) that the doctrine of *stare decisis* requires a later court to follow a precedent established in an earlier case. Enright highlights three aspects of the doctrine:

- Courts normally follow their own previous decisions, although they are not bound to do so.
- Courts must follow the decisions of higher courts within a hierarchy, unless the authority can be distinguished in some way. Higher courts can overrule decisions of lower courts.
- Where a court is not bound to follow a decision of another court it may still consider it as persuasive.

The term *ratio decidendi* is less significant when you are analysing the arguments and decisions of courts of the highest authority, such as the High Court of Australia or the Supreme Court of the United Kingdom (formerly known as the House of Lords), where the judges are generally free to change the rules laid down in previous cases.

7 Note that the justification for this rule is sometimes referred to as the 'principle' of finality.

8 See Stapleton, 'The Golden Thread at the Heart of Tort Law: Protection of the Vulnerable' (2003) at 242–4.

In these cases, the arguments and the reasoning used to justify the statements of the law are the most important aspects to focus on and the distinction between ratio and obiter is less important. However, if you are reading a case that has been decided by the local courts in your jurisdiction, the distinction would have much more bite, because these courts are all bound by the decisions of those made above them in the hierarchy.

3.1.6 Different legal arguments serve different legal goals

You should be alert to the themes and issues that appear in torts cases and look out for useful examples of judicial reasoning that you can use in your own arguments on similar issues. As you read the cases, you will begin to recognise that there are different patterns of legal reasoning, and it helps you to understand the arguments if you realise that each kind of legal argument tends to serve a different goal, as Table 3.1 explains.

Table 3.1 Six types of legal argument[9]

Arguments	**Legal goals**
Arguments can be based on a rule set down in an authoritative precedent case.	These arguments promote consistency, fairness, stability and certainty in the law.
Arguments can be based on principle.	These arguments allow the law to pursue sound moral goals.
Arguments can be based on policy.	These arguments allow the law to adjust to changing conditions and to achieve useful social, economic or political ends.
Arguments can be based on custom, tradition or longstanding practice.	These arguments accord with community expectations and promote social cohesiveness.
Arguments can be based on the actual words of a statute.	These arguments promote objectivity.
Arguments can be based on the intention of those who created a statute.	These arguments promote parliamentary sovereignty and respect the will of the people's democratically elected representatives.

The most common legal arguments that you will encounter in your torts courses will be those based on precedent, principle, policy and custom. However, given the increasing frequency of statutory intervention, you will encounter the other two types of arguments as well. You should remember that conflicts commonly occur between these different kinds of arguments – for example, arguments based on precedent may conflict with arguments based on principle or policy. When this happens, the judges may have to choose between stability and certainty in the law and the desirability of pursuing moral goals and/or achieving useful social, economic or political ends.

9 Wilson Huhn suggests in *The Five Types of Legal Argument* (2002) that there are five different kinds of legal argument and identifies the different types of values that each tends to serve (at 16). The six examples given in Table 3.1 have been adapted from Huhn's model.

Case example

The House of Lords had to decide the standing rules in the tort of private nuisance in *Hunter v Canary Wharf Ltd* (1997). Competing goals were relied upon by the majority and the minority judges in this case.

The frequency of conflicts between the different kinds of legal arguments creates a degree of uncertainty in the law, and an appreciation of how this uncertainty arises will add to your understanding of the cases that you read and improve the quality of your own analysis in case notes, essays and legal problem-solving exercises.

3.2 The nature of legal argument

3.2.1 Law is a culture of argument

Tort law is embedded in a culture of argument that uses principles and policy considerations to justify the construction and application of rules of conduct that will guide us in the pursuit of justice and the resolution of disputes. It takes time and effort to develop the skills and the knowledge needed to participate in this creative culture of argument. However, once you have mastered the art of legal argument you will be able to apply this skill effectively in a wide range of situations – not just in the legal environment. There are two distinct kinds of arguments that you need to master, and each one relates to tort law's two primary tasks.

- Tort law's first task is to lay down the law for the guidance and benefit of the community as a whole, so you need to learn how to construct persuasive and purposeful arguments about *what the law of torts ought to be.*
- The second task is to resolve individual disputes, so you also need to learn how to construct persuasive arguments that *apply the law of torts to solve practical legal problems.*

3.2.2 Legal arguments are purposeful arguments

The law of torts serves the community; it reflects the community's values, it responds to the community's changing needs and it must conform to the community's sense of justice. Consequently, you will gain a deeper understanding of how to argue about the proper state of the law of torts if you can point out that your suggestion for reforming the law will better reflect these wider goals and functions. Your arguments will be strengthened if you can relate them to a convincing and compelling purpose that will help you to persuade others of the correctness of your client's point of view.

Examples

- If your argument is about advancing sound moral principles – explain how it does this by relating it to one of tort law's *guiding principles* listed in Table 1.1.
- If your argument is about better serving the needs of the community – explain how by relating it to one of the *functions* of the law of torts listed in section 2.2.3 of Chapter 2.

- If your argument is consistent with the demands of the law itself – explain how it upholds one or more of the *legal goals and values* outlined in this chapter.
- If your argument is appealing to a broader sense of justice – explain how by relating it to the demands of *corrective* or *distributive justice* discussed in section 2.1 of Chapter 2.

3.2.3 Lawyers consider both sides of an issue

It is easy to spot someone who has learned how to argue like a lawyer. Good lawyers always consider both sides of an issue and test their own position for strengths *and* weaknesses. The nature of legal reasoning, the structure of the adversarial system and the requirements of professional practice make it crucial not only to develop your own arguments but also to anticipate and try to defeat any possible counterarguments that your opponents may make. You need to develop this special 'double vision' and learn how to see matters from the standpoint not only of the early bird but also of the worm. This, too, is a skill that needs practice. So, when you are reading cases, you should pay attention not only to the reasoning put forward by the majority judges but also to the counter-reasoning developed by the minority judges; and when you are constructing your own arguments in problem-solving exercises, moots and essays, you should take a critical approach that considers both sides of an issue and seeks out any alternative approaches to the law and any other interpretations of the facts.

As you saw in section 3.2 above, lawyers and judges can choose from a large menu of arguments and counterarguments that are derived from a range of different sources. It is critical to realise that these different arguments – based on precedent, principles, policy considerations and the nature of justice – may not all point in the same direction. Consequently, there will always be counterarguments to deal with when you are arguing about the proper state of the law, so remember to look for them. Furthermore, when you must apply the law to the facts of a case, and when you are interviewing your clients and advising them about their case, you always need to stop and consider two questions:

- Do you have all the relevant facts?
- How can the facts be interpreted – and are there any counterinterpretations?

Success as a lawyer (and as a law student) depends on your ability to construct an argument about the law that can withstand any counterarguments and an interpretation of the facts that will be more persuasive than any counterinterpretations.

3.2.4 Legal arguments exploit ambiguity and uncertainty

One of the lawyer's greatest skills lies in identifying and dealing with ambiguity and uncertainty – either in the law itself or in the facts of a problem. In fact, as Christopher Enright points out, legal issues often arise out of ambiguity.[10] Many of the cases that you will discuss in your torts classes have been selected because they offer classic examples of occasions when the law was uncertain. Chapter 1 explained why a certain degree of

10 Enright, *Legal Technique* (2002), ch 12. See also Enright, *Studying Law* (1991).

ambiguity is unavoidable in a subject like the law of torts; however, students sometimes find it difficult to deal properly with ambiguity at first.

Example

Students may try to fill in the gaps in the facts of a problem question without realising that their lecturers have deliberately created the ambiguity in order to find out whether the students can spot the uncertainty, identify the issue and construct an argument that responds to it correctly.

To be a good lawyer, you have to stop seeing things from only one perspective and train yourself to recognise that the Mona Lisa might be either happy or sad.

The way to deal with ambiguity in either the law or the facts is to 'answer both ways' or 'argue in the alternative'. You must recognise that whenever the *law* is uncertain or unclear or whenever the *facts* are unclear or missing, the case may turn out differently depending on which view of the law the court takes and what the true facts are. So, whenever you come to the point of uncertainty, you must work out where the alternative paths may lead – and be prepared to follow both of them – to find out whether they will be successful or not. Once you recognise that uncertainty offers a lawyer one of the best opportunities to demonstrate the art of legal argument, you will learn not only how to *spot* ambiguity, but also how to *create* ambiguity where at first there may appear to be complete certainty.

3.2.5 Legal arguments are made in words

Although a certain degree of uncertainty in the law is unavoidable, and despite the fact that lawyers are trained to detect and exploit ambiguity, you must recognise that too much ambiguity and uncertainty in your own arguments is counterproductive. Lawyers and law students must strive to:

- be as precise as possible in their statements of the law;
- be as accurate as possible in their description of the facts; and
- use clear, uncluttered language in their arguments about the law.

Keep legalese and jargon to a minimum. Do not try to show off. Avoid useless generalisations that serve only to leave your intended audience languishing in a fog of uncertainty. Vagueness in communication and in argument is the enemy of the law; so you should be picky, precise and pernickety – and learn to think before you speak or write. Law is laid down and communicated in words and your assessment exercises are all conducted in words, so learn how to use them well. Work on your spelling, sentence structure and grammar. Easy writing makes for hard reading; so, do the work for your clients and your assessors and do not make them struggle to decipher your meaning. The law is sometimes complex and confusing, and this is all the more reason to let your cleverness reveal itself through clarity – and not through convolution. If you experience difficulty, find help and take the time to fix the problem. Try your university's study support service or consult one of these excellent books on this topic:

- *Grammar for Lawyers* (2007) by Michael Meehan and Graham Tulloch; and
- *Legal Skills* (2006) by Bobette Wolski, David Field and John Bahrij.

3.2.6 Legal arguments are structured arguments

Tort law is structured, and early mastery of the structure principle is one of the keys to success as a torts student. The structure principle has three distinct aspects:

- The analysis of a torts case is structured on the elements, the defences and the remedies.
- Legal arguments are structured arguments.
- Legal writing is structured writing.

Your legal arguments must have a clear and logical structure and your assignments, when they contain these arguments, must also have a clear and well-ordered structure. The next section recommends a flexible and adaptable method, known as 'FIRO', which will give structure to your torts assignments. It also explains another method, known as 'HIRAC', that will help you structure the legal arguments that will appear in your problem-solving exercises. FIRO structures *assignments*, whereas HIRAC structures legal *arguments*.

In some assessment tasks, particularly in torts problem-solving assignments, you will need to use both methods of giving structure to your work. Each of these methods is explained in detail in sections 3.3 and 3.4.

3.3 The structure of legal argument

3.3.1 Introducing FIRO: How to structure an assignment

FIRO is a useful tool for structuring a range of legal assessment tasks. Most written and oral assignments should move through three key stages:

- The beginning – or introduction – identifies the **F**acts and the **I**ssues.
- The middle – or body – of the assignment presents the arguments and explains the **R**easoning used to deal with those issues.
- The end – or conclusion – identifies the **O**utcome of the reasoning process and explains its significance.

This general organising structure can be adapted for essays, problem questions, case notes, moots and oral presentations. This section demonstrates, in a general way, how to use FIRO for three of the most common tasks in torts courses, and how to structure an answer to a problem question. Chapter 4 will show you how to construct a case note, an essay and an oral presentation.

3.3.1.1 Structuring common assessment tasks with FIRO

The beginning identifies the facts and the issues, the middle explains the reasoning and the end explains the significance of the outcome.

Facts

Facts identify the reason why the dispute, debate or question has arisen.

- In a problem question: Identify the key facts about the dispute.
- In a case note: Identify the key facts about the dispute.

- In an essay: Identify the factual background to the topic that makes this question important.

Issues

- In a problem question: Identify the legal issues relating to the state of the law and/or its application to the facts.
- In a case note: Identify the legal issues relating to the state of the law and/or its application to the facts.
- In an essay: Identify the issues arising from the question and explain how you will deal with them.

Note: In some assignments you may also consider adding a quick statement of your preferred conclusion into your introduction to assist the reader to follow your reasoning.

Reasoning

Present the arguments and the counterarguments about the issues, using HIRAC where appropriate to give structure to the reasoning.

- In a problem question: Deal with each issue that arises, covering the plaintiff's case, the defendant's case and the remedies, using HIRAC to structure your argument on the issues. Remember: there may be more than one issue.
- In a case note: Explain the steps in the judges' reasoning, including both majority and minority judges.
- In an essay: Present the arguments, provide evidence, cite sources and rebut any counterarguments.

Outcome

- In a problem question: Identify the likely result and remedy.
- In a case note: Identify the result, the ratio and its significance.
- In an essay: Identify the desired outcome and its significance.

3.3.2 Introducing HIRAC: How to argue an issue

The arguments that you make in your torts problem-solving exercises also need to be structured. There are different mnemonic formulas that can assist you to structure your arguments on these issues so that you can 'argue like a lawyer'.[11] Five of these organising methods (HIRAC, IRAC, ILAC, MIRAT and FIRO) are compared in Table 3.2, where the acronyms are explained. These methods attempt to demystify the process of legal argument, but, as Kathy Laster points out in *Law as Culture* (2001) at 195, HIRAC is not a foolproof system that can be applied automatically or unthinkingly. Legal argument requires a certain amount of flexibility, imagination and creativity and no formula can capture everything that you need for success. There are times when the highly stylised HIRAC approach can help you – and there are times when you simply have to abandon the formula and set out to develop your own style and adapt the method to suit the circumstances. By the time

11 For a discussion of the HIRAC formula, see Laster, *Law as Culture* (2001) at 194. For the IRAC method, see Krever, *Mastering Law Studies and Exam Techniques* (2011) at 64. ILAC is found in Brogan and Spencer, *Surviving Law School* (2007) at 90 and MIRAT can be found in Wade, 'Meet MIRAT' (1990–91).

you graduate, you will have absorbed the deeper structure of legal argument and will be able to employ it without needing to slavishly follow such a step-by-step guide.

Table 3.2 Comparison of legal argument organising methods

HIRAC	IRAC	ILAC	MIRAT	FIRO
Heading	–	–	**M**aterial facts	**F**acts
Issue	**I**ssue	List the **I**ssues	**I**ssues of law and policy	**I**ssues
Rule	**R**ule	List the **L**aw	**R**ules and **R**esources	**R**easoning
Application	**A**pplication	Make the **A**rgument	**A**rguments/**A**pplication	**O**utcome
Conclusion	**C**onclusion	Make a **C**onclusion	**T**entative conclusion	–

You can see that each of these approaches reminds you to do much the same thing:

- Identify the issues that arise from the facts.
- Identify the relevant law.
- Present the arguments and the counterarguments, applying the law to the facts.
- Come to a conclusion on the issue.

The next subsection will explain in more detail how to use the HIRAC method to argue out an issue, and Part 2 will give further examples of how to answer practical problem-solving exercises. However, you should understand that HIRAC is *not* the method of answering legal problem-solving questions – it is a method of structuring a legal argument on a given issue. As you will see in section 3.4 below, the art of legal problem solving involves much more than HIRAC. Section 3.3.1.1 above outlines the FIRO structure and shows you where the HIRAC method fits into that larger scheme. Section 3.3.2.1 explains how to use the HIRAC formula to argue out a legal issue. Section 3.4 will give more detailed advice on how to put them together to produce a good answer to a problem-solving question and that advice is summarised at the end of this chapter.

3.3.2.1 Structuring a legal argument using HIRAC

Heading

- Headings identify the content of the discussion and 'signpost' the structure.
- A heading is usually a keyword from an element of a tort or a defence – for example, 'Intentional act', 'Breach of duty' or 'Contributory negligence'. If you are using IRAC instead of HIRAC, use the issue as your heading and underline the keywords. (See example below.)

Issue

- Identify the legal issue by linking the relevant facts to the relevant law. An issue is often phrased as a question – for example, 'Did Dr Dullwit (D) breach his duty to the patient, Ms Jones (P), by failing to advise her of the risk that she could lose the sight in her good eye as a result of the elective surgery on her blind eye?'

Rule (or law)

- State the law that will be used to resolve the issue, but remember that the law consists of rules, principles, policies and other standards and tests for liability, so the term 'rule' is used here as a shortcut for all of the relevant law.
- The law must be precisely stated and must be accompanied by an authority, either a case authority or a statute. For example:

> At common law, a doctor has a duty to advise the patient of all material risks inherent in the proposed treatment: that is, if in the circumstances of the particular case, a reasonable person in the patient's position, if warned of the risk, would be likely to attach significance to it, or if the medical practitioner is or should reasonably be aware that the particular patient, if warned of the risk, would be likely to attach significance to it. (*Rogers v Whitaker* (1992))

- If the law is unclear or has been criticised, you may need to include an argument on the proper state of the law by identifying the options and discussing them in more detail before applying the law to the facts.

Application, analysis and arguments

- Turn to the facts and explain whether the legal rule, standard or test can be satisfied on the facts of the problem.
- This part, which applies the law to the facts, should normally be the longest part of your answer.
- Be alert for any ambiguity or uncertainty in the facts and 'argue both ways'.
- Always consider both sides of the issue: are there any counterarguments on the law, or counterinterpretations of the facts that could be made?

Conclusion

- Finally, come to a conclusion on the issue (if it is possible to do so).
- If your conclusion is only tentative because the facts or the law are unclear, identify the most significant findings of fact or law that will make the critical difference to the outcome in this case.

3.4 Answering torts problem-solving questions

3.4.1 Overview

Legal problem-solving questions are the most common form of assessment in torts courses. Consequently, the art of legal problem-solving is one of the most important skills to master. These questions require you to analyse a set of facts and:

- identify the torts – or causes of action – that may arise;
- identify the legal issues that may be raised;
- identify the relevant law that can be used to resolve those issues; and then
- apply the relevant law to the facts by producing a set of arguments and counterarguments that lead to a possible solution to those issues.

The rest of this section explains how to work with the law, the facts and the arguments. It will give you advice on how to diagnose the issues and structure an answer to a torts problem-solving exercise. Before we embark on this discussion, there are two important pieces of advice to take on board:

- Remember that a tort is conduct by one person that can harm another person.
- Structure your analysis around the three main aspects of a torts case: the elements, the defences and the remedies associated with each cause of action.

3.4.2 Torts have a double focus on conduct and its effects

All torts have a double focus: they consist of conduct by one person that has an adverse effect on another person. The typical pattern of a torts case begins when a defendant (D) wrongfully harms a plaintiff (P) and ends when the law requires the defendant to compensate the plaintiff for that harm. So, being able to put the 'conduct and effect' pairs together is a basic skill that you need to learn. This technique is vitally important. In fact, if you identify these two aspects clearly and precisely from the facts right at the start, you are halfway to understanding a torts case and well on the way to writing a good answer to any problem question. Why? The answer lies in the 'bilateral' nature of tort law, which continually requires you to focus on both the conduct and its effects when you are arguing out the elements and defences and again when you try to find the proper remedy. You need to know what the conduct is, so that you can apply the law to work out if it is wrongful – and you need to identify the effect so that you can work out what the proper remedy will be. Linking the conduct and effect in each case will help you to identify the tort that the plaintiff can use to obtain their remedy and the issues that need to be argued out, so it also helps you to diagnose the problem. As you will see, if you can identify the critical facts correctly at the beginning, you improve your chances of getting the analysis right at the end.

The answer to the questions 'What did the defendant do?' and 'What harm did it cause?' must be answered by focusing on the facts, and not on the law. The following sentences show the difference between a purely factual description of a case and the legal conclusion that might result from applying the law of negligence to those facts.

Case example

- Stevenson (D), a manufacturer of soft drinks, allowed a snail to get into an opaque bottle before he filled it with ginger beer, which resulted in a consumer, Donoghue (P), suffering gastroenteritis and shock when she drank the contents.
- The defendant was negligent and should pay damages to the plaintiff.[12]

Learn to separate the two accounts of the case. Your first focus should always be on the facts – and only then should you move on to the second step and work out the legal significance of those facts. People go to lawyers because they are upset about the way someone else has treated them and hope the law will offer them a solution to their problems.

12 *Donoghue v Stevenson* (1932).

However, your clients will not walk into your office with their problems neatly packaged and laid out in clear legal terms. A lawyer's job is to translate the story of facts into a plausible and convincing story of law – but it is important to understand the difference between these two views of the world. Students often find this difficult at first, so it is important to practise the skill consciously every time you read a case or analyse a problem question. In time, it will become second nature and it will help you at every step of your journey through your torts course. We will return to this matter in subsequent subsections, where it will become clear just how important it is. In the meantime, hold on to this thought: look at the facts first and link the conduct and the effects together – then look at the law.

3.4.3 Use a three-stage analysis: Elements, defences and remedies

The next tip is to structure your analysis following the three main stages of a case:

- The first stage focuses on whether a plaintiff can prove a prima facie case by showing that every element of the tort is satisfied.
- The second stage focuses on whether the defendant can avoid a finding of liability by raising any of the available defences to the tort.
- The third stage considers the appropriate remedy.

Remember that each tort consists of a set of elements. To win the case, the plaintiff must prove every element. If the defendant can argue successfully that one of the elements has not been made out, the plaintiff will lose. Each tort also has a set of defences that may allow the defendant to escape liability. To win the case, the defendant only has to prove the existence of one of those defences. Finally, each tort has its own set of remedies, and the onus is on plaintiffs to prove that they qualify under the rules. Defendants will try to argue that the conditions set down by those rules have not been satisfied. Bear in mind that the rules on the onus of proof in tort law vary, depending on the tort.

3.4.3.1 The onus of proof in tort law

The general rule is that the plaintiff must prove all of the elements of the tort, whereupon the onus shifts to the defendant to prove lawful justification or a defence. This rule applies for the following torts:

- action on the case for physical injury;
- action on the case for nervous shock;
- action for severe emotional distress (possible new tort);
- conversion;
- detinue;
- defamation;
- negligence;
- nuisance; and
- privacy torts (possible new torts).

If the defendant is unable to avoid liability, the onus is on the plaintiff to prove their entitlement to a remedy.

3.4.3.2 The trespass torts

In the trespass torts, the onus is on the plaintiff to prove only the direct interference with the protected interest, whereupon the onus shifts to the defendant to avoid liability by disproving fault or proving a lawful justification or a defence. So, the trespass torts are an exception to the general rule that the plaintiff must prove all of the elements of the tort. The following are the trespass torts:

- battery;
- assault;
- false imprisonment;
- trespass to goods; and
- trespass to land.

If the defendant is unable to avoid liability, the onus is on the plaintiff to prove their entitlement to a remedy.

It is worth remembering that the term 'defence' can be used in different ways in each of the three different stages of a torts case. It is most commonly used to refer to the *classic defences* (eg self-defence, necessity, etc in the intentional torts, or truth, qualified privilege, etc in defamation), but sometimes a defendant's *counterargument* on the *elements* or the *remedies* is called a 'defence'. To avoid confusion, this book will refer to 'the elements of a tort' and 'the ingredients of a defence', and will restrict use of the term 'defence' to the classic defences. A consideration of each of the three stages of a case should appear in a full answer to a problem question. However, before you can write and structure your answer you have to diagnose the problem.

3.4.4 How to diagnose the problem and write an introduction

Diagnosing a problem question is done in two parts. First, you have to identify the parties to any possible causes of action and the relevant torts. Then you have to identify the issues. Once you have completed these tasks you can write an effective introduction. (Remember: the **FIRO** structure begins with the **F**acts and the **I**ssues.)

Examples

- To diagnose the *tort* and the *parties*, you have to focus on the facts. Identify and link the conduct and its effects first, and then find a tort that will offer the plaintiff a remedy.
- To diagnose the *legal issues*, work your way methodically through the elements of the tort, the ingredients of any relevant defences, and the rules relating to any available remedies.

To do these tasks successfully you need a 'look-up chart' that serves as a checklist of the torts and their elements, the defences and their ingredients, and the rules on awarding damages. There is a 'Look-up' section at the end of Chapter 7 containing a number of figures that set out the elements of the intentional torts and the defences to them. Remember that the same set of facts can give rise to more than one tort.

The best way to identify the tort is to work backwards from the harm or damage suffered by any person in your problem question. Remember: people consult a lawyer either because they want a remedy for the harm or loss that they have suffered (or may suffer in the future) or because they have been sent a letter demanding a remedy. So, the first step is to look for harm. The person who suffers the harm will usually become the plaintiff. The person whose conduct led to that harm will usually become the defendant. Once you have identified these four crucial facts, you need to work out which torts can best be used to give a remedy to the plaintiff. This requires knowledge of the focal points of each tort that is covered in your course. In the *trespass torts* each tort has a particular focus that will help you to diagnose the appropriate tort.

Examples

- The harm of physical contact with the body relates to the tort of **battery.**
- The harm of mental apprehension of physical contact relates to the tort of **assault.**
- The harm of total confinement relates to the tort of **false imprisonment.**
- The harm of possession of goods relates to the tort of **trespass to goods.**
- The harm of exclusive possession of land relates to the **tort of trespass to land.**

If the question focuses on the tort of *negligence*, you should not only look for harms, but you should also classify the kind of harm done: is it physical harm to the person or to property, pure mental harm (or psychiatric harm), pure economic loss, etc? Then you should look at the way the harm was caused, the context in which it occurred and the person or legal body that caused it: was it a case of an act or an omission, product liability, professional negligence, occupier's liability, a rescue, a misstatement, a public authority, etc? The combination of these facts – that is, the kind of harm that has been caused, the way that the harm was caused and the context in which it occurred – will lead you to identify the species of negligence (and then the specific issues peculiar to the case).

Figure 3.2 The 'six-point plan'

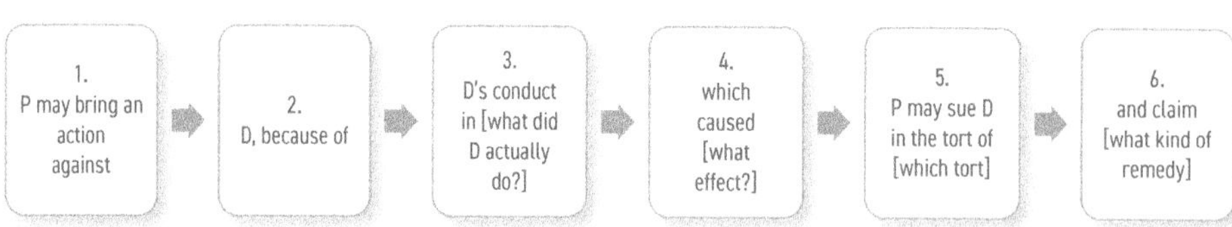

These crucial pieces of information can then be woven into a useful sentence that will go straight into the first paragraph of your introduction to your problem-solving answer. You can remember this sentence as the 'six-point plan', which is laid out in Figure 3.2 and which answers some important factual questions.

Example

- *Who* is upset with *whom?* This usually identifies the parties: the plaintiff and the defendant.
- *Why* are they upset? This directs you to the *conduct* and its *effects.*
- *What* do they want? This directs you to the *remedy* for those harmful effects.
- *How* can they get it? This directs you to the *tort* that may provide the remedy.

Once you have identified the possible torts, you need to work out what the issues are so you can complete your introduction. Two different kinds of issues may arise: some arise because the law itself may be uncertain, others arise because there may be some uncertainty about how the law should be applied to the facts of the problem. The first kind of issue is purely legal, and your checklist or summary of the law should identify areas where the law may be uncertain. Issues of the second kind are more difficult to identify. If the issue does not immediately jump into your mind as you read the facts of the problem, you can use your checklist to identify the issues by a process of elimination.

Begin your analysis by working in a methodical way through the elements of the tort to see if they can be satisfied on the facts. Then move to the next stage, where you focus on any possible defences and work out if they can be made out. Finally, look at the rules relating to the remedies and see if they can be satisfied. It is this systematic linking of law and facts together that allows you to diagnose the issues. This is a vitally important step in problem solving, not only because it helps you to write an effective and efficient introduction using the FIRO formula, but also because, once you have identified the number of issues that you have to argue out in depth using the HIRAC method, you can plan the rest of your answer. In exams, this is a critically important step because it helps you to allocate your time efficiently: if you have 40 minutes to discuss four issues, you know that you have only 10 minutes to do each one. (This approach also offers you some insurance if you run out of time in an exam, because your examiners will still be able to give you credit for identifying the issues, even if they cannot give you all the marks for arguing them out in full detail.)

Bear in mind that not every element of a tort or every defence will necessarily give rise to an arguable issue. However, at the diagnostic stage you do have to consider all of them and check them off one by one. If you *cannot be sure* whether one of these elements or ingredients can be satisfied on the facts of the case, then it is likely that you *have found an issue.* Later on, when you write up your answer you will have to discuss it in detail using the HIRAC method. On the other hand, if you can quickly see that one of the elements or ingredients can *easily be established,* this suggests that it is *not an issue* that needs to be given the in-depth HIRAC treatment. Once you have identified which aspects of the dispute will be in contention, you can add a list of those issues to your introduction and commence writing the body of your answer. Remember: *uncertainty* is the key that will help you to identify the issues that have to be argued out using the full HIRAC method. It may often be the case that some of the elements of the torts and some of the ingredients of the defences will be very easy to establish on the facts of your problem question, while others may require a more complicated discussion. As you develop your skills and confidence in problem solving, you will learn when to be brief and when to go into greater depth of argument and analysis. Here is a quick summary of the matters that should be included in an introduction.

Example

Petunia (P) wishes to sue Jemima (D) in the tort of battery for her conduct in 'stabbing Petunia with a knife', causing 'a deep wound' and a 'significant loss of blood' and resulting in Petunia having 'extensive medical treatment' and 'losing four weeks off work'. Petunia seeks damages for the invasion of her right to bodily integrity and for her consequent economic losses. Petunia will not have any difficulty in establishing a prima facie case as the facts indicate that 'Jemima ran screaming at Petunia and plunged the knife into her belly'. The real issue is whether Jemima was acting lawfully in self-defence.

Do not introduce the answer by repeating all of the facts of the problem, or by giving a long-winded essay on the history of the tort. Above all, do not be vague – it will not score any marks to say: 'Petunia is upset with Jemima for her outrageous and tortious conduct and wants redress.' Remember that you probably do not need to include any other information in an introduction to a problem question. Do not waste time or words rewriting all of the facts of the problem question. Select only the important ones; get to the point efficiently and move on to the discussion of the issues.

3.4.5 How to structure the body of the answer

The structure of a torts case should be mirrored in the structure of your answer to a problem-solving question. At each stage, be aware of the onus of proof (see section 3.4.3.1 above) and factor it into the pattern of your discussion: when you are considering the elements and the remedies, the plaintiff's arguments should be followed by the defendant's counterarguments; when you are considering the defences, the defendant's arguments should come first and be followed by the plaintiff's counterarguments. This is the pattern:

- *Stage 1: Elements*
  Plaintiff's arguments
  Defendant's counterarguments
- *Stage 2: Defences*
  Defendant's arguments
  Plaintiff's counterarguments
- *Stage 3: Remedies*
  Plaintiff's arguments
  Defendant's counterarguments.

Many problem-solving questions ask you to advise one of the particular parties, whereas others ask you to discuss the issues that arise from the set of facts from a more general perspective. However, if you use this standard organising structure, you can see why it does not really matter which of the parties you have been asked to advise – your answer should follow the same basic arrangement whether you have been asked to advise the plaintiff or the defendant. It is a common error to assume that you should provide only one side of a case when you have been asked to 'Advise X'. Remember, when you are advising your clients, you should always explain both the strengths and the weaknesses of their case so they can make an informed decision. Problem-solving questions offer you the chance to demonstrate your skills, and one of those skills is the ability to see both sides of an argument.

At the first stage of analysis, you need to remember that every element must be satisfied before a prima facie case can be made out. However, at the second stage, only one of the available defences needs to be made out for the defendant to escape liability. This means that while your answer *must* methodically consider every one of the elements, you do not need to methodically discuss every one of the defences. Instead, discuss only the defences that are open on the facts. This is the difference between *diagnosing* a problem and *answering* a problem. You need to run through all of relevant law as you diagnose the problem to find out which parts need to be discussed in detail, but when you are writing the answer you do not have to treat everything in the same depth.

- Remember: *every* element must be addressed at stage 1, but you must use HIRAC to discuss in depth *only* those elements that give rise to an arguable issue.
- Remember: only the *relevant* defences need to be discussed at stage 2, but *every* ingredient of the relevant defence must be considered. Use HIRAC only for the ingredients of the defence that give rise to an arguable issue.

3.4.6 HIRAC: How to formulate the issues

Legal rules are usually formulated in general terms so they can be applied not just to the case at hand but also to other cases. So, when you attempt to resolve a particular dispute by applying the law to the specific facts of a problem question, you have to link:

- the relevant *generally* stated law to
- the relevant *specific* facts in the problem.

This linking procedure shows you how to formulate the issues in a problem question. Issues can be posed as a question, and are based on the relevant rule or standard, as illustrated by process outlined in section 3.3.2.1 above. It is at this point, where you have to link the facts and the relevant legal rule together, that you will reap the full benefits of having taken the time to identify carefully the conduct and the effects from the facts. To formulate the issue, you often have to 'plant' the facts of your particular legal problem into the generally stated elements of the law. This technique is best explained by an example. Here are the elements of the tort of deceit, taken from the High Court case of *Magill v Magill* (2006) at [114]:

1. The defendant made a false representation/statement.
2. The defendant made the representation with the knowledge that it was false (or was reckless or careless as to whether the representation was false or not).
3. The defendant made the representation with the intention that it be relied upon by the plaintiff.
4. The plaintiff must have acted in reliance on the representation.
5. The plaintiff suffered damage which was caused by reliance on the false representation.

Using the FIRO structure and the 'six-point plan' we can write an introduction.

Case example

The plaintiff, Liam Magill, was upset with the defendant, his former wife Meredith Magill, because she wrote his name down in the section titled 'father' on the birth registration certificates for her second and third children, who were born during the course of the marriage. This led him to believe that he was their father. After DNA testing proved that he was not the father of these two children, he sued her in the tort of deceit claiming compensatory and punitive damages for personal injury (consisting of anxiety and depression), lost earnings that flowed from his injury (lost income) and other financial losses related to the time and costs associated with the upkeep of the children.

There are two main issues in this case. The first is the general question of whether the tort of deceit, which was developed in a business or commercial setting, could properly be used in a case of paternity fraud set in a domestic environment. The remaining issues relate to whether Mr Magill could prove the five elements of the tort on the facts of the case.

Assuming that each of the five elements of the tort of deceit could give rise to an arguable issue in this case, we can now easily identify those issues by combining the law and the facts. Note that some of the following examples are written as statements, whereas others illustrate the question format.

Examples

1. Did Mrs Magill make a false representation that Mr Magill was the father of the two children when she wrote his name down in the section titled 'father' on the birth registration forms and gave them to him to sign?
2. The second issue is whether, when Mrs Magill wrote Mr Magill's name on the birth registration forms as 'father', she knew that the representation was false (or was reckless as to the truth of that fact).
3. The third issue is whether Mrs Magill intended that Mr Magill should rely on the representation that he was the father, which was written on the birth registration forms.
4. The fourth issue is whether Mr Magill acted in reliance on the false representation written on the birth registration forms.
5. Did Mr Magill suffer the damage of personal injury (consisting of anxiety and depression), lost earnings that flowed from his injury (lost income) and other financial losses related to the time and costs associated with the upkeep of the children as a result of relying on the false representation contained on the birth registration forms?

The task of identifying and linking the conduct and the effects is deceptively simple. In fact, your selection and description of the facts can make the difference between winning and losing. When you are identifying the conduct being complained of by the plaintiff, there will often be a range of different alternatives that you can choose from. Some will be broad and some may be narrower. For example, in *Magill* the conduct was narrowly identified as writing Mr Magill's name down in the section titled 'father' on the birth registration forms. When you read the case, you can see why this tactical decision was so significant and how it determined the way that the case was argued. Mr Magill lost his case in the High Court, in part because of the narrow grounds upon which he based his claim. The result may have turned out differently if a wider description of Mrs Magill's conduct had been used. As an exercise, try reformulating the issues in this case if Mrs Magill's conduct had been described more widely as encouraging him by her words and conduct to believe that he was the father of the children before, during and after the birth of the two children.

3.4.7 HIRAC: Applying the rules to the facts

Once you have identified the relevant tort and its elements and begin to apply the law to the facts of your problem question, you should identify the relevant legal rules. Not all legal rules are the same; some are easy to apply and others require more work. Each different kind of rule requires a different response in problem-solving questions.

Examples

Bright-line rules

These are the easiest rules to apply – so long as you have all of the facts! To make your task more difficult, your lecturer may leave some of the critical facts out of the problem question (see the 'Missing facts' example below).

Fuzzy rules

These fuzzy rules are the most difficult to apply – because even reasonable people may disagree on whether something is reasonable. (A parent's idea of a 'reasonably tidy' bedroom may differ greatly from a teenager's.) Remember that when you are applying a fuzzy rule, you may need to refer to some factual examples from the case law to assist you in arguing out the rule's application. (You will see how to make a useful summary of the law in Chapter 4.)

Complicated rules – or rules with exceptions

You need to be careful here; avoid jumping straight in to apply this kind of rule to the facts. Make sure that your summary of the law includes all the relevant exceptions and definitions so that you do not miss them.

Unclear, out-of-date or criticised rules

When you are dealing with these kinds of rules, you may need to present an argument about the proper state of the law before you go ahead and apply the law to the facts. These arguments should be based on the underlying principles, policy matters, or purposes of the tort. Remember to consider any counterarguments and be aware that when you apply an uncertain rule to the facts, you need to 'answer both ways' (as illustrated below).

Identifying the relevant law is often straightforward; however, there will be occasions when the law is uncertain and in these cases you may need to resolve any difficulties with the rules first before you go on to apply the law to the facts.

The facts that you may find in a torts problem question also come in varying types, and, just like the different rules, different fact patterns require different responses.

Examples

Missing facts

In a 'missing fact' scenario, the essential fact that you need to resolve the issue may not be included – or may have been deliberately left out to test you. So, when you realise that you cannot find all the information that you need, you must 'answer both ways'. It will not earn any marks to say:

> The facts do not enable me to apply this rule; therefore, more information will be needed and it will be up to the court to decide.

In this situation you need to use your knowledge of the cases to explain the kinds of facts that you would be looking for, and then, using your imagination, provide examples of the specific facts that, if found, would win the case and examples of facts that would lose it. Be careful not to assume facts – this is a common student error. When your lecturer goes to the trouble of leaving a fact out, you should not assume facts to fill the gaps – but if you do, at least say clearly that you have done so.

Implied facts

Sometimes you are not told the key fact that you need, but instead you are given some other facts that allow you to 'put two and two together'. So, be on the alert for facts that allow you to deduce the existence of other critical facts or allow you to make an argument suggesting that they could exist.

Facts that point in different directions

Law teachers often plant facts in a problem question that favour one party, and then include more facts that allow the opposite party to make a counterargument. (This is often the case when you are being tested on a fuzzy rule that includes the concept of reasonableness within it.) In these problems where the facts run in different directions, you should be careful to look at both sides of the arguments that can be made. Always look for what each side will argue and do not content yourself with taking only one side of the facts: part of advising your clients involves telling them both the strengths and weaknesses of their case.

Tricky or provocative facts

Students sometimes take a dislike to one of the characters in a problem question – or feel sorry for another character. Be careful here, as the law may actually favour the unattractive character; if you let your emotions get in the way you may blind yourself to the arguments. You should also be very careful not to jump to conclusions on the basis of stereotypes or generalisations about people.

Bad facts

Sometimes you simply have a bad fact staring you in the face. You can try to argue your way around it, but it may just be that this is a situation where you can easily apply a rule, come quickly to a conclusion and then get on to the next issue. On the other hand, sometimes a fact looks 'bad' only because the rule that you are trying to apply is 'bad' or in need of updating. If you can get the rule changed (perhaps by arguing for an exception), then the fact may not look so bad at all. So, do not give up if the facts appear to be against you. Use your skills and imagination to come up with something to argue.

Learn how to read the facts carefully: work out exactly what they tell you and what they leave uncertain. Never assume, generalise, or fill in the gaps in the facts. Do not create certainty by making up facts or generalising about stereotypes. Become hard-nosed when you read the facts and imaginative when you seek out the possibilities:

- Work out what you *do know* for a fact.
- Work out what you *don't know* at all.
- Use your imagination to work out the possibilities that *could exist* so that you can come up with arguments and counterarguments on the issues.

The methods of dealing with certainty and uncertainty in your problem-solving exercises are explained in the next subsection.

3.4.8 Dealing with certainty – and uncertainty

If one of the elements of a tort or one of the ingredients of a defence can clearly be made out on the facts, you should explain briefly why it is clear – with a quick reference to the facts – and then move on to the 'live' issues that require full discussion. It helps to use short quotes from the facts of the problem when you are dealing with an element that is clearly made out. Do not waste time using the full **HIRAC** style to elaborate upon matters that are simple and clear. If there is no real issue, *prove the point* and move on (but do not leave it out).

Case example

Percy v Dr Kojak **(a hypothetical action in battery: treatment without consent)**

It is clear that the elements of bodily contact, intention and directness can be satisfied as the facts state that 'Dr Kojak injected Percy with a vitamin B supplement and administered mouth-to-mouth resuscitation'. The real issue is whether Dr Kojak can establish the defence of necessity, and while this may be relatively simple in the matter of the resuscitation because 'Percy was unconscious', I would advise Dr Kojak that there would be difficulties in arguing that the vitamin B injection was necessary – as opposed to being merely convenient at the time (*Murray v McMurchy* (1949)).

If either the law or the facts are unclear or uncertain, you should 'answer in the alternative' or 'answer both ways'. This means that you must consider both of the alternatives that are open as a result of the uncertainty. Remember that lecturers use different methods to create ambiguity in the facts of a problem question, including leaving facts out, inserting facts that assist both sides or including vague facts that can be interpreted in different ways. When the facts are ambiguous, answer both ways.

Example

The facts do not make it clear whether or not Petunia can actually smell the offal stored next door. If it can be established that the smell is so strong as to make an ordinary person retch – if, for example, the offal had rotted into an advanced state of decomposition, that would clearly satisfy the test laid down in *Halsey v Esso Petroleum* (1961): 'more than would affect a sensitive person'. On the other hand, if it is merely a background 'meaty' smell that betrays no hint of decomposition or rotting, it is unlikely to be sufficient to meet the *Halsey* test.

Note that when the facts in a problem question do not give you enough information to come to a firm conclusion, it becomes important to answer both ways and use your knowledge of the cases to suggest alternative possibilities – try to come up with one possibility that satisfies the rule and would lead to liability and one possibility that would not. There will be times when you do not have enough information to make a definite answer, so learn how to use these opportunities to show off your knowledge and legal skills. When there is uncertainty about the facts, do not make assumptions.

Examples

Do not say things like this:

- *It is likely that* Peter did consent.
- *He is probably* an adult, so he is able to consent.
- The doctor *probably would have* advised Peter of the material risks.

Avoid jumping to these conclusions and learn instead how to acknowledge uncertainty in the facts and answer both ways by giving an example and a counterexample from the range of possibilities.

Example

It *is possible that* Peter is an adult, in which case he is legally able to consent, but on the other hand, he *may be* under the age of 18, in which case he must satisfy the test for competence laid down in *Gillick v West Norfolk and Wisbech Area Health Authority* (1986).

Sometimes, the law is uncertain – for example when a novel case arises that has not been considered by the courts before. In other cases, the law may seem clear and certain, but as times change the law may become outdated and need to be changed to keep up with changes in social conditions and expectations. In these circumstances, you may need to create ambiguity or uncertainty where previously there was none, in order to make out your case. To do this, you need to use your imagination to envision what the law should be in order to best serve the community's needs, and then use your skills in legal argument to come up with a convincing argument that will persuade the court to adopt your view of the matter.

How to cope with uncertainty in the **facts**: be aware of when to flick the switch from 'It *is* the case that ...' to 'It *is possible* that ...'.

How to cope with uncertainty in the **law**: be aware of when to flick the switch from 'The law has always been ...' to 'The law should be ...'.

If there is ambiguity or uncertainty in the facts, you must answer both ways. If there is uncertainty in the law, you need to identify the source of the uncertainty and consider the options open to the court. This will usually involve a discussion of decided cases and may require an argument based on the underlying principles, policies and purposes of the law. After you have discussed the alternatives, make sure that you also explain what difference the decision on the law will make to the particular case at hand. A brief worked example is provided in section 3.4.8.1. Note that the conclusion in this example could equally well have pointed to a completely different outcome – without affecting the mark at all. This is because there is as yet no authoritatively 'correct answer' to this issue in Australia and there are persuasive arguments on both sides. You have the opportunity in these cases to suggest the answer that you think is the most persuasive and, provided you give a reason for your preference, your answer will be lawyerly and will score marks. Once you have completed section 8.1 of Chapter 8, on private and public nuisance, and read the cases on standing to sue, you should be able to expand and rewrite the final conclusion to this issue in a completely different way. An excellent answer would canvass the pros and cons of the two arguments before coming to a conclusion.

3.4.8.1 Sample of the HIRAC method where the law is unclear

- **H**eading: Standing
- **I**ssue: The issue is whether Petunia, as a person merely living on the land, has standing to sue in private nuisance.
- **R**ule (with authority): Identify uncertainty in the rule and explain the alternatives. The law in Australia is currently unclear. The courts in Canada in the cases of *Motherwell v Motherwell* (1976) and *Devon Lumber v MacNeill* (1987) have accepted that a plaintiff will have standing to sue if they 'normally live on the land' or have a 'substantial link to the land' as a member of the family that owns the land. The House of Lords decision in *Hunter v Canary Wharf Ltd* (1997) refused to follow the Canadian decisions and affirmed the traditional position that only those with a proprietary interest in the land and the right to exclusive possession may sue. The High Court of Australia has not made an authoritative decision on this issue.
- **A**pply to facts and argue: Answer both ways. Consider alternative points of view. If the Australian court were to adopt the formulation of the law laid down in *Hunter*, Petunia would not have standing to bring the action because the facts state that she is a 'mere licensee' living in her daughter's home. On the other hand, if the court were to follow the reasoning in the Canadian case of *Motherwell v Motherwell*, she would be entitled to maintain the action for nuisance in her own right, given the fact that she is 'normally living' on the affected land as a member of the family that owns the land.
- **C**onclusion: Identify the crucial factor affecting the decision. The arguments given by the House of Lords in *Hunter* on the nature of the tort of private nuisance suggest

it should be seen as a 'tort to land' rather than a 'tort to the person' and so only those with recognised interests over land should be entitled to bring an action in private nuisance. These highly persuasive arguments would likely be accepted in Australia and so I would advise Petunia that she would most likely not have standing to sue and that any action should be brought by the person who owns the land – her daughter, Primula.

3.4.9 HIRAC: Using cases in your arguments

You will be using the cases in your problem-solving arguments at two different points:

- at the '**R**ule' part of your argument, when you use a case as an authority for your statements of the law; and
- at the '**A**pplication' part of your argument, when you apply the rule from the authority to the facts of the problem question.

It helps to be aware of the facts of the authorities because this knowledge may help you to show off your legal skills when you turn to the application part of the answer. If there are significant similarities or differences between the facts of an authority and the facts of your problem question, you will be able to add depth to your answer by, for example, distinguishing the cases. It also helps to consider matters from the perspective of both parties to the dispute, and to follow an argument with a counterargument (and then with a 'counter-counterargument'). This technique is shown in the worked example given in Chapter 4, which shows you how to use your summary of the case law to help you argue out an issue in depth.

3.4.10 HIRAC: Coming to a conclusion

There are times when you should not trust your own tentative conclusions (the ones that appear at the end of your discussion of a particular issue). So, for example, in a defamation question, it would normally be a tactical error to trust your own judgement that the plaintiff does not have a prima facie case and then, on the basis of this conclusion, make the decision not to continue after the end of the first stage and consider whether the defendant might have a valid defence. If there are facts in the problem question suggesting that there is an arguable defence, you should continue to the next stage and consider whether it can be made out, regardless of whether your tentative conclusion after discussing the elements was that there may not be a prima facie case.

Example

For an instructive illustration of this approach to answering in the alternative and considering all the possibilities that are open on the facts of a case, see the decision of Hunt J in *Church of Scientology California Inc v Reader's Digest Services* (1980). The judge identifies the uncertainty in the law relating to interlocutory injunctions, explores the relative merits of the alternatives, resolves the uncertainty in the law by giving a reason why one alternative is to be preferred to the other, applies that law to the facts and comes up with a tentative conclusion on the issue that would in itself be enough to dispose of the case. However, because the matter was 'one upon which minds may well differ', his Honour went on (at 356) to discuss the remaining aspects of the case 'in case I am held elsewhere to be wrong in that conclusion'.

In a tort such as defamation, where the defences play such an important role, it would normally be an error to end the answer after the first stage. However, in a question on the tort of battery, there may be no defences open on the facts of the problem; in that case it would be safe to draw a conclusion at that point.

It may not always be possible to come to a positive conclusion at the end of your answer. In many problem questions your conclusions may have to remain tentative because the facts are unclear or the law is unsettled. In these circumstances, you should identify the most significant findings of fact or law that will make the difference in your particular case.

3.4.11 Signposting

This chapter has recommended that you begin your career as a law student by adopting a highly stylised method of structuring your answers to torts problem-solving questions. This method encourages you to use headings to assist you to work in a methodical fashion through the steps that will lead you to success – and to use those headings to reveal the structure of your arguments. You can also use a number of standard phrases that will help to reveal to your assessors that you are using the legal method.

Examples

- When you have stated the law with its authority and you turn to apply the law to the facts, you can use the standard phrase 'on the facts' to signal that you are moving from one stage to the next.
- When you are introducing a counterargument, use the wording 'on the other hand' or 'however' to indicate that a different point of view is coming up.
- When you are completing your discussion, use the phrase 'in conclusion' to signal that the end is near.

You can see a longer worked answer that illustrates the use of these standard phrases in section 4.2.5 of Chapter 4.

3.4.12 Beyond HIRAC

Once your understanding of the legal method develops, you will be able to let go of this highly stylised approach to structuring your answers to legal problem-solving questions. In fact, there are times when a slavish application of the HIRAC approach can hamper your ability to answer a question efficiently. For example, in an exam, when time is at a premium, you may not be able to use the full HIRAC method for every issue. However, once you understand that the key to dealing with a legal issue is to apply the law to the facts of a problem, you can avoid repetition and save time (and words) by 'telescoping' or combining two or more of the HIRAC steps into one. So, rather than first defining the elements of a tort and then applying the law to the facts in two separate sentences, you can demonstrate your understanding by folding the facts into your general statement of the law in a single step.

Examples

- Patrick may argue that Julia has committed an assault because, by deliberately leaping out in front of him and intentionally yelling abuse close to his face, she directly created in his mind a reasonable apprehension of imminent physical contact. The mere fact that she may have thought he was an escaped bank robber does not give her a lawful justification for her conduct because mistake is not a defence to the intentional torts (*Rendell v Associated Finance Pty Ltd* (1957)).
- It is clear that the elements of trespass to goods are made out, because Julia has physically moved all of the items. 'Mere asportation' is enough to make out trespass, provided Patrick was in possession (*Penfolds Wines Pty Ltd v Elliott* (1946)). Patrick will also argue that she has converted the two items, because by hiding them so that he cannot find them she has deprived him of his right of use and possession (*Penfolds Wines Pty Ltd v Elliot*).

Once your technique evolves and you internalise the method, you will be able to use this more fluid style without having to stop to remind yourself of the steps. Your answers will flow more naturally and you will need less time to make them. But remember that it takes time and practice, so do not be discouraged if it feels artificial at first – and do not put off the attempt or delay until you feel that you know exactly how to write the perfect answer. The secret is to dive in head first, keep on trying and aim to improve each time.

3.4.13 Structuring an answer to a problem question using FIRO

A suggested structure for a torts problem-solving answer can be found in the following example. However, it is important to realise that this structure, like the **HIRAC** method of argument, may need to be modified to fit the circumstances. A typical variation would be needed if the problem question included multiple parties. In that case, you would need to organise your answer suit by suit, identifying each time who is suing whom. You may sometimes be asked to write up your answer in the form of an internal office memorandum, and the **FIRO** structure can easily be adapted to this purpose, simply by adding the following headings before you begin.

Example

Internal memorandum

TO: [Insert name of recipient – that is, the person who asked you to write the memo.]

FROM: [Insert your name.]

DATE: [xx/xx/xxxx]

SUBJECT: [Remember to give a detailed and precise title; do not be vague.]

The *beginning* or introduction should outline succinctly the facts and the issues arising. In a memorandum it is often a good idea to note your recommendation in the introduction as well, so the person receiving it has a clear idea of the answer in their mind while they are reading the memo.

The *middle* should examine the issues and contain your reasoning.

The *end* should contain your recommended outcome.

Structuring a problem answer using FIRO

The beginning: Identify the facts and issues

Facts

Identify the key facts using the 'six-point plan'.

- The conduct by the defendant: describe in factual terms *what* the defendant did.
- The effects on the plaintiff: describe in factual terms *how* it affected the plaintiff.
- The tort to be used and the remedy desired: *how* might the law aid the plaintiff?

Issues

Identify the issues raised by the case

Some issues focus on the state of the law itself: What should the law be?

Some issues focus on the proper application of the law to the facts in the case.

The middle: Explain your reasoning in three stages

Reasoning

1. The plaintiff's prima facie case: Making out the elements (onus on the plaintiff).
    - Identify the elements of the relevant tort (or torts) and the authorities that establish it (or them).
    - Consider each element in turn and explain whether it can be made out on the facts. If an element is easily made out and there is no issue to argue, quickly explain why and move on to the important issues.
    - If there is a live issue to be argued, use HIRAC to structure the argument. For example:
        - Element 1 (no issue)
            - This element is satisfied because ... [explain why].
        - Element 2 [issue to be argued fully using HIRAC]
            - The plaintiff will argue ...
            - The defendant will counterargue ...
        - Come to a tentative conclusion: Can the plaintiff make out a prima facie case?
2. The defence case: Avoiding liability (onus on the defendant).
    - Identify any possible defences open on the facts.
    - Consider each defence and use the HIRAC method to outline the defendant's arguments and the plaintiff's counterarguments. (Note the reversal of the pattern in stage 1, above.)

    - Defence (issue to be argued fully using HIRAC)
    - The defendant will argue ...
    - The plaintiff will counterargue ...
  - Come to a tentative conclusion: Can the defendant make out a defence?
3. The remedies: Consider any issues arising from the relevant law.

The end: Identify the probable outcome and explain its significance

Outcome

- Suggest an outcome: Who will win the dispute and what remedy would they get?
- If the conclusion is only tentative, identify why that outcome is likely by explaining the key findings of fact or law that will determine that outcome.
- Explain the outcome's significance: Will the plaintiff (or the defendant) get what they originally wanted?

Conclusion

This chapter has explained the function of rules, principles and policy in legal argument and provided you with some advice on how to approach the task of legal problem solving. The next chapter will explain how to organise your study so that you can acquire these skills and achieve success in your torts courses.

REFERENCES

CASES

Breen v Williams (1996) 186 CLR 71
Burnie Port Authority v General Jones Pty Ltd (1994) 179 CLR 520
Cattanach v Melchior (2003) 215 CLR 1
Chappel v Hart (1998) 195 CLR 232
Church of Scientology of California Inc v Reader's Digest Services [1980] 1 NSWLR 344
Cole v Turner (1704) 6 Mod Rep 149; (1704) 87 ER 907
Devon Lumber v MacNeill (1987) 45 DLR (3rd) 300
Donoghue v Stevenson [1932] AC 562
Gillick v West Norfolk and Wisbech Area Health Authority [1986] AC 112
Halsey v Esso Petroleum [1961] 1 WLR 683
Hunter v Canary Wharf Ltd [1997] AC 655; [1997] 2 All ER 426
Magill v Magill (2006) 226 CLR 551
Motherwell v Motherwell (1976) 73 DLR (3rd) 62
Murray v McMurchy (1949) 2 DLR 442
Overseas Tankship (UK) Ltd v Morts Dock & Engineering Co Ltd [1961] AC 388 ('*The Wagon Mound (No 1)*')
Penfolds Wines Pty Ltd v Elliott (1946) 74 CLR 204
Rendell v Associated Finance Pty Ltd [1957] VR 604

Robinson v Kilvert (1889) 41 Ch D 88
Rogers v Whitaker (1992) 175 CLR 479
Rylands v Fletcher (1866) LR 1 Ex 265; (1868) LR 3HL 330
Sullivan v Moody (2001) 207 CLR 562
Tame v New South Wales (2002) 211 CLR 317

ARTICLES AND BOOKS

Boyle, J, 'The Anatomy of a Torts Class' (1985) 34 *American University Law Review* 1003.
Brogan, M & Spencer, D, *Surviving Law School*, 2nd ed (2007) Oxford University Press, Melbourne.
Dworkin, R, *Taking Rights Seriously* (1977) Duckworth, London.
Enright, C, *Legal Technique* (2002) Federation Press, Sydney.
Enright, C, *Studying Law* (1991) Branxton Press, Acton.
Huhn, W, *The Five Types of Legal Argument* (2002) Carolina Academic Press, Durham North Carolina.
Kennedy, D, 'A Semiotics of Legal Argument' (1991) 42 *Syracuse Law Review* 75.
Krever, R, *Mastering Law Studies and Exam Techniques*, 7th ed (2011) Butterworths, Sydney.
Laster, K, *Law as Culture* (2001) The Federation Press, Leichhardt.
MacAdam, A & Pyke, J, *Judicial Reasoning and the Doctrine of Precedent in Australia* (1998) Butterworths, Sydney.
MacCormick, N, *Legal Reasoning and Legal Theory* (1994) Oxford University Press, New York.
Mason, A, 'Policy Considerations', in Blackshield, T, Coper, M & Williams, G (eds), *Oxford Companion to the High Court of Australia* (2001) Oxford University Press, South Melbourne, 535.
Meehan, M & Tulloch, G, *Grammar for Lawyers* (2007) Butterworths, Sydney.
Osborn's Concise Law Dictionary (1983) Sweet & Maxwell, London.
Stapleton, J, 'The Golden Thread at the Heart of Tort Law: Protection of the Vulnerable', in Cane, P (ed), *Centenary Essays for the High Court of Australia* (2003) LexisNexis Butterworths, Sydney, 242.
Wade, J H, 'Meet MIRAT: Legal Reasoning Fragmented into Learnable Chunks' (1990–91) 2 *Legal Education Review* 283.
Wolski, B, Field, D & Bahrij, J, *Legal Skills: A Practical Guide for Students* (2006) Lawbook Co, Sydney.

4 STUDY STRATEGIES

Introduction

Torts is a foundational subject – one of the essential 'Priestley Eleven' topics prescribed for every law student.[1] However, while every law student must study torts, not every torts student has the same experience. More than 30 different universities in Australia offer this subject, in courses of different lengths, focusing on different torts delivered by different methods, and assessed in different ways. The most common form of assessment is the open-book exam, which requires students to answer hypothetical problem-solving questions and discuss essay-type questions. No matter how these courses are designed and delivered, every torts student's journey has common aspects, and this chapter aims to help you to navigate your way through your own particular course by focusing on the issues that concern all students. This book is written primarily for students who may not yet have developed the full range of study techniques that lead to success in their legal studies. Torts is a fascinating subject of study but, because it is frequently taught in the first year of law, students sometimes struggle – not because they cannot understand the law or because they are not interested in the law, but because they do not know how to

1 For more information and background on the 'Priestley Eleven' see Brogan and Spencer, *Surviving Law School* (2007) at 32–8.

study the law effectively. This chapter explains how to organise your study so that you can achieve the results that you deserve.

4.1 Manage your time effectively

4.1.1 Make a plan

One of the best tips is to work steadily throughout the term. Time management skills are critical, not only because many torts courses prescribe a heavy case-reading load, but also because the primary method of assessment in torts courses is the practical problem-solving question. For most students this is the hard part – but only at first. These questions require more than the regurgitation of knowledge; they require you to apply your knowledge to resolve a factual scenario that you may not have seen before. This means you have to organise your study so you can read the cases, construct a useful, assessment-focused summary of the law and still leave enough time for practising writing up answers to problem-solving questions before exam time. It takes time to develop these skills, so you need to start early in the term and work purposefully through to the end. A calendar is essential. Write in all of your classes and assessment deadlines and work backwards from those dates to ensure you can complete everything in time.

4.1.2 Be there: Class time is quality time

Promise yourself that you will never miss a lecture, tutorial, seminar or workshop. Remember that lectures give you only one half of the puzzle – the other half is contained in the problem-solving tutorials and workshops where you learn how to apply the law to a new set of facts. So, it helps to go to every class. Be there every time; nothing is better than spending quality time with the person who is setting and marking your assessment tasks. Get to know your teachers. You certainly do not have to agree with everything they say, but do bear in mind that you will be writing assignments and exams that they will be marking – so find out how to interest them and engage with them. Learn what makes them tick. Begin by reading all the course materials very carefully so that you can find out what your teachers are looking for. If lecturers go to the trouble of putting their expectations and assessment criteria down in writing, it makes sense to pay attention so you can deliver what they want. Furthermore, if you have already demonstrated your interest and engagement with the material in classes, you will then feel much more confident if you need to make an appointment with the teaching staff to discuss anything you do not understand. You can help yourself to succeed if you listen to what they say and identify the aspects of the law that seem to interest them most. Why? Because they are likely to focus on those aspects in their assessment.

Lectures, seminars, tutorials and workshops are opportunities to network, not just with the teaching staff, but with other torts students. Sometimes your study friends are your best teachers. Law is a discourse – so get into the habit of discussing it with your teachers, your family, your friends and your fellow students. If you have difficulty seeing matters from different perspectives, team up with students who take a different view of the world – they can help you to see a different side to an issue. And while you will be on your own in the exam, working with others during the term is a good way to discuss the law and brainstorm issues. Remember, however, that while study groups may help, they do not work for everybody. In particular, be aware that there is a fine line between networking and collusion, so you should always be careful to write up your answers independently of others to ensure that you submit work that is truly your own.

4.1.3 Be a reflective learner: Know yourself

Studying law can be an intense experience, especially in your first year, so it is important to assess your own circumstances and make a realistic study plan. Once you have settled on a study plan, you need to review your progress and revise the plan regularly. The key message is to prepare, practise, review and aim to improve at each step of your path through your law degree.

4.1.4 Work steadily throughout the term and prepare for classes

Do not fall behind in your study. Torts courses generally move at a smart pace, and once you fall behind it is difficult to catch up. It is obviously important to meet your assessment deadlines, but you also need to make time to put together a concise assessment-focused summary of the relevant law and then practise using it to build up your skills and prepare for the exams. You should try to complete your summary of each topic soon after the classes on that topic end so that you can use it to prepare for your problem-solving tutorials or seminars. Then put it away until swot vac and move on to the next topic. Table 4.1 contains a suggested study plan that you can modify to suit your own needs and circumstances. It is based on the lecture-tutorial teaching model, but it can be adapted to other teaching methods. The goal is to get yourself into a working rhythm that will ensure that you work steadily towards completing the work for each topic as you go. This leaves time for revision during swot vac. If you leave the task of making the summary for the end of term you will not have enough time to practise past exam questions. (And you will need to do this!)

It is very important to practise the art of legal problem solving. Generally, the first time you attempt to write up an answer to a problem question under exam conditions, you get about halfway through it. As you improve your skills in diagnosis and learn how to write using the legal method, you get faster and you begin to feel more comfortable. Early practice will yield other benefits: you will begin to see the patterns that tend to recur in the problem questions (which helps you to diagnose issues in the exam) and you can seek feedback on your technique from your tutors and lecturers (which will help you to improve even more). All this will increase your confidence when you sit down to do the exam.

Many students do not know how to study law when they begin their torts courses. They may enjoy the subject and they may have a good work ethic – but they do not know how to focus their study efforts. Consequently, they end up doing too much work or getting discouraged because they do not quite know what they need to do. Experienced students know that they have to get straight to work in the first week on making an efficient, focused summary of the law that will help them to prepare for the problem-solving questions in the exam. The next section of this chapter explains how to master this important study strategy.

Table 4.1 Adopt a study routine

<table>
<tr><th></th><th>Before: Prepare</th><th>After: review</th></tr>
<tr><td>Lectures</td><td>• Familiarise yourself with the material before each content module begins by reading the relevant chapter of Connecting with Australian Tort Law. At this point do not take any detailed notes – just aim for a general overview of the area.
• You will then be able to focus better on your lecturer's interpretation of the cases and the law, and you will recognise the case names and technical terms that you will hear in the class. This means that you will get more out of the lecture and be able to take a better set of notes.
Tip: During the lecture your main priority should be to make notes on the relevant legal rules and principles. You can always check the facts later.</td><td>Take a moment after the lecture to review the material – ask yourself:
• What was this lecture about? How does this topic fit into the course?
• Was there anything you did not understand? If so, deal with it (before the exam).
• Identify what you can do to resolve any problems:
o consult textbooks and/or read the cases;
o discuss the issues with your friends or study group;
o consult the tutor or lecturer.
Tip: You will find that your teachers will be more willing to help you if you have already tried to help yourself.</td></tr>
<tr><td>Tutorials</td><td>• Reread your lecture notes and the cases listed in your study materials.
• Make a summary of the relevant law (see section 2 below).
• Use your summary to prepare an answer to the problem question: see Chapter 3.
Tip: Take a dot-point answer to the tutorial and make notes during the class.</td><td>• Check over and improve your summary and your problem question structure.
• After the class, make time to sit down and write up a full answer under exam conditions.
Tip: The art of legal problem solving takes time to develop, so make time to practise.</td></tr>
<tr><td>Exams</td><td>Use your summary to practise writing up answers to tutorial questions or past exam questions during swot vac and if necessary get feedback from your lecturer or tutor.
Tip: Do not put yourself in the position where you write up your first ever answer to a problem question in the exam.</td><td>Review your performance once you have your results back and make an appointment to see your assessors for feedback if necessary.
Tip: Do not engage in post-exam agony sessions with your friends.</td></tr>
</table>

4.2 Making a summary of the law

4.2.1 You need an assessment-focused summary

One of your primary tasks as a torts student is to make a summary of the law that will help you to write up answers to the problem-solving questions that you will encounter in your assignments and exams. The first thing to remember is that a summary is *not* a transcript of your lectures or a collection of case briefs. It is a tool that is designed to help you answer legal problem-solving questions. So, it has to be put together in such a way that it will help you to:

- diagnose the torts and the issues in the problem;
- structure your answer correctly; and
- argue out the issues effectively using **HIRAC**.

The basic premise behind making a summary is that you should do as much as possible *before* the exam so that you can cover as much as possible *during* the exam. It makes sense to write up the law that you will be applying in advance – because this will save you time during the exam. It makes sense to plan out an answer in advance – because this will allow you to spend more time on the diagnosis and the arguments. If you know that you will be using **HIRAC** to argue out the issues, then it makes sense to anticipate what the **I**ssues might be, and to have the **H**eadings and the **R**ules all ready to go before you even enter the exam room. Several design principles will help you to make a useful summary:

- the *structure* principle;
- the *reversal* principle;
- the *precision* principle; and
- the *'tip of the iceberg'* principle.

4.2.2 The structure principle

A good problem-solving summary will be structured – just as the law of torts is structured. It should include two main sections. The first section must contain a concise checklist of all the relevant law arranged under the right headings so that you can diagnose the appropriate torts and identify the issues, as described in Chapter 3. This section will include all of the elements of the torts, the ingredients of the defences and the rules about the remedies. All of the relevant law (ie the rules, principles and policy) must be listed under each of these headings. The law needs to be succinctly stated and must always be accompanied by an authority. You will use these propositions of law when you are putting HIRAC into practice to argue out an issue. When you get to that point in your answer, you will simply copy the law and its authority directly into the body of your answer. While you are writing it down, you can be thinking ahead about how you will apply it to the facts.

The second section of the problem-solving summary will contain a sample layout – or generic answer plan – that you have worked out in advance. The answers to torts questions generally follow a predictable pattern of elements, defences and remedies, and they generally give rise to a predictable set of issues. This means you can save time in the exam by working out how to structure your answer beforehand. Then all you need to do on the day is adapt it to the particular problem that you find. Part 2 helps you to construct and adapt these answer plans for each of the main areas of tort law. One of the main benefits of putting a basic answer plan together in advance is that it forces you to think about the kind of issues you may need to address, and, once you have anticipated an issue, you will be better equipped to spot it in the exam. The other benefit of planning out an answer in advance is that it saves precious time in the exam – and you can spend that extra time on developing deeper arguments when you are applying the law to the facts, arguing out the issues and considering any counterarguments. A well-designed summary will maximise your chances of doing well on the exam by giving you extra time to spend on the two most important parts of any problem-solving answer:

- the correct identification of the issues; and
- the application of the law to those issues with supporting analysis and argument.

Making the summary has many benefits. By putting the summary together, you teach yourself the law and reinforce your knowledge. By anticipating the issues, you improve your diagnostic skills. By organising your answer in advance, you save time and allow yourself to spend the maximum time possible on collecting all the marks available for making the arguments that apply the law to the facts. To make an effective summary that yields all of these benefits you must become a structure seeker and a rule hunter, and Part 2 helps you to understand the best way to give structure not only to your summaries of the law of torts but also to your answers to problem questions.

Where should you begin when you sit down to make your summary of the law? If your course is taught in the lecture-tutorial method, you will be able to find most of the relevant legal rules, principles and policies in your lecture notes and study materials. In fact, when you are taking lecture notes you should listen very carefully and prioritise your efforts into getting all of the relevant law noted down. When you make the first part of the summary, you should begin with your lecture notes, which will probably provide you with many of the legal propositions that you need. Use your study materials to find the headings and then ensure that you put all of the relevant rules, principles and policy together in a logical pattern under those headings. If anything is missing, you should look at your casebook or textbook and then read a selection of the cases to expand your knowledge. Use your summary to help you to prepare for the tutorial and put together a sample answer to the problem question using one of the methods suggested in Chapter 3.

Your tutorials or seminars will help you to make the second section of the summary, which contains the answer plan. Pay careful attention to the way that your tutor guides the discussion in your problem-solving classes. Note how they structure the analysis of the problem question and compare the structure of your own answer (and the suggested structure in this book) with your tutor's version. After the class, go back to your summary and improve it. Then, once you have made the final version of your summary, which you know will satisfy your own teachers in your own torts course, sit down and write up a full answer to the problem question under exam conditions. If you want feedback, make an appointment to see your tutor or lecturer and show them both your summary and your answer. You will find that once you have made the effort and done the work, they will be happy to help you improve it.

This subsection has explained why you should make a summary and shown you how to put it together. Your summary will be the result of a joint effort made by you and your teachers – each complements the other. Your study materials will give you the structure and headings for the first part of the summary and your lectures will give you the legal rules, principles and policies that will go into it. Your tutorials will help you to put an answer plan together and once you practise using the summary, you can go back to your teachers and make sure you are on the right track.

4.2.3 The reversal principle

It is a common mistake to make a summary of the law simply by typing out a full transcript of material covered in classes. However, apart from taking up a lot of time, a transcript will not help you to find the law easily, identify the issues or structure an answer.

Lecturers usually give you a summary of the facts of a case and then move on to discuss the relevant law that emerged from it. However, your summary should not follow this pattern. Instead, your summary should reverse the pattern: focus *first* on noting down the law in a succinct and generally stated form and *then* on listing some factual examples to illustrate the rule in operation. When you list the rules, you should state the general proposition of law and then supply the case or statute authority in brackets afterwards.

Case examples

- The defendant must perform a positive physical act (*Platt v Nutt* (1988)).
- Passive conduct will not suffice (*Innes v Wylie* (1884)).
- If the contact or interference is the result of the plaintiff's own act the defendant will not be liable (*Platt v Nutt* (1988)).

The reason you should reverse your lecture pattern is directly related to the basics of legal argument. If you want to argue an issue out using the HIRAC method, you have to formulate the issue, state the relevant law and then apply the law to the facts of the problem question. This method does not require you to waste time by telling a long story about the facts of the authority case – it requires you to state the law succinctly, give an authority for it and then apply it to the facts of the present case. You will use the facts of the authority only if your arguments need to distinguish or liken the facts of your case to the authority case. So, your summary needs to contain a succinct summary of the law for the '**R**' part of HIRAC and it will help if you include a couple of factual examples that will assist you to recognise any common fact patterns and make any useful arguments (in the '**A**' part of HIRAC). When you are including examples from the cases, try to contrast one example with a 'counterexample'. These factual examples are particularly helpful:

- when you are looking for arguments and counterarguments;
- when you have to answer both ways if the facts are unclear; or
- when you have a fuzzy rule to cope with.

This technique is especially important when you are dealing with a fuzzy rule, which contains the concept of unreasonableness within it. Because even reasonable people may disagree on the issue of reasonableness, you need to include a few helpful examples from the cases so that you can use them to argue out the application of the rule (and show off your knowledge). Two sets of case examples follow: the first relates to the trespass torts, the second to the tort of private nuisance.

Case examples

Directness (in the trespass torts)

The defendant's act must directly result in physical contact with the plaintiff (*Scott v Shepherd* (1773)).

The law sometimes adopts an 'extended notion' of directness, so in cases where contact is the result of a third person acting not voluntarily but out of necessity for their own safety, the original actor will be held to have directly caused the contact (*Scott v Shepherd* (1773)).

Example

- The contact caused by throwing the squib into the marketplace and others instinctively throwing it away in the agony of the moment was sufficiently direct (*Scott v Shepherd* (1773)).

Counterexample

- In *Hutchins v Maughan* (1947) it was held that laying of the bait by D caused no harm directly to the dogs. It was caused by P consciously choosing to go down to the land after he had been warned. Contrast this with the previous case – here there was no conscious act or choice nor a heat-of-the-moment action.

But: the Court did say that if D had thrown the bait right down to the feet of the dogs, that might have been enough (*Hutchins v Maughan* (1947)).

Malice in the tort of private nuisance

Malice is relevant to determining unreasonableness in private nuisance (*Hollywood Silver Fox Farm v Emmett* (1936)).

If D does something deliberately to harm his neighbour, he is more likely to be held liable in nuisance if it is done only for the purpose of annoyance and he is not a legitimate user of D's land (*Christie v Davey* (1893)).

Not all retaliatory measures are unreasonable, provided they are directed at alleviating the nuisance and are not malicious, spiteful or aiming to harm (*Fraser v Booth* (1949)).

Examples

- Retaliating against the pigeons by squirting them with a hose and letting off firecrackers to alleviate the effects of the nuisance was *not* malicious (*Fraser v Booth* (1949)).
- Retaliating against a neighbour *to upset them* is malicious. For example:
    - Deliberately shooting guns to upset the silver foxes at breeding time was held to be malicious (*Hollywood Silver Fox Farm v Emmett* (1936)) – but ordinary noise might not be – for instance, legitimate noise caused by shooting rabbits on a farm to reduce their numbers and damage they might cause.
    - Banging on trays and shrieking to annoy musicians next door was malicious, but the ordinary noise caused by continuing music lessons was not (*Christie v Davey* (1983)).

4.2.4 The precision principle

The summary must state the law as precisely and succinctly as possible. Do not try to restate the rule or principle in your own words. Instead try to use the words laid down by the judge in the relevant case authority – or the parliament in the relevant statute. It also helps to use small quotations or key phrases taken from the judgments to weave into your own arguments. This demonstration of 'inside knowledge', when coupled with the citation of the relevant authority, shows that you have actually read the case and reminds the person marking your work that you know how to argue like a lawyer. So, if a judge has used a particularly pithy or memorable phrase in their formulation of the law, take it and work it into your own arguments. An example of this technique can be found in the problem-solving sample provided at the end of this section.

4.2.5 The 'tip of the iceberg' principle

How long should your summary be? This will depend on your own learning style as well as your available time and resources. Some people have a lot of time and like to be comprehensive. Others are pressed for time and have to fit their law studies into a busy life. Some have a good memory for detail and the gift of being able to think on their feet; others like to have everything written down in detail. So, the summary that you make will vary depending on your own personal circumstances. Some students will not feel comfortable unless they have a large, comprehensive summary; others can get away with something more compact. There is no single 'perfect' summary that suits every torts course and every torts student. For example, the summary you make for a closed-book exam would be very different from the one you would make for an open-book exam.

There are three critical features of a good problem-solving summary. The first is to make sure that you *do not overcrowd* it with too many facts. If you cannot help yourself, consider making two versions: a long, 'facty' version during the semester and a shorter 'tip of the iceberg' version in the study break. It can be a good revision exercise to use your swot vac time to reduce a larger summary down to a smaller, exam-focused 'tip of the iceberg' version. The smaller summary can be very helpful – especially if you consider how much law you really need to cover in the time allocated to each question in an exam (usually 40 to 60 minutes per question). The second is to make sure that you can *find* the law easily. So, make sure you are familiar with your summary, and use highlighters and tabs to help you to navigate your way through it. Practising past exams in swot vac also helps you to reacquaint yourself with a summary that has been made earlier in the semester. The final piece of advice is to *use* your summary. Use it to prepare for problem-solving exercises and practise using it again to prepare for exams so that you know it works. If you follow this advice you will feel confident when you go into your exams and you will know that you have given yourself the best possible chance to do well.

Your summary should allow you to construct a well-organised answer to a problem-solving question that demonstrates your knowledge of the law and your skills in legal argument. A sample that illustrates many of the design principles and legal problem-solving skills that have been described and recommended in Chapter 3 and this chapter follows. Once you have learned how to make a summary and used it to write up answers to problem-solving questions, you will feel much more comfortable as a law student and you will be able to apply these essential skills not just in your torts course, but in all the other courses that you will study during your law degree.

Example

Extract from the facts of a problem question on private nuisance

Penny Persimmon lives on Sandy Bay Road (a main street going through a mixed inner-city neighbourhood containing a commercial shopping district and good quality residential housing, schools and churches). The man who lives next door is Jack 'Spam' Sparrow, a wealthy IT professional who constantly worries about his low popularity with women. To make himself seem cool and fashionable, Spam renovated his home by installing a massive digital screen covering the whole front wall of the house. This enormous screen continuously shows pictures from underwear catalogues featuring celebrities like Miranda Kerr, Kylie Minogue, Elle McPherson and Pamela Anderson. Penny, who does not like seeing the pictures flickering next door and who feels very uncomfortable about their content, asked Spam to turn off the screen. He refused and she has come to you for legal advice.

Advise Penny.

The law

Write this out in your summary, as recommended in this chapter.

Concise statement of the rules from the case law:

> The test for 'moral nuisance' is whether the conduct is likely to offend ordinary reasonable people living in the district (*Laws v Florinplace* (1981), considering the effects on the minds of children and visitors, the usages of civilised society and the character of the neighbourhood (*Thompson-Schwab v Costaki* (1956)).

Case examples

- Sex centre and porn cinema in Pimlico (London) – the nature of this type of business could not be disregarded (*Laws v Florinplace*).
- The sight of prostitutes and their clients entering and leaving a brothel in the neighbouring premises was held offensive enough to be a nuisance in a 'good class residential street' in London (*Thompson-Schwab v Costaki*).

A sample argument on one of the issues in this nuisance problem

Penny (P) v Spam (D): Moral nuisance

The issue is whether Spam's conduct in continuously showing pictures of celebrities from underwear catalogues on a massive digital screen on the front of his house amounts to an unreasonable and substantial interference with Penny's use and enjoyment of land because it is morally offensive.

> *This first sentence states the issue. Note that this answer uses signal phrases to signpost the HIRAC components and includes small extracts from the facts to describe the conduct of the defendant, Spam, and its effects on Penny, the plaintiff.*

The test to be applied is whether the conduct is 'likely to offend ordinary reasonable people living in the district' (*Laws v Florinplace*), taking into account the effects on the minds of children and visitors and the usages of civilised society and the character of neighbourhood (*Thompson-Schwab v Costaki*).

The second sentence states the law to be applied and gives the authorities.

On the facts, Penny will point out that these pictures show half-naked women and that such pictures are not suitable for showing in the vicinity of Sandy Bay Road, which is a predominantly residential, respectable, well-to-do neighbourhood, containing schools and churches. It is a place where families with children walking or driving down the main access road would not expect to be confronted with semi-naked female bodies – by contrast with an area like the beach in summer time.

This paragraph applies the rule from the authorities directly to the facts from P's perspective. It uses the standard phrase 'on the facts' to signal that the application of the law to the facts is beginning.

On the other hand, Spam will argue that the women are not fully naked but are wearing underwear. He could point out that they are not selling sex but are selling clothing, and that such advertising pictures are commonly seen every day in newspapers, in magazines, on television and on billboards (some of which may be located in the commercial district of Sandy Bay). This suggests that they do not offend community standards and that showing them is not unreasonable.

This paragraph provides a counterargument on the facts, from D's perspective. It uses the standard phrase 'on the other hand' to signal that a counterargument is beginning.

Spam's operation of his screen can be distinguished from such cases as *Laws v Florinplace*, where the conduct complained of was the running of a cinema showing pornographic films, and *Thompson-Schwab v Costaki*, where the sight of prostitutes and their clients going in and out of a brothel was held to be offensive to those living in the district. Showing everyday pictures of celebrities advertising underwear is not as morally offensive as the overtly sexual conduct occurring in these two case authorities, which, in the case of the brothel, is possibly illegal, and, in the case of the pornographic cinema, is very likely to be contrary to the moral standards of respectable Sandy Bay residents.

These are counterarguments using the facts of the authorities and attempting to distinguish them from the facts in the current case.

The mere fact that Penny does not like seeing these pictures is not enough to prove that they are offensive or unreasonable. Penny may simply be complaining about a trivial matter that must be judged, not according to her 'dainty, fastidious and elegant' notions, but according to the standards of ordinary and reasonable people in the district (*Walter v Selfe* (1851)). Given that Spam's activities are neither illegal nor offensive by community standards, Penny may just have to 'give and take' and be prepared to be annoyed (*Bamford v Turnley* (1860)).

These are counterarguments raising other aspects and relevant factors from the law of nuisance, using case references when the precedents are being used. Note the use of small phrases taken from the authority cases, which are woven into the arguments – thereby adding weight to the arguments and proving to the assessor that the student is familiar with the cases.

However, Penny can counterargue by pointing out that while the pictures may not be as intrinsically morally offensive as the conduct in *Laws v Florinplace* and *Thompson-Schwab v Costaki*, the fact that the pictures are 'massive' and are being shown in public 'continuously' makes the conduct unreasonable and that the time, duration and frequency of the operation of the screen as well as the size of the pictures and the fact that it is permanent rather than temporary should be taken into account, as in the case of *Andreae v Selfridge & Co Ltd* (1938). Furthermore, a massive flickering picture of a woman in underwear on a large screen is more confronting than a small picture on a page of a newspaper or catalogue, which is viewed in private and which can be turned over at will. This is especially true given that the screen is located not just in the public view, but on a main road. It is not necessary for Spam to show these pictures in public, and therefore his 'leisurely pursuit' of 'coolness' and popularity should not be held to outweigh Penny's rights to enjoy her home (*Lester-Travers v City of Frankston* (1970)).

These are counterarguments by P, addressing the arguments raised by D, and referring to other aspects and relevant factors from cases in the law of nuisance. Use of the standard phrase 'however' signals the start of another line of argument.

In conclusion, it must be noted that Sandy Bay is a mixed district that contains both a commercial shopping area as well as a residential zone. The facts do not state exactly where Spam's screen is located. If it were to be situated near the commercial part of Sandy Bay Road, where there are already a number of large advertising signs and commercial activities taking place, it may be that a court would not find that such an activity as showing electronic pictures of this kind would be out of keeping with the nature of the locality (*St Helen's Smelting Co v Tipping* (1865)).

This is a tentative conclusion, identifying the crucial finding of fact that will determine whether or not the conduct is unreasonable in the locality. Use of the standard phrase 'in conclusion' signals that the end of the analysis has been reached.

4.3 Case-reading strategies

4.3.1 Reading torts cases

It is important to learn the art of legal argument from the experts, as demonstrated in the case law. There are three reasons why you are expected to read so many cases:

- Cases contain the law and explanations of how it has developed, so reading them will improve your *knowledge* and *understanding* of the law.
- Every case tells the story of how a practical legal problem was solved by the application (and sometimes the creation) of a legal rule or principle, so reading cases will improve your *legal problem-solving skills*.
- The judges give reasons for their decisions, so you will learn how to *argue like a lawyer* by identifying issues and following the steps in the legal reasoning used by the judges to resolve those issues.

4.3.2 Prepare to read a case – and read with purpose

Before you read a case you should remind yourself why you have been asked to read it. Check your class notes to see what the lecturer emphasised about the case, and glance over your textbook to find out why it is important. There are three common reasons why a case may be selected for law students to read:

- The case may be a 'landmark' case which changed the law by making a new rule – or by changing or abolishing an old one.
- The case may have established a new principle or policy application.
- The case may give a useful example of how the law applied to a particular set of facts.

Remember that you do not always have to read or understand every part of every case on your reading list. Some torts cases are extremely long and complicated and may also include discussion and analysis of other aspects of the law that are not directly relevant to your particular course. So, while reading cases is an important part of your legal education, there are times when you can legitimately reduce your reading load.

Example

It is often a good idea to begin reading the cases in reverse chronological order. If the most recent case has changed the law in any significant way, you will often find a judgment that contains a helpful summary of the earlier cases.

Some students enjoy using a casebook that includes only edited extracts from the cases, whereas others prefer to read fewer cases but to read them in their entirety. This is a matter of personal preference, so do not worry if your reading habits differ from those of your fellow students.

4.3.3 Look for the legal argument

When you read cases where the law was changed or developed, you need to know what the old law was, and identify the reasons advanced to justify changing or modifying the law. You will usually need to answer at least two questions:

- How did the judge define the issues in the case?
- How did the judge resolve the issues?

As you go through the cases and prepare notes, ask yourself how the judges have justified their decisions and read with these questions in mind.

4.3.3.1 Arguments based on the doctrine of precedent

- Did the judge rely on other cases? How did they *use* those cases?
- Did the judge distinguish an earlier case?
- Did the judge read an existing rule more narrowly or more broadly?
- Did the judge declare that an earlier case was wrongly decided, or is now out of date?

4.3.3.2 Arguments designed to change or extend the law

- Did the judge make a new rule or interpret the existing law in a new way?
- Did the judge add an exception to an existing rule or apply it in a different way?
- Did the judge make a radical change in the law or merely take an incremental step?
- Did the judge reason by analogy?

- Did the judge appeal to principle?
- Did the judge appeal to policy?

Some cases contain dissenting judgments. In these cases, you have access to a helpful set of arguments and counterarguments that you may be able to use in your own problem-solving exercises or in answering an essay question in an exam. So, for example, in *Hunter v Canary Wharf Ltd* (1997) the House of Lords dealt with the issue of standing to sue in the tort of nuisance, and the case contains two sets of arguments on an issue that has not yet come before the Australian High Court. After reading this case, you should be aware of both sets of arguments and you should be able to explain why you prefer one over the other.

4.3.4 Constructing a case note using FIRO

As you read torts cases you should adopt a methodical approach to record your understanding of the arguments that the judges have used to resolve the issues. Remember that the judges tend to follow a very similar pattern in their judgments and they usually:

- explain the facts leading to the dispute;
- explain how the case reached the particular point in the court hierarchy;
- identify the issues arising from the dispute, which may relate to the state of the law itself or the way the law should be applied to the facts of the case;
- canvass the alternatives;
- give reasons for preferring one alternative to another; and
- come to a conclusion.

Whether you are reading a judgment in a case or making your own arguments in essays or problem-solving exercises, you will be focusing over and over again on the same recurring features of the legal method as you progress through your torts studies. Just like the judges and the lawyers who appear before them, you will be identifying the legal issues arising from fact patterns; justifying the form of the relevant law by constructing convincing legal arguments; and then applying the law to the facts of the case to come up with a conclusion. You will learn how to do this by reading and analysing the cases and the FIRO formula can assist you to construct a useful case note, as the list below shows.

The beginning should identify the facts and the issues.

- Facts: Identify the basic aspects of the dispute.
  - The conduct by the defendant: describe in factual terms what the defendant did.
  - The effects on the plaintiff: describe in factual terms how it affected the plaintiff.
  - The tort used and the remedy desired: how was the law called in aid of the plaintiff?
- Issues: Identify the issues raised by the case.
  - Some issues focus on the state of the law itself: what should the law be?
  - Some issues focus on the proper application of the law to the facts in the case.
  - Note the history of the litigation: how did the case reach the court and how did the lower court(s) court decide the issues?

The middle should explain the reasoning.

- **R**easoning: Explain the reasoning used by the majority judges to resolve the issues. Explain the arguments made by any minority judges. Make sure that you:
  - identify the steps in the reasoning – by breaking it up into its components; and
  - classify the nature of the reasoning – are the arguments based on precedent, principles, rules, policies, analogies, etc?

The end should identify the outcome and explain its significance.

- **O**utcome: Note the outcome on the facts.
  - Who won the dispute? Identify the reason for that outcome (or legal ratio of the case).
  - Explain the significance of the case: place it in its legal context and identify the goal that the decision best serves.

4.4 Essay strategies

4.4.1 Constructing an essay using FIRO

The FIRO approach can also be used to organise your torts essays. A torts essay will usually focus on a particular area of the law that may be uncertain, controversial or especially difficult, and the question will often be designed to allow you to display a deeper knowledge of the case law, an ability to analyse and critically discuss the law, and skills in arguing about the proper form of the law using principles, policy and appropriate references to the views of academic articles and books. It will strengthen your essays if you can demonstrate that you can identify the relevant issues, argue logically and clearly about those issues, consider the options and counterarguments, and explain the significance of the issues and their proper resolution. Remember that your reading should be purposeful and analytical. As you read, try to classify the content of the material into categories – have you found an *issue* to discuss, a good *argument* to use, a helpful *counterargument,* or some useful *evidence* to support a proposition? Think carefully about the quotations that you use. A quotation is best employed:

- as an authority for a factual or legal proposition; or
- to introduce an issue or set up a counterargument.

The list below shows how to structure an essay using FIRO.

The beginning should identify the facts and the issues.

- **F**acts: Identify the factual background to the topic that makes this question important. There may be a current debate about a topic in:
  - the legal world (eg judges in cases or legal academics in books and articles);
  - the political arena; or
  - the media.

  Define any special terms and identify any parameters or boundaries of the debate.

- **I**ssues: Identify the issues raised by the question. Many issues focus on the state of the law itself.
  - What is wrong with the current law?
  - What should the law be?
  - What are the options?

Explain how you will tackle the issues. Remember, your goal is to introduce both:

- the topic (how it came about and why is it important); and
- the essay itself (and how you will structure it).

The middle should explain your reasoning.

- **R**easoning: Put forward your arguments, making sure that you:
  - identify the steps in your reasoning – break it up logically and make sure that it flows from paragraph to paragraph;
  - classify the nature of your reasoning and explain whether your arguments are based on precedent, principles, rules, policies, analogies, etc;
  - provide evidence for your arguments;
  - give references to the arguments of others wherever you make use of them; and
  - rebut any possible counterarguments.

The end should identify your desired outcome and explain its significance.

- **O**utcome: Summarise by restating your preferred outcome to the debate.
  - Restate the reason why this outcome is so desirable.

Explain the significance of your preferred outcome: place it in a wider context. See Chapter 2 for a summary of the functions of tort law and Table 3.1 in Chapter 3 for six types of legal argument.

4.4.2 Plagiarism, referencing and academic integrity

Plagiarised work will normally result in disciplinary action. The issue of plagiarism is vitally important for two reasons: the first is academic, the second is professional. Law students should understand that plagiarism can have very serious consequences, not only during their time at university but also in their future profession of law. This is because a finding of plagiarism (or other academic misconduct) is a serious matter that must be disclosed to the relevant admitting authority upon a graduate's application for admission to the legal profession, and it has the potential to delay admission or even prevent it altogether.

If you are unsure about what plagiarism is, you should read Anita Stuhmcke's excellent discussion of this subject (which includes tips on how to avoid it) in chapter 4 of *Legal Referencing* (2005). Stuhmcke identifies and explains at 43–45 four different ways to fall foul of the rules against plagiarism:

a stealing words is plagiarism;
b making summaries and changing words is plagiarism;
c stealing phrases and stealing thoughts is plagiarism; and
d unacknowledged paraphrasing is plagiarism.

The golden rule is: if you are in doubt, put in a reference – you will get credit for scrupulous acknowledgement of your sources. Lawyers and judges have traditionally given great respect to the use of authorities so it is a good idea to develop this professional attitude to the citation of sources early in your law career.

Generative AI is creating its own set of problems. Please make sure you are across your university's policies on the appropriate use of this type of tool. Generative AI tools can be permitted, partially permitted or fully prohibited depending on the type of assignment. This part of the book aims to help you to develop skills that will serve you *regardless* of generative AI. In some circumstances, you may be allowed and willing to use these tools to supplement your studies. When you do, make sure you always double check the results, and do not trust a result that is generated by generative AI (whether it is an answer to a question or a summary of a case, statute or of your lecture notes) without thoroughly double checking it for accuracy.

Law has its own system of referencing for cases, legislation, books and articles, etc, so you need to learn *how* to reference as well as *when* to reference. Different law schools adopt different referencing systems, so you need to check your study materials to make sure that you know how to follow the appropriate style. One of the most commonly used systems is the *Australian Guide to Legal Citation* (AGLC), which is published by the Melbourne University Law Review Association. You will note that this book does not comply with the AGLC method of referencing; rather, it adopts a more efficient method of referencing that does not clutter the page with too many footnotes and citations that may distract you from focusing on the contents as you read.

Consult your study materials and your university's student website for up-to-date information about the policy on plagiarism and use of generative AI. Make a point of reading these materials carefully. Do not assume that you already know what plagiarism is. Ignorance will not be accepted as an excuse.

Visit the AGLC website, where you can find an electronic copy of the latest referencing rules. The electronic version is 'read only' so you should consider buying a hard copy of the book for ease of reference.

If you have any doubts about referencing, you should contact your teaching staff, who will be able to advise you. Once you learn how to comply with these rules you will be well prepared for your torts study and for all of the other subjects that you will study during the rest of your time at law school.

4.4.3 An essay checklist

Many students feel much more comfortable when they are asked to write an essay than they do when they have to answer a problem question. This is because essay writing is a skill that they are likely to have developed before starting at law school. However, some reminders may be of assistance:

- Analyse the question before you embark on your research or start writing your answer. Then read with purpose, looking for ammunition.
- Remember that an introduction should serve two purposes: it should introduce the topic and the issues it raises as well as introduce the essay itself.

- Structure your essay in a logical way. Make sure it flows from paragraph to paragraph and make sure you have linked the sections. Use headings to make the structure clear to the reader.
- Have a point of view and express it clearly.[2] Do not simply reproduce the views of others – make your own argument in your own voice.
- Justify your views by providing a reasoned argument and evidence to back up your propositions. Consider any counterarguments and try to rebut them.
- If you have made use of the views of other writers, make sure that you have *acknowledged* them properly and *referenced* them properly.
- Do not conceal your sources by using the passive construction and hiding the true source of the idea by mentioning the author only in the footnotes. Instead, include the author's name in the sentence openly and put the reference in the footnotes. See the example below.
- Focus your answer directly on the question. An essay is not an invitation to tell the marker everything that you have found out about the topic. It requires you to focus your analysis and ruthlessly discard irrelevant material.
- Write a proper conclusion. A conclusion is not just a restatement of what you have already written. It should explain the significance of the argument that you have advanced in the body of the essay, either by placing it into a wider context or by linking the suggested resolution of the specific issues to some wider goal or purpose.
- Check the assessment criteria and learning outcomes so that you are sure that you know what the marker is looking for.
- Ensure that you have complied with the formalities – or you may lose marks.
- Read your own essay before you hand it in. (Try reading it out loud.)

Example

Not: It is argued that Australian tort law is in need of reform.

Rather: Luntz argues that Australian tort law is in need of reform.

4.5 Oral presentation strategies

4.5.1 Communication is an essential skill

Law graduates, like all graduates, need good communication skills in the workplace. Oral communication skills are required in almost every form of employment, so whether you intend to enter the legal profession or you plan to look for employment in the public service or the private sector, communication is a skill you will need to master. Interestingly, as David Weisbrot notes, one of the most common complaints about lawyers is not that they do not know the law, but that they do not know how to communicate, either with

2 Use plain English and avoid 'legalese': see O'Brien, 'Judicial Attitudes to Plain Language and the Law' (2009) and the other articles and books referred to in that article.

their clients, with judges or with other lawyers.[3] Studies have identified two main areas of dissatisfaction: problems interacting with clients and problems interacting with other professionals. You need communication skills not only in the workplace (and in job interviews) but also in everyday life. Bruce Elder points out that communication skills are central to human life because of the huge impact that they have on 'a person's happiness, success and sense of personal worth' and he reminds us never to underestimate their importance:[4]

> The unemployment queues are full of people whose services are no longer required, not because of incompetence, but because of misunderstandings in the workplace which led to major communications breakdowns and unpleasant conflicts. And the courts, particularly the divorce courts, are full of people telling each other that they couldn't communicate their emotions and feelings to each other.

Communication is conveying or interchanging thoughts, opinions, knowledge, information or meanings by speech, writing, signs or conduct. The process of communication requires at least two parties and a message:

- the sender of the message; and
- the receiver of the message.

Successful oral communication depends on:

- understanding yourself and finding the best communication style to match your personality, your strengths and your weaknesses;
- realising that communication occurs at both the verbal and non-verbal levels;
- learning how to prepare and construct a clear and effective message;
- knowing how to engage with your audience; and
- learning how to manage nerves and performance anxiety.

Advocacy is a special kind of communication. It is the art of persuasion – or convincing listeners to accept and adopt a particular position, belief, attitude or point of view. Legal advocates may seek to persuade their audience of the correctness of:

- their version of the *facts* of a particular case; and/or
- their view of the proper *response* to the facts of a particular case.

Richard Crawford defines persuasion in *The Persuasion Edge* (1989) as the process of seeking 'to induce co-operation from others'; he explains (at 1) that:

> Persuasion is the fuel which powers the engines of commerce and industry, government, religion, education, the justice system and all other human institutions. Persuasion is a part of the daily lives of teachers, shopkeepers, parents, social workers, entertainers, journalists, politicians, and all others who interact in personal or professional ways with people.

3 Weisbrot, 'What Lawyers Need to Know, or What Lawyers Need to Be Able to Do: An Australian Experience' (2002), text at footnotes 34–8.

4 Elder, *Communication Skills* (1994) at 2.

Successful legal advocacy requires the following skills and attributes:

- successful communication, including:
  - understanding yourself (your strengths and weaknesses);
  - understanding your message; and
  - understanding your audience;
- preparation and hard work;
- knowledge of the subject matter and the decision-making process;
- integrity, respect, courtesy and a sense of duty;
- imagination coupled with common sense; and
- courage, confidence and patience.

Oral presentations are designed not only to test your knowledge of the law but also to help you to develop these two essential skills of communication and advocacy. One of the most common student concerns is fear of public speaking, yet, despite their fears, an overwhelming majority of law students want to learn how to communicate more effectively and how to cope with nerves. Another challenge arises from the fact that students must learn to use the law's technical terminology and jargon, but at the same time, they need to be able to communicate clearly, precisely, naturally and without overindulging in jargon and 'legalese'.

At first you may feel uncomfortable when you have to use unfamiliar legal language and conform to the rather artificial rules of legal etiquette – and this can add to the anxiety that you might encounter when doing legal presentations and moots at law school. Performance anxiety is common, however, and is experienced not only by students doing class presentations, but by practising professionals as well. The secret is to learn how to control your performance despite the sensation of anxiety – not in hoping and waiting for the anxiety to disappear. By learning to accept your nerves and focus instead on controlling *what you do* instead of trying to control *how you feel* you will be able to improve your performance each time you have to do a presentation.

4.5.1.1 Five top tips[5]

1. Learn to live with your nerves – rather than fight them.
2. Focus on controlling what you do – rather than trying to control how you feel.
3. Be yourself. Develop your own style – rather than adopting an artificial style.
4. Speak naturally – and avoid using a word-for-word script if you possibly can.
5. Slow down your delivery – rather than racing through the presentation.

4.5.2 Constructing an oral presentation using FIRO

It is important to approach your presentation in a methodical way. Before the presentation you need to *prepare, plan and practise*. During the presentation you need to pay attention to your *performance* skills (see section 4.5.3 below). After the presentation is over, it is important to take some time to *review* your performance and work out how to improve for the next time (see section 4.5.5 below).

5 This list of affirmations has been adapted from the examples given in Berger, McCroskey and Richmond, 'Communication Apprehension and Shyness' (1984).

The first step is to *prepare* by identifying the issues that arise from your topic and then doing the research to gather your ammunition. The second step is to *plan* your presentation by constructing a clear, logical and effective message and putting it into an organised structure. The FIRO approach can be adapted to organise your oral presentations. Never speak from a word-for-word script. Plan out your presentation and write up your notes in advance but avoid the temptation to write down every single word. Your presentation notes should consist of a set of headings, key sentences and dot points (ie a skeleton outline). Use setting out, numbering, headings, dot points and highlighters to emphasise the structure of your presentation and your argument. When you are doing the presentation, it helps to have a clearly visible layout with headings and numbered points so that you can see quickly where you are (and how far you have to go). A continuous stream of words on a page does not help at all: it is too easy to lose your place, and it will alienate and irritate your audience if all you do is read to them.

The list below shows how to structure an oral presentation using FIRO.

The beginning should identify the facts and the issues.

- **Facts:** Identify your presentation topic very succinctly and clearly. Explain, giving good factual reasons, why it is an important or worthwhile topic. Your aim in the introduction should be to grab the audience's attention and to interest them in your topic by helping them to understand why they should care about it. Think about how you can relate the topic to something they already care about – or how you can trigger their interest in something that they may never have thought about before. For example, you could:
  - convince the audience that there is a problem that needs to be solved by giving them some interesting factual information; or
  - use a little factual story or vignette to illustrate the problem or the topic.
- **Issues:** Identify the issues raised by the topic and, if necessary, place them into context. Explain how you will tackle the issues, so that the audience can follow your presentation. Remember, your goal in the introduction is to introduce both:
  - the topic (how it came about, why is it important, why they should care about it); and
  - the structure of the presentation itself.

The middle should explain the reasoning.

- **Reasoning:** Put forward the arguments that can solve the problem. Address the issues that you have identified in your introduction, making sure that you:
  - identify the steps in your reasoning – break it up logically and make sure that it flows from section to section;
  - provide evidence for your arguments; and
  - provide signposts as you go through each step, so that the audience can follow you more easily.

  Note: This should be the longest part of your presentation.

The end should identify the outcome and explain its significance.

- **Outcome:** Summarise by restating:
  - the desirable outcome of the debate; or
  - the suggested solution to the problem.

  Explain its significance: place it in a wider context by identifying what implications it has:
  - for the state of the law and its development; and/or
  - for the wider community.

The third step is to *practise* so that you feel comfortable with your material and can adjust the timing. It helps to do a trial run-through of your presentation in front of trusted family members or friends so that they can give you some constructive feedback. Once you have adjusted your presentation you are ready to *perform*.

4.5.3 Performance tips

The key to a good performance is control. You may not be able to control your feelings, but you can learn to control what you do. There are four key aspects for beginners to focus on:

1. Control your breathing.
2. Control the speed, volume and tone of your voice.
3. Control your body by maintaining a positive, steady and open posture.
4. Control where you look by maintaining eye contact with your audience.

Beyond these four crucial aspects, you can build your confidence in many ways and deliver a good performance.

4.5.3.1 Make sure you connect with your audience

Make frequent eye contact

This makes you look confident: do not seek refuge in looking down and reading your notes, because that will make you look less confident as well as being much less engaging. One of the (many) reasons you should avoid reading from a script is that it encourages you to focus too much on your notes and not enough on your audience.

Concentrate on how the audience is going

The key issue is not how *you* feel, but whether the *group* is getting the message. Many people feel bad inside while speaking in public, but no one else knows how you are feeling. (They cannot look into your secret heart!) Realise that your fear does not have to show – and take comfort from the fact that you are the only one who will ever know how you really felt.

Smile

Smiling makes you feel relaxed and inspires confidence. (Smiling also relaxes your throat.)

Try to 'read' your audience during the presentation

The audience's responses will tell you whether they are following you. Communication is a continuous loop and you are just one part of the circle.

Share your message – not your symptoms!

Learn how to 'float' by dissociating yourself just a little from your nerves and from the whole event. Try to monitor yourself as you present – as if you were an outside observer.

Attitude is important

Be positive. Remember that your audience and your teachers want you to succeed.

4.5.3.2 Use your voice well

Hydration is important

Drink water in the hour before the presentation so that your throat does not dry out – this often happens with nerves. Avoid coffee and alcohol on the day of the presentation as they can both dry out the throat. Take a bottle of water with you and use it if you need it. No one will mind if you stop for a sip of water.

Breathe deeply (from your diaphragm)

Relax your body, ease neck tension and warm up your voice in the morning.

Slow down

Speaking too quickly is one of the most common errors, so make a conscious effort to slow down so that the audience (who may never have heard the material before) can follow your words. Do not let nerves make you speed up. Learn to 'use the pause' to emphasise your points: this comes with conscious practice. Have a friend in the audience who can let you know if you are going too fast. Remember that a measured and controlled performance is a convincing performance. (To prove this to yourself, try reading this paragraph out loud as fast as you can – and then read it more slowly, incorporating some meaningful pauses. Note the difference between the two effects.) A controlled performance is an authoritative and convincing performance.

Vary the pitch, tone and speed of your presentation

Raise your voice to emphasise the important issues, and use the pause, as suggested above. A pause gives you time to think, to breathe and to relax a little – and it keeps the audience awake. You do not have to fill in every second with speech.

Watch your inflection

Many Australians use a rising inflection at the end of sentences (which has the effect of making a statement sound like a question). This speech pattern makes you seem uncertain of yourself and an audience will not find your presentation convincing. So, listen to yourself as you present and avoid using a rising inflection unless you are actually asking a question.

Project your voice

Project your voice but do not try to push it out (or you might strain it). Visualise your voice floating out to the middle of the room and you will automatically speak at the right volume. Don't focus on your throat: focus on where you want your voice to *go* (not where it is coming *from*).

Smooth out your voice

If your voice is jittery, consciously try to smooth out your delivery and caress the audience with your voice: this helps to eliminate the kinks and wobbles. Love your audience – and imagine yourself absorbing energy from them.

Eliminate irritating 'fillers' and 'powerless speech' patterns

Make a point of listening to yourself and editing out all of those irritating 'fillers' that add nothing to your message: 'um', 'er', 'uh', 'ah', 'well', 'like', 'sort of', 'OK', 'ya know', 'whatever', etc. They make you seem much less authoritative and much more uncertain of yourself.

4.5.3.3 Pay attention to style

Look at the audience and consciously talk directly to them

Scan slowly around the room as you speak and try to include all parts of the room. Do not focus only on one person or one side of the room.

Hold your body well and maintain a positive stance

Poor posture makes you look unconvincing – and it strangles your breathing and your voice. Do not slouch – keep the body open, not hunched or closed. Use gestures well: face, hands and shoulders. (Do not overdo it – or you'll look like you are conducting an orchestra!) Avoid fidgeting or displaying irritating or distracting body language: no fidgeting, fiddling, hand or foot tapping, no hands in pockets, no grooming of hair or skin, no scratching.

The pen is your enemy

Do NOT hold a pen while you speak; it will be almost impossible not to fiddle with it. If you must take one, make sure that you put it well away from you. It is very distracting for the audience if you constantly fiddle with a pen (or any other item like reading glasses, for example).

Make the most of your own personality

Diversity is important; without it life would be boring. There is no single way to be successful as a presenter. Legal audiences like thoughtful, calm and respectful presentations better than a big, flashy, overdramatic performance. Do not try to be something that you are not: the audience can usually sense if you are being fake. If you are true to yourself, the audience will believe you. If you try to trick them they will not trust your message. Try to find your own style, based on your strengths and personality. If you are enthusiastic – let it show. If you are quiet and thoughtful – use that.

Look professional and wear nice clothes

This will increase your confidence. Dress with care and you will feel careful; dress like a professional and you will feel like a professional. Do not be too casual in your dress or you might be too casual in your manner. Lose the hat and the sunglasses and any other physical barriers between you and your audience. Do not chew gum.

4.5.3.4 Content and method

Avoid memorising a word-for-word script

It leads to an artificial performance. It is also nerve-wracking and often just as bad as reading a word-for-word script. Aim for a natural speaking style (without using slang).

Signpost as you go

Make it clear when you are making transitions and moving through the presentation, so that your audience feels like they know where they are and can follow you through the presentation. Here are some useful phrases:

- This is a case about ...
- There are three reasons why this is important: ...
- There are three key issues: ...
- The first issue arose because ...
- The judge dealt with this issue by ...
- The most important issue in this case was ...
- Turning to the second problem, ...
- In summary, ...
- The significance of this case is ...
- So, to conclude, ...

Pay attention to time

Try never to run *over* or *under* time. But always make the best use of your time. Modern life is increasingly busy and as the old saying goes, 'time is money'. It is also disrespectful of your audience (and any other speakers) if you run over time. You should prepare well in advance and practise your presentation, so that you can ensure that it will fill the allocated time efficiently and not go on too long. Take a watch or mobile phone and use it to time your performance.

PowerPoint presentations

Many students use PowerPoint presentations. There are some basic rules about the effective use of these slides on the internet. (Just type 'using PowerPoint' into your search engine and then type in 'how not to use PowerPoint'.) The greatest sin is to put too much text onto a slide and then to turn your back on the audience so that you can read every word out to them. Old but gold, the comedian Don McMillan made a very entertaining video titled 'Life after Death by PowerPoint' which illustrates many of the common mistakes (and this is still valid today!): <www.youtube.com/watch?v=lpvgfmEU2Ck>.

Develop your skills: Think about your future

- What kind of job do you want when you graduate?
- What communication skills will you need to get that job?
- Take a moment to analyse yourself: what are your key strengths?
- What aspects of your communication skills do you need to work on?

4.5.4 Handling nerves and performance anxiety

Many people claim they are more afraid of public speaking than they are of dying, and indeed, as Dorothy Leeds explains in *Powerspeak* (1988) at 9–15, the nature of the classic symptoms of performance anxiety suggests that it is triggered by the same 'fight or flight response' that fills the body with adrenalin when we are confronted by a perceived attack or threat to our survival. The sense of panic and unease and the release of chemicals in the body can cause the nervous speaker to experience a number of symptoms including a dry mouth, a racing heart, shaking hands, knees or legs, perspiration attacks, blushing, 'butterflies' in the stomach, 'heart in the mouth', feeling sick, and an urgent need to go to the toilet. Some people experience a 'freezing' sensation where the mind seems to go blank. Others stutter and their voice shakes.

You can learn many different strategies to help you to cope with performance anxiety. Careful and thorough preparation is one of the most effective ways to build your confidence but remember that most advocates and performers have learned how to live with their nerves. You can do it too. Over the next few years at law school, you can improve your skills – if you start learning the techniques now and practise applying them. Do not wait until the nerves go away: for most of us they never do – we just learn to do it *with* the nerves. The secret is to accept that your nerves exist and focus instead on controlling what you *do* instead of trying to control *how you feel*. Remember that no one may ever be able to tell that you felt anxious.

If you admit your fears and accept your nerves, they will become less powerful. Nerves indicate that your task is important – and for lawyers, the task of communication and advocacy *is* important, so you will often experience nerves. The best advice is that you should not try to 'fight them' or be tempted to wait until they go away. Rather, you should learn how to live with them, so that they become your familiar companions. People who meditate have a technique for dealing with unwanted thoughts that interrupt their meditation, and you can adapt it to deal with unwanted nerves: simply allow yourself to notice the nerves but then return to the task without castigating yourself for being nervous. (You can talk and perspire at the same time!) Say to yourself, 'Oh, there they are again'. And then just keep going. Reinterpret nerves as a source of energy and use the adrenalin to get yourself up for a performance. There are a number of self-help techniques that you can learn to help you to cope with performance anxiety.

4.5.4.1 Self-help techniques

Visualisation

In the days leading up to the presentation, use the power of your imagination to rehearse. Imagine yourself giving the presentation in a positive way and 'see' yourself speaking in a loud, clear, assured voice. Get into the habit of projecting this image onto the screen in your inner mind. Once you see it often enough, the reality will begin to match the image.

Systematic desensitisation

If you are very fearful of public speaking, make a point of speaking up in tutorials and seminars to desensitise yourself and get used to it *before* you have to do a full presentation. Use your tutorial as your therapy group and see it as a chance to get some practice in speaking in public – where it will not count for marks. Start by making a promise to yourself to say two things in every class, then build up to becoming an active participant. Make a deal with a friend in your class that you will both do this and then go out and celebrate afterwards. Reward yourselves and turn it into a fun activity – or at least a shared challenge.

Learn how to consciously relax the tension in your body while you are speaking in classes. (Practise relaxing when you are doing the visualisation exercises as well so that you associate relaxed awareness with speaking in public.)

Eliminate negative thinking

Replace negative thoughts with positive thoughts or affirmations: do not allow the bad thoughts to dominate. Consciously replace them with positive thoughts.

- I can't do this. → I can do this. This is no big deal.
- I hate this. → This is easier than I thought.
- I'll go blank. → I have prepared good notes.
- I don't understand it. → I have prepared this well.
- This is hard. → This is not so difficult. I can enjoy it.
- I don't have the gift. → With practice, I can learn this skill.
- I'll sound stupid. → They don't know as much as I do.
- I'll look stupid. → No one can tell how I feel inside.
- Everyone is watching me. → I'll be able to explain it to them.
- No one will understand me. → I'll slow down: it helps.
- I'll never be able to do it. → This is my chance to improve.

You can adapt these methods to use in a range of settings where you experience performance anxiety (eg to prepare for exams or job interviews).

4.5.5 Review your performance

When you start out, do not compare yourself with professional communicators like television presenters, film actors or experienced barristers. Remind yourself that everyone starts as a beginner and gets better with effort, analysis and practice. One of the keys to improvement is to review your own performance. Make a plan to develop your skills and to document your progress. Do not worry if you don't yet have these skills: you can learn all of them with practice. We know that employers look for graduates who want to develop their own expertise, who can learn on the job and who constantly seek to improve their skills throughout their working lives. The following quotation from a leading law firm's employment website explains the kind of attitude that they expect in their employees:

> We are looking for people who will thrive in our high performance culture, who share our values and who want to grow and develop professionally. A willingness to learn is important because we encourage our people to value learning as a lifelong activity.

So, become a lifelong learner and take the opportunity to build up your skills while you are at university. If you document your progress, you will be able to use the experience in your first job interview as an illustration of how you have improved yourself and worked to overcome your problems.

Review your performance in regard to style, attitude, preparation and reflection.

Style

- Voice*:* Were you too fast/too slow, too soft? Did you use too many 'ums' and 'ers'? Consider the cause – too excited and eager, too nervous, did not realise or even notice?
- Eye contact: Were you looking up or looking down at your notes too much?
- Body language: Were you fidgety or still, hunched or open, using too many/few gestures?

Attitude

- Were you being true to yourself – or trying to act a part?
- Were you scared, unconfident, combative or aggressive?
- Were you too flashy, overacting, overdramatic, or playing for laughs?
- Were you confident, calm, controlled, engaging, knowledgeable, polite and respectful?

Preparation

- Did your notes help or hinder?

Reflect

- What will you do next time to improve your performance?

Read everything you can about communication and advocacy, and go to watch experienced performers in public lectures, courtrooms, comedy clubs, etc. Bear in mind, as you watch the presentations of your classmates (and your lecturers or performers on television), that you can always learn something from every presentation, no matter how brilliant or how bad the presentation is. So, if you are enjoying a presentation, ask yourself what it is about that presentation that makes it so effective – and steal the trick from them. If a presentation is not working, do not tune out. Instead, ask yourself what feature is destroying the presentation – and learn how to avoid it in your own presentations. If you adopt an analytical and inquiring approach not only to your own presentations, but to the presentations of others as well, you will improve your own understanding and performance.

The comedian Jerry Seinfeld once said that most people attending a funeral would rather be in the casket than standing up the front giving the eulogy. If you feel this way and think that you would benefit from some extra practice and advice, you might consider joining a Rostrum group or Toastmasters International. These groups will help you to develop skills in public speaking, chairmanship of meetings and leadership. There are also many useful sources of information and assistance on public speaking on the internet. Don't forget about the numerous resources that universities develop and share with their students, as well as the activities, competitions and mentorship programs put in place by student organisations.

4.6 Exam strategies

4.6.1 Preparation is the secret of success

Your first experience of a law exam can be daunting – especially if it is a problem-solving exam and you have not developed your skills during the term. However, if you have followed the advice in Chapter 3 and this chapter, you should approach your law exams with confidence. If you have worked steadily throughout the term and made – and road tested – a summary of the law, you will be ready for the exam. If you have used your summary to answer tutorial questions and then asked for feedback from the teaching staff, you will know what they expect, and you will be able to deliver the answers that they are looking for. If you have practised tutorial questions or past exam papers under exam conditions, you will know exactly what is needed to cover the necessary material in the time that is allocated to the questions and so time management will not be a problem. You will be familiar with the kinds of issues that may arise (so you can spot them more easily) and you will be experienced in constructing an answer that states the relevant law, applies it to the facts, and considers both the arguments and the counterarguments that could arise. If you make the effort, you can make your own luck.

4.6.2 Revision

Everyone deals with exam stress in different ways. If you have left everything to the last week before the exam, you will not be able to avoid stress. However, if you have studied well during the term, your experience during the days before the exam may well be intense, but it need not be completely nerve-wracking. Some tips for the revision week follow.

4.6.2.1 Maintain a sense of control

Work out a plan and stick to it. List all the topics that you want to cover and allocate a set period for each task. This will give you confidence that you will get everything done and it will also help you to become 'time aware', which is a useful attribute at exam time. If you work in set blocks of time during swot vac you will help yourself to keep control of time during the exam. Do not allow yourself to get bogged down on one particular topic. Keep moving.

4.6.2.2 Include some recreation in your program

You need regular breaks to keep yourself fresh and to allow your brain time to process all the information that you are revising. So, make sure that you include some rest and recreation in your revision program. It will also help you to stay 'on task' if you know that you have a break already programmed.

4.6.2.3 Less is more

Do not try to do too much during the pre-exam study week. It is better to do less and really understand it than to overload yourself with detail and become exhausted and overwhelmed. Work steadily during the term to keep yourself on track for a productive pre-exam study week.

4.6.2.4 Your main task is to practise answering questions

The main task is to practise writing up exam answers, so make sure you have completed your summary during the term, then use the time in the pre-exam study week to refresh your understanding of the law and get into exam mode. Remember that the first time you attempt a problem question, you get only about halfway through it. After you work your way through some more questions, you learn how to cover all the relevant points efficiently and in enough depth in the allotted time. You must learn how to get to the point quickly and economically – so you need to practise this and get up to speed. Get feedback from the teaching staff to improve your answers.

4.6.2.5 Follow your tutorial or seminar program

If you work on your tutorial or seminar questions, you will come across many of the issues that tend to crop up in exams, and this makes spotting the issues in the exam and arguing them out much easier. The questions in an exam are often designed to mirror the work that you should have done during the term, so bear this in mind during the revision period.

4.6.2.6 Vary your revision program

It may help to program some time for group study, when you get together with other students to brainstorm the issues in past exam questions. Then go home and practise writing up the answer on your own. This will improve your confidence and build some social activity into your exam preparation – even if it is only law-focused activity! However, if the group study does not help, cancel it and focus on your own agenda.

4.6.3 During the exam

There are some basic rules for success in exams.

4.6.3.1 Follow the instructions

Read the instructions carefully. Under the pressure of the exam, you can sometimes make mistakes, so you need to focus carefully and make sure that you follow the instructions. Make sure that you understand the exact number of questions that you have to answer and work out how long you have to answer each one. If you have any doubts, ask for clarification.

4.6.3.2 Never go over time

It can be very tempting to go over time in a question, but you must resist the temptation. It is the most common error made by beginners in exams and is the worst mistake that you can make. The horrible feeling that you experience when you have left yourself only 15 minutes to do a 40-minute question is so distressing that most students rarely make this mistake more than once – but it is better never to make it all. Make sure you manage your time, and practise doing so!

4.6.3.3 Plan your answer before launching

It is always worthwhile taking some time to plan out your answer before you start writing. It is tempting to let your eager pen bite into the paper as soon as the invigilator allows you to begin, but this too is a temptation that must be resisted. This is especially important in a law exam, where identifying and addressing the legal issues is so important. There are two reasons for this claim: first, you cannot manage your time effectively if you have not identified the issues before you start writing; and second, you can insure yourself against losing marks if you follow the FIRO format for constructing your answer. If you introduce your problem question by identifying both the critical facts *and* the issues carefully and succinctly, you can probably convince the marker that you understand the problem (and the relevant law) by the end of the first two paragraphs. Then it is not a matter of whether you will pass, but only a matter of how well you will do.

4.6.3.4 The 'open-book' exam trap

It can be tempting to take too much material into an open-book exam. But realistically you do not have a lot of time in an exam to do extensive research and you need to prepare and use your materials carefully. In some ways it can help to treat an open-book exam like a closed-book exam; make sure that you understand the material – and then use your summary as a record of that understanding and a trigger to your memory. If you must take a lot of material into the exam, you have to be able to find your way around it with ease, so be organised. You need a concise summary of the law that will fit comfortably on the desk and that you know how to use.

4.6.4 Advice on problem-solving questions

Problem-solving questions have their own set of rules to follow.

4.6.4.1 Make sure you get the law right

In an open-book exam, you receive very little credit for getting the law right. This is because an open-book exam is designed to reveal your depth of skills in issue spotting, legal argument and analysis. By the same token, you may be penalised if you get the law wrong, particularly in an open-book exam, where you are allowed to take all your notes and summaries in with you. So, get into the habit of being very careful to get the law correct when you are making your summary.

4.6.4.2 Get to the point

Do not waste words. Do not introduce your question by rewriting all the facts of the problem (stick to the 'six-point plan') and do not allow yourself to digress by telling long-winded stories of the facts from the cases.

You are writing for an expert – so you do not have to give an introductory paragraph on the background of the law. Time is always at a premium in law exams, so learn how to get to the point and address it. Do not repeat yourself – just say things once and move on. Remember too that you can cross-reference *within* an answer. You score most marks for identifying issues and arguing them out, so focus your efforts on these two aspects.

4.6.4.3 Use HIRAC carefully

Remember that you do not have to use HIRAC for every point you make. There are times when you need to be brief and there are times when you need to go into depth. Remember, the longest part of any answer should always be the '**A**pplication' part, so if you get to the end of a long problem question and you have not gone into some depth of argument and counter-argument at any stage, then you have probably missed the point of the question. Check to see if you have jumped to a conclusion where there may have been an arguable issue.

4.6.4.4 Cite an authority for every proposition of law – and then use the law

Some students manage to write an answer to a problem question without citing a single case. This is a fundamental error. You must always cite a case or statute as your authority for the law, but remember that you do not have to give full citations in an exam. Furthermore, if you write a proposition of law down in your answer, you should also make sure that you *apply it* to the facts – if you do not use it, then it is probably not worth putting it down in the first place.

4.6.4.5 Use the authorities correctly

It often helps your answer if you can use the authorities not only as the source of the legal rules and principles, but also in your application and arguments. So, once you have cited your authority, stop and think: consider whether there are any significant similarities and/or differences between the facts of the authority and the facts in the problem questions. If so, you should point them out and weave them into your discussion of the issue.

4.6.4.6 Use the legal method (and do not fake it)

Some students who have not practised using the HIRAC method of structuring their arguments on an issue try to dress up their answers with the HIRAC style. However, there is more to HIRAC than structure; you must actually deliver upon your promise, so avoid answers like this:

> Heading: Battery
>
> Issue: Was there a battery?
>
> > *(This is not specific enough: what is the conduct?)*
>
> Rule: There must be a positive act.
>
> > *(No authority cited.)*
>
> Application: On the facts, P will argue that there was a positive act. On the other hand, D will argue that there was no positive act.
>
> > *(These statements are not arguments or counterarguments, they are simply two restatements of the rule urging alternative conclusions without arguing for them.)*
>
> Conclusion: It will be up to the court to decide.
>
> > *(This is not a conclusion – and it is very annoying!)*

4.6.4.7 Be precise and careful

You need to be precise in your statements of the law. Vague approximations are not convincing. You also need to check your facts. Under the stress of the exam, you can misremember the facts, so always double-check them before you commit to paper.

4.6.4.8 Do not jump to conclusions

This is a common failing. If you think that something is obvious or clear, you must explain *why* you reached that conclusion and show *how* it can be argued, even if only briefly. Remember, you always need to explain your reasoning. The reason why you need to show your 'working out' is because it is the argument that scores you marks, and not necessarily the conclusion. Jumping to a conclusion is almost always a mistake because your assessors are not always testing your ability to resolve the case. They are testing your knowledge of the law and your ability to construct legal arguments using that knowledge. Try to see the issues as an opportunity to show off these skills. Don't always race to a conclusion.

4.6.4.9 Avoid overenthusiastic use of the word 'clearly'

Be very careful when you use this word. It is a red rag to a lawyer – and a marker! If you say that something is clear, always explain why it is clear by referring to the relevant facts from the exam paper. Remember that if there seem to be a lot of facts provided on a particular aspect of the question, then that is probably an indication that you need to argue and counterargue the issue. Think about how each fact could be used and ask yourself why it might have been included. If you are not using the facts that have been provided in the question, you should consider whether you have missed an arguable issue.

4.6.4.10 Do not assume facts

Lecturers often leave facts out so that you can show off your skills by answering both ways. If you assume facts (and this is a risk), you must at least say that the facts are unclear and then identify what facts you have assumed. However, it is better not to assume them at all.

4.6.4.11 Reveal your structure

Make your structure clear to the marker so that they will be reassured that you know what you are doing. Use the headings and standard phrases that will help the marker see that you are on track and remember to underline case names and statutes (but do not waste time by giving full citations). This is especially important if your handwriting deteriorates under the stress of the exam. Make it easy for your markers to recognise what you are doing and to give you marks.

4.6.4.12 You can save time

You do not have to write up a problem question in the same way that you would write an essay – you can write it more like a report – and use headings and layout to show the steps in your answer. Do not waste time and words by repeating any particular sentences or paragraphs: just cross-reference. Remember too that you can use abbreviations for the names of the parties (use either P and D or perhaps their initials: PL v JD) and for the names of statutes (use *CLA* instead of writing out *Civil Liability Act* each time you refer to it).

4.6.5 Advice on essay questions

Some exams contain essay-style questions as well as problem-solving questions. As mentioned above, students do not usually find these questions to be too stressful, mainly because they have answered this type of question in exams before. If your exam contains both kinds of questions and you are one of those students who always seems to run out of time in exams, then doing an essay question can be a godsend. This is because you can more easily tailor an essay question to the available time without losing too many marks. By contrast with problem questions, which generally require you to cover a designated set of issues, an essay question can be answered either in depth or very concisely. So, if time management is a problem for you in exams, reserve an essay question for last, and then write a very pointed, waffle-free answer. Some more advice for answering essay questions follows.

4.6.5.1 Make sure that you answer the actual question

The main problem with essay questions is that students often tend to respond to the keywords in the question and then proceed to write down everything that they know about the general topic, without thinking about the actual question that was asked and taking care to address it.

4.6.5.2 Do not 'flood'

It is tempting in an open-book exam to try to 'flood' an essay answer with prepared material, but remember that you do not get marks for the length of your answer and too much irrelevant material will detract from your answer.

4.6.5.3 Select the relevant material and discard the irrelevant material

If you have an essay question, you have to be able to select from your prepared notes only the relevant material that will answer the actual question that is asked. If you do this, you can sometimes answer the question in a few succinct and direct pages and still get a good mark. If, on the other hand, you write down everything you know and cover 8 to 10 pages, but include too much irrelevant detail without focusing on the important parts in enough detail, you might receive only a low pass. It is better to have good, signposted notes and to select from those notes only the relevant material.

4.6.5.4 Be careful how you use a prepared answer

It is also tempting to write out an answer to a question that you had hoped might be on the exam but that did not actually appear. This is always a risk. Another temptation is simply to write out your tutorial or seminar notes on the topic – this can be a problem if the class topic focused on one aspect of a particular matter, but the exam question requires something different. It can also be a problem if you rely only on your lecture notes, because the essay may well require extra depth – or a different focus.

4.6.5.5 Critical discussion is important

If you are asked to critically discuss an issue, you must be able to come up with arguments *and* counterarguments. It will not be enough to regurgitate the facts and the law from your notes of the relevant cases – you will have to address the particular issues, think on your feet and demonstrate your ability to see both sides of the matter. Then, having done so, you can suggest which is the correct argument and give your reasons for that view.

4.6.5.6 Spell it out!

Many students manage to cover the correct material in their essay answers but do not appear to understand (or at least do not explain clearly enough) how that material is relevant to the question. So, always make your point clear and spell out why the material that you refer to in an essay question is relevant by linking it to the question.

Conclusion

Part 1 of this book has attempted to explain the law of torts and help you to understand how to organise your study so that you can achieve the results that you are aiming for. However, you should not judge yourself by your results. While getting good marks is nice, remember that getting good marks does not mean that you are a good person, or that you will necessarily be a good lawyer – good people and future great lawyers do not always get good marks. We pass this advice on to you because, having been both torts students and torts teachers for many years now, we know how true it is. You should not judge yourself a success or a failure by your results. Rather you should judge yourself by your efforts and the good faith you put into your work, both of which are more important than getting good marks. Many law students feel under extreme pressure to do well – and many outsiders simply do not understand how difficult it is. Your fellow students and your teachers do know how difficult it is to excel in the study of law, and while excellence is worth striving for, it is not measured exclusively in relation to marks – teachers and future employers know this. So be humble if you do well, and do not feel ashamed if you have not done as well as you were aiming for. If you have put in the best effort that you could in the circumstances, the work will always pay off in the long run.

REFERENCES

CASES

Andreae v Selfridge & Co Ltd [1938] Ch 1; [1937] 3 All ER 255
Bamford v Turnley (1860) 3 B & S 66; 122 ER 27
Christie v Davey [1893] 1 Ch 316
Fraser v Booth (1949) 50 SR (NSW) 113
Hollywood Silver Fox Farm v Emmett [1936] 2 KB 468; [1936] 1 All ER 825
Hunter v Canary Wharf Ltd [1997] AC 655; [1997] 2 All ER 426
Hutchins v Maughan [1947] VLR 131
Innes v Wylie (1844) 1 Car & K 257; 174 ER 800
Laws v Florinplace [1981] 1 All ER 659
Lester-Travers v City of Frankston [1970] VR 2
Platt v Nutt (1988) 12 NSWLR 231
Scott v Shepherd (1773) 2 Black W 892; 96 ER 525

St Helen's Smelting Co v Tipping (1865) 11 HLC 642; 11 ER 1483
Thompson-Schwab v Costaki [1956] 1 All ER 652; [1956] 1 WLR 335
Walter v Selfe (1851) 4 De G & Sm 315; 64 ER 849

ARTICLES, BOOKS AND OTHER RESOURCE

Berger, B A, McCroskey, J C & Richmond, V P, 'Communication Apprehension and Shyness', in Tinally, W N, Beardsley, R S & Cultiss, F R (eds), *Communication in Pharmacy Practice: A Practical Guide for Students and Practitioners* (1984) Lea & Febiger, Philadelphia, PA, 128.

Brogan, M & Spencer D, *Surviving Law School*, 2nd ed (2007) Oxford University Press, Melbourne.

Crawford, R, *The Persuasion Edge* (1989) Professional Education System, Wisconsin.

Elder, B, *Communication Skills* (1994) Macmillan, Melbourne.

Leeds, D, *Powerspeak* (1988) Judy Piatkus Ltd, London.

Melbourne University Law Review Association Inc and Melbourne Journal of International Law, *Australian Guide to Legal Citation*, 4th ed (2018) <https://law.unimelb.edu.au/mulr/aglx/about>.

O'Brien, K, 'Judicial Attitudes to Plain Language and the Law' (2009) 32 *Australian Bar Review* 204.

Stuhmcke, A, *Legal Referencing*, 3rd ed (2005) Butterworths, Sydney.

Weisbrot, D, 'What Lawyers Need to Know, or What Lawyers Need to Be Able to Do: An Australian Experience' (2002) 2001 ALWD Conference Proceedings, 1 *Journal of the Association of Legal Writing Directors* 21.

THE TORTS

Our approach to the torts

Well over a hundred years ago, the common law was described as 'chaos with a full index'.[1] The law of torts in particular developed in a haphazard way over hundreds of years – without the guidance of any accepted unifying theory that could either define the parameters of this expanding body of law or give a standard structure to each of the 'loose federation of causes of actions'[2] known as 'torts'. Consequently, an 'elements approach' has generally been taken to teaching this subject. This approach treats each tort as a separate entity, focusing on its specific list of elements and then moving on to the defences associated with each action.

While this 'torts as recipes'[3] approach to the subject has benefits, it also has limitations. For example, considering each tort as a separate entity does not help us to build a theory of tort law or to recognise common patterns in the law. In addition, there is no universally agreed-upon list of elements for each tort. In fact, some texts do not provide a list of elements at all. Many judges and commentators have pointed out that the division of a tort into elements is adapted mainly 'for convenience and to promote consistency of approach and accurate analysis', and that these elements are often interrelated and 'not entirely free standing'.[4] In other words, although the elements approach proceeds on the basis that each tort consists of several, well-defined elements, in reality the elements often bleed into one another, presenting a more complicated story.

1 Postema, 'Introduction: Search for an Explanatory Theory of Torts' (2001) at 1, citing Sir Thomas Holland.
2 Cane, *Tort Law and Economic Interests*, 2nd ed (1996) at 447.
3 Cane, *The Anatomy of Tort Law* (1997) at 2–10.
4 Kirby J in *Neindorf v Junkovic* (2005) at [50].

To address these problems, this book supplements the elements approach with a 'torts typology' approach, which treats each tort as a member of the same family (rather than as a separate entity). It does this by sorting and explaining the law that constitutes each tort using the same four conceptual aspects: conduct, effect, fault and circumstances. By using this standard analytical tool, we seek to impose some structure onto the apparent chaos of the law of torts. We hope that this will help you to create a sense of order for yourself.

Our torts typology, which is laid out in the list below, mirrors the advice given in Chapter 3, which encouraged you – as far as possible – to separate the factual facets of a case (for example, what the defendant *did* and what *effects* it had on the plaintiff) from its legal or normative facets (which explain why the conduct is viewed by the community as an actionable wrong). The first two aspects in the torts typology list identify the 'conduct and effect' pairs that you need to look for when solving torts problems, and together they explain the primarily *factual* matters that must be identified and proved by the plaintiff. The third aspect is primarily *normative* (*values-based*) because it contains the tests for fault. The final aspect, 'circumstances', specifies any other conditions that need to be satisfied before the defendant can be found legally liable to compensate the plaintiff, and it contains both factual and normative components. It is here that the two criteria of reasonableness and objectivity are generally incorporated into the assessment. This aspect also contains the requirement that there be no lawful justification for the conduct. This normative aspect is common to every tort, and it is included to emphasise the fact that a tort is a matter of wrongdoing, not simply an act of harm-doing. Its inclusion reminds you to consider any possible defences to the tort.

A torts typology

- **Conduct:** is primarily a factual aspect.
  - This aspect tells you what kind of conduct to look for in a problem question and clarifies whether there must be a positive act or whether an omission will suffice.
  - It helps you to identify the defendant.
  - Your task in any problem-solving exercise is to look at the facts in a problem question and write down as clearly as possible exactly what conduct was being complained about and who did it.
- **Effect:** is primarily a factual aspect.
  - This aspect tells you what kind of adverse effects to look for in a problem question. It explains whether the tort is:
    - a rights-based tort that is actionable per se; or
    - a harm-based tort that requires proof of actual damage before liability will be imposed.
  - It also explains whether the effect must be directly caused or whether an indirectly caused or consequential effect is acceptable.
  - It helps you to identify the plaintiff and the remedy.
  - Your task in any problem-solving exercise is to look at the facts and write down as clearly as possible who has been harmed, and the nature and extent

of the harmful effects. You then consider the appropriate remedies that may be claimed by the plaintiff to make good the harm that has been caused. See section 2.3.3.2 of in Chapter 2 for remedies.

- **Fault:** is primarily a normative aspect.
  - This aspect tells you what the tests for fault are.
  - These tests normally relate to the defendant's intention, knowledge or state of mind and identify whether the standard to be applied is objective or subjective.
  - Your task in any problem-solving exercise is to cite the relevant legal test (with its authority) and apply it to the facts of your problem question, using any other relevant cases to assist in your arguments.
- **Circumstance:** is an aspect which may include normative or factual tests.
  - This aspect identifies any other circumstances that must be proved or legal tests or limits that must be satisfied before the defendant will be held to be legally liable for their conduct. Most of these extra tests involve limits based on reasonableness or an objective person standard, but they may also include statutory requirements and limitations.
  - Your task in any problem-solving exercise is to cite the relevant legal tests (with authorities) and apply them to the facts of your problem question, using any other relevant cases to assist in your arguments.

While we consider this torts typology to be a useful tool to help you to navigate your way through the complexities of torts law, we acknowledge the practical utility of the elements approach. Consequently, each chapter continues to set out traditional lists of elements alongside our torts typology. The chapters also contain the same propositions of law as more traditional textbooks – they are simply cut up in a *different* way, in order to show you more clearly how the law of torts works. This approach has been designed to help you to:

- understand the nature of tort law better, by allowing you to analyse, compare and contrast each tort using the same conceptual categories each time;
- learn how to approach practical problem-solving exercises, by explaining how to recognise each tort on the facts and encouraging you to adopt a structured methodology that starts with the facts and then moves to the law; and
- prepare for professional practice, by assisting you to draft a statement of claim that includes the particulars or to write up a defence to a claim.

This method of exploring and understanding the essential aspects of the torts also expands upon the first two dimensions of the definition of a tort given in Chapter 1: wrongdoing and harm. Conceptually, a tort is *conduct* by one person that causes an *adverse or harmful effect* on another person, which is seen by the community to be blameworthy and *wrongful* in all the *circumstances*. So, the chapters in Part 2 explain exactly what kinds of conduct and effects to look for in your problem-solving exercises and consider all the circumstances that must exist before a defendant will be found legally liable to compensate the plaintiff or to provide the plaintiff with some other remedy.

By cutting up every tort in the same way each time, this method of analysis helps us to build a theory of tort law and recognise common patterns – or exceptions to those patterns. It also allows us to classify the members of the wider family of torts in different ways, depending on which organising concept we are most interested in. So, for example, we might begin by classifying the torts by the category of adverse or harmful effect, and then we could see how the groupings change if we adopt a fault-based criterion instead. It would also be possible to adopt a more complicated, two-part categorisation, by making an initial classification based on one element and then using another element to create subgroupings within the first group. For example, we could make the first cut by using the conduct element and then use a harm-based criterion to create a second set of sub-groups. This approach to analysing each tort can also be useful when you need to identify the relative merits of alternative causes of action in any given practical problem-solving question. For example, you can more easily compare and contrast a 'negligent trespass' to the person, land or goods with the classic negligence action to see which offers the better option.

This typology also aligns closely with the FIRO structure outlined in Chapter 3, which was designed to help students develop and present structured legal arguments. The first two aspects of the typology – conduct and effect – correspond to the 'Facts' and 'Issues' stages of FIRO, where students identify what happened and what kind of harm resulted. The third aspect – fault – guides the 'Reasoning' stage, helping students to apply relevant rules and assess the defendant's mental state or degree of care. The final aspect – circumstances – connects with both the 'Reasoning' and 'Outcome' stages, ensuring that students consider any contextual limits on liability, including justification or statutory authorisation. Together, the typology and FIRO framework offer a consistent and integrated method for analysing tort problems and constructing coherent legal arguments.

Structure of chapters

Most of the chapters in Part 2 begin in the same way – by defining the tort, listing its elements, noting the rules on the onus of proof and identifying the key principles behind the tort. The chapter then gives you an overview of the relevant law (structured according to the torts typology), notes any particular defences and remedies and, where relevant, notes any critique of the tort or possible developments in the area. The major exception is found in the discussion of the tort of negligence, which is covered in six chapters (Chapters 10–15). The discussion of each tort concludes with a section giving you advice on problem solving.

Chapters 5 and 6 also each contain a section titled 'Some helpful cases for your summary' that includes an 'Active reading' task asking you to link each case to an element of the tort. This feature drops out after these two chapters, and is replaced by another 'Active reading' feature that is linked to the new 'Summary points' feature that appears in the later chapters. Chapters 5–9 also each include a 'Case to remember' feature, which aims to support your learning in the early chapters. This feature drops out after Chapter 9, by which stage we hope you have learned how to make your own case summaries. At the end of each chapter you will find sample problem questions and other exercises that will allow you to test your understanding of the content of each tort, and to develop your legal writing and/or oral communication skills.

This chapter structure has been carefully designed to help you to build your basic skills in:

- recognising and clearly identifying the conduct and its effects;
- working out the appropriate remedies;
- identifying the issues;
- stating the appropriate rules and principles; and
- constructing arguments and counterarguments that apply the law to the facts to resolve the issues.

A warning

You need to remember that the law of torts is an uncertain body of law. As you saw in Chapter 1:

- there is no agreement on the definitions of many of the most basic and ancient torts (such as battery);
- there is no agreement on the elements of many of the torts;
- there is no agreement throughout the common law world on the content and scope of the law of torts;
- many of the crucial standards and tests that determine whether or not a tort has been committed are vague and uncertain; and
- the line between the elements and the defences is sometimes very difficult to draw.

Furthermore, it is very likely that for any proposition of law that is cited in a given torts case, you will be able to find another case either from Australia or some other common law country – generally the United Kingdom, Canada, New Zealand and the United States – which points towards a different view of the law.

You should also be aware that uncertainty in tort law does not arise only from case law. In many jurisdictions, the *Civil Liability Acts* contain provisions that have generated significant interpretive uncertainty. Despite being legislative in form, many of these statutory provisions use open-ended language that still requires judicial clarification. As a result, even the statutory framework intended to bring clarity has itself become a source of ongoing legal debate and variation between states and territories.

Consequently, each torts teacher constructs a slightly different 'universe' of the law of torts for you to work within, and this means you may need to modify the definitions and elements that have been supplied in this book to match your lecturer's approach. Consult your study materials and find your own lecturer's version of the definition and set of elements for each tort and make sure that you find a case or statute to cite as an authority for each of them.

A final thought: remember that you should adopt a critical approach to each tort and to every legal test you find. An unquestioning approach to the law does not serve the community properly – and the law of torts cannot develop unless it is challenged!

REFERENCES

CASE

Neindorf v Junkovic [2005] HCA 75; (2005) 222 ALR 631

BOOKS

Cane, P, *The Anatomy of Tort Law* (1997) Hart Publishing, Oxford.
Cane, P, *Tort Law and Economic Interests*, 2nd ed (1996) Clarendon Press, Oxford.
Postema, G J, 'Introduction: Search for an Explanatory Theory of Torts', in Postema, G J (ed), *Philosophy and the Law of Torts* (2001) Cambridge University Press, Cambridge, 1.

TRESPASS TO THE PERSON

5

Introduction

The trespass torts are some of the oldest causes of action in the common law. These torts create a number of fundamental common law rights protecting our personal dignity, our desire for autonomy, and our interests in the physical integrity of our bodies and the exclusive possession of land and goods. This chapter examines the nature of these torts and focuses on the three forms of trespass to the person: battery, assault and false imprisonment. It also briefly considers the potential development of a tort of privacy. Chapter 6 looks at the torts of trespass to land, trespass to goods, conversion and detinue.

5.1 The trespass torts

5.1.1 The nature of the trespass torts

One way in which trespass can be defined is by focusing on the adverse effects of the relevant conduct. From this perspective, trespass is an unjustified positive act that directly and either intentionally, recklessly or negligently interferes with the person, land or goods of another person. The various trespass torts differ in the nature of the adverse effect required, and each has its own distinctive focal point:

- battery – physical contact or interference with the body;
- assault – mental apprehension of imminent physical interference;
- false imprisonment – total restraint of liberty by confinement;
- trespass to land – interference with exclusive possession of land;
- trespass to goods – interference with exclusive possession of goods.

Another way of defining trespass is to emphasise the rights-based nature of these torts. From this perspective, trespass is an unjustified positive act that directly and either intentionally, recklessly or negligently invades another person's defined rights to bodily and mental integrity, freedom from confinement or the exclusive possession of land and goods.

Because the trespass torts protect fundamental common law rights, they do not require proof of any element of actual damage – they are actionable per se. As Brennan J pointed out at 236 in *Secretary, Department of Health and Community Services v JWB and SMB (Marion's Case)* (1992), 'each person has a unique dignity which the law respects and which it will protect'. It is for this reason that the trespass torts are sometimes called the 'dignitary torts', and why they impose liability for any direct and unjustified interference with a protected interest, even if that interference causes no harm.

5.1.2 The directness requirement: Trespass vs action on the case

One of the key features of the trespass torts is that they involve a *direct* interference with the plaintiff's rights. This is what differentiates trespass from an 'action on the case', which involves an *indirect* interference with the plaintiff's interests. You can refresh your memory of the difference between the trespass torts and actions on the case by consulting sections 2.2.4.1 and 2.2.4.2 of Chapter 2. The distinction between direct and indirect interference was the Court's focus in *Scott v Shepherd* (1773) (see the following 'A case to remember').

A case to remember

***Scott v Shepherd* (1773) 2 Black W 892; 96 ER 525**

Topic

Directness

Facts

D threw a lighted firework (known as a squib) into a crowded marketplace. It landed on a market stall and the stallholder instinctively threw it away. It then landed on the next stall and the second stallholder also instantly threw it away. It exploded and blinded P in one eye.

Issue

Was the contact with the P's body the direct and immediate result of D's conduct (making it a case of trespass to the person) or was it indirect (making it a case of 'action on the case')?

Significance

It was held by the majority of the Court that the physical contact was a sufficiently direct effect of D's conduct. The acts by the stallholders were not new or intervening causes of the contact. This 'extended' conception of directness applies where the contact is the result of another person acting out of a compulsive necessity for their own safety. In such circumstances the original actor will be held to have directly caused the contact.

Counterexample

This can be contrasted with *Hutchins v Maughan* (1947), a case of trespass to goods. In that case D warned P that he had laid poisoned bait in a particular area. Despite that warning, P took his sheepdogs to that place where they ate the bait and died. It was held that the harmful contact with the dogs was not sufficiently direct to constitute trespass. The real cause of the contact between the dogs and the bait was the consciously chosen act of intervention by P, who took the dogs to the baited area. Herring CJ did suggest that it would have been direct enough for a trespass action if D had thrown the baits to the dogs.

Where the defendant has *indirectly* harmed the plaintiff, the plaintiff will generally sue them for negligence (which is addressed in Chapters 10–15). However, if the indirect harm was caused *intentionally*, the plaintiff could also bring an action for one of the following torts:

- Action on the case for the intentional infliction of physical injury: This requires proof of a positive act by the defendant which indirectly caused actual physical injury to the plaintiff. The defendant must have intended to inflict the injury or been reckless about causing it (*Bird v Holbrook* (1828)).
- Action on the case for the intentional infliction of psychiatric injury or nervous shock: This requires proof of a positive act by the defendant which indirectly caused nervous shock or psychiatric injury to the plaintiff. The defendant must have wilfully intended to shock the plaintiff or been reckless about doing so. In addition, the defendant's conduct must have been 'calculated' or objectively likely to cause nervous shock or psychiatric injury (*Wilkinson v Downton* (1897); *Nationwide News v Naidu* (2007)).

While it is theoretically possible for a plaintiff to bring an action in these torts, in practice suits for action on the case are very rare (and so are not discussed in detail in this book). This is because the law in this area has largely been subsumed by advances in the tort of negligence. This has led some to doubt about whether there is even a need for these torts any more (see, eg, *Carrier v Bonham* (2001) at [27]; *Magill v Magill* (2006) at [117]). However, others have suggested that they remain necessary – and should even be expanded. For example, it has been suggested that the tort of action on the case for the intentional infliction of psychiatric injury or nervous shock should be extended to cover intentionally caused emotional distress, as is the case in many parts of the United States (see, eg, *Giller v Procopets* (2008), Maxwell P at [31] (dissenting)).

Develop your skills

The dissenting judgment of Blackstone J in *Scott v Shepherd* (1773) offers an early and insightful illustration of the conceptual uncertainties that continue to shape tort law. While the majority of the Court held the defendant liable for battery despite the intervening actions of third parties, Blackstone J argued that the necessary directness for trespass was lacking. To explore this tension, read Blackstone J's dissent alongside the majority's reasoning. Then write a short commentary analysing how the case highlights ongoing debates in tort law – particularly the distinction between trespass and negligence, and the legal significance of intervening acts. In your response, consider how each judgment characterises the causal link between the defendant's conduct and the plaintiff's injury, and reflect on which approach you find more persuasive and why.

5.1.3 Features of the trespass torts

The trespass torts share several common features, which we can classify using our torts typology.

5.1.3.1 Conduct

There must be a positive act by the defendant. It will generally not be sufficient for the defendant to have engaged in merely passive conduct, or to have failed to act in a certain way.

5.1.3.2 Effect

The defendant must have directly interfered with the relevant right. If the defendant only indirectly interfered with the right, the plaintiff will need to rely on one of the harm-based actions on the case. The mere invasion of the relevant right is sufficient. There is no need to prove damage. If damage does occur, this will increase the amount of damages that are payable.

5.1.3.3 Fault

The defendant's conduct must have been voluntary (directed by their will or conscious mind). Involuntary conduct, such as may occur while sleepwalking or during an epileptic seizure, is not considered blameworthy.

The defendant will be liable as long as they acted intentionally, recklessly or negligently (meaning carelessly). They will only escape liability if they were 'utterly without fault' (or had a lawful justification for their conduct). This low fault threshold is justified by the importance of the rights that these torts protect.

It is important to note that the concept of 'negligence' holds a different meaning in this context than it does in the tort of negligence. When used in relation to the trespass torts, negligence refers to mere carelessness in committing the act that constitutes the trespass. It does not require proof that the defendant breached a duty of care.

The defendant does not need to have exhibited ill will or hostility towards the plaintiff. This also emphasises the rights-based nature of the torts. The primary focus is on the plaintiff's rights, not the defendant's intention or attitude. If the defendant did exhibit ill will or hostility, this may be relevant to an award of aggravated or exemplary damages.

5.1.3.4 Circumstances

There must be no lawful justification for the conduct. This acknowledges the fact that sometimes there is a legitimate reason for invading a person's rights, such as when the police make a lawful arrest.

5.1.4 The onus of proof

The trespass torts largely take a common approach to the onus of proof. For each tort, the plaintiff generally only needs to prove that the defendant directly interfered with the relevant right. It is then for the defendant to disprove fault or otherwise justify their conduct (for example, by raising a defence: see section 5.1.7 below).[1] This approach flows from and emphasises the rights-based nature of these torts. The protected rights are so important that any direct invasion must be justified by the defendant.

5.1.5 Remedies

If an action for one of the trespass torts is successful, the defendant will be liable for all the direct consequences that flow from the tort. The test of reasonable foreseeability of harm used to limit damages in cases of negligence (see Chapter 10) does not apply to these torts. This more plaintiff-friendly approach to damages (as opposed to the more defendant-friendly test used as a limit in negligence) also points to the importance of the rights that these torts protect. One tip for remembering this approach to damages is to remind yourself that if the tort requires a *direct* interference with rights, then liability is imposed for all of the *direct* consequences of that interference.

In addition, equitable remedies such as injunctions may also be available in appropriate cases. In the context of trespass, injunctions are particularly useful in preventing ongoing or threatened future interferences - for example, restraining repeated unauthorised physical contact, preventing unlawful detention or stopping a continuing intrusion onto land. Because these torts protect rights that are *actionable per se*, a plaintiff may be able to obtain an injunction even where no actual harm has yet occurred, provided there is a risk of future violation of their legal rights.

5.1.6 Importance of the trespass torts

The trespass torts emerged in the late 12th century, at a time when the intentional interference with the body, land or goods of another citizen was seen as a breach of the King's peace. They created rights against other citizens that entitled the victim to ask for a remedy in the King's courts. These rights to bodily integrity, exclusive possession of land and goods, dignity, autonomy, freedom and liberty were zealously protected by the common law judges, and eventually they assumed an even greater significance; they

1 For historical reasons, there is a limited exception to this rule, which applies where the relevant events occurred on a highway. In such cases, it is for the plaintiff to prove the fault element.

created rights that protected individuals from interferences or invasions carried out not only by other citizens but also by the Crown, the executive government and the agents or officials of the state.

The importance of the trespass torts has been emphasised by the High Court of Australia ('High Court') on many occasions, including in the following cases:

- *Trobridge v Hardy* (1955): trespass to the person and false imprisonment;
- *Halliday v Nevill* (1984): trespass to land;
- *Plenty v Dillon* (1991): trespass to land;
- *Ruddock v Taylor* (2005): false imprisonment;
- *New South Wales v Ibbett* (2006): assault and trespass to land;
- *Kuru v New South Wales* (2008): trespass to land.

The judges in these cases have been quick to remind us that any interference with a person's body and liberty constitutes a grave infringement of the most elementary and important of all common law rights, to assert that 'everyone's home is their castle' and to insist that the common law will protect individuals from improper action by police.

5.1.7 Defences to the trespass torts

In certain circumstances, although the defendant committed the conduct that ordinarily constitutes a trespass tort, they may be able to escape liability by raising a defence. As noted in Chapter 7 (which considers defences in detail), defences play a critical role in tort law by allowing courts to balance individual rights with broader considerations of justice and social policy. For example, a person who acts in self-defence may interfere with another's rights in a way that would ordinarily be unlawful, but their actions may be justified by the circumstances.

Some defences, such as self-defence and necessity, have a long common law history, while other defences have been created by statute. For example, an Act may provide police with the power to:

- arrest and confine a person (battery, assault and false imprisonment);
- enter land without the occupier's consent (trespass to land); or
- confiscate goods (trespass to goods).

The courts have made it clear that any statutory authority that allows a person 'to engage in what otherwise would be tortious conduct' must be 'clearly expressed in unmistakable and unambiguous language': *Coco v The Queen* (1994), Mason CJ, Brennan, Gaudron and McHugh JJ at 436.

Where a defendant claims that their conduct was lawfully justified, this will need to be carefully assessed. This may require judges to weigh the relative importance of the principles underlying the trespass torts against some very important matters of public policy, such as detecting and preventing crime and maintaining border security and migration laws. This can lead judges to engage in careful and sometimes politically controversial exercises in statutory interpretation of a wide range of legislation covering such matters as police powers, migration, mental health, anti-terrorism and surveillance.

So, although the trespass torts may not be litigated in our courts with any great frequency, they remain important in modern Australian society as a way of vindicating our fundamental common law rights, especially in the jurisdictions that do not have a statutory Bill or Charter of Rights.

Although the various defences to the trespass torts are discussed in Chapter 7, we mention the issue of 'lawful justification' when discussing each trespass tort to remind you to consider any possible defences that may arise on the facts.

5.1.8 Using trespass case authorities

Because the trespass torts share a number of common features and elements, the cases from one trespass tort (such as battery) are often cited as authorities for the other trespass torts (such as trespass to land).

Case example

The 'extended' interpretation of the directness rule in the trespass to the person case of *Scott v Shepherd* (1773) (see 'A case to remember', section 5.1.2 above) is equally relevant to the other trespass torts.

Many texts and cases also cite old English precedents. Australian tort law has, however, diverged in many significant ways from its English origins, so you need to check the cases carefully before you use them in your arguments.

Another feature that has created a degree of uncertainty in this area of the law is the fact that some torts – battery, assault and false imprisonment, for example – are criminal offences as well as torts. Consequently, judges in torts cases may use terminology and cite principles and case authorities from the criminal law. However, you need to remember that the doctrines, principles and rules from criminal cases (especially English criminal cases) are not always directly and universally transferrable to tort law.

Case examples

- In *Roy v O'Neill* (2020) the High Court held that the law concerning the scope of the implied licence to enter land that was set out in the criminal case of *Barker v The Queen* (1983) *was applicable* to the tort of trespass to land: see Bell and Gageler JJ at [39]; Keane and Edelman JJ at [71]–[73].
- In *Ashley v Chief Constable of Sussex Police* (2008) the House of Lords held that the criminal law rule on mistaken belief in self-defence *was not applicable* in a torts case, because the purposes of tort law and criminal law, and their conceptions of justice, are different. Each requires that a different balance be struck between the right that every person has not to be subjected to physical harm and the right of another to self-defence: see Lord Scott of Foscote at [18].

5.2 Battery

5.2.1 The nature of battery

Battery is an unjustified act by one person that intentionally, recklessly or negligently causes direct and immediate physical contact or interference with the body of another person. The elements of battery are as follows:

1. There must be a positive act by the defendant.
2. The defendant's act must directly cause physical contact or interference with the plaintiff's body.
3. The defendant must have intended to cause the contact with the plaintiff, or been reckless or negligent about causing it.

The onus always lies on the plaintiff to prove the first two elements on the balance of probabilities: *McHale v Watson* (1964). The onus of proving the third element depends on whether or not the events occurred on a highway. Where they did, it is for the plaintiff to prove that the contact was intentional, reckless or negligent: *Venning v Chin* (1974). In all other cases, the onus is on the defendant to prove, on the balance of probabilities, that they were 'utterly without fault': *Weaver v Ward* (1616); *Croucher v Cachia* (2016).

It is possible for the defendant to argue that the contact was lawfully justified (for example, that they were making a lawful arrest or were acting in self-defence). Where they do, the onus will be on them to prove the relevant matter on the balance of probabilities. Defences to the intentional torts are addressed in Chapter 7.

One circumstance in which contact will be lawfully justified is where the defendant validly consented to that contact. This includes both explicit and implicit consent. In *Collins v Wilcock* (1984) Goff LJ noted that people implicitly consent to contact which is an inevitable and acceptable part of ordinary everyday life (such as bumping into someone on a train), and so such 'everyday contact' does not constitute battery.

There is some dispute about whether lack of consent is an element of battery (which must be proved by the plaintiff) or whether consent is a defence to the tort (which must be proved by the defendant). In England and New Zealand, the former approach has been taken: *Freeman v Home Office (No 2)* (1984); *S v G* (1995). By contrast, in Australia consent has generally been considered to be a defence: *McNamara v Duncan* (1979); *Marion's Case* (1992), McHugh J. However, in *White v Johnston* (2015) Leeming JA of the New South Wales Court of Appeal undertook an extensive consideration of the authorities and concluded that there was no binding authority on this issue in Australia. In his Honour's opinion, the correct view was that lack of consent was an element of the cause of action. Some cases have followed Leeming JA's approach (see, eg, *A v B* (2021)), while others have not (see, eg, *Tinnock v Murrumbidgee Local Health District (No 6)* (2017)). This matter, which is considered in more detail in Chapter 7, has not yet been resolved by the High Court.

There is no minimum level of force that must be applied for a battery to be committed – even the slightest touch can constitute a battery – and the touch need not be body to body. It is sufficient for the defendant to have touched the plaintiff through their clothes, or to have caused an object or force to come into contact with the plaintiff. For example, batteries have been committed by causing a sniffer dog to touch the defendant (*Darby v Director of Public Prosecutions* (2004)), by spraying CS gas at the defendant (*Binsaris v Northern Territory* (2020)) and by using a car (*Irlam v Byrnes* (2022)). There is also no requirement for the contact to be violent or motivated by hostility or ill will (*Collins v Wilcock* (1984)).

Given the multiplicity of ways that people can touch each other, battery encompasses a wide variety of conduct that may range from a vicious beating to medical treatment without consent or to a gentle and loving (but unwanted) caress. The key to recognising a possible battery in a problem question is to bear in mind that any act that causes any physical contact with, or application of force to, another human being may be unlawful, regardless of whether the *motive* is aggressive or well meaning, whether the *contact* is violent or gentle, or whether the *effect* is hurtful or not. The issue is not whether the contact was destructive or even offensive, but whether it was justified. Many cases – for example, *Collins v Wilcock* (1984) at 1177 and *Marion's Case* (1992) at 233 – cite Blackstone, who first explained this:

> The law cannot draw the line between different degrees of violence, and therefore totally prohibits the first and lowest stage of it; every man's person being sacred, and no other having a right to meddle with it, in any the slightest manner.[2]

5.2.2 Guiding principles

The tort of battery protects both the physical integrity of our bodies and our right to control access to our bodies. This follows from the tort's guiding principles, which promote respect for the unique dignity of each person and uphold our rights to physical bodily integrity, self-determination and autonomy.

Case examples

- 'The fundamental principle, plain and incontestable, is that every person's body is inviolate': *Collins v Wilcock* (1984) Goff LJ at 1177.
- The 'right to bodily integrity is a person's right not to have his or her body touched or interfered with without consent': *Falconer v Commissioner of Police (WA) (No 2)* (2024) Buss P and Vaughan JA at [116].
- On the principles of autonomy and dignity, see *Marion's Case* (1992), Mason CJ, Dawson, Toohey and Gaudron JJ at 233; Brennan J at 265–6; McHugh J at 309–10.

2 Blackstone's *Commentaries on the Laws of England* (1765–69).

5.2.3 Overview of the tort of battery

5.2.3.1 Conduct

- There must be a positive act by the defendant. Engaging in merely passive conduct or omitting or failing to act will not suffice (*Innes v Wylie* (1844); *Platt v Nutt* (1988)).

5.2.3.2 Effect

- The defendant's conduct must directly cause physical contact or interference with the plaintiff's body. The contact must be direct. If it is indirect, consider using another tort such as action on the case or negligence (*Carter v Walker* (2010)).
- There must be actual physical contact. If the contact is only threatened or feared, the appropriate tort is assault (*Barber v Goodstart Early Learning* (2021)).
- Battery is a rights-based tort that is actionable per se – there is no need for the contact to cause damage. The mere invasion of the right is enough (*Carter v Walker* (2010)).
- There is no need for the defendant's own body to touch the plaintiff. It is sufficient if the defendant's act directly and immediately causes an object or force to contact the plaintiff or causes the plaintiff to come into contact with an object (*Darby v Director of Public Prosecutions* (2004); *Binsaris v Northern Territory* (2020)).
- The plaintiff does not need to have been aware of the contact at the time it was made. For example, a battery may be committed on a sleeping or unconscious person (*Darby v Director of Public Prosecutions* (2004); *Binsaris v Northern Territory* (2020)).

5.2.3.3 Fault

- The defendant must have intended the act of physical contact or interference with the plaintiff's body, or been reckless or negligent (in the sense of being careless) about causing it (*Williams v Milotin* (1957); *Venning v Chin* (1974)).
- The defendant's act must have been voluntary (directed by the will or conscious mind) (*Morriss v Marsden* (1952); *Carter v Walker* (2010)).
- The defendant does not need to have intended to cause harm or to have acted with hostility or ill will towards the plaintiff (*Collins v Wilcock* (1984); *Marion's Case* (1992)).
- The defendant will not be liable if they can show that they were 'utterly without fault' (*Weaver v Ward* (1616); *Croucher v Cachia* (2016)).

5.2.3.4 Circumstances

- There must be no lawful justification for the conduct. Contact will be justified if it is an inevitable and acceptable part of ordinary everyday life and is reasonable in the circumstances (*Collins v Wilcock* (1984); *Rixon v Star City* (2001)).
- Conduct may be justified by common law principles or statutory provisions authorising physical contact. These include powers to:
  - arrest a person (with or without warrant);
  - prevent a person breaching the peace; and
  - detain a person under mental health legislation.
- Any statutory sources of lawful justification must be 'clearly expressed in unmistakable and unambiguous language' (*Coco v The Queen* (1994)).

LEGISLATION ALERT!

Consult your study materials to see:

- whether there is any legislation in your jurisdiction that changes the way battery is defined. For example, in Queensland courts have applied the definition of assault in s 245 of the *Criminal Code Act 1899* (Qld) (*Origliasso v Vitale* (1952)); and
- what powers police officers or other authorised individuals have in your jurisdiction to arrest or detain people.

5.2.4 Defences

The defences to the tort of battery are explained in Chapter 7. Some possibilities include that the defendant was defending themselves or another person, that the contact was necessary in the circumstances, or that the plaintiff consented to being touched.

A case to remember

***Collins v Wilcock* [1984] 1 WLR 1172**

Topics

The inviolability principle; fault; lawful justification; the 'everyday contact' exception; police powers; self-defence.

Facts

A police officer, when participating in a crackdown on sex workers accosting clients on public streets, tried to question a woman who appeared to be soliciting. The woman ignored the repeated questions and swore at the officer. The officer tried to restrain her by taking hold of her arm. The woman responded by scratching the police officer, who arrested her and charged her with assaulting a police officer in the execution of her duty. Note: both parties applied bodily force to the other.

Issues

- Which of the two applications of bodily force was a battery?
- Was the police officer acting in the course of her duty when she applied bodily force to the sex worker and, if not, did she have any other lawful justification for her conduct?

Significance

The Court held that the police officer's conduct was not justified by the relevant law on police powers of arrest (because the officer intended to *caution* the sex worker, not to *arrest* her when she touched her body). Nor was the contact covered by any of the other possible exceptions to the broad rule that 'any touching of another person, however slight, may amount to a battery'. For example, it did not fall within the scope of the exception that applies to the 'exigencies of daily life', which covers the inoffensive, inevitable and acceptable contacts of ordinary everyday life, such as touching a person to attract their attention, jostling in a busy street or slapping the back of a friend at a party by way of greeting. This was because the police officer's contact was not done to attract the sex worker's attention, but to hold her for cautioning.

Goff LJ explained the underlying principle of the tort: the inviolability of the body.

5.2.5 Remedies

The full range of nominal, compensatory (including aggravated) and exemplary damages may be awarded: see section 2.3.3.2 of Chapter 2. Once the action is made out, the defendant will be liable to compensate the plaintiff for all of the direct consequences of the tort.

Equitable remedies such as injunctions may also be available in battery cases. This will be particularly relevant in situations involving ongoing personal abuse, where damages alone may be insufficient to protect the plaintiff's bodily integrity and autonomy. The availability of injunctions reflects the court's broader commitment to preventing further violations of rights, rather than merely compensating for past harm.

Note that in most jurisdictions, the limitations imposed by the *Civil Liability Acts* on damages for personal injuries do not apply to harm caused by *intentional* acts. This may make it important to determine whether a battery was committed intentionally, recklessly or negligently (see, eg, *Croucher v Cachia* (2016); *Public Trustee v Atileo* (2023)).

LEGISLATION ALERT!

Consult your study materials to see which legislation governs the application of the *Civil Liability Acts* to the trespass torts in your jurisdiction.

5.2.6 Possible developments in the law

The rules of battery differ in different countries, and it is possible that in the future Australian tort law will follow some of the developments seen overseas.

Case examples

Below are overseas developments in battery law that may be embraced by Australian courts.

- The directness requirement could be abolished, as is the case in some parts of the United States. For example, in *Mink v University of Chicago* (1978) the plaintiff took some medication which the defendant had placed onto a table with the intention of the plaintiff taking it. The defendant was held liable in battery, even though the contact was indirect.
- Negligence could be abolished as a fault state, as is the case in England: *Letang v Cooper* (1965). This would mean that the contact would need to be either intentional or reckless. While this suggestion has been explicitly rejected in Australia (*Williams v Milotin* (1957); *Venning v Chin* (1974)), in *Platt v Nutt* (1988) Kirby J found merit in the suggestion.

- The burden of proving that the defendant was at fault could be shifted to the plaintiff, as is the case in England: *Fowler v Lanning* (1959).
- Consent could be considered an element of the tort (for the plaintiff to disprove), rather than a defence (for the defendant to prove), as is the case in England (*Freeman v Home Office (No 2)* (1984)) and New Zealand (*S v G* (1995)). See Leeming JA in *White v Johnston* (2015).

5.2.7 Some helpful cases for your summary

- In *Cole v Turner* (1704) it was explained that 'the least touching in anger' is a battery, that a gentle touch in a narrow passageway is not a battery, but that a touching done in a 'rude, inordinate manner' will be a battery.
- In *Innes v Wylie* (1844) it was held that a policeman standing passively 'like a wall', preventing an excluded patron from entering a club, had not committed a battery on the patron, as battery requires a positive act.
- In *Platt v Nutt* (1988) D slammed a glass door shut and P, who was standing next to the door, put her arm up instinctively to protect herself and connected with the door. The Court held that D was not liable for battery, as it was P's own act which had caused the contact. The result would have been different if D had intended to hit P with the door.
- In *Re F (Mental Patient: Sterilisation)* (1990) Goff LJ explained that an attitude of hostility is not an element of the tort of battery.
- In *Rixon v Star City* (2001), a case about unlawful arrest, assault, battery and false imprisonment, it was held that an employee's touching of a patron on the shoulder and asking him to identify himself was covered by the 'everyday contact' exception because it did not go beyond what is generally acceptable in the ordinary conduct of daily life.
- In *Darby v Director of Public Prosecutions* (2004), where a police dog handler allowed his sniffer dog to nudge a person's genital area and push its nose into their trouser pocket, the application of physical force was held to be a direct effect of the dog handler's conduct. The handler had used the dog as an instrument to commit battery.
- In *New South Wales v Ouhammi* (2019) the defendant slammed a door on the plaintiff's thumb. Brereton J noted that for the defendant to prove that they were 'utterly without fault' (as is required to negate the tort of battery), it was not sufficient for them 'merely to negative negligence in the sense of a breach of duty of care or a failure to exercise reasonable care and skill'. They must show that 'the exercise of ordinary care and caution on [their] part *could not possibly* have prevented the physical contact' ([99]–[100], emphasis in original).
- In *Binsaris v Northern Territory* (2020) prison officers used CS gas on detainees in a youth detention centre. As the use of this gas was not authorised by statute, it was held to be a battery.
- In *Davis v Viglianti* (2024) D intentionally induced P to climb through a window which he knew had been installed with a razor blade trap. P did so and injured himself. While D had not installed the trap, his conduct in luring P to climb through the window with the intention of causing him injury made the contact sufficiently direct to constitute battery.

Active reading

Link each of the cases listed in section 5.2.7 above to one of the elements of the tort.

5.2.8 Problem-solving tips

This section offers tips on how to approach and answer problem questions involving battery, highlighting the key steps and issues to look for when applying the principles covered in this chapter.

1. Before you begin, open your mind and think about all the different levels of conduct that battery could encompass – and get used to the idea that the tort is not restricted to cases where one person violently 'batters' another. Begin by looking for the *harmful or adverse effect*: read the facts carefully and identify anyone whose body has been touched or who has suffered any application of force to the body. They will most likely become the plaintiff. Then look to see whose *conduct* led to that contact – they will most likely become the defendant.

   Remember that D does not have to physically touch P's body; it will be enough that D set in motion a force or object that comes directly into contact with P. The application of bodily force, contact or interference does not have to touch P's skin – it would be enough if it contacts P's clothes. So, violently snatching P's bag from P's grasp or pouring water over P could suffice.
2. Check to see whether D committed a positive act, and the contact was sufficiently 'direct and immediate'. If the case is similar to *Scott v Shepherd* (1773) ('A case to remember', section 5.1.2 above), apply its method of reasoning. If the contact may have been too indirect or consequential, consider whether a different tort (such as action on the case or negligence) may be more appropriate.
3. Check whether D was at *fault*, remembering that this element will be satisfied if the contact was voluntary and:
   - D intended the contact;
   - D intended the act and was reckless as to contact; or
   - D intended the act and was careless as to contact.

   This means that it does not matter whether D planned the precise method of causing the contact – or even whether D intended to make contact with any particular person. As long as D intended the act that caused the contact with P, and was either reckless or careless about the contact that eventuated, D is at fault.

   Remember that the onus of proving fault will depend on whether the case occurred on a highway. If it did, then P will need to prove that D was at fault: *Venning v Chin* (1974). If it did not, then it will be for D to prove that they were 'utterly without fault': *Weaver v Ward* (1616); *Croucher v Cachia* (2016). Remember, too, that D need not act with a hostile motive: *Re F (Mental Patient: Sterilisation)* (1990).
4. Consider whether the contact was an inevitable and acceptable part of ordinary everyday life, as explained in *Collins v Wilcock* (1984) and *Rixon v Star City* (2001). If it was, then there will not be a battery even if P did not consent.

5. Check to see whether any of the relevant *defences* may apply (see Chapter 7). Note that a police officer (and in some limited circumstances, an ordinary citizen) making an arrest may be able to claim lawful authority as a defence to a claim of battery: see *Collins v Wilcock* (1984). However, if there were no grounds for a lawful arrest, or excessive force was used, the conduct will be a battery: see, for example, *Cruse v Victoria* (2019).
6. If there was more than one application of bodily force, such as occurred in *Collins v Wilcock* (where one person responded to another person's touch), make sure that you discuss each event strictly in time order. This is important because if the first touching is a battery, the second touching may be covered by a defence (such as self-defence); however, if the first event is lawfully justified, then the second event may be an unlawful battery.
7. Identify all of the direct consequences of the contact that may have occurred and work out from section 2.3.3.2 of Chapter 2 the remedies that may apply. If the conduct was outrageous or otherwise warrants some measure of condemnation by the courts, consider whether punitive or exemplary damages may be claimed.
8. Consider whether the battery was accompanied by an assault.

5.3 Assault

5.3.1 The nature of assault

Assault is an unjustified act by one person that directly and either intentionally, recklessly or negligently causes another person to reasonably apprehend imminent physical contact or interference with their body. The elements of assault are as follows:

1. There must be a positive act by the defendant.
2. The defendant's act must directly cause the plaintiff to reasonably apprehend imminent physical interference with their body.
3. The defendant must have intended to cause the plaintiff's apprehension, or been reckless or negligent about causing it.

The onus always lies on the plaintiff to prove the first two elements on the balance of probabilities: *McHale v Watson* (1964). Once the plaintiff has proved these elements, the onus shifts to the defendant to prove that they were 'utterly without fault' (*Weaver v Ward* (1616); *Croucher v Cachia* (2016)), that their conduct was lawfully justified or that they had a valid defence (see Chapter 7).

In contrast to the tort of battery, which requires us to respect the bodies of other people, the tort of assault requires us to respect their minds. It creates a right for people to be free from the mental disturbance or anxiety that can be caused if they anticipate a physical attack. Perhaps equally importantly, it also triggers the right to self-defence, which entitles the victim to pre-empt the threatened battery, provided any action taken is necessary, reasonable and proportionate (see Chapter 7). For this reason, the plaintiff's apprehension of an imminent battery must be reasonable.

There are various ways in which a person can commit an assault – they can do so by conduct, gestures, words or even silence (see, eg, *R v Ireland* (1998)). The court will need to consider all of the circumstances in which the person acted and spoke, to determine whether they caused the plaintiff to apprehend imminent physical interference with their body, and whether that apprehension was reasonable.

In most cases, assaults will involve the threat of physical violence through conduct such as punching, stabbing or shooting. However, this need not be the case. For example, a threat to spray someone with water or gas could constitute an assault, as could a threat to lightly touch them. The key issue is whether the plaintiff apprehended some kind of direct interference with their body, no matter what medium is used and no matter how slight it may be.

In some cases, such as *Tuberville v Savage* (1669), conduct which may on the surface seem to be an assault (such as a threatening gesture) will be negated by the accompanying words, which make it clear that there is no real threat of imminent physical contact. However, a conditional threat (eg 'give me your money or I'll shoot you') may constitute an assault if it is reasonable for the plaintiff to believe that physical contact will occur if the stated condition is not met (see, eg, *Police v Greaves* (1964); *Rosza v Samuels* (1969)).

A case to remember

Tuberville v Savage (1669) 1 Mod 3; 86 ER 291

Topics

Conditional threats; effect of words accompanying a threatening gesture; reasonableness of apprehension.

Facts

The plaintiff (P) placed his hand on his sword and said to the defendant (D): 'If it were not assize time, I would not take such language from you.' D responded to this provocation, attacked P and wounded him.

Note: 'Assize time' refers to the fact that the King's judges were on circuit in the town, hearing cases and dispensing justice.

Issue

Had P, by making the threatening gesture and saying those words, committed the tort of assault against D (thereby entitling D to launch a pre-emptive strike on him in self-defence)? In particular, was D's anticipation of an imminent physical attack reasonable given the words uttered by P as he made the gesture?

Significance

This case established the rule that sometimes the words that accompany a threatening gesture can negate or defuse an apparent assault. In this case, the conduct did not amount to an assault because the words that accompanied the threatening gesture made it clear that P had no intention of attacking D. P was saying in effect, 'I will not attack you because the judges are in town'. Therefore, D's apprehension of an imminent attack was not reasonable in the circumstances, and as P's conduct was not an assault, D was not entitled to act in self-defence.

Counterexample

A different type of conditional threat was made in *Police v Greaves* (1964). In that case, police officers were intimidated into retreating from investigating a domestic violence case by a somewhat inebriated man who, after opening the front door and pointing a carving knife at the police, said: 'Don't you bloody move. You come a step closer and you will get this straight through your ... guts ... Get off this ... property before you get this in your guts.' The Court held that this was an assault, despite the fact that the pointing of the knife was accompanied by a conditional threat. Unlike in *Tuberville v Savage* (1669), the words spoken by the defendant did not negate the threat. The officers had a reasonable belief that he had both the ability and the present intention to carry out his purpose.

Like all the trespass torts, assault is actionable per se: there is no need for the plaintiff to have suffered any actual damage. The mere apprehension of interference with the body is sufficient, provided it is reasonable. This means that it is not necessary for the defendant to have actually carried out the battery. While assault and battery often occur in close succession, each tort can be committed independently.

Examples

Imagine that a school teacher throws a whiteboard duster at a student.

- If the duster hits the student, who was not looking and did not see it coming, that would be battery but not assault.
- If the student saw the duster flying towards them, and managed to dodge out of the way, that would be assault but not battery.
- If the student saw the duster flying towards them, but could not manage to escape in time and it hit them, that would be both assault and battery.

As the focus of the tort is on the plaintiff's mental integrity, the defendant does not need to have actually intended to carry out the battery. It is sufficient if the plaintiff reasonably believed they were going to, and the defendant intended to cause them to have that belief, or was reckless or careless about creating such an apprehension: *Barton v Armstrong* (1969). In fact, the defendant doesn't even need to have been able to carry out the threatened battery. For example, it would be an assault to threaten the plaintiff with an unloaded gun, even though they could not actually be shot, if the plaintiff *reasonably believed* they could be shot: *R v St George* (1840).

In assessing the reasonableness of the plaintiff's fear, it will usually be necessary to determine whether a reasonable person in their circumstances would have apprehended imminent physical contact. However, if the defendant knew that the plaintiff was exceptionally timid, and intentionally acted in a way to cause them to apprehend battery, that will be an assault. In such circumstances, it will not matter that a reasonable person would not have feared contact: *MacPherson v Beath* (1975).

To constitute an assault, the plaintiff must have reasonably apprehended *imminent* physical contact. This does not need to be fear of an immediate battery – a fear of 'relatively imminent violence' is sufficient: *Zanker v Vartzokas* (1988), White J at 14. However, fear of being attacked at some unspecified time in the future is not sufficient.

You need to be aware that in some cases judges may refer to an 'assault' when the conduct under consideration is really a battery. This occurs because the criminal law often uses the single term 'assault' to cover conduct that in the law of torts is separated into the separate torts of assault and battery. Other cases and texts sometimes use the compendium term 'assault and battery' to describe an unlawful act of physical contact alone. You should therefore take great care when reading cases to understand precisely how the term 'assault' is being used.

5.3.2 Guiding principles

The tort of assault protects our right to mental integrity. This follows from the tort's guiding principles, which, like battery, promote respect for the unique dignity of each person and uphold our rights to self-determination and autonomy.

5.3.3 Overview of the tort of assault

5.3.3.1 Conduct

- There must be a positive act, gesture or threat made by the defendant. Depending on the circumstances, words alone or even silence can constitute an assault (*Barton v Armstrong* (1969); *R v Ireland* (1998)).
- A conditional threat can constitute an assault, if the plaintiff could reasonably believe that the threatened conduct will be imminently carried out if the condition is not complied with (*Police v Greaves* (1964); *Rosza v Samuels* (1969)).
- However, there is no assault if the words accompanying the threat make it clear that the threatened interference will not be imminently carried out (*Tuberville v Savage* (1669)).

5.3.3.2 Effect

- The defendant's act must directly cause the plaintiff to apprehend imminent physical interference with their body. The act need not cause actual damage, nor must it be followed up with an act of battery. The mere apprehension of imminent physical interference with the body is sufficient, provided it is reasonable[3] (*Barton v Armstrong* (1969); *Zanker v Vartzokas* (1988)).
- The plaintiff does not need to be scared or fearful. It is sufficient if they apprehend or anticipate imminent physical interference with their body.
- The plaintiff does not need to apprehend immediate physical contact. An apprehension of relatively imminent physical contact is sufficient (*Zanker v Vartzokas* (1988)).

3 See section 5.3.3.4.

5.3.3.3 Fault

- The defendant must have intended to cause the plaintiff's apprehension, or been reckless or negligent (in the sense of being careless) about causing it. The defendant does not need to have intended to carry through with the threat. It is sufficient that they intended to cause the plaintiff to believe they would, or were reckless or negligent about causing such apprehension (*Barton v Armstrong* (1969); *ACN 087528774 Pty Ltd (formerly Connex Trains Melbourne Pty Ltd) v Chetcuti* (2008)).

5.3.3.4 Circumstances

- The plaintiff's apprehension of imminent physical interference must have been reasonable in the circumstances. The defendant does not need to have had the means or intention to carry out their threat. It is sufficient if they reasonably appeared to have had the means and intention to do so (*Stephens v Meyers* (1830); *R v St George* (1840)).
- If the plaintiff only apprehended the interference because they were peculiarly sensitive or exceptionally timid, the claim may nevertheless be successful if the defendant knew of the special sensitivity (*Bunyan v Jordan* (1937); *MacPherson v Beath* (1975)).
- There must be no lawful justification for the conduct. An assault may be justified by common law principles or statutory provisions authorising the threatened physical interference. See the discussion of defences to battery above and in Chapter 7.

5.3.4 Defences

The defences to the tort of assault are explained in Chapter 7. One commonly raised defence is self-defence: the defendant will argue that they were defending themselves (or another person). In addition, it may be argued that the assault was authorised. For example, a police defendant may claim that they were executing a lawful arrest.

5.3.5 Remedies

The full range of nominal, compensatory (including aggravated) and exemplary damages may be awarded: see section 2.3.3.2 of Chapter 2. Once the action is made out, the defendant will be liable to compensate the plaintiff for all of the direct consequences of the tort. Equitable remedies such as injunctions may also be available in assault cases. This will be particularly relevant in situations involving ongoing harassment or threats.

5.3.6 Possible developments in the law

In section 5.2.6 above we considered various potential developments concerning the law of battery. Similar reforms could also be made to the law of assault. In addition, over time it is possible that the law of torts will develop to address the fact that the current law has been shaped by a predominantly male perspective, which has often failed to adequately consider the lived experiences and vulnerabilities of those outside this demographic. This male-centric viewpoint tends to prioritise physical harm and overt aggression as the primary criteria for assault, overlooking the nuanced and often psychological dimensions of fear, intimidation and coercion that disproportionately affect women and marginalised groups. In the area of criminal law, there have been significant developments to address these concerns, recognising the broader scope of harm that can arise from non-physical threats and power imbalances. It is possible that similar progress will occur in tort law, leading to a more just and comprehensive approach to assault.

5.3.7 Some helpful cases for your summary

- In *Stephens v Meyers* (1830) it was held at 735 that 'it is not every threat, when there is no actual physical violence, that constitutes assault, there must be, in all cases, the means of carrying the threat into effect'.
- In *R v St George* (1840) it was held that threatening another person with an unloaded pistol could be an assault, even though there were no means to carry out the threat. This was because the victim was unaware of the fact the pistol was not loaded, and so reasonably apprehended the imminent application of physical contact.
- In *Barton v Armstrong* (1969) Taylor J explained at 454–5 that a series of telephoned threats made at night, in circumstances that induced an atmosphere of drama and suspense, could reasonably give rise to an apprehension of imminent physical harm, given the development of technology that allowed for the remote detonation of explosives. He noted that whether words alone can constitute an assault will depend on all the circumstances.
- In *Rosza v Samuels* (1969) one taxi driver (P) threatened to punch another taxi driver (D). In response, D pulled out a knife and said, 'I will cut you to bits if you try it'. D then made a move towards getting out of his taxi. Although this threat was conveyed in conditional terms, it was held to be an assault: this was not a case like *Tuberville v Savage* (1669) where the words negated the threat. This was not considered to be an act of self-defence as D could have protected himself from being punched simply by locking his door.
- In *MacPherson v Beath* (1975) Bray CJ suggested at 177 that if the defendant 'intentionally puts in fear of immediate violence an exceptionally timid person known to him to be so', the unreasonableness of the fear may not prevent a finding of liability.
- In *Thomas v National Union of Mineworkers* (1986) the plaintiffs were mine workers who continued to work during a strike and had to cross picket lines formed by striking miners. The plaintiffs were transported to work in buses that were escorted by the police. As they passed through the picket lines, the striking miners engaged in aggressive and threatening behavior, including shouting threats and making violent gestures. This was not held to be an assault, as the plaintiffs were never directly at risk of harm due to the protective measures that were in place. Even though the striking miners made violent threats, their lack of capacity to carry out the threats was fatal to the claim.
- In *Zanker v Vartzokas* (1988) D was driving a young woman (P) home. He offered her money for sexual favours, but she refused and asked to be let out of the car. Instead of doing so, D accelerated and said, 'I am going to take you to my mate's house. He will really fix you up'. This was held by White J at 14 to be an assault because 'a present fear of relatively imminent violence' was instilled in the woman's mind 'from

the moment the words were uttered' and she was in 'immediate and continuing fear' for as long as she was imprisoned in the car by D.

- In *R v Ireland* (1998) the defendant made repeated silent telephone calls of a menacing nature. It was held that this could constitute an assault – that silent, heavy breathing could cause someone to reasonably apprehend the possibility of imminent violence.
- In *ACN 087528774 Pty Ltd (formerly Connex Trains Melbourne Pty Ltd) v Chetcuti* (2008) the Victorian Court of Appeal elaborated upon the elements of assault in a case involving a confrontation between ticket inspectors and a commuter.
- In *Balven v Thurston* (2013) it was held that conveying threats via text message or social media can constitute an assault, as long as the threat is reasonably perceived by P to be imminent.
- In *Barber v Goodstart Early Learning* (2021) the plaintiff was threatened with termination of their employment if they did not get the flu vaccination. It was held that this did not constitute an assault, as there was no threat of forcible vaccination, and so no threat of imminent physical contact.
- In *Zey v New South Wales (No 2)* (2024) the plaintiff was in her house, behind a closed and locked glass door. The police came to her door to discuss the way she had parked her car. Although the police conducted themselves in a calm and reasonable manner, the plaintiff claimed that she felt unsafe and under threat. The Court held that this did not constitute an assault, as the glass door separated her from the police, preventing the possibility of an imminent application of physical contact. In addition, there was no evidence that the police had acted in a way that would have caused her to reasonably apprehend a threat of force.

Active reading

Link each of the cases listed in section 5.3.7 above to one of the elements of the tort.

5.3.8 Problem-solving tips

This section offers tips on how to approach and answer problem questions involving assault, highlighting the key steps and issues to look for when applying the principles covered in this chapter.

1. Remember that the *harmful or adverse effect* in the tort of assault focuses on the plaintiff's (P) state of mind. Look at the facts to see if any person may have thought they were about to suffer any kind of unwanted physical interference, bearing in mind that it does not necessarily have to be violent contact. This person may become the P, and the person whose *conduct* gave rise to that apprehension will become the defendant (D).
2. Check for a direct causal link between D's conduct and P's apprehension, bearing in mind that (a) it may be possible to adopt an 'extended' notion of directness

based on *Scott v Shepherd* (1773) and (b) that it is not necessary for the two parties be in close physical proximity, as long as there is apprehension of imminent physical interference: see *Barton v Armstrong* (1969).

3. Check for missing facts. If there is any application of bodily force (any actual battery) in the problem question, make sure you consider whether it was also possible for P to have apprehended the imminent application of bodily force. If so, add a claim of assault to the battery claim.
4. Note that while some cases and texts state that P must 'fear' an imminent physical attack, a better way of thinking about this tort is to recognise that it requires P to have a reasonable *apprehension* or *anticipation* of imminent physical interference. So, even if P is not actually afraid of being hurt by D (perhaps because P is much stronger than D), there may still be a case of assault. Note, however, that P's state of fear may nevertheless be relevant to the reasonableness of any response or act of self-defence they take.
5. Remember that P must have anticipated a 'relatively imminent' battery; therefore it will not suffice if the threat was of a future application of force, no matter how reasonable it was for P to be afraid of that future event. Think also about the meaning of 'imminent': check *Zanker v Vartzokas* (1988). Clearly, a threat of a beating in two months' time is not a threat of imminent harm, but what about a threat that P will be beaten up in 10 minutes – or 10 hours?
6. Check whether P's apprehension was reasonable in the circumstances and *argue the facts*. The inclusion of the fuzzy term 'reasonable' in this rule means you need to look carefully at the facts and consider both the arguments and counterarguments that could be made. This is the issue most likely to arise in a problem question on assault.
7. Be very careful about how you deal with any conditional threats that accompany a threatening gesture. The mere fact that the words take the form of a condition does *not* necessarily mean that the words will 'unmake' the threat. Look at *Tuberville v Savage* (1669) and its accompanying counterexample, *Police v Greaves* (1964) ('A case to remember', section 5.3.1 above) and use them to help you to analyse the statements and argue your case. Check to see whether, on the facts, D had any lawful right to impose the condition, and whether D exhibited any intention to carry the threat out.
8. Check the *defences*, especially the rules on self-defence. If P reasonably apprehends a battery, they may take reasonable measures in self-defence. Note that the rules of the tort and of the defence both contain the 'fuzzy' requirement of reasonableness, which always gives rise to fertile sources of argument.

5.4 False imprisonment

5.4.1 The nature of false imprisonment

False imprisonment is an unjustified act by one person that directly and either intentionally, recklessly or negligently causes a total restraint of another person's physical liberty. The elements of false imprisonment are as follows:

1. There must be a positive act by the defendant.
2. The defendant's act must directly cause the plaintiff to be totally restrained or confined within a delimited area.
3. The defendant must have intended to cause the plaintiff's restraint or confinement, or been reckless or negligent about causing it.

The onus of proof lies on the plaintiff to prove the first two elements: *Myer Stores Ltd v Soo* (1991). The plaintiff must also generally provide some evidence to suggest that their detention was unlawful: *AKW22 v Commonwealth (No 2)* (2023). However, it is then for the defendant to prove that they were 'utterly without fault' (*Weaver v Ward* (1616); *Croucher v Cachia* (2016)) or that they had a valid defence (see Chapter 7).

It is sometimes said that this tort protects our freedom of movement: see, for example, *Ruddock v Taylor* (2005), Kirby J at [137]. However, as Coleridge J pointed out in *Bird v Jones* (1845) at 669, this tort does not create a right *to go* wherever we please; rather, it protects our right *to leave* a particular place and to be free from confinement.

This tort can be committed either by physical conduct or by words alone. Importantly, it requires the plaintiff to be *totally* confined – if they are free to leave in some way, they are not imprisoned. While this means that the plaintiff must have been confined to a delimited area from which there was no reasonable means of escape, it does not require confinement in a physical structure like a prison. For example, in *Meering v Graham-White Aviation* (1919) the Court held that it is false imprisonment to use intimidation or threats to make a person remain in an open field; and in *Myer Stores Ltd v Soo* (1991) (see below) the plaintiff was falsely imprisoned by being 'actively escorted' through the Myer department store to a security office. While not yet authoritatively determined, it seems likely that false imprisonment can also occur through chemical means, where a person's physical liberty is restrained by the non-consensual administration of sedatives, tranquilisers or other substances that render them immobile.

A case to remember

Myer Stores Ltd v Soo [1991] 2 VR 597

Topics

Nature of the defendant's conduct; the plaintiff's knowledge of restraint; damages.

Facts

The plaintiff was a regular customer of Myer's Lonsdale Street store. He was told by a store security officer, who was accompanied by two police officers, that he 'looked like' a person who had been caught on a video surveillance camera stealing some Waterford crystal. The security officer and the two police officers asked him to accompany them to the security office to sort things out. The plaintiff refused and asked to be interviewed where he was. The defendants did not use any physical force against the plaintiff, but he was 'actively escorted' to the office where he was held against his will and interviewed for one hour before being allowed to leave. After a fruitless search of the plaintiff's home by police, he was later asked to go to the police station for a further interview. The plaintiff did so and was exonerated. He sued the police officers, the security officer and his employer (Myer Stores) for false imprisonment.

Issues

Had the plaintiff been wrongfully deprived of his liberty either in the security office or later at the police station? Or did the lack of any use of physical force, the fact that the door of the security office remained open, and the plaintiff's apparent consent to accompany the officers to the office and to voluntarily attend the police station provide a defence?

Significance

It was held that by 'actively escorting' the plaintiff to the office and by 'passively' making it known to him that they intended to ask him questions about shoplifting, the police officers and the security officer had made it clear to the plaintiff that he had 'no option' but to comply with their instructions. It was reasonable for the plaintiff to assume that if he did not accompany the officers, that they would have used force and that he would not have been allowed to leave. Consequently, that conduct did amount to false imprisonment. However, the plaintiff was not falsely imprisoned when he went to the police station to clear his name, as that was a voluntary choice that he made.

The Court held that the defendant will be liable for false imprisonment if they personally imprisoned the plaintiff, caused their agent to imprison the plaintiff or were 'active in promoting and causing the imprisonment'. Consequently, in this case the police officers, the security officer and Myer Stores (as the security officer's employer) were all liable.

The Court explained that damages for false imprisonment are awarded to compensate for the loss of dignity, mental suffering, disgrace and humiliation and any attendant loss of social status, damage to reputation, physical injury, illness, anxiety, depression or discomfort. The plaintiff was awarded both nominal damages and aggravated damages.

In some cases, while the plaintiff may not have been able to readily exit the location, it may be argued that with some effort they could have left – and so they were not totally confined. For example, perhaps they could have broken a window and climbed out of it or jumped off the roof. The key issue in these cases is whether the means of escape was 'reasonable'. In *McFadzean v CFMEU* (2007) the Court held that in making this determination, it must consider four factors: the threat or danger the escape would have posed to the plaintiff; the threat or danger it would have posed to property; the distance the plaintiff would have had to travel and the time it would have taken to escape; and the legality of the alleged means of escape.

Case examples

- It is false imprisonment to lock a person on a balcony from which they can leave only by jumping from a dangerous height, or to lock them in a moving car which they would need to leap out of in order to escape (as occurred in *Zanker v Vartzokas* (1988)).

- It is false imprisonment to hold a person in a restaurant to compel them to pay for a bottle of wine: *Bahner v Marwest Hotels Co* (1970).
- It is false imprisonment to actively promote the unlawful detention of another person. For example, in *Dickinson v Waters Ltd* (1931) the manager of a shop who told a police officer to arrest the plaintiff for shoplifting was found liable for false imprisonment of the plaintiff.
- It is false imprisonment to use psychological domination, coercion or threats to compel a person to go to a particular place against their will: *Symes v Mahon* (1922).
- It is false imprisonment to continue to detain a prisoner after their designated release date: *Cowell v Corrective Services Commissioner of New South Wales* (1988).
- It is false imprisonment to fail to ensure that an arrested person is brought to court for a bail hearing as soon as practicable, where that is required by legislation in the jurisdiction: *McLaughlin v New South Wales (No 2)* (2023), affirmed in *New South Wales v McLaughlin* (2024).
- It is not false imprisonment to prevent a person from crossing a bridge, provided they are at liberty to leave by a different route: *Bird v Jones* (1845).
- It is not false imprisonment to prevent a person from leaving a location if, when they entered the location, they voluntarily accepted a lawful and reasonable condition for exiting, but then failed to meet that condition: *Robinson v Balmain New Ferry Co* (1906).

Many false imprisonment cases involve people who have been arrested by the police. The determination of such cases will generally depend on whether the arrest was lawful. This will require careful consideration to be given to the arrest powers in the relevant jurisdiction. Where an arrest has been made without a warrant, it will generally be necessary to prove that there were reasonable grounds for believing that an offence had been committed, and that it was reasonably necessary to arrest the plaintiff – although the precise requirements in this regard vary according to jurisdiction. It is for the defendant to prove that the arrest was lawful: *Zaravinos v New South Wales* (2004).

LEGISLATION ALERT!

Consult your study materials to see what powers police officers have in your jurisdiction to arrest or detain people.

5.4.2 Guiding principles

The guiding principle behind the tort of false imprisonment promotes the individual liberty, dignity and autonomy of each human being. This tort exists to vindicate and protect every person's fundamental common law and constitutional right to be free from unjustified imprisonment caused not only by other private citizens, but equally importantly, from any unlawful imprisonment ordered by the executive government or its agents. Consequently, it is a tort of strict liability, and mistake – or acting in good faith – is no defence: Kirby J in *Ruddock v Taylor* (2005) at [139]–[140].

Case examples

- In *Trobridge v Hardy* (1955) Fullagar J maintained at 152 that the 'mere interference with the plaintiff's person and liberty constituted *prima facie* a grave infringement of the most elementary and important of all common law rights'.
- In *Re Bolton; Ex parte Beane* (1987) Deane J explained at 528–9 that it 'cannot be too strongly stressed that these basic matters are not the stuff of empty rhetoric. They are the very fabric of the freedom under the law which is the *prima facie* right of every citizen and alien in this land. They represent a bulwark against tyranny.'
- In *Ruddock v Taylor* (2005) Kirby J explained at [137] that the tort of false imprisonment 'reflects the fundamental interest of the common law in protecting individual liberty and freedom of movement' and pointed out that it is 'especially significant' that under Australia's constitutional law 'the executive may not interfere with the liberty of an individual without valid authorisation'.
- In *Lewis v Australian Capital Territory* (2020) Gageler J noted at [24]: 'Through the tort, the "right to personal liberty" is protected by the common law – not from all restraints, but from those restraints for which "lawful authority" cannot be shown' (references omitted).

5.4.3 Overview of the tort of false imprisonment

5.4.3.1 Conduct

- There must normally be a positive act or statement by the defendant (or the defendant's agent). Words alone may be sufficient (*Myer Stores Ltd v Soo* (1991); *Symes v Mahon* (1922)).
- A continuation of a previous act of imprisonment may also suffice (*Cowell v Corrective Services Commissioner of New South Wales* (1988)).

5.4.3.2 Effect

- The defendant's conduct must directly cause a total restraint of the plaintiff's liberty by confining the plaintiff to a delimited area.
- The confinement must be total (*Bird v Jones* (1845); *McFadzean v CFMEU* (2007)).
- The confinement must have been directly caused by the defendant's conduct. If it is indirect, consider using another tort such as action on the case or negligence (*Carter v Walker* (2010)).
- The confinement may be caused solely by the plaintiff's submission to the defendant's power, if the plaintiff reasonably thought that, in the circumstances, there was no reasonable alternative but to comply (*Symes v Mahon* (1922); *Myer Stores Ltd v Soo* (1991)).
- This tort is actionable per se: the mere invasion of the right to liberty is sufficient (*South Australia v Lampard-Trevorrow* (2010); *Lewis v Australian Capital Territory* (2020)).
- The plaintiff does not need to have been aware of the imprisonment at the time (*Murray v Ministry of Defence* (1988); *Public Advocate v BC* (2019)).

5.4.3.3 Fault

- The defendant must have intended to cause the plaintiff's confinement, or been reckless or negligent (in the sense of being careless) about causing it. There is no requirement that the defendant must have intended to cause harm or act with hostility or ill will towards the plaintiff (*Cowell v Corrective Services Commissioner of New South Wales* (1988); *Abdulrahim v Adult Parole Board of Victoria* (2023)).

5.4.3.4 Circumstances

- There must be no reasonable means of escape (*Bird v Jones* (1845); *McFadzean v CFMEU* (2007)).
- There must be no lawful justification for the conduct. Confinement may be justified if the plaintiff voluntarily accepted a lawful and reasonable condition for exiting a location, but then failed to meet that condition (*Robinson v Balmain New Ferry Co* (1906)).
- A person may not be confined merely because of a breach of contract (*Bahner v Marwest Hotels Co* (1970)).
- Confinement may be justified by common law principles or statutory provisions authorising detention. These include powers to:
  - arrest a person (with or without warrant);
  - prevent a person breaching the peace; and
  - detain a person under mental health legislation.
- Any statutory sources of lawful justification must be 'clearly expressed in unmistakable and unambiguous language' (*Coco v The Queen* (1994)).

5.4.4 Defences

Defences to the trespass torts are explained in Chapter 7. The most commonly raised defence in this context is statutory authorisation: that the plaintiff was being lawfully arrested or detained.

5.4.5 Remedies

While the full range of nominal, compensatory (including aggravated) and exemplary damages may be awarded in false imprisonment cases (see section 2.3.3.2 of Chapter 2), damages are generally awarded to vindicate personal liberty rather than as compensation for loss per se: *CPCF v Minister for Immigration and Border Protection* (2015) at [155]. However, as is the case for all of the trespass torts, once the action is made out, the defendant is liable to compensate the plaintiff for all of its direct consequences: *Watson v Marshal and Cade* (1971). Equitable remedies such as injunctions may also be available in false imprisonment cases. This will be particularly relevant where the detention is ongoing.

For a useful discussion on the application of the compensatory principle to false imprisonment cases, see *Lewis v Australian Capital Territory* (2020). For a good discussion of nominal, aggravated and exemplary damages in the context of false imprisonment, see *Myer Stores Ltd v Soo* (1991) and *New South Wales v Delly* (2007). These cases explain that if the defendant's conduct is neither bona fide nor justifiable, aggravated damages may be awarded to compensate the plaintiff for the added humiliation and insult caused by the defendant's conduct during any trial of the matter, any further persistence in publicising untrue facts about the plaintiff, and any refusal to apologise to the plaintiff. Exemplary damages may be awarded to punish the defendant for antisocial behaviour and to deter others from similar conduct.

5.4.6 Possible developments in the law

Like the rules of battery, the rules of false imprisonment differ in different countries, and it is possible that Australian tort law will follow some of the developments seen overseas. Certain aspects of the current law have also been criticised and may be amended in the future.

Case examples

- The English case of *Letang v Cooper* (1965) decided that the form of negligent trespass to the person would no longer be available. As noted above, this view has been rejected in Australia in *Williams v Milotin* (1957) and *Venning v Chin* (1974), but Kirby J in *Platt v Nutt* (1988) found merit in the suggestion. If this approach were to be followed in Australia, a plaintiff would be restricted to bringing a case of negligent false imprisonment under the tort of negligence. As negligence is not actionable per se (unlike the tort of false imprisonment), this would require the plaintiff to prove they had been harmed by the imprisonment: *Campbell v Northern Territory (No 3)* (2021) at [430]. This could be difficult, as 'mere' mental distress is not considered sufficient (see Chapter 13). However, it is possible that the court may consider that 'a deprivation of a person's liberty effects an injury upon that person': *New South Wales v Madden* (2024) Bell CJ at [146]; see also *McLoughlin v Grovers* (2001) Hale LJ at [57].
- The case of *Robinson v Balmain New Ferry Co* (1906) held that it was not false imprisonment to confine a man who refused to pay a lawfully imposed exit fee of one penny to leave a wharf because (a) he had consented to the fee as a condition of entry and could not revoke it, and (b) he could have left the wharf by taking a ferry. This decision has been criticised on several grounds, including that it prioritises the rights of businesses to impose contractual conditions over the individual's right to freedom of movement: see, for example, Barker et al, *The Law of Torts in Australia* (2012) at 77 and Balkin and Davis, *Law of Torts* (2013) at 54. It is possible that the law in this regard will be revisited in the future.

5.4.7 Some helpful cases for your summary

- In *Symes v Mahon* (1922) D was a police officer who wanted P to accompany him on a train to a police station in Adelaide to answer a criminal charge (which was later found to be baseless). He made it clear to P that he would be arrested unless he cooperated. P reluctantly agreed to D's demand, and travelled with him to Adelaide on the train, but in a different compartment. It was held by Murray CJ at 453 that even though P and D had travelled in separate compartments it was false imprisonment, because P had completely 'submitted himself to the defendant's power, reasonably thinking that he had no way of escape'.

- *Louis v Commonwealth* (1987) is authority for the proposition that confinement in a continent the size of Australia is not sufficient to make out the tort of false imprisonment. In this case, an aircraft company was liable for false imprisonment after it carried people from Hong Kong to Australia against their will, in response to an informal request from the local authorities. There was no lawful justification because the request fell short of the formal direction required under Hong Kong law. Once those people were at liberty to move around in Australia or leave the country, however, they were no longer 'imprisoned'.
- In the criminal law case of *R v Garrett* (1988) the victim was held to be falsely imprisoned where their confinement was induced by threats made against the safety of a third party.
- *Murray v Ministry of Defence* (1988) is authority for the proposition that knowledge of confinement is not a requirement of the tort of false imprisonment.
- *McFadzean v CFMEU* (2007) contains a very useful summary of the law of false imprisonment, with helpful examples given at [23]–[113]. This includes an explanation of the four factors that must be considered when determining whether a reasonable means of escape exists (threat or danger to the self, threat or danger to property, distance and time, and legality).
- In the landmark case of *Trevorrow v South Australia (No 5)* (2007), where a member of the Stolen Generation was awarded damages for being taken unlawfully from his family and placed in care for 10 years at the age of 13 months, it was affirmed that knowledge of confinement is not required to make out the tort of false imprisonment, and that it was no defence to argue that the officers of the state had acted in accordance with their perceived statutory duty. However, in the subsequent appeal (*South Australia v Lampard-Trevorrow* (2010)), the South Australian Court of Appeal explained at [277]–[309] that the placement of the plaintiff in foster care, where he was given ordinary care, nurture and supervision, and where he 'had the same freedom of movement, or absence of freedom as the case may be, as other children of a like age', did not amount to confinement in the necessary sense.
- In *Haskins v Commonwealth* (2011) the High Court held at [54]–[68] that there could not be an action for false imprisonment between two members of the armed services, as such an action 'would be destructive of discipline'.
- In *CPCF v Minister for Immigration and Border Protection* (2015) Keane J at 631 affirmed that the person who imposes the restraint, as well as the person who directs them to do so, may both be liable for the tort.
- In *New South Wales v Robinson* (2019) the High Court held that it was false imprisonment for the police to arrest someone merely for the purpose of asking them questions or making investigations to see whether it would be proper or prudent to charge them. This was because in New South Wales, legislation provides that a police officer can only arrest someone without a warrant if they suspect on reasonable grounds that they are committing or have committed an offence, and are satisfied that it is reasonably necessary to make such an arrest for one of the reasons

listed in the Act. Where they do so, they must have an intention to charge the person, and must take them before a magistrate (or other authorised officer) as soon as is reasonably practicable to answer that charge.

- In *Public Advocate v BC* (2019) the Court held that detaining a 95-year-old man with dementia in a locked residential unit was false imprisonment, even though he did not know about the detention and lacked the capacity to understand what was happening.
- In *Lewis v Australian Capital Territory* (2020) Gageler J noted at [25] that people whose status or prior conduct has rendered them 'especially vulnerable to detention' (such as non-citizens and convicted offenders) are not 'outlaws'. They are 'entitled to expect that if, when, and for so long as, detention occurs in fact it will occur only in accordance with law. If the person is in fact detained for any period otherwise than in the exercise of lawful authority, the person is entitled to maintain an action for wrongful imprisonment in which the person is entitled to obtain an award of compensatory damages if the compensatory principle is satisfied'.
- In *Campbell v Northern Territory (No 3)* (2021) the defendant was lawfully detained in a youth detention centre, but was unlawfully moved to an isolation unit within that centre. The Court held that the imposition of a more stringent form of detention than was authorised constituted false imprisonment.
- In *Royal Caribbean Cruises Ltd v Rawlings* (2022) the Court noted that a medical practitioner has a defence to a claim for false imprisonment where the detention is necessary for the plaintiff's protection or the protection of others; and held at [35] that it is also a defence for the master of a ship to detain a person if they reasonably believe that their detention is 'necessary for the preservation of order and discipline, or for the safety of the vessel or persons or property on board'.
- In *Stradford (A Pseudonym) v Judge Vasta* (2023) it was held that a judge who sentenced the plaintiff to imprisonment, when they did not have the power to do so, had committed false imprisonment. The officers of Queensland Police and of Queensland Corrective Services who were involved in the plaintiff's detention and imprisonment were also held to have committed the tort of false imprisonment. However, this decision was overturned by the High Court in *Queensland v Stradford (A Pseudonym)* (2025). The Court held that as the judge was acting in a judicial capacity, he was protected by judicial immunity; and the police, correctional officers and security guards had a legal duty to enforce court orders that appeared valid on their face.
- In *Eastlake v Capner* (2024) the defendant had a history of acting violently and coercively towards the plaintiff. In the course of one particularly violent incident, it appeared that there were times during which the plaintiff could have escaped. However, the Court held that she was nonetheless falsely imprisoned because the combination of the prior violence and coercion meant that she was unable to leave.
- In *Reeves v New South Wales* (2024) the plaintiff was held in police custody for questioning. He indicated that he did not want to respond to any questions, but the police continued to ask him questions for 16 minutes. While at first instance it

was held that this constituted false imprisonment, this was overturned on appeal. The Court held that this was a legitimate part of the investigation period, during which police were authorised to detain the plaintiff.

Active reading

Link each of the cases listed in section 5.4.7 above to one of the elements of the tort.

5.4.8 Problem-solving tips

This section offers tips on how to approach and answer problem questions involving false imprisonment, highlighting the key steps and issues to look for when applying the principles covered in this chapter.

1. Look for the *harmful or adverse effect*. Is there any evidence that a person has been confined or prevented from leaving any premises or place? They will become the plaintiff (P).
2. Check how the confinement came about. Whose *conduct* or words led to the confinement? This person may become the defendant (D). It is also always worth checking to see if there is any possible claim against any employer of D under the doctrine of vicarious liability (see Chapter 16): in some cases it is possible for there to be more than one person who may be liable. For example, the person who physically confined P, the person whose statement or words actively promoted, caused and induced that person to confine P, and their employers could all potentially be liable. (See *Myer Stores Ltd v Soo* (1991), 'A case to remember', section 5.4.1 above.)
3. Remember that confinement must be total. However, it need not be in a building or a prison. It could be in a completely open space, as long as P has surrendered to the will of D, thinking reasonably that there is no alternative. The confinement may be for a very short time – no minimum period is specified in the case law. The length of confinement may reduce the award of damages, but even a short period of imprisonment of an innocent person may be a serious matter that warrants a significant award of damages.
4. Similarly, there is no requirement that P be aware of the confinement; but any lack of awareness may also affect the award of damages.
5. Remember that this tort contains a number of 'fuzzy' rules – for example, those requiring that there be no *reasonable* means of escape; that P must believe *reasonably* that force will be used against them or that they have no alternative but to comply with D's demands; and that D may be bound by a *reasonable* condition of entry. These rules require you to argue the facts of your particular problem question, and to explain whether in the circumstances they can (or cannot) be made out. Remember, too, that you may not have all of the facts – so consider if there are any missing facts and answer in the alternative if necessary.
6. If the imprisonment was brought about by indirect means, you may need to consider first whether you can mount an argument based on the 'extended' notion of

directness discussed in *Scott v Shepherd* (1773). If this argument fails, you should consider the alternative of bringing an action in negligence, but the problem will then become whether the imprisonment caused any actual damage. If the event led only to emotional distress, D may not be liable. In this scenario, P's claim may fall between the rights-based trespass torts (which are actionable per se but where the harm must be caused directly by a positive act) and a harm-based action on the case like negligence (which allows for indirect causation and may impose liability for an omission, but which insists on actual damage).

5.5 Development of the trespass torts: A new tort of privacy?

Although most of the trespass torts are very old, development is still possible. For example, we noted in section 5.1.2 above that in *Giller v Procopets* (2008) Maxwell P suggested that the tort of action on the case for the intentional infliction of psychiatric injury or nervous shock should be extended to cover intentionally caused emotional distress. While this suggestion was not taken up by the other judges in that case, it is possible that other courts may act upon this suggestion.

Another area where development is possible is in relation to a tort of privacy. For many years it was thought that the development of such a tort was precluded by the High Court's judgment in *Victoria Park Racing and Recreation Grounds v Taylor* (1937). However, in *Australian Broadcasting Corporation v Lenah Game Meats Pty Ltd* (2001) the High Court seems to have opened the door to the future development of the tort, with Callinan J at [335] suggesting that 'the time is ripe for consideration whether a tort of invasion of privacy should be recognised' (see also Gleeson J at [40]; Gummow and Hayne JJ at [132]). Such an approach has been taken in some states in the United States, which have recognised a set of common law tort actions based on the invasion of privacy.

While the High Court opened this door over 20 years ago, there has been limited development in the area, with courts taking differing viewpoints. For example, the existence of a tort of privacy was recognised by Skoien DCJ in the Queensland District Court in *Grosse v Purvis* (2003) and by Hampel J in the Victorian County Court in *Jane Doe v Australian Broadcasting Corporation* (2007). However, it has not been recognised in several other cases, including *Giller v Procopets* (2008), *Kostov v Nationwide News Pty Ltd (No 1)* (2018) and *Norkin v University of New England* (2022). In *Smethurst v Commissioner of Police* (2020) the High Court again noted that the door remains open (Kiefel CJ, Bell and Keane JJ at [48], [86]–[90]; Edelman J at [241]–[244]), but did not need to determine the issue.

The concept of a tort of privacy was firmly rejected by the House of Lords in *Wainwright v Home Office* (2003) on the grounds that, while privacy is an important value that underpins many other causes of action, it is too vague a concept to form the basis of a stand-alone tort and is not precise enough to justify or help to identify the full set of specific rules and exceptions that would need to be applied in concrete cases. These difficulties led the House of Lords to conclude that it would be more appropriate for Parliament to introduce any legal measures aimed at protecting privacy. The development of the law in this area is further complicated not only by the fact that some jurisdictions already have rights to privacy based on statute (eg the

Human Rights Act 1998 (UK)), but also by the fact that privacy is partially protected by the equitable cause of action for breach of confidence. Privacy therefore attracts several different sources of legal protection (statute, tort law and equity).

Some suggestions for the development of the law can be found in the Australian Law Reform Commission report *For Your Information: Australian Privacy Law and Practice* (2008) at 74.83, which recommended the introduction of a statutory cause of action for serious invasions of privacy, including:

- interference with the plaintiff's home or family life;
- unauthorised surveillance of the plaintiff;
- interference with or misuse or disclosure of the plaintiff's correspondence; and
- disclosure of sensitive facts about the plaintiff's private life.

At the time of writing this chapter, the Commonwealth Government had just introduced a Bill into Parliament which, if enacted, will create such a tort (Privacy and Other Legislation Amendment Bill 2024 (Cth)). The Explanatory Memorandum to that Bill states at [15]–[18]:

> The statutory tort for serious invasions of privacy would provide a flexible framework to address current and emerging privacy risks and provide individuals with the ability to better protect themselves and seek compensation for a broader range of serious invasions of privacy, including physical privacy, as well as misuse of information.
>
> Individuals would have a cause of action if they suffer an invasion of their privacy, either by an intrusion into their seclusion or by misuse of information, when: a person in their position would have had a reasonable expectation of privacy in all the circumstances; the invasion of privacy was intentional or reckless; and the invasion of privacy was serious. Where one or more competing public interests are identified by a defendant (for example, the public interest in freedom of expression), the plaintiff must also satisfy the court that the public interest in protecting their privacy outweighs those competing public interests.
>
> The statutory tort would include a range of defences and exemptions for legitimate activities that are essential in a free, safe and democratic society. This is intended to protect the vital public interest in press freedom, including the role of journalists in fostering informed public debate, to promote accountability and transparency, and serve as a platform for diverse opinions and voices. The defences and exemptions also recognise that legitimate activities of government may be privacy intrusive but are necessary and justifiable to ensure the proper administration of government (including law enforcement) and keep the community safe and secure.
>
> The statutory tort provides for a range of remedies including compensation. It also specifies some other modifications for the purposes of the tort, including a cap on damages, ensuring that summary judgment can be issued in all jurisdictions, and a role for the Information Commissioner to intervene with the leave of the court, or to assist as amicus curiae.

For further discussion of the development of a tort of privacy, see Gligorijevic (2021) and Lerch (2021).

Conclusion

This chapter has provided you with an introduction to the rights-based trespass torts, with a specific focus on battery, assault and false imprisonment. We have explored the essential elements and legal principles that underpin each of these torts, emphasising their role in protecting fundamental rights such as bodily integrity, personal autonomy and freedom from unlawful restraint. We have also considered some possible developments in the area, such as the creation of a tort of privacy. Our discussion of the trespass torts continues in the next chapter, which looks at trespass to land and goods.

Test your understanding

Problem solving

You can attempt these problems now, by referring to Figure 5.1 and applying your knowledge of the cases in this chapter. You will, however, be able to answer these problems more fully after you have covered the defences in Chapter 7.

Use these examples as an opportunity to practise spotting the torts, identifying the conduct and the effects clearly from the facts and diagnosing some of the possible issues.

Problem 1

Robert has claimed that a famous Australian sports star, Boko, hit him during an altercation at a local hotel. Robert claimed that Boko elbowed him in the jaw after he tried to take a photograph of him at The Lucky Punter Hotel. 'I was shocked because I was a huge fan, but not now,' Robert said. Robert explained that he had arrived at The Lucky Punter at about 5.30 pm last Sunday to have a few drinks with his girlfriend. 'I saw Boko and, although I never asked for his permission, I put my arm around him, not aggressively, and took a photo on my phone,' he said.

Robert said that Boko (who can be seen in the photo with his head down and wearing a cap with the brim pulled very low) was out with his teammates trying to forget the fact that they had just lost a grand final that day. Robert said: 'It wasn't my intention to offend him, and I wasn't trying to upset the guys he was drinking with, but as I took the photo, Boko just elbowed me in the jaw with his right elbow without saying anything. I asked, "What was that for?" and said that I was his biggest fan. He said, "I'm here to drink with my mates, not to spend time with arrogant creeps like you."'

Problem 2

During a game of AFL football, Des Docker ran past another player, Adam Eagle, who gave Des a fiercely hostile look and rudely raised his middle finger in the air. Des punched him in the stomach. Adam then noticed a tattoo of a female face on Des' arm. He taunted Des about the girl, suggesting in very vulgar terms that he had engaged in sexual intercourse with her the night before. He said that she was a 'slut'. Des Docker was outraged at this because the tattoo was a picture of his six-year-old daughter Matilda. He accused Adam Eagle of being a paedophile and struck Adam repeatedly and wrestled with him.

Problem 3

John works as a delivery driver for a small logistics company. One afternoon, he arrives at a remote warehouse to drop off a package. The warehouse manager, Steve, is the only person on site. After some casual conversation, Steve suddenly becomes agitated, accusing John of delivering a damaged package the week before. Without warning, Steve locks the warehouse door behind them, pocketing the only key. He tells John that he's not leaving until he admits to the alleged mistake and agrees to compensate the company. John insists that he had nothing to do with any damaged package, but Steve remains adamant and refuses to let him go.

John notices that there is a small window high up on the warehouse wall through which he could escape. The window is narrow and reaching it would require stacking boxes and climbing up. Even if he managed to get out, it's about a three-metre drop to the ground outside, and John is worried he could hurt himself. So he decides not to try and leave.

Steve continues to block the door, making it clear that John isn't free to leave until he complies with Steve's demands. After about half an hour of tense discussion, during which John repeatedly asks to be let out, Steve finally relents and unlocks the door.

Figure 5.1 Torts to the person: Battery, assault and false imprisonment

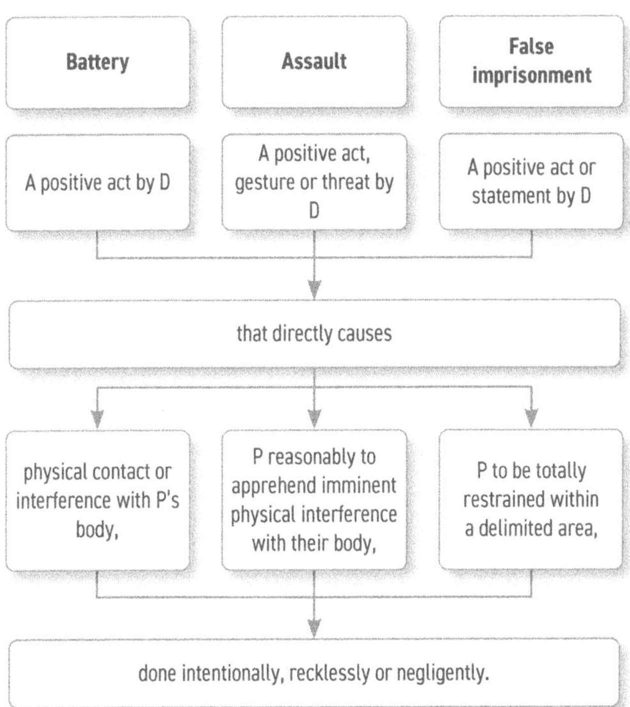

Always check for battery *and* assault. After determining the elements, consider whether any defences are available (see Chapter 7).

Tip 1. Start by looking for the *harmful* or *adverse effects*, then look to see whose *conduct* caused them. Deal with each event in time order.

Tip 2. Some torts are *linked*, or can be argued in the alternative:

- If you have a possible battery, consider whether there may also have been an assault.
- If you have difficulty arguing directness, consider an action for another tort such as negligence or action on the case.

REFERENCES

CASES

A v B [2021] NSWDC 491
Abdulrahim v Adult Parole Board of Victoria (2023) 71 VR 169; [2023] VSC 432
ACN 087528774 Pty Ltd (formerly Connex Trains Melbourne Pty Ltd) v Chetcuti [2008] VSCA 274; (2008) 21 VR 559
AKW22 v Commonwealth (No 2) [2023] FCA 332
Ashley v Chief Constable of Sussex Police [2008] 1 AC 962
Australian Broadcasting Corporation v Lenah Game Meats Pty Ltd (2001) 208 CLR 199
Bahner v Marwest Hotels Co (1970) 6 DLR (3rd) 322
Balven v Thurston [2013] NSWSC 21
Barber v Goodstart Early Learning (2021) 305 IR 38; [2021] FWC 2156
Barker v The Queen (1983) 153 CLR 338
Barton v Armstrong [1969] 2 NSWR 451
Binsaris v Northern Territory (2020) 270 CLR 549; [2020] HCA 22
Bird v Holbrook (1828) 4 Bing 628; 130 ER 911
Bird v Jones [1845] 7 QB 742; 115 ER 668
Bunyan v Jordan (1937) 57 CLR 1
Campbell v Northern Territory (No 3) [2021] FCA 1089
Carrier v Bonham [2001] QCA 234; [2002] 1 Qd R 474
Carter v Walker (2010) 32 VR 1
Coco v The Queen (1994) 179 CLR 427
Cole v Turner (1704) 6 Mod Rep 149; (1704) 87 ER 907
Collins v Wilcock [1984] 1 WLR 1172
Cowell v Corrective Services Commissioner of New South Wales (1988) 13 NSWLR 714
CPCF v Minister for Immigration and Border Protection (2015) 255 CLR 514
Croucher v Cachia [2016] NSWCA 132
Cruse v Victoria (2019) 59 VR 241; [2019] VSC 574
Darby v Director of Public Prosecutions [2004] NSWCA 431; (2004) 61 NSWLR 558
Davis v Viglianti [2024] FedCFamC2G 505
Dickinson v Waters Ltd (1931) 31 SR (NSW) 593

Eastlake v Capner [2024] QSC 136
Falconer v Commissioner of Police (WA) (No 2) [2024] WASCA 47
Fowler v Lanning [1959] 1 QB 426
Freeman v Home Office (No 2) [1984] 2 WLR 130
Giller v Procopets (2008) 24 VR 1
Grosse v Purvis [2003] QDC 151 (Skoien SJDC, 16 June 2003)
Halliday v Nevill (1984) 155 CLR 1
Haskins v Commonwealth (2011) 244 CLR 22; [2011] HCA 28
Hutchins v Maughan [1947] VLR 131
Innes v Wylie (1844) 1 Car & K 257; 174 ER 800
Irlam v Byrnes (2022) 108 NSWLR 285; [2022] NSWCA 81
Jane Doe v Australian Broadcasting Corporation [2007] VCC 281
Kostov v Nationwide News Pty Ltd (No 1) [2018] NSWSC 1822
Kuru v New South Wales (2008) 236 CLR 1
Letang v Cooper [1965] 1 QB 232
Lewis v Australian Capital Territory (2020) 271 CLR 192; [2020] HCA 26
Louis v Commonwealth (1987) 87 FLR 277
MacPherson v Beath (1975) 12 SASR 174
Magill v Magill (2006) 226 CLR 551
McFadzean v CFMEU [2007] VSCA 289; (2007) 20 VR 250
McHale v Watson (1964) 111 CLR 384
McLaughlin v New South Wales (No 2) [2023] NSWDC 525
McLoughlin v Grovers [2001] EWCA Civ 1743
McNamara v Duncan (1979) 26 ALR 584
Meering v Graham-White Aviation (1919) 122 LT 44
Mink v University of Chicago 460 F Supp 713 (ND Ill 1978)
Morriss v Marsden [1952] 1 All ER 925
Murray v Ministry of Defence [1988] 2 All ER 521
Myer Stores Ltd v Soo [1991] 2 VR 597
Nationwide News v Naidu [2007] NSWCA 377; (2007) 71 NSWLR 471
New South Wales v Delly [2007] NSWCA 303
New South Wales v Ibbett (2006) 229 CLR 638
New South Wales v Madden [2024] NSWCA 40
New South Wales v McLaughlin [2024] NSWCA 137
New South Wales v Ouhammi (2019) 101 NSWLR 160; [2019] NSWCA 225
New South Wales v Robinson (2019) 266 CLR 619; [2019] HCA 46
Norkin v University of New England [2022] NSWSC 819
Origliasso v Vitale [1952] St R Qd 211
Platt v Nutt (1988) 12 NSWLR 231
Plenty v Dillon (1991) 171 CLR 635
Police v Greaves [1964] NZLR 295
Public Advocate v BC (2019) 133 SASR 353; [2019] SAASCFC 58
Public Trustee v Atileo [2023] TASSC 33
Queensland v Stradford (A Pseudonym) [2025] HCA 3

R v Garrett (1988) 50 SASR 392
R v Ireland [1998] AC 146; [1997] 4 All ER 225
R v St George (1840) 9 C & P 483; 173 ER 921
Re Bolton; Ex parte Beane (1987) 162 CLR 514
Re F (Mental Patient: Sterilisation) [1990] 2 AC 1
Reeves v New South Wales [2024] NSWCA 125
Rixon v Star City (2001) 53 NSWLR 98
Robinson v Balmain New Ferry Co (1906) 4 CLR 379; [1910] AC 295
Royal Caribbean Cruises v Rawlings (2022) 107 NSWLR 51; [2022] NSWCA 4
Rosza v Samuels [1969] SASR 205
Roy v O'Neill [2020] HCA 45; (2020) 272 CLR 291
Ruddock v Taylor [2005] HCA 48; (2005) 221 ALR 32
S v G [1995] 3 NZLR 681
Scott v Shepherd (1773) 2 Black W 892; 96 ER 525
Secretary, Department of Health and Community Services v JWB and SMB (1992) 175 CLR 218 (*Marion's Case*)
Smethurst v Commissioner of Police [2020] HCA 14; (2020) 272 CLR 177
South Australia v Lampard-Trevorrow [2010] SASC 56; (2010) 106 SASR 331
Stephens v Meyers (1830) 4 C & P 350; 172 ER 735
Stradford (A Pseudonym) v Judge Vasta [2023] FCA 1020
Symes v Mahon [1922] SASR 447
Thomas v National Union of Mineworkers [1986] Ch 20
Tinnock v Murrumbidgee Local Health District (No 6) [2017] NSWSC 1003
Trevorrow v South Australia (No 5) [2007] SASC 285
Trobridge v Hardy (1955) 94 CLR 147
Tuberville v Savage (1669) 1 Mod 3; 86 ER 291
Venning v Chin (1974) 10 SASR 299
Victoria Park Racing and Recreation Grounds v Taylor (1937) 58 CLR 479
Wainwright v Home Office [2003] UKHL 53; [2004] 2 AC 406
Watson v Marshal and Cade [1971] 124 CLR 621
Weaver v Ward (1616) Hob 134; 80 ER 284
White v Johnston (2015) 87 NSWLR 779
Wilkinson v Downton [1897] 2 QB 57
Williams v Milotin (1957) 97 CLR 465
Zanker v Vartzokas (1988) 34 A Crim R 11
Zaravinos v New South Wales (2004) 62 NSWLR 58; [2004] NSWCA 320
Zey v New South Wales (No 2) [2024] NSWDC 289

ARTICLES, BOOKS AND OTHER RESOURCE

Australian Law Reform Commission, *For Your Information: Australian Privacy Law and Practice* (2008).
Balkin, R P & Davis, J L R, *Law of Torts*, 5th ed (2013) LexisNexis Butterworths, Sydney.
Barker, K, Cane, P, Lunney, M & Trindade, F, *The Law of Torts in Australia*, 5th ed (2012) Oxford University Press, Melbourne.

Blackstone's *Commentaries on the Laws of England* (1765–69) <www.lonang.com/exlibris/blackstone/>.

Gligorijevic, J, 'A Common Law Tort of Interference with Privacy for Australia: Reaffirming ABC v Lenah Game Meats' (2021) 44 *University of New South Wales Law Journal* 673.

Lerch, J, 'The Judicial Law-Making Function and a Tort of Invasion of Personal Privacy' (2021) 43 *Sydney Law Review* 133.

6 TRESPASS TO LAND AND PERSONAL PROPERTY

Introduction

In Chapter 5 we started our consideration of the trespass torts, examining the nature of those torts and focusing on the three forms of trespass to the person: battery, assault and false imprisonment. In this chapter we conclude our examination of the trespass torts, focusing on the torts of trespass to land and trespass to goods. We also consider two closely related torts that involve an interference with personal property: conversion and detinue.

These complicated and technical areas of tort law have a special relationship with the law of property, so before you study these four torts (and before you read the cases in the area) you need to become familiar with some new concepts (discussed in section 6.1 below). This area of the law also contains special and sometimes highly technical definitions, some of which can go beyond the ordinary everyday meanings of words (eg 'land') and others that you may never have heard of before (eg 'bailment'). Land is defined in section 6.2.1 below, and the terms 'trespasser', 'licensee' and 'invitee' are explained in Table 6.1. Bailment, and the associated definitions of 'bailee' and 'bailor', are explained in Table 6.2.

6.1 Essential concepts

6.1.1 Torts, possession and property law

Tort law is closely intertwined with property law, though the relationship is complex. Real property law defines 'land' and governs the relationships between people and land. By contrast, personal property law addresses the relationships between people and tangible goods (sometimes called 'chattels') as well as intangible assets like intellectual property. Once property law establishes rights and interests in land and goods, tort law comes into play to protect individuals from certain invasions of those rights by others. Fundamentally, tort law addresses actions by one person that harm another, and in this context, it specifically deals with actions that infringe upon another person's rights over land and goods in their possession.

You will learn more about this complex topic in your Property Law courses, but one of the most important distinctions you need to understand right now is the difference between *ownership* of land and goods on the one hand, and *possession* of land and goods on the other. This distinction is critical, because tort law is primarily concerned with protecting the possession of land and goods rather than with protecting the ownership of land and goods. As the High Court of Australia ('High Court') pointed out in *New South Wales v Ibbett* (2006) at [29]:

> It is well established that the tort [of trespass to land] protects the interest of the plaintiff in maintaining the right to exclusive possession of her place of residence, free from uninvited physical intrusion by strangers. It is not the concern of the law here to protect title in the sense of ownership.

Although the trespass torts are primarily concerned with possession rather than ownership, it will usually be the case that the right to possession of land or goods is held by the owner of the land or goods. However, an owner can temporarily dispose of their possessory interest in land or goods – for example, by granting a lease to a tenant. Once a lease exists, the tenant gains the right to possession of the leased land or goods and can use the law of torts to protect that right. This includes being able to sue the owner for trespass if they enter the leased land or interfere with the leased goods without consent or lawful justification.

In order to have possession of land or goods, a person does not need to be physically present on the land or be physically holding onto the goods. In this regard, the law draws a distinction between actual and constructive possession, both of which are sufficient to give legal rights over the property:

- Actual possession occurs when a person is in physical occupation of land or has physical control over goods. This includes when a person is living on their land, when they are carrying their backpack, or when they have their car parked in their garage and have the keys in their pocket.
- Constructive possession occurs in certain special circumstances when the law deems a person to be in possession even though they may not have actual physical *control* over goods or land. This includes when a person has left their land to travel overseas, if they accidentally leave their backpack on the beach or if their car is tipped into the sea (as occurred in *Proudman v Allen* (1954)).

The fact that tort law is so strongly focused on protecting possession means that a squatter who is exercising full factual possession and control over some piece of land – or a thief who is exercising full physical possession and control over stolen goods – is entitled to sue any third person who invades their possession (except of course the true owner). The reason for this intriguing feature of the law lies in the origins of these very old torts, which developed at a time when one of the law's key goals was to maintain 'law and order' and to discourage any violent breaches of the peace. So, a person in possession of land or goods was seen as having a legitimate 'possessory title', which they could maintain against all the world except the true owner. As Donaldson LJ pointed out in *Parker v British Airways Board* (1982) at 1009, this approach prevents a 'free-for-all

Table 6.1 Entering land: Invitees, licensees and trespassers

	Definition	**Notes**	**Examples**
Invitees	An invitee is someone who is invited onto land for special purposes – usually material, pecuniary or business purposes.	An occupier of land must take reasonable care to ensure that the premises are safe for invitees, particularly in relation to any dangers the occupier knows or ought to know about.	A doctor who is called in to treat someone in the home; a contractor entering to repair something on the land; a customer entering a shop.
Licensees	A licensee is someone who is not invited onto land for special material, pecuniary or business purposes, but who is allowed by the occupier to remain on the land for other purposes, often social or personal.	A licence to be on land may be express or implied (or contractual in nature), and the occupier may revoke the licence and ask the person to leave.	Children living in a home with their parents; visitors known to the occupiers; members of the public seeking to speak with the occupiers or to enter for some other innocent and lawful purpose (such as to collect for charity); a person who has bought a ticket to the races.
Trespassers	A trespasser is someone who is on land without lawful justification.	–	A person entering without bona fide motives (such as a person who enters to steal from the property or harm a person on it); a squatter who exercises factual possession of land; a licensee or invitee who exceeds the scope of their invitation or licence to be on the land or who, having been asked to leave, remains on land after a reasonable time to leave has expired.

in which the physically weakest would go to the wall'. It is often said that 'possession is nine tenths of the law' and in the law of torts, it is almost always the full ten-tenths.

6.1.2 Presence on land: The categories of entrant

The law has traditionally classified the people who enter land into different categories, each of which is treated differently, depending on their relationship with the owner of the land and the conditions under which they enter or remain on the land. So, in addition to understanding the differences between owners of land and other occupiers of land with a recognised legal interest in possession of land (like tenants under a lease), you also need to be aware of these special categories of entrant. (They will also be relevant to our discussion of the torts of private nuisance and negligence.) Note that a person who enters land under one category may shift into another category, depending on the circumstances, including their own subsequent conduct and the attitude of the occupier of the land who may change the conditions of entry.

6.1.3 Goods: The notion of bailment

Just as the law contains different categories to describe the people who enter or remain on land, it also contains different categories to describe the relationships between people and goods. Many of those categories depend on the notion of bailment, which

Table 6.2 Bailment

	Definition	**Examples**
Bailment	When the owner of goods gives temporary possession of the goods to another person, without transferring ownership.	The temporary placement of a painting in an art gallery for exhibition; the delivery of goods to a customer under a hire-purchase arrangement.
Bailor	The owner who gives possession of the goods to another person.	An artist who places their painting in a gallery for exhibition; a supplier who provides goods to a customer under a hire-purchase arrangement.
Bailee	The person receiving possession of the goods.	An art gallery that receives a painting for temporary exhibition; a customer who takes possession of goods under a hire-purchase arrangement.
Bailment for a term	Bailment for a defined period that is specified in the bailment agreement.	An artist places a painting in a gallery for a two-month exhibition, under an agreement that the painting will be returned at the end of that period.
Bailment at will (also known as a 'revocable bailment')	Bailment which is not for a fixed term, and which can be ended by the bailor or bailee whenever they choose.	An artist places a painting in a gallery for display without specifying a timeframe. The artist can ask for the painting back at any time, or the gallery can return it whenever they wish.

itself depends on the distinction between ownership and possession of goods. The common law developed many specialised categories of bailment, each with its own rules and remedies. Remember that these rules can be varied by a contractual agreement between the parties to the bailment. This is a very complicated area of law, but two of the most common kinds of bailment - bailment at will and bailment for a term - are defined in Table 6.2.

6.2 Trespass to land

6.2.1 The nature of trespass to land

Trespass to land is an unjustified act by one person that directly and either intentionally, recklessly or negligently causes physical interference with another person's exclusive possession of land. The elements of trespass to land are as follows:

1. The plaintiff was exercising exclusive possession of land or had a right to do so.
2. The defendant committed a positive act that directly caused physical interference with the plaintiff's (right to) exclusive possession of the land.
3. The defendant intended to cause that interference, or was reckless or negligent about causing it.

As is the case for the battery, the onus always lies on the plaintiff to prove the first two elements on the balance of probabilities. The onus of proving the third element depends on whether or not the events occurred on a highway. Where they did, it is for the plaintiff to prove that the interference was intentional, reckless or negligent: *Nickells v City of Melbourne* (1938). In all other cases, the onus is on the defendant to prove, on the balance of probabilities, that they were 'utterly without fault' (*Weaver v Ward* (1616); *Croucher v Cachia* (2016)).

It is possible for the defendant to argue that the interference was lawfully justified (eg that they had a search warrant for the property). Where they do, the onus will be on them to prove the defence on the balance of probabilities.

Because the ownership and possession of land was fundamentally important in English social history as one of the early sources of wealth, position and power, common law judges have been ferocious in protecting these rights. Any interference with possession of land is, therefore, a matter of strict liability. It will not be a defence for the plaintiff to argue that they thought they were walking across public land or to argue that they honestly believed that they were allowed to be on the land.

This tort protects the possessor's right to enjoy their land, control access to it and decide for themselves whether or not any other person may enter the land or physically interfere with it. Remember that this tort is not necessarily designed to protect owners of land - it protects anyone who has a recognised interest in the exclusive possession of land, which may include tenants holding a lease over the land or even squatters or trespassers who have taken over the exclusive factual possession of the land.

The law contains an extended definition of 'land' that is wider than the ordinary everyday meaning of the word. In addition to the ground, rocks and soil, the common law definition of land includes:

- buildings attached to the land;
- trees, plants, and uncut crops growing in the land;
- the land underneath the soil for considerable depth; and
- the airspace reasonably required for ordinary use of the land and the structures upon it.

Trespass to land is most obviously committed when the defendant physically enters the plaintiff's land against their will. However, it is not necessary for the defendant's body to enter the land at all. The tort can be committed by directly causing *any* physical interference with the land, no matter how slight. The tort can even be committed by preventing a person who has the right to immediate possession of the land from being able to exercise their right to physically access the land. For example, if the plaintiff and the defendant co-own a house together, and the defendant changes the locks so that the plaintiff cannot enter, the defendant has committed trespass to land – as they have prevented the plaintiff from being able to use and enjoy the house. This type of trespass to land is known as 'ouster'.

Case examples

- Trespass to land can be committed by pushing, driving or throwing something (or someone) onto the land. For example, in *Watson v Cowen* (1959) D was held liable for pushing earth onto P's property with a bulldozer.
- In *Davies v Benison* (1927) D shot and killed P's cat, which was sitting on a shed on P's land. The passage of the rifle pellet through P's airspace was held to be trespass to land.
- In *Kelsen v Imperial Tobacco Co* (1957) D's advertising sign protruded eight inches into the airspace over property leased by P. Although P had no plans to use that airspace, it was held to be trespass to land.
- In *Di Napoli v New Beach Apartments* (2004), to provide structural support for works on its land, D inserted 10 rock anchors which extended under the subsurface of P's land. This was held to constitute trespass to land.
- In *Johnson v Buchanan* (2012) D was found liable for trespass to his neighbour's land by allowing his arm to protrude over the fence dividing their properties.

While the potential scope of trespass to land is very broad, there are some kinds of conduct that will not amount to trespass.

Case examples

- Orbiting satellites or aircraft passing at a great height do not constitute trespass to land. This is because an owner's right to control the airspace above their land is limited to such a height as is necessary for the ordinary use and enjoyment of the land plus any buildings upon it: *Bernstein of Leigh (Baron) v Skyviews* (1977).
- Taking a photograph of land from adjoining land is not trespass to land: *Bathurst City Council v Saban* (1985). Note, however, that constant surveillance of another person's land may be a private nuisance (see Chapter 8).

- Allowing the roots of a tree to grow into another's land is not trespass, but it may constitute the tort of private nuisance (see Chapter 8).
- Some jurisdictions have passed legislation precluding liability in trespass for aircraft flown over properties at a reasonable height (see, eg, *Damage by Aircraft Act 1964* (WA) s 4). While this legislation clearly applies to vehicles such as airplanes and helicopters, it is currently unclear whether it also applies to drones.

LEGISLATION ALERT!

Consult your study materials to see whether there is any legislation in your jurisdiction that precludes liability in trespass for aircraft flown over property at a reasonable height. Consider whether it applies to drones.

This area of the law has developed some very complicated terminology and rules about the conduct that can amount to trespass to land. The types of trespass to land are summarised below.

6.2.1.1 Trespass *ab initio*

Trespass *ab initio* is a legal doctrine that applies when a person who initially had lawful authority to enter or use someone else's property subsequently abuses that authority or commits an unlawful act. This unlawful act retroactively invalidates the original permission, making the entire entry or use of the property a trespass from the beginning: *Six Carpenters Case* (1610); but see doubts expressed in *Barker v The Queen* (1983).

6.2.1.2 Residual trespass

Residual trespass occurs when someone lawfully enters a property, but remains on the property after their permission or right to be there has expired. This includes a licensee who overstays a time limit, or a person who has been asked to leave the premises but has failed to do so within a reasonable time: *Cowell v Rosehill Racecourse Co Ltd* (1937).

6.2.1.3 Continuing trespass

A continuing trespass occurs when the interference with another person's property continues over a period of time. Unlike a single, isolated act of trespass, a continuing trespass involves an ongoing violation that persists until the trespasser either leaves or stops the wrongful activity, or the situation is otherwise resolved. An example of a continuing trespass would be where a building intrudes into the airspace over another person's land. The trespass continues as long as the building remains in place: *Lord v McMahon* (2015). Where there is a continuing trespass, a successor in title may sue over conduct that occurred before they gained title: *Konskier v Goodman* (1928); *Kelsen v Imperial Tobacco Co* (1957).

6.2.2 Guiding principles

The guiding principles of trespass to land promote respect for the right to privacy in the home and the occupier's right to enjoy possession of land free from any interference or harassment. The autonomy right created by this tort prevents any invasion of land or physical contact with land without consent or other lawful justification, as Mason CJ, Brennan, Gaudron and McHugh JJ pointed out in *Coco v The Queen* (1994) at 435:

> Every unauthorised entry upon private property is a trespass, the right of a person in possession or entitled to possession of premises to exclude others from those premises being a fundamental common law right.

The tort is especially concerned to protect the possession of property and the privacy and security of the occupier: *Plenty v Dillon* (1991). These rights, which were asserted and protected very early in English law, remain important today.

Case examples

- In *Semayne's Case* (1604) the Court held that 'the house of every one is to him as his castle and fortress, as well as for his defence against injury and violence, as for his repose' (quoted by Mason CJ, Brennan and Toohey JJ in *Plenty v Dillon* (1991) at 639).
- In *Southam v Smout* (1964) Lord Denning MR at 320 adopted an old quotation from the Earl of Chatham, saying:

  > 'The poorest man may in his cottage bid defiance to all the forces of the Crown. It may be frail – its roof may shake – the wind may blow through it – the storm may enter – the rain may enter – but the King of England cannot enter – all his force dares not cross the threshold of the ruined tenement.' So be it – unless he has justification by law. [Quoted by Gaudron and McHugh JJ in *Plenty v Dillon* (1991) at 649.]

- In *Halliday v Nevill* (1984) Brennan J pointed out at 9 that in many trespass to land cases there is a clash between the principles of individual privacy and security, and the wider public policy that is concerned to enforce the criminal law and enable police officers to apprehend and arrest suspected criminals: 'It is a contest between public authority and the security of private dwellings.'
- In *New South Wales v Ibbett* (2006) the Court held at [38]:

  > The common law fixes … a line between the interests of the individual in personal freedom of action and the interests of the State in the maintenance of a legally ordered society. An action for trespass to land and an award of exemplary damages has long been a method by which, at the instance of the citizen, the State is called to account by the common law for the misconduct of those acting under or with the authority of the Executive Government.

- The majority judgment in *Kuru v New South Wales* (2008) emphasised at [37] 'the strong principle of Australian law defensive of the quiet enjoyment by an occupier of that person's residence' which 'defends an important civil right in our society'.

These statements highlight the significant conflict that often arises in this area between an individual's right to privacy and security on their land and the broader community's interest in maintaining law and order. However, this is not the only conflict. Another key issue arises when law enforcement officers exceed their lawful authority, creating a tension between the need to deter police misconduct and the community's interest in apprehending criminals.

6.2.3 Overview of the tort of trespass to land

6.2.3.1 Conduct

- There must normally be a positive act by the defendant. Ordinarily, trespass to land cannot be committed by omission (*Plenty v Dillon* (1991)).
- However, a person commits trespass if they fail to leave land within a reasonable time after their permission to be on the land has been revoked, even if their initial entry onto the land was lawful (*Cowell v Rosehill Racecourse Co Ltd* (1937); *Kuru v New South Wales* (2008)).

6.2.3.2 Effect

- The defendant's conduct must directly cause physical contact with land or an interference with the plaintiff's exclusive possession of land. It need not cause actual damage. This tort is actionable per se. The mere interference with possession or invasion of the right is sufficient (*Dumont v Miller* (1873); *Southport Corporation v Esso Petroleum Co Ltd* (1954); *Johnson v Buchanan* (2012)).
- The contact must be direct. If it is indirect, consider using another tort such as action on the case, negligence or nuisance.

6.2.3.3 Fault

- The defendant must have intended to cause the physical interference with the plaintiff's exclusive possession of land, or been reckless or negligent (in the sense of being careless) about causing it. There is no requirement that the defendant must intend to invade the land of another or even realise that the land is in possession of another (*Basely v Clarkson* (1681)).
- The defendant's act must be voluntary (directed by the will or conscious mind). For example, involuntary entry that occurs during an epileptic seizure is not trespass (*Public Transport Commission of New South Wales v Perry* (1977)).

6.2.3.4 Circumstances

- To be able to sue, the plaintiff must have the right to exclusive possession of the land or be exercising exclusive possession of the land. This is a question of fact. 'Mere licensees' may not bring an action, but those who exercise exclusive factual possession may (*Western Australia v Ward* (2002); *Glavinic v Commonwealth* (2023)).
- A landlord out of possession may be sued by a tenant in possession (*Newington v Windeyer* (1985); *Haddrick v Lloyd* (1945); *Moore v Devanjul Pty Ltd (No 5)* (2013)).

- It is unclear whether native title rights give sufficient title to sue in trespass. It has been suggested that this is arguable (*Buurabalayji Thalanyji Aboriginal Corporation v Onslow Slat Pty Ltd (No 2)* (2018)).
- There must be no lawful justification for the conduct. Entry to land will be lawfully justified if permission to enter the land was expressly or implicitly given by the plaintiff (*Halliday v Nevill* (1984); *Plenty v Dillon* (1991)).
- A person who exceeds the scope of their licence or who goes beyond any lawful authority to be on land commits a trespass (*Barker v The Queen* (1983) 153 CLR 338; *Roy v O'Neill* (2020)).
- Permission is limited to those who enter with bona fide motives (*Lincoln Hunt v Willesee* (1986)).
- Police officers have no greater rights than ordinary members of the public to enter land, unless they have lawful justification (*Halliday v Nevill* (1984); *Plenty v Dillon* (1991); *Kuru v New South Wales* (2008)).
- Any statute that authorises entry must do so in clear, unmistakable and unambiguous language (*Coco v The Queen* (1994)).

6.2.4 Defences

The defences to the tort of trespass to land are explained in Chapter 7. This is a tort of strict liability, and mistake will not be a defence. The question of lawful authority is an important matter, particularly as it relates to police powers: see *Halliday v Nevill* (1984); *Plenty v Dillon* (1991); *Coco v The Queen* (1994); *New South Wales v Ibbett* (2006); and *Kuru v New South Wales* (2008).

A key case in this regard is *Halliday v Nevill* (1984). In that case, the majority in the High Court explained at 6–7 that whether an occupier has given another permission to enter land is a question of fact. Such permission can sometimes be implied by law, allowing any member of the public to enter, as long as there is no obstruction or indication that entry is forbidden. This implied licence applies to police officers in the same way it applies to any member of the public with a legitimate reason to enter the property. Examples of when an implied licence might be assumed include:

- stepping into a driveway to avoid an obstruction on the road;
- entering a property to communicate with someone in the house; and
- retrieving property that has blown onto the land or a small child who has run onto the land.

For further discussion of the implied licence to enter land, see *Roy v O'Neill* (2020) at [11]–[20] (Kiefel CJ), [66]–[83] (Keane and Edelman JJ) and [31]–[50] (Bell and Gageler JJ (dissenting)). In that case, Keane and Edelman JJ at [79] noted that while police (like all other members of the public) may have an implied licence to enter land, in the absence of any other specific powers they will be trespassers if '(i) the sole purpose for their entry onto the premises is outside the scope of any implied licence, (ii) they remain on the land after the licence is revoked, or (iii) they act in a manner inconsistent with the licence'.

6.2.5 Remedies

Once liability for trespass is established, the plaintiff is entitled to damages as a matter of right, covering all direct consequences of the trespass, whether foreseeable or not. As noted by Mason CJ, Brennan and Toohey JJ in *Plenty v Dillon* (1991) at 645, when damages are awarded for trespass (rather than for a separate tort), 'the plaintiff is entitled to some damages in vindication of his right to exclude others from the land'.

The full range of nominal, compensatory (including aggravated) and exemplary damages may be awarded: see section 2.3.3.2 of Chapter 2. In *New South Wales v Ibbett* (2006), the High Court explained at [38]–[40] that exemplary damages serve a 'valuable purpose' by marking the court's disapproval of any oppressive, arbitrary or outrageous use of executive power, and by 'vindicating the strength of the law'. Aggravated damages may compensate for harassment, affront or humiliation caused to anyone on the land with the permission of the occupier, which in itself is 'an infringement of the right of the plaintiff to enjoy exclusive and quiet possession': *New South Wales v Ibbett* (2006) at [31]. For two examples of awards for aggravated damages which compensated the plaintiff for humiliation, distress and hurt to feelings, see *Greig v Greig* (1966) and *TCN Channel Nine Pty Ltd v Anning* (2002).

The plaintiff may also use the 'self-help' remedy of physical 'ejectment' if a trespasser forcibly enters their land, or if a licensee refuses to leave within a reasonable time after being asked: *Delaney v TP Smith Ltd* (1946). This remedy is strictly limited because it involves the use of force, but the courts do make allowances for the fact that the plaintiff may act in the heat of the moment. If the trespasser entered peacefully, they must be given a *reasonable* time to leave, and any force used must be *reasonably* necessary. If the trespasser entered forcibly, the plaintiff may use force without needing to request the trespasser to leave first. See Chapter 7 for further discussion of the self-help remedies.

Other remedies available to the plaintiff include:

- a declaration of right acknowledging the plaintiff's title to the land;
- an equitable injunction (if the trespass is likely to continue and the usual conditions for awarding an injunction are met). For a useful summary of the law in this area, see *Break Fast Investments Pty Ltd v PCH Melbourne Pty Ltd* (2007); and
- statutory remedies for any loss or damage caused by aircraft.

LEGISLATION ALERT!

Consult your study materials to see which legislation governs damage done by aircraft in your jurisdiction.

6.2.6 Some helpful cases for your summary

- *Haddrick v Lloyd* (1945) illustrates the operation of the rule that a tenant in possession under a lease has standing to sue a landlord who enters without consent, as well as any person invited on to the land by the landlord.

- *Coles-Smith v Smith* (1965) illustrates the operation of two rules: (1) that the wife of the owner of land may invite other people onto that land, but (2) if those people exceed the scope of their licence they become trespassers.
- In *Bernstein of Leigh (Baron) v Skyviews* (1977) Griffiths J explained that an owner's right to control the airspace above their land is limited to such a height as is necessary for the ordinary use and enjoyment of the land plus any buildings upon it.
- In *Newington v Windeyer* (1985) McHugh JA pointed out that the fact that the plaintiffs were not the registered owners of the land upon which the defendant had entered did not prevent them from bringing a case of trespass to land. They could protect their factual possession of the land, which they had exercised for a period of over 50 years, because their conduct in acting as if they were the owners gave them a possessory title.
- *Lincoln Hunt v Willesee* (1986) established the rule that where there is an implied invitation to the public to enter premises, it is limited to people entering with bona fide motives, and not those who may enter to rob or to harass.
- In *Plenty v Dillon* (1991) the police entered land to serve a summons after permission had been denied by the occupier. The majority in the High Court affirmed the fundamental principle that every invasion of private property, unless justified by law, is a trespass; and affirmed the earlier rule (from *Halliday v Nevill* (1984)) that police officers have no special right to enter except where specially authorised by law. Here, the relevant statute did not allow entry to serve a summons – it only allowed entry to arrest a person. Consequently, the police were held to be trespassing.
- In *Kuru v New South Wales* (2008) three important rules about police powers were summarised in the majority judgment of Gleeson CJ, Gummow, Kirby and Hayne JJ at [43]:

  > First, a person who enters the land of another must justify that entry by showing either that the entry was with the consent of the occupier or that the entrant had lawful authority to enter. Secondly, except in cases provided for by the common law and by statute, police officers have no special rights to enter land. And in the circumstances of this case it is also important to recognise a third proposition: that an authority to enter land may be revoked and that, if the authority is revoked, the entrant no longer has authority to remain on the land but must leave as soon as is reasonably practicable. [References omitted.]

- In *Lord v McMahon* (2015) Slattery J stated that the defence of consent to trespass to land requires that the plaintiff gave the defendant 'leave or licence' to enter the land, and noted that oral leave or licence is sufficient.
- In *James v North Star Pastoral Pty Ltd* (2019) the defendant mistakenly built a fence that extended two metres onto the plaintiff's land. Although this was an honest mistake, they were nevertheless held to be liable, as mistake is not a defence to trespass to land. It also didn't matter that the trespass was of a trifling nature: the fact that it interfered with the plaintiff's possession was sufficient.
- In *Roy v O'Neill* (2020) Mr Johnson and Ms Roy lived together in a unit. There was a domestic violence order (DVO) against Ms Roy, preventing her from being in Mr

Johnson's presence while intoxicated. The police did a welfare check on Mr Johnson, walking up the path to the unit where he lived and knocking on his door. Through the door they saw Ms Roy, who appeared to be intoxicated, so they asked her to do a breath test. It was argued that their conduct constituted a trespass, as the police do not have an implied licence to enter land for the purpose of exercising coercive powers (such as requiring a person to do a breath test). In a 3:2 decision the High Court held that the police were not trespassing. While the majority agreed that the police do not have an implied licence to enter land for the *sole* purpose of exercising coercive powers, that was not what had occurred here. The police had entered the 'curtilage' of the unit (ie the land immediately surrounding it) for the purpose of checking on Mr Johnson's welfare and assessing Ms Roy's compliance with the DVO. This fell within the scope of the implied licence to enter land.

- In *R v Southwell* (2022) the defendant entered the relevant premises for the purposes of assaulting the occupant. This was held to be a trespass, as the defendant's purpose lay entirely outside the scope of any licence to enter that had been granted by the occupant.
- In *Romani v New South Wales* (2023) the police jumped a locked gate which had a sign excluding police from entry in the absence of consent. As they were not lawfully authorised to enter the property without consent, they were trespassing. While the owner of the property had standing to sue them, the owner's daughter (who lived in the family home as a licensee) did not.
- In *BA v The King* (2023) the defendant was a co-tenant of an apartment with his former partner. When the relationship ended, the defendant stopped paying rent, moved out and returned the keys. Some time later he returned, demanding to be let in. When his former partner refused to do so, he kicked down the door and entered the property. In a 4:3 decision, the majority of the High Court held that this was not a trespass, as the defendant remained a co-tenant, which gave him a right to exclusive possession of the land. His former partner had no right to exclude him from the property.

Active reading

Link each of the cases listed in section 6.2.6 above to one of the elements of the tort.

Test your understanding and develop your skills

Case notes

Read the key cases of *Halliday v Nevill* (1984) and *Plenty v Dillon* (1991). Try to construct a report on each case, using the 'FIRO' format.

6.2.7 Problem-solving tips

This section offers tips on how to approach and answer problem questions involving trespass to land, highlighting the key steps and issues to look for when applying the principles covered in this chapter. Further tips are provided in section 6.8 below.

1. Before you begin, open your mind and think about all of the different levels of conduct that trespass to land could encompass – and get used to the idea that the tort is not restricted to cases where one person forcibly enters another person's land against their will. Remind yourself again of the legal definition of land, so that you will remember to look not only for physical entry to land, but also for any physical interferences to buildings, structures, growing plants and airspace.
2. Then look for any *harmful interference:* read the facts carefully and identify anyone whose land or possession of land has been interfered with. They will most likely become the plaintiff (provided they have standing to sue). Then look to see whose *conduct* led to that contact – they will become the defendant. When you consider who has standing to bring the action look for:
   - an owner in possession;
   - a tenant in possession under a lease (who may sue the landlord);
   - any person who has a recognised interest in the land that gives them a right to exclusive possession (eg the holder of a *profit a prendre*); or
   - any squatter or person exercising exclusive factual possession of land.
3. Consider whether any person has consent or lawful authority to be on land, bearing in mind that this is a question of fact and that such consent or authority can be:
   - expressly given by the defendant;
   - implicitly given by the defendant;
   - implied by law (ie the common law); or
   - expressly given in clear and unmistakable terms by statute.

   Then consider the scope of that consent or authority, and whether it has been revoked or exceeded in any way.
4. Be alert for any opportunity to argue that a continuing trespass has occurred and consider the possibility of a trespass *ab initio* or a continuing trespass. Check to see whether the defendant may have:
   - entered without bona fide motives or lawful authority;
   - remained on land after a request to leave;
   - left any items on land after they have left;
   - exceeded the scope of their licence or lawful authority to be on land; or
   - committed any act of wrongdoing while on land.
5. Consider any remedies. Check to see whether any possible self-help remedies may have given rise to a counter-suit by the defendant. For example, if the plaintiff has exceeded what is reasonable in the circumstances when ejecting a trespasser, then they may be subject to a battery claim.

6.3 Introduction to the personal property torts

The remainder of this chapter focuses on three torts that protect people's rights and interests in personal property: trespass to goods (section 6.4), conversion (section 6.5) and detinue (section 6.6). Before we look at each of these torts in detail, it is important to understand what is covered by the term 'personal property' (and thus protected by these torts) and have a sense of the differences between the three torts.

6.3.1 Personal property

'Personal property' generally refers to tangible (ie physically touchable), moveable items, such as vehicles, clothing and furnishings. These items are often referred to as 'goods' or 'chattels'. Importantly, this category excludes land and items permanently attached to it (such as plants), which are classified as 'real property' (see the definition of land in section 6.2.1 above). However, if an item is 'severed' from land (eg a plant is dug up), it will become personal property.

Purely intangible assets, such as money in a bank account, intellectual property rights (eg internet domain names and internet protocol (IP) addresses) and digital assets (eg computer files and e-tickets) are not currently considered to be personal property for the purposes of tort law. This means that while you can use the personal property torts to sue a person who takes your physical concert tickets without permission, you can't use them to sue someone who takes your electronic tickets. Given advances in technology, and the increasing use of digital assets, it has been suggested that the law in this regard should be reformed. This issue is discussed further in section 6.7.1 below.

The question of whether human tissue or biological samples can be deemed personal property has emerged as a contentious issue. In *Doodeward v Spence* (1908) the High Court determined that a human corpse is not property, and so cannot be subject to personal property tort actions. However, the Court also held that a body part that has undergone the application of 'work or skill' – a process that adds a unique characteristic to the item – may be treated as property. Subsequently, it has been held that body parts dissected or preserved for scientific purposes may qualify as personal property (*R v Kelly* (1999)), as may stored sperm (*Robin v Public Trustee (ACT)* (2015); *Re Creswell* (2019)). However, the precise boundaries of this rule remain unsettled. For instance, it is not clear whether genetic samples qualify as personal property. This issue is further addressed in section 6.7.2 below.

6.3.2 Trespass to goods, conversion and detinue

There are three separate intentional tort actions that deal specifically with personal property:

- **Trespass to goods** applies where the defendant directly causes an unauthorised interference with goods in the plaintiff's possession.

- **Conversion** applies where the defendant seriously interferes with the plaintiff's possession of goods, in a manner repugnant to the plaintiff's right to possess those goods.
- **Detinue** applies where the defendant wrongfully retains possession of the plaintiff's goods despite a rightful demand for their return.

As noted in section 6.1.1 above, these torts are primarily concerned to protect the plaintiff's *possession* of personal property rather than their *ownership* of that property. This means that in order to bring one of these actions, a plaintiff will generally only need to demonstrate actual or constructive possession of the property (or, in some cases, a right to immediate possession of the property).

It can be seen from these brief descriptions of the personal property torts that while they are somewhat similar, their focus differs: trespass to goods is concerned with the *physical state of goods* that are in the plaintiff's possession; conversion is concerned with the *plaintiff's right to possess or control goods*; and detinue is concerned with the defendant's *failure to respond to the plaintiff's demand to return the goods*. This difference in focus is reflected in issues such as who has standing to sue, the elements of the torts, and the remedies that are available.

Despite these differences, however, there is a considerable degree of overlap between the torts, and in many cases it will be possible to bring more than one action. Consider these examples:

- Many cases of conversion will also involve a trespass to goods – because a person who has seriously interfered with the plaintiff's possession of goods, in a manner repugnant to the plaintiff's right to possess those goods, is also likely to have directly caused an unauthorised interference with goods in the plaintiff's possession.
- Most cases of detinue will also involve conversion – because one of the methods of seriously interfering with the plaintiff's possession of goods, in a manner repugnant to the plaintiff's right to possess those goods, is to refuse to return them.

However, there will be some cases where the torts do not overlap, and it will be important to carefully select the appropriate action. Consider these examples:

- If the defendant simply moves goods around without the plaintiff's consent, they will have committed trespass to goods but not conversion or detinue.
- If the defendant cannot return goods to the plaintiff because they have accidentally lost them, this will constitute detinue but not trespass to goods or conversion.

Therefore, when there appears to have been an interference with a person's personal property it is essential that you work through the elements for each of the three torts, to determine which one (or more) of them is relevant in the circumstances. You can compare and contrast these torts as they are presented in Figures 6.1–6.3, which are at the end of the chapter.

A further important distinction between conversion and detinue lies in the assessment of the value of the goods for the purpose of awarding damages. In conversion, damages are typically assessed as at the date of the wrongful act, which can disadvantage a plaintiff if the goods subsequently appreciate in value. By contrast, in detinue, damages are usually assessed as at the date of judgment, reflecting the ongoing nature of the defendant's wrongful retention. This means that if the goods have appreciated significantly over time, a plaintiff may prefer to sue in detinue rather than conversion. Conversely, if the goods have depreciated in value, conversion is likely to be preferable.

The leading Australian case on both trespass to goods and conversion of goods is *Penfolds Wines Pty Ltd v Elliott* (1946), which is definitely a 'case to remember' because it is used as authority for most of the legal rules that govern these two torts. This is a notoriously difficult case because it is almost impossible to extract a ratio.[1] There were three issues before the High Court and different combinations of judges decided each issue differently. The reason why this case is so often cited is because of the lengthy exposition of the law given by Dixon J – but you should be careful when reading the case because, while all the judges agreed there was no trespass to goods, Dixon J was in the *minority* on the issue of conversion, and in the *majority* on the issue of awarding an injunction. This case is so significant that you need to become familiar with it before you go any further. It also gives you some indication of the complexity of the issues that these cases can raise.

A case to remember

Penfolds Wines Pty Ltd v Elliott (1946) 74 CLR 204

Topics

Trespass to goods; conversion; bailment; standing to sue; injunctions.

Facts

The plaintiff, Penfolds Wines (P), sold its wine in specially marked bottles, which made it clear that it was selling its customers only the wine and not the bottle – the bottles were supposed to be returned to P after the wine had been consumed. Mr Elliott, the defendant (D), ran a hotel where he sold bulk wine to his customers if they brought in containers for him to fill. His brother, who had bought and drunk some of P's wine, took the empty bottles to the hotel and left them with D so that he could fill them with the bulk wine. This method of reusing Ps bottles was widespread, and P didn't like it. In P's view it had bailed the bottles to its customers on condition that they did not use them for any purpose other than using them to store the wine that they had purchased, and this was a breach of the bailment agreement. In an attempt to discourage the practice, P brought a test case (in relation to three bottles) against D asking for damages and an injunction restraining him (among other things) from placing any other liquor in any of P's bottles. P was not awarded an injunction, and so it took its case to the High Court.

1 See Fleming, *The Law of Torts* (2011) at 73, and Balkin and Davis, *Law of Torts* (2013) at 77.

Issues

- Did D, by filling the bottles with wine, commit trespass to goods against P by interfering with their possession of those goods?
- Did D, by filling the bottles with wine, act in a manner that was in effect a denial of P's title to the bottles, and so commit the tort of conversion?
- If D had committed either (or both) of these torts, was it appropriate in the circumstances to award P an equitable injunction as a remedy?

Decision

1. All the judges agreed that there was no trespass to goods. This was because at no point did D interfere with P's possession of the bottles. This was due to the fact that P had consented to D's brother having the bottles (having bailed them to him), and his brother had subsequently consented to D having the bottles. So even though P did not authorise the use of its bottles for the purpose of buying and selling any other wine, D was in possession of them with his brother's consent – and thus was not directly interfering with any property in P's possession.
2. The High Court split 3:2 on the issue of conversion. All the judges were in broad agreement that 'the essence of conversion is a dealing with a chattel in a manner repugnant to the immediate right of possession of the person who has the property or special property in the chattel' (Dixon J at 229). They also all agreed that a person can sue for conversion if they have a right to immediate possession of the goods, which was the case here. However, they disagreed on whether D's conduct was a sufficiently serious interference with P's interests to amount to conversion. The majority (Latham CJ, McTiernan and Williams JJ) held, in separate judgments, that D's conduct in filling the bottles with his own wine for the purposes of his own trade, accompanied by the belief that he was entitled to do so, was an exercise of dominion over the bottles that amounted to a sufficiently serious denial of P's title to the goods. He had, therefore, converted the goods to his own use. The minority (Dixon J, with whom Starke J agreed) held that there was no act (and no intent) inconsistent with P's right to possession, and expressed the view that as a matter of policy there was no reason why putting goods to a 'temporary and harmless use' should be a civil wrong.
3. There was also a (different) 3:2 split on whether it was appropriate to award an injunction in these circumstances, with the majority holding that it was not. Dixon J did not support an injunction because he had decided that D had not committed any wrong at all by using the bottles; obviously, if there was no trespass and no conversion there were no grounds for awarding any remedy. Starke J held that, even assuming that there had been a conversion of the bottles, there was no evidence of any systematic or substantial practice of dealing with P's bottles that would justify an injunction. McTiernan J did not support an injunction because the evidence showed that, at most, there was a conversion of only three bottles, and without any evidence of a threatened further material infringement by D, this was not enough to justify an injunction.

So in the end, Penfolds failed in its aim. The company lost its appeal, even though it did establish a case of conversion and was entitled to collect common law damages. It should not surprise you to learn that Penfolds now charges for its bottles.

6.4 Trespass to goods

6.4.1 The nature of trespass to goods

Trespass to goods is an unjustified act by one person that intentionally, recklessly or negligently causes direct physical interference with another person's exclusive possession of goods. The elements of trespass to goods are as follows:

1. The plaintiff was in exclusive possession of goods (or, in limited circumstances, was entitled to immediate possession: see section 6.4.2 below).
2. The defendant committed a positive act that directly caused physical interference with the plaintiff's possession of the goods.
3. The defendant intended to cause that interference, or was reckless or negligent about causing it.

The onus of proof lies on the plaintiff to prove the first two elements. It is then for the defendant to prove that they were 'utterly without fault', or that they had a valid defence (see Chapter 7).

The purpose of this tort is to protect a possessor's right to control access to goods and to decide whether any other person may move the goods or otherwise physically interfere with them. Trespass to goods can range from minor interferences with possession to very serious infringements.

Examples

The following acts can constitute trespass to goods if done without authorisation or consent:

- simply moving another person's goods from one place to another (eg moving their bag from one room to another);[2]
- using another person's goods (eg borrowing their backpack, reading their torts textbook, riding their horse or driving their car);
- damaging another person's goods (eg scratching the paintwork of their car);
- destroying another person's goods (eg eating their apple, blowing up their car, killing their pet rabbit).

One issue that has yet to be determined is whether a 'mere touch' can amount to trespass to goods.[3] Allowing recovery for certain kinds of touching (eg of an item in a museum) would be consistent with the rules used in other trespass actions like battery and trespass to land, where mere physical contact with the body or land is sufficient to make out a case. However, there is no clear authority on the issue. While there are some cases that indicate that mere touching will be sufficient (eg *Cressy v Johnson* (2009); *Slaveski v Victoria* (2010)), in *Sheridan v Australian Pacific Airports (Melbourne) Pty Ltd* (2021) Gorton J suggested at [80] that simply touching a car may not be enough.

2 This is known as 'mere asportation'.
3 See, eg, Davies et al, *Focus Torts* (2024) at 919–20.

However, this could be accounted for by making an analogy with the 'everyday contact' rule in battery, which allows an exception for innocent contact that is considered to be an inevitable and acceptable aspect of ordinary everyday life.

6.4.2 Guiding principles

The guiding principles of trespass to goods emphasise respect for the physical integrity of personal property and the autonomy of those who possess it. This tort protects the plaintiff's right to exclusive possession, meaning they have the authority to prevent others from interfering with the goods. As Dixon J stated in *Penfolds Wines Pty Ltd v Elliott* (1946) at 227, 'the gist of the action of trespass must be the wrong to the right of possession'.

Unlike property law, which focuses on ownership, this tort protects anyone who has exclusive possession or a right to immediate possession of goods, regardless of ownership. This means that individuals who possess, but do not own, goods may have standing to sue. This includes:

- finders of lost goods (*Parker v British Airways Board* (1982));
- thieves or possessors of stolen goods (*Costello v Chief Constable of Derbyshire Constabulary* (2001));
- trustees of goods in the possession of a beneficiary (*Barker v Furlong* (1891));
- executors of deceased estates (*Tharpe v Stallwood* (1843)); and
- bailees in possession of goods owned by another (*Penfolds Wines Pty Ltd v Elliott* (1946)).

In *Penfolds Wines Pty Ltd v Elliott* (1946) at 226–8, Dixon J noted that in some circumstances owners who have a legal entitlement to immediate possession, but who are not currently in possession, may also have standing to bring an action. This includes bailors who have given possession of goods to a bailee under a bailment at will, who may bring an action:

- against a third party, if that third party has violated the bailee's possession of the goods; or
- against the bailee in certain circumstances (eg if the bailee destroys the goods).

6.4.3 Overview of the tort of trespass to goods

6.4.3.1 Conduct

- There must be a positive act by the defendant. An omission is not sufficient.

6.4.3.2 Effect

- The defendant's conduct must directly cause a physical interference or infringement of the plaintiff's exclusive possession of goods. The interference must be with tangible, moveable items which are considered to be 'goods'. It cannot have been an interference with purely intangible assets, such as money in a bank account, intellectual property rights or digital assets (*Hoath v Connect Internet Services Pty Ltd* (2006)).

- The interference must be direct. Indirect actions, such as locking goods in a room, are not sufficient (*Hartley v Moxham* (1842)).
- The conduct need not cause damage to the plaintiff's goods. Like all trespass torts, trespass to goods is actionable per se (*Penfolds Wines Pty Ltd v Elliott* (1946); *Hutchins v Maughan* (1947); *William Leitch & Co v Leydon* (1931); *Kirk v Gregory* (1876)).

6.4.3.3 Fault

- The defendant must have intended to cause the physical interference or infringement of the plaintiff's possession of goods, or been reckless or negligent (in the sense of being careless) about causing it.
- The defendant's act must have been voluntary (directed by the will or conscious mind) (*Morriss v Marsden* (1952); *Beals v Hayward* (1960)).
- The defendant does not need to have intended to invade the plaintiff's possession, or even to have known that the goods belonged to someone else. It is sufficient that they intended to cause the physical interference with the goods (*Penfolds Wines Pty Ltd v Elliott* (1946)).
- The defendant will not be liable if they can show that they were 'utterly without fault' (*National Coal Board v Evans* (1951)).

6.4.3.4 Circumstances

- The plaintiff must usually have been in actual or constructive possession of the goods at the time of the trespass. In some circumstances it may be enough if the plaintiff was entitled to immediately exercise physical control and possession of the goods (*Penfolds Wines Pty Ltd v Elliott* (1946); *Tallot v City of Stirling* (2017)).
- The plaintiff does not need to be the true owner of the goods. A thief or finder of goods in possession has a possessory title that is good against all the world except the true owner (*Armory v Delamirie* (1722); *Parker v British Airways Board* (1982); *Costello v Chief Constable of Derbyshire Constabulary* (2001)).
- There must be no lawful justification for the conduct. There will be no trespass to goods if the plaintiff's actions were done with the consent of the person in possession (*Penfolds Wines Pty Ltd v Elliott* (1946)).
- Conduct may be justified by common law principles or statutory provisions authorising physical contact. These include powers to seize or confiscate goods.

6.4.4 Defences

The defences to the personal property torts are addressed in Chapter 7. Trespass to goods is a tort of strict liability, and mistake will not be a defence. The question of lawful authority is an important matter, particularly as it relates to police powers and the entitlement to impound and retain goods reasonably believed to be stolen: *Costello v Chief Constable of Derbyshire Constabulary* (2001). The common law 'self-help' remedies of 'distress' and 'recaption of chattels', which allow a person to seize goods in possession of another in certain limited circumstances, may also be raised as defences (see section 6.4.5).

6.4.5 Remedies

The full range of nominal, compensatory (including aggravated) and exemplary damages may be awarded: see section 2.3.3.2 of Chapter 2. Once the action is made out, the defendant will be liable to compensate the plaintiff for all of the direct consequences of the tort. Equitable remedies such as injunctions may also be available. This will be particularly relevant in situations where the trespass is ongoing or repeated.

Plaintiffs may also be entitled to resort to the 'self-help' remedy of 'recaption of chattels', which allows a person who has been deprived of possession to recover the goods immediately, without having to wait upon taking legal action. Like all self-help remedies, recaption of chattels is subject to a reasonableness test: see *Toyota Finance Australia Ltd v Dennis* (2002). The plaintiff may also be able to rely on the remedy of 'distress', which allows people, in limited circumstances, to seize goods belonging to a debtor to compel payment of the debt.[4] This remedy has, however, been abolished in several jurisdictions due to concerns about its potential abuse. The self-help remedies are discussed further in Chapter 7.

LEGISLATION ALERT!

Consult your study materials to see whether there is any legislation in your jurisdiction that abolishes the remedy of distress.

6.4.6 Some helpful cases for your summary

- In *Hutchins v Maughan* (1947) D laid poisonous baits on unfenced land. P's dogs ate the poisoned baits and died. This was held not to be trespass to P's goods (his dogs) as the interference with his possession of those goods was not sufficiently direct. Herring CJ pointed out at 133 that each case must be 'determined on its own facts' and suggested at 134 that it would have been direct enough for a trespass action if D had thrown the baits to the dogs.
- In *National Coal Board v Evans* (1951) D was contracted to excavate a trench by an owner of land. In doing so, D inadvertently damaged P's underground electrical cable. It was held that D was 'utterly without fault' because they did not know about the cable, nor should they have known about it. In the absence of either intention or negligence, D could not be liable for trespass to goods.
- *Southport Corporation v Esso Petroleum Co Ltd* (1954), an English case where oil discharged from a ship was carried by the tide to P's land, contains two useful - and contrasting - interpretations of the directness rule.
- In *Wilson v Lombank Ltd* (1963) P purchased a car from a person who did not own it (and so did not become the legal owner). When P left the car at a garage for repairs it was spotted by D, who wrongly thought it belonged to them and drove it away. When D realised it was not their car, they returned it to the true owner. P sued D for trespass to goods and won. Although the car was not physically with them at the time it

4 See Barker et al, *The Law of Torts in Australia* (2012) at 133–7.

was taken, it was still considered to be in their (constructive) possession when it was at the garage. The fact that they did not own the car did not matter; nor did it matter that the car had been returned to the true owners. It was sufficient that P had a better right to possess the car than D (who had no rights to it).

- *Costello v Chief Constable of Derbyshire Constabulary* (2001) reaffirmed the rule that possession – whether gained lawfully or not – gives a title that is good against all the world except the true owner. P was found in possession of a car believed to have been stolen. It contained a 'car ringing' kit that had been used to grind off the original engine identification number. The police established that P knew the car had been stolen, but were unable to establish the identity of the true owner. They refused to return the car to P. The Court held that although P's title to the car was frail, P was entitled to have it protected. In the contest between P's possessory title and any public policy considerations relating to illegality and possession of stolen goods, P's title took precedence. P's title was therefore stronger than that of the police, and so P was entitled to the car.
- In *Slaveski v Victoria* (2010) a police officer picked up documents and handed them to other officers. It was held that as those other officers had no authority to handle the documents (such as a search warrant), this 'mere asportation' constituted trespass to goods.

Active reading

Link each of the cases listed in section 6.4.6 above to one of the elements of the tort.

6.4.7 Problem-solving tips

Problem-solving tips for all of the personal property torts can be found in section 6.8 below.

6.5 Conversion

6.5.1 The nature of conversion

Conversion of goods is an unjustified and deliberate act of dealing with goods, which causes such a serious interference with those goods that it deprives the true owner or possessor of the goods of their right to use them, control them or exercise dominion over them.

In *Bunnings Group Ltd v CHEP Australia Ltd* (2011), Allsop J acknowledged at 124 that the 'framing of a precise definition of the tort of conversion has been described as "well nigh impossible"', but went on to note:

> The essential elements ... involve an intentional act or dealing with goods inconsistent with or repugnant to the rights of the owner, including possession and any right to possession. Such an act or dealing will amount to such an infringement of the possessory or proprietary rights of the owner if it is an intended act of dominion or assertion of rights over the goods.

Given the difficulties involved in framing the elements of this tort, it is not possible to set them out with any certainty. However, in general terms it can be said that the tort requires the following:

1. The plaintiff was in possession of goods or had a right to immediate possession of them.
2. The defendant deliberately acted in a way that was so inconsistent with (or 'repugnant' to) the plaintiff's (right to) possession of the goods that it effectively excluded the plaintiff from the use and possession of those goods.
3. The defendant intended to cause the plaintiff to lose dominion over the goods, or was reckless about causing their loss of dominion.

The onus of proof lies on the plaintiff to prove all of the elements of the tort. If they can do so, the onus shifts to the defendant to raise a valid defence.

Many acts which constitute trespass to goods will also amount to conversion. However, this will not always be the case. This is because liability for trespass to goods can be imposed for relatively minor interferences with goods (eg minor damage or 'mere asportation'), whereas conversion is reserved for more serious interferences where the defendant has acted as if they have the right of ownership of the goods. Because one way of converting goods is to refuse to deliver them up after a demand has been made by the person with a right to possess them, this tort also strongly overlaps with the tort of detinue (see section 6.6 below).

Conversion of goods can be committed in a wide variety of ways.

Examples

- Intentionally *destroying* goods – for example, throwing P's essay into the sea, eating their apple, blowing up their car, killing their pet rabbit or burning their money. Note that 'mere damage' may not be enough for a case of conversion (although it will be trespass to goods). To be conversion, the damage must either result in the destruction of the goods, or it must be sufficiently serious to be considered a denial of P's title.
- *Changing the nature* of goods – for example, diluting P's whisky with water or fermenting their apple juice into cider. Note that this requires the goods to have been essentially changed. Simply doing something, such as bottling P's wine to preserve it, is not sufficient (as it does not change the nature of the wine): see *Philpott v Kelley* (1835).
- Intentionally *taking possession* of another person's goods or making it impossible for them to exercise their right to possession – for example, taking away a pen that happens to belong to P, pawning P's jewellery, stealing their torts textbook or hiding their backpack so that they cannot find it.
- *Making use* of another person's goods for your own purposes without permission – for example, riding P's horse to another town, taking their car for a drive, using P's milk crates to store D's goods or persistently filling P's bin with D's rubbish. Note that the use must occur in such a way that it substantially interferes with P's right to immediate possession. It will not be sufficient if it is a minor interference of short duration.

- Unreasonably *refusing to deliver* goods after a lawful and reasonable demand by P – for example, refusing to return P's car after it has been put in for a service or refusing to return P's coat after borrowing it. Note: this overlaps with the tort of detinue (see section 6.6 below).
- Wrongfully *selling and delivering* another person's goods to a third party – for example, auctioning P's car without their consent or selling a computer that had been borrowed from P. Note that in these cases, both the vendor and the purchaser will have committed conversion. This will be the case even if the purchaser had no idea that the goods belonged to P and had bought them in good faith.
- *Misdelivering goods* – for example, delivering online shopping to the wrong house. Note that there must be a positive act of misdelivery – merely allowing a third person to take goods away is not conversion: see *Ashby v Tolhurst* (1937).

It is not the case, however, that all acts which have the effect of dispossessing the plaintiff of their goods amount to conversion.

Examples

- Simply stating that the plaintiff does not have title to their goods is not sufficient. To constitute conversion the statement must be accompanied by a positive act of dealing with the goods.
- Carelessly losing someone else's goods is not conversion. The relevant conduct must be intentional or reckless. Note that where a subsequent demand for the lost goods is made (and necessarily refused, as the goods have been lost) this may constitute detinue.
- Merely moving goods without intending to deprive the owner of the goods is not conversion: *Fouldes v Willoughby* (1841).
- Refusing to repay a debt is not conversion (because a debt is intangible).

Conversion is a complex tort with uncertain boundaries and there is no precisely defined set of tests that specify how long the interference must last for or how extensive the interference must be. (Recall that in the case of *Penfolds Wines Pty Ltd v Elliott* (1946), the judges were divided 3:2 over whether it was conversion to put someone else's bottles to a harmless and temporary use by filling them with wine.)[5] It is important, therefore, to argue the facts of your case and use your knowledge of the authorities to strengthen your arguments. The use of analogy with decided cases is a particularly useful technique when discussing the tort of conversion.

6.5.2 Guiding principles

The guiding principle behind the tort of conversion is the protection of others' property rights. As Dixon J noted in *Penfolds Wines Pty Ltd v Elliott* (1946) at 224 and 229, the

5 Note that textbooks differ in their interpretation of the outcome of this case. For example, Davies et al (*Focus Torts* (2024) at 926) argue that 'the defendant was not guilty of conversion'. By contrast, Balkin and Davis (*Law of Torts* (2013) at 77) and Fleming (*The Law of Torts* (2011) at 73) maintain that there was conversion, though no injunction was granted.

personal property torts collectively guard against infringements on both possession and ownership. Trespass to goods involves an interference with possession, whereas conversion is defined as an action that is 'repugnant to the immediate right of possession of the person who has the property or special property in the chattel'. Thus, the core of conversion lies in respecting the rights of the 'true owner', with its essential basis being the intent to deprive the owner of their right to possess the goods or to significantly impair that right.

While the primary purpose of the tort of conversion is to protect the rights of the true owner, legally owning the property is not a requirement to bring an action for conversion. It is sufficient for the plaintiff to be in actual possession of the goods at the time of the interference or to have the right to immediate possession. Consequently, as we saw was the case in relation to trespass to goods (see section 6.4.2 above), individuals with lesser possessory interests – such as finders of goods, licensees, or even those in possession of stolen goods – can also sue. However, a person who only has a right to *future* possession (rather than *immediate* possession) does not have standing to sue.

When the relevant goods have been bailed, standing to sue will depend on the nature of the bailment and the conduct of the bailee.

Case examples

- In the case of a *bailment at will*, both the bailee and the bailor have a right to bring an action in conversion against a third party: *Kahler v Midland Bank Ltd* (1950); *Glass v Hollander* (1935). The bailee can sue because they have actual possession and the bailor can sue because they have the legal right to immediate possession: *Perpetual Trustees & National Executors of Tasmania Ltd v Perkins* (1989).
- In the case of a *bailment for a term*, unless the bailee's conduct has brought the bailment to an end (see below), only the bailee (and not the bailor) can sue a third party during the term of the bailment: *Howe v Teefy* (1927). Provided that the bailment has not been terminated, the bailee can also sue the bailor if they convert the goods: *City Motors (1933) Pty Ltd v Southern Aerial Super Service Pty Ltd* (1961).
- If the *bailee's conduct has brought the bailment to an end* (eg by acting in a way that is wholly inconsistent with the terms of the bailment), the bailor will have a right to immediate possession of the goods, and will be able to bring an action for conversion against the bailee or a third party: *Penfolds Wines Pty Ltd v Elliott* (1946). This rule may be modified by the terms of the bailment or by statutory provisions. See also *Citicorp Australia Ltd v BS Stillwell Ford Pty Ltd* (1979) and *Flowfill Packaging Machines Pty Ltd v Fytore Pty Ltd* (1993).

6.5.3 Overview of the tort of conversion

6.5.3.1 Conduct

- The defendant must have engaged in deliberate conduct. They must have positively dealt with the goods. An omission is not sufficient (*Penfolds Wines Pty Ltd v Elliott* (1946); *Kuwait Airways Corporation v Iraqi Airways Co* (2002)).

6.5.3.2 Effect

- The defendant's conduct must have been so inconsistent with (or 'repugnant' to) the plaintiff's right to immediate possession of the goods that it effectively excluded the plaintiff from the use and possession of those goods. The right to possession must be to a tangible, moveable item which is capable of being possessed at law. It cannot be a purely intangible asset, such as money in a bank account, an intellectual property right or a digital asset (*Hoath v Connect Internet Services Pty Ltd* (2006)).
- The conduct (and its effects) must be so serious that the defendant should be treated as having taken ownership of the goods, and therefore 'may justly be required to pay its full value' (Fleming, *The Law of Torts* (2011) at 66–7).
- There is no requirement that the defendant's conduct *directly* exclude the plaintiff from the use and possession of those goods. This reflects the origin of conversion as a form of 'action on the case' (rather than a trespass tort) (*Penfolds Wines Pty Ltd v Elliott* (1946)).

6.5.3.3 Fault

- The defendant must have intended to cause the plaintiff to lose dominion over the goods, or have been reckless about causing their loss of dominion. Mere negligence or carelessness will not normally suffice (*Payne v Dwyer* (2013)).
- The defendant does not need to have acted in bad faith or to have known that the goods belonged to someone else. It is sufficient that they intended to act in a way that was sufficiently inconsistent with the plaintiff's right to immediate possession (*Hollins v Fowler* (1875); *Penfolds Wines Pty Ltd v Elliott* (1946); *Moorgate Mercantile Co Ltd v Finch & Read* (1962); *Payne v Dwyer* (2013)).

6.5.3.4 Circumstances

- At the time the goods were converted, the plaintiff must have been in possession of the goods or had the right to immediate possession. A right to future possession is not sufficient (*Penfolds Wines Pty Ltd v Elliott* (1946); *Perpetual Trustees & National Executors of Tasmania Ltd v Perkins* (1989); *Chairman, National Crime Authority v Flack* (1998)).
- A thief or finder of goods in possession has a possessory title that is good against all the world except the true owner (*Armory v Delamirie* (1722); *Parker v British Airways Board* (1982); *Costello v Chief Constable of Derbyshire Constabulary* (2001)).
- There must be no lawful justification for the conduct (*Penfolds Wines Pty Ltd v Elliott* (1946)).

6.5.4 Defences

The defences to the personal property torts are addressed in Chapter 7. Given that the aim of the tort of conversion is to protect property rights, it is a tort of strict liability and mistake (even an honest and reasonable, but mistaken, belief that the defendant owns the goods or is entitled to possess the goods) will not be a defence: see *Rendell v Associated*

Finance Pty Ltd (1957). Defendants also generally cannot raise the defence of '*jus tertii*', arguing that some third party has a better title to the goods than the plaintiff. The dispute is usually seen as a contest between the relative strength of the plaintiff's and defendant's titles - but some cases have suggested otherwise (see, eg, *Edwards v Amos* (1945); *Esanda Finance Corporation v Gibbons* (1999)) and there are exceptions to this rule.[6]

6.5.5 Remedies

Nominal, compensatory (including aggravated) and exemplary damages may be awarded: see section 2.3.3.2 of Chapter 2. Typically, damages are measured as the full market value of the goods at the date of the conversion.[7] However, exceptions exist to address the disadvantage this may cause to plaintiffs. For instance, in cases where the market value of the goods increases between the date of conversion and the trial, plaintiffs have sometimes been permitted to claim the increased value as special damages. This approach was applied in *Graham v Voigt* (1989), where the plaintiff recovered the higher value of nine valuable stamp albums that had appreciated between the date of the conversion and the date of the trial.

Plaintiffs may also recover damages for consequential losses, provided these losses are foreseeable and not too remote. For example, in *Graham v Voigt* (1989) the plaintiff was entitled to compensation not only for the loss of his stamp collection, which he had been building since 1940, but also for the distress caused by his inability to pass the collection on to his daughter – a loss that was deemed reasonably foreseeable.

The damages awarded will not include any increase in the value of the goods attributable to the defendant's repairs or additions. This is because the compensation principle dictates that plaintiffs are only compensated for their actual loss and do not receive a windfall.

6.5.6 Some helpful cases for your summary

- In *Armory v Delamirie* (1722) P found a ring and took it to D, a goldsmith, for valuation. D removed the stone and refused to return it. It was held at 664 that P, as a finder of the goods, had a right to possession superior to all the world except the true owner and, in the absence of the stone, P was awarded damages as if it was a jewel 'of the finest water'.
- In *Doodeward v Spence* (1908) the High Court held that P, who exhibited a preserved stillborn two-headed foetus in a jar in his travelling show, was entitled to maintain an action in conversion against D, a policeman who had seized the item. This was because a person who has by 'lawful exercise of work or skill so dealt with a part of a human body that it has acquired some attributes differentiating it from a mere corpse' gains 'a right to possession of it': Griffith CJ at 414.

6 See Barker et al, *The Law of Torts in Australia* (2012) at 124–5, 139–45 and Balkin and Davis, *Law of Torts* (2013) at 69–70, 85–92.

7 This differs from detinue, where damages are calculated according to the value of the goods at the time of trial. Consequently, plaintiffs are often advised to use conversion in a falling market and detinue in a rising market.

- In *Ashby v Tolhurst* (1937) D, who was a car park attendant, negligently allowed a third party to drive P's car away. This was not conversion as D had not intended to deal with the car in a manner that was inconsistent with P's right to immediate possession – he had simply been careless.
- In *Citicorp Australia Ltd v BS Stillwell Ford Pty Ltd* (1979) D purchased P's car from a car yard in good faith, not knowing of P's existence or their right to the car. This was nevertheless held to be conversion, as D had intentionally interfered with P's title (by buying the car and taking possession of it) in a way that was inconsistent with P's right to immediate possession.
- In *Parker v British Airways Board* (1982) P found a gold bracelet in the British Airways first-class lounge at Heathrow. He gave it in to the desk with his name and address and requested its return if it remained unclaimed. When British Airways sold the item and retained the money, P sued. The English Court of Appeal held that P, as a finder of the goods who had acted honestly, was entitled to maintain an action in conversion, even though the item had been found on premises occupied by BA. This was because BA, as an occupier of premises, had not demonstrated an intention to exercise control over the premises and the things within it sufficient to establish possession of the bracelet before P found it. Consequently, BA did not have better title to the bracelet than P. Lord Donaldson's decision contains a useful list of rules on the rights and obligations of finders of goods and the rights and obligations of occupiers at 1017–18, which in general provide as follows:
  - If the good is found *on the surface of the land* (eg on the floor of a building), the finder will have better title than the occupier, unless the occupier has manifested an intention to exercise exclusive control over the area where it was found.
  - If the good is found *attached to or under the land*, the occupier will have a better title than the finder.
- In *Perpetual Trustees & National Executors of Tasmania Ltd v Perkins* (1989) the Supreme Court of Tasmania ordered the return of two heirloom family portraits to the Ps, two sisters who had lent the portraits to their brother Bill. Bill had given the portraits to another brother, David, who had then left them to his son, Tim, in his will. After David's death, Tim and his mother, Beryl, had sold one portrait to the Art Gallery of South Australia while Beryl had kept the other. The Court found this to be conversion, as the Ps, having lent the portraits to Bill under a bailment at will, retained the right to immediate possession. Their title was superior to both Tim's and the Art Gallery's, entitling them to the return of both portraits.
- In *Chairman, National Crime Authority v Flack* (1998) police officers on a drug raid impounded a briefcase containing a substantial sum of money after they found it in flat occupied by P (who had no knowledge of the briefcase's presence or contents). It was established that other persons had regular access to the flat. The investigation did not lead to any charges. The Federal Court of Australia held, by a majority of 2:1, that P was entitled to the return of the case and the money on the grounds that P, as the occupier of the premises where the items were found, had a right to possession, which was good against all the world except the true owner of the goods. Heerey J at 26, following *Parker v British Airways Board* (1982), applied

the rule that 'the occupier of a private home will ordinarily manifest the necessary intention to control chattels therein', even if there are goods on the premises that have been hidden there by others without the occupier's knowledge.

- In *Bunnings Group Ltd v CHEP Australia Ltd* (2011) Bunnings had over 60 000 CHEP pallets, which they received from suppliers who had hired them from CHEP. Bunnings used the pallets to display, store, and transport goods. In 2006, CHEP demanded that Bunnings sign a hire agreement for the pallets, but Bunnings refused. CHEP then obtained court orders for their return. The Court found that simply possessing the pallets or using them to store the goods they arrived with did not amount to conversion. However, using the pallets to transport Bunnings' own goods or store other goods was inconsistent with CHEP's ownership rights and constituted conversion.
- In *Sell Your Gold Pty Ltd v Australian Diamond Trading Corporation Pty Ltd* (2018) P bailed five diamonds to a diamond dealer on consignment for sale. In breach of the terms of bailment, the dealer gave the diamonds to D as security for a loan. D later returned the diamonds to the dealer, but the dealer never returned them to P. P sued D for conversion (for temporarily possessing the diamonds) but lost. The Court held that mere unauthorised possession of goods is not sufficient – to constitute conversion, an innocent possessor (such as D) must do something more, such as dealing with the goods in some way (eg by selling and delivering them) or exercising ownership over them (eg by refusing to return them to the true owner upon request). That had not occurred here: D had simply possessed the diamonds for a short time.

Active reading

Link each of the cases listed in section 6.5.6 above to one of the elements of the tort.

6.5.7 Problem-solving tips

Problem-solving tips for all of the personal property torts can be found in section 6.8 below.

6.6 Detinue

6.6.1 The nature of detinue

Detinue is an unjustified and unreasonable refusal to yield possession of goods to a person who, having the legal right to immediate possession, has made a clear and proper demand for the goods. The elements of detinue are as follows:

1. The plaintiff had a right to immediate possession of goods that are or were in the defendant's possession.
2. The plaintiff made a proper demand of the defendant for the return of the goods.

3. The defendant wrongfully refused to return the goods to the plaintiff, depriving the plaintiff of their possession.
4. The defendant's refusal was intentional.

Once the plaintiff has proved that the goods were in the defendant's possession and that a proper demand has been made for their return, the onus shifts to the defendant to disprove fault or raise a defence. So, for example, if the defendant no longer has possession of the goods, they must prove that their inability to deliver them was not due to any carelessness on their part: *Houghland v RR Low (Luxury Coaches) Ltd* (1962).

Detinue developed very early in the history of the common law and its significance as a personal property tort lies in the unique remedy it offers: it allows the plaintiff to ask the court to order the defendant to *return the goods* (rather than to simply pay for them, as is the case for trespass to goods and conversion).

As noted above, detinue overlaps with conversion because one way to commit conversion is to refuse to deliver up goods up after a demand has been made by the person with a right to possess them. Detinue can also be committed by a refusal to return goods – or even by an inability to return goods – but you need to remember that not every failure to give goods immediately to their owner will amount to detinue.

Examples

- Refusing to give back borrowed goods after the owner has asked for their return is detinue.
- Failing to give back goods because they have been carelessly lost is also detinue (but will generally not be conversion): *Houghland v RR Low (Luxury Coaches) Ltd* (1962).
- Asking for extra time to check the situation may not amount to detinue. This will depend on whether that delay amounts to an unreasonable refusal to return the goods.
- Refusing to return goods after a vague or unclear demand for their return will not be detinue. The defendant must know what goods are being demanded and where or to whom they should be returned.

A key feature of the tort of detinue is that it is triggered by the plaintiff's demand for the return of goods, with the cause of action only arising once the demand is made. This allows a plaintiff who is out of time to sue under other causes of action, such as conversion or breach of contract, to create a new cause of action simply by making a demand for possession – even if the goods have already been destroyed or lost. Detinue is therefore particularly important because it not only enables plaintiffs to seek the return of specific goods, but also provides an alternative pathway to a remedy when other legal avenues are no longer available.

LEGISLATION ALERT!

Consult your study materials to see which legislation in your jurisdiction governs the limitations periods for the personal property torts.

6.6.2 Guiding principles

The guiding principles of the tort of detinue emphasise respect for a person's entitlement to possess goods and aim to prevent the unlawful detention of goods without lawful justification. This tort is concerned with protecting the right to reclaim possession, rather than ownership, as Dixon CJ clarified in *City Motors (1933) Pty Ltd v Southern Aerial Super Service Pty Ltd* (1961) at 485: 'the right asserted is to regain possession'.

The rules on standing to sue in detinue are similar to those in conversion (see section 6.5.2 above) and are similarly influenced by the rules surrounding bailment. The plaintiff must have a right to immediate possession, whether through ownership, bailment, or another legal basis. A person with a future right to possession does not have standing. The essence of the contest was summarised by Isaacs and Rich JJ in *Russell v Wilson* (1923) at 547:

> [A] wrongdoer is, according to Lord Campbell, 'one who takes them' (the goods) 'from him' (the possessor), 'having no title in himself'. The expression 'having no title in himself' must, we think, mean no legal right superior to the title of possessor. If the person taking the goods has a superior right, then to the extent of that superior right, and to that extent only, must the possessory title yield. The absolute owner, his rights being unqualified by any circumstance, would of course be justified in taking and keeping or demanding the goods, because his title is superior.

More recently, McDougall J explained in *CHEP Australia Ltd v Bunnings Group Ltd* (2010) at 183 that detinue involves 'the wrongful refusal to deliver up goods to a person having the immediate right to the possession of those goods'. This wrongful refusal distinguishes detinue from other personal property torts, such as conversion or trespass to goods.

6.6.3 Overview of the tort of detinue

6.6.3.1 Conduct

- The defendant must have refused to comply with a demand made by the plaintiff to yield possession of goods. The refusal may be constituted by a statement or by conduct, so either a positive act of refusal or a failure to deliver will suffice (*John F Goulding v Victorian Railways Commissioners* (1932); *Crowther v AGC Ltd* (1985); *CHEP Australia Ltd v Bunnings Group Ltd* (2010)).

6.6.3.2 Effect

- The defendant's conduct must have deprived the plaintiff of the possession of the goods (*John F Goulding v Victorian Railways Commissioners* (1932)).

6.6.3.3 Fault

- The defendant must have intended the refusal. There is no requirement that the defendant must have intended to deprive the plaintiff of the goods, only that the plaintiff intended the refusal (*John F Goulding Pty Ltd v Victorian Railways Commissioners* (1932)).

6.6.3.4 Circumstances

- The plaintiff must be lawfully entitled to demand the goods – by virtue of having a right to immediate possession of the goods, which is superior to that of the defendant (*Russell v Wilson* (1923); *The Premier Group Pty Ltd v Followmont Transport Pty Ltd* (2000)).
- The defendant's refusal to return the goods must have been wrongful. A refusal will be wrongful if it was unreasonable in the circumstances – such as where the defendant improperly gave away the goods, carelessly lost them or intentionally destroyed them (*John F Goulding Pty Ltd v Victorian Railways Commissioners* (1932); *Howard E Perry & Co Ltd v British Railways Board* (1980)).
- A refusal to return goods will not be unreasonable if:
  - the defendant never had possession of the goods (*Jones v Dowle* (1841));
  - the plaintiff's demand was unclear or equivocal, or if the plaintiff is otherwise able to obtain the goods for themselves (*Lloyd v Osborne* (1899); *Flowfill Packaging Machines Pty Ltd v Fytore Pty Ltd* (1993));
  - the defendant merely seeks some extra time to clarify matters such as title. However, it will be unreasonable if there is no doubt about the plaintiff's title to the goods (*Clayton v Le Roy* (1911); *Flowfill Packaging Machines Pty Ltd v Fytore Pty Ltd* (1993)).
- There must be no lawful justification for the conduct.

6.6.4 Defences

The defences to the personal property torts are explained in Chapter 7. Many of the issues raised in relation to trespass to goods (see section 6.4.4 above) and conversion (see section 6.5.4 above) also apply to detinue.

6.6.5 Remedies

As noted above, detinue is the appropriate tort to use when the plaintiff wishes to regain possession of specific goods, but other remedies are also available.

Examples

- If the goods are of specific personal value to the plaintiff, they may claim the return of the goods plus damages for their detention. This is known as 'specific restitution'.
- If the goods are of no specific personal value (or if they have been destroyed or lost), the plaintiff may claim the full value of the goods plus damages for their detention.
- In some cases, the plaintiff may claim *either* the return of the goods *or* recovery of their value, and leave it to the defendant to decide which they would prefer.

The full range of nominal, compensatory (including aggravated) and exemplary damages may be awarded: see section 2.3.3.2 in Chapter 2. In *Egan v State Transport Authority* (1982) at 531–3, White J in the Supreme Court of South Australia justified an award of exemplary damages in detinue because of the 'ignominy surrounding the peremptory and overbearing' exercise of power (on an erroneous basis) by the defendant who seized and detained the plaintiff's bridge construction equipment and plant, and the traumatic effects of that exercise of power on the plaintiff's reputation, business and capacity to work.

6.6.6 Some helpful cases for your summary

- In *Jones v Dowle* (1841) Baron Parke at 9 made the rule that 'detinue does not lie against him who never had possession of the chattel, but it does against him who once had, but improperly parted with possession of it'.
- In *Lloyd v Osborne* (1899) a demand for delivery of some sheep was so vague in its terms that it was held that it was not unreasonable for the defendant to fail to give possession of the sheep to the plaintiff. The demand did not specify either *where* the sheep were to be delivered or *to whom* they were to be delivered.
- In *Clayton v Le Roy* (1911) Fletcher Moulton LJ pointed out at 1051 that the rule is that 'a man does not act unlawfully in refusing to deliver up property immediately upon demand made. He is entitled to take adequate time to inquire into the rights of the claimant'.
- In *John F Goulding Pty Ltd v Victorian Railways Commissioners* (1932), a case of misdelivery of goods (which gave rise to claims in both detinue and conversion), the High Court held that time begins to run in a case of conversion at the point when the misdelivery occurs, but that time begins to run in a case of detinue at the point when the demand is made (which can be much later than the time of the original misdelivery).
- In *Houghland v RR Low (Luxury Coaches) Ltd* (1962) P had deposited her luggage with D for a coach journey, but on arrival at the final destination the suitcase could not be found. The Court held that the 'act of refusal' for the purposes of detinue can be a mere inability to return the goods. In these circumstances, the burden was on D to show that there was no negligence on their part in the care which they took of the goods. (Note that this would not necessarily be enough to establish conversion.)
- In *Howard E Perry & Co Ltd v British Railways Board* (1980) D acknowledged P's title to a consignment of steel, but refused to deliver it during a steelworkers' strike, because they were afraid that any delivery of the steel would result in industrial action by their own railway workers. This refusal, which was based only on their fear of the consequences to their own business, was not reasonable in the circumstances. The Court ordered D to deliver the steel to P.
- In *Egan v State Transport Authority* (1982) White J explained at 520 that regardless of whether D intended to deprive P permanently of the goods, the 'very failure to restore the possession' of the goods to P rendered D liable.
- In *Crowther v AGC Ltd* (1985) Bollen J doubted at 69 and 102 that it 'was an immutable rule' that there must always be a demand followed by a refusal. Provided P can prove that D has demonstrated an intent not to deliver up the goods 'come what may', then the 'absence of demand will not defeat the plaintiff's claim'.
- In *Flowfill Packaging Machines Pty Ltd v Fytore Pty Ltd* (1993) Young J reviewed a wide range of authorities and held that the 'reasonable time to investigate' rule

applies only where D has a bona fide doubt as to P's title, and does not apply in any case where there is no doubt about P's title to the goods. In this case, P's claim for detinue failed because (1) the demand for the items was too uncertain in its terms and (2) in the circumstances, P would have been able to repossess the goods without interference.

- *The Premier Group Pty Ltd v Followmont Transport Pty Ltd* (2000) contains a helpful discussion of the problems posed by a 'chain of bailments'.

Active reading

Link each of the cases listed in section 6.6.6 above to one of the elements of the tort.

6.6.7 Problem-solving tips

Problem-solving tips for all of the personal property torts can be found in section 6.8 below.

6.7 Possible developments in the law

The torts of trespass to goods, conversion and detinue have traditionally focused on the protection of tangible personal property. However, advances in technology, evolving societal values and increasing recognition of new forms of property raise significant questions about the scope and future direction of these torts. This section explores potential developments in the law, including issues surrounding digital data and intangible assets, body parts and biological materials, and clarifying the bounds of the torts.

6.7.1 Digital data and intangible assets

A significant question for the future is whether the personal property torts should apply to unauthorised access to computer systems, or interferences with digital data and intangible assets (such as internet domain names, IP addresses and cryptocurrencies), when the conduct does not involve any physical interaction with computer hardware (eg activities conducted entirely over the internet). This would include actions like hacking, data harvesting, and deploying spyware or ransomware.[8]

At present, in Australia there are two key problems with using the personal property torts in relation to such conduct:

- Trespass to goods must be direct but this conduct will often be indirect (eg occurring from a remote location and/or time).
- The personal property torts only apply to tangible items and on the surface these forms of conduct appear to relate to intangible assets.

8 See Spinello, *CyberEthics* (2003) at 196–203 for a discussion of internet trespass; and Fitzgerald et al, *Internet and e-Commerce Law: Technology, Law and Policy* (2007) for a discussion of the wider issues.

Courts in the United States have considered whether such conduct can constitute trespass to goods.[9] However, there are two differences between Australian and American law that make it difficult to borrow directly from the American cases. First, the directness requirement has been dropped from American trespass law, meaning that the courts in the United States have not needed to grapple with this issue. Second, unlike in Australia, where the tort of trespass to goods is actionable per se, in the United States the tort requires proof of harm to the physical condition, quality, or value of the good. Consequently, the case law in the United States mainly deals with the issue of whether this conduct leads to any kind of recognisable physical harm - an issue that is not important in the Australian context.

In the absence of legislative reform - such as removing the requirements for directness or tangibility - it seems unlikely that the personal property torts will be extended to cover interferences with digital data or intangible assets. However, such an extension is not entirely impossible. Courts could potentially rely on the broader notion of directness found in cases like *Scott v Shepherd* (1773) and *Southport Corporation v Esso Petroleum Co Ltd* (1954) to argue that digital interference is sufficiently direct. It could also be held that there is an interference with tangible goods where the tangible computer equipment housing the information has been 'invaded' by incoming electrons, as suggested by Radin ('Information Tangibility' (2004) at 10). Alternatively, Radin's more radical argument that electronic information itself could be recognised as a tangible object capable of being interfered with ('Information Tangibility' (2004) at 24) might be accepted.

While these arguments are theoretically possible, they face significant challenges. Australian courts have repeatedly declined to extend personal property torts to intangible assets. Consider the following examples:

- In *Joukhoador v Commissioner of Police* (2020) Beech-Jones J held at [55] that information is not property and, therefore, cannot be possessed. A similar conclusion was reached in *Chandrasekharan v Commonwealth (No 3)* (2020) at [144].
- In *Hoath v Connect Internet Services Pty Ltd* (2006) the New South Wales Supreme Court refused to extend the tort of conversion to cover internet domain names and IP addresses.
- In *OBG Pty Ltd v Allan* (2008) the House of Lords, by a 3:2 majority, declined to extend conversion to intangible items like 'choses in action', maintaining its traditional focus on physical 'choses in possession'.

However, recent Australian case law suggests a potential shift. In *CME Blasting & Mining Equipment Ltd v Rock Tool Refurbishment Solutions Proportionately Ltd (No 2)* (2022), Besanko J refused to grant summary judgment against claims of conversion and detinue for unauthorised use of software, stating at [98] that he was not satisfied the claims lacked a reasonable prospect of success. Although this decision did not establish liability, it signals a potential willingness by courts to reconsider the application of the personal property torts to intangible assets in certain circumstances.

9 See the discussion in Mendelson, *The New Law of Torts* (2018) at 235; and Davies et al, *Focus Torts* (2024) at 920–1.

Calls for reform have also been growing. For example, Davies et al (*Focus Torts* (2024)) argue at 932 that excluding intangible property is indefensible in an increasingly digital society, where 'some valuable forms of property are entirely electronic, as in the case of cryptocurrencies and non-fungible tokens (NFTs)'. They highlight the inconsistency in treating the interception of a cheque as conversion (because of its physical form) but not applying the same principle to intercepted electronic payments. These criticisms have been echoed in *OBG Pty Ltd v Allan* (2008), where the dissenting judgments by Lord Nicholls and Baroness Hale presented compelling arguments for reform. Lord Nicholls held at [220]–[241] that the law has outgrown the need for outmoded, artificial and unhelpful legal fictions and should jump the gap between tangibles and intangibles. Similarly, Baroness Hale advocated at [308]–[318] for tortious remedies to protect any recognised form of property, irrespective of its tangible or intangible nature. These perspectives provide a foundation for future reconsideration of the issue.

6.7.2 Body parts and biological materials

The question of whether human body parts and biological materials can be considered 'tangible movable objects' subject to the personal property torts has become increasingly significant with advances in medical technology. Categories such as frozen human embryos, sperm and eggs, which can now be created and stored through in vitro fertilisation (IVF) technology, challenge traditional legal rules. It has been suggested that the law should evolve to protect plaintiffs seeking to maintain control over these valuable items.

As noted in section 6.3.1 above, traditionally the common law did not recognise the human body, excised body parts or bodily products as property capable of being the subject matter of the personal property torts. An exception existed only where a person's 'lawful exercise of work or skill' upon a body transformed it into 'property' capable of sustaining a cause of action: *Doodeward v Spence* (1908) Griffith CJ at 414; *Dobson v North Tyneside Health Authority* (1997). Moreover, the common law position has been that individuals cannot 'possess' their own body or its parts: *Moore v Regents of the University of California* (1990); *R v Bentham* (2005). This precludes an action based on a legal right to possession of body parts.

However, recent developments in Australian and international jurisprudence indicate a shift in the area. Courts have increasingly recognised that, in defined circumstances, human body parts or products can be owned or possessed in law. For example, several Australian cases have recognised rights over posthumously extracted sperm: see, eg, *Bazley v Wesley Monash IVF Pty Ltd* (2011); *Re Estate of Edwards* (2011); *Re H, AE (No 3)* (2013); and *GLS v Russell-Weisz* (2018). These cases reflect a growing willingness to reconsider traditional restrictions and acknowledge certain biological materials as property under specific conditions. While this area remains legally complex and contentious, these developments suggest an evolving approach that could ultimately expand the scope of the personal property torts.

6.7.3 Clarifying the law

In *Kuwait Airways Corporation v Iraqi Airways Co* (2002) at [39], Lord Nicholls highlighted the near impossibility of precisely defining the tort of conversion. Later, in

OBG Pty Ltd v Allan (2008), he criticised the tort's reliance on traditional fictions and formalisms, arguing that these outdated concepts contribute to its complexity. In the United Kingdom, efforts to address these issues have included legislative reforms, such as abolishing the tort of detinue (which overlapped with conversion) under the *Torts (Interference with Goods) Act 1977* (UK).

The complexity and inconsistency in the personal property torts, particularly conversion, have also led to calls for legislative reform in Australia. For example, in *Sell Your Gold Pty Ltd v Australian Diamond Trading Corporation Pty Ltd* (2018), the Victorian Court of Appeal emphasised the difficulty in determining whether an act constitutes a sufficient interference with an owner's rights to amount to conversion. The Court described the concepts of 'repugnancy' and 'dominion' as abstract and elusive (at [88]), warning that such vagueness risks idiosyncratic rulings and potential injustice. The Court urged legislative reform to clarify the law and address concerns such as the overlap between conversion and detinue, and the strict liability nature of conversion, which can unfairly penalise innocent parties acting in good faith. To date, however, no Australian Parliament has taken up this suggestion.

6.8 Problem-solving tips

This section offers tips on how to approach and answer problem questions involving all the personal property torts, highlighting the key steps and issues to look for when applying the principles covered in this chapter.

1. Begin by reminding yourself of the definition of personal property and recall the controversial categories of goods. Then refresh your memory of the elements and the focal points of each of the three personal property torts by referring to Figures 6.1–6.3 – bearing in mind that the torts overlap. Always double-check your first diagnosis in case you missed an overlap.
   - **Trespass to goods:** *Interfering with exclusive possession of goods.* Remember that the interference may range from a very minor interference to a very major interference (which may also amount to conversion of goods). The key focus of this tort is on the right to *exclusive possession*, which means that the plaintiff has the right to exclude others from physically interfering with the goods. So look for any touching of or contact with goods as a minimum and work up from there.
   - **Conversion:** *A deliberate dealing with goods that is so serious that it denies the rights of the person entitled to exercise dominion over the goods, and the defendant should be treated as if they have taken ownership of the goods.* Remember that the tests for conversion are not completely clear and that you may need to use your knowledge of decided cases to assist your arguments. The two key points for your arguments in this tort will focus on the kinds of dealing with goods and the degree of seriousness of that dealing.
     a. *Dealing* with goods may involve:
        - destroying goods;
        - changing the nature of goods;

- taking possession of goods;
- withholding/refusing to give possession of goods (may overlap with detinue);
- using goods for the defendant's own purposes;
- disposing of goods by sale; or
- misdelivery of goods.

b. When discussing *seriousness*, look for:
- length of the interference – how long did it last?
- degree of the interference – how extensive (or damaging) are the effects of the defendant's meddling on the goods?
- expense and inconvenience caused – how has the owner of the goods been affected?
- intention of the defendant to exercise dominion – is there any evidence that the defendant intended to take control of the goods?

- **Detinue:** *Unreasonably refusing to yield possession of goods after a lawful request.* Remember that in detinue, a refusal to comply with the demand must be intentional or deliberate, but it may be technical in the sense that it may have arisen from an inability to deliver possession of the goods, which itself may have been caused by carelessness. So, always take care to distinguish between the defendant's act of refusal and the earlier conduct that led to the refusal (which may be completely separate). The key focus is on the fuzzy concept of *unreasonableness,* so look carefully at the problem question to see if there are any features that allow you to argue the facts for and against reasonableness. Here are some examples:
  - Nature of the defendant's possession – how did it originate?
  - Nature of the plaintiff's demand – has there been a demand and was it specific and clear in its terms? If there was no demand, can you argue for an exception to be made on the facts of your case?
  - Nature of the refusal – was it qualified or justified in some way? Look at the facts and the case authorities to support your arguments.
  - Inability to deliver possession – what facts led to the defendant's inability? Is there any evidence of fault or carelessness by the defendant?

  Remember that if for any reason an action in conversion may not be successful (eg if the limitations period has expired) then you may need to advise your client that they could trigger a new cause of action in detinue by making a demand for the goods. So, detinue can be a route to a remedy, even if no demand has yet been made by the plaintiff on the facts.

2. Having refreshed your memory, read the problem question and look for the *harmful effects.* You are looking for any physical interferences with goods or any refusal to give possession of goods to another. Once you have identified any interferences, work out whose *conduct* caused those interferences and identify the defendant. Then work out who the proper plaintiff is by referring to Figures 6.1–6.3, remembering that this is complicated by the bailment rules.
3. List the causes of action in time order and then, using the individual tables of elements, work your way through the elements to resolve them. Refer to section 2.3.3.2 of Chapter 2 to work out the appropriate remedies.

4. If any party appears to have resorted to a 'self-help' remedy, check to see whether they have exceeded what is reasonable in the circumstances, remembering that if they have exceeded what is reasonable, they may have committed some other tort.
5. Remember that the precise boundaries of the personal property torts are uncertain, so you need to be familiar with the decided cases and will often have to argue by analogy.

Conclusion

In this chapter we have concluded our exploration of the trespass torts, focusing on trespass to land and trespass to goods, as well as the related torts of conversion and detinue. These torts are designed to protect possession rather than ownership, emphasising the importance of an individual's right to control access to and use of their land or goods. In the case of trespass to land, the law safeguards the exclusive possession of land from unauthorised interference. The tort's principles reflect a balance between respecting an individual's privacy and property rights and broader societal interests, such as law enforcement or public access. The personal property torts further illustrate the emphasis on protecting possession over ownership. Each tort addresses specific forms of interference with goods, ranging from minor physical disruptions to significant acts that undermine the possessor's rights. The distinctions between these torts are critical, as they determine the appropriate legal action and remedies. However, the overlaps between the torts, as well as the evolving nature of personal property (such as digital assets), reveal ongoing challenges in applying these principles in modern contexts. In the next chapter, we will complete our examination of the intentional torts by exploring the defences available to these actions.

Test your understanding

Problem solving

Now that you have covered the torts to land and goods, as well as all of the intentional torts, you are ready for some more problem solving. This is a 'spot the tort' question that will test your diagnostic skills. Once you have completed the chapters on defences to the intentional torts and principles of damages, you may be able to identify some extra issues in this problem.

Mei Lei, a wealthy socialite, was crazy about dogs. She owned two champion pedigree poodles named Moet (a male) and Chandon (a female). She regularly entered the poodles in dog shows each year and bought them every luxury, including special 'Pampered Poodle Chow' to eat and very expensive jewelled collars. Moet's collar spelled the letter 'M' in diamonds and Chandon's collar spelled 'C' in rubies.

Each day Mei Lei's gardener, Rolf, took the dogs for a walk. Rolf loved the dogs, but his wife Raimonda (Mei Lei's cook) secretly hated them, and one day last year she added a powerful drug to the dogs' Poodle Chow. Once they ate it, they suffered for two weeks with vomiting and diarrhoea. Both dogs were so sick that Mei Lei thought they would die. The vet was called and had to visit the dogs every day for two weeks. The bills piled up, but Mei Lei did not care about the expense.

Even though Moet and Chandon survived, Mei Lei became so obsessed with losing the dogs that she took them to a special animal IVF clinic, Furry Friends Genetics (FFG), and asked them to extract and store genetic material from both animals so that she could clone them if anything ever happened to them again. The material was frozen and lodged with FFG for storage. Mei Lei, who suspected Raimonda of having had something to do the dogs' illness, told Rolf that Raimonda was strictly forbidden from having any more contact with them.

Two weeks later, Raimonda offered to help Rolf by taking the dogs for their early morning walk. Rolf, who was halfway down the driveway when he was hit by a blinding migraine, accepted Raimonda's offer, handed the dogs' leads to his wife and went to bed. Raimonda, a fitness freak, forced Moet and Chandon to run for two hours until they were exhausted – even though they needed to be in top condition so that they could be entered into a show that afternoon. On the way back she took the dogs to the Poodle Salon to have their coats cut, shampooed and styled for the competition and was taking them home when Sally, a small eight-year-old girl who loved dogs, asked if she could pat them. Raimonda refused permission, because once the dogs had been prepared for the competition their coats could not be touched; however, Sally patted them both gently and kissed them before she could be stopped.

Sebastian, a local drug user who was desperate for money, spotted the dogs' jewelled collars and decided that he needed them more than the dogs did. While Raimonda was distracted by Sally, he raced over, grabbed the leads roughly out of Raimonda's hands and dragged the terrified pooches into a side street. He tried to force the collars off the animals, but they bit him, so Sebastian repeatedly kicked their heads until they were unconscious, pulled the collars off the dogs and shoved their bodies under some boxes so that no one could see them.

Sebastian threw the leads over the fence and into the backyard of one of the houses in the street. As he was walking away with the collars, he was accosted by Rolf who, feeling guilty about leaving the dogs with Raimonda, had set out to the salon to find them. Rolf demanded that Sebastian give him the collars and tell him where the dogs were. He managed to get hold of Chandon's collar, but Sebastian took it back, eluded his grasp, pushed him over and escaped to the park where he found Marshall, his dealer, and quickly organised a deal by trading Moet's collar for heroin. He continued his journey to the jeweller, where he sold Chandon's collar and pocketed the cash.

Meanwhile, Raimonda rushed into the side street and searched everywhere for the dogs; she ran into a nearby property and searched the garden, pushing through the bushes trying to find the animals; she threw the rubbish bins in the street aside looking for any trace of the poodles and finally she searched through the park, where she saw Marshall, who was wearing Moet's collar and showing off the diamond 'M' to his friends. She grabbed him and ripped the collar from his neck, but even though she searched Marshall's backpack, she could not find Chandon's collar anywhere. She did find Marshall's stash of drugs and money and so she took them, intending to give them to the police when she reported the attack on the dogs and the theft of their collars.

Eventually, after searching for two days, Rolf found the dogs and took them back to Mei Lei, who called the vet again and collapsed in hysterics. Raimonda called the doctor, who, after trying every method to calm her down, was forced to sedate her by injecting her with drugs. Chandon died from her injuries after six months of experimental treatment. Moet responded to the treatment and his life was saved, but he never recovered fully from the brain damage sustained in the attack and his personality changed – he became an aggressive and vicious dog – and finally, one year after these events, Mei Lei had to have him put down.

Mei Lei, who had always wanted to breed Moet and Chandon's puppies, decided that she would use the genetic material stored at FFG to fulfil her dream. She went to the clinic and asked to see a consultant about her options, but was told the bad news that FFG's refrigerators had failed a few weeks earlier because FFG had forgotten to have the equipment serviced. Half of their items, including all of Chandon's genetic material, had been defrosted and all of the other items, including Moet's remaining genetic material, had been sent to another storage depot across town. She phoned the depot and asked for Moet's samples, but was told that until she paid the storage fees, she could not collect them.

Desperately upset at the news that she could not breed the puppies, Mei Lei was on her way across town to visit the other depot so that she could at least retrieve the samples and make a clone of Moet when she spotted Chandon's collar in the window of a jeweller's shop. Mei Lei, her eyes blinded by tears, rushed into the store and demanded to be given her property. The assistant, Jasmine, who was taken aback by Mei Lei's distraught appearance, was not sure whether she should hand over the collar, so she told Mei Lei that she would have to check with her boss first. Mei Lei, who was by now beyond patience, began yelling at Jasmine, calling her a 'stupid, arrogant fool'. She pushed her way past Jasmine, ran behind the counter and tried to grab Chandon's collar from the display, but she slipped and fell through the plate glass window. Jasmine called an ambulance and Mei Lei, recovering in hospital, received a bill from the store manager requiring her to pay for the broken window and offering to negotiate with her on the matter of recovering Chandon's collar.

A month after this ordeal, Mei Lei organised for FFG to produce a clone of Moet. Unfortunately, when the puppy was born it was clear that it had not been produced from Moet's genetic material. Further investigations by FFG revealed that an animal rights campaigner known only as 'Snoop Puppy' had hacked into their computer system and scrambled the identity codes of all of their samples – and Mei Lei's new puppy was not a champion poodle, but was instead the clone of someone else's pet, 'Ruffy', a mongrel cross-breed of no distinguished pedigree at all.

Identify and discuss each tort committed, and any remedies that may be claimed.

Trespass to goods

Distinguishing focus

- Interference with the plaintiff's exclusive possession (ie the right to exclude others from physical interference with the goods). For example:
  - mere 'asportation' of goods;
  - damaging goods.
- Query: Is mere touching enough?

Title to sue

- At the time of the interference with the goods, the plaintiff must have either had:
  - possession (actual or constructive) of the goods; or
  - (in some limited circumstances) a right to immediate possession of them. For example, a bailor may sue:

- a third party who invades the bailee's possession; or
- the bailee (eg if the bailee destroys the goods).

See Figure 6.1.

Figure 6.1 Trespass to goods

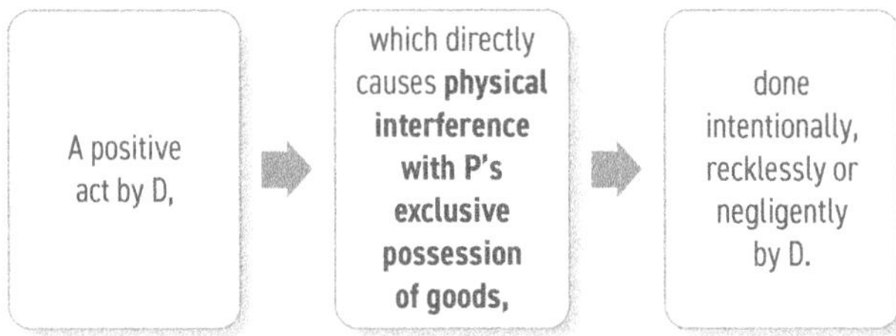

Conversion

Distinguishing focus

- Inconsistent and serious dealing. For example:
  - destroying goods;
  - changing the nature of goods;
  - taking, withholding or refusing to give possession of goods;
  - using goods for the defendant's purposes;
  - disposing of goods by sale;
  - misdelivery of goods.

Title to sue

- At the time of the conversion, the plaintiff must have either had:
  - possession (actual or constructive) of the goods, or
  - a right to immediate possession of them – for example:
    - bailment at will – bailee and bailor may sue;
    - bailment for a term – bailee may sue; bailor may sue only if the bailee destroys the bailment.

See Figure 6.2.

Figure 6.2 Conversion

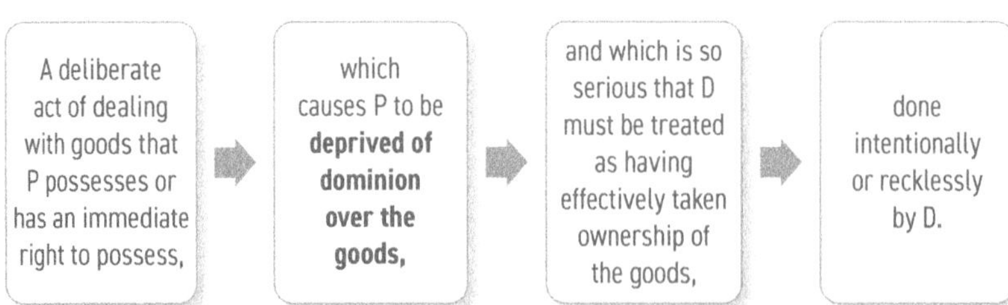

Detinue

Distinguishing focus

- Unreasonable refusal to yield possession of goods to the plaintiff after a demand. For example:
  - detaining goods if the goods are in the defendant's possession;
  - failing to return goods, if the defendant has wrongfully lost or destroyed the goods.

Title to sue

- At the time of demand, the plaintiff must have a superior title to the defendant, which gives a right to immediate possession of the goods. For example:
  - bailment at will – bailee and bailor may sue:
  - bailment for a term – bailee may sue, and bailor may sue only if the bailee destroys the bailment.

See Figure 6.3.

Figure 6.3 Detinue

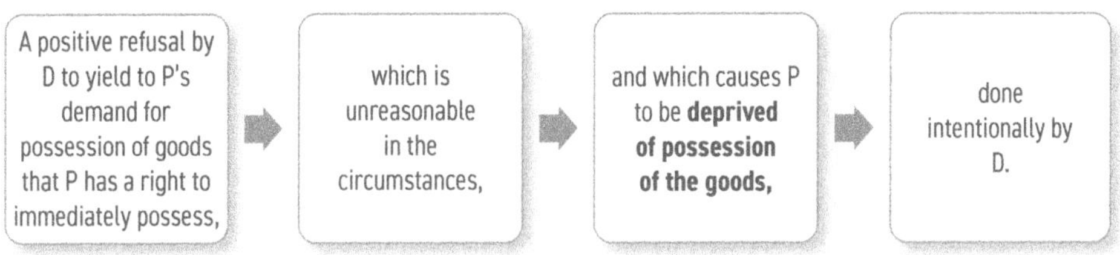

After checking the elements, consider whether any defences are available (see Chapter 7).

REFERENCES

CASES

Armory v Delamirie (1722) 1 Stra 505; 93 ER 664
Ashby v Tolhurst [1937] 2 KB 242
BA v The King (2023) 275 CLR 128; [2023] HCA 14
Barker v Furlong [1891] 2 Ch 172
Barker v The Queen (1983) 153 CLR 338
Basely v Clarkson (1681) 3 Lev 37; 83 ER 565
Bathurst City Council v Saban (1985) 2 NSWLR 704
Bazley v Wesley Monash IVF Pty Ltd [2010] QSC 118; [2011] 2 Qd R 207
Beals v Hayward [1960] NZLR 131
Bernstein of Leigh (Baron) v Skyviews [1977] 3 WLR 136
Break Fast Investments Pty Ltd v PCH Melbourne Pty Ltd (2007) VSCA 311; (2007) 20 VR 311
Bunnings Group Ltd v CHEP Australia Ltd (2011) 82 NSWLR 420; [2011] NSWCA 342

Buurabalayji Thalanyji Aboriginal Corporation v Onslow Slat Pty Ltd (No 2) [2018] FCA 978
Chairman, National Crime Authority v Flack (1998) 86 FCR 16; 156 ALR 501
Chandrasekharan v Commonwealth (No 3) [2020] FCA 169
CHEP Australia Ltd v Bunnings Group Ltd [2010] NSWSC 301
Citicorp Australia Ltd v BS Stillwell Ford Pty Ltd (1979) 21 SASR 142
City Motors (1933) Pty Ltd v Southern Aerial Super Service Pty Ltd (1961) 106 CLR 477
Clayton v Le Roy [1911] 2 KB 1031
CME Blasting & Mining Equipment Ltd v Rock Tool Refurbishment Solutions Proportionately Ltd (No 2) [2022] FCA 632
Coco v The Queen (1994) 179 CLR 427
Coles-Smith v Smith [1965] Qd R 494
Costello v Chief Constable of Derbyshire Constabulary [2001] 1 WLR 1437
Cowell v Rosehill Racecourse Co Ltd (1937) 56 CLR 605
Cressy v Johnson [2009] VSC 52
Croucher v Cachia [2016] NSWCA 132
Crowther v AGC Ltd (1985) Aust Torts Reports 80-709
Davies v Benison (1927) 22 Tas LR 52
Delaney v TP Smith Ltd [1946] KB 393
Di Napoli v New Beach Apartments [2004] NSWSC 52
Dobson v North Tyneside Health Authority [1997] 1 WLR 596
Doodeward v Spence (1908) 6 CLR 406
Dumont v Miller (1873) 4 AJR 152
Edwards v Amos (1945) 62 WN (NSW) 204
Egan v State Transport Authority (1982) 31 SASR 481
Esanda Finance Corporation v Gibbons [1999] NSWSC 1094
Flowfill Packaging Machines Pty Ltd v Fytore Pty Ltd (1993) Aust Torts Reports 81-244
Fouldes v Willoughby (1841) 8 M & W 540; 151 ER 1153
Glass v Hollander (1935) 35 SR (NSW) 304
Glavinic v Commonwealth [2023] ACTSC 361
GLS v Russell-Weisz [2018] WASC 79; 52 WAR 413
Graham v Voigt (1989) 89 ACTR 11
Greig v Greig [1966] VR 376
Haddrick v Lloyd [1945] SASR 40
Halliday v Nevill (1984) 155 CLR 1
Hartley v Moxham (1842) 114 ER 675
Hoath v Connect Internet Services Pty Ltd (2006) 229 ALR 566
Hollins v Fowler (1875) LR 7 HL 757
Houghland v RR Low (Luxury Coaches) Ltd [1962] 1 QB 694
Howard E Perry & Co Ltd v British Railways Board [1980] 1 WLR 1375
Howe v Teefy (1927) 27 SR (NSW) 301
Hutchins v Maughan [1947] VLR 131
James v North Star Pastoral Pty Ltd [2019] NTSC 72
John F Goulding Pty Ltd v Victorian Railways Commissioners (1932) 48 CLR 157
Johnson v Buchanan (2012) 223 A Crim R 132

Jones v Dowle [1841] 9 M & W 19; 152 ER 9
Joukhoador v Commissioner of Police [2020] NSWSC 227
Kahler v Midland Bank Ltd [1950] AC 24
Kelsen v Imperial Tobacco Co [1957] 2 QB 334
Kirk v Gregory [1876] 1 Ex D 55
Konskier v Goodman [1928] 1 KB 421
Kuru v New South Wales (2008) 236 CLR 1
Kuwait Airways Corporation v Iraqi Airways Co [2002] 2 AC 883; [2002] UKHL 19; 3 All ER 209
Lincoln Hunt v Willesee (1986) 4 NSWLR 457
Lloyd v Osborne (1899) 20 LR (NSW) 190
Lord v McMahon [2015] NSWSC 1619
Moore v Devanjul Pty Ltd (No 5) [2013] QSC 323.
Moore v Regents of the University of California 51 Cal 3d 120, 793 P 2d 479 (1990)
Moorgate Mercantile Co Ltd v Finch & Read [1962] 1 QB 701
Morriss v Marsden [1952] 1 All ER 925
National Coal Board v Evans [1951] 2 KB 861
New South Wales v Ibbett (2006) 229 CLR 638
Newington v Windeyer (1985) 3 NSWLR 555
Nickells v City of Melbourne (1938) 59 CLR 219
OBG Pty Ltd v Allan [2008] 1 AC 1
Parker v British Airways Board [1982] QB 1004; [1982] 2 WLR 503
Payne v Dwyer [2013] WASC 271
Penfolds Wines Pty Ltd v Elliott (1946) 74 CLR 204
Perpetual Trustees & National Executors of Tasmania Ltd v Perkins (1989) Aust Torts Reports 80-295
Philpott v Kelley (1835) 3 Ad & El 106; 111 ER 353
Plenty v Dillon (1991) 171 CLR 635
Proudman v Allen [1954] SASR 336
Public Transport Commission of New South Wales v Perry (1977) 137 CLR 107
R v Bentham [2005] UKHL 18; [2005] 1 WLR 1057
R v Kelly [1999] QB 621
R v Southwell [2022] SADC 72
Re Estate of Edwards (2011) 81 NSWLR 198; [2011] NSWSC 478
Re H, AE (No 3) (2013) 118 SASR 259; [2013] SASC 196
Re Creswell [2019] 1 Qd R 403
Rendell v Associated Finance Pty Ltd [1957] VR 604
Robin v Public Trustee (ACT) (2015) 10 ACTLR 300
Romani v New South Wales [2023] NSWSC 49
Roy v O'Neill (2020) 272 CLR 291; [2020] HCA 45
Russell v Wilson (1923) 33 CLR 538
Scott v Shepherd (1773) 3 Black W 892; 96 ER 525
Sell Your Gold Pty Ltd v Australian Diamond Trading Corporation Pty Ltd [2018] VSCA 355
Semayne's Case (1604) 5 Co Rep 9; 77 ER 194
Sheridan v Australian Pacific Airports (Melbourne) Pty Ltd [2021] VSC 440

Six Carpenters Case (1610) 8 Co Rep 146; 77 ER 695
Slaveski v Victoria [2010] VSC 441
Southam v Smout (1964) 1 QB 308
Southport Corporation v Esso Petroleum Co Ltd [1954] 2 QB 182
Tallot v City of Stirling [2017] WASCA 126
TCN Channel Nine Pty Ltd v Anning [2002] NSWCA 82; (2002) 54 NSWLR 333
Tharpe v Stallwood (1843) 5 Man & G 760; 134 ER 766
The Premier Group Pty Ltd v Followmont Transport Pty Ltd [2000] 2 Qd R 338
Toyota Finance Australia Ltd v Dennis [2002] NSWCA 369
Watson v Cowen [1959] Tas SR 194
Weaver v Ward (1616) Hob 134; 80 ER 284
Western Australia v Ward [2002] HCA 28; 213 CLR 1
William Leitch & Co v Leydon [1931] AC 90
Wilson v Lombank Ltd [1963] 1 WLR 1294

BOOKS AND RESEARCH PAPER

Balkin, R P & Davis, J L R, *Law of Torts,* 5th ed (2013) LexisNexis Butterworths, Sydney.
Barker, K, Cane, P, Lunney, M & Trindade, F, *The Law of Torts in Australia,* 5th ed (2012) Oxford University Press, Melbourne.
Davies, M, Malkin, I & Voon, T, *Focus Torts,* 10th ed (2024) LexisNexis Butterworths, Sydney.
Fitzgerald, B, Fitzgerald, A, Beale, T, Lim, Y & Middleton, G, *Internet and e-Commerce Law: Technology, Law and Policy* (2007) Lawbook Co, North Ryde.
Fleming, J G, *The Law of Torts,* 10th ed (2011) Law Book Co, North Ryde.
Mendelson, D, *The New Law of Torts,* 3rd ed (2014) Oxford University Press, Melbourne.
Radin, M J, *Information Tangibility* (2003) Stanford Law School, Public Law Research Paper No 48, available at SSRN <http://ssrn.com/sol3/papers.cfm?abstract_id=357060> or doi: <10.2139/ssrn.357060>.
Spinello, R A, *CyberEthics* (2003) Jones and Bartlett, Sudbury Massachusetts.

DEFENCES TO THE INTENTIONAL TORTS

7

Introduction

We have seen in the previous two chapters that the intentional torts are designed to protect fundamental rights, such as personal autonomy, bodily integrity, and property interests. The courts have repeatedly emphasised the importance of protecting those rights, and have even provided plaintiffs with an avenue for remedies in the absence of any damage. This does not, however, mean that a plaintiff will always succeed if they can prove all the elements of a particular tort. This is because the defendant may have a defence available to them. Defences provide a framework for recognising that, in certain circumstances, actions that might otherwise constitute a tort are justifiable or excusable.

Defences play a critical role in tort law by allowing courts to balance individual rights with broader considerations of justice and social policy. For example, a person who acts in self-defence or under necessity may interfere with another's rights in a way that would ordinarily be unlawful, but their actions may be justified by the circumstances. Similarly, defences like consent or statutory authorisation reflect the idea that liability should not arise where the plaintiff has permitted the interference or where the defendant is acting in accordance with the law. Without defences, the law would be overly rigid, punishing conduct that, in context, may be entirely reasonable or socially acceptable.

In this chapter we begin by discussing the distinction between a denial of liability and a defence. A *denial of liability* challenges whether the plaintiff has proven the elements of the tort, whereas a *defence* assumes that the elements are satisfied but provides a justification or excuse for the defendant's actions. We then examine 13 key defences to intentional torts:

- *consent* – where the plaintiff agrees to the conduct;
- *necessity* – where the defendant acts to prevent a greater harm;
- *self-defence, defence of another* and *defence of property* – where the defendant uses defensive force to protect themselves, a third party or their property;
- *infancy* and *incapacity* – where the defendant's youth or lack of capacity in a particular respect provides a defence;
- *statutory authorisation* – where the defendant's conduct is permitted by law;
- *recaption of goods, re-entry on land, ejectment of trespassers,* and *distress* – where the defendant is permitted to take the law into their own hands and help themselves directly to a remedy without having to go through the courts; and
- *discipline* – where certain relationships justify lawful chastisement.

We also consider two potential procedural barriers to liability: *illegality* (where the plaintiff's unlawful conduct may bar recovery) and *limitation of actions* (where the claim is brought outside the prescribed time period). Finally, we briefly address two matters which do not constitute defences to the intentional torts: *mistake* and *provocation.*

7.1 Distinguishing denials and defences

In tort law, it is essential to distinguish between denials of liability (or simply 'denials') and defences, as they serve different purposes and operate in distinct ways. A denial challenges the plaintiff's ability to establish one or more of the elements of a tort. For example, in battery the plaintiff must prove that the defendant caused physical contact or interference with the plaintiff's body, and a denial might assert that the defendant never touched the plaintiff. By contrast, a defence assumes that the plaintiff has proven all the elements of the tort but provides a legal reason why the defendant should not be held liable. For example, in a battery case the defendant might acknowledge that they touched the plaintiff but claim that they did so in self-defence.

7.1.1 Denials

In Chapters 5 and 6 you have seen that each intentional tort is comprised of specific elements that must be satisfied for liability to arise. In tort law, the onus of proof is normally on the plaintiff to prove all of the elements – but as we have seen, the trespass torts are an exception to this rule, because the plaintiff only needs to prove that the defendant directly interfered with them in the relevant way, and then the onus shifts to defendant to prove a lack of fault (unless the case is covered by the 'highway exception', in which case the plaintiff must also prove that the defendant was at fault). It is important to note that even if the burden shifts to the defendant to prove that they were 'utterly without fault' (*Weaver v Ward* (1616)), the fault element remains part of the tort, meaning that disproving it constitutes a denial of the tort rather than a defence.

When the defendant denies liability, they are arguing that one or more elements of the tort have not been met. Denials of liability can take several forms. For example, in a trespass to land claim the defendant may deny:

- that the relevant conduct occurred – by arguing that they never interfered with the plaintiff's exclusive possession of land;
- that they were at fault – by arguing that they did not act intentionally, recklessly or negligently; or
- that the circumstances required for the tort to be established have been met – by arguing that the plaintiff did not have the right to exclusive possession of the land in question.

In everyday language, people often refer to such denials as 'raising a defence', but this is technically inaccurate. Denials merely challenge whether the tort has been established in the first place, whereas defences accept that the tort is proven but provide a justification or excuse for the conduct. This confusion is particularly common regarding the so-called 'defence' of inevitable accident. Inevitable accident is not a defence at all but a denial of the elements of a tort – it is merely another way of saying that the defendant was entirely blameless for their conduct. As discussed in Chapters 5 and 6, none of the intentional torts can be established where the defendant was 'utterly without fault': *Weaver v Ward* (1616); *Croucher v Cachia* (2016).

Case examples

- In *Weaver v Ward* (1616), a case of assault and battery brought after the defendant discharged his musket and wounded the plaintiff, the Court pointed out at 284 that a person should be excused from liability for trespass if they are 'judged utterly without fault', and gave the following illustration:

> If a man by force take my hand and strike you, or if here, the defendant had said that the plaintiff had ran across his piece when it was discharging, or had set forth the case with the circumstances, so as it appeared to the Court that it was inevitable, and that the defendant had committed no negligence to give occasion to the hurt.

- In *Stanley v Powell* (1890) the Court held that the plaintiff could not recover damages after being struck in the eye by pellets that ricocheted off a tree when the defendant fired at a pheasant. The Court found that the force applied was neither intentional nor the result of negligence on the defendant's part, and so no liability arose.
- In *National Coal Board v Evans* (1951) the defendant, a contractor hired by a third party to plough a trench accidentally damaged an underground cable belonging to the plaintiff. The Court held that the defendant was 'utterly without fault' (Cohen CJ at 874, Singleton LJ at 879, Morris LJ at 881) because he neither knew nor could reasonably have suspected the cable's presence. In the absence of an intention to make contact with the cable, negligence in doing so, or any knowledge of its existence, the defendant was not liable.
- In the 'sexual battery' case of *Scalera v Non-Marine Underwriters, Lloyd's of London* (2000), McLachlin J in the Supreme Court of Canada explained at 11 that in the rights-based torts of trespass, a defendant can avoid liability on the grounds of being 'utterly without fault' by proving 'a lack of intention or negligence'.

There is some debate about whether consent constitutes a denial or a defence. Some argue that consent negates the wrongful interference required to establish a tort, making it a denial. However, Australian courts generally treat consent as a defence, placing the burden on the defendant to establish it (see section 7.2 below). This chapter adopts that approach, treating consent as a defence.

7.1.2 Defences

Defences concede that the plaintiff has proven the elements of the tort but provide a reason why liability should not attach to the defendant's conduct. As noted above, the defences exist because we recognise that there are times when a person may be justified in invading the rights of others. This means our common law rights are not absolute; a degree of flexibility and contextual judgement is built into the system of rights and obligations that the law of torts constructs and enforces. The elements of each tort specify the conditions under which, *as a general rule*, we should not invade the rights of others. The defences identify the conditions under which, in the light of all the *particular circumstances* of an individual case, a defendant will not be blamed for invading them.

A classic example may be found in the right of self-defence. It is clearly a battery to shoot another person intentionally, but if the defendant was acting reasonably in self-defence we do not hold them liable to compensate the injured plaintiff. We absolve the defendant of blame and cast the true blame for the events upon the plaintiff who was initially at fault by making the threat or attack.

There are many different defences to the intentional torts, but it is possible to group them according to their underlying reasoning, as set out in Table 7.1.

Each of these defences has its own set of elements, all of which must be proven to make out the defence. The onus of proof is on the defendant to prove a defence on the balance of probabilities. If they can do so, then they win – and the case is over. However, if the defence fails (and all the elements of the torts have been proven), the onus shifts to the plaintiff to prove their losses and claim a remedy.

Table 7.1 Classification of intentional torts

	Definition	Example	Relevant defences
Justifications	These defences apply where the defendant's conduct is considered to be right or acceptable given the circumstances.	A person who is being attacked may be justified in using proportionate defensive force.	Self-defence; defence of another; defence of property; necessity.
Excuses	These defences acknowledge that the defendant acted wrongfully, but hold that the defendant should nevertheless be excused for some reason.	It may be excusable for a very young child to hit someone, if they don't understand what they are doing.	Infancy; incapacity.
Authorised acts	These defences apply because the defendant was authorised to engage in the relevant conduct. They could have been authorised by the plaintiff (who consented to the conduct) or by law.	–	Consent; statutory authorisation; the self-help remedies (recaption of goods; re-entry on land; ejectment of trespassers; distress).

7.2 Consent

Consent is a complete defence to intentional torts. Grounded in the principle of autonomy, the rationale for this defence is that the plaintiff has authorised the defendant's conduct, and so it would be unreasonable for a plaintiff to seek compensation if the defendant has acted within the bounds of their permission (ie within the scope of the consent). However, this will only be the case if the consent was valid. As we discuss further below, this requires the plaintiff to have been capable of giving consent, to have understood what they were consenting to, and to have voluntarily given their consent.

7.2.1 The onus of proving consent

There is a lack of clarity about whether consent operates as a defence or as a denial of liability, and thus about who bears the onus of proving or disproving consent. In *Secretary, Department of Health and Community Services v JWB and SMB (Marion's case)* (1992), McHugh J in obiter considered both international and local cases on the issue, determining that the Australian position is that consent is a defence, and that it must be proved by the defendant on the balance of probabilities. This approach has also been taken by the New South Wales and Australian Capital Territory Courts of Appeal (*Dean v Phung* (2012) at [59]–[62]; *Moon v Whitehead* (2015) at [14]), as well as by the Supreme Court of Canada (*Scalera v Non-Marine Underwriters, Lloyd's of London* (2000)). However, commentators have argued that consent is such a critical aspect of all the trespass torts that the absence of consent should be included as an element in their definitions and should be proved by the plaintiff.[1] This is the approach that has been taken in the United Kingdom and New Zealand (*Freeman v Home Office (No 2)* (1984); *S v G* (1995)) and was also the view adopted by Leeming JA, after detailed consideration of the history of the law in the area, in *White v Johnston* (2015).

A case to remember

White v Johnston (2015) 87 NSWLR 779

Topics

Battery; consent.

Facts

The plaintiff, a war veteran whose dental treatment was being paid for by the Department for Veterans' Affairs, had received a significant amount of treatment from the defendant, a dentist. Although the defendant had obtained the plaintiff's consent for the work, the plaintiff claimed that it was completely unnecessary and ineffective, and that the defendant's sole motivation for performing the work was to obtain financial compensation from the Department. The plaintiff argued that since the dental work had been undertaken solely for non-therapeutic purposes, the consent she gave was invalid, and the work carried out therefore constituted a battery.

Issues

- Where a patient consents to treatment, but does not know that the medical practitioner is motivated solely by an unrevealed non-therapeutic purpose, is the consent valid?
- Who bears the onus of proof in establishing consent?

Decision

The judge at first instance held that the plaintiff's consent was invalid and the dental work constituted a battery. The defendant appealed, and the New South Wales Court of Appeal allowed the appeal. It held that where a medical practitioner is motivated solely by an unrevealed non-therapeutic purpose, there can be no valid consent to the treatment; but that in this case there was no evidence that the defendant was solely motivated by non-therapeutic purposes in each and every instance of the treatment given.

Although that settled the issue on appeal, Leeming JA went on to consider the broader issue of who bears the onus of proof in establishing consent. Noting that there was no binding authority on the issue, his Honour considered a number of cases but ultimately followed the authority of *Christopherson v Bare* (1848), in which it was held that consent was an element of the cause of action rather than a defence. Leeming JA further noted at [124]–[125]:

> The modern academic commentator who has, in my view, considered the question most carefully, is of the same view: 'It is tentatively concluded, therefore, that to

1 See, for example, Goudkamp, *Tort Law Defences* (2013) at 67.

plead consent in proceedings in trespass is to offer a denial rather than a defence': J Goudkamp, *Tort Law Defences* (Hart Publishing, Oxford, 2013) p 67.

If it be the case, as I think *Christopherson v Bare* establishes it was, that an absence of consent was of the gist of assault and battery, such that the legal burden of proving so is for the plaintiff, has the law changed? Alternatively, should it change? I do not consider that the law has changed or that it should.

Leeming JA concluded at [107] that 'where a patient's consent is said to have been rendered invalid by reason of the fraud, or conduct tantamount to fraud, the onus remains with the patient to establish fraud'.

The conflict in the authorities on who bears the onus of proof for establishing consent leaves the law in an unsatisfactory position, which is unlikely to be resolved until the High Court of Australia ('High Court') has an opportunity to address the issue. In the meantime, it seems that the more widely accepted view is that consent is a defence – which is the approach we have taken in this chapter. In some jurisdictions there are also legislative provisions that bear on this issue. For example, in Queensland, lack of consent is an element of battery.

LEGISLATION ALERT!

Consult your study materials to see whether there is any legislation in your jurisdiction that specifies that absence of consent is an element of any of the intentional torts. An example is s 245 of the *Criminal Code Act 1899* (Qld).

7.2.2 Express and implied consent

Consent may be express or implied. Express consent is explicitly given, either verbally or in writing, and clearly authorises specific conduct. For example, a patient who signs a form to approve a medical procedure, or who verbally agrees to participate in a scientific study, gives express consent. By contrast, implied consent arises from the conduct or circumstances of the plaintiff, where consent is reasonably inferred even though it is not explicitly stated. For instance, players in a game of Australian Rules football or rugby understand in broad terms that they will be subject not only to contact as allowed by the rules (eg being tackled), but also to 'commonly encountered infringements of the rules' (eg being pushed in the back). In *Giumelli v Johnston* (1989) King CJ noted at [4] that by knowingly taking part in the sport, participants implicitly consent to both kinds of contact. They do not, however, consent to the intentional infliction of physical harm.

As noted in section 6.2 of Chapter 6, implied consent is often a key issue in trespass to land cases, as people often enter other people's land without their explicit permission (eg when a post officer comes to your door to leave a parcel). Whether implied consent exists in that context is a question of fact and will generally depend on whether there is any obstruction or indication that entry is prohibited. In *Halliday v Nevill* (1984) the

Court noted that some examples of an implied licence to enter land include stepping into a driveway to avoid an obstruction, entering to speak with someone in the house, or retrieving property that has blown onto the land or a small child who has run onto it. This implied licence applies to police officers in the same way it applies to any member of the public with a legitimate reason to enter the property. However, as noted in *Roy v O'Neill* (2020), police and others exceed the scope of the implied licence if they enter for purposes outside the licence, remain after it is revoked or act inconsistently with it.

Case examples

- In *Halliday v Nevill* (1984) the High Court considered whether police officers entering a driveway without explicit permission committed trespass to land. The Court held that an occupier's permission to enter land could be implied if there were no barriers, signs, or other indications prohibiting entry. The implied licence applies to members of the public, including police officers, provided their purpose for entry coincides with the ordinary use of the property, such as approaching the house to communicate with the occupants.
- In *Giumelli v Johnston* (1989) the plaintiff and the defendant were playing in an AFL match. When the plaintiff had the ball, the defendant did a 'hip and shoulder' bump, which is permitted by the rules. It was held that this did not constitute battery, as people who participate in a football match are taken to consent to the infliction of such physical force as is permitted by the rules of the game (as well as to some bodily contact outside the rules of the game).

To successfully raise the defence, the defendant must prove that they acted within the scope of the consent given. This requires the court to carefully consider what the plaintiff agreed to (if consent was express) or the boundaries of consent that can be implied from the circumstances. If the defendant exceeded the scope of what was agreed to, the consent will not shield them from liability. Additionally, consent can be revoked at any time, and any action taken after consent has been withdrawn constitutes an unauthorised interference. This reinforces the principle that consent is tied to the plaintiff's autonomy and must be respected throughout the interaction.

7.2.3 Valid consent

Even if the plaintiff appears to have clearly and explicitly consented to the defendant's conduct, that does not necessarily mean the defendant will be able to successfully raise consent as a defence. For the defence to succeed, the defendant must also demonstrate that the consent was valid, by proving that:

- the plaintiff was competent (ie had capacity to consent);
- the plaintiff understood in broad terms the nature of what was being proposed; and
- the plaintiff's consent was voluntary.

You should bear in mind that these ingredients overlap to a certain degree and that there are occasions where it is lawful to proceed without a plaintiff's consent, such as in the case of necessity; see section 7.3 below.

7.2.3.1 Competence (capacity)

The first component of valid consent is that it must be given by a person who is competent (ie has the mental capacity to consent). Special rules apply to the question of competence, depending on whether the plaintiff is an adult or a child under the age of 18, and whether common law rules have been supplemented by legislation. In general, adults are presumed to have capacity, but this presumption can be rebutted by proving facts that indicate either a permanent loss of capacity (eg due to a brain injury) or a temporary loss of capacity (eg caused by drugs or alcohol). Special rules apply in the case of children. Some legislation allows substituted consent in cases of incapacity.

LEGISLATION ALERT!

Consult your study materials to see whether there is any legislation in your jurisdiction that governs consent (eg *Consent to Medical Treatment and Palliative Care Act 1995* (SA)).

Many important cases about consent have arisen from disputes about medical treatment. This is because medical practitioners must obtain the consent of their patients to all medical procedures – since without a valid consent the treatment (as a direct and intentional contact with the body) will amount to a battery.

Case examples

The capacity of adults

- In *Re C* (1994) doctors wished to amputate the gangrenous foot of a patient in a secure mental health facility who was experiencing paranoid schizophrenia, but the patient (who experienced delusions that he was a famous doctor who could cure himself) refused to give consent, saying, 'I would rather die with two feet than live with one'. Thorpe J reviewed the authorities at 294–6 and decided that the doctors had to respect the patient's wishes. His Honour explained at 294:

  > Prima facie every adult has the right and capacity to decide whether or not he will accept medical treatment, even if a refusal may risk permanent injury to his health or even lead to premature death. Furthermore, it matters not whether the reasons for the refusal were rational or irrational, unknown or even non-existent.

  The two tests for rebutting the presumption of competence laid down in this case (at 295) are:

  1. Does the plaintiff understand the nature, purpose and effects of the proposed treatment?
  2. Can the plaintiff comprehend the information, believe it, and weigh it to make a choice?

- The Canadian case of *Beausoleil v Communaut* (1964) explained that a purported consent that is given after ingesting sedating drugs may be vitiated.
- The case of *Re B (Adult: Refusal of Treatment)* (2002) contains a very helpful summary at [100] listing the rules governing the capacity to consent to (and refuse) medical treatment. In Australia the principles relating to refusal of treatment have been considered in a number of

cases, such as *Hunter and New England Area Health Service v A* (2009) and *Brightwater Care Group (Inc) v Rossiter* (2009).

The capacity of children

- In *Gillick v West Norfolk and Wisbech Area Health Authority* (1986) a mother sought a declaration that it would be unlawful for a doctor to prescribe contraceptive medical treatment to any of her daughters aged under 16. The House of Lords held by a 3:2 majority that there was no 'fixed age rule' governing the capacity of a child to consent to medical treatment. Rather, the test is whether the particular child has developed to a point where they have a 'sufficient understanding and intelligence' to enable them 'to understand fully what is proposed': see Lord Scarman at 189 and Lord Fraser at 169. If the child has not achieved this capacity, then the parents may consent on behalf of the child, provided the treatment is for the child's benefit and protection; however, the parents' capacity to decide diminishes gradually as the child's capacities and maturity grow.
- The majority of the High Court approved the 'Gillick test' in *Secretary, Department of Health and Community Services v JWB and SMB* (*Marion's Case*) (1992), a case that considered the lawfulness of a sterilisation operation that had been proposed for a girl with cognitive impairment. The majority judges maintained that 'there is no fixed age rule' (at 237) and held that parents can consent to *some*, but not *all*, treatment so long as it is in the best interests of the child (at 240). Mason CJ, Dawson, Toohey and Gaudron JJ explained at 240 that the principle to be applied is whether the treatment is for the 'welfare of the child as objectively assessed' and maintained that there are some kinds of intervention that constitute such a serious invasion of a child's bodily integrity that they are beyond the ordinary scope of the parental power to consent. In these cases, the courts must be consulted.
- In *X v Sydney Children's Hospital Network* (2013) the New South Wales Court of Appeal considered the refusal of a 17-year-old defendant, who suffered from Hodgkin's Disease, to consent to a blood transfusion on religious grounds. The Court granted a declaration authorising doctors to administer a blood transfusion. The defendant and his parents appealed. In dismissing the appeal, Basten JA noted at 60:

> The interest of the state in preserving life is at its highest with respect to children and young persons who are inherently vulnerable, in varying degrees. Physical vulnerability diminishes (usually) with age and is at its height with respect to babies. Intellectual and emotional vulnerability also diminish with age but, as the facts of this case illustrate, may be a function of experience (including but by no means limited to education) as well as age. Vulnerability lies at the heart of the disability identified by legal incapacity.

7.2.3.2 Understanding

The second component of valid consent is that the plaintiff must broadly understand the nature of what the defendant proposes. This does not mean the plaintiff must comprehend every risk or detail of the proposed conduct; it is sufficient if they have a general understanding of what is going to happen.

Case examples

- In the criminal case of *R v Williams* (1923) a young and naive girl, who was not aware of the nature of sexual intercourse, was persuaded to have sex with her church choir master on the basis that this proposed 'treatment' or 'surgical operation' would improve her breath production and singing voice. Her apparent consent to allowing him to have intercourse with her was vitiated not only by his fraud as to the effects of the act (see section 7.2.3.3 below), but also by the fact that she did not appreciate or understand the true nature of what was being proposed: see 341 and 347.
- In the medical cases of *Chatterton v Gerson* (1981) at 443 and *Rogers v Whitaker* (1992) at 490, the courts held that once a patient understands a medical procedure's nature in broad terms, their consent to battery remains valid, even if they were not informed of all the material risks. In such situations, a plaintiff can only succeed by proving negligence, rather than battery (see section 14.6 of Chapter 14).

7.2.3.3 Voluntariness

The final component of the defence specifies that the consent must be voluntary – that is, freely given. If an apparent consent is produced by fraud, undue influence, the use or threat of physical force or economic duress, it is vitiated and the defence will fail. Fraud is the most difficult issue raised by this ingredient of a valid consent, and as Stephen J pointed out in *R v Clarence* (1888) at 42–3, the statement that 'fraud vitiates consent' is too wide. In fact, not every kind of fraud will invalidate consent. The usual formulation of the rule specifies that fraud will vitiate consent only if it is fraud as to the nature or character of the act itself, or fraud as to the identity of the defendant. This means that:

- if the defendant pretends to be the plaintiff's partner, sneaks into their bed and engages in sexual intercourse with them, they will have committed battery as they have defrauded the plaintiff about their identity, negating consent;[2]
- if the defendant pretends to be wealthy to seduce the plaintiff into consenting to sexual intercourse, they have not committed battery, as the fraud relates to their attributes rather than their identity.

In recent years, one issue that has come before the courts is whether an employer commits battery against an employee by requiring them to undergo vaccination (such as against influenza or COVID-19) under threat of dismissal or other negative consequences (such as demotion or disciplinary sanctions). It has been argued that the coercion involved in such measures negates any purported consent to the physical act of the vaccination. In *Falconer v Commissioner of Police (WA) (No 2)* (2024) the Court acknowledged that such measures could be coercive, and that the 'use of coercion to bring about vaccination stands in tension with the precepts of personal autonomy and the right to bodily integrity' (Buss P and Vaughan JA at [130]). However, whether such measures negate any purported consent to the vaccination (which would consequently be considered a battery) requires careful consideration of the circumstances, the consequences for the defendant and any underlying statutory authority. See also *Kassam v Hazzard* (2021).

2 In many jurisdictions this will also be a criminal offence, such as rape.

Case examples

- In *R v Clarence* (1888) the Court for Crown Cases Reserved decided by a majority of 9:4 that a woman's consent to have sexual intercourse with her husband was not vitiated by his failure to disclose that he was infected with a venereal disease. She understood the nature of the act (sexual intercourse) and was deceived only as to the health risks of the act. Stephen J at 44 formulated the rule as requiring fraud 'as to the nature of the act itself, or as to the identity of the person who does the act'.
- In *Papadimitropoulos v The Queen* (1957) the High Court of Australia held that the plaintiff's consent to sexual intercourse was not invalidated by the defendant's fraudulent misrepresentation that a ceremony they had participated in was a valid marriage. Although the plaintiff was induced to agree to intercourse by her mistaken belief that she was married to the defendant, the Court determined at 261 that her consent was valid. The Court reasoned that consent is only vitiated if the mistake relates to the identity of the person or the nature of the act itself, not its moral or social character. The plaintiff's mistaken belief that she was engaging in 'marital intercourse' rather than 'fornication' was insufficient to invalidate her consent: see 254 and 261.
- In *R v Richardson* (1999) Diane Richardson was a dentist who treated several patients who were unaware that her dentistry licence had been suspended. They claimed this was a battery, on the basis that they had consented to treatment by a qualified dentist, not a suspended one. This argument was not accepted by the Court, which held that consent is only negated where a person is mistaken about the nature and character of the relevant act, or about the identity of the person committing it. Here, the patients understood that they were going to be treated by Diane Richardson, which meant that the treatment was consensual (and thus not a battery). The fact that they did not know about her suspension was not sufficient to negate consent – that was not a matter that went to the 'identity of the person' who was treating them. See also *Tinnock v Murrumbidgee Local Health District (No 6)* (2017).
- In *R v Tabassum* (2000) three women allowed the defendant to touch their breasts because they mistakenly thought he was medically qualified, when in fact he had an indecent purpose. It was held that their consent was vitiated, as they were mistaken about the quality of the act. This meant that they did not understand what they were consenting to.
- In *Falconer v Commissioner of Police (WA) (No 2)* (2024) the Court considered whether a mandatory vaccination scheme constituted battery. Buss P and Vaughan JA stated at [133]:

> [T]he focus must be on the relevant measure's impact on the plaintiff's consent. Absent a real or genuine choice as to whether to vaccinate there is ... an infringement or impairment of the right to bodily integrity. Conversely, where, despite the application of pressure, there remains a real or genuine choice as to whether to vaccinate, there is no infringement or impairment of the right to bodily integrity. Whether this is the case in a particular situation requires close consideration of the legal and practical operation of the measure.

7.3 Necessity

The defence of necessity is an intriguing defence because it allows a defendant who is facing an extreme emergency of either a private or public nature to deliberately invade the rights of a completely innocent plaintiff without having to pay them any form of compensation.

Examples

- *Private necessity:* A doctor may amputate the arm of an unconscious victim trapped in the wreckage of a motor vehicle accident to save them from being killed in a threatened explosion.
- *Public necessity:* A fire fighter may enter land and pull down another person's house to prevent the spread of a fire that is threatening great damage to life and property.

In *Proudman v Allen* (1954) Hannan JA noted that this defence serves an important policy purpose: it encourages individuals to act to protect life or property in emergencies without fear of legal liability. However, because of its potential to infringe on the rights of others, the defence is strictly limited by legal tests of urgency, necessity and proportionality. The defendant must prove each of the following elements:

1. There was imminent danger to person or property.
2. It was reasonably necessary for the defendant to act to preserve the person or property.
3. The steps the defendant took were reasonable and proportionate.

Even if all of these elements are met, the defendant will be precluded from relying on the defence if the danger was brought about by their own fault: *Rigby v Chief Constable of Northamptonshire* (1985); *Simon v Condran* (2013).

The first element focuses on the threat faced at the time of the defendant's actions. There must be a real and immediate danger to the defendant or a third party, or to somebody's land or goods. The danger must be a sudden emergency rather than a prolonged or general hardship. For example, actions motivated by long-term issues such as homelessness, hunger or climate change do not meet this requirement: *Southwark London Borough Council v Williams* (1971); *Rolles v Commissioner of Police* (2020).

Unlike self-defence (see section 7.4 below), it is insufficient for the defendant to simply have *believed* that a danger exists; there must be an actual, objective threat: *New South Wales v McMaster* (2015). This is judged based on the circumstances as they appeared to the defendant at the time of the event. Even if a later analysis reveals that the threatened conduct would not have eventuated, the defence will be available if the defendant's perception of imminent peril was reasonable. For example, if a fire reasonably appears to threaten a town, and the defendant trespasses to create a firebreak, the defence will apply even if the fire later changes direction and would not have actually damaged the town: *Cope v Sharpe (No 2)* (1912).

The second element requires the defendant to demonstrate that their actions were reasonably necessary to avert the danger. This will depend on the specific facts of the case, including the urgency and gravity of the situation. This element will not be met where the conduct was merely convenient or expedient – it must be *necessary* to prevent the threatened harm: *Murray v McMurchy* (1949).

The third element ensures that the defendant's actions were a reasonable and appropriate response to the danger they sought to address. The law does not require their actions to have succeeded in averting the threat; what matters is that their actions were proportionate to the threatened harm: *Proudman v Allen* (1954).

Case examples

- In *Mouse's Case* (1609) a ferryman threw passengers' luggage overboard during a tempest in order to lighten his barge and save the passengers from drowning. Mouse sued for damages for the loss of his casket, but the English court held that the action was justified by the need to save lives.
- In the infamous English case *R v Dudley and Stephens* (1884), shipwrecked sailors killed and ate a cabin boy to survive. The English Court of Appeal pointed out that the defence of necessity has clear limits. As a matter of both principle and policy, the Court held at 287–8 that killing an innocent person to save one's own life can never be justified.
- The Canadian case of *Murray v McMurchy* (1949) established that the defendant's actions must be necessary, not merely convenient. In this case, a doctor performing a caesarean delivery also sterilised the unconscious patient without her prior consent. The doctor justified the sterilisation by citing suspected tumours in her uterus, which made future pregnancies inadvisable, and argued it was more convenient for everybody to perform the procedure during the caesarean. The Court rejected the defence of necessity, holding (at 444–5) that while the operation may have been convenient, it was not immediately necessary for the patient's health at that time.
- In *Proudman v Allen* (1954) the defendant, in attempting to avert a collision, steered the plaintiff's car into the sea. Although this caused more damage than the initial threat posed, the Court upheld the defence of necessity. Hannan JA reviewed earlier authorities and explained that the law requires the defendant to act in a 'proper and reasonable manner', taking only those actions that a reasonable person would consider appropriate in the face of 'urgent necessity' and 'imminent danger'. Although here the defendant's intervention caused more damage than the original threat, he had acted reasonably in an urgent situation to prevent harm, so the defence was open to him.
- In *Southwark London Borough Council v Williams* (1971) a group of squatters, acting in an 'orderly manner' and out of 'great despair', occupied vacant houses owned by the local council. The Court of Appeal rejected the defence of necessity, with Lord Denning affirming at 743 that the defence could only apply in cases of 'great and imminent danger'. He further emphasised at 744 that the doctrine must be narrowly limited to uphold law and order. Similarly, Edmund Davies LJ noted at 746 that necessity is confined to 'urgent situations of imminent peril', warning that without such constraints it could easily become a 'mask for anarchy'. Megaw LJ added at 747 that decisions on policy issues, such as the allocation and use of housing, should remain the responsibility of elected political bodies rather than the courts.

- In *Re F (Mental Patient: Sterilisation)* (1990) Lord Goff explained (at 75) that the doctrine of necessity in a case of medical emergency imposed two requirements: first, there must be 'a necessity to act when it is not practicable to communicate with the assisted person' (eg when the person is unconscious); and second, 'the action taken must be such as a reasonable person would in all the circumstances take, acting in the best interests of the assisted person'.
- *Re A (Children) (Conjoined Twins: Surgical Separation)* (2000) involved conjoined twins who were going to die if they were not separated. However, separating the twins was going to hasten the death of one of them, creating potential legal liability for the surgeons. The Court authorised the surgery on the basis of necessity: it was held that the harm to be inflicted (the death of one child) was not be disproportionate to the harm that would be avoided (the death of both children). See also *Queensland v Nolan* (2001).
- In *Simon v Condran* (2013) the Court prevented a woman who had chased her dog onto her neighbour's property to rescue it from a dog fight from relying on the defence of necessity, as she had been negligent in allowing the dog onto that property. She was precluded from relying on the defence as her own conduct had brought about the emergency.
- In *New South Wales v McMaster* (2015) police attended the scene where a violent home invasion had taken place shortly before. A man who was the brother and son of the two victims was shot by one of the police officers after running at the other officer with a curtain rod. He sued the state of New South Wales, alleging the police officers were vicariously liable for battery. The Court of Appeal held that the defences of both necessity and self-defence were available in these circumstances.
- In *Rolles v Commissioner of Police* (2020) the defendant was a climate change protestor who was charged with criminal trespass. He claimed that his actions were necessary to avert global climate change. He lost, as the Court did not consider this to be a sufficiently sudden or exceptional emergency to justify his actions.
- In *Hannam v New South Wales (No 9)* (2022) the plaintiff was intoxicated and was at risk of falling or jumping off the balcony of a building. To prevent this from happening, the defendant (who was a police officer) tasered him. The defence of necessity was successful, with the Court holding that the defendant had not committed battery in these circumstances.
- In *Royal Caribbean Cruises Ltd v Rawlings* (2022) the plaintiff was a passenger on a ship who was accused of sexual assault against another passenger. The ship's captain detained the plaintiff in his cabin to prevent him from having further contact with the alleged victim or her family. While this was held to constitute false imprisonment, the ship's captain was able to successfully raise the defence of necessity. It was held that his actions were reasonably necessary for the safety of people on board the ship.

Active reading

Link each of the cases listed above to one of the elements of the defence.

7.4 Self-defence

The defence of self-defence is available when a defendant demonstrates that they acted reasonably to protect themselves against an imminent threat posed by the plaintiff. As Lord Scott of Foscote pointed out in the case of *Ashley v Chief Constable of Sussex Police* (2008) at [18], the defence balances conflicting rights:

> [E]very person has the right in principle not to be subjected to physical harm by the intentional actions of another person. But every person has the right also to protect himself by using reasonable force to repel an attack or to prevent an imminent attack. The rules and principles defining what does constitute legitimate self-defence must strike the balance between these conflicting rights.

While the defences of self-defence and necessity are similar, in that both seek to avert harm, self-defence is used when the need to act is triggered by the plaintiff's own prior act of wrongdoing, rather than by an externally caused emergency.

Self-defence is a defence in both criminal and civil law. In criminal law, the High Court in *Zecevic v Director of Public Prosecutions (Vic)* (1987) at 661 stated the test for self-defence to be whether the defendant:

> believed upon reasonable grounds that it was necessary in self-defence to do what he did. If he had that belief and there were reasonable grounds for it ... then he is entitled to an acquittal.

Although this is a criminal law case, this test – which includes both subjective and objective aspects – has been widely cited and adopted in torts cases (eg *Carter v Walker* (2010); *Illert v Northern Adelaide Local Health Network Inc* (2016)). While different texts break down the elements in slightly different ways, in general it appears that the defendant must prove that:

1. the defendant believed the plaintiff posed a threat of imminent harm to them;
2. the defendant believed it was necessary to use the force they used to protect themselves from that threat; and
3. there were reasonable grounds for the defendant's belief that it was necessary to use the force they used to protect themselves.

The first element relates to the defendant's state of mind – they must have believed that the plaintiff posed an imminent threat to them. This includes threats of physical harm, sexual violence and false imprisonment. If the threat was to another person or to property, the defences of 'defence of another' (see section 7.5 below) or 'defence of property' (see section 7.6 below) should be used instead. While the threat need not be immediate (ie about to happen in the next few seconds), it must be imminent. This generally requires the threat to have been so pressing that the defendant lacked a proper opportunity to consider alternative responses, such as calling the police.

Because this element relates to the defendant's beliefs, it doesn't matter if the threat did not actually exist. This element will be satisfied so long as the defendant genuinely *believed* there was a threat of imminent harm. However, if there were no reasonable grounds for that belief, the defendant will not be able to establish the third element (see below) and the defence will fail. They may also have difficulty persuading the judge that they actually held that belief.

In cases involving family violence, courts have recognised that the defendant's prior experiences can significantly influence their perception of an imminent threat. Defendants who have endured sustained abuse or coercive control may reasonably perceive a threat as imminent, even when it might not appear so to an outsider. The courts can consider the defendant's history with the plaintiff, including patterns of violence or intimidation, to assess whether their belief in the threat was genuine: *Ray v Southon* (2022) at [14].

The second element relates to the defendant's belief that it was necessary to use force to respond to the threat. It requires the defendant to prove that their actions were motivated by a genuine need to protect themselves, rather than by an ulterior purpose such as retaliation. It also requires the defendant to show that they believed the specific level of force they used was required in the circumstances, and that they hadn't gone beyond what they considered necessary. This can include pre-emptive action – the defendant is not required to wait for the plaintiff to strike first: *LO v Northern Territory* (2017).

The third element requires the defendant to prove that there were reasonable grounds for their belief that it was necessary to do what they did. This is an objective requirement that involves consideration of all of the surrounding circumstances. The court must not only determine whether there was a reasonable basis for the defendant to have used force in the circumstances, but also whether the force used was in reasonable proportion to the threat posed by the plaintiff. The court will assess proportionality by considering matters such as the nature of the threat faced by the defendant, the type of force they used and whether less harmful alternatives were available. For example, if someone was threatening to punch the defendant, hitting them may be considered proportionate but shooting them may not.

The courts are mindful of the pressure and urgency defendants face during such situations. They do not expect the defendant to precisely calibrate their actions to the perceived danger – they just want to ensure that they have not responded with excessive force (*Watkins v Victoria* (2010)). Factors such as whether the defendant used a weapon, the number of blows they inflicted or whether the threat was already neutralised will be relevant to this assessment. Courts will also consider whether there were realistic alternatives to using force, such as fleeing or seeking help. However, they recognise that defendants may not have the time or ability to fully evaluate all options. They also understand that in some circumstances (such as those involving a history of family violence) fleeing may not avert the threatened harm.

Some jurisdictions have enacted a statutory version of self-defence which applies to both civil and criminal cases.

LEGISLATION ALERT!

Consult your study materials to see whether there is any legislation in your jurisdiction that governs the defence of self-defence. An example is s 271 of the *Criminal Code Act 1899* (Qld).

Case examples

- In *Fontin v Katapodis* (1962) P hit D with a wooden T-square. D retaliated by throwing a piece of plate glass at P, which injured his hand. McTiernan J examined at 181–2 the rules on self-defence and pointed out that where the response by D is out of all reasonable proportion to the emergency confronting them, and where D had no need to stand their ground and could easily have avoided the threat by escaping, the defence was not available (see also Owen J at 186).
- In *McClelland v Symonds* (1951) Scholl J explained at 162 that any blows inflicted by a defendant on a helpless plaintiff after a threat had been extinguished would amount to a battery.
- In *Hall v Fonceca* (1983) it was held that a mistaken but nevertheless honest and reasonable belief in the need for self-defence would ground the defence, provided that the defendant acts reasonably in response to the perceived threat.
- In *Ashley v Chief Constable of Sussex Police* (2008) Lord Scott decided at [18] that 'for civil law purposes an excuse of self-defence based on non-existent facts that are honestly but unreasonably believed to exist must fail'.
- In *South Australia v Crossley* (2020) the Ds were police officers who used capsicum spray on P when arresting him. It was held that they had exceeded the bounds of reasonable self-defence, given the threat that P posed at the time of the spraying.

7.5 Defence of another

The defence of 'defence of another' operates similarly to self-defence, but applies when the defendant has used reasonable force to protect *someone else* (rather than themselves) from an imminent threat of harm. To rely on this defence, the defendant must establish the following elements:

1. The defendant believed that the plaintiff posed an imminent threat of harm to a third party.
2. The defendant believed it was necessary to use the force they used to protect the third party from that threat.
3. There were reasonable grounds for the defendant's belief that it was necessary to use the force they used to protect the third party.

As is the case for self-defence, the reasonableness of the defendant's belief and actions is central to the defence. Courts will consider factors such as the immediacy and severity of the threat, the nature of the response, the use of any weapons and whether there were alternative ways to avert the harm. Any use of excessive force will not be protected by this defence.

While this defence was originally restricted to cases where the defendant was protecting someone with whom they had a specific relationship, such as a spouse or child, this is no longer the case. The law now provides that everyone has the right to defend any other person from unlawful force, irrespective of their relationship: *Pearce v Hallett* (1969); *R v Portelli* (2004); *May v Thomas* (2014).

As with self-defence, many jurisdictions now have statutory versions of this defence, which may apply in civil as well as criminal cases.

LEGISLATION ALERT!

Consult your study materials to see whether there is any legislation in your jurisdiction that governs 'defence of another'. An example is s 52 of the *Civil Liability Act 2002* (NSW).

Case examples

- In *Goss v Nicholas* (1960) D attacked P in the belief that P was about to attack a third person – a stranger who was unrelated to D. Crawford J reviewed the authorities at 134–44 and concluded that the defence of another would be lawful if D had reasonable grounds for believing danger existed, and D's use of force was proportionate to the danger posed.
- In *Corowa v Winner* (2019) three men who had earlier threatened to kill D and his family went to his house armed with a gun and fence palings. D was in his car at the time and could have escaped. However, his fiancée and grandmother were in the front yard of the house. To protect his family, D drove into one of the men, badly injuring him. He successfully raised defence of another, as it was held that his actions were reasonably necessary to protect his fiancée and grandmother.

7.6 Defence of property

A defendant may also use reasonable force to protect their property from an imminent threat of harm. The elements of this defence are similar to the elements for self-defence and defence of another. The defendant must prove that:

1. they believed that the plaintiff posed an imminent threat to their property;
2. they believed it was necessary to use the force they used to protect their property from that threat; and
3. there were reasonable grounds for their belief that it was necessary to use the force they used to protect their property.

Once again, the reasonableness of the defendant's belief and actions is central to the defence – and courts will consider the same kind of factors (eg the urgency, magnitude and imminence of the threat). It should be borne in mind, however, that in this context the defendant is protecting *property* rather than a *person*. This will affect the court's assessment of proportionality. For example, it is unlikely to be considered reasonable to use lethal force solely to protect property.

Although not entirely clear, it is generally believed that this defence is limited to protecting one's own property. If the defendant's conduct was committed to protect someone else's property, the defence of necessity may instead be applicable (see section 7.3 above).

As with self-defence and the defence of another, some jurisdictions now have statutory versions of this defence, which may apply to civil cases.

LEGISLATION ALERT!

Consult your study materials to see whether there is any legislation in your jurisdiction that governs the defence of property. An example is s 277 of the *Criminal Code Act 1899* (Qld).

Case examples

In *Shaw v Hackshaw* (1983) and *Hackshaw v Shaw* (1984), the courts considered the lawfulness of a farmer's actions after he shot at a car parked by a thief during the night, injuring the thief's passenger. The farmer had been experiencing repeated petrol thefts and acted in an attempt to protect his property. Although the case was ultimately decided on other grounds, both the Supreme Court of Victoria and the High Court acknowledged the farmer's right to take reasonable action in defence of his property. However, the judges disagreed on whether the defence applied to the specific facts of the case. It is unclear whether it would be lawful to go so far as to take a life in such circumstances.

7.7 Infancy and incapacity

Defendants may sometimes argue that they should be absolved of blame because they were a child, or because they were experiencing mental health problems at the time of the relevant conduct. These kinds of claims are often accepted as defences in criminal cases, but mere 'insanity' or 'infancy' will not of itself excuse a defendant from civil liability. The law of torts, as a victim-focused practice, generally favours placing the loss on the person whose intentional conduct caused the invasion of another's rights, rather than on an innocent plaintiff (always provided the defendant was able to form an intention to act). This means that that the mere fact that a defendant was young, or did not know that their conduct was wrong, will not exempt them from liability (unlike at criminal law): *Morriss v Marsden* (1952); *Carrier v Bonham* (2001).

There are, however, some circumstances where the defendant's age or mental health condition may excuse them from tortious liability:

- If they were so young that they were unable to understand the nature of the act they committed.
- If their mental health condition caused them to behave involuntarily (eg they were acting in a state of dissociative automatism). This is a reflection of the general principle that a person cannot be held liable for involuntary acts: see Chapter 5.
- If their mental health condition meant that they did not understand the nature and quality of what they were doing.

Case examples

Infancy

- In *Smith v Leurs* (1944) a 13-year-old boy was found to be liable for firing 'a quantity of gravel and some apricots' at a group of boys with his shanghai and hitting one in the face. Mayo J explained at 217 that children of seven years and upwards are in general liable to compensate others for their own wrongs.
- In *Hart v Attorney-General (Tas)* (2006), a Tasmanian case decided in 1959 which was re-reported in 2006, both P and D were six years old. D chased P and slashed her face with a razor blade that he had found outside their primary school, saying, 'I'll get you' just before he did so. Burbury CJ reviewed the authorities at 3–5 (citing cases where children as young as four and five were held liable) and held at 4 that 'infancy is no defence'. D was liable in battery, notwithstanding his youth, because he intended the contact – and no other 'specific intention' was necessary: at 3. It did not matter that D was unable to appreciate the seriousness of his conduct or its consequences: at 3.
- In *McHale v Watson* (1964) Windeyer J suggested at 386 that children would be liable for their own torts if they were 'old enough to know better'.

Incapacity

- In *Weaver v Ward* (1616) the Court explained at 284 that 'if a lunatick hurt a man, he shall be liable in trespass'.
- In *Morriss v Marsden* (1952) D attacked P while experiencing schizophrenia. Because his mental illness prevented him from understanding that his actions were wrong, he was not criminally liable for his actions. However, he was held to be liable for assault and battery. Stable J held at 928 that as long as D understood the 'nature and quality of his act', the fact that his mental illness rendered him incapable of knowing that the act was wrong was not a defence in tort.
- In *Carrier v Bonham* (2001) D attempted to throw himself under the bus driven by P whilst experiencing schizophrenia. As a result, P experienced post-traumatic stress disorder (PTSD) and had to give up his job. All three members of the Queensland Court of Appeal agreed that D's mental illness did not afford a defence. The judges pointed out that the approach of the law of torts differs from that of the criminal law, with McMurdo P stating at [5] that 'the reason is that the civil courts are concerned, not to punish him, but to give redress to the person he has injured'.

7.8 Statutory authorisation

It is a defence to show that the defendant's action has been authorised by statute. For example:

- a police officer who arrests someone may have a defence to assault, battery and false imprisonment if the arrest was authorised;

- a police officer who enters a person's home and removes their goods may have a defence to trespass to land, trespass to goods, conversion or detinue if their actions were authorised by a search and seizure warrant.

In such circumstances it is important to look closely at the authorising legislation and the terms of any warrants that have been issued, to ensure that the defendant's actions fall within their scope and comply with any specified requirements (such as that the force used is reasonable).

In *Coco v The Queen* (1994) the High Court emphasised that where a statute is relied on as authority for otherwise tortious conduct, it must be clearly expressed in unmistakeable and unambiguous language.

Case example

In *Binsaris v Northern Territory* (2020) prison officers used CS gas on detainees in a youth detention centre. The detainees alleged that this constituted battery, but the police claimed it was authorised by statute. The Court looked closely at the terms of the relevant statutory provisions, which only permitted the use of a weapon (such as the CS gas) to maintain order in a prison or police prison – not in a youth detention centre. Consequently, as the use of this gas was not authorised by statute it was held to be a battery.

7.9 Self-help remedies

On rare occasions people are allowed to take the law into their own hands and help themselves directly to a remedy without having to go through the courts. These 'self-help remedies' include the following:

- *Recaption of goods*: A person entitled to possession of goods may reclaim them if they are wrongfully taken.
- *Re-entry on land*: A person entitled to immediate possession of land may re-enter it if unlawfully occupied.
- *Ejectment of trespassers*: A landowner may remove a trespasser using reasonable force.
- *Distress*: A landlord may seize a tenant's goods for unpaid rent.

Edmund Davies LJ explained in *Southwark London Borough Council v Williams* (1971) at 475 that the law regards these self-help remedies 'with the deepest suspicion' and permits them 'only in very special circumstances'. For example, they are all limited by a requirement to act reasonably. Notice must be given, as well as a reasonable time to comply, unless the other person has entered forcibly or is threatening to use force. In such cases, these requirements can be dispensed with. Any force used must be no more than is reasonably necessary in the circumstances. Any excessive or disproportionate use of force may give rise to liability.

Because of the risks involved in allowing people to take the law into their own hands, most jurisdictions have legislation that restricts the availability of these self-help remedies.

LEGISLATION ALERT!

Consult your study materials to see whether there is any legislation in your jurisdiction that limits the availability of self-help remedies. An example is s 80 of the *Residential Tenancies Act 1987* (WA).

Case examples

- In *Cowell v Rosehill Racecourse Co Ltd* (1937) P was asked to leave D's racecourse but refused to do so, making him a trespasser. D physically ejected him from the racecourse and was sued for battery. D successfully raised the defence of re-entry of land. The High Court held that D was entitled to use reasonable force to abate P's trespass to their land.
- In *Horkin v North Melbourne Football Club Social Club* (1983) the plaintiff's licence to be in the after-match room of the North Melbourne Football Club was revoked. He was physically ejected and sued for battery. He won, as it was held that the club had used excessive force to eject him, and the defence of ejectment of trespassers only permits the use of reasonable force.
- In *Toyota Finance Australia Ltd v Dennis* (2002) P's husband hired a car from D under a hire-purchase agreement. He fell behind in his payments, which under the agreement entitled D to repossess the car. D attempted to do so, but P resisted. There was a struggle for the car keys, in the course of which D grabbed and pulled on P's arm. D was sued for assault and battery. They argued that they were entitled to use force to regain possession of the vehicle, but they lost. In a 2:1 decision, the New South Wales Court of Appeal held that the defence of recaption of goods is limited to cases where the initial possession of the goods was unlawful, which was not the case here – P's husband was initially entitled to possession of the goods under the hire-purchase agreement, and only later lost that right (due to non-payment). In such circumstances, D needs to use other legal mechanisms (such as suing for detinue) to recover their goods.

7.10 Discipline

Discipline – or lawful chastisement – is a longstanding but controversial defence. Traditionally, certain relationships granted one party the right to impose moderate discipline or corporal (bodily) punishment on another, provided it was reasonable. These relationships historically included:

- parents and children;
- teachers and students;
- husbands and wives; and
- captains of ships and passengers or crew.

However, societal and legal shifts have significantly narrowed the application of the defence. The rights of husbands to physically chastise their wives are no longer recognised (*R v Reid* (1973)), and in most jurisdictions corporal punishment by teachers in schools is now prohibited by statute. The use of corporal punishment on children is controversial. While the defence is still recognised at common law, it is confined within strict limits. In *R v Terry* (1955) at 116, Scholl J held that the defendant must prove that:

1. their response to the child's wrongdoing was moderate;
2. their response had a proper relation to the age, physique and mentality of the child; and
3. their response was carried out with reasonable means or instrument.

The defence of discipline shares similarities with the defences of necessity and self-defence, focusing on the reasonableness and proportionality of the response. This is a question of fact to be assessed in light of all relevant circumstances, including:

- the child's age, health, and temperament;
- the parent's motive, attitude, and emotional state;
- the proportionality of the punishment to the child's wrongdoing; and
- whether a weapon or implement was used.

If the defendant goes beyond what is reasonable in the circumstances, the defence will not succeed. Cases where the defence is raised are rare, as it is uncommon for a child to sue their parent for battery. However, the defence may arise in cases where children, supported by their parents, bring actions against third parties who have disciplined them.

Case example

In *Lumb v Police* (2008) a childcare worker was convicted of assaulting a four-year-old child under her care. The incident occurred when the child refused to come inside as instructed. In response, the worker roughly picked up the child, carried her by the arms with her legs off the ground, and dropped her from a height of 45–60 centimetres on two occasions, causing the child to land forcefully. The worker raised the defence of discipline but failed, with the Court holding that the force used was not reasonable 'bearing in mind the age of the child, the behaviour sought to be addressed, ... the nature of the admonition and the [defendant's] behaviour'.

7.11 Procedural barriers to liability

In this section we consider two potential procedural barriers to liability: illegality and limitation of actions. Although these areas are sometimes treated like defences, they are conceptually different:

- *Defences* acknowledge that the defendant has committed the tort, but hold that the defendant should not be held liable for some reason (eg because their conduct was justifiable, excusable or authorised).
- *Procedural barriers* rely on broader legal principles or procedural rules to prevent the plaintiff's claim being adjudicated, regardless of the merits of the plaintiff's claim.

7.11.1 Illegality

A defendant may argue that the plaintiff's claim should be dismissed on the grounds that it arose out of the plaintiff's participation in an unlawful act. This argument is traditionally framed by the Latin maxim *ex turpi causa non oritur actio* (no cause of action arises out of a base – ie wrongful – act). However, the application of this rule to Australian tort law has been questioned. In *Smith v Jenkins* (1970), Windeyer J criticised the early cases in the area as 'conflicting', and stated at 414 that the rule 'has no place in our law' and should be limited to areas such as contracts and conveyances. Kitto J held at 403 that the principle applies only when *both* parties have knowingly participated in an illegal act, resulting in no legal rights arising between them due to their mutual participation. This approach to illegality was taken in the early Irish case of *Hegarty v Shine* (1878); however, the judges in that case precluded liability not only where the joint conduct was *illegal*, but also where the harm complained of by the plaintiff arose out of *immoral* conduct (ie fornication). This extension of the principle to merely immoral conduct is unlikely to be followed today.

Some jurisdictions have passed laws restricting people who are injured while engaging in unlawful acts from succeeding in tortious claims.

LEGISLATION ALERT!

Consult your study materials to see whether any legislation in your jurisdiction governs the entitlement of a plaintiff who has been injured in the course of committing an unlawful act to succeed in a claim for damages. An example is s 54 of the *Civil Liability Act 2002* (NSW).

Case examples

- In *Hegarty v Shine* (1878) the Irish Court of Appeal dismissed the plaintiff's claim on the grounds that it arose out of her own 'immoral life', and that for reasons of public policy and public decency (see 294, 299 and 301) it was correct to follow the views expressed by Fitzgerald J in the earlier case (at 276) that 'no polluted hand shall touch the pure fountains of justice'.
- In *Revill v Newbery* (1996) the defendant, a landowner who had been repeatedly targeted by vandalism and theft, shot a burglar. The case addressed the relevance of the plaintiff's illegal conduct in tort law. The English Court of Appeal held that a plaintiff who engaged in criminal activity is not automatically excluded from seeking compensation for injuries sustained. At 577 and 579, the Court emphasised that even those involved in unlawful acts do not become 'outlaws' who are 'debarred by the law from recovering compensation for any injury which [they] might sustain'. This decision reinforced the principle that illegal conduct does not wholly preclude a claim in tort, though it may be relevant to issues such as contributory negligence or the availability of certain defences.

A significant development in the doctrine of illegality occurred in English law with *Patel v Mirza* (2017). The United Kingdom Supreme Court, led by Lord Toulson, endorsed a policy-based approach, focusing on whether applying the doctrine would produce inconsistency and disharmony in the law or bring the legal system into disrepute. While *Patel v Mirza* was a case involving unjust enrichment, it has sparked academic debate, including Goudkamp's (2017) analysis in 'Does Patel v Mirza Apply in Tort?', on whether this approach could influence other areas of private law, including tort law.

7.11.2 Limitation of actions

A defendant may sometimes argue that the plaintiff's claim is barred because it was initiated after the legally prescribed time period for bringing such claims had expired (eg *Stingel v Clark* (2006); *Prince Alfred College Inc v ADC* (2016)). Limitation periods are set out in statutes (eg *Limitation Act 2005* (WA)) and vary depending on the type of claim (eg personal injury, contract or property disputes). The defendant must specifically plead the limitation period as a defence, as it is not automatically applied by the court. If the plaintiff is out of time, the court will not be able to hear the case, regardless of its merits. However, in some circumstances the court may be able to extend the limitation period.

LEGISLATION ALERT!

Consult your study materials to see which legislation governs the limitations periods in your jurisdiction. Note any differences between actions brought 'in tort' and actions brought for personal injury.

Defendants relying on this argument must clearly demonstrate when the cause of action accrued and that the claim was filed outside the applicable period. It is important to bear in mind that a single event or set of facts can give rise to liability under more than one tort - and that time may begin to run at a different point for each cause of action. For example, time for the tort of conversion begins to run when the goods are dealt with by the defendant, but time for the tort of detinue begins to run when the demand for the return of goods is made (see Chapter 6).

Case example

In *Wilson v Horne* (1999), a case involving child sexual abuse, the defendant was found liable for both battery and negligence. The liability for battery arose during the period from 1973 to 1980, corresponding to the time of the original physical contact between the defendant and the plaintiff. In contrast, the liability for negligence arose in 1994, when the plaintiff was diagnosed with PTSD arising from the abuse.

7.12 Non-defences

7.12.1 Mistake

In criminal law, an honest and reasonable mistake of fact can sometimes operate as a defence. However, this is not the case in tort law, where mistake of fact or law is not recognised as a defence: *Rendell v Associated Finance Pty Ltd* (1957); *Egan v State*

Transport Authority (1982). This means that even if the defendant honestly and reasonably believed they were entitled to act as they did, they will still be held liable. For example, a person who mistakenly enters land believing it to be their own will be liable for trespass to land (*Basely v Clarkson* (1681)) and an auctioneer who mistakenly sells goods believing they are entitled to do so will be liable for conversion (*Consolidated Co v Curtis & Son* (1892)).

7.12.2 Provocation

Provocation is generally not a defence to liability for intentional torts, such as assault and battery. Defendants remain liable for compensatory damages even if their actions were a heated response to highly provocative conduct by the plaintiff. However, in *Fontin v Katapodis* (1962) the High Court ruled that provocation by the plaintiff may operate to reduce an award of exemplary or aggravated damages: see Owen J at 186–7 and McTiernan J at 184.

In some jurisdictions, statutory provocation provisions may apply to civil cases of assault and battery, allowing provocation to be raised as a defence.

LEGISLATION ALERT!

Consult your study materials to see whether there is any legislation in your jurisdiction that allows the defence of provocation to be raised in relation to the intentional torts. An example is ss 245–247 of the *Criminal Code* (WA).

Case example

In the section on self-help remedies (section 7.9 above) we noted that in *Horkin v North Melbourne Football Club Social Club* (1983) D was unable to rely on the defence of re-entry to land, as they had not used reasonable force to eject P from the premises. The Court awarded compensatory damages, noting at 162 that the provocation offered by P was no defence. P's provocative conduct did, however, operate to prevent any award of aggravated or exemplary damages.

7.13 Final problem-solving tips

When you are faced with an intentional torts problem in an exam or assignment, it can be easy to feel overwhelmed by the range of possible causes of action and defences. The following problem-solving tips are designed to give you a structured way to approach the question, diagnose the relevant issues, and present your answer clearly and efficiently.

7.13.1 Tips on diagnosis

Refer to Figures 7.1–7.6 in the 'Look up' section at the end of this chapter to help diagnose the possible torts, the parties, the damage done (if any) and the issues. Remember: look for the adverse or harmful effects and then work out whose conduct caused those effects. Remember also that some torts tend to go together or are linked. For example:

- assault and battery often occur together;
- the tortious actions relating to goods can overlap on the facts, so check for all possibilities.

7.13.2 Tips on writing the introduction

When you are introducing an intentional torts problem with several torts, you have to get to the point. You should adapt the 'six-point plan' in your introduction by listing the parties, the torts and the conduct. An illustration follows.

> There are three possible suits arising on these facts:
>
> *Rosalie v Jim* in assault and battery for the latter hitting the former with a branch of a tree.
>
> *Prue v Penny* in battery for the latter punching the former in the arm (possible self-defence).
>
> *Martin v Ian* in trespass to goods and possibly conversion for hiding his laptop.

Note that the generic formula is:

'AAA' (P) v 'BBB' (D) in the tort of 'XXX' for 'YYY'.

AAA = insert name of the plaintiff

BBB = insert name of defendant

XXX = insert name of the specific tort

YYY = identify the positive act carried out by D from the facts

Add a brief statement about damages being sought to complete the introduction. You can find the remedies in section 2.3.3.2 of Chapter 2.

7.13.3 Tips on writing the body of the answer (remember FIRO)

Take each suit in turn.

1. Identify the tort, then turn back to its overview table to look for the issues.
2. Briefly explain which of the elements are easily made out, and then spend more time on any aspects that may be in doubt using HIRAC to argue the issues out, using your knowledge of the cases.
3. Consider any defences, and then move on to the next suit and repeat the process.

(Read Chapter 3, where you can find further advice and examples.)

In an exam you can save time (and words) by using the sentence in the relevant figure at the end of this chapter that covers all of the elements instead of writing out each element separately. Remember: you can cross-reference within an answer. This means that you do not need to write out the same definition of the elements of the torts more than once. If a similar issue arises in two different causes of action, you can also cross-reference.

7.13.3.1 Defences

For a defence to succeed, the defendant (D) must establish all of its elements on the balance of probabilities. Recall that there is some uncertainty about whether consent operates as a true defence (to be proved by the defendant) or whether lack of consent is part of the tort itself (to be proved by the plaintiff (P) – see section 7.2.1 of Chapter 7).

Inevitable accident

The claim that D's action was an 'inevitable accident' is not a true defence – it is a denial of liability. However, it is often treated as a defence.

D will not be liable if they were utterly without fault. This will be the case if they acted involuntarily, or (depending on the tort) if their conduct was not intentional, reckless or negligent.

Consent

- P explicitly or implicitly consented to D's conduct.
- P had the capacity to consent.
- P broadly understood the nature of what D proposed.
- P's consent was voluntary (ie it was not produced by force, threats, duress, undue influence or fraud as to the nature of the act or the identity of D).
- D's conduct was within the scope of what P consented to.

Necessity

- There was imminent danger to person or property.
- It was reasonably necessary for D to act to preserve the person or property.
- The steps D took were reasonable and proportionate.
- D did not bring about the danger by their own fault.

Self-defence

- D believed that P posed a threat of imminent harm to them.
- D believed it was necessary to use the force they used to protect themselves from that threat.
- There were reasonable grounds for D's belief that it was necessary to use the force they used to protect themselves.

Defence of another

- D believed that P posed an imminent threat of harm to a third party (T).
- D believed it was necessary to use the force they used to protect T from that threat.
- There were reasonable grounds for D's belief that it was necessary to use the force they used to protect T.

Defence of property

- D believed that P posed an imminent threat to their property.
- D believed it was necessary to use the force they used to protect their property from that threat.

- There were reasonable grounds for D's belief that it was necessary to use the force they used to protect their property.

Infancy

- D was so young that they were unable to understand the nature of the act they committed.

Incapacity

- D was experiencing a mental health condition that:
  - caused them to act involuntarily; or
  - meant that they did not understand the nature and quality of what they were doing.

  The mere fact that D did not know that their conduct was wrong is not a defence.

Statutory authorisation

- D's actions were authorised by statute (eg they were undertaking an authorised arrest).

  Look closely at the authorising legislation and the terms of any warrants that have been issued, to ensure that D's actions fell within their scope and complied with any specified requirements.

Self-help remedies

Self-help remedies include the following:

- Recaption of goods: A person entitled to possession of goods may reclaim them if they are wrongfully taken.
- Re-entry on land: A person entitled to immediate possession of land may re-enter it if unlawfully occupied.
- Ejectment of trespassers: A landowner may remove a trespasser using reasonable force.
- Distress: A landlord may seize a tenant's goods for unpaid rent.

These remedies are generally limited by a requirement to:

- give P notice and a reasonable time to comply; and
- act reasonably and proportionately.

Discipline

- D's response to the child's wrongdoing was moderate.
- D's response had a proper relation to the age, physique and mentality of the child.
- D's response was carried out with reasonable means or instrument.

7.13.3.2 Procedural barriers

Illegality

P's claim may be barred if it arose out of their participation in an unlawful act. However, the application of this principle to the intentional torts has been doubted. It is possible the barrier only applies when both parties have knowingly participated in an illegal act together.

Limitation of actions

P's claim may be barred because it was initiated after the legally prescribed time period for bringing such claims had expired. Carefully consider when the relevant cause of action accrued.

7.13.3.3 Non-defences

Mistake

Mistake of fact or law is *not* a defence.

Provocation

Provocation is not a defence to the intentional torts at common law. However, it may operate to reduce an award of exemplary or aggravated damages.

Conclusion

As you have seen in this chapter, the defences contain many fuzzy rules that offer you the opportunity to show off your skills in arguing the facts. They require you to focus very carefully on the circumstances of the individual case, and to construct arguments and counterarguments based around the themes of reasonableness and fault, in order to decide the question of whether the defendants were justified in acting as they did. On a deeper level, the defences also require you to address a fundamental legal question: under what conditions can we justify holding a person accountable for causing one of 'life's misfortunes'?[3] Once you have worked your way through all the elements and made out a prima facie case, you have established that the defendant invaded the plaintiff's protected interests. If any damage has also been done, the plaintiff will also have suffered a loss on top of that invasion of their rights. The issue then becomes whether a defendant who appears to have done something that the law forbids should be held liable for causing that misfortune – or whether the misfortune should be left solely as a matter for the plaintiff to deal with.

The role of the defences in the intentional torts is critical to determining whether the courts will uphold the wrongfulness of the defendant's conduct or whether they will excuse the conduct and leave the loss where it falls. They require you to go beyond the facts and to focus on the essential values and principles that underpin the intentional torts. Familiarity with these goals, values and principles will assist you to construct strong, purposeful arguments that engage directly with the essential concepts of fault, wrongdoing and responsibility. So, before you begin the problem-solving questions below, take a moment to familiarise yourself once more with the contents of the following tables:

3 See section 2.3 of Chapter 2, explaining Jules Coleman and Arthur Ripstein's characterisation of the law of torts as a debate about 'who owns life's misfortunes'.

- Table 1.1 'Tort law's guiding principles'
- Table 3.1 'Six types of legal argument'.

You should also check through the previous two chapters to remind yourself of the guiding principles that justify the existence and shape of each tort, so that you can think about how to use those principles to strengthen your arguments about the proper application of the defences in any given case. At the end of this chapter there is a 'Look-up' section comprised of Figures 7.1–7.6: these flow charts contain the key elements of each tort and the essential ingredients of each of the defences. Taken together, the elements of the torts and the defences to those torts specify the conditions under which one person will justly be held liable to compensate another for their wrongful conduct. Once you appreciate the way the elements and defences combine to strike a balance – not only between the competing rights of the parties, but also between the competing goals of the community – you will understand better tort law's unique conception of interpersonal wrongdoing and the complicated system of interlocking rights and obligations that it constructs to deal with that wrongdoing.

If you take a moment to compare and contrast the nature of the rules contained in the elements and the defences you will see how – and why – the law needs to undertake that balancing exercise. The elements of the trespass torts consist predominantly of bright-line rules that construct a perfect world where no one is allowed to directly invade the protected rights of others. They represent the world that we want to live in. The defences recognise that we do not live in that ideal world. They force us to take a more pragmatic view and recognise that as human beings who live together, we have to take the reality of our own nature into account and deal with the fact that as a community we must achieve some kind of balance between our competing goals and interests. The defences recognise that it is impossible to make a simple set of bright-line rules that can cover all of the tricky situations and ethical dilemmas that we face as human beings. The fuzzy rules found in many of the defences do most of the hard moral work in the intentional torts, and this why they will challenge you to take your skills in legal argument to a higher level of complexity and sophistication.

The key to mastering those skills lies in developing your understanding of the deeper challenge that the law of torts must face: how do we justify and apply a set of rules that governs and guides human conduct? Once you understand that the answer to this question involves balancing our desire for idealism with our need for pragmatism, you will realise that the elements and the defences are two sides of the same coin. After you have completed the chapters on the torts of nuisance, negligence and defamation, you will see how the law of torts faces the same conundrum every time, but weighs the balance between the elements and the defences – and between clear bright-line rules that are easy to apply and complex fuzzy rules that are dominated by the ubiquitous concept of reasonableness – slightly differently in each case. You will also understand why the arguments about the law of torts will never be concluded, and why we will never be completely satisfied with the particular balance that each generation draws between idealism and pragmatism. It is because these two defining but distinct aspects of human nature can never be completely reconciled.

Test your understanding

Problem solving

Refer to Figures 7.1–7.6 at the end of this chapter to help diagnose the relevant torts and any possible defences.

Problem 1

Paloma is a tenant in a block of flats. Her landlord, Darien, wanted to rent the flat to his friend Arthur as soon as the lease expired (on 8 April). On 7 April, Darien and Arthur went around to the flat to inspect it and, because the door was wide open, they went straight in without knocking. Paloma, who was busy packing for her move – and who was expecting the removalists to arrive – did not see them enter the flat.

Arthur looked into the bedroom of Paloma's son, Manuel. He spotted a huge model of a spaceship that Manuel has spent six months making out of 'Konstructo', a connecting toy lent to Manuel by his cousin Pablo. Being an inquisitive type, Arthur could not resist pulling some of the pieces apart to see how the spaceship was held together, and the whole model fell to pieces. Paloma heard the noise of the Konstructo crashing onto the floor and rushed terrified into the bedroom, shrieking, 'What do you think you are doing? Get out of here, you vandal!' She pushed the two men out of the room and wondered what on earth she was going to say to Manuel, who was planning to enter his model into a Konstructo competition that weekend. She decided to go to the police to see what could be done about the situation.

On her way to the police station, Paloma began to feel very unwell. Thinking that it would be safer to pull off the road, she drove hurriedly into one of two empty parking bays nearby. There was a notice on the fence which read:

> Private Parking! Trespassers will be prosecuted and any vehicle left on the premises is liable to be towed away or wheel-clamped.

The notice would have been visible to anyone standing up in the car park, but Paloma, who had been violently sick on the footpath soon after getting out of the car, and who had then rushed into a nearby building to ask for assistance, did not see the sign.

After having made her complaint about Darien to the police, Paloma wearily trudged back to her car, only to discover that it had been wheel-clamped. She found the parking attendant, Lionel, and demanded her car back, but he refused to release the car unless she paid $500. A tired and angry Paloma, who felt too weak to walk the distance to get a taxi, pleaded with Lionel to make an exception, but after arguing for 15 minutes, she paid under protest and went home. Paloma, who is outraged at what she says is the invasion of her home, the destruction of Manuel's Konstructo spaceship, and the high-handed attitude of Lionel, the parking attendant, seeks your legal advice.

Your research reveals the following provisions in your local *Residential Tenancy Act*.

> 24 Right of entry
>
> 1. Subject to this section, an owner of premises must not enter the premises without the tenant's permission.

2. An owner of residential premises may enter the premises at any time without the tenant's permission if it is reasonably believed that –
   a. the tenant is ill or injured and is unable to give permission;
   b. a denial of immediate access is likely to result in damage to all or part of the premises;
   c. there is a risk to the tenant or another person present on the premises;
   d. damage has occurred to the premises; or
   e. it is reasonably believed that the premises have been abandoned.
3. An owner of residential premises may enter the premises by giving at least 24 hours notice to the tenant if entry is for one of the following reasons:
   a. to meet commitments under the residential tenancy agreement;
   b. if it is reasonably suspected that the tenant has failed to comply with any provision of the residential tenancy agreement;
   c. to ensure that repairs have been properly carried out; or
   d. to carry out routine inspections once every 3 months.
4. An owner of residential premises may enter the premises without the approval of the tenant to show the premises to one prospective tenant only and any persons accompanying the prospective tenant on the giving of not less than 48 hours notice in writing to the tenant, and within one month before the expiry of the agreement.

What advice would you give Paloma?

Problem 2

Medea had a job at the Fragrant Garden, an outlet that specialised in selling imported scented flowering plants and seed stock. Earlier this year, Medea was accompanying Jason up to the second floor of the shop to show him the latest seed imports from Greece. Jason was a regular customer who always asked Medea out on a date whenever he came to the shop. This time, as the lift doors closed, Jason moved over very close to Medea, and began whispering into her ear. He told Medea all the sexually intimate things that he had done with his previous girlfriend, Gloria – in quite graphic detail – and said he would like to do the same with her if she came out on a date with him that night. Medea, who had been sexually assaulted as a young girl, panicked and kneed Jason in the groin. She then dashed out of the lift in such a rush that she cannoned into Petunia, a co-worker waiting with a crowd of others to get into the lift. Petunia fell over and knocked a valuable vase out of the hands of Flossie, who was on her way to set up a new display in the Fragrant Garden's display window.

Medea became so upset at the thought of encountering Jason again that she left her job and changed her phone number. She began to suffer flashbacks about the events in the lift and the event triggered a recurrence of her nightmares about her previous sexual assault. They become so frequent that she had to consult a doctor. Jason, who could not get his attraction to Medea out of his mind, found out where she lived and started to hang around her house at night, regularly leaving handwritten messages and presents in her letterbox for her to find in the morning. Medea became very worried about Jason's behaviour, so she borrowed her father's rifle and kept it under her bed. One night, six weeks later, Medea saw Jason outside her house again and rang the police from her bedroom. A little while after making the call she heard a rattle at the front door. Medea grabbed the rifle and yelled out, 'Go away – I've called the police!' It was dark and she could not see very well. She thought that she heard someone inside her hallway and so she used the rifle – firing twice before she heard a scream and stopped. She turned on the lights and saw Talos, a policeman, who had been sent out to investigate her call, lying on the floor of her hall, writhing in pain from a wound to his upper chest.

Discuss the claims that could be made on these facts. Would your answer differ if the person on the floor of Medea's hall turned out to be Jason instead of Talos? (This problem question is an elaboration of the discussion in Conaghan and Mansell, The Wrongs of Tort *(1998) at 170.)*

Problem 3

Your client, Peter, has come to you seeking legal advice. Some years ago, at his annual health check with Dr Xavier, the latter had suggested an 'IAC' examination. Peter, who had never heard of the test, was initially reluctant but Dr Xavier, who had treated Peter as his family doctor for over 12 years, explained that the new test could reveal the existence of a virulent new strain of highly infectious anal colitis with 100 per cent accuracy. He had added that not only would Peter be helping others by participating in the special screening program that he was conducting, but that it would also be in Peter's best interests to take the test in order to eliminate any question of incipient infection. After a lengthy discussion, Peter consented. The test revealed no health problems.

This year, however, Peter became aware that Dr Xavier had been brought before the Australian Medical Practitioners Board after it came to light that, by comparison with other doctors, he had been overzealous in his use of the screening test. Despite the fact that the infection was almost never found in males who had not engaged in anal sexual intercourse, Dr Xavier had screened all of his male patients. On hearing that the examination may have been unnecessary, Peter, who has always been an intensely private, physically modest, shy person, began experiencing devastating flashbacks of the invasive examination. These flashbacks led to a severe, but rare, psychiatric condition that has disabled him since that time. Peter, who has never engaged in anal sex, tells you that giving consent would have been out of the question had he known that he was unlikely to have contracted the infection.

Discuss Peter's chances of success in any legal action against Dr Xavier, identifying any facts that you would need to ascertain in order to advise him fully. (Once you have completed the chapters on negligence, you will be able to return to this question and discuss a different set of issues.)

Look up: Intentional torts, defences and procedural barriers (Figures 7.1–7.6)

Figure 7.1 Battery

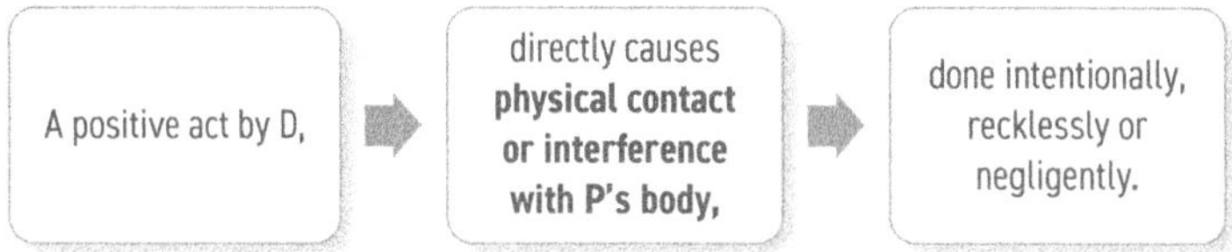

Figure 7.2 Assault

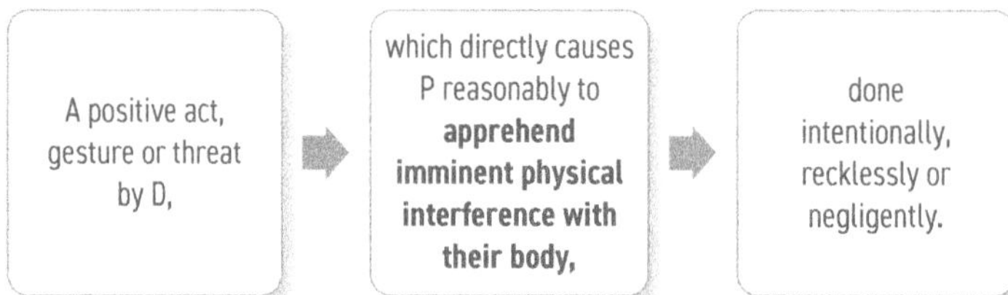

Figure 7.3 False imprisonment

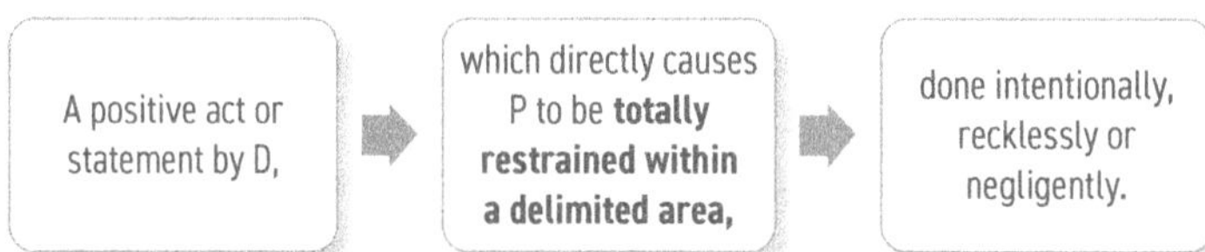

Figure 7.4 Trespass to goods

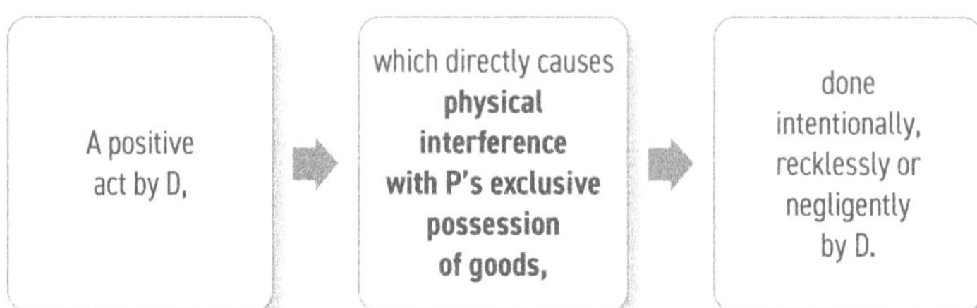

Figure 7.5 Conversion

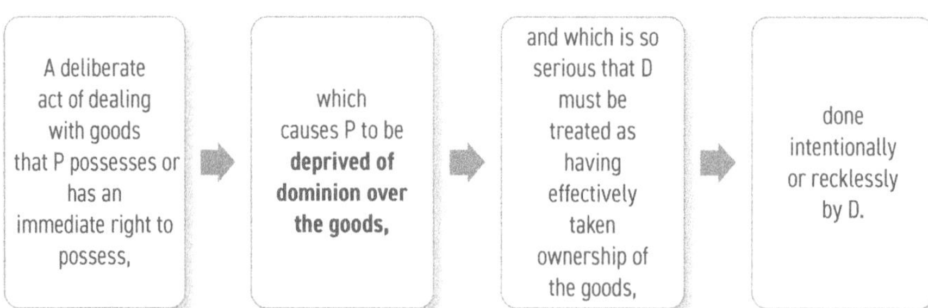

Figure 7.6 Detinue

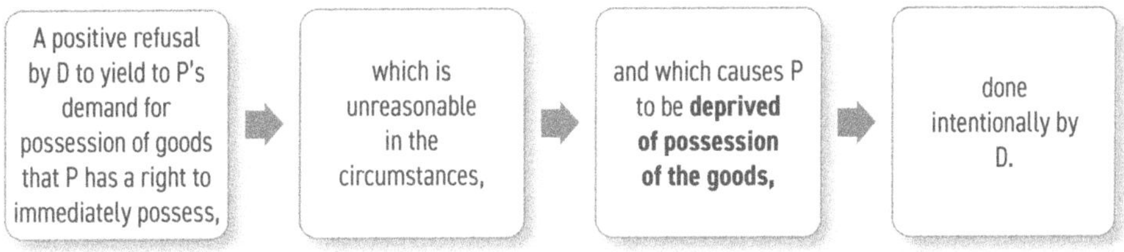

REFERENCES

CASES

Ashley v Chief Constable of Sussex Police [2008] 1 AC 962
Basely v Clarkson (1681) 83 ER 565
Beausoleil v Communaut (1964) 53 DLR (2nd) 65
Binsaris v Northern Territory (2020) 270 CLR 549
Brightwater Care Group (Inc) v Rossiter [2009] WASC 229
Carrier v Bonham [2001] QCA 234; [2002] 1 Qd R 474
Carter v Walker (2010) 32 VR 1
Chatterton v Gerson [1981] QB 432
Christopherson v Bare (1848) 11 QB 473
Coco v The Queen (1994) 179 CLR 427
Consolidated Co v Curtis & Son [1892] 1 QB 495
Cope v Sharpe (No 2) [1912] 1 KB 496
Corowa v Winner [2019] QDC 135
Cowell v Rosehill Racecourse Co Ltd (1937) 56 CLR 605
Croucher v Cachia [2016] NSWCA 132
Dean v Phung [2012] NSWCA 223
Egan v State Transport Authority (1982) 31 SASR 481
Falconer v Commissioner of Police (WA) (No 2) [2024] WASCA 47
Fontin v Katapodis (1962) 108 CLR 177
Freeman v Home Office (No 2) [1984] QB 524
Gillick v West Norfolk and Wisbech Area Health Authority [1986] AC 112
Giumelli v Johnston [1989] SASC 1880
Goss v Nicholas [1960] Tas R 133
Hackshaw v Shaw (1984) 155 CLR 614
Hall v Fonceca [1983] WAR 309
Halliday v Nevill (1984) 155 CLR 1
Hannam v New South Wales (No 9) [2022] NSWSC 648
Hart v Attorney-General (Tas) (2006) 14 Tas R 1
Hegarty v Shine (1878) 14 Cox's Criminal Cases 145; (1878) 4 LR IR 288
Horkin v North Melbourne Football Club Social Club [1983] 1 VR 153
Hunter and New England Area Health Service v A (2009) 74 NSWLR 88
Illert v Northern Adelaide Local Health Network Inc [2016] SASC 186

Kassam v Hazzard [2021] NSWSC 1320
LO v Northern Territory [2017] NTSC 24
Lumb v Police [2008] SASC 198
May v Thomas [2014] WASCA 176
McClelland v Symonds [1951] VLR 157
McHale v Watson (1964) 115 CLR 199
Moon v Whitehead [2015] ACTCA 17
Morriss v Marsden [1952] 1 All ER 925
Mouse's Case (1609) 12 Co Rep 63; 77 ER 1341
Murray v McMurchy (1949) 2 DLR 442
National Coal Board v Evans [1951] 2 KB 861
New South Wales v McMaster (2015) 91 NSWLR 666
Papadimitropoulos v The Queen (1957) 98 CLR 249
Patel v Mirza [2017] AC 467
Pearce v Hallett [1969] SASR 423
Prince Alfred College Inc v ADC (2016) 335 ALR 1
Proudman v Allen [1954] SASR 336
Queensland v Nolan [2001] QSC 174
R v Clarence (1888) 22 QBD 23
R v Dudley and Stephens (1884) 14 QBD 273
R v Portelli (2004) 10 VR 259
R v Reid [1973] 1 QB 299
R v Richardson [1999] QB 444
R v Tabassum [2000] EWCA Crim 90
R v Terry [1955] VLR 114
R v Williams [1923] 1 KB 340
Ray v Southon [2022] NSWCA 267
Re A (Children) (Conjoined Twins: Surgical Separation) [2000] 4 All ER 961
Re B (Adult: Refusal of Treatment) [2002] 2 All ER 449
Re C [1994] 1 WLR 290
Re F (Mental Patient: Sterilisation) [1990] 2 AC 1
Rendell v Associated Finance Pty Ltd [1957] VR 604
Revill v Newbery [1996] 2 WLR 239; [1996] 1 All ER 291
Rigby v Chief Constable of Northamptonshire [1985] 2 All ER 986; [1985] 1 WLR 1242
Rogers v Whitaker (1992) 175 CLR 479
Rolles v Commissioner of Police [2020] QDC 331
Roy v O'Neill (2020) 272 CLR 291; [2020] HCA 45
Royal Caribbean Cruises Ltd v Rawlings (2022) 107 NSWLR 51; [2022] NSWCA 4
S v G [1995] 3 NZLR 681
Scalera v Non-Marine Underwriters, Lloyd's of London (2000) 185 DLR 1
Secretary, Department of Health and Community Services v JWB and SMB (1992) 175 CLR 218 *(Marion's Case)*
Shaw v Hackshaw [1983] 2 VR 65
Simon v Condran [2013] NSWCA 388

Smith v Jenkins (1970) 119 CLR 397
Smith v Leurs [1944] SASR 213
South Australia v Crossley [2020] SASCFC 128
Southwark London Borough Council v Williams [1971] 1 Ch 734
Stanley v Powell [1890] 1 QB 86
Stingel v Clark [2006] HCA 37; (2006) 228 ALR 229
Tinnock v Murrumbidgee Local Health District (No 6) [2017] NSWSC 1003
Toyota Finance Australia Ltd v Dennis (2002) 58 NSWLR 101
Watkins v Victoria (2010) 27 VR 543
Weaver v Ward (1616) Hob 134; 80 ER 284
White v Johnston (2015) 87 NSWLR 779
Wilson v Horne [1999] Aust Torts Reports 81-504
X v Sydney Children's Hospital Network (2013) 85 NSWLR 294
Zecevic v Director of Public Prosecutions (Vic) (1987) 162 CLR 645

ARTICLE AND BOOKS

Conaghan, J and Mansell, W, *The Wrongs of Torts,* 2nd ed (1998) Pluto Press, London.
Goudkamp J, 'Does Patel v Mirza Apply in Tort?' [2017] (July/August) *Personal Injury Law Journal* 1.
Goudkamp, J, *Tort Law Defences* (2013) Hart Publishing, Oxford.

8 NUISANCE

Introduction

Nuisance is a tort that responds to interferences with the use and enjoyment of land, or with rights shared by the community at large. It is a flexible cause of action, capable of addressing diverse harms such as smoke, noise, odours and obstruction of access to public places. Although often categorised under tort law, nuisance has long straddled the boundaries between private law, public law and regulatory regimes.

There are two kinds of tortious nuisance actions, each with a distinct focus and legal framework:

- *The tort of private nuisance* focuses on the use and enjoyment of land (or some right over or interest in land). It is a civil wrong giving rise to an ordinary tort suit between two persons.
- *The tort of public nuisance* focuses on conduct that obstructs defined public rights or threatens the common rights of a substantial number of people in a relatively wide area. Cases of public nuisance are generally brought by the Attorney-General to protect the broader public interest. However, in limited circumstances individuals can bring an action if they have suffered 'special' or 'particular' damage that goes beyond the harm experienced by the general public.

There is also a criminal offence of public nuisance, which focuses on similar issues to the tort of public nuisance, but instead of the Attorney-General bringing a civil action, the state prosecutes individuals under relevant criminal law statutes.

In modern legal systems, the boundaries of nuisance are increasingly shaped by legislation. For example, planning laws, pollution control statutes, environmental regulations and airport zoning schemes often interact with or override common law nuisance principles. These types of legislative regimes may limit the scope of nuisance by authorising certain conduct, prescribing alternative remedies or displacing common law actions altogether. As a result, the availability and utility of nuisance claims often depend on navigating the complex interface between common law and statutory regulation.

This chapter primarily focuses on the tort of private nuisance, but it also provides a brief overview of the tort of public nuisance.

8.1 The place of nuisance in tort law

Nuisance occupies a unique position in tort law, protecting interests in land by addressing interferences that are not covered by other torts, such as trespass to land and negligence. Its development alongside trespass reflects its historical roots in the common law, with both torts evolving to safeguard different aspects of land ownership and use. Trespass focuses on direct physical interference with possession, while nuisance generally addresses indirect interferences affecting the use, enjoyment or condition of land. By contrast, negligence addresses a failure to exercise reasonable care resulting in harm. These distinctions are explored further below (and summarised in Figures 8.1–8.3).

The tort of nuisance existed long before the modern tort of negligence, and for some years it was doubted whether the emergence of the tort of negligence had left it any real role to play – until the environmental movement breathed new life into the tort, and others who wanted to reform the law began to see it as one way to offer protection from invasions of privacy and other antisocial conduct like harassment and stalking.

8.1.1 Nuisance vs trespass to land

There are several key differences between nuisance and trespass to land:

- Trespass to land requires a direct act that interferes with the plaintiff's exclusive possession of land, such as entering or physically placing objects on the land without permission. By contrast, nuisance typically involves indirect interferences, such as noise, smells or vibrations, which affect the use or enjoyment of the land rather than its possession.
- Trespass to land protects the right to exclusive possession, ensuring the plaintiff can control access to their property. By contrast, nuisance focuses on broader rights, such as the ability to enjoy land free from unreasonable interference.
- Trespass to land is actionable per se. By contrast, nuisance requires proof of material damage to property or substantial interference with amenity, or a threat of damage or substantial interference which the action seeks to prevent.

Although nuisance is often described as *requiring* an indirect interference, this is not entirely accurate. Nuisance can also arise from direct interferences with amenity, such as intentionally creating loud noise to irritate neighbours: see, for example, *Christie v Davey* (1893). However, nuisance typically addresses indirect interferences, whereas trespass to land always requires a direct interference. Importantly, these torts are mutually exclusive; the same conduct cannot simultaneously form the basis for both. If there is a direct interference with the right to exclusive possession of land, the appropriate action is trespass to land: see Chapter 6.

8.1.2 Nuisance vs negligence

Nuisance and negligence share some common features. For example:

- they may arise either from an act or an omission (a failure to act); and
- they are both uncertain areas of law dominated by the concept of reasonableness.

However, the two torts differ in several ways:

- Negligence assesses whether the defendant's conduct fell below an objective standard of care, while nuisance considers whether the interference with the plaintiff's land was unreasonable.
- Negligence requires proof of fault, whereas nuisance is a tort of strict liability (meaning a defendant may be liable even if they exercised reasonable care to avoid the interference).
- Negligence focuses on the defendant's failure to meet an objective standard, whereas nuisance involves balancing the rights of landowners to use their land against the impact on neighbours.

Trespass to land, private nuisance and negligence are illustrated in Figure 8.1, Figure 8.2 and Figure 8.3.

Figure 8.1 Trespass to land

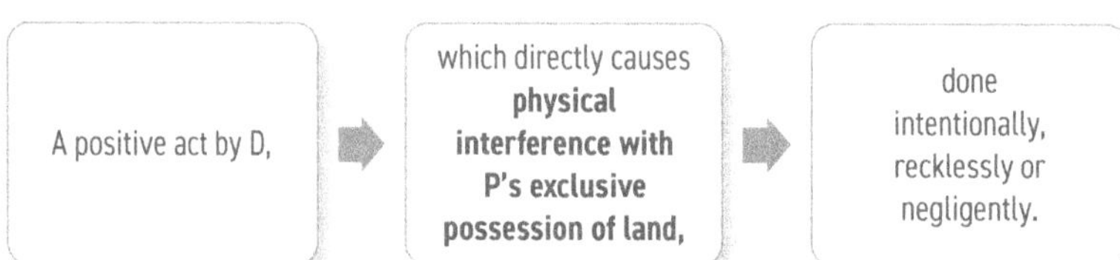

Figure 8.2 Private nuisance

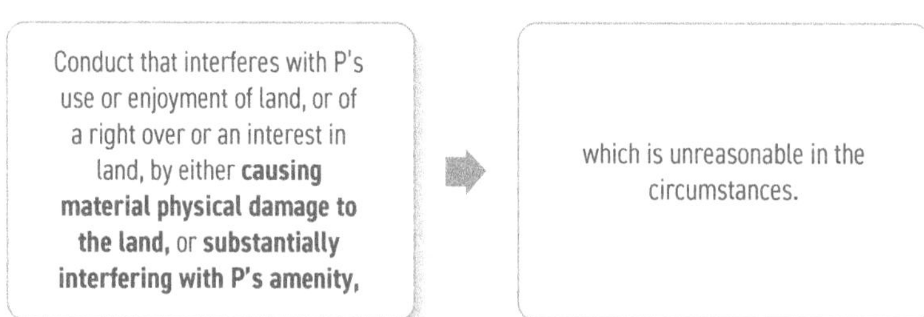

Figure 8.3 Negligence

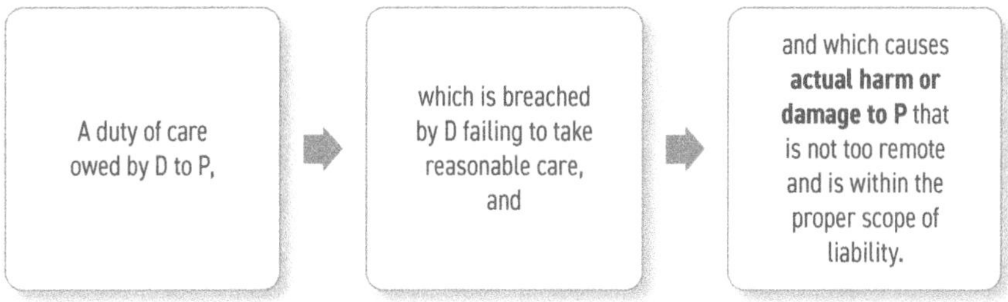

8.2 Private nuisance

8.2.1 The nature of private nuisance

The law of private nuisance is uncertain: its definition is elusive, its precise scope is unclear and its role in the modern law of torts has been challenged by the rise of negligence. In 1867, Ehle CJ sent a warning in *Brand v Hammersmith and City Railway* (1867) at 247 that is as true today as it was over 150 years ago.

> *This cause of action is immersed in undefined uncertainty;* there is no standard by which to measure degrees of annoyance, or to estimate the effect of circumstances; each neighbour is a source of some annoyance; proximity necessitates mutual forbearance; the degree of forbearance to be required is measured by the sensibility to feelings of delicacy of the tribunal which has to decide the case, and cannot be foreseen till that decision is given. The maxim, '*sic utere tuo at alienum non lædas,*' [use your own property in such a way that you do not harm another's] is no help to decision, as it cannot be applied till the decision is made; and the use of the word 'nuisance' in the discussion prolongs the dispute, because it means both annoyance that is actionable, and also that which is not actionable; and where the question is, whether an annoyance is actionable, the word nuisance introduces an equivocation which is fatal to any hope of a clear settlement. [Emphasis added.]

This warning emphasises how important it is to remember that there is a critical distinction between the factual conduct and the legal label given to that conduct.

While the precise bounds of the tort of private nuisance are unclear, in general terms it is an action that forbids conduct that causes an unreasonable and substantial interference with another person's use and enjoyment of land or an interest in land. The elements of the tort are as follows:

1. The defendant's conduct interfered with another person's use or enjoyment of land, or of a right over or an interest in land (eg an easement), by either:
   a. causing material physical damage to the land; or
   b. substantially interfering with their amenity.
2. The interference was unreasonable in all the circumstances.

Although the first element is framed in terms of the defendant's *conduct,* it is important to note that this does not need to be a positive act. As discussed in section 8.2.9 below, the defendant can be liable for failing to act in certain circumstances. For example, a person can be held liable for failing to prevent a fire from spreading onto their neighbour's property: *Goldman v Hargrave* (1966).

While nuisance is considered to be a single tort, in reality it encompasses two separate categories of interference: material damage and substantial interference with amenity. These categories are treated differently, with the Court holding in *St Helen's Smelting Co v Tipping* (1865) that distinct legal tests apply depending on the type of nuisance involved:

- In material damage cases, it is presumed that the interference was unreasonable in all the circumstances, and thus that the second element is satisfied. The onus shifts to the defendant to prove (if they can) that the interference was reasonable.
- In interference with amenity cases, it is for the plaintiff to prove that the interference was unreasonable in all the circumstances.

Consequently, when considering a nuisance situation, it is crucial to first determine whether the alleged nuisance has caused material damage or merely interfered with amenity, as this will decide which approach to take. Where a case involves both material damage and interference with amenity, the court will deal with each claim separately, applying the relevant legal test. An example of this can be seen in the leading case of *Halsey v Esso Petroleum* (1961) (see 'A case to remember' below). This case is important because it summarises many of the tests from the earlier case law that you will use in problem solving. It also serves as a reminder that conduct giving rise to a private nuisance may also in some cases amount to a public nuisance. The action was described by the judge (at 688) as a case where 'the little man' asked for legal protection from the activities of 'a large and powerful neighbour'.

A case to remember

***Halsey v Esso Petroleum* [1961] 1 WLR 683**

Topics

Public and private nuisance; pollution by airborne acid deposits, vibrations, noise and smell by day and night; defence of prescription.

Facts

Halsey (P) owned a house in a residential area. Since 1896, Esso Petroleum (D) had operated an oil depot across the road in an industrial area. The *conduct* complained of by P was that D stored large quantities of oil at the depot for distribution throughout the city at night by 'exceptionally heavy oil tankers' and used steam boilers in a boiler house to heat and manufacture fuel oil. The *effects* on P were as follows:

- *Pollution:* Noxious sulphuric acid smoke, acid smuts and drops of oil emitted from the depot's boiler chimneys caused material physical damage, including corrosion of the paintwork on P's car parked on the street, damage to curtains inside the house and holes in laundry hanging outside.

- *Smell:* The heated oil emitted odours ranging from a 'general background of occasional oily smells' to a 'vile' and 'pungent nauseating smell'.
- *Noise:* The depot's boilers produced noise levels of 63 decibels ('loud') day and night, while nighttime convoys of up to 18 tankers generated noise reaching 83 decibels ('very loud'), causing P's doors and windows to vibrate and disrupting his sleep.

Issues

1. Was the conduct causing the noise, smell and airborne acid deposits sufficiently substantial and unreasonable to amount to a private nuisance?
2. Could the damage to the car, which took place on the public road and was not therefore an interference with P's use and enjoyment of his own land, amount to a public nuisance?
3. Could Esso claim the defence of prescription, given that they had operated the depot for over 20 years?

Reasoning

On the issue of *pollution* by noxious acid smoke, acid smuts and oil droplets, Veale J summarised the relevant law from previous authorities, and at 689–90 cited *St Helen's Smelting Co v Tipping's* (1865) distinction between:

- conduct that causes 'material injury' to property; and
- conduct that produces 'sensible personal discomfort'.

Veale J noted that nuisances causing personal discomfort must be assessed in light of the locality, while material physical injury to property is considered inherently unreasonable regardless of the location. Consequently, the acid deposits that damaged washing drying on P's land constituted a private nuisance. However, the oil droplets, being infrequent and non-damaging, did not amount to a private nuisance given the industrial nature of the locality.

Regarding the damage to the paintwork of P's car, Veale J explained at 692 that it was not a private nuisance because the car was parked outside P's land. However, it was deemed a public nuisance, because the acid smuts affected a widespread area and P suffered 'special damage' (ie more than an ordinary member of the public).

In relation to *interferences with amenity* (such as smell and noise) generally, Veale J noted:

- The test is whether the effect is 'an inconvenience materially interfering with the ordinary physical comfort of human existence' (at 691).
- 'It is no answer to say that the best known means have been taken to reduce or prevent the noise complained of, or that the cause of the nuisance is the exercise of a business or trade in a reasonable and proper manner' (at 691).
- There is 'no absolute standard' to be applied – it is 'always a question of degree' to be considered in the light of 'all the relevant circumstances' (at 691).
- 'What might be a nuisance in one area is by no means necessarily so in another' (at 691–2).
- 'In an urban area, everyone must put up with a certain amount of discomfort and annoyance from the activities of neighbours, and the law must strike a fair and reasonable balance between the right of the plaintiff on the one hand to the undisturbed enjoyment of his property, and the right of the defendant on the other hand to use his property for his own lawful enjoyment' (at 692).

- The standard to be applied is that of 'the ordinary reasonable and responsible person who lives in [the] particular area' (at 692).

On the issue of smell, Veale J explained that 'injury to health is not a necessary ingredient'. Whether a smell constitutes a nuisance 'depends on the whole of the circumstances, including the character of the neighbourhood and the nature, intensity and frequency of the smell'. In this case, the heated oil's pungent and nauseating smell, which was 'far beyond any triviality' and 'more than would affect a sensitive person', was deemed an actionable nuisance. However, the general background oily smell was *not* sufficiently substantial or unreasonable to amount to an actionable nuisance, given the locality (at 696).

On the issue of noise, Veale J held that the test was whether the noise was so loud that it would interfere with ordinary conversation or prevent sleep at night by an ordinary person wanting to rest (at 696–7). The noises from the boilers and the trucks satisfied both tests and were a private nuisance. The noise from the concentration of the tankers into the area at night was also a public nuisance from which P suffered special damage.

The *defence of prescription* failed because it requires the conduct being complained of to have continued for at least 20 years – but here, although D had operated the depot for that long, the acts causing the nuisance had only occurred for a few years (at 696).

8.2.2 Examples of nuisance

Private nuisance covers a very wide range of conduct committed by private individuals or large corporations that can cause an equally wide range of effects. To understand nuisance, you should begin by thinking about all the different things we might want to do in our homes and on our land, and consider all the ways that we can be harmed or annoyed by the conduct of our neighbours. The cases demonstrate that, beyond the easy cases of physical damage (eg caused by fire, flood or subsidence), our enjoyment or use of land can be interfered with in many diverse ways. These interferences can impact all our senses – sight, sound, smell, touch and even our sense of morality – demonstrating the far-reaching scope of this tort.

Case examples

People have been successful in nuisance cases involving various conduct, such as the following:

- The use of a large pestle and mortar by a confectioner to break up and pound loaf sugar: *Sturges v Bridgman* (1879).
- The activities of the Salvation Army, which carried out Sunday services accompanied by brass bands, shouting and clapping from 7.00 am to 9.30 pm: *McKenzie v Powley* (1916).
- The keeping of pigeons: *Fraser v Booth* (1949).
- A dairy's use of horses to deliver milk, giving rise to flies emanating from the stables, the smell of manure and urine, and the noise of horses and other early-morning activities: *Munro v Southern Dairies Ltd* (1955).
- The irritations and physical damage caused by cricket ovals and golf courses: *Bolton v Stone* (1951); *Miller v Jackson* (1977); *Lester-Travers v City of Frankston* (1970).

- Forms of 'moral nuisance', including the operation of clinics treating sexually transmitted diseases, funeral parlours, brothels and sex shops: *Laws v Florinplace* (1981).
- Breathing problems and asthma caused by dust from a lumber mill: *Devon Lumber v MacNeill* (1987).
- Harassing phone calls and physical stalking: *Khorasandjian v Bush* (1993).
- Floodlights and motion activated surveillance cameras aimed at the plaintiff's property: *Raciti v Hughes* (1995).
- Wind turbines operating at a wind farm: *Uren v Bald Hills Wind Farm* (2022).

However, not all adverse effects on a neighbour will necessarily amount to an actionable nuisance. For example, in *Hunter v Canary Wharf Ltd* (1997) the plaintiffs complained (among other things) about the interference with their television reception that was caused by the construction of what was then Britain's highest building. While some of the judges recognised that the ability to receive television signals was an important aspect of modern life that could be protected by the tort, it was held that the cause of the interference must be taken into account in determining whether a nuisance has been committed. If the interference resulted from electrical emanations caused by the defendant's activities that may be sufficient. However, in this case the interference arose from the 'mere presence' of a lawfully constructed building under an approved planning scheme. This did not meet the requirements for nuisance.

8.2.3 The guiding principle of 'give and take'

In *Bamford v Turnley* (1860), Baron Bramwell pointed out at 33 that private nuisance is animated by the 'give and take' or 'live and let live' principle, which aims to balance two competing private interests against each other: the right of a person to use their land as they see fit, and the right of their neighbour to use and enjoy their land without unreasonable interference. This balancing process emphasises that private nuisance is not a rights-based tort like trespass, but a tort that is dominated by the ubiquitous (and fuzzy) concept of reasonableness – and focuses on what is reasonable as between one neighbour and another. As Lord Millett maintained in *Southwark London Borough Council v Tanner* (2001) at 20, the 'governing principle is good neighbourliness, and this involves reciprocity'.

8.2.4 Overview of private nuisance

8.2.4.1 Conduct

- There must be either:
  - a positive act by the defendant; or
  - a failure by the defendant to rectify a state of affairs on land occupied by them that was caused by another person or an act of nature (*Sedleigh-Denfield v O'Callaghan* (1940); *Goldman v Hargrave* (1966); *De Jager v Payneham & Magill Lodges Hall Inc* (1984); *Hunter v Canary Wharf Ltd* (1997)).

- Note that the defendant may be either the person whose conduct created the nuisance *or* the person who occupies or owns the land from which it emanated (see under 'Fault' below).

8.2.4.2 Effect

- The act or omission by the defendant must cause either:
  - material physical damage to another's land; or
  - substantial interference with the use or enjoyment of another's land (*St Helen's Smelting Co v Tipping* (1865); *Hargrave v Goldman* (1963)).

8.2.4.3 Fault

- The defendant must have either:
  - intended the act that created the damage/state of affairs; or
  - authorised, adopted or continued that state of affairs.
- The defendant does not need to have intended to cause the damage or to have interfered with the plaintiff's use or enjoyment of their land (*Sedleigh-Denfield v O'Callaghan* (1940)).
- A person implicitly authorises a nuisance by allowing their property to be used for a purpose that carries a specific risk of that nuisance (*De Jager v Payneham & Magill Lodges Hall Inc* (1984)).
- A person adopts a nuisance by making use of whatever it is that constitutes the nuisance (*Sedleigh-Denfield v O'Callaghan* (1940)).
- A person continues a nuisance when they know about it, or ought to know about it, but do not take reasonably prompt and efficient steps to remedy it (*Sedleigh-Denfield v O'Callaghan* (1940) *Lippiatt v South Gloucestershire Council* (1999)).
- In determining whether the defendant has taken reasonable steps to remedy a state of affairs caused by a natural hazard, the court will take into account the defendant's personal circumstances (*Goldman v Hargrave* (1966); *Leakey v National Trust* (1980)).

8.2.4.4 Circumstances

- The interference must be unreasonable in all the circumstances (*St Helen's Smelting Co v Tipping* (1865)). The plaintiff must have standing to sue.
- The law in Australia is uncertain in this regard:
  - Some cases have held that the plaintiff must have a recognised interest in the land – for example, the right to possession of the land (as an owner or lease holder) or exclusive factual possession (eg as a squatter) (*Oldham v Lawson (No 1)* (1976); *Hunter v Canary Wharf Ltd* (1997); *Pemberton v Southwark London Borough Council* (2000)).
  - Other cases have held that a person 'normally living' on a property may sue, at least in relation to interference with comfort and amenities, provided the plaintiff is exercising a 'right to occupy the family home' or P's occupancy amounts to a 'substantial link' to the land (*Motherwell v Motherwell* (1976); *Khorasandjian v Bush* (1993); *Animal Liberation (Vic) Inc v Gasser* (1991)).

- The kind of damage must be reasonably foreseeable (*Overseas Tankship (UK) Ltd v The Miller Steamship Co* (1967) (*'The Wagon Mound (No 2)'*); *Gales Holdings Pty Ltd v Tweed Shire Council* (2013)).
- There must be no lawful justification for the conduct. It will be a defence if Parliament authorised the defendant's conduct and its adverse effects on the plaintiff (*Manchester Corporation v Farnsworth* (1930); *Southern Properties (WA) Pty Ltd v Executive Director, Department of Conservation and Land Management* (2012)).

8.2.5 Material damage

One of the two primary categories of private nuisance is nuisance involving material damage. As noted above, the legal approach to these cases is distinct from cases involving interference with amenity, with unique tests and burdens of proof applied.

Material damage cases are guided by the principles established in *St Helen's Smelting Co v Tipping* (1865), where Lord Westbury clarified that actual physical damage to property is almost inherently unreasonable, regardless of the locality. Consequently, to succeed in a material damage claim, the plaintiff only needs to demonstrate that the defendant's conduct caused the damage. Once established, the onus shifts to the defendant, who must prove that the interference was reasonable: *Kraemers v Attorney-General (Tas)* (1966); *Corbett v Pallas* (1995). This will generally be difficult to establish, making material damage cases much easier to win than interference with amenity cases.

A person's property can be materially damaged in many ways: for example, their house can be burned down, their basement can be flooded or vibrations can cause their walls to crack. Cases have made it clear that the damage does not need to be to buildings. Nuisance cases have been successful where the defendant's conduct has caused material damage to vegetation (*St Helen's Smelting Co v Tipping* (1865)) or goods (*Halsey v Esso Petroleum* (1961)) on the plaintiff's land. Where the plaintiff has suffered material damage, they will often be able to purse a negligence claim as well as a nuisance claim – these actions are not mutually exclusive.

8.2.6 Interference with amenity

The second category of private nuisance is nuisance involving interference with amenity. Unlike cases involving material damage, this category focuses on personal inconvenience and discomfort, rather than physical harm to property. It often involves sensory disturbances or other intrusions that discompose or injuriously affect the senses or the nerves: *St Helen's Smelting Co v Tipping* (1865) at 1486.

There are various ways in which a person's use and enjoyment of land can be interfered with, including by the following disturbances:

- Loud or persistent noises: *McKenzie v Powley* (1916); *Uren v Bald Hills Wind Farm* (2022).
- Offensive odours: *Munro v Southern Dairies Ltd* (1955).
- Offensive sights: *Laws v Florinplace* (1981).
- Lights: *Raciti v Hughes* (1995).
- Surveillance: *Raciti v Hughes* (1995).
- Infestations of flies or other pests: *Munro v Southern Dairies Ltd* (1955).

- Balls flying into the yard: *Bolton v Stone* (1951).
- Dust: *Devon Lumber v MacNeill* (1987).
- Smoke: *Pittman v Newport* (2022).
- Electronic interference: *Hunter v Canary Wharf Ltd* (1997).
- Blocking entry to the property ('besetting' it): *Fertility Control Clinic v Melbourne City Council* (2015).
- A persistent threat of catastrophic harm (eg a large boulder sitting above the plaintiff's property which could fall at any time): *Frost v Northern Beaches Council* (2022).

However, there are some forms of conduct which might annoy a person, but which do not constitute a nuisance. For example, in *Victoria Park Racing and Recreation Grounds v Taylor* (1937) the defendant built a tower to observe and broadcast races held on the plaintiff's property. The plaintiff argued that being observed in this fashion constituted nuisance, but he lost. The High Court of Australia ('High Court') held that merely being observed does not interfere with one's use or enjoyment of their property. The fact that it interfered with his business interests (as people stopped going to the races) was irrelevant. This should be distinguished from being constantly surveilled, which can constitute a nuisance. For example, in *Raciti v Hughes* (1995), where motion-activated floodlights and cameras intrusively monitored a neighbour's backyard, there was held to be a substantial interference with the plaintiff's amenity which constituted a nuisance.

A similar issue was recently addressed in the United Kingdom case of *Fearn v Board of Trustees of the Tate Gallery* (2023). In that case the Tate Modern art gallery had built a viewing platform which was approximately 30 metres away from a block of luxury flats. The plaintiffs, who were residents of the flats, complained that visitors to the platform could see directly into their homes, often taking photographs or staring into their living spaces. They argued that this amounted to a substantial and unreasonable interference with their use and enjoyment of their property. In a split decision, the United Kingdom Supreme Court held that there was a nuisance. In the majority's view, the visual intrusion from the platform went beyond what could be considered the ordinary use of land and substantially interfered with the plaintiffs' enjoyment of their property. They characterised the platform as creating a 'constant visual intrusion' that was highly disruptive. It is unclear whether, in light of the High Court of Australia's judgment in *Victoria Park Racing and Recreation Grounds v Taylor* (1937), Australian courts would take the same approach.

There are two steps involved in resolving a case involving interference with amenity. First, you need to determine whether the alleged interference is *substantial* (see section 8.2.7). This requires you to consider whether it is more than a trivial interference with the plaintiff's use and enjoyment of their land. If it is, you must then determine whether it is *unreasonable in the circumstances*, taking into account the relevant factors identified in previous cases and looking at the matter from both points of view (see section 8.2.8 below). This involves balancing the competing rights of the plaintiff to enjoy their land and the defendant to use their property.

8.2.7 Substantial interference

For an interference with amenity claim to succeed, the interference with the plaintiff's amenity must be more than trivial – it must be substantial. This is an acknowledgement of the fact that when people live together in a community, they will often do things that annoy each other – and we don't want them constantly taking each other to court! For example, if you live in an apartment building, you may occasionally make noise late at night as you rummage around in your fridge for something to eat. That shouldn't provide grounds for your neighbour to sue you, even if they get irritated by it. Legal redress should be limited to matters that *substantially* interfere with the use or enjoyment of land.

This restriction makes sense if you think about what the tort is trying to do – which is to balance the interests of the plaintiff to enjoy their property against the defendant's interests in lawfully using their property. You don't want to penalise any little interference with the plaintiff's amenity, or that would unjustly impede the defendant's rights to use their land. You only want to prevent conduct which significantly affects their life, and which is unreasonable in the circumstances.

In determining whether an interference is substantial, the court considers how it affects ordinary, everyday living. In the words of the Court in *Walter v Selfe* (1851) at 322, it has to be something that materially interferes with 'the ordinary physical comfort of human existence, not merely according to elegant or dainty modes and habits of living, but according to plain and sober and simple notions obtaining among English people'.

Whether conduct constitutes a substantial interference is going to depend on the specific nature of the nuisance. For example, if it is noise, you need to consider how loud it is, how frequent it is and when it occurs. By contrast, if it is smell, you need to consider the nature of the smell, its intensity and its frequency. This is a question of fact, and you need to remember not only that there are no absolute 'bright-line' rules in this area of the law, but also that the issues of substantiality and unreasonableness (discussed in section 8.2.8 below) do overlap to a certain extent. As Murray CJ explained in *McKenzie v Powley* (1916) at 15, this kind of nuisance is 'emphatically a question of degree'. To begin, you need to focus on what the victims can see, hear, smell, inhale and feel – using both their physical senses and their moral senses. Then you need to go on to consider the flow-on effects that those sensory perceptions may lead to. What do they prevent the victims from doing – and what kinds of embarrassment, upset, pain and discomfort do they force the victims to suffer? Focus on the facts and the inferences that you can draw from those facts. The cases give some guidance.

Case examples

Noise

Consider whether the conduct:

- interferes with ordinary conversation or prevents sleep at night by an ordinary person wanting to rest (*Halsey v Esso Petroleum* (1961) at 696);
- is 'exceptive', unusual or excessive (*McKenzie v Powley* (1916) at 17–18 and 30–3); or
- causes 'the loss of even one night's sleep' (*Munro v Southern Dairies Ltd* (1955) at 335).

Smell

Consider the whole of the circumstances, including the 'character of the neighbourhood, the nature, intensity and frequency of the smell', bearing in mind that while the plaintiff does not have to show that the smell interfered with health, it must be 'more than would affect a sensitive person' (*Halsey v Esso Petroleum* (1961) at 496).

Moral nuisance, harassment and besetting

Consider the whole of the circumstances, including whether:

- the conduct is likely to offend ordinary reasonable people in the district, taking into account the nature of the business (*Laws v Florinplace* (1981) at 665–6);
- the conduct interferes with the plaintiff in the 'comfortable and convenient enjoyment of his land', taking into account the 'usages of civilised society', the character of the neighbourhood, and the effect on the minds of the plaintiff's children and the feelings of visitors (*Thompson-Schwab v Costaki* (1956) at 654 and 656, a case where residents complained about being able to see prostitutes and clients entering and leaving a brothel located in their street);
- the conduct is objectionable, harassing and 'plainly calculated to harm' (*Khorasandjian v Bush* (1993) at 679);
- people are intimidated and surrounded 'with hostile demeanour' and 'put in fear of safety' by conduct 'plainly calculated to put people in fear' (besetting) (*Animal Liberation (Vic) Inc v Gasser* (1991) at 58–9).

8.2.8 Unreasonable interference

The cases also make it clear that ordinary everyday conduct by one person will *not* amount to a private nuisance, unless the conduct is also unreasonable in all the circumstances – even if it does cause a substantially adverse effect on another person's use and enjoyment of land.

Case example

In *Southwark London Borough Council v Tanner* (2001) the plaintiffs were tenants in a block of flats built in 1919 and run by the local council. They complained about the fact that the inadequate sound insulation between the flats allowed them to hear all the noises created by the day-to-day living of the neighbours. Lord Hoffmann identified the conduct and the effects at 7:

> The tenants can hear not only the neighbours' televisions and their babies crying but their coming and going, their cooking and cleaning, their quarrels and their love-making. The lack of privacy causes tension and distress.

However, even though the effects of the neighbours' conduct amounted to a substantial interference with the plaintiffs' use and enjoyment of their flats, Lord Hoffmann concluded at 15 that 'the normal use of a residential flat' could not 'possibly be a nuisance to the neighbours. If it were, we would have the absurd position that each, behaving normally and reasonably, was a nuisance to the other.' Lord Millett, citing *Bamford v Turnley* (1860), explained (at 20) that it is 'no answer to an action for nuisance to say that the defendant is only making reasonable use of his land'. Rather, activities that would otherwise be actionable will be exempted under the reasonableness rule if the conduct is both 'necessary for the common and ordinary use and occupation of land and houses' and 'done with proper consideration for the interests of neighbouring occupiers'.

Reasonableness is to be judged according to the standards of the ordinary, reasonable person living in the district. This means that plaintiffs are not entitled to recover where they are affected by the defendant's conduct solely because they are:

- unduly sensitive to noise, smell or any other form of interference (*Munro v Southern Dairies Ltd* (1955) at 335); or
- carrying on 'an exceptionally delicate trade' (*Robinson v Kilvert* (1889) at 97; *McKinnon Industries v Walker* (1951) at 581). However, there may be an exception to this rule if the defendant's conduct interferes with the health and safety of people involved in the plaintiff's business (see *Onus v Telstra Corporation Ltd* (2011)).

Case examples

- In *Robinson v Kilvert* (1889) the plaintiff stored special brown paper in their factory. The alleged nuisance was heat that came from the defendant's property, which dried out the paper, making it weigh less. Because the paper was priced by weight, this caused the plaintiff economic loss. Their nuisance action was unsuccessful, because it was held that the heat wouldn't have been a problem for the ordinary person. It was only a problem for them because they were abnormally sensitive to heat.
- In *Onus v Telstra Corporation Ltd* (2011) the plaintiff operated an airfield on their land. The defendant planned to build a 35-metre tower on their land next door, which would interfere with the safety of people flying to and from the plaintiff's airfield. While the tower would not have interfered with the ordinary person's use of their land, it was nevertheless held to constitute a nuisance as it posed a danger to aviation safety.
- In *Marsh v Baxter* (2015) the plaintiffs were organic farmers affected by GM contamination of their crops by their GM-farming neighbour. The defendant's conduct wouldn't have affected an ordinary person's use of their land, so it wasn't considered unreasonable. The Western Australian Court of Appeal noted at 127 that '[a]n interference which "alone causes harm to something of an abnormal sensitiveness does not of itself constitute a nuisance."'.

It is important to note that the plaintiff can recover if the defendant's conduct *would* substantially and unreasonably interfere with ordinary people's use and enjoyment of land, but they suffer *additional damage* because they are particularly sensitive or vulnerable. For example, if ordinary people would have been substantially and unreasonably affected by the heat radiating from the defendant's factory in *Robinson v Kilvert* (see above), the plaintiff may have been able to recover the additional damages they suffered because of the damage to their paper. This would be a question of remoteness of damage rather than liability (with the 'eggshell skull' rule applying). However, if the conduct wouldn't substantially and unreasonably interfere with ordinary people, then the plaintiff cannot recover.

When judges consider whether an interference is unreasonable, they weigh the substance of the interference together with several 'relevant factors' (discussed below), such as the location of the conduct, and its duration and frequency. For example, the plaintiff may have established that the noise of a neighbour's renovations is extremely loud; however, if those renovations are only temporary, then the plaintiff may have to 'live and let live' and tolerate the annoyance under the 'give and take' principle. But if the defendant is doing their renovations at 4 am, the plaintiff doesn't need to put up with that – there are bounds to what is reasonable. The point is that people who live near each other have to put up with a certain amount of irritation from their neighbours, but only what is reasonable given all of the circumstances.

It is important to bear in mind that the 'relevant factors' discussed below are not essential *elements* of the action – they are just matters that may be relevant to determining whether an interference was unreasonable. This means that you do not necessarily need to work your way through *every* one of them in your answer to every problem – rather, you should focus only on those that are pertinent on the facts.

8.2.8.1 The nature of the defendant's activity

In determining whether the defendant's conduct amounts to a nuisance, the nature of their activities is an important consideration. The courts assess whether the activity is reasonable based on the ordinary usages of people living in the particular locality: *Sedleigh-Denfield v O'Callaghan* (1940) at 903. For instance:

- if it is something that is ordinarily done by people in the area, and is done with proper consideration for their neighbours, it is unlikely to be considered unreasonable (see, eg, *Southwark London Borough Council v Tanner* (2001));
- if it is a trade that needs to be carried out, and that by necessity must cause some level of inconvenience, it also may not be unreasonable (see, eg, *Lester-Travers v City of Frankston* (1970)).

The fact that an activity is lawful, charitable or socially useful does not preclude it from being classified as a nuisance. For instance, in *McKenzie v Powley* (1916), the noise created by the Salvation Army's activities was held to be a nuisance, as was the operation of a suburban dairy in *Munro v Southern Dairies Ltd* (1955), despite its value to the community. However, the social utility of the defendant's conduct can be a relevant, though not decisive, factor. For example, in *Uren v Bald Hills Wind Farm* (2022), the Court considered the social utility of generating clean energy in its assessment of whether the operation of a wind farm amounted to a nuisance; however, it ultimately concluded that because the wind turbines interfered with the plaintiff's sleep they were a nuisance, despite their utility.

8.2.8.2 Location of the events

While the locality of the neighbourhood in which the nuisance occurs is not relevant in material damage cases (as all damage is presumptively unreasonable, regardless of where it occurs), the location of the conduct is often highly relevant in interference with amenity cases. As the Court noted in *Sturges v Bridgman* (1879) at 865, what constitutes a nuisance in one area may not constitute a nuisance in another.

The key thing to note here is that the assessment of reasonableness is not to be determined merely by abstract consideration of the defendant's conduct, but by reference to its circumstances. If the conduct is in keeping with the character of the neighbourhood, it may not be a nuisance: *St Helen's Smelting Co v Tipping* (1865). For example, if you live in an area with a lot of background traffic noise, sounds emanating from a nearby pub may not be considered a nuisance: *Ammon v Colonial Leisure Group Pty Ltd* (2019). By contrast, if you live in a rural area that is usually quiet at night, the sound of nearby wind turbines may be considered unreasonable: *Uren v Bald Hills Wind Farm* (2022).

8.2.8.3 Time, duration and frequency of the interference

The time of day or night at which the interference occurs may be a relevant factor. For example, an activity that may be perfectly reasonable at midday may be completely unreasonable at midnight. Courts are particularly concerned to protect the sleep of people living in residential areas, often finding that causing the loss of even one night's sleep is unreasonable: see, for example, *Andreae v Selfridge & Co Ltd* (1938). The duration and frequency of the conduct may also be relevant. Courts tend to give more leeway to temporary activities (eg construction work), with nuisance cases generally relating to ongoing states of affairs. However, even temporary activities may be found to be unreasonable, depending the circumstances. For example, it would usually be unreasonable to begin construction work at 3 am, unless there was an emergency.

8.2.8.4 Permits, licences and standards

An issue that sometimes comes up in nuisance cases is whether compliance with permits or licences shields a defendant from liability. For example, a defendant may hold a council permit to operate a particular business, or a licence to carry out an activity, and may argue that because they complied with the terms of the permit or licence their actions were not unreasonable. This is not, however, how the law in this area works. The mere fact that a person acted in compliance with a permit or license does not mean that their acts are reasonable. They still have an obligation to act in a reasonable manner, regardless of their permit or license – and if their conduct constitutes an unreasonable interference with the plaintiff's use and enjoyment of land, then it will be a nuisance regardless of the permit or licence: *Lawrence v Fen Tigers* (2014).

A similar approach is taken in relation to standards (eg noise or pollution standards).

- If the defendant's conduct was *within* the standards, that may provide an indication that their conduct is reasonable, but it is not conclusive. The reasonableness of their conduct is still going to need to be judged by reference to factors such as time of day, frequency, duration and location.
- If the defendant's conduct *exceeded* the standards, that also is not going to be conclusive. While it may indicate that their conduct was unreasonable, again that needs to be determined by reference to all the circumstances: *De Gruchy v The Owners – Units Plan No 3989* (2020); *Uren v Bald Hills Wind Farm* (2022).

8.2.8.5 Malicious motives

In most nuisance cases the defendant will not have acted with ill will towards the plaintiff: they will merely have engaged in conduct that happens to have an adverse effect on them. However, it will occasionally be the case that the defendant's conduct will be specifically done in order to annoy the plaintiff. Where this is the case, their malicious motive may make their conduct unreasonable, even if it might not have been deemed so otherwise.

Case examples

- In *Christie v Davey* (1893) the plaintiff was a music teacher who lived in a semi-detached house in London. She would frequently sing and play instruments – which very much bothered her neighbour (the defendant). The defendant retaliated by deliberately banging pots and pans every time the music started. While this might not typically amount to a nuisance, the Court held that because it was done with malice to 'vex and annoy' the plaintiff, it was unreasonable and constituted a nuisance.
- In *Hollywood Silver Fox Farm v Emmett* (1936) the plaintiff operated a silver fox farm, prominently displaying a sign with its name. The defendant, a neighbouring landowner and property developer, objected to the sign, fearing it would lower the value of his property. After the plaintiff refused to remove it, the defendant began shooting a gun on his land to frighten the breeding vixens, causing them to eat their young and significantly disrupting the plaintiff's business. Although the defendant claimed he was shooting to control rabbits, the Court found his actions were motivated by malice. This malicious intent made his conduct unreasonable and a nuisance, even though shooting on his land might otherwise have been lawful.

8.2.8.6 Precautions taken by the defendant

In determining whether the defendant's conduct was unreasonable, the court may take into account any precautions the defendant has taken to minimise interference with the plaintiff's use and enjoyment of their land. However, even where all reasonable precautions have been taken, the defendant may still be liable if the activity still causes a substantial interference: *Lester-Travers v City of Frankston* (1970). For example, in *Bonnici v Kur-ring-gai Municipal Council* (2001) stormwater from the council's drainage system flowed onto the plaintiff's land. The council had taken various measures to try to address the problem, but was unsuccessful. The Court held that allowing the water to flow onto the plaintiff's property constituted a nuisance, even though the council had taken all reasonable steps to mitigate the problem.

This is one key area where nuisance differs from negligence. In negligence, if the defendant has acted with all reasonable care, they won't be liable – even though they may have caused harm. By contrast, in nuisance, a person who has acted with reasonable care may still be liable, if their conduct caused a substantial interference and was considered to be unreasonable in all the circumstances.

If there is a simple precaution that the defendant *could* have taken to minimise the nuisance, but they did not take it, their conduct is likely to be considered unreasonable. For example, in *Painter v Reed* (1930) the alleged nuisance was excessive noise caused by the plaintiff's neighbour breaking in horses. This was a rural area, and breaking in horses was the defendant's business – so some leeway needed to be given. However, the defendant was doing this at 4 am, because that's when it suited them. It would have been simple for the defendant to have waited a few more hours, when the noise would not have been so bothersome. Their failure to take that simple but reasonable precaution meant that their conduct was held to be unreasonable.

When considering the issue of precautions, there are various factors the court will need to consider, such as the cost of the precaution and the extent to which it would reduce the interference. If the precaution is going to be prohibitively expensive, and is unlikely to make much difference, then the court won't give the defendant's failure to take it much weight.

8.2.8.7 Impact on health or safety

If the defendant's conduct impacts on the plaintiff's health or safety, that may also be a relevant factor. This can be seen in the case of *Pittman v Newport* (2022), which brings together many of the issues we have considered.

Case example

In *Pittman v Newport* (2022), P lived above D in a high-density residential building near the ocean. D frequently smoked cigarettes on his unenclosed balcony, with the smoke travelling up to P's apartment. This substantially affected P: it irritated his eyes, caused headaches, sneezing and coughing, and lingered in his apartment, disrupting his sleep and leading to stress and irritability. To mitigate the impact, P avoided using his balcony, kept his doors and windows shut, and even blocked his door, but the smoke still infiltrated. The situation worsened to the point where P was unable to work from home, leading to the loss of his job.

P sued D in nuisance. It was accepted that the interference was substantial, but the key question was whether it was unreasonable. D argued that smoking cigarettes is lawful, and it is reasonable for a homeowner to be able to smoke on their balcony. By contrast, P argued that the impact on their use and enjoyment of their property was so bad that it was unreasonable for D to continue acting in this way.

The Court noted that the law permits a person to use their land in a manner that interferes with the use by a neighbour of their land, provided this interference is not unreasonable. In applying the unreasonableness test, it is necessary to consider the context in which that test is to be applied. In this case, it was an apartment in a medium-rise residential block located in a residential neighbourhood among other apartment blocks. This is a relatively high-density type of communal living. The Court noted that in such a context, there is a degree of give and take required of the occupants – they can't reasonably expect to be unaffected by their neighbour's use of their own land.

The Court held that it is also necessary to consider the nature of the D's activities and the nature of the nuisance. Here, D was smoking cigarettes, which exposed P to second-hand cigarette smoke. In this regard, the Court noted a number of facts:

- Smoking is legal, although as a society we frequently limit where people can smoke.
- The second-hand smoke was having a significant impact on P's health.

- There is no safe level of exposure to tobacco smoke – any exposure can pose a serious health risk due to its carcinogenic properties.
- The potential for the second-hand smoke to cause such serious harm was causing P to feel distressed and anxious.
- D had done nothing to address the problem, whereas P had taken various steps to try to limit the impact of the smoke. This included never using their balcony, which was unreasonable to expect of a person who lives near the ocean with a view.

Given all these circumstances, the Court held that the smoking constituted a substantial and unreasonable interference with P's use of their apartment. The judges stated at [118] that '[w]hile communal living requires give and take, exposure to actual discomfort and disease and potential additional serious health risk is well beyond the reciprocity required of the plaintiffs and permitted for the defendant, having regard to contemporary notions of comfort and safety'.

The Court ordered that D not be permitted to smoke on their balcony or permit anyone else to do so, nor to smoke inside their house if that was likely to result in smoke entering P's property.

8.2.9 Creating, authorising, adopting or continuing a nuisance

For the defendant to be held liable for nuisance, it must be possible to attribute the cause of the relevant nuisance (eg the noise or the smell) to them in some away. In most cases this won't pose a problem, as the defendant will have created the nuisance by committing some kind of positive act, such as playing music loudly or heating pungent oil. As long as they did that act intentionally, they will be potentially liable. This is the case even if they didn't intend to damage the plaintiff's property or interfere with their amenity – they only need to have intended to commit the relevant act: *Sedleigh-Denfield v O'Callaghan* (1940).

The defendant does not, however, need to have personally created the nuisance to be held liable. In certain circumstances they can also be held liable for allowing a nuisance to emanate from their land. This can be a nuisance caused by a third party or by a natural hazard.

Case examples

- In *Bank of New Zealand v Greenwood* (1984) the defendant occupied land that had a building on it that reflected a lot of light into the plaintiff's property. The defendant hadn't built the building but was nonetheless liable for the nuisance it caused – as it owned the land from which it emanated.
- In *Goldman v Hargrave* (1966) lightning struck a tree on the defendant's property, starting a fire. The defendant knew about the fire, but failed to do anything about it – and the fire spread to their neighbours' properties, causing damage. The defendant was held liable for nuisance, even though they hadn't created the risk.

One circumstance in which the defendant can be held responsible for a nuisance they didn't personally create is where they *authorised the nuisance*. This could be explicit (eg they expressly permit someone to operate noisy machinery on their property) or implicit (eg they rent their land to a business that will inevitably make a lot of noise). The defendant will *not* have implicitly authorised a nuisance where they simply rented out their property to a tenant who goes on to disturb the neighbours: in such circumstances it is the tenant who will be liable (see, eg, *Peden Pty Ltd v Bortolazzo* (2006)). The defendant will only be responsible if they hired out the property for a *purpose that carried with it a special risk of nuisance* (ie the nuisance was a natural and inevitable consequence of the purpose for which it was rented). For example, in *De Jager v Payneham & Magill Lodges Hall Inc* (1984) the defendant owned a hall that they hired out for functions – which obviously carries with it a risk of creating noise. Neighbours frequently complained about the noise of people using the hall, so the defendant installed a volume regulation device on the PA system. But the people who hired the hall kept finding ways to neutralise the device and to continue playing loud music. The defendant was held liable for this nuisance, on the basis that they had implicitly authorised it by hiring the hall out for a purpose which would naturally and inevitably result in such a nuisance.

The other circumstance in which the defendant can be held responsible for a nuisance they didn't personally create is where they *adopted or continued the nuisance*. The defendant 'adopts' a nuisance by using whatever it is that constitutes the nuisance. For example, in *Sedleigh-Denfield v O'Callaghan* (1940) council workers had trespassed onto the defendant's land and constructed a faulty drain, which ended up flooding their neighbour's property. While the defendant had not authorised this work, they were aware that it had been done – and they used the drains, thereby adopting the nuisance. So as a result, they were held liable for it.

By contrast, the defendant 'continues' a nuisance when they know about it, or ought to know about it, but do not take reasonably prompt and efficient steps to remedy it. For example, in *Lippiatt v South Gloucestershire Council* (1999) the defendant was a local council which owned land that travellers illegally camped on. The travellers caused a nuisance to the plaintiff (eg by blocking access to their field). The council was held liable for their conduct, as they knew they were there and did nothing to remove them – in fact, they even installed some toilets for them.

In *Goldman v Hargrave* (1966) the Privy Council held that in determining whether the defendant has taken reasonable steps to remedy a state of affairs caused by a natural hazard – such as lightning striking a tree on the defendant's property, causing a fire – the court should take into account the defendant's personal circumstances. This includes their knowledge of what has happened and their ability to deal with the situation, as well as their financial and material resources.

If a person is not aware of a nuisance emanating from their property, and there is no evidence to suggest they should have known of it, then they won't held be liable for it. For example, in *Montana Hotels Pty Ltd v Fasson* (1987) a broken downpipe in the defendant's building caused structural damage to the plaintiff's hotel next door. The defendant was not aware of the broken downpipe, and there was nothing to suggest that they should have been aware of it. Consequently, they were not held liable in nuisance for the damage it had caused. However, once they were made aware of the problem, they had an obligation to fix it in order to prevent further damage.

It should be noted that where a landholder has authorised, adopted or continued a third party's nuisance, the plaintiff can *either* sue the landholder or the person who created the nuisance. For example, in *Fennell v Robson Excavations* (1977) an excavation company did some work on a developer's land. That work caused erosion on the neighbour's property when there were heavy rains. While the neighbour could have sued the developer, by the time the damage occurred they had gone out of business. So instead, they sued the excavation company (and won).

8.2.10 Standing to sue

To bring an action in private nuisance, the plaintiff must have standing to sue. It is clear that people who have a recognised interest in land, such as owners and leaseholders, have standing, as do owners of dominant tenements (ie people who have the benefit of an easement) and people in exclusive possession of property (including squatters).

Case examples

- In *Pemberton v Southwark London Borough Council* (2000) the plaintiff was a tolerated trespasser exercising an exclusive right to occupy a flat. His exclusive possession of the flat gave him a sufficient interest in the premises to sustain an action in private nuisance.
- In *Turvey v Crotti* (2018) the plaintiff had an easement over land owned by the defendant. The defendant placed and locked gates that restricted her access to the easement and the plaintiff sued for nuisance. The Court confirmed that as the owner of the dominant tenement the plaintiff had sufficient standing to sue.

It is not clear, however, whether mere licensees or occupiers are able to bring an action in private nuisance. Courts have taken two divergent approaches to this issue. One approach treats nuisance as a tort to land, requiring the plaintiff to have a recognised legal interest in the land to be able to sue: *Oldham v Lawson (No 1)* (1976); *Hunter v Canary Wharf* (1997); *Hampshire Automotive Centre Pty Ltd v Centre Com (Sunshine) Pty Ltd* (2019). Under this approach, mere licensees or occupiers do not have standing to sue, unless they have exclusive possession of the land.

Case examples

- In the English case of *Malone v Laskey* (1907) it was held that a mere licensee with no proprietary or possessory interest in the land had no standing to bring the case.
- In *Oldham v Lawson (No 1)* (1976) the Victorian Supreme Court followed *Malone v Laskey*, holding that a husband living in a house owned by his wife was a mere licensee, and so was unable to bring an action in private nuisance.
- In *Hunter v Canary Wharf Ltd* (1997) the House of Lords, by majority (Lord Cooke dissenting), affirmed the rule that a plaintiff suing in private nuisance must have a recognised interest in land.

The other approach views nuisance as a tort that protects personal interests in the use and enjoyment of land. Under this approach, the courts have allowed nuisance actions by individuals who normally live on the property, provided they can demonstrate a substantial link to the land: *Motherwell v Motherwell* (1976); *Animal Liberation (Vic) Inc v Gasser* (1991); *Bald Hills Wind Farm Pty Ltd v South Gippsland Shire Council* (2020).

Case examples

- In *Motherwell v Motherwell* (1976), a Canadian harassment case, a wife living with her husband (who owned the house) was entitled to sue in nuisance on the grounds that she had a right to live in the matrimonial home with her husband and children. The Court relaxed the standing rules to allow a person 'normally living' on a property to sue where there is 'substantial occupancy': see 77–8.
- This decision was followed in *Devon Lumber v MacNeill* (1987), a Canadian dust case, where the right of two children to occupy the family home with their parents was accepted by the Court as sufficient to justify their entitlement to bring an action in nuisance.
- In the English case of *Khorasandjian v Bush* (1993), the plaintiff, a young woman living with her mother, was held by a majority to have sufficient standing to bring an action. This decision was overruled in *Hunter v Canary Wharf Ltd* (1997).
- In *Animal Liberation (Vic) Inc v Gasser* (1991), plaintiffs who operated a travelling circus on land under a licence were granted an injunction to stop picketing activities by Animal Liberation, even though they were mere licensees who lacked exclusive possession.

The High Court of Australia has not yet addressed this issue, leaving the law in an unclear state for now. We consider this issue in more detail in section 8.2.13 below.

8.2.11 Defences to private nuisance

By contrast with the intentional torts, which have a large range of defences that focus on the reasonableness of the defendant's conduct (see Chapter 7), the number of defences to private nuisance is limited. This is because the main focus of the arguments when proving the elements of nuisance is normally on whether the interference was unreasonable *as between the two parties*. So, given that this issue will have been fully considered when proving the tort, it does not need to be raised again in any detail at the defence stage. (Note, however, that it may become relevant at the *remedies* stage if the plaintiff asks for the equitable remedy of an injunction.)

In practice, there is really only one defence that is commonly raised in private nuisance cases: statutory authorisation. We discuss this defence in detail below. However, there are three other possible defences to nuisance which should be mentioned for the sake of completeness:

- *Consent:* In theory, it is possible for a person to consent to a nuisance: see, for example, *Kiddle v City Business Properties* (1942). This does not, however, arise in practice – presumably because it requires the plaintiff to have consented to either having material damage caused to their property (which is unlikely) or to having their amenity substantially and unreasonably interfered with (which is also unlikely). If consent were to be raised as a defence, all of the requirements discussed in section 7.2 of Chapter 7 would apply.

- *Prescription:* The common law contains a defence of prescription, which was raised unsuccessfully in *Halsey v Esso Petroleum* (1961). This defence allows people who have continued their activities as of right for a period of 20 years, without complaint by any person adversely affected by the interference, to continue committing the nuisance. Time begins to run only once an actionable nuisance exists – that is, once another person is adversely affected by the defendant's conduct. This defence is extremely difficult to establish and has rarely been successfully raised in Australia.
- *Contributory negligence:* As will be seen in Chapter 15, historically contributory negligence was a complete defence, meaning that if the plaintiff contributed even minimally to the harm they suffered, they would be barred from recovering damages. Around Australia, this approach has been reformed by legislation which allows for apportionment of damages (ie damages are reduced in proportion to the plaintiff's contribution to the harm). However, in some jurisdictions (such as Western Australia) the apportionment legislation appears to only apply to negligence claims. This means that the common law may still apply to nuisance cases, providing a complete defence where the plaintiff has contributed to the harm they have suffered: see, for example, *Przetak v Metropolitan (Perth) Passenger Transport Trust* (1961). However, this theoretical position has not been tested in recent cases; and in practice, courts tend to apportion damages for nuisance in a manner similar to negligence claims.

Note that it will be rare that a case is time barred under the relevant *Limitations of Action* legislation, because nuisance is almost always an ongoing state of affairs.

LEGISLATION ALERT!

Consult your study materials to see:

- whether the legislation covering contributory negligence applies to nuisance in your jurisdiction; and
- what the limitation period for nuisance is in your jurisdiction.

It may be considered that the fact that the plaintiff 'came to the nuisance' (ie the defendant was already committing the relevant conduct before the plaintiff arrived in the area) should be a defence. For example, if the defendant has been operating noisy machinery in a factory for many years before the plaintiff moves next door, it may be thought that the plaintiff should be precluded from complaining about that noise. However, this is not the approach taken in the law of nuisance. The courts have held that if the defendant is substantially and unreasonably interfering with the plaintiff's use and enjoyment of their land, that will constitute a nuisance – regardless of when the plaintiff moved in: see, for example, *Sturges v Bridgman* (1879). It may, however, be relevant to the issue of whether a court will grant the plaintiff an injunction: see section 8.2.12.

8.2.11.1 Statutory authorisation

The defence of statutory authorisation applies where Parliament has authorised the defendant's conduct, as well as its adverse effects on the plaintiff: *Manchester Corporation v Farnsworth* (1930). It is unlikely that this will be explicitly stated – it would be unusual for Parliament to pass an Act that provides that it intends to deprive a person of their right to sue for nuisance. Instead, it will generally be a matter of interpreting the relevant statutory provision. In this regard, the Court in *Southern Properties (WA) Pty Ltd v Executive Director, Department of Conservation and Land Management* (2012) held that there are two questions that need to be considered:

1. Did the statute *require* the defendant to undertake the relevant activity, or did it simply *permit* them to do so?
2. Was the defendant's conduct authorised?

The way the second question is approached will be determined by the answer to the first question:

- If the activity was *required*, it will have been authorised unless it was not conducted with reasonable care. In such cases, all the defendant needs to show is that they exercised reasonable care in carrying out the activity.
- If the activity was merely *permitted*, the defendant must prove that the nuisance was an inevitable consequence of the performance of the duty. This is a stricter test, which considers matters such as the decision to undertake the activity, and the circumstances and manner in which it was undertaken.

Case examples

- In *Manchester Corporation v Farnsworth* (1930) the defendant was permitted to build an electrical generating plant. The plant emitted poisonous fumes that affected the plaintiff. The defendant raised the defence of statutory authorisation but failed – because it was held that it was *not* an inevitable consequence of building the plant that it emit poisonous fumes. They could not prove that they had used all 'reasonable diligence' to do all that was 'practically feasible', according to the state of scientific knowledge at the time, to avoid causing a nuisance to their neighbours: see 183 and 195. In other words, they could have built the plant in a way that prevented the poisoning.
- In *York Bros (Trading) Pty Ltd v Commissioner of Main Roads* (1983), a case of public nuisance, the defendant built a bridge that blocked traffic on a navigable river. They failed in the defence of statutory authorisation because, although they had been authorised to build bridges by an Act of Parliament, it would have been possible for them to build the bridge at a height that did not obstruct river traffic.
- In *Southern Properties (WA) Pty Ltd v Executive Director, Department of Conservation and Land Management* (2012) the defendant was required to carry out a prescribed burn. The smoke

affected the plaintiff's grapes, making them useless for making wine. The defendant successfully raised the defence of statutory authorisation. As they were required to do the burn, all they needed to show was that they had carried it out with reasonable care – which they could do. There was no way they could have done the burn without the smoke, and they couldn't control its impact on the plaintiff's grapes.

This defence adds another reminder to you of the importance, in any nuisance problem-solving question, of identifying clearly from the facts both the conduct being complained of and the effects on the plaintiff. The cases show that if it was possible for the defendant, using all reasonable diligence, to perform the authorised activity without causing the adverse effect on the plaintiff, the defence will not succeed.

8.2.12 Remedies for private nuisance

There are three different kinds of remedy available to a plaintiff in a nuisance case:

- common law damages;
- an injunction (an equitable remedy); and
- the self-help remedy of abatement.

Compensatory damages are available as of right under the usual common law principles. Plaintiffs can also be compensated for any loss in the value of their land as a result of the nuisance. However, unless plaintiffs are complaining about an isolated happening that caused physical damage, they will rarely be seeking a simple award of damages. More often, plaintiffs will want to regain the use and enjoyment of their land, and so the remedy most commonly sought in a nuisance case is either:

- a prohibitive injunction, ordering the defendants to stop their activities; or
- a mandatory injunction, ordering the defendants to do something to remedy the state of affairs on their land.

In some cases, plaintiffs may bring an action because they are afraid that a state of affairs on neighbouring land may cause a nuisance in the future. In such cases they will seek a *quia timet* injunction to prevent the threat of imminent danger. In other cases, plaintiffs may ask for an interim order known as an interlocutory injunction, which may be replaced by a final or perpetual order once the case is decided. Unlike the award of common law damages, however, injunctive relief is an equitable remedy, and this means that it is not available as of right – but is awarded at the discretion of the court. So, even though a plaintiff may win the case by proving all the elements of the action, they are not necessarily guaranteed to get the remedy that they want.

Case example

In the controversial case of *Miller v Jackson* (1977), the plaintiffs wanted an injunction forbidding the playing of cricket on the ground that adjoined their property. They won their case in nuisance (and negligence), but a majority of the judges denied them an injunction – in part because the plaintiffs had come to the nuisance and built their house next to the ground knowing that cricket had been played there for over 70 years, and also because the public interest in continuing to play cricket had to be balanced against the plaintiff's private interest in enjoying their land free from the incursions of cricket balls.

The courts aim to do justice to both parties when they exercise the discretion to award an injunction, and this task requires them to weigh up the relative rights of the parties using the following factors as a guide:

- Would damages be an adequate remedy?
- Can the damages be estimated in money?
- Is the activity trivial or occasional?
- Is the activity ongoing or is it over?
- Has the plaintiff behaved badly? (Plaintiffs seeking equity must come with 'clean hands'.)
- Would the injunction order the defendant to desist from action or to engage in positive action?
- Would an injunction be unduly vexatious or oppressive to the defendant?

An important issue is whether the injunction asked for by the plaintiff is clear and precise in its terms – and this is another reason why you need to be very careful at the very beginning of any nuisance problem-solving exercise to identify clearly *from the facts* both the conduct being complained of and the effects of the conduct on the plaintiff. (You will not get an injunction ordering the defendants 'to stop causing a nuisance'.) If the court decides not to grant an injunction, the plaintiff may be awarded damages in lieu of the injunction to cover future interferences.

The final remedy is the 'self-help' remedy of abatement, which allows people affected by a nuisance to deal with the matter themselves without going through the courts. All self-help remedies that entitle one person to invade the protected rights of another are limited by a requirement to act reasonably (see section 7.9 of Chapter 7), and the remedy of abatement is no different. Notice must normally be given of the intention to enter another's land to abate (or put an end to) the nuisance, and a reasonable time should generally be given to the defendant to deal with the nuisance, unless it is an emergency threatening immediate danger to life or health where it would be unreasonable to expect the plaintiff to wait. However, abatement is a risky enterprise that risks counter-suits in trespass to land and/or trespass to goods, and there are some cases that have held that once a plaintiff has abated a nuisance, they may not thereafter seek a remedy from the courts: *Traian v Ware* (1957).

Case example

In *Traian v Ware* (1957) the plaintiff complained that the defendant had trespassed onto their land and cut a bank of earth to allow the escape of flood water. The defendant claimed that they were acting to abate a threatened danger. The judge pointed out that the law does not favour the remedy of abatement in preference to legal action, and requires strong reason to justify it, especially when it involves entering the land of another. In this case the defendant's action in trespassing on the plaintiff's property, without giving them notice or requesting that they abate the danger themselves, was 'unauthorised and high-handed', so the defendant was liable in damages for the trespass.

LEGISLATION ALERT!

Consult your study materials to see whether there are any legislative measures limiting the use of nuisance law to claim a common law remedy in your jurisdiction. An example is the *Trees (Disputes Between Neighbours) Act 2006* (NSW).

Note also that a plaintiff is entitled to recover damages only for harm that is of a reasonably foreseeable kind. The law on this issue of 'remoteness of damage' is the same as the law that applies in the tort of negligence (see Chapter 13).

8.2.13 Possible developments in the law

The tort of private nuisance is complicated, not only because there are two different kinds of nuisance that are established in different ways using different tests for fault, but also by the fact that there is a wider than usual range of possible defendants that extends beyond the occupier of the land from which the nuisance has emanated. Furthermore, there is also uncertainty in Australia about who should properly bring the action. So, the identity of both the proper plaintiff and the best defendant may not always be easy to establish. The relevant law is fuzzy, its application is difficult, its relationship to the tort of negligence has not been adequately settled and the theoretical underpinning of the tort is unclear.

Some have argued that cases of material physical damage should be dealt with only under the tort of negligence. This would mean that all indirectly caused physical damage would be covered by a single tort that uses one objective test for fault and would leave only non-physical interferences with the use and enjoyment of land for the tort of private nuisance to deal with.

Others have argued that the courts or Parliament should clarify whether private nuisance is a 'tort to land' or a 'tort to the person'. As we saw in section 8.2.10 above, the law in this regard is currently unclear. Under the 'tort to land' approach (see, eg, *Oldham v Lawson (No 1)* (1976); *Hunter v Canary Wharf Ltd* (1997)), the suffering of those actually living on the land does not of itself entitle them to bring an action; rather, it is evidence that the amenity of the land has been adversely affected, and so it entitles only the person with an interest in the land to bring an action. Under the 'tort to the person' approach (see, eg, *Motherwell v Motherwell* (1976); *Animal Liberation (Vic) Inc v Gasser* (1991)), the suffering of the victims does entitle them to bring an action, provided they have a substantial link to the land.

The High Court has not had the opportunity to hear a case on either of these issues, so the future of the law of nuisance in Australia is uncertain: it is caught between several possible directions that have been canvassed in the case law and in academic commentary.

Case examples

The courts in Australia might adopt these approaches:

- Require claims for material physical damage (either to the person or property) to rely on the tort of negligence, restricting private nuisance to cases of non-physical interferences with the use and enjoyment of land: see Newark, 'The Boundaries of Nuisance' (1949); and Gearty, 'The Place of Nuisance in a Modern Law of Torts' (1989).
- Keep both forms of private nuisance, but restrict the tort to actions that protect only those with a recognised interest in land: see the majority judgment in *Hunter v Canary Wharf Ltd* (1997); and Cane, 'What a Nuisance!' (1997).
- Set the tort free from its early origins and give it a wider scope as a tort protecting any person whose enjoyment of land has been adversely affected: see the minority judgment by Lord Cooke in *Hunter v Canary Wharf Ltd* (1997); *Motherwell v Motherwell* (1976); *Devon Lumber v MacNeill* (1987); the majority judgment in *Khorasandjian v Bush* (1993); and the American *Restatement of Torts*: *Restatement 2d*, §821E.
- Widen the scope of the tort to allow it to be used to offer protection from other forms of antisocial conduct, such as sexual harassment and stalking, or develop a new tort of harassment: see *Khorasandjian v Bush* (1993); Conaghan, 'Harassment and the Law of Torts: *Khorasandjian v Bush*' (1993) and 'Gendered Harms and the Law of Tort: Remedying Sexual Harassment' (1996); Nolan, 'Square Pegs in a Round Hole' (1994–95); Piotrowicz, 'Private Lives and Private Nuisance in English Law: *Khorasandjian v Bush*' (1993); and Stanton, 'Harassment: An Emerging Tort?' (1993).

Develop your skills

Prepare an oral presentation on *Hunter v Canary Wharf Ltd* (1997)

The issue of standing to sue in private nuisance raises many critical practical and theoretical issues about the nature of the tort. Using the guide in section 4.5 of Chapter 4, prepare a ten-minute oral presentation on *Hunter v Canary Wharf Ltd* (1997) that covers both the majority view and the dissenting judgment of Lord Cooke. This case is well worth reading because of the fundamental issues about the tort of private nuisance that it discusses, and the quality of the reasoning given by both the majority and the dissenting decision of Lord Cooke.

8.3 Public nuisance

8.3.1 The nature of public nuisance

Public nuisance is both a common law crime that protects the community as a whole and a tort that protects individual members of the community who suffer special damage over and above that suffered by the wider public. Lord Bingham pointed out in *R v Rimmington* (2006) at 468 that in an 'unpoliced and unregulated society, in which local government was rudimentary or non-existent', the crime of public nuisance once had an important role to play in dealing with conduct that is now covered by a wide array of statutory offences that control and regulate matters of public health and safety. *Rimmington* contains a helpful discussion of the history of both the crime and the tort of nuisance, from its early inceptions where it controlled obstructions of the highways, threats to health or safety by disease-ridden persons, vicious animals or sewerage disposal ('filth'), and the selling of food unfit for human consumption, through to modern times where it has been used to prosecute defendants who have organised acid house parties attended by thousands of people or who pose other threats to public amenities or security – for example, by making hoax bomb calls.

The crime is prosecuted by the state; a tort case is brought by the Attorney-General, either on their own initiative (*ex officio*) or in a 'relator' action (*ex relatione*) after representation by a specific member of the public. Lord Denning explained in *Attorney-General v PYA Quarries Ltd* (1957) at 190–1 that public nuisance:

> is a nuisance which is so widespread in its range or so indiscriminate in its effect that it would not be reasonable to expect one person to take proceedings on his own responsibility to put a stop to it, but that it should be taken on the responsibility of the community at large.

The central and defining feature of public nuisance is the requirement that the defendant's conduct interfere with public rights held in common by members of the community *as a group* (by contrast with private nuisance where the interference is with private rights to occupy and enjoy land held by persons *as individuals*). The elements of the crime and the tort are the same, and as you can see in sections 8.3.1.1 and 8.3.1.2, public and private nuisance may overlap on the facts of any given case (as occurred in *Halsey v Esso Petroleum* (1961)).

There is no precise definition of the 'public' or any set number of people that must be affected by the defendant's conduct, so you need to argue the facts of your case, bearing in mind that the 'common injury' to a 'representative cross-section' of the community or a 'class of Her Majesty's subjects' *does* have to be widespread, but does *not* have to affect every member of the public: *Attorney-General v PYA Quarries Ltd* (1957); *R v Rimmington* (2006).

8.3.1.1 Private nuisance

Elements

- The conduct interferes with another person's use or enjoyment of land, or of a right over or an interest in land, by either:
  - causing material physical damage to the land; or
  - substantially interfering with the person's amenity.
- Such conduct is unreasonable in the circumstances.

To sue in the tort of private nuisance the plaintiff must have either:

- a recognised interest in land; or
- a substantial link to land (the law is uncertain).

8.3.1.2 Public nuisance

Elements

- The conduct interferes with the public, by either:
  - causing material physical damage to members of the public enjoying public rights; or
  - substantially interfering with defined public rights to free access, health, safety, comfort, etc.
- Such conduct is unreasonable in the circumstances.

To sue in the tort of public nuisance the plaintiff must be either:

- the Attorney-General (or the Director of Public Prosecutions); or
- a person who has suffered special or particular damage over and above that suffered by the general public.

The test for determining the defendant's responsibility for the nuisance is the same in both private and public nuisance (see section 8.2.9 above). The principle of 'give and take' and the concept of reasonableness that dominate the tort of private nuisance also govern the tort of public nuisance. The range of possible interferences is similarly wide.

Case examples

- Noise, dust, vibrations and the risk of physical injury from the projection of stones and splinters caused by the defendant's quarrying operations: *Attorney-General v PYA Quarries Ltd* (1957).
- Noise caused by oil tankers and property damage to a car parked in the street caused by acid smuts: *Halsey v Esso Petroleum* (1961).
- Personal injury caused by a golf ball hitting a taxi's windscreen on a public street, damaging the eye of the driver: *Castle v St Augustine's Links Ltd* (1922).
- Financial loss caused to a farmer who had to take a longer route to market because the defendant had blocked a public right of way: *Smith v Wilson* (1903).
- Delay and inconvenience caused by the defendant's blocking of a public highway: *Walsh v Ervin* (1952).
- Inconvenience and disruption caused by queues of people attracted to the defendant's business: *Silservice v Supreme Bread* (1949).
- Health risks (including smell and the risk of illness from flies and mosquitoes) caused by the unsanitary condition of sheep and cattle saleyards located near a residential district: *Attorney-General v Abraham* (1949).

Note the decision of the High Court in *Brodie v Singleton Shire Council* (2001), where Gaudron, McHugh and Gummow JJ decided (at [55] and [129] in a joint judgment) that in cases where roads have fallen into disrepair due to inaction by highway authorities, 'the tort of public nuisance ... has been subsumed into the tort of negligence'.

8.4 Problem-solving tips

Because of the complexity of the tort of nuisance, many tips on problem-solving have been included in the sections discussing the law. Learning how to apply the law of nuisance will help you to develop your skills in problem solving and legal argument to a higher level because applying the tests and relevant factors requires:

- detailed knowledge of the facts of previous cases; and
- a careful analysis of the facts of your case, which must be:
  - considered in the light of the fuzzy concept of reasonableness; and
  - the guiding principle of 'give and take'.

8.4.1 Identifying the matters the plaintiff is complaining about

Before you begin, make a summary of the law in a checklist format, including any factual examples and counterexamples from the cases, where available.

Begin your diagnosis (as always) by looking for any *harmful or adverse effects*, remembering that you are looking for either existing harms or threatened future harms. Remind yourself of the different kinds of interferences that you will be looking for in a private nuisance action (noting that the third kind of interference is rarely assessed in torts exams):

- Physical damage:
  - fire, flood, noxious/dangerous substances;
  - earth movement, subsidence, etc.
- Interferences with the use and enjoyment of land:
  - smells, noises, vibrations, lights, dust, any other sensory irritations;
  - interference with the plaintiff's activities;
  - offensive sights or conduct that upset the plaintiff;
  - any other intangible emanations from the land – for example, electrical interferences.
- Remember to check for any possible public nuisances: Look for any interferences that may attract a claim in public nuisance on the grounds that the defendant's conduct has interfered with a public right; see section 8.3 above.

Then track back to the *conduct* so that you can construct the usual 'conduct and effect pairs' by identifying anyone:

- whose positive act created the nuisance; or
- who authorised, adopted or continued the nuisance.

This helps you to identify the range of possible defendants.

Note also whether the original cause was human or natural.

Finally, classify each 'conduct and effect' pair under its appropriate species of nuisance, so that you know who has the onus of proof on the issue of reasonableness (see section 8.2.1 above), and can start thinking about what kind of factors you may need to consider to determine whether the interference was substantial and unreasonable.

8.4.2 Identifying remedies

Once you have listed the matters that the plaintiff is complaining about, you can quickly identify the *remedies* they will claim (see section 8.2.12 above).

8.4.3 Writing your introduction

Now you are ready to write your introduction, using a modified version of the 'six-point plan'. You will have to modify it by adding an extra level of classification to your pairs so that for each matter the plaintiff complains of, you note the *conduct*, its *effect* and the *kind of nuisance*. For example, Peter is upset with Julia because of her conduct in:

- roasting coffee beans every day, causing a burning *smell* (private nuisance, interference with amenity);
- playing her trombone for five hours each night, causing the plaintiff to lose sleep because of the *noise* (private nuisance, interference with amenity);
- allowing a large crack in the soil to develop on her land, threatening to cause *subsidence* on the plaintiff's land (private nuisance, material damage); and
- attracting long queues of customers to her coffee shop, causing a blockage of the footpath (public nuisance).

Taking the time to make this list is critical. If you classify each complaint carefully, you set yourself up to apply the right legal rules and reach a sound conclusion. If you skip this step, the rest of your answer will quickly go off track. This is why:

- If you do not classify the effects by 'kind of nuisance' you will not know how to apply the correct law or argue your case properly, because each different kind of nuisance has a different set of tests.
- If you do not identify the conduct clearly, you will not know how to word your injunction.
- If you do not identify the effects on the plaintiff, you will not know what amount of compensatory damages to claim.
- If you do not clearly identify the conduct and its effects, you will not be able to work out which defences (if any) may apply.

Finish your introduction by identifying the remedies that will be sought. Be precise and not too general.

8.4.4 Writing the body of your answer

The next step is to write the body of your answer by taking each 'conduct and effect pair' and discussing it before moving on to the next one. In other words, argue your case 'nuisance by nuisance' rather than 'factor by factor'. If you have a lot of different kinds of interferences, you will get too confused if you construct your answer 'factor by factor'. We suggest that you begin your discussion by seeing whether the effect of the interference on the plaintiff is substantial, and then considering whether it was unreasonable. Construct arguments and counterarguments that weave in appropriate references to the relevant factors and your knowledge of the cases – always bearing in mind that the crucial issue in a case of private nuisance is *reasonableness* as between the two parties, considered in the light of all the *circumstances* and the dominating principle of *'give and take'*. This is fuzzy law, so argue the facts and look at the matter from both points of view. Remember also that the mere fact that the plaintiff is upset is not of itself proof of a substantial and unreasonable interference – because the matter is judged according to the standards of ordinary reasonable persons living in the neighbourhood.

8.4.5 Useful tips

- Remember that the relevant factors set out in section 8.2.8 above are *not* elements; they should be discussed only if they are actually relevant. For example, if there is no indication of malice in the facts of the problem question, do not raise it.
- Remember to consider the issue of whether the plaintiff has standing to sue, bearing in mind that the law on private nuisance in Australia is unclear. This means that you should argue 'both ways'. The lack of clarity in the law means that the victim of the interference may not always be a proper plaintiff. So, check the property rights held by the people affected by the interference and work out who is the best person to bring the action. If you have a case of public nuisance, check to see whether the plaintiff has suffered any special damage.
- Be careful in applying the defence of statutory authorisation: remember that before the defence will be successful, the statute must not only authorise the *conduct* of the defendant but the *effects* of the defendant's conduct on the plaintiff. If the activity was required, it will have been authorised unless it was not conducted with reasonable care. If the activity was merely permitted, the defendant must prove that the nuisance was an inevitable consequence of the performance of the duty. Again, argue the facts. This defence applies to both public and private nuisance.
- Consider remedies carefully and remember that although the plaintiff may win the case on the merits, they may not necessarily get an injunction.
- There are lots of examples of nuisance problem solving in Chapters 3 and 4.

Conclusion

In this chapter we have explored the tort of nuisance. This tort plays a critical role in balancing the rights of individuals to enjoy their land with the rights of others to use their property. Through the doctrines of private and public nuisance, the law seeks to mediate conflicts that arise from diverse and often competing interests, emphasising reasonableness and the necessity of mutual accommodation in a shared environment. In the next chapter, we turn our attention to the tort of defamation, exploring its role in protecting individuals' reputations while balancing freedom of expression.

Test your understanding

Problem solving

Problem 1

Angela and Roberto Casa have come to you for legal advice because they are outraged by the conduct of their 80-year-old neighbour Dorothy Domus, whose increasingly bizarre behaviour is causing great distress to the Casas' 10-year-old daughter Janella. The Casa family, who migrated to your city from Italy in 2004, have been living with and caring for their elderly aunt, Romana Mano, since that time.

Ever since they moved in, Dorothy has yelled abuse at the Casa family whenever she sees one of them walking past the side fence between the houses, accusing Roberto of being 'an Italian pimp' and Angela and Janella of being prostitutes, and telling them to 'go back to Italy'. She put a large hand-drawn picture of the Casa family in her front window labelled 'die, foreign scum', which was easily visible from the road.

One year ago, Dorothy told little Janella that she was a high-ranking witch and that she had cast spells on the Casa family that would bring them all bad luck and make their pet cat Tombalino die. Since then, Dorothy has been drawing white chalk outlines of human bodies and cats with the letters 'RIP' inside them all over the footpath, the road and even on the driveway of the house where the Casa family lives. Dorothy regularly calls Romana's phone and pretends to be ringing Emergency Services, saying that she wants to report that a terrible accident has happened and asking for an ambulance to be sent to the street immediately.

Janella is now terrified of Dorothy. She cannot sleep at night if the phone rings because of her fear of the vivid nightmares about Tombalino's death and traffic accidents that she experiences after the calls. Angela and Roberto Casa tell you that they cannot afford to move out or buy their own house and say that they cannot cope any more.

Discuss all tort actions arising from these facts.

Hint: This question is not only about nuisance – it contains other torts that you have already studied in previous chapters and may involve the extension of some of those torts. It is based on a true story that was published in the newspapers in England. It has been included to emphasise the fact that, unlike law school problem questions, real disputes rarely come neatly packaged into one category of tort law.

Problem 2

Penny Persich is looking after her parents' home while they are away working in Antarctica. The house is on Bella Vista Road (a main street going through a mixed inner-city neighbourhood containing a commercial shopping district and good quality residential housing, schools and churches). The man who lives next door is Jack 'Spam' Sparrow, a wealthy IT professional who constantly worries about his low popularity with women. To make himself seem cool and fashionable, Spam built himself a magnificent modern home. He installed a massive digital screen, which forms the whole of the front wall of the house. This enormous screen constantly shows pictures from underwear catalogues featuring celebrities like Miranda Kerr, Kylie Minogue, Elle McPherson and Pamela Anderson.

Penny does not like seeing the pictures flickering next door and she feels very uncomfortable not only about their content, but also about the men who congregate in groups on the footpath to watch the display. Some days she cannot get out of her driveway to get to work because of the crowds. She asked Spam to turn off the pictures but Spam, who thought Penny was being uncool, refused her request and began bombarding her every day with emails advertising underwear as a joke.

An environmental activist and animal lover named Storm lives on the other side of the Persich house. Storm has recently converted his back yard into a vegetable garden. He collects large piles of organic fertiliser made from a mixture of blood, bone and manure, with the aim of making his vegetables (which he sells to a local health food shop) the best in the neighbourhood. Storm has also installed a new henhouse, which contains some hens and a rooster named Roger. Roger the rooster crows every day at sunrise for five minutes. This wakes Storm's dog Harry, a tiny chihuahua, who barks frantically for half an hour or so, until Storm yells out several times at the top of his voice, 'Shut up Harry!' and everything returns to normal.

Penny is a nurse who works late shifts. She normally arrives home at 3.00 am each working night and, because she does not fall asleep until 4.00 am at the earliest, has developed an obsessive hatred of Roger and Harry. She cannot bear to hear the crowing and barking or the sound of Storm yelling. To stifle the noise she has timed her CD player to blast out 'Who Let the Dogs Out?' by the Baha Men followed by her favourite Ricky Martin songs from sunrise till 12.00 noon because it is the only thing that soothes her to sleep and keeps her from being disturbed by her obsession with the noise next door. This music unsettles Storm's hens, who stop laying.

Storm's 12-year-old son, Cloud, was inspired by 'Spam' Sparrow's example down the street and built himself a very rough-looking cubby house in a large tree which overlooks the block where Penny lives. Cloud now spends much of his day in the tree house looking into the front yard of the Persich house and, because he hates Ricky Martin's music, he has painted a pretend screen on the wall of the tree house, and has drawn a crude picture of a girl in her underwear on it, which has upset Penny because she believes it is meant to be a portrait of her.

Penny, who is desperately upset by all these events, comes to you for legal advice. You discover that the state *Domestic Animals (Welfare, Health and Safety) Act 2002* contains a provision that allows 'the keeping of no more than ten chickens and one rooster on any suburban block situated in the greater metropolitan district'.

Advise Penny fully about any nuisance actions that may arise from these facts.

(This question is also based on true stories collected from Australian newspapers. You will note that it bears some similarity to the worked example used in Chapter 4, but it is not identical. Remember: your teachers may sometimes recycle problem questions, but they usually change some of the facts, so be careful not to recycle your prepared answers without checking carefully!)

REFERENCES

CASES

Ammon v Colonial Leisure Group Pty Ltd [2019] WASCA 158
Andreae v Selfridge & Co Ltd [1938] Ch 1; [1937] 3 All ER 255
Animal Liberation (Vic) Inc v Gasser [1991] 1 VR 51

Attorney-General v Abraham [1949] NZLR 461
Attorney-General v PYA Quarries Ltd [1957] 2 QB 169
Bald Hills Wind Farm Pty Ltd v South Gippsland Shire Council [2020] VSC 512
Bamford v Turnley (1860) 3 B & S 66; 122 ER 27
Bank of New Zealand v Greenwood [1984] 1 NZLR 525
Bolton v Stone [1951] AC 850
Bonnici v Kur-ring-gai Municipal Council (2001) 121 LGERA 1
Brand v Hammersmith and City Railway (1867) LR 2 QB 223
Brodie v Singleton Shire Council (2001) 206 CLR 512
Castle v St Augustine's Links Ltd (1922) 38 TLR 615
Christie v Davey [1893] 1 Ch 316
Corbett v Pallas (1995) Aust Torts Reports 81-329
De Gruchy v The Owners – Units Plan No 3989 [2020] ACTSC 65
De Jager v Payneham & Magill Lodges Hall Inc (1984) 36 SASR 498
Devon Lumber v MacNeill (1987) 45 DLR (3rd) 300
Fearn v Board of Trustees of the Tate Gallery [2023] UKSC 4
Fennell v Robson Excavations [1977] 2 NSWLR 486
Fertility Control Clinic v Melbourne City Council [2015] VSC 424
Fraser v Booth (1949) 50 SR (NSW) 113
Frost v Northern Beaches Council [2022] NSWSC 1214
Gales Holdings Pty Ltd v Tweed Shire Council (2013) 85 NSWLR 514
Goldman v Hargrave (1966) 115 CLR 458
Halsey v Esso Petroleum [1961] 1 WLR 683
Hampshire Automotive Centre Pty Ltd v Centre Com (Sunshine) Pty Ltd (2019) 60 VR 579
Hargrave v Goldman (1963) 110 CLR 40
Hollywood Silver Fox Farm v Emmett [1936] 2 KB 468; [1936] 1 All ER 825
Hunter v Canary Wharf Ltd [1997] 2 AC 655; [1997] 2 All ER 426
Khorasandjian v Bush (1993) 3 All ER 669; [1993] QB 727
Kiddle v City Business Properties [1942] 1 KB 269
Kraemers v Attorney-General (Tas) [1966] Tas SR 113
Lawrence v Fen Tigers [2014] UKSC 13
Laws v Florinplace [1981] 1 All ER 659
Leakey v National Trust [1980] QB 485
Lester-Travers v City of Frankston [1970] VR 2
Lippiatt v South Gloucestershire Council [1999] 4 All ER 149
Malone v Laskey [1907] 2 KB 14
Manchester Corporation v Farnsworth [1930] AC 171
Marsh v Baxter (2015) 49 WAR 1
McKenzie v Powley [1916] SALR 1
McKinnon Industries v Walker [1951] 3 DLR 57
Miller v Jackson [1977] QB 966; [1977] 3 WLR 20
Montana Hotels Pty Ltd v Fasson [1987] VR 147
Motherwell v Motherwell (1976) 73 DLR (3rd) 62
Munro v Southern Dairies Ltd [1955] VLR 332

Oldham v Lawson (No 1) [1976] VR 654
Onus v Telstra Corporation Ltd [2011] NSWSC 33
Overseas Tankship (UK) Ltd v The Miller Steamship Co [1967] 1 AC 617 ('*The Wagon Mound (No 2)*')
Painter v Reed [1930] SASR 295
Peden Pty Ltd v Bortolazzo [2006] 2 Qd R 574
Pemberton v Southwark London Borough Council [2000] 3 All ER 924
Pittman v Newport [2022] NSWCATCD 173
Przetak v Metropolitan (Perth) Passenger Transport Trust [1961] WAR 2
R v Rimmington [2006] 1 AC 459
Raciti v Hughes Unreported, SC (NSW) Equity Division, Young J, 19 October 1995; BC9501706; (1995) 7 BPR 14, 837
Robinson v Kilvert (1889) 41 Ch D 88
Sedleigh-Denfield v O'Callaghan [1940] AC 880
Silservice v Supreme Bread (1949) 50 SR (NSW) 127
Smith v Wilson [1903] 2 IR 45
Southern Properties (WA) Pty Ltd v Executive Director, Department of Conservation and Land Management (2012) 42 WAR 287
Southwark London Borough Council v Tanner [2001] 1 AC 1
St Helen's Smelting Co v Tipping (1865) 11 HLC 642; 11 ER 1483
Sturges v Bridgman (1879) 11 Ch D 852
Thompson-Schwab v Costaki [1956] 1 All ER 652; [1956] 1 WLR 335
Traian v Ware [1957] VR 200
Turvey v Crotti [2018] NSWSC 1959
Uren v Bald Hills Wind Farm [2022] VSC 145
Victoria Park Racing and Recreation Grounds v Taylor (1937) 58 CLR 479
Walsh v Ervin [1952] VLR 361
Walter v Selfe (1851) 4 De G & Sm 315; 64 ER 849
York Bros (Trading) Pty Ltd v Commissioner of Main Roads [1983] 1 NSWLR 391

ARTICLES AND OTHER RESOURCE

Cane, P, 'What a Nuisance!' (1997) 113 *Law Quarterly Review* 515.
Conaghan, J, 'Gendered Harms and the Law of Tort: Remedying Sexual Harassment' (1996) 16 *Oxford Journal of Legal Studies* 407.
Conaghan, J, 'Harassment and the Law of Torts: *Khorasandjian v Bush*' [1993] 1 *Feminist Legal Studies* 189.
Gearty, C, 'The Place of Nuisance in a Modern Law of Torts' [1989] *Cambridge Law Journal* 214.
Newark, F H, 'The Boundaries of Nuisance' (1949) 65 *Law Quarterly Review* 480.
Nolan, D, 'Square Pegs in a Round Hole: The Need for a New Tort' (1994–95) 5 *Kings College Law Journal* 124.
Piotrowicz, R W, 'Private Lives and Private Nuisance in English Law: *Khorasandjian v Bush*' (1993) 1 *Torts Law Journal* 207.
Restatement (Second) of Torts § 821E (1979) American Law Institute.
Stanton, K M, 'Harassment: An Emerging Tort?' (1993) 1 *Tort Law Review* 179.

DEFAMATION

9

Introduction

Defamation is different from many of the other torts, not only because it contains concepts that do not arise elsewhere, but also because in no other tort do the defences play such a significant role in litigation. As you can see in Figure 9.1, the elements of the tort (represented by the outermost line of the 'doughnut') set a wide circle of protection that shields a person's *private interest* in their reputation – but this protection is cut down to a large extent by the defences, most of which reflect the importance of a countervailing *public interest* in free communication of information and opinion. To succeed in a defamation action, the plaintiff must be able to bring their case into the central zone (but note that the balance between the two zones has varied over time).

There are good reasons to study nuisance and defamation consecutively, and it is instructive to compare and contrast the two torts:

- Both torts can be committed either by a positive act or by a failure to correct a state of affairs created by a third party.
- Both torts protect intangibles (nuisance focuses on the use and enjoyment of land and defamation on a person's interest in their good name and reputation).
- Both torts deal with competing interests; however, while nuisance involves deciding between the competing *private interests* of two individual parties, the law of defamation must strike a balance between the competing *private interests* of individual plaintiffs in the protection of their reputation and the *wider public interest* of the community as a whole in freedom of speech.

Figure 9.1 Defamation

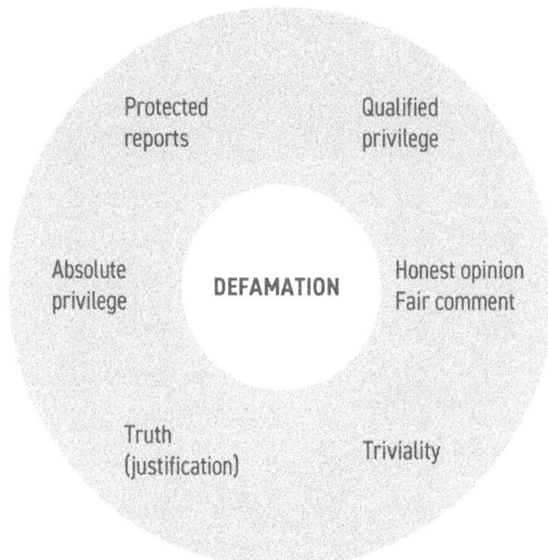

Defamation is a highly technical and complicated tort with intricate rules of procedure and pleading. Consequently, this chapter offers only an overview of this tort, which challenges practitioners to develop not only specialised legal knowledge but also high levels of ingenuity, creativity and language skills. This chapter focuses on outlining the law, rather than on giving factual examples of defamation, so you should make a point of reading a selection of cases to familiarise yourself with the way that lawyers draw out the defamatory imputations from the published matter.

Difficulties for plaintiffs

One problem facing litigants in this area is the fact that the contest between a private individual whose reputation has been harmed and a powerful, well-resourced media group is not an even one. It may be very difficult for a private individual to obtain a legal remedy. The difficulties encountered by plaintiffs who become 'entangled in pleading difficulties' and seemingly endless interlocutory proceedings against which they must struggle with 'great expenditure of time and labour' were discussed by Hutley JA in *Hepburn v TCN Channel Nine Pty Ltd* (1983) at 692:

> The law of defamation is one of the shields that the citizen has against excesses by the media. To be effective for this purpose, the hearing of the complaint should follow closely after the event. Moreover, I do not consider a court should disregard the fact that in most defamation proceedings against the media, there is an enormous disparity of resources and specialized legal skill ...

Kirby J took a similar view in *Favell v Queensland Newspapers Pty Ltd* (2005) at [20]:

> Defamation procedure in Australia, including pre-trial applications of the kind that occurred in this case, have become unnecessarily complex. A plaintiff who alleges that it has been defamed must run a gauntlet of interlocutory proceedings

> ... which ... are illustrated by the numerous skirmishes in *Hepburn*, the repeated reports of other cases and the proceedings in the instant case. The result may be satisfactory to most lawyers who specialise in [defamation law]. It cannot but be discouraging to a plaintiff with a legitimate complaint forced into a system of interlocutory hearings which may occasionally even be used to exhaust or discourage those on the receiving end of defamation ... [References omitted.]

In many cases plaintiffs find that defending their reputation carries a high cost, not only in money and time, but also because of the risk of spreading negative publicity and the findings uncovered by defendants running a truth defence to a much wider audience. Examples of such controversial cases are *Costello v Random House Pty Ltd* (1999), *Abbott v Random House Pty Ltd* (1999) and, more recently, *Roberts-Smith v Fairfax Media Publications Pty Ltd (No 41)* (2023) and *Lehrmann v Network Ten Pty Ltd* (2024). In the latter case, when referring to aborted criminal proceedings against the plaintiff, Lee J's line from the judgment achieved an equally wide audience: 'having escaped the lions' den, Mr Lehrmann made the mistake of going back for his hat'. While defendants are said to publish at their own peril, the tort of defamation is equally onerous for plaintiffs who encounter the perils of litigation.

Additionally, plaintiffs will often enter litigation wanting to receive a public apology that will vindicate their reputation, but while the new defamation laws (see below) encourage the making of apologies and offers to make amends, they do not give the courts the power to order such remedies.

Reforms to the law of defamation

The law of defamation in Australia is a combination of common law and statute. Defamation law was different in every state and territory prior to 2006, but the Uniform Defamation Laws ('uniform defamation legislation' or uniform legislation'), which came into effect in all jurisdictions on 1 January 2006, resulted in a relatively uniform approach being adopted throughout all states and territories. At the end of 2019, however, the Australian Council of Attorneys-General (CAG) announced a plan for a major overhaul of Australia's defamation laws. The need for the review came about because of the impact of modern technology, specifically digital media, on defamation law, as well as concerns that an imbalance had arisen in favour of the protection of plaintiffs' individual reputations over freedom of speech, particularly in matters of public interest. Following the review, CAG agreed to adopt the *Model Defamation Amendment Provisions 2020* (*MDAP*). The legislation proposed a number of significant changes, such as requiring a plaintiff to prove serious harm in order to establish defamation and requiring them to issue a concerns notice before commencing proceedings. The changes also provided for two new defences: peer-reviewed matters published in academic or scientific journals, and responsible communication of matters of public interest. Additionally, the *MDAP* introduced a single publication rule for online defamation, which means that a defamation action can only be brought within one year of the first publication of the defamatory material, even if it remains accessible online. In addition to the common law's goal of protecting a person's reputation, the objects of the new defamation regime are to promote uniformity in the law, protect freedom of expression on matters of public interest and importance, provide effective and fair remedies, and promote prompt and non-litigious dispute resolution.

Unfortunately, adoption of the reforms has been anything but uniform across the states and territories. At the time of writing (October 2025), two jurisdictions (Western Australia and the Northern Territory) are yet to adopt the 'serious harm' requirement of the first-stage reforms. Additionally, further reforms from the second-stage review of the *MDAP* came into effect on 1 July 2024 but only in New South Wales and the Australian Capital Territory. These reforms extend the defence of absolute privilege to apply to publications of defamatory matter to police forces or services[1] and protect digital intermediaries from liability by exempting them when they provide passive technical services such as caching or search results.[2] If the adoption of reforms continues to be inconsistent, there is a danger that Australia's relatively uniform defamation law could revert to its pre-2006 state, with the concomitant danger that plaintiffs engage in 'forum-shopping' if they have a choice of jurisdiction in which to commence proceedings.

LEGISLATION ALERT!

Given the current lack of uniformity in the Uniform Defamation Laws and the state of flux in the adoption of the *MDAP* reforms, it is important that you consult your study materials to find the appropriate provisions in your jurisdiction – and fill in the gaps left in the text to make sure you know which provisions apply.

Download a copy of the relevant defamation legislation in your jurisdiction:

- *Civil Law (Wrongs) Act 2002* (ACT) ch 9;
- *Defamation Act 2005* (NSW);
- *Defamation Act 2005* (Qld);
- *Defamation Act 2005* (SA);
- *Defamation Act 2005* (Tas);
- *Defamation Act 2005* (WA);
- *Defamation Act 2005* (Vic);
- *Defamation Act 2006* (NT).

Develop your skills

Prepare a case note on *Chesterton* (2009)

Before you begin this chapter, read the decision in *Radio 2UE Sydney Pty Ltd v Chesterton* (2009) of the High Court of Australia and then construct a report on the case, using the 'FIRO' method explained in Chapter 4.

1 *Model Defamation Amendment (Absolute Privilege) Provisions 2023.*
2 *Model Defamation Amendment (Digital Intermediaries) Provisions 2023.*

The joint judgment of French CJ, Gummow, Kiefel and Bell JJ reviewed some of the most significant aspects of the law of defamation, including:

- the major test for defamation and the 'hypothetical referee' at [3]–[9] and [32]–[49];
- a critique of the general test at [39] and [49];
- the topic of true innuendo at [51]–[52]; and
- the distinction between defamation and the tort of injurious falsehood at [10]– [12].

See section 4.5 of Chapter 4 on preparing an oral presentation.

Prepare an oral presentation on *Chesterton* (2009)

Using the advice given in section 4.5 of Chapter 4, prepare an oral presentation on this case.

9.1 The elements of defamation

9.1.1 The nature of defamation

Defamation is the unjustified conduct by the defendant that communicates to a third party some matter that has the capacity to diminish the plaintiff's reputation or to lower their standing in the community and the esteem in which they are held by others. The elements are as follows:

1. The published matter must contain a defamatory imputation.
2. The imputation must be about the plaintiff.
3. The matter containing the imputation must be published by the defendant to a third party.
4. The publication has caused, or is likely to cause, serious harm to the reputation of the plaintiff (this fourth element does not yet apply in Western Australia or the Northern Territory).

Defamation is therefore not a bilateral but a *trilateral* tort that requires the involvement of at least three persons for liability to be established: someone who *makes* the communication, someone who is the *subject* of the communication and someone who *receives* the communication. Of course, the rise of social media has made it infinitely easier to disseminate defamatory comments to many people. The tort is not complete until the defamatory matter is received by the third party in a comprehensible form, and it occurs in that place: *Dow Jones and Co Inc v Gutnick* (2002). The onus lies on the plaintiff to prove all the elements of defamation on the balance of probabilities, whereupon the onus shifts to the defendant to prove a defence.

The focus of the tort of defamation is on protecting a person's interests in all aspects of their personal, professional and business reputation and in their entitlement to be treated respectfully by others in the community as a person of honour, dignity and good character who is worthy of esteem and social inclusion: see the joint judgment in *Radio 2UE Sydney Pty Ltd v Chesterton* (2009) at [1]–[12]. Defamation is a tort of strict liability; all that is required by the fault element is the intention to publish, not any intention to harm the reputation of another. For this reason, a person is said to publish at their own peril: Lord Mansfield in *R v Woodfall* (1774) at 916. At common law only separate legal entities (natural persons or artificial legal persons such as corporations) have standing to bring an action for defamation; however, the capacity of corporations or public bodies to bring an action in defamation was limited under the uniform laws. Note also that the Uniform Defamation Laws abolished the distinction between libel and slander.

LEGISLATION ALERT!

Consult your study materials and note the provisions in the defamation legislation in your jurisdiction on:

- libel and slander; and
- limits on standing.

9.1.2 Guiding principles

Two key principles dominate the tort of defamation and each protects important, but competing, interests. The law must strike a balance between protecting the private interest that an individual plaintiff has in their reputation as a person of honour, dignity and worth and, at the same time, ensure that the law does not place unreasonable limits on freedom of expression and the discussion of matters of public importance (as the objects clause of the uniform defamation legislation makes clear).

Case examples

- In *Uren v John Fairfax & Sons Pty Ltd* (1966), Windeyer J traced the history of the tort and explained at 149–51 that the fundamental principles of liability in defamation are to compensate the plaintiff for any damage done to their intangible interests in their honour and reputation, to vindicate the plaintiff to the public, and to console them for any indignity and humiliation caused by the defendant's wrong.
- The Full Court of the High Court of Australia ('High Court') in *Lange v Australian Broadcasting Corporation* (1997) ('*Lange*') reiterated at 568 that the 'purpose of the law of defamation is to strike a balance between the right to reputation and freedom of speech' and at 559 that 'freedom of communication on matters of government and politics is an indispensable incident of that system of representative government which the Constitution creates'.
- In *Chakravarti v Advertiser Newspapers Ltd* (1998), Kirby J pointed out at 575–6 [134] the universal value that the international community places on two competing, fundamental (but not absolute) human rights, namely:
  - the protection of a person's honour and reputation, which is a right recognised by the *Universal Declaration of Human Rights 1948*, art 12; and

  - the importance attached to freedom of communication, which is another fundamental right that is upheld by both the *Australian Constitution* and the *International Covenant on Civil and Political Rights 1966*, art 19.2.
- Stewart J in *Rosenblatt v Bear* (1966) at 92 explained that defamation law reflects the 'basic concept of the essential dignity and worth of every human being – a concept at the root of any decent system of ordered liberty'.

LEGISLATION ALERT!

Consult your study materials and note the objects clause in the defamation legislation in your jurisdiction.

9.1.3 Overview of the tort of defamation

9.1.3.1 Conduct

The conduct that needs to be proved is *publication:* The defendant must either communicate or facilitate the communication of some matter to a third party: *Pullman v Water Hill & Co* (1891); *Urbanchich v Drummoyne Municipal Council* (1991); *Godfrey v Demon Internet Ltd* (2001); *Fairfax Media Publications Pty Ltd v Voller* (2021); *Google LLC v Defteros* (2022).

Publication occurs when, and in the place where, the matter is received by the third party in a comprehensible form (*Dow Jones and Co Inc v Gutnick* (2002).

9.1.3.2 Effect

The matter published by the defendant must contain a defamatory imputation about the plaintiff – that is, one that has the capacity to produce one or more of the following effects:

- Diminish the plaintiff's reputation by lowering them in the estimation of ordinary, reasonable and decent people in the community or inducing such people to think less of the plaintiff. Reputation includes all aspects of a person's standing in the community, including their character, office, trade, business or profession, all of which may be disparaged *(Sim v Stretch* (1936); *Slatyer v Daily Telegraph Newspaper Co Ltd* (1908); *Radio 2UE Sydney Pty Ltd v Chesterton* (2009); *Cornes v The Ten Group Pty Ltd* (2011)).
- Expose the plaintiff to derision or ridicule, even though it may not suggest moral blame (*Parmiter v Coupland* (1840); *Boyd v Mirror Newspapers Ltd* (1980); *Berkoff v Burchill* (1996)).
- Induce others to shun, avoid or exclude the plaintiff from society, even though it may not suggest moral blame (*Youssoupoff v Metro-Goldwyn-Mayer Pictures Ltd* (1934)).

The defamatory imputation must cause the plaintiff to suffer serious harm (in jurisdictions in which this is a requirement).

9.1.3.3 Fault

The defendant must have intended to publish or communicate the matter to a third party or been reckless or careless about doing so. Liability will depend on whether communication of the matter was reasonably foreseeable and on the state of the defendant's knowledge, either proved or inferred, of the conditions likely to prevail in any place where the matter may be communicated to others (*Theaker v Richardson* (1962); *Byrne v Deane* (1937); *Google Inc v Duffy* (2017)).

Given that this is a tort of strict liability, there is no requirement that the defendant must intend the damage to the plaintiff's reputation. Neither does it matter that the defendant did not know or could not have known all the facts that allow the defamatory imputation reasonably to be drawn by others – or that the damage done to the plaintiff was of a kind which the defendant could not have foreseen (*E Hulton & Co v Jones* (1910); *Cassidy v Daily Mirror* (1929); *Morgan v Odhams Press Ltd* (1971)).

9.1.3.4 Circumstances

Standing must be proved, specifically that the plaintiff is entitled to bring the action. Under the uniform defamation legislation, limits are placed on the standing of deceased persons, corporations and public bodies to sue.

LEGISLATION ALERT!

Consult your study materials and note the provision on standing in the defamation legislation in your jurisdiction. There must be no lawful justification for the conduct. Remember that the defences play a significant role in this tort.

9.1.4 Element 1: The matter must contain a defamatory imputation

The first element requires the plaintiff to prove that the matter published by the defendant contained an imputation that is defamatory. This involves three steps:

1. The plaintiff must identify the '*matter*' (or thing) that has been published by the defendant.
2. The plaintiff must identify the *imputations* contained in the matter.
3. The plaintiff must prove that the imputations are *defamatory*.

9.1.4.1 Step 1: The plaintiff must identify the 'matter' that has been published by the defendant

The 'matter' is the vehicle that delivers the defamatory message. It refers to the thing produced by the defendant that conveys or communicates some suggestion about the plaintiff to others. This thing – or 'matter' – can be a physical item (eg a book, letter, newspaper, cartoon or statue) or an intangible thing (eg an orally delivered speech or song). Matter can be published in either a permanent or temporary form. The term is defined in the uniform defamation legislation to include spoken or written words, pictures, gestures, anything communicated by the print or electronic media, or 'any other thing by means of which something may be communicated to a person'. It is important in problem solving to note the nature of the matter, because the law recognises that people respond differently to different modes of communication.

LEGISLATION ALERT!

Consult your study materials and note the provision defining 'matter' in the defamation legislation in your jurisdiction.

9.1.4.2 Step 2: The plaintiff must identify the imputations allegedly contained in the matter

The 'imputation' is the suggestion about the plaintiff that is conveyed by the matter. Griffith CJ explained in *Hall-Gibbs Mercantile Agency Ltd v Dun* (1910) at 91–2 that 'impute' is an ordinary English word that refers to 'any act or condition asserted of or attributed to a person'. These suggestions about the plaintiff may be conveyed directly by the natural meaning of the words (eg 'Patrick is a thief and a murderer') or they may be conveyed indirectly through insinuation, irony or innuendo. So, to extract the imputations you need to be careful, creative and precise. Consider first the natural or ordinary meaning of any words used, bearing in mind that it includes any inferences that an ordinary reasonable and fair-minded reader would draw from them: *Charleston v News Group Newspapers* (1995) at 69. Then consider whether there is any innuendo. In defamation law there are two types of innuendo:

1. 'Popular' or 'false' innuendo (which is based on the meaning that an ordinary person would understand using their everyday general knowledge of popular culture).
2. 'Legal' or 'true' innuendo (which is the meaning that is conveyed only to a limited group of people who have extrinsic knowledge of particular facts that are not stated in the published matter). In this kind of 'legal' or 'true' innuendo, the essential requirement of the plea is that the meaning is not within the general knowledge of the public, so the plaintiff must provide evidence of those special facts, known to those to whom the matter was published, which, when combined with the published material, gives rise to the imputation: *Radio 2UE Sydney Pty Ltd v Chesterton* (2009) at [51]; *Cornes v The Ten Group Pty Ltd* (2011) at [94].

Case example

- In *Grubb v Bristol United Press Ltd* (1963) at 336–7, Davies LJ gave an example of words that can yield two imputations: 'The advertising of Mr X is in extremely bad taste and indeed grossly vulgar.' The first imputation, that Mr X has bad taste and uses vulgar advertising, is based purely on the natural and ordinary meaning of the words taken at face value. The second imputation, that Mr X is guilty of professional misconduct, is based on a 'legal' or 'true' innuendo, because it could be drawn out only by those who also had the special extrinsic knowledge that (a) Mr X is a barrister, and (b) that under the professional ethics of the bar, barristers are forbidden to advertise.

- In the case of 'popular' or 'false' innuendo the plaintiff relies not on the natural meaning of the words, but on their acquired or secondary meaning in popular culture. So, to say that someone is a 'few sandwiches short of a picnic' does not literally mean that they have forgotten to pack enough food for everyone at their outdoor gathering; rather, it means that they are not very bright.

9.1.4.3 Step 3: The plaintiff must prove that the imputations are defamatory

Extracting the imputations is creative work – but showing that they carry a defamatory 'sting' can be the most testing part of a defamation case because, as Lord Atkin pointed out in *Sim v Stretch* (1936) at 1240, 'judges and textbook writers alike have found difficulty in defining with precision the word "defamatory"'. The tests for defamation were considered in depth by the High Court in *Radio 2UE Sydney Pty Ltd v Chesterton* (2009). The joint judgment explained at [4] that an imputation will be defamatory if it has the capacity to:

- diminish or lower the plaintiff's reputation (the 'general test');
- expose the plaintiff to ridicule or derision, or display them in a 'ridiculous light'; or
- induce others to shun, avoid or exclude the plaintiff from society (also known as the 'social exclusion' test).

The general test for loss of reputation is the most important – and the most difficult to apply. The other two tests are more straightforward, because they are more factual in focus and do not involve any ascription of moral blame to the plaintiff. It was established in *Jones v Skelton* (1963) and *Favell v Queensland Newspapers Pty Ltd* (2005) that the question of whether the words being complained of are capable of conveying a defamatory meaning is a question of law that is decided by the judge; and whether the words do in fact convey a defamatory meaning is a question for the finder of fact (either a jury, if there is one, or a judge if there is not).

LEGISLATION ALERT!

Consult your study materials and note whether jury trials are available in the defamation legislation in your jurisdiction.

Remember too that any given matter may give rise to imputations that satisfy more than one test. Furthermore, the plaintiff does not have to prove in evidence that any of these adverse effects has actually occurred in order to establish that the imputations are defamatory. Given the intangible nature of the harm done by defamation, the focus of the tests is on the likelihood, tendency or capacity of the imputations to lead to any of these adverse consequences.

The 'social exclusion' test

An imputation will be defamatory if it tends to induce others to shun, avoid or exclude the plaintiff from society. This test does not require any suggestion of moral blame attaching to the plaintiff and the cases give several illustrations of its application where it was suggested that a plaintiff was either insane, suffered from a 'loathsome' or contagious disease, had been raped or dishonoured – or even that they 'stink' and suffered from 'the itch': *Villers v Monsley* (1769). In that case it was held that it is defamatory to suggest that the plaintiff is either insane, as in *Morgan v Lingen* (1863), or suffers from any serious sexually transmissible or serious contagious disease even though it did not suggest any moral wrongdoing by the plaintiff: see also *Berkoff v Burchill* (1996).

Case example

- In *Youssoupoff v Metro-Goldwyn-Mayer Pictures Ltd* (1934) the matter being complained of was a scene in a film entitled *Rasputin, the Mad Monk* which showed a Russian princess being 'ravished' against her will by Rasputin. The Court held that, even though the imputation that the plaintiff had been raped by Rasputin did not suggest any moral discredit on the plaintiff's part, it was defamatory because it had a tendency to lead others to shun, avoid or exclude her from society.
- This loss of social reputation or respectful consideration from others discussed by Slesser LJ in *Youssopoff v Metro-Goldwyn-Mayer Pictures Ltd* (1934) at 587 was seen as analogous to other cases where it was held that it is defamatory to suggest that the plaintiff is either insane, as in *Morgan v Lingen* (1863), or suffers from any serious sexually transmissible or serious contagious disease (like leprosy or the plague) even though it did not suggest any moral wrongdoing by the plaintiff: see also *Berkoff v Burchill* (1996).

The 'ridiculous light' test

An imputation will be defamatory if it displays the plaintiff in a ridiculous light or exposes the plaintiff to public ridicule or derision. This test, like the 'social exclusion' test, does not require any suggestion of moral blame.

Case examples

- In *Berkoff v Burchill* (1996) the defendant, a film critic, commented twice on the plaintiff, an actor and director. The first article described him as 'hideous looking' and a second article said that Frankenstein's monster looked 'a lot like Stephen Berkoff, only marginally better looking'. It was held by the majority that this imputation could variously expose the plaintiff to ridicule, cause others to shun or avoid him or lower his standing in the estimation of the public. It is worth reading Lord Millett's dissenting judgment, which described the case as 'frivolous' and pointed out that 'the line between mockery and defamation may sometimes be difficult to draw'.
- *Ettingshausen v Australian Consolidated Press Ltd* (1991) concerned a well-known Australian rugby player who successfully sued over a magazine photograph that showed him showering naked after a game. Given that a particular part of the blurry picture was capable of being

interpreted as showing his genitals, it was held to be defamatory because it exposed the plaintiff to 'more than a trivial degree of ridicule'. This case reviews other 'ridicule' cases.

- In *Boyd v Mirror Newspapers Ltd* (1980), D published an article about P, a rugby player, under the headline 'Boyd is Fat, Slow and Predictable', which said, 'As the player wearing No 9 jersey for the Sea Eagles waddled into the sunshine, I couldn't believe it was Les Boyd.' Hunt J held that an imputation must either be disparaging of P, must induce others to shun and avoid P, or must display P in a ridiculous light (even though it may not suggest any fault or moral blame on P's part). So, the mere description of P as 'fat and slow' was not enough on its own because it did not suggest that P was morally to blame for his own condition; nor was it enough to make others shun or avoid P, or capable of displaying him in a ridiculous light. By contrast, D's expression of incredulity at the sight of P 'waddling' onto the field was capable of yielding a defamatory imputation under the 'ridiculous light' test.
- *Zbyszko v New York American Inc* (1930) concerned a newspaper article on the theory of evolution that was illustrated with a photo of a 'hideous looking' gorilla placed next to a photo of the plaintiff, with the caption: 'Stanislaus Zbyszko, the wrestler: not fundamentally different from the gorilla in physique.' McAvoy J pointed out at 413 that it was 'not necessary that words impute disgraceful conduct to the plaintiff. If they render him contemptible or ridiculous, he is equally entitled to redress'. This case is discussed in *Berkoff v Burchill* (1996).

The 'general test' for defamation

An imputation will be defamatory if it has the capacity to diminish a plaintiff's personal, official, business or professional reputation by lowering them in the estimation of ordinary, reasonable and decent members of the community or inducing such people to think less of the plaintiff. Aspects of this general test were discussed by the High Court in *Slatyer v Daily Telegraph Newspaper Co Ltd* (1908) and it was given its current form by the joint judgment in *Radio 2UE Sydney Pty Ltd v Chesterton* (2009) after a review of the perceived shortcomings of earlier versions of the test. One of the original tests for defamation, which was given by Parke B in *Parmiter v Coupland* (1840) at 108, looked at whether the imputation was 'calculated to injure the reputation of another, by exposing him to hatred, contempt, or ridicule'. This test was seen as too narrow. Another early version, which asked whether the imputation would 'tend to lower the plaintiff in the estimation of right-thinking members of society generally', was used by Lord Atkin in *Sim v Stretch* (1936) at 1240, but this 'right-thinking' formula had been criticised as ambiguous by Griffiths CJ as early as in 1908 in *Slatyer v Daily Telegraph Newspaper Co Ltd* (1908) at 7. The joint judgment noted at [40] that this formula 'most clearly implies a standard of decency in a person' and explained at [38]:

> The expression 'right-thinking' should not be taken to refer to the application by the hypothetical referee of moral or social standards, those referable to general character. Such an approach might also limit the application of the general test. It should be understood as a rejection of a wrong standard, one not held by the community. It should be taken to describe a person who shares the standards of the general community and will apply them.

The joint judgment retained the focus of the earlier tests on injury to reputation and went on to elaborate upon both the nature and scope of the term 'reputation' as well as the nature of the notional group in the community known as the 'hypothetical referee' that supplies the basis for judgment that a plaintiff's reputation has been injured. It explained at [36] and [10] that the concept of reputation 'comprehends all aspects of a person's standing in the community' including their 'private character' and their 'office, profession, business or trade' and maintained that the general test applies to all these aspects. It also pointed out at [38]–[41] that 'it is important to distinguish between the general test for defamation and any general community standards which may be relevant in a particular case' because the general test does not 'import particular standards, those of a moral or ethical nature, to the assessment of the imputations' – rather it provides a 'benchmark by which some views would be excluded from consideration as unacceptable'. The judgment concluded at [36]:

> [T]he general test for defamation should apply to an imputation concerning any aspect of a person's reputation. A conclusion as to whether injury to reputation has occurred is the answer to the question posed by the general test, whether it be stated as whether a person's standing in the community, or the estimation in which people hold that person, has been lowered or simply whether the imputation is likely to cause people to think less of a plaintiff.

The positive qualities of the 'hypothetical referee' or the 'hypothetical audience' and its approach to the task have been explained in many cases. Other cases have explained that certain approaches would be rejected by the hypothetical referee and made it clear that not every unpleasant comment made about another person will necessarily be defamatory. These positive and negative characterisations of the hypothetical referee are a helpful source of arguments and counterarguments to use when you apply the test in any problem-solving exercises.

Case examples

The positive attributes of the hypothetical referee

- The Privy Council in *Jones v Skelton* (1963) explained at 1371 that 'the test of reasonableness guides and directs the court in its function of deciding whether it is open to a jury in any particular case to hold that reasonable persons would understand the words complained of in a defamatory sense'. This was adopted and applied by the joint judgment of Gleeson CJ, McHugh, Gummow and Heydon JJ in *Favell v Queensland Newspapers Pty Ltd* (2005) at [9].
- In *Lewis v Daily Telegraph Ltd* (1964) at 258, Lord Reid described the audience as able to 'read between the lines' in the light of their 'general knowledge and experience of worldly affairs' and at 260 as ordinary people who are not 'avid for scandal'. They are also 'fair-minded': Lord Morris of Borth-y-Gest at 268.
- Gummow and Hayne JJ, citing *Boyd v Mirror Newspapers Ltd* (1980), referred to them as 'ordinary decent folk' in *John Fairfax Publications Pty Ltd v Gacic* (2007) at [53].

- In *Reader's Digest Services Pty Ltd v Lamb* (1982), Brennan J pointed out at 506 that the hypothetical referees are not only 'taken to have a uniform view of the meaning of the language used' but that they are also taken to share 'moral or social standards' that are 'common to society generally'.
- The joint judgment in *Radio 2UE Sydney Pty Ltd v Chesterton* (2009) explained at [38], [40] and [53] that the hypothetical audience, as ordinary, decent and reasonable people, will apply 'whatever community standards were appropriate and relevant to the imputations' and will reject any wrong standards not held by the community.
- In *Trkulja v Google LLC* (2018), Kiefel CJ, Bell, Keane, Nettle and Gordon JJ stated [at 31] that the exercise of determining whether something is defamatory is 'one of attempting to envisage a mean or midpoint of temperaments and abilities and on that basis [deciding] the most damaging meaning that ordinary reasonable people at the midpoint could put on the impugned words or images considering the publication as a whole'.

Interpretations that will be rejected by the hypothetical referee

- In *Cassidy v Daily Mirror* (1929) Greer LJ maintained at 350 that 'unduly suspicious' interpretations will be rejected.
- In *Slatyer v Daily Telegraph Newspaper Co Ltd* (1908) Griffith CJ agreed at 7 that any 'perverse minded or unreasonable interpretations' will be rejected.
- In *Byrne v Deane* (1937) Slesser LJ explained at 833 that whereas members of the 'criminal classes' might regard a person who had given information about a possible crime to the police with disfavour, no 'right-thinking' person would adopt that standard.
- Lord Morris of Borth-y-Gest explained in *Jones v Skelton* (1963) at 1370 that any 'meanings which can only emerge as the product of some strained, or forced, or utterly unreasonable interpretation' must also be rejected: see also the joint judgment in *Favell v Queensland Newspapers Pty Ltd* (2005) at [9].
- A mere display of 'words of heat' and 'mere vulgar abuse' that are 'uttered in anger' will not necessarily be defamatory in the eyes of an ordinary reasonable person: Croom-Johnson J in *Cleghorn v Sadler* (1945) at 327; *Mundey v Askin* (1982); Heydon J in *Radio 2UE Sydney Pty Ltd v Chesterton* (2009) at [69]. So, for example, vulgar abuse directed at an umpire by a spectator at a football match may not necessarily give rise to a cause of action, given the context in which it is uttered and heard.

Critique of the general test for defamation

The joint judgment in *Radio 2UE Sydney Pty Ltd v Chesterton* (2009) noted at [39] that the general test has been criticised as being ambiguous, unclear, circular and difficult to apply. It questioned whether the test may need to be developed further in the future to avoid the problem caused by the current requirement that the standard must be one that is 'common to society, rather than one which reflects an attitude of a section of it', as noted by Brennan J in *Reader's Digest Services Pty Ltd v Lamb* (1982) at 507. The joint judgment explained at [49]:

> Questions have been raised concerning the notion of there being one general community standard with respect to all topics; and as to whether standards applied by the

> courts in some cases are in reality those of the general community. ... And it has been suggested that sectional attitudes may be valid, when regard is had to the cultural diversity of countries such as Australia.

The joint judgment left the issue of 'sectional attitudes' and the meaning of the term 'community' open for further consideration, but the fact is that reasonable and decent people in the Australian community do disagree on many social and ethical matters. The way to answer such criticisms, and others levelled by Kirby J at the 'ludicrous elaborations' and 'judicial verbiage' surrounding the 'fiction' of the ordinary reasonable person test in *Favell v Queensland Newspapers Pty Ltd* (2005) at [23], may be found in the following cases.

Case examples

- In *Hepburn v TCN Channel Nine Pty Ltd* (1983), a case where the plaintiff, a doctor, objected to being called an 'abortionist' on a current affairs television program, Glass JA pointed out at 693–4 that the law should 'recognize that there are many subjects in a pluralist society upon which contradictory attitudes exist' and that it would be futile to expect judges to arbitrate between them. His Honour reviewed authorities that supported both allowing and denying liability in such circumstances of disagreement and suggested that it should be enough to satisfy the test if an imputation had the capacity to lower the plaintiff in the estimation of 'an appreciable and reputable section of the community'.
- Hunt J suggested in *Krahe v TCN Channel Nine Pty Ltd* (1986) at 544 that where the plaintiff relies upon the existence of a particular attitude which is held by one group within the community but not by the general community, the plaintiff should 'plead that sectional attitude as an extrinsic fact or circumstance' and 'proceed upon the basis that publication in a defamatory sense is alleged only in relation to the publication to members of that particular group'.

So, under the test proposed in *Hepburn* (1983):

- if it is possible to identify a section or group of people in the community that is appreciable in size (ie reasonably substantial in numbers); and
- that group is a reputable and decent group of people (and not a perverse-minded group); and if
- that group would tend to think less of the plaintiff on hearing the imputations,

then, as *Radio 2UE Sydney Pty Ltd v Chesterton* (2009) explains, it would *not* be a matter of whether the fact-finder agrees that this group's views are morally correct and should be preferred over the views of those who disagree; the result would be that the imputation is defamatory. To summarise, the *Hepburn* (1983) approach searches for a standard that is commonly found *in* the community – not necessarily one that is common *to all* in the community.

Develop your skills

Prepare an oral presentation on *Hepburn* (1983)

Using the advice given in section 4.5 of Chapter 4, prepare an oral presentation on *Hepburn v TCN Channel Nine Pty Ltd* (1983).

Try a problem-solving exercise

Imagine a scenario where the defendant, a climate activist, decides to reveal that Pietro, a prominent local politician, has been active in an online climate change denial forum under the username 'Mr Skeptik'.

In addition to *Hepburn* (1983) and *Youssoupoff* (1934), you may find some assistance in the following article and cases:

- Baker, 'Defamation and the Moral Community' (2008);
- *Rivkin v Amalgamated Television Services Pty Ltd* (2001);
- *Kelly v John Fairfax Publications Pty Ltd* (2003); and
- *John Fairfax Publications Pty Ltd v Rivkin* (2003), Kirby J at [140]–[143].

Interpreting the meaning

The search for the meaning of any published matter is aided by considering the mode of publication and the surrounding context, circumstances and time in and at which the matter is published: *Charleston v News Group Newspapers* (1995) at 68. The nature of the publication is to be considered, and it is assumed that a reader of a book or article published in a permanent form will be able devote more time and effort to digest the meaning of the matter by contrast with the more fleeting experience of listening to a radio broadcast: *Morosi v Broadcasting Station 2GB Pty Ltd* (1980). It is also accepted that different kinds of newspapers may well have different readerships, and that readers of 'sensationalist' newspapers may not always read as carefully as others: *Morgan v Odhams Press Ltd* (1971); *Charleston v News Group Newspapers* (1995). As we saw above, the fact that different sections of the community do not always share one single moral standard causes difficulties when we are applying the test for defamation, and similar problems occur when we try to establish a single meaning for any given published matter. Despite the fact that different people might easily derive different meanings from the same passage of words, defamation law requires the fact-finder to take the publication as a whole and determine one single 'right' meaning when considering whether it is defamatory: *Slim v Daily Telegraph* (1968) at 171–4; *Charleston v News Group Newspapers* (1995) at 69–71; *Mirror Newspapers Ltd v World Hosts Pty Ltd* (1979) at 368. This approach to determining the meaning of a publication has been criticised by Kirby J, who argued in *Chakravarti v Advertiser Newspapers Ltd* (1998) at [134] that it denies plaintiffs a remedy and 'ignores the realities' of modern media and 'the way in which ordinary people receive and are intended to receive' these communications.

One commonly encountered problem occurs when a publication, such as a book, article, television program or radio show, appears to send mixed messages about the plaintiff. Some parts might contain material that is negative and highly defamatory if taken in isolation and others may contain other material that appears to paint the plaintiff in a positive light. The plaintiff may object to the inclusion of the unpleasant and poisonous material – but the defendant will claim that the positive material undoes the effect of the 'poison'. The plaintiff, however, cannot base a claim on an isolated passage taken out of context. To assist with the challenge of extracting 'one single meaning'[3] and solving the 'bane and antidote'[4] problem, the courts have given guidance on how the ordinary reasonable reader, listener or viewer of average intelligence might extract a defamatory 'sting' from any given matter.

Case examples

- The law recognises that ordinary, reasonable people do not analyse matters in the same way that lawyers do. Lord Reid explained in *Lewis v Daily Telegraph Ltd* (1964) at 259 that the hypothetical reader must avoid not only any 'unusually suspicious' interpretations but also those that are 'unusually naïve'. As Lord Devlin pointed out at 285, the 'layman reads in an implication much more freely' than a lawyer and so, as Hunt J explained in *Fahrquar v Bottom* (1980) at 386, if the words published are 'imprecise, ambiguous, loose, fanciful, or unusual' a wide degree of latitude will be given.
- The test allows for 'a certain amount of loose thinking': *Morgan v Odhams Press Ltd* (1971) at 1245.
- Pictures and headlines can be used to help interpret the imputations contained in the accompanying text: *Bickel v John Fairfax & Sons Ltd* (1981) at 488. In *Hepburn v TCN Channel Nine Pty Ltd* (1983) at 685 the illustration in a backdrop shown during a television program was taken into account.
- Those who print defamatory headlines are 'playing with fire': *Charleston v News Group Newspapers* (1995) at 72. In *Hockey v Fairfax Media Publications Pty Ltd* (2015), the headline 'Treasurer for Sale' was held to be defamatory when it was posted on Twitter without a link to the full newspaper article, which would have put the headline in context.
- The matter complained of must be read as a whole to determine one single 'right' meaning: Lord Reid in *Slim v Daily Telegraph* (1968) at 171–4; *Charleston v News Group Newspapers* (1995) at 68–71. However, this 'does not mean that either the court or the jury must give equal significance to each part of the publication': *Mirror Newspapers Ltd v World Hosts Pty Ltd* (1979) at 646.
- McHugh J explained in *John Fairfax Publications Pty Ltd v Rivkin* (2003) at [27] that the 'emphasis that the publisher supplies by inserting conspicuous headlines, headings and captions is a legitimate matter that readers do and are entitled to take into account' and that 'contrary statements in an article do not automatically negate the effect of other defamatory statements in the article', citing *Savige v News Ltd* (1932) and *Sergi v Australian Broadcasting Commission* (1983).

3 *Slim v Daily Telegraph* (1968) at 171.
4 *Morosi v Broadcasting Station 2GB Pty Ltd* (1980) at 419.

- The 'bane and the antidote must be taken together': *Chalmers v Payne* (1835) at 68; *Charleston v News Group Newspapers* (1995) at 68. So, a disclaimer or denial of any intention to harm any living persons is not enough on its own to prevent the publication from defaming the plaintiff, because it must be taken as a whole: *Fahrquar v Bottom* (1980) at 387–8; *Australian Broadcasting Corporation v Hanson* (1998) at 8.
- In the case of a television or radio broadcast, an ordinary reasonable listener or viewer of average intelligence is 'deemed to have listened to the whole of what was broadcast'; nevertheless, the law accepts that they may not have 'devoted the same degree of concentration' to it as they would to a written document. However, the plaintiff 'cannot succeed because some viewers or listeners may have left the room momentarily or had their attention distracted, and thus missed the qualifying passages in the whole matter that was broadcast': *Gordon v Amalgamated Television Services Pty Ltd* (1980) at 413, citing *Morosi v Broadcasting Station 2GB Pty Ltd* (1980) at 419–20.
- Hunt J explained in *Fahrquar v Bottom* (1980) at 388 that there will be rare occasions where:

  > [i]f the imputation arises by way of inference only, and the matter complained of itself contains an express disclaimer of any intention to convey such an imputation; or if the refutation consists of a statement of fact destructive of the entire basis upon which the imputation relies, then the matter complained of, taken as a whole, will be incapable of conveying the imputation refuted.

- The fact that an imputation is made in a fictional setting will not prevent it from being defamatory. See the cases of *E Hulton & Co v Jones* (1910) for defamation of a natural person and *Sungravure v Middle East Airlines Airliban SAL* (1975) for defamation of an airline's reputation.
- The time in history when *words* are used will be taken into account, so in *Slazengers (Ltd) v C Gibbs & Co* (1916) it was suggested that during the First World War it may have been defamatory to describe a company as 'German' and in *Cross v Denley* (1952) it was possibly defamatory to call a person a communist during the Cold War. See also *Slatyer v Daily Telegraph Newspaper Co Ltd* (1908) where the word in question was a 'socialist'.
- In *Trkulja v Google LLC* (2018), the High Court determined that search engine results and auto-completions are capable of being defamatory.

9.1.5 Element 2: The imputation must be about the plaintiff

Plaintiffs must prove that the defamatory matter was published 'of and concerning' them or was 'reasonably referable' to them, so if the plaintiff is identified clearly and expressly in the published matter this element is satisfied. In other cases where the plaintiff is not identified by name – or if a name is mentioned that could refer to a number of people, or a group is mentioned without naming individuals – the test is whether ordinary reasonable persons would reasonably believe that the matter referred to the particular plaintiff: *E Hulton & Co v Jones* (1910); *Lee v Wilson* (1934); *Morgan v Odhams Press Ltd* (1971). Because defamation is designed to protect individual persons, a group may not sue to protect their collective reputation, but any individual who is reasonably identifiable as a member of that group may bring an action, provided the group is small enough to enable the plaintiff to be identified and any extrinsic facts enabling the identification are proved: *Bjelke Petersen v Warburton* (1987). The 'extravagance' of the accusation is also relevant: Lord Porter in *Knupffer v London Express Newspapers Ltd* (1944) at 124.

Case examples

- In *E Hulton & Co v Jones* (1910), P succeeded in an action against D, who, unaware of P's existence, had published a humorous fictional piece about a man with an invented name (Artemus Jones), which by coincidence was also P's real name.
- Greer LJ explained in *Youssoupoff v Metro-Goldwyn-Mayer Pictures Ltd* (1934) at 585 that although D had not used P's real name, they 'used a description of her that could apply to no one but the plaintiff'. Similarly, if D referred to the 'Prime Minister of Ruritania' that would be sufficient to identify P, even if the name was never mentioned. See also *Consolidated Trust Co v Browne* (1948) for a similar example.
- In *Lee v Wilson* (1934), an article mentioned a 'Detective Lee' and alleged he had taken bribes. There were three officers named 'Lee' in the police force, and two sued. Dixon J said at 295 that, regardless of the intention of the writer, if defamatory words, capable of relating to more than one person, are found actually to disparage each of them among the respective groups of the community which know them, because the words are reasonably understood to refer to each of them, then they may all maintain actions.
- In *Lloyd v David Syme* (1986) an article suggested that the West Indies cricket team, which was touring Australia, had 'taken a dive' in a one-day match. The article did not refer to the captain by name and, even though he had not played in the match, he did recover damages for defamation, because the group was limited in size, and Lloyd, as captain, was well known.
- Likewise, in *Bjelke Petersen v Warburton* (1987), members of the Queensland ministerial cabinet were entitled to bring an action to protect their reputation against an allegation that some 'Ministers have their hands in the till' on the grounds that the group of 18 ministers was 'sufficiently narrow for each member of the class to complain that the words complained of may reasonably be taken to refer to him or her': Kneipp J at 467. Another test was 'whether a sensible man, having knowledge of the relevant circumstances, and reading casually, not expecting a high degree of accuracy of a contestant in the political arena would reasonably identify the plaintiffs as the persons defamed': Connolly J at 470, citing *Morgan v Odhams Press Ltd* (1971) and *Lewis v Daily Telegraph Ltd* (1964).

9.1.5.1 Standing to sue

At common law, only living plaintiffs with legal personality have standing to bring an action in defamation (because a person's interest in their reputation dies with them). The uniform defamation legislation in most jurisdictions (but not all) repeats this rule. Under the uniform legislation there are now statutory limits on the entitlement of public bodies and large corporations to bring an action to protect their trading reputation, but those limits do not prevent plaintiffs who work for such a body from bringing actions to protect their personal reputations, provided they can satisfy the identification rules.

LEGISLATION ALERT!

Consult your study materials and note the standing rules in the defamation legislation in your jurisdiction.

Case examples

- Under the uniform defamation legislation, a case like *McDonald's Corporation v Morris & Steel* (1997) could not be brought in Australia. This case, which was known as the 'McLibel' case, became the longest-running defamation case in England. It achieved huge publicity when two unrepresented environmental activists were sued for making statements about the fast-food chain.
- In *Council of the Shire of Ballina v Ringland* (1994), a majority of the New South Wales Court of Appeal followed the House of Lords decision in *Derbyshire County Council v Times Newspapers Ltd* (1993), which decided that at common law an incorporated local government authority whose members are popularly elected may not maintain an action for defamation because it would stifle the democratic right to free political comment. Individual members of such bodies may sue. See also *Jones v Skelton* (1963).
- Although actions may not be brought on behalf of deceased persons, any living plaintiff whose personal reputation has been defamed indirectly by the publication of matter about a deceased family member may bring an action: *Livingstone-Thomas v Associated Newspapers Ltd* (1969); *Krahe v TCN Channel Nine Pty Ltd* (1986).

9.1.5.2 Strict liability

Defamation is a tort of strict liability; all that is required is an intention to publish the material and there is no requirement that the defendant must intend to harm the reputation of a defined individual. In *R v Woodfall* (1774) at 916, Lord Mansfield said, 'Whatever a man publishes, he publishes at his peril' and Lord Reid pointed out in *Morgan v Odhams Press Ltd* (1971) at 1242:

> It does not matter whether the publisher intended to refer to the plaintiff or not. It does not even matter whether he knew of the plaintiff's existence. And it does not matter that he did not know or could not have known the facts which caused the readers with special knowledge to connect the statement with the plaintiff. Indeed, the damage done to the plaintiff by the publication may be of a kind which the publisher could not have foreseen.

9.1.6 Element 3: Publication by the defendant to a third party

The term 'publication' in defamation law refers to the 'communication of the defamatory matter to a third person': *Pullman v Water Hill & Co* (1891) Lopes LJ at 529, Lord Esher at 527. This conduct attracts liability because it creates the possibility of harming the plaintiff's reputation or lowering their standing in the community (which are things that can exist only in the perceptions of others). Publication may either be the result of a direct positive act by the defendant, or it may be facilitated by the defendant's omission or failure to deal with a continuing state of affairs created by another person: *Byrne v Deane* (1937). To be liable for their conduct in publishing defamatory matter by a positive act, the defendant must have either intended the act of publication or been reckless or negligent in allowing publication to someone who could understand the material. The test for liability in cases of unintended publication focuses on the reasonable foreseeability of communication and the state of the defendant's knowledge, either proved or inferred, of the conditions likely to prevail in any place where the matter may be communicated to others: *Theaker v Richardson* (1962). Publication does not occur until it is received by the third party in a comprehensible form: *Dow Jones and Co Inc v Gutnick* (2002). Whether or not publication has taken place is a question of fact that depends on all the circumstances in each case: *Byrne v Deane* (1937); *Fairfax Media Publications Pty Ltd v Voller* (2021); *Google LLC v Defteros* (2022).

Case examples

- In *Byrne v Deane* (1937), where a poem was placed by a third party on a wall in the premises of a golf club owned by D, there was publication by D who had not removed it. A failure to remove defamatory matter from public display was also considered in *Godfrey v Demon Internet Ltd* (2001), where D, an internet service provider, was held to have published defamatory matter posted on its news server by an unknown third party because D allowed it to remain for a short period of about a fortnight even though D had been asked by P to remove it. In each case, the decision was based on D's knowledge and power to remove the matter from public display.
- In *Urbanchich v Drummoyne Municipal Council* (1991), a case where posters had been put up on bus shelters under D's control, Hunt J went further and suggested, at 69 and 193–4, that D would not be liable unless P could establish that D had accepted responsibility for the continued display of the matter in some way (either expressly or by inference).
- In *Pullman v Water Hill & Co* (1891), the defendant dictated a letter to a secretary who typed it and sent it to a firm where it was opened by a clerk who was following common business practice. This amounted to publication to both the secretary who typed the letter and the clerk who opened and read it. Lord Esher pointed out at 527 that if a letter is sent to and read only by the person about whom it was written, it would not amount to publication 'for you cannot publish a libel of a man to himself'. The judges explained that a defendant would *not* be liable for publishing the letter if, for example, the defendant had locked the letter in a desk and a thief had broken in and read it (at 527), or if the letter had been marked 'Private' but someone other than the addressee had nevertheless opened and read it (at 529).
- In *Huth v Huth* (1915), there was no publication when a butler had acted in breach of his duty by opening and reading a letter addressed to a person staying with his employer.
- By contrast, in *Theaker v Richardson* (1962), publication was found to have occurred when a husband opened and read an unstamped document that looked like a circular addressed to his wife, which had been left by the defendant on their doormat. Harman LJ said at 159 that 'the question of publication of a libel contained in a letter will depend on the state of the defendant's knowledge, either proved or inferred, of the conditions likely to prevail in the place to

which the libel is destined'. So, because the document was, in the circumstances, likely to be read by the husband (which could 'quite easily and naturally happen in the ordinary course of events'), publication had occurred.

- More recently, in *Fairfax Media Publications Pty Ltd v Voller* (2021), P sued D for failing to remove defamatory comments made by members of the public about P under news stories on D's Facebook pages. The High Court held the media companies were liable for defamatory comments made by third-party users on their social media pages. Importantly, per Kiefel CJ, Keane and Gleeson JJ [at 55] 'facilitating, encouraging and thereby assisting the posting of comments by the third-party Facebook users rendered [the media companies] publishers of those comments'.
- In *Google LLC v Defteros* (2022), P, a criminal lawyer, sued D for failing to remove search results that included a headline and hyperlink to a newspaper article which P alleged defamed him. At first instance and on appeal, D was found liable as publisher of the article; however, this decision was overturned by the High Court. A majority of the justices (5:2) found that merely providing a search result and a hyperlink did not amount to publication of the content, as the hyperlink had merely facilitated access to the article and did not in any way endorse or adopt the defamatory article.

At common law, the original publisher can also be liable for any further republication of the material if it is authorised or is the natural or probable consequence of their own conduct: *Sims v Wran* (1984); *Selecta Homes and Building Co Pty Ltd v Advertiser-Weekend Publishing Co Pty Ltd* (2001). Any person who republishes defamatory matter will also be independently liable; however, both the common law and the uniform defamation legislation allow for a defence of innocent dissemination that protects those who republish such material as a subordinate distributor, provided they neither knew, nor ought reasonably to have known, that the matter was defamatory. The cases are discussed in *Godfrey v Demon Internet Ltd* (2001).

LEGISLATION ALERT!

Consult your study materials and find the innocent dissemination provision in your jurisdiction's defamation legislation, as well as the definition of a subordinate distributor.

9.1.7 Element 4: Serious harm

In jurisdictions where the uniform defamation legislation has been amended to incorporate the first stage of the *MDAP* provisions (ie all jurisdictions other than Western Australia and the Northern Territory), serious harm is now an element of a cause of action in defamation. The element requires that the plaintiff prove they have suffered 'serious harm' to their reputation,[5] otherwise no liability will attach to the defendant

5 For example, *Defamation Act 2005* (NSW) s 10A.

in relation to the defamatory matter. Serious harm is not defined in the uniform legislation and is a matter for the judge to determine.[6]

In *Newman v Whittington* (2022), Sackar J referred to the United Kingdom Supreme Court decision of *Lachaux v Independent Print Ltd* (2020), which interpreted an analogous provision in the United Kingdom's *Defamation Act 2013* (and on which the *MDAP* provisions had been modelled), noting at 64 that the term 'serious harm' is:

> to be determined by reference to the actual facts about its impact and not just to the meaning of the words.

Before defamation proceedings can be commenced, a plaintiff must first send the defendant a concerns notice, which must set out in writing the defamatory implications, as well as the serious harm the plaintiff is alleging. Proceedings cannot then be commenced until 28 days after the plaintiff has served the notice. The purpose of the concerns notice is to encourage parties to resolve their issues and avoid a trial.

LEGISLATION ALERT!

Consult your study materials and find the serious harm provisions in your jurisdiction's defamation legislation.

9.2 The defences to defamation

9.2.1 The nature of the defences to defamation

Once a plaintiff has established a prima facie case by proving the three elements of defamation, the onus shifts to the defendant to escape liability by proving a defence. Given the range and wide scope of the defences, there are many situations where defamatory matter is lawfully published. Remember too that more than one defence may apply. Most of these defences are justified because of the wider public interest in freedom of speech and free communication of opinions and information on matters of public interest, as discussed in section 9.1.2 above. The defences are classified in Table 9.1. Innocent dissemination has already been mentioned in section 9.1.6 above. The uniform defamation legislation provides statutory defences that sit side by side with those created by the common law but note that they do not always share the same names. Due to the current lack of uniformity in defamation law, remember to check your study materials to confirm which of the following defences are available in the defamation legislation in your jurisdiction.

9.2.2 Triviality

The defence of triviality now only exists in Western Australia and the Northern Territory following the introduction of the 'serious harm' requirement in all other

6 For example, *Defamation Act 2005* (NSW) s 10A(3).

Table 9.1 The defences to defamation

Type of defence	**Defence**	**Notes**
A defence based on harm	*Triviality*	D must prove that the circumstances of publication were such that P was unlikely to sustain any harm.
A defence based on fault	*Innocent dissemination* (both common law and statute)	This defence amounts to a denial of fault (or blameworthiness) on the part of D and it focuses mainly on D's state of mind (ie lack of knowledge or any negligence in the circumstances).
Absolute defences	*Truth* (common law) *Justification* (statute) *Absolute privilege* (common law and statute)	These defences exist in both the uniform defamation legislation and at common law. They provide a complete defence and so the motive of D in making the publication is irrelevant. For *Truth* or *Justification,* D must prove that the imputations are substantially true. For *Absolute privilege* (common law and statute), D must prove that the matter was published on an occasion of absolute privilege, eg in parliamentary or judicial proceedings.
Limited defences	*Qualified privilege* (common law) *Fair comment* (common law) *Honest opinion* (statute) *Public documents and reports* (common law and statute) • D must prove that the matter was, or was contained in: + a fair report of any proceedings of public concern; or + a public document. *Publication on a matter of public interest* (statute) • D must prove the matter concerns an issue of public interest; and + D reasonably believed that the publication of the matter was in the public interest.	These defences offer limited protection for specific purposes only and the state of mind of the defendant is relevant (so, depending on the defence, malice or dishonesty may destroy it). For qualified privilege, D must prove that the matter was published reasonably for a legitimate purpose to a person with a special interest in receiving it: common law 'duty–interest' qualified privilege; the extended '*Lange*' (1997) privilege relating to free political speech; or the statutory version of qualified privilege.

Table 9.1 (cont.)

Type of defence	Defence	Notes
	Scientific or academic peer review (statute) • D must prove the material has been published in a scientific or academic journal; and the material + must have undergone a peer review process before publication; and + D must demonstrate that they have acted honestly in publishing the material for the information of the public or the advancement of education.	For fair comment or honest opinion, D must prove that the matter was an expression of an honest opinion on a matter of public interest and was based on proper material, ie facts that are substantially true, privileged or protected.
Consent	Consent – sometimes known 'leave or licence' or '*volenti*' – is also a defence to defamation.	It may be express or implied but must be clear and unequivocal. (It is not discussed in this chapter. See section 7.3 of Chapter 7 and section 15.2 of Chapter 15.)

jurisdictions. Triviality is a question of fact in all the circumstances. Relevant 'circumstances of publication' may be: the nature of the defamatory matter; the manner and time of its publication; and the nature, knowledge and size of the audience to whom it was published. Emotional distress is not sufficient to constitute harm; the plaintiff must establish actual reputational damage: *Smith v Lucht* (2016).

9.2.3 Truth (Justification)

The law presumes that defamatory imputations are false, so it is a complete defence both at common law and under the uniform legislation if the defendant can prove that the 'stings' contained in the imputations are true or substantially true. This defence is not defeated by proof of malice. Note that the concept of substantial truth is also relevant to the defences of fair comment/honest opinion.

Case examples

- Minor mistakes or inaccuracies in the published matter will not prevent the defence of truth being made out – because the factfinder is directed to look at the substance of the 'sting' and decide whether it is true: Lord Shaw in *Sutherland v Stopes* (1925) at 79. So, if the allegation is that X took Y's saddle from the stable and sold it the next day, whereas X took it from the harness room and sold it a week later, then the substance of the sting will still be true: at 79.

- If the imputation describes P's character as 'maliciously and corruptly untruthful' and 'a dishonest, calculating liar', as in *Penton v Calwell* (1945), or as a 'libellous journalist', as in *Wakley v Cooke* (1849), the defence of truth will not be made out unless D proves P has lied or libelled on more than one occasion because the sting lies in the characterisation of P's personality.
- If D has reported that there are rumours about P, D must prove that the rumours themselves are in substance true, not merely that it is true that there are rumours: *Lewis v Daily Telegraph Ltd* (1964). Likewise, if D publishes a report that P is being investigated or charged with a crime that is accompanied by an account of the suspicious circumstances that may have aroused the interest of the authorities and point towards actual guilt, then D must be able to prove that the allegation is true: *Favell v Queensland Newspapers Pty Ltd* (2005).
- The English practice of '*Polly Peck*' pleading (claiming that while D cannot prove the truth of all of the defamatory allegations in a published matter, D can nevertheless prove the truth of a more abstract but 'common sting' carried by all of the imputations) was disapproved by Brennan CJ and McHugh J in *Chakravarti v Advertiser Newspapers Ltd* (1998) at [7]–[13] as contravening fundamental principles of common law pleading.
- See *Roberts-Smith v Fairfax Media Publications Pty Ltd (No 41)* (2023) and *Lehrmann v Network Ten Pty Ltd* (2024) for two recent well-known examples where the truth defence was successfully raised by media companies.

9.2.3.1 Contextual truth

The uniform defamation legislation provides that a defendant may defend the publication by proving, first, that the imputations being complained of were accompanied by other imputations that are substantially true, and second, that the imputations being complained of do not 'further harm the reputation of the plaintiff because of the substantial truth of the contextual imputations'.[7] This prevents plaintiffs from choosing to sue only over a minor untrue imputation, which, if it is considered in context, has been overshadowed by other much more serious imputations, which are true. An example is where the defendant says that the plaintiff shoplifted a chocolate frog (untrue) on the way to committing an armed robbery where he shot and killed a bank customer in cold blood (both true). In *Fairfax Media Publications Pty Ltd v Zeccola* (2015), it was held that a contextual imputation may be pleaded in defence to a specific imputation even though it relates to the same subject matter, as long as it differs in substance. Also see *Fairfax Media Productions Pty Ltd v Kermode* (2011).

9.2.4 Absolute privilege

It is a defence to defamation if the defendant can prove that the imputations were published on an occasion of absolute privilege. This is a complete defence which is not defeated by malice, and it exists in both the common law and the uniform defamation legislation. The occasions of absolute privilege derive either from the importance

7 For example, *Defamation Act 2005* (NSW) s 26.

attached to the need for free and fearless speech in particular forums – or from the desire to protect candour in the communication between people in certain kinds of relationships. In these circumstances, the defendant is allowed to defame without fear of litigation, regardless of motive and regardless of the truth of the imputations. Under the uniform legislation and at common law, absolute privilege applies to the proceedings, reports, documents and evidence given in a parliamentary body or in an Australian court (including certain tribunals and other statutory bodies). It also protects certain proceedings as specified by state and territory legislation. The privilege protects advocates, litigants, witnesses and other participants in those proceedings. At common law there are other categories of absolute privilege, but while the categories are not closed, the courts are reluctant to extend them.

Case examples

- At common law, a defamatory imputation made by one spouse to another has been protected, either on the traditional grounds that as husband and wife are viewed by the law as 'one person' there can be no publication in those circumstances, or on the grounds that 'social policy' or 'public policy' indicates that free communication between spouses should be protected: *Wennhak v Morgan* (1888), Manisty J at 639.
- Communications made between solicitors and clients as part of consultations concerning anticipated litigation are protected: *More v Weaver* (1928), Scrutton LJ at 524–5, citing *Browne v Dunn* (1893), Lord Herschell at 72, Lord Bowen at 80.
- Some communications between high officers of state, government officials, ministers and diplomats, which are made in the course of their duty, are protected, but the extent and scope of the protection is uncertain: *Chatterton v Secretary of State* (1895); *Fayed v al-Tajir* (1988); *Mann v O'Neill* (1997).
- The communication must take place inside the court or parliament in order for the defendant to successfully claim absolute privilege: see, for example, *O'Shane v Harbour Radio Pty Ltd* (2013).

9.2.5 Public documents and reports of proceedings of public concern

The uniform defamation legislation, like the common law, provides defences to those who publish certain public documents or reports of proceedings of public concern, but this protection is not absolute. The legislative protection is limited by the requirements that the defendants must publish fair summaries or extracts of the reports or proceedings and the defences will be defeated if the matter was 'not published honestly for the information of the public or the advancement of education'.[8] In *Belbin v Lower Murray Urban and Rural Water Corporation* (2012), it was held that an informal letter written by a Minister in the Victorian government to a group of former customers, explaining

8 For example, *Defamation Act 2005* (NSW) s 28(3).

the decision to close down the First Mildura Irrigation Trust, did not contain 'the relevant official character or quality' and was therefore not a public document: at 94. 'Fair' means accurate and not slanted, biased, distorted or unbalanced: see, for example, Gleeson CJ and Gummow J in *Rogers v Nationwide News Pty Ltd* (2003) at [9]–[24] and *Jones v Fairfax* (1986). Proceedings of public concern may include proceedings of such bodies as courts, parliaments, local government bodies, international organisations, law reform bodies, learned societies, ombudsmen, sport or recreation associations, public meetings, shareholders meetings and trade associations.

9.2.6 Qualified privilege

Both the common law and the new legislative regime give limited protection – or qualified privilege – to publication of defamatory matter for certain recognised public or private purposes provided the defendant has acted in good faith and not misused the privilege: see *Horrocks v Lowe* (1975). Qualified privilege does not offer absolute protection – the scope of the privilege is limited by the special purposes that justify allowing the defendant to damage the plaintiff's reputation. So, by contrast with absolute privilege – where publication is protected regardless of motive or the truth of the imputations – the defence of qualified privilege is more strictly limited. Since the introduction of the new laws, there are now three kinds of qualified privilege:

1. the old common law 'duty-interest' qualified privilege;
2. the extended *'Lange'* (1997) qualified privilege covering free political speech; and
3. the new statutory version of qualified privilege.

In all of these categories, the privilege will be defeated by malice.

9.2.6.1 Common law 'duty-interest' qualified privilege

At common law there are three main sub-categories of qualified privilege. Their existence depends on whether the person publishing the material has either:

- a legal, social or moral interest or duty to communicate something to another person (*Adam v Ward* (1917) at 334);
- a legitimate interest of their own to protect (*Horrocks v Lowe* (1975) at 149); or
- information on a subject of legitimate public interest of such a nature that for the convenience, welfare and benefit of society the defendant has a duty to publish (*Toogood v Spyring* (1834) at 193; *Australian Broadcasting Corporation v Comalco Ltd* (1986) at 534).

In each case, there must also be either a reciprocal 'duty and interest relationship' between the defendant and every person who receives the information, or both must share a common interest in the information. This reciprocity is essential and any wider publication that goes beyond the confines of the relationship will destroy the defence (*Adam v Ward* (1917) at 334; *Lange v Australian Broadcasting Corporation* (1997) at 572).

Case examples

- Some occasions where D may claim the defence include D writing a reference about P for a potential employer; D complaining to P's supervisor about poor service given by P in order to seek redress; D providing a credit report on P to a potential lender; D protecting D's own reputation from an attack by P or others; D warning the authorities about P's suspicious behaviour in planting a suspected bomb or making a security threat; D discussing the conduct of a CEO with fellow shareholders at a meeting; or local council members who are speaking 'freely and frankly, boldly and bluntly, on any matter which they believe affects the interests or welfare of the inhabitants': *Horrocks v Lowe* (1975) at 152.
- In *Loveday v Sun Newspapers Ltd* (1938), a newspaper published parts of a letter written by the secretary of a District Unemployed Relief Council attacking the local council over its treatment of the plaintiff, a worker. It also published a reply by the council's town clerk that was defamatory of the plaintiff. Both the town clerk and the newspaper could claim qualified privilege. Latham CJ explained at 513 that normally there is no general entitlement for 'a newspaper to publish a defamatory statement of fact about an individual merely because the statement is made in the course of dealing with a matter of public interest'. However, as Starke J explained at 515:

  > A man who attacks another in or through a newspaper cannot complain if that other repels or refutes the attack for the purpose of vindicating himself. He has appealed to the public and provoked or invited a reply. A person attacked has both a right and an interest in repelling or refuting the attack, and the appeal to the public gives it a corresponding interest in the reply.

- The Full Court of the New South Wales Court of Appeal in *Morosi v Mirror Newspapers Ltd* (1977) at 778 explained as follows:

  > The occasions of privilege are not closed. In 1868, Cockburn CJ affirmed the adaptability of the law of privilege to meet 'the varying conditions of society', and 'the requirements and habits' of the current age: *Wason v Walter* (1868) ...
  >
  > The common law does not place newspaper editors or journalists in any different position to that of other citizens ...
  >
  > A publication in a newspaper is not the subject of qualified privilege merely because it gives the public information concerning a matter in respect of which the public is interested. Something more is needed which is said in some circumstances to constitute a duty, and in other circumstances an interest, on the part of the newspaper to communicate the information.

  So, the mere fact that the public may have been interested to find out about an alleged sexual relationship between a married government Minister and his personal private secretary (who was also married) did not create the required duty–interest relationship that gave qualified protection to mass publication of the story by the newspaper.

- Likewise, in *Australian Broadcasting Corporation v Comalco Ltd* (1986), the ABC could not claim qualified privilege for publishing a TV program across Australia criticising Comalco for the adverse social effects of its mining operations at Weipa in Queensland on the local

Aboriginal people, because not every person receiving the information had a recognised or legitimate interest in receiving it. This meant there was no duty to publish despite the public's general interest in the socially important topic.

- In *Aktas v Westpac Banking Corporation Ltd* (2010), Westpac (the defendant) wrongfully failed to honour cheques issued by the plaintiff. Despite the fact that there were sufficient funds to cover the cheques, the defendant, when communicating with customers who tried to cash the cheques, used the phrase 'refer to drawer', which is used in Australia to indicate that there are insufficient funds to meet the cheque. In a 3:2 majority decision, French CJ, Gummow and Hayne JJ cited *Toogood v Spyring* (1834) and decided at [31]–[42] that the defence of qualified privilege could not be made out by the bank on this occasion because there was no 'benefit or advantage to society' (at [35]) or any public interest (at [42]) to be promoted in allowing the bank to make such a communication to those who presented the cheques. Allowing the privilege would run counter to the 'large and powerful interest' that the community has in maintaining 'an efficient and stable banking system' and in seeing banks observe the need for 'accuracy and reliability of transactions' (at [42]).

The defence failed in both *Morosi v Mirror Newspapers Ltd* (1977) and *Australian Broadcasting Corporation v Comalco Ltd* (1986) because of the strict rule requiring the existence of a corresponding duty–interest relationship between the publisher and every receiver of the information and, in fact, only in 'exceptional cases has the common law recognised an interest or duty to publish defamatory matter to the general public': *Lange v Australian Broadcasting Corporation* (1997) at 569. However, because this limitation came to be seen as an 'unreasonable restraint' (at 570), the defence has now been extended by the High Court in a series of cases culminating in the *Lange* decision in 1997 and it has recently been given even greater scope in the uniform defamation legislation. In both of these newer versions, the reciprocal duty–interest relationship requirement has been relaxed but, at the same time, a reasonableness test has been imposed.

9.2.6.2 The '*Lange*' category of qualified privilege

In *Lange v Australian Broadcasting Corporation* (1997), the Full Court of the High Court extended the categories of qualified privilege to allow freedom of communication on matters of government and politics on the grounds that such political debate and discussion is 'an indispensable incident' of the system of representative government and free elections created by the *Constitution*: see 559–60, 568. The Court held at 560 that the 'interest that each member of the Australian community has in such a discussion extends the categories of qualified privilege' but insisted at 561 that the freedom is 'not absolute' and so, in these extended cases where the defence is not normally available because of the duty–interest rule, it is limited by a reasonableness test. The test is whether 'the defendant's conduct in making the publication was reasonable in all the circumstances of the case' at 573:

> As a general rule, a defendant's conduct in publishing defamatory material will not be reasonable unless the defendant had reasonable grounds for believing

the defamatory imputation was true, took proper steps so far as they were reasonably open to verify the accuracy of the material, and did not believe the imputation to be untrue. The privilege will be defeated if the plaintiff proves that the publication was actuated by ill will or other improper motive.

9.2.6.3 The statutory version of qualified privilege

The statutory version of the defence also abandons the reciprocity rule and allows publication of defamatory matter if the defendant can prove that:

a. the recipient has an interest or apparent interest in having information on some subject; and
b. the matter is published to the recipient in the course of giving to the recipient information on that subject; and
c. the conduct of the defendant in publishing that matter is reasonable in the circumstances.

The uniform legislation gives a non-exhaustive list of matters that the court may take into account when deciding the question of reasonableness, including:

a. the extent to which the matter published is of public interest;
b. the extent to which the matter published relates to the performance of the public functions or activities of the person;
c. the seriousness of any defamatory imputation carried by the matter published;
d. the extent to which the matter published distinguishes between suspicions, allegations and proven facts;
e. whether it was in the public interest in the circumstances for the matter published to be published expeditiously;
f. the nature of the business environment in which the defendant operates;
g. the sources of the information in the matter published and the integrity of those sources;
h. whether the matter published contained the substance of the person's side of the story and, if not, whether a reasonable attempt was made by the defendant to obtain and publish a response from the person;
i. any other steps taken to verify the information in the matter published; and
j. any other circumstances that the court considers relevant.

The legislative regime broadens the allowable subject matter of the published information (by contrast with the *Lange* (1997) privilege, which limits the protection to discussion of government and political matters only). It focuses less on the interest of the person receiving the information and more on the reasonableness of the defendant's conduct in publishing it. This means that the statutory privilege may be used by the mass media to defend publication of information more widely than has previously been allowed, but the requirement of reasonableness will nevertheless provide a limit on the kinds of information that can be disseminated.

Case example

In *Chappell v TCN Channel Nine Pty Ltd* (1988), Hunt J considered an earlier version of statutory qualified privilege that also imposed a reasonableness test. In this case, a national current affairs television program was restrained from airing an interview with a woman who claimed to have had an affair with a former Australian cricket captain, and who proposed to reveal details of his 'unusual' sexual activities. Hunt J decided at 170–1 that the defence of qualified privilege would fail on two grounds: first, because publication of such private material was not a legitimate matter of public interest; and second, because the form in which the defendant intended to present the information could not conceivably be seen as reasonable in the circumstances. (See section 9.2.7 below on public interest.)

9.2.6.4 Malice

Both at common law and under the extended and legislative versions of qualified privilege, the defence will be defeated if it is 'actuated by malice'. The High Court considered the issue in *Roberts v Bass* (2002), a case where a member of the South Australian Parliament sued two defendants over the distribution of a mock postcard and pamphlets during an election campaign (ie the person who prepared the material, and another who distributed the material). The judgments of Gleeson CJ at [8]–[15] and Gaudron, McHugh and Gummow JJ at [75]–[104], building on the English authority of *Horrocks v Lowe* (1975), explained the rules on malice in detail:

- 'A purpose or motive that is foreign to the occasion and actuates the making of the statement is called express malice.' Presumed or implied malice 'arises on proof of a false and defamatory statement': [75]; see also [10].
- A defendant may have mixed motives, but the defence will not be destroyed unless malice is the 'dominant' motive: [75], [104].
- 'Improper motive in making the defamatory publication must not be confused with the defendant's ill will, knowledge of falsity, recklessness, lack of belief in the defamatory statement, bias, prejudice or any other motive than duty or interest for making the publication': [76].
- The fact that the defendant's views might be 'wrong-headed, or prejudiced, or carelessly formed, or even irrational, would not constitute, or demonstrate, malice': [13].
- 'If the defendant knew the statement was untrue when he or she made it, it is almost invariably conclusive evidence of malice. That is because a defendant who knowingly publishes false and defamatory material almost certainly has some improper motive for doing so, despite the inability of the plaintiff to identify the motive': [77].
- Recklessness alone or recklessness combined with other factors may justify the finding of malice. To constitute malice it must be 'so gross as to constitute wilful blindness': [84].
- A 'mere lack of belief in the truth of the communication is not to be treated as if it was equivalent to knowledge of the falsity of the communication and therefore as almost conclusive proof of malice' and 'recklessness, short of wilful

blindness, is not enough to destroy the privilege. It must be accompanied by some other state of mind': [87].

- Carelessness 'never provides a ground for inferring malice': [103].
- Even if the defendant's dominant motive in attacking the plaintiff is to damage the latter's electoral prospects, or to cause political damage to them, this in itself is not proof of malice, even if the attack is expressed with 'vigour' or 'pungency': [11], [74].

Case examples

- In *Roberts v Bass* (2002), the High Court held by majority that the defendant, who merely distributed the campaign material and who honestly believed in its truth, was not acting with malice as his dominant purpose; but that the case of the other defendant who prepared the material (and who fabricated parts of it) should be reheard to decide whether he had used the occasion for an improper purpose.
- The New South Wales Court of Appeal upheld a trial judge's finding that malice had destroyed the defence in *Lindholdt v Hyer* (2008). The defendant, who despised the plaintiff, and who used extreme language ('the little Hitler running Premier Cabs') as part of a determined campaign against him, had exhibited a reckless disregard for the truth and so this ill will precluded a finding of fair comment.
- See also the comments of the High Court in the case of *Cush v Dillon* (2011) on the issue of malice.

Note that malice is also relevant to the common law defence of fair comment.

9.2.7 Fair comment (Honest opinion)

9.2.7.1 Fair comment

The common law defence of fair comment protects the expression of defamatory opinions on matters of public interest, provided those opinions are honestly held and not actuated by malice. The defence recognises the important community role played by the free expression of critique, opinion, debate and commentary. It covers publications of theatre, television, book and restaurant reviews as well as commentary, discussion and editorials on sport, politics, art, music, other public affairs (and the conduct of those who participate in them) and anything (eg advertisements, events or speeches) put before the public for consideration or scrutiny. As Gleeson CJ pointed out in *Channel Seven Adelaide Pty Ltd v Manock* (2007) at [3], provided all conditions are satisfied, the defence protects even 'obstinate, or foolish, or offensive statements of opinion' in the name of freedom of speech. This defence grew out of the older defence of qualified privilege and the crucial concepts of 'public interest' and 'malice' are common to both.

The concept of substantial truth, found in the defence of truth (justification), is also relevant to fair comment. The ingredients of the common law defence of fair comment are as follows:

1. the imputation must be a *comment* (a statement of opinion, not of fact);
2. the comment must be on a matter of *public interest*;

3. the comment must be based on *true or privileged facts* stated or referred to with sufficient clarity in the published material, or, if the facts are not stated, they must be notorious (well known); and
4. the comment must be *fair* in the sense that it is an honest opinion that could reasonably have been made upon the facts by a fair-minded person.

These ingredients are based on the analysis found in the judgment of Gleeson CJ and the joint reasons of Gummow, Hayne and Heydon JJ in the High Court case of *Channel Seven Adelaide Pty Ltd v Manock* (2007). A general summary can be found at [168] in the judgment of Kirby J, who dissented. In particular, the case clarified three of the four ingredients listed above:

- *Ingredient 1:* It is the defamatory imputations that attract the defence and not the entire published matter that contains them, so the imputation must be reasonably capable of being regarded only as comment: at [83].
- *Ingredient 3:* The comment or opinion must be supported by facts that are either expressly stated or referred to with sufficient clarity in the published material to form a proper substratum of fact upon which the comment or opinion can be based. If not stated, the facts must be notorious. It is not enough that they are merely 'indicated': see [4]–[5] and [47]–[49]. (Note, Kirby J dissented.)
- *Ingredient 4:* The comment must be fair in the sense that it must be an honest opinion that could reasonably have been made upon the facts by a fair-minded person: [3]–[6], [90].

9.2.7.2 Comment versus fact

The first step is to begin with the imputations and classify them as either fact or comment. Gleeson CJ at [3] defined a comment as 'an expression of an opinion, or inference, or evaluation, or judgment'. The joint majority judgment of Gummow, Hayne and Heydon JJ explained at [35] that 'a comment can be made by stating a value judgment and can also be made by stating a fact if it is a deduction from other facts'. The test the majority adopted is whether the ordinary, reasonable recipient of a communication would understand that a statement of fact was being made, or that an opinion was being offered: at [36]. Making the distinction is not an easy task, especially when facts and comments are mixed or intermingled together: at [3], [41]. However, this step is significant because later steps require the defendant to prove that any *facts* are true, substantially true or covered by privilege; sufficiently stated, notorious or referred to in the matter published; and form an adequate foundation upon which the opinion is based. By contrast, *comments* do not have to be true, but must be fair (honestly held).

Case examples

- In *Channel Seven Adelaide Pty Ltd v Manock* (2007), the plaintiff objected to an advertisement aired on television that promoted an upcoming program. It included pictures of the plaintiff and was 'very brief and was calculated to have a strong impact': at [11]. The words in the promo were as follows:

> The new Keogh facts. The evidence they kept to themselves. The data, the dates and the documents that don't add up. The evidence changed from one court to the next.

The majority in the High Court decided that the promo, standing alone, did not sufficiently distinguish between facts and comments and it did not state, include or refer with sufficient clarity to the facts from which any comment could reasonably have been drawn.

- In *O'Shaughnessy v Mirror Newspapers Ltd* (1970), D, a theatre reviewer, published a review of P's production of Shakespeare's *Othello*, describing it as a 'disaster' and referring to the 'waste and dishonesty' of the production. The joint judgment in the High Court held at 174 that D had not confined herself to facts truly stated but wrote what could be regarded as a defamatory statement of fact (ie that P had dishonest motives). The judges explained at 174 that an imputation that P is dishonest is not always construed as an assertion of fact (because it would depend on the wording and context). However, 'if what was written had been no more than comment it only had to be fair, but, if it were fact, it had to be correct' (in which case D would have to *prove* that P was actually dishonest).

Whether an imputation is classified as a fair comment rather than a statement of fact will depend on an analysis of the subject of the published matter, the actual words used, the context in which they were used, the existence of any qualifying or cautionary language (eg 'It seemed to me that ...'), the inclusion of a disclaimer, and whether the words were accompanied by other supporting facts that allow the receiver of the material to realise that the imputation is actually a comment or opinion.

9.2.7.3 A matter of public interest

Any imputation that is classified as a comment must be on a matter of public interest. In *Bellino v Australian Broadcasting Corporation* (1996), Dawson, McHugh and Gummow JJ explained at 369 that at common law, the concept 'meant the actions or omissions of a person or institution engaged in activities that either inherently, expressly or inferentially invited public criticism or discussion'. However, Brennan CJ, who insisted at 192 that 'public interest' is a 'key concept' that 'must be broad and flexible', preferred the definition in *London Artists Ltd v Littler* (1969):

> Whenever a matter is such as to affect people at large, so that they may be legitimately interested in, or concerned at, what is going on; or what may happen to them or to others; then it is a matter of public interest on which everyone is entitled to make fair comment.

Gaudron J also disagreed with a narrow interpretation and argued at 241–2 that public interest 'is capable of broad contemporary application' and 'must be construed according to ordinary usage'. In *Australian Broadcasting Corporation v Comalco Ltd* (1986), Smithers J said at 54 that the defence is founded on 'a legitimate and proper interest as opposed to interest due to idle curiosity or a desire for gossip'. So, the mere fact that some members of the public might be interested in hearing about salacious details of a plaintiff's private life does not mean that the issue is one of 'public interest' that justifies comment.

Case example

In *Chappell v TCN Channel Nine Pty Ltd* (1988), discussed in section 9.2.6.3 above, Hunt J said at 167 that a plaintiff's private life could become a matter of public interest only if it 'affects the performance of his public duties' or if the matter had been made public by the plaintiff himself. On the facts, the plaintiff had not made his sexual conduct a public issue himself and nor did the alleged sexual activity affect his performance of any of his public duties, so the imputations did not relate to a matter of public interest.

9.2.7.4 Facts upon which the opinion is based

As noted in section 9.2.7.1 above, the joint majority judgment in *Channel Seven Adelaide Pty Ltd v Manock* (2007) made it clear that the comment or opinion must be supported by facts (sometimes known as a 'substratum' of facts) that satisfy both of the following conditions (see [4]–[5], [47]–[49] of the judgment):

- The facts must be true, substantially true, or covered by privilege.
- The facts forming the basis for the opinion must be either expressly stated in the published material or referred to with sufficient clarity in the material. If not stated or referred to, the facts must be notorious (well known). It is not enough that they are merely 'indicated' (Kirby J dissented on this point).

Gleeson CJ explained that these conditions are necessary so that the person to whom the comment is published can identify it as comment on the facts and assess its foundation for themselves: at [5]–[6], citing *Pryke v Advertiser Newspapers Ltd* (1983). In some scenarios, however, it is not necessary for the receiver of the material to have full access to the facts, because, as Gleeson CJ pointed out at [8], 'certain forms of conduct are of such a nature as to invite comment'. A person who puts their work or ideas before the public is seen as inviting public critique. So, a person reviewing a play, for example, does not have to include a complete video of the production so that those who receive the review can form their own opinion about the comment – but the facts of the production must be sufficiently referred to and the critique must be clearly identifiable as comment and not as fact: see [7]–[8].

9.2.7.5 A comment must be fair

The majority reasons in *Channel Seven Adelaide Pty Ltd v Manock* (2007) explain that a comment is fair if it is an honest opinion that could reasonably have been made upon the facts by a fair-minded person: at [90]. In this context, Gleeson CJ explained at [3] that 'fair' does not require the *opinion* itself to be an objectively reasonable one: it focuses instead on the process that formed the opinion and the link or connection between the foundation of facts and the opinion. So the test is not whether the fact-finder agrees with the comment, or whether reasonable people might disagree with it. Instead it asks whether the opinion (even an offensive or prejudiced opinion) could reasonably have been based on those facts by an honest person: at [3], [6].

9.2.7.6 Malice defeats the common law defence

If the defendant is actuated by malice, the defence will be defeated: see the summary of the law in section 9.2.6.4 above.

9.2.7.7 Publishing an opinion

Although many of the cases dealing with this defence concern reviews published in newspapers, you should remember that anyone can make a fair comment on a matter of public interest. As Diplock J pointed out in *Silkin v Beaverbrook Newspapers Ltd* (1958) at 517–20, we are all entitled to comment on matters of public interest, and a newspaper reporter or editor has 'the same rights, neither more nor less, than every other citizen'. Those who publish the opinions of others (eg letters to the editor or opinion pieces published in a newspaper) are also able to claim the defence of fair comment - or honest opinion, as discussed below.

9.2.7.8 Statutory defence of honest opinion

The uniform defamation legislation contains three statutory defences of honest opinion that match the common law defence. However, there are two significant differences: the statutory defence dispenses with the requirement that the opinion be 'fair' in the common law sense; and malice is not relevant. The critical test is the honesty of the opinion. The statutory defences protect those who publish their own honest opinions as well as those who publish the honestly held opinions of others (eg employees or agents of the defendant, or other commentators). The ingredients of the basic defence are as follows:

a. the matter was an expression of opinion of the defendant rather than a statement of fact;
b. the opinion related to a matter of public interest; and
c. the opinion is based on proper material.

An opinion is based on 'proper material' if it is based on material that:

a. is substantially true;
b. was published on an occasion of absolute or qualified privilege (either under the uniform legislation or at general law); or
c. was published on an occasion that attracted the protection of a defence of honest opinion, the defence for publication of public documents, or the defence for fair reports of proceedings of public concern.

The uniform legislation also explains that not all of the material contained in the published matter must be 'proper material'. It will be enough if 'the opinion might reasonably be based on such of the material as is proper material'.[9] The defence will be defeated if, and only if, the opinion was not honestly held by the defendant at the time

9 For example, *Defamation Act 2005* (NSW) s 31(6).

the matter was published; or in the case where the defendant has published the opinions of others, where the defendant did not believe that the opinion was honestly held by the employee or agent, or had reasonable grounds to believe that the opinion was not honestly held by the commentator.

LEGISLATION ALERT!

Consult your study materials and find the provisions on honest opinion in the defamation legislation in your jurisdiction.

9.2.8 New defences

Consistent with the stated desire to protect freedom of expression on matters of public interest and importance, two new defences to defamation were created by the first stage of the *MDAP* reforms: the defence of publication on a matter of public interest and the defence of scientific or academic peer review.

The defence of publication on a matter of public interest is available to the defendant if the matter concerns an issue of public interest and the defendant reasonably believed that the publication of the matter was in the public interest. It is the reasonableness of the defendant's belief that is key to this defence. As stated by Lee J in *Russell v Australian Broadcasting Commission (No 3)* (2023) at [322]:

> [T]his element of the defence is not made good by showing that a notional reasonable person in the respondent's position could have believed that publication was in the public interest. The respondent must prove this element by adducing evidence that the publisher turned the publisher's actual or attributed mind to the issue and did hold the relevant belief.

(See also [259]–[308] for Lee J's discussion of the history leading up to the creation of the defence.)

The defence of scientific or academic peer review was intended to protect authors, academics and publishers from defamation claims, provided they adhere to rigorous peer-review standards. To establish the defence, the material must have been published in a scientific or academic journal and undergone a peer review process before publication. In addition, the publisher must demonstrate that it has acted honestly in publishing the material for the information of the public or the advancement of education.

LEGISLATION ALERT!

Consult your study materials and find the provisions on the two new defences in the defamation legislation in your jurisdiction. (They are not yet available in Western Australia or the Northern Territory.)

9.3 Remedies

9.3.1 Damages for defamation

The two main remedies for defamation are damages and injunctions. A plaintiff is entitled to damages as of right, and at common law an award of damages may include compensatory, aggravated and exemplary damages: see section 2.3.3.2 of Chapter 2. See also the case involving actor Rebel Wilson, *Wilson v Bauer Media Pty Ltd* (2017) and *Bauer Media Pty Ltd v Wilson (No 2)* (2018), in relation to damages. In *Uren v John Fairfax & Sons Pty Ltd* (1966), Windeyer J explained at 149–51 that defamation aims to compensate plaintiffs for any damage done to their honour and reputation, to vindicate them in the eyes of the public, and to console them for any indignity and humiliation caused by the defendant's wrong. Damages may be awarded to cover not only the hurt, distress and humiliation caused by the publication and any damage to the plaintiff's reputation, but also any consequent economic losses, particularly if the material has damaged the plaintiff's prospects of employment or ability to pursue their profession, business or public office. The conduct of the defendant after the publication is also relevant; see, for example, *Carson v John Fairfax & Sons Ltd* (1993) and *Herald & Weekly Times Ltd & Bolt v Popovic* (2003).

Under the uniform defamation legislation there are some significant changes to the law, including caps and limits on both the extent and kinds of damages that may be awarded and rules on the factors relevant to the mitigation of damages. Note also that the limitations period is generally reduced to one year.

LEGISLATION ALERT!

Consult your study materials, and find and note down the provisions on damages in the defamation legislation in your jurisdiction.

s [......] Damages to bear rational relationship to harm

s [......] Damages for non-economic loss limited

s [......] State of mind of defendant generally not relevant to awarding damages

s [......] Exemplary or punitive damages cannot be awarded

s [......] Factors in mitigation of damages

s [......] Damages for multiple causes of action may be assessed as single sum

Limitations period [......]

9.3.2 Injunctions

In addition to an award of damages, a plaintiff may sometimes seek an injunction preventing any future publication once the trial of the matter has been concluded. More commonly, a plaintiff may ask the courts for an interlocutory injunction restraining either a threatened publication that they fear is defamatory, or any further republication before a trial of material that has already been published. The High Court case of *Australian Broadcasting Corporation v O'Neill* (2006) gave extensive consideration to the law governing interlocutory injunctions. The majority in that case made it clear that the power to make such an order, which interferes with the right of free speech, will only rarely be exercised and the discretion must be used with 'exceptional caution': Gleeson CJ and Crennan J at [19], [30]–[32]; and Gummow and Hayne JJ at [65]–[73]. Gleeson CJ and Crennan J at [19] identified some of the relevant issues:

> Foremost among those considerations is the public interest in free speech. A further consideration is that, in the defamation context, the outcome of a trial is especially likely to turn upon issues that are, by hypothesis, unresolved. Where one such issue is justification, it is commonly an issue for jury decision. In addition, the plaintiff's general character may be found to be such that, even if the publication is defamatory, only nominal damages will be awarded.

Develop your skills

Make a look-up chart for defamation

Using the advice given in section 4.2 of Chapter 4, and following the figures in the 'Look-up' section at the end of Chapter 7, make yourself a look-up chart for the topic of defamation.

9.4 Problem-solving tips

This section offers tips on how to approach and answer problem questions involving defamation, highlighting the key steps and issues to look for when applying the principles covered in this chapter.

1. Before you begin, learn how to extract defamatory imputations from different kinds of material by reading some of the cases listed in your study materials. Download a copy of the defamation legislation in your jurisdiction and familiarise yourself with its contents.
2. Make a summary of the relevant law to use in diagnosing a problem question. Make sure that you include all of the three elements of defamation and all of the ingredients of the defences – and give an authority for each.
3. Begin your diagnosis (as always) by looking for the *harm*, remembering that in defamation the harm is *intangible* and the focus is on the *capacity* to:
   - diminish or lower the plaintiff's personal, professional, business or official reputation by making people think less of the plaintiff;
   - expose the plaintiff to ridicule or derision, or display the plaintiff in a 'ridiculous light'; or
   - induce others to shun, avoid or exclude the plaintiff from society.
4. Continue the diagnosis by identifying the *matter* (or vehicle) that conveyed any defamatory suggestions about the plaintiff. Remember that 'matter' is defined very widely; so, do not restrict yourself only to words in written publications. Note the nature of the matter because this will be useful when you are arguing

about the meaning of the imputation (by reference to its nature, context and mode of publication) and also when you have to apply the defences.

5. Identify the defendant who *published* the matter by communicating it to a third person. Remember that communication can be the result of an act or an omission and that you should also look for any republication or further dissemination as well.
6. Consider the *remedies* and then you are ready to construct the answer.
7. Begin your *introduction* in the usual way by using the 'six-point plan' to identify who is suing whom and why – and noting the issues that may arise:

Example

Sample introduction

Paul (P) may sue Rania (D1) in defamation for her conduct in posting the following words on the internet: 'Paul has the lights on but nobody's home. He stole a packet of Smarties on his way to commit an armed robbery where he shot a bank customer in cold blood.' He may also sue Raimondo (D2) for allowing the posting to remain on his internet server for a week before taking it down. He is seeking compensatory damages for the loss of his reputation and the consequent economic loss that he suffered when his boss sacked him as a result of the post.

The elements that the plaintiff must prove are ... The issues in this case are ...

8. In the *body* of your answer, you should take each publication in turn by working your way through the three elements and then moving straight on to consider any of the relevant defences. Then go on to the next publication (if there is one) and repeat the process. It is often a mistake in a defamation question that contains more than one publication to try to do them together, because you may get confused over the imputations and because different defences may apply to each publication. Unless the publications contain exactly the same imputations it is better to keep them separate – but remember that you can save time in the second part of the answer by cross-referencing to the first whenever practicable. You do not need to repeat the law.
9. When you are working through the *elements*, remember that the plaintiff's arguments should be followed by the defendant's counterarguments on each element. The first element will probably take up the bulk of your answer at this point because you must:
   - identify the matter published;
   - list all of the imputations that it conveys and explain how they can be drawn out from the matter; and then
   - explain how they are defamatory by applying the relevant test(s).
10. You must identify the content of the *imputations* by identifying the 'sting' contained in the material in clear factual terms. This may be easy in cases where

the words are obvious on their face, but it may be more difficult if you have a case of innuendo or a combination of words, headlines and pictures. So, note whether you are relying on:

- the natural ordinary meaning of any words (if so, state it);
- the false or popular innuendo (if so, explain it); or
- the legal or true innuendo (if so, identify the extrinsic knowledge required to yield the imputation).

This step is *critical* to your success in a problem question. If you do not specify the imputations clearly, you will most likely fail the question – because you will not be able to argue out the first element of the tort properly *or* apply the defences. For example, if you try to apply the defence of truth, you have to know what the sting is before you can consider exactly what the defendant has to prove is true (or substantially true) and what evidence might be used to for proof. If you try to argue fair comment, you have to be able to explain whether the imputations are comments (which have to be honestly held) or whether they are facts (which have to be true, privileged or notorious and referred to properly in the published matter). You are most likely to go astray in cases of innuendo, so be especially careful to look for and to specify any hidden meanings, because if you miss them, you may miss all of the other issues that flow from them.

11. *Missing facts:* Be careful in a problem question if you have not been given the entire contents of the matter that has been published. Consider whether you may have been given only the 'bane' and ask yourself whether there may also have been some 'antidote' or whether one piece may have been taken out of context. What could the missing facts contain that would either help or hinder your case? Do not make assumptions about any missing facts.
12. When you are discussing the meaning of the imputations and whether they can be drawn from the published material, keep in mind the descriptions of the 'hypothetical referee' given in section 9.1.4 above, and weave them into your arguments where relevant.

Examples

Descriptors the defendant will try to use

'Perverse', 'avid for scandal', 'unusually suspicious', 'unusually naïve'; this is a 'strained', or 'forced' or 'utterly unreasonable interpretation'; 'the antidote undoes the effect of the bane'; 'merely words of vulgar abuse'.

Descriptors the plaintiff will try to use

The test allows for 'a certain amount of loose thinking'; D is 'playing with fire'; 'the words are imprecise', 'ambiguous', 'loose', 'fanciful', or 'unusual, and so a wide degree of latitude will be given'; 'the audience can read between the lines'; 'the antidote is not enough to undo the effect of the poison'.

13. Once you have worked your way through all three elements, come to a tentative conclusion: can the plaintiff make out a prima facie case?
14. When you work out which *defences* are to be applied, bear in mind that the onus shifts to the defendant and that you do not have to write about every defence. Consider only those that are open on the facts. However, remember that more than one defence might apply to any given imputation (and conversely that any particular defence may apply to some, but not all of the imputations).

    Keep in mind that much defamatory material is lawfully published and that different defences may apply to different imputations. Try to find at least one arguable defence for each imputation. It is a mistake to ignore the defences in a defamation question because they play such a large role in the tort. (So, if you were to come to a tentative conclusion that the imputations being complained of by the plaintiff are not defamatory, it would be a mistake to stop your answer at that point. You need to go on, because you can be almost certain that every defamation question in a torts exam will require you to consider some of the defences.)

Test your understanding

Problem solving

Paul Plodder is a well-known local football star who is playing in his final season as captain of 'The Mighty Avengers' – one of the best known of all Australian football teams. Near the end of the season rumours began to circulate that the police had interviewed a number of 'prominent Australian sportsmen' in relation to charges of indecent assault on a young supporter at an end-of-season trip last year. During the last match of the season, Plodder came under close attention from the league's most suspended player, Tony 'Hitman' Hardy, a notorious sledger and eye-gouger. Throughout the match Hardy quietly needled Plodder, asking him if he was the 'paedo' that the police were searching for. Plodder told Hardy to shut up and focus on the game and as their tempers rose the two engaged in some pushing and shoving behind play.

By the end of the game Plodder had become more and more agitated and frustrated by the Hitman's constant abuse and close-checking tactics. When Hardy finally repeated his suggestion that Plodder was the 'footy paedo' within the vicinity of one of his Avenger team-mates, he lost control completely, pushed Hardy once more and swung at him, intending to silence him for the rest of the game. Hardy dodged the blow and Plodder landed a punch instead on one of Hardy's team-mates who had run in to separate the two men. At this point, a full-scale melee broke out on the field, which involved the enthusiastic participation of most of the players from both teams. When the game was over Hardy came up to Plodder and said, 'Look mate, let's just let bygones be bygones and leave what's happened during the game on the playing field.'

In a large feature article that appeared in *The Sunday City Courier* the next day, well-known journalist Isabella Islington reported on the rumours of inappropriate conduct by sportsmen that had swept the nation and the violence that had occurred during Plodder's last game. Under the headline 'Thugs, Criminals or Just Complete Idiots?' she went on to attack the 'appalling moral standards of Australian footballers and their fans who relish the violence and the bloodlust and who use on-field violence to fuel off-field misconduct that places the young football fans of our nation in fear', concluding that 'it was a sad day for football, a sad day for the Avengers, and a sad way for one of the game's legends to bow out of sport'. The newspaper also published the feature article on its public Facebook page. The article received many 'angry reacts' and comments from members of the public, with one commentator writing that Plodder was a 'filthy rapist'.

Plodder comes to you seeking legal advice. He is very worried about losing his reputation as the 'Gentle Giant of Aussie Football' and the implications that these events may have on his future now that he has retired from sport.

Advise Plodder fully about any possible tort actions that may arise.

Hint: this question contains some other torts as well as defamation, so use it as an opportunity to do some revision.

Conclusion

In this chapter, you've seen how the law of defamation must simultaneously protect individual reputation and preserve freedom of expression, while taking into account the changing nature of communication in the modern era. The Australian defamation law framework has seen significant changes in recent years, with the 2020 *MDAP* amendments the most consequential. These amendments were an attempt to address some of the challenges posed by the digital age as well as reflecting the ongoing challenge of balancing individual reputations with the principle of free expression. However, as a result of the amendments, Australia now faces a somewhat uneven national legal framework. At the time of writing (October 2025) Western Australia and the Northern Territory continue to operate under the original 2006 Uniform Defamation Laws. New South Wales and the Australian Capital Territory have implemented two waves of legislative reforms and the remaining jurisdictions have, to date, only enacted the first phase of the reforms. Only time will tell whether this inconsistent approach across the country is temporary or a more permanent state of affairs.

REFERENCES

CASES

Abbott v Random House Pty Ltd (1999) 94 FCR 296
Adam v Ward [1917] AC 309
Aktas v Westpac Banking Corporation Ltd [2010] HCA 25; (2010) 241 CLR 79
Australian Broadcasting Corporation Ltd v Comalco Ltd (1986) 12 FCR 510
Australian Broadcasting Corporation v Hanson [1998] QCA 306
Australian Broadcasting Corporation v O'Neill (2006) 227 CLR 57
Bauer Media Pty Ltd v Wilson (No 2) [2018] VSCA 154
Belbin v Lower Murray Urban and Rural Water Corporation [2012] VSC 535
Bellino v Australian Broadcasting Corporation (1996) 185 CLR 183

Berkoff v Burchill [1996] EWCA Civ 564; [1996] 4 All ER 1008
Bickel v John Fairfax & Sons Ltd [1981] 2 NSWLR 474
Bjelke Petersen v Warburton [1987] 2 Qd R 465
Boyd v Mirror Newspapers Ltd [1980] 2 NSWLR 449
Browne v Dunn (1893) 6 R 67
Byrne v Deane [1937] 1 KB 818
Carson v John Fairfax & Sons Ltd (1993) 178 CLR 44
Cassidy v Daily Mirror [1929] 2 KB 331
Chakravarti v Advertiser Newspapers Ltd (1998) 193 CLR 519
Chalmers v Payne (1835) 2 Cr M & R 156; 150 ER 67
Channel Seven Adelaide Pty Ltd v Manock (2007) 232 CLR 245
Chappell v Mirror Newspapers Ltd (1984) Aust Torts Reports 80-691
Chappell v TCN Channel Nine Pty Ltd [1988] 14 NSWLR 153
Charleston v News Group Newspapers [1995] 2 AC 65
Chatterton v Secretary of State [1895] 2 QB 189
Cleghorn v Sadler [1945] 1 KB 325
Consolidated Trust Co v Browne (1948) 49 SR (NSW) 86
Cornes v The Ten Group Pty Ltd (2011) 114 SASR 1
Costello v Random House Pty Ltd (1999) 137 ACTR 1
Council of the Shire of Ballina v Ringland (1994) 33 NSWLR 680
Cross v Denley (1952) 52 SR (NSW) 112
Cush v Dillon [2011] HCA 30; (2011) 279 ALR 631
Derbyshire County Council v Times Newspapers Ltd [1993] AC 534
Dow Jones and Co Inc v Gutnick (2002) 210 CLR 575
E Hulton & Co v Jones [1910] AC 20
Ettingshausen v Australian Consolidated Press Ltd (1991) 23 NSWLR 443
Fahrquar v Bottom [1980] 2 NSWLR 380
Fairfax Media Productions Pty Ltd v Kermode [2011] NSWCA 174
Fairfax Media Publications Pty Ltd v Voller (2021) 273 CLR 346; 392 ALR 540; [2021] HCA 27
Fairfax Media Publications Pty Ltd v Zeccola (2015) 91 NSWLR 341
Favell v Queensland Newspapers Pty Ltd [2005] HCA 52; (2005) 221 ALR 186
Fayed v al-Tajir [1988] QB 712; [1987] 3 WLR 102
Godfrey v Demon Internet Ltd [2001] 1 QB 201
Google Inc v Duffy [2017] SASCFC 130
Google LLC v Defteros (2022) 403 ALR 434; [2022] HCA 27
Gordon v Amalgamated Television Services Pty Ltd [1980] 2 NSWLR 410
Grubb v Bristol United Press Ltd (1963) 1 QB 309
Hall-Gibbs Mercantile Agency Ltd v Dun (1910) 12 CLR 84
Hepburn v TCN Channel Nine [1983] 2 NSWLR 682
Herald & Weekly Times Ltd & Bolt v Popovic [2003] VSCA 161
Hockey v Fairfax Media Publications Pty Ltd (2015) 237 FCR 33; [2015] FCA 652
Horrocks v Lowe [1975] AC 135
Huth v Huth [1915] 3 KB 32
John Fairfax Publications Pty Ltd v Gacic (2007) 230 CLR 291

John Fairfax Publications Pty Ltd v Rivkin [2003] HCA 50; (2003) 201 ALR 77
Jones v Fairfax (1986) 4 NSWLR 466
Jones v Skelton [1963] 1 WLR 1362
Kelly v John Fairfax Publications Pty Ltd [2003] NSWSC 586
Knupffer v London Express Newspapers Ltd [1944] AC 116
Krahe v TCN Channel Nine Pty Ltd (1986) 4 NSWLR 536
Lachaux v Independent Print Ltd [2020] AC 612
Lange v Australian Broadcasting Corporation (1997) 189 CLR 520
Lee v Wilson (1934) 51 CLR 276
Lehrmann v Network Ten Pty Ltd [2024] FCA 369
Lewis v Daily Telegraph Ltd [1964] AC 234
Lindholdt v Hyer [2008] NSWCA 264; (2008) 251 ALR 514
Livingstone-Thomas v Associated Newspapers Ltd (1969) 90 WN (Pt 1) NSW 223
Lloyd v David Syme [1986] AC 350
London Artists Ltd v Littler [1969] 2 QB 375
Loveday v Sun Newspapers Ltd (1938) 59 CLR 503
Mann v O'Neill (1997) 191 CLR 204
McDonald's Corporation v Morris & Steel [1997] EWHC 366 (QB)
Mirror Newspapers Ltd v World Hosts Pty Ltd (1979) 141 CLR 632
More v Weaver [1928] 2 KB 520
Morgan v Lingen (1863) 8 LT 800
Morgan v Odhams Press Ltd [1971] 1 WLR 1239
Morosi v Broadcasting Station 2GB Pty Ltd [1980] 2 NSWLR 418
Morosi v Mirror Newspapers Ltd [1977] 2 NSWLR 749
Mundey v Askin [1982] 2 NSWLR 369
Newman v Whittington [2022] NSWSC 249
O'Shane v Harbour Radio Pty Ltd [2013] NSWCA 315
O'Shaughnessy v Mirror Newspapers Ltd (1970) 125 CLR 166
Parmiter v Coupland (1840) 6 M & W 105; (1840) 151 ER 340
Penton v Calwell (1945) 70 CLR 219
Pryke v Advertiser Newspapers Ltd (1983) 37 SASR 175
Pullman v Water Hill & Co [1891] 1 QB 524
R v Woodfall (1774) *Lofft* 776; [1790] Eng R 1949; 98 ER 914
Radio 2UE Sydney Pty Ltd v Chesterton (2009) 238 CLR 460
Reader's Digest Services Pty Ltd v Lamb (1982) 150 CLR 500
Rivkin v Amalgamated Television Services Pty Ltd [2001] NSWSC 432
Roberts v Bass (2002) 212 CLR 1
Roberts-Smith v Fairfax Media Publications Pty Ltd (No 41) (2023) 417 ALR 267
Rogers v Nationwide News Pty Ltd (2003) 216 CLR 327
Rosenblatt v Bear, 383 US 75 (1966)
Russell v Australian Broadcasting Commission (No 3) [2023] FCA 1233
Savige v News Ltd [1932] SASR 240
Selecta Homes and Building Co Pty Ltd v Advertiser-Weekend Publishing Co Pty Ltd (2001) 79 SASR 451

Sergi v Australian Broadcasting Commission [1983] 2 NSWLR 669
Silkin v Beaverbrook Newspapers Ltd [1958] 2 All ER 516
Sim v Stretch [1936] 2 All ER 1237
Sims v Wran [1984] 1 NSWLR 317
Slatyer v Daily Telegraph Newspaper Co Ltd (1908) 6 CLR 1
Slazengers (Ltd) v C Gibbs & Co (1916) 33 TLR 35
Slim v Daily Telegraph [1968] 2 QB 157
Smith v Lucht [2016] QCA 267
Sungravure v Middle East Airlines Airliban SAL (1975) 134 CLR 1
Sutherland v Stopes [1925] 1 AC 47
Theaker v Richardson [1962] 1 All ER 229
Toogood v Spyring (1834) 1 CM & R 181; 149 ER 1044
Trkulja v Google LLC (2018) 356 ALR 178; [2018] HCA 25
Urbanchich v Drummoyne Municipal Council (1991) Aust Torts Reports 81-127
Uren v John Fairfax & Sons Pty Ltd (1966) 117 CLR 118
Villers v Monsley (1769) 2 Wilson 403; 95 ER 886
Wakley v Cooke (1849) 4 Ex 511; 154 ER 1316
Wason v Walter (1868) LR 4 QB 73
Wennhak v Morgan (1888) 20 QBD 635
Wilson v Bauer Media Pty Ltd [2017] VSC 521
Youssoupoff v Metro-Goldwyn-Mayer Pictures Ltd (1934) 50 TLR 58
Zbyszko v New York American Inc, 239 NYS 411 (1930)

ARTICLE

Baker, R, 'Defamation and the Moral Community' (2008) 13(1) *Deakin Law Review* 1.

10 INTRODUCTION TO NEGLIGENCE

Introduction

The tort of negligence is the primary tool adopted by common law systems for deciding when and under what circumstances it is appropriate to shift a loss from the person who suffers a loss to the person who caused it. It does so by imposing liability on a defendant who, when placed in circumstances where there is a reasonably foreseeable and not insignificant risk of harm to another person, unjustifiably fails to take reasonable care, either:

- to avoid *causing* that harm; or
- in some circumstances, to *prevent* that harm from occurring,

provided it is thought right to impose a legal duty to take such care on the defendant. Because of its general focus on wrongdoing that causes harm, negligence is the most wide-ranging and commonly litigated tort. It is also the most uncertain. Its boundaries are blurry and its underlying rationale broad. Giving clear guidance on many of the essential tests for imposing liability is therefore complex, as negligence's compass can vary from great moral dilemmas to very mundane calculations. Guido Calabresi, in his seminal work *The Costs of Accidents* (1970), put it clearly when he said: 'Our society is not committed to preserving life at any cost ... lives are spent not only when the quid pro quo is some great moral principle, but also when it is a matter of convenience.' Since its beginning in *Donoghue v Stevenson* (1932) in the English House of Lords and its recognition in Australia in *Grant v Australian Knitting Mills Ltd* (1936), the tort has developed over almost a century. However, while there is now broad agreement in the common law world on the basic elements of duty of care, breach of duty and causation of harm, there remains significant disagreement on the best way to impose principled limits on this imprecise and ever-growing tort of negligence and to explain how it should fit together with other forms of tort liability.

Negligence is the most intellectually and morally challenging of all the torts. It was called into being by the social, political and economic changes in society that were brought about by the Industrial Revolution of the 19th and early 20th centuries. It continued to expand in new directions because of the more sophisticated financial systems and market economies that developed in its wake, and is now grappling with the existential questions of the 21st century, such as climate change and the digital revolution. These changes continue to make it possible for people to harm others in ways that were inconceivable in earlier times. The need for this form of tort liability grew out of the perceived inability of the older causes of action to deal with new, more devastating and potentially more widespread, mass harms that new technologies could cause. The birth of negligence in the 1930s (and its subsequent expansion during the rise of the welfare state) was accompanied by a deeply felt fear of its limitless scope – a fear that still dominates the debates over the tort's future to this day – and one that may never be resolved because of the inherent features of this tort.

The 'pendulum' of negligence

Since 2002, the law of negligence in Australia has been governed by a combination of common law and statute, and the substance of the law can vary between each of the states and territories in Australia. The legislative intervention of 2002 that modified and limited the common law was motivated by a growing sense that judges had shifted the balance of the 'negligence pendulum' too far in a 'rampant pro-plaintiff' direction and that a shift back towards a principle of taking personal responsibility was needed to end a growing 'culture of blame' and bring the tort back into a more defendant-friendly state of equilibrium.[1] A more immediate trigger for the reforms of 2002 to the law of negligence was the so-called 'insurance crisis' that occurred after the terrorist attacks of 11 September 2001. A series of events led to perceptions that Australia could not afford to fund the growing number of increasingly large negligence payouts and claims that 'the absence of insurance or availability of insurance only at unaffordable rates' was threatening 'the basic fabric of community life', leading to the closure of hospitals, the refusal of doctors to continue in some forms of medical practice, and the cancellation of community

1 The swings of the 'negligence pendulum' have been tracked by Justice David Ipp, the Chair of the Panel of Eminent Persons, which was asked by the state and federal governments to conduct the Review of the Law of Negligence: see 'Policy and the Swing of the Negligence Pendulum' (2003); 'Themes in the Law of Torts' (2007); and 'The Politics, Purpose and Reform of the Law of Negligence' (2007). See also Cane, 'Reforming Tort Law in Australia: A Personal Perspective' (2003); Spigelman, 'Negligence: The Last Outpost of the Welfare State' (2002); and the special 2002 edition of vol 25, issue 3 of the *University of New South Wales Law Journal* devoted to the Forum entitled 'Reform of the Law of Negligence: Balancing Costs and Community Expectation'.

gatherings and social events.[2] The issue came to the attention of the general public with the decision in *Simpson v Diamond* (2001), which saw a plaintiff in a medical malpractice case being awarded damages of over $14 million.[3] Given that damages awards for negligence are funded mostly by insurance companies, parliaments acted on the rising fear that the rights of plaintiffs could be worth very little if defendants could not obtain insurance. In 2002, the Commonwealth, state and territory governments appointed a panel of eminent persons chaired by Justice David Ipp to review the law of negligence. Once the panel delivered its Final Report (known as the Ipp Report) in October of that year,[4] governments around Australia implemented changes designed to limit liability, extend the scope of the defences, and introduce caps and thresholds on damages awards (the latter being the prime motivator for the legislative intervention). Unfortunately, in places they ignored the panel's appeal for uniform changes and, as a result, negligence law in Australia has increased in complexity since the reforms.[5]

LEGISLATION ALERT!

Given the significant differences between the civil liability statutes, you will need to consult your study materials to find the appropriate legislation in your jurisdiction – the legislation of all the Australian jurisdictions is listed below.

- *Civil Law (Wrongs) Act 2002* (ACT)
- *Civil Liability Act 2002* (NSW)
- *Personal Injuries (Liabilities and Damages) Act 2003* (NT), *Personal Injuries (Civil Claims) Act 2003* (NT)
- *Civil Liability Act 2003* (Qld), *Personal Injuries Proceedings Act 2002* (Qld)
- *Civil Liability Act 1936* (SA)
- *Civil Liability Act 2002* (Tas)
- *Civil Liability Act 2002* (WA), *Volunteers and Food and Other Donors (Protection from Liability) Act 2002* (WA)
- *Wrongs Act 1958* (Vic)

The challenges that existed at the beginnings of negligence still bedevil the tort today. Therefore, this chapter begins by explaining how the common law developed to meet those challenges. When you begin negligence problem solving, however, you must remember to check whether the common law has been modified or limited by any statutes in your jurisdiction, and to make sure that your summary reminds you to use the

2 Ipp, 'Negligence – Where Lies the Future?' (2003) at 156.
3 The sum was reduced to nearly $11 million on appeal in *Diamond v Simpson (No 3)* (2003), making it the highest award of damages for this type of claim.
4 The report can be found online: <https://treasury.gov.au/review/review-of-the-law-of-negligence>.
5 Joachim Dietrich describes the 'reforms' as 'retrograde' and characterised by 'prejudice' and 'sloppy drafting' in 'Duty of Care under the "Civil Liability Acts"' (2005) at 39–40.

current legislative provisions in preference to any pre-existing common law rules. Since the legislative reforms of 2002, applying the law of negligence in Australia is as much an exercise in statutory interpretation as it is an application of the common law. In the words of Kirby J in *Neindorf v Junkovic* (2005) at 42:

> [W]here a statute of relevant operation has been enacted, it is the duty of Australian courts to start their analysis of the legal liability of parties affected not with the pre-existing common law but with the statutory prescription ... Where Parliament has spoken, it is a mistake to start with common law authority.

Yet, as you will see, the common law is still relevant to the interpretation of those very statutory provisions that now govern negligence in all states and territories. This intricate interplay between common law and statute adds a further layer of complication to negligence, one that requires particular care and attention when approaching a problem question. Over 20 years have passed since the adoption of these statutes, yet a cursory glance at everyday negligence cases in lower courts reveals how deeply entrenched common law-based reasoning is in the judiciary.

10.1 The history and challenge of negligence

10.1.1 Historical development

Negligence was called into existence because technology and the forms of enterprise that arose out of the Industrial Revolution made it possible for people to cause harm to others in ways that the older torts were not designed to deal with. In a pattern familiar to legal historians, advances in technology drove advances in the law, and a new legal response was needed to cope with new problems caused by human ingenuity, endeavour and development. Lawyers seeking compensation for plaintiffs who were injured in workplace accidents in unsafe factories, or by unregulated mass transportation systems, or by manufactured goods that were mass-produced and distributed to unprecedentedly large numbers of consumers, asked judges to push the law's protection in directions never before contemplated. It is no coincidence that the three landmark cases that changed the law in the common law world dealt with products of the Industrial Revolution designed for mass production and wide distribution.

Case examples

- The first case in the United States, *MacPherson v Buick Motor Co* (1916), concerned a mass-produced motor car.
- The landmark case in the United Kingdom, *Donoghue v Stevenson* (1932), dealt with a factory-produced bottle of aerated ginger beer.
- The first case in Australia, *Grant v Australian Knitting Mills Ltd* (1936), concerned mass-produced underwear: the defendant had distributed more than 4.5 million pairs of the woollen long-johns in issue.

Some judges, like Lord Buckmaster and Lord Tomlin in *Donoghue v Stevenson* (1932), viewed these attempts to change the law with horror, contempt and outrage; others, like Lord Atkin and Lord Macmillan, used their legal ingenuity to overcome the legal obstacles that appeared to stand in the way of dealing with emerging threats to public health and safety. It is difficult to understand just how radical these suggestions were at the time, because nowadays we take for granted all of the safety standards that control those who employ us, who manufacture the goods that we consume or who provide us with the services that we rely on. But it is a mistake to treat the judges who dissented in the case of *Donoghue v Stevenson* (1932) with the same disdain that they showed for the pioneers who brought about the birth of the tort of negligence, because many of the problems that caused their misgivings still remain unresolved today – even though lawyers, judges and scholars have been working on this tort for over a century.

The difficulty that plagues the tort of negligence lies in the fact that we can harm each other indirectly. One person's conduct can set off a complex chain of cause and effect that can travel across space, time and even national boundaries to end up harming a complete stranger. In some cases the resulting harm can be caused by the combination of different people acting at different times and in different places. You need to learn how to recognise this recurring fact pattern – not only because it could very well arise to complicate your *practical* problem-solving exercises, but also because it is the same one that causes *theoretical* problems for judges who are being asked to extend the tort's protection to 'novel cases' which do not fit any clear precedent. Of course, many negligence cases involve only two parties, but the following selection of leading cases will provide a snapshot of some of the complicated multiparty fact patterns that have caused ongoing debates about the content and scope of the tort of negligence in the highest courts in England and Australia.

Case examples

- In *Donoghue v Stevenson* (1932), a decomposing snail was sealed inside a dark opaque bottle of ginger beer produced in Stevenson's factory and distributed to a cafe owner named Minchella. Minchella sold it to a customer who bought it for a friend, May Donoghue, who drank half of the contents before discovering the snail and becoming ill. The issue was whether the manufacturer, Stevenson (D), owed the ultimate consumer, Donoghue (P), a duty to take reasonable care in the manufacture and bottling of the ginger beer.
- *Chapman v Hearse* (1961) concerned a car being driven by Emery which was hit by a second car driven by Chapman. Chapman was catapulted out of his vehicle and lay injured on the road. Dr Cherry, who happened to be passing, stopped to help Chapman, but was killed when he was hit by a third car driven by Hearse. Dr Cherry's estate sued Hearse, who joined Chapman to the action. One of the issues was whether Chapman, whose negligence caused the first collision, owed a duty of care to Dr Cherry, who came to his rescue.
- In *Distillers Co (Biochemicals) Ltd v Thompson* (1971), an English company, Distillers (D), bought a drug named thalidomide, which had been developed and manufactured in Germany by a German company. It was packaged by D in England and then marketed and sold in Australia under the name Distaval by an Australian company. A pregnant woman whose doctor had

prescribed the drug to her for morning sickness purchased it from a pharmacy in New South Wales and subsequently gave birth to a disabled child, P, who sued D.

- In *Jaensch v Coffey* (1984), Jaensch (D) was driving a car that hit a motorcycle being driven by a policeman named Coffey, who was seriously injured. His wife, who did not witness the collision itself, developed a psychiatric illness after being called into the intensive care ward, witnessing his injuries and subsequently being told that his condition, which was bad, had taken a turn for the worse. Mrs Coffey (P) sued D, who had injured her husband, and the issue was whether he owed her a duty of care to avoid causing her psychiatric injury.
- In *Voth v Manildra Flour Mills Pty Ltd* (1990), Voth (D), an American accountant working in Missouri, gave incorrect taxation advice to Manildra Milling Corporation, a Kansas corporation carrying on business in the United States. This corporation was a wholly owned subsidiary of Honan Holding USA, which was in turn a subsidiary of Honan Investments Pty Ltd, an Australian company. Honan Investments also owned and operated another Australian company named Manildra Flour Mills Pty Ltd, which was incorporated in New South Wales and which entered into transactions with Manildra Milling. As a result of D's negligent advice to Manildra Milling, the Australian companies Manildra Flour Mills and Honan Investments (Ps) suffered financial losses. They sued D in Australia and the High Court of Australia ('High Court') had to decide where the tort had taken place – and which law would govern the case.
- In *Perre v Apand Pty Ltd* (1999), Apand Pty Ltd (D) supplied diseased potato seeds sourced from Victoria to Virgara Brothers in Adelaide. Virgara Brothers supplied the seeds to Sparnons, who were farmers in rural South Australia. The potatoes were subsequently found to be infected with bacterial wilt. As a result of quarantine rules, the Perres (P), who also grew and processed potatoes within the quarantine zone, were prevented from selling their (healthy) potatoes to the lucrative Western Australian markets, and so suffered an economic loss.
- In *Harriton v Stephens* (2006), Dr Stephens (D) failed to diagnose and adequately inform Mrs Harriton that she had contracted rubella while pregnant with her daughter Alexia (P), who was born with severe disabilities – a known risk to the foetus of a pregnant woman affected by rubella. There was little doubt that, in the circumstances, D's conduct in failing to diagnose and warn was negligent towards the mother. The question was whether his duty could and should extend to the harm suffered by the unborn child (P) as a result of such negligence.
- The plaintiffs in *Adeels Palace Pty Ltd v Moubarak* (2009) went to a restaurant run by Adeels Palace Pty Ltd (D) on New Year's Eve. After a dispute on the dance floor, another patron left the restaurant, armed himself with a gun and returned to the restaurant, where he shot the two plaintiffs. The victims (Ps) of the gunman sued D, claiming it had been negligent in not providing sufficient security.
- The plaintiffs (Ps) in *Wicks v State Rail Authority of New South Wales* (2010) were members of the New South Wales police force who were called to a rescue effort after a passenger train carrying almost 50 people came off the tracks at high speed. They were the first to arrive and were so confronted by the scene of death and injury in the wreckage of the train and the danger that faced them and the survivors of the crash that they subsequently developed psychological and psychiatric conditions. They sued the State Rail Authority of New South Wales (D).
- In *Amaca Pty Ltd v Ellis* (2010), a man died of lung cancer. He had been smoking nearly one packet of cigarettes per day for about 26 years. During that time, he had also been exposed

to 'respirable asbestos fibres' from asbestos cement pipes in the course of two successive employments. While it was accepted that both smoking and inhaling asbestos fibres can cause lung cancer, the challenge was determining with reasonable certainty what, in the particular circumstances of the case, had materially caused the cancer. The man's wife (P), who was his executor, sued both employers and the manufacturer of the cement pipes.

This sample of leading cases illustrates the complexity of the tort of negligence and the multiparty fact patterns that mark it out from other simpler areas of liability, where the legal relationship between the plaintiff and the defendant is mapped upon the physical tracks of a single act that directly links the parties. We can contrast these more complicated negligence scenarios with those found in the rights-based trespass torts, which, because they require a *positive* act that *directly* invades the plaintiff's rights and causes a *narrowly defined effect* on the plaintiff, almost always give rise to more simple, two-party scenarios that take place between people in close physical proximity (see Figure 10.1).[6]

As you saw in the earlier chapters, the trespass torts covered only directly caused rights invasions, and so plaintiffs who had been *indirectly harmed* by another person's conduct could bring an action only in restricted circumstances. Before the birth of negligence as a distinct tort, plaintiffs had to fit their case into one of a limited number of recognised causes of action:

1. *other torts* – including the tort of deceit (or fraud), and the 'actions on the case' for the intentional infliction of physical harm or nervous shock;
2. *contract* – a plaintiff linked to a defendant by a contract could sue for a breach of a contractual duty to take reasonable care;
3. *special duty categories* – certain recognised relationships between the plaintiff and the defendant imposed a duty to take reasonable care on a defendant who carried out a particular role – for example, occupiers, common carriers, surgeons, smiths, innkeepers; or
4. *dangerous goods* – a person who was in charge of dangerous goods also came under a special duty to compensate those who were injured by those goods (eg explosives or poisons).

Figure 10.1 Before *Donoghue v Stevenson*

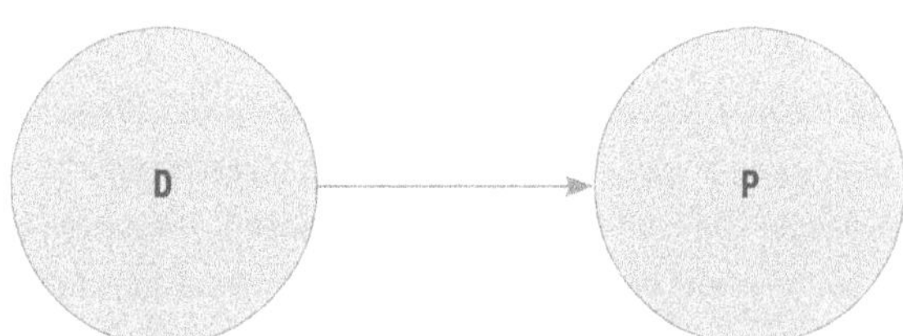

6 A notable exception involving a three-party scenario, which was dealt with by extending the concept of directness, is found in *Scott v Shepherd* (1773), discussed in section 5.1 of Chapter 5.

Before *Donoghue v Stevenson* liability had to be based on:

- the trespass torts (direct rights invasion);
- breach of a contract between the plaintiff and the defendant; or
- special duty categories based on the relationship between the defendant and the plaintiff.

Before *Donoghue v Stevenson* indirectly caused harm was also covered by:

- other torts of intentional wrongdoing; or
- strict liability for control of dangerous goods.

Figure 10.2 As new technology developed

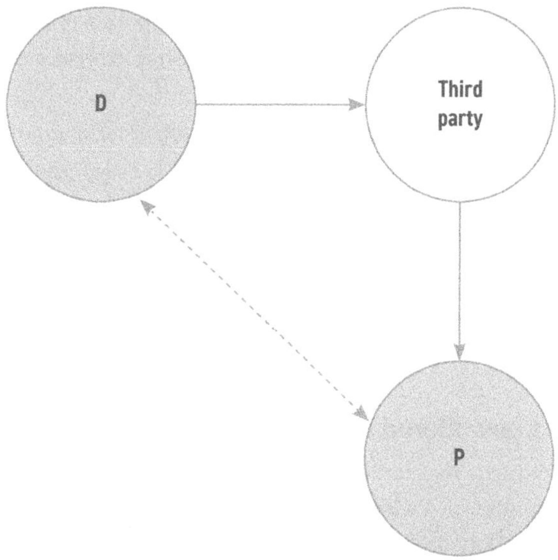

As new technology developed, new, *indirect*, ways of causing harm to another developed that did not fit established categories. The solid lines in Figure 10.2 show the tracks of harm. The dashed line shows the new legal relationship needed.

The fact pattern involving indirectly caused harm that arose in *Donoghue v Stevenson* in 1932 was not new. It is illustrated in Figure 10.2. This pattern of indirectly caused harm had troubled the law for some time, but judges had either found a way around it or had refused to allow liability in such cases. As discussed below, however, there were three significant multiparty cases that did not fit into the pre-existing patterns, where judges had nevertheless imposed liability on defendants who had indirectly been the cause of harm to a plaintiff. These cases became critically important when the case of *Donoghue v Stevenson* (1932) came to be decided by the House of Lords and formed the basis for recognising the new tort of negligence.

10.1.1.1 Tort-based solutions

Initially, the problem of *indirectly* caused harm had been dealt with by extending the law of torts. However, liability was imposed only in cases where the defendant's conduct carried an obvious hallmark of moral wrongdoing in the form of fraud or a wilful intention to cause physical injury or shock.

Case examples

- **The tort of deceit: *Pasley v Freeman* (1789).** In cases of fraud, P could recover damages by using the tort of deceit if they could show that they were a victim of a fraudulent representation intentionally made by D. In *Pasley v Freeman* (1789), a three-person scenario, D persuaded P to sell goods on credit to an insolvent third party on the faith of D's fraudulent representation that the third party was a trustworthy person of financial substance. D had made this false statement intentionally and with knowledge that it was untrue, intending P to act on it.
- **Action on the case: the tort in *Bird v Holbrook* (1828).** If D intentionally caused physical injury through indirect means, liability would be imposed, as in the case of *Bird v Holbrook* (1828), a two-party case, where D set a spring gun on his land with the express intention of shooting any trespassers.
- **Action on the case: the tort in *Wilkinson v Downton* (1897).** If D wilfully intended to shock, upset or terrify P by engaging in conduct that was 'calculated' to cause psychiatric injury or illness (nervous shock) and succeeded in causing that injury, liability would be imposed as in the case of *Wilkinson v Downton* (1897), a two-party case, where D told a woman a false story that her husband had been badly injured in an accident.

See section 5.4 of Chapter 5 on *Bird v Holbrook* (1828) and *Wilkinson v Downton* (1897).

10.1.1.2 Contract law offered a partial solution

Inadvertent wrongdoing – that is, harm that arose indirectly as a result of a negligent failure to take reasonable care without being (necessarily) characterised by any kind of fraud or wrongful intention – posed a more difficult problem. Before *Donoghue v Stevenson* (1932), the best option was to show that the parties were linked together in a direct one-to-one *contractual* relationship, arising from an agreed bargain between them. So, if the plaintiffs had purchased defective goods directly from a manufacturer themselves, they could then rely on a contractual warranty of fitness for purpose or a contract-based duty to take reasonable care. Critically, however, the doctrine of privity prevented any third parties, who were characterised as 'strangers to the contract', from benefitting from a contractual duty to take reasonable care, so this option was often closed off for plaintiffs who had been damaged indirectly in a multiparty scenario. Both of the following cases fitted the fact pattern in Figure 10.2 – and in both cases the judges refused to impose liability because the circumstances did not fit into any of the recognised categories that imposed liability for indirectly caused harm.

Case examples

- *Winterbottom v Wright* (1842) was a three-party scenario where P lost because he was not privy to a contract with the negligent D. P was injured when driving a coach owned by his employer that had been carelessly manufactured by D. P's employer was a party to the contract with the manufacturer but P was a stranger to the contract, so D was not liable to P. Abinger CB pointed out at 404 and 405 that the doctrine of privity was an important limiting device that was necessary to prevent 'an infinity of actions':

> Unless we confine the operation of such contracts as this to the parties who entered into them, the most absurd and outrageous consequences, to which I can see *no limit*, would ensue. [Emphasis added.]

Alderson B said at 405:

> The only safe rule is to confine the right to recover to those who enter into the contract: if we go one step beyond that, there is no reason why we should not go fifty.

Rolfe B sympathised with the plaintiff's unfortunate position, but said at 406 that the Court could not assist him, because, as has been frequently observed, 'hard cases ... are apt to introduce bad law'.

- *Le Lievre v Gould* (1893) was another multiparty scenario where the Ps lost because there was no contract between themselves and D. D was an architect and surveyor, who, with 'gross' negligence, issued building progress certificates to his employer. D's employer, a builder, used the certificates to borrow money on a mortgage, but the mortgagees (Ps) who advanced money on the basis of the carelessly drawn certificates sued D for his professional negligence after they sustained losses. The Court held that there was no fraud on the part of D and no contract between the Ps and D that justified imposing a duty on D. Smith LJ also distinguished an earlier case relied on by the Ps, saying at 504 that it had no application in these circumstances:

> The decision of *Heaven v Pender* was founded upon the principle, that a duty to take due care did arise when the person or property of one was in such proximity to the person or property of another that, if due care was not taken, damage might be done by one to the other. *Heaven v Pender* goes no further than this, though it is often cited to support all kinds of untenable propositions. [References omitted.]

Lord Esher MR (formerly Brett MR) also maintained at 497 that although *Heaven v Pender* (1883) had shown that 'under certain circumstances, one man may owe a duty to another, even though there is no contract between them' (eg where 'one man is near to another, or near the property of another'):

> The question of liability for negligence cannot arise at all until it is established that the man who has been negligent owed some duty to the person who seeks to make him liable for his negligence. What duty is there when there is *no relation between the parties by contract*? A man is entitled to be as negligent as he pleases towards the whole world if he owes no duty to them. [Emphasis added.]

10.1.1.3 Special categories of duty

As noted by Lord Esher MR in *Le Lievre v Gould* (1893), the law did contain a concept of negligence as a duty owed and neglected, but unless the parties were linked together in a contractual relationship, a duty to take reasonable care was normally imposed only in a strictly limited number of special categories where the plaintiff and the defendant were otherwise linked together in a defined one-to-one relationship (as illustrated in Figure 10.1).

Examples

- Occupiers of premises owed a duty to licensees or invitees who were lawfully present on the premises.
- Common carriers owed a duty to take care to avoid harming people and goods being carried.
- Surgeons, smiths and innkeepers owed a duty to their patients, customers and guests.

10.1.1.4 Dangerous goods

A defendant in control of dangerous goods also came under a special duty.

Examples

- If D had been in control of goods that were recognised as being inherently dangerous in themselves (eg a noxious or flammable substance like a poison, gas, chemical or an explosive like gunpowder; or a dangerous device like a loaded gun or other 'implements of destruction') D would be under a duty to P and be liable for any indirectly caused harm.
- In certain exceptional cases, D would also be liable if the goods were not dangerous *per se*, but were goods known by D to be in a dangerous condition.

10.1.1.5 Three anomalous early cases

In three important cases judges had appeared to apply the law more flexibly, without insisting that a duty to take reasonable care for the safety of another could be derived only from a contract or one of the special categories. These cases fit the fact pattern illustrated in Figure 10.2, but the judges nevertheless imposed liability on the defendants. When you read *Donoghue v Stevenson* (1932), you should pay close attention to the starkly different interpretations that the minority and majority judges placed on these cases – and the different conclusions that they drew from the reasons behind these three decisions.

Case examples

Anomalous cases

- *Langridge v Levy* (1837) was a three-party scenario where P won. P was injured and his hand was amputated after a gun that he was using exploded. The gun had been supplied by D to P's father under a contract of sale. P argued that D had claimed that the gun was safe and that he and his father had relied on D's claims about its safety and quality. D argued that P was not a party to the contract, but despite this, liability was imposed by judges who cited *Pasley v Freeman* (1789) and based their decision on the fact that D had made false claims about the safety and provenance of the gun and had *known at the time of purchase* that the gun was to be used by both P and his father, which constituted deceit.

- *George v Skivington* (1869) was a three-party scenario where P won. P was harmed after using a hair wash that had been purchased by her husband from the manufacturer (D). Again, despite the fact that P was not a party to the contract, the judges cited *Langridge v Levy* (1837) and allowed liability because P's husband had told D that he was buying it for his wife, P, at the time of purchase.
- *Heaven v Pender* (1883) was a multiparty scenario where P won. P was a painter who was employed by a contractor, Grey, to paint a ship (owned by another party) that was in a dry dock owned by D. P was injured in a fall caused by a faulty rope supplied by D as part of a wooden stage on which the painting took place, but there was no contract between P and D. Two judges imposed liability on the recognised grounds that D, as an occupier, owed a duty to P (ie they saw the case as falling into the fact pattern illustrated in Figure 10.1), but Brett MR (later Lord Esher MR) imposed liability on different grounds (which better fitted the fact pattern in Figure 10.2). Brett MR defined negligence at 507 in terms referencing the three traditional elements of duty, breach and damage:

  > Actionable negligence consists in the neglect of the use of ordinary care or skill towards a person to whom the defendant owes the duty of observing ordinary care and skill, by which neglect the plaintiff, without contributory negligence on his part, has suffered injury to his person or property.

  At 507–8, Brett MR defined the issue as:

  > [W]hat is the proper definition of the relation between two persons other than the relation established by contract, or fraud, which imposes on the one of them a duty towards the other to observe, with regard to the person or property of such other, such ordinary care or skill as may be necessary to prevent injury to his person or property.

  After surveying the earlier cases and categories, Brett MR proposed a novel and wider basis for imposing a duty (ie the foreseeability principle) at 509:

  > The proposition which these recognised cases suggest, and which is, therefore, to be deduced from them, is that whenever one person is by circumstances placed in such a position with regard to another that every one of ordinary sense who did think would at once recognise that if he did not use ordinary care and skill in his own conduct with regard to those circumstances he would cause danger of injury to the person or property of the other, a duty arises to use ordinary care and skill to avoid such danger.

This more general basis for imposing a duty of care was not supported by other judges, and the reasoning was subject to criticism in subsequent cases like *Le Lievre v Gould* (1893), noted above. By 1932, however, the increasing volume of cases seeking redress for indirectly caused harm created a more urgent need for legal protection for those who were not protected by the law of contract. Partly because of the high reputation of Lord Esher MR (formerly Brett MR) and partly because one of the examples that he had used at 510 in *Heaven v Pender* (1883) when illustrating the operation of the foreseeability principle included the case of a person who supplied goods for the use of others in circumstances where there was no opportunity for them to discover any defect, this basis for imposing liability was picked up again when Mrs Donoghue's lawyers argued for a new approach to the emerging problem of how best to protect the public from the negligent manufacture of consumer goods. The idea of using the foresight of a person of 'ordinary sense' who could recognise the risk to another person if they did not use 'ordinary care and skill to avoid such danger', which had been raised 49 years before *Donoghue v Stevenson* (1932), then came into direct conflict with the concerns emphasised 90 years earlier by the judges in *Winterbottom v Wright* (1842) who had insisted that, absent fraud or intentional wrongdoing, liability for negligence must be kept within the safe limits set by contract.

A case to remember

Donoghue v Stevenson

Facts

The special challenge posed by *Donoghue v Stevenson* (1932) lay in the facts that the case involved multiple parties and that the harm was caused indirectly by an ordinary, everyday object (a bottle of ginger beer) that contained another ordinary, everyday object (a snail). The decomposing snail had been sealed inside a dark opaque bottle of ginger beer that was manufactured in Stevenson's factory and then distributed to a cafe owner named Minchella. Minchella sold it to a customer, who bought it for a friend, May Donoghue, who drank half of the contents before discovering the remains of the snail and becoming ill. Because the factory workers had sealed the dark bottle before sending it on to its ultimate destination, the cafe, Mrs Donoghue had been unable to protect herself by inspecting its contents before drinking the ginger beer. These facts made it the perfect vehicle to extend the law, because Mrs Donoghue could not bring her case into any of the pre-existing pockets of recognised liability. She had been given the drink by her friend and so, because she was not in any contractual relationship, either with the manufacturer Stevenson or with the cafe owner Minchella, neither owed her a contractual duty. The bottle was not the kind of thing that was dangerous per se; nor was it known to be defective. There had been no fraud that could attract the tort of deceit or any wrongdoing by any other party that could attract the operation of the intentional torts, and Mrs Donoghue did not fall into any of the other special duty categories that might have linked her in a legally recognised relationship with Stevenson, the manufacturer.

Issue

Mrs Donoghue's problem forced her lawyers to ask the judges for an extraordinary legal solution. The judges were asked to recognise a new category of negligence based on the relationship between manufacturer and consumer. This relationship would impose a duty on the manufacturer to take reasonable care to see that the article was not injurious to health. The defendant argued that there was no cause of action open on the pleadings, because a manufacturer did not owe such a duty to a consumer unless there was a contract between them. The judge at first instance in Scotland dismissed this argument and sent the case to trial on the facts. The defendant appealed against this decision and the judges in the Scottish Second Division upheld the appeal 3:1, dismissing the action and absolving the defendant of any blame. The plaintiff appealed to the House of Lords and the issue was whether this novel duty, allegedly owed by the manufacturer, Stevenson, to the ultimate consumer, Donoghue, to take reasonable care in the manufacture and bottling of the ginger beer, had any basis in law.

Reasoning

The case was decided in the House of Lords by a majority of 3:2 in the plaintiff's favour. The two dissenting judges relied on the weight of authority in the previous cases, like *Winterbottom v Wright* (1842) and *Le Lievre v Gould* (1893), which had denied liability in analogous situations, and disposed of the handful of anomalous cases noted above that appeared to support the plaintiff's case. They declared in very emphatic and sometimes sarcastic terms that they would not countenance any further exception to the old rules or any introduction of a new category of duty. They intimated that abandoning the doctrine of privity would open a floodgate of claims that would place an intolerable burden on industry and invite disaster.

Examples of reasoning in *Donoghue*

- **Lord Buckmaster** began by explaining at 567:

  > The law applicable is the common law, and, though its principles are capable of application to meet new conditions not contemplated when the law was laid down, these principles cannot be changed nor can additions be made to them because any particular meritorious case seems outside their ambit.

  Lord Buckmaster refused to extend the law by adopting the justification for imposing liability in *Heaven v Pender* (1883) posited by Brett MR, saying at 577–8:

  > The principle of tort lies completely outside the region where such considerations apply, and the duty, if it exists, must extend to every person who, in lawful circumstances, uses the article made. There can be no special duty attaching to the manufacture of food apart from that implied by contract or imposed by statute. If such a duty exists, it seems to me it must cover the construction of every article, and I cannot see any reason why it should not apply to the construction of a house. If one step, why not fifty? Yet if a house be, as it sometimes is, negligently built, and in consequence of that negligence the ceiling falls and injures the occupier or any one else, no action against the builder exists according to the English law, although I believe such a right did exist according to the laws of Babylon.

- **Lord Tomlin** agreed with Lord Buckmaster and expressed concern at 600 about the 'alarming consequences' that might flow if the case succeeded and the doctrine of privity of contract was allowed to be 'ripped open' by a tort action. Lord Tomlin emphasised the impossibility of imposing proper limits on the action if the case succeeded in setting a precedent, saying at 599–600:

  > I think that if the appellant is to succeed it must be upon the proposition that every manufacturer or repairer of any article is under a duty to every one who may thereafter legitimately use the article to exercise due care in the manufacture or repair. It is logically impossible to stop short of this point. There can be no distinction between food and any other article.

The three judges who decided the case in the plaintiff's favour justified their decision to allow this novel kind of tort liability by, first, pointing to the public good that would be achieved by requiring manufacturers to take care that their products were safe; then highlighting the cases like *Langridge v Levy* (1837) and *George v Skivington* (1869) where indirectly caused harm had been allowed in three-party scenarios; and finally, building on the principle of reasonable foreseeability of harm first introduced by Lord Esher MR (then Brett MR) in *Heaven v Pender* (1883). The key task faced by the majority judges in adopting and adapting this new justification lay in addressing the misgivings raised by the dissenting judges over whether it was possible to keep this new form of tort liability under control, both at the stage of imposing the duty and at the stage of limiting the scope of the duty by ruling out harm that was too remote from the breach. This task was begun by Lord Atkin, who emphasised the notion of proximity or nearness first introduced by Brett MR in *Heaven v Pender* (1883) as a limit on the circumstances that would give rise to a duty. It was taken up by Lord Macmillan, who suggested the concept of control as another relevant limiting factor.

Examples of reasoning in *Donoghue*

- **Lord Atkin** began by explaining, at 579, that the issue was important 'both because of its bearing on public health and because of the practical test which it applies to the system under which it arises'. After noting the difficulty of finding any 'statements of general application defining the relations between parties that give rise to the duty', his Honour suggested at 580 that 'the duty which is common to all the cases where liability is established must logically be based upon some element common to the cases where it is found to exist'. Commenting that the test framed by Brett MR in *Heaven v Pender* (1883) was 'demonstrably too wide', Lord Atkin then pointed out that 'if properly limited, [the test] would be capable of affording a valuable practical guide'. In a well-known passage at 580 Lord Atkin explained the origin of the now famous 'neighbour principle':

  > [I]n English law there must be, and is, some *general conception of relations giving rise to a duty of care*, of which the particular cases found in the books are but instances. The liability for negligence, whether you style it such or treat it as in other systems as a species of 'culpa,' is no doubt based upon a *general public sentiment of moral wrongdoing for which the offender must pay*. But acts or omissions which any moral code would censure cannot in a practical world be treated so as to give a right to every person injured by them to demand relief. In this way rules of law arise which *limit the range of complainants and the extent of their remedy*. The rule that you are to love your neighbour becomes in law, you must not injure your neighbour; and the lawyer's question, Who is my neighbour? receives a restricted reply. You must *take reasonable care to avoid acts or omissions which you can reasonably foresee would be likely to injure your neighbour*. Who, then, in law is my neighbour? The answer seems to be – persons who are *so closely and directly affected by my act* that I ought reasonably to have them in contemplation as being so affected when I am directing my mind to the acts or omissions which are called in question. [Emphasis added.]

Lord Atkin suggested at 581 that once the *Heaven v Pender* doctrine was 'limited by the notion of proximity' introduced in *Le Lievre v Gould* (which he described at 582 as 'the necessary qualification of proximate relationship'), it could keep the tort of negligence under proper control:

> I think that this sufficiently states the truth if *proximity be not confined to mere physical proximity*, but be used, as I think it was intended, to extend to such *close and direct relations* that the act complained of directly affects a person whom the person alleged to be bound to take care would know would be directly affected by his careless act. [Emphasis added.]

Lord Atkin agreed that something more than mere foreseeability of harm was needed when moving away from a limit based on the privity of a contractual relationship, and devised a limiting concept based on a relationship of proximity, which he found in *Heaven v Pender* and *Le Lievre v Gould* (1893).

Lord Atkin stated at 582 that if a consumer were to have no remedy against a negligent manufacturer it would be not only 'a grave defect in the law' but also 'contrary to principle'; however, he concluded at 583:

> I do not think so ill of our jurisprudence as to suppose that its principles are so remote from the ordinary needs of civilized society and the ordinary claims it makes upon its members as to deny a legal remedy where there is so obviously *a social wrong*. [Emphasis added.]

The key to Lord Atkin's analysis of the previous case law lay in the fact that he did not take the previous cases at face value (at 594–5):

> With all respect, I think that the judgments in the case err by seeking to confine the law to *rigid and exclusive categories* and by not giving sufficient attention to the *general principle* which governs the whole law of negligence in the duty owed to those who will be immediately injured by the lack of care. [Emphasis added.]

After discussing at some length the outcomes and reasoning from previous cases to show how they could be reconciled with the imposition of a duty owed by a manufacturer to a consumer and expressing his satisfaction at 598 that the 'fundamental principles of the common law' had led to a similar development in the United States, Lord Atkin at 599 finally pronounced the rule that heralded a new form of negligence liability – one that was based not simply on the recognition of a new category but on the wider 'neighbour principle':

> My Lords, if your Lordships accept the view that this pleading discloses a relevant cause of action you will be affirming the proposition that by Scots and English law alike a manufacturer of products, which he sells in such a form as to show that he intends them to reach the ultimate consumer in the form in which they left him with no reasonable possibility of intermediate examination, and with the knowledge that the absence of reasonable care in the preparation or putting up of the products will result in an injury to the consumer's life or property, owes a duty to the consumer to take that reasonable care.

- **Lord Thankerton** at 603 agreed with Lord Atkin that 'a relationship of duty' should be inferred from the fact that the manufacturer, by placing the drink on the market, 'has intentionally so excluded interference with, or examination of, the article by any intermediate handler of the goods between himself and the consumer that he has, of his own accord, brought himself into *direct relationship with the consumer*' (emphasis added).

He agreed with the judgment given by Lord Atkin and pointed out at 603:

> The English cases demonstrate how impossible it is to catalogue finally, amid the ever varying types of human relationships, those relationships in which a duty to exercise care arises apart from contract, and each of these cases relates to its own set of circumstances, out of which it was claimed that the duty had arisen.

- **Lord Macmillan** explained at 609 that the topic of negligence engaged 'two rival principles of the law'; the first was 'the well established principle that no one other than a party to a contract can complain of a breach of that contract' and the other was 'the equally well established doctrine that negligence apart from contract gives a right of action to the party injured by that negligence'. He agreed at 614 that Lord Esher's principles were 'sound guides' and pointed out at 615 that 'where the retailer is merely the vehicle of transmission of the products to the consumer' there was no reason to see the damage as 'too remote' from the manufacturer's negligence. He continued at 618–19:

> The law takes no cognizance of carelessness in the abstract. It concerns itself with carelessness only where there is *a duty to take care and where failure in that duty has caused damage*. In such circumstances carelessness assumes the legal quality of negligence and entails the consequences in law of negligence.
>
> What, then, are the circumstances which give rise to this duty to take care? In the daily contacts of social and business life human beings are thrown into, or place themselves in, an infinite variety of relations with their fellows; and the law can refer only to the *standards of the reasonable man* in order to determine whether any particular relation gives rise to a duty to take care as between those who stand in that relation to each other. The grounds of action may be as various and manifold as human errancy; and the conception of legal responsibility may develop in adaptation to altering social conditions and standards. The criterion of judgment must adjust and adapt itself to the changing circumstances of life. *The categories of negligence are never closed.* [Emphasis added.]

Lord Macmillan located the source of the duty (at 620) in the fact that a manufacturer 'who for gain engages in the business of manufacturing articles of food and drink intended for consumption by members of the public in the form in which he issues them' both *intends* and *contemplates* that they will be consumed and therefore:

> he places himself in a relationship with all the potential consumers of his commodities, and that relationship which he assumes and desires for his own ends imposes upon him a duty to take care to avoid injuring them.

He agreed at 620 that 'liability can only arise where a *reasonable man would have foreseen and could have avoided* the consequences of his act or omission' (emphasis added) and suggested at 622:

> It must always be a *question of circumstances* whether the carelessness amounts to negligence, and whether the injury is not too remote from the carelessness.
>
> It may be a good general rule to regard *responsibility as ceasing when control ceases*. [Emphasis added.]

The significance of *Donoghue v Stevenson* (1932) can not be overstated. This case justified the recognition of a new category of duty based on the relationship between manufacturer and consumer. By setting out a principle of general application, Lord Atkin released the concept of negligence from the confines of the contractual doctrine of privity and the rigid categories previously recognised by the law of torts. *Donoghue v Stevenson* transformed the way that judges saw the legal status of the parties and the rights and obligations arising from their relationships. Before this case, a plaintiff who had been harmed indirectly in a multiparty scenario was often seen as a stranger who stood outside the relationships that attracted the law's protection. After this case, plaintiffs like May Donoghue were seen not as illegitimate, almost invisible 'third parties' that the law could not recognise, but as legitimate plaintiffs in their own right, who were directly owed a duty of care by the person whose original negligence set in motion the chain of cause and effect that led to the harm that they had suffered. Instead of tracking the legal relationships through the (indirect) physical tracks of harm, the majority judges traced the legal basis of the duty of care directly to the nature and special features of the more abstract relationship between the defendant and the plaintiff to find a new form of proximity or closeness existing between them.[7] Once the contract-based idea of privity was replaced by the tort-based idea of proximity as a new way of linking the two parties in a direct legal relationship, the fact that the plaintiff had been harmed indirectly through the involvement of some third party no longer mattered. Figure 10.3 illustrates the shift in perception that occurred in *Donoghue v Stevenson* (1932).

Figure 10.3 The foreseeability progression

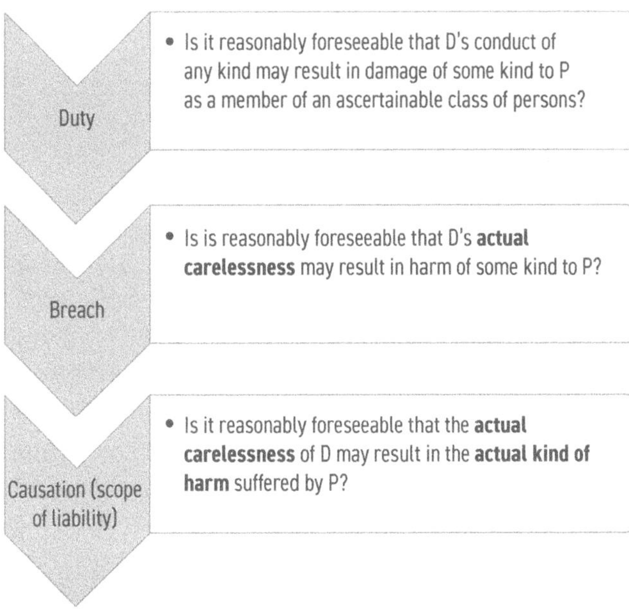

7 Windeyer J called it proximity in 'the metaphysical sense' in *Hargrave v Goldman* (1963) at 64.

The justifying power of the 'neighbour principle' in the case of *Donoghue v Stevenson* (1932) gave birth to the modern tort of negligence. However, the victory won by May Donoghue did not end the debate over the issues that had delayed the recognition of the new tort. Because the theoretical problems that were highlighted by the dissenting judges in that case did not disappear, the conversation that had begun well before *Donoghue v Stevenson* (1932) over the limits and justification of the duty to take reasonable care did not end – and in fact, those debates have intensified with the passage of time, increasingly complicated patterns of relationships have emerged and different kinds of harm (like pure economic loss and psychiatric injury) have been given recognition. You will recognise the threads of those conversations when you read the cases that are discussed in the following chapters, and as you read them, your familiarity with *Donoghue v Stevenson* (1932), and cases like *Heaven v Pender* (1883) that went before it, will help you to understand and participate in the debates that have continued to this day.

10.1.2 The challenge of negligence

The preceding story of the birth of negligence has introduced you to some of the continuing themes that dominate the case law. The tort has taken decades to develop into its current form, and although a degree of clarity has begun to emerge as the judges have gradually defined the elements and explained the relevant tests for liability, the 'staggering march of negligence'[8] since its inception appears to have confirmed some of the fears expressed by the dissenting judges in *Donoghue v Stevenson* (1932), while at the same time providing unexpected avenues for compensation and vindication to otherwise powerless victims. Some of the reasons for the tort's complexity have already been identified in section 10.1.1 above; however, several features make it a particularly difficult tort to recognise, limit, understand and apply.

Examples

- **Scope and focus:** Negligence has an exceptionally wide focus on harm that can overlap with other causes of action in both contract and tort. This leads to debates over how to reconcile it with other pre-existing pockets of tort liability. In some cases, negligence has subsumed other areas of liability – for example, occupiers liability and the tort based on *Rylands v Fletcher* (1866) – but the future of the tort and its relationship with the other torts like nuisance, defamation and the intentional torts (both the trespass torts and the special actions on the case) is uncertain. Different solutions have been found in different countries.

  Beyond this problem lies the further difficulty of justifying principled sources of limits on the extent of liability. This problem is caused by the fact that both the test of reasonable foreseeability for duty and the 'but for' test for causation set the net of possible liability too wide. In the words of Lord Buckmaster (see above): 'If one step, why not fifty?'

8 Weir, 'The Staggering March of Negligence' (1998) discusses the extensions of the tort. See also Spigelman, 'Negligence: The Last Outpost of the Welfare State' (2002), discussing the 'imperial march' of negligence.

- **Acts and omissions:** Negligence allows liability for both acts and omissions, so not only is its scope much more extensive than other torts, but, from a practical viewpoint, it is also much more difficult to define the conduct being complained of. For example, an omission, which is conduct that by definition has *not* occurred, is much harder to specify from the facts than a positive act that *has* actually occurred. To understand why omissions pose such a difficult task, try this exercise: write down clearly and precisely all the things that you *did not do* on your birthday last year.
- **Causation covers both direct and indirect consequences of the defendant's conduct:** Negligence can apply to indirectly caused harm, with the result that the difficult issue of causation arises more frequently in this tort than in any other. Part of the problem lies in the fact that the 'but for' test for factual causation (or 'necessary condition', as rephrased in civil liability legislation) cannot do enough on its own to limit liability and so it must be supplemented with other more imprecise normative considerations. Given that the effects of the defendant's conduct can theoretically carry on forever, the need to limit the extent of the defendant's liability for the harm that ripples out from any given event leads to further difficulties.
- **Justification:** Negligence has very wide and imprecise moral and policy justifications that do not provide a limit on the circumstances that attract liability. This makes the law uncertain and potential defendants can find it difficult to organise their enterprises so as to avoid liability. The lack of a clear justification can lead judges to resort to (often unstated or broadly defined) notions of 'policy' or 'principle', which in turn leads to further debates over tort law's role in responding to social wrongs. This is compounded by difficulties in deciding *how* we should draw an appropriate line between our moral code and our legal code – and in deciding on *who* (the judges or the elected representatives of the public) should be trusted to draw that line. As we will see, this issue is becoming particularly evident in negligence claims involving climate change and environmental harm.
- **Types of harm:** Negligence developed as a response to the Industrial Revolution, which created countless new sources of risk in people's everyday lives. Obvious examples are the widespread risk to road users' safety brought by the proliferation of automobiles, or work-related accidents linked to industrial labour. Yet, the harms resulting from these new activities shared the common denominator of being ascribable to relatively easily identifiable accidents. As science, technology and society progressed, new and more complex types of harm emerged. These include what Jane Stapleton in *Disease and the Compensation Debate* (1986) has named 'man-made' diseases (such as the conditions induced by asbestos or chemicals or adverse reactions to pharmaceuticals), the intricate category of *pure mental harm* (in which the victim is not personally involved in an accident), the financially motivated category of *pure economic loss*, the *loss of cultural identity* in cases involving vulnerable minorities, and the compounding effects of climate change on future generations. It is unclear that a remedy born out of the need to provide compensation for accidents causing physical injury is necessarily well suited to these varied and sophisticated types of loss. Yet it remains to this day the only general remedy for wrongdoing available to victims.
- **Core concept:** Negligence relies heavily on the vague concept of reasonable foreseeability that changes its focus in each of the three elements of duty, breach and causation. The inclusion of the notoriously fuzzy concept of reasonableness means that the tests in the elements of breach and causation are incapable of laying down precise rules of conduct and so these issues must be argued out in each case in the light of its particular facts.

These features of the tort of negligence mark it out from the other forms of trespass torts, for example, which can be kept within clear boundaries. This is not only because they require a positive act that directly invades the plaintiff's rights and causes a narrowly defined effect, but, given the fundamental rights that they protect, the trespass torts are also much less controversial and more obviously justifiable than negligence. Similarly, the torts of nuisance and defamation also focus on a defined harm, so even though they both allow for indirectly caused harm, their narrow harm focus helps to limit their scope. For these reasons, many of the difficult questions that arise in the tort of negligence (like duty, causation and remoteness) arise much less frequently in those torts. Table 10.1 contrasts some of these distinguishing features of negligence with those of the rights-based trespass torts and shows how, on almost every point of comparison (except for the nature of the duty owed), negligence is much broader than trespass.

Negligence challenges our sense of moral or social justice and asks a big question about how best to respond to wrongdoing that causes harm – and the answer is not easily found, because, as Lord Macmillan pointed out, the grounds of action are as 'various and manifold as human errancy' (see above). Because it asks such a big question, this tort also asks much more of a plaintiff than the other torts, both from the normative point of view and the factual point of view. Consequently, negligence requires a more creative and imaginative approach to problem solving by comparison with other torts. Negligence asks the plaintiff not only to justify *why* a defendant should have taken reasonable care to avoid causing or allowing harm to befall them in the circumstances, but also to explain *what*, on the facts, the defendant should have done and to show *how*, if the defendant had done the right thing, it would have made a critical difference to the plaintiff's ultimate fate. Once these matters have been decided, the plaintiff then has to identify *what* the defendant needs to do to put the plaintiff into the hypothetical position they would have been in if the defendant had behaved as they should have done, to *quantify and prove* their losses in money terms, and to justify *why* the defendant's liability should extend to cover those kinds of losses.

Negligence is a challenge because its principal driver – the notion of reasonable foreseeability of harm to others – cannot do enough on its own to keep liability within fair bounds. Furthermore, negligence is a tort that cannot draw in advance a clear bright line between what is allowed and what is not allowed. Unlike the trespass torts (which can issue a simple command like 'do not touch'), negligence can only issue guidance that is qualified and incomplete. This is so, not only because the command 'do not harm others' simply does not always match our moral intuitions about what is right and wrong, but also because such a prohibition would be impossible to comply with, would paralyse us from action too often, would conflict with other important goals and would constrict our freedom of action too much. Even the addition of a reasonableness criterion does not completely solve the problem, because a command such as 'do what is reasonable in the circumstances' is still incapable of drawing a clear line dividing the conduct that is permissible from that which is forbidden. The intentional torts, which deal with absolutes, offer us a clear black-and-white choice between acting and not acting at all – but negligence requires us to choose where to draw a line on a grey scale containing an infinite number of shades. This is why the 'pendulum of negligence' will never find an obvious

Table 10.1 Distinguishing trespass and negligence

	Rights-based trespass torts	**Negligence**
Justification	Protecting defined fundamental rights to bodily integrity, integrity of possession, autonomy and dignity.	Responding to a 'general public sentiment of moral wrongdoing for which an offender must pay' (Oliver Wendell Holmes Jr).
Conduct	Must be a positive act only.	Either a positive act or an omission.
Focal point	Each tort has a single clearly defined focus, eg land, goods, physical contact with the body, apprehension of bodily contact, or physical confinement.	Generally defined to include a wide range of harm, including physical damage, damage to property, psychological injury and economic loss.
Causation	Must encompass direct causation only.	Either direct or indirect causation based on causing or failing to prevent harm.
Common fact pattern	Primary rights invasions that almost always occur in a two-party scenario involving people in close physical proximity.	Extends beyond two-party scenarios to cover multiple-person fact patterns and more complicated relationships between people, places and events.
Common type of rules	'Bright line' rules that issue clear and absolute 'black-and-white' orders, eg 'Do not touch.'	Fuzzy rules that depend on the assessment of individual circumstances, eg 'Do what is reasonable.'
Nature of the duty	Universal duties owed to all, but limited by the nature of the protected right.	Specific duties owed only to ascertainable classes of persons.
Remoteness of consequences	Effects tracked through direct consequences.	Effects tracked through reasonably foreseeable consequences.
Insurance	It is not possible to insure against committing an intentional tort.	Insurance is available because negligence is an inadvertent form of wrongdoing.

point of equilibrium and why the tort will always require contextual judgement, where each situation is assessed in the light of the facts to determine whether the defendants have responded reasonably in the circumstances that they encountered at the time.

10.2 Critique of negligence

10.2.1 Abolishing or modifying negligence

Negligence is a tort without obvious limits. It seeks to answer some very challenging questions, and the answers that the judges have given to these questions have not satisfied everyone. We noted in Chapter 1 that the law of torts covers a wide range of causes of action that are labelled as torts because they do not fit better into any other category of the law. The discussion of the origins of this tort shows that negligence is the paradigm tort – the ragbag inside the ragbag – that was invented to fill a gap in the law. For these reasons, the tort has been subject to trenchant criticism, not only from the insurance groups, whose businesses support the existence of the tort, but also from practitioners and judges who work within the legal system, those like academics and politicians who observe the tort from outside, and interest groups that critique the legal system from specific angles.

Negligence will always be subject to some criticism, and some of the specific suggestions for improving the substantive law are considered in Chapters 11–14, which cover the elements, and Chapter 15, which covers the defences. However, some critics have argued that some parts of the tort of negligence should be abolished and replaced either by private insurance or by a no-fault compensation scheme covering all forms of personal injury, regardless of whether the injuries have been the result of negligence or are simply characterised as accidental.

Examples

- In the New South Wales Court of Appeal case of *Reynolds v Katoomba RSL All Services Club Ltd* (2001), Spigelman CJ suggested at [26] that the tort of negligence could be seen as 'the last outpost of the welfare state'. The Chief Justice reported in a later article that one of Australia's most respected torts scholars, Professor Harold Luntz, had responded by saying:

  > No welfare state would ever have created a system so irrational, expensive, wasteful, slow and discriminatory.[9]

- The authors of successive editions of *Atiyah's Accidents, Compensation and the Law* (Patrick Atiyah, who wrote the original version and Peter Cane, who wrote the most recent version in 2006) both argue that, when viewed from a wider 'legal and social landscape' (at xv), it is clear that the tort of negligence, which relies on an incoherent and flawed account of fault, should be replaced by a fairer, more efficient no-fault compensation scheme. They criticise the fault principle chiefly on the grounds that the compensation payable by a defendant often bears no relation to their degree of fault and that a fault-based system often leaves many victims without any compensation. In *The Damages Lottery* (1997), Atiyah suggested that a no-fault road accident scheme combined with new, more widespread forms of personal first-party insurance would offer a better solution. Atiyah's central claim is that public resources would be better spent by diverting them out of the cumbersome, sometimes irrational and unfair system of tort law and devoting them to a less wasteful, more modest and more certain system that can deliver better outcomes to more victims of misfortune. Atiyah was an early critic of the 'blame culture' and 'paternalist ideology' associated with the welfare state and the law of negligence (see 176), and his views in *The Damages Lottery*, where he advocated a shift towards personal responsibility, have been very influential. Despite the fact that his more radical solution of abolishing negligence-based damages for accidental personal injury and increasing reliance on first-party insurance has not attracted any great support, his emphasis on the principle of personal responsibility has certainly found an echo in recent Australian cases.

9 Spigelman, 'Negligence: The Last Outpost of the Welfare State' (2002) at 432, citing Luntz, *Assessment of Damages for Personal Injury and Death* (2002) at x.

- John Keeler discusses Atiyah's views in 'Thinking through the Unthinkable: Collective Responsibilities in Personal Injury Law' (2001), noting the reasons behind negligence law's resilience in the face of calls for its abolition, and explaining how it serves a useful purpose in 'expressing important corrective justice values'. He concludes by suggesting, at 385–6, that a greater concern for the way that issues of distributive and corrective justice can be related to the realities of modern society would provide critics 'with a better evaluation of the force of the arrangements they seek to change'.
- Conversely, others have argued that the law of torts, and negligence in particular given its wide and ever-expanding scope, perform a significant function in advancing society. Leslie Bender (1988) makes the argument that tort law should be seen as a 'tool for social equality and justice struggle, rather than as a purely compensatory regime'. In two classic contributions by American scholars Peter Schuck and Kip Viscusi, tort law is respectively described as an instrument for the pursuit of the public interest in *Tort Law and the Public Interest* (1991), and as a means of achieving regulatory goals in the absence of public options in *Regulation through Litigation* (2002). All of these accounts capture what can be described as a hidden function of tort law and negligence in particular: the ability to serve interests that go beyond the individual parties involved. Arguably, it is precisely because it lacks clearly defined boundaries that negligence can be adaptive enough to perform this social role.
- The New Zealand government has abolished most forms of negligence liability for personal injuries and replaced them with a no-fault accident compensation scheme, which is administered by the Accident Compensation Corporation. It is discussed by Geoffrey Palmer in 'Financing and Delivering: New Zealand's Accident Compensation Scheme' (2023).
- Stephen D Sugarman argues in 'Doing Away with Tort Law' (1985) that tort law is a 'bizarre system' of compensation. This article was published in a special edition of the *California Law Review*, which also contains many other articles from the Symposium on Alternative Compensation Schemes and Tort Theory. See also Robert Abel's article 'A Critique of Torts' (1994), which argues that our method of awarding damages in negligence serves only to reproduce inequality, commodify our experience and encourage inefficient safety levels.
- In 'The Future of Negligence' (2007), John Smillie advocates a complete 'statutory abolition of the tort of negligence without putting anything in its place' on the grounds that it would be 'fairer, more rational and more cost-effective than the current regime of fault liability backed by third-party insurance', which he argues is morally indefensible and practically inefficient.
- See also *Tort Theory* (1993), an edited collection by Ken Cooper-Stephenson and Elaine Gibson, which contains an extensive collection of criticism from many different perspectives, including the feminist, economic, critical legal studies and postmodernist approaches to negligence. The book also includes a chapter by Bruce Feldthusen, 'If This Is Torts, Negligence Must Be Dead', who discusses the 'impotence of personal injury law' (at 394).
- The quest for a rational and self-contained tort of negligence is a chimeric enterprise that continues to torment legal scholars. In his contribution titled 'Rationalising Tort Law for the Twenty-First Century' (2017), Ken Oliphant candidly admits that 'the common law's whole approach to the duty of care concept is so completely incoherent that it precludes any effort to communicate or discuss its nature and role in intelligible terms'. While perhaps overly dramatic, this observation captures a real measure of unrest. As a matter of fact, one must acknowledge that there

is an inherent tension within the tort of negligence that speaks to two very different but equally essential aspects of the legal profession: the lawyer's insatiable search for certainty and coherence, and the advocate's demand for justice and fairness.

- More recently, Mark Geistfled in his contribution 'Unifying Principles within Pluralist Tort Adjudication' (2024) has attempted to provide a more positive account, suggesting that reasoning by analogy in tortious adjudication can form the basis for the coherent incremental development of 'unifying categorical principles with the potential to converge into a single integrated rationale for tort law'.

Not all critics of the tort go so far as Atiyah and Smillie, who argue that, at its core, the tort of negligence is unstable, incoherent and morally indefensible. Some, like David Ibbetson (2003), who accept that the existence of the tort can be justified by reference to moral values or economic efficiency, simply argue that there is 'a degree of unavoidable uncertainty on its outer boundaries' and suggest ways of improving our understanding of why those outer boundaries are uncertain and exploring solutions that will improve the clarity of the tort.

Examples

- David Ibbetson states frankly in 'How the Romans Did for Us: Ancient Roots of the Tort of Negligence' (2003) at 475 that 'the law of negligence is in a mess' and suggests that an understanding of the tort's roots can explain how 'the over-precision of duties of care' and the 'under-precision of the other elements of the tort' (that are based on abstract concepts like carelessness, reasonableness, foreseeability etc) are in fact 'opposite sides of the same coin'.
- James Gordley, who takes up the debate on the issue of whether negligence law contains an acceptable account of fault, argues in 'The Common Law in the Twentieth Century: Some Unfinished Business' (2000) at 1817 that negligence law in the common law world, which was formed out of an 'amalgam of inherited rules, civil law borrowings, and the rationalizations of 19th and early 20th century jurists', is 'neither traditional nor rational'. He argues that 'we must reject the compromise and weed out the relics of the older common law' and at 1847 advocates scrapping our traditional list of torts and redesigning our tort law to more closely resemble the civil law approach found in Europe with the goal of ensuring that we 'should hold defendants liable only in cases where they are genuinely at fault'.
- The legal systems of Europe referred to by James Gordley (which are known as the 'civil law systems' and are modelled on the *Napoleonic Code* of 1804) take a different approach to negligence. As Peter Cane explains in *The Anatomy of Tort Law* (1997) at 3, the civil law approach differs from the common law's 'torts as recipes' approach by deriving the law from 'a few very general provisions' and a generally stated 'principle of personal responsibility for damage caused by faulty conduct'. The French *Code Civil*, art 382, reads: 'Any act whatever of man, which causes damage to another, obliges the one by whose fault it occurred, to compensate it.'
- Allan Beever argues in *Rediscovering the Law of Negligence* (2007) that we should not be captured by the lure of policy-based justifications for the current state of the law of negligence (which he too describes as 'a mess'). Beever argues that, because the law of negligence gains

internal coherence from corrective justice and the principles that underpin it, 'the law is able to determine liability without any appeal to policy whatsoever' and he concludes at 514:

> The modern law of negligence is a mess because we have forgotten what its principles actually are. The modern approaches create this mess by distorting the principles of the law. They then seek to tidy the mess by distorting the principles of the law by inventing policies to determine the scope of liability. But those policies increase the mess by moving us further from the principles of the law. In consequence there is a new mess that attracts new policies that create more mess ... None of this is necessary.

- Harold Luntz and Christian Witting make radically different arguments. In 'Tort Law, Policy and the High Court of Australia' (2007), Witting describes the role of policy in the Court's decision-making process as 'a logical inevitability'. This is so because, as Luntz puts it in 'The Use of Policy in Negligence Cases in the High Court of Australia' (2007) at 59, 'policy arguments may come into play when a decision cannot be made according to established rules, which, I have suggested, will be in nearly every case that comes before the High Court'.

The stark contrast between the position of Beever and those of Luntz and Witting is yet another example of the uncertain contours of the tort of negligence. While this is symptomatic of a measure of chaos that can at times create difficulties, it also signals a level of vitality and adaptability that has virtually no match in any other legal field.

10.2.2 Gender bias, race bias and social power

While the legal systems of other countries offer a source of critique of our own common law approach to the tort of negligence, another criticism is that gender- and race-based biases have not disappeared from tort law.

Examples

- Leslie Bender argues in 'A Lawyer's Primer on Feminist Theory and Tort' (1988) that the reasonableness standard in negligence is dominated by a masculine ethic of self-interested and antisocial calculation of utilities and the maximisation of efficiency and profit. She suggests that greater recognition of a feminist ethic of care and concern for the needs and welfare of others would change the face of negligence law (eg by imposing a duty to rescue). Bender also argues that replacing the 'reasonable man' with the 'reasonable person' standard does not eradicate the term's ingrained sexism. See also Bender's 'Tort Law's Role as a Tool for Social Justice Struggle' (1998).
- Martha Chamallas argues in 'The Architecture of Bias: Deep Structures in Tort Law' (1998) at 467 that 'contemporary tort law devalues or undervalues the lives, activities, and potential of women and people of colour'.
- Joanne Conaghan explores these themes further in 'Tort Law and the Feminist Critique of Reason' (1996), where she critically discusses feminist scholarship that critiques tort law's claims both to justice, fairness and decency on the one hand and to rationality and objectivity on the other.

- Reg Graycar has focused on 'the ways in which important issues of social power – in particular, issues of gender or racial hierarchy, and disability – are dealt with' in modern torts scholarship, with a special focus on the issues raised by Harold Luntz in his influential teaching text *Torts: Cases and Commentary* (2002) and subsequent editions. Her article is essential reading: 'Teaching Torts as if the World Really Existed: Reflections on Harold Luntz's contribution to Australian Law School Classrooms' (2003); see also Graycar's 'Judicial Activism or Traditional Negligence Law? Conception, Pregnancy, and Denial of Reproductive Choice' (2006).
- See also Mayo Moran's book, *Rethinking the Reasonable Person: An Egalitarian Reconstruction of the Objective Standard* (2003), which contains a lengthy scholarly critique of the objective reasonableness standards of the law (both criminal and tort law). Moran concludes at 315 that it is critical to the legitimacy of the reasonable person standard 'to distinguish sharply between its normative and non-normative content' because there is a 'deep tension between what is reasonable and what is customarily done'. Her book analyses the problem of the 'reasonable person' and critically discusses the case law dealing with the reasons why judges treat men and women, girls and boys, the able and the disabled in different ways (depending on their sometimes distorted and sexist views of what is appropriately 'normal' and 'ordinary' on the one hand or 'abnormal' and 'extra-ordinary' on the other).

Joanne Conaghan and Wade Mansell also provide a critique, not only of the tort of negligence but of other torts as well, in *The Wrongs of Tort* (2006). They make an important point when they explain at 2–3 that 'the whole process of critique is a value-laden enterprise'. They maintain that it is 'impossible' to adopt a 'neutral disinterested point of view' and suggest that the fact that the law's values may be unstated, implicit or uncontentious does not mean that the law is value-free. These writers emphasise that the goal of engaging in critique is not to uncover which legal position is 'correct' but to help us to understand more clearly which solution to any legal issue is to be preferred by revealing more openly what the underlying values may be, regardless of whether they are classified as political, social, economic, feminist, environmental, etc. They argue that dressing up an argument by labelling it as being based on 'common sense' can retard the proper development of the law, because it is only by recognising that tort law, and negligence in particular, 'expresses a partial and contingent point of view' that we can be 'free to imagine the possibility of alternative arrangements and ultimately, to pursue them'. You can contrast this view with that of Alan Beever, discussed above, who maintains that policy should have no place in negligence, to realise how far apart different positions on the fundamentals of this tort can go.

10.3 New challenges to negligence in the digital age

The tort of negligence was born out of the social necessity to address the numerous new sources of risk created by the Industrial Revolution. Whether in the form of car accidents, industrial work-related injuries or defective manufactured products, the development of new technologies and scientific knowledge has been a key driver of the evolution of legal systems, and particularly the rules that dictate liability. In *The Fourth Industrial Revolution* (2016) Klaus Schwab discusses the disruptive technologies that are affecting our lives in the 21st century, from the internet of things (IoT), to virtual reality (VR), artificial intelligence (AI) and machine learning (ML). These technologies feed off and contribute to the expansion of unprecedented data pools and data networks – a phenomenon widely described as 'Big Data'. Schwab explains that the characteristic of this historical time, which sets it apart from previous periods (and previous industrial revolutions), is the pace of technological progress, coupled with the pervasiveness and invasiveness of these technologies. Indeed, countless aspects of our everyday lives are now decisively, if not exclusively, determined by the operation of algorithms, in ways that pose radical challenges to our society. Whether you are applying for a visa, seeking unemployment benefits, undergoing diagnostic procedures for complex medical conditions or filing a tax return, AI and ML algorithms are increasingly likely to be involved. In more recent times, the deployment of large language models and generative AI, such as ChatGPT, have further complicated the field. This shift towards automation, algorithmic decision-making, and generative AI can be particularly problematic.

Examples

- Frank Pasquale, in *The Black Box Society* (2015), explains that the algorithms that connect the dots between large datasets (fed by such diverse inputs as the invisible electronic footprints we leave behind when we browse the internet, use our mobile devices, connect to a mobile network, or go for a run wearing a fitness watch) are far from neutral. Behind a cloak of secrecy and technical complexity lies a web of vested interests, incentives and biases that raise alarming questions about the fairness and accountability of algorithmic decision-making.
- In *Made by Humans* (2018), Ellen Broad provides a succinct and compelling explanation of the structural problems of AI and algorithmic decision-making. The people designing these technologies are a restricted group: those with the means and education to do so. The preconceptions, biases and values of these people will inform the ways in which AI is designed and deployed. So, in addition to the risks of corporate interests discussed by Pasquale, there is an additional, subtle risk of entrenching unconscious biases.
- In the American case *State of Wisconsin v Loomis* (2016), the Supreme Court of Wisconsin allowed the use of a proprietary risk assessment tool (known as 'COMPAS') to determine whether Mr Loomis was at risk of recidivism. The algorithm, developed by the company Northpointe Inc, was later shown to be racially biased: the rates at which COMPAS incorrectly classified white and black offenders as being at risk of recidivism differed significantly. At trial, Northpointe was allowed to keep the algorithm's methodology secret, due to its proprietary nature, effectively making a review of the decision in Loomis' case impossible.
- The progress of AI is matched by the unwieldy development of the literature in the field. While it would be impossible to provide a full account of this development here, a good reference is Lim and Morgan's *The Cambridge Handbook of Private Law and Artificial Intelligence* (2024), which provides useful explainers as to what AI is, and what it means for core fields of private law, such as the law of torts.

The law of negligence is not immune to the complex challenges set by the digital age for at least two sets of reasons. First, because with the rise of autonomous systems, the exercise of allocating liability for wrongdoing results in a further layer of complication: who is ultimately liable? And second, because – as we have seen and will further discuss below – negligence is permeated by the notions of reasonableness and foreseeability. Conversely, AI systems operate on the basis of dry criterion-based rationality and the processes that lead to algorithmic outputs tend to be intrinsically opaque.

Examples

- A good example of the first set of problems (identifying who is ultimately liable) is the conundrum faced by legal systems across the world in cases of accidents involving autonomous vehicles (AVs). Some models of AV maintain an interaction between a human and the machine, in which case, when an accident occurs, the decisive question for the purpose of allocating liability revolves around the level of control maintained by the human – the issue being to establish whether that control can be characterised as 'meaningful'. Other AVs are driverless, and in those cases the question of liability can be mindboggling. In the absence of a human driver, courts and commentators are struggling to provide clear answers. Who should be liable? The manufacturer of the car? The software developers? The IT personnel who service the car? Now imagine a further layer of intricacy: the driverless car finds itself in a traffic situation in which it is confronted with a version of the classic 'trolley problem': a choice between staying the course and injuring its passenger, swerving to the right and injuring a pedestrian walking their dog, or swerving to the left and injuring a family coming home from the park. How does a machine make that decision and how is a court supposed to review that decision to establish fault?
- Commentators are divided about the appropriate course of action under current laws. Some, like Tom Mackie in 'Proving Liability for Highly and Fully Automated Vehicle Accidents in Australia' (2018), suggest that the solution lies with Australia's special provisions for product liability. Alternatively, Mark Brady et al in 'Automated Vehicles and Australian Personal Injury Compensation Schemes' (2017) suggest that the most appropriate way would be to adopt a special no-fault compensation scheme for injured parties. Others maintain that the law of negligence should continue to operate, but the question remains: who is the appropriate defendant?
- In 'Algorithmic Torts: A Prospective Comparative Overview' (2019), Marta Infantino and Weiwei Wang provide a broader overview of the myriad algorithmic-related activities that are multiplying around us and discuss in general terms the increased risks of harm that ensue from this proliferation of digital technologies, and the potential role of tort law in addressing it.

The second issue, how to reconcile the logic of negligence with the logic of AI, is even more challenging. The problem is pressing, because AI is creeping into legal practice and steadily establishing itself as a solid alternative to traditional legal actors and methods, particularly through the advent of generative AI. This is true in a range of areas, from the use of AI in law firms to replace the traditional work of paralegals and junior associates, to the practice of outsourcing online dispute resolution to algorithmic decision-making, to the controversial use of algorithmic predictions in criminal sentencing or preventive policing. The involvement of AI in negligence cases in the not so distant future is not a far-fetched proposition. But these are extremely complex issues, so as you embark upon your legal studies while the fourth industrial revolution maintains its disruptive pace, you should bear a few questions in mind.

Examples

Questions to bear in mind

- Negligence, as we continue to stress, is at times irrational, unpredictable and prone to value-laden judgements that affect its consistency. Could the use of AI and algorithms, which operate on the basis of a criterion-based logic, bring a measure of certainty, efficiency and predictability to impose some order on the chaos?
- Negligence was born and subsequently developed out of the ingenuity of sharp legal minds faced with the challenge of adapting the law to emerging social needs. Would AI and its ML processes be able to match (or even surpass) the creativity of a human legal mind? Or would relying on algorithms create the risk of entrenching bad, inadequate or undesirable decisions?
- Negligence requires a plaintiff to prove causation. This effectively means providing a plausible explanation, which must be more likely than its alternatives, as to what happened in the individual case at hand. The finder of fact in a negligence case will weigh the possible explanations brought to their attention and, on the basis of all the evidence and circumstances of the case, issue a *judgment*. AI, on the other hand, works in a radically different fashion. It does not seek explanations – it provides *predictions* by drawing correlations and identifying patterns emerging from the aggregate data that it feeds off. Predictions also form the basis for the creation of outputs by generative AI and large language models. Is it possible to reconcile these very different forms of logic?
- A defining characteristic of the functioning of AI and algorithms is that it can be extremely difficult, if not impossible, to review in detail how the machine comes to a specific conclusion in an individual case. As you will see, each element of negligence is rife with tests that strive to ensure that each step in the decision-making process is properly motivated and explained. Is it desirable and justifiable to move away from this traditional method, even if we were to accept that an AI system is statistically more likely to 'get it right'?

In considering these questions (and more!) you should reflect on Frank Pasquale's book, *New Laws of Robotics* (2020), where he makes the compelling argument that the first general 'new law' of robotics should be that AI and robotic systems should complement, never replace, the craft and judgement of professionals.

10.4 The steps in a negligence case

10.4.1 The three elements of negligence

Negligence is a legal term that does not map neatly on to the everyday meaning of the word. As Lord Wright explained soon after *Donoghue v Stevenson* (1932) in *Lochgelly Iron and Coal Co v McMullan* (1934) at 25, negligence in its technical sense 'means more than heedless or careless conduct'. The elements of the tort, first identified by Brett MR in *Heaven v Pender* (1883) at 507, were elaborated upon by Deane J in *Jaensch v Coffey* (1984) at 586, and more recently can be seen clearly in the structure of the High Court's decision in *Adeels Palace Pty Ltd v Moubarak* (2009). The three elements of negligence are as follows:

1. *Duty of care:* The defendant must owe a duty of care to the plaintiff.
2. *Breach:* The defendant must have fallen short of the standard of reasonable care. (Sometimes this is called 'breach of duty' or 'breach of the standard'.)
3. *Causation of harm:* The defendant's negligence must have caused the plaintiff to suffer actual harm of a recognised kind, which is within the appropriate scope of the defendant's liability and is not too remote.

Although the tort is traditionally divided into elements and into different questions of law and fact so that the analysis can proceed in a structured way, you must remember that:

- these elements and issues tend to bleed together and the answers to the questions posed by the tort of negligence are 'not entirely freestanding', as Kirby J pointed out in *Neindorf v Junkovic* (2005) at [50]; and
- 'each element can be defined only in terms of the others', as Brennan J explained in *John Pfeiffer Pty Ltd v Canny* (1981) at 241–2.

The cause of action is not complete (and the limitation period does not begin to run) until actual damage of a recognised kind has been suffered by the plaintiff. The High Court decided in *John Pfeiffer Pty Ltd v Rogerson* (2000) and *Regie National des Usines Renault SA v Zhang* (2002) that a torts case will be governed by the law of the place of the tort (the *lex loci delicti*), and the approach to locating a tort was discussed in *Voth v Manildra Flour Mills Pty Ltd* (1990).[10] The onus lies on the plaintiff to prove all of the elements on the balance of probabilities, whereupon the onus shifts to the defendant to prove a defence.

The wrong that this tort aims to prevent is the failure to live up to an objective standard of reasonable care that is owed to others, which causes actual harm to another. The issue of fault in negligence is not determined by asking whether, from a subjective point of view, the defendants have done the best that they could in the circumstances; rather, the tort offers everyone in the community a higher degree of protection by holding the defendants to an objective standard that requires them to do what a reasonable person in their position would have done in response to the risk of harm. This means we can go about our daily lives generally trusting that the law will protect our entitlement to be treated by others with reasonable care. However, as discussed, it is not always clear when a duty of care will be imposed. McHugh J pointed out in *Perre v Apand Pty Ltd* (1999) at [88] that while the law 'is one of the most important means by which a Western society remains socially cohesive', its effectiveness 'is seriously diminished' when lawyers 'cannot confidently advise what the law is or how it applies to the diverse situations of everyday life'. A similar sentiment was recently expressed by Edelman J in the case of

10 These rules come from the area of law known as 'conflict of laws' or 'private international law': see Davies et al, *Nygh's Conflict of Laws in Australia* (2019).

Mallonland Pty Ltd v Advanta Seeds Pty Ltd (2024), in which he appears to trace the contours of the future of the tort in Australia, as discussed in Chapters 11 and 14.

10.4.2 The five steps in a negligence case

As we saw in section 10.4.1 above, negligence in the legal sense has traditionally been divided into the three elements of duty, breach and causation. In fact, a negligence case, when considered in its full context, actually moves through five different steps, each of which directs our focus more widely or more narrowly into a different aspect of the case. The elements also raise a mix of legal and factual questions – each of which requires a different approach in argument.

1. **Duty:** The element of duty is a *limiting element* that has a *general focus* on the nature of the relationship between the parties and the circumstances that justify imposing a legal duty of care on the defendant. Whether a duty of care exists is predominantly a question of *law*, so you should direct your arguments to the important rules, principles and policy matters that have been identified by the courts in any relevant precedents.
2. **Breach:** This is the *fault element* and it has a more *specific focus* on assessing the reasonableness of the defendant's conduct in the circumstances. It requires a more detailed assessment of the facts and circumstances of the case. This element involves two sub-steps. The first is to set the standard of reasonable care. This is a question of *law*, so you should direct your arguments to the relevant rules, principles and policy matters that have been identified in the precedents. The second is to determine whether or not the defendant has breached that standard. This is predominantly a question of *fact*, and so you should direct your arguments towards the evidence in your particular case.
3. **Causation:** This element focuses on two connected aspects: making the link between the defendant's wrongful conduct and the harm suffered by the plaintiff, and resolving the issue of whether it is reasonable to hold the defendant liable for the full extent of that harm (referred to as 'remoteness of damage' at common law or as 'appropriate scope of liability' in the statutes). The first aspect is a question of *fact*, so you should focus your arguments on the specific evidence in your particular case. The second aspect is a *limiting* device that raises a question of *law*, so you should direct your arguments to the relevant rules, principles and policy matters identified by the courts in the precedent cases.
4. **Defences:** This step shifts the focus on to assessing the plaintiff's conduct and asks whether the plaintiff should be disentitled to a remedy, either in full or in part.
5. **Damages:** Once the extent of the defendant's liability has been set, the final step is to measure the relevant harm suffered by the plaintiff and reduce it to a certain sum of money that the defendant must pay to the plaintiff.

These steps are laid out in more detail in the list below, which presents the standard approach to the tort of negligence. Please remember that the tort exists as a whole, and so while it is analytically useful to break it down into separate elements, all the pieces need to be in place for an action to be successful. As such, you will see, for example, that some cases start the analysis by identifying whether a recognisable harm has been suffered (a step that typically takes place at the causation stage). You also need to be aware that the element of causation effectively comprises three sub-elements: harm, factual causation, and scope of liability. Once again, remember that negligence is a tort that poses special challenges!

The five steps in a negligence case are outlined below.

1. **Duty:** A limiting element
   - Task: Justifying the existence of a duty of care owed by D to P by reference to the circumstances and nature of the relationship between them.
   - Essential question: Who is D's neighbour? (a question of law)
   - The law's answer*:* D owes a duty to P if P is a person, or a member of a class of persons, whom D can reasonably foresee could be injured if D does not take reasonable care (*Donoghue v Stevenson* (1932), *Chapman v Hearse* (1961)) and either:
     - P and D fit into an established duty relationship; or
     - there are other salient features of the relationship between them that justify the imposition of a duty (*Sullivan v Moody* (2001)); and
     - there are no other features of the case that justify an immunity.
2. **Breach:** The fault element
   - Task: Setting and applying the standard of reasonable care owed by D to P to determine whether D was at fault and should be blamed for their conduct.
   - Essential question: How should D have treated their neighbour?
     - What standard of conduct should D have complied with? (a question of law)
     - Did D actually meet that standard? (a question of fact)
   - The law's answer: D must take the precautions that:
     - a reasonable person in D's position would have taken at the time; and
     - were in response to a reasonably foreseeable and not insignificant risk of harm (*Civil Liability Acts, Wyong Shire Council v Shirt* (1980)).
3. **Causation:** A limiting element
   - Task: Justifying the extent of D's legal liability for the harm that their wrongful conduct has caused.
   - Essential question: How much of the harm to P should D have to pay for?
     - Did P suffer a recognisable form of harm? (a question of fact and law)
     - Would it have made a difference to P's fate if D had done the right thing? (a question of fact)
     - How far should D be held responsible for the harm that their wrongdoing has caused to P? (a question of law)
   - The law's answer: D should be liable for all the harm:
     - that is of a kind recognised by law as damage; and
     - that D has caused in the sense that their wrongful conduct was either a necessary condition (or 'but for' cause) of the occurrence of the harm to P (*Civil Liability Acts, March v Stramare* (1991)); or, in exceptional cases, where D's wrongful conduct materially contributed to the harm suffered by P (*Amaca Pty Ltd v Booth* (2011)); and

    - that is within the proper scope of liability in the sense that it is harm of a kind that is reasonably foreseeable as a consequence of the breach even if the manner and extent of the harm was not reasonably foreseeable (*Civil Liability Acts, The Wagon Mound (No 1)* (1961), *The Wagon Mound (No 2)* (1967)).

4. **Defences:** A limiting role
   - Task: Justifying why D should be relieved of all or part of the liability for their wrongdoing.
   - Essential question: *Should P share part of the blame for the harm that has occurred?*
   - The law's answer: The extent of D's liability will be reduced:
     - completely, if P has voluntarily accepted the physical and legal risk inherent in the situation (*Scanlon v American Cigarette Co (Overseas) Pty Ltd (No 3)* (1987), *Insurance Commissioner v Joyce* (1948)) or is taken to be aware of an obvious risk and took no reasonable steps to avoid it (*Civil Liability Acts*); or
     - completely, if P has voluntarily engaged with D in a joint illegal enterprise (*Jackson v Harrison* (1978), *Miller v Miller* (2011)) or was engaged in criminal conduct at the time (*Civil Liability Acts*)); or
     - in proportion to P's relative degree of fault, if P also contributed to the occurrence of the harm by failing to take reasonable care for their own safety (*Civil Liability Acts*, apportionment legislation).
5. **Damages:** A measuring role and a limiting role
   - Task: Justifying the quantum of damages.
   - Essential question: How much money should D pay to P in compensation?
   - The law's answer: D must pay P a sum of money that will, as nearly as possible, put P in the position they would have been in had they not sustained the harm, provided that:
     - P has not failed unreasonably to mitigate their loss (*Todorovic v Waller* (1981), *Medlin v State Government Insurance Commission* (1995)); and
     - P's losses are within the limits set in the *Civil Liability Acts.*

10.4.3 Lord Atkin's 'neighbour principle'

The dominating concept of reasonable foreseeability changes its focus in each of the three elements of negligence. This concept, which is contained in Lord Atkin's 'neighbour principle', begins by looking at the *persons* who are linked together in a relationship by a duty of care. Then it moves on to consider the *risks* that the defendant should have responded to, and finally, it looks at the *kind of harm* that flows from the defendant's negligence.

- *Duty: Who* is D's neighbour? The focus of reasonable foreseeability in the element of duty is on whether P is a person, or a member of an ascertainable class of persons, whom D can reasonably foresee could be injured if D does not take reasonable care.
- *Breach: How* should D have treated their neighbour? The focus of reasonable foreseeability in the element of breach is on the nature and degree of the risks that D must respond to.
- *Causation: How much* of the harm to P should D have to pay for? The focus of reasonable foreseeability in the element of causation is on the kind of harm suffered by P.

An alternative way to look at foreseeability is to imagine it as a funnel asking questions that become more specific with each element.

The law of torts can be described as the law of reasonableness, a concept that dominates the tort at all levels. It seeks to define and justify the standards of reasonable conduct that govern the way that we should treat each other and then to respond reasonably when those rules are broken. Unlike the intentional torts and the torts of nuisance and defamation that we have already discussed in this book, negligence responds to the concepts of harm and wrongdoing, interpreted in broad and almost undefinable terms.

The idea that we should avoid conduct that we can foresee might harm our neighbours is a fundamentally moral concept, but it is also one that is intrinsically unlimited. Our desire to avoid being harmed by others is a fundamentally important one, but any attempt to lay down an absolute rule that requires us to avoid *every* act or omission that could possibly lead to harm would force us to deny another equally fundamental human desire – for freedom, autonomy and liberty of action. So the judges and the politicians, who are required by their positions in their two separate arms of government to secure our welfare, guard our safety, protect our rights and do justice to the communities they serve, must engage in a process of balancing these competing desires. This need to negotiate a path between our need for security and our desire for liberty – and between our recognition of our factual vulnerability to harm and our moral sense of responsibility when we cause harm – ensures that the pendulum of negligence will never find a satisfying point of equilibrium, because our individual and collective moral compasses are in continuous evolution.

The goal of justice, which is itself the manifestation of the human desire for balance, remains elusive. The impossibility of achieving perfect justice forces us to call upon our other human sense of reasonableness to fill the gap in the law. This is why negligence is dominated by the concept of reasonableness and why it will always be subject to criticism. It explains why the themes of harm and vulnerability, fault and responsibility, and autonomy and liberty recur all the way through the case law. Chapters 11, 12 and 13 cover the three elements of the tort: duty of care, breach and causation. Chapter 15 explores the defences. You will see how Lord Atkin's neighbour principle is used to structure the law in each of the three elements of negligence, and how the idea of taking reasonable care to avoid causing harm also appears in the defence of contributory negligence. Chapter 14 considers some of the deeper challenges posed by the tort of negligence as regards particular types of defendants (such as public authorities or health professionals) or harm (such as mental harm and pure economic loss). Chapters 11 and 14 show how judges and legislators have identified further sets of principles that aim to respond to the challenges posed by this tort, which was called into being by human ingenuity and development – and which demands an equal degree of legal ingenuity from the judges who have the challenging task of developing this frustrating, mysterious and most challenging of all the torts.

10.5 Recap and looking ahead

This chapter has introduced the tort of negligence, which imposes liability on a defendant who, when placed in circumstances where there is a reasonably foreseeable and not insignificant risk of harm to another person, unjustifiably fails to take reasonable care, either:

- to avoid *causing* that harm; or
- in some circumstances, to *prevent* that harm from occurring,

provided it is thought right to impose a legal duty to take such care on the defendant.

The three elements of negligence are as follows:

1. *Duty:* D must owe a duty of care to P.
2. *Breach:* D must have fallen short of the standard of reasonable care. (Sometimes this is called 'breach of duty' or 'breach of the standard'.)
3. *Causation:* D's negligence must have factually caused P to suffer actual harm of a recognised kind, which is within the appropriate scope of D's liability.

Each of these elements poses its own set of difficulties, and you need to remember that the issues they raise tend to recur throughout the different stages of a negligence case. This is because the essential task in the tort of negligence is to explain why it is reasonable to impose liability on the defendant in the circumstances. While these elements seem fairly short in number and fairly straightforward in their focus (duty, breach and causation), there are many challenges associated with each step. You can see this by looking at section 10.4.2 above, which presents the five steps in a negligence case list, taking you through a negligence case from start to finish, and section 10.5.1 below, which analyses the tort of negligence using the 'torts typology' used in other chapters of this book. As we have discussed, the concept of reasonableness dominates the elements of negligence. This feature means that most of the hard work in a negligence case is done before you get to the defences (unlike the intentional torts, where the concept of reasonableness appears most often at the defences stage of the analysis). Notice in section 10.5.1 that this tort contains an extensive set of limiting devices that are used to control the extent of liability. The need for these limits stems from the fact that both the 'neighbour principle' of reasonable foreseeability of harm and the 'but for' test of causation of harm set the net of liability too wide.

10.5.1 Negligence: Overview of the tort

10.5.1.1 Duty

- The 'duty of care' limit: D must owe a duty of care to P.
- P must be a person, or a member of a class of persons, whom D can reasonably foresee could be injured if D does not take reasonable care (*Donoghue v Stevenson* (1932); *Chapman v Hearse* (1961)).
- **And** P and D must fit into an established duty relationship; **or** in 'novel' cases, special rules must be satisfied (see Chapter 11).
- To justify imposing a duty in special cases, the relevant principles must be balanced and sufficient salient features of the relationship between P and D must be present.
- Positive indicators may include:

  - that P is vulnerable to D and cannot otherwise protect themselves – for example, because of the presence of 'salient features' such as:
    - reliance by P and an assumption of responsibility by D;
    - D has special control over matters affecting P; or
    - D has special knowledge of matters affecting P (*Perre v Apand Pty Ltd* (1999); *Sullivan v Moody* (2001)).
- Negative indicators: No duty will be imposed if it would create undue:
  - interference with autonomy or personal freedom of action or speech;
  - disrespect for personal responsibility;
  - indeterminate liability, uncertainty or difficulty in defining or complying with the duty or in measuring the damages; or
  - incoherence or inconsistency in the duties (*Bryan v Maloney* (1995); *Perre v Apand Pty Ltd* (1999); *Sullivan v Moody* (2001); *Graham Barclay Oysters Pty Ltd v Ryan* (2002); *Harriton v Stephens* (2006); *CAL No 14 Pty Ltd v Motor Accidents Insurance Board* (2009)).
- Note that no duty will be imposed if the case comes within a recognised immunity category.
- The 'recognised damage' limit: The harm must be of a kind that is recognised by the law (see Chapter 13) (*Jaensch v Coffey* (1984); *Harriton v Stephens* (2006)).
- The 'scope of liability' or 'remoteness of damage' limit: The harm must be within the appropriate scope of liability, and it must not be too remote (ie it must be harm of a kind that was reasonably foreseeable) (see Chapter 13) (*Civil Liability Acts*; *Wagon Mound (No 1)* (1961); *Wagon Mound (No 2)* (1967)).
- There must be no lawful justification for the conduct.
- Note: The courts are not always consistent when classifying the above propositions of law and so they can appear, and reappear, in discussions of duty, harm, remoteness or the defences.

10.5.1.2 Conduct

P must be able to identify either:

- a positive act by D; or
- in some circumstances, an omission or failure to act by D (*Donoghue v Stevenson* (1932)).

10.5.1.3 Fault

- D must have been negligent in the legal sense: P must prove that D's conduct fell short of the standard of reasonable care because D failed to take the precautions that a reasonable person in D's position would have taken at the time in response to a reasonably foreseeable and not insignificant risk of harm (see Chapter 12) (*Donoghue v Stevenson* (1932); *Wyong Shire Council v Shirt* (1980); *Civil Liability Acts*).
- Relevant circumstances always include:
  - probability that the harm would occur if care was not taken;
  - likely seriousness of the harm which may result;
  - burden of taking the precautions to avoid the risk of harm; and
  - social utility (usefulness) of the risk-creating activity.

- Relevant circumstances may also include:
  - professional or customary standards;
  - statutory standards;
  - anticipated carelessness by P;
  - expectation that P knows of obvious risks; and
  - intoxication (legislation) etc.

10.5.1.4 Effect

D's conduct must directly or indirectly cause harm (see Chapter 13), either:

- because the conduct was a necessary condition (or 'but for' cause) of the occurrence of the harm suffered by P (*Civil Liability Acts*; *March v Stramare* (1991)); or
- in some exceptional cases, because the conduct is proved to have materially contributed to the harm suffered by P (*Civil Liability Acts*; *Amaca Pty Ltd v Ellis* (2010); *Amaca Pty Ltd v Booth* (2011)).

Note: Limits on the kind of harm apply – see 'Duty' above.

LEGISLATION ALERT!

Consult your study materials and note down the relevant rules in your jurisdiction (which may be either statutory or based on the common law).

Download a copy of the relevant legislation:

- *Civil Law (Wrongs) Act 2002* (ACT)
- *Civil Liability Act 2002* (NSW)
- *Personal Injuries (Liabilities and Damages) Act 2003* (NT), *Personal Injuries (Civil Claims) Act 2003* (NT)
- *Civil Liability Act 2003* (Qld), *Personal Injuries Proceedings Act 2002* (Qld)
- *Civil Liability Act 1936* (SA), which amended the old *Wrongs Act* of 1936
- *Civil Liability Act 2002* (Tas)
- *Wrongs Act 1958* (Vic)
- *Civil Liability Act 2002* (WA), *Volunteers and Food and Other Donors (Protection from Liability) Act 2002* (WA)

The factors collected under 'Duty' in section 10.5.1.1 above are indicative of the limits of negligence. As such, they appear in different elements of the tort – but you need to remember that, in essence, they are all performing the same function, which is to limit the imposition and extent of liability in negligence. It should not surprise you to find that the courts can shift from classifying some of these devices as relevant to the analysis of either duty, breach, harm, the extent of liability, or in some cases, the defences.

The imposition of these 'control devices' has been explained either as a response to the perceived need to confine the tort's 'twentieth century expansiveness' or as an 'inevitable' result of its origins as an action on the case: *Hargrave v Goldman* (1963), Windeyer J at 63. Gummow J explained in *Pyrenees Shire Council v Day* (1998) at [125] that the 'broad concepts which found the modern law of negligence' are 'expressed in major premises which, if unqualified, may extend liability beyond the bounds of social utility and economic sustainability'. However, when you begin your analysis of the tort of negligence, it helps to remember the advice given by Gummow and Kirby JJ who said in *Tame v New South Wales* (2002) at [185] that the assessment of whether or not a duty of care should be imposed on a defendant is 'necessarily fluid', and that:

> the *assessment of reasonableness,* which informs *each element* of the cause of action, is inherently adapted to the vindication of meritorious claims in a tort whose hallmark is *flexibility of application.* [Emphasis added.]

Once you realise that the rules of negligence are aimed at promoting arguments about whether it is reasonable to impose liability and you understand that those arguments should be informed by the key principles underlying the tort, you will be much better equipped to navigate your way through that complexity.

Conclusion

This chapter has introduced the tort of negligence, which imposes liability on a defendant who, when placed in circumstances where there is a reasonably foreseeable and not insignificant risk of harm to another person, unjustifiably fails to take reasonable care, either:

- to avoid *causing* that harm; or
- in some circumstances, to *prevent* that harm from occurring,

provided it is thought right to impose a legal duty to take such care on the defendant.

The chapter has outlined the three elements of negligence: duty, breach and causation. Chapter 11 considers the element of duty, Chapter 12 focuses on breach, and Chapter 13 on causation. Chapter 14 discusses special circumstances arising out of the nature of the defendant or the nature of the harm. Chapter 15 covers defences.

Test your understanding

Analyse the judgments in *Donoghue v Stevenson* (1932)

Read the case of *Donoghue v Stevenson* (1932) and then:

- using Table 3.1 as a guide, identify the rules, the principles and the relevant policy justifications that you find in both the dissenting and the majority judgments; and
- using Table 3.2 as a guide, identify the different kinds of argument that the judges used in their reasons.

Develop your skills

Prepare an oral presentation on *Donoghue v Stevenson* (1932)

Using the advice given in section 4.5 of Chapter 4, prepare a 10-minute oral presentation on *Donoghue v Stevenson* (1932), making sure that you explain clearly the differences between the majority and minority judges.

Essay writing

- Explain in 1000 words how the judges in *Donoghue v Stevenson* (1932) used the precedent cases in the light of the old American legal proverb quoted by James Gordley in 'The Common Law in the Twentieth Century' (2000) at 1818: 'Law is made by what judges do, not by what they say.'
- Choose one of the quotations below and write a 1500-word essay that critically discusses the issues it raises:
  - 'The modern law of negligence is a mess.'
  - 'The fact that the tort of negligence is unstable does not mean that it is necessarily morally indefensible.'

REFERENCES

CASES

Adeels Palace Pty Ltd v Moubarak (2009) 239 CLR 420
Amaca Pty Ltd v Booth (2011) 246 CLR 36
Amaca Pty Ltd v Ellis (2010) 240 CLR 111
Bird v Holbrook (1828) 4 Bing 628; 130 ER 911
Bryan v Maloney (1995) 182 CLR 609
CAL No 14 Pty Ltd v Motor Accidents Insurance Board (2009) 239 CLR 390
Chapman v Hearse (1961) 106 CLR 112
Diamond v Simpson (No 3) [2003] NSWCA 373
Distillers Co (Biochemicals) Ltd v Thompson [1971] AC 458
Donoghue v Stevenson [1932] AC 562
George v Skivington (1869) LR 5 Ex 1
Graham Barclay Oysters Pty Ltd v Ryan (2002) 211 CLR 540
Grant v Australian Knitting Mills Ltd [1936] AC 85
Hargrave v Goldman (1963) 110 CLR 40
Harriton v Stephens (2006) 226 CLR 52
Heaven v Pender (1883) 11 QBD 503
Insurance Commissioner v Joyce (1948) 77 CLR 39
Jackson v Harrison (1978) 138 CLR 438
Jaensch v Coffey (1984) 155 CLR 549
John Pfeiffer Pty Ltd v Canny (1981) 148 CLR 218
John Pfeiffer Pty Ltd v Rogerson (2000) 203 CLR 503

Langridge v Levy (1837) 2 M&W 519; 150 ER 863
Le Lievre v Gould [1893] 1 QB 491
Lochgelly Iron and Coal Co v McMullan [1934] 1 AC 1
MacPherson v Buick Motor Co 111 NE 1050 (NY, 1916)
Mallonland Pty Ltd v Advanta Seeds Pty Ltd [2024] HCA 25; (2024) 418 ALR 639
March v Stramare (1991) 171 CLR 506
Medlin v State Government Insurance Commission (1995) 182 CLR 1
Miller v Miller (2011) 242 CLR 446
Neindorf v Junkovic [2005] HCA 75; (2005) 222 ALR 631
Overseas Tankship (UK) Ltd v Morts Dock & Engineering Co Ltd [1961] AC 388 ('*The Wagon Mound (No 1)*')
Overseas Tankship (UK) Ltd v The Miller Steamship Co [1967] 1 AC 617 ('*The Wagon Mound (No 2)*')
Pasley v Freeman (1789) 3 TR 51; 100 ER 450
Perre v Apand Pty Ltd (1999) 198 CLR 180
Pyrenees Shire Council v Day (1998) 192 CLR 330
Regie National des Usines Renault SA v Zhang (2002) 210 CLR 491
Reynolds v Katoomba RSL All Services Club Ltd (2001) 53 NSWLR 43
Rylands v Fletcher (1866) LR 1 Ex 265; (1868) LR 3HL 330
Scanlon v American Cigarette Co (Overseas) Pty Ltd (No 3) [1987] VR 289
Scott v Shepherd (1773) 2 Black W 892; 96 ER 525
Simpson v Diamond [2001] NSWSC 925
State of Wisconsin v Loomis 881 NW 2d 749 (Wis, 2016).
Sullivan v Moody (2001) 207 CLR 562
Tame v New South Wales (2002) 211 CLR 317
The Wagon Mound (No 1) (1961) see *Overseas Tankship (UK) Ltd v Morts Dock & Engineering Co Ltd* [1961] AC 388
The Wagon Mound (No 2) (1967) see *Overseas Tankship (UK) Ltd v The Miller Steamship Co* [1967] 1 AC 617
Todorovic v Waller (1981) 150 CLR 402
Voth v Manildra Flour Mills Pty Ltd (1990) 171 CLR 538
Wicks v State Rail Authority of New South Wales (2010) 241 CLR 60
Wilkinson v Downton [1897] 2 QB 57
Winterbottom v Wright (1842) 10 M&W 109; 152 ER 402
Wyong Shire Council v Shirt (1980) 146 CLR 40

ARTICLES, BOOKS AND REPORTS

Abel, R, 'A Critique of Torts' (1994) 2 *The Tort Law Review* 99.
Atiyah, P, *The Damages Lottery* (1997) Hart Publishing, Oxford.
Beever, A, *Rediscovering the Law of Negligence* (2007) Hart Publishing, Oxford.
Bender, L, 'A Lawyer's Primer on Feminist Theory and Tort' (1988) 38 *Journal of Legal Education* 3.
Bender, L, 'Tort Law's Role as a Tool for Social Justice Struggle' (1998) 37 *Washburn Law Journal* 249.
Brady, M, Burns, K, Leiman, T & Tranter, K, 'Automated Vehicles and Australian Personal Injury Compensation Schemes' (2017) 24 *Torts Law Journal* 32.
Broad, E, *Made by Humans* (2018) Melbourne University Press, Melbourne.

Calabresi, G, *The Costs of Accidents* (1970) Yale University Press, New Haven.

Cane, P, *Atiyah's Accidents, Compensation and the Law*, 7th ed (2006) Cambridge University Press, Cambridge.

Cane, P, 'Reforming Tort Law In Australia: A Personal Perspective' (2003) 27 *Melbourne University Law Review* 649.

Cane, P, *The Anatomy of Tort Law* (1997) Hart Publishing, Oxford.

Chamallas, M, 'The Architecture of Bias: Deep Structures in Tort Law' (1998) 146 *University of Pennsylvania Law Review* 463.

Conaghan, J, 'Tort Law and the Feminist Critique of Reason', in Bottomley, A (ed), *Feminist Perspectives on the Foundational Subjects of Law* (1996) Cavendish, London, 47.

Conaghan, J & Mansell, W, *The Wrongs of Tort*, 2nd ed (2006) Pluto Press, London.

Cooper-Stephenson, K & Gibson, E (eds), *Tort Theory* (1993) Captus University Publications, North York, Ontario.

Davies, M, Bell, A S, Brereton, P L G & Douglas, M, *Nygh's Conflict of Laws in Australia*, 10th ed (2019) LexisNexis Butterworths, Sydney.

Dietrich, J, 'Duty of Care under the "Civil Liability Acts"' (2005) 13 *Torts Law Journal* 17.

Feldthusen, B, 'If This Is Torts, Negligence Must Be Dead', in Cooper-Stephenson, K & Gibson, E (eds), *Tort Theory* (1993) Captus University Publications, North York Ontario, 394.

Geistfeld, M A, 'Unifying Principles within Pluralist Tort Adjudication', in Burns, K, Gardner, J & Morgan, J (eds), *Torts on Three Continents* (2024) Oxford University Press, Oxford.

Gordley, J, 'The Common Law in the Twentieth Century: Some Unfinished Business' (2000) 88 *California Law Review* 1817.

Graycar, R, 'Judicial Activism or Traditional Negligence Law? Conception, Pregnancy, and Denial of Reproductive Choice', in Freckelton, I & Petersen, K (eds), *Disputes and Dilemmas in Health Law* (2006) Federation Press, Sydney, 436.

Graycar, R, 'Teaching Torts as if the World Really Existed: Reflections on Harold Luntz's Contribution to Australian Law School Classrooms' (2003) 27 *Melbourne University Law Review* 677.

Ibbetson, D, 'How the Romans Did for Us: Ancient Roots of the Tort of Negligence' (2003) 26 *University of New South Wales Law Journal* 475.

Infantino, M & Wang, W, 'Algorithmic Torts: A Prospective Comparative Overview' (2019) 29 *Transnational Law & Contemporary Problems* 1.

Ipp, D, 'Negligence – Where Lies the Future?' (2003) 23 *Australian Bar Review* 158.

Ipp, D, 'Policy and the Swing of the Negligence Pendulum' (2003) 77 *Australian Law Journal* 732.

Ipp, D, 'The Politics, Purpose and Reform of the Law of Negligence' (2007) 81 *Australian Law Journal* 456.

Ipp, D, 'Themes in the Law of Torts' (2007) 81 *Australian Law Journal* 609.

Ipp, D, Cane, P, Sheldon, D & Macintosh, I, *Review of the Law of Negligence: Final Report* (2002) <https://treasury.gov.au/review/review-of-the-law-of-negligence>

Keeler, J, 'Thinking through the Unthinkable: Collective Responsibilities in Personal Injury Law' (2001) 30 *Common Law World Review* 349.

Lim, E & Morgan, P, *The Cambridge Handbook of Private Law and Artificial Intelligence* (2024) Cambridge University Press, Cambridge.

Luntz, H, *Assessment of Damages for Personal Injury and Death*, 4th ed (2002) LexisNexis Butterworths, Sydney.

Luntz, H, 'The Use of Policy in Negligence Cases in the High Court of Australia', in Bryan, M (ed), *Private Law in Theory and Practice* (2007) Routledge, London, 85.

Luntz, H, Hambly, D, Burns, K, Dietrich, J, Foster, N, Grant, G & Harder, S, *Torts: Cases and Commentary*, 8th ed (2017) LexisNexis Butterworths, Sydney.

Mackie, T, 'Proving Liability for Highly and Fully Automated Vehicle Accidents in Australia' (2018) 34 *Computer Law & Security Review* 1314.

Moran, M, *Rethinking the Reasonable Person: An Egalitarian Reconstruction of the Objective Standard* (2003) Oxford University Press, Oxford.

Oliphant, K, 'Rationalising Tort Law for the Twenty-First Century', in Barker, K, Fairweather, K & Grantham, R (eds), *Private Law in the 21st Century* (2017) Hart Publishing, Oxford.

Palmer, G, 'Financing and Delivering: New Zealand's Accident Compensation Scheme', in Baehler, K J (ed), *The Oxford Handbook of Governance and Public Management for Social Policy* (2023) Oxford University Press, Oxford, 442.

Pasquale, F, *New Laws of Robotics* (2020) Harvard University Press, Cambrudge MA.

Pasquale, F, *The Black Box Society* (2015) Harvard University Press, Cambridge MA.

Schuck, P, *Tort Law and the Public Interest: Competition, Innovation and Consumer Welfare* (1991) W W Norton, New York.

Schwab, K, *The Fourth Industrial Revolution* (2016) Crown Publishing, New York.

Smillie, J, 'The Future of Negligence' (2007) 15 *Torts Law Journal* 300.

Spigelman, J J, 'Negligence: the Last Outpost of the Welfare State' (2002) 76 *Australian Law Journal* 432.

Stapleton, J, *Disease and the Compensation Debate* (1986) Oxford University Press, Oxford.

Sugarman, S D, 'Doing Away with Tort Law'(1985) 73 *California Law Review* 555.

Viscusi, K, *Regulation through Litigation* (2002) AIE-Brookings, Washington DC.

Weir, T, 'The Staggering March of Negligence' in Cane, P & Stapleton, J (eds), *The Law of Obligations: Essays in Celebration of John Fleming* (1998) Clarendon Press, Oxford, 97.

Witting, C, 'Tort Law, Policy and the High Court of Australia' (2007) 31 *Melbourne University Law Review* 569.

NEGLIGENCE: DUTY OF CARE

11

Introduction

The element of duty of care is covered in three sections. Section 11.1 covers the role and nature of duty – what it is there for and what it covers. Section 11.2 deals with the law on the established categories of negligence (duties and immunities). Section 11.3 discusses the methodology of negligence in cases involving novel fact scenarios, where a duty is not pre-established and needs to be developed from scratch.

Because of the complexity of this area of the law, this chapter introduces a new 'Summary points' feature at the ends of sections 11.1 and 11.3. It summarises the matters you should take into account when approaching a problem question and asks you to engage in an active reading exercise, linking each point with a case in that section.

11.1 The role and nature of the duty of care

11.1.1 The limiting role of duty

Duty is a limiting element. It can be described as the entry point of negligence: without a duty owed there can be no liability. Its rules have been designed so that 'a duty of care will be imposed when it is reasonable in all the circumstances to do so', as Kirby J concluded in *Graham Barclay Oysters Pty Ltd v Ryan* (2002) at [244]. Duty has many complicating factors, but happily, not all cases display them. Cases in negligence are traditionally divided into two main classes: those that fall into an established or recognised duty category, and are therefore more easily dealt with, and the 'novel' cases, which raise more difficult issues and require the more detailed analysis that the High Court of Australia ('High Court') laid down in *Sullivan v Moody* (2001), and again in *Harriton v Stephens* (2006). We will look at the established categories of duty and immunity first, then move on to discuss the methodology of negligence in cases involving novel fact scenarios. The more difficult topics covered in Chapter 14 include omissions, public authorities, pure psychiatric injury (or pure mental harm), negligent misstatements, pure economic loss and medical negligence. The easiest type of case is one where the plaintiff and the defendant are in a recognised relationship and the defendant, by a positive act, has caused physical harm directly to the plaintiff. This scenario (which closely resembles the direct one-to-one fact patterns that we commonly see in the trespass torts) is not difficult to deal with, as Kirby J pointed out in *Harriton v Stephens* (2006) at [63]:

> Most tort actions fall within a recognised duty of care category. Of the actions that fall outside, or lie on the boundary of, an established duty category, the test of *reasonable foreseeability will ordinarily provide guidance in determining whether a duty is in fact owed.* This is not because satisfying this test is sufficient to establish a duty of care. This Court has repeatedly affirmed that this is not the case. Rather, it is because, *in so far as physical injuries arising from a positive act are concerned,* it is accepted that if the reasonable foreseeability test is satisfied, the elusive additional component of a duty of care will generally exist. [Emphasis added and footnote references omitted.]

11.1.2 The 'neighbour' test: Reasonable foreseeability of harm

The test of reasonable foreseeability in the duty element focuses on linking the defendant with the plaintiff in a relationship of 'neighbourhood'. It imposes a duty of care on the defendants when they should reasonably have foreseen that the plaintiff might be harmed if they act without care (or fail to act with care) in the circumstances, as Lord Atkin pointed out in *Donoghue v Stevenson* (1932) at 580:

> The rule that you are to love your neighbour becomes in law, you must not injure your neighbour; and the lawyer's question, Who is my neighbour? receives a restricted reply. You must take reasonable care to avoid acts or omissions which you can reasonably foresee would be likely to injure your neighbour. Who, then, in law is my neighbour? The answer seems to be – persons who are so closely and directly affected by my act that I ought reasonably to have them in contemplation as being so affected when I am directing my mind to the acts or omissions which are called in question.

The neighbour principle was accepted in Australian law in *Grant v Australian Knitting Mills Ltd* (1936), a case where an Adelaide doctor contracted acute dermatitis caused by the undetectable presence of sulphites in a pair of 'Golden Fleece' woollen long-johns manufactured by Australian Knitting Mills. The Privy Council explained the importance of whether the plaintiff was able to discover the cause of the risk in this case of manufacturer's liability at 105:

> The principle of Donoghue's case can only be applied *where the defect is hidden and unknown to the consumer,* otherwise the directness of cause and effect is absent: the man who consumes or uses a thing which he knows to be noxious

> cannot complain in respect of whatever mischief follows, because it follows from his own conscious volition in choosing to incur the risk or certainty of mischance ... The presence of the deleterious chemical in the pants, due to negligence in manufacture, was a *hidden and latent defect*, just as much as were the remains of the snail in the opaque bottle: it could not be detected by any examination that could reasonably be made. Nothing happened between the making of the garments and their being worn to change their condition. The garments were made by the manufacturers for the purpose of being worn exactly as they were worn in fact by the appellant: it was not contemplated that they should be first washed. [Emphasis added and references omitted.]

The focus at the duty stage is on the foreseeability of causing harm to the plaintiff and the two critical issues are: *who* is the person to whom a duty is owed ('Who is my neighbour?'); and *whether* the duty should be imposed in the circumstances. As noted above, in cases where a defendant's positive act directly causes physical harm, the test of reasonable foreseeability is normally a sufficient guide to liability, but in cases where the harm is caused indirectly, the question of reasonable foreseeability may be more complex. So, the rule laid down by the High Court in *Chapman v Hearse* (1961) at 120–1 explained that the plaintiff does *not* have to show that the complex chain of cause and effect that led to the harm was reasonably foreseeable; rather it need only be shown that it was reasonably foreseeable that the defendant's conduct might cause harm to a particular class of persons that includes the plaintiff:

> But one thing is certain and that is that in order to establish the prior existence of a duty of care with respect to a plaintiff subsequently injured as the result of a sequence of events following a defendant's carelessness it is not necessary for the plaintiff to show that the *precise manner* in which his injuries were sustained was reasonably foreseeable; it is sufficient if it appears that *injury to a class of persons of which he was one* might reasonably have been foreseen as a consequence. [Emphasis added.]

Case example

In *Chapman v Hearse* (1961), a car being driven by Emery was hit by a second car negligently driven by Chapman (D1). Chapman was catapulted out of his vehicle as a result of the collision and lay injured on the road. Dr Cherry, who was on his way home from golf, saw the accident and stopped to help Chapman but he was killed when he was hit by a third car negligently driven by Hearse (D2).[1] When deciding that D1, who caused the original event, did owe a duty to Dr Cherry, the High Court did not accept the argument that he could not have foreseen the precise sequence of events that led to the doctor's death. It was enough that D1, as a driver, should have foreseen as a more general matter that a carelessly caused collision might lead to 'the attendance on the

1 Note that the parties in this case are the two negligent drivers whose conduct, added together, led to the death of Dr Cherry. Chapman (D1) argued that he did not owe a duty to Dr Cherry and should not have to contribute anything towards the damages owed by Hearse (D2) to Dr Cherry's estate.

roadway, at some risk to themselves, of persons fulfilling a moral and social duty to render aid to those incapacitated or otherwise injured' (at 120).

In this case, we can categorise the relationship between D1 (the first driver who created the initial danger) and Dr Cherry as a relationship between an injured driver and a person giving aid, whereas the relationship between Dr Cherry and D2 (the second driver who actually killed him) was between a driver and a person present on the road. Both drivers owed Dr Cherry a duty of care, but in each case Dr Cherry belonged to a different but nevertheless still reasonably foreseeable 'class of persons'.

If injury to the plaintiff (either as a known individual or as a member of a class of persons) is not reasonably foreseeable, a duty will not be imposed and the victim is classed as an 'unforeseeable plaintiff'. Furthermore, the breach of a duty owed to one person will not necessarily translate into a breach of a duty owed to another. In every case, the test of reasonable foreseeability must be individually satisfied.

Case examples

- In the case of *Palsgraf v Long Island Railway Co* (1928), a man carrying a small parcel was running to board a moving train. Because he seemed about to fall, two railway employees tried to help him (one by shoving him and the other by pulling him), but in the scuffle the man dropped his parcel. The package contained fireworks, which exploded upon hitting the rails, and the shock caused a set of heavy scales to fall on the plaintiff, who was standing on the platform many feet away. Cardozo J, at 341, cited Pollock – who said that 'negligence in the air' would not be enough to impose a duty – and explained that although the railway workers may have owed a duty to the man who had been carrying the package to take reasonable care to avoid causing *him* any physical injury or to avoid damaging his goods, they did not owe any such duty to the plaintiff, because it was not reasonably foreseeable that their actions could have caused her any injury:

  > Relatively to her it was not negligence at all. Nothing in the situation gave notice that the falling package had in it the potency of peril to persons thus removed.

  So, in the absence of a 'wrong to herself' the plaintiff could not succeed because there was 'merely a wrong to someone else'.

- In the more recent case of *Sydney Water Corporation v Turano* (2009), the High Court found against Mrs Turano, the widow of a man who had been killed in 2001 when a tree was blown onto his car while he was driving on Edmonson Avenue in Austral. The root of the tree had been significantly damaged by an infection triggered by a slow leakage of water from a water main installed 20 years earlier by Sydney Water. The Court concluded, at 53, that the plaintiff in this case was not foreseeable:

  > [I]njury to road users as the result of the tree's eventual collapse was not a *reasonably* foreseeable consequence of laying a water main, as the primary judge held. Alternatively, it may be expressed as a conclusion that in the absence of control over any risk posed by the tree in the years after the installation of the water main there

was not a sufficiently close and direct connection between Sydney Water and Mrs Turano, a person present on Edmonson Avenue in 2001, for her to be a 'neighbour' within Lord Atkin's statement of the principle. [Emphasis in original.]

11.1.3 The scope of a duty

In *Sydney Water Corporation v Turano* (2009), the High Court agreed at [47] with Gummow J, who had said in the earlier case of *Roads and Traffic Authority (NSW) v Dederer* (2007) at [43]:

> First, duties of care are not owed in the abstract. Rather, they are *obligations of a particular scope*, and that scope may be more or less expansive depending on the relationship in question. Secondly, whatever their scope, all duties of care are to be discharged by the exercise of reasonable care. They do not impose a more stringent or onerous burden. [Emphasis added.]

This means that you must be careful in problem-solving exercises not only to consider whether a duty is owed, but also to go one step further to identify the basic content of the duty. A duty is not a general all-encompassing 'duty of care'; it is a duty to take reasonable care to avoid causing a foreseeable kind of injury to a particular person or an ascertainable class of persons in identifiable circumstances.

The High Court has emphasised in many cases, including *Sydney Water Corporation v Turano* (2009) at [45], that the general inquiry at the duty stage should be posed at a 'higher level of abstraction' than at subsequent stages. In the words of French CJ, Gummow, Hayne, Crennan and Bell JJ: 'the concept is to be understood and applied with due regard to the consideration that, in the context of the issue as to duty of care, it is bound up with the question of whether it is reasonable to require a person to have in contemplation the risk of injury that has eventuated'. In essence, the element of duty has a more general focus than the subsequent element of breach. Kirby J explained in *Harriton v Stephens* (2006) at [69]–[70] why this 'relatively general level of abstraction' was needed:

> (1) the duty concept is already overworked and unduly complex; (2) particularising the duty of care to too great a level of specificity carries with it the risk of eliding questions of law and fact; and (3) making specific enquiries at the duty stage subverts the traditional structure of the cause of action in negligence, which is designed to pose increasingly specific questions as each successive element falls for decision. ...
>
> Furthermore, defining the content of the duty of care to an excessive degree would diminish the precedential value of decisions on duty. Decisions that cast duties of care in narrow terms are of limited assistance to litigants and to judges in future cases. As a matter of practicality, it is desirable that determinations on points of law be framed with a sufficient degree of generality to make them useful in later cases where the facts are necessarily different but where the concepts will necessarily be the same.

Kirby J had already explored the scope of duty issue in *Neindorf v Junkovic* (2005), concluding at [55]:

> Generally speaking, each of the constituent elements of the tort of negligence – duty, breach and damage – considered seriatim, progressively increases the specificity of the inquiry into how the incident occurred and the way in which damage was sustained. The broadest and most general level of analysis occurs at the duty stage. Here, the inquiry is primarily concerned with whether injury to the plaintiff or a class of persons to whom the plaintiff belongs, was reasonably foreseeable. With respect to the breach element, the inquiry is directed, in part, to whether a reasonable person in the defendant's position would have foreseen the risk of injury to the plaintiff. Finally, the damage element is the most specific. The issue here is whether the damage sustained as a result of the breach of duty was of a kind which was reasonably foreseeable. Attempts to force more content into the duty element, by defining the obligation created with greater specificity, turns the traditional analysis of the tort of negligence on its head. It blurs the distinction between its constituent elements. It may also lead to the decision as to breach being pre-empted. This Court should avoid such an error.

In *Graham Barclay Oysters Pty Ltd v Ryan* (2002), McHugh J explained at [106] that formulating the duty in overly specific terms can lead to error 'because it is likely to mix a question of law (whether a duty existed) with a question of fact (whether a breach occurred)'.

Case examples

- In *Vairy v Wyong Shire Council* (2005), McHugh J gave the following example to illustrate the difference between the general nature of the *duty question* and the more specific level of inquiry needed to answer the *question of breach* at [26]:

  > [T]he duty owed by motorists to other users of the highway, for example, is expressed in terms of the duty to take reasonable care for the safety of other users of the highway having regard to all the circumstances of the case. The duty is not subdivided into categories such as a duty to keep a proper lookout or sound a warning or to keep a safe distance away from the car in front. In the particular circumstances of the case, failure to do one or more of these things may constitute a breach of the duty to take reasonable care. But they are not themselves legal duties for the purpose of the law of negligence.

- Similarly, in *CAL No 14 Pty Ltd v Motor Accidents Insurance Board* (2009), the High Court criticised the fact that the 'duty alleged was framed by reference to the particular breach that was alleged and thus by reference to the course of the events that had happened', with the result that this over-specific formulation of the duty 'merged the separate inquiries about duty of care and breach of duty': Hayne J at [68]. His Honour also cited several recent cases where similar warnings had been made, including:

- *Romeo v Conservation Commission (NT)* (1998) at [163]–[164];
- *Vairy v Wyong Shire Council* (2005) at [29], [54], [60]–[61], [122]–[129];
- *Mulligan v Coffs Harbour City Council* (2005) at [50]; and
- *Roads and Traffic Authority (NSW) v Dederer* (2007) at [65].

- In *CAL No 14 Pty Ltd v Motor Accidents Insurance Board*, a patron in a hotel bar, who feared that he might be caught by a rumoured police breathalyser operation, asked the licensee of the hotel whether he could leave his wife's motorcycle (which he had been riding) in the hotel's storeroom. He gave the keys to the licensee for safekeeping, and the two men made a joint plan that the licensee would ring the patron's wife to ask her to come and collect the patron later when he wanted to go home. After drinking between seven and eight cans of bourbon and cola over a period of three hours, the patron was then refused any further service. He then changed his mind about the plan and decided to drive himself home. He insisted three times that he was 'right to drive', agitatedly refused to give the licensee his wife's telephone number, demanded the return of the keys and subsequently died after crashing the motorcycle on the journey home. His blood alcohol reading was 0.253. His widow sued the licensee, arguing that he owed a duty of care to her husband not to serve him too much alcohol and to follow through with the plan by preventing him from riding home on the motorcycle.

  The joint judgment of the High Court criticised at [32] and [37] the overly specific formulation of the duty in this case, which was defined in very narrow terms as a duty to carry out the plan 'selected prospectively by Mr Scott and the Licensee' and which focused on 'a particular chain of circumstances leading towards Mr Scott's death' by contending that 'there was a duty to take care to prevent that chain of circumstances from occurring by preventing Mr Scott from riding the motorcycle'. The joint judgment pointed out at [31] that the content of the duty had to be formulated in much more general terms:

  > There is no doubt that the Proprietor and the Licensee owed Mr Scott various duties to take reasonable care – for example, a duty to take reasonable care to ensure that the premises were physically safe, and a duty to take reasonable care to ensure that equipment in operation, like gambling machines and kegs, did not injure him.

  The correct and more general formulation of the duty question was identified at [46]:

  > Do publicans owe a duty to take care not to serve customers who have passed a certain point of inebriation? And do they owe a duty to take positive steps to ensure the safety of customers who have passed that point after they leave the publican's premises? [References omitted.]

  Having formulated the duty question, the joint judgment concluded at [52] and [57] that 'save in exceptional circumstances', publicans owe 'no general duty of care at common law to customers which requires them to monitor and minimise the service of alcohol or to protect customers from the consequences of the alcohol they choose to consume'.

- In *Karpik v Carnival plc* (2023), the Federal Court of Australia ('Federal Court') had cause to reiterate the point. The case involved the Ruby Princess cruise ship, and the mental harm suffered by one of their passengers in witnessing their spouse contracting COVID-19 and getting severely ill from the virus. Mrs Karpik, sued the Carnival plc, owners of the Ruby Princess, alleging (among other things, including several breaches of the *Australian Consumer Law*) that they were negligent in their management of the outbreak aboard the ship. While acknowledging that a duty of care would be owed to passengers to take reasonable care for their health and safety, the respondent put forward detailed arguments as to why such a duty should not extend to the facts of the case. Specifically, they sought to 'cast the duty posited by Mrs Karpik as a duty to "prevent the spread of contagious diseases" or a duty to "protect patrons from one another", each characterisation of which they say is foreclosed' (at [526]). The Federal Court rejected the argument at [527]–[528]:

> Each of those characterisations is wrong as it is addressed at an inappropriate level of specificity. *By characterising the relevant duty with such specificity, the determination of Mrs Karpik's case would be circumvented by having the issues decided at the duty stage in circumstances where the crux of the dispute in the negligence case is whether they failed to take reasonable care and whether that failure caused her harm.*
>
> The question of the existence or non-existence of a duty of care is to be considered at a higher level of abstraction, or generality, than questions of breach. That higher level of abstraction involves expressing the duty in terms of a want of reasonable care. [Emphasis added and references omitted.]

The Court concluded that the duty owed to Mrs Karpik and passengers of the Ruby Princess was simply 'to take reasonable care for her health and safety', and for abundance of clarity, Stewart J added at [559]: 'I consider that to be a sufficient description of the duty. However, for the avoidance of doubt, that duty extends to the risk of harm caused by COVID-19 infection.'

These cases show that you have to be very careful in defining the nature of the duty owed by a defendant to a plaintiff. The key takeaway is that you should not define the duty in terms of the specific breach. Rather, in your problem-solving exercises you should keep the duty question at the appropriate level by focusing on identifying the general nature of the relationship between the parties and the general nature of the harm that might be risked to the general class of persons that includes the plaintiff, bearing in mind three sources of advice from the High Court. The first tip was given in *Sutherland Shire Council v Heyman* (1985), where Brennan J stated at 487 that 'a postulated duty of care must be stated in reference to the *kind of damage* that a plaintiff has suffered and in reference to the plaintiff or a *class* of which the plaintiff is a member' (emphasis added) because 'the actual nature of the damage suffered is relevant to the existence and extent of any duty to avoid or prevent it'. The second warning came from Gummow J in *Vairy v Wyong Shire Council* (2005), who emphasised at [73] that the duty must not be so wide that it is 'devoid of meaningful content'. The third tip came from Hayne J in *Modbury Triangle Shopping Centre Pty Ltd v Anzil* (2000), who pointed out at [103] that it is unhelpful to formulate the duty 'too broadly: for example, by asking did the defendant owe *any* duty of care to the plaintiff?' Hayne J suggested at [105] that in cases:

> where the extent of the relevant duty is not clear, it is useful to begin by considering the damage which the plaintiff suffered, and the particular want of care which is alleged against the defendant. Asking then whether that damage, caused by that want of care, resulted from the breach of a duty which the

> defendant owed the plaintiff, may reveal more readily the scope of the duty upon which the plaintiff's allegations of breach and damage must depend.

The High Court provided guidance on the difficult task of defining the scope of a duty of care stemming from the decision in *Kuhl v Zurich Financial Services Australia Ltd* (2011), where French CJ and Gummow J explained at [22]:

> Different classes of care may give rise to different problems in determining the nature or scope of a duty of care. In many cases a duty formulated as being one to take 'reasonable care' may suffice for the finding of duty in that particular case ... But where the relationship falls outside of a recognised relationship giving rise to a duty of care, or the circumstances of the case are such that the alleged negligent act or omission has little to do with that aspect of a recognised relationship which gives rise to a duty of care, a duty formulated at too high a level of abstraction may leave unanswered the critical questions respecting the content of the term 'reasonable' and hence the content of the duty of care. These are matters essential for the determination of this case, for without them the issue of breach cannot be decided. The appropriate level of specificity when formulating the scope and content of the duty will necessarily depend on the circumstances of the case.

As discussed, this was recently reiterated by the Federal Court in *Karpik v Carnival plc* (2023), and again by the New South Wales Court of Appeal in *Bondi Beach Foods Pty Ltd v Chadwick* (2023), with Leeming JA explaining at [68] and [69]:

> Duties of care do not ordinarily exist contingently on 'the particular circumstances of the case'. Instead, it is the particular circumstances of the case which mean that they have or have not been breached.
>
> [The defendant] wished to submit that it owed no duty to prevent harm 'in the particular circumstances of the case' ... That is an example of an over-specification of duty.

To support his reasoning, Leeming JA referred to this useful passage by James Goudkamp, from his article 'Breach of Duty: A Disappearing Element of the Action in Negligence?' (2017) at 482:

> Judges, by over-specifying the content of the duty of care element, routinely treat breach cases as though they were duty cases. ... Judges who proceed in this way typically utter formulae such as: 'no duty of care was owed by the defendant in the present case to do ϕ because the reasonable person in the defendant's position would not have done ϕ.' However, the structure of that phrase reveals immediately that the duty of care element is not in play at all. The very fact that the court is discussing what the reasonable person in the defendant's person would have done indicates that the dispute is actually about the breach element, that being the only element of the action in negligence that is concerned with the satisfactoriness of the defendant's conduct.

11.1.4 Summary points

11.1.4.1 Formulating a duty of care

When you are formulating the duty of care in a problem question, ensure that you identify clearly the following:

1. *Who* is the known *person* or ascertainable *class of persons* that the defendant should reasonably foresee could suffer harm as a result of their conduct? This can often be done by identifying the *relationship* between the defendant and the plaintiff, either by consulting the list of established categories noted below in section 11.2.1 or by identifying the circumstances that brought the two parties together. (Make sure that the defendant is not protected by an immunity, noted in section 11.2.2.)
2. *What* is, in broad and general terms, the *kind of damage* that the plaintiff could suffer?
3. *What* is the *content* of the duty (ie under what kind of circumstances should the defendant take care when acting or refraining from acting in certain ways)? Remember that you should not classify the nature of the duty:
   - too *broadly*, so that it is devoid of content; or
   - too *narrowly* on the facts of the case, so that it merges the separate steps of duty and breach.

Active reading

Link each of these summary points to a case authority in section 11.1 above.

LEGISLATION ALERT!

The *Civil Liability Acts* adopted in most states and territories since 2002 have divisions or sections titled 'Duty of Care'. Be advised that this is an inaccurate phrasing because the content of these sections refers to the breach of duty. As the High Court said in *Adeels Palace Pty Ltd v Moubarak* (2009) at 13, with regard to the New South Wales legislation: 'Although s 5B appear[s] beneath the heading "Duty of care", that heading is apt to mislead ... [That provision is] evidently directed to questions of breach of duty'.

The duty of care in negligence claims must still be established on the basis of the common law, except for cases of mental harm, which have to be established under the specific tests provided by civil liability legislation in most states and territories. Also note the special provisions for public authorities, which complement (without replacing) the common law tests. Both mental harm and public authorities are discussed in Chapter 14.

The method of formulating the duty in terms of the relationship between the parties and the nature of the harm risked is illustrated in the following discussion of the established duty categories.

11.2 Established categories of duty and immunity

The easiest cases are those where the facts fit into either one of the established duty categories or one of the established categories of immunity. In the years since *Donoghue v Stevenson* (1932) established the category of manufacturers' liability and Lord Macmillan pointed out (at 619) that the 'categories of negligence are never closed', the courts have gradually added to the categories of relationships that will attract liability so long as the test of reasonable foreseeability is satisfied.

Examples

- Manufacturers or producers of goods and products owe a duty to consumers.
- Employers owe a duty to employees.
- Motorists and road users owe a duty to others on or near the road.
- Occupiers of premises owe a duty to others present or near the premises.
- Proprietors of licensed premises owe a duty to others present in the premises.
- Occupiers who carry out dangerous activities on their land owe a duty to others on or near the premises.
- Professionals owe a duty to clients or patients, for example: doctors, dentists and other medical practitioners owe a duty to patients; and lawyers, accountants, auditors, engineers, architects, etc owe a duty to clients.
- Parents owe a duty to children.
- Doctors owe a duty to unborn plaintiffs (within limits).
- School authorities/teachers owe a duty to students.
- Hospitals owe a duty to patients.
- Prison authorities owe a duty to prisoners.
- Bailees of goods owe a duty to the bailors of the goods.

The rules relating to these established categories are explained below.

Test your understanding

Practise identifying the duty relationships

Remember that a single plaintiff could be categorised as belonging to more than one kind of relationship at the same time. Using the examples above, make a list of the possible duty relationships that a person who leaves her home and drives to her local hospital to consult with a doctor about an operation that is to be carried out in the future may fall into.

11.2.1 Established categories of duty

11.2.1.1 Manufacturers or producers of goods and products

We have seen in *Donoghue v Stevenson* (1932) that the modern law of negligence stems from a case of a defective product: a ginger beer bottle with a dead snail inside. Since then, manufacturers or producers of goods and products owe a duty to take reasonable care to avoid causing injury to the ultimate consumer or user of the manufactured goods or products: *Donoghue v Stevenson* (1932); *Grant v Australian Knitting Mills Ltd* (1936). The High Court had the opportunity to reflect on the scope of the duty owed by manufacturers in *Robinson Helicopter Company Inc v McDermott* (2016). Here, the plaintiff suffered serious injuries in a helicopter crash caused by a safety defect. The defect was the result of incorrect assembly, contrary to instructions given in the manufacturer's maintenance manual. The High Court found that it was open to the trial judge to find, as he did, that the manual was adequate. This serves as a reminder that the test is whether the instructions accompanying a product are clear and comprehensive having regard to the *foreseeable reader*.

LEGISLATION ALERT!

In Australia, the *Competition and Consumer Act 2010* (Cth) introduced the *Australian Consumer Law* (*ACL*) in sch 2. The provisions of the *ACL* create a regime of strict liability (ie liability without fault, where the plaintiff needs to show a defect in the product, a harm, and a causal link between a defect and the harm without also having to demonstrate the fault of the manufacturer). This regime runs in parallel to the common law without superseding it. This provides consumers with a range of choices and possible avenues to seek remedies.

Since the first decision in *Donoghue v Stevenson* (1932), the liability of manufacturers and producers has evolved significantly, to the point that it can now be identified as a discrete area of tort law. In many jurisdictions, the liability of manufacturers has been the subject of specific statutory provisions that override general tort law rules for quite some time (eg Directive 85/374/EEC on product liability in the European Union, or the Second and Third *Restatements of Torts* in the United States). An early advocate of the move away from general negligence law to specific strict liability regimes for product liability was Jane Stapleton in *Product Liability* (1994). A recent analysis can be found in Duncan Fairgrieve and Richard S Goldberg, *Product Liability* (2020), and for a closer look at Australia you can read the relevant chapters by Jeannie Paterson in *Corones' Australian Consumer Law* (2023). While the ACL has become the natural choice for Australian plaintiffs injured by defective products, the recent class action decided in favour of the plaintiffs by the Full Court of the Federal Court in *Ethicon Sàrl v Gill* (2021) is a reminder to manufacturers that fault-based liability remains very much alive, and that manufacturers continue to owe a duty of care in negligence to end users, even in the heavily regulated space of consumer and therapeutic goods.

11.2.1.2 Employers

Employers owe a duty to take reasonable care for the safety of their employees to avoid causing them injury. The duty of an employer is known as a personal, 'non-delegable' duty that requires the employer to provide the employee with a safe system of work, safe plant and equipment, and competent supervisory staff and co-workers: *Hamilton v Nuroof* (1956); *Smith v Charles Baker & Sons* (1891); *Kondis v State Transport Authority* (1984); *Bankstown Foundry Pty Ltd v Braistina* (1986); *Stevens v Brodribb Sawmilling Co Pty Ltd* (1986). This is further discussed in Chapter 16. Note, however, that special rules apply if the injury is pure mental harm: *New South Wales v Fahy* (2007), further discussed in Chapter 14. The Australian approach to an employer's liability for mental harm used to be very narrowly defined, as seen in the case of *Koehler v Cerebos (Australia) Ltd* (2005). The recent High Court decision in *Kozarov v Victoria* (2023) has extended the scope of an employer's duty of care in situations where the employer reasonably ought to have awareness of the risk of mental harm to their employee as a result of the discharge of their employment duties.

The scope of the duty of care owed by an employer is particularly broad, and can go as far as including, in certain circumstances, illegal acts of third parties causing harm to the plaintiff in the course of employment: *Chomentowski v Red Garter Restaurant Ltd* (1970).

In *Czatyrko v Edith Cowan University* (2005), the High Court at 12 took the opportunity to restate the principles established in *Hamilton v Nuroof* (1956) and summarise the duty of care owed by employers to their employees:

> An employer owes a non-delegable duty of care to its employees to take reasonable care to avoid exposing them to unnecessary risks of injury. If there is a real risk of an injury to an employee in the performance of a task in a workplace, the employer must take reasonable care to avoid the risk by devising a method of operation for the performance of the task that eliminates the risk, or by the provision of adequate safeguards. The employer must take into account the possibility of thoughtlessness, or inadvertence, or carelessness, particularly in a case of repetitive work.

When dealing with work-related injuries, always keep in mind that workers are normally entitled to be compensated under statutory schemes. However, because these schemes do not provide full compensation (as common law damages do), an incentive still exists for workers to sue their employers in negligence in cases of serious injury. State and territory legislation has curtailed the rights of workers to bring claims in negligence, which are now available only when the injury exceeds statutory minimum thresholds.

LEGISLATION ALERT!

Consult your study materials for any statutes in your jurisdiction that establish special provisions for the compensation of work-related injuries.

11.2.1.3 Motorists and road users

Motorists and road users owe a duty to take reasonable care for the safety of passengers, other road users, potential rescuers and other people present on the highway or in premises adjoining the highway to avoid being the cause of injury, either to those persons or to their property: *Chapman v Hearse* (1961); *Cook v Cook* (1986), *Imbree v McNeilly* (2008). Once again, the duty owed by motorists and road users to their fellow road users is a broad one, which may include, in certain circumstances, the negligent acts of third parties when the risk of such negligence is initially created by them: *Chapman v Hearse* (1961). They also owe a duty to third parties to avoid causing them pure psychiatric injury in certain circumstances: *Jaensch v Coffey* (1984), further discussed in section 14.3 of Chapter 14.

Also remember that, while the existence of a duty of care for road users is uncontroversial, its scope is broad but not unlimited. *Simmonds-Thatcher v Kamari* (2021) illustrates how it would be excessively broad to include within the scope of this existing category of duty instances where a pedestrian might suddenly come into the path of an oncoming vehicle. The Court reflected at [51]: 'If drivers were required to anticipate in any and all circumstances that a pedestrian might suddenly stray onto the road, traffic would come to a standstill.' Note that this is arguably one of those cases lamented by the Federal Court in *Karpik v Carnival plc* (2023) (discussed above), where a court decides a case at the duty stage by excessively narrowing the scope of a duty of care, when really the relevant question ought to be whether the duty, broadly defined, has been breached.

Remember also the discussion in Chapter 10 about autonomous vehicles (AVs). AVs raise new issues about the nature and scope of this category of duty, which will require courts to reflect upon such elements as the level of control maintained by human drivers. Where that control is minimal or, in more extreme cases, involving fully driverless AVs, absent, the development of principles and criteria to identify the liable party will be needed.

11.2.1.4 Occupiers of premises

Occupiers of premises owe a duty to take reasonable care to ensure that people entering are not exposed to risks of physical injury arising from the condition of the premises: *Australian Safeway Stores v Zaluzna* (1987). However, the scope of this duty does not necessarily extend to removing all potential hazards from their land: *Neindorf v Junkovic* (2005). Occupiers also owe a duty to take reasonable care to remove, reduce or prevent hazards that risk causing damage to other premises in the neighbourhood, depending upon their knowledge of the hazard, their ability to foresee the consequence of not checking or removing it, and their ability to remove it (*Goldman v Hargrave* (1966)), and socially accepted standards of behaviour (*Smith v Littlewoods Ltd* (1987)). Note, however, that a landowner's duty as an occupier of the land does not normally extend to taking reasonable care to prevent physical injury to an injured employee resulting from the criminal behaviour of third parties on that land, unless:

- some of the salient features like special vulnerability, special knowledge or an assumption of responsibility are present: *Modbury Triangle Shopping Centre Pty Ltd v Anzil* (2000) (see section 11.3.6 below); or

- statutory regimes (eg liquor licensing laws) impose a duty to take reasonable care to prevent injury to persons present on the premises from the violent conduct of other patrons: *Adeels Palace Pty Ltd v Moubarak* (2009).

In general, note that the scope of an occupier's duty does not extend to *all* risks, particularly when such risks arise from commonly encountered objects or natural hazards: *Graham v Welch* (2012).

In *Thompson v Woolworths (Qld) Pty Ltd* (2005), the High Court restated the point that an occupier is someone exercising a 'measure of control' over the premises, which is to be appreciated in light of the facts of the case. While the relationship between the occupier and the entrant may be of relevance (in particular, whether the entrant is an invitee, a licensee or a trespasser), the approach rigidly based on categories of entrants is not the law in Australia. The duty is owed to entrants in general, as established in *Australian Safeway Stores v Zaluzna* (1987), where the High Court determined that the occupier's liability towards entrants should be governed by the general common law of negligence.

Landlords also owe a duty to take reasonable care to avoid foreseeable risk of injury to their prospective tenants and members of their household. The precise scope and nature of the duty is not yet clear, but it is accepted that it will extend to known defects and faulty repairs that they authorise. The landlord's duty is limited to defects that they know or ought to know about; it does not extend to a common law requirement to periodically inspect property and engage experts to inspect for latent defects of which they would have no knowledge. In general, it will assist in imposing a duty if they have sufficient control over the premises, or other 'salient features' exist: *Northern Sandblasting Pty Ltd v Harris* (1997); *Jones v Bartlett* (2000).

LEGISLATION ALERT!

Consult your study materials for any statutes in your jurisdiction that modify the rules on occupiers' liability.

In particular, take notice of the following provisions, which do not have a significant impact on the common law method of identifying who an occupier is and when a duty is owed as established in *Australian Safeway Stores v Zaluzna* (1987), but introduce elements of significance for establishing an occupier's standard of care and breach of duty, as further discussed in Chapter 12.

- Australian Capital Territory: *Civil Law (Wrongs) Act 2002*, pt 12.1
- Northern Territory: *Civil Liability Act 2002*, s 9
- South Australia: *Civil Liability Act 1936*, pt 4
- Victoria: *Wrongs Act 1958*, pt IIA
- Western Australia: *Occupiers' Liability Act 1958*

The complicated relationship between the common law, the special provisions for occupiers liability and the general civil liability legislation has been thoroughly analysed by

Peter Handford and Brenda McGivern in 'Two Problems of Occupiers' Liability' (Parts I and II) (2015).

A number of leading cases covering important aspects of the breach inquiry are in fact occupiers' liability cases, which goes to show that this particular category of liability and the general common law of negligence share a close and interdependent relationship. Note also that a statutory or public authority having the care, control and management of land to which the public has access owes each member of the public who enters the land a duty to take reasonable care to avoid causing them injury, provided that the other relevant factors pertaining to the duty question are present: *Romeo v Conservation Commission (NT)* (1998); *Vairy v Wyong Shire Council* (2005). Public authorities are further discussed in Chapter 14.

11.2.1.5 Proprietors of licensed premises

Proprietors of licensed premises owe those present on the premises a duty to take reasonable care to ensure that the premises are physically safe, and that equipment is safe, and in some circumstances, publicans may owe a duty to third parties who may be damaged by reason of the intoxication of other customers present on the premises: *Adeels Palace Pty Ltd v Moubarak* (2009). This was restated in *Brighten v Traino* (2019), which emphasises that the occupier of licensed premises owes a duty to take positive steps to protect patrons from injury caused by other patrons. However, as pointed out by Martin Davies and Ian Malkin in *Focus: Torts* (2024) at 494, they do not, save in exceptional circumstances, owe 'a general duty of care at common law to customers which requires them to monitor and minimise the service of alcohol or to protect customers from the consequences of the alcohol they choose to consume': *Cole v South Tweed Heads Rugby League Football Club Ltd* (2004); *CAL No 14 Pty Ltd v Motor Accidents Insurance Board* (2009).

11.2.1.6 Occupiers who carry out dangerous activities on their land

Occupiers who carry out dangerous activities on their land owe a personal, non-delegable duty to their neighbours to avoid causing injury to persons or property: *Burnie Port Authority v General Jones Pty Ltd* (1994). This is further discussed in Chapter 16 with reference to non-delegable duties.

11.2.1.7 Medical practitioners

Doctors owe patients a duty to take reasonable care in the provision of diagnosis, treatment and advice: *Rogers v Whitaker* (1992). The liability of health professionals is further discussed in Chapter 14.

11.2.1.8 School authorities and teachers

The early case of *Williams v Eady* (1893) suggested that teachers owe a duty of care to students to take such precautions for safety as a reasonable parent would have done in the circumstances. However, the High Court modified the duty in 1977 so that a teacher 'should take such measures as in all the circumstances were reasonable to prevent physical injury' to a pupil: see Murphy and Aickin JJ in *Geyer v Downs* (1977) at 102, citing

Victoria v Bryar (1970) at 141. This is further discussed in Chapter 16 with reference to non-delegable duties.

The duty was restated by the High Court in *Roman Catholic Church Trustees for the Diocese of Canberra and Goulburn v Hadba* (2005). School authorities owe a personal, non-delegable duty to their pupils to ensure that reasonable care is taken of them while they are on the school premises during hours when the school is open for attendance: *Ramsay v Larsen* (1964); *Commonwealth v Introvigne* (1982). Note that the 'temporal ambit of the duty'[2] extends to the period before classes are due to start, where it is (or ought to be) known that school premises are in use at that time, requiring the school to provide an adequate system of supervision.

11.2.1.9 Hospitals

Hospitals undertaking the care, supervision and control of patients owe them a personal, non-delegable duty of care to ensure that reasonable care is taken to avoid injury: *Ellis v Wallsend District Hospital* (1989). Note the limitations on the liability of mental health facilities for harm caused by patients in their care: *Hunter and New England Local Health District v McKenna* (2014). This is further discussed in Chapter 16 with reference to non-delegable duties of hospitals.

11.2.1.10 Legal practitioners

Solicitors owe a duty of care to their clients to exercise reasonable care in the provision of their professional services, which in some cases may also extend to encompass a duty owed to third persons – an example is a duty of disclosure to beneficiaries under a will: *Hawkins v Clayton* (1988); *Hill v Van Erp* (1997); *Astley v Austrust* (1999); *Badenach v Calvert* (2016). The content of the duty will depend on the instructions given by the client and the extent to which the defendants have held themselves out as 'practising a highly skilled and exacting profession': *Midland Bank v Hett, Stubbs and Kemp* (1979) at 402–3, cited by Mason CJ and Wilson J in *Hawkins v Clayton* (1988) at 544. Solicitors' duties are further discussed in Chapter 14.

11.2.1.11 Prison authorities

The High Court has explained that prison authorities owe a duty to exercise reasonable care for the safety of prisoners in custody based on the fact that they have deprived them of their personal liberty and assumed control over them, and bearing in mind that violence from other prisoners is 'often on the cards': *New South Wales v Bujdoso* (2005) at 44; *Howard v Jarvis* (1958). It is also worth noting that prison authorities will normally not have a duty to prevent harm caused by prisoners who have escaped beyond the immediate vicinity of the prison's premises: *New South Wales v Godfrey* (2004). Note that privately owned prisons owe the same duty of care to prisoners as government prisons do: *GEO Group Australia Pty Ltd v O'Connor* (2019). This includes taking positive steps to separate inmates at known risk of violence from other inmates.

2 *Geyer v Downs* (1977) 138 CLR 91, Stephen J at [6].

11.2.1.12 Bailees of goods

Bailees owe a duty to bailors to take such care of the goods as is reasonable in the circumstances: *Hobbs v Petersham Transport Co* (1971); *Pitt Son & Badgery Ltd v Proulefco* (1984).

Given that the categories of negligence are never closed, it may be necessary in a novel problem-solving exercise to argue by analogy from these established categories and to supplement your case with arguments based on the relevant principles and salient features present in those cases, as recommended in *Sullivan v Moody* (2001). These are analysed in detail in section 11.3 below.

11.2.2 Established categories of immunity

Just as the courts have recognised established categories of duty, there are also several categories of immunity from liability, many of which have been justified on grounds of 'public policy' because the rule is designed to achieve or recognise some greater public good.

Examples

- Armed forces in wartime operations
- Police officers and prosecutors
- Parole boards
- Child protection agencies
- Fire brigades and coastguards
- Government officials exercising discretionary policy-making functions
- Barristers and trial advocates
- University examiners
- Statutory immunities (*Civil Liability Acts*)

Many of these immunities are supported by the necessity to preserve the coherence of the law (considered in detail in section 11.3 below), which requires judges to respect the proper distinction between the roles of the judiciary and the other branches of government.

11.2.2.1 Armed forces in wartime operations

The armed forces do not owe a duty of care to members of the public when engaged in active operations against the enemy in time of warfare: *Shaw Savill & Albion Co Ltd v Commonwealth* (1940); *Groves v Commonwealth* (1982). This immunity is justified on the basis that it would be improper for the courts of law to attempt to control or interfere in matters of public security that must be directed by the executive government and its military officers. So, in *Shaw Savill & Albion Co Ltd v Commonwealth* (1940), Dixon J explained at 361 that to impose civil liability for negligence during 'all active operations against the enemy in time of warfare' is 'opposed alike to reason and to policy'. Starke J said at 355–6:

> In my judgment, there is no doubt that the Executive Government and its officers must conduct operations of war, whether naval, military, or in the air, without the control or interference of the courts of law. Acts done in the course of such operations are not justiciable and the courts of law cannot take cognizance of them.

Remember that this immunity is limited in scope and does not apply in cases where defence personnel engage in activities that cannot be classified as active operations against the enemy. This means that activities that could theoretically be performed by civilians and do not entail military actions or operative decisions fall beyond the scope of the immunity: *Groves v Commonwealth* (1982). It is also worth noting that the Supreme Court of the United Kingdom has further limited the scope of the 'combat immunity' by excluding instances of injuries or death by 'friendly fire' that could have been prevented by providing armed forces with adequate equipment and training: *Smith v Ministry of Defence* (2014).

11.2.2.2 Police officers and prosecutors

Members of the police force do not owe a duty of care to members of the public, potential victims or the accused in investigating a crime: *Tame v New South Wales* (2002); *Cran v State of New South Wales* (2004). In *Tame v New South Wales* (2002), McHugh J said at [124]–[125] that it would be 'preposterous to suggest that an officer has a duty of care' when taking down statements or investigating criminal activity. Gleeson CJ said at [26]:

> The primary duty of a police officer filling out such a report is to make available to his or her superiors, honestly and frankly, the results of the observations, inquiries and tests that were made. It would be inconsistent with such a duty to require the police officer to take care to protect from emotional disturbance and possible psychiatric illness a person whose conduct was the subject of investigation and report.

This extends to individual members of the public who might suffer injury through a police force's careless failure to apprehend a dangerous criminal. This immunity is justified on the grounds that the 'conduct of a police investigation involves a variety of decisions on matters of policy and discretion, including decisions as to priorities in the deployment of resources': McHugh J in *Sullivan v Moody* (2001) at [57], citing *Hill v Chief Constable of West Yorkshire* (1989), Lord Keith at 63. It is also justified because of the possibility that the duty owed by the officers to their employer might be incompatible with the posited duty owed to the members of the public, or as Lord Keith also noted in *Hill v Chief Constable of West Yorkshire* (1989) at 63, because a duty could lead to a police officer adopting a 'detrimentally defensive frame of mind'.

More recently, however, the United Kingdom Supreme Court significantly changed the scope of this 'immunity' in *Robinson v Chief Constable of West Yorkshire Police* (2018). In *Robinson*, a bystander who was injured in the course of an arrest negligently performed by the police was deemed to be owed a duty of care by the officers who were performing the arrest. It is not yet clear whether this decision will have any impact on Australian law. Interestingly, this possibility had already been entertained in Australia in *Australian Capital Territory v Crowley* (2012), where the Court found at [311] that a police officer may owe a duty of care to a bystander even when they do not owe one to a suspect:

> We think a member of the police force might be in control (in the relevant sense) of a group of bystanders at a scene, but not in control of an alleged offender or suspect. Therefore ... it is possible, subject to other considerations, that a member of the police force may owe a duty of care to a bystander, but not to an alleged offender or suspect.

In any event, the immunity given to the police is never an 'absolute blanket immunity'. It does not necessarily extend to a case where one police officer negligently exposes another police officer to unnecessary risk of injury or where the police have assumed a particular responsibility to a particular member of the public: *Costello v Chief Constable of Northumbria Police* (1999).

A similar immunity exists to protect prosecution services making charges: *Elguzouli-Daf v Commissioner of Police* (1995). This immunity is justified on the grounds that it might require prosecutors to weigh the private interests of the victim against their general public duties, and because the effectiveness of the prosecution services could be inhibited because of the risk that prosecutors would act to protect themselves from actions for negligence and the expenditure of valuable time and scarce resources in dealing with such claims.

11.2.2.3 Parole boards

A parole board (or officers of a Department of Correctional Services) does not owe a duty of care to members of the public at large as to the manner in which it exercises its powers to release convicted persons; however, where information becomes available that reveals that there may be a breach of a parole condition and that breach is reasonably foreseeable by the defendant as being likely to cause harm to a particular person or persons, then a duty of care may be imposed: *Swan (By His Next Friend) v South Australia* (1994). However, see also *X v South Australia (No 2)* (2005) (suggesting that there were limits on the exception to that proposition, given the reliance in the earlier case on the doctrine of proximity) and the subsequent decision of the Court of Appeal in *X v South Australia (No 3)* (2007). See also the decision of the Supreme Court of New Zealand in *Couch v Attorney-General* (2008).

11.2.2.4 Child protection agencies

Child protection agencies investigating suspected abuse are immune from suit if, in the interests of protecting a child or in pursuing their duty to their employers, they negligently accuse a person of abusing a child: *Sullivan v Moody* (2001). Note that the immunity refers to duties owed to the public at large, not to the children under the agencies' responsibility (to whom a duty can be owed): *South Australia v Lampard-Trevorrow* (2010). In 2015, the Royal Commission into Institutional Responses to Child Sexual Abuse listed a number of factors to be taken into account when establishing whether a child protection agency owes a duty of care in negligence to a child. These include: (1) the statutory scheme under which the agency operates; (2) the degree of control exercised by the agency over the risk of harm; (3) the vulnerability of those who depend on the exercise of the agency's powers; and (4) the consistency of a duty of care with the statutory scheme.[3]

11.2.2.5 Fire brigades, coastguards and emergency services

Fire brigades are not under a common law duty to members of the public to answer a call for help or to take care when doing so; however, if a brigade by their negligence creates a danger that causes a particular plaintiff's injury, the immunity from suit would not apply: *Capital & Counties plc v Hampshire City Council* (1997). This rule also applies to coastguards responding to emergency calls: *OLL Ltd v Secretary of State for Transport* (1997), and to police services and other emergency services answering an emergency call: *Alexandrou v Oxford* (1993). However, the immunity does not apply to ambulance services who have received a specific emergency telephone call, because of the unlikelihood of any conflict of duties arising and because other issues of public policy do not support the granting of an immunity: *Kent v Griffith* (2001).

11.2.2.6 Government officials exercising discretionary policy-making functions

Government officials and public authorities are under no duty of care in relation to decisions which involve, or are dictated by, financial, economic, social or political factors or constraints; however, this governmental immunity will not necessarily apply to government officials or public authorities engaged in operational activities: *Sutherland Shire Council v Heyman* (1985); *Brodie v Singleton Shire Council* (2001); *Graham Barclay Oysters Pty Ltd v Ryan* (2002). In *Minister for the Environment v Sharma* (2022), the Full Court of the Federal Court firmly reiterated that courts cannot meddle in matters of 'high policy'. This governmental immunity was traditionally justified on the grounds that 'the King can do no wrong' but more recently has been justified because of the distinction that the courts make between the proper roles of the legislature, the executive and the judiciary. The liability of public authorities is further discussed in Chapter 14.

LEGISLATION ALERT!

Consult your study materials for any statutes in your jurisdiction that modify the rules on the liability of public authorities.

11.2.2.7 Barristers and trial advocates

Trial advocates are immune from liability for negligence to their client in the conduct of a case in court, or in work out of court that leads to a decision affecting the conduct of a case in court (ie work 'intimately connected' with court proceedings): *Giannarelli v Wraith* (1988); *D'Orta-Ekenaike v Victoria Legal Aid* (2005); *Atwells v Jackson Lalic*

3 *Redress and Civil Litigation Report* (2015) at 461.

Lawyers Pty Ltd (2016). This immunity is controversial and is not always recognised in other jurisdictions (eg in England in *Arthur JS Hall & Co (a Firm) v Simons* (2002), Lord Hoffman suggests, at 707, that the immunity should be 'abolished altogether'; see also *Chamberlains v Lai* (2007) in New Zealand). Generally speaking, the immunity is justified on the basis that finality in litigation is needed to conserve public confidence in the administration of justice and the important public interest in ensuring that cases, which have been concluded, are not endlessly open to re-litigation. It is also justified on the grounds that advocates owe a duty to the court as well as to their clients. In *Giannarelli v Wraith* (1988), Mason CJ at 555 identified this duty as underpinning a barrister's immunity from a suit in negligence for the conduct, preparation or management of a case for and during a trial:

> So the barrister's immunity, if it is to be sustained, must rest on considerations of public policy. ... The peculiar feature of counsel's responsibility is that he owes a duty to the court as well as to his client. His duty to his client is subject to his overriding duty to the court. In the performance of that overriding duty there is a strong element of public interest.

For a long time, as underlined by the Western Australia Court of Appeal in *Alpine Holdings Pty Ltd v Feinauer* (2008) at [84], a controversial aspect remained: 'where the line is to be drawn as to the application of the immunity in relation to advice given in connection with the settlement of legal proceedings'. The High Court has had the chance to revisit the issue in the case of *Atwells v Jackson Lalic Lawyers Pty Ltd* (2016), where the plaintiffs, upon legal advice from the defendants, had accepted unfavourable terms of settlement. The Court restated the purpose of the advocate's immunity, which is grounded in the necessity of ensuring that the certainty of finality of judicial decisions is not undermined by subsequent attacks. No other social purpose can be offered for further extending the immunity, considering that it comes at the expense of equality before the law. In *Atwells,* the Court decided that the settlement agreement was indisputably not the result of the exercise of judicial power; so the immunity could not extend to actions in association with the settlement agreement. This was subsequently confirmed by the High Court in *Kendirjian v Lepore* (2017), where the plaintiff received damages lower than a previous offer of settlement, which had been rejected on the basis of advice given by the defendant law firm. The advice given by a barrister about a settlement offer in a personal injury case does not activate the advocate's immunity, because there is no material difference between negligent advice given about the amount of likely damages and negligent advice given to reject an offer of a disclosed amount. In these circumstances, the position of a barrister is akin to that of a solicitor providing negligent advice.

11.2.2.8 University examiners

The courts will decline jurisdiction over disputes between students and a university's examiners and will not act as a court of appeal from decisions involving matters of academic judgement: *Thomson v London University* (1864); *Thorne v University of London* (1966); *Clark v University of Lincolnshire and Humberside* (2000); *Griffith University v Tang* (2005).

11.2.2.9 Statutory immunities (*Civil Liability Acts*)

The civil liability legislation has introduced – or in some cases, reintroduced – some other statutory immunities, as Joachim Dietrich has explained in 'Duty of Care under the "Civil Liability Acts"' (2005), including those protecting 'good Samaritans' and volunteers engaging in community work without remuneration, and road authorities. Some of these statutory immunities are further analysed in Chapter 14 in the discussion of liability for omissions and the liability of public authorities. Dietrich is very critical of some of these expanded immunities, describing them as 'contrary to the development of a principled, general law of negligence' (at 25), unnecessary (at 27), sometimes 'meaningless' and 'nonsensically drafted' (at 31), 'harsh and misconceived' (at 36) and 'knee-jerk' responses (at 38). He argues (at 30) that the South Australian rules on the immunity of road authorities in s 42 of the *Civil Liability Act 1936* (SA) have 'potentially appalling consequences'. The South Australian legislation provides a blanket immunity from negligence claims for road authorities in cases of failure to maintain roads or to take action to minimise risks of harm resulting from failure to maintain roads, as opposed to other states and territories where such immunity does not cover instances in which the authorities had actual knowledge of the particular risk (eg *Civil Liability Act 2002* (WA) s 5Z(2)).

LEGISLATION ALERT!

Consult your study materials for any statutes in your jurisdiction that add to or modify any immunities from liability in negligence.

The immunities discussed above make it possible to argue by analogy if a new case raises similar issues that would warrant recognition of a new category of immunity, or challenges the existence of an existing category of immunity. The principles discussed in section 11.3 below provide guidance on how to justify any modifications to these rules. The most important thing to remember is that the special rules and categories of immunity (and their limits and exceptions), like much of the law on duty, are subject to change if a meritorious case arises. A court can be persuaded to develop the law in a different direction if the relevant principles and policy justifications are compelling. So, just as the recognised categories of negligence are 'never closed', the immunities and the 'no duty' categories are not set in stone.

11.2.3 Parents, children and the unborn plaintiff

Children may sue their parents. As Barwick CJ pointed out in *Hahn v Conley* (1971) at 283–4, the relationship of parent and child of itself does not impose a general duty of care; however, while 'the moral duties of conscientious parenthood do not as such provide the child with any cause of action when they are not, or badly, performed or neglected', a parent, like any other person having the care of a child, may 'in particular situations and because of their nature or elements' owe a duty 'to take reasonable care to protect the child against foreseeable danger' and to avoid leading the child 'into danger by their actions'.

Parents are not automatically liable for the torts of their children unless they have been personally at fault, as Dixon J explained at 262 in *Smith v Leurs* (1945):

> It appears now to be recognized that it is incumbent upon a parent who maintains control over a young child to take reasonable care so to exercise that control as to avoid conduct on his part exposing the person or property of others to unreasonable danger.

11.2.3.1 Duty to the unborn and other birth-related claims

An unborn plaintiff has no standing to sue, and a foetus has no interest in existence that can override the interests of the mother. However, this does not mean that no duty is owed to the foetus, as Kirby J explained at [66] in *Harriton v Stephens* (2006), citing *Watt v Rama* (1972) and *X and Y (By Her Tutor X) v Pal* (1991):

> Originally, the common law accepted a principle that, because legal personality arises at birth, duties cannot be owed to a person before that person is born. However, it is now established that health care providers owe a duty to an unborn child to take reasonable care to avoid conduct which might foreseeably cause pre-natal injury. Such a duty has been held to exist even before conception. Once the child is born, the damage accrues in law and the child is able to maintain an action for damages.

So, a child may sue their mother or any other person for injuries suffered before birth, provided they were a member of a class of persons whom the defendant could reasonably have foreseen were put at risk by their conduct: *Watt v Rama* (1972); *Lynch v Lynch* (1991). However, in other jurisdictions (eg Canada), the courts have decided that, for reasons of public policy and concerns about autonomy and privacy, a pregnant woman does not owe a legal duty of care towards her foetus or subsequently born child to avoid negligently causing injuries before birth: *Dobson (Litigation Guardian of) v Dobson* (1999).

While medical practitioners could be liable for negligently harming a foetus subsequently born alive, they do not owe a duty to an already disabled foetus to prevent it from being born at all: *Harriton v Stephens* (2006). In this case, which falls into the awkwardly named category of 'wrongful life' claims, a child who was born with severe congenital disabilities sued her mother's doctor for failing to diagnose the fact that her mother had been exposed to the rubella virus. Crennan J explained at [252] and [254] why the law could not impose a duty of care on the doctor to prevent the child being born disabled:

> A comparison between a life with disabilities and non-existence, for the purposes of proving actual damage and having a trier of fact apprehend the nature of the damage caused, is impossible ...
>
> A duty of care cannot be stated in respect of damage which cannot be proved by persons alleging such a duty has been breached, and which cannot be apprehended by persons said to be subject to the duty, and which cannot be apprehended or evaluated by a court (or jury).

In stark dissent, Kirby J noted at [104] that the law routinely faces and engages with the comparison between existence and non-existence (eg where it allows withdrawal of life-sustaining treatment from terminally ill patients, or the decriminalisation of suicide). He explained further at [85] that although comparing existence with non-existence may defy the logic of the compensatory principle that lies at the heart of negligence law,

> the life of legal systems derived from the common law of England has not been fashioned by logic alone. It is the product of experience, judgment and opinion offered by judges.

The principle established in *Harriton v Stephens* was upheld by the New South Wales Court of Appeal in *Waller v James* (2015), where the negligence of the doctor consisted of failing to advise the parents of a child conceived via IVF of the hereditary nature of a disease suffered by the child's father. Note the contrast between the decision in *Harriton v Stephens* and that in *Cattanach v Melchior* (2003). In *Cattanach v Melchior*, which falls into the separate but also awkwardly named category of 'wrongful birth' claims, two parents sued Dr Cattanach for his negligent advice, which had caused them to become parents of an unplanned child. The High Court held that the negligent doctor was liable for the costs of rearing and maintaining a healthy child. Note, however, that by virtue of subsequent legislative reform in some jurisdictions, medical practitioners will not be liable in damages for the cost of upkeep for any healthy but unplanned child, conceived as a result of negligence. 'Wrongful life' and 'wrongful birth' claims are further discussed in Chapter 14.

LEGISLATION ALERT!

Consult your study materials for any relevant statutory provisions in your jurisdiction.

11.2.4 Critique: Is duty the 'fifth wheel on the coach'?

Some commentators have argued that the concept of a duty of care is a superfluous element of the tort. In *Hargrave v Goldman* (1963), Windeyer J at 63 canvassed this issue:

> As long ago as 1897 Holmes J suggested that the idea of a duty of care was a superfluous addition to the requirement of reasonable care: (1897) 10 *Harvard Law Review* p 47. And Professor Buckland, fittingly enough as a Roman lawyer, thought the duty of care 'an unnecessary fifth wheel on the coach, incapable of sound analysis and possibly productive of injustice'. He realized, however, that it was 'certainly a part of our law': (1935) 51 *Law Quarterly Review* 637. Sir Percy Winfield took the same view in an article in the (1934) 34 *Columbia Law Review*, pp. 41–66 reprinted in his *Select Legal Essays* (1952) pp. 70–95. The matter is now beyond purposeful debate, except as an exercise in juristic philosophy. The concept of a duty of care, as a prerequisite of liability in negligence, is embedded in our law by compulsive pronouncements of the highest authority. And it

> may well be that it could not be otherwise, if the law of negligence is to have symmetry, consistency and defined bounds, and its application in particular cases is to be reasonably predictable.

This passage, written over half a century ago, was referred to with approval by Hayne J in *Modbury Triangle Shopping Centre Pty Ltd v Anzil* (2000) at [99]. His Honour also recommended an article, 'Duty of Care: Peripheral Parties and Alternative Opportunities for Deterrence' (1995), by Jane Stapleton, who pointed out at 303–4 that the duty concept serves a valuable purpose by allowing the courts to signal both the 'relevant systemic factors' pointing *towards* the imposition of liability as well as those 'countervailing systemic factors' that tend towards *refusing* liability.[4] Given that the rules on duty will never be completely clear, this is perhaps the best advice that you can take from our discussion of the element of duty, and it is mirrored in the approach taken by the High Court in *Sullivan v Moody* (2001), a case analysed in depth in section 11.3.

11.3 The methodology to establish new duties

The tort of negligence is dominated by the concepts of reasonable foreseeability and fault laid down by Lord Atkin in *Donoghue v Stevenson* (1932). However, as shown in Chapter 10 – and as will become increasingly clear in Chapters 12 and 13 when discussing breach and causation – these foundational concepts cannot provide any clear limits on the extent of liability in negligence. Consequently, this tort contains an important set of 'control devices' that allow judges to move the boundaries of the tort in accordance with the 'felt necessities of the time'.[5] Historically, the two most important methods of controlling the reach of the tort of negligence have been located in the elements of duty and causation. The concept of the 'duty of care' provides judges with a preliminary and critical source of control, and the element of causation, which uses the notions of 'recognised harm' and 'scope of liability', provides another. All of the limiting devices are questions of law and are therefore matters for the judge to decide.

At the birth of negligence in 1932, the judges were conscious of this tension between keeping liability within principled bounds and ensuring that the law could adapt to changing social needs and conditions. This is particularly true for the purpose of establishing a duty of care in a 'novel' fact scenario – that is, a situation in which the parties involved do not fall within an established category of duty (such as those described above: eg road users, doctor–patient). This section will describe the High Court's principles and methods, which the Court has developed to deal with these difficult cases. It will give some examples used by the High Court to illustrate the origin and importance of these principles and methods and an indication of how they are deployed in practice. Chapter 14 will look into six special topics in negligence which pose specific sets of challenges.

4 See also McBride, 'Duties of Care – Do They Really Exist?' (2004) and Howarth, 'Many Duties of Care – or a Duty of Care? Notes from the Underground' (2006).

5 Holmes, *The Common Law* (1881) at 1.

11.3.1 The inadequacy of reasonable foreseeability of harm

The need to find a principled source of limits for the tort of negligence has preoccupied judges since the neighbour principle was first suggested as the basis for imposing a duty of care. Most judges and commentators have agreed for some time that 'something more' than the reasonable foreseeability of harm is required, but few have agreed on what that elusive 'something' might actually be. The High Court explained in *Sullivan v Moody* (2001) at [42] why some limits must be placed on the tort and why the mere foreseeability of harm is not enough on its own to justify imposing a duty:

> If it were otherwise, at least two consequences would follow. First, the law would subject citizens to an intolerable burden of potential liability, and constrain their freedom of action in a gross manner. Secondly, the tort of negligence would subvert many other principles of law, and statutory provisions, *which strike a balance of rights and obligations, duties and freedoms.* [Emphasis added.]

In the years leading up to *Sullivan v Moody* (2001), the High Court judges considered two alternative sources of limits in their search for a supplement to the neighbour principle that could provide some guidance for lower courts and some certainty for litigants, and would also preserve an appropriate balance in the law. The first option was to develop the concept of 'proximity' that was introduced by Brett MR in *Heaven v Pender* (1883) and taken up by Lord Atkin in *Donoghue v Stevenson* (1932); the second option was to allow an overt consideration of policy matters. Despite the fact that both approaches had attracted some judicial support, there was never a time when all of the judges in the High Court agreed on any single option, and both options were eventually rejected in *Sullivan v Moody* (2001) after a lengthy period of disagreement within the High Court over the best approach to the problem.[6]

11.3.2 The evolution of the law elsewhere

Introducing some meaningful limits to the exceedingly broad requirement of foreseeability has been a complex exercise for jurisdictions across the common law world. Before analysing the evolution of the Australian approach, it is worth briefly taking stock of how the law elsewhere has dealt with the matter of establishing a duty of care – in particular, the trajectory of the English common law as developed by the House of Lords (now the United Kingdom Supreme Court), with which the High Court has always engaged in a dialogue, whether implicitly or explicitly.

In *The Duty of Care in Negligence* (2018), James Plunkett offers a comprehensive historical analysis of the way that the concept has evolved. This history revolves around a few essential cases that have shaped, reshaped and refined the approach to the duty of

6 A brief summary of the High Court's search for a methodology can be found in *Graham Barclay Oysters Pty Ltd v Ryan* (2002), Kirby J at 622–9, [229]–[249]. See also Todd, 'A Methodology of Duty' (2004) at 221–41; Witting, 'Duty of Care: An Analytical Approach' (2005); and Beever, *Rediscovering the Law of Negligence* (2007) at 168–204. For a very critical take on the duty of care in English common law, see Ken Oliphant, 'Rationalising Tort Law for the Twenty-First Century' (2017).

care in England, with repercussions across the common law world. The first milestone case in which the developing test to establish a duty aimed to create an explicit control device over the potential overreach of foreseeability was *Anns v Merton LBC* (1978). In this case, building contractors had negligently dug the foundations of a building, disregarding the requirements laid out in the building plan approved by local authorities. Years later, the building was starting to show significant structural defects, allegedly due to the negligently dug foundations. A group of lessees of the building sued the defendant owner for failure to adequately supervise the contractors and to ensure that they complied with the building plan. The judgment was delivered by Lord Wilberforce, who at 752 laid out the test for duty of care:

> [T]he question has to be approached in two stages. First one has to ask whether, as between the alleged wrongdoer and the person who has suffered damage there is a sufficient relationship of proximity or neighbourhood such that, in the reasonable contemplation of the former, carelessness on his part may be likely to cause damage to the latter, in which case a prima facie duty of care arises. Secondly, if the first question is answered affirmatively, it is necessary to consider whether there are any considerations which ought to negative, or to reduce or limit the scope of the duty or the class of person to whom it is owed or the damages to which a breach of it may give rise.

The test quickly became known as the 'two-stage test' and effectively required the plaintiff to show that some foreseeable damage had occurred ('proximity' in this judgment is effectively used as a synonym of foreseeability). It was then for the defendant to bring evidence and a plausible explanation as to why a duty *should not* exist. This is intuitively quite harsh on defendants, and almost creates a 'presumption of duty' provided a plaintiff can meet the (rather undemanding) threshold of proving foreseeability. The two-stage test was never popular (and never adopted) in Australia, because of its vague contours and the excessive burden it placed on defendants. However, it did have a significant influence in other jurisdictions, and in particular in Canada, where it was adopted by the Supreme Court in *City of Kamloops v Nielsen* (1984), and confirmed (albeit with some limitations) in *Cooper v Hobart* (2001).[7]

The two-stage test soon became unpopular with defendants and courts. In particular, defendants lamented the heavy burden of a test requiring them to demonstrate that they *ought not to owe a duty* in new cases arising – a counterintuitive requirement in a fault-based tort system based on the premise that it is for the plaintiff to build their case. By 1990, the time was ripe to move past the vagaries of *Anns v Merton LBC* (1978), and the House of Lords seized the opportunity in *Caparo Industries plc v Dickman* (1990) to substantially revisit the test for the duty of care. This case revolved around the reliance placed by the plaintiff on an audit report prepared by the defendant. The facts are quite

7 In *The Duty of Care in Negligence* (2018), Plunkett discusses how, after *Cooper v Hobart*, Canada has effectively adopted a three-stage test, along the lines of that developed by the United Kingdom House of Lords in *Caparo Industries plc v Dickman* (1990).

complex and are not necessary to understand the relevance of the case, which lies in Lord Bridge's analysis at 617 of the constitutive elements of the duty of care:

> What emerges is that, in addition to the foreseeability of damage, necessary ingredients in any situation giving rise to a duty of care are that there should exist between the party owing the duty and the party to whom it is owed a relationship characterised by the law as one of 'proximity' or 'neighbourhood' and that the situation should be one in which the court considers it fair, just and reasonable that the law should impose a duty of a given scope upon the one party for the benefit of the other.

The case introduces a novel 'three-stage test', in which a plaintiff has to show:

- *foreseeability* as defined in *Donoghue v Stevenson* (1932) – a broad and unspecific foreseeability of harm to a person in the plaintiff's position (or to the class of persons the plaintiff belongs to);
- *proximity*, which is no longer a synonym of foreseeability as in *Anns*, but rather qualifies the relationship between plaintiff and defendant as sufficiently close to warrant imposition of a duty[8] (the exact characteristics of proximity would vary from case to case – uncontroversial in cases of directly inflicted physical injury, much more controversial in cases of, for example, mental harm); and
- that it is *fair, just and reasonable* that a duty be owed in the circumstances.

This last limb of the test is the most controversial, as it explicitly requires courts to establish a duty of care on the basis of policy considerations. In *The Duty of Care in Negligence* (2018) at 55, Plunkett suggests that arguments based on *policy* are informed by consideration of 'the consequences that the imposition of a duty would have on the community'. This is in contrast with considerations of *principle*, which conversely focus on the fairness and desirability of a duty being imposed 'as between the parties before the court'. We shall see in section 11.3.3 below that this contrast between policy and principle has been at the core of the development of the test for establishing a duty of care in Australia, where the High Court has adopted a very distinctive approach.

In *Robinson v Chief Constable of West Yorkshire Police* (2018) (discussed above), the United Kingdom Supreme Court significantly departed from its established case law by explicitly stating that there is no single test to be used for establishing a duty of care. The approach, the Court noted at [21], should rather be based, in the manner characteristic of the common law, on precedent, and on the development of the law incrementally and by analogy with established authorities. The Court restated this at [100]:

> In cases where the question whether a duty of care arises has not previously been decided, the courts will consider the closest analogies in the existing law, with a view to maintaining the coherence of the law and the avoidance of

8 Witting describes it as the pre-existing 'factual relationship between the parties', in 'What Are We Doing Here? The Relationship between Negligence in General and Misstatements in English Law' (2015) at 39.

> inappropriate distinctions. They will also weigh up the reasons for and against imposing liability, in order to decide whether the existence of a duty of care would be just and reasonable.

This increased reliance on reasoning by analogy could be interpreted as narrowing the margin of manoeuvre left to courts, limiting their ability to reason on the basis of policy and imposing greater reliance on principle. Yet, as noted above, *Robinson v Chief Constable of West Yorkshire Police* (2018), while departing from the three-stage approach of *Caparo Industries plc v Dickman* (1990), also makes significant inroads into the traditional 'police immunity' category, in a turn that reads very much like policy-based decision-making: police should be liable for the harm they negligently cause in the course of their operations.

11.3.3 Proximity in Australia

The Australian trajectory has developed in parallel to that in the United Kingdom briefly sketched above. Lord Atkin turned to the concept of proximity in an attempt to find a principled reason to limit the wide harm-based scope of the neighbour principle. In the mid-1980s, this concept was developed by Deane J, who suggested that proximity could provide the unifying touchstone or determining test for imposing a duty of care. It bears noting that 'proximity' as understood by Deane J was a much more nuanced concept than 'proximity' as described in *Anns v Merton LBC* (1978) by Lord Wilberforce. Indeed, in *Jaensch v Coffey* (1984), Deane J at 584–5 identified three ways that a 'relationship of proximity' might be established, including physical proximity, circumstantial proximity and causal proximity:

> Lord Atkin did not seek to identify the precise content of the requirement of the relationship of 'proximity' which he identified as a limitation upon the test of reasonable foreseeability. It was left as a broad and flexible touchstone of the circumstances in which the common law would admit the existence of a relevant duty of care to avoid reasonably foreseeable injury to another. It is directed to the relationship between the parties in so far as it is relevant to the allegedly negligent act of one person and the resulting injury sustained by the other. It involves the notion of nearness or closeness and embraces *physical* proximity (in the sense of space and time) between the person or property of the plaintiff and the person or property of the defendant, *circumstantial* proximity such as an overriding relationship of employer and employee or of a professional man and his client and *causal* proximity in the sense of the closeness or directness of the relationship between the particular act or cause of action and the injury sustained. [Emphasis added.]

This 'extended notion' of proximity dominated – and in some cases distorted[9] – the reasoning in the High Court's decisions on negligence for many years, until it was rejected by the High Court in *Sullivan v Moody* (2001). After reviewing the older cases

9 See, for example, the case of *Gala v Preston* (1991) discussed in Chapter 15.

of *Donoghue v Stevenson* (1932), *Heaven v Pender* (1883) and *Le Lievre v Gould* (1893), the judges in *Sullivan v Moody* (2001) at [48] rejected proximity because of its imprecision and its inability to offer any 'practical guidance' or any 'explanation of a process of reasoning':

> As Professor Fleming said 'no one has ever succeeded in capturing in any precise formula' a comprehensive test for determining whether there exists, between two parties, a relationship sufficiently proximate to give rise to a duty of care of the kind necessary for actionable negligence. The formula is not 'proximity'.

In *Miller v Miller* (2011) at [59] the High Court reiterated that the 'demise of proximity as a useful informing principle in this area is now complete' and went on to explain at [60] that 'it is important to remember why proximity has been discarded from the Australian judicial lexicon':

> The expression is one which has been found not to be useful. It is not useful because it neither states, nor points to, any relevant principle that assists in the resolution of disputed questions about the existence of a duty of care, beyond indicating that something more than foreseeability of damage is necessary. Instead, 'proximity' was used as a statement of conclusion. And, because it was used as a statement of conclusion, it is important to look to the reasoning that lay behind the conclusion, rather than the bare fact that the conclusion was expressed by using the terms 'proximity' or 'relationship of proximity'.

'Proximity' continues to be explicitly rejected as the appropriate formal concept to apply to the duty inquiry in novel fact scenarios in Australian negligence law, such as in *Brookfield Multiplex Ltd v Owners Corporation Strata Plan 61288* (2014) at [20]–[21] (a case of pure economic loss).

Although proximity is no longer seen as 'the' answer to the duty question, the reasoning behind the proximity principle continues to be important because it directs our focus to the relationship between the parties. This focus eventually led to a new approach that seeks to identify the 'salient features' of the duty relationship. It led to the recognition of other features, including that of vulnerability, which grew out of the reaction against proximity's inadequacies and which is now prominent in the High Court's new methodology of duty. Proximity has faded as a grand theory of negligence in Australia, but the search for convincing reasons for viewing the parties as linked together in a legally significant relationship – which began in *Donoghue v Stevenson* (1932) – continues, because, as the High Court pointed out in *Miller v Miller* (2011) at [46], citing Gummow and Hayne JJ in *Graham Barclay Oysters Pty Ltd v Ryan* (2002) at [145], the 'totality of the relationship between the parties' is 'the proper basis upon which a duty of care may be recognised'. Interestingly, the idea of proximity occasionally resurfaces in complex cases, such as in *Minister for the Environment v Sharma* (2022), where Beach J referred to the insufficient 'closeness' between the Minister and the children potentially affected by the Minister's decision.

11.3.4 Policy in Australia

Having abandoned proximity as the key supplement to the foreseeability principle, the High Court in *Sullivan v Moody* (2001) at [49] also rejected the second option of using policy considerations:

> The question as to what is fair, and just and reasonable is capable of being misunderstood as an invitation to formulate policy rather than to search for principle. The concept of policy, in this context, is often ill-defined. There are policies at work in the law which can be identified and applied to novel problems, but the law of tort develops by reference to principles, which must be capable of general application, not discretionary decision-making in individual cases.

This decision is an explicit rejection of the three-stage approach developed by the United Kingdom House of Lords in *Caparo Industries plc v Dickman* (1990), and of the third limb of the test in particular. The three-stage test had been strongly advocated for by Kirby J in *Pyrenees Shire Council v Day* (1998), but even so, in *Sullivan v Moody* (2001) a unanimous High Court (Kirby J not sitting in that case) decided that *Caparo Industries plc v Dickman* (1990) was not the law in Australia, and that policy-based decision-making should be rejected altogether. Most recently, this was reiterated by Allsop CJ in *Minister for the Environment v Sharma* (2022).

Since *Sullivan v Moody* (2001), the High Court appears to have given up the search for a single solution that will answer all the problems associated with developing and limiting the tort of negligence. The High Court's jurisprudence in this area now appears to be focused on developing a 'methodology of balance'. This approach does not create a single 'test'; nor does it elevate any one particular feature of the relationship between the parties or any single principle to a place of dominance. Rather, it seeks to identify the relevant or 'salient' features present in the case and to evaluate them in the light of established case law, with the goal of striking 'a balance of rights and obligations, duties and freedoms'. This was summarised by the Court in *Sullivan v Moody* (2001) at [50]:

> The relevant problem will then become the focus of attention in a judicial evaluation of the factors which tend for or against a conclusion, to be arrived at as a matter of principle.

This is, in theory, a welcome development because the abandonment of the doomed search for the 'ultimate test' frees the High Court from its internal disagreement. However, the current 'methodology of balance' has not always offered a clear picture in over 20 years of operation. It is at times difficult to draw a meaningful distinction between policy-based and principle-based reasoning in controversial cases: see, for example, *Harriton v Stephens* (2006), noted in section 11.2.3.1 above. So, while we know that the 'something extra' (in addition to mere foreseeability) is not to be found in a single solution, the Australian 'multi-faceted'[10] approach to negligence cannot always offer to litigants the level of certainty they would ideally wish for.

10 This label was used by Gummow and Hayne JJ in *Graham Barclay Oysters Pty Ltd v Ryan* (2002) at [149]. The 'multi-factorial' approach in *Sullivan v Moody* has been criticised by Witting as a 'serious error' in 'The Three-Stage Test Abandoned in Australia – or Not?' (2002).

11.3.5 The current Australian approach: *Sullivan v Moody* and the 'methodology of balance'

Two of the key goals articulated by the High Court in *Sullivan v Moody* (2001) are:

- to preserve a proper *balance* between the rights of plaintiffs and the duties of defendants (at [42]); and
- to maintain the coherence of the law and the appropriate *balance* between the imposition of a duty in negligence and the existence of other overlapping statutory or tortious duties (at [53]–[55]).

The step-by-step guidance given by the High Court in *Sullivan v Moody* (2001) points to the following main matters for consideration:

1. Consider the common characteristics in the established categories – see [51].
2. Consider the negative indicators present in the 'no duty' categories – see [53].
3. Identify and balance the relevant principles or 'salient features' – see [49] and [53].
4. Ensure that any new step presents a coherent development of compatible legal duties in the law, more widely considered – see [54]–[55].

The new approach begins by identifying the *factual* similarities and differences between the new case and the previous cases that have both allowed and denied liability (steps 1 and 2); it then moves on to consider the wider source of principles in the cases dealing with negligence, where the relevant 'salient features' underpin a form of reasoning by principled rather than factual analogy (step 3); and finally, it takes an even wider view that checks whether the proposed new duty fits within a consistent pattern of duties that the law already imposes on the parties with the aim of generating a *coherent development* in the law (step 4).

11.3.5.1 Step 1: Common characteristics (or 'salient features') in established categories

The first step identified by the High Court in *Sullivan v Moody* (2001) at [51] requires us to look at the previous case law to 'identify the relevant characteristics that are common to the kinds of conduct and relationship between the parties which are involved in the case for decision' and then to compare them with 'the kinds of conduct and relationships which have been held in previous decisions of the courts to give rise to a duty of care'.[11] These relevant characteristics, or positive indicators, have also been referred to as 'salient features' in other cases.

Case examples

- *Graham Barclay Oysters Pty Ltd v Ryan* (2002), Gummow and Hayne JJ at [149]
- *Perre v Apand Pty Ltd* (1999), Gummow J at [198]–[201]

11 This first step is taken from Lord Diplock in the leading English case of *Home Office v Dorset Yacht Co Ltd* (1970) at 1058.

- *Caltex Oil (Australia) Pty Ltd v The Dredge 'Willemstad'* (1976), Stephen J at 576–7
- *Harriton v Stephens* (2006), Kirby J at [64]

This approach appears to echo the views of Brennan J, who stated in *Sutherland Shire Council v Heyman* (1985) at 481 that 'the law should develop novel categories of negligence incrementally and by analogy with established categories' of liability, and McHugh J, who said in *Perre v Apand Pty Ltd* (1999) at [93]–[95] that the 'best solution is to proceed incrementally from the established cases and principles' and 'by reference to the reasons why the material facts in analogous cases did or did not found a duty' and 'the few principles of general application that can be found in the duty cases'. Note, however, that the 'incremental approach' has been disapproved by Gummow J in *Crimmins v Stevedoring Industry Finance Committee* (1999) at [160] and *Perre v Apand Pty Ltd* (1999) at [199].

The essential difference between the 'incremental approach' of Brennan J and the High Court's preference for 'salient features' can be summarised as follows. Reasoning *incrementally* requires the court to focus on concrete precedents rather than general rules. This means the analogy courts can draw between novel scenarios and established cases is quite narrowly constrained. Reasoning on the basis of *salient features*, on the other hand, requires the court to isolate the principles emerging from established precedents, and apply them to the novel scenario. The margin for manoeuvre is thus broader, because principles can be relevant in situations that are factually very different. This will become clearer when we discuss key salient features below.

11.3.5.2 Step 2: Negative indicators or 'control mechanisms'

The second step recommended in *Sullivan v Moody* (2001) at [53] is to consider the guidance offered by the reasons in previous cases where the 'conduct and relationships may have been held not to give rise to a duty of care'. This is consistent with the approach taken by Deane J in *Jaensch v Coffey* (1984) at 586, which directed attention to 'any statutory provision or other common law rule ... which operates to preclude the implication of such a duty of care to the plaintiff in the circumstances of the case'. A similar approach that allowed for the operation of appropriate control mechanisms was advocated by Gummow J in *Perre v Apand Pty Ltd* (1999) at [201]. The 'no duty' categories are discussed in section 11.2.2 above.

11.3.5.3 Step 3: Principled development

The High Court maintained in *Sullivan v Moody* (2001) at [49] that the law of negligence should be developed 'by reference to principles, which must be capable of general application' and said at [53] that, where possible, the development of negligence should not 'cut across other legal principles as to impair their proper application'. This approach is fundamental to all areas of the law and we explore some of the key principles of negligence, or 'salient features' as they are most commonly called, that are used in novel cases in section 11.3.6 below.

11.3.5.4 Step 4: Coherent development of compatible legal duties

The final step is to ensure that the recognition of any new duty maintains the overall 'coherence of the law' and promotes the desirable goal of achieving consistency and imposing 'compatible' duties on defendants: *Sullivan v Moody* (2001) at [54]–[55]. This is an outward-looking aspect, which takes the court's focus beyond the tort of negligence itself and looks to other sources of existing legal duties and their underlying justifications. This aspect of the High Court's negligence jurisprudence has been taken up in later cases: for example, Gummow and Hayne JJ in *Graham Barclay Oysters Pty Ltd v Ryan* (2002) at [149]; *CAL No 14 Pty Ltd v Motor Accidents Insurance Board* (2009) at [41]–[42]; and *Miller v Miller* (2011) at [15]–[16] and [24]–[29]. We consider several different applications of the 'coherence principle' in section 11.3.10 below.

Note that while it is analytically useful to separate the various steps as outlined above, in practice you will find that courts at times merge them (or some of them) into a holistic appraisal of the novel fact scenario. If you reflect on the decisions you read, you will always be able to recognise the steps that lead to a court's conclusion. In your problem-solving tasks, you need to be aware of the relevance of each step as developed by the High Court in *Sullivan v Moody*, but you don't necessarily need to get too hung up on this structure. In general, both when reading cases and tackling your own problem solving, you should always be able to point to the three main moves described in Figure 11.1.

Figure 11.1 Essential questions in duty of care (novel fact scenario)

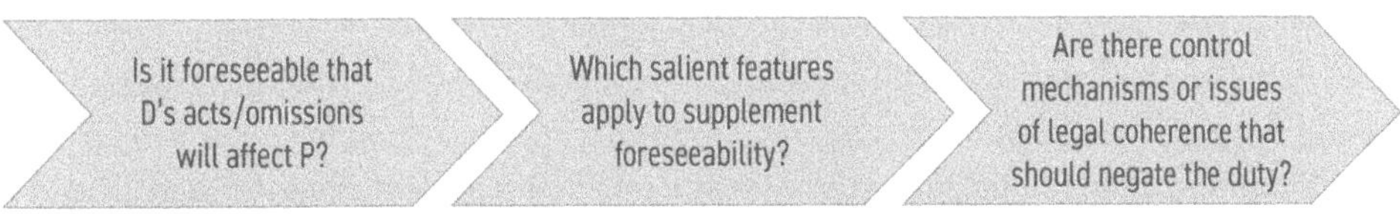

Develop your skills

Case analysis

Read the case of *Sullivan v Moody* (2001) and then undertake the following:

- Using the problem-solving tips given in section 15.9 of Chapter 15, write a 'six-point plan' that introduces the facts and issues in the case.
- Using Table 3.1 in Chapter 3 as a guide, identify the rules, the principles and the relevant policy justifications that were used in the arguments put to the High Court by the two parties and then identify those that were used in the judgment itself.
- Using Table 3.2 in Chapter 3 as a guide, identify the different kinds of argument that the judges used in their reasons.
- Explain the three reasons why the judges in this case maintained that foreseeability of harm alone is not sufficient to give rise to a duty of care.

- How did the appellants in this case attempt to get around the problem caused by the rule that those who investigate crimes on behalf of the state do not normally owe a duty of care to potential suspects? Why did this argument fail?
- Explain why the judges rejected 'proximity' as the test for the existence of a duty of care.
- Explain what the *Caparo* test is and why the judges in *Sullivan v Moody* (2001) rejected it.
- How did the judges in this case use the precedent cases of *Donoghue v Stevenson* (1932), *Heaven v Pender* (1883) and *Le Lievre v Gould* (1893)?

Prepare an oral presentation on *Sullivan v Moody* (2001)

Using section 4.5 of Chapter 4 as a guide, prepare a 10-minute oral presentation summarising the issues in this case and explaining the steps in the reasoning used by the judges to resolve those issues.

11.3.6 Key salient features in negligence

In *Sullivan v Moody* (2001), the High Court rejected policy-based reasoning and insisted that the tort of negligence be developed by reference to principles. As we saw in Chapter 10, there are two primary principles in negligence that were first articulated by Lord Atkin in *Donoghue v Stevenson* (1932) and that are applied in every case: the first is the 'neighbour principle' and the second is the fault principle, which requires a defendant to meet a standard of reasonable care. To supplement the neighbour principle, Australian courts now refer to 'salient features'. You should think of 'salient features' as principled rather than factual analogies between cases. So, for example, while cases involving car drivers will often share sufficient factual analogies as to warrant reference to the established category of road users, sometimes the analogy can be more subtle. For example, while the facts of two cases may be very different, they might still involve plaintiffs that are particularly vulnerable, or situations where a defendant exercises a high degree of control over the source of harm. These similarities are not factual as such. They are better understood as principled analogies that emerge from established patterns in the case law.

Some of the most important salient features are identified below. The first two are already familiar to you from Chapter 10, and the others are outlined in this section.

You should remember that some judges refer to some of these features as principles, or even as legal policies, and that the line between a 'principle' and a 'policy' justification can sometimes be blurry: see section 3.1 of Chapter 3. Jane Stapleton in 'The Golden Thread at the Heart of Tort Law: Protection of the Vulnerable' (2003) doubts at 135 that there is any 'compelling account of the difference between principle and policy'. She argues at 136 that such terminology is meaningless and often 'masks the substance of a judge's reasoning process' and suggests at 137 that judges should 'simply describe these concerns neutrally as "legal concerns"'.[12]

12 Since the emphatic rejection of policy as a solution to the development of negligence in *Sullivan v Moody* (2001), the use of 'policy' as a label appears to have diminished somewhat, but see Ipp, 'Policy

Below is a snapshot of key salient features, supplemented by a more in-depth analysis of each of these identified key salient features in the sections to follow.

Examples

Key salient features in brief

Proximity

- Proximity is 'directed to the relationship between the parties in so far as it is relevant to the allegedly negligent act of one person and the resulting injury sustained by the other' and involves a 'nearness or closeness' that embraces physical proximity, circumstantial proximity and causal proximity (*Jaensch v Coffey* (1984), Deane J at 584–5).
- Note: Proximity appears in many cases, but was abandoned in *Sullivan v Moody* (2001) and *Miller v Miller* (2011) as a key control mechanism to establish a duty of care, as discussed above. It is still occasionally referred to when relevant to the circumstances, such as in *Minister for the Environment v Sharma* (2022).

Vulnerability and degree of control

- If the relationship between the plaintiffs and the defendants is characterised by vulnerability in the special sense that the plaintiffs are vulnerable to harm as a result of the defendants' conduct and they are unable to protect themselves by taking any other measures (eg by reason of ignorance or social, political or economic constraints), then significant weight will be given to protecting the plaintiff by imposing a duty of care on the defendant (*Esanda Finance Corporation Ltd v Peat Marwick Hungerfords* (1997), Toohey and Gaudron JJ at 263–4; *Woolcock Street Investments Pty Ltd v CDG Pty Ltd* (2004), Gleeson CJ, Gummow, Hayne and Heydon JJ at [23]–[24], [31]–[32] and McHugh J at [80]).
- Vulnerability may be indicated by the following salient features:
    - *control* by the defendant (D) over events or matters affecting the plaintiff (P);
    - D's *special knowledge* of important matters affecting P; or
    - *reliance* by P on D and an *assumption of responsibility* by D to P.

  See, for example, *Perre v Apand Pty Ltd* (1999), Gleeson CJ at [10]–[11], Gaudron J at [37], and McHugh J at [118] and [124]–[125].
- Vulnerability focuses on the plaintiff. Its counterpart is the degree of control exercised by the defendant over the source of harm. A plaintiff may be vulnerable, but if a defendant has little control over the source of harm, courts will be reluctant to find a duty of care. This is particularly true in cases involving a public authority as a defendant (eg *Graham Barclay Oysters Pty Ltd v Ryan* (2002); *Stuart v Kirkland-Veenstra* (2009)).

and the Swing of the Negligence Pendulum' (2003), who seems to have persisted in using the word 'policy' to describe many considerations that would be better labelled as principles because of their moral foundations. See also Beever, *Rediscovering the Law of Negligence* (2007) and Witting, 'Tort Law, Policy and the High Court of Australia' (2007).

Autonomy and personal responsibility

- 'One of the central tenets of the common law is that a person is legally responsible for their choices. It is a corollary of that responsibility that a person is entitled to make those choices for themselves without unjustifiable interference from others. In other words, the common law regards individuals as autonomous beings entitled to make, but responsible for, their own choices' (*Perre v Apand Pty Ltd* (1999), McHugh J at [114] and [115]).
- The corollary of autonomy is personal responsibility; however, a person's freedom to make their own choices is not absolute and may be limited 'to the extent necessary for the maintenance of society' (*Perre v Apand Pty Ltd* (1999), McHugh J at [114] and [115]; *Agar v Hyde* (2000), Gaudron, McHugh, Gummow and Hayne JJ at [90]; see also Gleeson CJ at [125]).

Certainty or indeterminacy

- The law should not impose liability if the duty is too uncertain in nature, is impossible to define or comply with, or gives rise to liability 'in an indeterminate amount for an indeterminate time to an indeterminate class'; however, it is 'not necessarily fatal to the recognition of a duty of care that the duty is owed to a class whose members cannot be identified with complete accuracy' (*Perre v Apand Pty Ltd* (1999), Gaudron J at [32], citing *Bryan v Maloney* (1995), Mason CJ, Deane and Gaudron JJ at 618, in turn citing Cardozo CJ in *Ultramares Corporation v Touche* (1931) at 444; see also *Sullivan v Moody* (2001) at [61] and *Harriton v Stephens* (2006), Crennan J at [254]).

Coherence

- A duty should not be imposed if it undermines the coherence of the law, by subverting 'many other principles of law, and statutory provisions, which strike a balance of rights and obligations, duties and freedoms'; for example,
  - if it would not be compatible with other duties that the parties owe;
  - if it is inconsistent with, or has a tendency to discourage, the due performance of other duties or responsibilities; or
  - if the asserted duty of care is inconsistent with the terms, scope and purpose of any relevant statute (*Sullivan v Moody* (2001) at [30], [42], [50], [53]–[55], [60]; *Graham Barclay Oysters Pty Ltd v Ryan* (2002), Gummow and Hayne JJ at [149]; *CAL No 14 Pty Ltd v Motor Accidents Insurance Board* (2009), Gummow, Heydon and Crennan JJ at [41]–[42]; *Miller v Miller* (2011) at [15]–[16] and [24]–[29]).
- This principle takes a number of forms and can apply either to:
  - *rule*-based coherence, which requires consistency with other duties imposed by tort law, criminal law, statute or any other wider areas of the law;
  - *role*-based coherence, which requires maintaining respect for a coherent division of roles between judges and legislators; or
  - *goal*-based coherence, which requires maintaining support for wider community goals and community goods, etc.

11.3.7 The salient feature of vulnerability

As a result of the growing dissatisfaction with proximity theory and the increasing focus by the High Court on the hallmarks of a duty relationship, proximity (while still occasionally referred to) has effectively been superseded by the feature of vulnerability, which is broad in nature and encompasses numerous aspects such as control, knowledge, reliance, and assumption of responsibility. If the relationship between the plaintiff and the defendant is characterised by vulnerability in the special legal sense that the plaintiff is vulnerable to harm as a result of the defendant's conduct and they are unable to protect themselves by taking any other measures (eg by reason of powerlessness, reliance, ignorance or social, political or economic constraints), then significant weight will be given to protecting the plaintiff by imposing a duty of care on the defendant. The development of vulnerability has been discussed by Jane Stapleton in two leading articles (1998 and 2003, listed in this chapter's References section). Early authorities for this principle can be found in the following cases.

Case examples

- *Esanda Finance Corporation Ltd v Peat Marwick Hungerfords* (1997), Toohey and Gaudron JJ at 263–4
- *Crimmins v Stevedoring Industry Finance Committee* (1999), McHugh J at [93]; *Perre v Apand Pty Ltd* (1999), Gleeson CJ at [10]–[11], McHugh J at [118], Gaudron J at [37]
- *Graham Barclay Oysters Pty Ltd v Ryan* (2002), McHugh J at [84], Gummow and Hayne JJ at [149]
- *Woolcock Street Investments Pty Ltd v CDG Pty Ltd* (2004), Gleeson CJ, Gummow, Hayne and Heydon JJ at [23]–[24], [31]–[32], and McHugh J at [80]

This vulnerability, which links the plaintiff and the defendant together in the legal sense and explains why the defendant should take reasonable care to avoid harming the plaintiff, can be recognised by several indicating factors, including the following:

- *Control:* The defendant has control over events or matters affecting the plaintiff – for example, if the defendant is a teacher in charge of pupils, a prison authority in charge of inmates or a carrier responsible for passengers.
- *Knowledge:* The defendant has special knowledge of important matters affecting the plaintiff.
- *Reliance* and *assumption of responsibility:* The plaintiff has relied on the defendant, especially if the defendant has also assumed responsibility for specific matters concerning the plaintiff.

Many of the judges referred to these special features in *Perre v Apand Pty Ltd* (1999).

Case examples

- Gleeson CJ, *Perre v Apand Pty Ltd* (1999) at [10]–[11]:

  > Moreover, knowledge (actual, or that which a reasonable person would have) of an individual, or an ascertainable class of persons, who is or are reliant, and therefore vulnerable, is a significant factor in establishing a duty of care.

- McHugh J, *Perre v Apand Pty Ltd* (1999) at [118]:

  > The vulnerability of the plaintiff to harm from the defendant's conduct is therefore ordinarily a prerequisite to imposing a duty. If the plaintiff has taken, or could have taken steps to protect itself from the defendant's conduct and was not induced by the defendant's conduct from taking such steps, there is no reason why the law should step in and impose a duty on the defendant to protect the plaintiff from the risk of pure economic loss.

  See also McHugh J at [124]–[125]:

  > Vulnerability will often include, but not be synonymous with, concepts of reliance and assumption of responsibility ... Reliance and assumption of responsibility are merely indicators of the plaintiff's vulnerability to harm from the defendant's conduct, and it is the concept of vulnerability rather than these evidentiary indicators which is the relevant criterion for determining whether a duty of care exists.

- Gaudron J, *Perre v Apand Pty Ltd* (1999) at [37]:

  > In *Hill* [*Hill v Van Erp* (1997)], both Gummow J and I saw the solicitor's control over the realisation of the intentions of the testatrix as a special factor warranting the imposition of a duty of care. And Dawson J, with whom Toohey J agreed, placed emphasis on the fact that 'the intended beneficiary's interests [were] totally and unavoidably dependent upon the proper performance of a function within the sole province of the solicitor' which, of course, is simply the corollary of the solicitor's control. [Footnote references deleted.]

The role of vulnerability in the law of negligence is not new. For example, even though vulnerability was not mentioned in those terms as a factor in the seminal cases of *Donoghue v Stevenson* (1932) and *Grant v Australian Knitting Mills Ltd* (1936), it is easy to look back now and see how the plaintiffs in both cases were vulnerable in the special legal sense to the defendants.

Case examples

- May Donoghue could not see through the opaque glass hiding the snail in the ginger beer bottle: *Donoghue v Stevenson* (1932).
- Dr Grant could not detect the hidden impurities in the woollen long-johns: *Grant v Australian Knitting Mills Ltd* (1936).

In both *Donoghue v Stevenson* (1932) and *Grant v Australian Knitting Mills Ltd* (1936), it was seen as reasonable to impose the duty not only because the manufacturers were in *control* of the process but also because they *knew* (and intended) that their products would be used by members of the public, who in turn reasonably *relied* on the manufacturers to take reasonable care when making the goods. So, once we are alerted to the feature of vulnerability, the insistence of the judges in those two landmark cases on the inability of the plaintiffs to protect themselves from the consequences of the defendants' failure to take reasonable care takes on new significance. The High Court judges, by looking back over earlier cases and identifying the relationship of vulnerability as a recurring feature, have in a sense re-created the process by which Lord Atkin arrived at the neighbour principle – and found a way of uniting the 'novel' cases with the established duty categories. The result is that vulnerability, which supplements the test of reasonable foreseeability of harm, gives us a stronger moral justification for imposing a duty.

Note that another feature that courts will recurringly refer to is that of degree of control over the source of harm. While partially overlapping with the idea of control described in this section (there is no doubt, for example, that the manufacturer of consumer products has control over the source of harm which contributes to the vulnerability of the plaintiff), the specific notion of degree of control over the source of harm can be more nuanced, and either reinforce the finding of a duty of care, or negate it. For example, in *Stuart v Kirkland-Veenstra* (2009), while the plaintiff could certainly be characterised as vulnerable, the defendants (two police officers) were found to have an insufficient degree of control over the direct source of harm to the plaintiff (in that case, the plaintiff themselves). The feature of degree of control over the source of harm can be very relevant in cases involving public authorities, and particularly when the conduct under scrutiny is an omission. This is further discussed in Chapter 14.

Examples

Certain cases discussed in Chapter 14 on omissions (section 14.1), public authorities or holders of statutory powers (section 14.2), professional liabilities of solicitors (section 14.5), cases of pure economic loss (section 14.5) and professional liability of doctors (section 14.6).

In sum, with reference to the relational aspect between parties that may prompt a court to find a duty of care in a novel fact scenario, the decision in *Osborne Park Commercial Pty Ltd v Miloradovic* (2019) at [133] offers a useful summary:

> Characteristics of a relationship which in the past have assumed some significance in the determination of the existence and content of a duty of care include (1) reliance by the plaintiff on the defendant; (2) an assumption of responsibility by the defendant; (3) the defendant's knowledge of and control over the conditions from which the risk of injury arises; (4) the plaintiff's dependence on the defendant to exercise reasonable care in the defendant's undertaking; (5) the vulnerability of the plaintiff to harm from the defendant's conduct; and (6) the physical, geographical, and commercial propinquity of the parties, in

> the activities of each in which one suffered, and the other caused, the harm. Some of these characteristics have been seen to be overlapping or corollaries of others. [References omitted.]

11.3.8 The salient features of autonomy and personal responsibility

Autonomy is another important salient feature that is commonly used by the High Court, both when imposing a duty and when refusing to recognise a duty. This feature is familiar, because, as seen in Chapter 5, it justifies the existence of the trespass torts, which protect our rights to liberty of movement (false imprisonment) and to control access to our bodies, land and goods (battery, trespass to land and trespass to goods). It also justifies the defence of consent in the intentional torts, as Chapter 7 explains. Autonomy plays a very similar role in the tort of negligence: not only it is a key feature that supports the imposition of a *duty* of care, but it is also a relevant consideration in the element of *breach* and the *defence* of voluntary assumption of risk, as discussed in Chapters 12 and 15 respectively. Autonomy is closely associated with its mirror image, personal responsibility, which has come into prominence, not only in the case law, but also in the legislation passed after the Ipp Review. The effect of these two salient features and the link between them has been explained by the courts in a series of cases.

Case examples

- McHugh J explained in *Perre v Apand Pty Ltd* (1999) at [114] and [115] how the 'common law's concern for the autonomy of the individual and its desire to give effect to the choices of the individual by not burdening his or her freedom of action' can justify some of the categories of immunity from duty (eg no duty to rescue, no general duty to avoid causing economic losses on a business competitor):

  > One of the central tenets of the common law is that a person is legally responsible for his or her choices. It is a corollary of that responsibility that a person is entitled to make those choices for him or her self without unjustifiable interference from others. In other words, the common law regards individuals as autonomous beings entitled to make, but responsible for, their own choices.
  >
  > ... In any organised society, however, individuals cannot have complete autonomy, for the good government of a society is impossible unless the sovereign power in that society has power in various circumstances to coerce the citizen. Nevertheless, the common law has generally sought to interfere with the autonomy of individuals only to the extent necessary for the maintenance of society.

- In *Agar v Hyde* (2000), a case where injured rugby players unsuccessfully sued the board responsible for making the rules of their sport, Gaudron, McHugh, Gummow and Hayne JJ explained at [90] how the twin features operate:

  > The decision to participate is made freely. That freedom, or autonomy, is not to be diminished. But with autonomy comes responsibility. To hold that the appellants owed a duty of care to Mr Worsley would diminish the autonomy of all who choose, for whatever reason, to engage voluntarily in this, or any other, physically dangerous

> pastime. It would do so because it would deter those who fulfil the kind of role played by the IRFB and the appellants in regulating that pastime from continuing to do so lest they be held liable for the consequences of the individual's free choice. The choices available to all would thus be diminished.

Gleeson CJ also referred to autonomy's role in *Agar v Hyde* (2000) at 15:

> People who pursue recreational activities regarded as sports often do so in hazardous circumstances; the element of danger may add to the enjoyment of the activity. Accepting risk, sometimes to a high degree, is part of many sports. A great deal of public and private effort, and funding, is devoted to providing facilities for people to engage in individual or team sport. This reflects a view, not merely of the importance of individual autonomy, but also of the public benefit of sport.

- Two cases of omissions explain why the common law does not impose a general duty to rescue another from the consequences of their own consciously chosen conduct: *Stuart v Kirkland-Veenstra* (2009) at [87]–[88] and [124] and *CAL No 14 Pty Ltd v Motor Accidents Insurance Board* (2009) at [54]. See the discussion of omissions in Chapter 14.
- Cases dealing with the duty owed by publicans to their customers who have suffered injury as a result of being intoxicated have emphasised personal responsibility: see *Cole v South Tweed Heads Rugby League Football Club Ltd* (2004) and *CAL No 14 Pty Ltd v Motor Accidents Insurance Board* (2009), where Gummow, Heydon and Crennan JJ summarised the point at [54]:

> Balancing the pleasures of drinking with the importance of minimising the harm that may flow to a drinker is also a matter *of personal decision and individual responsibility*. It is a matter more fairly to be placed on the drinker than the seller of drink. [Emphasis added.]

These two features have been used increasingly by the High Court at the duty stage, and it is important to understand that autonomy and personal responsibility can function either as a bridge to liability or as a wall that prevents liability from being imposed. They can work either in favour of a plaintiff or in favour of the defendant. The value of autonomy and its corollary, personal responsibility, must therefore be weighed in the balance when judges decide whether a defendant should owe a duty of care to a plaintiff, and they can give us two different, but opposing answers to the duty question.

- It will be a positive factor weighing in favour of imposing a duty of care if the duty would enhance and support a plaintiff's exercise of their autonomy.
- It will be a negative factor that weighs against imposing a duty of care on the defendant if that duty might conflict with the plaintiff's exercise of their autonomy, or might unduly hamper the defendant's exercise of their autonomy, or might unduly free a plaintiff from the consequences of the exercise of their autonomy.

These two features play an important part in the law of negligence and, as is further discussed in Chapters 12 and 15, the requirement that each person is expected to take some responsibility for their own safety is raised not only at the duty stage of a negligence case. These principles are also weighed in the balance when the element of *breach* is assessed and they re-emerge in a different guise at the *defence* stage, where the defence of voluntary assumption of risk allows the defendant to avoid liability for their negligence if the plaintiff has voluntarily assumed the legal liability for a particular risk of harm. This principle is relevant to the provisions on obvious risk in the civil liability legislation; this is also discussed in Chapter 15. So, as you will see, liability may not be imposed in cases where the plaintiff has consciously engaged in conduct that carries an obvious physical risk, including risky sports and dangerous recreational pursuits (eg diving or rugby), on the grounds that they must take personal responsibility for the consequences of their own autonomous choices.

Case examples

- *Mulligan v Coffs Harbour City Council* (2005), a diving case
- *Romeo v Conservation Commission (NT)* (1998), a case where the plaintiff fell off a cliff late at night after drinking at a party
- *Agar v Hyde* (2000), a case about playing rugby
- *Woods v Multi-Sport Holdings Pty Ltd* (2002), an indoor cricket case, where Gleeson CJ at [40] said:

> In some cases ... a court is not confronted with a risk that is quite unlikely to occur; it is dealing with an activity which carries with it the possibility of injury, including serious injury, in a number of different forms. The appellant was not a child, and he was not being compelled to play the game. He was an adult who chose, for his personal enjoyment, to play. That the activity is risky is plain to anyone who understands what it involves, including the respondent.

Autonomy and personal responsibility have been used in a wide variety of cases, as you will see in Chapter 14, including cases dealing with failure to rescue, compulsive gamblers, pure mental harm, pure economic loss, and advice on material risks of medical treatment.

As the negligence pendulum has swung back towards a more defendant-friendly position, autonomy and personal responsibility have become more prominent in cases that refuse to impose a duty of care. However, the law has traditionally drawn back from imposing liability on two other more general grounds: for example, in circumstances where the suggested rule might create too much *uncertainty* and in cases where the rule might lead to *incoherence* in the law more widely considered. These two features are not unique to tort law. Rather, they are principles of more general application that happen to have a particular bite in the law of negligence – perhaps because negligence itself is so prone to uncertainty and charges of incoherence, as previously discussed.

11.3.9 The salient feature of certainty

As a broad principle, certainty requires that legal rules, which can interfere so greatly with the lives and liberty of individual citizens, must be clear, precise and capable of certain application. In negligence, the salient feature of certainty justifies declining to impose liability if:

- the duty is too uncertain in nature;
- it is impossible to define or comply with; or
- it may lead to liability 'in an indeterminate amount for an indeterminate time to an indeterminate class'.

However, judges have pointed out that it is 'not necessarily fatal to the recognition of a duty of care that the duty is owed to a class whose members cannot be identified with complete accuracy': Gaudron J in *Perre v Apand Pty Ltd* (1999) at [32], citing *Bryan v Maloney* (1995), Mason CJ, Deane and Gaudron JJ at 618, in turn citing Cardozo CJ in *Ultramares Corporation v Touche* (1931) at 444. See also *Sullivan v Moody* (2001) at [61] and *Harriton v Stephens* (2006) at [254].

The feature of certainty (which could also be called the feature of 'uncertainty') gives support to the 'indeterminacy' argument which has been raised in many 'novel' or hard cases in the history of negligence law. If the potential class of plaintiffs cannot be identified, or the duty itself cannot be complied with or defined with sufficient clarity to enable a defendant to anticipate or calculate the likely extent of the risk and their liability – or if that liability may extend without limit – then these matters are all treated as factors that tend against imposing a duty of care. The risk of indeterminate liability was recently restated by Beach J in *Minister for the Environment v Sharma* (2022). However, the mere fact that a defendant's conduct may potentially cause extensive or great harm is not enough to attract the operation of the principle and deny liability. So, you need to remember that the arguments based on certainty should be distinguished from traditional 'floodgates' arguments, which focus on the potential volume of claims, and not on the essential indeterminacy, indefinability or incomprehensibility of the potential liability. You also need to distinguish this usage of 'certainty' from the level of certainty that is required under the burden of proof in a civil case, where plaintiffs do not have to prove their case to a standard of total certainty but must persuade the fact-finder only on the balance of probabilities. In essence, the feature of certainty rules out indefinable liability but not extensive liability.

Case examples

- In *Harriton v Stephens* (2006), where a child who was born with severe congenital disabilities sued her mother's doctor for failing to diagnose the fact that her mother had been exposed to the rubella virus, Crennan J explained at [252] and [254] why the law could not impose a duty of care on the doctor to prevent the child being born disabled:

> A comparison between a life with disabilities and non-existence, for the purposes of proving actual damage and having a trier of fact apprehend the nature of the damage caused, is impossible. [252]
>
> A duty of care cannot be stated in respect of damage which cannot be proved by persons alleging such a duty has been breached, and which cannot be apprehended

> by persons said to be subject to the duty, and which cannot be apprehended or evaluated by a court (or jury). [254]

- See also the judgments of the minority judges in the 'wrongful birth' case of *Cattanach v Melchior* (2003): Gleeson CJ and Hayne and Heydon JJ.

Certainty is also applied in the element of causation (see section 13.1.4 of Chapter 13,) and to the question of damages (see Chapter 17). The fear of uncertainty – or the need for a definite end to litigation – also appears to justify the traditional immunity given to a barrister from a suit in negligence for the conduct, preparation or management of a case for and during a trial.

Case example

In *Giannarelli v Wraith* (1988), Wilson J at 574 stated:

> The common law principle of immunity from civil action for in-court negligence thus derives support from the fundamental principle favouring finality of litigation.

Certainty appears in many cases discussed in Chapter 14, including cases on pure omissions, public authorities, pure psychiatric injury, statements and pure economic loss.

11.3.10 The salient feature of coherence of the law

Closely related to that of certainty is the salient feature of coherence of the law, which is based on the ideal that the decisions made by our judges should be aimed at producing a coherent set of rules that are consistent with previous judicial and legislative decisions and the reasons and goals that underpin them. These decisions, which take place against a backdrop of pre-existing, generally conceived moral and political values, should be ordered into a coherent scheme and applied in a consistent and principled manner.[13] Coherence requires that different parts of the law should not impose contradictory duties on citizens. In other words, the law should speak clearly, consistently, and with one voice. The High Court explained in *Sullivan v Moody* (2001) at [42] that a duty should not be imposed if it undermines the coherence of the law, by subverting 'many other principles of law, and statutory provisions, which strike a balance of rights and obligations, duties and freedoms'.

Case examples

- A duty should not be imposed if it would 'so cut across other legal principles as to impair their proper application' or if it would not be compatible with other duties that the parties owe, or is 'inconsistent with, or [has] a tendency to discourage the due performance' of other duties or responsibilities: *Sullivan v Moody* (2001) at [30], [42], [50], [53]–[55]; *CAL No 14 Pty Ltd v Motor Accidents Insurance Board* (2009), Gummow, Heydon and Crennan JJ at [41]–[42].

13 See MacCormick, *Legal Right and Social Democracy* (1982) at 27–32.

- A duty should not be imposed if the asserted duty of care is inconsistent with the terms, scope and purpose of any relevant statute: *Graham Barclay Oysters Pty Ltd v Ryan* (2002), Gummow and Hayne JJ at [149].

The coherence principle, which has been invoked in many cases since *Sullivan v Moody*, is most often applied at the duty stage and it can also be seen to support many of the categories of immunity from duty (see section 11.2 above).

Case examples

- In *Sullivan v Moody* (2001), a case on the immunity of child protection agencies investigating allegations of abuse, the High Court explained at [55] and [60]:

> More fundamentally, however, these cases present a question about coherence of the law ... A duty of the kind alleged should not be found if that duty would not be compatible with other duties which the respondents owed. [55]
>
> People may be subject to a number of duties, at least provided they are not irreconcilable. A medical practitioner who examines, and reports upon the condition of, an individual, might owe a duty of care to more than one person. But if a suggested duty of care would give rise to inconsistent obligations, that would ordinarily be a reason for denying that the duty exists. Similarly, when public authorities, or their officers, are charged with the responsibility of conducting investigations, or exercising powers, in the public interest, or in the interests of a specified class of persons, the law would not ordinarily subject them to a duty to have regard to the interests of another class of persons where that would impose upon them conflicting claims or obligations. [60]

- In the 'wrongful birth' case of *Cattanach v Melchior* (2003) Callinan J explained at [295]:

> Hitherto, the classes of defendants enjoying immunities have done so essentially for public purposes, and in at least a well understood, if not always unquestioned, public interest. For example the immunity of advocates, of judges, of parliamentarians for various purposes, of the instrumentalities entitled to the shield of the Crown and, until very recently, of highway authorities, fall into this category. [References omitted.]

- In the 'wrongful life' case of *Harriton v Stephens* (2006) Crennan J explained at [249]:

> To superimpose a further duty of care on a doctor to a foetus (when born) to advise the mother so that she can terminate a pregnancy in the interest of the foetus in not being born, which may or may not be compatible with the same doctor's duty of care to the mother in respect of her interests, has the capacity to introduce conflict, even incoherence, into the body of relevant legal principle.

- In the older case of *Giannarelli v Wraith* (1988), Mason CJ at 555 identified one of the sources of a barrister's immunity from a suit in negligence for the conduct, preparation or management of a case for and during a trial:

> The peculiar feature of counsel's responsibility is that he owes a duty to the court as well as to his client. His duty to his client is subject to his overriding duty to the court. In the performance of that overriding duty there is a strong element of public interest.

The necessity to preserve coherence allows the judges to take a progressively wider view, depending on the kind of case. So, in some cases it requires consistency with other duties imposed by the law of *torts* or the law of *contract* or *trusts*; in others it may require consistency with the duties imposed by a legislative regime in a relevant *statute* (especially those governing a public authority); and in others it may require consistency with *criminal law* duties.

Case examples

- In both *Sullivan v Moody* (2001) and *Tame v New South Wales* (2002) – cases on pure psychiatric injury – judges in the High Court held that the proposed duty in negligence would be incompatible with the balance of rights and duties struck by the tort of defamation.
- In *CAL No 14 Pty Ltd v Motor Accidents Insurance Board* (2009), the joint judgment explained at [39]–[42] that the proposed duty on the publican would be incompatible with duties imposed by other torts (including assault, battery and false imprisonment), the law of bailment, the legislative regimes governing the service of alcohol in licensed premises, and the Tasmanian criminal law.
- The joint judgment of French CJ, Gummow, Hayne, Crennan, Kiefel and Bell JJ in *Miller v Miller* (2011) noted at [15] that 'the principles applied in relation to the tort of negligence must be congruent with those applied in other areas of the civil law (most notably contract and trusts)'. This case dealt with the effect of joint illegal enterprise on the duty issue.

11.3.10.1 Role-based coherence

The feature of coherence can also extend to justify what might be called 'role-based' coherence, which requires the judges to respect the distinction between the role properly played by judges and the wider policy-based role played by the legislature. So, when judges refuse to impose liability in negligence on the grounds that the decision would be better made by Parliament, they are maintaining respect for a coherent division of roles among the community's law-making bodies, each of which is entitled to take into account a different set of considerations.

Case examples

- Kirby J explained in *Cattanach v Melchior* (2003) at [137]:

  > The setting of such bounds by a legislature can be arbitrary and dogmatic. Subject to any constitutional restrictions, Parliaments, motivated by political considerations and sometimes responding to the 'echo-chamber inhabited by journalists and public

> moralists', may impose exclusions, abolish common law rules, adopt 'caps' on recovery and otherwise act in a decisive and semi-arbitrary way. Judges, on the other hand, have the responsibility of expressing, refining and applying the common law in new circumstances in ways that are logically reasoned and shown to be a consistent development of past decisional law. Of course, in a general way, judges should take the economic outcomes of their decisions into account. But they have no authority to adopt arbitrary departures from basic doctrine. Least of all may they do so, in our secular society, on the footing of their personal religious beliefs or 'moral' assessments concealed in an inarticulate premise dressed up, and described, as legal principle or legal policy.

- In *Winnipeg Child and Family Services (Northwest Area) v G (DF)* (1997), a Canadian case, McLachlin J explained at [18]–[20] that, while the courts can extend common law principles to suit new circumstances, they will not extend the common law 'where the revision is major and its ramifications complex':

> There are sound reasons supporting this judicial reluctance to dramatically recast established rules of law. The court may not be in the best position to assess the deficiencies of the existing law, much less problems which may be associated with the changes it might make. The court has before it a single case; major changes in the law should be predicated on a wider view of how the rule will operate in the broad generality of cases. Moreover, the court may not be in a position to appreciate fully the economic and policy issues underlying the choice it is asked to make. Major changes to the law often involve devising subsidiary rules and procedures relevant to their implementation, a task which is better accomplished through consultation between courts and practitioners than by judicial decree. Finally, and perhaps most importantly, there is the long-established principle that in a constitutional democracy it is the legislature, as the elected branch of government, which should assume the major responsibility for law reform.

- In *Minister for the Environment v Sharma* (2022), Allsop CJ explained at [246]:

> [Matters of] high policy-making ... are not only the natural province of the Executive and Parliament, but also ... comprise the foundation of the (public or political) duty of consideration and policy formulation by at least the Executive on this subject.

The menu of public 'goods' or goals available to judges and politicians does overlap, and there is no clear borderline separating the public goods that a judge may legitimately take into account and those which are best left to politicians to introduce. However, while all would agree that imposing thresholds or caps on damages awards is beyond the legitimate reach of judges (even allowing that it might give rise to a socially or economically desirable outcome), there are some issues, such as the award of damages for the birth of a healthy but unplanned child after a failed sterilisation procedure, that divide judges, as the case of *Cattanach v Melchior* (2003) showed. The same goes with the future harm that may be caused to current and future generations of children by the decision of the executive branch that will have an impact on climate change, as in *Minister for the Environment v Sharma* (2022).

The same case exemplifies how maintaining respect for a coherent distribution of roles between the judiciary and the other branches of government leads judges to refuse to make decisions that would intrude on the policy-making role of government. This is often the case when decisions might interfere with budgetary matters or force government authorities to redirect public expenditure. Such matters are traditionally seen as political issues that require a different kind of balancing of public priorities and goals and so this discretion is one that the courts are not generally willing to interfere with. But be aware that courts make a distinction between policy issues and 'operational' matters in the liability of public authorities, the latter being challengeable. This is further discussed in Chapter 14.

11.3.10.2 Goal-based coherence

The ideal of coherence also allows judges to take into account wider community goals, shared values and common community interests like the free communication of opinion, wisdom and experience, the maintenance of security, public safety and other 'good' things.

Case examples

- Brennan J, in *San Sebastian Pty Ltd v Minister Administering the Environmental Planning and Assessment Act 1979* (1986) at 272, suggested that one of the reasons judges had been slow to impose a duty of care in negligent misstatement cases was to maintain the value of free communication:

  > To impose a legal duty of care on the unsolicited and voluntary giving of any information and advice on serious or business matters would *chill communications* which are a valuable source of wisdom and experience for a person contemplating a course of conduct. [Emphasis added.]

- In *Shaw Savill & Albion Co Ltd v Commonwealth* (1940), Dixon J explained at 361 that to impose civil liability for negligence during 'all active operations against the enemy in time of warfare' is 'opposed alike to reason and to policy'. Starke J said at 355–6:

  > In my judgment, there is no doubt that the Executive Government and its officers must conduct operations of war, whether naval, military, or in the air, without the control or interference of the courts of law. Acts done in the course of such operations are not justiciable and the courts of law cannot take cognizance of them.

Some of these shared public values, such as the value of autonomy and freedom of action, are so important that they have achieved the status of stand-alone principles; but others, such as maintaining public order, can be dealt with under the broader umbrella of coherence.

11.3.11 Principles, salient features, and their limits

The law of negligence needs limits, but it is not obvious where those limits should be drawn. After acknowledging that there is no definitive test for imposing or limiting the duty of care, the High Court has turned towards identifying salient features that can assist in deciding these questions and has developed a step-by-step methodology for dealing with the problem posed by the challenging tort of negligence. Many of these features will come into high relief when we look at the 'novel' cases; however, if you read any of the leading negligence cases, you will see that these features also support many of the (now) uncontroversial existing categories of negligence. They assist the judges to construct a balanced set of rules that can shield the vulnerable and secure our protection from unreasonably caused harm, while at the same time protecting many of our most fundamental interests in autonomy and freedom of action.

The features highlighted in this chapter are prominent patterns in the case law that ensure the law of negligence has a sound principled basis upon which it can evolve. They provide us with a useful menu of arguments to use in the difficult cases that fall at the boundaries of negligence, and, to the extent that they have replaced the older 'foreseeability plus proximity' test and excluded the resort to overt policy-based justifications, they represent an advance in negligence theory. But whether they can provide us with a predictable and certain body of rules is another question. Principles and salient features are at best vague guides, which often point us in different directions. They must be weighed in the balance, and hard choices must be made when they conflict. So the step taken in *Sullivan v Moody* (2001) has taken us forward, but the fact that the new approach to recognising new duty categories focuses so strongly on principled analogies means that we may not have reached our final destination. In the recent High Court decision in *Mallonland Pty Ltd v Advanta Seeds Pty Ltd* (2024), Edelman J in his separate judgment foreshadowed the possibility of a new approach to establishing duties in novel scenarios - one that is less reliant on salient features and more narrowly confined to incrementalism.

Like the 'neighbour principle' that they supplement, the features of vulnerability, certainty, coherence, autonomy and personal responsibility (and please note that these are just the most common ones - the list is not closed!) are not in and of themselves capable of providing us with a clear source of limits on this expanding tort. To find this source of limits we will need to look further. One suggestion, made by Allan Beever in *Rediscovering the Law of Negligence* (2007), is to focus on the nature of negligence as a system of corrective justice that is based on protecting our primary rights.[14] Beever concludes at 512–4 that this conception of negligence can provide us with a 'simple and elegant account of a kind of moral responsibility' that can 'determine liability without any appeal to policy whatever'. Beever's solution, which resolves the problem of finding a principled source of limits by focusing on the tort's essential and enduring structure as corrective justice, is indeed elegant and rewarding to read. It also rules out some of the extensions of the law of negligence made by the High Court, and therefore provides us with a stimulating source of critique of the current state of Australian negligence law that warrants careful attention. By contrast, Harold Luntz and Christian Witting have both made the opposite argument that *some* degree of policy-based reasoning, particularly in

14 See also Stevens, who argues in *Torts and Rights* (2007) that the law of torts is not a 'free-standing subject' but is rather a mechanism for vindicating primary rights.

difficult decisions that reach the High Court, is a logical inevitability, as noted in Chapter 10. The very nature of negligence, which requires courts to assess when losses should shift from wrongdoer to victim, is imbued with inner conflict between the search for fairness and justice in the individual case and the broader quest for social justice. It is a conflict that may very well never be entirely resolved.

In Chapters 12 and 13 we will look into the second and third elements of negligence: breach and causation. We will return to the key salient features identified in this chapter in Chapter 14 where we will look at their application in a series of special topics of negligence. As the 'pendulum' of negligence swung towards greater protection for plaintiffs over the 20th century, some of the previous categories of immunity and some of the older rules that restricted the kinds of harm for which liability was available were relaxed. The most important thing to note about these special rules and categories of immunity (and the exceptions to them that qualify and limit the immunity) is that they are, like much of the law on duty of care, subject to change if a meritorious case arises and if, in light of the relevant principles and salient features, a court can be persuaded to develop the law in a different direction. So, just as the recognised categories of negligence are 'never closed', the immunities and the 'no duty' categories are, likewise, not set in stone.

Where a case does not fall clearly within one of the recognised duty categories (or perhaps if a case appears to be ruled out by one of the traditional immunities, but the immunity rule is in need of modification), the approach currently favoured by Australian courts involves applying the broad foreseeability test as developed by Lord Atkin in *Donoghue v Stevenson*. Further, it involves curtailing the excessively expansive nature of that test by identifying the factual similarities and differences between the new case and previous cases that have both allowed and denied liability, as outlined in *Sullivan v Moody* (2001). Taking those positive and negative indicators or 'salient features' into account, the aim is to construct an argument that balances relevant principles and features to generate a coherent development in the law. An important limitation of this approach is that it risks curtailing the ability of the tort to adapt to fast-changing societal circumstances.

Case to remember

Minister for the Environment v Sharma (2022)

Climate change litigation is one of the contemporary societal developments that is pushing the boundaries of tort law globally. Climate change challenges the tenets of negligence across all elements, from duty of care down to causation and scope of liability. The decision in *Minister for the Environment v Sharma* (2022) by the Full Court of the Federal Court provides an excellent example of the inherent difficulties encountered by the tort of negligence as it currently stands in Australia when confronting a wicked problem like climate change. We will continue our exploration of this tort in Chapters 12, 13 and 14, which discuss breach, causation and the liability of public authorities respectively. For now, it is important to get a sense of the facts and main arguments for and against the finding of a duty of care – the process is revealing of the limitations of the approach to establishing duties in novel fact scenarios described in this chapter.

Facts

The case is an appeal from *Sharma v Minister for the Environment* (2021),[15] in which Bromberg J in the Federal Court handed down a historic decision in the first climate change negligence claim raised in Australia. The claim was commenced in connection with a coal mine expansion. Vickery Coal Pty Ltd had applied to significantly expand the scope of an existing mining approval in regional New South Wales. Due to its environmental implications, under the *Environment Protection and Biodiversity Conservations Act 1999* (Cth) (*EPBCA*), the proposal could not proceed without the explicit approval of the Minister for the Environment. At this point, eight children initiated a representative class action seeking an injunction to stop the Minister from breaching what they identified as a duty of care in negligence. Specifically, the alleged duty was one owed by the Minister to exercise her function in a way that would avoid causing harm to the children in the form of mental and physical harm, economic harm, and property damage, which was likely to arise in the future as a consequence of climate change.

Decision at first instance

Bromberg J was persuaded that a duty should be owed by the Minister as claimed by the plaintiffs. The reasoning encompassed acknowledgement that it should be reasonably foreseeable to the Minister that her action (in this case the approval of the coal mine expansion) would cause future harm to the children. The other factors, or salient features, that weighed in favour of this finding follow familiar patterns described in this chapter. In essence, the Minister was found to have *knowledge* of the risk of harm stemming from climate change (at [286]) and the [*EPBCA*] placed her in a position of *control* in respect of the source of risk of that harm (at [284]), as she was to make a positive decision with regard to the approval. The children were *vulnerable* due to their powerlessness and inability to protect themselves from the prospective harm (at [296]) and they were *reliant* on the Minister to protect them (at [299]).

The heavy moral undertones of the judgment became explicit at [293] and [312] where Bromberg J reflected on the core issues at stake, prompting him to find a duty of care should be owed by the Minister:

> *It is difficult to characterise in a single phrase the devastation that the plausible evidence presented in this proceeding forecasts for the Children.* As Australian adults know their country, Australia will be lost and the World as we know it gone as well. The physical environment will be harsher, far more extreme and devastatingly brutal when angry. As for the human experience – quality of life, opportunities to partake in nature's treasures, the capacity to grow and prosper – all will be greatly diminished. Lives will be cut short. Trauma will be far more common and good health harder to hold and maintain. None of this will be the fault of nature itself. *It will largely be inflicted by the inaction of this generation of adults, in what might fairly be described as the greatest inter-generational injustice ever inflicted by one generation of humans upon the next.* [At [296]; emphasis added.]

15 The formal citation is *Sharma by her litigation representative Sister Marie Brigid Arthur v Minister for the Environment* [2021] FCA 560.

> They bear no responsibility for the unparalleled predicament which they now face. *That innocence is also deserving of recognition and weight in a consideration of the relationship between the children and the government they look to for protection.* [At [312]; emphasis added.]

Decision on appeal

The Full Court of the Federal Court overturned Bromberg J's decision at first instance. In three separate judgments, Allsop CJ, Beach J and Wheelahan J found insurmountable obstacles to the finding of a duty of care owed by the Minister. Allsop CJ considered the risk of harm resulting from approving the coal mine extension to be reasonably foreseeable (at [300]–[333]), but considered that the relationship between the children and the Minister was that of 'the governing with the governed', and therefore not one giving rise to a duty of care in negligence (at [266]). He implicitly engaged with the idea of 'role-based coherence', as discussed above, to emphasise that questions of high policy exceed the remit of the judicial role (at [246]). He also found that a duty of care in negligence would be inconsistent with the statutory purpose of the *EPBCA* (at [267]–[268]) for the following reason: 'The duty would create a form of mandatory consideration beyond the considerations in respect of the decision in question provided for by the EPBC Act on its proper construction. The EPBC Act does not contain as an overall purpose the safety of human life.'

Beach J emphasised the insufficient 'closeness', whether temporal, geographical or causal, between the Minister and the children as an ascertainable class of people that could 'reasonably be considered to be "so closely and directly affected" by any act of the Minster with respect to her exercise of statutory power in the present context' (at [701]). In addition to this lack of closeness, Beach J also highlighted the risk of indeterminate liability attached to the finding of a duty in the case (at [704]). He reasoned along similar lines as Allsop CJ's finding that there was no 'special vulnerability' characterising the relationship between the Minister and the children as opposed to the general population, and therefore no real way to confine the class of potential plaintiffs.

Wheelahan J, in addition to reiterating issues of coherence and indeterminacy raised by Allsop CJ and Beach J, went one step further. He highlighted that '[r]easonable foreseeability of injury is not just a salient feature: it is a necessary element of a duty of care' (at [869]), and on that basis proceeded to explain why he was not persuaded it would be reasonably foreseeable that the approval of the coal mine extension would cause personal injury to the children given the current understanding of causation in negligence. This judgment is worth reading as it exemplifies how the tort of negligence exists as a whole, despite being analytically divided into the three distinct elements of duty, breach and causation. You cannot have a cause of action without a foreseeable and recognisable harm, something that is normally addressed at the stage of causation, as discussed in Chapter 13. In complex cases courts sometimes will make a decision at the duty stage if it transpires that the harm is either unforeseeable or not cognisable at law (contrast Wheelahan's reasoning with that of Crennan J in *Harriton v Stephens* (2006)).

While both the first instance and appellate decisions are long judgments, the *Sharma* litigation is worth reading to understand the complexities of negligence, and how difficult it can be to neatly distinguish matters of principle from matters of policy.

11.3.12 Summary points

11.3.12.1 The methodology of balance

In addition to the neighbour principle as established in *Donoghue v Stevenson* (1932), which continues to apply and set the broad test of foreseeability, the methodology of balance set down in *Sullivan v Moody* (2001) involves the following steps:

1. Consider the common characteristics in established categories - see [51].
2. Consider the negative indicators present in the 'no duty' categories - see [53].
3. Identify and balance the relevant salient features - see [49] and [53]; and section 11.3.6 above.
4. Ensure that any new step presents a coherent development of compatible legal duties in the law, more widely considered - see [54]–[55] and section 11.3.6 above.

The **positive** indicators that might justify imposing a duty include the following:

- The case exhibits features that are similar or analogous to the features that characterise the established cases.
- There is a relationship of proximity between the parties in a physical, temporal, circumstantial or causal sense.
- The plaintiffs are vulnerable to the defendants in the special legal sense that they cannot otherwise protect themselves - for example, because of the presence of one or more of the following characteristics:
  - reliance by the plaintiff and an assumption of responsibility by the defendant;
  - the defendant has special control over matters affecting the plaintiff; or
  - the defendant has knowledge of matters affecting the plaintiff.
- The duty would support or assist the plaintiff in exercising their autonomy or encourage the taking by the plaintiff or the defendant of personal responsibility for their own choices and conduct.
- The duty would aid the free communication of opinion, wisdom and experience; the maintenance of security; public safety; and/or any other shared community goals.

The **negative** indicators that point against imposing a duty include the following:

- The case exhibits similar features to those characterising the cases of immunity where a duty has been denied.
- The facts of the case do not exhibit a sufficient degree of control over the source of harm on the part of the defendant.
- The duty would interfere unduly with the autonomy or personal freedom of action or speech of one of the parties.
- The duty would derogate from the principle of personal responsibility.
- The duty would create indeterminate liability, uncertainty or undue difficulty in defining and complying with the duty or in measuring the damages.
- The duty would lead to incoherence or inconsistency in the duties imposed by the law - for example, if it:

    - would cut across other legal principles or impair their proper application;
    - would discourage the due performance of other duties or responsibilities imposed by the law of torts, contract, equity or the criminal law; or
    - is inconsistent with the terms, scope and purpose of any relevant statute.
- The proposed change in the law would be better made by Parliament or the executive because of its policy implications and would therefore preserve a coherent division of roles among the community's law-making bodies.
- The duty would impair: the free communication of opinion, wisdom and experience; the maintenance of security; public safety; and/or any other shared community goals.

Active reading

Link each of these summary points to a case authority in section 11.3 above.

Test your understanding and develop your skills

Arguments, counterarguments and their application

Exercise 1

Using the key salient features in negligence in section 11.3.6 above as a guide, make a list of arguments and counterarguments that could be raised in a case where a child, who has been born disabled because of her mother's drug abuse during pregnancy, sues the mother for damages.

Exercise 2

Read the case of *CAL No 14 Pty Ltd v Motor Accidents Insurance Board* (2009).

- Read section 15.9 of Chapter 15 and use the tips provided in that section as a guide to write a 'six-point plan' that introduces the facts and issues in the case.
- Using the key salient features in negligence in section 11.3.6 above as a guide, classify the arguments discussed by the judges in the case.

How might those arguments differ if:

- Mr Scott had been encouraged to 'drink up and have some fun' by the barman, who pressed drinks upon him?
- Mr Scott showed visible signs of extreme drunkenness and fell down several times while wheeling the motorcycle out of the storeroom?
- the publican knew that Mr Scott had been previously convicted of driving under the influence of alcohol and had been involved in several motorbike accidents?

Exercise 3

Read the facts of *Robinson v Chief Constable of West Yorkshire Police* (2018).

- Using the key salient features in negligence in section 11.3.6 above as a guide, map the arguments that could inform the reasoning of the High Court in a hypothetically similar case.

Conclusion

Duty of care is the entry point of negligence, and its key limiting factor. For someone to be held liable in negligence, they must first have owed a duty of care to the plaintiff. The issue of duty is often resolved by way of analogy, relying on established categories of duties that emerge from the case law. It is uncontroversial that road users owe a duty of care to fellow road users, or that manufacturers owe a duty to consumers, or that occupiers owe a duty to entrants, etc. Remember though that duties are always of a limited scope. So while the existence of established categories is not controversial, their scope can come into question depending on the circumstances.

When there is no established category to rely on, courts will establish a duty of care based on the mechanism devised by the High Court in *Sullivan v Moody* (2001). Provided that the foreseeability requirement of the 'neighbour principle' is satisfied, they will rely on 'salient features' to justify whether or not a duty should be found.

The element of duty focuses on the relationship between the plaintiff and the defendant, thereby answering a question of law. The next chapter is dedicated to the element of breach, which focuses on the conduct of the defendant (and to a lesser extent of the plaintiff), thereby answering a question of fact.

REFERENCES

CASES

Adeels Palace Pty Ltd v Moubarak (2009) 239 CLR 420
Agar v Hyde (2000) 201 CLR 216
Alexandrou v Oxford [1993] 4 All ER 328
Alpine Holdings Pty Ltd v Feinauer [2008] WASCA 85
Anns v Merton LBC (1978) AC 728
Arthur JS Hall & Co (a firm) v Simons [2002] 1 AC 615
Astley v Austrust (1999) 197 CLR 1
Atwells v Jackson Lalic Lawyers Pty Ltd (2016) 259 CLR 1
Australian Capital Territory v Crowley (2012) 7 ACTLR 142
Australian Safeway Stores v Zaluzna (1987) 162 CLR 479
Badenach v Calvert (2016) 257 CLR 440
Bankstown Foundry Pty Ltd v Braistina (1986) 160 CLR 301
Bondi Beach Foods Pty Ltd v Chadwick [2023] NSWCA 265
Brighten v Traino [2019] NSWCA 168

Brodie v Singleton Shire Council (2001) 206 CLR
Brookfield Multiplex Ltd v Owners Corporation Strata Plan 61288 (2014) 254 CLR 185
Bryan v Maloney (1995) 182 CLR 609
Burnie Port Authority v General Jones Pty Ltd (1994) 179 CLR 520
CAL No 14 Pty Ltd v Motor Accidents Insurance Board (2009) 239 CLR 390
Caltex Oil (Australia) Pty Ltd v The Dredge 'Willemstad' (1976) 136 CLR 529
Caparo Industries plc v Dickman (1990) 2 AC 605
Capital & Counties plc v Hampshire City Council [1997] QB 1004
Cattanach v Melchior (2003) 215 CLR 1
Chamberlains v Lai [2007] 2 NZLR 7
Chapman v Hearse (1961) 106 CLR 112
Chomentowski v Red Garter Restaurant (1970) 92 WN (NSW) 1070
City of Kamloops v Nielsen [1984] 2 SCR 2
Clark v University of Lincolnshire and Humberside [2000] 3 All ER 752
Cole v South Tweed Heads Rugby League Football Club Ltd (2004) 217 CLR 469
Commonwealth v Introvigne (1982) 150 CLR 258
Cook v Cook (1986) 162 CLR 376
Cooper v Hobart [2001] 3 SCR 537
Costello v Chief Constable of Northumbria Police [1999] ICR 752; [1999] 1 All ER 550
Couch v Attorney-General [2008] NZSC 45, [2008] 3 NZLR 275
Cran v State of New South Wales (2004) 62 NSWLR 95
Crimmins v Stevedoring Industry Finance Committee (1999) 200 CLR 1
Czatyrko v Edith Cowan University (2005) 214 ALR 349
D'Orta-Ekenaike v Victoria Legal Aid (2005) 223 CLR 1
Dobson (Litigation Guardian of) v Dobson [1999] 2 SCR 753; (1999) 174 DLR (4th) 1
Donoghue v Stevenson [1932] AC 562
Elguzouli-Daf v Commissioner of Police [1995] QB 335
Ellis v Wallsend District Hospital (1989) 17 NSWLR 553
Esanda Finance Corporation Ltd v Peat Marwick Hungerfords (1997) 188 CLR 241
Ethicon Sàrl v Gill (2021) 288 FCR 338
Gala v Preston (1991) 172 CLR 243
GEO Group Australia Pty Limited v O'Connor [2019] NSWCA 323
Geyer v Downs (1977) 138 CLR 91
Giannarelli v Wraith (1988) 165 CLR 543
Goldman v Hargrave (1966) 115 CLR 458; [1967] 1 AC 645
Graham Barclay Oysters Pty Ltd v Ryan (2002) 211 CLR 540
Graham v Welch [2012] QCA 282
Grant v Australian Knitting Mills Ltd [1936] AC 85
Griffith University v Tang (2005) 221 CLR 99
Groves v Commonwealth (1982) 150 CLR 113
Hahn v Conley (1971) 126 CLR 276
Hamilton v Nuroof (1956) 96 CLR 18
Hargrave v Goldman (1963) 110 CLR 40
Harriton v Stephens (2006) 226 CLR 52

Hawkins v Clayton (1988) 164 CLR 539
Heaven v Pender (1883) 11 QBD 503
Hill v Chief Constable of West Yorkshire [1989] AC 53
Hill v Van Erp (1997) 188 CLR 159
Hobbs v Petersham Transport Co (1971) 124 CLR 220
Home Office v Dorset Yacht Co Ltd [1970] AC 1004
Howard v Jarvis (1958) 98 CLR 177
Hunter and New England Local Health District v McKenna (2014) 253 CLR 270
Imbree v McNeilly (2008) 236 CLR 567
Jaensch v Coffey (1984) 155 CLR 549
Jones v Bartlett (2000) 205 CLR 166
Karpik v Carnival plc (The Ruby Princess) [2023] FCA 1280
Kendirjian v Lepore (2017) 259 CLR 275
Kent v Griffith [2001] 1 QB 36
Koehler v Cerebos (Australia) Ltd (2005) 222 CLR 44
Kondis v State Transport Authority (1984) 154 CLR 672
Kozarov v Victoria (2023) 273 CLR 115
Kuhl v Zurich Financial Services Australia Ltd (2011) 243 CLR 361
Le Lievre v Gould [1893] 1 QB 491
Lynch v Lynch (1991) 25 NSWLR 411
Mallonland Pty Ltd v Advanta Seeds Pty Ltd [2024] HCA 25; (2024) 418 ALR 639
Midland Bank v Hett, Stubbs and Kemp (1979) Ch 384
Miller v Miller (2011) 242 CLR 446
Minister for the Environment v Sharma (2022) 291 FCR 311
Modbury Triangle Shopping Centre Pty Ltd v Anzil (2000) 205 CLR 254
Mulligan v Coffs Harbour City Council (2005) 223 CLR 486
Neindorf v Junkovic [2005] HCA 75; (2005) 80 ALJR 341; (2005) 222 ALR 631
New South Wales v Bujdoso (2005) 227 CLR 1
New South Wales v Fahy (2007) 232 CLR 486
New South Wales v Godfrey (2004) Aust Torts Reports 81-741
Northern Sandblasting Pty Ltd v Harris (1997) 188 CLR 313
OLL Ltd v Secretary of State for Transport [1997] 3 All ER 897
Osborne Park Commercial Pty Ltd v Miloradovic (2019) 54 WAR 1
Palsgraf v Long Island Railway Co, 248 NY 339; 162 NE 99 (1928)
Perre v Apand Pty Ltd (1999)198 CLR 180
Pitt Son & Badgery Ltd v Proulefco (1984) 153 CLR 644
Pyrenees Shire Council v Day (1998) 192 CLR 330
Ramsay v Larsen (1964) 111 CLR 16
Roads and Traffic Authority (NSW) v Dederer (2007) 234 CLR 330
Robinson Helicopter Company Inc v McDermott (2016) 337 ALR 550
Robinson v Chief Constable of West Yorkshire Police [2018] AC 736
Rogers v Whitaker (1992) 175 CLR 479
Roman Catholic Church Trustees for the Diocese of Canberra and Goulburn v Hadba (2005) 221 CLR 161

Romeo v Conservation Commission (NT) (1998) 192 CLR 431
San Sebastian Pty Ltd v Minister Administering the Environmental Planning and Assessment Act 1979 (1986) 162 CLR 340
Sharma by her litigation representative Sister Marie Brigid Arthur v Minister for the Environment [2021] FCA 560
Shaw Savill & Albion Co Ltd v Commonwealth (1940) 66 CLR 344
Simmonds-Thatcher v Kamari [2021] VSCA 133
Smith v Charles Baker & Sons [1891] AC 325
Smith v Leurs (1945) 70 CLR 256
Smith v Littlewoods Ltd [1987] AC 241
Smith v Ministry of Defence [2014] 1 AC 52
South Australia v Lampard-Trevorrow [2010] SASC 56; (2010) 106 SASR 331
Stevens v Brodribb Sawmilling Co Pty Ltd (1986) 160 CLR 16
Stuart v Kirkland-Veenstra (2009) 237 CLR 215
Sullivan v Moody (2001) 207 CLR 562
Sutherland Shire Council v Heyman (1985) 157 CLR 424
Swan (By His Next Friend) v South Australia (1994) 62 SASR 532
Sydney Water Corporation v Turano (2009) 239 CLR 51
Tame v New South Wales (2002) 211 CLR 317
Thompson v Woolworths (Qld) Pty Ltd (2005) 221 CLR 234
Thomson v London University (1864) 33 L J Ch 625
Thorne v University of London [1966] 2 QB 237
Ultramares Corporation v Touche 255 NY 170 (174 NE 441) (1931)
Vairy v Wyong Shire Council (2005) 223 CLR 422
Victoria v Bryar (1970) 44 ALJR 174
Waller v James (2015) 90 NSWLR 634
Watt v Rama [1972] VR 353
Williams v Eady (1893) 10 TLR 41
Winnipeg Child and Family Services (Northwest Area) v G (DF) [1997] 3 SCR 925
Woods v Multi-Sport Holdings Pty Ltd (2002) 208 CLR 460
Woolcock Street Investments Pty Ltd v CDG Pty Ltd (2004) 216 CLR 515
X and Y (By Her Tutor X) v Pal (1991) 23 NSWLR 26
X v South Australia (No 2) (2005) 91 SASR 258
X v South Australia (No 3) (2007) 97 SASR 180

ARTICLES, BOOKS AND REPORTS

Beever, A, *Rediscovering the Law of Negligence* (2007) Hart Publishing, Oxford.
Davies, M & Malkin, I, *Focus: Torts*, 10th ed (2024) LexisNexis, Sydney.
Dietrich, J, 'Duty of Care under the "Civil Liability Acts"' (2005) 13 *Torts Law Journal* 17.
Fairgrieve, D & Goldberg, R, *Product Liability*, 3rd ed (2020) Oxford University Press, Oxford.
Goudkamp, J, 'Breach of Duty: A Disappearing Element of the Action in Negligence?' (2017) 76(3) *The Cambridge Law Journal* 480
Handford, P & McGivern, B, 'Two problems of Occupiers' Liability – Part One: The Occupiers' Liability Acts and the Common Law' (2015) 39 *Melbourne University Law Review* 128.

Handford, P & McGivern, B, 'Two problems of Occupiers' Liability – Part Two: The Occupiers' Liability and Civil Liability Legislation (2015) 39 *Melbourne University Law Review* 507.

Holmes, O W, *The Common Law* (1881) Little, Brown and Co, Boston.

Howarth, D, 'Many Duties of Care – or a Duty of Care? Notes from the Underground' (2006) 26 *Oxford Journal of Legal Studies* 449.

Ipp, D, 'Policy and the Swing of the Negligence Pendulum' (2003) 77 *Australian Law Journal* 732.

Ipp, D, Cane, P, Sheldon, D & Macintosh, I, *Review of the Law of Negligence: Final Report* (2002) <https://treasury.gov.au/review/review-of-the-law-of-negligence>.

Luntz, H, 'The Use of Policy in Negligence Case in the High Court of Australia', in Bryan, M (ed) *Private Law in Theory and Practice* (2007) Routledge, London, 55

Luntz, H, Hambly, D, Burns, K, Dietrich, J, Foster, N, Grant, G & Harder, S, *Torts: Cases and Commentary,* 8th ed (2017) LexisNexis Butterworths, Sydney.

MacCormick, N, *Legal Right and Social Democracy* (1982) Clarendon Press, Oxford.

McBride, N, 'Duties of Care: Do They Really Exist?' (2004) 24 *Oxford Journal of Legal Studies* 417.

Oliphant, K, 'Rationalising Tort Law for the Twenty-First Century', in Barker, K, Fairweather, K & Grantham, R (eds), *Private Law in the 21st Century* (2017) Hart Publishing, Oxford, 67.

Paterson, J M, *Corones' Australian Consumer Law,* 5th ed (2023) Thomson Reuters.

Plunkett, J, *The Duty of Care in Negligence* (2018) Hart Publishing, Oxford.

Royal Commission into Institutional Responses to Child Sexual Abuse, *Redress and Civil Litigation Report* (2015) <www.childabuseroyalcommission.gov.au/redress-and-civil-litigation>

Stapleton, J, 'Duty of Care Factors: A Selection from the Judicial Menus', in Cane, P & Stapleton, J (eds), *The Law of Obligations: Essays in Celebration of John Fleming* (1998) Clarendon Press, Oxford, 59.

Stapleton, J, 'Duty of Care: Peripheral Parties and Alternative Opportunities for Deterrence' (1995) 111 *Law Quarterly Review* 301.

Stapleton, J, *Product Liability* (1994) Butterworth & Co, London.

Stapleton, J, 'The Golden Thread at the Heart of Tort Law: Protection of the Vulnerable' (2003) 24 *Australian Bar Review* 135.

Stevens, R, *Torts and Rights* (2007) Oxford University Press, Oxford.

Todd, S, 'A Methodology of Duty' in Cane, P (ed), *Centenary Essays for the High Court of Australia* (2004) Butterworths, Sydney, 221.

Witting, C, 'Duty of Care: An Analytical Approach' (2005) 25 *Oxford Journal of Legal Studies* 33.

Witting, C, 'The Three-Stage Test Abandoned in Australia – or Not? (2002) 118 *Law Quarterly Review* 214.

Witting, C, 'Tort Law, Policy and the High Court of Australia' (2007) 31 *Melbourne University Law Review* 22.

Witting, C, 'What Are We Doing Here? The Relationship between Negligence in General and Misstatements in English Law', in Kit Barket, Ross Grantham & Warren Swain (eds), *The Law of Misstatements: 50 Years on from Helder Bryne v Heller* (2015) Hart Publishing, Oxford, 237.

12 NEGLIGENCE: BREACH

Introduction

In this chapter, the element of breach is covered in four sections. Section 12.1 discusses the nature of breach as an element of the tort of negligence – what it is there for and what it covers. Section 12.2 discusses the standard of care – a question of law. Section 12.3 explains what courts take into account to assess the conduct of a defendant – a question of fact. Section 12.4 discusses the ways in which breach of duty can be proved.

Two sets of 'Summary points' summarise the matters that you should take into account when approaching a problem question. They appear at the end of the discussion of the nature and role of breach (section 12.1) and again at the end of the chapter.

Note that these 'Summary points' ask you to engage in an active reading exercise: your task is to link each of the summary points with a case in the section.

12.1 Introducing breach

12.1.1 Breach is the fault element

The element of breach is the fault element. It directs us to consider whether the defendant has acted wrongfully and should be blamed for their conduct. This second element of the tort of negligence requires an assessment: did the defendant respond to a reasonably foreseeable risk of harm to another person by taking the precautions that a reasonable person in their position would have taken in the circumstances existing at the time? Like the element of duty, the element of breach also focuses on the two concepts of reasonableness and foreseeability of the harm that could flow from the defendant's conduct. In the duty element, the essential question is: 'Who is the defendant's neighbour?' – the question focuses on the relationship between plaintiff and defendant. In the element of breach, however, where the courts take a more specific and contextualised approach, the essential question is: 'How should the defendant have treated their neighbour?' – and so the focus moves to the conduct of the defendant. At this point, the court must weigh the relevant facts together to decide whether, on balance, the defendant has met the standard of reasonable care.

Negligence, like all torts, is conduct by one person who wrongfully and unreasonably causes adverse effects on another. The element of breach brings us to the critical point of considering whether a defendant's conduct was unreasonable in the circumstances of the case. The issue of fault in negligence is not determined by asking whether, from a subjective point of view, the defendant *as an individual* has done the best that they could in the circumstances; rather, the tort strives to offer everyone in the community an equal degree of protection by holding each defendant to an objective standard that requires them to do what a reasonable person in their position would have done in response to the risk of harm. As Alderson B pointed out, long before *Donoghue v Stevenson* (1932), in *Blyth v Birmingham Waterworks Co* (1856) at 784, negligence is:

> the omission to do something which a reasonable [person], guided upon those considerations which ordinarily regulate the conduct of human affairs, would do, or doing something which a prudent and reasonable [person] would not do.

The element of breach is the tool that courts use in a negligence claim to assess the conduct of a defendant against the objective parameter known as 'standard of care'. It raises two different issues. The first task involves setting the standard of reasonable care. This is a *question of law* for the judge, so the arguments at this point are based on the rules, principles and policy matters that have been identified in the statutes and cases. This ensures that the judge sets a standard that is in line with the appropriate goals of negligence. These kinds of decisions set a precedent for similar cases in the future, so once the standard of care is set in one specific category of liability, it will generally be applied without too much debate in subsequent cases until the time comes when a judge is persuaded that the law should be changed. In Chapter 14 you will read more about the standard of care for medical practitioners as an example of this kind of development in the law.

The second task is to apply the standard to the facts of the case at hand. This raises a *question of fact* that does not set a precedent for future cases. In jurisdictions where juries are still used in civil cases, this issue is one for the jury who must decide the matter based on the evidence presented by the plaintiff who must prove their case on the civil standard – on the balance of probabilities. In jurisdictions where civil juries have been abolished, the judge, as fact-finder, decides this issue. So, the first task of identifying the standard of care involves looking at any relevant legislation and precedents in previous cases to find out the appropriate level of reasonable care. The second task involves assessing the evidence in the particular case to decide whether the defendant's conduct has either reached that level or fallen below it. This factual analysis takes us back once again to the concept of reasonable foreseeability that we encountered in the element of duty. However, while the focus of reasonable foreseeability in the duty element is on the *persons* who are linked together by a duty of care, the focus of reasonable foreseeability in the element of breach shifts to the *nature of the risks* that the defendant should have responded to and the *kinds of precautions* that they should have taken in response to that risk.

12.1.2 The negligence 'calculus'

The law requires the defendant to comply with an objective standard. Since the Ipp reforms were enacted in the period 2002 to 2004, the law in this area mandates consideration of four factors, three of which were mentioned long ago by an American judge in the case of *United States v Carroll Towing Co* (1947). In that case, Learned Hand J identified at 173 'three variables' that were to be linked by the judge in 'algebraic terms', namely: the probability of the harm occurring (P), the gravity of the injury or harm (L), and the cost or burden of adequate precautions against the risk (B). The 'Hand formula', or 'negligence calculus' as it came to be known, suggested that 'liability depends on whether B is less than L multiplied by P, ie whether B is less than PL' (at 173). While this mathematical *method* has never been accepted in either the English or Australian courts,[1] these *factors* are widely used by the courts (and are now mandated by the civil liability legislation). They were discussed by the famous English authority on torts, Professor R F V Heuston, in an influential article published to mark the 25th anniversary of the birth of negligence, '*Donoghue v Stevenson* in Retrospect' (1957). Heuston's survey of the cases yielded an extra factor, namely the 'comparative social utility of the conduct of both parties' (at 17), and versions of these four factors have now found their way into the new legislation.

The leading Australian common law judgment on the element of breach was delivered by Mason J in the High Court of Australia ('High Court') in the case of *Wyong Shire Council v Shirt* (1980) at 47–8:

> A risk of injury which is quite unlikely to occur ... may nevertheless be plainly foreseeable. Consequently, when we speak of a risk of injury as being 'foreseeable' we are not making any statement as to the probability or improbability of its occurrence, save that we are implicitly asserting that the risk is not one that is far-fetched or fanciful. Although it is true to say that in many cases the greater the degree of probability of the occurrence of the risk the more readily it will be perceived to be a risk, it certainly does not follow that a risk which is unlikely to occur is not foreseeable.
>
> In deciding whether there has been a breach of the duty of care the tribunal of fact must first ask itself whether a reasonable man in the defendant's position would have foreseen that his conduct involved a risk of injury to the plaintiff or to a class of persons including the plaintiff. If the answer be in the affirmative, it is then for the tribunal of fact to determine *what a reasonable man would do by way of response to the risk*. The perception of the reasonable man's

1 See Gilles, 'The Emergence of Cost–Benefit Balancing in English Negligence Law' (2002), and Witting, 'The Hand and *Shirt* Tests of Breach and the Civil Liability Acts' (2009).

> response calls for a consideration of the *magnitude* of the risk and the *degree of the probability* of its occurrence, along with the *expense, difficulty and inconvenience* of taking alleviating action and any other *conflicting responsibilities* which the defendant may have. It is only when these matters are *balanced out* that the tribunal of fact can confidently assert what is the standard of response to be ascribed to the *reasonable man placed in the defendant's position.* [Emphasis added and references omitted.]

The guidance supplied by the '*Shirt* calculus' has been applied in all cases in Australia since 1980, notwithstanding some criticism in *New South Wales v Fahy* (2007) about the appropriateness of the word 'calculus', as Gummow and Hayne JJ said at [57]:

> This approach to questions of breach of duty has come to be known as the '*Shirt* calculus'. The description may be convenient but it may mislead. Reference to 'calculus', 'a certain way of performing mathematical investigations and resolutions', may wrongly be understood as requiring no more than a comparison between what it would have cost to avoid the particular injury that happened and the consequences of that injury. *Shirt* requires a more elaborate inquiry that does not focus only upon how the particular injury happened. It requires *looking forward to identify what a reasonable person would have done, not backward to identify what would have avoided the injury.* [Emphasis added and references omitted.]

A similar criticism of the use of the term 'calculus' had been voiced by Gleeson CJ and Kirby J in *Mulligan v Coffs Harbour City Council* (2005) at [2]:

> A calculus is a method of calculation. What is involved in the process to which Mason J was referring [in *Wyong Shire Council v Shirt* (1980)] *is not a calculation; it is a judgment* ... Moreover, depending upon what may be involved in the concept of conflicting responsibilities, in some contexts ... to treat what was said in *Shirt* as an inflexible formula could produce a distinctly unreasonable result. [Emphasis added.]

Like the common law, the legislation requires judges to determine the issue of breach by considering whether the defendant has taken the precautions that a reasonable person would have taken. The reforms recommended by the Ipp Report were not followed uniformly by the legislatures, so there can be variations of standards and tests applied in different states and territories throughout Australia. The law in this area is a complicated combination of the old common law as modified by the legislation. The precise effect of the civil liability legislation is relatively well understood because the High Court has decided a series of cases dealing with these provisions. Bear in mind, however, as you study the way that these cases have shaped the components of the element of breach, that they might apply only in their own states, and that the lessons learned from any given case will not necessarily assist those bringing similar cases in other jurisdictions where the wording of the statutes is different. So, you need to be careful to check the precise words of your local statute, noting not only any particular definitions, but also any limits on the application of the statutory provisions. This is particularly true for the provisions that cover the standard of care for professionals, which have a significant degree of variation across states.

LEGISLATION ALERT!

Consult your study materials and note the statutory provisions in your jurisdiction on breach.

- Check the definitions section, particularly the definition of negligence (if applicable).
- Note any limits on the application of the statute.

In the Northern Territory the common law in *Wyong Shire Council v Shirt* (1980) still applies.

12.1.2.1 The rule on breach

The rule on breach is very similar under the common law and the civil liability legislation, with a few discrepancies that will be highlighted as we move forward. In all cases, the plaintiff must prove that the defendant's conduct fell short of the standard of reasonable care by adducing evidence showing, on the balance of probabilities, that the defendant failed to take the precautions that a reasonable person in the defendant's position would have taken in the circumstances at the time, in response to a reasonably foreseeable and not insignificant risk of harm. The legislative provisions here, while not identical in each state, are very similar.

Legislative example

***Civil Liability Act 1936* (SA)**

31 - Standard of care

(1) For determining whether a person (the defendant) was negligent, the standard of care required of the defendant is that of a reasonable person in the defendant's position who was in possession of all information that the defendant either had, or ought reasonably to have had, at the time of the incident out of which the harm arose.

32 - Precautions against risk

(1) A person is not negligent in failing to take precautions against a risk of harm unless:

  (a) the risk was foreseeable (that is, it is a risk of which the person knew or ought to have known); and

  (b) the risk was not insignificant; and

  (c) in the circumstances, a reasonable person in the person's position would have taken those precautions.

(2) In determining whether a reasonable person would have taken precautions against a risk of harm, the court is to consider the following (among other relevant things):

  (a) the probability that the harm would occur if precautions were not taken;

(b) the likely seriousness of the harm;

(c) the burden of taking precautions to avoid the risk of harm;

(d) the social utility of the activity that creates the risk of harm.

Note that some states do not have a specific provision explicitly establishing the standard of care, but move directly to the principles governing what a reasonable person would have done in the circumstances.

Legislative example

***Civil Liability Act 2002* (WA)**

5B. General principles

(1) A person is not liable for harm caused by that person's fault in failing to take precautions against a risk of harm unless –

(a) the risk was foreseeable (that is, it is a risk of which the person knew or ought to have known); and

(b) the risk was not insignificant; and

(c) in the circumstances, a reasonable person in the person's position would have taken those precautions.

(2) In determining whether a reasonable person would have taken precautions against a risk of harm, the court is to consider the following (amongst other relevant things) –

(a) the probability that the harm would occur if care were not taken;

(b) the likely seriousness of the harm;

(c) the burden of taking precautions to avoid the risk of harm;

(d) the social utility of the activity that creates the risk of harm.

All of the matters listed by these legislative provisions must be considered; however, the legislation does not provide either an identical list in every jurisdiction, or a completely exhaustive list of all of the things that will be relevant to the balancing exercise that has to be undertaken by the courts. Some statutes also specify some extra rules, and the legislation clearly anticipates that there will be 'other relevant things' a court should take into account. These 'other relevant things', which have been held by the common law cases to be important factors, include: professional or customary standards in any given area of enterprise; relevant statutory standards; and the common law requirement that the defendant must anticipate (to a certain degree) foreseeable carelessness on the part of the plaintiff. This third factor has now been modified by some of the legislative provisions to take account of the principle of personal responsibility – a recent emphasis appearing in both the courts and the parliaments. A court is now entitled to take this principle into account. Plaintiffs should take responsibility for their own choices and conduct by being aware of and responding properly to any inherent and obvious risks. So, to summarise, if we combine all of the legislatively mandated considerations with some of the pre-existing common law factors, there are now several key aspects to any assessment of the element of breach. It is important to consider each of these matters in turn, bearing in mind that the court's aim is not to look back with the wisdom of hindsight in order to hold a defendant liable because they did not do everything necessary to prevent every kind of harm that was in fact suffered by the plaintiff. Rather, the court's task is to put themselves into the position of a reasonable person at the time before the harm occurred, and decide what a reasonable person would have done in the face of the risks that existed at that time, after weighing all of the relevant matters in the balance. These are two very different bases for assessing liability: the first resembles a regime of strict liability for causing harm; the second strives to create a fair and balanced system of fault, as objectively assessed.

12.1.3 Summary points

12.1.3.1 Approaching the breach question

As a preliminary step when you are tackling the element of breach in a problem question, you should ensure that you clearly identify the following:

1. *Who* is the defendant? (there may be more than one in multiparty litigation)
2. *What* is the standard of care for each defendant? (a question of law)
3. *What* is the specific conduct which is to be assessed against the relevant standard(s) of care? (a question of fact)

Active reading

Link each of these summary points to a case in section 12.2.

12.2 The nature of the 'reasonable person'

12.2.1 Characteristics of the 'reasonable person' and variations of the standard

One of the differences between the common law as laid down in *Wyong Shire Council v Shirt* (1980) and the 2002 legislation is the statutory recognition of the change in societal norms and expectations that prompted courts to move from the 'reasonable man' in *Wyong Shire Council v Shirt* to the 'reasonable person'. You can refer back to Chapter 10 on the gender biases of negligence and the critique of the 'maleness' of the reasonable person.

The reasonable man was formerly described in England as the 'man on the Clapham omnibus' or in Australia as a person travelling on the 'Bondi tram' to indicate that the courts should hold the defendant to a standard that is not dictated by reference to the extraordinary, but to a person of 'ordinary intelligence and experience' (*Glasgow*

Corporation v Muir (1943) at 457 (or of 'ordinary prudence' (*Vaughan v Menlove* (1837) at 493). The presumed attributes of this reasonable person were famously listed by Lord Macmillan in *Glasgow Corporation v Muir* (1943) at 457:

> The standard of foresight of the reasonable [person] is, in one sense, an impersonal test. It eliminates the personal equation and is independent of the idiosyncrasies of the particular person whose conduct is in question ... The reasonable [person] is presumed to be free both from over-apprehension and from over-confidence, but there is a sense in which the standard of care of the reasonable [person] involves in its application a subjective element. It is still left to the judge to decide what, in the circumstances of the particular case, the reasonable [person] would have had in contemplation, and what, accordingly, the party sought to be made liable ought to have foreseen. Here there is room for a diversity of view ... What to one judge may seem far-fetched may seem to another both natural and probable.

In *Australian Principles of Tort Law* (2017), Pam Stewart and Anita Stuhmcke argue at 218 that it is 'impossible to formulate rules as to how a reasonable person will behave in all the factual situations' that may come to the attention of courts. While in broad terms the standard of the reasonable person requires individuals to act in their everyday lives as generic 'good citizens', what this means in each individual case is left to the appreciation of the finder of fact. This is as true today as it was in the days of Lord Macmillan.

The legislative shift away from the 'reasonable man' to embrace the 'reasonable person' constitutes a move towards the reduction of structural gender bias in the operation of the law of negligence.[2] However, the issue of bias is more complex. It involves the multiple ways in which judges formulate their understanding of what constitutes the fictitious notion of a reasonable person. Gender is one aspect of bias; another major contributor is the largely monocultural and upper-class nature of the judiciary, as implicitly suggested by Joachim Dietrich and Ian Field in 'The "Reasonable Tort Victim"' (2017). Digging deeper into the issue of potential unconscious biases of decision-makers, Kylie Burns has conducted several studies in which she has identified 'social facts' as a key element of judicial decision-making (see, eg, Burns (2018)). In 'The Australian High Court and Social Facts: A Content Analysis Study' (2012), Burns defines social facts as 'general statements about the nature and behaviour of people and institutions and the nature of society' – and as such, they form part of a broadly shared common sense. She cites, as an early example of a social fact, this observation by Starke J of the High Court in *Australian Knitting Mills Ltd v Grant* (1933) at [409]–[410]:

> Woollen undergarments are commonly used, in Australia and elsewhere ... But untoward results or accidents cannot, with the greatest of care, be wholly eliminated, in any industrial process.

2 See section 10.2 of Chapter 10 and, among others, Wendy Parker, 'The Reasonable Person: A Gendered Concept?' (1993).

While these social facts are not normally predominant in judicial reasoning, they nevertheless inevitably inform such reasoning, particularly in hard cases presenting novel issues. There is therefore a risk that outdated or biased commonsensical notions will influence decisions, particularly where the judiciary is lacking in diversity.

While you should remember these complex issues and read cases and commentaries with a critical eye whenever claims of objectivity are laid out, you should also remember that the law of negligence holds a defendant to a standard based on an ideal *reasonable person*. This standard strives to be as objective as it can by looking into what a *reasonable person in the defendant's position* would have done in the circumstances of the case. There are, however, occasions where some (but not all) of the subjective features of the specific defendant are factored into the assessment. Issues that are often raised include those discussed below.

12.2.1.1 Age of the defendant (children)

The courts will take into account the fact that a child does not have same knowledge and experience as an adult, but you should note that the same allowance is not applied to those of advanced age.

Case examples

- In *McHale v Watson* (1966), a 12-year-old boy injured a nine-year-old girl. He threw a sharpened steel rod at a post that was roughly four feet away from where the girl was standing, but it ricocheted off the post and hit her eye. The judges in the High Court took the boy's lack of maturity into account. He was not held to the standard of an ordinary 'person' but to the standard of an ordinary reasonable child of similar age, with ordinary experience and intelligence.
- Note, however, that the nature of the activity will have an impact on judicial reasoning, and that in some circumstances courts will be less forgiving. In *Zanner v Zanner* (2010), an 11-year-old boy injured his mother while parking her car at home. The boy's foot slipped onto the accelerator and caused the impact. Tobias JA in the New South Wales Court of Appeal stated at [60]:

> The act of negligence in the present case was the failure of [the child] to keep his foot on the brake and to prevent it slipping onto the accelerator. That was not an activity whose importance would be beyond the understanding of an 11 year old.

12.2.1.2 Disabled defendants suffering from mental illness or physical impairment

The courts do not take into account the fact that a person may be suffering from a debilitating mental illness or disability. This approach mirrors the position found in the defences to the intentional torts, as discussed in Chapter 7, and the test used to assess contributory negligence (discussed in section 15.6 of Chapter 15): *Town of Port Hedland v Hodder (No 2)* (2012).

Case example

In *Carrier v Bonham* (2002), D, who suffered from chronic schizophrenia, attempted to throw himself under the bus driven by P, with the result that P suffered PTSD and had to give up his job. All three members of the Queensland Court of Appeal agreed that D's mental illness did not afford a defence to any intentional tort, or to a claim in negligence. McMurdo P said at [8]:

> Whilst a child's actions in a negligence claim can be judged by the objective standard to be expected of an ordinary reasonable child of comparable age, the action of an adult lacking capacity because of mental illness in a negligence claim cannot be similarly judged by any objective standard of an ordinary reasonable person suffering from that mental illness; if the mental illness has deprived the person of capacity then the person has also been deprived of rationality and reasonableness. The standard of care must be the objective standard expected of the ordinary person.

Note that, in the case of a physical impairment suffered by a defendant, a distinction must be drawn. On the one hand, there are existing physical impairments giving rise to a risk to others, which a defendant is aware of – in these cases the person's negligent conduct consists of failing to protect others against such risks, as discussed by Harold Luntz et al in *Torts: Cases and Commentary* (2017) at 230. On the other hand, impairments may arise unexpectedly and suddenly, in circumstances where no reasonable person could have taken precautions against them (eg the case of a motorcyclist who is stung by a wasp and who then crashes into a car). In these situations, the court will decide, in the circumstances of the case, whether or not the defendant had an opportunity to take precautions: *Roberts v Ramsbottom* (1980); *Smith v Lord* (1962); *Scholtz v Standish* (1961).

12.2.1.3 Experience and skill of the defendant (beginners, professionals and specialists)

Ordinary people are not expected to have special knowledge or advanced skills, so if a plaintiff has agreed to employ a defendant knowing that they possess only a particular level of skill, the defendant will not necessarily be held to a higher standard.

Case examples

- As Latham CJ explained at 46 in *Insurance Commissioner v Joyce* (1948) and Mason, Wilson, Deane and Dawson JJ noted at 382 in *Cook v Cook* (1986), if a person were to ask a blacksmith, rather than a jeweller, to repair a watch, then the blacksmith would not be held to the standard of a watchmaker's skill, though he would be held to the standard of the ordinary skilled blacksmith repairing a watch.
- In the case of *Philips v William Whitely Ltd* (1938), a woman asked a jeweller in a department store to pierce her ears. Following the method that he had used about 150 times before, the jeweller washed his hands, disinfected the needle and passed it through a flame, but he did not sterilise it in the same way that a doctor would have done. After the plaintiff developed

an infected abscess in her neck, she sued, arguing that the jeweller should have conformed to the same standard as a doctor, but she was unsuccessful because the jeweller was not to be held to the higher standard that would be applied to a doctor, but only to the ordinary standard expected of a jeweller.

If a person who is inexperienced decides to undertake an ordinary activity that requires ordinary care and skill, then their inexperience will not necessarily be factored into the attributes of the 'reasonable person'. The case of *Cook v Cook* (1986) decided that an inexperienced learner driver, who crashed into a telegraph pole after being encouraged by the plaintiff to drive, would be held to the standard of an ordinary *learner* driver. However, the High Court's decision in *Imbree v McNeilly* (2008) overturned the decision in *Cook v Cook* (1986) and decided that learner drivers should be held to the same standard of care as any other ordinary reasonable driver on the road. Gummow, Hayne and Kiefel JJ said at [53] that 'the standard is objective' and that it 'does not vary with the particular aptitude or temperament of the individual'. Their Honours concluded at [54]:

> Knowledge of inexperience can thus provide no sufficient foundation for applying different standards of care in deciding whether a learner driver is liable to one passenger rather than another, or in deciding whether that learner driver is liable to a person outside the car rather than one who was seated in the car, in the adjoining seat. The other passenger will ordinarily know that the driver is a learner driver; the road user outside the car can see the L-plates. Yet it is not disputed that the learner driver owes each of those persons a standard of care determined by reference to the reasonable driver.

The High Court decided in this case that while the fact that the plaintiff knew that the defendant driver of the car was an inexperienced and unlicensed teenager should not alter the standard of care required of the driver, it would be relevant to the issue of contributory negligence on the part of the plaintiff, who was supervising him while he drove.

Special rules apply to professionals such as engineers, architects, doctors and lawyers, who must 'exercise reasonable professional care and skill' to the standard 'of the ordinary skilled person exercising and professing to have that special skill', as the High Court explained in *Rogers v Whitaker* (1992) at 483 and 492. So, a person practising as a professional will be held to the standard of the ordinary skilled professional regardless of whether they are a complete novice who has been in the profession for one day or an experienced professional who has worked in the field for many years.

Case example

In *Wilsher v Essex Area Health Authority* (1987), a junior doctor, who was treating a premature baby, mistakenly inserted a catheter into the baby's umbilical vein rather than his artery. The defendants argued that the fact of the doctor's inexperience should have been taken into account, but the English Court of Appeal did not accept that the standard should be set to the personal experience of each individual doctor. Rather, as Mustill J pointed out at 751, it should be set by reference 'to the post which he occupies' and the 'degree of skill appropriate to the task which he undertakes'.

Specialists within a profession are also held to a higher standard. If defendants have held themselves out as having a special skill or a higher than usual level of skill over and above that of an ordinary professional – for example, a medical practitioner who specialises in ophthalmology, as was the case in *Rogers v Whitaker* (1992) – then they will be held to that higher standard of a skilled specialist. This common law principle has been given statutory expression in some of the civil liability legislation, which requires the assessment of breach to be based on what could reasonably be expected of a person professing to have that skill, and the 'relevant circumstances at the date of the alleged negligence'.

LEGISLATION ALERT!

Consult your study materials and note the statutory provisions in your jurisdiction covering the standard of care owed by persons professing to have a particular skill. Note that the Western Australian legislation has specific provisions dedicated to health professionals, but not to professionals more generally.

Consult your study materials and note any statutory provisions in your jurisdiction that define 'a professional'.

The test for breach of the standard of care for persons who are members of a profession has also been given statutory form in many Australian jurisdictions; this is discussed further in section 12.3.3 below. The special rules that are applied to health professionals are outlined in Chapter 14.

12.2.1.4 Intoxication

The ordinary reasonable person is normally taken to be sober; however, some of the civil liability statutes have modified the law. For example, s 31(2) of the *Civil Liability Act 1936* (SA) allows that the reasonable person standard may be modified to take account of the fact that a defendant was intoxicated due to the use of drugs taken in accordance with the prescription or instructions of a medical practitioner. Other legislation in states like Victoria, New South Wales and Queensland explicitly addresses the issue of the plaintiff's intoxication, to clarify that when a plaintiff is of diminished capacity due to intoxication, this does not 'of itself increase or otherwise affect the standard of care owed to the person': see, for example, *Civil Liability Act 2002* (NSW) s 49.

LEGISLATION ALERT!

Consult your study materials and note any relevant statutory provisions in your jurisdiction.

The examples given in section 12.2.1 show that there are limits on the extent to which the reasonable person can be modified to reflect the subjective features of the defendant. This is because the more that the individual defendant's subjective features are built into the description of the reasonable person, the more likely it is that the defendant will be found to have conformed with that personalised standard – and the less likely it is that the plaintiff will be protected by the law.

12.2.2 The time of assessment and the problem of hindsight

Both the common law and the statutes require the plaintiff to prove on the balance of probabilities that the defendant failed to take the precautions that a reasonable person in their position would have taken in the circumstances as they existed *at the time of the alleged breach*. The assessment of breach must not be influenced by hindsight, and it should not take into account any changes or developments that may have occurred after the event. The defendant is held to have knowledge only of the information available at the time of the alleged breach.

Case examples

- In *Roe v Minister of Health* (1954), the defendant, an anaesthetist, injected two patients with nupercaine contaminated with phenol steriliser that had entered the sealed ampoules through fine, invisible and undetectable cracks. The contaminated nupercaine caused the two patients to suffer paraplegia. The English Court of Appeal held that the defendant had not breached his duty of care because it was not known at the time that nupercaine could be contaminated by this mechanism. Lord Denning said at 833–4 that although it is 'easy to be wise after the event' it was not right to 'look at the 1947 accident with 1954 spectacles'.
- See also cases concerning the state of scientific knowledge of the HIV virus and the avoidance of hindsight: for example, *H v Royal Alexandra Hospital for Children* (1990) and *E v Australian Red Cross Society* (1991).
- The case of *Derrick v Cheung* (2001) concerned a driver who was travelling at between 45 and 50 kph on an ordinary street that had a speed limit of 60 kph. A small toddler of 21 months, who had escaped unnoticed from a nearby house, dashed out from between two parked cars, and the driver was unable to avoid hitting the child. The High Court explained at [13] that even though the driver may have been able to avoid hitting the child if her 'speed had been slower by a few kilometres per hour', this fact, which had been established after the event, could not justify imposing a duty on the driver to drive at that slower speed:

  > Few occurrences in human affairs, in retrospect, can be said to have been, in absolute terms, inevitable. Different conduct on the part of those involved in them almost always would have produced a different result. But the possibility of a different result is not the issue and does not represent the proper test for negligence.

In the same vein, the High Court has repeatedly emphasised that when breach is being assessed, the question must be posed prospectively, and it must be answered in the light only of the knowledge and information available at the time to a reasonable person in the defendant's position – and not with the misleading 'wisdom of hindsight': see *Neindorf v Junkovic* (2005), Hayne J at [97]; *Vairy v Wyong Shire Council* (2005), Hayne J at [126]; *Sydney Water Corporation v Turano* (2009) at [46]; *Adeels Palace Pty Ltd v Moubarak* (2009) at [31]; and *CAL No 14 Pty Ltd v Motor Accidents Insurance Board* (2009), Hayne J at [68]. The matter is summed up by Gummow J in *Roads and Traffic Authority (NSW) v Dederer* (2007) at 18: 'breach must be assessed prospectively, not retrospectively'.

Case examples

- In the diving case of *Vairy v Wyong Shire Council* (2005), a plaintiff suffered a catastrophic spinal injury after diving from a height of about 1.5 metres into the sea from a rocky platform and hitting his head on the sand bed. He argued that the council had breached the standard of reasonable care by failing to put up a sign prohibiting diving from the platform or warning of its dangers. The majority in the High Court found that the council had not been negligent, and Hayne J at [126] said that the judgment must be made by seeking 'to identify what the response would have been by a person looking *forward at the prospect of the risk* of injury' (emphasis added).
- In *Neindorf v Junkovic* (2005), the plaintiff, who was attending a garage sale held on an ordinary suburban house block, tripped over a crack in a concrete driveway. She unsuccessfully sued the occupier of the land for her injuries. Hayne J discussed the problem of hindsight at [97]:

  > It is only when the particular event of the respondent's stumble is known to have happened that it appears reasonable to take steps to reduce or eliminate the danger presented by unevenness in the driveway surface. Only with that knowledge does it appear reasonable to point out or cover that irregularity. But that is to look at the problem with hindsight. That is not the question the statute (or the common law) presents. That question is what would have been the reasonable response of the occupier before the accident happened.

- In *Sydney Water Corporation v Turano* (2009), the plaintiffs were injured in 2001 when a tree fell onto their car. They sued the Sydney Water Corporation, the statutory authority that had laid a nearby water main 20 years earlier in 1981. The High Court said at [46]:

  > It was not necessary that the precise sequence of events leading to Mrs Turano's injury be foreseen. However, it was necessary to show that *in 1981* it was foreseeable by Sydney Water that laying a water main in a bed of sand in this location involved a risk of injury to road users.

- The plaintiffs in *Adeels Palace Pty Ltd v Moubarak* (2009) were shot in a restaurant (Adeels Palace) after a dispute on the dance floor. The victims of the gunman sued Adeels Palace Pty Ltd, claiming that the company had been negligent in not providing sufficient security. The High Court, denying liability, said at [31]:

  > [A]ll of those questions fell to be answered, and the probability of harm and other considerations mentioned in s 5B(2) assessed, prospectively, not with the wisdom of hindsight. That is, they were to be assessed *before* the function began, not by reference to what occurred that night.

- In *Caledonian Collieries Ltd v Spiers* (1957), a train of freight trucks loaded with coal was travelling out of control at high speed on a private railway line. A man was killed at a level crossing when the train collided with his car. The man's wife sued the owners of the line, arguing that they were negligent in not providing catch-points that would have allowed the runaway train to be safely diverted. The High Court noted at 225 that while the fact that the defendant had acted to install catch-points within a fortnight after the fatality was admissible as evidence showing that it was practicable to take the precautions, it was not *of itself* 'an admission by the appellant that reasonable care in the management of the line required such a provision'.

Some jurisdictions have given statutory form to this common law rule – and others have introduced legislative rules that an apology after the event does not constitute an admission of liability (and some make such expressions of regret inadmissible evidence).

LEGISLATION ALERT!

Consult your study materials and note any relevant statutory provisions in your jurisdiction.

These warnings against an assessment of breach that asks only 'What *could* the defendant have done to avoid the harm?' must also be read in conjunction with the warnings that have been given by the High Court on the error that ensues if the 'question of the scope or content of the conceded duty of care' is merged improperly with 'the question of breach': Gummow J in *Vairy v Wyong Shire Council* (2005) at [98]. The combination of conflating the duty and breach issues and then asking, with the 'wisdom' (or bias) of hindsight, whether there was anything that the defendant could have done to avoid the harm will lead to error – because the issue in the second element is not the question of *factual causation* (which is analysed in the third element of negligence) but the question of *fault*, which must be found in an objective assessment (as much as possible) of the responses of a reasonable person in the position of the defendant before the harm occurred. This assessment involves answering the questions now encapsulated in the civil liability legislation and the common law and weighing the answers in the balance.

Test your understanding

Analyse the 'reasonable person' standard.

- Outline the factors that make the standard an objective one.
- Outline the reasons why the standard cannot be completely objective.
- Outline the justifications for varying or not varying the standard of care in specific circumstances.

12.3 The nature of the reasonable response

The common law still governs the process that leads to the formulation of a duty of care, whether in established categories or novel fact scenarios, as discussed in Chapter 11. Conversely, establishing whether a duty has been breached is, in all states and territories with the sole exception of the Northern Territory (where the common law still applies), a matter governed by the civil liability legislation. As recently noted by Mark Leeming in *The Statutory Foundations of Negligence* (2019) at 41, 'there is substantial resemblance to the principles (sometimes unfortunately described as the "calculus") stated by Mason J in *Wyong Shire Council v Shirt*'.

The provision on breach of duty follows the same structure in every state and the Australian Capital Territory with very small variations to the opening words.

Legislative example

The most common formulation is that of s 5B of the *Civil Liability Act 2002* (NSW):

(1) A person is not negligent in failing to take precautions against a risk of harm unless:

- (a) the risk was foreseeable (that is, it is a risk of which the person knew or ought to have known), and
- (b) the risk was not insignificant, and
- (c) in the circumstances, a reasonable person in the person's position would have taken those precautions.

(2) In determining whether a reasonable person would have taken precautions against a risk of harm, the court is to consider the following (amongst other relevant things):

- (a) the probability that the harm would occur if care were not taken,
- (b) the likely seriousness of the harm,
- (c) the burden of taking precautions to avoid the risk of harm,
- (d) the social utility of the activity that creates the risk of harm.

Other states have small variations to the wording of subsection (1), which do not have significant implications for the meaning and operation of the section (eg s 5B of the *Civil Liability Act 2002* (WA), which states, 'A person is not liable for harm caused by that person's fault in failing to take precautions against a risk of harm unless ...' – the rest of the provision is identical).

Note the comment of the High Court in *Adeels Palace Pty Ltd v Moubarak* (2009) at [13] with regards to the New South Wales provision (but the same applies to other civil liability statutes):

> Although s 5B appear[s] beneath the heading 'Duty of care', *that heading is apt to mislead* ... [That provision is] evidently *directed to questions of breach of duty* ... [Emphasis added.]

We will now examine each of these aspects in turn: (1) Was the risk foreseeable? (2) Was the risk 'not insignificant'? and (3) What precautions would a reasonable person have taken?

12.3.1 Was the risk foreseeable?

An ordinary reasonable person does not take precautions against unforeseeable risks. This means a defendant is not required to respond to every imaginable or theoretically possible risk, but only to those that are foreseeable by the reasonable person. As Lord Normand said in *Bolton v Stone* (1951) at 861–2: 'It is not the law that precautions must be taken against every peril that can be foreseen by the timorous.' Foreseeability of the risk is a question of fact and can be assessed only in the light of the circumstances of each particular case. As Mason J explained in *Wyong Shire Council v Shirt* (1980) at 47–8, it is critical to understand that the '*foreseeability* of the risk of injury and the *likelihood* of that risk occurring are two different things' and to remember that a 'risk of injury which is quite unlikely to occur ... may nevertheless be plainly foreseeable'.

Case example

The facts of *Palsgraf v Long Island Railway Co* (1928) provide an illustration of a risk that may have been a theoretical possibility, but which, the Court decided, was not a foreseeable one in the circumstances. The facts of the case are recounted in Chapter 11. If the Railway had been put on notice – for example, if packages of exploding fireworks had regularly been dropped onto the tracks in the past and caused other objects to fall, or if the brass scales had a tendency to fall over in strong winds and other bystanders had been hurt on a regular basis – then the risk may have been classified as foreseeable.

To answer this question, therefore, you always have to look carefully at the facts of your case and, referring to the common sense, intelligence and experience of an ordinary person, explain why the risk, even if small or even unlikely, was nevertheless foreseeable. Note that the requirement of foreseeability at the breach stage asks a different question from the one asked at the duty stage. As Glass CJ put it in *Minister Administering the Environmental Planning and Assessment Act 1979 v San Sebastian Pty Ltd* (1983) at 296:

> The breach question requires proof that it was reasonably foreseeable as a possibility that *the kind* of carelessness charged against the defendant might cause damage of *some kind* to the plaintiff's person or property.

Case examples

- In *Coles Supermarkets Australia Pty Ltd v Bridge* (2018), P slipped and fell on the wet surface of D's car park while pushing his trolley. At the time of the incident, P had removed one hand from the trolley to answer his mobile phone. Tests carried out after the accident suggested that the surface of the car park significantly contributed to the risk of slipping. D argued that breach should be assessed prospectively and not retrospectively; yet, as recognised by Leeming and Payne JJA of the New South Wales Court of Appeal, formulating the risk of harm must involve an exercise of hindsight, to the extent that it must encompass the risk which is claimed to have materialised and caused the damage in question. This risk should not be formulated so generally that it extends beyond the class in question. So, in the circumstances, the risk was that a customer pushing a trolley through D's car park might slip and fall – a risk of which D ought to have known.

Note that the fact that P was on the phone at the time was relevant to contributory negligence, not breach of duty.

- In *Horne v JK Williams Contracting* (2023), a cyclist (P) was injured after hitting at night a water-filled orange-coloured barricade that was placed on the verge of a roadway along a construction site. P brought a claim against the contractor responsible for the construction site (D), alleging the barricade was not visible enough. However, one of the issues accepted at trial was that the streetlight at the time were not operating at full capacity, and this was beyond the control of D. The New South Wales Court of Appeal agreed with the trial judge that, in the absence of any evidence that D knew or ought to have known the streetlights were not operating properly, the risk of a cyclist colliding with the barricade at night was not a foreseeable one: 'If the risk did not arise during daylight hours, it would not have arisen if the area were adequately lit at night-time' (at [31]).

The test of foreseeability has been described as setting a rather low threshold by the High Court. In *Tame v New South Wales* (2002), McHugh J put it bluntly at [99]: 'Given the undemanding nature of the current foreseeability standard, an affirmative answer to the question whether damage was reasonably foreseeable is usually a near certainty.' Yet, cases can fall at that hurdle, either because sometimes a risk is genuinely not reasonably foreseeable, as in the cases described above, or because the risk is not appropriately identified or characterised. As explained by Gummow J in *Roads and Traffic Authority (NSW) v Dederer* (2007) at [238]: 'the assessment of breach depends on *the correct identification of the relevant risk of injury*' (emphasis added). For a risk to be foreseeable it must be properly identified and framed, or a court will not be able to assess whether the conduct of the defendant was in breach of their standard of care. It is also essential not to characterise the risk of harm too narrowly or rely on hindsight for the purpose of identification.

Case examples

- In *Bondi Beach Foods Pty Ltd v Chadwick* (2023) Mr Chadwick (P) was seriously injured when he was struck repeatedly with a stool by another patron who was attending the same beachfront bar, The Bucket List in Bondi Beach. P sued both Bondi Beach Foods Pty Ltd (D1) as the owner and operator of The Bucket List and its security contractor for the damage he suffered as a result of the assault. On appeal before the New South Wales Court of Appeal, D1 argued that the risk of harm had been incorrectly identified as it had been characterised too broadly by P. In dismissing this ground, Leeming JA observed at [66]:

> The primary judge adopted a slightly wider risk of harm. Rather than the risk of physical injury from patrons who were objectively manifesting signs of intoxication or anti-social behaviour, his Honour simply characterised the risk as physical injury from an intoxicated person. There is no error in adopting that wider characterisation.

Note that a risk of harm being deemed foreseeable doesn't imply a finding of breach. As Leeming JA observed in the same paragraph:

> However, it is difficult to point to any precautions that a reasonable licensee could take against the risk that a patron who manifests no signs of intoxication or anti-social behaviour, but who nevertheless is intoxicated, might without warning inflict harm on another patron.

- In *Liprini v Hale* (2020), the same court dealt with a plaintiff's claim in negligence against his solicitors' firm for failure to initiate proceedings concerning the plaintiff's mother's estate before participating in mediation, where all claims arising under that estate were resolved. A complex chain of events then led to the plaintiff to suffer a substantial financial loss, prompting them to sue their solicitors. Fatal to the plaintiff's initial claim and subsequent appeal was their failure to establish the critical question of the risk of harm. The New South Wales Court of Appeal noted that it was not clear what risk of harm had existed at the time the conduct (ie participating in mediation before initiating proceedings), or at what point the risk arose, against which the precaution of commencing proceedings against the mother's estate should have been taken. McCallum observed at [131] that 'the appellant's case on that issue was overly informed by hindsight'.

12.3.2 Was the risk 'not insignificant'?

Ordinary, reasonable people do not take precautions against *unforeseeable* risks; and neither do they always take precautions against every *foreseeable* risk. The foreseeable risk must also be one that is 'not insignificant'. One of the main legislative changes in this area is found in the description of the risk to which the reasonable person must respond. Under the older approach from *Wyong Shire Council v Shirt* (1980), quoted above, the foreseeable risk was sometimes described as one that was 'not far-fetched or fanciful'. In light of the criticism that the pendulum of negligence had swung too far in favour of plaintiffs, the Ipp Report recommended that it be replaced with the phrase 'not insignificant', which was chosen to indicate 'a risk that carries a higher degree of probability of harm': see [7.15] in chapter 7 of the Final Report (2002). So, while the risk does not have to be as high as a 'significant' risk, the plaintiff must convince the court that it was 'not insignificant' (and the defendant will counterargue by suggesting that it was 'far-fetched or fanciful'). It is sometimes difficult to keep the discussion of whether a risk is 'foreseeable' separate from the issue of whether it is also 'not insignificant', and in fact these two considerations are often blended together in the cases. However, the High Court, when considering the new section of the New South Wales legislation in *Adeels Palace Pty Ltd v Moubarak* (2009), made it clear that both of these steps must be clearly taken and articulated.

Case examples

- In *Bolton v Stone* (1951), the plaintiff, a woman standing on a road outside her home, was hit by a cricket ball that had been hit out of the adjacent cricket ground. She sued the committee and members of the cricket club, arguing that they had not taken sufficient precautions to prevent the escape of cricket balls from the oval. In the light of the evidence that only about six balls had been hit out of the ground in the previous 28 years, the House of Lords decided that the risk, while foreseeable, was too small and therefore not significant enough to require the club to have taken precautions. Lord Oaksey said at 863:

  > The standard of care in the law of negligence is the standard of an ordinarily careful man, but in my opinion an ordinarily careful man does not take precautions against every foreseeable risk. He can, of course, *foresee the possibility of many risks, but life would be almost impossible if he were to attempt to take precautions against every risk which he can foresee.* He takes precautions against risks which are reasonably likely to happen. Many foreseeable risks are extremely unlikely to happen and cannot be guarded against except by almost complete isolation. The ordinarily prudent owner of a dog does not keep his dog always on a lead on a country highway for fear it may cause injury to a passing motor cyclist, nor does the ordinarily prudent pedestrian avoid the use of the highway for fear of skidding motor cars. It may very well be that after this accident the ordinarily prudent committee man of a similar cricket ground would take some further precaution, but that is not to say that he would have taken a similar precaution before the accident. [Emphasis added.]

- In *Wyong Shire Council v Shirt* (1980), an inexperienced water-skier became a quadriplegic after falling off his skis in shallow water. The justices of the High Court disagreed on whether the risk of harm to the plaintiff was reasonably foreseeable and discussed the formulation of the 'not far-fetched or fanciful' test of risk. The majority held that, notwithstanding the fact that the water was clearly shallow in the area where the skier had fallen, the fact that there was an ambiguous sign erected by the council saying 'Deep Water', near a deeper channel further out in the lake, meant that the risk of harm was foreseeable and not too remote a possibility. Wilson J dissented and held that there was no real or foreseeable risk. Murphy J, who agreed with the majority (and who described the decision in *Bolton v Stone* as having been decided on the basis of 'policy considerations concerning English cricket'), pointed out at 49:

  > Most traffic and industrial accidents result from circumstances in which the chance of an accident occurring is extremely slight. Under modern urban conditions, most people habitually drive carelessly. One needs only to observe peak-hour traffic in and out of a city to notice that almost every car is driven unsafely close to the car in front; speed limits are also habitually exceeded. The chances of an accident from any breach of traffic rules is very slight, but, if harm does result (and if the court concerns itself with 'foreseeability'), it is treated as foreseeable.

- In *Drinkwater v Howarth* (2006) the plaintiff was injured when his friend, who was being escorted out of a hotel by two security officers, was pushed and fell, knocking the plaintiff to the ground. In discussing s 5B of the *Civil Liability Act 2002* (NSW), Basten JA said at [16] that '[a] risk which is much more than far-fetched or fanciful may not differ materially from a risk which is not insignificant' and suggested at [21]:

> [T]here is a danger in seeking to take each limb of s 5B separately in considering how it should operate. It is clear from the report of the committee which recommended the change to the foregoing common law principles that in changing the terminology from not far-fetched or fanciful they were concerned to ensure that attention was given to other aspects of the risk.

Again, at [25], Basten JA clarified that it may well be the case that no material difference exists between the two formulations in any given case:

> [I]n this case there is no possibility of a different result of applying a test that the risk in question be not insignificant, from applying the test as formulated in *Shirt*, namely that the risk be not far-fetched or fanciful.

- In *Electro Optic Systems Pty Ltd v New South Wales* (2014), Jagot J, quoting Macfarlan JA in *Shaw v Thomas* (2010), restated at [226] that the statutory 'not insignificant' test 'imposes a more demanding standard [than that of the common law] but not by much'.
- The fact that the not-insignificant test remains undemanding is further exemplified by the decision of the New South Wales Court of Appeal in *Bunnings Group Ltd v Giudice* (2018) where the respondent Ms Giudice tripped and fell to the ground upon entering a children's play area at Bunnings, the appellant, upon which she suffered significant physical injury. The Court found that the risk of injury was so obvious as to be insignificant. Note that obvious risks are normally dealt with in dedicated provisions of civil liability statutes (s 5H in New South Wales), but in the absence of any reliance on that section by Bunnings, the Court found at [55]–[56] that 'based on the exiguous evidence adduced at trial, it has not been shown that the risk of harm was not insignificant'. While it would not be prudent to infer that, on this basis, any obvious risk will be deemed insignificant, this is a factor that courts can factor into the assessment.

The High Court warned in *Adeels Palace Pty Ltd v Moubarak* (2009) at [11] that unless the Court's attention is 'directed first to the *Civil Liability Act*' and then to any other relevant legislation, 'there is serious risk that the inquiries about duty, breach and causation will miscarry'. The Court noted at [28] that once it is accepted that a risk 'was not insignificant', the question then becomes whether a reasonable person in the position of the defendant would have taken the precautions that the plaintiffs allege should have been taken. The judges emphasised at [35] and [38] that it is critically important to articulate clearly why 'a risk of that kind should have been foreseen' and 'why a reasonable person would have taken that step', and concluded at [39]:

> The absence of consideration at trial of the matters prescribed by s 5B of the *Civil Liability Act* may have been reason enough to conclude that the question of breach of duty was not determined properly by the trial judge.

Note that some jurisdictions have attempted to unpack the meaning of the phrase 'not insignificant' in the statutes (see, eg, s 48(3) of the *Wrongs Act 1958* (Vic)).

LEGISLATION ALERT!

Consult your study materials and note any relevant statutory provisions in your jurisdiction.

12.3.3 What precautions would a reasonable person have taken?

A reasonable person is expected to take precautions against a foreseeable and not insignificant risk after weighing several factors in the balance. As noted above, these factors originated in the common law, and four of them are now mandated by the civil liability legislation. So, as the High Court emphasised in *Adeels Palace Pty Ltd v Moubarak* (2009) at [40], the plaintiff has to identify the precautions that they argue should have been taken in response to the risk of harm, and then give evidence showing, on the balance of probabilities, why the defendant should be held liable for failing to take them. From the outset, it bears noting that the statutory test asks what precautions a reasonable person *would* have taken in the circumstances, not what precautions they *might* have taken: see Basten JA in *Fabre v Lui* (2015) at [34].

Remember that, as discussed above, the standard of care (ie the precautions that a reasonable person in the defendant's position is expected to take in the presence of a foreseeable and not-insignificant risk of harm) will vary from that of the ordinary person, to the ordinary skilled professional, or be adjusted when the defendant is a child etc. And remember too that the emphasis that the civil liability legislation places on the circumstances of the case can be a decisive factor.

Case example

In *Reardon v Seselja* (2021), the normal standard of care of road users in light of the extraordinary nature of the circumstances. In this case, D's car was the object of a 'terrifying and unexpected attack unprovoked by anything done by the occupants' of D's car, such that it was reasonable for D to have been frightened for their safety and have been in a state of panic (at [50]). Consequently, irrespective of whether D had known of P's approaching car behind him, the 'immediacy and extent' of the crisis were such that it was not unreasonable for him to slowly reverse his car without first checking his rear-view mirror, and to then reverse at a higher speed upon reacting to the assailant 'unexpectedly grabbing his driver's door' (at [51]). As observed by the Court of Appeal of the Australian Capital Territory, this was a case that allowed an opportunity for calm reflection. The agony of the moment meant the defendant's actions were not negligent in the circumstances (at [53]).

The following subsections show how the factors incorporated in the statutes are weighed in the balance – the operation that has become known as the 'negligence calculus' from *Wyong Shire Council v Shirt* (1980) – but remember that the expression 'calculus' in this context is something of a misnomer.

12.3.3.1 The probability that the harm would occur if precautions were not taken

A risk of harm that is plainly foreseeable may be ignored if, when balanced against the other factors, the probability of it occurring is too small to warrant a response.

Case examples

- In *Bolton v Stone* (1951), the cricket case noted above, the House of Lords decided that the risk of harm, while foreseeable and of a serious kind, was nevertheless too unlikely to occur to require the club to have taken precautions. The plaintiffs 'argued that 'as soon as one ball had been driven into the road in the ordinary course of a match' it would have been enough to impose a duty on the defendants to take steps to prevent such an occurrence. Lord Reid responded to this argument at 866–7:

  > If the true test is foreseeability alone I think that must be so ... [but it] would take a good deal to make me believe that the law has departed so far from the standards which guide ordinary careful people in ordinary life. In the crowded conditions of modern life even the most careful person cannot avoid creating some risks and accepting others ... In my judgment the test to be applied here is whether the risk of damage to a person on the road was so small that a reasonable man in the position of the appellants, considering the matter from the point of view of safety, would have thought it right to refrain from taking steps to prevent the danger.

  Lord Reid took into account the remoteness of the risk in deciding that there had been no breach, saying that it was 'extremely small' but pointed out at that if the risk had been any higher he would have decided otherwise:

  > If cricket cannot be played on a ground without creating *a substantial risk*, then it should not be played there at all. [Emphasis added.]

  Lord Normand said at 862 that while the 'serious injury which a cricket ball might cause must not be left out of account', the other critical issue was the fact that the number of balls likely to be hit out of the ground was 'almost negligible' and the probability of anyone being hit was therefore 'very slight'.

  Note that, under the civil liability legislation, this case is also used to illustrate the preliminary requirement that a risk of harm be not-insignificant – in the sense that this is a case where an Australian court today is likely to find the risk to be too small and thus insignificant.

- The facts of *Roads and Traffic Authority (NSW) v Dederer* (2007) were that a 14-year-old boy dived head first off a bridge into shallow water, despite the presence of warning pictograms prohibiting diving on each end of the bridge and signs forbidding climbing on the bridge. He suffered catastrophic injuries. He argued that the RTA and local council should have done more to prevent him from being able to dive off the bridge, but a majority of 3:2 in the High Court found that the defendants had not breached the standard of reasonable care. Gummow J noted at [70] and [71] that even though 'the risk of injury was reasonably foreseeable', the 'magnitude of the risk was self-evidently grave', and the harm of 'partial paralysis is among the worst kinds of injuries imaginable', these factors had to be balanced by the fact that 'the *probability of that injury occurring was, however, low*' (emphasis added).

- In *Rogers v Whitaker* (1992), a doctor was held to be in breach of his duty to take reasonable care to advise his patient (who had one blind eye and one good eye) of an exceptionally small chance, rated as 1 in 14 000, that as a result of elective cosmetic surgery on her blind eye, she could develop a rare condition that could lead to blindness in her remaining good eye. Sometimes a reasonable person must respond to a very unlikely risk where the circumstances of the case warrant it – see more on a doctor's duty to warn in Chapter 14.
- In *Farriss v Axford* (2023), the plaintiff, Mr Farriss, started a claim in negligence for injuries suffered to his left hand when it became caught in the electric anchoring mechanism of a boat he had chartered. After failing at first instance, he lodged an appeal and the New South Wales Court of Appeal upheld the initial decision and rejected, among other things, the plaintiff's argument that the absence of any prior incidents was of little probative value, and further underlined that the appeal failed to consider evidence that the mechanism was subject to routine surveyance and inspection. In the absence of prior incidents and in light of routine controls, the Court found the probability of harm to be extremely low.

12.3.3.2 The likely seriousness of the harm

The likely seriousness of the harm is one of the most important factors that often carries great weight. As the cases have explained, however, the defendant will not always be expected to respond in every case where the harm risked is very serious, if the other factors outweigh that seriousness. So, if the seriousness of the harm is high, but if the likelihood of it occurring is very small, and the burden of taking precautions to avoid it would be disproportionately high, then depending on the circumstances, the reasonable person may not always respond to that risk.

Case examples

- *Paris v Stepney Borough Council* (1951) was a case where the House of Lords recognised, in a majority decision of 3:2, a breach of the duty to take reasonable care owed by an employer to an employee. In this case a worker was employed to knock metal bolts off the chassis of a car with a steel hammer. He was not given any protective eye goggles. This worker was particularly vulnerable because he was effectively blind in one eye due to serious injuries suffered during World War Two. When a metal splinter broke off the chassis and damaged his remaining eye, he sued the employer for negligently failing to provide him with goggles. Lord Normand at 381 illustrated the issue of the seriousness of the harm risked by quoting *Winfield on Tort:* 'No reasonable man handles a stick of dynamite and a walking stick in the same way.' His Honour at 383 emphasised the 'disastrous consequences' if a particle of metal flew into the employee's eye, concluding:

> Blindness is so great a calamity that even the loss of one of two good eyes is not comparable; and the risk of blindness from sparks of metal is greater for a one-eyed man than for a two-eyed man, for it is less likely that both eyes should be damaged than that one eye should, and the loss of one eye is not necessarily or even usually followed by blindness in the other.

- In the Australian case of *Caledonian Collieries Ltd v Spiers* (1957), noted above, Dixon CJ, McTiernan, Kitto, and Taylor JJ said at 223 that installing catch-points was the only way to ensure that 'the danger to road traffic could be averted' and, given the dangers that a runaway freight train posed, decided at 225 that even though this measure may have been 'drastic', a reasonable person would have acted to give users of the level crossing this protection.

The cases make it clear that a reasonable person does not always have to act to prevent even a serious harm.

Case example

In *Romeo v Conservation Commission (NT)* (1998), an intoxicated 14-year-old girl, who had drunk 150 ml of rum while attending a night-time beach party, fell six and a half metres from the top of a cliff onto a beach in a nature reserve and suffered serious paraplegia. She argued that the Conservation Commission should have put up fences and warning signs along the two-kilometre length of the cliff. The High Court held that the Commission was not in breach, primarily because the likelihood of the harm occurring was low. Even though the harm of falling off the cliff face was obviously a serious harm, the probability of it occurring was actually low, considered in the light of the fact that people ordinarily take reasonable care when in the vicinity of dangerous cliffs. Brennan CJ pointed out at [51] that there is a 'tension' between the approach that focuses on 'the degree of probability of the occurrence of an accident' and other decisions of the High Court that:

> place this factor on the scales, to be weighed against the seriousness of the foreseeable risk and the expense, difficulty and inconvenience of precautions which could be taken.

Kirby J at [128], citing *The Wagon Mound (No 2)* (1967) at 642–3, explained that there were times when, despite the 'magnitude of the risk', a reasonable person:

> would be entitled, in a proper case, to accept that the risk of a mishap such as occurred was so remote that 'a reasonable man, careful of the safety of his neighbour, would think it right to neglect it.'

Note, however, that Kirby J said in the later case of *Neindorf v Junkovic* (2005) at [74] and [75]: 'If I could expunge the quoted passage from my reasons in *Romeo*, I would gladly do so' because it may lead to the 'mischief' that 'contributory negligence, of whatever proportion, becomes again a complete defence to an action framed in negligence'. See Chapter 15 on contributory negligence.

Both *Romeo v Conservation Commission (NT)* (1998) and *Caledonian Collieries Ltd v Spiers* (1957) concerned circumstances where the seriousness of the harm involved was high, but in each case the court came to a different conclusion on the facts. In *Romeo v Conservation Commission (NT)* (1998) the other factors outweighed the seriousness of the harm, whereas in the circumstances in *Caledonian Collieries Ltd v Spiers* (1957), the seriousness of the harm carried more weight. These examples show that each case must be considered on its own merits – and that the balancing exercise is not easy, and its results can be unpredictable.

12.3.3.3 The burden of taking precautions to avoid the risk of harm

Many of the High Court cases discussed above have emphasised the importance of weighing the burden of taking precautions in the balance, and as the pendulum of negligence has been moved back towards a more defendant-friendly position, this factor has assumed increased importance.

Case examples

- In *Romeo v Conservation Commission (NT)* (1998), the justices noted the huge costs that would be incurred by the Conservation Commission if the entire cliff face in the conservation area had to be signposted and fenced, and Kirby J at [132] took into account the 'expense, difficulty and inconvenience of alleviating conduct and the other proper priorities of the Commission'.
- In *Graham Barclay Oysters Pty Ltd v Ryan* (2002), the Ps contracted hepatitis after eating D's oysters. The oysters had been contaminated following heavy rains in Wallis Lake, where they were grown. The heavy rain had caused sewage to overflow in the lake, exposing the oysters to pollutants. The Ps sued the producer (and the local council) for failing to take adequate precautions in preventing a hepatitis outbreak. There had been no such outbreak in over 100 years of D farming oysters. The High Court confirmed that while a duty of care was owed to the Ps, it had not been breached by D, who had followed its standard testing procedures. The burden of taking precautions against the risk of a hepatitis outbreak would have been unreasonable in the circumstances.
- In *Neindorf v Junkovic* (2005), where the plaintiff who was visiting a suburban garage sale tripped over a crack in the pathway, the judges were divided over the issue of breach. Gleeson CJ, Hayne, Callinan and Heydon JJ at [111] and [117] preferred the view of Doyle CJ in the earlier appeal case, who had said:

  > If a duty of care is imposed in respect of such a hazard, it applies to each and every hazard on those parts of private property where visitors can reasonably be anticipated. Removing or neutralising all such hazards could be a significant burden on the occupier of a property. It would be an ongoing task.

  Gleeson CJ and Hayne J also found that a reasonable person in the defendant's position would not have taken any precautions against this ordinary everyday 'hazard', but Kirby J dissented and stated at [70] that the identified precautions were 'so modest, inexpensive and obvious' that 'it would not have been a large burden' on the defendant.

- In *Roads and Traffic Authority (NSW) v Dederer* (2007), where a 14-year-old boy was injured after diving off a bridge, Gummow J said at [78]:

  > Though grave, the risk faced by Mr Dederer was of a very low probability, and a reasonable response to that risk did not demand the measures suggested by him. Those measures lacked evidential support; were of doubtful utility; would have caused *significant expense* in the case of the modifications to the handrail and fencing; and were in some cases contrary to express findings of fact. [Emphasis added.]

- In *Karpik v Carnival plc* (2023), noted in Chapter 11, the fact that the respondent decided to cancel cruises five days after the facts of the case prompted the Court to infer that cancelling a cruise was not unduly burdensome for the respondent. In fact, cancelling the specific cruise that the plaintiff suffered the damage on at the last minute would have been far less burdensome than the respondent's subsequent actions in cancelling all cruises a few days later. The respondents also later had to refund the passengers of the relevant cruise in full, such that the financial outcome of undertaking the cruise was significantly more burdensome than abstaining from the cruise (at [607]). Thus, a reasonable cruise operator would have cancelled the cruise in the circumstances, and not doing so amounted to a breach of duty.

These burdens are not always expressed in financial terms, and there are times when the social costs and the adverse effects of a particular precautionary measure on the daily life of the community are also taken into account.

Case examples

- Asquith LJ illustrated this point in *Daborn v Bath Tramways Motor Co Ltd* (1946) at 336:

  > As has often been pointed out, if all the trains in this country were restricted to a speed of five miles an hour, there would be fewer accidents, but our national life would be intolerably slowed down.

- See also *Derrick v Cheung* (2001), noted above, and the cricket case of *Bolton v Stone* (1951), also noted above, where Lord Oaksey pointed out at 863 that 'life would be almost impossible' if everyone had to take precautions against every risk that they can foresee.

Note that many of the civil liability statutes have specifically added provisions allowing the court to take into account the financial and other resources of a public authority, as further discussed in Chapter 14.

LEGISLATION ALERT!

Consult your study materials and note any relevant statutory provisions in your jurisdiction.

12.3.3.4 The social utility of the activity that creates the risk of harm

The social utility (usefulness) of the defendant's conduct is now a mandatory factor under the civil liability legislation, and it is also a relevant factor under the common law. As noted above, Heuston's survey of the cases in 1957 identified (at 17) the 'comparative social utility of the conduct of both parties' as an important consideration; and Mason J, in *Wyong Shire Council v Shirt* (1980) at 48, referred to 'any other conflicting responsibilities which the defendant may have'.

Case examples

- In *Daborn v Bath Tramways Motor Co Ltd* (1946), an ambulance driver (P) trying to turn right was injured when a bus driver (D) hit the ambulance when overtaking it from behind. It was argued on behalf of D that P should have taken more care when signalling her right turn, because she was driving one of many American left-hand drive vehicles that were used as ambulances in wartime England during the Blitz in the Second World War. However, the English Court of Appeal did not accept that P was contributorily negligent. Lord Asquith noted at 336 'the necessity in time of national emergency of employing all the transport resources that were available' and explained that the 'purpose to be served, if sufficiently important, justifies the assumption of abnormal risk'.
- Lord Singleton approved of this passage in *Watt v Hertfordshire County Council* (1954) at 838 and Lord Denning also said in that case at 838:

  > It is well settled that in measuring due care you must balance the risk against the measures necessary to eliminate the risk. To that proposition there ought to be added this: *you must balance the risk against the end to be achieved.* If this accident had occurred in a commercial enterprise without any emergency there could be no doubt that the servant would succeed. But the commercial end to make profit is very different from the human end to save life or limb. [Emphasis added.]

  The plaintiff in *Watt v Hertfordshire County Council* (1954) was a fireman who was seriously injured when a heavy jack that was needed in an emergency rescue effort fell on him during the journey to the scene. He argued that his employers should have taken more care of his safety, but the English Court of Appeal held that the employers were justified in taking abnormal risks when trying to 'save life or limb'.

Even though the same principle was invoked in both *Daborn v Bath Tramways Motor Co Ltd* and *Watt v Hertfordshire County Council*, as discussed in the examples above, in *Daborn* the victim of the accident was protected by the fact that she had been driving an ambulance to assist the war effort, while in *Watt* the victim was not protected, because his employer was seeking to achieve a valuable social end. In other words, the risk must be balanced against the end to be achieved, and this principle has also been invoked in Australia.

Case example

In *E v Australian Red Cross Society* (1991), where a plaintiff contracted the HIV virus through a contaminated blood transfusion, Wilcox J found that, in the light of the state of scientific knowledge at the time, the Red Cross (the defendant) had not breached its duty to take reasonable care by failing to introduce screening tests. In weighing the burden of taking these precautions against the known seriousness of the risk, Wilcox J noted at [277] and [288] that, even though the decision forced the plaintiff to 'bear the costs of protecting the wider public interest', the cost to society would have been the 'wasting of something like 5 per cent of all donations' with a 'serious effect on the blood supply' and so the defendant was entitled to 'give priority to the interests of all blood users'.

Note that activities undertaken by individuals within the scope of a family relationship may also be considered of great social utility by courts.

Case example

In *Hoffman v Boland* (2013), the grandmother was carrying her daughter's five-month-old baby down the stairs at night when she fell, causing injury to the infant. The judges in the New South Wales Court of Appeal disagreed on whether the grandmother owed a duty of care while she had the physical care and control of her granddaughter. However, all judges agreed that, in any case, she had taken appropriate precautions to guard against the risk of a fall. Basten JA explained at [138] that the act of the grandmother in taking control of the crying child to offer relief to the mother had 'a very high social utility', which contributed to the finding of no breach: 'Domestic assistance of this kind ... goes to the very heart of what family members do for each other.' The question remains open whether a non-family member would be found to be in breach of their duty under similar circumstances.

12.3.3.5 'Other relevant things': Professional or customary standards

Evidence of standards commonly observed in a particular area of enterprise may be given as evidence of breach, but as Latham CJ pointed out in *Mercer v Commissioner for Road Transport and Tramways (NSW)* (1936) at 589:

> The mere fact that a defendant follows common practice does not necessarily show that he is not negligent, though the general practice of prudent men is an important evidentiary fact. A common practice may be shown by evidence to be itself negligent.

The role of industry and customary practices was considered again by the High Court in *Woods v Multi-Sport Holdings Pty Ltd* (2002), which dealt with a sporting accident. The High Court confirmed that reference to industry standards does not of itself decide whether the standard of care has been breached; nevertheless, such standards are relevant and must be adequately taken into account.

This approach was applied by the New South Wales Court of Appeal in *Erwin v Iveco Trucks Australia Ltd* (2010), which again raised the question of industry practice in the case of an allegedly defective truck. Sackville AJA stated at [110]:

> [I]n the absence of evidence that the industry practice itself was deficient or that potential safety issues had been identified at the time but not acted upon, the respondent's adherence to the industry norm is a *strong indication* that a reasonable person in the respondent's position would not have adopted additional precautions to guard against the risk. [Emphasis added.]

A related but separate question is whether a professional has breached their standard of care. The civil liability legislation in most jurisdictions now gives protection to the members of certain professions who have acted in a manner that accords with the standards adopted by others in the same profession, provided that these practices are not 'irrational' (or in some statutes 'unreasonable'). This is often referred to as the 'peer professional opinion' defence. The precise scope and wording of these provisions vary, and you should note the wording of your own statute carefully.

Legislative example

***Civil Liability Act 2002* (Tas)**

22 Standard of care for professionals

(1) A person practising a profession ('a professional') does not breach a duty arising from the provision of a professional service if it is established that the professional acted in a manner that (at the time the service was provided) was widely accepted in Australia by peer professional opinion as competent professional practice.

(2) Peer professional opinion cannot be relied on for the purpose of this section if the court considers that the opinion is irrational.

(3) The fact that there are differing peer professional opinions widely accepted in Australia concerning a matter does not prevent any one or more (or all) of those opinions being relied on for the purpose of subsection (1).

(4) Peer professional opinion does not have to be universally accepted to be considered widely accepted.

(5) This section does not apply to liability arising in connection with the giving of (or the failure to give) a warning, advice or other information in relation to the risk of harm associated with the provision by a professional of a professional service to a person.

Note that, in states and territories that have adopted it, the 'peer professional opinion' operates as a *defence*, and not as a substitute for the elements to be taken into account when establishing breach. This was explained by the New South Wales Court of Appeal in *South Western Sydney Local Health District v Gould* (2018). So, technically, when a professional is involved, you should consider whether they have breached their standard of care, taking into account the elements listed in the previous sections (*probability and severity of harm*, *burden of taking precautions*, and *social utility*), and *then* consider whether a defence would apply on the basis of a widely accepted 'peer professional opinion'. In practice, however, the rule can have an overriding effect, and prompt courts to implicitly make findings as to the general rules on breach, while focusing their reasoning on the relevance of the peer professional opinion to the specific circumstances of the case.

Case example

In *Johnson v Firth* (2021), P sued their solicitor (D) for prematurely reaching a settlement, thereby having their client's (P) claim substantially undervalued. However, Brereton JA considered P's stated 'dire financial circumstances and desire for an early settlement' as well as the fact that 'the offer ultimately accepted was far from being so unreasonable as to require a warning against acceptance' (at [65]). On this basis his Honour concluded that D had 'conducted the claim "in a manner which would be widely accepted in Australia, and in New South Wales as competent and professional" for the purposes of (NSW) *Civil Liability Act 2002*, s 50' (at [52] quoting the judgment at first instance).

LEGISLATION ALERT!

Consult your study materials and note any statutory provisions in your jurisdiction covering the liability of professionals, and make sure that you check the scope and definitions in the legislation.

In Chapter 14 you will find more detail on the operation of this rule (and its alternatives) for health professionals. Also note that the current formulation of breach in civil liability legislation, whereby courts are to determine whether a reasonable person in the defendant's position would have taken precautions, has arguably reduced the practical relevance of this rule, as discussed by Marco Rizzi in 'Health Professionals' Standard of Care and Breach of Duty in Western Australia' (2020).

12.3.3.6 'Other relevant things': Statutory standards

Any relevant statutory standards will also be weighed in the balance to assist in the determination of breach. However, these statutory rules, like the professional practices noted above, may not always provide a definitive answer because, as the High Court pointed out in *Sibley v Kais* (1967) at 427, the 'common-law duty to act reasonably in all the circumstances is paramount'. In this case the High Court explained that the road rules contained in the *Road Traffic Code 1965* (WA) were 'not definitive of the respective duties of the drivers of vehicles' and nor was the breach of those regulations 'conclusive as to the performance of the duty owed'. Similarly, in *Lowns v Woods* (1996), a case mostly known for its unusual finding that the defendant owed the plaintiff a duty to rescue, the statutory standards imposed on medical practitioners by the *Medical Practitioners Act 1938* (NSW) (in force at the time) had a significant role in the finding of the Court. In sum, you should remember that reference to statutory standards is never of itself determinative of breach nor of diligent conduct. It is simply one factor that courts are to take into account in the overall 'calculus'. See Chapter 14 for more discussion on the duty to rescue and the role of statutory standards.

12.3.3.7 'Other relevant things': Carelessness by the plaintiff

The requirement that the defendant, as a reasonable person, should take into account the well-known fact that others do not always act reasonably or take care for their own safety has been part of the negligence 'calculus' for many years. However, recent times have seen changes in this area of the law as criticisms of the 'welfare state' mentality among 'pro-plaintiff judges' have taken hold. These changes have occurred in both the common law cases and in the statutes. The difference in approach can be seen by comparing the outcome and the reasoning in the two High Court cases of *McLean v Tedman* (1984) and *Romeo v Conservation Commission (NT)* (1998).

Case examples

- In the case of *McLean v Tedman* (1984), which was described in 2007 by the Chair of the Ipp Review as 'the high point of the nursemaid theory',[3] an employer was held liable to an employee, a garbage collector who was hit by a car when crossing the road without paying proper attention while carrying a loaded rubbish bin. The employer was found to be negligent in failing to take suitable precautions against the foreseeable risk of injury which arose from the practice of garbage collectors running across busy streets. Mason, Wilson, Brennan and Dawson JJ said at 311:

  > In such a situation it is not an acceptable answer to assert that an employer has no control over an employee's negligence or inadvertence. The standard of care expected of the reasonable man requires him to take account of the possibility of inadvertent and negligent conduct on the part of others.

- By the time that *Romeo v Conservation Commission (NT)* (1998) was decided, the majority judges took a very different view of the relevance of a plaintiff's carelessness in the face of a clearly obvious risk. Despite the fact that the apportionment legislation allowed a proportionate deduction of damages depending on the degree of a plaintiff's contributory negligence, the majority in the High Court took into account, when denying liability altogether, the fact that the risk of falling off a cliff was a 'perfectly obvious' risk that posed a danger which anyone exercising reasonable care for their own safety would clearly recognise: Brennan CJ at [25]; also Kirby J at [123]. Toohey and Gummow JJ explained at [50] that while a defendant had to take into account 'the possibility that one or more of the persons to whom the duty is owed might fail to take proper care for his or her own safety', this did not mean that they were obliged to ensure 'that those coming onto the Reserve would not suffer injury by ignoring an obvious danger'.

3 Ipp, 'Themes in the Law of Torts' (2007) at 610.

Many of the other cases discussed in this chapter also follow this trend. See, for example, the two diving cases of *Vairy v Wyong Shire Council* (2005) and *Roads and Traffic Authority (NSW) v Dederer* (2007) and the discussion of the dangers of self-induced intoxication and drink-driving in *CAL No 14 Pty Ltd v Motor Accidents Insurance Board* (2009). The obviousness of the risk and carelessness of the plaintiff were also relevant in *Bunnings Group Ltd v Giudice* (2018) and *Brodie v Singleton Shire Council* (2001). See also *Woods v Multi-Sport Holdings Pty Ltd* (2002), *Bus v Sydney City Council* (1989) at 90 and *Nagle v Rottnest Island* (1993) at 431. The civil liability legislation has made important changes to the law on the relevance of both 'inherent' and 'obvious' risks in different circumstances (eg recreational activities), which affect the way in which courts have traditionally tackled the issue of breach and the defences of voluntary assumption of risk and contributory negligence. It is important to note that, while the common law once approached the issue of obvious and inherent risks *alternatively* as a matter of breach *or* as relevant to the defences of voluntary assumption of risk and contributory negligence, the wording of the civil liability legislation suggests that obvious and inherent risks now constitute statutory defences to negligence, as further discussed in Chapter 15.

LEGISLATION ALERT!

Consult your study materials and note any relevant statutory provisions in your jurisdiction.

Case to remember

Tapp v Australian Bushmen's Campdraft & Rodeo Association Ltd (2022)

Facts

The case stemmed from an accident that occurred during a campdrafting competition, which involves horseback riders working with cattle. The plaintiff, Ms Tapp, who was an experienced rider and a participant in the competition, suffered serious injuries when her horse slipped on the surface of the arena. Both rider and horse fell to the ground. Importantly, prior to Ms Tapp's fall, four other competitors had also fallen from their horses, prompting the organisers to disrupt the competition to assess the arena due to concerns about the slippery ground. This notwithstanding, the competition proceeded, and Ms Tapp was injured.

Issues

The key issue was whether the defendant, the Australian Bushmen's Campdraft & Rodeo Association, had breached its duty of care under s 5B of the *Civil Liabiltiy Act 2002* (NSW), and whether the risk of harm had been an obvious risk from a recreational activity, against which the same act provides a statutory defence under s 5L. Defences to negligence are discussed in Chapter 15. For the purpose of establishing breach, the High Court was to determine whether the risk had been characterised at the appropriate level of generality, and whether the circumstances of s 5B(2) had been appropriately balanced.

Reasoning

With regard to the first point, the appropriate level of generality, Gordon, Edelman and Gleeson JJ in light of the specific facts of the case concluded at [125]:

> [T]he risk should be characterised as the substantially elevated risk of physical injury by falling from a horse that slipped by reason of the deterioration of the surface of the arena ... no more precision than this was necessary in characterising the relevant risk in this case.

With regard to the complex balancing act codifed under s 5B(2), their Honours succinctly outlined their reasoning at [127]:

> In short: (i) the relevant risk was substantially elevated, so that a reasonable person in the position of the Association could have foreseen a probability that harm would occur if the competition were not stopped until members of the Committee ... had taken precautions beginning with inspecting the arena to be satisfied that the ground of the arena was reasonably safe; (ii) the likely seriousness of the harm was at the level of physical injury that could be catastrophic; (iii) the burden of taking precautions to avoid the risk of harm was the simple act of stopping the event to inspect the arena and consider the safety of the ground of the arena; and (iv) these matters could not be outweighed by the social utility of continuing the event so that contestants who had already competed on worse ground were not at a competitive disadvantage.

You should read paragraphs [120] to [143] of the majority judgment by Gordon, Edelman and Gleeson JJ, as it is an excellent illustration of how courts are expected to engage with key elements of s 5B: namely, the proper characterisation of the risk of harm (at [120]–[125]), and the balancing of the relevant circumstances under s 5B(2) – in other words, the 'negligence calculus' as revised in the civil liability legislation (at [126]–[143]).

12.4 Proof of breach

A final aspect to consider is that of proving breach of duty. The rule in negligence claims is that the plaintiff bears the *onus* of proving *on a balance of probabilities* that the defendant's conduct was in breach of their duty of care. It is important to note two preliminary matters:

1. The *onus* of proof rests on the plaintiff: there is no presumption of fault in negligence; when you bring a claim, you have to prove it.
2. The *standard* of proof is on a balance of probabilities: a plaintiff must show that a certain reconstruction of events is more likely than any alternative one. This is fundamentally different from (and significantly lighter than) the standard of proof in criminal law, which requires the prosecution to prove their case beyond reasonable doubt.

You will find that, quite often, *direct evidence* of a defendant's negligence is hard to come by. A classic example of direct evidence is an eyewitness who can provide first-hand information about the event. When direct evidence is unavailable, parties and courts will have to rely on the broader circumstances of the case to establish whether or not, on a balance of probabilities, a defendant's conduct has fallen below the required standard of care.

12.4.1 Use of inferences

When direct evidence is unavailable, courts and parties have to make inferences about the actual unfolding of the events. An inference is a form of logical reasoning by which, from one fact that is established, you can deduce one that is not. This deductive process was formally adopted by the High Court in *Holloway v McFeeters* (1956). In that case, a man was killed in a hit-and-run accident. No direct evidence was available to ascertain what had happened. The evidence that the plaintiff (the man's wife) was able to provide the Court was limited to: a statement from a witness who had interacted with the victim shortly before the accident and could therefore testify to his state; and a number of physical clues, specifically tyre marks and debris from a motor vehicle, and evidence of the state of the victim's body, which had suffered a violent impact. The majority (Williams, Webb and Taylor JJ) explained at 483:

> It is clear that it is a mistake to think that because an event is unseen its cause cannot be reasonably inferred ... Inferences from actual facts that are proved are just as much part of the evidence as those facts themselves.

This finding was subsequently restated in cases such as *Jones v Dunkel* (1959) and *TNT Management Pty Ltd v Brooks* (1979), both of which were road accident cases. All of these cases made reference to the older decision by the High Court in *Bradshaw v McEwans Pty Ltd* (1951), and specifically to the following decisive passage of the reasoning by Dixon, Williams, Webb, Fullagar and Kitto JJ at 5:

> We are concerned with probabilities, not with possibilities. The difference between the criminal standard of proof in its application to circumstancial [sic] evidence and the civil is that in the former the facts must be such as to exclude reasonable hypotheses consistent with innocence while the latter you need only circumstances raising a more probable inference in favour of what is alleged. In questions of this sort where direct proof is not available it is enough in the circumstances appearing in the evidence give rise to a reasonable and definite inference: they must do more than give rise to conflicting inferences of equal degrees of probability so that the choice between them is mere matter of conjecture. But if circumstances are proved in which it is reasonable to find a balance of probabilities in favour of the conclusion sought then though the conclusion may fall short of certainty it is not to be regarded as a mere conjecture or surmise.

And at 6:

> All that is necessary is that according to the course of common experience the more probable inference from the circumstances that sufficiently appear by

> evidence or admission, left unexplained, should be that the injury arose from the defendant's negligence. By more probable is meant no more than that upon a balance of probabilities such an inference might reasonably be considered to have some greater degree of likelihood.

Note that while the case law on inferential proof derives mostly from road accident claims, the principles developed in such cases are applicable to negligence claims in general: *Lithgow City Council v Jackson* (2011); *Seltsam Pty Ltd v McGuiness* (2000). Inferential reasoning can also be used in less physical and more abstract contexts, such as in *Karpik v Carnival plc* (2023), noted above, where the Court inferred its finding as to the burden of taking precautions against a foreseeable risk of harm.

12.4.2 *Res ipsa loquitur*

Res ipsa loquitur ('the thing itself speaks') is a method of proof that has been accepted by courts in a limited number of situations. The idea is simple: the harmful event (the *res*, or 'thing') is in and of itself proof of negligent conduct, so the simple fact that the accident happened will suffice to demonstrate that the conduct of the defendant must have fallen below the standard of care. *Res ipsa loquitur* was first applied in the case of *Scott v London & St Katherine Docks Co* (1865) at 667:

> [W]here the thing is shown to be under the management of the defendant or his servants, and the accident is such as in the ordinary course of things does not happen if those who have the management use proper care, it affords reasonable evidence, in the absence of explanation by the defendants, that the accident arose from want of care.

The factors that justify the use of this method of proof are rigidly limited in order to avoid the risk of abuses that would effectively reverse the onus of proof by shifting it from the plaintiff to the defendant. In particular, the High Court clarified in *Schellenberg v Tunnel Holdings Pty Ltd* (2000), per Gleeson CJ and McHugh J at [25], that *res ipsa loquitur* is available when:

- there is an 'absence of explanation' as to how the accident happened;
- the accident is one that would not ordinarily occur without negligence; and
- the act or thing that causes the accident must have been under the defendant's control.

In *Schellenberg v Tunnel Holdings Pty Ltd* (2000), a hose that carried compressed air to a grinding device operated by the plaintiff came loose and injured him. The plaintiff filed a claim in negligence against his employer and relied on *res ipsa loquitur* to prove breach by alleging that the fact that the hose had separated from the fitting was 'in itself evidence of negligence'. On appeal to the High Court, the applicability of the maxim to the circumstances was denied (Gaudron J dissenting), on the following grounds:

- The cause of the accident was known, insofar as it was not controversial that the plaintiff had been hit by the hose – the question thus becoming whether the hose had detached because of the defendant's negligence: Gleeson CJ and McHugh J at [27].

- The Court also found that there could have been multiple and equally plausible alternative explanations of the accident other than the defendant's negligence (eg a latent defect): Kirby J at [118].
- Finally, the thing that caused the accident could not be said to be under the defendant's control, as the plaintiff himself was operating it and therefore had some agency in the unfolding of events: Gleeson CJ and McHugh J at [49].

Note that *res ipsa loquitur* will very rarely be relied upon. For example in cases involving complex machinery, it will generally be inapplicable: *City Elevator Services v Burrows* (2004); *Dimitrelos v 14 Martin Place Pty Ltd* (2007). In *Schellenberg v Tunnel Holdings Pty Ltd* (2000), Gleeson CJ and McHugh J even pondered, at [46], whether or not to abolish the use of *res ipsa loquitur* in Australian tort law altogether. The Court eventually decided not to do so; as Gleeson CJ and McHugh J explained at [47], there is no 'need to subsume the maxim into the general body of tort law: it is already fully consonant with it'. But remember that its use will be limited and depends very much on the facts.

Test your understanding and develop your skills

Exercise 1

Read the reasoning of Mason CJ in *Wyong Shire Council v Shirt* (1980) and contrast it with the reasoning of Gordon, Edelman and Gleeson JJ in *Tapp v Australian Bushmen's Campdraft & Rodeo Association Ltd* (2022). Reflect on the following aspects:

- How, if at all, has the mechanism to establish the standard of care evolved from the common law to the relevant statutory formulations enshrined in civil liability legislation?
- How have the elements of the 'negligence calculus' evolved from the common law to the relevant statutory formulations enshrined in civil liability legislation? What are the differences that are likely to matter in practice?

Exercise 2

Read the reasoning supporting the decision in *Karpik v Carnival plc* (2023), and pay particular attention to the paragraphs dedicated to inferential reasoning. Reflect on the following questions:

- What distinguishes possibility from probability in the context of proving breach?
- Why does this distinction matter in practice?

12.4.3 Summary points

12.4.3.1 Assessing breach

1. Who is the 'reasonable person' in the problem question? Identify the relevant attributes of 'a reasonable person in the defendant's position' by reference to the facts of the case at hand, by considering:

- whether the defendant is a child or an adult;
- the nature of the role that the defendant has assumed and the kind of task that the defendant has undertaken;
- the knowledge (if any) that the plaintiff has of the defendant's level of experience;
- whether the defendant has held themself out as possessing special skills and experience, or is a member of a profession, or a specialist within a profession;
- the information available to the defendant at the time of the events; and
- any other relevant matters identified by the legislation or the common law.

2. How would a reasonable person have responded in the problem question? Identify in factual terms the precautions that the defendant should have taken in response to the risk, in the light of the rules that:
   - the risk must have been *foreseeable*;
   - the risk must have been *not insignificant*; and
   - the *precautions* must be the ones that a reasonable person would have taken in the circumstances, after balancing the following factors.

   First, consider the four mandatory factors from the legislation:

   a. the *probability* that the harm would occur if precautions were not taken;
   b. the *likely seriousness* of the harm;
   c. the *burden of taking precautions* to avoid the risk of harm;
   d. the *social utility* of the activity that creates the risk of harm.

   Second, consider the 'other relevant things' from the case law, including:

   a. any professional or customary standards in the area;
   b. any relevant statutory standards; and
   c. the common law requirement that the defendant must anticipate foreseeable carelessness on the part of the plaintiff – which is now counterbalanced by the legislative requirements that a plaintiff should be aware of inherent risks and obvious risks.

3. Finally, you should consider which elements of proof are available to demonstrate or refute breach of duty in the circumstances of the case.

Active reading

Link each of these summary points to a case in section 12.4 above.

Conclusion

In the traditional formulation of the three elements of negligence, breach stands between duty and causation (see Figure 12.1). This position is not only traditional, but it is also fitting, because it marks the fact that the element of breach has a focus on the facts of the case that is not only more specific and contextual than the duty element but is also less specific than the third and final element of causation. So, while the element of fault provides the tort with its normative heart, the next element of causation takes us one step closer to the body of the tort by looking even more directly at the facts and making the link between the defendant's wrongful conduct and the harm suffered by the plaintiff. In a pleasing symmetry, the element of causation also takes us back to the place that we started and closes the circle of negligence by considering whether or not and why the defendant should be held liable for causing any or all of that harm.

Figure 12.1 Essential steps in breach of duty

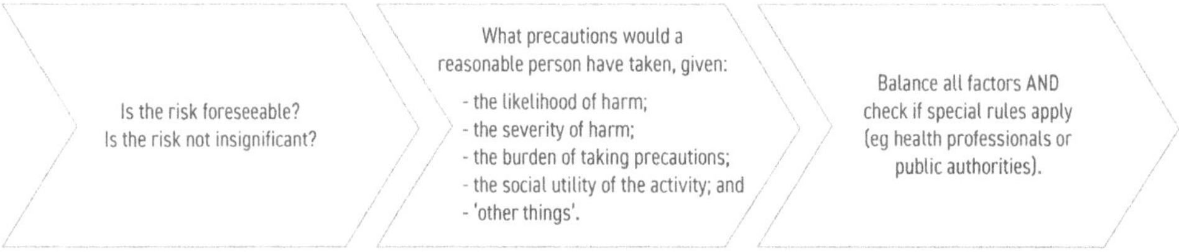

REFERENCES

CASES

Adeels Palace Pty Ltd v Moubarak (2009) 239 CLR 420
Australian Knitting Mills Ltd v Grant (1933) 50 CLR 387
Blyth v Birmingham Waterworks Co (1856) 11 Exch 78; 156 ER 1047
Bolton v Stone (1951) AC 850
Bondi Beach Foods Pty Ltd v Chadwick [2023] NSWCA 265
Bradshaw v McEwans Pty Ltd (1951) 217 ALR 1
Brodie v Singleton Shire Council (2001) 206 CLR 512
Bunnings Group Ltd v Giudice [2018] NSWCA 144
Bus v Sydney City Council (1989) 167 CLR 78
CAL No 14 Pty Ltd v Motor Accidents Insurance Board (2009) 239 CLR 390
Caledonian Collieries Ltd v Spiers (1957) 97 CLR 202
Carrier v Bonham [2002] 1 Qd R 474; [2002] 1 Qd R 474
City Elevator Services v Burrows [2004] NSWCA 26
Coles Supermarkets Australia Pty Ltd v Bridge [2018] NSWCA 183
Cook v Cook (1986) 162 CLR 376
Daborn v Bath Tramways Motor Co Ltd [1946] 2 All ER 333
Derrick v Cheung [2001] HCA 48; (2001) 181 ALR 301
Dimitrelos v 14 Martin Place Pty Ltd [2007] NSWCA 85
Donoghue v Stevenson [1932] AC 562
Drinkwater v Howarth [2006] NSWCA 222
E v Australian Red Cross Society (1991) 27 FCR 310
Electro Optic Systems Pty Ltd v New South Wales [2014] ACTCA 45
Erwin v Iveco Trucks Australia Ltd [2010] NSWCA 113; (2010) 267 ALR 752
Fabre v Lui [2015] NSWCA 157

Farriss v Axford [2023] NSWCA 255
Glasgow Corporation v Muir [1943] 1 KB 205
Graham Barclay Oysters Pty Ltd v Ryan (2002) 211 CLR 540
H v Royal Alexandra Hospital for Children (1990) Aust Torts Reports 81-000
Hoffman v Boland [2013] NSWCA 158; (2013) Aust Torts Reports 82-134
Holloway v McFeeters (1956) 94 CLR 470
Horne v JK Williams Contracting [2023] NSWCA 58
Imbree v McNeilly (2008) 236 CLR 567
Insurance Commissioner v Joyce (1948) 77 CLR 39
Johnson v Firth [2021] NSWCA 237
Jones v Dunkel (1959) 101 CLR 298
Karpik v Carnival plc [2023] FCA 1280
Liprini v Hale (2020) 103 NSWLR 275
Lithgow City Council v Jackson (2011) 244 CLR 352
Lowns v Woods (1996) Aust Torts Reports 81-376
McHale v Watson (1966) 115 CLR 199
McLean v Tedman (1984) 155 CLR 306
Mercer v Commissioner for Road Transport and Tramways (NSW) (1936) 56 CLR 580
Minister Administering the Environmental Planning and Assessment Act 1979 v San Sebastian Pty Ltd [1983] 2 NSWLR 286
Mulligan v Coffs Harbour City Council (2005) 223 CLR 486
Nagle v Rottnest Island (1993) 177 CLR 423
Neindorf v Junkovic [2005] HCA 75; (2005) 222 ALR 631
New South Wales v Fahy (2007) 232 CLR 486
Overseas Tankship (UK) Ltd v The Miller Steamship Co [1967] 1 AC 617 ('*The Wagon Mound (No 2)*')
Palsgraf v Long Island Railway Co, 248 NY 339; 162 NE 99 (1928)
Paris v Stepney Borough Council [1951] 1 AC 367
Philips v William Whitely Ltd [1938] 1 All ER 566
Reardon v Seselja [2021] ACTCA 4
Roads and Traffic Authority (NSW) v Dederer (2007) 234 CLR 330
Roberts v Ramsbottom (1980) 1 WLR 823
Roe v Minister of Health [1954] 2 QB 66
Rogers v Whitaker (1992) 175 CLR 479
Romeo v Conservation Commission (NT) (1998) 192 CLR 431
Schellenberg v Tunnel Holdings Pty Ltd (2000) 200 CLR 121
Scholtz v Standish [1961] SASR 123
Scott v London & St Katherine Docks Co [1865] 3 H&C 596
Seltsam Pty Ltd v McGuiness [2000] *NSWCA* 29; (2000) 49 NSWLR 262
Shaw v Thomas [2010] *NSWCA* 169; (2010) Aust Torts Reports 82-065
Sibley v Kais (1967) 118 CLR 424
Smith v Lord [1962] SASR 88
South Western Sydney Local Health District v Gould [2018] NSWCA 69; (2018) 97 NSWLR 513

Sydney Water Corporation v Turano (2009) 239 CLR 51
Tame v New South Wales (2002) 211 CLR 317
Tapp v Australian Bushmen's Campdraft & Rodeo Association Ltd (2022) 273 CLR 454
The Wagon Mound (No 2) (1967) see *Overseas Tankship (UK) Ltd v The Miller Steamship Co* [1967] 1 AC 617
TNT Management Pty Ltd v Brooks (1979) 23 ALR 325; 53 ALJR 267
Town of Port Hedland v Hodder (No 2) [2012] WASCA 212; (2012) 294 ALR 315
United States v Carroll Towing Co, 159 F2d 169 (1947)
Vairy v Wyong Shire Council (2005) 223 CLR 422
Vaughan v Menlove (1837) 3 Bing (NC) 468; 132 ER 490
Watt v Hertfordshire County Council [1954] 1 WLR 835
Wilsher v Essex Area Health Authority [1987] QB 730; [1988] AC 1074 (House of Lords)
Woods v Multi-Sport Holdings Pty Ltd (2002) 208 CLR 460
Wyong Shire Council v Shirt (1980) 146 CLR 40
Zanner v Zanner [2010] NSWCA 343; 79 NSWLR 702

ARTICLES, BOOKS AND REPORTS

Burns, K, '"In This Day and Age": Social Facts, Common Sense and Cognition in Tort Law Judging in the United Kingdom' (2018) 45(2) *Journal of Law and Society* 226.

Burns, K, 'The Australian High Court and Social Facts: A Content Analysis Study' (2012) 40 *Federal Law Review* 317.

Dietrich, J & Field, I, 'The "Reasonable Tort Victim": Contributory Negligence, Standard of Care and the "Equivalence Theory"' (2017) 41(2) *Melbourne University Law Review* 602.

Gilles, S G, 'The Emergence of Cost–Benefit Balancing in English Negligence Law' (2002) 77(2) *Chicago-Kent Law Review* 489.

Heuston, R F V, '*Donoghue v Stevenson* in Retrospect' (1957) 20(1) *Modern Law Review* 1.

Ipp, D, 'Themes in the Law of Torts' (2007) 81 *Australian Law Journal* 456.

Ipp, D, Cane, P, Sheldon, D & Macintosh, I, *Review of the Law of Negligence: Final Report* (2002) <https://treasury.gov.au/review/review-of-the-law-of-negligence>.

Leeming, M, *The Statutory Foundations of Negligence* (2019) The Federation Press, Alexandria.

Luntz, H, Hambly, D, Burns, K, Dietrich, J, Foster, N, Grant, G & Harder, S, *Torts: Cases and Commentary*, 8th ed (2017) LexisNexis Butterworths, Sydney.

Parker, W, 'The Reasonable Person: A Gendered Concept?' (1993) 23 *Victoria University of Wellington Law Review* 105.

Rizzi, M, 'Health Professionals' Standard of Care and Breach of Duty in Western Australia: A Requiem for the "Peer Professional" Test at a Time of Uncertainty' (2020) 26(2) *Torts Law Journal* 179.

Stewart, P & Stuhmcke, A, *Australian Principles of Tort Law*, 4th ed (2017) The Federation Press, Annandale.

Witting C, 'The Hand and *Shirt* Tests of Breach and the Civil Liability Acts' (2009) 17 *Torts Law Journal* 242.

13 NEGLIGENCE: CAUSATION

Introduction

Causation is arguably the most complex of the elements of negligence. It is covered in three sections in this chapter. Section 13.1 covers the criteria for identifying a recognisable harm and the nature of causation in tort law – that is, what type of explanation does it look for? Section 13.2 covers the evolution of the methods adopted by Australian courts to identify factual causation. Section 13.3 discusses the difficult normative challenge of putting a limit on the extent (or 'scope') of a defendant's liability.

Because this area of the law of negligence is extremely complex, the chapter includes three sets of 'Summary points' and two 'Test your understanding' features. At the end of the chapter, you will find an appendix with the provisions on causation adopted in the civil liability legislation of each Australian state and territory.

13.1 The problem of harm and the nature of the causal inquiry

13.1.1 The problem of harm: A search for limits

The element of causation focuses squarely on the issue of harm.[1] Whereas the element of duty asks us to explain *why* defendants should take reasonable care to avoid acts and

1 It is often said that 'damage is the gist of negligence': see Stapleton, 'The Gist of Negligence' (1988); Nolan, 'New Forms of Damage in Negligence' (2007); *Tabet v Gett* (2010), Gummow J at [16], and Luntz et al, *Torts: Cases and Commentary*, 8th ed (2017), 333. Note that the statutes now use the term 'particular harm' rather than 'damage'.

omissions that they can reasonably foresee might harm their neighbour, and the element of breach asks us to explain *how* the defendants should have behaved in the circumstances, the element of causation asks us first to show *whether* the plaintiff's harm would have been avoided if the defendant had done the right thing, and then to justify *how far* to extend the defendant's liability to compensate the victim for the harm that their conduct has caused. Negligence, like all torts, is conduct by one person that wrongfully and unreasonably causes an adverse effect on another person, and the element of causation brings us to the three critical tasks of:

- defining the harm that is recognised as an adverse effect;
- linking the conduct of the defendant to the harm suffered by the plaintiff; and
- deciding how far the defendant should be held liable for causing that harm.

This element is the most specific and factual of all the elements of negligence, and given that its focus is on harm, it is in one sense the primary element of the tort: if the plaintiff had not suffered any harm or damage, there would be no complaint in the first place. But although this element is the most factual of all, it does not escape the structural uncertainties that bedevil this tort, because as the High Court of Australia ('High Court') said in *Amaca Pty Ltd v Ellis* (2010) at [6], the court's task can sometimes require it 'to reduce to legal certainty a question of causation to which no other conclusive answer can be given'.

Like the element of duty, the element of causation also serves a limiting role. This limiting task is necessary both at the beginning and at the end of a negligence case, because both the 'neighbour test' of foreseeability of harm, which is used in the duty element, and the 'but for' test, which is used in the element of causation of harm, can allow the scope of the tort to go beyond what we intuitively feel is right. So, these 'factual' tests are both supplemented by normative (or value-based) limits that use the concept of reasonableness and the appeal to principles and other values as 'control devices'. In a familiar pattern, the ubiquitous concept of reasonable foreseeability is used to justify the limits – and in this element the focus is on the foreseeability of the *kind of harm* that the plaintiff has suffered. See Figure 10.3 in Chapter 10 on the 'foreseeability progression' in negligence.

In the past, the element of causation was traditionally seen as consisting of two aspects – causation and remoteness – and both aspects were seen as involving the use of value judgements or 'normative' considerations. The conflation of factual and normative considerations was summarised by Mason J in *March v Stramare* (1991) at 518 in his conclusion, which he drew '[a]s a matter of both logic and common sense'. The Ipp Report (2002) at 108 squarely rejected the conflation on this basis:

> The current law in Australia (as laid down by the High Court) appears to be that whether negligent conduct caused the harm in question is to be answered by the application of 'common sense'. A problem with this approach is that it gives courts and parties to negligence claims very little guidance about when negligent conduct will be considered to have caused harm.

The approach adopted in the Ipp Report was to neatly divide the factual and normative components of the causal inquiry. As a result, the issue of causation in the civil liability regime is now seen as a purely factual question and only the issue of 'remoteness' or 'scope of liability' continues to be seen as involving questions of normative value. As restated by Mark Leeming in *The Statutory Foundations of Negligence* (2019) at 70, the two inquiries are separate and must be undertaken in turn. Note that, while some common law cases that predate the civil liability statutes remain relevant today, the law on causation and remoteness has been changed significantly by those statutes, and so you need to be careful to read and refer to these old cases coherently with the current context.

Legislative example

***Civil Liability Act 2002* (NSW) s 5D(1)**

(1) A decision that negligence caused particular harm comprises the following elements –

(a) that the negligence was a necessary condition of the occurrence of the harm ('factual causation');

(b) that it is appropriate for the scope of the negligent person's liability to extend to the harm so caused ('scope of liability').

Note that all states and territories have similar provisions with minor variations, with the exception of the Northern Territory where the common law applies – see Appendix 13.1.

13.1.2 Summary points

13.1.2.1 The element of causation

Under the current statutory approach to the element of causation, a defendant will be liable to compensate a plaintiff for the harm that they have suffered only if three conditions are satisfied:

1. The harm must be of a *kind that is recognised* by law as damage ('particular harm').
2. The defendant must have *factually caused* the harm in the sense that their wrongful conduct was either:
   - a necessary condition (or 'but for' cause) of the occurrence of the harm suffered by the plaintiff; or
   - (in some exceptional circumstances) the defendant's wrongful conduct has materially increased the plaintiff's harm.
3. The harm must fall within the *appropriate scope of liability* in the normative sense that it is not too remote – that is, first, it must be harm of a *kind* that is reasonably foreseeable as a consequence of the breach, even if the *extent* of the harm was not reasonably foreseeable; and second, there must be no alternative and more proximate cause.

Active reading

Link each of these summary points to a case authority or statute discussed in this chapter. Each of these conditions comes from the common law, but in most states and territories they have also been incorporated (with some substantive modifications) by the civil liability legislation. Make sure you note whether the legislation in your jurisdiction contains a definition of harm that must be used where the statute applies.

Legislative example

Civil Liability Act 2002 (WA) s 3

Terms used

In this Act, unless contrary intention appears –

harm means harm of any kind, including the following –

(a) personal injury;

(b) damage to property;

(c) economic loss;

personal injury includes –

(a) death; and

(b) pre-natal injury; and

(c) impairment of a person's physical or mental condition; and

(d) disease; ...

Note that most states and territories identify types of damage to which the statute does not apply (eg *Civil Liability Act 2002* (WA) s 3A). So, for example, should an employee sue their employer in negligence for injuries that would be covered by workers compensation schemes, the civil liability statutes in most states and territories will not apply. The case will be dealt with on the basis of common law rules, which therefore continue to be very relevant.

You should also apply the specific statutory form of factual causation and scope of liability adopted in your jurisdiction. Note that the relevant provisions also specify that the plaintiff always bears the burden of proving, on the balance of probabilities, any fact relevant to the issue of causation.

LEGISLATION ALERT!

Consult your study materials and note the statutory provisions in your jurisdiction on the definition of harm.

Consult your study materials and note the relevant causation provisions in your jurisdiction.

13.1.3 Recognising a 'particular harm'

The element of causation, like the element of duty, serves a linking role in the tort of negligence. Just as the defendant's duty is not called into being unless there is a reasonably foreseeable risk of harm to the plaintiff, the tort is not complete unless the wrongful conduct of the defendant actually causes the plaintiff to suffer some harm. A cause of action in negligence does not crystallise unless and until the plaintiff and the defendant are linked together by the doing and suffering of some actual harm which 'leaves the plaintiff worse off as a result', as Crennan J explained in *Harriton v Stephens* (2006) at [251]. Further, Hayne and Bell JJ said, in *Tabet v Gett* (2010) at [66]:

> For the purposes of the law of negligence, 'damage' refers to some difference to the plaintiff. The difference must be detrimental. What must be demonstrated ... is that a difference has been brought about and that the defendant's negligence was a cause of that difference. The comparison invoked by reference to 'difference' is between the relevant state of affairs as they existed *after* the negligent act or omission, and the state of affairs that *would have existed* had the negligent act or omission not occurred. [Emphasis added.]

This method of comparing the state of affairs that *does exist 'after* the negligent act or omission' with the imaginary 'state of affairs that *would have existed* had the negligent act or omission not occurred' is central to the issue of causation, and a moment's thought will reveal that this exercise, while it is focused on the facts, is not necessarily a simple 'factual' task.

Although the harm that negligence seeks to remedy is very broadly defined in the civil liability legislation (and includes physical injury, mental harm, death or 'loss of life', economic loss and loss/harm of any kind, depending on the wording), at common law not all adverse effects on a plaintiff are necessarily recognised as damage by the courts, and some kinds of harm are treated as special cases. As Gleeson CJ noted in *Cattanach v Melchior* (2003) at [23], and Crennan J said in *Harriton v Stephens* (2006) at 225, proving that actual loss or damage has been suffered requires proof that there has been 'an interference with an interest that has been recognised as capable of protection by law'. This 'recognised damage' limit prevents a plaintiff from recovering damages in negligence if they have suffered certain kinds of adverse effects.

Case examples

- Pure emotional distress, sorrow or grief that does not amount to a recognised psychiatric illness is not compensable: *Mount Isa Mines Ltd v Pusey* (1970); *Tame v New South Wales* (2002). Note that, in this sense, the civil liability legislation introduced on the basis of the Ipp Report recommendations adopts a more restrictive approach than the common law, which referred to a 'recognisable psychiatric illness'. Mental harm is further discussed in Chapter 14.
- Losses that result from a rational and voluntary decision to engage in criminal activity are not compensable: *State Rail Authority of New South Wales v Wiegold* (1991).
- In *Harriton v Stephens* (2006) Crennan J, with whom Gleeson CJ and Gummow J agreed, said at [277] that life itself, with or without disabilities, 'is not actionable'. More specifically, because establishing harm requires courts to recognise that the plaintiff is somehow worse off as a

result of the defendant's negligence, doing so in 'wrongful life' cases is, in the view of Crennan J, impossible. In *Harriton v Stephens*, had the defendant doctor not been negligent, the mother would most likely have opted for an abortion. This means that for a court to find actual damage, they would need to compare a life with disabilities with no life at all, and decide that non-existence is preferable to a life of disability. As Crennan J explained at [252]:

> A comparison between a life with disabilities and non-existence, for the purposes of proving actual damage and having a trier of fact apprehend the nature of the damage caused, is impossible.

- Under some of the civil liability legislation, the award of damages arising from the birth of an unplanned but healthy child born as a result of the negligence of a doctor is not allowed – contrast this with the High Court decision in *Cattanach v Melchior* (2003).
- In the absence of any actual physical injury (ie difference) to a plaintiff, the mere loss of a chance of a better *medical* outcome does not count as damage: *Tabet v Gett* (2010), recently reaffirmed in cases such as *Phelan v Melbourne Health* (2019) and *Williams v Fraser* (2022). Note, however, that a loss of a chance of a better *financial* outcome can constitute recognised damage: *Sellars v Adelaide Petroleum NL* (1994); *Johnson v Perez* (1988).
- The common law traditionally refused to allow that death could give rise to a cause of action: *Baker v Bolton* (1808); *Rose v Ford* (1937); *Fitch v Hyde-Cates* (1982). This was because the courts held that the death of a human being could not be complained of as an injury by a third party and because of the old rule that any cause of action in tort died with the deceased plaintiff. The effect of these rules was reversed by statutes that were enacted first in England and later in Australia, which allowed for the survival of a deceased's cause of action for the benefit of their dependents in cases where a defendant had wrongfully caused the death. Note the difference between the statutes that allow for the survival of a deceased's cause of action for the benefit of the *estate* of the deceased, and the statutes that provide for an independent personal cause of action against the defendant for any *dependents of the deceased*.[2]
- A particularly complex scenario involves the prospective harm of climate change. In *Minister for the Environment v Sharma* (2022), discussed in Chapter 11, Allsop CJ made a number of observations at [295], [297] and [298] with reference to the difficulties of imposing a duty of care in negligence in the absence of a readily foreseeable harm:

> I have already referred to the *unusualness in the law of tort of a duty of care being imposed in the absence of damage or likely threatened damage* from the tortious conduct. Not only is it unusual, but also it has, in these circumstances, the vice of *separating the imposition of the duty from the existence of the cause of action or damage* of such immediate direct threat as to justify a conclusion of the threat of a cause of action. ...
>
> Here duty is sought to be imposed *decades before any foreseeable harm* which could have any connection whatsoever to the act in question referable to the duty imposed.
>
> A duty is being imposed decades before one knows whether there will be a cause of action. This is not to say that the risk of catastrophic global warming is

2 Mendelson, *The New Law of Torts* (2010), ch 3, 'Survival Actions and Wrongful Death'.

> only hypothetical and not real. It is, however, to say that *a duty is being imposed under the law of torts not only before any damage occurs, but decades before one can even begin to assess the causal contribution*, if any, of this decision to any harm. [Emphasis added.]

The reasoning of Allsop CJ is very much in line with the reasoning of Crennan J in *Harriton v Stephens*, albeit on a reverse timeline, insofar as it continues to uphold a narrow conception of harm, which is identified through a hypothetical counterfactual instead of on its own merits.

- Just as the recognised categories of negligence are never closed and are subject to change if a meritorious case arises, the types of recognised damage also evolve in time. This will become apparent in Chapter 14, when we discuss pure mental harm and pure economic loss.
- Finally, you should be aware that there is a *de minimis* rule – that is, a minimum amount of damage that is required for an action in negligence to be successful: *Alcan Gove Pty Ltd v Zabic* (2015).

LEGISLATION ALERT!

Consult your study materials and note the legislation in your jurisdiction dealing with liability for wrongful death and the survival of actions.

The limitations period does not begin to run until actual damage of a recognised kind has been suffered by the plaintiff.

LEGISLATION ALERT!

Consult your study materials and check the legislation in your jurisdiction relating to limitations periods for negligence, noting whether there are any special rules for cases of personal injury.

13.1.4 The problem of causation and scope of liability

The concept of causation has caused philosophers a great deal of pain, but as the High Court has reminded us, lawyers need not suffer to the same extent as philosophers because 'the legal concept of causation differs from philosophical and scientific notions of causation': *March v Stramare* (1991) Mason CJ at 509. One difference lies in the fact that a lawyer's question about causation is always far more precise and much more limited in scope than either the scientist's or the philosopher's – and it is not even asked until it has first been proved that the defendant has fallen short of the standard of reasonable care. As Gemma Turton puts it in *Evidential Uncertainty in Causation in Negligence* (2016) at 33:

> 'Causation' in everyday language is used flexibly to mean different things in different circumstances. In contrast, the law requires greater consistency and precision in the definition of causation.

In this respect, Gaudron J pointed out in *Chappel v Hart* (1998) at [7]:

> Questions of causation are not answered in a legal vacuum. Rather, they are answered in the legal framework in which they arise. For present purposes, that framework is the law of negligence. And in that framework, it is important to bear in mind that that body of law operates, if it operates at all, to assign a duty to take reasonable steps to prevent a foreseeable risk of harm of the kind in issue.

So, while philosophers may ponder the *general meaning* of the concept of 'causation' and while scientists may seek to identify *all* of the causes of a particular event in order to explain it fully, a lawyer asks a much narrower and more purposeful question. The High Court pointed out at [39] in *Amaca Pty Ltd v Ellis* (2010), a case where a man died of lung cancer, the question that the courts ask is not 'Why did Mr Cotton develop lung cancer?' Rather, it asks a more confined question: 'Is it more probable than not that the negligence of the defendant was a cause of Mr Cotton's cancer?' As Mason CJ explained at 509 in *March v Stramare* (1991):

> In law, on the other hand, problems of causation arise in the context of ascertaining or apportioning legal responsibility for a given occurrence. The law does not accept John Stuart Mill's definition of cause as the sum of the conditions which are jointly sufficient to produce it. Thus, at law, a person may be responsible for damage when his or her wrongful conduct *is one of a number of conditions* sufficient to produce that damage. [Emphasis added and references omitted.]

This passage from *March v Stramare* (1991) represents a critically important step forward in the history of the courts' analysis of causation, and this approach, which seeks only to identify whether the defendant's wrongdoing was *'a' cause* of the plaintiff's harm (rather than *'the' single cause*), has now found its way into the civil liability legislation. The common law approach to causation laid down by Mason CJ in *March v Stramare* (1991) also recognised at [516] that the element of causation raises not only factual questions, but also other questions that must be 'tempered by the making of value judgments and the infusion of policy considerations'. This approach to causation, which combined the factual and the normative aspects together into one question, continued to be used until the civil liability legislation took a further step, with a view to keep the two apart. So, now the analytical process that makes the first factual or 'causal' link between the wrongdoing and the harm is separated from the second process, which takes the evaluative or 'normative' considerations into account to determine the extent and scope of the defendant's liability. As a result of these two developments, the law of causation in Australia reached an important new phase in its development, and in 2009 the first cases that were to be decided under the new statutory approach began to reach the High Court. These two steps, which are now known as 'causation' and 'scope of liability', are illustrated in Figure 13.1.

The task of the factual causation test is to tell us how to make the links (represented by the black arrows in Figure 13.1) between one event and another. The task of the normative scope of liability test is to tell us how many of the links in this chain of cause and effect that extend outward from the time when the harm is first suffered by the plaintiff E should be

Figure 13.1 Causation and scope of liability

A, B, C, D: represent the events that lead up to the time when P suffers harm at [E].
[E] is the moment when P first suffers a recognised form of harm and the cause of action accrues.
F, G, H, I: represent further harms that the plaintiff may suffer as time goes on.
The black arrows represent the 'links' of factual causation.
The task of the 'scope of liability' test (which incorporates what used to be referred to as 'remoteness') is to decide where the chain of liability should end.

A → B → C → D → [E] → F → G → H → I → ?

included when we are tallying up the damages bill. The reason why we need the second test is that the test of factual causation cannot tell us when to stop counting the harm that may flow from a defendant's wrongful conduct (which could theoretically continue on forever). Each test has its own challenges, which are explored in the rest of this chapter.

To use a different metaphor, factual causation is the 'flick of the first tile' in a domino effect. Scope of liability is the normative judgment that establishes the number of fallen tiles for which the 'flicker' should be held liable.

As you continue to learn about causation and its various steps, you should always maintain a critical lens and interrogate to what extent is it actually possible to separate the factual from the normative in a blurry tort like negligence. This issue will continue to surface as we progress in the chapter and discuss complex cases.

13.2 Factual causation

13.2.1 The 'necessary condition' or 'but for' test

Two tests are commonly used to determine the question of factual causation. The common law test, known as the 'but for' test, was explained in *March v Stramare* (1991), discussed below. The statutory test, known as the 'necessary condition' test, uses a slightly different formulation of words. One of the first cases to go to the High Court under the new legislation was *Adeels Palace Pty Ltd v Moubarak* (2009). In that case, the High Court considered the version of the test contained in s 5D of the *Civil Liability Act 2002* (NSW), which is broadly similar in effect to the provisions in other jurisdictions (but in some cases, is slightly different in wording – see Appendix 13.1).

Legislative example

Civil Liability Act 2002 (NSW) s 5D(1)

(1) A determination that negligence caused particular harm comprises the following elements:

(a) that the negligence was a necessary condition of the occurrence of the harm (*factual causation*); and

(b) that it is appropriate for the scope of the negligent person's liability to extend to the harm so caused (*scope of liability*).

The High Court in *Adeels Palace Pty Ltd v Moubarak* (2009) pointed out at [42] that this statute 'divides the determination of whether negligence caused particular harm into two elements: factual causation and scope of liability' and emphasised at [44] that the applicable statutory provision 'must be applied'. The Court explained at [45] how the first element of factual causation 'is determined by the "but for" test: but for the negligent act or omission, would the harm have occurred?' This means the two different versions of

Figure 13.2 The 'but for' test

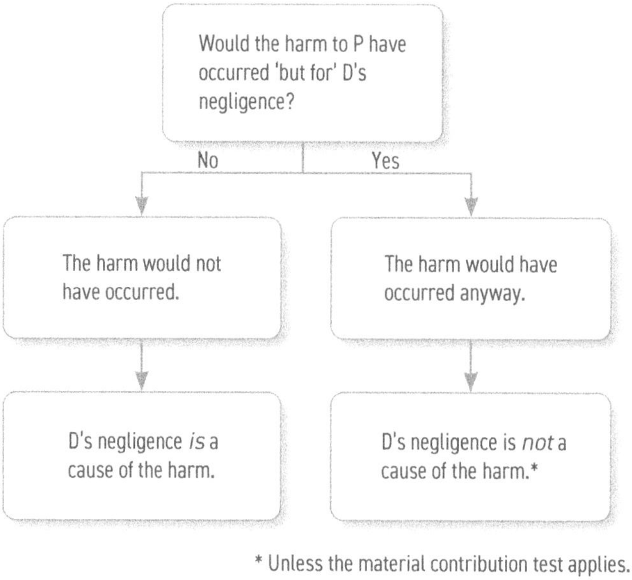

Figure 13.3 The 'necessary condition' test

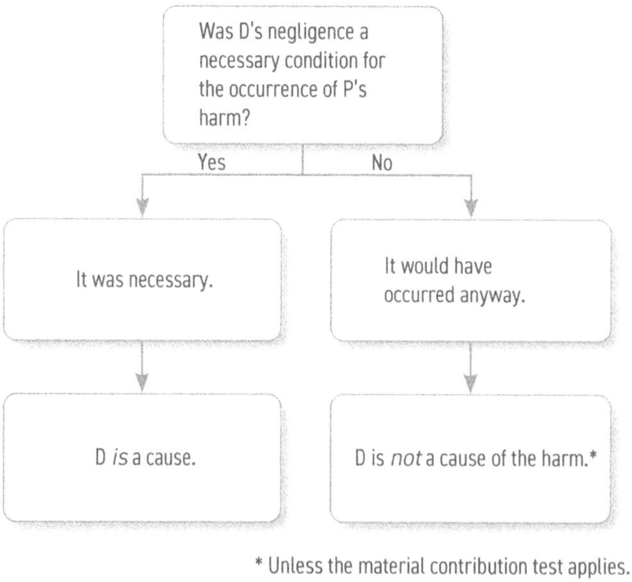

the test can be treated as equivalents, despite the difference in wording. So, if we apply the statutory version of the test to Figure 13.1, A will be counted as a cause of B if the happening of A was a necessary condition of the occurrence of B, and so on through the chain. Another way of formulating the test, as the High Court pointed out, is to say that A will be counted as a cause of B if the occurrence of B would not have happened 'but for' the prior occurrence of A. The two tests give the same outcome, but the statutory version of the test asks a better question that gives us a more intuitively appropriate answer. This is because under the statutory version of the test, a *positive* answer leads to a *positive* finding of causation, as you can see from Figures 13.2 and 13.3.

The High Court applied the test to the facts in *Adeels Palace Pty Ltd v Moubarak* (2009), and concluded at [53] that the 'but for' test of factual causation had not been satisfied.

Case example

The plaintiffs in *Adeels Palace Pty Ltd v Moubarak* (2009) went to a restaurant run by Adeels Palace Pty Ltd (D) on New Year's Eve. After a dispute on the dance floor, another patron left the restaurant, armed himself with a gun and returned to the restaurant, where he shot the two plaintiffs. The victims (Ps) of the gunman claimed that D had been negligent in not providing sufficient security. The High Court held that the Ps had not established the element of causation because they had not proved that if D had provided more security it would have made any difference to the final fate of the Ps, and said at [53]:

> It was not shown to be more probable than not that, but for the absence of security personnel (whether at the door or even on the floor of the restaurant), the shootings would not have taken place. That is, the absence of security personnel at Adeels Palace on the night the plaintiffs were shot was not a necessary condition of their being shot. Because the absence of security personnel was not a necessary condition of the occurrence of the harm to either plaintiff, s 5D(1) was not satisfied.

The High Court also determined that the case did not fit into the category of 'exceptional cases' provided for by s 5D(2) that could be decided by the application of other 'established principles' (ie the 'material contribution' test).

One of the problems associated with the factual test of causation is the difficulty of deciding how far back in time we should go when looking for a cause of the harm. It is sometimes said that if we keep going back in time, we could theoretically go all the way back to the Big Bang and the origins of the universe. Yet, this is not really a problem if we remember that as lawyers we are not interested in causation in the abstract. We are interested only in finding an answer to a confined question, and our question about causation does not even arise *unless and until* we have a person who has already been proved to be a wrongdoer. So, lawyers do not have to keep going back in time seeking out the ultimate cause of everything (or every cause of anything). We simply have to work out whether the wrongdoers will be liable for their conduct, and this means that we rarely have to worry about any items on our chain of cause and effect that may have occurred *before* the first act of wrongdoing on our list.

Case example

If we look again at the facts of the case of *Chapman v Hearse* (1961), noted in Chapter 11, and apply the 'necessary condition' or 'but for' test to the facts of the case, we might be tempted to think that the fact that Dr Cherry had decided to go out to play golf on the day that he died could be counted as one of the 'but for' causes of his eventual tragic death. This is because he would not have been travelling home past the site of the first accident that night, if he had not gone to the golf course that day. However, because his decision to play golf was not an act of wrongdoing, we can discard it from our list of relevant prior events that led up to the death, and focus only on the two acts of wrongdoing that did lead to his death: the first act was Chapman's (D1) negligent conduct in rear-ending the car being driven by Emery, and the second was the negligent driving by Hearse (D2), who was driving too fast in the conditions that night to be able to stop in time to avoid hitting Dr Cherry who was on the road treating D1. If we apply the tests to their conduct, we find that the death of Dr Cherry would not have occurred unless D1 and D2 had both been negligent that night, and so we can understand why the courts held that both men were to be counted as having caused the death – and why both of them had to contribute towards the damages bill.

This is an important point to understand, because any given harm can often be the result of the conduct of more than one person (including the plaintiff), or even a combination of human-caused and natural events.

Case example

In *March v Stramare* (1991) the harm suffered by P had two relevant causes. The first was the conduct of D, who wrongfully parked his vegetable truck in the middle of a six-lane street late at night so that he could unload it. He left the hazard lights on as a warning to other road users. The second relevant cause was the conduct of P himself who was drunk and was speeding along the same road at 1.00 am. He did not see the truck until it was too late to avoid hitting it. Both P and D were clearly at fault, and the High Court, after applying the 'but for' test of causation, decided that both were to be seen as *a cause* of the harm being complained of by the plaintiff. The High Court restored the trial judge's apportionment of damages (of 30 per cent to D who created the initial hazard, and 70 per cent to P who was driving without proper care).

March v Stramare (1991) was a turning point in the law of causation, and while the law has changed since that time, the essential point that Mason CJ made in that case, after analysing the previous rather confused state of the law on causation, remains valid today. The reason for the confusion was that in earlier times the common law provided that any contributory negligence by the plaintiff was a complete defence that destroyed the plaintiff's case, even if they were only 10 per cent to blame for the harm that they suffered. This was very harsh for the plaintiffs, who had to shoulder all of the costs, even though someone else may have been 90 per cent to blame. Later legislative action overturned the common law rule and introduced the apportionment of liability legislation, which allowed judges to divide the cost of the damages bill between the two parties according to their relative degrees of fault. Before this happened, however, the judges had invented another way around the problem by applying the 'last clear opportunity' rule in deserving cases. As Mason CJ explained in *March v Stramare* at 511–4, the judges would allow a careless plaintiff to succeed if the defendant had the 'last clear opportunity' or the 'last clear chance' to avoid the harm. In these cases, the defendant was held to be '*the* effective cause' of the harm, but this rule could also have an unfair outcome, because a defendant, who may have been only partly to blame for the accident, then had to pay for 100 per cent of the cost. Neither of these 'all or nothing' outcomes sat well with the community's sense of justice and so, when the case of *March v Stramare* (1991) reached the High Court, Mason CJ reviewed the law and identified the solution at [512]:

> [T]he courts are no longer as constrained as they were to find *a single cause* for a consequence and to adopt *the* 'effective cause' formula. These days, courts readily recognise that there are concurrent and successive causes of damage on the footing that liability will be apportioned as between the wrongdoers. [Emphasis added.]

So, when you are problem solving, you need to remember that there may well be more than one person to blame for the harm that the plaintiff has suffered, and to bear in mind that if there are several wrongdoers, each of them may be counted as a cause if they satisfy the test.

Test your understanding

Applying the old rules

- Read the case *March v Stramare* (1991) and explain the significance of the apportionment legislation.
- Work out who would have won if the old version of the 'contributory negligence' rule had been applied to the facts of the case.
- Work out who would have won if the 'last clear opportunity' rule had been applied to the facts of the case.

Determining causation can become quite a difficult task, but it is not an issue in every case. If the defendant, by a positive act, has caused physical harm directly to the plaintiff, the issue will rarely arise at all. For example, if the defendant carelessly drives off the road and hits the plaintiff who is innocently walking down the footpath, the issue of causation is clearly and obviously made out. The problem of causation really arises when the cases become more complicated and where the conduct by the defendant is an omission rather than a positive act. However, one of the strengths of the 'but for' test is that it can help us to rule out certain events that should not count as causes, as occurred in *Adeels Palace Pty Ltd v Moubarak* (2009), noted above, and in *Barnett v Chelsea & Kensington Hospital Management Committee* (1968), discussed below.

Case example

In *Barnett v Chelsea & Kensington Hospital Management Committee* (1968), a night watchman drank some tea that was poisoned with arsenic. Feeling unwell, he went to the local hospital and requested treatment. The nurse phoned the duty doctor, who, feeling unwell himself, told her to tell the man to go home to bed and call his own doctor. Five hours later the watchman died. It was established in evidence that even if the watchman had been admitted and treated with the antidote when he had presented at the hospital, he could not have been saved. This was because there was so much poison in his body that no amount of care could have made any difference. The judge therefore found that, while the doctor was clearly in breach of his duty to treat the patient, the element of causation could not be made out on the facts, and so no liability was imposed. Remember that factual evidence is critical to establish factual causation.

The doctor in this case, who had done the wrong thing by failing to treat the patient, did not have to pay damages to the night watchman's widow because his wrongdoing made no real difference to the watchman's final fate. The critical piece of evidence was the fact that no antidote would have saved the patient. If nothing would have saved the patient, then the doctor's failure to treat him could not be counted as 'a cause' of the death. The only cause of the death was the person who originally poisoned the tea. On the other hand, if the poison had not taken such a deadly hold on the patient and a timely application of the antidote would have saved him, then the doctor's negligence would have been counted as one of two causes of the death and then liability would have been imposed. This is why the question of causation is described as a question of fact – because we need factual evidence to help us to work out what would have happened on the balance of probabilities if the defendant had done the right thing.

The reasoning process used in cases where causation is an issue requires us to use our imagination to make a comparison between two different states of affairs. We compare what we know *did happen* with the state of affairs that we imagine *would have happened* in a parallel factual universe where we keep everything the same, except the single fact of the defendant's wrongdoing. We change the script and try to imagine what would have happened if the defendant had done the right thing, and then compare the outcome of our thought experiment with the known outcome of the case at hand. If both outcomes are identical, we can decide that the element of causation has not been satisfied. But if the outcomes differ and it seems that the harm would have been avoided if the defendant had done the right thing, we can conclude that causation has been established. Tables 13.1 and 13.2 illustrate the process. It is critically important in problem solving to identify at the breach stage of your analysis the actual nature of the precautions that the defendant should have taken on the facts of the case *before* you try to apply the 'but for' test of causation. This is because the test requires you to compare and contrast what *did* happen with what is *likely to have happened* if the defendant had taken those precautions. So, the breach analysis leads into the 'but for' analysis of causation.

In *Barnett v Chelsea & Kensington Hospital Management Committee* (1968), the test showed that the conduct of the defendant was not 'a cause' of the harm. Table 13.1

Table 13.1 *Barnett v Chelsea & Kensington Hospital Management Committee*

What did occur in the case:	What would have happened:
a. P, a watchman, drinks a cup of tea that is poisoned with arsenic.	A. P, a watchman, drinks a cup of tea that is poisoned with arsenic.
b. P becomes sick, attends hospital and requests treatment.	B. P becomes sick, attends hospital and requests treatment.
c. Doctor, *in breach of duty, fails to treat P.*	C. Doctor, *in conformity with duty, treats P,* but poison is so strong that no treatment would have worked.
d. P *dies* from arsenic poisoning.	D. On balance of probabilities, P *would have died* from arsenic poisoning.

At point c/C: Crucial finding of fact: Treatment would *not* have worked.
At point d/D: Crucial comparison between what did happen and what would have happened if the doctor had followed his duty to treat the patient.
Conclusion: Given the identity of outcomes on balance of probabilities, factual causation is not established.

illustrates the reason why the issue of causation is a question of fact: because the only way to decide the matter is by weighing the evidence. A similar scenario occurred more recently in *Ziaee v Rubino* (2023), which involved a patient who suffered harm because of a long waiting period before being treated by a specialist. The plaintiff lamented the failure of their GP to follow up on their referral to the specialist. The Australian Capital Territory Court of Appeal was not persuaded that the failure to follow up constituted a breach to begin with. But even if it had, the Court at [67] found nothing in the evidence departing from 'the normal operation of a significantly overstretched public health system'. The reason for the delay was a product of the ordinary operation of priority classification rules. This meant that following up on a referral would not have resulted in seeing a specialist any sooner, thereby defeating the 'but for' test.

If there is not enough evidence the case fails altogether (as in *Adeels Palace Pty Ltd v Moubarak* (2009)), but in *Barnett v Chelsea & Kensington Hospital Management Committee* (1968) the evidence was clear, just as it was in another contrasting medical case, *Rogers v Whitaker* (1992), where the element of causation was made out and the case succeeded (see Table 13.2).

Case example

In *Rogers v Whitaker* (1992), a doctor was held to have fallen short of his duty to take reasonable care to advise a patient (who was blind in one eye) of an exceptionally small chance (1 in 14 000) that as a result of elective cosmetic surgery on her blind eye, she could develop a rare condition called sympathetic ophthalmia that could lead to blindness in her good eye. The patient was particularly worried throughout the course of her consultations with the doctor about anything happening to her good eye, and she established in evidence that she would not have gone ahead with the operation had she been told that there was any chance, however small, that her one remaining eye could be affected.

Table 13.2 *Rogers v Whitaker*

What did occur in the case:	What would have happened:
a. P, who is blind in one eye, seeks advice from her doctor, D. Doctor informs P of cosmetic operation that will improve the appearance of her blind eye.	A. P, who is blind in one eye, seeks advice from her doctor, D. Doctor informs P of cosmetic operation that will improve the appearance of her blind eye.
b. P asks incessant questions about the operation because of her fear that something might happen to her good eye.	B. P asks incessant questions about the operation because of her fear that something might happen to her good eye.
c. D, *in breach of duty, fails to advise P* of a tiny, but real, risk of sympathetic ophthalmia.	C. D, *in conformity with duty, does tell P* of a tiny, but real, risk of sympathetic ophthalmia.
d. P *goes ahead* with operation.	D. Operation would *NOT have occurred.*
e. Sympathetic ophthalmia occurs and P *becomes blind* in both eyes.	E. P *would have retained sight* in the good eye.

At point c/C: Crucial finding of law: D had a duty to advise P of small, but material risk.
At point d/D: Crucial finding of fact: This P would *not* have gone ahead with the cosmetic operation if D had followed his duty and advised her of the risk.
At point e/E: Crucial contrast between what did happen and what would have happened if the doctor had followed his duty to advise the patient.
Conclusion: Given the disparity *of outcomes on the balance of probabilities, factual causation* is *established.*

The High Court decision in *Tapp v Australian Bushmen's Campdraft & Rodeo Association Ltd* (2022), discussed in Chapter 12, is a recent restatement of this approach. A reasonable person in the plaintiff's position would not have had any concerns about the safety of the grounds and would not have inspected them. Therefore, 'but for' the negligence of the defendant failing to maintain or, at a minimum, warn of the condition of the grounds, the plaintiff would not have fallen and suffered harm. Or, to use the statutory language, the negligence of the defendant was a necessary condition for the fall and subsequent injuries to the plaintiff.

13.2.2 Complex scenarios: Multiple sufficient causes (or 'causal overdetermination')

The 'but for' test is certainly attractive in its simplicity; however, there are circumstances in which it is liable to produce irrational results. Katy Barnett and Sirko Harder discuss the issue of causal overdetermination in *Remedies in Australian Private Law* (2019). This is the situation in which the defendant's negligent conduct *and* another wrongful or non-wrongful event 'were each sufficient to bring about the plaintiff's harm, or would each have been sufficient if the other harm had not occurred' (at 81). If we adopt Barnett and Harder's model, causal overdetermination can be of two types: duplicative causation or pre-emptive causation.

13.2.2.1 Duplicative causation

To understand duplicative causation, take, for example, the following situation, which is adapted from the facts of *Summers v Tice* (1948), noted below in section 13.2.3.3 below. Three friends set out on a hunting party in the course of which two of them fire one pellet each. Unfortunately for their third companion, both pellets lodge in his right eye, causing him blindness in that eye. It is proved that while both pellets hit the eye, each on its own would have been sufficient to cause the blindness. In this scenario the 'but for' test yields a misleading result, because it suggests – given the identity of outcomes if we conduct the thought experiment – that neither shooter was a 'necessary condition' of the loss of the eye in the circumstances. If Shooter 1 had not shot his gun, then the harm to the victim would have occurred anyway (because the other shot was enough on its own to cause the blindness). Likewise, if Shooter 2 had not shot his gun, then the harm to the victim would still have occurred anyway. Both shots constitute sufficient causes of the harm, and therefore both would fail on a strict application of the 'but for' test.

A similar problem exists when, instead of two independent positive actions, the harm is caused by two independent omissions. This type of situation was dealt with by the New South Wales Court of Appeal in *Elayoubi v Zipser* (2008), which is discussed in detail by Barnett and Harder at 83–4. The Court held that when both independent causes are wrongful acts, both are to be considered factual causes of the harm. Basten JA summarised the rationale for this decision at [57]:[3]

> If the negligence of the two tortfeasors each contributes to the indivisible harm suffered by the victim, each is liable for the harm suffered. If neither were negligent, no harm would have been caused. If either one were negligent and the other not, in each case the negligence would have caused the harm. But a conclusion that if both were negligent and the harm eventuated, neither was responsible for that harm, invites a question as to whether the reasoning process has gone awry.

You should note that under the civil liability legislation, which mandates a strict application of the 'but for' or 'necessary condition' test, this type of reasoning, essentially grounded on fairness and public policy, would be difficult to justify, and would need to rely on the application of subsection (2) of the statutory provisions on factual causation.

Legislative example

Civil Liability Act 2002 (NSW) s 5D(2)

(2) In determining in an exceptional case, in accordance with established principles, whether negligence that cannot be established as a necessary condition of the occurrence of harm should be accepted as establishing factual causation, the court is to consider (amongst other relevant things) whether or not and why responsibility for the harm should be imposed on the negligent party.

3 In situations where one of the sufficient causes is negligent and the other is not (which Basten JA adverted to only in passing), it could be argued that the defendant should not be liable. That result would be coherent with situations involving pre-emptive causation in which the pre-empted event (second in time) is not negligent.

Note that most states and territories have similar provisions, with minor variations in Victoria and Western Australia (which make reference to an 'appropriate case'), and a more limited scope of application in the Australian Capital Territory and South Australia.

See the detailed discussion in section 13.2.4 below on the application of the exception, and Appendix 13.1.

LEGISLATION ALERT!

Consult Appendix 13.1 and your study materials and note the scope of application of the exception to the 'necessary condition' test in the legislation in your jurisdiction.

13.2.2.2 Pre-emptive causation

The second category of causal overdetermination eventuates when, once again, there are two sufficient causes of some or all of the harm suffered by the plaintiff, but this time one cause pre-empts the other (pre-emptive causation). This type of situation is best understood by reference to three classic decisions by United Kingdom courts: *Performance Cars Ltd v Abraham* (1962), *Baker v Willoughby* (1970) and *Jobling v Associated Dairies Ltd* (1982).

Case examples

- In *Performance Cars Ltd v Abraham* (1962), the plaintiff's car was damaged in two successive collisions within a two-week interval. Each collision alone would have been sufficient to cause the damage to the car, and the car had not been repaired at the time of the second collision. In this instance, the first accident pre-empted the second – the second driver had not caused any additional damage and therefore was not liable, despite having negligently caused an accident. The principle here is that the pre-empted event cannot be considered a factual cause of the harm (which has in fact already happened), whether or not the pre-empting event is negligent. In Australia, Barwick CJ used similar reasoning in *Dillingham Construction Pty Ltd v Steel Mains Pty Ltd* (1975).
- In *Baker v Willoughby* (1970) P was hit by a car in an accident that left him with a stiff ankle, reduced mobility and a reduced earning capacity. After the accident, but before the trial, P was shot by a robber in the same leg, which at that point had to be amputated. D argued at trial that the shooting had superseded the initial harm caused by the accident and, therefore, they should be liable to compensate P only for the physical injury and loss of earnings suffered as a result of the initial accident up until the shooting happened. The House of Lords rejected this argument, holding D liable for the initial damage suffered by P even after the time of the shooting. The principle here appears to be that, when both events are wrongful, the pre-empting event (the one that chronologically happens first) is to be regarded as a cause of the harm – a principle restated in *Dimond v Lovell* (2002).
- In *Jobling v Associated Dairies Ltd* (1982), the plaintiff, Mr Jobling, suffered a slipped disk as a result of falling on the floor at work due to his employer's negligence. As a result of his injury his earning capacity was reduced to half of what he was making before the accident. Four years later, but before the trial, Mr Jobling was diagnosed with a pre-existing spinal condition, not

caused by the accident, which would eventually make him completely unable to work. In this case, the House of Lords held that damages would be owed by the employer only until the onset of the disease. The principle here is that when the pre-empted event (or the event subsequent in time) is *not* a wrong, the first wrongdoer will only be liable for the damages occurring as a result of the pre-empting event (first in time) up until the onset of the pre-empted event (second in time). This was accepted in Australia in *K-Mart Australia Ltd v McCann* (2004).

13.2.3 Proving factual causation and the issue of 'evidentiary gaps'

As with breach of duty (Chapter 12), the onus of proving factual causation rests again on the plaintiff. This approach was summarised in the Ipp Report (2002) at 117:

> **Recommendation 29**
> The Proposed Act should embody the following principles:
> *Onus of proof*
>
> **(a)** The plaintiff always bears the onus of proving, on the balance of probabilities, any fact relevant to the issue of causation.

This recommendation has been adopted in the civil liability legislation in all states and territories except the Northern Territory.

LEGISLATION ALERT!

Consult your study materials and identify the statutory provisions in your jurisdiction on the onus of proof of causation.

Discharging the onus of proof of causation can sometimes be a relatively straightforward exercise. For example, in a road traffic accident, once the negligence of the defendant driver has been established and the harm has eventuated, proving causation is usually uncontroversial. In more complex cases, the availability of evidence will be decisive: see, for example, *Rogers v Whitaker* (1992). As discussed above, it was easy for the plaintiff in that case to prove causation, because the evidence showed that she would have done nothing to jeopardise her good eye and would not have accepted even an infinitesimal risk. However, in cases involving a higher degree of evidentiary uncertainty, a straight application of the 'but for' test can be problematic. We will look at three evidentiary issues that can give rise to particularly thorny issues at the causal stage of a negligence claim.

13.2.3.1 The plaintiff's own evidence

When the negligence of a defendant involves an omission – for example, a failure to warn – establishing causation requires the plaintiff to establish on the balance of probabilities what would have happened in the hypothetical alternative scenario in which the defendant had not been negligent. The Ipp Report (2002) at 118 made the following recommendation:

Recommendation 29

The Proposed Act should embody the following principles:

Factual causation

(i) For the purposes of sub-paragraph (ii) of this paragraph, the plaintiff's own testimony, about what he or she would have done if the defendant had not been negligent, is inadmissible.

(ii) Subject to sub-paragraph (i) of this paragraph, when, for the purposes of deciding whether allegedly negligent conduct was a factual cause of the harm, it is relevant to ask what the plaintiff would have done if the defendant had not been negligent, this question should be answered subjectively in the light of all relevant circumstances.

This provision has been adopted in most jurisdictions, with the exception of South Australia, the Australian Capital Territory and the Northern Territory – see Appendix 13.1. You should note that this difference should not have any notable practical repercussions given the similar attitude adopted by the common law towards the plaintiff's own evidence. The essential point is that a plaintiff cannot rely on their own appreciation of what they would have done differently with the benefit of hindsight. This issue was central in two medical negligence claims in *Rosenberg v Percival* (2001) and *Wallace v Kam* (2013), both of which are discussed in greater detail in Chapter 14. In *Rosenberg v Percival,* Kirby J at [158] quoted an article by Shane Monks, 'The Concept of Informed Consent in the United States, Canada, England and Australia: A Comparative Study' (1993) at 233:

> When determining whether a reasonable patient would attach significance to a risk, the court should bear in mind that reasonable people accept not insignificant risks on a regular basis, eg driving cars and playing contact sport.
>
> When deciding whether the patient would have undergone treatment if the risk had been disclosed, the court should assess the plaintiff's testimony carefully ... If a reasonable person would have undergone treatment, regardless of disclosure, then in the absence of personal characteristics or circumstances which would explain a refusal, it must be difficult for a court to conclude that the plaintiff would have rejected the treatment no matter what the plaintiff now genuinely believes that he or she would have done.

A similar point was made few years later by the Full Court of Western Australia in *Prast v Town of Cottesloe* (2000). The case involved a bodysurfer who was rendered tetraplegic by a wave that had thrown him on the ocean bed near the shore at Cottesloe Beach. The plaintiff alleged that the Town of Cottesloe had breached its duty to provide adequate warnings about the risks to surfers presented by the shallow waters and rocky ocean bed near the shore. Ipp J took this opportunity to explain at [47]:

> [I]n deciding upon the hypothetical question as to what would have occurred had the defendant done certain things, objective factors are generally more important than the plaintiff's subjective testimony in hindsight.

And again at [54]:

> The test for causation remains a subjective one although ... appropriate weight must be given to all relevant objective factors.

Evidence of what the plaintiff would have done in the circumstances had the defendant not been negligent is highly relevant – and this explains the reference made by Ipp J to the subjective nature of the causal test in cases involving a failure to warn. But the sole testimony of the plaintiff, given with the benefit of hindsight, will be inadmissible. Indeed, what the plaintiff would have done differently, while a subjective matter, should be proved by reference to the circumstances of the case and objective factors, such as the abundant evidence presented by the plaintiff in *Rogers v Whitaker* (1992) noted above.

13.2.3.2 The use of inferences

A second evidentiary dilemma for plaintiffs seeking to prove factual causation is the use of inferences. The thrust of the reasoning that justifies the use of inferences for the purpose of proving breach (discussed in Chapter 12) applies equally to the use of inferences in proof of causation. This is unsurprising, since both breach and factual causation deal with questions of fact, and, as suggested by Sandy Steel in *Proof of Causation in Tort Law* (2015) at 66, '[t]here is a sense in which all of our conclusions about matters of fact involve inductive inference'. The matter has been tackled by the High Court in several cases.

Case examples

- In *Chappel v Hart* (1998), a medical negligence case, which is further discussed in section 14.6 of Chapter 14, McHugh J explained at [34] that in cases involving a failure to warn where a plaintiff proves that the defendant has breached their duty to warn of a risk, and the risk eventuates, a prima facie case of causal connection can be inferred. This reasoning was further developed by McLure J in *City of Stirling v Tremeer* (2006) at [80]:

  > As I understand the law in Australia, once a plaintiff demonstrates that a breach of duty has occurred followed by injury within the area of the foreseeable risk, a *prima facie* causal connection will be established and the defendant has an evidential burden to show that the breach had no effect. However, once there is evidence sufficient to displace the plaintiff's prima facie case, it remains for the plaintiff upon the whole of the evidence to satisfy the tribunal of fact of the extent of the injury caused by the defendant's negligence.

  As clarified by Harold Luntz et al in *Torts: Cases and Commentary* (2017) at 285, the fact that courts *can* draw inferences to establish causal links does not *compel* them to do so.

- The matter was further discussed in *Amaca Pty Ltd v Booth* (2011), a difficult asbestos case noted in section 13.2.4 below. While maintaining that the onus of proof rests on the plaintiff (as mandated by the civil liability legislation), French CJ sanctioned the use of logical inferences, explaining at [43]:

> [I]f the association between two events is shown to have a causal explanation, then the conclusion may be open, if the second event should occur, that the first event has been at least a contributing cause of that outcome. An after-the-event inference of causal connection may be reached on the civil standard of proof, namely, balance of probabilities, notwithstanding that the statistical correlation between the first event and the second event indicated, prospectively, no more than a 'mere possibility' or 'real chance' that the second event would occur given the first event.

This means that the causal inquiry is to be carried out with the benefit of hindsight, in the sense that it is only after the fact that it is possible to assess whether a certain conduct was a necessary condition for the harmful event to occur. The fact that an event is *unlikely* to be triggered by a certain action or omission does not mean that, in the circumstances, the event was not in fact caused by such action or omission, and a court can reach this conclusion on the basis of logical inferences.

Note: You must be careful to distinguish the fact that *causation is established with the benefit of hindsight* from the limitations placed on the admissibility of the *plaintiff's own evidence, given with the benefit of hindsight*, as to what they would have done had the tortfeasor not been at fault, as discussed above. Consider too that, as discussed in *Brocklands Ptd Ltd v Tasmanian Networks Pty Ltd* (2020) and again in *East Metropolitan Health Service v Ellis* (2020) (further discussed in Chapter 14), it is sufficient that *a* breach of duty caused the harm, without the need to specify *which* exact breach did so where multiple breaches have been shown to occur. It is sufficient for a court to be satisfied, on the balance of probabilities, that the harm suffered by a plaintiff was caused by one or more of the breaches of duty by the defendant, even if the court is not (or cannot be) satisfied that the harm was caused by any one particular breach.

- In *Strong v Woolworths Ltd* (2012) P, who had an amputated leg, slipped and fell when one of her crutches came in contact with a fried potato chip that was lying on the floor of a shopping mall outside a Big W store operated by D. As a result of the fall, she suffered a serious back injury. At the time, D had no system in place for the inspection and cleaning of the area, which was found to be in breach of its duty of care as occupier of the premises. At trial, it was also found that an adequate system would have required inspections to take place every 20 minutes. The question for the Court was therefore whether, on a balance of probabilities, the chip had been on the floor long enough to be caused by D's negligence. As the accident occurred at 12.30 pm, the question was whether the chip had reached the floor after 12.10 pm (in which case even an adequate system would not have prevented the fall) or earlier (which would satisfy factual causation). The New South Wales Court of Appeal found in favour of D on the basis that there was no evidence to support the inference that the chip had been there for a long period of time. Of relevance to the Court of Appeal's reasoning was the fact that the incident had taken place in a food court at lunch hour, suggesting that the chip had probably been there for a short amount of time. In their joint majority judgment, French CJ, Gummow, Crennan and Bell JJ reversed the Court of Appeal's decision on the basis that (at [38]):

  > The evidence did not permit a finding of when, in the interval between 8.00am and 12.30pm, the chip came to be deposited in that area. In these circumstances, it was an error for the Court of Appeal to hold that it could not be concluded that the chip had

> been on the ground for long enough for it to be detected and removed by the operation of a reasonable cleaning system. The probabilities favoured the conclusion that the chip was deposited in the longer period between 8.00am and 12.10pm and not the shorter period between 12.10pm and the time of the fall.

This interesting decision implies that, where circumstances warrant it, in the face of an otherwise insurmountable evidentiary gap, a causal link may be inferred on the basis of probabilistic reasoning. So, in this case, in the absence of any other element of proof, the probability of a chip falling in an interval of 4 hours and 10 minutes is to be considered higher than that of the same chip falling in a shorter interval of less than 20 minutes. You should note, however, that both the decision of the Court of Appeal and that of the High Court rely, explicitly or implicitly, on an assumption (or 'social fact', to use Kylie Burns' terminology discussed in Chapter 12). The Court of Appeal assumed that it was more likely than not that chips would be consumed at lunchtime. The High Court, in dismissing this finding as speculation, implicitly relied on the different assumption that people are equally likely to consume chips at any point in time between 8 am and 12.30 pm. This case is an excellent illustration of the inherent difficulties that courts will encounter when they try to neatly separate the factual from the normative in establishing causation. While certainly attractive in the abstract, the two-steps approach of the civil liability legislation ('necessary condition' first, and then 'scope of liability') does not always stack up to the complexity and imperfection of real-life scenarios.

- In *Karpik v Carnival plc* (2023), noted in Chapter 11, the issue was whether the negligence of D had caused P's husband to become infected with COVID-19. D's argument was to the effect that its negligence had merely increased the probability of harm occurring without in fact causing it (a method of establishing factual causation developed in the United Kingdom under the case of *Fairchild v Glenhaven Funeral Services Ltd* (2003), which has not been accepted in Australia, as further discussed below). The Full Court of the Federal Court of Australia rejected the argument in light of the circumstances of the case, as well as relevant expert testimonies, and restated at [818]:

> [I]t is uncontroversial that expert evidence that expresses itself in the form of possibilities and risks, rather than probabilities, can be relevant and support an inference of causation.

13.2.3.3 Multiple wrongdoers

A situation that poses serious challenges to the operation of the 'but for' test is the scenario in which multiple wrongdoers *could* have individually or cumulatively caused the harm and there is simply no conclusive way to identify who *actually* caused or contributed to the harm and who did not.

Case example

In *Summers v Tice* (1948), three men went quail hunting. A quail was flushed out from the undergrowth and two men (Ds) fired their shotguns loaded with pellets. P was hit in the eye by one pellet and in the lip by another pellet, which meant either that one D had hit him with two pellets or that both Ds had hit him with one pellet each. It could not be established which of the Ds had caused the injuries. The Court decided that in the face of the uncertainty over who had actually injured P, P could recover damages from both Ds, and held at 88 that 'reasons of policy and justice' justified shifting 'the burden to each of defendants to absolve himself if he can'. A very similar case, which had significant influence in the subsequent development of the rules of causation in the common law world, was *Cook v Lewis* (1951) – a case from Canada resolved in the same way.

We have looked at a hypothetical scenario adapting these facts in section 13.2.2 above as an example of 'duplicative causation'. The difference with the actual case of *Summers v Tice* (1948) is that, in the hypothetical scenario, it was established that both hunters had fired one pellet each, and both had hit the plaintiff's eye. Conversely, the difficulty for the plaintiff in *Summers v Tice* (1948) was that he could not prove on the balance of probabilities *who* had caused his injuries. In the hypothetical scenario, characterised by duplicative causation, there is 'causal overdetermination' (each event is a sufficient cause of the harm); but in the *Summers* scenario there is an 'evidentiary gap', in the sense that both events could have *alternatively* caused the harm. The Court simply could not know with any certainty whether one single shooter had caused the injury or whether two wrongdoers had each contributed to the injury. The judges had the choice of dismissing the case for lack of proof or finding another way around the problem – and so they used their sense of fairness to engineer a result, because, in the absence of all the facts, the 'but for' test could not provide an answer to the problem.

This logical conundrum is particularly intricate in the cases dealing with what Jane Stapleton calls 'human-made diseases', such as asbestosis or adverse reactions to chemicals or pharmaceuticals, which have led the courts to develop the 'material contribution' test as an exception to the rule requiring plaintiffs to satisfy the 'but for' test in cases involving multiple wrongdoers and presenting otherwise insurmountable evidentiary gaps.[4]

13.2.4 The 'material contribution' test

Given the weaknesses of the 'but for' test, particularly in the presence of multiple sources of harm (whether wrongfully caused or not), and the recognised need to supplement the test either with special exceptions or with value judgments, policy and 'common sense', the courts developed an alternative test of causation, which has become known as the 'material contribution' test. This alternative test has now been given explicit statutory recognition in the civil liability legislation of South Australia and the Australian Capital Territory, while in other states and territories it is applicable to the extent that it is recognised as an 'established principle': see Appendix 13.1. It can

4 The point is eloquently made by Stapleton in 'Compensating Victims of Diseases' (1985) at 248: 'The bias to accidents is readily explained for, although the law of torts does not formally sanction preferential treatment of accident victims, its conceptual machinery dramatically favours this class in practice. As a consequence effective tort liability is principally confined to cases of traumatic injury.'

generally be used either when there is some recognised form of relevant evidential uncertainty or in cases where there are multiple sufficient causes. It is important, however, to distinguish between cases where the fact of uncertainty completely destroys a plaintiff's case (as happened in *Amaca Pty Ltd v Ellis* (2010)) and other cases where a different kind of uncertainty triggers the use of the alternative (and exceptional) material contribution test.

Case example

In *Amaca Pty Ltd v Ellis* (2010), Mr Cotton died of lung cancer. He had worked for two employers who had exposed him to asbestos, which is known to cause cancer. He had also smoked between 15 and 20 cigarettes a day for over 26 years, which is also known to cause cancer. The evidence could not prove with any certainty whether the cancer had been caused either by the asbestos alone, or by the smoking alone, or by the combination of both the smoking and the asbestos exposure. After identifying the question to be asked at [40], which was 'Is it more probable than not that the negligence of the defendant was a cause of Mr Cotton's cancer?', the High Court said at [70]:

> The answer to the question can be expressed in several different ways. All depend upon the basic and unpalatable fact that no scientific or medical examination can now say, with certainty, what caused Mr Cotton's cancer or lung cancer in any other particular case. As explained at the outset of these reasons, despite this uncertainty, the courts must, and do, 'reduce to legal certainty [a question] to which no other conclusive answer can be given'. The courts do that by asking whether it is more probable than not that X was a cause of Y. Saying only that exposure to asbestos *may have been a cause of Mr Cotton's cancer is not a sufficient basis* for attributing legal responsibility. Observing that a small percentage of cases of cancer were probably caused by exposure to asbestos does not identify whether an individual is one of that group. And given the small size of the percentage, the observation does not, without more, support the drawing of an inference in a particular case. [Emphasis added.]

The High Court explained that the problem in Mr Cotton's case was caused by 'the limits of knowledge about what causes cancer' and held that this lack of proof was enough to dispose of the case altogether. It was not a case where it was appropriate to invoke the exception: see the discussion in [12] and [66]–[68] for the High Court's views on the material contribution test.

The 'material contribution' test was developed in a series of cases from England and Scotland beginning in 1956 and culminating with the seminal House of Lords decision in *Fairchild v Glenhaven Funeral Services Ltd* (2003). You will notice that many of these cases concern workplace exposure to dust-borne particles and so you must check very carefully which of the statutory rules apply because some jurisdictions have passed special provisions for recovery in dust-related cases.

LEGISLATION ALERT!

Consult your study materials and note any relevant statutory provisions in your jurisdictions on specific types of damage that may be excluded from the application of the civil liability legislation.

Note also whether there are any limits or conditions that must be satisfied before the test can be applied.

Case example

In *Bonnington Castings Ltd v Wardlaw* (1956), a worker employed by the Bonnington foundry suffered from a dust-borne respiratory disease caused by the cumulative effects of inhaling silica over a period of eight years. The silica in the workplace came from two different sources: from swing grinders and from a pneumatic hammer. The grinders were fitted with a dust extraction plant but it was not properly maintained by the foundry; in this respect the foundry owners were in breach of their statutory duty. However, at the time, there were no reasonable means of protection from the dust emanating from the hammer, so the foundry was not in breach in respect of this source of the risk. Lord Reid said at 620:

> In my judgment, the employee must in all cases prove his case by the ordinary standard of proof in civil actions: he must make it appear at least that on a balance of probabilities the breach of duty caused or *materially contributed to* his injury. [Emphasis added.]

Lord Reid concluded at 622 that while it was 'sufficiently proved that the dust from the grinders made a substantial contribution', it was also 'probable that much the greater proportion of the noxious dust which he inhaled over the whole period came from the hammers' and decided at 623 as follows:

> I cannot avoid the conclusion that the proportion which came from the swing grinders was not negligible ... and therefore did help to produce the disease. That is sufficient to establish liability.

The words used by Lord Reid in *Bonnington Castings Ltd v Wardlaw* (1956) (in the example above) were picked up in subsequent cases where there was some uncertainty about causation.[5] In fact, the High Court was asked by the plaintiff to take that case into account when deciding *Amaca Pty Ltd v Ellis* (2010), but the judges explained at [67] that it was important to recognise the context in which *Bonnington Castings Ltd v Wardlaw* (1956) was decided:

5 Bailey, 'Causation in Negligence: What is a Material Contribution?' (2010) argues at 174 that there is a 'fundamental ambiguity at the heart' of this case and suggests that it is unclear whether the 'material contribution' rule as applied to these facts involved an *application* of the but-for principle or an *exception* to that rule. He concludes at 184 that '*Bonnington Castings* should be confirmed as a case applying conventional and not unconventional principles'.

> [T]he question in the case was not what was the most probable source of the pursuer's disease: dust from one source or the other. The question was whether dust from the poorly maintained equipment was *a* cause of his disease when the medical evidence was that pneumoconiosis is caused by a gradual accumulation of silica particles inhaled over a period of years.

Given the very different facts in both cases, the issues were therefore very different and so *Bonnington Castings Ltd v Wardlaw* (1956) did not offer any assistance to the plaintiff in *Amaca Pty Ltd v Ellis* (2010). As the High Court explained at [68], whereas the issue in *Bonnington Castings Ltd v Wardlaw* (1956) was 'whether one source of an injurious substance contributed to a gradual accumulation of dust that resulted in disease', the issue in *Amaca Pty Ltd v Ellis* (2010) was 'whether one substance that *can* cause injury *did* cause injury.' This suggests that the application of the material contribution test referred to in the statutes will need to be very carefully scrutinised by the courts, in the light of the facts of the case, the precise wording of the relevant statutes on causation, and the analysis of the earlier cases dealing with 'material contribution'.[6]

Case example

McGhee v National Coal Board (1973) concerned a worker (P) who suffered from dermatitis as a result of being employed to empty kilns at a brickworks. The medical evidence established that dermatitis is caused by the cumulative effect of repeated abrasions by the dust on the skin. P argued that if his employer (D) had provided adequate shower facilities, he would not have contracted the disease. Instead he had to ride home on his bicycle 'caked with sweat and dust' and this prolonged his exposure to the danger. D admitted negligence in not providing the showering facilities but argued that causation had not been made out. The medical evidence could not establish for certain that, if P been able to wash immediately, he would not have contracted the disease, but, given the fact that the evidence did show that exposure to the dust does cause dermatitis (albeit in a way that was not completely understood) and that the provision of showering facilities would have materially reduced his exposure and therefore his chances of getting the dermatitis, the House of Lords held that causation was made out and that P could recover damages. Lord Reid said at 4 that 'in cases like this we must take a broader view of causation' and at 5 concluded that there was no substantial difference between saying that D '*materially increased the risk of injury* to the plaintiff' and saying that what D did 'made *a material contribution* to his injury'. Lord Wilberforce asked at 6 why a defendant should be held liable in these circumstances, and answered:

> First, it is a sound principle that where a person has, by breach of a duty of care, created a risk, and injury occurs within the area of that risk, the loss should be borne by him unless he shows that it had some other cause. Secondly, from the evidential point of view, one may ask, why should a man who is able to show that his employer should have taken certain precautions, because without them there is

6 An excellent discussion of the cases can be found in Beever, *Rediscovering the Law of Negligence* (2007) at 453–92.

> a risk, or an added risk, of injury or disease, and who in fact sustains exactly that injury or disease, have to assume the burden of proving more: namely, that it was the addition to the risk, caused by the breach of duty, which caused or materially contributed to the injury?

In *McGhee v National Coal Board* (1973) and *Bonnington Castings Ltd v Wardlaw* (1956) the workers had both been exposed by a single defendant to two different sources of risks that accumulated together to cause them harm. The next case, which failed, concerned a case where the plaintiff suffered from five conditions. Four of these conditions occur naturally, and only the fifth had been caused by the negligence of the defendant.

Case example

In *Wilsher v Essex Area Health Authority* (1987), a prematurely born baby was negligently treated by a junior doctor. The baby became blind, but it could not be established in evidence which of five different conditions possibly suffered by the baby had caused the harm. Given that the incorrect treatment by the doctor was only one of five possible causes of the harm, causation was not established. The House of Lords distinguished the earlier cases and refused to apply the 'material contribution' test, holding that the plaintiff had not proved on the balance of probabilities that the negligence of the defendant was a cause of the harm.

Fairchild v Glenhaven Funeral Services Ltd (2003), which is specifically mentioned in the civil liability legislation of South Australia, concerned plaintiffs who had been exposed to the same kind of danger by consecutive employers (rather like the case of *Summers v Tice* (1948), above, where the plaintiff had been exposed to two identical risks of pellet damage, but it could not be proved whose pellet did the damage).

Case example

In *Fairchild v Glenhaven Funeral Services Ltd* (2003), several cases were brought to the House of Lords by plaintiffs who had developed the respiratory disease mesothelioma after being been exposed to asbestos by a series of different employers (the defendants). It was established in evidence that inhaling just one fibre of asbestos (the 'single fibre' theory) could lead to the disease, and it was proved that the defendants had been negligent, but the plaintiffs were unable to prove on the balance of probabilities which of their employers had caused them to inhale the deadly fibre(s) that triggered their cancer. Building on the earlier cases, the House of Lords allowed liability on the grounds that proof of the fact that each defendant's wrongdoing had *materially increased the risk* of contracting the disease was sufficient to satisfy the causal requirements. Lord Bingham explained at [2] that a 'modified approach to proof of causation was justified' in the circumstances despite the 'rock of uncertainty' on which the case was based at [9]. Lord Nicholls emphasised at [43]:

> The principle applied on these appeals is emphatically not intended to lead to such a relaxation whenever a plaintiff has difficulty, perhaps understandable difficulty, in discharging the burden of proof resting on him. Unless closely confined in its application this principle could become a source of injustice ... The reason must be sufficiently

weighty to justify depriving the defendant of the protection this test normally and rightly affords him, and it must be plain and obvious that this is so. Policy questions will loom large when a court has to decide whether the difficulties of proof confronting the plaintiff justify taking this exceptional course. It is impossible to be more specific.

The significance of *Fairchild v Glenhaven Funeral Services Ltd* (2003) was that it imposed liability on all the employers, even though it had not been proved that any one of them had caused the disease. The decision pushed the test of 'material contribution to harm' as developed in the earlier cases to a broader notion of 'material increase in risk'. The problem is that it was 'impossible to be more specific' about the conditions that triggered the exceptional departure from the usual 'but for' approach. This is an ongoing challenge for Australian courts, and the answer is still being crafted in accordance with statutory requirements, alongside the progress of scientific knowledge. Some initial assistance in the qualification to the *Fairchild v Glenhaven Funeral Services Ltd* approach was provided by Lord Hoffmann in another dust case, *Barker v Corus UK Ltd* (2006) at [24]:

> In my opinion it is an essential condition for the operation of the exception that the impossibility of proving that the defendant caused the damage arises out of the existence of another potential causative agent which operated in the same way. It may have been different in some causally irrelevant respect, as in Lord Rodger's example of the different kinds of dust, but the mechanism by which it caused the damage, whatever it was, must have been the same. So, for example, I do not think that the exception applies when the claimant suffers lung cancer which may have been caused by exposure to asbestos or some other carcinogenic matter but may also have been caused by smoking and it cannot be proved which is more likely to have been the causative agent.

This advice was not needed by the High Court in *Amaca Pty Ltd v Ellis* (2010), where the facts were very similar to the example given by Lord Hoffmann in *Barker v Corus*, because the plaintiffs in that case 'expressly disavowed' any reliance on the *Fairchild v Glenhaven Funeral Services Ltd* (2003) line of authority, and restricted themselves only to arguments based on *Bonnington Castings Ltd v Wardlaw* (1956). The High Court said at [68]:

> Questions of material contribution arise only if a connection between Mr Cotton's inhaling asbestos and his developing cancer was established. Knowing that inhaling asbestos *can* cause cancer does not entail that in this case it probably *did*. For the reasons given earlier, that inference was not to be drawn in this case. Questions of what is a material contribution do not arise.

The most interesting Australian case to engage with the 'material contribution' test is the High Court decision in *Amaca Pty Ltd v Booth* (2011), another case with facts not dissimilar to those in *Fairchild v Glenhaven Funeral Service Ltd* (2003). In this case, the Court has arguably adopted the stricter version of the material contribution test, limiting it to the narrower 'material contribution to harm' of the earlier cases and moving away from the broader 'material increase in risk' developed by the House of Lords. While this may very well be due to the evolving nature of the expert evidence that supports complex mesothelioma claims, the net result is a more restrictive and demanding legal principle.

Case example

In *Amaca Pty Ltd v Booth* (2011), P was a retired motor mechanic diagnosed with mesothelioma. He had worked for almost 30 years with brake linings containing asbestos, a significant proportion of which were manufactured by Amaca Pty Ltd (D). Before beginning work as a mechanic, P had been exposed to asbestos on three different occasions. Compared to his exposure while working as a mechanic, the previous exposures had been brief. It could not be established that he would not have developed the disease without the exposure during his work with asbestos brake linings, and it could not be established whether it was the exposure to D's brake linings that eventually triggered the mesothelioma.

However, instead of reasoning along the lines of the House of Lords in *Fairchild v Glenhaven Funeral Services Ltd*, the High Court took a different direction, based on the scientific evidence presented to the Court, which differed significantly from that relied upon eight years earlier by the House of Lords. Indeed, as stated by French CJ, Gummow, Hayne and Crennan JJ at [79]: 'The "single fibre" theory was not accepted in the evidence in the present case as representing current expert opinion', which was rather to the effect that 'the development of mesothelioma and its probability of development will be influenced by the number of fibres' inhaled. For this reason, the High Court concluded that D was liable because, on the balance of probabilities, the asbestos brake lining it manufactured had materially contributed to P's mesothelioma. This is the key difference: the contribution is *not simply to the increased risk* that harm might occur, but rather a *contribution to the harm itself.*

You should note that separating a 'material contribution to harm' from a 'material increase in risk' has important implications, especially in terms of the types of harm that can give rise to a negligence claim in the presence of multiple sources of harm. Where the harm is somehow *divisible,* identifying a material contribution to harm will be much easier than in a situation where the harm is *indivisible,* which will always require courts to reason at a higher level of abstraction.

Case example

In *Kuhl v Zurich Financial Services Australia Ltd* (2011), P's arm was caught in a powerful vacuum hose for about 30 seconds, as a result of which he suffered significant physical injuries. The evidence showed that there were three concurring causes of P's injuries, summarised by Heydon, Crennan and Bell JJ at [100] as:

- the forces operating at the moment his arm was sucked into the hose;
- the forces operating on his arm until the arm was pulled out; and
- the 'reverse' forces applied by P and his workmates in order to extract his arm from the hose.

The evidence supported a finding that, while the initial sucking of the arm could not be attributed to the negligence of D, the absence of a safety system (such as the installation of a 'break box') to stop the machine in cases of accidental sucking was indeed negligent. The question for the Court was therefore whether the injuries had occurred as a result of the non-negligent initial sucking of the arm, or rather as a result of the prolonged sucking and reverse force applied by P and his workmates (both of which were attributable to D's negligence). Heydon, Crennan and Bell JJ concluded at [103]:

> The probabilities are that a not insignificant amount of the plaintiff's injuries would have occurred after the initial few seconds in which his arm was sucked into the hose. In the circumstances there is no bar to the conclusion that the plaintiff's damage was caused by the breach of duty.

In *Adeels Palace Pty Ltd v Moubarak* (2009), the High Court at [54] considered the broader circumstances that may trigger the application of the 'exceptional case' rule (or 'appropriate case' rule in other states and territories – see Appendix 13.1):

> Section 5D(2) makes provision for what it describes as 'an exceptional case'. But the Act does not expressly give content to the phrase 'an exceptional case'. All that is plain is that it is a case where negligence cannot be established as a necessary condition of the harm; the 'but for' test of causation is *not* met. In such a case the court is commanded 'to consider (amongst other relevant things) whether or not and why responsibility for the harm should be imposed on the negligent party'. But beyond the statement that this is to be done 'in accordance with established principles', the provision offers no further guidance about how the task is to be performed. Whether, or when, s 5D(2) is engaged must depend, then, upon whether and to what extent 'established principles' countenance departure from the 'but for' test of causation.

The Court then emphasised at [55] that 'the "but for" test is now to be (and has hitherto been seen to be) a *necessary* test of causation in all but the undefined group of exceptional cases contemplated' by the legislation. It remains to be seen how the courts will develop the principles that justify taking that exceptional step away from the 'but for' test that is normally a prerequisite to establishing liability. What we do know from the cases that have reached the High Court is that the lower courts must clearly address each of the legislative tests and must explain in their reasoning why they have or have not departed from the strictly factual 'but for' or 'necessary condition' test, not only in each case, but also for each defendant. This rule requiring an overt explanation of the reasons justifying the decision in each case will assist in the future clarification of the conditions that justify the exceptions.

So far, it appears that the notion of 'material contribution to harm' is to be preferred to the broader 'material increase in risk' (except perhaps in those jurisdictions that explicitly mention *Fairchild v Glenhaven Funeral Services Ltd* (2003) in their *Civil Liability Acts*, such as South Australia). Katy Barnett and Sirko Harder note in *Remedies in Australian Private Law* (2019) at 90–1:

> [S]ince the enactment of [the civil liability] provisions, the High Court of Australia has still not decided on whether a material increase in risk establishes factual causation at common law, and intermediate appellate courts continue to reject the concept, leaving the decision to the High Court.

Leaving the matter to the common law was an explicit choice made in the Ipp Report (2002) at [7.33]. Unfortunately, the common law has been, so far, rather indecisive in this matter. In *Strong v Woolworths Ltd* (2012) noted above, the majority of the High Court at [26] summarised the discussion:

> Whether negligent conduct resulting in a material increase in risk may be said to admit of proof of causation in accordance with established principles under the common law of Australia has not been considered by this Court. Negligent conduct that materially contributes to the plaintiff's harm but which cannot be shown to have been a necessary condition of its occurrence may, in accordance with established principles, be accepted as establishing factual causation, subject to the normative considerations to which s 5D(2) requires that attention be directed.

Until the matter is determined conclusively by the High Court, the safest assumption is that cases involving a *material contribution to harm* will be successful if proved on the balance of probabilities, while a mere *increase in risk* will probably not suffice. In the strong words of French CJ in *Amaca Pty Ltd v Booth* (2011) at [41]:

> Causation in tort is not established merely because the allegedly tortious act or omission increased a risk of injury. The risk of an occurrence and the cause of the occurrence are quite different things.

13.3 Scope of liability: Closing the circle of negligence

13.3.1 Limiting the scope of liability and 'remoteness'

In the older cases such as *March v Stramare* (1991), the issue of causation was treated as being a fusion of both factual (or evidence-based) assessment and normative (or value-based) considerations of fairness. However, while both normative and factual matters are still taken into consideration under the new legal regime, the old 'fused' approach to the topic of causation has now been ended by the civil liability legislation. This means that all of the normative or value-based 'policy considerations' that once used to be expressed in *causal terminology* like 'breaks in the chain of causation', '*novus actus interveniens*' (Latin for 'new intervening act') or 'remoteness of damage' are to be kept separate from the issue of factual causation and must instead be relevant to the second issue raised by the element of causation, namely, the 'appropriate scope of liability'.

Once the court has decided that the plaintiff has proved that the defendant's conduct was a necessary condition of the harm that they have suffered (or in exceptional cases, that it had materially contributed to the harm occurring), the task is then to work out how much of the harm must be considered when setting the 'scope of liability'. This change makes good sense, because the causal language used in the earlier cases (and the frequent references to a 'common sense' application of the 'but for' test) tended to distract attention from the fact that the judges were deciding the matter not on factual grounds, but on other equally valid but nevertheless normative grounds. These value-based aspects of the law will now be addressed more openly as the judges explain in each case 'whether or not and why' (as expressed in the judgments and in the legislation) the defendant's liability should be either extended or curtailed in appropriate cases.

The issue of the appropriate 'scope of liability' takes us back to the familiar concept of reasonable foreseeability. The basic rule, which was originally laid down in *Overseas Tankship (UK) Ltd v Morts Dock & Engineering Co Ltd* (1961) ('*The Wagon Mound (No 1)*') and was somewhat blurred in the subsequent case of *Overseas Tankship (UK) Ltd v The Miller Steamship Co* (1967) ('*The Wagon Mound (No 2)*'),[7] is that the defendant will be liable to compensate the plaintiff for all the harm that they have caused, provided that it is harm of a kind that is reasonably foreseeable as a result of the defendant's negligence. This rule of remoteness abandoned the old trespass-based directness test used in the older case of *Re Polemis* (1921), which made a defendant liable for all the direct consequences flowing from their wrongful conduct. Viscount Simonds said in *The Wagon Mound (No 1)* at 423:

> For, if some limitation must be imposed upon the consequences for which the negligent actor is to be held responsible – and all are agreed that some limitation there must be – why should that test (reasonable foreseeability) be rejected which, since he is judged by what the reasonable man ought to foresee, corresponds with the common conscience of mankind, and a test (the 'direct' consequence) be substituted which leads to nowhere but the never-ending and insoluble problems of causation.

After explaining that the *extent of the liability* should be confined by the same principle that justified *imposing the duty* in the first place, Viscount Simonds maintained at 426 that 'the essential factor in determining liability is whether the damage is of such a kind as the reasonable man should have foreseen' and added:

> But if it would be wrong that a man should be held liable for damage unpredictable by a reasonable man because it was 'direct' or 'natural,' equally it would be wrong that he should escape liability, however 'indirect' the damage, if he foresaw or could reasonably foresee the intervening events which led to its being done ... Thus foreseeability becomes the effective test.

This *Wagon Mound* rule uses the reasonable foreseeability of the *kind of harm* to justify limiting the *extent* of a defendant's liability for their breach of the duty to take reasonable care to avoid causing harm. It has been elaborated upon and supplemented by several sub-rules in subsequent authorities as judges have attempted to give some substance to the notion of 'reasonable foreseeability' and to explain how it applies in this context. These cases will continue to be relevant in the wake of the civil liability legislation, which provides that the decisions on the scope of liability should take into account 'other relevant things'. You should note, however, that the judges in many of these cases (which were decided during the years when the tort of negligence was still emerging from its

7 The second *Wagon Mound* case 'somewhat blurred' the issue because it combined matters that we now try to keep separate – that is, matters relating to duty, breach, causation and remoteness. It has taken 40 years of experience to unravel the tangled questions addressed by this case.

rather tangled origins) sometimes use the language of causation to express conclusions, which nowadays would be recast in the normative language of values prescribed by the new civil liability regime. So, decisions which suggested that a particular harm should be excluded because the 'chain of causation' had been 'broken' by a 'new intervening cause' ('*novus actus interveniens*') or 'superseding cause' would now be described differently as part of the court's task of explaining whether or not and why it is appropriate that the defendant's liability should either extend *to include* a particular harm or – equally importantly – why it should be curtailed *to exclude* a particular kind of harm.

One of the problems in the tort of negligence is caused by the fact that there may be a significant delay between the time when the defendant's wrongdoing takes place and the time when the plaintiff suffers harm of a recognised kind. In that intervening period, other complicating events may occur that add to the harm or exacerbate it. In other cases, one form of harm may lead to other forms of harm. In circumstances where subsequent events supersede or follow upon the original event, it is sometimes argued that 'it may be right as a matter of common sense to hold that the breach was not a cause of damage' in cases 'where an abnormal event intervenes between the breach and damage': McHugh J in *Henville v Walker* (2001) at [106]. However, as Mason CJ explained in *March v Stramare* (1991) at 518–9:

> As a matter of both logic and common sense, it makes no sense to regard the negligence of the plaintiff or a third party as a superseding cause or novus actus interveniens when the defendant's wrongful conduct *has generated the very risk of injury* resulting from the negligence of the plaintiff or a third party and *that injury occurs in the normal course of things.* In such a situation, the defendant's negligence satisfies the 'but for' test and is properly to be regarded as a cause of the consequence because there is no reason in common sense, logic or policy for refusing so to regard it. [Emphasis added.]

Despite the use of causal language in this case, the legal proposition that it contains will continue to be relevant if a defendant raises the 'scope of liability' by arguing that their liability should not extend to include certain harms that occurred after their own wrongful conduct. But if their conduct has generated the very risk of injury that subsequently occurred, then their liability will extend to include it, unless other good reasons of principle indicate otherwise. The analysis that follows does not use the old method of classifying the rules in this area of the law, nor does it use the old language of 'causes'; rather, it attempts to account for the reasons behind the decisions in ordinary language and to explain them in terms of principle.

Most of the special rules in this area of the law can be classified according to whether they relate either to conditions existing *at the time* the tort occurred (as shown by event E in Figure 13.1 above) or to *subsequent events* that took place after the cause of action accrued (as shown by points F, G, H, I, etc in Figure 13.1). At each of these points, some of the sub-issues that may be raised include:

- the unusual *way* that the harm occurred;
- the unusual *nature* or *extent* of the harm suffered by the plaintiff;
- the unusual nature or *special vulnerability* of the plaintiff ('eggshell skull' rule);

- subsequent harms that occurred because of a *choice made by the plaintiff* – these may be classified as being (a) outside the 'appropriate scope of liability' (or in the old terminology, classified as a 'new intervening act') if the plaintiff's conduct is seen as an unreasonable response; or (b) as being within the 'appropriate scope of liability' (or in the old terminology, classified as being 'caused by the defendant's initial act of wrongdoing') if the plaintiff's conduct is seen as a reasonable or forced response to the initial harm;
- *naturally caused events* (which sometimes are still referred to as 'acts of God') where the plaintiff was unlucky because they were in the wrong place at the wrong time, and where the perceived coincidence absolves the defendant of further liability; and
- other subsequent harms caused by the *wrongful conduct of a third person* which may be classed as being outside the 'appropriate scope of liability' (or in the old terminology, classified as a 'new intervening act').

13.3.2 Summary points

There are typically two situations in which it would not be appropriate for the scope of the defendant's liability to extend to the harm suffered by the plaintiff, even when a factual link exists between the harm and the defendant's negligence. They occur when:

1. there is a **more proximate cause that is** both independent of the defendant's negligence and causally related to the loss suffered as to interrupt and restart the chain of causation (*novus actus interveniens*); or when
2. the harm is of an **unforeseeable kind** (remoteness).

Active reading

As you read sections 13.3.3, 13.3.4 and 13.3.5 below, tie each case to the first type or the second type of situation.

13.3.3 Conditions existing at the time the tort occurred

There are two issues that can arise out of the initial harm-causing event that brings the cause of action into existence: the first issue that is sometimes raised by defendants relates to the unusual *way* that the harm may have occurred, and the second relates to the special *nature of the plaintiff* that may make them more than usually vulnerable to suffering from unusual harms. In both of these scenarios, the rule from the *Wagon Mound* cases imposes liability on the defendant for all the harm that they have caused, provided it is damage *of a kind* that is reasonably foreseeable as a consequence of the breach, even if the full *extent of the harm* was not reasonably foreseeable. This means that the defendant will be liable for all the foreseeable kinds of harm that they have caused by their breach – even if that harm is caused in an unusual or even bizarre way – and even if their victim suffers harm to an unexpected or unusual degree.

Case examples

The unusual way the harm occurred

- *Hughes v Lord Advocate* (1963) concerned a case where two boys, aged eight and 10, were badly burnt one night after they went into a tent that had been placed over an open manhole. It had been left by workers who had been maintaining underground telephone equipment earlier that day. The men had negligently left burning paraffin lamps hanging on the tent, and after one of the boys knocked a lamp into the manhole it exploded, causing the boys to suffer serious burns. It was argued that the boys should not recover damages for their injuries because the lamp had behaved in an unpredictable way (by exploding), but the House of Lords allowed recovery.

  Lord Reid said at 845 that the defendant would still be liable even though 'the damage may be a good deal greater *in extent* than was foreseeable', and explained that a defendant could 'only escape liability if the damage can be regarded as differing *in kind* from what was foreseeable'. Lord Guest added at 855 that 'it was not necessary that the precise details leading up to the accident should have been reasonably foreseeable' (in words very similar to the later Australian case of *Chapman v Hearse* (1961) discussed in section 13.2.1).

  So, even though the damage in this case was caused by a known source of danger that had behaved unpredictably, it nevertheless caused physical injury in the form of burns, which was damage of a kind that is reasonably foreseeable if a burning lamp is left unattended in a place where small boys can get hold of it.
- See also *Haley v London Electricity Board* (1964) where a blind man, who was walking with his cane along a footpath, fell into a trench dug by Post Office workers and suffered physical injuries that caused him to become deaf. He was successful in recovering damages because the possibility that he could suffer physical injuries from the breach was foreseeable, even though the precise sequence of events that led to the damage to his hearing on that day was not.
- *Chapman v Hearse* (1961) also made it clear at 120–1 that a wrongdoer is responsible for all damage of the same type or kind as that which was reasonably foreseeable, even if the particular damage, or its extent, was not reasonably foreseeable, or if that damage was caused in an unexpected or unforeseeable manner.

The 'eggshell skull' rule specifies that the defendants 'must take their victims as they find them' and this rule applies even if the victim is especially vulnerable to that harm because of a pre-existing physical, psychological, cultural or social susceptibility. In *Commonwealth v McLean* (1996), Handley and Beazley JJA defined this rule at 406:

> The 'egg shell skull' principle makes a defendant liable for damage of an unforeseeable extent, but not for unforeseeable damage of a different kind. Under this principle a defendant is liable for additional damage of a foreseeable kind suffered by a plaintiff who has some special vulnerability.

Case examples

The unusual nature or extent of the harm (the 'eggshell skull' rule)

- In *Smith v Leech Brain & Co Ltd* (1962) a man, who was employed to lower articles into a tank containing molten metal with an overhead crane, was struck by a piece of molten metal on his lower lip, causing a burn. The burn developed into cancer which killed him three years later. It was established that the cancer had developed in tissues that already had a pre-malignant condition and that 'but for' the burn, the cancer might never have developed. It was decided that the physical burn injuries suffered by the workman were of a kind that was reasonably foreseeable. Liability for the subsequent cancer death was imposed because, as Lord Parker CJ said at 414, '[i]t has always been the law of this country that a tortfeasor takes his victim as he finds him'. He quoted from an earlier case, *Dulieu v White & Sons* (1901), where it was said at 679:

  > If a man is negligently run over or otherwise negligently injured in his body, it is no answer to the sufferer's claim for damages that he would have suffered less injury, or no injury at all, if he had not had an unusually thin skull or an unusually weak heart.

- In *Shorey v PT Ltd* (2003), Kirby J reaffirmed at [44]:

  > The principle is that a negligent defendant must take its victim as it finds her and must pay damages accordingly ... If such symptoms were genuine and a consequence of the subject trauma, the apparent disproportion between cause and effect is not an exculpation for the negligent party. It does not render the damage 'unforeseeable' or otherwise outside the scope of the damages that may be recovered.

13.3.4 Subsequent events

The 'eggshell skull' rule is also applied if, at a time *after* the initial harm was incurred and the cause of action has accrued, some other event occurs that adds to the harm suffered by the plaintiff, or if some other, different or unusual, harm subsequently develops. In some cases the continued existence of a plaintiff's original condition of vulnerability justifies the application of this rule, whereas in others it is justified because the plaintiff has incurred a new vulnerability as a direct result of the initial injuries caused by the tortfeasor.

Case examples

The unusual nature or extent of subsequent harm

- In *Haber v Walker* (1963) liability was imposed (by a majority in the Supreme Court of Victoria) on a defendant whose negligence caused a man to suffer severe and extensive physical and psychological injuries. After he became severely depressed and distressed by his appearance, his mental and physical impairment and his incapacity to earn enough money to support his family, this psychiatrically vulnerable victim committed suicide 17 months after the initial accident. His widow brought an action against the tortfeasor. The reasons for the decision were expressed in causal language, but the outcome turned on the fact that in the opinion of the majority, the victim's actions were not properly to be classified as voluntary. Given that the accident had caused the depression, the victim's new vulnerability to mental illness, that led to his suicide, was seen as properly attributable to the defendant (and so the victim's conduct did not amount a 'new intervening act' that broke 'the chain of causation').

- A similar decision was reached in the case of *Medlin v State Government Insurance Commission* (1995). Here a university professor saw his capacity to work reduced as a result of an accident. He could still work but was unable to meet the university's research requirements and therefore decided to retire early. The question before the High Court was whether the decision to retire was a voluntary intervening act by the plaintiff that broke the chain of causation. The Court found that the decision could not be characterised as voluntary in the circumstances, and therefore the chain of causation remained uninterrupted.
- In *Nader v Urban Transit Authority of New South Wales* (1985) a 10-year-old boy was injured while getting off a bus that was negligently driven by the defendant. He suffered minor physical injuries, but subsequently developed Ganser Syndrome, which is a recognised psychiatric illness. It was accepted by a majority in the New South Wales Court of Appeal that some of the symptoms of the syndrome could be said to have had an organic basis and that the condition and its continuation were partly a reaction to the overprotectiveness of the child's parents and partly due to the failure of the parents to obtain appropriate treatment. Given that psychiatric illness of some kind was reasonably foreseeable as a consequence of the physical injury, it did not matter that the particular psychiatric illness was rare. McHugh JA said at 537:

> I think that the defendant must take the plaintiff with all his weaknesses, beliefs and reactions as well as his capacities and attributes, physical, social and economic. If the result of an accident is that a ten-year-old boy reacts to his parents' concern over his injuries and develops an hysterical condition, no reason of justice, morality or entrenched principle appears to me to prevent his recovery of compensation.

- This decision was followed in the controversial case of *Kavanagh v Akhtar* (1998), where the plaintiff, a Muslim woman, suffered a shoulder injury as a result of the defendant's negligence. As a consequence of that injury, she was unable to care properly for her long hair, so eventually she cut it off. She did not, however, obtain her husband's consent first, and so because her conduct was contrary to the principles and customs of their religion, her husband became very angry, ceased having marital relations with her and ultimately left her after the marriage broke down. The plaintiff suffered psychiatric illness as a result, but the defendant, whose negligence had caused the initial physical injury, argued that liability should not extend to include this harm, which it was argued was caused by her own unreasonable choice to cut her hair. The Court of Appeal held for the plaintiff, on the grounds that a psychiatric injury was a foreseeable consequence of a physical injury. The fact that it was caused by an unforeseeable step taken by the plaintiff, which was followed by an unforeseeable response by her husband, was irrelevant. Mason P said at 601:

> The principle that a tortfeasor takes the victim as he or she is found is not absolute and unqualified. However, I see no reason why the appellant should not take the respondent in the family and cultural setting that she lived (cf *Nader* at 537). Equality

> before the law puts a heavy onus on the person who would argue that the 'unusual' reaction of an injured plaintiff should be disregarded because a minority religious or cultural situation may not have been foreseeable.

- A similar conclusion was reached again by the New South Wales Court of Appeal in *Gittani Stone Pty Ltd v Pavkovic* (2007), where the manner in which the defendant's employee ended up suffering physical harm was deemed irrelevant provided that physical harm was foreseeable in the circumstances.
- In *Pyne v Wilkenfeld* (1981), the plaintiff was injured in a traffic accident caused by the defendant's negligent driving. She suffered whiplash injuries and had to wear a collar on her neck as part of her treatment. The collar obscured her vision and she later tripped on an uneven part of a footpath and injured her knee. Given that she had not been guilty of any contributory negligence, liability for the subsequent injury was imposed, because as Zelling J explained at 442:

> The reason why she could not see the unevenness in the surface which caused her to fall was that her head and neck were held high as a cervical collar always does, and she could not see immediately in front of her.

The plaintiff in *Pyne v Wilkenfeld* (1981), noted above, had incurred a new temporary vulnerability as a direct result of the initial injuries caused by the tortfeasor, and, given that she was not careless with her own safety, liability was imposed. There are, however, other cases where a plaintiff who has unreasonably disregarded their own safety has had to bear the consequences of their own foolishness, and other cases where the subsequent injury to a plaintiff is not seen as properly within the scope of the defendant's liability because the unlucky plaintiff was simply in the wrong place at the wrong time.

Case examples

Unlucky coincidence and fault of a third party

McKiernan v Manhire (1977) was a case where a plaintiff had been knocked down by a negligently driven car. After she had been treated and sent to a convalescent hospital to recover, she tripped on a step in the office and broke her hip. Bright J held that, while the hospital was liable for failing to warn her of the odd placing of the step, the original tortfeasor should not bear any liability for the subsequent injury even though the patient would not have been in the convalescent hospital but for the original tortfeasor's wrongdoing. Bright J did suggest at 576, however, that if she had fainted because of her weakened state and incurred the injury, then the original tortfeasor would be liable.

Unreasonable conduct by the plaintiff

In *McKew v Holland and Hannen & Cubitts* (1969) D was liable for injuring P's leg. Subsequently P (who needed to use crutches to walk) attempted to get down a steep staircase that had no handrail, without waiting for assistance. He fell, fracturing his ankle. D, although responsible for initially injuring P, was held not to be liable for the subsequent injury. Lord Reid explained at 1623:

> But if the injured man acts unreasonably he cannot hold the defendant liable for injury caused by his own unreasonable conduct. His unreasonable conduct is *novus actus interveniens*. The chain of causation has been broken and what follows must be regarded as caused by his own conduct and not by the defender's fault or the disability caused by it ... A defender is not liable for a consequence of a kind which is not foreseeable. But it does not follow that he is liable for every consequence which a reasonable man could foresee.

Lord Reid used the language of causation to express the value judgement that the plaintiff, who voluntarily chose to do something that was unreasonable in the circumstances, should have to take personal responsibility for the consequences. Mason CJ discussed this case in *March v Stramare* (1991) at 517:

> The decision may be explained by a value judgment that it would be unjust to hold the defendant legally responsible for an injury which ... was the immediate result of unreasonable action on the part of the plaintiff. But in truth the decision proceeded from a conclusion that the plaintiff's injury was the consequence of his independent and unreasonable action.

This basis for curtailing a defendant's liability was considered in the next case, where the defendant argued that the plaintiff's autonomous decision to risk incurring a subsequent harm should preclude her from recovering damages for that harm.

Case example

The case of *Harvey v PD* (2004) concerned a plaintiff (P) whose doctor (D) negligently failed to advise her of the rules relating to consent that governed the sharing of information about HIV test results. As a result, P remained in ignorance of her fiancé's HIV positive health status. After P's fiancé fraudulently assured her that he was HIV negative, she married him and conceived a child. Both P and the child were found to be HIV positive. P subsequently divorced her husband, and then, knowing of her HIV status, conceived a second child with another partner. She claimed in negligence against D, seeking damages to cover, among other things, the future costs of raising both children once she became incapable of doing so herself.

The judges in the New South Wales Court of Appeal allowed the costs for the first child (given that P was vulnerable to suffering this particular loss caused by her husband's 'not unforeseeable' deceit) but refused to award damages for the upkeep of the second child, reasoning that P's voluntary and independent decision to have the second child and the possibility of indeterminate liability both pointed against recovery and both had to be 'weighed in the balance': Ipp J at [225].

13.3.5 Subsequent acts of third parties

The final set of cases explains the relevance of wrongful conduct by third parties that causes the plaintiff to suffer additional harm. These wrongful acts can be further divided into those that are 'the free, deliberate and informed act or omission of a human being, intended to exploit the situation created by defendant' (McHugh J in *Bennett v Minister of Community Welfare* (1992) at [13]) and that do curtail liability (and that were formerly described as 'new intervening acts'), and those that are reasonably foreseeable, which do not absolve the defendant from liability.

Case examples

Subsequent negligent medical treatment

In *Mahony v J Kruschich (Demolitions) Pty Ltd* (1985) P was injured when he was working on a power station demolition job. His employer (D) was negligent. P then suffered additional harm when his doctor negligently treated him. The High Court said at 528–9:

> A negligent tortfeasor does not always avoid liability for the consequences of a plaintiff's subsequent injury, even if the subsequent injury is tortiously inflicted. It depends on whether or not the subsequent tort and its consequences are themselves properly to be regarded as foreseeable consequences of the first tortfeasor's negligence. A line marking the boundary of the damage for which a tortfeasor is liable in negligence may be drawn either because the relevant injury *is not reasonably foreseeable* or because the chain of causation is broken by a novus actus interveniens.
>
> When an injury is exacerbated by medical treatment, however, the exacerbation may easily be regarded as *a foreseeable consequence for which the first tortfeasor is liable*. Provided the plaintiff acts reasonably in seeking or accepting the treatment, negligence in the administration of the treatment need not be regarded as a novus actus interveniens which relieves the first tortfeasor of liability for the plaintiff's subsequent condition. [Emphasis added.]

The High Court also explained at 529–30, however, that this rule does not apply if there is 'gross negligence':

> However, in the ordinary case where efficient medical services are available to an injured plaintiff, the original injury does not carry the risk of medical treatment or advice that is 'inexcusably bad', or 'completely outside the bounds of what any reputable medical practitioner might prescribe' or 'so obviously unnecessary or improper that it is in the nature of a gratuitous aggravation of the injury' or 'extravagant from the point of view of medical practice or hospital routine'. In such a case, it is proper to regard the exacerbation of a plaintiff's condition as resulting *solely from the grossly negligent medical treatment or advice* and the fact that the plaintiff acted reasonably in seeking and accepting the treatment or in following the advice will not make the original tortfeasor liable for that exacerbation. [Emphasis added and references omitted.]

Subsequent criminal wrongdoing by a third party

- In *Baker v Willoughby* (1970), noted in section 13.2.2.2 above, the unlucky plaintiff (P) was hit by the first defendant (D1) while crossing a road. P suffered injuries to his left leg, causing stiffness. He sued D1 but before the case was heard, P was shot in the same leg during an armed robbery and consequently the leg was amputated. The case reached the House of Lords, who held that the later injury and the later amputation of the leg should not reduce the extent of D1's liability to pay the full cost for his initial wrongdoing. Lord Reid said at 493:

> These cases exemplify the general rule that a wrongdoer must take the plaintiff (or his property) as he finds him: that may be to his advantage or disadvantage. In the present case the robber is not responsible or liable for the damage caused by the respondent: he would only have to pay for additional loss to the appellant by reason of his now having an artificial limb instead of a stiff leg.

- In *State Rail Authority of New South Wales v Chu* (2008), the plaintiff fell after slipping on wet steps at a train station, breaking her ankle. Subsequently, she was the victim of a sexual assault about five weeks after the accident and the trial judge found that her reduced mobility (which hindered her capacity to escape) made her more vulnerable to the sexual predator who attacked and assaulted her. He held that the State Rail Authority was liable in damages for the subsequent effects of the assault. On appeal by the State Rail Authority, the New South Wales Court of Appeal held that the sexual assault was plainly a '*novus actus interveniens*' which broke the chain of causation following the original negligence by the State Rail Authority. Hodgson J at [50] and [54] quoted *Mahony v J Kruschich (Demolitions) Pty Ltd* (1985, noted above) as well as citing the following comments of McHugh J in *Bennett v Minister of Community Welfare* (1992) at 429–30:

  > The causal connection between a defendant's negligence and the plaintiff's damage is negatived by the subsequent conduct of another person only when that conduct is 'the free, deliberate and informed act or omission of a human being, intended to exploit the situation created by defendant'.

  Hodgson J, with whom the other judges *State Rail Authority of New South Wales v Chu* agreed, concluded at [55] that the criminal act committed by the 'assailant was clearly a "free, deliberate and informed act"' and held that this justified overturning the conclusion of the trial judge.
- The New South Wales Court of Appeal reached a different conclusion in *Chomentowski v Red Garter Restaurant Ltd* (1970), where the defendant employer was found liable for the injuries suffered by their employee as a result of being robbed while carrying the day's earnings in cash to a bank across town. The criminal act of third parties was found not to have broken the chain of causation, though you should note that this has to do with the very special nature of the employer–employee relationship and the very broad scope of the employer's duty of care, as discussed in Chapter 11.

This overview of the case law reveals a series of indicators. While the cases are not completely consistent, the exact nature of the statutory requirement that courts must explain 'whether or not and why' liability should be imposed remains very much linked to the development of the common law. As the High Court explained in the medical negligence case of *Wallace v Kam* (2013) at [22], the civil liability provision on scope of liability 'guides but does not displace common law methodology. The common law method is that a policy choice once made is maintained unless confronted and overruled'.

13.3.6 Summary points

13.3.6.1 Scope of liability

1. Harm is generally classed as being *within* the 'appropriate scope of liability' if:
   - it is not 'too remote' in the sense that it is harm of a kind that is reasonably foreseeable, even if it occurred in an unforeseeable way;
   - the 'eggshell skull' rule applies, that is, the victim suffered harm to an unusual extent because they were unusually vulnerable because of a pre-existing physical, psychological, cultural or social susceptibility;
   - the defendant's wrongdoing created a new vulnerability in the plaintiff that led to an additional, but still foreseeable, harm, provided the plaintiff has not been unreasonably careless of their own safety; or
   - the defendant's wrongdoing resulted in injuries that rendered the plaintiff vulnerable to negligent medical treatment (unless the treatment is grossly negligent, in which case the harm will be outside the scope of liability).
2. Harm is generally classed as being *outside* the 'appropriate scope of liability' if:
   - the harm is of a kind that is not reasonably foreseeable;
   - the harm has been caused by a conscious act of wrongdoing by a third party that was a free, deliberate and informed act or omission intended to exploit the situation created by the defendant;
   - the additional harm was the result of the plaintiff's own unreasonable lack of care for their own safety;
   - the additional harm was consciously risked by the plaintiff who voluntarily chose to proceed with a certain course of action with full knowledge of the possible consequences, and so should accept personal responsibility for that exercise of their autonomy;
   - the additional harm was the result of a third party's subsequent, unrelated and independent act of negligence (but see above, on the exception made in cases of gross medical negligence); or
   - the additional harm can be classed as an unlucky coincidence, in the sense that the defendant's wrongdoing simply secured the plaintiff's presence in a place and at a time when another harm-causing event (eg a natural disaster) occurred.

Active reading

Link each of these summary points to a case in section 13.3.6 above.

Figure 13.4 Essential steps in causation

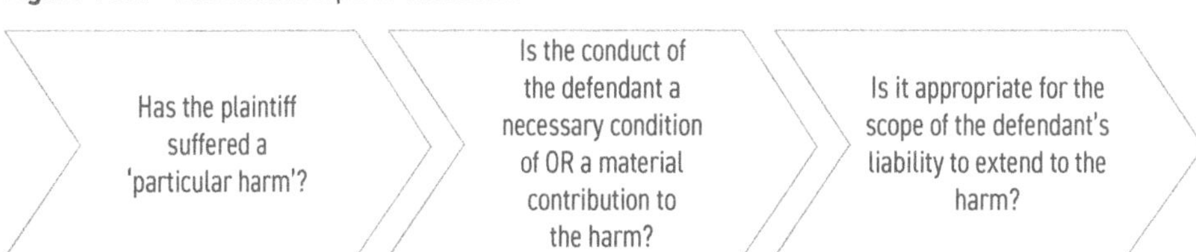

13.3.7 Critique of causation

The courts' approach to the element of causation has been the subject of sustained criticism throughout the common law world over many years. The focus of much of this criticism has been on the shortcomings of the 'but for' test. Other criticism has centred on the unhelpful merging of the factual issue of causation and the normative reasons for curtailing liability together under the single umbrella term of 'causation' (see Figure 13.4). One of the most influential Australian critics is Jane Stapleton, who has written extensively on the topic of causation and who is regarded as one of the leading authorities on this subject in the common law world. This influential criticism was referred to extensively in the Ipp Report (2002), which led to the passing of the legislation in most jurisdictions that now requires the courts to keep the two issues of factual causation and scope of liability separate. Some of Stapleton's most important articles are noted below.

Examples

- 'Unpacking "Causation"' (2001).
- 'Legal Cause: Cause-in-Fact and the Scope of Liability for Consequences' (2001).
- 'Cause-in-Fact and the Scope of Liability for Consequences' (2003).
- 'Choosing What We Mean by "Causation" in the Law' (2008).
- 'The Two Explosive Proof-of-Causation Doctrines Central to Asbestos Claims' (2009).
- 'The Risk Architecture of the Third Restatement of Torts' (2009).
- 'Factual Causation' (2010).

Conclusion

Once the scope of the defendant's liability has been determined, the elements of the tort are complete, and the onus shifts to the defendant to raise a defence. In the past, the defences have been overshadowed by the elements of negligence, and in fact most of the battles in this tort occur at the first stage where the question of liability is at stake – and where most of the important limiting devices are located. The fact that the concept of reasonableness has already been considered in every element explains why the defences have assumed a less significant role in this tort (by contrast with the intentional torts, for example, where the concept of reasonableness rarely features in the elements but is built into many of the defences). However, as you will see in Chapters 14 and 15, the statutory provisions have revamped the role of defences to negligence in particular areas.

For now, remember the progression of the tort: (1) establish a duty of care, (2) establish whether the conduct of the defendant had fallen below the required standard of care and (3) establish whether the conduct of the defendant caused a particular harm that falls within the scope of their liability (see Figure 13.5).

Test your understanding

Prepare for problem solving

Students can find causation particularly tricky and so it is useful to try and map the process of problem solving for this element. Always remember that no template is ever going to fit every possible case and every possible factual scenario! However, by and large, once you have established a breach of duty and need to tackle causation, you can aim to proceed by tackling the following questions (the provisions are from the *Civil Liability Act 2002* (WA)):

a. Identify the 'particular harm' or harms (damage) – s 5C.
    i. Is the harm more than trivial?
    ii. Is the harm recognised at law and compensable?
b. Establish factual causation – s 5C(1) and (3).
    i. Was the fault of D a necessary condition for the harm (s 5C(1)(a))?
    ii. If so, is there an evidentiary gap that requires relying on inferences?

    or, if the necessary condition test is not viable due to the nature of the harm suffered (ie not simply because of a lack of evidence):

    iii. Did the fault of D materially contribute to the harm (s 5C(2))?
    iv. If the case has multiple tortfeasors, can you satisfy the necessary condition test against one defendant?
        1. If yes, you can move on to scope of liability.
        2. If no, consider: **pre-emptive causation** (second event is pre-empted by the first, where it is possible to determine which D's fault caused the harm); **duplicative causation** (both Ds did a wrongful act and it is impossible to determine which conduct caused the harm); or **material contribution to harm** (where final harm is the result of cumulative effect of separate conducts).
    v. If relevant, consider what P would have done absent fault of D (s 5C(3)(a)).
c. Establish scope of liability – ss 5C(1)(b) & 5C(4).
    i. Are there any intervening causes (*novus actus interveniens*)? This is asking whether there is a more proximate cause of the ultimate injury than the original negligent act of the defendant. Consider:
        1. where the intervening act was of a third party, whether the act was reasonably foreseeable;
        2. where the intervening act was of the P, whether the act was so unreasonable as to make it unforeseeable;
        3. where the intervening act was of the P, whether the act was involuntary; or
        4. where the intervening act was of the P, whether it is truly an intervening act or an action better dealt with as contributory negligence.

    Note: the act of P must be free, deliberate and informed.

ii. Is the loss too remote in the sense that it is unforeseeable? Remember:
   1. The kind of harm suffered needs to be reasonably foreseeable.
   2. The manner in which the harm occurred, and the extent of the harm are irrelevant if harm is of a foreseeable kind.
   3. The 'eggshell skull' rule applies where the extent of the harm is due to the unusual vulnerability of the P because of pre-existing psychological, physical, cultural or social susceptibilities. Note that such vulnerability is irrelevant provided it is not the sole reason for suffering harm.

Figure 13.5 Progression of the causal inquiry

Note: References are to the *Civil Liability Act 2002* (WA). Refer to Appendix 13.1 for the equivalent provisions in the other Australian jurisdictions.

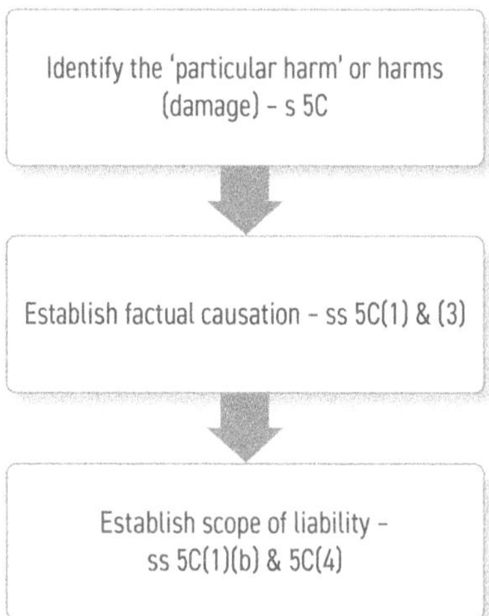

APPENDIX 13.1 CAUSATION PROVISIONS IN AUSTRALIAN CIVIL LIABILITY LEGISLATION

New South Wales

Civil Liability Act 2002

5D General principles

(1) A determination that negligence caused particular harm comprises the following elements:

(a) that the negligence was a necessary condition of the occurrence of the harm (***factual causation***), and

(b) that it is appropriate for the scope of the negligent person's liability to extend to the harm so caused (***scope of liability***).

(2) In determining in an exceptional case, in accordance with established principles, whether negligence that cannot be established as a necessary condition of the occurrence of harm should be accepted as establishing factual causation, the court is to consider (amongst other relevant things) whether or not and why responsibility for the harm should be imposed on the negligent party.

(3) If it is relevant to the determination of factual causation to determine what the person who suffered harm would have done if the negligent person had not been negligent:

  (a) the matter is to be determined subjectively in the light of all relevant circumstances, subject to paragraph (b), and

  (b) any statement made by the person after suffering the harm about what he or she would have done is inadmissible except to the extent (if any) that the statement is against his or her interest.

(4) For the purpose of determining the scope of liability, the court is to consider (amongst other relevant things) whether or not and why responsibility for the harm should be imposed on the negligent party.

Victoria

Wrongs Act 1958

51 General principles

(1) A determination that negligence caused particular harm comprises the following elements:

  (a) that the negligence was a necessary condition of the occurrence of the harm (*factual causation*); and

  (b) that it is appropriate for the scope of the negligent person's liability to extend to the harm so caused (*scope of liability*).

(2) In determining in an appropriate case, in accordance with established principles, whether negligence that cannot be established as a necessary condition of the occurrence of harm should be taken to establish factual causation, the court is to consider (amongst other relevant things) whether or not and why responsibility for the harm should be imposed on the negligent party.

(3) If it is relevant to the determination of factual causation to determine what the person who suffered harm (the *injured person*) would have done if the negligent person had not been negligent, the matter is to be determined subjectively in the light of all relevant circumstances.

(4) For the purpose of determining the scope of liability, the court is to consider (amongst other relevant things) whether or not and why responsibility for the harm should be imposed on the negligent party.

Tasmania

Civil Liability Act 2002

11 General principles

(1) A decision that a breach of duty caused particular harm comprises the following elements:

(a) the breach of duty was a necessary condition of the occurrence of the harm (*factual causation*);

(b) it is appropriate for the scope of the liability of the person in breach to extend to the harm so caused (*scope of liability*).

(2) In deciding in an exceptional case, in accordance with established principles, whether a breach of duty – being a breach of duty that is established but which can not be established as satisfying subsection (1)(a) – should be accepted as satisfying subsection (1)(a), the court is to consider (among other relevant things) whether or not and why responsibility for the harm should be imposed on the party in breach.

(3) If it is relevant to deciding factual causation to decide what the person who suffered harm would have done if the person who was in breach of the duty had not been so in breach –

(a) the matter is to be decided subjectively in the light of all relevant circumstances, subject to paragraph (b); and

(b) any statement made by the person after suffering the harm about what he or she would have done is inadmissible except to the extent (if any) that the statement is against his or her interest.

(4) For the purpose of deciding the scope of liability, the court is to consider (among other relevant things) whether or not and why responsibility for the harm should be imposed on the party who was in breach of the duty.

South Australia

Civil Liability Act 1936

34 General principles

(1) A determination that negligence caused particular harm comprises the following elements:

(a) that the negligence was a necessary condition of the occurrence of the harm (*factual causation*); and

(b) that it is appropriate for the scope of the negligent person's liability to extend to the harm so caused (*scope of liability*).

(2) Where, however, a person (the *plaintiff*) has been negligently exposed to a similar risk of harm by a number of different persons (the *defendants*) and it is not possible to assign responsibility for causing the harm to any one or more of them –

(a) the court may continue to apply the principle under which responsibility may be assigned to the defendants for causing the harm[8]; but

(b) the court should consider the position of each defendant individually and state the reasons for bringing the defendant within the scope of liability.

(3) For the purpose of determining the scope of liability, the court is to consider (amongst other relevant things) whether or not and why responsibility for the harm should be imposed on the negligent party.

8 See *Fairchild v Glenhaven Funeral Services Ltd* [2002] 3 WLR 89.

Western Australia

Civil Liability Act 2002

5C General principles

(1) A determination that the fault of a person (the *tortfeasor*) caused particular harm comprises the following elements:

(a) that the fault was a necessary condition of the occurrence of the harm (*factual causation*); and

(b) that it is appropriate for the scope of the tortfeasor's liability to extend to the harm so caused (*scope of liability*).

(2) In determining in an appropriate case, in accordance with established principles, whether a fault that cannot be established as a necessary condition of the occurrence of harm should be taken to establish factual causation, the court is to consider (amongst other relevant things) –

(a) whether and why responsibility for the harm should, or should not, be imposed on the tortfeasor; and

(b) whether and why the harm should be left to lie where it fell.

(3) If it is relevant to the determination of factual causation to determine what the person who suffered harm (the *injured person*) would have done if the tortfeasor had not been at fault –

(a) subject to paragraph (b), the matter is to be determined by considering what the injured person would have done if the tortfeasor had not been at fault; and

(b) evidence of the injured person as to what he or she would have done if the tortfeasor had not been at fault is inadmissible.

(4) For the purpose of determining the scope of liability, the court is to consider (amongst other relevant things) whether and why responsibility for the harm should, or should not, be imposed on the tortfeasor.

Australian Capital Territory

Civil Law (Wrongs) Act 2002

45 General principles

(1) A decision that negligence caused particular harm comprises the following elements:

(a) that the negligence was a necessary condition of the happening of the harm (*factual causation*);

(b) that it is appropriate for the scope of the negligent person's liability to extend to the harm so caused (*the scope of liability*).

(2) However, if a person (the *plaintiff*) has been negligently exposed to a similar risk of harm by a number of different people (the *defendants*) and it is not possible to assign responsibility for causing the harm to 1 or more of them:

(a) the court may continue to apply the established common law principle under which responsibility may be assigned to the defendants for causing the harm; but

(b) the court must consider the position of each defendant individually and state the reasons for bringing the defendant within the scope of liability.

(3) In deciding the scope of liability, the court must consider (among other relevant things) whether or not, and why, responsibility for the harm should be imposed on the negligent party.

REFERENCES

CASES

Adeels Palace Pty Ltd v Moubarak (2009) 239 CLR 420
Alcan Gove Pty Ltd v Zabic (2015) 257 CLR 1
Amaca Pty Ltd v Booth (2011) 246 CLR 36
Amaca Pty Ltd v Ellis (2010) 240 CLR 111
Baker v Bolton (1808) 1 Camp 493
Baker v Willoughby [1970] AC 467
Barker v Corus UK Ltd [2006] 2 AC 572
Barnett v Chelsea & Kensington Hospital Management Committee [1968] 1 QB 428; [1968] All ER 1068
Bennett v Minister of Community Welfare (1992) 176 CLR 408
Bonnington Castings Ltd v Wardlaw [1956] AC 613
Brocklands Ptd Ltd v Tasmanian Networks Pty Ltd [2020] TASFC 4
Cattanach v Melchior (2003) 215 CLR 1
Chapman v Hearse (1961) 106 CLR 112
Chappel v Hart (1998) 195 CLR 232
Chomentowski v Red Garter Restaurant Ltd (1970) 92 WN (NSW) 1070
City of Stirling v Tremeer (2006) 32 WAR 155
Commonwealth v McLean (1996) 41 NSWLR 389
Cook v Lewis [1951] SCR 830
Dillingham Construction Pty Ltd v Steel Mains Pty Ltd (1975) 132 CLR 323
Dimond v Lovell [2002] 1 AC 384
Dulieu v White & Sons [1901] 2 KB 669
East Metropolitan Health Service v Ellis [2020] WASCA 147
Elayoubi v Zipser [2008] NSWCA 335; (2008) Aust Torts Reports 81-895
Fairchild v Glenhaven Funeral Services Ltd [2003] 1 AC 32
Fitch v Hyde-Cates (1982) 150 CLR 482
Gittani Stone Pty Ltd v Pavkovic [2007] NSWCA 355; (2007) Aust Torts Reports 81-924
Haber v Walker [1963] VR 339
Haley v London Electricity Board [1964] 3 All ER 185
Harriton v Stephens (2006) 226 CLR 52
Harvey v PD (2004) 59 NSWLR 639

Henville v Walker (2001) 206 CLR 459
Hughes v Lord Advocate [1963] AC 837
Jobling v Associated Dairies Ltd [1982] AC 794
Johnson v Perez (1988) 166 CLR 351
K-Mart Australia Ltd v McCann [2004] NSWCA 283
Karpik v Carnival plc (The Ruby Princess) (Initial Trial) [2023] FCA 1280
Kavanagh v Akhtar (1998) 45 NSWLR 588
Kuhl v Zurich Financial Services Australia Ltd (2011) 243 CLR 361
Mahony v J Kruschich (Demolitions) Pty Ltd (1985) 156 CLR 522
March v Stramare (1991) 171 CLR 506
McGhee v National Coal Board [1973] 1 WLR 1
McKew v Holland and Hannen & Cubitts [1969] 3 All ER 1621
McKiernan v Manhire (1977) 17 SASR 571
Medlin v State Government Insurance Commission (1995) 182 CLR 1
Minister for the Environment v Sharma (2022) 291 FCR 311
Mount Isa Mines Ltd v Pusey (1970) 125 CLR 383
Nader v Urban Transit Authority of New South Wales (1985) 2 NSWLR 501
Overseas Tankship (UK) Ltd v Morts Dock & Engineering Co Ltd [1961] *AC* 388 ('*The Wagon Mound (No 1)*')
Overseas Tankship (UK) Ltd v The Miller Steamship Co Pty Ltd [1967] 1 AC 617 ('*The Wagon Mound (No 2)*')
Performance Cars Ltd v Abraham [1962] 1 QB 33
Phelan v Melbourne Health [2019] VSCA 205
Prast v Town of Cottesloe (2000) 22 WAR 474
Pyne v Wilkenfeld (1981) 26 SASR 441
Re Polemis [1921] 3 KB 560
Rogers v Whitaker (1992) 175 CLR 479
Rose v Ford [1937] AC 826
Rosenberg v Percival (2001) 205 CLR 434
Sellars v Adelaide Petroleum NL (1994) 179 CLR 332
Shorey v PT Ltd [2003] HCA 27; 77 ALJR 1104; 197 ALR 410
Smith v Leech Brain & Co Ltd [1962] 2 QB 405
State Rail Authority of New South Wales v Chu [2008] NSWCA 14; [2008] Aust Torts Reports 81-940
State Rail Authority of New South Wales v Wiegold (1991) 25 NSWLR 500
Strong v Woolworths Ltd (2012) 246 CLR 182
Summers v Tice, 33 Cal 2d 80; 199 P 2d 1 (1948)
Tabet v Gett (2010) 240 CLR 437
Tame v New South Wales (2002) 211 CLR 317
Tapp v Australian Bushmen's Campdraft & Rodeo Association Ltd (2022) 273 CLR 454
Wallace v Kam (2013) 250 CLR 375
Williams v Fraser [2022] NSCWA 200
Wilsher v Essex Area Health Authority [1987] QB 730
Ziaee v Rubino [2023] ACTCA 7

ARTICLES, BOOKS AND REPORT

Bailey, S H, 'Causation in Negligence: What Is a Material Contribution?' (2010) 30 *Legal Studies* 167.

Barnett, K & Harder, S, *Remedies in Australian Private Law*, 2nd ed (2019) Cambridge University Press, Cambridge.

Beever, A, *Rediscovering the Law of Negligence* (2007) Hart Publishing, Oxford.

Ipp, D, Cane, P, Sheldon, D & Macintosh, I, *Review of the Law of Negligence: Final Report* (2002) <https://treasury.gov.au/review/review-of-the-law-of-negligence>.

Leeming, M, *The Statutory Foundations of Negligence* (2019) The Federation Press, Alexandria.

Luntz, H, Hambly, D, Burns, K, Dietrich, J, Foster, N, Grant, G & Harder, S, *Torts: Cases and Commentary*, 8th ed (2017) LexisNexis Butterworths, Sydney.

Mendelson, D, *The New Law of Torts*, 2nd ed (2010) Oxford University Press, Melbourne.

Monks, S, 'The Concept of Informed Consent in the United States, Canada, England and Australia: A Comparative Study' (1993) 17 *University of Queensland Law Journal* 222

Nolan, D, 'New Forms of Damage in Negligence' (2007) 70 *Law Quarterly Review* 59.

Stapleton, J, 'Cause-in-Fact and the Scope of Liability for Consequences' (2003) 119 *Law Quarterly Review* 388.

Stapleton, J, 'Choosing what we mean by "Causation" in the Law' (2008) 73 *Missouri Law Review* 433.

Stapleton, J, 'Compensating Victims of Diseases' (1985) 5(2) *Oxford Journal of Legal Studies* 248.

Stapleton, J, 'Factual Causation' (2010) 38 *Federal Law Review* 483.

Stapleton, J, 'Legal Cause: Cause-in-Fact and the Scope of Liability for Consequences' (2001) 54 *Vanderbilt Law Review* 941.

Stapleton, J, 'The Gist of Negligence' (1988) 104 *Law Quarterly Review* 213 and 'The Gist of Negligence – Part II' (1988) 104 *Law Quarterly Review* 389.

Stapleton, J, 'The Risk Architecture of the Third Restatement of Torts' (2009) 44 *Wake-Forest Law Review* 1309.

Stapleton, J, 'The Two Explosive Proof-of-Causation Doctrines Central to Asbestos Claims' (2009) 74 *Brooklyn Law Review* 1011.

Stapleton, J, 'Unpacking "Causation"', in Cane, P & Gardner, J (eds), *Relating to Responsibility: Essays in Honour of Tony Honoré on his Eightieth Birthday* (2001) Hart Publishing, Oxford, 145.

Steel, S, *Proof of Causation in Tort Law* (2015) Cambridge University Press, Cambridge.

Turton, G, *Evidential Uncertainty in Causation in Negligence* (2016) Hart Publishing, Oxford.

SPECIAL TOPICS IN NEGLIGENCE

14

Introduction

The tort of negligence is dominated by the concepts of reasonable foreseeability and fault laid down by Lord Atkin in *Donoghue v Stevenson* (1932). However, as shown in Chapters 10–13, these foundational concepts cannot provide neatly defined limits on the extent of liability in negligence. Consequently, this tort contains an important set of 'control devices' (discussed in Chapters 11 and 13) that allow judges to move the boundaries of the tort in accordance with the 'felt necessities of the time'.[1] Chapter 10 explained that, at the birth of negligence in 1932, judges were conscious of the tension between keeping liability within principled bounds and ensuring that the law could adapt to changing social needs and conditions. This difficulty continues and is especially apparent in a range of cases rendered particularly complex either by the nature of the parties involved or the nature of the harm suffered, with this chapter discussing:

- the challenges associated with imposing liability in cases of 'pure omissions' or 'nonfeasance' as opposed to positive conduct or 'misfeasance' (section 14.1);
- the traditional immunity of public authorities, which has been gradually relaxed over time (section 14.2);

1 Holmes, *The Common Law* (1881) at 1.

- the traditional reluctance to impose liability in negligence for psychiatric injury or mental harm, which has seen many swings in the negligence pendulum (section 14.3);
- the difficulties in allowing liability for losses caused not by physical conduct but by 'mere words' or statements (section 14.4);
- the relaxation of the traditional rule denying liability for conduct that causes pure economic loss (section 14.5); and
- the difficulties of establishing liability for health professionals, which has seen different courts take more proactive or more deferent approaches (section 14.6).

The source of the reluctance to impose liability in some of these cases has varied. The concern in cases of omissions and statements focused on the *nature of the conduct* that led to the claim, whereas the issue in cases of pure economic loss or pure mental harm arose from concerns about the *nature of the harm* itself, and finally, in cases of medical negligence and public authorities, the concerns focused on the *nature of the defendant*. Traditional reluctance to allow liability in such cases has gradually been overcome, but the search for a principled justification for extending the categories of negligence has taken a long time. While many distinctions between special categories and other established categories of duty are arguably blurring, some commentators, such as Danuta Mendelson, have suggested that 'at least some of the special categories ... have now effectively developed into discrete causes of action' or 'sub-species' which 'should be allowed to develop in their own right' under the general principle of coherence laid down by the High Court of Australia ('High Court') in the landmark case of *Sullivan v Moody* (2001): see *The New Law of Torts* (2010) at 497.

This chapter on special topics in negligence will look at some examples where the High Court has justified either expanding or denying liability in negligence. Each section summarises the approaches that have emerged in each of these special areas and will alert you to the relevance of the civil liability legislation as enacted by states and territories in response to the Ipp Report (2002). Before you begin this chapter, it may be useful to revisit Chapter 11, particularly the section on key salient features in negligence.

14.1 Omissions and rescue

14.1.1 The problem of omissions

A tortfeasor can be liable both for a positive act of 'misfeasance' (a positive act of wrongdoing) and in some circumstances for culpable 'nonfeasance' (not doing anything). The law has traditionally drawn a distinction between misfeasance and nonfeasance and Deane J maintained in *Sutherland Shire Council v Heyman* (1985) at 502 that the distinction between a failure to act and positive action 'remains a fundamental one'. However, while all acts of misfeasance are by definition wrongful, nonfeasance may be characterised either as innocent or as culpable, depending on the circumstances.[2] All of the trespass

2 Allan Beever analyses the traditional distinction between misfeasance and nonfeasance and between acts and omissions in *Rediscovering the Law of Negligence* (2007) at 203–10 and concludes at 209: 'While one event can rightly be described as both an action and an omission, no event can be both

torts include an element requiring a positive act by the defendant, and so liability in trespass will not be imposed in cases of omissions or failures to act; but liability in tort does not always depend on the proof of a positive act carried out by the defendant.

Examples

- Liability may be imposed in the tort of private nuisance if a defendant fails to rectify a state of affairs that causes material physical damage to another's land or an unreasonable interference with another's use and enjoyment of land (or a right over or interest in land): see Chapter 8.
- Liability may be imposed in the tort of defamation if a defendant by an omission allows or enables the communication of defamatory matter: see Chapter 9.

A tort is wrongful conduct by one person that has the capacity to harm another person, and we can wrong a person by what we actually *do to them* as well as by the things that *we fail to do for them*. The fact that the term 'conduct' can encompass both positive acts and culpable failures to act makes it an especially useful term in the law of negligence. Given that liability in negligence is imposed on the basis that a person is at fault because they have failed to do what a reasonable person would have done in the circumstances, this tort responds both to positive acts of wrongdoing as well as culpable failures to act. But there are several difficulties associated with imposing liability for omissions.

Case examples

- Applying the test of causation in cases of negligent omissions can be more difficult than in clear cases of positive acts. There is a conceptual difficulty in seeing how a non-doing can 'cause' anything, but this can be resolved by the application of the 'but for' or 'necessary condition' test – as assessed on the balance of probabilities. The question becomes: is it more likely than not that the harm to the plaintiff would have occurred but for the negligent conduct (ie failure to act) of the defendant? See the discussion of *Adeels Palace Pty Ltd v Moubarak* (2009) and of two further cases in Tables 13.2 and 13.3 in Chapter 13, all concerned with negligent omissions.
- It is also difficult to establish the location of an omission, which is by definition an act that has not taken place at all. The significance of locating the place of an omission lies in the fact that the law of the *place* of a tort provides the rules that are used to assess liability for the tort, as the High Court decided in *John Pfeiffer Pty Ltd v Rogerson* (2000) and *Regie National des Usines Renault SA v Zhang* (2002). The High Court discussed the method for locating an omission in *Voth v Manildra Flour Mills Pty Ltd* (1990).

misfeasance and nonfeasance.' Danuta Mendelson explores the history of this distinction in *The New Law of Torts* (2010) at 499–504 and explains that 'the reasons for existence of a *duty to act* are different from reasons for the existence of a *duty to take care when acting*'.

Another difficulty in this area is caused by the fact that a person's conduct can often be described either in terms of what they did (an act) – or in terms of what they did not do (an omission). Driving is a traditional example that is often used to illustrate the options we have when we choose how to characterise a defendant's conduct. We could describe the conduct of a defendant who crashed into a fence either as the omission to apply the brakes properly or as an act of driving too fast. But this is not really a problem in cases like driving where the defendant is engaging in a positive course of conduct, but has failed to take care while doing so. The same scenario occurred in *Donoghue v Stevenson* (1932), where the defendant was carrying out a positive course of conduct in manufacturing and distributing bottles of ginger beer.

Case example

With respect to *Donoghue v Stevenson* (1932), we can describe the defendant Stevenson's conduct as carelessly carrying out the positive acts of making and distributing bottles of ginger beer; but we could also describe it as carelessly *failing to prevent* the snail from getting into the bottle or not checking inside the bottle before filling it with ginger beer (two omissions).

Nothing turned on the fact that the defendant did not himself put the snail into the bottle by a positive act; nor was there any issue about whether liability could justly be imposed in the face of his 'nonfeasance' (the omission to check the bottle for snails). The issue was whether he was liable for failing to take reasonable care to prevent snails from getting into his bottles during his positive course of conduct. So, in these cases, although we could focus on two different ways of describing his conduct, they are in essence two sides of the same coin – namely, the failure to take reasonable care.

Negligence is conceptualised as a failure to reach a standard of reasonable care. So, provided the defendant has engaged in a positive course of conduct, no issue arises if they failed to take any particular step carefully by omitting to do something that a reasonable person would have done in the circumstances. In fact, identifying the precautions that the reasonable person would have taken (and that the defendant did not take) is a critical step in establishing the element of breach, as seen in Chapter 12. It is only when the precaution is itself embarking on a positive course of conduct that we encounter the true difficulty of dealing with an omission. The mere fact that a defendant did not perform an act is not the problem; the real problem lies in deciding when to impose a duty to act in circumstances where a defendant is *not* already engaged in a positive course of conduct – but where, if they did act, they could prevent an already existing and potentially harmful chain of events from continuing. These are the cases of 'pure' omissions, and in these cases the common law has traditionally been reluctant to insist that one person should take positive action to prevent foreseeable harm to another.

Negligence does impose liability for certain kinds of nonfeasance, but the challenge is (as always) to find a principled way to delineate innocent nonfeasance, morally wrongful nonfeasance and legally wrongful nonfeasance. This difficulty was alluded to by Lord Atkin in *Donoghue v Stevenson* (1932) at 580, when he explained that our moral code does not always map directly onto our legal code. Jeffrie Murphy put the point more forcefully when he noted that while a person who sits idly by watching a child drown in a case of easy rescue is a 'piece of moral slime' who should 'be shunned by all decent people', that person has, nevertheless, committed no legal wrong.[3] It helps to overcome the difficulty, however, to remember that liability in negligence is always a question of reasonableness in all the circumstances, and to bear in mind that our assessments of reasonableness in cases of omissions are guided by the identifiable patterns in the case, which the High Court has variably referred to as 'salient features' or 'other factors' in the context of establishing duties of care in novel scenarios.

14.1.2 Relevant salient features

The law of negligence will sometimes insist that a defendant should act positively to intervene and change the course of an already existing situation. This is uncontroversial where defendants themselves have created the potentially harmful situation, but it is more controversial where the defendant is not responsible for creating the danger, but is nevertheless in a position to appreciate, respond to and avert it. In these cases of pure omissions, the test of reasonable foreseeability of harm is clearly satisfied, but the courts have always insisted that 'something more' than mere foreseeability is needed to justify imposing a duty to engage in a positive act of intervention. The three most important principles that must be balanced in these cases of pure omissions are explained as follows:

- The feature of *autonomy* and its corollary, that of *personal responsibility*, may operate either to impose or to deny a duty, depending on the circumstances. In cases of pure omissions, the value of protecting the defendant's autonomy will point against the imposition of a duty to act: *Stuart v Kirkland-Veenstra* (2009), Gummow, Hayne and Heydon JJ at [87]–[88] and [90]; *CAL No 14 Pty Ltd v Motor Accidents Insurance Board* (2009), Gummow, Heydon and Crennan JJ at [38], [52] and [54]–[55]; and *Stovin v Wise* (1996), Lord Hoffmann at 943–4.
- The feature of *vulnerability* may be relevant in cases where the ancillary features of control and/or specific knowledge and/or assumption of responsibility by the defendant, and/or reliance by the plaintiff, exist. In cases of pure omissions, the value of the plaintiff's special vulnerability justifies making an exception to the rule and imposing a duty to act: *Stuart v Kirkland-Veenstra* (2009), Gummow, Hayne and Heydon JJ at [87]–[88] and [90]; *CAL No 14 Pty Ltd v Motor Accidents Insurance Board* (2009), Gummow, Heydon and Crennan JJ at [54]. See also *Sutherland Shire Council v Heyman* (1985), Mason J on reliance at 641 and 648.
- The feature of *certainty* requires that liability must not be too uncertain in nature or give rise to indeterminate liability. In these cases, the problem of indeterminate liability points against imposing a duty, unless the class of persons to whom the duty is owed is clearly ascertainable: *Stovin v Wise* (1996), Lord Hoffmann at 943–4,

3 Murphy, 'Blackmail: A Preliminary Inquiry' (1980), cited by Feinberg, *Harm to Others* (1984) at 130. See also Honoré, 'Are Omissions Less Culpable?' (1999) at 41–66. A vigorous argument in favour of a duty to rescue was put forward the same year by Ernest Weinrib, 'The Case for a Duty to Rescue' (1980).

discussing *Hargrave v Goldman* (1963). Given that there are so many foreseeable harms in the world that we could in fact help to avert, a general duty to intervene would be so uncertain, extensive and indeterminate in its scope that no person could possibly comply with it.

14.1.3 Key cases

14.1.3.1 No general duty to rescue

The starting point in cases of pure omissions is that the law will not normally impose a duty to engage in a positive course of conduct either to save another from a situation of danger or from the dangerous conduct of third parties. As many judges have pointed out, this means there is no liability for failing to save or rescue another unless special circumstances exist. The High Court has affirmed this rule many times in a series of cases, which include *Hargrave v Goldman* (1963) and *Sutherland Shire Council v Heyman* (1985).

Case examples

- In *Hargrave v Goldman* (1963) (see also the Privy Council decision of *Goldman v Hargrave* (1966)), the High Court held that the owner and occupier of a 600-acre grazing property in Western Australia had a duty to take reasonable steps to extinguish a fire that had been started by a lightning strike on a tree on his land, so as to prevent it from spreading to his neighbour's land. Windeyer J said at 66:

  > The dictates of charity and of compassion do not constitute a duty of care. The law casts no duty upon a man to go to the aid of another who is in peril or distress, not caused by him. The call of common humanity may lead him to the rescue. This the law recognizes, for it gives the rescuer its protection when he answers that call. But it does not require that he do so. There is no general duty to help a neighbour whose house is on fire.

- This statement by Windeyer J was approved of in *Sutherland Shire Council v Heyman* (1985), by Gibbs CJ at 444:

  > Similarly, there is no general duty to warn another who is running into a position of danger, or to assist a person who is in peril or distress, and 'the general rule is that one man is under no duty of controlling another man to prevent his doing damage to a third'. [References omitted.]

  Mason J noted the 'the common law's general reluctance to require an individual to take positive action for the benefit of others' at 468, and said at 461 that the rule applies unless:

  > a person, by practice or past conduct upon which other persons come to rely, creates a self-imposed duty to take positive action to protect the safety or interests of another or at least to warn him that he or his interests are at risk.

  Mason J also noted at 468 that there are exceptions to the rule that were based on the fact of reliance:

> Even so, we need to recall that in other jurisdictions the failure of an employer (*Harris v Pennsylvania Railroad Co* (1931)), an occupier (*Ayres & Co v Hicks* (1942)) and a boat operator (*Horsley v MacLaren* ('*The Ogopogo*') (1971)) to go to the rescue of an employee, a guest and a passenger constitutes negligence though the peril was not the fault of the defendant.

Brennan J pointed out at 479:

> I can be liable only for an injury that I cause to my neighbour. If I do nothing to cause it, I am not liable for the injury he suffers except in those cases where I am under a duty to act to prevent the injury occurring ... Foreseeability of an injury that another is likely to suffer is insufficient to place me under a duty to him to act to prevent that injury. Some broader foundation than mere foreseeability must appear before a common law duty to act arises. There must also be either the undertaking of some task which leads another to rely on its being performed, or the ownership, occupation or use of land or chattels to found the duty.

Deane J explained at 502 that a duty to act will be imposed only in exceptional cases, but that otherwise:

> The common law imposes no prima facie general duty to rescue, safeguard or warn another from or of reasonably foreseeable loss or injury or to take reasonable care to ensure that another does not sustain such loss or injury.

Similar statements of the rule can be found in *Pyrenees Shire Council v Day* (1998), McHugh J at [101] (the case concerned a local council's liability for failing to ensure that a chimney, which it knew was defective, was properly dealt with); and in the rugby case of *Agar v Hyde* (2000), Gaudron, McHugh, Gummow and Hayne JJ at [68]. The basis of principle that underpinned this rule and its exceptions was explained in the English case of *Stovin v Wise* (1996) and again in the Australian cases of *CAL No 14 Pty Ltd v Motor Accidents Insurance Board* (2009) and *Stuart v Kirkland-Veenstra* (2009).

Case examples

- In *Stovin v Wise* (1996) Lord Hoffmann explained at 943–4 why 'something special' is required before liability will be imposed for pure omissions, and why the principles of autonomy and certainty must be taken into account:

> One can put the matter in political, moral or economic terms. In political terms it is less of an invasion of an individual's freedom for the law to require him to consider the safety of others in his actions than to impose upon him a duty to rescue or protect. A moral version of this point may be called the 'why pick on me?' argument. A duty to prevent harm to others or to render assistance to a person in danger or distress may apply to a large and indeterminate class of people who happen to be able to do something. Why should one be held liable rather than another? In economic terms, the efficient allocation of resources usually requires an activity should bear its own costs.

Lord Hoffmann pointed out that imposing a duty on one neighbour to act to prevent danger to another neighbour in the circumstances of *Hargrave v Goldman* (1963) complied with the certainty principle because the class of persons to whom the duty was owed was clearly ascertainable (and was fairly imposed because such a duty is mutual).

- In *Stuart v Kirkland-Veenstra* (2009), a case where a widow unsuccessfully sued the police for failing to prevent her husband from committing suicide, Crennan and Kiefel JJ pointed out at [124] that the 'common law does not recognise a duty to rescue another person' and Gummow, Hayne and Heydon JJ explained at [87]–[88] and [90] how the 'primacy' given to the value of personal autonomy supports the rule that there is no general duty to prevent another from self-harm, unless the plaintiff exhibits a special vulnerability of the legally recognised kind:

> Personal autonomy is a value that informs much of the common law. It is a value that is reflected in the law of negligence. The co-existence of a knowledge of a risk of harm and power to avert or minimise that harm does not, without more, give rise to a duty of care at common law. As Dixon J said in *Smith v Leurs*, '[t]he general rule is that one man is under no duty of controlling another man to prevent his doing damage to a third'. It is, therefore, 'exceptional to find in the law a duty to control another's actions to prevent harm to strangers.' And there is no general duty to rescue. [References omitted.] ...
>
> When a duty to control the actions of another is found it will usually be because the person to be controlled is not autonomous. Thus, the duty of care which a gaoler owes a prisoner is owed because the prisoner is deprived of personal liberty and the gaoler has assumed control of the prisoner's person. The prisoner does not have autonomy. [References omitted.]

Gummow, Hayne and Heydon JJ also identified at [112]–[116] another consideration 'of critical significance', which lay in the fact that it 'was not the officers who controlled the source of the risk of harm to Mr Veenstra; it was Mr Veenstra alone who was the source of that risk'. This factor was of 'predominant importance' because it meant that Mr Veenstra's apparent factual vulnerability (in the normal sense of the word) could not amount to the special kind of 'vulnerability' that justifies imposing a duty (which requires that the source of the risk to the plaintiff be caused by or be within the control of the defendant and that the plaintiff have no other way of protecting themselves from the risk).

The courts have refused to impose a duty to rescue, arguing that any unwarranted or 'interfering paternalism' that would force a defendant to act to save a plaintiff from the consequences of their own freely chosen decisions would impair the autonomy of both parties and deny the value of freedom, individualism and personal responsibility upon which the common law is based: *CAL No 14 Pty Ltd v Motor Accidents Insurance Board* (2009), Gummow, Heydon and Crennan JJ at [54].

Case examples

- In *CAL No 14 Pty Ltd v Motor Accidents Insurance Board* (2009), the High Court held that a proprietor of licensed premises did not owe a duty to protect a customer from the consequences of the alcohol that they voluntarily chose to consume. Gummow, Heydon and Crennan JJ explained at [54]:

> Balancing the pleasures of drinking with the importance of minimising the harm that may flow to a drinker is also a matter of personal decision and individual responsibility.

However, the judgment also pointed out at [38] that the principle of autonomy may conflict with, and therefore need to be balanced against, the vulnerability principle – for example, if a plaintiff 'is not autonomous, or fully autonomous':

> This conflict does not arise where for some supervening or overriding reason a person who is owed the putative duty is not autonomous, or fully autonomous – because, for example, some control must be exercised by the defendant over another person who either was vulnerable before the control was first exercised, or has become vulnerable by reason of the control having begun to be exercised. That is so for pupils in relation to their teachers, wards in relation to their guardians, prisoners in relation to the risk of fire caused by the negligence of gaolers, prisoners in relation to the risk of harm from other prisoners not properly restrained by gaolers, patients in relation to hospitals, crowds in relation to those charged with the duty to control them, and employees in relation to their employers. [References omitted.]

- A similar approach was used to justify denying liability in *Reynolds v Katoomba RSL All Services Club Ltd* (2001), a case where a gambler unsuccessfully sued a club for failing to prevent him losing money while gambling. Spigelman CJ (citing Lord Hoffmann in *Reeves v Commissioner of Police of the Metropolis* (2000) at 368) said at [24]–[27] that the courts 'should be very slow indeed to recognise a duty to prevent self-inflicted economic loss' because losing money when gambling 'is an inherent risk in the activity and cannot be avoided'. Spigelman CJ added at [24] that the significance of autonomy lies in the fact that:

> there is a difference between protecting people against harm caused to them by third parties and protecting them against harm which they inflict upon themselves. It reflects the individualist philosophy of the common law. People of full age and sound understanding must look after themselves and take responsibility for their actions.

See also *Politarhis v Westpac Banking Corporation* (2009).

A duty to rescue will be imposed if the defendant is under a statutory or common law obligation to act: *Hargrave v Goldman* (1963); *Stuart v Kirkland-Veenstra* (2009), noted above.

Case example

In *Adeels Palace Pty Ltd v Moubarak* (2009), the High Court pointed out at [21] and [25] that the *Liquor Act 1982* (NSW) imposed a duty on the licensee to prevent harm arising 'from violence and other anti-social behaviour'.

14.1.3.2 Liability to rescuers

If the defendants have created a danger, however, they will be liable if any third-party attempts to rescue a victim and is injured in the process – provided the test of reasonable foreseeability is satisfied.

Case examples

- Cardozo J said in *Wagner v International Railway Co* (1921) that 'danger invites rescue'.
- *Haynes v G Harwood & Sons* (1935) concerned a case where the defendant's servant negligently left some horses in a public highway and the plaintiff, a policeman, was injured when he attempted to prevent a horse from bolting after a child had thrown a stone at it.
- See also *Chapman v Hearse* (1961), the case where a doctor went to the rescue of an injured driver.
- Lord Denning said in *Videan v British Transport Commission* (1963) at 669:

  > If a person by his fault creates a situation of peril, he must answer for it to any person who attempts to rescue the person who is in danger. He owes a duty to such a person above all others. The rescuer may act instinctively out of humanity or deliberately out of courage. But whichever it is, so long as it is not wanton interference, if the rescuer is killed or injured in the attempt, he can recover damages from the one whose fault has been the cause of it.

- In *Horsley v MacLaren* ('*The Ogopogo*') (1971), the Supreme Court of Canada considered the liability of a boat owner who invited some guests onto his cabin cruiser, two of whom drowned on the trip. The first guest accidentally fell overboard, and another went to his rescue after it seemed that the owner's rescue tactics were going to fail. All members of the Court affirmed the duty on the part of the host as the owner and operator of the cabin cruiser to do the best he could to effect the rescue of his guests, but both claims failed (in part because the Court held by a majority of 3:2 that the owner had not failed to take reasonable care in attempting to rescue the first guest).

Note that the civil liability legislation introduced in the aftermath of the Ipp Report (2002) added extra protection for 'good Samaritans' who are acting as rescuers or assisting others in need as a result of an emergency.

LEGISLATION ALERT!

Consult your study materials and note any relevant statutory provisions in your jurisdiction.

14.1.3.3 Special circumstances and special relationships

In other cases, and regardless of whether the defendant has caused the original source of danger, the affirmative duty to rescue is derived from other special relationships existing between the defendant and plaintiff that are marked out by the salient features that indicate vulnerability, including reliance, an assumption of responsibility, control and knowledge. Note that some of these categories of special relationships reflect the early 'pockets of duty' categories, discussed in Chapter 10.

Case examples

- **Innkeepers and guests, carriers and passengers, bailees and bailors, occupiers and invitees:** These are very old categories that impose a duty to take positive steps to protect others from harm. See also the categories noted above in *CAL No 14 Pty Ltd v Motor Accidents Insurance Board* (2009) at [38].
- **Gaoler and prisoner:** In *Howard v Jarvis* (1958) at 183, and *New South Wales v Bujdoso* (2005) at [32] and [45], the High Court emphasised the importance of the control exercised by the gaoler over the prisoners and the conditions in which they are confined. This focuses attention on the special vulnerability and powerlessness of the prisoners and their inability to protect themselves from harm while in gaol.
- **Employer and employee:** This is a recognised special relationship that gives rise to a duty to take affirmative action, as noted in *Modbury Triangle Shopping Centre Pty Ltd v Anzil* (2000), Gleeson CJ at [26] and *CAL No 14 Pty Ltd v Motor Accidents Insurance Board* (2009), Gummow, Heydon and Crennan JJ at [38]. This liability is grounded in the employer's control of the workplace and the reliance that the employee must place on the employer to guard their safety.
- **School authorities/teachers and students:** The cases of *Richards v Victoria* (1969) and *Victoria v Bryar* (1970) emphasise the factor of control, which justifies imposing a positive duty to engage in affirmative acts to prevent harm to students. See also *Cox v New South Wales* (2007), where a school was liable for failing to take proper steps to prevent bullying which resulted in psychological harm to the vulnerable plaintiff. School authorities owe a personal, non-delegable duty to their pupils to ensure that reasonable care is taken of them while they are on the school premises during hours when the school is open for attendance and during school trips, etc: *Geyer v Downs* (1977); *Ramsay v Larsen* (1964); *Commonwealth v Introvigne* (1982). See also *Graham v New South Wales* (2001) and Mason P in *Lepore v New South Wales* (2001), who cited *Geyer v Downs* (1977) and *Trustees of the Roman Catholic Church for the Diocese of Bathurst v Koffman* (1996) when explaining at [37] that there 'will be times when it may be difficult to determine whether a pupil is within the umbrella of a non-delegable duty' – for example, when the pupil is 'at school well outside ordinary hours' or 'outside school premises'.
- **Cases imposing liability on a doctor to assist non-patients:** In *Lowns v Woods* (1996) the New South Wales Court of Appeal held by a majority of 2:1 that a doctor came under a duty to leave his rooms to attend the plaintiff, a boy who was suffering an epileptic fit but who was not (and had never been) his patient. Given that the boy's sister had asked the doctor to come to treat her brother, and in the light of the provisions of s 27(2) of the *Medical Practitioners Act 1938* (NSW), the majority held that the doctor was in a relationship of physical, circumstantial and causal proximity to the plaintiff that justified imposing the duty in the circumstances.[4]

4 See Day, 'Medical Negligence – the Duty to Attend Emergencies and the Standard of Care: *Lowns & Anor v Woods & Ors*' (1996); and Gray and Edelman, 'Developing the Law of Omissions: A Common Law Duty to Rescue?' (1998).

Test your understanding

Use the new methodology of negligence to construct arguments

Read the facts of *Lowns v Woods* (1996) and *BT v Oei* (1999). Using the methodology of negligence developed in the aftermath of the decision in *Sullivan v Moody* (2001), formulate arguments for and against imposing a duty of care on the doctors in these cases.

14.1.3.4 Duty to control third parties or protect the plaintiff from third parties

Just as there is no general common law duty to rescue another, there is no general duty to protect another person by controlling the conduct of third parties, unless there is a relevant pre-existing relationship that imposes such a duty – for example, in the cases where parents are in control of children, prison authorities are in control of prisoners and teachers are in control of pupils, or there has been an undertaking or assumption of responsibility. In *Smith v Leurs* (1945) Dixon J said at 262:

> It is, however, exceptional to find in the law a duty to control another's actions to prevent harm to strangers. The general rule is that one man is under no duty of controlling another man to prevent his doing damage to a third. There are, however, *special relations* which are the source of a duty of this nature. It appears now to be recognized that it is incumbent upon a parent who maintains control over a young child to take reasonable care so to exercise that control as to avoid conduct on his part exposing the person or property of others to unreasonable danger. [Emphasis added.]

A landowner's duty as an occupier of land does not normally extend to taking reasonable care to prevent physical injury to an injured entrant resulting from the criminal behaviour of third parties on that land, unless:

- a 'special relationship' or vulnerability exists, as indicated where the salient features of special knowledge, reliance, control or an assumption of responsibility are present: *Modbury Triangle Shopping Centre Pty Ltd v Anzil* (2000), *CAL No 14 Pty Ltd v Motor Accidents Insurance Board* (2009); or
- a statutory regime such as the liquor licensing laws imposes a duty to take reasonable care to prevent injury to persons present on the premises from the violent conduct of other patrons: *Adeels Palace Pty Ltd v Moubarak* (2009). Remember that the existence of a statutory duty may be indicative of a duty of care in negligence, but is not in and of itself determinative.

Case examples

- In *Modbury Triangle Shopping Centre Pty Ltd v Anzil* (2000), P (an employee of a video store) had been attacked by a third party in the shopping centre car park after leaving work one night.

The lights in the car park were off. P argued that D (the shopping centre) was negligent in not leaving the car park lights on. The High Court held by a majority of 4:1 that D did not owe P a duty to take reasonable care to prevent injury to P resulting from the criminal behaviour of third persons on D's land: Gleeson CJ at [29] and [36]; Gaudron J at [42]–[43], Hayne J at [108]–[118]; Callinan J at [147]. Gleeson CJ pointed out at [28] that 'if people were under a legal duty to prevent foreseeable harm to others, the burden imposed would be intolerable' and said at [26]:

> Leaving aside contractual obligations, there are circumstances where the relationship between two parties may mean that one has a duty to take reasonable care to protect the other from the criminal behaviour of third parties, random and unpredictable as such behaviour may be. Such relationships may include those between employer and employee, school and pupil, or bailor and bailee. But the general rule that there is no duty to prevent a third party from harming another is based in part upon a more fundamental principle, which is that the common law does not ordinarily impose liability for omissions. [References omitted.]

- In *Adeels Palace Pty Ltd v Moubarak* (2009), the plaintiffs went to a restaurant run by Adeels Palace Pty Ltd (the defendant) on New Year's Eve. After a dispute on the dance floor, another patron left the restaurant, armed himself with a gun and returned to the restaurant, where he shot the two plaintiffs. The victims of the gunman unsuccessfully sued, claiming that the defendant had been negligent in not providing sufficient security. The High Court noted the provisions of the *Liquor Act 1982* (NSW), reviewed the cases including *Smith v Leurs* (1945), *Modbury Triangle Shopping Centre Pty Ltd v Anzil* (2000), *Stuart v Kirkland-Veenstra* (2009) and *CAL No 14 Pty Ltd v Motor Accidents Insurance Board* (2009), and concluded at [24]:

  > Several considerations set the present case apart from *Modbury* and point to the conclusion that Adeels Palace owed each plaintiff a relevant duty of care. First, the complaint that was made in these cases was that the occupier of premises failed to control access to, or continued presence on, its premises. Secondly, the premises concerned were licensed premises where liquor was sold. They were, therefore, premises where it is and was well recognised that care must be taken lest, through misuse and abuse of liquor, 'harm [arise] from violence and other anti-social behaviour'. And thirdly, the particular duty ... is a duty to take reasonable care to prevent or hinder the occurrence of events which, under the *Liquor Act*, the licensee was bound to prevent occurring – violent, quarrelsome or disorderly conduct.

- Two English cases that also consider the 'special relation' that must exist before a duty is owed are *Home Office v Dorset Yacht Co Ltd* (1970), which imposed a duty on officers supervising boys from a 'borstal' or reform institution (who escaped and caused damage to the plaintiff's yacht) to take reasonable care to prevent the boys from escaping; and *Costello v Chief Constable of Northumbria Police* (1999), a case where a police inspector accompanying a colleague for her protection was in breach of a duty of care when she came under attack and he did nothing to help her.
- See also the cases concerning the liability of parole authorities: *Swan (By His Next Friend) v South Australia* (1994), *X v South Australia (No 2)* (2005) and *X v South Australia (No 3)* (2007).

14.1.4 Summary points

14.1.4.1 Pure omissions and rescue

1. The most important features in this area of the law are autonomy, vulnerability and certainty.
2. A failure to act (an omission) during a positive course of conduct is not treated as a 'pure omission'. Rather, it is treated as part of the breach (ie the failure to do what a reasonable person would have done in the circumstances).
3. There is no general duty to engage in an affirmative course of action to save another from a foreseeable harm or to protect a plaintiff from the conduct of a third party unless one of the recognised exceptions apply.
4. The exceptions include circumstances where:
    - there is a special relationship existing between the parties (eg employer and employee, carrier and passenger, innkeeper and patron, bailee and bailor, occupier of premises and person present on premises, school and student, gaoler and prisoner, hospital and patient, crowd controller and crowd);
    - the defendant has created the danger to the plaintiff;
    - the defendant has assumed a responsibility or given an undertaking to the plaintiff;
    - a statute imposes a duty on the defendant (indicative of a duty of care, not determinative); and
    - the balance of circumstances suggests that the value of autonomy is outweighed by the special vulnerability of the plaintiff (provided that the duty does not give rise to indeterminate liability).
5. If a defendant has created a danger by their own negligence, they will be liable if any third party attempts to rescue a victim and is injured in the process.
6. Some statutes create a special immunity for 'good Samaritans': check your study materials for any relevant provisions in your jurisdiction.
7. Note that other issues may arise to complicate the question of liability for a pure omission – for example, in cases where the defendant is a public authority (section 14.2) or where that omission leads to pure economic loss (section 14.5).

Active reading

Link each of these summary points to a case discussed in section 14.1 above.

14.2 Public authorities

14.2.1 The problem of public authorities

The law traditionally held that 'the King can do no wrong', but this old doctrine of Crown immunity 'disappeared early' in Australia's legal history after legislation was passed that 'deprived the Crown of its former immunity from liability for civil wrong' and paved the way for suits against public authorities or holders of statutory powers: see Dixon J in *Commissioner of Railways (WA) v Stewart* (1936) at 535–6 on the Western Australian legislation passed in 1898, and Gleeson CJ in *Graham Barclay Oysters Pty Ltd v Ryan* (2002), at [11], on the New South Wales legislation passed in 1857. Many cases that we have already discussed in the chapters on negligence involved suits brought against a wide range of governments (state, territory and Commonwealth), local councils and other public bodies constituted by statute. The increasing frequency of these cases can be accounted for both by the rapid expansion in the numbers and activities of these statutory authorities during the 20th century and the fact that public bodies are perceived to have 'deep pockets', which can make litigation attractive to plaintiffs. But the pendulum of negligence has swung back against such plaintiffs; many governments passed legislation in 2002 that gave public authorities a new 'policy defence' designed to reduce the number of successful claims.

The difficulties associated with imposing a duty of care on a public authority were explained by Mason J in *Sutherland Shire Council v Heyman* (1985) at 456:

> These problems are referable mainly to the character of a public authority as a body entrusted by statute with functions to be performed in the public interest or for public purposes. Some adjustment therefore needs to be made to accommodate the application of the principles and concepts of negligence to the acts and omissions of such a body.

In *Crimmins v Stevedoring Industry Finance Committee* (1999), McHugh J explained at [79] that negligence law is 'often an inapposite vehicle' for examining the choices and judgements made by public bodies who must perform their functions 'with limited budgetary resources' and who must therefore make 'difficult policy choices and discretionary judgments'. This theme was taken up by Gleeson CJ in *Graham Barclay Oysters Pty Ltd v Ryan* (2002) at [6], who pointed out that although 'citizens blame governments for many kinds of misfortune', a different set of considerations must apply when people seek compensation from public funds:

> They are claiming against a body politic or other entity whose primary responsibilities are to the public. And, in the case of an action in negligence against a government of the Commonwealth or a State or Territory, they are inviting the judicial arm of government to pass judgment upon the reasonableness of the conduct of the legislative or executive arms of government; conduct that may involve action or inaction on political grounds. Decisions as to raising revenue, and setting priorities in the allocation of public funds between competing claims on scarce resources, are essentially political.

Judges are reluctant to trespass upon the proper role of elected law-makers and officials who are entrusted with the task of setting policy, exercising their discretionary decision-making powers that involve balancing 'financial, economic, social or political factors or constraints' and allocating limited resources out of the public budget for public purposes: see *Sutherland Shire Council v Heyman* (1985), Mason J at 469; *Graham Barclay Oysters Pty Ltd v Ryan* (2002), Gleeson CJ at [12]. These public matters of governmental policy require the balancing of a different set of criteria for a different set of public purposes, with the result that these matters are 'inappropriate as subjects of curial judgment about reasonableness', as Gleeson CJ pointed out in *Graham Barclay Oysters Pty Ltd v Ryan* (2002) at [13], citing Lord Diplock in *Home Office v Dorset Yacht Co Ltd* (1970) at 1067. The most recent restatement of such reluctance appears in Allsop CJ's reasoning in *Minister for the Environment v Sharma* (2022), discussed in Chapter 11, in which he describes the issue at [246] in the following terms:

> Here, if the duty is to be imposed, *the considerations and judgements attending the decision will involve an evaluation of the adequacy of national and State policies taken within the framework of international agreement and whether such policy or policies was or were adequate and whether it or they should be persisted with or remade.* Such policy or policies and such agreement draw out and are based on multi-disciplinary considerations including environmental, climatic, economic, social and political considerations. These are not only the natural province of the Executive and Parliament, but also, by their nature and character as attending the safety and wellbeing of all Australians, and (on the uncontested evidence) the wellbeing of the world and humanity, *comprise the foundation of the (public or political) duty of consideration and policy formulation* by at least the Executive on this subject. [Emphasis added.]

These concerns about the appropriateness of using the tort of negligence to hold public bodies accountable for their acts or omissions are directly related to the different roles played by judges and legislators and the different conceptions of justice that direct their decisions. Judges, when deciding negligence cases, are primarily concerned with doing *corrective justice*, whereas legislators and public officials have a wider duty that requires them to take questions of *distributive justice* into account when deciding on the general distribution of benefits and burdens, resources and opportunities among different members of the community. Consequently, judges are aware that their role gives them limited scope to engage in essentially political decisions aimed at securing the health, welfare and security of the community. The need to maintain a coherent division in roles accounts not only for many of the immunities noted earlier, but also for many of the other difficulties that judges encounter when deciding these cases involving public authorities.

Case examples

- It is difficult to draw an appropriate distinction 'between discretionary and non-discretionary powers, between policy and operational decisions and between powers and duties' which may themselves be subject to particular limits, as Gaudron J explained in *Crimmins v Stevedoring Industry Finance Committee* (1999) at [27]. It will often require a careful reading of the statute that sets up the authority to distinguish between a statute that confers a power to act and a statute that imposes a duty to act: see Kirby J at [243] in *Graham Barclay Oysters Pty Ltd v Ryan* (2002).
- Further, a long-lasting debate continues to evolve with regard to a rather blurry conceptual distinction between policy decisions, which fall beyond the scope of judicial remit, and operational ones, which on the other hand fall within this scope. The matter was discussed by

the High Court in *Brodie v Singleton Shire Council* (2001), and reprised by the Full Federal Court of Australia in *Minister for the Environment v Sharma* (2022), where Allsop CJ explained again at [246]:

> Debate took place in relation to ... *the so-called policy/operational divide* ... we are not dealing here with the distinction at all. We are not dealing with decisions of authorities in the allocation of budgets or in the choice of policy as to planning and constructions of roads. We are dealing with core, indeed, high policy-making. There are many fields, as Gaudron, McHugh and Gummow JJ said in *Brodie* 206 CLR at 560 [106] where so-called policy cannot be used to hide a breach of requirements of the law. If a road authority wishes to rely upon policy questions and resource allocation as a justification for not repairing a plainly dangerous bridge of which it is aware, it can propound its case at the point of considering breach of duty and will be judged by reference to considerations amenable to, and suitable for, judicial determination: *Brodie* at 560 [106]. [Emphasis added.]

- Another complication may occur if the facts of a case also give rise to a claim under the separate tort of breach of statutory duty. This tort provides a different basis for imposing liability, and requires the proof of a different set of elements, which include the extra requirements noted by Lord Browne-Wilkinson in *X (Minors) v Bedfordshire County Council* (1995) at 731:

  > The principles applicable in determining whether such statutory cause of action exists are now well established, although the application of those principles in any particular case remains difficult. The basic proposition is that in the ordinary case a breach of statutory duty does not, by itself, give rise to any private law cause of action. However, a private law cause of action will arise if it can be shown, as a matter of construction of the statute, that the statutory duty was imposed for the protection of *a limited class of the public* and that Parliament *intended to confer on members of that class a private right* of action for breach of the duty. [Emphasis added.]

  For further elaboration of the elements of the tort of breach of statutory duty, see:
  - Mendelson, *The New Law of Torts* (2010), ch 19 at 692; and
  - Stewart and Stuhmcke, *Australian Principles of Tort Law*, 4th ed (2017), ch 19 at 558.
- The issues relating to public authorities can be complicated even further in cases where the authority has been sued:
  - for an omission (section 14.1); or
  - for making a statement (section 14.4); or
  - for causing a pure economic loss (section 14.5) or mental harm (section 14.3).
- Many cases concerning the liability of public authorities were decided during the period between 1984 and 2001, when the High Court was divided over the proper methodology to be used in these special or 'novel' categories of duty. Consequently, they are not only extremely long, but in many cases it is very hard to find a clear line of reasoning to apply in new cases because different judges used different methodologies and gave different reasons for their decisions – as occurred in *Crimmins v Stevedoring Industry Finance Committee* (1999), where seven judges took 370 paragraphs and 120 pages to explore the issues.

The best way to navigate through these difficulties is to return to first principles and to adopt the *Sullivan v Moody* (2001) approach to the duty question.

14.2.2 Relevant salient features

Three important features are regularly referred to in the complex cases dealing with the liability of public authorities:

1. The feature of *coherence* is one of the most important ones in this area: *Sullivan v Moody* (2001) at [30], [42], [50], [53]–[55] and [60]; *Graham Barclay Oysters Pty Ltd v Ryan* (2002), Gummow and Hayne JJ at [149]; *Electricity Networks Corporation v Herridge Parties* (2022). At the general level it supports the respect for a coherent division of roles between judges on the one hand and legislators and policy makers on the other, as discussed in section 14.2.1 above. The notion of coherence also lends support to any posited duty of care if the duty might enhance or maintain support for other wider community goals – and supports denying a duty if it would run counter to these wider goals, as Brennan J suggested in *San Sebastian Pty Ltd v Minister Administering the Environmental Planning and Assessment Act 1979* (1986) at 272.
   On a more detailed level, coherence supports denying a duty if:
   - it would not be compatible with other duties that the authority or its officers owe;
   - it is inconsistent with, or has a tendency to discourage, the due performance of other duties or responsibilities; or
   - the asserted duty of care is inconsistent with the terms, scope and purpose of any relevant statute: see above references to *Sullivan v Moody* (2001).
2. The feature of *vulnerability* supports imposing a duty in cases where public authorities have a great degree of control over (and/or specific knowledge of) a situation that places the plaintiff into a position of special vulnerability or where the plaintiffs have specifically and reasonably relied on the public authority and cannot protect themselves in any other way, which can suggest an assumption of responsibility by the public authority: *Sutherland Shire Council v Heyman* (1985), Mason J at 641 and 648; *Graham Barclay Oysters Pty Ltd v Ryan* (2002); McHugh CJ at [84], Gummow and Hayne JJ at [149], citing the following cases:
   - *Howard v Jarvis* (1958) at 183;
   - *Burnie Port Authority v General Jones Pty Ltd* (1994) at 550–2, 556–7;
   - *Crimmins v Stevedoring Industry Finance Committee* (1999) at [44]–[46], [91]–[93], [100];
   - *Sullivan v Moody* (2001) at [55]–[62]; and
   - *Tepko Pty Ltd v Water Board* (2001) at [47] and [76];

   More recently see the decision of the High Court in *Electricity Networks Corporation v Herridge Parties* (2022), reiterating the centrality of these features.
3. The feature of *certainty*, which requires that liability must not be too uncertain in nature or give rise to indeterminate liability, is also relevant to cases concerning the liability of public authorities. In these cases, the potential indeterminacy of liability points against imposing a duty, unless the class of persons to whom the

duty is owed is ascertainable: *Sutherland Shire Council v Heyman* (1985), Mason J at 465; *Sullivan v Moody* (2001) at [61]; see also *Stovin v Wise* (1996), Lord Hoffmann at 943–4. So, if as Gummow and Hayne JJ pointed out in *Graham Barclay Oysters Pty Ltd v Ryan* (2002) at [185], 'the practical content of any such duty would be elusive', this 'supports the conclusion that it does not exist'. Gleeson CJ said in *Crimmins v Stevedoring Industry Finance Committee* (1999) at [5]:

> In some cases, the difficulty of formulating the practical content of a duty to take reasonable steps to avoid foreseeable risks of harm, for the purpose of measuring the performance of an authority against such a duty, may be a reason for denying the duty.

So, provided the suggested duty does not infringe either the necessity of coherence or that of certainty, and if it is supported by the presence of salient features of sufficient weight (including control, knowledge, reliance and/or assumption of responsibility), then the vulnerability of the plaintiff will point in favour of imposing a duty, and the issue then becomes whether the other elements of breach and causation can be made out.

14.2.3 Key cases

The case law on public authorities is complicated, and for the reasons noted above, rather confusing. Consequently, this subsection will focus on identifying the unifying themes from the leading cases that support the High Court's methodology of establishing a duty.

Case examples

- *Sutherland Shire Council v Heyman* (1985) concerned a case where the Ps, who purchased a house in 1975 built by others in 1970, sued a local council (D) for losses caused by subsidence in 1976 of inadequate footings. The Ps argued that D had failed to ensure that the foundations were properly laid. Three judges in the High Court denied liability on the grounds that D did not owe a duty to the Ps because, although D had approved the plans, there was no evidence that the Ps had either made inquiries of D or relied upon D having inspected the footings when they decided to buy the house. The other judges held that there was no evidence of breach. Note that this case also contains an important discussion of the problem of pure omissions.

  Mason J noted at 458 that it was 'well settled that a public authority may be subject to a common law duty of care when it exercises a statutory power or performs a statutory duty' but went on to explain at 459:

  > Generally speaking a public authority which is under no statutory obligation to exercise a power comes under no common law duty of care to do so. But an authority may by its conduct place itself in such a position that it attracts a duty of care which calls for exercise of the power. A common illustration is provided by the cases in which an authority in the exercise of its functions has created a danger, thereby subjecting itself to a duty of care for the safety of others which must be discharged by an exercise of its statutory powers or by giving a warning.

When denying the existence of a duty in this case, Mason J emphasised the following points:

- The mere foreseeability of either physical damage or an economic loss is not enough to found a duty (at 466; see also Brennan J at 479).
- A public authority must be free to 'make policy-making decisions and discretionary judgments': at 457–8. It is important to make a distinction between 'policy-making and discretionary' decisions and 'operational' decisions: at 468–9. Note that the relevance of this distinction has been doubted in later cases.
- The importance of 'reliance or dependence' in establishing a duty of care (at 466 and 461) and, on the facts of the case, the significance of the lack of any specific inquiry or reliance (at 466). See also Brennan J at 486 and 494, and Deane J at 498 and 508–9. Note, however, that the idea of a more general reliance, discussed at 463–4, was not followed in later cases that emphasise the need for specific factual reliance.
- The common law's 'concern about endless indeterminate liability' is relevant if the claim against a public authority is for a pure economic loss: at 465.

- *Pyrenees Shire Council v Day* (1998) is an extremely complicated and lengthy case that concerned a local council's liability for failing to ensure that a chimney, which council staff knew was defective, was properly dealt with so as to avoid danger of fire. While liability was imposed on the defendant council by the High Court and the two plaintiffs recovered damages for their losses, the case was dominated by disagreement over the appropriate methodology of duty and there is very little agreement between the judges other than the conclusion by a majority of three that the concept of general reliance that was introduced by Mason J in *Sutherland Shire Council v Heyman* (1985) 'is not sound' and could not provide the basis of liability: see Brennan CJ at [19], Gummow J at [157]–[165] and Kirby J at [225]–[232].
- In *Crimmins v Stevedoring Industry Finance Committee* (1999), D, a public authority given the power to secure 'the expeditious, safe and efficient performance of stevedoring operations', was found (by a majority of 5:2) to owe a duty to P, a waterside worker who contracted the dust-borne disease of mesothelioma, an asbestos-related respiratory disease. This case saw a measure of agreement emerge from the High Court on the relevance of the important 'salient features' that indicate vulnerability on the part of P to the conduct of D, including:
  - the knowledge of the special risk to P and the power of D to control or minimise the risk; and
  - the inability of P to protect their own interests in the circumstances.

  See Gaudron J at [43]–[46]; McHugh J at [51], [93], [100]–[101]; Gummow J at [166]; Kirby J at [233]; Hayne J at [276]–[277]; and Callinan J at [357].
- The case of *Brodie v Singleton Shire Council* (2001) saw a majority of 4:3 in the High Court overturn the old common law immunity of highway authorities for 'nonfeasance', and introduced the distinction between policy and operational decisions as a way to engage with a public authority's decision-making without encroaching into that authority's ability to exercise its powers with autonomy. After reviewing many earlier cases, Gaudron, McHugh and Gummow JJ noted the 'fundamental importance' of a public authority's control over a source of risk, saying at [103]–[104]:

> Whatever may be the general significance today in tort law of the distinction between misfeasance and non-feasance, it has become more clearly understood that, on occasions, the powers vested by statute in a public authority may give it such *a significant and special measure of control over the safety of the person* or property of citizens as to impose upon the authority a duty of care ... It is often the case that statutory bodies which are alleged to have been negligent because they failed to exercise statutory powers have no control over the source of the risk of harm to those who suffer injury. Authorities having the control of highways are in a different position. They have physical control over the object or structure which is the source of the risk of harm. This places highway authorities in a category apart from other recipients of statutory powers. [Emphasis added.]

- In *Dansar Pty Ltd v Byron Shire Council* (2014), the plaintiff had lodged an application for residential development consent. The Byron Shire Council initially refused on the basis that it would result in a sewerage load in excess of the current load, and the plaintiff suffered pure economic loss as a result of the delay. The question before the New South Wales Court of Appeal was whether a common law duty of care can be owed in respect of one role of a public authority if it conflicts with another role of the public authority. Meagher JA explained at [181] that a public authority acting in its capacity as both a sewerage authority and a consent authority did not owe a duty of care to a developer to avoid economic loss resulting from the refusal or delay of consent, because this duty would be incompatible with the authority's obligation to give paramount consideration to the exercise of both those statutory functions.

The landmark case of *Sullivan v Moody* (2001) saw the High Court develop a new approach to the duty problem. It provided the Court with a perfect opportunity to consider the issue because it came after a lengthy period of debate in the earlier cases, which had seen an emerging degree of agreement over the relevance of many of the salient features, and because the claim involved one of the special duty areas – namely, the liability for negligently causing pure psychiatric injury. In the absence of Kirby J, who had campaigned for many years for the English three-stage '*Caparo* test', the High Court was able to issue a short, 65-paragraph judgment containing succinct reasoning that supported a unanimous decision and a new approach to the problem of finding principled limits on the tort of negligence. In this case, which is noted again in section 14.3 on pure psychiatric injury, the High Court identified at [55]–[60] two important features that relate directly to the liability of public authorities: coherence and certainty. The Court pointed out at [53] that if a duty 'would so cut across other legal principles as to impair their proper application' it would 'lead to the conclusion that there is no duty of care of the kind asserted', and continued at [55] and [60]:

> More fundamentally, however, these cases present a question about coherence of the law. Considering whether the persons who reported their suspicions about each appellant owed that appellant a duty of care must begin from the recognition that those who made the report had other responsibilities. A duty of the kind alleged should not be found if that duty would not be *compatible with other duties* which the respondents owed. [Emphasis added.] [55]

> ... The circumstance that a defendant owes a duty of care to a third party, or is subject to statutory obligations which constrain the manner in which powers or discretions may be exercised, does not of itself rule out the possibility that a duty of care is owed to a plaintiff. People may be subject to a number of duties, at least provided they are not irreconcilable ... But if a suggested duty of care would give rise to *inconsistent obligations*, that would ordinarily be a reason for denying that the duty exists. Similarly, when public authorities, or their officers, are charged with the responsibility of conducting investigations, or exercising powers, in the public interest, or in the interests of a specified class of persons, the law would not ordinarily subject them to a duty to have regard to the interests of another class of persons where that would impose upon them *conflicting claims or obligations*. [Emphasis added.] [60]

The Court also pointed out at [61] the significance of the problem of uncertainty, noting that 'there is also a question as to the extent, and potential indeterminacy, of liability'. This approach to the issue of duty was taken up in later cases. The succinctness of the High Court in cases involving public authorities was lost in the next case of *Graham Barclay Oysters Pty Ltd v Ryan* (2002) (which took 332 paragraphs and 129 pages to deliver). It was found again in more recent times in the case of *Electricity Networks Corporation v Herridge Parties* (2022) (which confines itself to 60 paragraphs and is well worth a read!), but note that this case involves a statutory corporation with a clear statutory purpose but no policy-making functions, which of course simplifies the process of establishing a duty of care.

Case example

In *Graham Barclay Oysters Pty Ltd v Ryan* (2002), a representative action was brought on behalf of people who contracted hepatitis A after eating contaminated oysters. They sued the oyster growers and distributors as well as the local council and the state of New South Wales for failing to exercise their powers to order sanitary surveys that might have identified the contamination and prevented their illness. Both claims against the public authorities failed on the grounds either that the bodies had not been in breach or that they did not owe a duty to the consumers. This case saw the continuation of the High Court's review of the salient features approach to the liability of public authorities.

McHugh J at [84] repeated his list of important features from an earlier judgment in *Crimmins v Stevedoring Industry Finance Committee* (1999) at [93], which was adapted from the chapter by Stephen Todd, 'Liability in Tort of Public Bodies' (1998) at 55, and which included: reasonable foreseeability of harm; the degree of control exercised by the public authority; the plaintiffs' vulnerability in the special sense of being unable to protect themselves; whether the defendant knew or ought to have known of the risk to the specific class of persons including the plaintiff; the exercise of 'core policy-making' or 'quasi-legislative' functions; and any relevant 'policy' considerations that would deny the existence of the duty.

Gummow and Hayne JJ (with whom Gaudron J agreed) noted at [146] that the existence of a duty of care owed by a statutory authority 'turns on a close examination of the terms, scope and purpose of the relevant statutory regime' and then summarised the focus of the 'multi-faceted' inquiry at [149]:

> The focus of analysis is the relevant legislation and the positions occupied by the parties on the facts as found at trial. It ordinarily will be necessary to consider the degree and nature of *control* exercised by the authority over the risk of harm that eventuated; the degree of *vulnerability* of those who depend on the proper exercise by the authority of its powers; and the *consistency* or otherwise of the asserted duty of care with the terms, scope and purpose of the relevant statute. In particular categories of cases, some features will be of increased significance. For example, in cases of negligent misstatement ... *reasonable reliance* by the plaintiff on the defendant authority ordinarily will be a significant factor in ascertaining any relevant duty of care. [Emphasis added and references omitted.]

Kirby J gave up the campaign for the English *Caparo* test and acknowledged at [243] and [249] the importance of the 'multi-factorial or "salient features" approach', noting the importance of the presence of control, which justified the imposition of the duty in the cases of *Crimmins v Stevedoring Industry Finance Committee* (1999) and *Brodie v Singleton Shire Council* (2001).

Callinan J at [321] also noted the importance of the features of 'vulnerability, power, control, generality or particularity of the class, the resources of, and demands upon the authority' but maintained that none of them should be decisive.

A summary of the relevant principles in this area can be found in the judgment of Ipp JA in *Amaca Pty Ltd v New South Wales* (2004) at [18]–[23], and more recently in the unanimous High Court judgment in *Electricity Networks Corporation v Herridge Parties* (2022).

14.2.4 Legislative intervention

The Ipp Report (2002) reported at [10.3] and [10.9] on a growing perception that the common law approach to the liability of public authorities was deficient. It was claimed that because the courts were imposing liability on public authorities for decisions made in 'good faith' either about the allocation of 'scarce resources between competing activities' or in the course of implementing a good faith 'political and social policy' after weighing the 'competing interests of the various groups affected', the common law approach was having a 'detrimental impact on the ability of public authorities to perform their functions in the public interest'. The Ipp Report concluded at [10.11]:

> First, courts are not well qualified, either in terms of expertise or procedure, to adjudicate upon the reasonableness of decisions that are essentially political in nature. Secondly, courts are inappropriate bodies to consider the reasonableness of such decisions because they are neither politically representative nor politically responsible. Thirdly, proper consideration of the reasonableness of such decisions may be very expensive and time consuming.

As a result of the recommendation of the Ipp Report that a new 'policy defence' was needed to remedy the problems caused by the deficiencies in the common law approach to the liability of public authorities, most jurisdictions in Australia (with the exception of South Australia and the Northern Territory) enacted legislation putting the recommendation into effect, supplemented by further provisions acknowledging the limited resources available to public authorities in the exercise of their (often very broad) public functions.

Legislative examples

Civil Law (Wrongs) Act 2002 (ACT) s 110

Principles about resources, responsibilities etc of public or other authorities

The following principles apply in deciding in a proceeding whether a public or other authority has a duty of care or has breached a duty of care:

(a) the functions required to be exercised by the authority are limited by the financial and other resources reasonably available to the authority for exercising the functions;

(b) the general allocation of the resources by the authority is not open to challenge;

(c) the functions required to be exercised by the authority are to be decided by reference to the broad range of its activities (and not only by reference to the matter to which the proceeding relates);

(d) the authority may rely on evidence of its compliance with the general procedures and applicable standards for the exercise of its functions as evidence of the proper exercise of its functions in the matter to which the proceeding relates.

Civil Liability Act 2002 (WA) s 5AA

Exercise of function or decision to exercise does not create duty

In proceedings to which this Part applies, the fact that a public body or officer exercises or decides to exercise a function does not of itself indicate that the body or officer is under a duty to exercise the function or that the function should be exercised in particular circumstances or in a particular way.

LEGISLATION ALERT!

Consult your study materials and note down the relevant statutory provisions in your jurisdiction (if any) introducing a policy defence.

Finally, many jurisdictions also acted to restore the old immunity that had been traditionally given to highway authorities to protect them from any liability for 'nonfeasance' or a failure to construct, maintain or repair a road, and which had been abolished by the High Court in *Brodie v Singleton Shire Council* (2001).

Legislative example

Civil Liability Act 1936 (SA) s 42(1)

Liability of road authorities

(1) A road authority is not liable in tort for a failure –

(a) to maintain, repair or renew a road; or

(b) to take other action to avoid or reduce the risk of harm that results from a failure to maintain, repair or renew a road.

The scope of the immunity varies across jurisdictions, and is in most cases slightly narrower in scope. See, for example, the provision of the *Civil Liability Act 2002* (NSW) s 45(1).

Legislative example

Civil Liability Act 2002 (NSW) s 45(1)

Special nonfeasance protection for roads authorities

(1) A roads authority is not liable in proceedings for civil liability to which this Part applies for harm arising from a failure of the authority to carry out road work, or to consider carrying out road work, unless at the time of the alleged failure the authority had actual knowledge of the particular risk the materialisation of which resulted in the harm.

The liability of road authorities is a very complex matter, and the legislative intervention adopted by most states and territories has arguably not succeeded in simplifying the law. Two cases from New South Wales illustrate the questions left open by the civil liability provisions.

Case examples

- In *Curtis v Harden Shire Council* (2014), resurfacing works had caused a section of a particular road to be covered in loose gravel, which led to a fatal motor accident. The council, acting in its capacity as a road authority for the purpose of the *Civil Liability Act 2002* (NSW), had failed to put up signs warning of a slippery surface, and failed to reduce the speed limit on the road. The question for the New South Wales Court of Appeal was whether the particular provision of s 43A (which has equivalents in most states and territories) would apply to the facts of the case. Section 43A provides that an act or omission involving an exercise or failure to exercise a special statutory power does not give rise to civil liability unless the act or omission is so unreasonable that no authority in question could consider the act a reasonable exercise of its power. Bathurst CJ explained that while s 43A applied, the council was nevertheless liable because it failed to live up to the reduced standard of care set by s 43A(3). The relevant test is that of a reasonable and responsible public authority, having particular expertise and functions.

In this case, there was no evidence that no road authority would have properly considered it appropriate to put up road signs, thus suggesting the conclusion that the failure to act was so unreasonable that no reasonable road authority would act similarly.

- In *Nightingale v Blacktown City Council* (2015), the plaintiff sustained injuries to his foot and ankle caused by stepping into a sunken area of a footpath. He sued the council in negligence for failure to carry out road work on the footpath. The New South Wales Court of Appeal had previously held in *North Sydney Council v Roman* (2007) that where a plaintiff is arguing that a road authority failed to carry out road work which caused their injury, a natural person with authority to carry out the road work on behalf of the road authority must have requisite actual knowledge of the need for road work. In *Nightingale v Blacktown City Council*, Basten JA at [40]–[48] placed emphasis on the requirement that there be actual knowledge of the particular risk, the materialisation of which resulted in the harm.

Note that while the reasoning in these decisions came from cases involving road authorities, it may also be applicable to public authorities in general, specifically because they involve an evaluation of what a *reasonable* authority would do in the circumstances, and the weight that actual knowledge of the existence of a risk has in that determination.

LEGISLATION ALERT!

Consult your study materials and note any relevant statutory provisions in your jurisdiction.

14.2.5 Summary points

14.2.5.1 Public authorities

1. The most important features in this area are coherence, certainty and vulnerability.
2. Any relevant statutes must be considered and their terms, scope and purpose carefully interpreted.
3. A holder of a statutory power does not come under a general duty to exercise that power, even if it is reasonably foreseeable that harm may ensue if they do not exercise it. Something more is required, and an adjustment must be made to accommodate the special nature and functions of a public authority.
4. It will weigh *against* imposing a duty if, in the circumstances:
   - the matter is not appropriate for judgement by the courts because it involves policy-making, 'quasi-legislative' or budgetary decisions about the use of limited public resources in the wider public interest involving an assessment of 'financial, economic, social or political factors or constraints' (*Sutherland Shire Council v Heyman* (1985), Mason J at 469), and so a refusal to impose a duty would preserve a coherent division of roles between the separate arms of government;
   - the duty on the authority is 'elusive' or would create indeterminate liability, uncertainty or undue difficulty in defining and complying with the duty or in measuring the damages;

- the duty on the authority would lead to incoherence or inconsistency in the duties imposed by the law – for example, if it:
  - would cut across other legal principles or impair their proper application;
  - would discourage the due performance of other duties or responsibilities imposed by the law of torts or the criminal law; or
  - is inconsistent with the terms, scope and purpose of any relevant statute;
- the authority is neither the source of the risk nor in control of the risk;
- the plaintiff is not in an ascertainable class of persons who might foreseeably suffer harm.

5. It will weigh in *favour* of imposing a duty if, in the circumstances:
   - the authority has itself created a risk or a danger;
   - the authority had assumed a responsibility to carry out a particular function for the benefit of the plaintiff;
   - the authority was in a position analogous to an employer;
   - the plaintiff was in a position of special vulnerability – for example, because:
     - the authority knew or ought to have known about the risk;
     - the authority had the power to control or minimise the risk;
     - the plaintiff was not in control of the risk and they had no other way of protecting themselves from the risk; or
     - the plaintiff had made specific inquiries of the authority or reasonably placed specific reliance on the authority.
6. In many jurisdictions, parliaments have provided for a new statutory 'policy defence' and reinstated the old immunity covering highway authorities for 'nonfeasance'.
7. The question of duty may be more complicated if the public authority has been sued for pure economic loss (see section 14.5 below) or mental harm (see section 14.3 below) or if the conduct being complained of is a pure omission (see section 14.1 above) or is a negligent misstatement (see section 14.4 below).

Active reading

Link each of these summary points to a case in section 14.2 above.

Develop your skills

Oral presentations, case notes and memorandums

Exercise 1: Oral presentation

Prepare a five-minute oral presentation on the topic 'What limits should be placed on the courts' ability to judge the acts and omissions of a public authority?'

Exercise 2: Case analysis

Write a case note on *Sutherland Shire Council v Heyman* (1985).

Exercise 3: Memorandum

Write a 1500-word internal office memorandum explaining to your senior partner why the plaintiffs in *Graham Barclay Oysters Pty Ltd v Ryan* (2002) failed to recover damages from the two public authorities.

Exercise 4: Impact of statutory provisions

Write a 500-word explanation of whether and how the special provisions for public authorities introduced by the civil liability legislation have facilitated or further limited a plaintiff's ability to sue a public authority.

14.3 Mental harm

The approach taken by the courts to liability for mental harm (also referred to as 'psychiatric injury' and originally known as 'nervous shock') has been complicated and subject to criticism.[5] Despite the fact that many steps have been taken over the last 30 years towards constructing a more principled approach to mental harm, the law in this area remains difficult to understand and challenging to apply. The problems associated with imposing liability for causing mental harm, which is the terminology adopted by the civil liability legislation, arise from the nature of the harm itself and from our incomplete understanding of the way it is caused. As *Donoghue v Stevenson* (1932) showed, these difficulties do not necessarily provide any great hurdle when the mental harm is either a consequence of, or accompanied by, a *physical injury*. They have, however, taken up a lot of judicial attention in cases where 'pure' psychiatric injury is the *only* harm suffered by a plaintiff. Judges who responded to these difficulties in the early cases by constructing barriers to liability have in turn caused more problems for later courts, which, with the benefit of better scientific knowledge and medical advice, have then had to justify dismantling those barriers many years later.

The history of the common law on pure mental harm in Australia can be divided into two parts. The first stage, which lasted from 1888 until 2002, saw the rise and fall of an approach based on imposing 'control devices'. The introduction of these barriers to liability began in *Victorian Railways Commissioners v Coultas* in 1888 and the gradual dismantling of almost all of those barriers was completed in 2002 in *Tame v New South Wales,* in which the High Court jointly decided two cases involving pure mental harm (the second of which is often cited as *Annetts,* in reference to the name of the plaintiffs in that case). The second stage began with many (but not all) parliaments enacting civil liability legislation in late 2002, which was meant to restate the common law of negligence liability for mental harm. This happened precisely at the time when the High Court was completing the common law's transition to

5 See Handford, *Mullany and Handford's Tort Liability for Psychiatric Damage* (2006) and Dietrich, 'Nervous Shock: *Tame v New South Wales* and *Annetts v Australian Stations Pty Ltd*' (2003).

its new approach to negligence. As a refresher, the High Court's approach was outlined in *Sullivan v Moody* (2001), in which the Court put renewed emphasis on the primary neighbour principle of *Donoghue v Stevenson* (1932) and supplemented it with salient features that had emerged in the negligence cases over the previous decades (see Chapter 11).

14.3.1 The problem of pure mental harm

The courts have traditionally treated cases of pure mental harm with extreme caution, if not outright suspicion.

Case example

In the first case of its type brought in Australia, *Victorian Railways Commissioners v Coultas* (1888), the plaintiff, a pregnant woman whose carriage was stuck on a railway track due to the negligence of a gatekeeper, was placed in 'imminent peril' of being killed by a train. She was not physically injured but she did suffer a 'severe nervous shock' and extreme terror, which caused her to become ill. Her claim was ultimately rejected by the Privy Council, and the Judicial Committee explained at 225–6 that the difficulty of allowing recovery in a case where the harm 'arises from mere sudden terror unaccompanied by any actual physical injury, but occasioning a nervous or mental shock' lay:

- first, in deciding whether such harm was reasonably foreseeable;
- second, in being able to prove that it was actually caused by the shock; and
- third, in opening up the possibility of a 'wide field' of 'imaginary claims'.

As many judges have subsequently pointed out, this reluctance can be partly explained by the state of medical knowledge existing at that time, but the barriers that the early judges put in place to deal with their doubts about psychiatric illness have taken many years to break down. Some of these doubts and difficulties have been collected and commented on in *Mount Isa Mines Ltd v Pusey* (1970) by Windeyer J at 402–5; in *Jaensch v Coffey* (1984) by Brennan J at 560 and 564–5 and by Deane J at 590–3; and in *Tame v New South Wales* (2002) by Gummow and Kirby JJ at [192] and Hayne J at [243]–[246].

Examples

- Pure mental harm is not 'real' harm (by contrast with physical injuries).
- Even if it is real harm, pure mental harm is too difficult to distinguish from mere emotional upset or distress, so it is not possible to draw a suitable line between the two.
- The 'Cartesian' distinction between mind and matter has had an 'obdurate influence' on legal thinking and the interrelation between the mind and the body is not well enough understood: Windeyer J in *Mount Isa Mines Ltd v Pusey* (1970) at 405.
- Pure mental harm is by its nature vague, unverifiable, unobservable, too easily faked and too difficult to prove. This means that allowing liability would open up the possibility of claims made by malingerers or worse, a flood of exaggerated, false or imaginary claims. The availability of damages would also provide an 'unconscious disincentive' to rehabilitation.

- If pure mental harm can be caused either by the hearing of bad news, the mere knowledge of upsetting facts or the mere dissemination through the media of footage of upsetting and shocking tragedies, it follows that the extent of liability will either be indeterminate or impose a disproportionate burden on defendants. As Gummow and Kirby JJ noted in *Tame v New South Wales* (2002) at [192] (quoting *Prosser and Keeton's Torts*), the fear is that such defendants would have to pay for 'the lacerated feelings' of every person disturbed by the danger they created 'including every bystander shocked at an accident, and every distant relative of the person injured, as well as all his friends'.

To this list, we can add the difficulty caused by the fact that the law is no longer uniform throughout Australia as a result of the civil liability legislation. This means that decisions in cases going to the High Court from one state are not necessarily of assistance in other jurisdictions unless the wording of the provisions matches. Two good examples can be found in the High Court case of *Wicks v State Rail Authority of New South Wales* (2010), which was based on the precise wording and history of the New South Wales legislation, and the High Court case of *King v Philcox* (2015), which was based on the specific provisions of the South Australian statute.

14.3.2 Controls on liability: 1888–2002

Uncertainty about psychiatric illness led judges to develop a number of control mechanisms that limited the liability of a defendant whose negligence may have led to psychiatric illness. These limits related to:

- the nature of the *harm* suffered by the plaintiff;
- the psychological *fortitude* of the plaintiff;
- the nature of the *event* that gave rise to the harm;
- the *causal mechanism* that led to the harm suffered by the plaintiff;
- the *physical proximity of the plaintiff* to the events and the victims; and
- the *relationships* between the plaintiff, the defendant and any victims.

Overarching all of these special barriers is the concept of reasonable foreseeability, which, as we know from *Donoghue v Stevenson* (1932) and *Chapman v Hearse* (1961), normally provides a primary control on imposing a duty of care. Many of these barriers have since been relaxed by the High Court, but given that some have subsequently returned in a slightly different form in the civil liability legislation, it is important to understand their sources and history. Some of these barriers, which began as strict limiting rules, have become relevant considerations. Others, which started out as strict limiting rules and then became relevant considerations at common law, have now returned once more as strict rules in the legislation.

LEGISLATION ALERT!

Consult your study materials and identify any relevant statutory provisions in your jurisdiction. Note the scope and coverage of the provisions and any exclusions.

14.3.2.1 The foreseeability of pure mental harm

Judges in the past used the foreseeability requirement as a means of denying liability.

Case example

In *Chester v Council of the Municipality of Waverley* (1939), the plaintiff was a mother who had been searching for hours for her seven-year-old son who had gone missing. He was eventually found drowned in a deep water-filled trench that had been left open and unfenced by council workers. The mother had not been present at the moment of his death but was present when his body was taken out of the trench. She became ill, but was unsuccessful in her claim against the council. Latham CJ said at 10:

> A reasonable person would not foresee that the negligence of the defendant towards the child would 'so affect' a mother ... Death is not an infrequent event, and even violent and distressing deaths are not uncommon. It is, however, not a common experience of mankind that the spectacle, even of the sudden and distressing death of a child, produces any consequence of more than a temporary nature in the case of bystanders or even of close relatives who see the body after death has taken place.

This Australian case echoed the earlier old-fashioned approach taken in *Victorian Railways Commissioners v Coultas* (1888), noted above. However, advances in medical science led to a reassessment of these decisions, and the older view that mental harm was by its very nature 'too remote' from the negligence of the defendant was abandoned. While the courts came to accept that mental harm could be reasonably foreseeable in many circumstances, they nevertheless insisted that reasonable foreseeability would not be enough on its own to found a duty and for many years they continued to use other rules to keep the liability within narrow limits. As Gaudron J explained in *Tame v New South Wales* (2002) at [45]:

> Whatever purpose those 'rules' might hitherto have served in the development of the law relating to pure psychiatric injury, they now serve to emphasise that, as with pure economic loss, something more than foreseeability of the likelihood of harm of the kind in issue is necessary before a defendant will be held to owe a duty of care to take reasonable steps to avoid a risk of that kind.

14.3.2.2 The nature of the harm suffered by the plaintiff

In all cases the courts have insisted that the harm suffered by the plaintiff must amount to 'serious mental harm' in the form of a 'recognised' or a 'recognisable' psychiatric illness,[6] thus ruling out any claims for 'mere' emotional distress, anxiety or grief: *Mount Isa Mines Ltd v Pusey* (1970), Windeyer J at 394 and 402, affirmed in *Tame v New South*

6 The possible differences between a 'recognised' and a 'recognisable' psychiatric illness in the civil liability era have been discussed by Des Butler in '*Gifford v Strang* and the New Landscape for Recovery for Psychiatric Injury in Australia' (2004) at 16–17.

Wales (2002), Gleeson CJ at [7], Gaudron J at [44], Gummow and Kirby JJ at [193], and Hayne J at [285]–[297]. In *Gifford v Strang Patrick Stevedoring Pty Ltd* (2003), Gummow and Kirby JJ noted at [88]:

> Australian law seeks to protect, in an appropriate case, the plaintiff's freedom from serious mental harm which manifests itself in a recognisable psychiatric illness.

This harm-based limit remains, both at common law and under the legislative regimes. Some jurisdictions have also applied this rule to claims for 'consequential' mental harm as well as to claims for 'pure' mental harm.

Legislative examples

- Under s 31 of the *Civil Liability Act 2002* (NSW), there is no liability to pay damages for pure mental harm resulting from negligence unless the harm consists of a recognised psychiatric illness.
- Under s 33 of the *Civil Liability Act 2002* (NSW), a court cannot make an award of damages for economic loss for consequential mental harm resulting from negligence unless the harm consists of a recognised psychiatric illness.

LEGISLATION ALERT!

Consult your study materials and note any relevant statutory provisions in your jurisdiction. Note any definitions.

14.3.2.3 A 'person of normal fortitude'

Before *Tame v New South Wales* (2002), it was thought that any plaintiff who was not a 'person of normal fortitude' was precluded from recovering damages. This common law requirement that the plaintiff must be a person of 'customary phlegm' or 'normal nervous strength' was highlighted in the 'pregnant fishwife' case of *Bourhill v Young* (1943) by Lord Porter at 117 and by Lord Wright at 110. It was mentioned with 'misgivings' by Windeyer J in *Mount Isa Mines Ltd v Pusey* (1970), who questioned at 405–7 the validity of the proposition and suggested that the idea of a person 'of normal emotional fibre' as distinct from one who is 'sensitive, susceptible and more easily disturbed' is 'imprecise and scientifically inexact'. Subsequently, four judges decided in *Tame v New South Wales* (2002) that, while the mental fortitude of a plaintiff may often be a relevant issue (eg when deciding the question of breach), the rule that the plaintiff must be a person of normal fortitude should not be a precondition for the imposition of a duty: Gleeson CJ at [16], Gaudron J at [59]–[62], Gummow and Kirby JJ at [197]–[203]. However, strong dissents were delivered by McHugh and Hayne JJ, who insisted that the concept of 'normal fortitude' had a role to play at the duty stage. This was picked up by many parliaments when the civil liability statutes were passed in 2002, though it was not linked to the specific plaintiff in the case, but rather was treated as an objective requirement of foreseeability. As explained, for example, by the Court of Appeal of the Western Australian Supreme Court in *Zaghloul v Bayly* (2021) at [94] with reference to the relevant Western Australian provision, a plaintiff need not show that they are themselves of normal fortitude. They rather need to make the case that *a* person of normal fortitude could foreseeably suffer from a recognised psychiatric illness in the circumstances of the case. Many of these statutes added a provision that the rule would not preclude the imposition of a duty in cases where the objective threshold would not be met, but the defendant knew, or ought reasonably to have known, that the plaintiff was a person of less than normal fortitude.

Legislative examples

Civil Liability Act 2002 (WA) s 5S(1)

(a) A person (the *defendant*) does not owe a duty of care to another person (the *plaintiff*) to take care not to cause the plaintiff mental harm unless the defendant ought to have foreseen that a person of normal fortitude might, in the circumstances of the case, suffer a recognised psychiatric illness if reasonable care were not taken.

Civil Liability Act 2002 s 5S(4)

(a) This section does not require the court to disregard what the defendant knew or ought to have known about the fortitude of the plaintiff.

LEGISLATION ALERT!

Note any statutory provisions in your jurisdiction on 'fortitude'.

14.3.2.4 The sudden nature of the shocking event and its effect on the plaintiff

Another limit, which remained until 2002, focused on the kind of event that caused the harm. To satisfy this rule, the event had to be an intrinsically traumatic event that gave the plaintiffs a 'sudden shock' which in turn disordered their senses and led to illness. In *Jaensch v Coffey* (1984), Brennan J explained at 566–7:

> The notion of psychiatric illness induced by shock is a compound, not a simple, idea. Its elements are, on the one hand, psychiatric illness and, on the other, shock which causes it ... I understand 'shock' in this context to mean the sudden sensory perception – that is, by seeing, hearing or touching – of a person, thing or event, which is so distressing that the perception of the phenomenon affronts or insults the plaintiff's mind and causes a recognizable psychiatric illness. A psychiatric illness induced by mere knowledge of a distressing fact is

> not compensable; perception by the plaintiff of the distressing phenomenon is essential. If mere knowledge of a distressing phenomenon sufficed, the bearers of sad tidings, able to foresee the depressing effect of what they have to impart, might be held liable as tortfeasors.

Brennan J noted at 565:

> Psychiatric illness caused in other ways attracts no damages, though it is reasonably foreseeable that psychiatric illness might be a consequence of the defendant's carelessness. The spouse who has been worn down by caring for a tortiously injured husband or wife and who suffers psychiatric illness as a result goes without compensation; a parent made distraught by the wayward conduct of a brain-damaged child and who suffers psychiatric illness as a result has no claim against the tortfeasor liable to the child.

While many of the exceptions noted by Brennan J remain a part of the common law rules, any requirement that the psychiatric condition must be caused by a 'sudden shock' was rejected in *Tame v New South Wales* (2002), by Gleeson CJ at [17]–[18], Gaudron J at [65]–[66], Gummow and Kirby JJ at [189]–[190] and [204]–[214], and Hayne J at [275]. The judgment in *Tame v New South Wales* actually covered two separate cases, the second of which, originally called *Annetts v Australian Stations Pty Ltd*, is still often cited by that alternative name. The '*Annetts* plaintiffs' had not experienced a single sudden shock, but rather, as loving and devoted parents of a missing boy, they had suffered through a prolonged nightmare of growing anxiety and stress that ended in tragic news.

Case example

The plaintiffs in *Annetts*, the second of the two cases decided in *Tame v New South Wales* (2002), were the parents of James, a 16-year-old boy who went to work as a jackaroo on a cattle station. They had allowed him to go only after being reassured by their son's employers that he would be well looked after and supervised. However, soon after arriving at the outback station, James and another young jackaroo were sent out on their own to look after a remote desert station without adequate supervision or training. The two boys left the station in an unroadworthy vehicle provided to them by their employers, which broke down. The boys became lost in the desert and their parents were notified that they were missing. Their bodies were not found for several months. During this period the plaintiffs were frantic with worry about their missing son, and after his remains had finally been found and it was established that the two boys had died of dehydration, exhaustion and hypothermia, they developed psychiatric illnesses. They sued their son's employers and the High Court held that they were owed a duty of care by the defendants. In their joint judgment, Gummow and Kirby JJ used some harsh words at [190] to criticise the 'control mechanisms' developed by the common law in over a hundred years of ruminations on mental harm since *Victorian Railways Commissioners v Coultas*:

> [T]he requirements of 'sudden shock' and 'direct perception' of a distressing phenomenon or its 'immediate aftermath' have operated in an arbitrary and capricious manner. Unprincipled distinctions and artificial mechanisms of this type bring the law into disrepute.

And on the problem of piecemeal adjustments to inadequate rules, their Honours maintained at [191]:

> [T]he emergence of a coherent body of case law is impeded, not assisted, by such a fixed system of categories. Rigid distinctions of the type required by the 'direct perception' rule inevitably generate exceptions and new categories, like the 'immediate aftermath' qualification, as the inadequacies of the recognised categories become apparent and 'hard cases' are accommodated. The old rule that 'nervous shock' sounded in damages only where it arose from a reasonable fear of immediate personal injury to oneself, and its subsequent relaxation to permit recovery where the plaintiff feared for the safety of another, illustrates the point. As the categories and exceptions proliferate, the reasoning and outcomes in the cases become increasingly detached from the rationale supporting the cause of action.

At common law, the fact that the plaintiff's illness *may* have been caused by a sudden shock will continue to be relevant, but there is no longer any requirement that the illness *must* have been caused by a sudden shock. Under the civil liability legislation, the fact that mental harm may have been caused by a sudden shock is now a relevant circumstance that a court must consider when deciding whether to impose a duty. Note that this circumstance is not of itself determinative of whether a duty will be owed.

LEGISLATION ALERT!

Note any statutory provisions in your jurisdiction on 'sudden shock'.

14.3.2.5 'Direct perception' and 'unaided senses'

Another limit was found in the rule that plaintiffs could recover damages only if their illness resulted from their own direct observation of the traumatic event or its immediate aftermath using their unaided or unmediated senses.

Case examples

- In *Hambrook v Stokes Brothers* (1925) a mother who had escorted her children part of the way to school was terrified for their safety when she saw a lorry rushing out of control around a bend into a narrow street where she knew that her children were walking. Bankes LJ explained at 152 that a cause of action would be established if the plaintiff's illness resulted from what 'she saw or realized by her own unaided senses, and not from what someone told her', and the shock was 'due to a reasonable fear of immediate personal injury either to herself or her children'.
- In *Jaensch v Coffey* (1984) a woman whose husband had been badly injured in a motor vehicle accident was called to the emergency ward in the hospital where she observed her husband's injuries and was subsequently told that he 'was pretty bad'. Later, she was summoned urgently back to the hospital after he had been taken to intensive care and 'had a change for

the worse'. Although he eventually recovered, she feared that he might die, and subsequently she developed a psychiatric illness. She successfully sued the driver who had negligently caused her husband's injuries. The fact that she had not witnessed the initial accident, but had only been present during its aftermath at the hospital, did not prevent liability from being imposed.

The old rigid rule had the effect of tying liability to the plaintiff's physical proximity in both time and space to the event or its immediate aftermath. This provided another limit on claims. The 'unaided senses' requirement was reduced to a relevant consideration at common law in *Tame v New South Wales* (2002), on the grounds that (like many of the other control mechanisms) it was arbitrary, capricious and unprincipled: see Gleeson CJ at [17], Gaudron J at [51], Gummow and Kirby JJ at [190] and [214]–[230] and the other references cited above under 'sudden shock'. This approach was confirmed in *Gifford v Strang Patrick Stevedoring Pty Ltd* (2003).

Case example

In *Gifford v Strang Patrick Stevedoring Pty Ltd* (2003) a worker was crushed to death by a reversing forklift truck. His three children, who did not live with him but had a very close relationship with him, did not see either the accident or the body but they all developed psychiatric problems as a result of hearing later that day about the horrific injuries that killed their father. They successfully sued their father's employer.

At common law, the question of whether a plaintiff has directly perceived the event or its aftermath may be raised as a relevant matter at the duty, breach or causation and remoteness stages of a case, depending on the circumstances. In many jurisdictions this consideration is now a relevant circumstance that must be considered under the civil liability legislation at the duty stage, where it is most often referred to as 'witnessing' the event 'at the scene' or being 'present at the scene'. In some jurisdictions, however, the plaintiff's presence at the scene has been resurrected as one of two strict limiting rules that also apply at the damages stage.

Legislative example

Wrongs Act 1958 (Vic)

- Under s 72(1)(b), 'whether the plaintiff witnessed, at the scene, a person being killed, injured or put in danger' is a circumstance that is relevant to the imposition of a duty of care.
- Under s 73, limits are applied to the award of damages:

  (1) This section applies to the liability of a person (the *defendant*) for pure mental harm to a person (the *plaintiff*) arising wholly or partly from mental or nervous shock in connection with another person (the *victim*) being killed, injured or put in danger by the act or omission of the defendant.

(2) The plaintiff is not entitled to recover damages for pure mental harm unless –

(a) the plaintiff witnessed, at the scene, the victim being killed, injured or put in danger; or

(b) the plaintiff is or was in a close relationship with the victim.

LEGISLATION ALERT!

Note any relevant statutory provisions in your jurisdiction, paying particular attention to the wording of the relevant circumstances, as well as any further limitations that may apply to the award of damages.

14.3.2.6 The distinction between 'primary' and 'secondary' victims

One of the difficulties in this area of negligence arises from the fact that psychiatric injury can be caused either directly or indirectly in two-party or multiparty scenarios, as the figures in this chapter show. There are several different fact patterns involving so-called 'primary' and 'secondary' victims.[7] The primary victim cases are the most straightforward. In these two-party cases a plaintiff may develop a psychiatric injury as a result of having been directly involved in a traumatic event caused by the defendant where they either:

- fear for their own safety; or
- see the defendant die or suffer traumatic injuries.

Case examples

P is directly terrified for their own safety

- In *Victorian Railways Commissioners v Coultas* (1888), noted above, the unsuccessful plaintiff was placed in 'imminent peril' of being killed by a train. She was not physically injured but she did suffer a 'severe nervous shock' and extreme terror which caused her to become ill.
- *Dulieu v White & Sons* (1901) concerned a pregnant woman who, while serving behind the bar of her husband's public house, was terrified for her own safety by an accident that occurred after a negligently driven pair-horse van crashed into the bar. She was not physically injured, but she did suffer a severe shock and subsequent serious illness. The judges in her case did not follow the precedent in *Victorian Railways Commissioners v Coultas* (1888), and she was allowed to recover damages.

7 McHugh J said in *Tame v New South Wales* (2002) at [93] that the distinction between primary and secondary victims originated in England and has not been recognised by the High Court in Australia, but the terminology is often used in the cases: see, for example, Gummow and Hayne JJ at [182].

P is directly involved in a traumatic accident caused by D

- In *Shipard v Motor Accident Commission* (1997), P, who was unhurt, was involved in a traffic accident in which a motor cyclist (D1) was decapitated when he negligently crashed into the large prime mover that P was driving. He successfully sued the Motor Accident Commission (D2) after developing a psychiatric injury. Doyle CJ said at 247 that many of the old control mechanisms that were introduced to limit recovery by secondary victims had no part to play in the case of primary victims.
- See also *Carrier v Bonham* (2002), where a bus driver (P) suffered PTSD after D tried to commit suicide by throwing himself into the path of the bus that P was driving. He successfully sued D.

The so-called 'secondary victim' cases arise when plaintiffs who have not been directly involved in a traumatic event nevertheless develop a psychiatric illness:

- indirectly, as a result of *personally witnessing its immediate aftermath*, perhaps because they were called to the scene as rescuers, coworkers or close relatives of the primary victims who were directly killed or injured in the event caused by the defendant; or
- even more indirectly, as a result of *being told later* about the horrific injuries or death of a primary victim who is a loved one or close family member.

The plaintiffs in these multiparty cases have not been faced personally or directly with a physical risk, but they have become ill because they either saw or heard about the trauma suffered by the 'primary victim'.

Case examples

P arrives after a traumatic event and witnesses its effects on the victim

- In *Chester v Council of the Municipality of Waverley* (1939), noted above, the unsuccessful plaintiff was the *mother* of the primary victim who arrived at the scene after her son's death.
- In *Mount Isa Mines Ltd v Pusey* (1970) the plaintiff went to the *rescue of two fellow employees* who had suffered extensive 'ghastly' and 'gruesome' burn injuries in a workplace explosion. He developed a serious mental illness because of what he had seen, and successfully sued his employer, whose negligence led to the accident suffered by the primary victims.
- In *Jaensch v Coffey* (1984), noted above, the successful plaintiff was a *wife* who was called to the hospital and who witnessed the injuries to the primary victim, her husband, that were caused by the defendant.

P is told about the horrific death of a close family member

- In *Tame v New South Wales* (2002), noted above, the successful plaintiffs in the *Annetts* case were the *parents* of the primary victim, the young jackaroo whose death was caused by his employers, the defendants.

- In *Gifford v Strang Patrick Stevedoring Pty Ltd* (2003), noted above, the successful plaintiffs were the three *children* of the primary victim, their father, whose death was caused by the negligence of his employer.

Fears of unlimited liability that might extend to include 'mere' bystanders who have stopped by to look at an accident out of curiosity – or others who may have seen coverage unfold on television – led the judges to impose limits on liability. The first, which required that the plaintiff actually witness the event with their own 'unaided senses', has already been discussed. A second test required that there must be a very close relationship between the 'primary victim' and the 'secondary victim' before a duty would be recognised. Some of the recognised relationships include close family or personal relationships, close working relationships between fellow employees, and the temporary relationship between a victim and a rescuer. However, as Brennan J noted in *Jaensch v Coffey* (1984) at 571, the categories 'are not closed' and in *Gifford v Strang Patrick Stevedoring Pty Ltd* (2003) McHugh J said at [48]:

> It is the closeness and affection of the relationship – rather than the legal status of the relationship – which is relevant in determining whether a duty is owed to the person suffering psychiatric harm. The relationship between two friends who have lived together for many years may be closer and more loving than that of two siblings. There is no policy justification for preventing a claim for nervous shock by a person who is not a family member but who has a close and loving relationship with the person harmed or put in peril.

At common law, therefore, the nature of the relationship must be examined, because as McHugh J said in *Gifford v Strang Patrick Stevedoring Pty Ltd* at [48] 'the reasonable foresight of the defendant extends to all those with whom the victim has or had a close and loving relationship'. Under the civil liability legislation, the relationship between the victim and the plaintiff and between the plaintiff and the defendant can be relevant not only at the duty stage, but also, in some jurisdictions, at the damages stage as well. Some statutes have reintroduced strict limits on the categories of plaintiffs who may recover damages that replicate the old common law limits in these multiparty cases.

Legislative example

Civil Liability Act 1936 (SA) s 33

(1) A person (the *defendant*) does not owe a duty to another person (the *plaintiff*) to take care not to cause the plaintiff mental harm unless a reasonable person in the defendant's position would have foreseen that a person of normal fortitude in the plaintiff's position might, in the circumstances of the case, suffer a psychiatric illness.

(2) For the purposes of this section –

(a) in a case of pure mental harm, the circumstances of the case to which the court is to have regard include the following:

(i) whether or not the mental harm was suffered as the result of a sudden shock;

(ii) whether the plaintiff witnessed, at the scene, a person being killed, injured or put in peril;

(iii) the nature of the relationship between the plaintiff and any person killed, injured or put in peril;

(iv) whether or not there was a pre-existing relationship between the plaintiff and the defendant;

(b) in a case of consequential mental harm, the circumstances of the case include the nature of the bodily injury out of which the mental harm arose.

Under s 53(1) of the *Civil Liability Act 1936* (SA), only those in two categories may be awarded damages:

> **(1)** Damages may only be awarded for mental harm if the injured person –
>
> **(a)** was physically injured in the accident or was present at the scene of the accident when the accident occurred; or
>
> **(b)** is a parent, spouse, domestic partner or child of a person killed, injured or endangered in the accident.

LEGISLATION ALERT!

There is a non-insignificant degree of variation across different jurisdictions in this matter, so make sure you are familiar with the exact wording of the legislation that applies to the facts presented to you.

The so-called 'secondary victim' cases (discussed in section 14.3.2.6 above) have raised issues and presented factual scenarios that at first glance appear to be very similar to those raised by the seminal case of *Donoghue v Stevenson* (1932): compare Figure 10.1 in Chapter 10 with Figure 14.1. The judges have been faced with a fear of liability without limits (eg Lord Buckmaster, one of the dissenting judges in *Donoghue v Stevenson* (1932) commented, 'If one step, why not fifty?') and a challenge of finding a way to justify imposing a duty in cases where 'something more' than the mere foreseeability of harm is required. Of course, the fact that harm has been caused indirectly does not rule out liability in negligence, which is a tort designed to deal with indirectly caused harms. But as we have seen, judges in the early cases like *Chester v Council of the Municipality of Waverley* (1939) were reluctant to allow liability. This was partly because they saw it as a derivative form of liability for a harm that seemed to be too remote from the defendant's initial negligence (if indeed they recognised it as harm at all). They refused to allow a secondary duty (owed to P2 in Figure 14.2) to be parasitic on the primary duty (owed to P1). This attitude is strikingly similar to the views of the dissenting judges in *Donoghue v Stevenson* (1932), who refused the plaintiff's claim because they saw it as an impermissible attempt to derive a secondary *tort-based* duty owed to a consumer (P2) from the primary *contract-based* duty owed by the manufacturer to a purchaser (P1). But, just as the majority judges in *Donoghue v Stevenson* (1932) found a way around the barrier posed by the doctrine of privity, so too have the judges in the High Court been able to find a way to drop the barriers to liability in cases of mental harm. They did this by reconceiving the basis for imposing a duty of care.

This process began in *Mount Isa Mines Ltd v Pusey* (1970), when Windeyer J insisted at 408 that this type of liability should not be seen as a 'by-product' of a primary liability to another person. Instead, the 'shock-producing event' should be considered as 'a tort to the plaintiff'. As Brennan J explained in *Jaensch v Coffey* (1984) at 560:

> The respective duties of care owed to the plaintiff and to the other person and the causes of action arising from their breach are independent one of the other. It is now settled law that the duty owed to one is not to be regarded as secondary to or derived from the duty owed to the other. [References omitted.]

Once the judges recognised that the question facing them in these cases of pure mental harm was whether or not the defendant owed an independent *legal* duty of care directly to the plaintiff, the special *factual* distinction between primary and secondary victims lost much of its former significance. By reconceiving the problem in this way, the judges could drop the artificial control devices and focus instead on developing 'the ordinary principles of negligence' which were enough on their own to justify the duty and 'circumscribe recovery', as Gummow and Kirby JJ pointed out in *Tame v New South Wales* (2002) at [195]. Once this breakthrough occurred, the closeness of the relationship between the primary victim and the plaintiffs simply became a fact to consider when applying the ordinary neighbour principle, as McHugh J explained in *Gifford v Strang Patrick Stevedoring Pty Ltd* (2003) at [51]:

> A person is a neighbour in Lord Atkin's sense if he or she is one of those persons who 'are so closely and directly affected by my act that I ought reasonably to have them in contemplation as being so affected'. If the defendant ought reasonably foresee that its conduct may affect persons who have a relationship with the primary victim, a duty will arise in respect of those persons. The test is, would a reasonable person in the defendant's position, who knew or ought to know of that particular relationship, consider that the third party was so closely and directly affected by the conduct that it was reasonable to have that person in contemplation as being affected by that conduct? [References omitted.]

Figure 14.1 Pure mental harm scenarios: Two-party cases

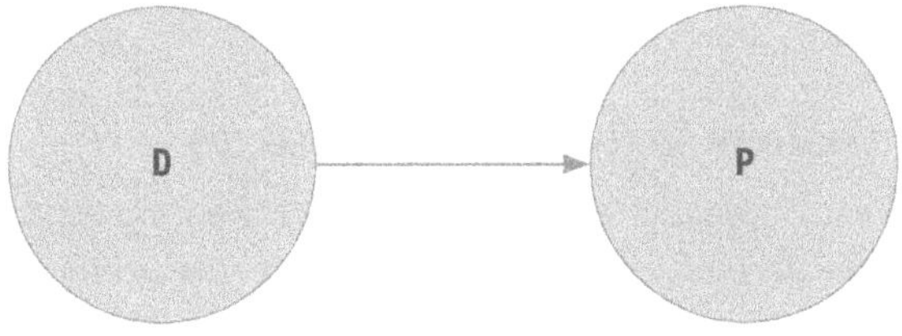

The solid line in Figure 14.1 shows the track of harm. Examples of two-party or 'primary victim' cases include *Dulieu v White & Sons* (1901), *Shipard v Motor Accident Commission* (1997) and *Carrier v Bonham* (2002).

Figure 14.2 Pure mental harm scenario: Multiparty cases

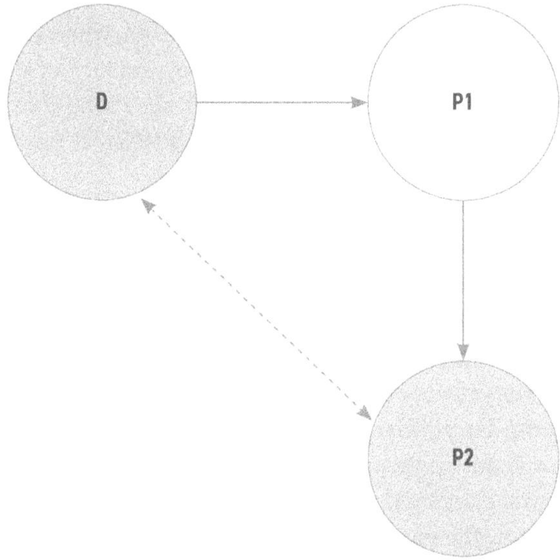

The solid lines in Figure 14.2 show the tracks of harm. The dotted line shows the new legal relationships. An example of a multiparty or 'secondary victim' case is *Mount Isa Mines Ltd v Pusey* (1970), which involved a coworker.

The emergence of this new principled approach to the problem of pure psychiatric injury was aided by the fact that very similar factual multiparty scenarios and theoretical issues had been thrown up by cases dealing with pure economic loss, as you will see in section 14.5 below. The significance of these two streams of negligence, which followed a similar path of development in the years leading up to the landmark case of *Sullivan v Moody* (2001), can be seen in the extensive cross-references to the pure economic loss cases found in the 'nervous shock' cases of *Sullivan v Moody* (2001) and *Tame v New South Wales* (2002). So, by 2003, when *Gifford v Strang Patrick Stevedoring Pty Ltd* (2003) confirmed the dismantling of the last of the artificial barriers, the relevant principles that were applied in cases of pure psychiatric injury included not only the foundational 'neighbour principle' from *Donoghue v Stevenson* (1932) but also the key features of vulnerability, certainty, coherence, autonomy and personal responsibility that now form the basis of a unified approach to the duty question in all cases of negligence.

14.3.3 Relevant salient features and key cases

The judges in *Sullivan v Moody* (2001) introduced a new methodology of duty that highlighted the significance of the foundational neighbour principle from *Donoghue v Stevenson* (1932) and supplemented it with salient features. As many judges have emphasised, it is critically important when answering the duty question in multiparty psychiatric injury cases to consider whether the plaintiffs are in a class of persons who are 'so closely and directly affected' by a defendant's conduct that they ought reasonably to have been in the defendant's contemplation.

Case examples

- *Sullivan v Moody* (2001) at [46]
- *Tame v New South Wales* (2002), Gleeson CJ at [9], Gaudron J at [46]–[54], McHugh J at [106]–[107]
- *Gifford v Strang Patrick Stevedoring Pty Ltd* (2003), McHugh J at [46]–[51], Gummow and Kirby JJ at [86], Callinan J at [118]

The High Court also explained in *Sullivan v Moody* (2001) at [42] why the mere foreseeability of harm, including pure psychiatric harm, is not enough on its own to establish a duty and why other principles must be considered:

> First, the law would subject citizens to an intolerable burden of potential liability, and constrain their freedom of action in a gross manner. Secondly, the tort of negligence would subvert many other principles of law, and statutory provisions, which strike a balance of rights and obligations, duties and freedoms.

The 'other principles of law' and any relevant 'statutory provisions' must therefore be weighed together at the duty stage of a pure psychiatric injury case. The key features in this area include the principles of coherence, certainty, vulnerability and autonomy.

14.3.3.1 Coherence

The feature of coherence is crucial in cases of pure mental harm as the landmark case of *Sullivan v Moody* (2001) shows at [30], [42], [50], [53]–[55] and [60]. The idea of coherence supports denying a duty if:

- it would not be compatible or reconcilable with other duties owed by the defendant;
- it is inconsistent with, or has a tendency to discourage, the due performance of other duties or responsibilities; or
- the asserted duty of care is inconsistent with the terms, scope and purpose of any relevant statute.

The principle of coherence can justify refusing to impose a duty.

Case examples

- In *Sullivan v Moody* (2001), the Ps were both fathers of children who had been examined for evidence of sexual abuse by the Ds who were medical practitioners and social workers employed by the Department of Community Welfare in South Australia. As a result of the Ds' examinations of the children, the Ps were accused of sexually abusing their children and both subsequently developed psychiatric illnesses. They sued the Ds (and the State of South Australia), arguing that their negligence in the conduct of the examinations of their children constituted a breach of a duty owed to them as the fathers of those children. The High Court unanimously rejected the claim that the Ds owed a duty to the fathers, despite the undisputable fact that it was reasonably foreseeable that they could suffer psychiatric harm if the Ds did not take care in investigating and reporting upon the allegations: see [25] and [42]. The High Court said at [53] and [54]:

> There are cases, and this is one, where to find a duty of care would so cut across other legal principles as to impair their proper application and thus lead to the conclusion that there is no duty of care of the kind asserted.
>
> More fundamentally, however, these cases present a question about *coherence of the law.* Considering whether the persons who reported their suspicions about each appellant owed that appellant a duty of care must begin from the recognition that those who made the report had other responsibilities. A duty of the kind alleged should not be found if that duty *would not be compatible with other duties which the respondents owed.* [Emphasis added.]

The High Court held that the proposed duty owed to the fathers must be denied because:

- it would be incompatible with the balance of rights and duties struck by the tort of defamation, which 'resolves the competing interests of the parties' on 'an altogether different basis' (at [54]);
- it would conflict with the defendants' obligations to conduct the investigation and exercise their powers in the public interest (at [60]);
- it could not be reconciled with the primary duties owed by the defendants to the children to consider their welfare as paramount because 'the interests of the children' and the interests of 'those suspected of causing their harm, are diverse, and irreconcilable' (at [55] and [60]–[62]);
- it would be inconsistent with 'the proper and effective discharge of the responsibilities' imposed on them by the statutory scheme (at [62]), and would 'have a tendency to discourage' the due performance by the defendants of their 'statutory duties' (at [30]).

- The plaintiff in *Tame v New South Wales* (2002) was a woman who had been the innocent victim in a traffic accident caused by the drunken driving of another member of the public. The defendant, a police officer who was investigating the accident, mistakenly wrote the blood alcohol reading of the drunken driver next to the name of the plaintiff. The error was subsequently corrected, but some time later the plaintiff found out. She became obsessed with the mistake and eventually developed a psychiatric disorder. The High Court unanimously held that the police officer did not owe her a duty in the circumstances, in part because of the application of the coherence principle. Gleeson CJ pointed out at [27] that in this case 'there is the same intersection with the law of defamation, and the same need to preserve legal coherence' and noted at [26]:

> The primary duty of a police officer filling out such a report is to make available to his or her superiors, honestly and frankly, the results of the observations, inquiries and tests that were made. It would be inconsistent with such a duty to require the police officer to take care to protect from emotional disturbance and possible psychiatric illness a person whose conduct was the subject of investigation and report.

See also Gaudron J at [56]–[57], who suggested that it 'would be incongruous and, perhaps, give rise to incompatible duties', and McHugh J, who discussed the coherence principle at [122]–[125] and concluded at [125] that it would be 'preposterous to suggest that an officer has a duty of care' when taking down statements or investigating criminal activity because it would 'defeat the whole purpose of intelligence recording if the officer were required to check the accuracy of the material recorded'.

Coherence can also weigh in favour of imposing a duty of care, particularly if the duty aligns with the defendant's other business interests and is consistent with the duties owed by the defendant to any other parties.

Case example

In *Gifford v Strang Patrick Stevedoring Pty Ltd* (2003), noted above, Gummow and Kirby JJ pointed out at [104] that the duty of care owed by the defendant to the children of their employee to avoid causing them pure psychiatric injury was wholly compatible with the other 'tortious and express or implied contractual duties' that they owed to the father as an employee to ensure his safety; and:

> [m]oreover, there is no inconsistency between the existence of a duty of care to the appellants and the legitimate pursuit by the respondent of its business interests ... The law requires an employer in the position of the respondent so to order its affairs as to avoid causing injury or death to its employees.

14.3.3.2 Certainty and indeterminate liability

The feature of certainty, which requires that liability must not be too uncertain in nature or give rise to indeterminate liability, is also relevant to cases of pure mental harm. In some cases, the potential indeterminacy of liability points against imposing a duty.

Case examples

- In *Sullivan v Moody* (2001), the High Court noted at [61]:

  > There is also a question as to the extent, and potential indeterminacy, of liability. In the case of a medical practitioner, the range of people who might foreseeably (in the sense earlier mentioned) suffer some kind of harm, as a consequence of careless diagnosis or treatment of a patient, is extensive.

  In that case the plaintiffs sought to avoid the problem by arguing that, as parents of the children, they were members of a limited and ascertainable class of potential plaintiffs, but the High Court said at [63] that this was 'unconvincing':

  > But, if it exists, why should it be so limited? If the suspected child abuser were a relative other than a parent, or a schoolteacher, or a neighbour, or a total stranger, why

> should that person be in a position different from that of a parent? The logical consequence of the appellants' argument must be that a duty of care is owed to anyone who is, or who might become, a suspect.

- In *Politarhis v Westpac Banking Corporation* (2009), the defendant bank (D) mistakenly made funds available to P, who had a gambling problem. D was unaware of the problem and subsequently P, who had used the extra funds to fuel his gambling habit, sued D. He argued that D's negligence had caused him to develop a mental disorder (and to suffer economic loss). Doyle CJ explained that the action failed on many grounds, including the issue of indeterminacy, and noted at [113]:

> To impose a duty of care in the present case and circumstances would impose a duty of care on lenders to take reasonable care to protect borrowers from causing psychological injury to themselves by their own choice as to the use of the money borrowed. If such a duty of care were to be imposed, it seems to me that a like duty should be imposed in respect of physical harm, such as harm attributable to spending the money on alcohol or drugs, or through over-eating.

On the other hand, as Gummow and Kirby JJ explained in *Tame v New South Wales* (2002) at [239], if 'the recognition of a duty of care does not raise the prospect of an intolerably large or indeterminate class of potential plaintiffs', that will weigh in favour of imposing a duty.

Case examples

- In *Tame v New South Wales* (2002), the plaintiffs in the *Annetts* case were the concerned parents of the young boy who wanted to leave his home in New South Wales to work as a jackaroo in the far north of Western Australia. Before they allowed him to take up the position, the parents had sought and obtained from Australian Stations assurances that James would be appropriately supervised. The employers undertook specifically to minimise the risk of harm to the boy and promised that he would be well cared for and supervised. The parents in this case, unlike the parents in *Sullivan v Moody* (2001), were clearly in a defined, ascertainable class of plaintiffs, and so the certainty principle weighed in favour of imposing the duty.
- It is interesting to compare and contrast this decision, which now forms the heart of the Australian approach to mental harm in negligence claims, with the leading case on secondary victims in the United Kingdom: *Alcock v Chief Constable of South Yorkshire Police* (1992). This case stemmed from the tragedy of the Hillsborough Football Stadium. During an FA Cup game, 96 spectators were killed and another 450 injured in the course of a human crush, which had been caused by the negligence of the local police who allowed too many spectators into the stadium. The game was being broadcast live on television and radio, with friends and relatives of the victims watching or hearing about the dramatic events as they unfolded. A number of such friends and relatives sued the South Yorkshire Police in negligence for the psychiatric injuries they suffered as a result of watching or hearing about the incident live. The first concern of the House of Lords was to avoid opening the floodgates of litigation, which prompted their

Lordships to adopt a series of strict control mechanisms, including in particular a requirement of physical proximity of the secondary victims to the 'shocking events', and the need to perceive such events with their own unaided senses.

This stark contrast between the leading Australian decision in *Tame v New South Wales* (2002) and its United Kingdom equivalent in *Alcock v Chief Constable of South Yorkshire Police* (1992) is a vivid example of the piecemeal way in which the common law tends to develop. The very different nature of the facts that inspired these two decisions (a single-family tragedy in Australia, and a mass tort in the United Kingdom) clearly had an impact on the very different rationales adopted by the High Court and the House of Lords. The restrictive approach of the United Kingdom has been subsequently reaffirmed in *White v Chief Constable of the South Yorkshire Police* (1999).

14.3.3.3 Vulnerability

The feature of vulnerability, which is of particular relevance in cases also involving the features of control, knowledge, reliance and assumption of responsibility (as discussed in Chapter 11), supports imposing a duty in cases where the defendant has such a great degree of control over a situation that the plaintiffs are placed into a position of special vulnerability or where the plaintiffs have specifically and reasonably relied on the defendant and cannot protect themselves from incurring the pure psychiatric injury in any other way: *Tame v New South Wales* (2002); *Gifford v Strang Patrick Stevedoring Pty Ltd* (2003).

Case examples

- In *Tame v New South Wales* (2002), noted above, the vulnerability principle weighed strongly in favour of imposing the duty in the second case because all the hallmarks of vulnerability in the special legal sense were present. As Gummow and Kirby JJ noted at [238]–[240]:
  - the parents (the Annetts) were not in a position to minimise the risk of harm to their son or to protect themselves from the risk of pure psychiatric injury;
  - the defendants controlled the conditions under which their son worked; and
  - the parents had reasonably relied upon the assurances from the defendants who undertook the responsibility of looking after their son.

  See also Gleeson CJ at [37] and Gaudron J at [54].
- In *Gifford v Strang Patrick Stevedoring Pty Ltd* (2003), noted above, the vulnerability principle also weighed in favour of imposing the duty. Gummow and Kirby JJ pointed out at [90] that this case 'shares important characteristics with the relationship at issue in Annetts' because the children:

  > had no way of protecting themselves against the risk of psychiatric harm which eventuated. The respondent controlled the conditions under which Mr Gifford worked and held a significant, perhaps exclusive, degree of control over the risk of harm to him and the risk of consequent psychiatric harm to the appellants. The respondent's control over the risk of harm was, in a legal and practical sense, direct rather than remote. [References omitted.]

It is very important to bear in mind that 'vulnerability' in this context can have two very different connotations. It can describe either the *relationship* between the plaintiff and the defendant or it can describe the *personality* of the plaintiff – and only the first type of 'relational vulnerability' comes under the umbrella of the salient feature of vulnerability. Vulnerability in the special legal sense described in *Tame v New South Wales* (2002) and *Gifford v Strang Patrick Stevedoring Pty Ltd* (2003) is a feature of the relationship that exists between the defendant and the plaintiff that justifies imposing a duty of care. On the other hand, the fact that the plaintiff may have a 'vulnerable personality' and therefore be particularly susceptible to suffering from some form of psychiatric illness raises the issue of whether a plaintiff is a person of 'normal fortitude' (which we discussed in section 14.3.2 above). Under the civil liability legislation, the issue of 'normal fortitude' is relevant to the question of duty, but only to the extent that it creates an objective threshold (without requiring the specific plaintiff to be of normal fortitude). Under the common law it may be relevant both to the elements of duty and breach.[8] Gleeson CJ suggested at [16] in *Tame v New South Wales* (2002) that this type of vulnerability is relevant to the issue of duty because the 'vulnerability or susceptibility of a particular plaintiff' makes it 'unreasonable to require a person to have in contemplation' that kind of injury. Gummow and Kirby JJ suggested in the same case at [200]–[201] that it would also be a relevant consideration in determining the issue of breach:

> Where the plaintiff's response to the defendant's conduct is so extreme or idiosyncratic as to render the risk of that response far-fetched or fanciful, the law does not require the defendant to guard against it.

These two different usages of the term 'vulnerability' must be kept separate, not only because each refers to a different aspect of the case, but also because each points in a different direction.

Case examples

- In *Tame v New South Wales* (2002), the particular factual or personal vulnerability of the plaintiff in the first case and her 'extreme and idiosyncratic' reaction to hearing that a mistake had been made on the accident report pointed away from imposing liability, whereas in the second case decided in that judgment, as in *Gifford v Strang Patrick Stevedoring Pty Ltd* (2003), the relationship of vulnerability in the special legal sense that existed between the plaintiffs and the defendants pointed towards imposing liability.
- In *Koehler v Cerebos (Australia) Ltd* (2005), noted below, McHugh, Gummow, Hayne and Heydon JJ noted at [35] that the 'relevant duty of care is engaged if psychiatric injury to the particular employee is reasonably foreseeable' and maintained at [36] that any attempt to:

  > qualify the operation of the [employment] contract as a result of information the employer later acquires about the vulnerability of the employee to psychiatric harm would be ... contradictory of basic principle.

8 Joachim Dietrich argues in 'Nervous Shock: *Tame v New South Wales* and *Annetts v Australian Stations Pty Ltd*' (2003) that the two cases left the law in a state of 'continuing uncertainty'.

14.3.3.4 Autonomy

The salient feature of autonomy has assumed great importance in cases of pure mental harm where it has been emphasised that a duty should not be imposed if doing so would impose an intolerable burden on the autonomy of individuals: *Sullivan v Moody* (2001); *Tame v New South Wales* (2002). In *Sullivan v Moody* (2001) the High Court insisted at [42] that the consequence of imposing a duty of care merely on the grounds that pure mental harm might be reasonably foreseeable would 'subject citizens to an intolerable burden of potential liability, and constrain their freedom of action in a gross manner'. This approach has been reaffirmed many times in subsequent cases. In *Tame v New South Wales* (2002), many judges pointed to the importance of the autonomy principle when imposing a duty of care. Gleeson CJ said at [5]–[6] that it was important to consider the effect of liability on 'the freedom and security with which people may conduct their ordinary affairs' and Gummow and Kirby JJ pointed out at [185] that the essential question of reasonableness in a negligence case 'reconciles the plaintiff's interest in protection from harm with the defendant's interest in freedom of action'. McHugh J linked the issue of autonomy with the 'vulnerable personality' issue and emphatically endorsed the role of autonomy in these cases, explaining at [110] that to repudiate the normal fortitude test 'ignores the right of citizens in a free society not to have their freedom of action and communication unreasonably burdened':

> To insist that the duty of reasonable care in pure psychiatric illness cases be anchored by reference to the most vulnerable person in the community – by reference to the most fragile psyche in the community – would place an undue burden on social action and communication. To require each actor in Australian society to examine whether his or her actions or statements might damage the most psychiatrically vulnerable person within the zone of action or communication would seriously interfere with the individual's freedom of action and communication. To go further and require the actor to take steps to avoid potential damage to the peculiarly vulnerable would impose an intolerable burden on the autonomy of individuals.

This theme was taken up in *Gifford v Strang Patrick Stevedoring Pty Ltd* (2003) by Gleeson CJ, who emphasised once more that requiring people to anticipate and guard against all kinds of foreseeable psychiatric injury to others would impose an unreasonable burden on human activity (at [9]).

14.3.3.5 Reasonableness

The majority in *Tame v New South Wales* (2002) rejected the traditional arbitrary, unprincipled and indefensible 'control mechanisms' to establishing a duty of care in cases of mental harm as definitive tests of liability. However, it is important to bear in mind that the concerns which gave rise to those barriers remain relevant to the issue of reasonableness, which as judges have repeatedly emphasised, provides an overarching control that must be considered in each of the elements of duty, breach and causation (including remoteness).

Case example

In *New South Wales v Fahy* (2007), the plaintiff was a female police officer who developed a psychiatric illness after being called in to assist a severely wounded victim of an armed hold-up. Although she had been working under the 'buddy system' with a fellow police officer, she was left without his support to deal with the victim, who was bleeding profusely and believed he was dying. Other officers present at the scene also walked away and failed to assist her. She argued that the police force had failed to observe or respond adequately to the trauma she suffered. By a majority of 4:3 the High Court held that the New South Wales police force had not failed to do what a reasonable police force would have done in the light of the foreseeable risk. The judgments in this case focus on the issue of the reasonable foreseeability of pure psychiatric injury in the circumstances and the reasonableness of the police force's response. They illustrate the difficulty of determining the question of reasonableness, particularly in cases like this one, where the duties required of an employee are inherently risky and stressful.

While the 'control mechanisms' have faded as strict common law rules and are now seen as raising questions that are to be resolved by applying the criterion of reasonableness in all the circumstances, you need to bear in mind that some of these rules have returned in the civil liability legislation.

14.3.4 Legislative intervention

At the same time that the High Court was moving to dismantle the older approach to the law on pure mental harm and replace it with a more defensible set of controls based on principle, many parliaments throughout Australia enacted statutes that altered the common law. As noted above, however, these statutes are not uniform. The general thrust of the legislation was to:

- reintroduce the concept of 'a person of normal fortitude' into the duty question as a precondition or limit;
- require the courts to consider the circumstances of the case when determining the duty question, including such matters as:
  - 'sudden shock';
  - witnessing at the scene a person being killed, injured or put in peril;
  - the relationship between the plaintiff and any person killed, injured or put in peril; and
  - any pre-existing relationship between the plaintiff and the defendant;
- treat 'consequential' mental harm and 'pure' mental harm in the same way; and
- reintroduce some limits on the categories of plaintiffs who could recover damages.

These measures were introduced because of the belief that the modern common law of negligence had become too plaintiff-friendly and needed to be reined in. So, when parliaments were searching for ways to limit the extent of liability in negligence, some of the older limits in the area of pure mental harm offered an obvious option and were easily revived.

Legislative example

Civil Liability Act 2002 (NSW) s 30 and s 32

30 Limitation on recovery for pure mental harm arising from shock

(1) This section applies to the liability of a person (*the defendant*) for pure mental harm to a person (*the plaintiff*) arising wholly or partly from mental or nervous shock in connection with another person (*the victim*) being killed, injured or put in peril by the act or omission of the defendant.

(2) The plaintiff is not entitled to recover damages for pure mental harm unless:

(a) the plaintiff witnessed, at the scene, the victim being killed, injured or put in peril, or

(b) the plaintiff is a close member of the family of the victim.

[Subsections (3)–(5) are omitted.]

32 Mental harm – duty of care

(1) A person (*the defendant*) does not owe a duty of care to another person (*the plaintiff*) to take care not to cause the plaintiff mental harm unless the defendant ought to have foreseen that a person of normal fortitude might, in the circumstances of the case, suffer a recognised psychiatric illness if reasonable care were not taken.

(2) For the purposes of the application of this section in respect of pure mental harm, the circumstances of the case include the following:

(a) whether or not the mental harm was suffered as the result of a sudden shock,

(b) whether the plaintiff witnessed, at the scene, a person being killed, injured or put in peril,

(c) the nature of the relationship between the plaintiff and any person killed, injured or put in peril,

(d) whether or not there was a pre-existing relationship between the plaintiff and the defendant.

(3) For the purposes of the application of this section in respect of consequential mental harm, the circumstances of the case include the personal injury suffered by the plaintiff.

(4) This section does not require the court to disregard what the defendant knew or ought to have known about the fortitude of the plaintiff.

LEGISLATION ALERT!

Most states and territories have introduced provisions relating to mental harm in their civil liability legislation.

Note the relevant provisions in your jurisdiction.

Where a statutory provision governs establishing a duty of care for mental harm is where your analysis should start. The reasoning emerging from the case law discussed so far will remain relevant as a useful interpretive tool for the relevant provisions.

Case example

The plaintiffs in *Wicks v State Rail Authority of New South Wales* (2010) were members of the New South Wales police force who were called to a rescue effort after a passenger train carrying almost 50 people came off the tracks at high speed. They were the first to arrive and were so confronted by the scene of death and injury in the wreckage of the train and the danger that faced them and the survivors of the crash that they subsequently developed psychological and psychiatric conditions. They sued the New South Wales State Rail Authority (the defendant). The defendant argued that the plaintiffs were precluded by s 30(2) from recovering damages because they had not 'witnessed at the scene, the victim being killed, injured or put in peril'. The High Court analysed the statute and decided that the plaintiffs had both witnessed others 'being injured' at [48] and 'being put in peril' at [49]. The Court noted at [44] that 'there are cases where death, or injury, or being put in peril takes place over an extended period', and emphasised at [50] the fact that:

> [a] person is put in peril when put at risk; the person remains in peril (is 'being put in peril') until the person ceases to be at risk.

The High Court noted the effect of the statutory provision on duty in s 32 of the New South Wales legislation in *Wicks v State Rail Authority of New South Wales* (2010) at [26]:

> Consistent with what was decided in *Tame* [*Tame v New South Wales* (2002)], s 32 assumes that foreseeability is the central determinant of duty of care. Consistent with *Tame*, 'shocking event', and the existence and nature of any connection between plaintiff and victim and between plaintiff and defendant, are considerations relevant to foreseeability, but none is to be treated as a condition necessary to finding a duty of care. But contrary to what was decided in *Tame*, s 32 provides that a duty of care is not to be found unless the defendant ought to have foreseen that a person of normal fortitude might, in the circumstances of the case, suffer a recognised psychiatric illness. [Reference omitted.]

The High Court emphasised at [22] that neither s 32 nor any other provision in the New South Wales statute 'identifies positively when a duty of care to another person to take care not to cause mental harm to that other should be found to exist'. Rather, the duty provision imposes a control on 'what otherwise would be a duty of care arising at common law'. The High Court also explained at [42] that s 30 of the New South Wales statute has the effect of creating 'a particular subset of cases' that are to be treated differently because the section places limits on the categories of victims who can recover damages in certain kinds of pure psychiatric injury cases. This means that in many of the jurisdictions covered by the civil liability legislation, there will be plaintiffs who, despite the fact that they were owed a duty of care by the defendant and have suffered a psychiatric injury as a result of the defendant's breach, will nevertheless be precluded from recovering any damages. To recover, the plaintiffs in these jurisdictions must not only satisfy the relevant rules (whether common law or statute), but they must also come within the extra statutory limits that control the categories of plaintiffs who may recover damages, as illustrated in Figure 14.3. Note that the wording and scope of these limiting provisions varies significantly between jurisdictions.

Figure 14.3 Pure psychiatric injury under the statutes

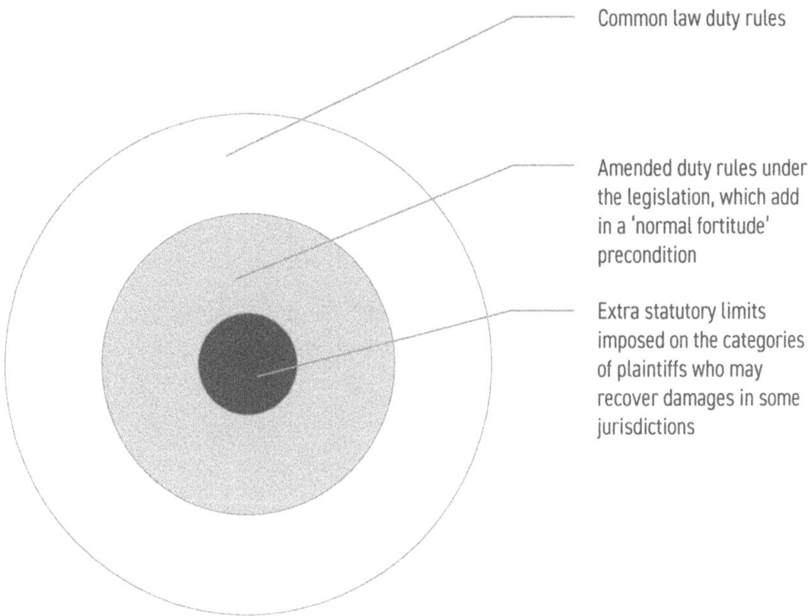

Case example

The interpretation of the wording 'witnessed at the scene' provided by the High Court in the case of *Wicks v State Rail Authority of New South Wales* (2010), noted above, is inapplicable in South Australia, as discussed by the High Court in *King v Philcox* (2015). In that case, a car negligently driven by the defendant collided with another car at an intersection. The passenger in the defendant's car died while trapped in the car. The plaintiff drove through the intersection while the cars were still at the scene of the accident. He discovered later that the deceased passenger in the defendant's car was his brother, and he suffered a major depressive disorder and PTSD because he did not know that his brother was in the car at the time he drove past the accident, and did not stop to offer assistance. The High Court held that the defendant owed the plaintiff a duty of care not to cause him mental harm, because such a duty can extend to a sibling of a victim in the same way that it can extend to a parent, spouse, child or rescuer of a victim. The relative closeness of such a relationship (eg in comparison to parent–child) would go to causation, rather than to existence of a duty of care. However, s 53(1) of the South Australian *Civil Liability Act 1936* defeated the claim, because it required that a plaintiff be 'present at the scene' of the accident when it occurs in order to claim damages.

14.3.5 A complex issue: Mental harm at work

A particularly intricate issue with liability for mental harm is how this type of matter plays out in the employment context. The issue is complex for two reasons.

The first reason is that, in most states and territories, any type of injury covered by statutory workers compensation schemes excludes the application of civil liability legislation. In these jurisdictions, any negligence claim brought against an employer for mental harm therefore requires a plaintiff to follow common law rules to establish a duty of care. Note that often these exclusions are not limited to mental harm but extend to any personal injury. The issue is, however, of relevance to mental harm, because most civil liability acts create specific rules to establish a duty of care, whereas for other types of personal injuries the general common law rules still apply.

LEGISLATION ALERT!

Check your materials to determine whether the application of the civil liability legislation of your jurisdiction is excluded in cases involving workers compensation or other statutory compensation schemes.

Legislative example

***Civil Liability Act 2003* (Qld)**

5 Civil liability excluded from Act

(1) This Act does not apply in relation to deciding liability or awards of damages for personal injury if the harm resulting from the breach of duty is or includes –

(a) an injury for which compensation is payable under the *WorkCover Queensland Act 1996*, other than an injury to which section 36(1)(c) or 37 of that Act applies; or

Example for paragraph (a) –
A worker employed under a contract of service with a labour hire company is injured at the premises of a host employer while driving a defective machine. The worker pursues claims for damages for civil liability against the labour hire company, the host employer and the manufacturer of the machine. The worker suffers a number of injuries but only 1 of them is accepted as an injury under the *WorkCover Queensland Act 1996*, section 34. This Act does not apply to any of the claims for damages.

(b) an injury for which compensation is payable under the *Workers' Compensation and Rehabilitation Act 2003*, other than an injury to which section 34(1)(c) or 35 of that Act applies; or

(c) an injury that is a dust-related condition; or

(d) an injury resulting from smoking or other use of tobacco products or exposure to tobacco smoke.

The second reason mental harm in the employment context is traditionally a complicated issue in Australia is that, for about two decades, the High Court has adopted a particularly restrictive approach following its decision in the case of *Koehler v Cerebos (Australia) Ltd* (2005).

Case example

The plaintiff in *Koehler v Cerebos (Australia) Ltd* (2005) was employed as a sales representative on a part-time contract. She repeatedly complained to her supervisor that she did not have enough time to perform her duties. After five months she developed a psychiatric illness and subsequently sued her employer (the defendant). The defendant argued, as recorded in the High Court judgment at 49, that coherence of the law 'dictates that nothing in the content of the common law duty of care can contradict what is called for in the contract of employment'. The claim was denied on the grounds that 'the risk of psychiatric injury to the appellant was not reasonably foreseeable' at [20], but McHugh, Gummow, Hayne and Heydon JJ discussed the content of the duty of care at [21]–[36] and stated at [29]:

> An employer may not be liable for psychiatric injury to an employee brought about by the employee's performance of the duties originally stipulated in the contract of employment.

The joint judgment then explained at [30]–[31] that to read into a contractual agreement a 'qualification to the effect that performance of the obligations is excused if performance would be beyond what is required by some external standard' would 'invite attention to fundamental questions of legal coherence'.

As such, finding that a duty of care is owed by an employer for the mental harm suffered by an employee is dependent on two concurrent factors, which, when read jointly, significantly confine the likelihood of an employer owing such a duty:

> Because the inquiry about reasonable foreseeability takes the form it does, seeking to read an [employee's] obligations under a contract as subject to a qualification which would excuse performance, if performance is or may be injurious to psychiatric health, encounters two difficulties. *First, the employer engaging an employee to perform stated duties is entitled to assume, in the absence of evident signs warning of the possibility of psychiatric injury, that the employee considers that he or she is able to do the job.* Implying some qualification upon what otherwise is expressly stipulated by the contract would contradict basic principle. Secondly, seeking to qualify the operation of the contract as a result of information the employer *later* acquires about the vulnerability of the employee to psychiatric harm would be no less contradictory of basic principle. The obligations of the parties are fixed at the time of the contract unless and until they are varied. [Emphasis added and references omitted.]

This particularly restrictive approach, which has effectively implied a substantial limitation on an employee's ability to sue their employer in negligence for mental harm suffered in the course of employment, has been criticised by Peter Handford in 'Liability for Work Stress: *Kohler* Ten Years On' (2015) at 179:

> [I]t remains curious that when in the context of psychiatric injury claims generally Australian common law has accepted that the general test that should be applied is one of reasonable foreseeability, and that other suggested limitations are hard to defend, it adopts a more restrictive approach in the work stress context.

However, a more recent flurry of cases has seen a change of course. It started with cases such as *Robinson v Queensland* (2017) and *Age Co Ltd v YZ (A Pseudonym)* (2019), where courts in Queensland and Victoria respectively demonstrated willingness to relax the barriers to recovery for work-related mental harm, particularly in cases involving highly stressful and emotionally challenging work.

Case examples

An example of an evolving approach to mental harm in the contest of high-stress work comes from the New South Wales Court of Appeal, in two cases of 2016 and 2022 respectively.

- In *New South Wales v Briggs* (2016), the respondent was a former police officer who suffered psychiatric injury caused by exposure to traumatic events in the course of duty. The New South Wales Court of Appeal held that the State was not liable, because Mr Briggs had not established any steps that the State could have taken that would have led him to avoid the harm or seek early treatment. The numerically large body of police officers and the particular system of work in question made it difficult to implement an alternative system of work to avoid this type of harm from occurring.
- In *New South Wales v Skinner* (2022) a police officer suffered a major depressive episode and PTSD after being exposed over several years to traumatic events at work. She also had endured other significant challenges, both personal and work-related, including the deaths of her father, who had ended his own life, and of two of her colleagues in 2007. The New South Wales Court of Appeal held that the evidence established how the police force had failed to provide adequate support for the plaintiff's psychiatric conditions while she was an officer and should have conducted a thorough mental health assessment in 2007 when it had at least constructive knowledge of her significant emotional challenges and depressive condition.

A further development for mental harm in the employment context came with the High Court decision in the case of *Kozarov v Victoria* (2022), which aligns with the more general approach to mental harm adopted in *Tame v New South Wales* (2002), at least for the purposes of employment that is by its nature 'inherently and obviously dangerous to the psychiatric health' (at [6]). Employment that does not fit within this description will remain constrained to the limitations of *Koehler v Cerebos (Australia) Ltd* (2005), which already placed great emphasis on 'the nature and extent of the work being done by the particular employee' (at [35]) in establishing the foreseeability of mental harm.

Case example

Kozarov v Victoria (2022) involved a plaintiff, Ms Kozarov, who had worked on serious sexual offences prosecutions. She was exposed to cases of significant violence and depravity while performing her duties as a prosecutor within the Specialist Sexual Offences Unit (SSOU) of the Office of Public Prosecutions of Victoria. In February 2012, Ms Kozarov was diagnosed with PTSD resulting from vicarious trauma that she had suffered in the course of employment, which:

> routinely involved interaction with survivors of trauma and exposure to their traumatic experiences including by attending court to instruct in sexual assault trials, meeting with child and adult alleged victims of sexual offences and their families, viewing explicit child pornography and preparing child complainants for cross-examination. (At [32].)

She was also later diagnosed with a major depressive disorder as a corollary of her PTSD and sued her employer for failure to prevent her mental harm. The matter reached the High Court, which ultimately found in favour of Ms Kozarov in a complex decision that sparked sufficient discussion as to warrant four separate judgments. Kiefel CJ and Kean J distinguished the case from *Koehler*, emphasising that it was clear from the circumstances of the case that the employer had a 'lively' awareness of the risk to Ms Kozarov. Specifically, their Honours found that while the SSOU had a vicarious trauma policy in place, none of the measures detailed in the policy had been adequately implemented at the time of the facts – which concurrently satisfied the requirements of foreseeability of harm and breach of duty. This included the possibility of rotating the employee to a different position. In this regard, Gageler and Gleeson JJ underlined how a reasonable person advised of risks of serious psychiatric injury may be expected, on the balance of probabilities, to accept a rotation to avoid those risks, thus dismissing the Court of Appeal's finding that Ms Kozarov had not given sufficient evidence that she would have accepted a rotation, had she been appropriately offered one. Even accepting that Ms Kozarov was particularly invested in her work and reluctant to leave the SSOU, Edelman J explained that an employer will not act in compliance with their duty to ensure a safe place of work by acquiescing in an employee's refusal to be rotated from a position that, by reason of some physical characteristic of the employee, involves a high risk of serious physical or psychiatric injury.

The decision of the High Court places great emphasis on the nature of the employment and the potential risks of mental harm inherent to the employment functions in question. There was no doubt in *Kozarov v Victoria* (2022) that the functions of a prosecutor in the specialist unit focused on sexual offences met the threshold. This is consistent with other cases such as *Age Co Ltd v YZ (A Pseudonym)* (2019), where the activities of a crime reporter were found to be inherently risky enough as to warrant the finding of a duty. It remains to be seen which other forms of employment will meet that threshold, and which on the other hand will remain constrained by the much more burdensome criterion, set in *Koehler v Cerebos* (2005), of a plaintiff having to show 'evident signs warning of the possibility of psychiatric injury'.

14.3.6 Summary points

14.3.6.1 Pure psychiatric injury (mental harm)

When you are working on a problem-solving exercise, you should adopt the correct approach, which will require you to be aware of the relevant statutory provisions in your jurisdiction, and of the approach adopted by the High Court in *Sullivan v Moody* (2001), *Tame v New South Wales* (2002) and *Wicks v State Rail Authority of New South Wales* (2010).

14.3.6.2 Aim

The aim of the law in this area is to protect the plaintiff from serious mental harm which manifests itself in a recognisable psychiatric illness. It rules out any claims based solely on severe emotional distress or grief.

14.3.6.3 Duty of care – statutory provisions

Apply the statutory pre-conditions laid down in your jurisdiction that apply to the element of duty. Remember that where the civil liability legislation has adopted specific rules for establishing a duty of care, you must follow the statutory scheme and use relevant case law for interpretative guidance. Remember that the 'normal fortitude' requirement does not apply to the specific plaintiff but rather creates a threshold of foreseeability.

14.3.6.4 Duty of care – common law

Alternatively, where the operation of statute is excluded (or there is no special statutory scheme) consider whether the common law would impose a duty, taking into account all the relevant principles and features, and bearing in mind that the overarching control device at common law is the reasonable foreseeability of the risk of pure psychiatric injury to a person or class of persons who were so 'closely and directly affected' by the defendant's conduct, in the circumstances, that the defendant ought to have had them in their contemplation at the time when they acted or refrained from acting.

The most important supplementing salient features in this area are coherence, certainty, vulnerability and autonomy.

It will weigh *against* imposing a duty if, in the circumstances:

- the suggested duty would lead to *incoherence* – for example, if:
  - it would not be compatible or reconcilable with other duties owed by the defendant;
  - it would be incompatible with the balance of rights and duties struck by the tort of defamation;
  - it is inconsistent with, or would have a tendency to discourage, the due performance of other responsibilities;
  - the suggested duty of care is inconsistent with the terms, scope and purpose of any relevant statute;
  - it would be incompatible with a set of duties agreed under a contract; or
- the suggested duty would lead to undue *uncertainty or indeterminacy* – for example, if:
  - the class of persons to whom the duty is owed is too uncertain, extensive or indeterminate; or
  - the suggested duty would unduly interfere with the *autonomy* of citizens or 'constrain their freedom of action in a gross manner' (the High Court in *Sullivan v Moody* (2001) at [42]).

It will weigh *in favour* of imposing a duty if, in the circumstances:

- the suggested duty would *not* create incoherence – for example, if:
  - the duty is compatible with other common law, contractual and statutory duties and responsibilities owed by the defendant; or
  - there is no inconsistency between the existence of the duty of care and the legitimate pursuit by the respondent of its business interests;
- the recognition of a duty of care would not raise the prospect of an intolerably large or *indeterminate* class of potential plaintiffs; or
- the plaintiff is *vulnerable* to the defendant in the special legal sense, and cannot protect themselves from incurring the pure psychiatric injury in any other way. This can be evidenced by the presence of other salient features such as control, knowledge, reliance and assumption of responsibility.

14.3.6.5 Breach and causation

Consider the other elements of breach and causation. These are still relevant in mental harm cases although you should consider that establishing a duty is the main control device in this area.

14.3.6.6 Statutory limits

Apply any relevant statutory limits on the categories of plaintiffs who are precluded from recovering damages.

Active reading

Link each of these summary points to a case in section 14.3 above.

Test your understanding

Problem solving

Mr Miller, the plaintiff, sued the defendant, Super Springs Water Ltd, for psychiatric injury sustained as a result of seeing some dead flies and a spider in a clear bottle of water supplied to him by Super Springs. In the course of replacing an empty bottle of drinking water with a full one, Mr Miller saw the dead creatures in the unopened replacement bottle. No member of his family consumed any of the water from the bottle, but Mr Miller became obsessed with the event and its 'revolting implications' for the health of his family, who had been drinking water supplied by Super Springs for the previous 15 years. Mr Miller developed a major depressive disorder with associated phobia and anxiety. He sued Super Springs for damages.

Discuss the liability of Super Springs, in the light of any relevant legislation in your jurisdiction.

14.4 Negligent misstatements

This section covers liability in negligence for cases where the conduct being complained of is the making of a written or oral statement and the resulting effect is pure economic loss (as opposed to any kind of physical damage or injury). *Negligent* misstatements (or misrepresentations) should be distinguished from *fraudulent* misrepresentations, which are dealt with under the tort of deceit. This section covers other forms of negligent conduct leading to pure economic loss.

14.4.1 The problem of words

The common law has traditionally been reluctant to impose liability in cases where the conduct giving rise to the complaint has been 'mere words' and where the harm is a 'pure economic loss' – that is, a financial loss or cost that has not flowed from any injury or damage to person or property. Courts have treated liability for negligent misstatements with suspicion for reasons that are sometimes paradoxical. In older times, when physical injury was the primary focus of the law's concern, a duty was not imposed because words were seen as harmless: 'sticks and stones may break my bones, but words can never hurt me'. But in modern times, it is the volatility and dangerousness of words that gives rise to caution because of the ease and rapidity with which information can be replicated and then transmitted across time and space to wide audiences.

Case examples

- In *Le Lievre v Gould* (1893), Bowen LJ refused to impose liability on an architect who issued a negligently prepared certificate, saying at 502 that the law 'does not consider that what a man writes is like a gun or other dangerous instrument'.
- The warning made in the well-known American case of *Ultramares Corporation v Touche* (1931) is repeated in almost every case dealing with pure economic loss. Cardozo CJ said at 444 that imposing a duty in negligence to avoid making careless statements could expose defendants to a potential liability 'in an indeterminate amount for an indefinite time to an indeterminate class'.
- In the landmark English case of *Hedley Byrne & Co Ltd v Heller & Partners Ltd* (1964), which decided that liability for statements was allowable under limited circumstances, Lord Pearce at 535 emphasised the potential dangers of words:

> The reason for some divergence between the law of negligence in word and that of negligence in act is clear. Negligence in word creates problems different from those of negligence in act. Words are more volatile than deeds. They travel fast and far afield. They are used without being expended and take effect in combination with innumerable facts and other words. Yet they are dangerous and can cause vast financial damage. ... If the mere hearing or reading of words were held to create proximity, there might be no limit to the persons to whom the speaker or writer could be liable. Damage by negligent acts to persons or property on the other hand is more visible and obvious; its limits are more easily defined, and it is with this damage that the earlier cases were more concerned.

Lord Reid explained at 482–3 why the law must treat negligent words and negligent acts differently:

> The most obvious difference between negligent words and negligent acts is this. Quite careful people often express definite opinions on social or informal occasions even when they see that others are likely to be influenced by them; and they often do that without taking that care which they would take if asked for their opinion professionally or in a business connection.

The second 'obvious difference' lay in the fact that 'a negligently made article will only cause one accident' whereas 'words can be broadcast with or without the consent or the foresight of the speaker or writer': at 483.

- In the Australian case of *Mutual Life & Citizens Assurance Co Ltd v Evatt* (1968), Barwick CJ noted at 567 another reason why the law had distinguished between damage caused by physical acts and damage caused by statements:

  > In the first, it is said that the injury and damage is direct and obvious without any intervening act whilst in the latter nothing results unless the hearer acts upon the utterance, the loss and damage in a real sense directly arising out of the hearer's own action.

  Barwick CJ concluded at 568 that there is no such 'radical difference' between damage caused by acts and words that might justify denying liability.
- Subsequent Australian cases have echoed these concerns: see, for example, *L Shaddock & Associates Pty Ltd v Parramatta City Council* (1981) Gibbs CJ at 231. In *San Sebastian Pty Ltd v Minister Administering the Environmental Planning and Assessment Act 1979* (1986), the joint judgment noted at 353–4 the 'propensity of negligent statements to generate loss which is purely economic' and added another concern, namely, the problem of the disparity between the degree of the defendant's wrongdoing and the magnitude of the resulting loss, suggesting that this might 'provoke doubts about the justice of imposing liability for it on the defendant'.

The misgivings about imposing liability for negligent misstatements have now been overcome, as the joint judgment in *San Sebastian Pty Ltd v Minister Administering the Environmental Planning and Assessment Act 1979* (1986) pointed out at 534:

> Conscious of the factors already mentioned, courts have sometimes dealt with the duty of care in relation to negligent misstatement without relating it to Lord Atkin's exposition in *Donoghue v Stevenson*. However, the correct view is that, just as liability for negligent misstatement is but an instance of liability for negligent acts and omissions generally, so the treatment of the duty of care in the context of misstatements is but an instance of the application of the principles governing the duty of care in negligence generally.

This area of law is further complicated by the fact that there are several other causes of action that may be available when the triggering conduct amounts to mere words.

Examples

- *Negligence:* words that cause physical harm to a person, goods or land

  If actual physical damage results from statements made negligently, liability may be imposed under the ordinary principles of negligence. Any consequential economic loss flowing from that harm will be compensable, provided it is within the proper scope of liability.

- *Action on the case:* words that are intended to shock

  If physical illness or 'nervous shock' is caused by statements that are 'calculated' to cause that nervous shock, the tort in *Wilkinson v Downton* (1897) may provide compensation.

- *Deceit:* fraudulent words that deceive another

  The tort of deceit (also known as fraudulent misrepresentation) imposes liability on a defendant who has caused damage to a plaintiff by knowingly making a false statement with the intention that it be relied upon by the plaintiff: *Pasley v Freeman* (1789). The governing principle of the tort of deceit is honesty: see *Magill v Magill* (2006).

- *Defamation:* words that lower the reputation of another

  If words published by a defendant lower the reputation of the plaintiff in the eyes of others, an action in defamation may lie.

- *Contract:* statements that evidence a breach of contract

  If statements are made in breach of a term of a contract specifying that reasonable care and skill will be used in performing the contractual obligations, an action in contract may lie, provided there is privity between the parties.

- *Equity:* statements that cause detriment

  If the defendant makes a statement that is in breach of a fiduciary duty or makes a statement that gives rise to a promissory estoppel, and the plaintiff suffers detriment, an action in equity may lie.

- *Statute:* words that are misleading and deceptive

  If the defendant has made statements in trade or commerce that amount to 'misleading or deceptive conduct', a plaintiff may rely on the statutory cause of action in s 18 of the *Australian Consumer Law* (*ACL*).

Test your understanding

Make a look-up chart

Make a look-up chart that lists the elements of the tort actions noted above and compare them to the statutory action under the *ACL*, s 18.

14.4.2 Relevant salient features

In addition to the standard negligence principles of reasonable foreseeability of harm and fault, the most important salient features in the area of negligent misstatements are certainty or indeterminacy, vulnerability, autonomy and coherence.

14.4.2.1 Certainty and indeterminacy

The fear of indeterminate liability is a key concern in cases of negligent misstatement, as noted in section 14.4.1 above, which justifies declining to impose liability if it may lead to liability 'in an indeterminate amount for an indeterminate time to an indeterminate class': Gaudron J in *Perre v Apand Pty Ltd* (1999) at [32], citing *Bryan v Maloney* (1995) Mason CJ, Deane and Gaudron JJ at 618, in turn citing Cardozo CJ in *Ultramares Corporation v Touche* (1931) at 444. In these cases, certainty requires that the defendant knows that the information or advice is being sought by or on behalf of a 'limited class', as noted by Lord Reid in *Hedley Byrne & Co Ltd v Heller & Partners Ltd* (1964) at 483, or 'an identified or identifiable class of persons': *Mutual Life & Citizens Assurance Co Ltd v Evatt* (1968), Barwick CJ at 570.

14.4.2.2 Vulnerability

If the relationship between the plaintiffs and the defendants is characterised by vulnerability in the special legal sense that the plaintiff is vulnerable to harm as a result of the defendant's conduct and they are unable to protect themselves by taking any other measures, this factor will weigh in favour of imposing a duty. The judges in *Hedley Byrne & Co Ltd v Heller & Partners Ltd* (1964) focused on the 'special relationship' between the plaintiff and the defendant. They justified imposing liability in misrepresentation cases, reasoning in part by analogy with the tort of deceit, where reliance is an essential element, and with other legally recognised categories where plaintiffs and defendants are in a special relationship marked out by vulnerability and reliance (eg fiduciary relationships, contractual relationships and cases of medical negligence). Likewise, in *Esanda Finance Corporation Ltd v Peat Marwick Hungerfords* (1997), Toohey and Gaudron JJ noted at 263–4 the parallels with other duties in negligence where a special relationship exists – for example, non-delegable duties. And in *San Sebastian Pty Ltd v Minister Administering the Environmental Planning and Assessment Act 1979* (1986) and *Esanda Finance Corporation Ltd v Peat Marwick Hungerfords* (1997), Brennan J used language and concepts that were strikingly similar to the language and concepts found in cases of equitable or promissory estoppel. So, it is unsurprising that the most common indicators of vulnerability in negligent misstatement cases are knowledge, reasonable reliance and an assumption of responsibility.

- *Knowledge:* If the defendant has special or exclusive knowledge of important matters affecting the plaintiff, then a duty will more readily be imposed (see, eg, *L Shaddock & Associates Pty Ltd v Parramatta City Council* (1981)). On the other hand, if that knowledge or information can be obtained from another source and the plaintiff could easily have protected themselves from suffering the loss by accessing other expert advice, then liability may not be imposed on the grounds that the plaintiff should have taken responsibility for protecting their own interests (see, eg, the majority judgments in *Tepko Pty Ltd v Water Board* (2001)).

- *Reliance and assumption of responsibility:* If the defendant has assumed responsibility for making a statement to the plaintiff and the plaintiff has reasonably relied on the defendant's statement, then it is more likely that liability will be imposed. On the other hand, if the defendant has disclaimed responsibility, it will weigh against imposing liability, but a disclaimer will not of itself be decisive because the question is whether it was reasonable in all the circumstances for the plaintiff to rely on the defendant's statement and whether the defendant could reasonably have foreseen that the statement would be relied upon by the plaintiff: see, for example, *Hedley Byrne & Co Ltd v Heller & Partners Ltd* (1964) at 486, 502 and 514; *Mutual Life & Citizens Assurance Co Ltd v Evatt* (1968), Barwick CJ at 570; and *Esanda Finance Corporation Ltd v Peat Marwick Hungerfords* (1997), Toohey and Gaudron JJ at 263–4.

Case examples

- The joint judgment in *San Sebastian Pty Ltd v Minister Administering the Environmental Planning and Assessment Act 1979* (1986) pointed out at 355:

> In cases of negligent misstatement, reliance plays an important role, particularly so when the defendant directs his statement to a class of persons with the intention of inducing members of the class to act or refrain from acting, in reliance on the statement, in circumstances where he should realize that they may thereby suffer economic loss if the statement is not true.

- In *Esanda Finance Corporation v Peat Marwick Hungerfords* (1997), Toohey and Gaudron JJ at 264 discussed the special features that indicate vulnerability, noting:

> [R]eliance is to be understood, in the context of the provision of information or advice, as an expectation, which is reasonable in the circumstances, that due care will be exercised in relation to that provision. Similarly ... assumption of responsibility should be understood ... as the assumption of responsibility for providing information or advice in circumstances where it is known, or ought reasonably be known, that it will or may be acted upon for a serious purpose, and loss may be suffered if it proves to be inaccurate.

- Many of the judges referred to these special features in *Perre v Apand Pty Ltd* (1999), another case of pure economic loss, discussed in further detail in section 14.5 below. Gleeson CJ said at [10]–[11]:

> In relation to the giving of advice or information, questions of reliance and actual foresight of the possibility of harm, (or, what is the same thing, the foresight that a reasonable person would have), are closely related. Moreover, knowledge (actual, or that which a reasonable person would have) of an individual, or an ascertainable class of persons, who is or are reliant, and therefore vulnerable, is a significant factor in establishing a duty of care.

14.4.2.3 Autonomy and personal responsibility

Autonomy and personal responsibility also justify holding a defendant liable for the consequences of their freely chosen decision to speak when they could have remained silent and when they know or intend that another should rely upon it.

Case examples

- The judges in *Hedley Byrne & Co Ltd v Heller & Partners Ltd* (1964) emphasised the point that the imposition of liability is justified in part by the fact that the defendant has voluntarily, knowingly or deliberately assumed a responsibility to the plaintiff: see, for example, Lord Morris at 494 and Lord Devlin at 53.
- In *Mutual Life & Citizens Assurance Co Ltd v Evatt* (1968) Barwick CJ pointed out at 570:

> But, though the willingness of the speaker to give or the giving of the information or advice can be described as an acceptance of the duty to be careful in the sense that having in the circumstances a choice to speak or to remain silent, or perhaps to speak with reservation, ... the speaker elects to speak and thus by his voluntary act attracts the duty to be careful both in preparing himself for what he says and in the manner of saying it.

On the other hand, if the two parties are in commercial competition with each other, autonomy may weigh against imposing a duty.

Case example

In *Woolcock Street Investments Pty Ltd v CDG Pty Ltd* (2004), also discussed in section 14.5 below on pure economic loss, McHugh J noted at [78] that the common law's concern to protect autonomy does not require a person who is 'legitimately protecting or pursuing' their own commercial interests 'to be concerned with the effect of his or her conduct on the economic interests of other persons'.

Personal responsibility can also justify denying liability if the plaintiffs have caused their own losses or if they could have protected themselves from that loss. In *Mutual Life & Citizens Assurance Co Ltd v Evatt* (1968), Barwick CJ noted at 568 that a loss would not be recoverable if it flowed from the independent judgement of the plaintiff. Furthermore, liability may be denied if the plaintiffs have chosen to rely on the defendant's statement when they could have protected themselves from the risk by seeking the information elsewhere and guaranteeing themselves some security by entering into a paid contract for professional advice (see, for example, the majority judgments in *Tepko Pty Ltd v Water Board* (2001)). In this scenario, vulnerability and personal responsibility together reinforce the conclusion that the defendant should not be liable.

14.4.2.4 Coherence

Coherence requires consistency both with the duties imposed in other areas of the law and with wider community values. Given that liability for negligent misrepresentations was developed by analogy with other areas of the law including tort law, contract and equity (as noted above), the step taken by the courts to recognise a duty to take reasonable care in the making of statements did not lead to any inconsistency in the law. However, one of the justifications for placing limits on that duty is based on goal-based coherence – in particular, the value of free communication of opinion, wisdom and experience.

Case example

In *San Sebastian Pty Ltd v Minister Administering the Environmental Planning and Assessment Act 1979* (1986) Brennan J suggested at 372 that one of the reasons why judges had been slow to impose a duty of care in negligent misstatement cases was to maintain the value of free communication:

> To impose a legal duty of care on the unsolicited and voluntary giving of any information and advice on serious or business matters would chill communications which are a valuable source of wisdom and experience for a person contemplating a course of conduct.

14.4.3 Key cases

The wider principles of negligence have given rise to a set of rules and special considerations that must be taken into account by the courts when deciding cases of negligent misrepresentations. The judges have insisted that 'something more' than mere foreseeability of harm is necessary: *Hedley Byrne & Co Ltd v Heller & Partners Ltd* (1964), Lord Reid at 483; *San Sebastian Pty Ltd v Minister Administering the Environmental Planning and Assessment Act 1979* (1986), Brennan J at 365. As the joint judgment in *San Sebastian Pty Ltd v Minister Administering the Environmental Planning and Assessment Act 1979* (1986) explained at 534, the 'special complications' that arise in negligent misstatement cases 'can only be unravelled in a variety of factual situations'. Most of the cases involve two-party scenarios (see Figure 14.4), but some cases also involve more complicated fact patterns where a statement is given by the defendant to one party and then that statement is passed on to the ultimate plaintiff who suffers detriment as a result of relying on the statement: see Figure 14.5.

Figure 14.4 Negligent misstatement scenario: Two-party cases

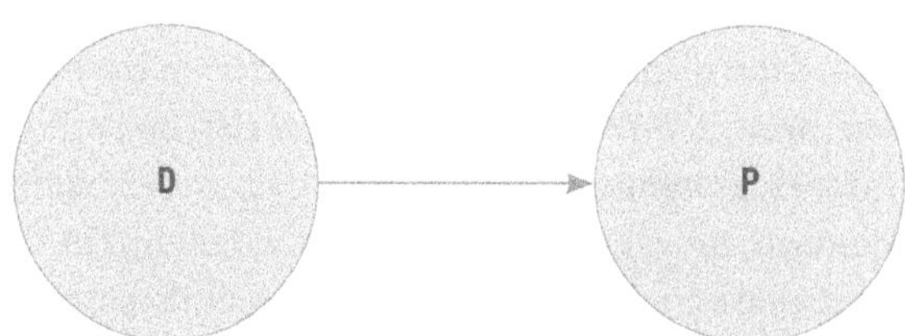

The solid line in Figure 14.4 shows the path of the statement. Examples of two-party cases include *Mutual Life & Citizens Assurance Co Ltd v Evatt* (1968) and *Tepko Pty Ltd v Water Board* (2001).

Figure 14.5 Negligent misstatement scenario: Three-party cases

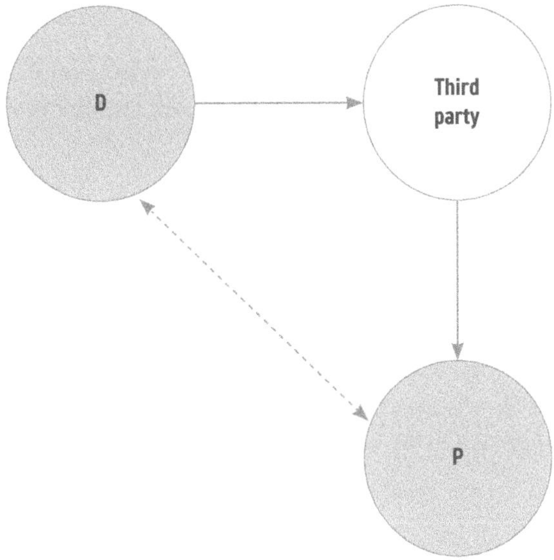

The solid lines in Figure 14.5 show the paths of the statement. The dotted line shows the new legal relationships and justifications needed.

Case example

Hedley Byrne & Co Ltd v Heller & Partners Ltd (1964) was the first case to accept that the making of a statement that caused pure economic loss could give rise to liability. The plaintiffs, a firm of advertising agents, had consulted a bank, Heller & Partners Ltd, about the creditworthiness of one of the bank's customers, Easipower, because they were contemplating entering into an advertising contract with that customer. The bank gave written advice saying that the customer was 'a respectably constituted company, considered good for its ordinary business arrangements' but added a disclaimer making it clear that the advice was issued 'without responsibility on the part of the bank or its officials'. The plaintiffs relied on the credit report, and subsequently lost money when Easipower was unable to pay its debts.

The House of Lords recognised that a duty in negligence could arise for a negligent (as opposed to a fraudulent) misstatement but held that liability would not be imposed in this case because of the disclaimer of responsibility. The duty of care may arise where the parties are in a special relationship (eg equivalent to contract) and the plaintiff reasonably relies on the defendant's special skill.

The following special considerations were noted by the judges in this case:

- Words expressed on a social, informal occasion will not attract a duty: Lord Reid at 482–3, Lord Devlin at 529.
- Where the parties are in a special relationship, a duty to take reasonable care may be imposed if the defendants, who possess a special skill, have voluntarily taken it upon themselves to give a statement to the plaintiffs, or have undertaken some responsibility, knowing that they were

being trusted or relied upon by the plaintiffs, provided that it is reasonable for the plaintiffs to rely on the statement in all the circumstances: Lord Reid at 486, Lord Morris at 502–3, Lord Hodson at 514, Lord Devlin at 529–30.

- If there is an express disclaimer of responsibility, it may not be reasonable to rely on the statement and so liability may not be imposed: Lord Reid at 492, Lord Morris at 504, Lord Pearce at 540, Lord Devlin at 529.

The first case of this type in Australia, *Mutual Life & Citizens Assurance Co Ltd v Evatt* (1968), followed the lead given by the House of Lords. The High Court recognised that liability could be imposed for a negligent misstatement and gave judgment for the plaintiff in a split decision of 3:2. Despite the fact that the decision by the High Court was overturned on appeal to the Privy Council, subsequent Australian cases have approved the views of Barwick CJ, who gave the most influential judgment that laid the foundation for the Australian approach to the law of negligent misstatements.

Case example

The plaintiff in *Mutual Life & Citizens Assurance Co Ltd v Evatt* (1968) held an insurance policy with MLC (the defendant). He consulted MLC for advice about a planned investment in one of MLC's subsidiary companies, HG Palmer Ltd, and requested information about its financial stability. Acting in reliance on the statement given by MLC that HG Palmer Ltd was financially stable, P made the investment and suffered a financial loss. The plaintiff ultimately lost the case in the Privy Council in a majority decision of 3:2 on the grounds that the defendant did not let it be known or claim that it possessed a 'special skill' in the giving of advice. The leading Australian judgment is that of Barwick CJ and the most important part of the judgment is found at 569–73:

> It seems to me, therefore, that whenever a person gives information or advice to another ... upon a serious matter ... and the relationship of the parties arising out of the circumstances is such that ... the speaker realizes or ought to realize that he is being trusted ... to give the best of his information or advice as a basis for action on the part of the other party and it is reasonable in the circumstances for the other party ... to act upon that information and advice, the speaker, choosing to give the information or advice in such circumstances, comes under a duty of care both to utilize with reasonable care the information and sources of information at his disposal and to employ with reasonable care what capacity he has for judgment in relation to the matter and to exercise reasonable care in the expression of what he is prepared to convey by way of information or advice.

Other special considerations mentioned by Barwick CJ were as follows:

- The duty of care is imposed by law and does not arise out of any consensual or unilateral assumption of duty: at 568 and 570.
- There is no reason to distinguish between information and advice: at 572.
- The defendant must give the information 'willingly and knowingly' to 'an identified or identifiable class of persons' in circumstances where the defendant is aware of the implications of making the statement: at 570.

- Given that the duty is imposed by law, the giving of a disclaimer of responsibility may not always prevent the imposition of liability because it will always depend on the circumstances: at 570.
- The loss will not be recoverable if it flows from the independent judgement of the plaintiff: at 568.
- No duty arises for statements that are made on social occasions when legal relationships would not be contemplated, but a duty may arise if the matter is a serious matter or an important business matter: at 569.
- It is not necessary for the defendant to possess or to claim a special skill in the giving of advice or information: at 574.

The need to consider 'all the circumstances' continues to be emphasised in the case law, and this means that you should pay careful attention to the facts when you are problem solving in this area. You should also note that many of the cases decided in the period between 1984 and 2001 were based in part on the doctrine of proximity, which has now been largely superseded by the vulnerability principle. Consequently, the discussion of the following cases will be confined to the relevant facts and current legal concerns.

Case example

The plaintiffs in *L Shaddock & Associates Pty Ltd v Parramatta City Council* (1981) were property developers who sought information about any planned road widening proposals from the Parramatta City Council before buying some land. Their solicitor made two inquiries. The first was an informal telephone inquiry to an unnamed person, who advised that there were no proposals. The second was a written application for a certificate from the Council, specifically asking about any proposed road widening or realignment proposals. Despite the fact that there were such plans, the council sent a certificate that did not mention them. Acting in reliance on that certificate, the plaintiffs bought the land and subsequently sued the council for the financial losses that they incurred as a result of the plans, which prevented them from developing the land as they had originally intended.

Despite the fact that the council did not hold itself out as possessing a special skill or competence, the High Court allowed the claim on the basis that, while it was *not* reasonable for the plaintiffs to have relied on the informal statement made on the telephone, it *was* reasonable for them to rely on the certificate. The relevant circumstances were identified by Gibbs CJ at 235–6:

- The 'Council was in a position to know better than anyone else whether any such proposals existed, and it commonly followed the practice of giving information as to that matter when requested'.
- 'The importance of certificates given under s 342AS for conveyancing purposes is obvious and well known.'
- The 'Council ought to have known that the road widening, if carried out, would adversely affect the use of the land for most conceivable purposes'.
- 'The Council ... followed the practice, in the course of exercising its functions, of making such information available.'

- 'The nature of the inquiry – made by a solicitor, for conveyancing purposes, on a form commonly used and prepared by law stationers – made clear the gravity of the inquiry and the importance attached to the answer.'

Mason J pointed out at 253 that 'the existence of a duty of care does not depend upon knowledge on the part of the speaker of the precise use to which the information will be put' but noted that it would be enough:

> if he knows, or ought to know, that the inquirer is requesting it for a serious purpose, that he proposes to act upon it and that he may suffer loss if it proves to be inaccurate.

The case of *Hedley Byrne & Co Ltd v Heller & Partners Ltd* (1964) did not 'place liability for negligent words on the same footing as liability for negligent acts', as Gibbs J noted in *Caltex Oil (Australia) Pty Ltd v The Dredge 'Willemstad'* (1976) at 549. However, in the next case, the High Court united the negligent misstatement cases with mainstream negligence.

Case example

San Sebastian Pty Ltd v Minister Administering the Environmental Planning and Assessment Act 1979 (1986) concerned property developers who sued New South Wales public planning authorities and a local council because they suffered losses after relying on information published by the defendants in a development planning scheme. They did not make any request for information, but relied on the scheme's published documents.

The High Court held that the authorities did not owe a duty to the developers in the circumstances. The joint judgment of Gibbs CJ, Mason, Wilson and Dawson JJ at 353–4 followed the approach taken by Barwick CJ in *Mutual Life & Citizens Assurance Co Ltd v Evatt* (1968) and reaffirmed at 355 that 'the element of reliance plays a prominent part in the ascertainment ... of a duty of care'. Having decided that the area of negligent misstatement should not be seen as a separate category standing outside the mainstream of negligence, the joint judgment summarised the earlier statement of the law at 356:

> [W]henever a person gives information or advice to another upon a serious matter in circumstances where the speaker realizes, or ought to realize, that he is being trusted to give the best of his information or advice as a basis for action on the part of the other party and it is reasonable in the circumstances for that other party to act on that information or advice, the speaker comes under a duty to take reasonable care in the provision of the information or advice which he chooses to give.

In *San Sebastian*, the plaintiffs had not asked the defendants for information, but the joint judgment maintained at 356 that, while it was 'by no means essential' for the plaintiff's reliance to be the result of a specific request:

> the existence of an antecedent request for information or advice certainly assists in demonstrating reliance, which is a cornerstone of liability for negligent misstatement.

The joint judgment identified at 359 the fact that 'proposals of this kind are subject to alteration, variation and revocation' and pointed out at 360 that there were two 'relevant characteristics' of the development scheme that supported the decision that no duty arose because it was not reasonable for the plaintiff to rely on the statements in all the circumstances.

> First, there is the element of impermanence and capacity for modification and revocation. Secondly, the plan does not diminish the overriding discretion of the responsible authority to depart from the proposals incorporated in the plan when determining individual applications for development approval.
>
> These characteristics point to the conclusion that, in the absence of indications to the contrary, it will not readily be inferred that a plan intended to serve as a guide to future development contains an assurance that it will be continuously and inflexibly applied in the future. Rather it is an expression of present intention and future expectation which would in ordinary circumstances deter developers and businessmen from relying on it as a solid and unchangeable foundation for development approvals.

Most cases of negligent misstatement arise out of two-party scenarios where a written or oral statement is made directly by the defendant to the plaintiff (or their agents) and the plaintiff relies upon that statement and suffers an economic loss. However, the courts have not ruled out liability in cases that involve more indirect fact patterns.

Case example

Esanda Finance Corporation v Peat Marwick Hungerfords (1997) was a three-party scenario where the plaintiff was unsuccessful. Peat Marwick Hungerfords (D), audited the accounts of a company named Excel. The information in D's audit report was given by Excel to Esanda Finance Corporation (P), who relied on the report and entered into a number of transactions with Excel. P sued D after suffering losses, claiming that the report was in breach of mandatory auditing standards and arguing that D should have foreseen that they might rely on that report.

The High Court decided unanimously that D did not owe a duty to P. None of the judges ruled out the possibility that liability may arise in a case where the information flowed indirectly to P through a third party, but they did emphasise that before a duty could be imposed, there must be something more than the mere foreseeability of a loss occurring in those circumstances. Brennan CJ noted at 252 that the 'mere foreseeability of the possibility' that a third party might rely on the report was insufficient to justify imposing a duty. Rather:

> in every case, it is necessary for the plaintiff to allege and prove that the defendant knew or ought reasonably to have known that the information or advice would be communicated to the plaintiff, either individually or as a member of an identified class, that the information or advice would be so communicated for a purpose that would be very likely to lead the plaintiff to enter into a transaction of the kind that the plaintiff does enter into and that it would be very likely that the plaintiff would enter into such a transaction in reliance on the information or advice and thereby risk the incurring of economic loss if the statement should be untrue or the advice should be unsound.

Toohey and Gaudron JJ accepted at 261 that the principle 'extends to a situation in which advice is communicated to a third party' but said at 265:

> [C]ommonsense requires the conclusion that a special relationship ... marked either by reliance or by the assumption of responsibility does not arise unless the person providing the information or advice has some special expertise or knowledge, or some special means of acquiring information which is not available to the recipient. Moreover, ordinary principles require that the relationship does not arise unless it is reasonable for the recipient to act on that information or advice without further inquiry.

The relevant considerations in this case were noted at 260, 262 and 266:

- P had not asked D for the information.
- D did not know that Excel was going to use the report to obtain finance.
- D did not know or intend that P was going to rely on the report; D did not prepare the report with the purpose of inducing P to enter into any transactions with Excel and D did not expressly or impliedly invite P to act on the reports.
- Nothing suggested that 'Esanda was not itself able to have accountants undertake the same task on its behalf as a condition of its entertaining the possibility of entering into financial transactions with Excel'.

McHugh J noted several policy reasons that justified a refusal to impose liability, including the possibility that there would be a reduction in demand for, supply of and quality of auditing services if liability in these kinds of cases was recognised: at 282–5.

Our final case shows that the courts will examine very carefully the alternative sources of advice available to the plaintiffs, the nature of the venture being carried out by the plaintiffs, and the habits and practices of the defendant in issuing information and advice.

Case example

Tepko Pty Ltd v Water Board (2001) was another case where the plaintiffs failed in their claim that the defendant, a public authority, owed them a duty to take reasonable care in the provision of information. Tepko Pty Ltd wanted to rezone and subdivide land and so it asked the Water Board for an estimate of the likely cost of connecting water services to the development. Tepko, which was in a difficult financial position, did not tell the Board that it needed the estimate to convince its bankers that its development plans were sound.

The Board had a policy of refusing to give these costings but eventually it did give an estimate 'in the order of $2.5 million'. This figure prompted the collapse of the funding arrangements for the development and Tepko's bank placed the company into receivership. The Board later discovered that the cost would have been substantially less than the estimated figure and so Tepko and others sued the Board, claiming that it had caused them to suffer financial losses. The High Court held by a 4:3 majority that the Board did not owe a duty to take reasonable care in giving the estimate.

The joint judgment of Gleeson, Gummow and Hayne JJ emphasised at [48] that a duty of care should not be imposed on 'a party who has no appreciation of, and could not be expected to appreciate, the implications of making an error'. In this case, the critical features were as follows:

- The Board did not know about the 'critical state' of the plaintiff's relationship with the bank, which meant that the Board did not appreciate either the seriousness of the inquiry or the possible consequences: at [48].
- The figure was a 'ball-park' figure, which, as any developer would have known, was given only as a 'starting point' at the beginning of a 'well-established' four-level costing process: at [37] and [49]. This meant that it was not reasonable in the circumstances for Tepko to rely on the costing: at [49].
- The defendant was 'plainly a reluctant participant' and Tepko 'at all material times had access to expert advice', which led to the conclusion that it was 'unreasonable to posit a duty' and that Tepko was not a 'vulnerable party' in the sense that they were 'unable to protect themselves against that harm': at [49]–[50].

Gaudron J noted at [76] that reliance must be reasonable in all the circumstances and at [81]–[82] that the statement must be given with knowledge or an assumption of responsibility. The fact that the Board provided only an uncertain and preliminary estimate meant that it could not be concluded that the Board (at [86]):

> knew or should have known that the appellants intended to act upon that cost estimate for any purpose, let alone a serious purpose. And because the Water Board indicated that it was prepared to enter into further discussions with the appellants, it cannot be concluded that it assumed any responsibility in relation to that estimate.

Gaudron J also concluded at [87]–[88] that reliance was unreasonable because the Board was not 'the sole repository of expertise' and Tepko had 'engaged their own experts and could have relied on their knowledge as to likely cost once the extent of the work was known'. The 'considerable uncertainty' and the 'speculative' nature of the venture required Tepko to 'carefully examine the detail of the course on which they were embarked and to rely on the professional advice available to them'.

These cases illustrate the difficulties that a plaintiff may encounter in a case of negligent misrepresentation: of all the plaintiffs, only those in *L Shaddock & Associates Pty Ltd v Parramatta City Council* were ultimately successful in recovering damages. For these reasons, many plaintiffs find that the statutory alternative offered by the *Australian Consumer Law* (*ACL*) offers a better path to a remedy.

14.4.4 Legislation

The importance of the legal treatment of negligent misstatements (or misrepresentations) has been significantly reduced since the passing of the *Trade Practices Act 1974* (Cth) (*TPA*), which introduced a new era of protection for consumers in Australia by imposing a regime of strict liability for conduct that is misleading or deceptive. In 2010 the *ACL* replaced the old statute. The *ACL* is located in sch 2 of the *Competition and Consumer Act 2010* (Cth), and it is also incorporated into the *Fair Trading Acts* in the states and territories across Australia.

Legislative example

Section 18 of the *ACL* provides:

> A person must not, in trade or commerce, engage in conduct that is misleading or deceptive or is likely to mislead or deceive.

This provision replaces the older provision in s 52 of the old *TPA*, which was drafted in the same terms except that the *TPA* referred to a 'corporation' rather than a 'person'.

There are several benefits in using the statutory causes of action, including:

- a plaintiff does not have to prove the element of duty;
- a plaintiff does not have to prove fault on the part of the defendant;
- in some circumstances, 'conduct that is misleading or deceptive or is likely to mislead or deceive' may include silence (ie a failure to speak); and
- the range of available remedies is more extensive.

You should note, however, that the statutes and the common law do not cover exactly the same ground, so it is important to be familiar with both options. Other legislation in some jurisdictions also expands the remedies available at common law and in equity for misrepresentation (see, eg, *Misrepresentation Act 1972* (SA) and *Civil Law (Wrongs) Act 2002* (ACT)).

LEGISLATION ALERT!

Consult your study materials and note any relevant statutory provisions in your jurisdiction.

14.4.5 Summary points

14.4.5.1 Negligent misrepresentation

1. Originally the courts treated liability for negligent misstatements as a separate category, but since *San Sebastian Pty Ltd v Minister Administering the Environmental Planning and Assessment Act 1979* (1986) it has been dealt with as another 'instance of liability for negligent acts and omissions generally'.
2. There are other important common law, equitable and statutory causes of action that also deal with liability for statements.
3. The most important salient features in this area of the law are certainty or indeterminacy, vulnerability, autonomy and coherence. These general features of negligence point towards imposing personal responsibility on a defendant who has failed to take reasonable care in making a statement if, in the circumstances:
   - the defendant has voluntarily assumed a responsibility to the plaintiff or has autonomously made a free choice to make a statement, knowing or intending that the plaintiff will rely on it;

- the defendant can reasonably foresee that the plaintiff is vulnerable to suffering a loss if they reasonably rely on the correctness of the statement in the circumstances; and
- the plaintiff is otherwise unable to protect themselves by seeking the information elsewhere;
- provided that:
  - the imposition of the duty is consistent with the other duties imposed on the defendant;
  - the imposition of the duty does not impose a new burden that unduly limits free competition and the free communication of ideas and information;
  - the duty is capable of certain definition;
  - the identity of the plaintiff either as an individual or as a member of a class of persons is readily ascertainable; and
  - the imposition of the duty will not expose the defendant to liability in 'an indeterminate amount for an indeterminate time to an indeterminate class'.

4. The main summary of the law on duty is found in the joint judgment in *San Sebastian* at 356, to the effect that:
   - whenever a person gives information or advice to another upon a serious matter in circumstances where the speaker realises, or ought to realise, that he is being trusted to give the best of his information or advice as a basis for action on the part of the other party; and
   - it is reasonable in the circumstances for that other party to act on that information or advice; then
   - the speaker comes under a duty to take reasonable care in the provision of the information or advice which he chooses to give.
5. The joint judgment in *San Sebastian* explained at 534 that the 'special complications' that arise in negligent misstatement cases 'can only be unravelled in a variety of factual situations'. The following are some of the relevant matters:

   The nature of the defendant and the reason why they made the statement
   - D willingly accepted or assumed responsibility for making the statement.
   - D made the statement with the intention of inducing P to act upon it.
   - D made the statement in response to a serious and specific request by P and was given reasons for the request that alerted D to the importance of the request and to the fact that reliance would be placed on the statement.
   - P made a request through a solicitor and for serious purposes.
   - D professed to have a special skill, expertise or competence in the matter.
   - D was the only supplier or repository of the information and had made it a practice to give that information on request.

   The nature of the relationship between the parties
   - There was a pre-existing legal, professional or other special relationship between the parties.
   - D knew, or was in a position to know, why P wanted the information and what P was going to do with that information.

The circumstances surrounding the making of the statement and the contents of the statement

- D's statement was made on a serious occasion – or was made on a casual or social occasion.
- D's statement was made on a serious matter or on a matter of business.
- D's statement was made by an authorised, identified person.
- D's statement was informally given over the phone – or was written on an official letter or document.
- The statement was made directly to P – or was passed indirectly to P through a third party without D's knowledge.
- Liability had been expressly disclaimed.
- The statement was qualified in some way, was clearly inconclusive or was made on a matter that was inherently impermanent and known to be changeable.
- The statement was a statement of future intention – or was a statement of fact.

The circumstances of the plaintiff

- P had other sources of independent advice – or was fully dependent on D for information.
- P's venture was inherently uncertain or speculative.
- P's loss flowed from their own independent decision.

6. In a problem question, you need to establish the three essential elements of the tort: duty, breach and causation. So, once you have argued out the element of duty, it is important to go on to identify the nature of the precautions that the defendant should have taken and to work your way through the standard aspects of breach (including the foreseeability, significance and probability of the risk), causation and any possible defences.
7. Note that other issues may arise to complicate the question of liability for a statement – for example, in cases where the defendant is a public authority or where that statement leads to pure psychiatric injury.

Active reading

Link each of these summary points with a case discussed in section 14.4 above.

Develop your skills

Case analysis and oral presentation

Read the minority judgments in *Tepko Pty Ltd v Water Board* (2001) and collect the arguments and 'relevant factual characteristics' used by the judges to justify their decision to impose a duty on the defendants in that case.

Prepare a five-minute oral presentation explaining whether you agree with the minority view or the majority view in this case, giving reasons for your choice.

14.5 Pure economic loss

The courts took quite some time after *Donoghue v Stevenson* (1932) to overcome their 'marked reluctance' to allow liability in cases where the harm caused by a defendant's conduct consists solely of economic or financial loss: Mason J in *Caltex Oil (Australia) Pty Ltd v The Dredge 'Willemstad'* (1976) at 584. After *Hedley Byrne & Co Ltd v Heller & Partners Ltd* (1964) paved the way for recovery of pure economic loss caused by statements, the courts began allowing liability for pure economic loss caused in other ways. Note that this section (14.5), should be read together with section 14.4 above because the legal concerns and principles in both are very similar: negligent misstatement is a form of pure economic loss.

This section covers four categories where claims for pure economic loss have been made on different grounds:

1. pure economic loss that is a consequence of material physical damage negligently caused by the defendant to a third party (also called 'relational loss' cases);
2. pure economic loss that arises when a plaintiff purchases a building that has been negligently constructed by the defendant for a previous owner (sometimes called 'transferred loss' cases);
3. pure economic loss that is an indirect consequence of negligently performed professional legal services that were contracted for by a third person;
4. pure economic loss suffered by plaintiffs who gamble.

Note that, while cases of pure economic loss are often classified in accordance with these four categories (in addition to negligent misstatements discussed above in section 14.4), novel fact scenarios may prompt courts to find liability for pure economic loss in cases that do not fit squarely into any of these categories.

Most of the cases covered in this section (with the exception of the gambling cases) arise out of complicated multiparty fact patterns involving indirectly caused losses. The cases where a public authority has been sued for causing a pure economic loss to a plaintiff are covered in section 14.2 above. Remember that this section should also be read in conjunction with section 14.4 above, which covers negligent statements.

Test your understanding

Explain why most of the cases in this area of pure economic loss arise out of multiparty fact patterns involving indirectly caused financial loss and relatively few arise from two-party factual scenarios.

14.5.1 The problem of pure economic loss

The problems associated with pure economic loss arise because the duty test laid down by Lord Atkin's harm-based neighbour principle and the 'but for' test of causation cannot provide a clear and obvious limit on the extent of liability in negligence. As Gibbs

J explained at 550 in the landmark case of *Caltex Oil (Australia) Pty Ltd v The Dredge 'Willemstad'* (1976), 'the world of commerce would come to a halt and ordinary life would become intolerable' if we were liable for every foreseeable adverse consequence of our acts and omissions. Gibbs J illustrated this point at 551 by pointing to the extensive losses that could ensue if a ship knocked down a bridge and cut off a large suburban area containing shops, homes and factories from its means of access to a city – or if a driver accidentally cut off the power supply to a large industrial area, causing workers to lose their income. His Honour labelled the burden of liability in such cases as 'out of all proportion' to the wrong and described the possible claims as 'unlimited in number and crippling in amount'. This fear of unlimited liability in negligence was not new. Lord Buckmaster, one of the dissenting judges in *Donoghue v Stevenson* (1932), raised similar concerns at the birth of negligence at 577, saying: 'If one step, why not fifty?' And in *Caltex Oil (Australia) Pty Ltd v The Dredge 'Willemstad'* (1976), Stephen J referred at 568–9 to the looming 'spectre' of indeterminate liability made famous by Cardozo CJ and the fears of a 'great influx of cases' as two of the reasons why judges in the past had imposed a 'Draconic' exclusory rule forbidding recovery for pure economic loss.[9]

In *Bryan v Maloney* (1995), Mason CJ, Deane and Gaudron JJ summarised at 618 the two primary concerns that lay behind the old rule denying liability:

> One policy consideration which may militate against recognition of a [duty] in a category of case involving mere economic loss is the law's concern to avoid the imposition of liability 'in an indeterminate amount for an indeterminate time to an indeterminate class'. Another consideration is the perception that, in a competitive world where one person's economic gain is commonly another's loss, a duty to take reasonable care to avoid causing mere economic loss to another, as distinct from physical injury to another's person or property, may be inconsistent with community standards in relation to what is ordinarily legitimate in the pursuit of personal advantage. [References omitted.]

Other concerns, as listed by McHugh J in *Woolcock Street Investments Pty Ltd v CDG Pty Ltd* (2004) at [88]–[104], are as follows:

- the reluctance to impose a responsibility to control third parties;
- a fear of outflanking the law of contract;
- the floodgates argument;
- a fear of disproportionate liability;
- the lack of a measurable standard of care; and
- circumventing the policy of limitation legislation.

The old exclusionary rule did at least offer some certainty, as McHugh J pointed out in *Perre v Apand Pty Ltd* (1999) at [87]. However, that certainty was lost in Australia in 1975 because the High Court made an exception to the rule when deciding in *Caltex Oil (Australia) Pty Ltd v The Dredge 'Willemstad'* (1976) that 'economic damage is, no less

9 Stephen J referred to the 'exclusory' rule, but later cases use the term 'exclusionary' rule.

than property damage, a very real detriment' worthy of protection: see Mason J at 591. The decision accepted the general rule against imposing liability, but allowed that a duty could exist in some circumstances. This case led the courts to spend most of the next 20 years not only searching for a principled approach to deciding the duty question for the 'novel' forms of negligence, but also seeking an acceptable 'control device' that would deal with the problem of indeterminate liability. The fact that the High Court could not agree on a methodology of negligence until 2001 means that the (very lengthy) cases in this area of the law are difficult to disentangle and time consuming to read, and so the discussion in this section will focus on highlighting the principles that finally emerged at the end of this period and on identifying the important factual matters that accounted for the decisions in these cases. In an interesting turn of events, in 2024 the High Court revisited the issue of pure economic loss in *Mallonland Pty Ltd v Advanta Seeds Pty Ltd* (2024), and after almost five decades of progressively opening up the field, returned to a much stricter approach.

14.5.2 Relevant salient features

The law in the area of pure economic loss has not developed to a position where 'there has been enunciated a governing principle applicable in all cases', as Gaudron J pointed out in *Perre v Apand Pty Ltd* (1999) at [25], concluding: 'Perhaps it never will.' In the same case, McHugh J also doubted that there would ever be a 'correct approach' to determining the wider duty question in negligence, saying at [76]: 'Perhaps none is possible.' These doubts were justified in the years leading up to *Sullivan v Moody* (2001), but since that time, the High Court has abandoned the search for a single unifying principle and articulated a 'multi-faceted' approach that seeks a balance both between the competing rights and duties of the parties and between the relevant principles and salient features emerging from the case law. In fact, it is largely because of the lengthy process of debate in the 'novel' cases dealing with pure psychiatric injury and pure economic loss that the new methodology emerged. Beyond the two controlling principles of reasonable foreseeability of harm and fault, the most important supplementing salient features in this area of the law are, once again, certainty or indeterminacy, vulnerability (with important caveats now in place after the decision in *Mallonland Pty Ltd v Advanta Seeds Pty Ltd* (2024)), autonomy and coherence.

14.5.2.1 Certainty and indeterminacy

Indeterminate liability is one of the most important considerations that leads the courts to reject a duty in cases of pure economic loss: see Gaudron J in *Perre v Apand Pty Ltd* (1999) at [32], citing Mason CJ, Deane and Gaudron JJ at 618 in *Bryan v Maloney* (1995), in turn citing Cardozo CJ in *Ultramares Corporation v Touche* (1931) at 444. This has now also been reaffirmed by Gaegeler CJ, Gordon, Steward, Gleeson, Jagot and Beech-Jones JJ in *Mallonland Pty Ltd v Advanta Seeds Pty Ltd* (2024) at [31]–[32]. However, in *Perre v Apand Pty Ltd* (1999) Gaudron J pointed out at [32] that 'it is not necessarily fatal to the recognition of a duty of care that the duty is owed to a class whose members cannot be identified with complete accuracy'. McHugh J explained at [107]–[108]:

> Liability is indeterminate only when it cannot be realistically calculated ... The number of claims or their size, therefore, does not of itself raise any issue of indeterminacy. Indeterminacy depends upon what the defendant knew or ought to have known of the number of claimants and the nature of their likely claims, not the number or size of those claims.

So, this principle points away from imposing a duty in cases where the liability is truly indeterminate (as opposed to large in extent), but will point towards imposing liability in cases where the plaintiff is either:

- a known identified individual (eg the disappointed beneficiary in *Hill v Van Erp* (1997));
- a reasonably foreseeable or obviously vulnerable victim (eg the plaintiff who was one of two parties known to use the oil pipeline in *Caltex Oil (Australia) Pty Ltd v The Dredge 'Willemstad'* (1976), or the subsequent owner of the house in *Bryan v Maloney* (1995)); or
- a member of an ascertainable or specific class of victims (eg the farmers within the 20 km exclusion zone in *Perre v Apand Pty Ltd* (1999)).

14.5.2.2 Vulnerability

Vulnerability, together with indeterminacy, has dominated the High Court's reasoning in pure economic loss cases for decades. If the relationship between the plaintiffs and the defendants is characterised by vulnerability in the special legal sense that the plaintiffs are unable to protect themselves from the risk by taking any other reasonable measures, then this feature will point strongly towards imposing a duty. This is even more pronounced if the plaintiff is known by the defendant to be vulnerable and the defendant has some special degree of control over matters affecting the plaintiff. Many of the judges in *Perre v Apand Pty Ltd* (1999) referred to these special features of control, knowledge and reliance that together indicate vulnerability.

Case example

- *Perre v Apand Pty Ltd* (1999), Gleeson CJ at [10]–[11]:

> Moreover, knowledge (actual, or that which a reasonable person would have) of an individual, or an ascertainable class of persons, who is or are reliant, and therefore vulnerable, is a significant factor in establishing a duty of care.

- *Perre v Apand Pty Ltd* (1999), McHugh J at [124]–[125]:

> Vulnerability will often include, but not be synonymous with, concepts of reliance and assumption of responsibility ... Reliance and assumption of responsibility are merely indicators of the plaintiff's vulnerability to harm from the defendant's conduct, and it is the concept of vulnerability rather than these evidentiary indicators which is the relevant criterion for determining whether a duty of care exists.

- *Perre v Apand Pty Ltd* (1999), Gaudron J at [37]:

> In *Hill*, both Gummow J and I saw the solicitor's control over the realisation of the intentions of the testatrix as a special factor warranting the imposition of a duty of care. And Dawson J, with whom Toohey J agreed, placed emphasis on the fact that 'the intended beneficiary's interests [were] totally and unavoidably dependent upon the proper performance of a function within the sole province of the solicitor' which, of course, is simply the corollary of the solicitor's control. [References omitted.]

On the other hand, if a plaintiff is not vulnerable in the special legal sense, then this finding can weigh decisively against imposing a duty.

Case examples

- In *Perre v Apand Pty Ltd* (1999) McHugh J said at [118]:

> The vulnerability of the plaintiff to harm from the defendant's conduct is therefore ordinarily a prerequisite to imposing a duty. If the plaintiff has taken, or could have taken steps to protect itself from the defendant's conduct and was not induced by the defendant's conduct from taking such steps, there is no reason why the law should step in and impose a duty on the defendant to protect the plaintiff from the risk of pure economic loss.

- In *Woolcock Street Investments Pty Ltd v CDG Pty Ltd* (2004), Gleeson CJ, Gummow, Hayne and Heydon JJ at [23]–[24] and [31]–[33], and McHugh J at [80], all identified the fact that the plaintiff was in a position to protect themself as one reason why no duty was imposed on the defendant in this case. McHugh J said at [80]:

> In this context, vulnerability to risk means not that the plaintiff was exposed to risk but that by reason of ignorance or social, political or economic constraints, the plaintiff was not able to protect him or herself from the risk of injury.

His Honour concluded at [90] that the plaintiffs' capacity to protect themselves 'from damage by means of contractual obligations' is one of the 'decisive' reasons for rejecting a duty of care in pure economic loss cases.

- In *Mallonland Pty Ltd v Advanta Seeds* (2024), Gaegeler CJ, Gordon, Steward, Gleeson, Jagot, Beech-Jones JJ at [39] summarised the current state of the law on vulnerability:

> The relevant vulnerability is the plaintiff's inability to protect him or herself from the economic loss that eventuated as a consequence of a defendant's carelessness, either entirely or in a way that would cast the consequence of loss on the defendant (for example, by contractual stipulations). A mere likelihood of suffering economic loss if reasonable care is not taken will not amount to vulnerability ... [The] capacity of a person to protect him or herself from economic loss by contractual agreement (or, by analogy, by any other reasonable means) is a reason, and often a decisive one, for rejecting the existence of a duty of care. [References omitted.]

14.5.2.3 Autonomy (and assumption of responsibility)

Autonomy is another important consideration that is now commonly used by the High Court when deciding whether to impose a duty. In cases of pure economic loss, the value of the defendant's 'commercial freedom' is one of the factors that justifies the general reluctance to impose a duty, but that freedom is not absolute. It must be weighed against the plaintiff's known vulnerability and considered in the light of any existing duties owed by the defendant in the circumstances. Relevant to the issue of autonomy is whether the defendant has 'assumed responsibility' in such a way that the plaintiff is legitimately relying on the defendant's actions.

Case examples

- McHugh J explained in *Perre v Apand Pty Ltd* (1999) at [114] and [115] how the 'common law's concern for the autonomy of the individual and its desire to give effect to the choices of the individual by not burdening their freedom of action' can justify the rule that there is no general duty to avoid causing economic losses on a business competitor:

  > One of the central tenets of the common law is that a person is legally responsible for his or her choices. It is a corollary of that responsibility that a person is entitled to make those choices for him or her self without unjustifiable interference from others. In other words, the common law regards individuals as autonomous beings entitled to make, but responsible for, their own choices.
  >
  > ... In any organised society, however, individuals cannot have complete autonomy, for the good government of a society is impossible unless the sovereign power in that society has power in various circumstances to coerce the citizen. Nevertheless, the common law has generally sought to interfere with the autonomy of individuals only to the extent necessary for the maintenance of society.

  McHugh J went on to point out at [123] that the vulnerability of the plaintiff may often justify impinging on that commercial freedom by imposing a duty, especially when the plaintiff could not have protected itself in contract.
- In *Woolcock Street Investments Pty Ltd v CDG Pty Ltd* (2004), McHugh J explained at [78]–[79] that 'the common law's concern for autonomy', which justifies protecting a defendant who is 'legitimately protecting or pursuing his or her commercial interests', did not carry great weight 'in the context of claims for damages for pure economic loss arising out of the defective design or construction of a building'. This was because:

  > [t]hose involved in the building are already under a duty to the first owner to avoid physical injury to the owner's person and property. Consequently, imposing a duty to avoid economic loss to the first or a subsequent owner is not inconsistent with the pursuit of the legitimate interests of those who design or construct the building.
- In *Mallonland Pty Ltd v Advanta Seeds* (2024), Gaegeler CJ, Gordon, Steward, Gleeson, Jagot and Beech-Jones JJ touched on a related matter, that of 'assumption of responsibility', which, when established, suggests that a defendant ought to be liable for the consequences of actions undertaken by the plaintiff in reliance of that assumption of responsibility. This can occur for

types of conduct that would normally be labelled as exercises of the defendant's autonomy. Their Honours explained at [33]–[34] that there were strict limitations on the notion of 'assumption of responsibility' and the ability of a defendant to demonstrate that they had disclaimed responsibility (as ended up being the case in *Mallonland*, noted below):

> Where a defendant has assumed a responsibility towards the plaintiff to take reasonable care to avoid economic loss to the plaintiff, a duty of care may well be established. The term 'assumption of responsibility' has been criticised as 'imprecise and beguiling but deceptively simple'. An assumption of responsibility is best understood as an undertaking (whether express or implied) by a person to take on a task or job for another person or class of persons, from which it can be inferred that the first person accepted that he or she would take reasonable care when engaging in that task or job.
>
> Where a duty to take reasonable care to avoid causing pure economic loss is said to arise out of an assumption of responsibility by a defendant to a particular person or class of persons, the defendant can negate or limit that assumption and thus the duty by words or conduct directed to that person or class. That is because such a negation or limitation amounts to a denial of an assumption of responsibility on the part of the defendant which the person or class cannot ignore or reject. For example, no duty to avoid causing pure economic loss will arise in connection with the provision of advice or information if the defendant 'had effectually disclaimed any responsibility for it'. [References omitted.]

So, in cases where the defendants' autonomy and their freedom to pursue their own interest have already been justifiably fettered by another pre-existing duty, the coherence principle will then weigh in favour of imposing a concurrent duty to avoid causing pure economic loss.

14.5.2.4 Coherence

Coherence is based on the ideal that judges' decisions should produce a coherent set of rules that is consistent with previous judicial and legislative decisions and the goals that underpin them. Citing *Sullivan v Moody* (2001), McHugh J explained at [102] in *Woolcock Street Investments Pty Ltd v CDG Pty Ltd* (2004) that while the law is too complex to be 'a seamless web', it is 'always relevant in determining whether to create, extend or formulate a duty in tort to consider whether it is consistent with other legal doctrines, principles and policies'. So, the feature of coherence requires the judges to avoid recognising any new duty if it would be *inconsistent* with the other duties already imposed on the defendant by other parts of the law. Conversely, the circumstances could weigh in favour of imposing a new duty to avoid causing pure economic loss to the plaintiff if that duty *is consistent* with an existing duty already owed by the defendant. This is particularly important in multiparty scenarios where the eventual plaintiff suffers as a result of the defendant's breach of a duty already owed to another person and where the new duty protects the eventual plaintiff from the same risk that was covered by the original duty.

Case examples

- In *Caltex Oil (Australia) Pty Ltd v The Dredge 'Willemstad'* (1976), the new duty imposed on the defendant, to avoid causing financial loss to the plaintiff who transported its oil through a pipeline owned by another party, was consistent with the defendant's pre-existing duty in negligence owed to the owner of the pipeline (which protected it from the risk of physical damage and consequential economic loss).
- In *Hill v Van Erp* (1997), the defendant solicitor owed a pre-existing duty to the testator who contracted with the solicitor to prepare her will in order to bestow a benefit on the beneficiary, and this duty was consistent with the new duty imposed by the Court on the solicitor to avoid causing pure economic loss to the plaintiff, the disappointed beneficiary.
- In *Perre v Apand Pty Ltd* (1999), the new duty owed by the defendant to avoid causing financial loss to the plaintiffs was consistent with the pre-existing duty in negligence and in contract to avoid providing another party in the same district with diseased potato seed stock.
- By contrast, in *Woolcock Street Investments Pty Ltd v CDG Pty Ltd* (2004), the new duty invoked by the plaintiff was not consistent with the pre-existing duty originally owed by the defendants to the third party, and so the extra duty was not recognised in the circumstances.
- In *Mallonland Pty Ltd v Advanta Seeds Pty Ltd* (2024), the alleged new duty to be owed by the defendant to avoid causing economic loss to the plaintiffs was inconsistent with the pre-existing disclaimer of liability asserted by the defendants.

14.5.2.5 Goal-based coherence

The ideal of coherence also allows judges to take into account wider community goals, shared values and common community interests like the free communication of opinion, wisdom and experience, the maintenance of security, public safety and other 'good' things. So, if a new duty is consistent with these goals and values, that factor will weigh in favour of imposing a duty and, conversely, if the new duty would be inconsistent with those defining values, it will weigh against imposing the duty.

Case example

In *Hill v Van Erp* (1997) McHugh J explained at 211 that one of the reasons for refusing to impose a general duty to avoid causing another person to suffer pure economic loss lay in the fact that any such duty would be inconsistent with one of the basic tenets underpinning our free enterprise society, which allows one person to compete with another with the aim of taking away their rival's market share and succeeding at the cost of the other. In words reminiscent of the objections raised by the dissenters in *Donoghue v Stevenson* (1932), McHugh J added that another reason for refusing a duty was the sense that it would be inconsistent with the law of contract to allow a plaintiff to 'be a free rider on the contract' between the defendant and another person. However, as McHugh J pointed out at [123] in *Perre v Apand Pty Ltd* (1999), when the assumptions underlying the law of contract are negated on the facts and when other principles weigh in favour of imposing liability, a duty can be justified:

One of the assumptions of the law of contract, for example, is that the parties can bargain to protect their interests. A plaintiff who is vulnerable – for whatever reason – cannot do this in any meaningful way. In its quest for corrective justice, the law of negligence may be able to fill the gap which the law of contract has left.

14.5.2.6 Role-based coherence

Coherence also requires that there be a principled division of roles between courts and legislators, and this ideal was invoked in the landmark case that recognised liability for pure economic loss consequent upon material physical damage negligently caused by the defendant to a third party.

Case example

In *Caltex Oil (Australia) Pty Ltd v The Dredge 'Willemstad'* (1976) Stephen J explained at 570 that the Court's job is to deliver what 'justice and morality' require. However, his Honour maintained at 580–1 that this does not extend to taking any policy-based considerations such as 'loss spreading' into account:

> The task of the courts remains that of loss fixing rather than loss spreading and if this is to be altered it is, in my view, a matter for direct legislative action rather than for the courts. It should be undertaken, if at all, openly and after adequate public inquiry and parliamentary debate and not worked towards covertly, in the course of judicial decision, by the adoption of policy factors which assume its desirability as a goal and operate to further its attainment.
>
> But there is, I think, no justification for the courts, when deciding actions in tort between private litigants, to make use of such views as policy determinants in the absence of any independent opportunity to test their soundness and without parliamentary sanction for the departure from pre-existing goals of the law of torts which their espousal involves.

14.5.3 Key cases

Cases dealing with pure psychiatric injury and pure economic loss offered the High Court the opportunity to develop a distinctive Australian approach to the duty question. Both of these controversial categories of negligence excite judicial concerns about uncontrolled liability, and both have compelled a search for 'something more' than reasonable foreseeability to ground the duty. The two categories are equally complicated in that both often arise out of complex multiparty factual scenarios, as Figures 14.2, 14.5 and 14.7 illustrate. On a deeper level, one of the most significant features uniting these two categories of case is the fact that both are concerned with a kind of harm that is not protected by a primary right. In contrast with the recognised right that we have to the physical integrity of our bodies, land and goods, we do not have (or at least did not used to have) any similar right to the integrity of our more 'incorporeal' interests in financial security or psychological equanimity. Rather, these interests have traditionally attracted only limited protection. One of the significant differences between the two categories lies in the fact that, while it is rare for one person to intend to create pure psychiatric injury, it is both common (and in many cases perfectly lawful) for one person to intend to cause economic loss to another. Consequently, the task of drawing a line between acceptable and unacceptable conduct causing pure economic loss is made all the more difficult. The task of finding that 'control mechanism or limitation' was first discussed in 1976 in the landmark case of *Caltex Oil (Australia) Pty Ltd v The Dredge 'Willemstad'*, which set up the first category (other than negligent misstatement) where liability for pure economic loss is allowed: relational economic loss.

Figure 14.6 Pure economic loss scenario: Two-party cases

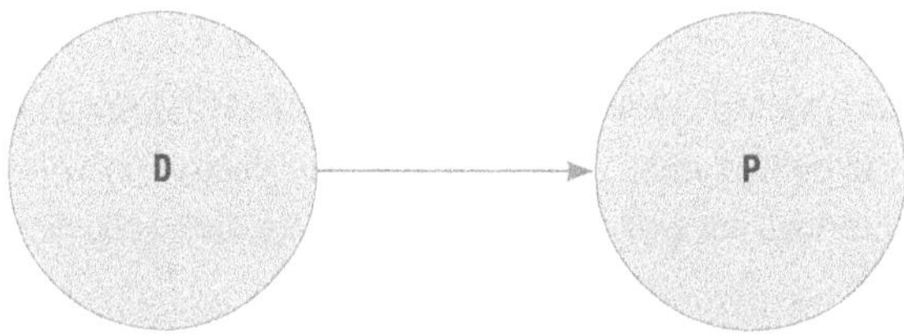

The solid line in Figure 14.6 shows the track of harm.

Figure 14.7 Pure economic loss scenario: Three-party cases

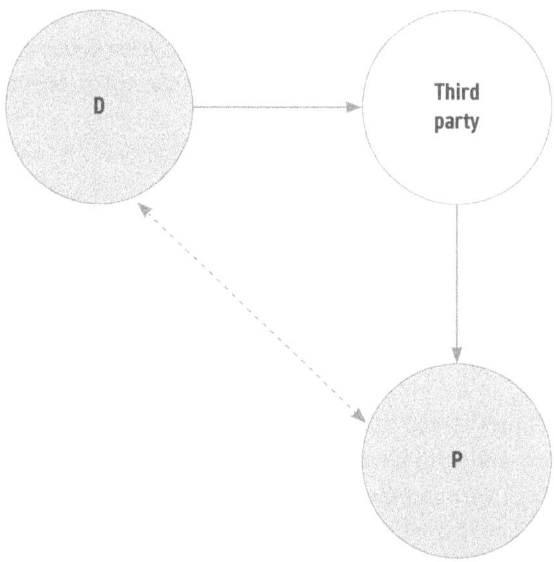

The solid lines in Figure 14.7 show the tracks of harm. The dotted line shows the new legal relationships and justifications needed. Examples of this legal relationship include *Caltex Oil v The Dredge* 'Willemstad' (1976), *Perre v Apand Pty Ltd* (1999), *Bryan v Maloney* (1995) *Hawkins v Clayton* (1988) and *Hill v Van Erp* (1997).

14.5.3.1 Economic loss flowing from material physical damage negligently caused to the property of a third person (or relational economic loss)

Liability for pure economic loss may be imposed on a defendant whose negligent conduct has caused two different categories of harm to two separate, but related plaintiffs. In these 'relational loss' cases, where the same activity initially causes direct material damage to one person's property and then indirectly causes a 'pure' economic loss to another closely related party, the issue is whether the court will recognise a duty owed by the defendant to the second plaintiff who suffered only that economic loss. There are three leading High Court cases under this category where the triggering event is the causing of material physical damage.

Case example

Caltex Oil (Australia) Pty Ltd v The Dredge 'Willemstad' (1976) arose out of a three-party scenario where Caltex Oil (P), successfully sued the dredge Willemstad (D), for causing it to suffer pure economic loss after D negligently fractured an oil-carrying pipeline that was owned by a third party, Australian Oil Refining Pty Ltd (AOR). P's depot and AOR's refinery were located opposite each other across Botany Bay. They were linked by a pipeline. AOR owned the pipeline but both parties used it in the course of their mutually related businesses of refining and distributing oil. The oil was sent to and from one establishment to the other through AOR's pipeline, but after D damaged the pipeline, P was forced to use a different and more costly method of transport. Both parties successfully sued D, but the issue in the High Court was whether D owed a duty to P to avoid causing it to suffer a pure economic loss.

The High Court decided unanimously that D did owe a duty to P in the circumstances. For the reasons outlined in section 14.5.1 above, four of the judges maintained that, as a general rule, one person does not owe a duty to another to avoid causing pure economic loss: see Gibbs J at 555, Stephen J at 558–9, Mason J at 592 and Jacobs J at 598. These judges allowed a modification to the rule in this case where the economic loss was the result of negligent conduct by D that caused material physical damage to the property of another. However, conscious of the problem of indeterminacy, the judges insisted that 'something more' was needed in such a case. Stephen J explained at 573–4 why 'an additional control mechanism is necessary':

> But if economic loss is to be compensated its inherent capacity to manifest itself at several removes from the direct detriment inflicted by the defendant's carelessness makes reasonable foreseeability an inadequate control mechanism.

Gibbs J stated at 555 that the exceptional feature justifying liability in this case was the fact that D had 'the knowledge or means of knowledge that the plaintiff individually, and not merely as a member of an unascertained class' was likely in the circumstances to suffer economic loss. Gibbs J also stressed at 555 that 'all the facts of the particular case will have to be considered' and noted, as 'material' details, the two facts that the 'property of the plaintiff was in physical proximity to the damaged property' and that P and the third party were 'engaged in a common adventure'.

Mason J also noted at 593 that the fact that D in this case could 'reasonably foresee that a specific individual, as distinct from a general class of persons, will suffer financial loss' is critical because it 'eliminates or diminishes the prospect' of indeterminate liability. So in this case, the fact that the pipeline was used only by AOR and P meant that the possibility of indeterminate liability was absent. Furthermore, as Gleeson CJ would point out in the later case of *Perre v Apand Pty Ltd* (1999) at [11], the 'obvious vulnerability' of the specific plaintiff (noted by the judges in *Caltex (Australia) Pty Ltd v The Dredge 'Willemstad'* (1976) at 555, 576–7 and 593) also illustrated 'the idea that in a given case, the degree (and nature) of foreseeability may have an important bearing on whether there is a duty of care'.

Stephen J noted at 570 that the fact that the detriment in these cases 'manifests itself in monetary terms' means that there is 'nothing about economic loss which makes it inherently unsuited to compensation by an award of damages'. Emphasising at 574 the need for a 'control mechanism based on notions of proximity', Stephen J pointed at 576–7 to 'a number of salient features' that would be characteristic of this type of pure economic loss and concluded that a duty was owed. The features noted by Stephen J were:

> acknowledgment that a duty of care was owed to AOR; the fact that Caltex was not less proximately concerned than was AOR in the continued integrity of the pipeline; the very nature of the pipeline, a major mode of conveyance of products to an identifiable recipient, whose use of its terminal was for the receipt of such products; the nature of the economic loss, direct and inevitably flowing from the severing of the pipeline and not in any sense a matter for speculation only ...

The next case of *Perre v Apand Pty Ltd* (1999) took the reasoning from *Caltex Oil (Australia) Pty Ltd v The Dredge 'Willemstad'* (1976) one step further, but *Perre v Apand Pty Ltd* (1999) is a long and testing case to read, because it contains seven separate judgments that took different approaches to the issue that dominated the High Court in the late 20th and early 21st centuries – namely, the search for a methodology of duty. Despite the fact that little progress was made on the issue of methodology in *Perre v Apand Pty Ltd* (1999), the High Court did make some progress towards solving the problem of indeterminacy in pure economic loss cases. This was possible because, by 1999, the new theme of vulnerability had emerged as a crucial factor in deciding whether to impose a duty. By adding this theme to the emerging focus on autonomy and 'commercial freedom', the High Court was able to advance the law. So, with the wisdom of hindsight provided by the later case of *Sullivan v Moody* (2001), which *did* resolve the bigger problem of methodology, it is now possible to face *Perre v Apand Pty Ltd* (1999) with considerably more confidence than was felt by those who read the case at the time it was delivered.

Case example

Perre v Apand Pty Ltd (1999) arose out of a multiparty scenario involving one defendant, Apand Pty Ltd (Apand), and several plaintiffs who were adversely affected by Apand's conduct in supplying diseased potato seed stock to Sparnons, who, like some of their neighbours in South Australia, grew potatoes for sale in the lucrative crisping market in Western Australia. The stock negligently supplied by Apand to Sparnons was infected with bacterial wilt. The quarantine rules governing the Western Australian market imposed a strict ban on the importation of any potatoes grown within 20 kilometres of any disease-affected land, and this meant not only that Sparnons, the primary victims, were unable to sell their potatoes in Western Australia, but also that several other plaintiffs in the district indirectly suffered financial losses as a result of Apand's negligence. The secondary victims included the Perres, who were growers, and others in the district who were potato processors. All plaintiffs were ultimately successful. The issue before the High Court was whether Apand owed a duty to avoid causing pure economic loss to the 'secondary' plaintiffs.

Common themes that emerged from the disparate judgments can be summarised under the four main salient features governing pure economic loss: namely, vulnerability, certainty, autonomy and coherence.

- *Vulnerability:* The plaintiffs were vulnerable to Apand in the sense that they were unable to protect themselves by contract or by physical barriers from the risk posed by the diseased stock. Apand, who supplied potato seed stock to 60 per cent of the Australian crisping industry, had knowledge of the risks of bacterial wilt and the rules governing the market and had full control over the condition of the stock sent to Sparnons: see Gleeson CJ at [11]–[13], Gaudron J at [37]–[42], McHugh J at [118]–[119] and [149]–[151], Gummow J at [216], Kirby J at [296], and Callinan J at [408] and [416].
- *Certainty:* It was possible for Apand to identify the plaintiffs as an 'ascertainable class of vulnerable persons' with sufficient certainty because of the operation of the 20 km quarantine rule. This meant that the concerns about indeterminate liability did not weigh against imposing the duty in these circumstances: see Gleeson CJ at [13]–[15], Gaudron J at [32]–[33], McHugh J at [106]–[129], Gummow J at [214], Kirby J at [296]–[298], Hayne J at [336]–[344] and Callinan J at [409]. McHugh J said that there is 'no reason to limit the existence of a duty to an "identified plaintiff"' (at [109]) or to a 'defined and small class' (at [139]).
- *Autonomy:* Apand's autonomy and commercial freedom were not unreasonably burdened by extending its liability for its conduct in supplying the diseased potato stock by imposing a duty on the plaintiffs, because Apand was already under a duty to take reasonable care in the original supply of seed stock to Sparnons: see McHugh J at [50] and [146]–[148], Kirby J at [300]–[301] and Callinan J at [421].
- *Coherence:* Imposing a new duty on Apand was consistent not only with their duties to Sparnons, but also with the fact that any deliberate supply of such diseased stock would have been illegal and would have exposed the defendants to liability under other torts. This, plus the fact that the new duty was also consistent with the law governing the deliberate interference with another's trade and the successive statutory provisions of the South Australian *Fruit and Plant Protection Acts*, suggested that the duty would not 'cut across accepted bases of economic organisation of this society or ... prevent ordinary commercial dealings', as Hayne J explained at [345]–[350]. See also McHugh J at [120]–[122] and Callinan J at [395] and [424].

McHugh J summed up the application of these crucial features at [50]:

> The losses suffered by the Perres were a reasonably foreseeable consequence of Apand's conduct in supplying the diseased seed; the Perres were members of a class whose members, whether numerous or not, were ascertainable by Apand; the Perres' business was vulnerably exposed to Apand's conduct because the Perres were not in a position to protect themselves against the effects of Apand's negligence apart from insurance (which is not a relevant factor); imposing the duty on Apand does not

expose it to indeterminate liability although its liability may be large; imposing the duty does not unreasonably interfere with Apand's commercial freedom because it was already under a duty to the Sparnons to take reasonable care; and Apand knew of the risk to potato growers and the consequences of that risk occurring.

The final case on relational loss is the decision of the High Court in *Mallonland Pty Ltd v Advanta Seeds Pty Ltd* (2024), which confirms the validity of *Caltex Oil (Australia) Pty Ltd v The Dredge 'Willemstad'* (1976), while at the same time re-establishing strict boundaries with respect to relational economic loss. Such boundaries had arguably become more relaxed in the aftermath of *Perre v Apand Pty Ltd* (1999) and the subsequent adoption of the salient feature methodology in *Sullivan v Moody*, particularly as a result of the prevalence of 'vulnerability' as a prominent salient feature of negligence cases.

Case example

Mallonland Pty Ltd v Advanta Seeds Pty Ltd (2024) involved several farmers who purchased grain sorghum seeds produced by Advanta Seeds from a third party. Some of the bags of seeds turned out to be contaminated with shattercane, a form of grass that is similar in appearance to sorghum, but is not useable for grain crops, and spreads widely and fast. It is also a competitor of sorghum and can cause significant long-term damage to sorghum cultivation. Indeed, eradication requires fields to be sprayed and left uncultivated for several growing seasons. At trial, it became apparent that shattercane found its way into the bags of grain sorghum seeds as a result of the producer's negligence in the production process of a specific batch of seeds. The ensuing contamination of the fields caused the farmers to incur the significant cost of applying insecticides and herbicides to the crops, and significant loss of revenue due to leaving the fields uncultivated for a number of years.

The bags of seeds purchased by the growers displayed a disclaimer drawing attention to the conditions of sale and use, as well as a product description guaranteeing a minimum of 99 per cent purity, but allowing the possibility of other seeds.

The High Court rejected the appeal brought by the unsuccessful farmers and took the opportunity to clarify the law on relational economic loss, particularly with respect to the relevance and meaning of vulnerability and assumption of responsibility in this space.

- *Vulnerability:* The farmers could not be said to be vulnerable. Edelman J describes vulnerability at [96] in the following terms:

  > a reference to the plaintiff's inability to protect itself from the consequences of a defendant's want of reasonable care, either entirely or at least in a way which would cast the consequences of loss on the defendant.

  In this sense, vulnerability cannot become a 'catch-all' salient feature that protects one from unfavourable economic consequences by the simple fact that a defendant has somehow contributed to that result. Vulnerability arises where a plaintiff is materially unable to protect itself, and this was not the case with the farmers, who at a minimum could have heeded the warning and disclaimer printed on the bags before sowing the seeds. Gageler CJ, Gordon, Steward, Gleeson, Jagot and Beech-Jones JJ explain at [39]:

> [A] matter that adherence to the required incremental and analogical approach has identified as relevant to the existence of a duty of care to avoid causing pure economic loss is a plaintiff's 'vulnerability' to the particular type of economic loss that eventuated. The relevant vulnerability is the plaintiff's inability to protect him or herself from the economic loss that eventuated as a consequence of a defendant's carelessness, either entirely or in a way that would cast the consequence of loss on the defendant (for example, by contractual stipulations). A mere likelihood of suffering economic loss if reasonable care is not taken will not amount to vulnerability. As McHugh J explained it in *Woolcock Street Investments Pty Ltd v CDG Pty Ltd*, a plaintiff may be unable to protect him or herself from the risk of economic loss by reason of 'ignorance or social, political or economic constraints'. Conversely, the capacity of a person to protect him or herself from economic loss by contractual agreement (or, by analogy, by any other reasonable means) is a reason, and often a decisive one, for rejecting the existence of a duty of care.

- *Assumption of responsibility:* Again, the term is to be understood to have a specific meaning. This is illustrated by Gageler CJ, Gordon, Steward, Gleeson, Jagot and Beech-Jones JJ at [33]–[34], quoted above. Not only can there be no assumption of responsibility in a situation where a disclaimer is explicitly provided (as was the case in *Mallonland*), but such an assumption will only exist in the very restricted perimeter of circumstances where an explicit or implicit undertaking is evident. This is to say that, for example, the simple fact of selling a product in the course of a commercial transaction cannot, in and of itself, amount to an assumption of responsibility by the producer of a certain good as to the consequences of the use of the product by subsequent buyers. So, while the overall approach laid out in *Caltex* remains valid, its interpretation, which had become expansive in the aftermath of *Perre* and the subsequent adoption of the salient features approach in *Sullivan v Moody* (2001), has now been significantly reined in.

In reading *Mallonland* you should note Edelman J's concurring judgment, in which his Honour puts into question the validity and usefulness of the salient features approach more generally, at least with reference to cases of pure economic loss. His most powerful critique comes at [103], where he challenges reliance on vulnerability by the High Court in *Perre:*

> As a matter of principle, vulnerability is also difficult to justify as a central salient feature. Even if the successful plaintiffs in *Perre* could all be said to have been vulnerable, why should they be able to recover at common law whilst the infant dependants of a deceased or severely injured tort victim cannot? Further, as Professor Stevens has powerfully argued:
>
> > 'If we consider the duty of care in the law of torts to be a duty owed to another imposed by law, is it acceptable to require parties in the real world to deduce their obligations one to another by deduction from such a subtle, indeed Byzantine, concept as that of vulnerability?' [Reference omitted.]

While the majority in *Mallonland* upheld *Caltex* and *Perre*, although in much narrower terms than what reliance on salient features had opened the door to in the aftermath of the latter, it is not impossible that the law might continue to develop – and quite likely in an increasingly restrictive manner.

14.5.3.2 Economic loss caused by the defendant to a subsequent purchaser of a defective building

The previous subsection explained that liability for pure economic loss may be imposed on a defendant whose negligent conduct has caused two different categories of harm to two separate, but related plaintiffs. In the 'transferred loss' cases, where the defendant's conduct takes the form of negligently constructing a defective building that indirectly causes a subsequent purchaser to incur a financial loss, the issue is whether the builder owes a duty to that subsequent purchaser. The main difference between the building cases and the *Caltex Oil (Australia) Pty Ltd v The Dredge 'Willemstad'* category of cases lies in the fact that in the latter, the quantum of the defendants' liability was extended and multiplied by the recognition of the new duty, whereas in the building cases the extent of liability does not increase if the extra duty is recognised. Rather, the initial quantum of damage is conserved when the potential loss is transferred from the initial owner of the house (who would have had a remedy) to a subsequent purchaser (who may be deprived of a remedy unless negligence law fills the gap). There are two leading High Court cases under this 'transferred loss' category where the triggering event is the negligent construction of a building; each gave rise to a different outcome and the critical feature in these cases was the issue of vulnerability and the nature of the plaintiff.

Case example

In *Bryan v Maloney* (1995), Maloney (P) bought a house in 1986 from the second owners, who had bought it from the initial owner, who had contracted with Bryan (D) to build the private dwelling in 1979. P successfully sued D for his negligent conduct in building the house with inadequate footings, which caused her to incur financial costs when the defects led to extensive cracking six months after purchase and she had to pay for repairs and reconstruction. The issue in the High Court was whether D owed a duty to P and the case, which was heard in 1994, was argued mainly on the basis of proximity theory. It was held by a 4:1 majority that D did owe a duty in these circumstances. Brennan J dissented and held that no duty was owed to such a remote purchaser.

The joint judgment of Mason CJ, Deane and Gaudron JJ noted at 618 the difficulties of indeterminate liability and the possible inconsistency in allowing liability for pure economic loss in a community that allows for and encourages conduct in 'legitimate pursuit of personal advantage'. The joint judgment then examined other leading cases where concurrent duties in both contract and negligence had been imposed on defendants that allowed third parties to sue, and concluded at 623–4 that there was no risk of indeterminate liability in this case, nor any inconsistency between imposing a duty and the 'legitimate pursuit by the builder' of his own financial interests, given that he already owed a duty at the time of building the house to the initial owner.

Further reasons in favour of classing the relationship as one of 'proximity' and imposing the duty on a 'stranger to the contract' were noted at 624–5 and included an 'assumption of responsibility' on the part of the builder at the time of building and 'known reliance' on the part of the owner; and the 'connecting link' between the two parties in the form of the house, which was a 'permanent structure to be used indefinitely' and which represents 'one of the most significant, possibly *the* most significant investment which the subsequent owner will make' during their lifetime.

The second case in this category was decided after the High Court had abandoned proximity theory and had developed a new methodology of duty in *Sullivan v Moody* (2001). Consequently, a new focus on vulnerability replaced the old focus on proximity seen in *Bryan v Maloney* (1995). A further point of distinction between the two cases noted by some of the judges was the fact that the building in *Bryan v Maloney* (1995) was a private dwelling whereas in *Woolcock Street Investments Pty Ltd v CDG Pty Ltd* (2004) it was a commercial office building.

Case examples

- *Woolcock Street Investments Pty Ltd v CDG Pty Ltd* (2004) concerned commercial business premises purchased by Woolcock Street Investments Pty Ltd (P), as an investment in 1992. The foundations of the building had been designed in 1987 for the initial owner by the first defendant, an engineering company, CDG Pty Ltd (D). P entered a contract of sale with the earlier owner that did not include a warranty that the building was safe from defect, and there was no assignment by the vendor of any rights that it had against the Ds. At the time that the building was constructed, the initial owners had refused to pay for any geotechnical investigations, despite the fact that the Ds had obtained a quotation for them.

  The building had serious structural defects which caused P to incur financial losses, and so it sued D and one of D's employees for their negligence in designing and constructing the building. The High Court held in a 6:1 decision (Kirby J dissenting) that no duty was owed by the Ds to P in the circumstances. There were two main reasons why P failed: the first was the finding that P was not vulnerable in the legal sense, and the second was the fact that the duty claimed by P was not the same as the duty owed by the defendants to the original owners of the building.

  - *Vulnerability:* P was not vulnerable to the Ds in the sense that it was unable to protect itself by contract from the risk posed by the inadequate foundations. P could, for example, have included a term warranting the soundness of the building in its contract with the vendors – or could have paid for an independent professional assessment of the building's structural integrity itself before entering the contract. Given that the purchase was for an investment, such measures could easily have been taken by P, but it chose not to protect itself in this way: see the joint judgment of Gleeson CJ, Gummow, Hayne and Heydon JJ at [23]–[24] and [31]–[32], McHugh J at [80]–[86] and [112]–[114], and Callinan J at [216]–[224].
  - *Inconsistency in the two duties:* The case was distinguished from *Bryan v Maloney* (1995) because, as the joint judgment pointed out at [25], the Ds did not owe 'the original owner of the land a duty to take reasonable care to avoid economic loss of the kind' claimed by P. Given that the original owners had chosen not to protect themselves by having the geotechnical investigations carried out, there was no original duty owed by CDG to take reasonable care to avoid exposing the original owners to the risk of that kind of economic loss: see the joint judgment at [25]–[30].
- In *Brookfield Multiplex Ltd v Owners Corporation Strata Plan 61288* (2014), the High Court was again faced with a claim for pure economic loss. Here Brookfield Multiplex Ltd (D),

was a builder who carried out construction of a strata apartment complex, and the Owners Corporation (P), was the manager of the common property and agent of the owners of the apartments. Latent defects were uncovered in the common property of the complex, as a result of which P sued D to recover damages for costs incurred in repairing these defects. The High Court took the opportunity to reaffirm that vulnerability is a key principle when deciding whether a duty of care is owed for pure economic loss in cases of latent defect to property. P was found to be insufficiently vulnerable in its relationship with D, because it had been in a position to take steps to protect itself from the risk of loss. In this sense, French CJ pointed out at [23]:

> It is in relation to vulnerability that there is a sharp distinction between *Bryan v Maloney* and the present case. That distinction is analogous to that made in the subsequent decision of this Court in *Woolcock Street Investments Pty Ltd v CDG Pty Ltd.*

The reasoning in these cases emphasises the importance of focusing very carefully on the facts and the relevant circumstances in any given problem. The importance of protecting home buyers has since been recognised by many legislatures in Australia. Statutes in almost all jurisdictions now give protection to subsequent purchasers of domestic buildings.

Legislative example

***Domestic Building Contracts Act 1995* (Vic) s 9**

Section 9 provides that warranties will 'run with the building':

> In addition to the building owner who was a party to a domestic building contract, any person who is the owner for the time being of the building or land in respect of which the domestic building work was carried out under the contract may take proceedings for a breach of any of the warranties listed in section 8 as if that person was a party to the contract.

LEGISLATION ALERT!

Consult your study materials and note any relevant statutory provisions in your jurisdiction that may modify or add to the common law rules.

14.5.3.3 Economic loss caused by negligent professional legal services

Liability for pure economic loss may be imposed on a defendant whose negligent conduct in providing professional legal services to a client causes pure economic loss to another person. The 'disappointed beneficiary' cases arise when a solicitor's negligent conduct in dealing with a client's will deprives a plaintiff of a benefit that the testator had intended to give to them. The difficulty in these cases is caused by the fact that 'the only person who has a valid claim has suffered no loss, and the only person who has suffered a loss, has no valid claim', as McHugh J pointed out in *Hill v Van Erp* (1997) at 215. The issue is whether the law of negligence should step in to fill the gap where the law of succession does not provide a remedy for the benefit lost under the failed testamentary gift. The decisions of the High Court in the two cases discussed in this category held that negligence should provide such a remedy by imposing a duty on the negligent solicitor to compensate the plaintiffs for their economic loss. These decisions, like the decision in *Donoghue v Stevenson* (1932), which also allowed a third-party 'stranger to the contract' to recover damages, were both decided by majority, and both have been subjected to criticism by the minority judges and some academic commentators.

Case examples

- The plaintiff in *Hawkins v Clayton* (1988) was the executor and residual beneficiary under a will prepared in 1970 by a solicitor working at the firm of Clayton Utz & Co (D) for their client, Mrs Brazier. D retained custody of the will but after Mrs Brazier's death in 1975, the firm took no steps to contact P. D did not inform him of Mrs Brazier's death or about the contents of her will until 1981. P, who had lost contact with the testator and who had not known of the death, subsequently incurred a fine for late lodgement of documents and discovered that the house that he had inherited, and which had been left uninhabited for six years, had fallen into disrepair. P sued D in negligence for its conduct in failing to take reasonable steps to inform him of his interest and duties under the will, which caused him to suffer financial losses. The High Court held by a 3:2 majority that D owed a duty to P and were liable to compensate him for the financial losses caused by the firm's unreasonable delay. This case was decided during the period when the High Court was divided over the proximity doctrine. Two of the majority judges, Deane and Gaudron JJ, used a proximity-based analysis of the case, but Brennan J, who had never followed the proximity approach, came to the same conclusion by a different method.

  The two key factors justifying the duty were the assumption of responsibility for the performance of professional work by the original solicitor as a 'specially qualified person possessing expert knowledge and skill' and reliance by the client on the solicitor to use that skill in performing that work, as Deane J pointed out at 578. The fact that D retained custody of the will within that context was held by Deane J at 580 to support the conclusion that they had 'effectively assumed the custodianship of the testatrix's testamentary intentions' and justified imposing a duty on the firm to take positive steps to find and inform P about the death and the contents of the will. See also Gaudron J at 593–7, who in addition to noting the relevance of reliance and an assumption of responsibility, also based the decision on the solicitor's position of control, the reasonable expectations of the parties, and the fact that D's negligent conduct caused an impairment of P's legal right to exercise his powers as the executor of the will.

- In *Hill v Van Erp* (1997), Van Erp (P) was named as a beneficiary under a will executed by her friend, the testator, after it had been prepared by the testator's solicitor, Hill (D). D had asked the husband of the intended beneficiary to witness the will, which invalidated the gift under the *Succession Act 1981* (Qld). The disappointed beneficiary sued D, claiming that her negligent conduct in asking her husband to witness the will had caused her to lose the financial benefit intended by the testator.

The High Court held, by a 5:1 majority (McHugh J dissenting), that D owed a duty to P and was liable to compensate her for the lost benefit. This case can be analysed using the four key salient features of vulnerability, certainty, autonomy and coherence.

- *Vulnerability as evidenced by D's control:* The intended beneficiary was 'particularly vulnerable' in the legal sense that she could not protect herself from the risk of suffering pure economic loss caused by D's negligence, because as Dawson J pointed out at 186, 'in the normal course the solicitor's error only becomes apparent after the death of the client' and at that point 'the hitherto concealed error becomes irreversible'. Both Gaudron and Gummow JJ emphasised the critical importance of the solicitor's control not only over whether the testamentary intentions and wishes of the client were put into effect but also over whether the intended beneficiary gained that benefit. This justified imposing a duty to take reasonable steps to avoid causing pure economic loss to the intended beneficiary: see Gaudron J at 198–9 and Gummow J at 232.
- *Certainty:* The concerns about indeterminate liability were absent because the identity of the beneficiary as a 'specific, identifiable individual rather than a member of an unascertained class' was known to D: see Brennan J at 171, Dawson J at 180, Gaudron J at 193 and 198, McHugh J at 215 and Gummow J at 235–6.
- *Autonomy:* D's 'legitimate pursuit of personal advantage' was not diminished by imposing a duty owed to P, and in fact would enhance that pursuit: see Gummow J at 236 and McHugh J at 215.
- *Coherence:* Imposing a new duty owed by the solicitor to the intended beneficiary was consistent with the pre-existing duty that she owed to the client: see Gaudron J at 193 and 199 and McHugh J at 215. Dawson J noted at 180:

  > [T]he recognition of a duty of care would not supplant or supplemen remedies available in other areas and would not disturb any general body of rules constituting a coherent body of law.

  McHugh J agreed at 215 that many of the factors identified by the other judges were present in the case, but concluded that imposing liability could not be justified because:

  > none of these reasons persuasively differentiates the present case from numerous other areas of social and business activity where a person is under no duty to prevent economic loss to another.

- In *Badenach v Calvert* (2016), a solicitor executed a will in accordance with the deceased's instructions. The will provided that the entire estate would pass to Mr Calvert. However, the deceased's daughter successfully obtained a court order that provision must be made for her under the *Testator's Family Maintenance Act 1912* (Tas). Mr Calvert brought an action against the solicitor for failing to advise the deceased about the possibility that their daughter might make a claim, and for failing to advise on options that would have prevented such a claim from being successful. The High Court clarified that, while advice about the possibility of the claim was clearly relevant, advice on how specifically to avoid such a claim was not. The solicitor could not have been expected to assume the deceased would need this advice. So, as explained by Gageler J at [56], the scope of the duty the solicitor owed Mr Calvert was not the same as the duty they owed the deceased and the former was narrower than the latter. This case was also distinguished from *Hill v Van Erp* (1997) because, while *Hill* was focused on the need to give effect to testamentary intention, this case was more generally about giving 'advice as to the client's property interests and future estate' (French CJ, Kiefel and Keane JJ at [45]).

The decisions by the High Court in the three categories of pure economic loss discussed in each of sections 14.5.3.1–14.5.3.3 have used the tort of negligence to fill a legal gap in cases where the law of contract and the law of succession would allow defendants to escape liability despite the fact that their conduct:

- was in breach of another legal duty owed by the defendant to a third party; and
- has caused reasonably foreseeable pure economic loss to another vulnerable person.

The next category of pure economic loss cases can be distinguished from the first three because no question of a breach of a legal duty to any third party is involved.

14.5.3.4 Pure economic loss suffered by plaintiffs who gamble

The final set of cases arise when a plaintiff who has lost money gambling seeks to hold another person liable for their losses. They argue either that the defendant should have prevented them from gambling or that the defendant has enabled their losses through their own negligent conduct. Note that both of these cases (in the examples below) were mentioned earlier in the chapter.

Case examples

- In *Reynolds v Katoomba RSL All Services Club Ltd* (2001), Reynolds (P), who had identified himself as a 'problem gambler' and had asked to be prevented from gambling, sued Katoomba RSL All Services Club Ltd (D), claiming that D's staff had caused him to incur extensive financial losses by their positive conduct in continuing to cash his cheques, and by their omissions in failing to advise him to resign his membership of the club so that he could then be excluded from the premises, and in failing to warn him of the lack of prudence in gambling when they saw him gambling.

  The New South Wales Court of Appeal held unanimously that D did not owe a duty to P to prevent him from losing money while gambling in D's club. Spigelman CJ relied heavily on the two concepts of autonomy and vulnerability that had been developed by the High Court in the years between *Caltex Oil (Australia) Pty Ltd v The Dredge 'Willemstad'* (1975) and *Perre v Apand Pty Ltd* (1999).

  - *Vulnerability:* P claimed that he was an 'especially vulnerable individual' because of his lack of personal control over his gambling problem and argued that D's staff had both knowledge of his susceptibility and overall control over his situation. However, the trial judge found that P had not been deprived of his ability to control his own actions. Spigelman CJ reviewed the cases on vulnerability at [20]–[28] and concluded at [46] that P was not vulnerable in the legal sense, pointing out at [48] that he could have protected himself by staying away from the club or resigning his membership.

- *Autonomy:* Spigelman CJ also emphasised the important principle of autonomy at [29]–[43], concluding at [46] and [49] that as 'an individual whose autonomy the common law respects' P 'must accept responsibility for his own actions'.

Spigelman CJ said at [25], in a much quoted passage:

> In many respects the tort of negligence is the last outpost of the welfare state. There have been changes over recent decades in the expectations within Australian society about persons accepting responsibility for their own actions. Such changes in social attitudes must be reflected in the identification of duty of care for purposes of the law of negligence. The recent authoritative statements in *Perre v Apand Pty Ltd* and *Agar v Hyde* give greater emphasis, in the development of the law of negligence, to the acceptance by individuals of a personal responsibility for their own conduct, than may have been given in the past.

- In *Politarhis v Westpac Banking Corporation* (2009), the bank (D) mistakenly increased the funds available to their customer (P), who had a gambling problem. P took advantage of the mistake, withdrew the money and lost it gambling. He sued D, claiming that its conduct in making the extra funds available had caused him to lose a large amount of money (and led to his pathological gambling addiction). The Full Court of the Supreme Court of South Australia held unanimously that none of the three elements of negligence could be made out on the facts. Doyle CJ concluded at [118]:

> [A]cknowledgment of the autonomy of the individual, and of the responsibility of the individual for decisions made and not made, are matters that tell against the imposition of a duty of care.

In this case, P was not vulnerable in the legal sense:

> Westpac did not know that Mr Politarhis was a gambler, or had a gambling problem. I agree that absent such knowledge, it seems impossible to impose a duty of care of the kind postulated. At the time of the borrowing Mr Politarhis was capable of acting rationally. It cannot be said that at that time he was in a position of particular vulnerability of which Westpac should have been aware. ... Mr Politarhis was in at least as good a position as Westpac to protect himself against the likelihood of loss through gambling. There is the circumstance that there is no indication of any reliance by Mr Politarhis on Westpac to protect his interests. Westpac had no means of control over the conduct of Mr Politarhis. It is impractical to postulate a duty which requires a lender to ascertain, before agreeing to lend, whether the potential borrower has a tendency or condition that is likely to lead to the borrowed money being squandered.

14.5.3.5 Novel fact scenarios involving pure economic loss

You should remember that the categories of pure economic loss discussed in this subsection are not closed and that the classification exists only as a matter of convenience. So, when a case that does not fit squarely within any of these categories comes to the attention of the courts, the decision will hinge, as in any novel fact scenario, on the principles of negligence.

Case example

In *Barclay v Penberthy* (2012), two individuals employed by the plaintiff died and three others were injured when a light aircraft piloted by one of the defendants crashed and caught fire soon after take-off. The employer of the individuals who died and were injured sued the defendants, claiming that their negligence had caused them pure economic losses. The High Court applied the principle of *vulnerability* developed in *Woolcock Street Investments Pty Ltd v CDG Pty Ltd* (2004). The pilot, Mr Penberthy, knew that his passengers were employees, flying for commercial purposes, and it should have been in his contemplation that their employer was a member of an ascertainable class of potential plaintiffs who would suffer economic loss as a result of his negligence. Indeed, the employer was found to be reasonably relying on the pilot's exercise of professional skills, making them vulnerable to any negligent performance of such skills. As it was established that the plane had crashed in part due to Mr Penberthy's negligence, the High Court was satisfied that Mr Penberthy owed the employer of the deceased and injured passengers a duty of care, as they were unable to protect themselves from the pure economic loss foreseeably stemming from the pilot's negligence.

Note that the other defendant, the company responsible for the faulty design of the aircraft, which was found to be the other cause of the crash, did not owe a duty to the employer of the deceased and injured passengers in the circumstances.

Develop your skills

Exercise 1: Active reading exercise – making a summary

Section 14.5 does not include a 'Summary points' feature. You can use this opportunity to test your personal skills development by constructing your own summary. Using the 'Summary points' feature in this chapter as a model, make your own set of summary points for this topic, ensuring that you connect each point to the relevant authorities in section 14.5. Add in any other cases included in your study materials under the appropriate headings and look to see whether they fit into the High Court's new approach by analysing them using the relevant principles discussed in this section.

Exercise 2: Case notes

Construct a case note of each of the following cases, using the principles laid down by the High Court to structure your analysis:

- *Johnson Tiles Pty Ltd v Esso Australia Pty Ltd* (2003);
- *Fortuna Seafoods Pty Ltd v The Eternal Wind* (2005);
- *Kakavas v Crown Melbourne Ltd* (2009).

Exercise 3: Legal research

Search for critical commentaries on the Australian approach to pure economic loss cases. You will find many useful references in the footnotes of the more recent cases.

Exercise 4: Essay writing

Write a 2000-word essay explaining why you agree or disagree with the Australian approach to cases of pure economic loss.

14.6 Medical negligence

14.6.1 The problem of professional negligence

The doctor–patient relationship is an established duty category. The content of the common law duty is identified in *Rogers v Whitaker* (1992), where Mason CJ, Brennan, Dawson, Toohey and McHugh JJ stated at 483:

> The law imposes on a medical practitioner a duty to exercise reasonable care and skill in the provision of professional advice and treatment. That duty is a 'single comprehensive duty covering all the ways in which a doctor is called upon to exercise his skill and judgment'; it extends to the examination, diagnosis and treatment of the patient and the provision of information in an appropriate case. [References omitted.]

At common law, the 'standard of reasonable care and skill required is that of the ordinary skilled person exercising and professing to have that special skill': *Rogers v Whitaker* (1992), Mason CJ, Brennan, Dawson, Toohey and McHugh JJ at 483. Chapter 12 explained that special rules apply to professionals, including doctors. While this aspect of medical negligence is uncontroversial, there are several areas of continuing debate in Australia. The first area concerns the focus of the test for whether a medical practitioner has breached the standard of reasonable care and the question of whether the court should defer to the opinions of the medical profession. The second relates to the problem of causation of harm and the question of whether certain outcomes (eg the birth of an unplanned child after an unsuccessful sterilisation operation or the loss of a chance of a better medical outcome) should be recognised as compensable forms of damage. The third, more general area of debate has focused on the content of the duty of care itself. On the issue of a doctor's liability for a 'pure omission' see *Lowns v Woods* (1996).

14.6.1.1 The test for breach of the standard of care

The main focus of debate in recent years has been on the test for whether a medical practitioner has breached the standard of reasonable care. The issue, which arises in all cases of professional negligence, is whether setting the standard ought to be a matter of medical opinion or legal judgment. Mason CJ, Brennan, Dawson, Toohey and McHugh JJ highlighted the source of the difficulty in *Rogers v Whitaker* (1992) at 483:

> At its basis lies the recognition that, in matters involving medical expertise, there is ample scope for genuine difference of opinion and that a practitioner is not negligent merely because his or her conclusion or procedure differs from that of other practitioners.

In many ways the history of the test for breach mirrors the development of most of the other special topics considered in this chapter because the approach taken in the early cases in England was first extended by the courts in Australia and then modified once more by the civil liability reforms. The original test that was laid down in England in 1957 focused on professional opinion as the source of the standard. Lord Scarman described the so-called '*Bolam* test', first laid down in *Bolam v Friern Hospital Management Committee* (1957), in *Sidaway v Governors of Bethlem Royal Hospital* (1985) at 881:

> The *Bolam* principle may be formulated as a rule that a doctor is not negligent if he acts in accordance with a practice accepted at the time as proper by a responsible body of medical opinion even though other doctors adopt a different practice. In short, the law imposes the duty of care: but the standard of care is a matter of medical judgment.

In the landmark case of *Rogers v Whitaker* (1992), the High Court of Australia rejected the '*Bolam* test' and refocused it into a more patient-friendly form. By reserving the right of the courts to make the final decision, the Court effectively (and controversially) refused to defer to medical opinion on the issue of breach. Mason CJ, Brennan, Dawson, Toohey and McHugh JJ noted at 489 that 'responsible professional opinion will have an influential, often a decisive, role to play'. However, they nevertheless concluded at 487 that the standard of care 'is not determined solely or even primarily by reference to the practice followed or supported by a responsible body of opinion in the relevant profession or trade'. Rather:

> the courts have adopted the principle that, while evidence of acceptable medical practice is a useful guide for the courts, it is for the courts to adjudicate on what is the appropriate standard of care after giving weight to 'the paramount consideration that a person is entitled to make his own decisions about his life'. [References omitted.]

The decision in *Rogers v Whitaker* (1992), which was a case about a doctor's breach of the duty to advise of material risks, was reaffirmed in *Naxakis v Western General Hospital* (1999), a case that concerned treatment rather than advice. Thirteen years later, parliaments in many jurisdictions used the civil liability legislation to modify the test again by moving it back into a more doctor-friendly position. The law is now a mix of common law and statute, and the most common result is that:

- in cases of examination, treatment and diagnosis, the standard used in the statutes is adapted from the '*Bolam* test' and is ultimately set by reference to the opinion and practices of the profession, provided that the opinion or practice is not irrational (or, in some jurisdictions, unreasonable); and
- in cases of advice about material risks inherent in any proposed treatment, the standard in both the common law and the statutes is determined by a two-limbed test modelled on the rule in *Rogers v Whitaker* (1992), which requires a doctor to give the patient all the information that either:

- a reasonable person in the patient's position would want to know (the objective limb or 'proactive' aspect of the duty to inform); or
- the particular patient would want to know (the subjective limb or 'reactive' aspect of the duty to inform).

You should note that in *Montgomery v Lanarkshire Health Board* (2015), the United Kingdom Supreme Court has abandoned the '*Bolam* test' in cases involving a doctor's duty to inform a patient of the risks related to medical procedures, and explicitly embraced the Australian approach. As noted by Lords Kerr and Reed at [87]:

> The correct position, in relation to the risks of injury involved in treatment, can now be seen to be substantially that adopted in *Sidaway* by Lord Scarman, ... subject to the refinement made by the High Court of Australia in *Rogers v Whitaker* ... An adult person of sound mind is entitled to decide which, if any, of the available forms of treatment to undergo, and her consent must be obtained before treatment interfering with her bodily integrity is undertaken. The doctor is therefore under a duty to take reasonable care to ensure that the patient is aware of any material risks involved in any recommended treatment, and of any reasonable alternative or variant treatments. The test of materiality is whether, in the circumstances of the particular case, a reasonable person in the patient's position would be likely to attach significance to the risk, or the doctor is or should reasonably be aware that the particular patient would be likely to attach significance to it.

LEGISLATION ALERT!

Consult your study materials and note any relevant statutory provisions in your jurisdiction that may modify the common law rules.

14.6.1.2 Complex cases: Wrongful life, wrongful birth and loss of a chance

Several controversial medical cases were decided by the High Court in the years after *Rogers v Whitaker* (1992). The first case, *Cattanach v Melchior* (2003), was a 'wrongful birth' action brought by the parents of an unplanned child who was conceived after a failed sterilisation operation. They succeeded in recovering damages from the doctor for the cost of raising their child to the age of 18. This case attracted a great deal of political and media comment and subsequently parliaments in some states brought in legislation that prevented any future awards of this kind. The next case, *Harriton v Stephens* (2006), was a 'wrongful life' action brought on behalf of a child against her mother's doctor. The plaintiff argued that the doctor's conduct in failing to detect the mother's rubella infection while she was pregnant with the plaintiff made it impossible for her mother to have sought a termination of the pregnancy, causing the plaintiff to be born with severe disabilities and facing a lifetime of suffering. The third case, *Tabet v Gett* (2010), was a 'loss of a chance of a better outcome' case that was brought by a plaintiff who sued her doctor on the grounds that his negligence had cost her the possibility, but not the probability, of a better medical outcome. Both cases offered the High Court the opportunity to recognise new forms of harm in negligence, but the High Court did not take up those opportunities and the plaintiffs were unsuccessful.

LEGISLATION ALERT!

Consult your study materials and note any relevant statutory provisions in your jurisdiction that may modify the common law rules. See, for example, the statutes that preclude the award of damages for the birth of a healthy child.

14.6.2 Relevant principles

The most important principles[10] that operate in the field of medical negligence are the principles of autonomy, vulnerability, certainty (or indeterminacy) and coherence. However, as you will see from the strongly expressed disagreement in many of the recent controversial cases, these principles do not necessarily point towards an obvious answer in the difficult cases where the judges are asked to push the boundaries of negligence by recognising new forms of duty or new forms of damage. This is because, unlike a rule (which prescribes a definite outcome), a principle carries only a relative weight that pushes us in a particular direction. The difficulty is that different judges assess the significance and degree of that weight differently when they put those principles in the balance.

14.6.2.1 Autonomy

The autonomy principle is one of the most important legal principles in the area of medical treatment. It not only justifies the requirement imposed by the tort of *battery* that a patient's consent must first be obtained before any medical treatment can proceed, but it also underpins the doctor's duty in *negligence* to warn a patient of material risks inherent in any proposed treatment.

Case examples

- In *Secretary, Department of Health and Community Services v JWB and SMB (Marion's Case)* (1992), McHugh J emphasised at 309–10 the importance that the common law places on respecting the autonomy and dignity of the patient:

> By doing so, the common law accepts that a person has rights of control and self-determination in respect of his or her body which other persons must respect.

10 It is appropriate to speak of 'principles' rather than 'salient features', as we are not discussing a situation where establishing a duty of care is controversial. So these are not relevant here for the purpose of establishing a duty of care in addition to foreseeability like in novel fact scenarios. Rather, they more holistically permeate the reasoning of courts in cases involving health professionals.

See also Mason CJ, Dawson, Toohey and Gaudron JJ at 233, and Brennan J at 265–6.

- In *Rogers v Whitaker* (1992) the joint judgment of Mason CJ, Brennan, Dawson, Toohey and McHugh JJ explained at 487 that 'the paramount consideration is that a person is entitled to make his own decisions about his life' and noted at 489 that the choice to undergo any proposed treatment 'is, in reality, meaningless unless it is made on the basis of relevant information and advice'. However, the judges also suggested in obiter at 490 that the duty to inform 'is subject to the therapeutic privilege'. The therapeutic privilege allows a doctor to withhold information from their patient if they believe on reasonable grounds that the knowledge itself would cause serious harm to the patient: see *Battersby v Tottman* (1984). The basis for this exception to a patient's right to make an autonomous choice was doubted by Gaudron J at 494.
- In *Chappel v Hart* (1998), the importance of respecting a patient's right to choose was one of the factors that led Kirby J to find in favour of the plaintiff who argued that if her doctor had warned her of a risk of permanent damage to her voice, she would have taken steps to have her operation carried out by a more experienced expert in the field. Kirby J said at [95] that a doctor's duty to patients extended to 'respecting their rights, including (where they so choose) to postpone medical procedures and to go elsewhere for treatment'. See also Gummow J at [65].

The 'wrongful birth' cases have also led to the development of a concept of 'reproductive autonomy' that is based on the freedom of parents to choose (and to limit) the size of their family: see *McFarlane v Tayside Health Board* (2000), Lord Millett at 114; and *Cattanach v Melchior* (2003), Gleeson CJ at [23], and Hayne J at [190], [191] and [216]. Many judges in these cases have noted that a parent's choice to keep the unplanned child rather than undergoing a termination or giving the child up for adoption must also be respected as an autonomous choice: see *Cattanach v Melchior* (2003), Kirby J at [113]–[114] and Hayne J at [220]–[222]. Similar views appear in the 'wrongful life' case of *Harriton v Stephens* (2006), Crennan J at [248] and Kirby J at [112]–[116]. As Kirby J noted in *Cattanach v Melchior* (2003) at [114]:

> Neither in this appeal nor in most other recent decisions on the issue has the argument been accepted that a plaintiff is disentitled to damages because she failed to procure a termination of her pregnancy or, upon birth of the child, failed to arrange for its adoption.

However, the courts' respect for each person's autonomy, which is normally used to justify imposing liability in this area, has also been used to justify a different conclusion. For example, Priestley JA concluded in the earlier 'wrongful life' case of *CES v Superclinics (Australia) Pty Ltd* (1995) at 84–5 that the fact that the mother had made a real and voluntary choice to keep her child, rather than choosing to mitigate her loss by placing the child for adoption, compelled the conclusion that the defendant was not legally responsible for the financial costs of rearing the child. So, in this case, respecting the plaintiff's right to choose led to the conclusion that she could not recover any costs of rearing the child after the date that she made her choice. These arguments illustrate the point that principles can often point in different directions.

14.6.2.2 Vulnerability

The vulnerability principle was developed primarily in the cases about pure economic loss and pure psychiatric injury. However, the principle also has a role to play in governing the legal relationship between a doctor and a patient, because as Brennan CJ noted at 83 in the case of *Breen v Williams* (1996), 'the relationship of doctor and patient is one where the doctor acquires an ascendancy over the patient and the patient is in a position of reposing trust in the doctor'. Vulnerability in the legal sense arises in many medical cases because doctors have far more knowledge and understanding of medical matters than their patients, who reasonably rely upon them for advice and guidance. This knowledge gap leading to reliance within a professional relationship underpins the requirement that doctors must advise patients of all material risks inherent in any proposed treatment. Without the knowledge of the possible risk, a patient may become vulnerable in the sense that they are unable to protect themselves from the consequences if the risk eventuates.

Case example

Thake v Maurice (1986) was a case where a doctor failed to advise a couple, who consulted him about limiting the size of their family, about the possibility that the healing processes of nature could restore the husband's fertility after a vasectomy. Three years after the operation, the wife became pregnant with her fifth child, but in ignorance of the possibility that her husband's vasectomy could have reversed itself, she mistook the signs of pregnancy for the menopause because she was convinced that it was impossible for her to conceive. Consequently, she did not discover the fact that she was pregnant until it was too late to have a termination. The plaintiffs were successful in their suit against the doctor.

The fact that the patients may also be in pain because of their particular medical condition, or may be confused or worried because of the effects of their illness or its continuing treatment, heightens the need for doctors to take reasonable care in advising patients to ensure that the advice is intelligible to the patient and is 'responsive to that patient's expressed concerns and questions', as Santow JA pointed out in *Johnson v Biggs* (2000) at [53].

Case examples

- In *Hookey v Paterno* (2009), a case where a patient sued a dental practitioner for negligence, Nettle and Redlich JJA emphasised the importance of tailoring the warning about possible risks inherent in the proposed treatment to the nature of the patient and her particular concerns because, as noted at [120], this patient was 'heavily reliant' on the advice of the professionals. They said at [116]:

  > In order to convey to the lay patient the gravity of the possible consequences of that risk, it was necessary to outline them in sufficient detail and simplicity to be comprehensible.

- The case of *Harvey v PD* (2004) concerned a plaintiff whose doctor negligently failed to advise her of the rules relating to consent that governed the sharing of information about HIV test results. As a result, she remained in ignorance of her fiancé's HIV positive health status. After her fiancé fraudulently assured her that he was HIV negative, she married him and conceived a child. Both the mother and the child were found to be HIV positive. The plaintiff subsequently divorced her husband, and then knowing of her HIV status, conceived a second child with another partner. She claimed in negligence against the doctor, seeking damages to cover, among other things, the future costs of raising both children once she became incapable of doing so herself.

Santow JA pointed out at [106] that 'vulnerability is an important factor if not a prerequisite for the protection afforded by the law of negligence' and concluded that this vulnerability justified imposing a duty on the doctor. However, the New South Wales Court of Appeal allowed recovery of damages only for the upkeep of the first child, reasoning that the plaintiff's voluntary and independent decision to have the second child and the possibility of indeterminate liability both pointed against recovery and both had to be 'weighed in the balance': Ipp JA at [225]–[236]; see also Santow JA at [140]–[147].

These cases also illustrate the difficulties associated with an argument based on principles. In *Harvey v PD* (2004) the patient's special vulnerability justified imposing a duty on the doctor to take reasonable care to discuss with his patient the question of mutual disclosure of the HIV test results, but the principles of certainty and autonomy were used to justify limiting the extent of the doctor's liability. Similarly, in *Cattanach v Melchior* (2003), Heydon J at [324] emphasised the 'special vulnerability' of children and used this feature of the case as a justification for denying the claim, but the majority judges disagreed and allowed the claim on the basis of the 'ordinary principles of negligence': see, for example, Kirby J at [151] and [179], and Callinan J at [296]. More recently, Kirby J reasoned in dissent in *Harriton v Stephens* (2006) at [72] that the disabled plaintiff in this case 'evidenced the important "salient feature" of vulnerability to harm' but the majority gave greater weight to the other principles of coherence, certainty and autonomy.

14.6.2.3 Certainty and indeterminacy

The certainty (or indeterminacy) principle weighs against imposing liability in cases where the extent of liability is indeterminate; however, as Mason CJ, Deane and Gaudron JJ noted at 618 in *Bryan v Maloney* (1995), a case of legal professional negligence, it is 'not necessarily fatal to the recognition of a duty of care that the duty is owed to a class whose members cannot be identified with complete accuracy'. The indeterminacy principle has been invoked in a number of recent medical negligence cases, but while the judges agree that the principle is an important one, they do not necessarily agree on how it applies in particular cases.

Case examples

- The indeterminacy principle, along with the principle of coherence, was invoked by Gleeson CJ in the 'wrongful birth' case of *Cattanach v Melchior* (2003) at [38] to justify the minority view that the doctor should not be liable to pay for the costs of raising the unplanned child. After pointing out at [32] that 'indeterminacy does not mean magnitude', Gleeson CJ concluded at [38]:

> The liability sought to be imposed is indeterminate ... It is based upon a concept of financial harm that is imprecise; an imprecision that cannot be concealed by an arbitrary limitation of a particular claim in subject matter or time. It is incapable of rational or fair assessment.

However, Callinan J took the opposite view, concluding at [282] that while the fact that 'the damages may be substantial, or that they may vary very much from case to case does not mean that they are indeterminate'. In a narrow 4:3 decision, the majority held that the damage alleged by the parents was capable of assessment and liability was imposed on the doctor.

- In *Harvey v PD* (2004), noted above, both Santow and Ipp JJA relied in part on the indeterminacy principle when justifying denying the doctor's liability to pay for the cost of raising the plaintiff's second child. Santow JA said at [147] that 'indeterminacy is itself a matter of degree' but distinguished the decision in *Cattanach v Melchior* (2003) in light of the fact that the degree of indeterminacy in *Harvey v PD* was 'considerable' given the concerns noted at [140] over the potential ambit of damage recovery and the possibility that 'each later birth would open up an even longer anticipated period of future incapacity'.
- Crennan J picked up the theme of indeterminacy in *Harriton v Stephens* (2006), concluding at [261] and [277] that 'the lack of certainty about the class of persons to whom the proposed duty is owed' weighed against allowing liability. Crennan J also considered at [252] and [254] that the calculation required by the claim was impossible:

> A comparison between a life with disabilities and non-existence, for the purposes of proving actual damage and having a trier of fact apprehend the nature of the damage caused, is impossible. ...
>
> A duty of care cannot be stated in respect of damage which cannot be proved by persons alleging such a duty has been breached, and which cannot be apprehended by persons said to be subject to the duty, and which cannot be apprehended or evaluated by a court (or jury).

This argument about the impossibility of making the required calculation in the wrongful life cases is linked very closely to the argument based on the principle of coherence.

14.6.2.4 Coherence

The controlling principle of coherence that was articulated in *Sullivan v Moody* (2001) has been invoked in the recent 'wrongful life' and 'wrongful birth' cases in both Australia and England.

Case examples

- The 'wrongful life' case of *Harriton v Stephens* (2006) illustrated the operation of the coherence principle. Crennan J, with whom Gleeson CJ and Gummow J agreed, cited the earlier case of *Sullivan v Moody* (2001) when explaining at [242]–[257] why the law could not impose a duty of care on the doctor to prevent the child being born disabled. Crennan J concluded at [276] that allowing the claim would introduce 'serious incoherence' into the 'well-established and well-known principles' that are 'integral to the body of doctrine' that is applied 'to all plaintiffs and defendants in actions in all other categories of negligence'. In addition to the matters noted above under the certainty principle, Crennan J also explained at [249]:

> To superimpose a further duty of care on a doctor to a foetus (when born) to advise the mother so that she can terminate a pregnancy in the interest of the foetus in not being born, which may or may not be compatible with the same doctor's duty of care to the mother in respect of her interests, has the capacity to introduce conflict, even incoherence, into the body of relevant legal principle.

Callinan J also noted in this case that there should be 'absolute coherence in the law' and pointed out at [205] that if the appellant were to succeed:

> coherence would require that a mother, who knew of, but failed to abort a foetus likely to emerge at full term seriously disabled, be liable to that child, a prospect that I suspect few would contemplate with equanimity.

- In the 'wrongful birth' case of *McFarlane v Tayside Health Board* (2000), the idea of coherence was used in the House of Lords to justify denying liability by Lord Millett at 108 and Lord Steyn at 83, who said: 'Coherence and rationality demand that the claim by the parents should also be rejected.' See also the judgments of the minority judges in *Cattanach v Melchior* (2003), including Gleeson CJ at [39] who considered that any imposition of liability in these cases 'was difficult to relate coherently to other rules of common law and statute'.
- In *Tabet v Gett* (2010) the trial judge held that the plaintiff, who was diagnosed with a brain tumour, had not proved on the balance of probabilities that her doctor's negligent failure to order a timely CT scan was a cause of the brain damage that she had suffered. However, the judge did accept, as an alternative form of damage, the fact that she had been deprived by the defendant's negligence of a chance (valued at 40 per cent) of achieving a better medical outcome. The High Court unanimously denied the patient's claim, and four of five judges rejected the proposition that 'the possibility (but not the probability) that the brain damage suffered by the [patient] would have been less catastrophic than it was' could amount to compensable damage: see Crennan J at [101].

  Gummow ACJ invoked the idea of coherence laid down in *Sullivan v Moody* (2001) as one of the reasons that justified rejecting the 'loss of a chance' doctrine in the field of medical negligence: at [18], [26] and [53]–[54]. Gummow ACJ said at [53] that if 'the act or omission complained of does not amount to interference with or impairment of an existing right', the process of recognising a new interest said to be harmed must be carried out 'in a coherent fashion' and 'requires a sense of the existing and inherent principles of the law'. His Honour rejected the contractual loss of a chance doctrine as providing an appropriate analogy at [47] and concluded at [46]:

  > [I]n personal injury cases the law of negligence as understood in the common law of Australia does not entertain an action for recovery when the damage, for which compensation is awarded consequent upon breach of duty, is characterised as the loss of a chance of a better outcome of the character found by the trial judge in this case.

Keifel J, with whom Hayne, Bell and Crennan JJ agreed, maintained at [143]–[152] that the standard of proof could not be lowered to recognise the 'radical' proposition that 'possible, rather than probable causation' could be a condition of liability because this fundamental change to the law of negligence 'simply denies proof of damage as necessary to an action in negligence'.

14.6.2.5 Role-based coherence

The principle of role-based coherence is also used in difficult medical cases to justify denying liability. Judges who sympathise with the plaintiff's plight, but who find themselves unable to find any compelling legal arguments that justify imposing a duty in these cases, sometimes fortify their decision by suggesting that imposing liability is a 'step too far' and is one that only Parliament should make.

Case examples

- The High Court refused to impose a general duty on a doctor to give a patient access to their medical records in *Breen v Williams* (1996). Gaudron and McHugh JJ stated at 115 that 'if change is to be made, it must be made by the legislature' on the grounds that 'in a democratic society' it is a 'serious constitutional mistake to think that the common law courts have authority to "provide a solvent" for every social, political or economic problem' unless the change in the law can be 'derived logically or analogically from other legal principles, rules and institutions'.
- In contrast, Kirby J used the same point to justify imposing liability in *Cattanach v Melchior* (2003), pointing out at [137]:

  > Judges, on the other hand, have the responsibility of expressing, refining and applying the common law in new circumstances in ways that are logically reasoned and shown to be a consistent development of past decisional law. But they have no authority to adopt arbitrary departures from basic doctrine. [References omitted.]

  Kirby J decided at [180] that an allowance for the cost of raising the child *did* fit within the existing body of principles and concluded therefore that to deny liability 'would be arbitrary' and as such, any denial of liability 'is the business, if of anyone, of Parliament not the courts'. (As noted in the introduction to this section, several parliaments did in fact deny liability in these cases.)
- Similar points were made in the 'loss of a chance of a better outcome' case of *Tabet v Gett* (2010) by Crennan J, who identified some of the policy issues in the case and said at [102]:

  > Policy considerations which tell against altering the present requirement of proof of causation in cases of medical negligence include the prospect of thereby encouraging defensive medicine, the impact of that on the Medicare system and private medical insurance schemes and the impact of any change to the basis of liability on professional liability insurance of medical practitioners. From the present vantage point, the alteration to the common law urged by the appellant is radical, and not incremental, and is therefore the kind of change to the common law which is, generally speaking, the business of Parliament.

The medical cases illustrate very clearly the dilemma posed by the High Court's methodology of balance. A focus on principles on its own does not always provide a clear or obvious solution in the hard cases that take us to the borders of the law. In these finely balanced cases where the principles point in different directions, different judges often give different weight to different principles and arrive at different outcomes. In some cases, the same principle can be used to justify opposed conclusions. There are several solutions to this problem. One option is to allow judges to take policy matters overtly into consideration, but this option has been rejected by the High Court in *Sullivan v Moody* (2001). Another option, put forward by Peter Cane in 'Taking Disagreement Seriously: Courts, Legislatures and the Reform of Tort Law' (2005) at 394, is to 'prefer statute law to common law and allow judges, in developing the common law, to give effect to their personal beliefs and values' in these hard cases where there is 'genuine, reasonable and intractable disagreement about values' and to decide matters simply by a majority vote. The third solution, put forward by Allan Beever in *Rediscovering the Law of Negligence* (2007), rejects policy-based decision-making and focuses instead on using the underlying structure of tort law as a rights-based system of corrective justice to help resolve these issues of principle.[11]

14.6.3 Key cases, basic rules and reforms

This subsection covers the basic rules that govern a medical practitioner's liability to a patient. It does not discuss the questions of duty and damage raised in the 'wrongful birth' and 'wrongful life' cases.

14.6.3.1 Breach of the duty to take reasonable care

As noted above, the common law test for breach does not defer to the legal profession as the ultimate source of the standard. This applies both in cases about advice, as laid down in *Rogers v Whitaker* (1992), and in cases about diagnosis and treatment, as laid down in *Naxakis v Western General Hospital* (1999).

Case examples

- *Rogers v Whitaker* (1992) concerned a patient (who had one blind eye and one good eye) who became almost totally blind after elective surgery on her blind eye. The specialist had conducted the operation with the required care and skill, but the patient argued that he was in breach of his duty to take reasonable care to advise her of an exceptionally small risk, rated as 1 in 14 000, that as a result of the surgery on her blind eye, she could develop a rare condition called sympathetic ophthalmia that could lead to blindness in her remaining good eye. The patient was particularly worried about anything happening to her good eye throughout the course of her consultations with the doctor, and she established in evidence that she would not have gone ahead with the operation had she been told that there was any chance, however small, that her one remaining eye could be adversely affected.

11 Beever discusses the birth cases in chapter 11 of *Rediscovering the Law of Negligence* (2007).

The defendant doctor argued that the '*Bolam* test' should apply and presented evidence from a body of reputable medical practitioners that they would not have given any warning in those circumstances. As noted above, the High Court rejected the '*Bolam* test', and Mason CJ, Brennan, Dawson, Toohey and McHugh JJ concluded at 487 that the standard of care 'is not determined solely or even primarily by reference to the practice followed or supported by a responsible body of opinion in the relevant profession or trade'. The patient-oriented test was laid down in the joint judgment at 490:

> The law should recognize that a doctor has a duty to warn a patient of a material risk inherent in the proposed treatment; a risk is material if, in the circumstances of the particular case, a reasonable person in the patient's position, if warned of the risk, would be likely to attach significance to it or if the medical practitioner is or should reasonably be aware that the particular patient, if warned of the risk, would be likely to attach significance to it.

The joint judgment also pointed out at 488 and 490 that several factors noted in the case of *F v R* (1983) should be considered by a medical practitioner when deciding whether to advise a patient about any given risk, including:

- the nature of the matter to be disclosed;
- the nature of the treatment;
- the desire of the patient for information;
- the temperament and health of the patient; and
- the general surrounding circumstances.

The joint judgment held, at 491, that the doctor should have warned this particular patient of the small but material risk, noting that the evidence showed that she had 'incessantly' questioned her doctor about any possible complications and was clearly very apprehensive about anything happening to her good eye. The judges also held that 'a reasonable person in the patient's position would be likely to attach significance to the risk'.

- In *G & C v Down* (2008), the trial judge held that the defendant, a doctor who advised his patient about the risks attendant on a proposed sterilisation by tubal ligation, had a duty to advise not only of his own failure rate, which was 1:2000, but also the general failure rate, which was 1:500. This failure to provide an adequate level of advice was held to be a breach; however, given that the trial judge found that this patient, even if warned, would have gone ahead with the procedure, the plaintiff lost on the issue of causation. On appeal in *G, PA & C, P v Down* (2009), Anderson J, with whom White and Kourakis JJ agreed, said at [66] that it is 'the relative risk of pregnancy between the contraception currently used and tubal ligation that is critical' to patients and concluded at [67] that the failure to refer to the published failure rates and the other information available at the time was a breach of the standard of reasonable care.

The common law position has been changed in many jurisdictions as a result of the civil liability reforms. The Ipp Report discussed this issue in chapter 3 and noted at [3.4] that there was 'a significant body of opinion, especially among the medical profession, in favour of reinstating the *Bolam* rule in its original form'. However, the Panel maintained that the law should deal with treatment and advice cases differently. After explaining at [3.36] that the approach in cases of advice about material risks inherent in the medical treatment should be based on 'the right of individuals to decide their own fate', the Ipp Report recommended at [3.69] in Recommendation 7 that the distinction between the 'proactive' duty to warn and the 'reactive' duty to warn should remain:

> The proactive duty to inform requires the medical practitioner to take reasonable care to give the patient such information as the reasonable person in the patient's position would, in the circumstances, want to be given before making a decision whether or not to undergo treatment.
>
> The reactive duty to inform requires the medical practitioner to take reasonable care to give the patient such information as the medical practitioner knows or ought to know the patient wants to be given before making the decision whether or not to undergo the treatment.

The Ipp Report also recommended at [3.19] in Recommendation 3 that a modified version of the '*Bolam* test' be adopted in cases of treatment:

> A medical practitioner is not negligent if the treatment provided was in accordance with an opinion widely held by a significant number of respected practitioners in the field, unless the court considers that the opinion was irrational.

The reason why the Ipp Report modified the '*Bolam* test' by adding the qualification about irrational opinions was to avoid the problem identified in [3.10] – namely, the problem of 'rogue experts' and 'localised practices that are not regarded with approval widely throughout the profession', which can 'give rise to results that would be unacceptable to the community'. The Ipp Report gave two examples of localised practices that were seen as irrational.

Case examples

- The first example was noted in the Ipp Report at [3.8]:

> The first is discussed in *Bolitho v City and Hackney Health Authority* (1998) by Lord Browne-Wilkinson, referring to *Hucks v Cole* (a 1968 case), in which 'a doctor failed to treat with penicillin a patient who had septic spots on her skin even though he knew them to contain organisms capable of leading to puerperal fever. A number of distinguished doctors gave evidence that they would not, in the circumstances, have treated [the patient] with penicillin'. Despite this body of supportive opinion, the Court of Appeal held the doctor to have been negligent because he had knowingly taken a risk of causing grave danger even though it could have been easily and inexpensively avoided. [References omitted.]

- The second example was discussed at [3.9]:

> The second instance concerns the events described in the *Report of the Committee of Inquiry into Allegations Concerning the Treatment of Cervical Cancer at National Women's Hospital and into Other Related Matters* (1988). The report arose out of a

> research programme, conducted over the course of almost 20 years, at the National Women's Hospital (Auckland, New Zealand). ... The programme involved leaving untreated women who returned positive Pap smears ... which may develop into invasive cancer ... The approach followed in the programme was accepted by many other practitioners, within and outside the hospital, and formed the basis for under graduate and post graduate teaching. According to the Report, several women died as a result of the failure to offer conventionally accepted treatment.

Many jurisdictions followed these recommendations, although some substituted the term 'unreasonable' for the word 'irrational'. Others have special rules about the requirement of a medical practitioner to advise a patient about obvious risks. More importantly, some jurisdictions interpret the standard of care of professionals as a defence, while other jurisdictions see it as an alternative standard of care. Recently, Courts of Appeal in New South Wales, Queensland and Western Australia, in interpreting the provisions of the civil liability legislation adopted in their states, have reached diverging conclusions on the nature of the special provisions on the liability of skilled professionals (or, in the case of Western Australia, health professionals).

Case examples

- The case of *Dobler v Halverson* (2007) examined the New South Wales provisions. Giles JA (with whom Ipp and Basten JJA agreed) explained the effect of the statutory version of the new rule in s 50 of the *Civil Liability Act 2002* (NSW) at [59], noting that its importance 'does not lie so much in questions of onus of proof as in who determines the standard of care' and concluding at [60]:

  > The plaintiff will usually call his expert evidence to the effect that the defendant's conduct fell short of acceptable professional practice, and will invite the court to determine the standard of care in accordance with that evidence. He will not be concerned to identify and negate a different professional practice favourable to the defendant, and s 50 does not require that he do so. The defendant has the interest in calling expert evidence to establish that he acted according to professional practice widely accepted by peer professional opinion, which if accepted will (subject to rationality) mean that he escapes liability.

- In *South Western Sydney Local Health District v Gould* (2018), the New South Wales Court of Appeal revisited this interpretation. In this case, the respondent child presented to a hospital with an open fracture of the left thumb. After the patient was discharged the next day following examination, gangrene developed in the thumb, leading to its amputation. In the circumstances, the Court found that the statutory 'standard of care for professionals', established under s 50 of the *Civil Liability Act 2002* (NSW), gives rise to a *defence*, if the defendant can call evidence establishing they acted in accordance with a widely accepted peer professional opinion (unless this opinion is either 'irrational' or 'unreasonable'). Note that the provision is treated as a defence even though the heading refers to a 'standard of care'. It is therefore the defendant who is required to demonstrate that they acted in accordance with such peer professional opinion. The relevance of this decision is that, if the provision provides a statutory defence rather than an alternative method of establishing breach, the onus is on the defendant and not the plaintiff.

- The Queensland Court of Appeal had reached a similar conclusion in the case of *Mules v Ferguson* (2015). In this case, the Court took the opportunity to set stringent parameters for the applicability of the defence, which depends on the facts of the case and cannot be established by way of generalisation, as explained by Boddice J at [191]:

  > That defence requires an identification of the particular conduct, and the group of peer opinion supporting that conduct as being widely accepted practice. The onus rests on the [defendant] to satisfy that defence. Whether the [defendant] met that onus required a consideration of the [defendant]'s conduct in the context of the presenting symptoms as found by the trial judge.

- The Western Australian Court of Appeal in *Child and Adolescent Health Service v Mabior* (2019) reached a different conclusion in interpreting s 5PB of the *Civil Liability Act 2002* (WA), which deals with the 'standard of care for health professionals'. Quinlan CJ, Murphy and Pritchard JJA clarified that, as the provision refers to a widely accepted 'practice' as opposed to 'opinion', the text is to be interpreted as establishing an alternative *standard of care* rather than a *defence*. This, in theory, implies that it should be incumbent on the plaintiff to show that the actions of the health professional *did not* act in accordance with a widely accepted practice. Note, however, that the practical difference between the two approaches is limited in the sense that, as noted by the Court at [330]–[332]:

  > [W]hile the onus is on the plaintiff in relation to whether the defendant breached any applicable standard of care, there must be some evidence as to the kind of practice referred to in s 5PB(1) before it arises for consideration. ...
  >
  > This leads to the second preliminary issue: namely, whether a defendant, seeking to contest liability on the basis that he or she acted in accordance with a practice that was widely accepted by the health professional's peers as competent professional practice at the time, is required to plead material facts concerning the applicability of s 5PB(1).
  >
  > The answer to that question is, generally, 'yes'.

- The New South Wales Court of Appeal returned to the question of what constitutes an established practice in *Dean v Pope* (2022). The approach taken by the Court was that it may not be necessary to identify *a* specific practice but rather a manner of acting recognised as competent professional practice at the relevant time. While this is a broader approach than that taken in Western Australia, the point remains that a defendant cannot simply call expert witnesses to testify that they would have acted in the same way as the defendant in the unique circumstances with which the defendant was confronted. This would be beyond the scope of the defence.

In sum, both approaches effectively require the health professional defendant to show that they acted in accordance with a widely accepted practice. You should also consider that, as explained by the Western Australian Court of Appeal in *Child and*

Adolescent Health Service v Mabior (2019) at [335], s 5PB is only applicable where there 'is evidence that there is a widely accepted practice supporting the defendant's conduct'. This seems to imply that where such evidence of a widely accepted practice is not available (eg in cases involving clinical scenarios that are unusual or highly dependent on non-generalisable individual characteristics), a health professional's conduct will be assessed on the basis of the general breach of duty provisions and principles (eg s 5B of the *Civil Liability Act 2002* (WA)).

LEGISLATION ALERT!

Consult your study materials and note any relevant statutory provisions in your jurisdiction that may modify the common law rules on breach.

14.6.3.2 Causation

The tests for causation are explained in Chapter 13, which includes tables showing the causation process in the leading cases of *Barnett v Chelsea & Kensington Hospital Management Committee* (1968) and *Rogers v Whitaker* (1992) (Tables 13.1 and 13.2 respectively). Two other leading cases that also raised the issue of causation in cases of an omission or a failure to advise of material risks are noted below.

Case example

Chappel v Hart (1998) concerned a patient who suffered paralysis of her right vocal cord and consequent partial voice loss after an operation by the defendant, an ear, nose and throat specialist, during which he had perforated her oesophagus. She claimed that she would have delayed the operation and consulted an expert in the field if he had advised her of the extremely rare, but real, risk of voice loss that was inherent in the surgery. The evidence established that, as a teacher-librarian, she had been very concerned about any adverse effects on her voice and had asked about any such risks.

The defendant contended that, in the light of the fact that the plaintiff's condition was relentlessly progressive and that she would inevitably have had to undergo the same operation at some time in the future, the case should not be conceptualised as a claim for physical injury but seen rather as a claim for the loss of a chance to have the surgery performed by another surgeon at another time. He argued further that his failure to advise her of the risk had not increased the objective likelihood that she might suffer such damage due to such a 'random event' and that, therefore, she had not suffered any real damage.

The High Court decided by a 3:2 majority that the claim was properly seen as an ordinary claim based on the causation of a physical injury by a failure to advise about material risks inherent in the treatment. The majority rejected the characterisation of the claim as one based on a loss of a chance (or exposure to a risk of harm) and held that the plaintiff had proved on the balance of probabilities that she would not have suffered the loss of her voice if the surgeon had advised her of the risk and she had delayed the operation. This outcome was based on two findings:

- The first factual finding was that while the *nature* of the risk did not change, the *degree* of risk varied depending on the level of experience of the surgeon, and therefore on the balance of probabilities the risk would have diminished if the plaintiff had been operated on later by a more experienced expert: see Gaudron J at [17]–[19] and Kirby J at [97].
- The second was the evidence that the risk of these rare complications occurring was, in any case, extremely small.

The extreme rarity of the risk eventuating meant that on the balance of probabilities, it was very likely that if the operation been carried out by another surgeon on another day, no complications would have occurred and the damage to the plaintiff's voice would have been avoided. The application of the 'but for' test as seen by the majority is illustrated in Table 14.1.

Test your understanding

Reasoning about causation

Read the case of *Chappel v Hart* (1998) and make a causation chart that reflects the reasoning that underpinned the minority judgments.

Table 14.1 *Chappel v Hart*

What did occur in the case:	What would have happened:
a. P, teacher-librarian, seeks advice from D about her throat problem, expresses concern about her voice and asks about any risks.	A. P, teacher-librarian, seeks advice from D about her throat problem, expresses concern about her voice and asks about any risks.
b. D, in breach of duty, *fails to advise P of rare, but possible complications.*	B. D, in conformity with the duty to advise, *tells P about rare, but possible complications.*
c. P, in ignorance of the risk, decides to go ahead with operation.	C. P *would not have gone ahead with the operation at that time.*
d. *Complications occur.*	D. A different operation would have occurred with a different surgeon and on the balance of probabilities *no complications would have occurred,* because of the small degree of risk.

At point c/C: crucial finding of fact: P would have delayed the operation and would have sought treatment at a later time with an experienced expert.
At point d/D: crucial comparison between what did happen and what would have happened if D had complied with his duty to advise P.
Conclusion: Given the disparity of the outcomes, factual causation is established on the balance of probabilities.

Case example

Rosenberg v Percival (2001) also considered the issue of causation and a failure to advise of risks, but in this case the plaintiff lost (see Table 14.2). The patient, an experienced nurse and university academic holding a PhD in nursing, sued her dental surgeon in negligence after she developed severe joint complications referred to as TMJ, which included permanent, severe and disabling pain, after he performed routine elective surgery on her jaw. She claimed that he had been negligent in carrying out the operation and said that if he had advised her of the risk of TMJ, she would not have undergone the operation. The surgeon had not been aware of the risk, which was rare.

The trial judge found on the evidence that the surgeon had not been negligent in diagnosing, treating or advising the patient, and went on to hold that this patient, even if warned of the risk, would nevertheless have gone ahead with the planned operation. This was based in part on the patient's intelligence, training and knowledge as an experienced nurse, her awareness of the general risks of surgery, her keenness to have the surgery and achieve the best possible result, the seriousness of her need for corrective surgery and her failure to ask specific questions about risk. Given that neither breach nor causation could be established, the plaintiff's case failed. On appeal, the Full Court of the Supreme Court of Western Australia held that there had been a negligent failure to advise the patient of a material risk and set aside the trial judge's finding that causation had not been established. On further appeal to the High Court, the decision of the trial judge was restored in a unanimous decision.

- *Subjective test:* The judges reiterated the point that in Australian law, the test of whether a patient would have undertaken treatment or surgery if advised of a material risk is a subjective test that asks whether this patient would have gone ahead with the course of action, not whether a reasonable person would have done so: see Gummow J at [87], McHugh J at [24] and [44], and Kirby J at [154].
- *Define the risk and the content of the warning:* Gummow J noted at [60] that the essential first step that must be taken when applying the rules on breach in a case of failure to advise is to define the risk 'by reference to the circumstances in which the injury can occur, the likelihood of the injury occurring, and the extent or severity of the potential injury' and to specify 'the content of any warning that could have been given'.
- *The problem of hindsight:* Gleeson CJ at [16] warned against using 'the prism of hindsight' when deciding the questions of causation or breach. Kirby J at [153]–[159] discussed the 'inherent unreliability of such self-serving testimony' and emphasised the need for the Court to scrutinise the plaintiff's testimony carefully to avoid an overly uncritical reliance on any such 'retrospective evaluation by that aggrieved patient who only stands to gain by affirming that he or she would not have proceeded with the treatment' and to 'reject absurd, self-interested assertions'.
- *Nature of the patient:* Callinan J explained at [210] how the nature of a patient can affect the assessment of breach:

> What this in practice may mean is that the more inquisitive, or demanding, or less or more sophisticated perhaps, or obsessive, or suspicious, or hypochondriacal the patient may be, the greater the need for identification of and elaboration upon the slightest risks because such a patient may be likely to attach significance to them.

It went against the plaintiff that she had not made inquiries about risks, unlike the plaintiffs in *Rogers v Whitaker* (1992) and *Chappel v Hart* (1988), who were able to prove that they had been particularly concerned about the risks that did in fact eventuate and would have acted to avoid them if advised.

Table 14.2 *Rosenberg v Percival*

What did occur in the case:	**What would have happened:**
a. P, a nursing academic, seeks advice from D about her jaw problem.	A. P, a nursing academic, seeks advice from D about her jaw problem.
b. D *does not tell P about possible TMJ complications.* *	B. D *tells P about possible TMJ complications.*
c. P decides to go ahead with the operation.	C. P *would have gone ahead with the planned operation anyway.*
d. *Complications occur.*	D. Given that exactly the same operation would have occurred, *the same complications would have occurred.*

* The judges in the High Court disagreed on the issue of breach, and the case was decided on the issue of causation.
At point c/C: crucial finding of fact: P would have gone ahead with the operation, even if warned of the risk of TMJ complications.
At point d/D: crucial comparison between what did happen and what would have happened if D had complied with his duty to advise P.
Conclusion: Given the identical nature of the outcomes, factual causation is not established on the balance of probabilities.

The problem of hindsight bias and self-serving testimony has been dealt with in some jurisdictions by parliaments that followed the recommendation by the Ipp Report at [7.40] that 'in determining causation, any statement by the plaintiff about what they would have done if the negligence had not occurred should be inadmissible'.

LEGISLATION ALERT!

Consult your study materials and note any relevant statutory provisions in your jurisdiction on the admissibility of statements made by a plaintiff.

14.6.3.3 Scope of liability

Many of the new 'scope of liability' provisions passed as part of the civil liability reforms require judges, when deciding the element of causation, to consider and explain 'whether or not and why' responsibility for compensating a plaintiff for any particular harm should be imposed on the negligent defendant. The Ipp Report gave an example derived from the case of *Chappel v Hart* (1998) of the way that such a provision could be used in a medical case.

Example

The Ipp Report collected the arguments for and against imposing liability at [7.50]:

> In favour of denying liability, it could be argued that in the absence of negligence on the part of the defendant in performing the operation, the harm suffered by the plaintiff was a mere coincidence for which the defendant ought not to be liable. On the other hand, it could be argued that even though the occurrence of the harm was a coincidence, it was the very risk about which the plaintiff had inquired. For that reason, the imposition of liability would be justified in order to reinforce the doctor's reactive duty to inform and the patient's interest in freedom of choice.

The High Court of Australia discussed the scope of a health professional's liability in the case of *Wallace v Kam* (2013).

Case example

Wallace v Kam (2013) was a case in which P unsuccessfully relied on *Rogers v Whitaker* (1992) in a negligence claim against a medical professional. In this case, D was a neurosurgeon who performed a surgical procedure on P. This procedure had two inherent risks, neither of which was brought to the attention of P. The first risk was temporary damage to P's thigh (a condition called 'neurapraxia'). The second was a one-in-20 chance of permanent and catastrophic paralysis. The first risk eventuated as a result of the operation. The second did not. It was apparent on the evidence that D's failure to warn of the risks was negligent. Yet the issue was whether it could be said that the scope of D's liability should extend to the harm suffered, since it was also established that P would have chosen to undergo the procedure anyway if warned only of the risk of that harm. The High Court decided that it would be inappropriate for D's liability to extend to the injury sustained by their patient where it was established that the patient would have decided not to undergo the procedure if warned of all material risks (both the neurapraxia and the paralysis), but would have gone ahead with the surgery if warned only of the risk that in fact eventuated (the neurapraxia). French CJ, Crennan, Kiefel, Gageler and Keane JJ explained at [36]:

> Consideration of a case involving the materialisation of one of a number of distinct risks of different physical injuries makes it necessary to return to the nature of the duty and the policy that underlies its imposition. The duty of a medical practitioner to warn the patient of material risks inherent in a proposed treatment is imposed by reference to the underlying common law right of the patient to choose whether or not to undergo a proposed treatment. However, the policy that underlies requiring the exercise of reasonable care and skill in the giving of that warning is neither to protect that right to choose nor to protect the patient from exposure to all unacceptable risks. The underlying policy is rather to protect the patient from the occurrence of physical injury the risk of which is unacceptable to the patient. It is appropriate that the scope of liability for breach of the duty reflect that underlying policy.

It follows from these cases that a patient cannot be compensated for the materialisation of a risk that they were willing to accept. Such a risk falls beyond the *scope* of the health professional's liability even though it can be argued that *factually*, in cases like *Wallace v Kam*, but for the negligence of the surgeon in failing to advise the patient of all material risks, the patient would have decided not to undergo a procedure, thereby avoiding harm.

14.6.4 Summary points

14.6.4.1 Medical negligence

1. Medical negligence has changed in recent years as a result of the civil liability reforms. This means that you need to cross-reference this section on medical negligence with the material on the elements of negligence in Chapters 11–13 and note any legislative measures that alter the common law in your jurisdiction.
2. In addition to the usual negligence principles of reasonable foreseeability of harm and fault, the most important principles in this area are the autonomy principle, the coherence principle, the certainty (or indeterminacy) principle and the vulnerability principle.
3. The element of duty reflects an established duty category and the content of the established duty includes diagnosis and treatment on the one hand, and advice about material risks inherent in the proposed treatment on the other.
4. The tests for determining whether a defendant has fallen short of the standard of reasonable care may differ, depending on the nature of the breach.
5. In discussing the issue of *breach in cases involving treatment and diagnosis,* it is important to consult your study materials to find out whether the civil liability legislation has reintroduced the modified '*Bolam* test' in your jurisdiction or whether the common law applies.
6. Where the civil liability legislation has introduced special provisions, identify whether the 'peer professional opinion' constitutes a defence or an alternative standard of care, and whether the onus of proof rests on the plaintiff or the defendant.
7. In discussing the issue of *breach in advice cases*, it is important to follow the procedure explained in *Rosenberg v Percival* (2001).
   - Identify and define the nature of the risk, considering:
     - the circumstances in which the injury or harm can occur;
     - the likelihood of the injury occurring; and
     - the degree of severity of the risked harm.
   - As part of explaining the precautions that a reasonable doctor should have taken, identify the content of the advice or warning that the doctor should have given to the patient in the light of the state of knowledge at the time.
   - Consider whether the risk was a material risk by applying the two-limbed test:
     - the objective limb (or 'reactive' duty); and
     - the subjective limb (or 'proactive' duty).

8. The factors noted in *Rogers v Whitaker* (1992) and the other cases will also provide assistance in deciding whether or not the doctor should have known that the patient needed to be given any particular advice:
   - the nature of the matter to be disclosed;
   - the nature of the treatment;
   - the desire of the patient for information;
   - the temperament and health of the patient; and
   - the general surrounding circumstances.
9. In discussing the issue of *causation in advice cases,* it is important to bear in mind the advice given in *Rosenberg v Percival* (2001).
   - The test of whether a patient would have gone ahead with treatment is a subjective one that asks whether this patient would have gone ahead with the treatment, but the court will take care not to accept self-serving testimony by an aggrieved patient who sees the events through the prism of hindsight.
   - The court will consider the following factors when assessing the evidence:
     - Was the treatment elective or essential?
     - Was the patient inquisitive, known to be worried about any particular kinds of risks – or careless of risk or determined to have the procedure?
     - Were there any other options available to the plaintiff?
     - What knowledge, if any, does the plaintiff already possess about medical matters?
     - What is the nature of the risk itself, and the extent and severity of the possible harm that may occur?
   - Remember also the key point of *Wallace v Kam* (2013): The liability of a doctor for failure to warn does not extend to harm from the materialisation of risks that the patient was willing to accept. This principle applies even where the failure to warn includes other risks, which the patient was not willing to accept but did not materialise.
10. The usual defences to negligence apply: see Chapter 15.

Test your understanding

Exercise 1: Active reading exercise

Link each of the summary points noted above with a case discussed in section 14.6 above.

Exercise 2: Problem solving

Your clients, Phil and his wife Caroline, were shocked this year when they discovered that Caroline was two months pregnant with their fourth child. This was despite the sterilisation procedure that Caroline had undergone shortly after the delivery of their third child two years earlier. The sterilisation procedure was performed by an obstetrician, Dr Liam Black.

During her third pregnancy, Caroline had raised the issue of sterilisation with Dr Black a number of times, explaining to him that they simply could not afford any more children. Dr Black agreed to perform a sterilisation after her third child was born and suggested that they discuss the various sterilisation options at Caroline's post-delivery check-up.

When Caroline was in labour with her third child two years ago, it became apparent that the baby was experiencing some distress. Although Caroline had delivered her previous two babies naturally, Dr Black informed her that she would need a caesarean to deliver this child. He also told her that since he was going to have to operate anyway, and if she was sure about sterilisation, he could 'put some clips on while he was in there'. Caroline nodded emphatically and told him to go ahead.

The clips Dr Black was referring to were 'Bleier' clips, small spring clips that attach to the fallopian tubes and close them shut, thus preventing pregnancy. The failure rate was known to be 0.8 per cent with the Bleier clips, but Dr Black had used the clips for years and had never known a patient to become pregnant. Recent medical journals, however, had reported studies showing that the Bleier clips could dislodge relatively easily and that the newer 'Pomeroy' clips had a much lower failure rate. In fact, most obstetricians had ceased using Bleier clips in recent years. In addition, it was well known that attaching the Bleier clips at the same time as a caesarean section delivery increased the risk of the clips dislodging, resulting in an even higher failure rate of 1.5 per cent.

Not wanting to worry Caroline during a difficult birth, Dr Black decided to go ahead with the procedure without informing her about the increased failure rate. At the post-delivery consultation, Dr Black briefly discussed the sterilisation procedure with Caroline, saying, 'The clips are on now. Remember they're not perfect but then, what is?' He did not advise her to undergo testing to make sure the procedure had been a success, and nor did he suggest that she take additional contraceptive precautions until she could get confirmation that the sterilisation had been effective. As far as Caroline and Phil were concerned at the time, they thought that they would not be able to have any more children.

Advise Phil and Caroline, who are struggling to make ends meet because of the burdens of caring for their family of six and want to sue Dr Black in negligence.

Conclusion

This chapter on special topics in negligence has looked at some key areas where the High Court has justified either expanding or denying liability in negligence and outlined how legislative provisions can influence these areas. The variety of situations covered in this chapter make it difficult to draw generalisable conclusions, but you should keep in mind that special rules can apply in the presence of particular categories of defendants, or in response to particular types of conduct, or particular types of harm (see Table 14.3).

Consider the foundational 'neighbour principle' and then the relevance of any of the important features and inquiries.

Table 14.3 Inquire: Special duty categories

	Important features	Cross-reference
Omissions and rescue	Autonomy and personal responsibility Vulnerability Certainty – indeterminacy	Is the harm *pure economic loss*? Is the harm a *pure psychiatric injury*? Is the defendant a *public authority*?
Public authorities	Coherence Certainty – indeterminacy Vulnerability	Is the harm *pure economic loss*? Is the harm a *pure psychiatric injury*? Was the conduct a *statement*? Was the conduct an *omission*?
Statements	Autonomy and personal responsibility Vulnerability Coherence Certainty – indeterminacy	Is the harm *pure economic loss*? Is the harm a *pure psychiatric injury*? Is the defendant a *public authority*?
Pure psychiatric injury	Coherence Certainty – indeterminacy Autonomy Vulnerability	Was the conduct a *statement*? Was the conduct an *omission*? Is the defendant a *public authority*?
Medical negligence	Autonomy Vulnerability Coherence	Was the conduct provision of *information*? Was the conduct a *diagnosis*? Was the conduct provision of *treatment*?
Pure economic loss	Autonomy and personal responsibility Vulnerability Certainty – indeterminacy Coherence	Was the conduct a *statement*? Was the conduct an *omission*? Is the defendant a *public authority*?

REFERENCES

CASES

Adeels Palace Pty Ltd v Moubarak (2009) 239 CLR 420

Agar v Hyde (2000) 201 CLR 216

Age Co Ltd v YZ (A Pseudonym) (2019) 60 VR 189

Alcock v Chief Constable of South Yorkshire Police [1992] 1 AC 310

Amaca Pty Ltd v New South Wales [2004] NSWCA 124; [2004] *Aust Torts Reports* 81-749

Ayres & Co v Hicks 40 NE 2d 334 (1942)

Badenach v Calvert (2016) 257 CLR 440

Barclay v Penberthy (2012) 246 CLR 258

Barnett v Chelsea & Kensington Hospital Management Committee [1968] 1 QB 428; [1968] 1 All ER 1068

Battersby v Tottman (1984) 35 SASR 524

Bolam v Friern Hospital Management Committee [1957] 1 WLR 582

Bolitho v City and Hackney Health Authority [1998] AC 232

Bourhill v Young [1943] AC 92
Breen v Williams (1996) 186 CLR 71
Brodie v Singleton Shire Council (2001) 206 CLR 512
Brookfield Multiplex Ltd v Owners Corporation Strata Plan 61288 (2014) 254 CLR 185
Bryan v Maloney (1995) 182 CLR 609
BT v Oei [1999] NSWSC 1082
Burnie Port Authority v General Jones Pty Ltd (1994) 179 CLR 520
CAL No 14 Pty Ltd v Motor Accidents Insurance Board (2009) 239 CLR 390
Caltex Oil (Australia) Pty Ltd v The Dredge 'Willemstad' (1976) 136 CLR 529
Carrier v Bonham [2002] 1 Qd R 474
Cattanach v Melchior (2003) 215 CLR 1
CES v Superclinics (Australia) Pty Ltd (1995) 38 NSWLR 47
Chapman v Hearse (1961) 106 CLR 112
Chappel v Hart (1998) 195 CLR 232
Chester v Council of the Municipality of Waverley (1939) 62 CLR 1
Child and Adolescent Health Service v Mabior [2019] WASCA 151
Commissioner of Railways (WA) v Stewart (1936) 56 CLR 520
Commonwealth v Introvigne (1982) 150 CLR 258
Costello v Chief Constable of Northumbria Police [1999] ICR 752; [1999] 1 All ER 550
Cox v New South Wales [2007] NSWSC 471; (2007) 71 NSWLR 225
Crimmins v Stevedoring Industry Finance Committee (1999) 200 CLR 1
Curtis v Harden Shire Council (2014) 88 NSWLR 10
Dansar Pty Ltd v Byron Shire Council (2014) 89 NSWLR 1
Dean v Pope (2022) 110 NSWLR 398
Dobler v Halverson [2007] NSWCA 335; (2007) 70 NSWLR 151
Donoghue v Stevenson [1932] AC 562
Dulieu v White & Sons [1901] 2 KB 669
Electricity Networks Corporation v Herridge Parties (2022) 276 CLR 271
Esanda Finance Corporation Ltd v Peat Marwick Hungerfords (1997) 188 CLR 241
F v R (1983) 33 SASR 189
Fortuna Seafoods Pty Ltd v The Eternal Wind [2005] QCA 405
G & C v Down [2008] SADC 135
G, PA & C, P v Down (2009) 104 SASR 332; [2009] SASC 217
Geyer v Downs (1977) 138 CLR 91
Gifford v Strang Patrick Stevedoring Pty Ltd (2003) 214 CLR 269
Goldman v Hargrave (1966) 115 CLR 458
Graham v New South Wales [2001] NSWCA 248
Graham Barclay Oysters Pty Ltd v Ryan (2002) 211 CLR 540
Hambrook v Stokes Brothers [1925] 1 KB 141
Hargrave v Goldman (1963) 110 CLR 40
Harris v Pennsylvania Railroad Co 50 F2d 866 (1931)
Harriton v Stephens (2006) 226 CLR 52
Harvey v PD (2004) 59 NSWLR 639
Hawkins v Clayton (1988) 164 CLR 539
Haynes v G Harwood & Sons [1935] 1 KB 146

Hedley Byrne & Co Ltd v Heller & Partners Ltd [1964] AC 465
Hill v Van Erp (1997) 188 CLR 159
Home Office v Dorset Yacht Co Ltd [1970] AC 1004
Hookey v Paterno [2009] VSCA 48; (2009) 22 VR 362
Horsley v MacLaren ('The Ogopogo') (1971) 22 DLR (3d) 545; [1972] SCR 44
Howard v Jarvis (1958) 98 CLR 177
Jaensch v Coffey (1984) 155 CLR 549
John Pfeiffer Pty Ltd v Rogerson (2000) 203 CLR 503
Johnson Tiles Pty Ltd v Esso Australia Pty Ltd [2003] Aust Torts Reports 81-692; [2003] VSC 27
Johnson v Biggs [2000] NSWCA 338
Kakavas v Crown Melbourne Ltd [2009] VSC 559
King v Philcox (2015) 255 CLR 304
Koehler v Cerebos (Australia) Ltd (2005) 222 CLR 44
Kozarov v Victoria (2022) 273 CLR 115
L Shaddock & Associates Pty Ltd v Parramatta City Council (1981) 150 CLR 225
Le Lievre v Gould [1893] 1 QB 491
Lepore v New South Wales [2001] NSWCA 112; (2001) 52 NSWLR 420
Lowns v Woods (1996) Aust Torts Reports 81-376
McFarlane v Tayside Health Board [2000] 2 AC 59
Magill v Magill (2006) 226 CLR 551
Mallonland Pty Ltd v Advanta Seeds Pty Ltd [2024] HCA 25; (2024) 418 ALR 639
Minister for the Environment v Sharma (2022) 291 FCR 311
Modbury Triangle Shopping Centre Pty Ltd v Anzil (2000) 205 CLR 254
Montgomery v Lanarkshire Health Board [2015] UKSC 11, [2015] 1 AC 1430
Mount Isa Mines Ltd v Pusey (1970) 125 CLR 383
Mules v Ferguson [2015] QCA 5
Mutual Life & Citizens Assurance Co Ltd v Evatt (1968) 122 CLR 556
Naxakis v Western General Hospital (1999) 197 CLR 269
New South Wales v Briggs (2016) 95 NSWLR 467
New South Wales v Bujdoso (2005) 227 CLR 1
New South Wales v Fahy (2007) 232 CLR 486
New South Wales v Skinner [2022] NSWCA 9
Nightingale v Blacktown City Council (2015) 91 NSWLR 556
North Sydney Council v Roman (2007) 69 NSWLR 240
Pasley v Freeman (1789) 3 TR 51; 100 ER 450
Perre v Apand Pty Ltd (1999) 198 CLR 180
Politarhis v Westpac Banking Corporation (2009) Aust Torts Reports 82-008; [2009] SASC 96
Pyrenees Shire Council v Day (1998) 192 CLR 330
Ramsay v Larsen (1964) 111 CLR 16
Reeves v Commissioner of Police of the Metropolis [2000] 1 AC 360
Regie National des Usines Renault SA v Zhang (2002) 210 CLR 491
Reynolds v Katoomba RSL All Services Club Ltd (2001) 53 NSWLR 43
Richards v Victoria [1969] VR 136
Robinson v Queensland [2017] QSC 165

Rogers v Whitaker (1992) 175 CLR 479
Rosenberg v Percival (2001) 205 CLR 434
San Sebastian Pty Ltd v Minister Administering the Environmental Planning and Assessment Act 1979 (1986) 162 CLR 340
Secretary, Department of Health and Community Services v JWB and SMB (1992) 175 CLR 218 ('*Marion's Case*')
Shipard v Motor Accident Commission (1997) 70 SASR 240
Sidaway v Governors of Bethlem Royal Hospital [1985] AC 871
Smith v Leurs (1945) 70 CLR 256
South Western Sydney Local Health District v Gould (2018) 97 NSWLR 513
Stovin v Wise [1996] AC 923
Stuart v Kirkland-Veenstra (2009) 237 CLR 215
Sullivan v Moody (2001) 207 CLR 562
Sutherland Shire Council v Heyman (1985) 157 CLR 424
Swan (By His Next Friend) v South Australia (1994) 62 SASR 532
Tabet v Gett (2010) 240 CLR 537
Tame v New South Wales (2002) 211 CLR 317
Tepko Pty Ltd v Water Board (2001) 206 CLR 1
Thake v Maurice [1986] 1 QB 644
Trustees of the Roman Catholic Church for the Diocese of Bathurst v Koffman (1996) Aust Torts Reports 81-399
Ultramares Corporation v Touche 255 NY 170, 174 NE 441 (1931)
Victoria v Bryar (1970) 44 ALJR 174
Victorian Railways Commissioners v Coultas (1888) 13 App Cas 222
Videan v British Transport Commission [1963] 2 QB 650
Voth v Manildra Flour Mills Pty Ltd (1990) 171 CLR 538
Wagner v International Railway Co, 133 NE 437 (1921)
Wallace v Kam (2013) 250 CLR 375
White v Chief Constable of the South Yorkshire Police [1999] 2 AC 455; [1998] 3 WLR 1509
Wicks v State Rail Authority of New South Wales (2010) 241 CLR 60
Wilkinson v Downton [1897] 2 QB 57
Woolcock Street Investments Pty Ltd v CDG Pty Ltd (2004) 216 CLR 515
X (Minors) v Bedfordshire County Council [1995] 2 AC 633
X v South Australia (No 2) (2005) 91 SASR 258
X v South Australia (No 3) (2007) 97 SASR 180
Zaghloul v Bayly [2021] WASCA 125

ARTICLES, BOOKS AND REPORTS

Beever, A, *Rediscovering the Law of Negligence* (2007) Hart Publishing, Oxford.
Butler, D, '*Gifford v Strang* and the New Landscape for Recovery for Psychiatric Injury in Australia' (2004) 12 *Torts Law Journal* 1.
Cane, P, 'Taking Disagreement Seriously: Courts, Legislatures and the Reform of Tort Law' (2005) 25 *Oxford Journal of Legal Studies* 393.

Cartwright, S R, *Report of the Committee of Inquiry into Allegations Concerning the Treatment of Cervical Cancer at National Women's Hospital and into Other Related Matters* (1988) Government Printing Office, Auckland.

Day, K, 'Medical Negligence – The Duty to Attend Emergencies and the Standard of Care: *Lowns & Anor v Woods & Ors*' (1996) 18 *Sydney Law Review* 386.

Dietrich, J, 'Nervous Shock: *Tame v New South Wales* and *Annetts v Australian Stations Pty Ltd*' (2003) 11 *Torts Law Journal* 1.

Feinberg, J, *The Moral Limits of the Criminal Law, Volume 1, Harm to Others* (1984) Oxford University Press, Oxford.

Gray, N & Edelman, J, 'Developing the Law of Omissions: A Common Law Duty to Rescue?' (1998) 6 *Torts Law Journal* 240.

Handford, P, 'Liability for Work Stress: *Kohler* Ten Years On' (2015) 39(2) *University of Western Australia Law Review* 150.

Handford, P, *Mullany and Handford's Tort Liability for Psychiatric Damage*, 2nd ed (2006) Law Book Co, Sydney.

Holmes, O W, *The Common Law* (1881) Little, Brown and Co, Boston.

Honoré, T, 'Are Omissions Less Culpable?', in *Responsibility and Fault* (1999) Hart Publishing, Oxford, 41.

Ipp, D, Cane, P, Sheldon, D & Macintosh, I, *Review of the Law of Negligence: Final Report* (2002) <https://treasury.gov.au/review/review-of-the-law-of-negligence>.

Mendelson, D, *The New Law of Torts*, 2nd ed (2010) Oxford University Press, Melbourne.

Murphy, J G, 'Blackmail: A Preliminary Inquiry' (1980) 63 *The Monist* 168.

Prosser, W, *Prosser and Keeton's Torts*, 5th ed (1984) West Group, St Paul MN.

Stevens, R, 'The Divergence of the Australian and English Law of Torts', in Degeling, S, Edelman, J & Goudkamp, J (eds), *Torts in Commercial Law* (2011) Thomson Reuters, 37

Stewart, P & Stuhmcke, A, *Australian Principles of Tort Law*, 4th ed (2017) Federation Press, Sydney.

Todd, S, 'Liability in Tort of Public Bodies', in Mullany, N & Linden, A (eds), *Torts Tomorrow: A Tribute to John Fleming* (1998) Law Book Co, North Ryde, 36.

Weinrib, E, 'The Case for a Duty to Rescue' (1980) 90 *Yale Law Journal* 247.

15 DEFENCES TO NEGLIGENCE

Introduction

Negligence governs the legal obligations individuals and organisations owe to others to avoid causing harm. Once liability is considered, however, there are defences available that can reduce or even eliminate a defendant's responsibility. These defences reflect the fact that the blame for that harm cannot – or should not – always be laid solely at the defendant's feet and that the actions of the plaintiff themselves can affect legal outcomes. In this chapter, we'll explore the key defences to negligence, such as voluntary assumption of risk (*volenti*), the statutory defence provisions that exist in various jurisdictions and contributory negligence. By examining the legal principles and significant cases behind these defences, you'll gain insight into how the courts deal with these defences and the impact they can have on liability.

15.1 The nature of the defences

Once a plaintiff has established a prima facie case by proving the three elements of negligence, the onus shifts to the defendant to escape liability by proving a defence. The defences are classified in a list below but you need to remember that they have been altered in significant ways by legislation. Some of these defences, such as 'voluntary assumption of risk', are known as complete defences because they totally absolve the defendant of liability, whereas others, such as the defence of contributory negligence (which is now dealt with under the apportionment legislation), are known as partial defences because they allow for the imposition of proportionate liability, depending on the plaintiff's relative degree of fault. As a result of the civil liability legislation, the differences between the defences are blurring. It is also important to note that there is very little uniformity in the rules on the defences as they have been given different forms in different jurisdictions, so you must be very careful to consult your study materials to identify the relevant defences in your jurisdiction. The civil standard of proof must normally be met in most of these defences, but in one rare situation noted below, the higher criminal law standard of proof has been adopted, again as a result of the civil liability reforms. Likewise, the onus of proof is normally on the defendant to raise and prove a defence, but in some circumstances the new legislation has introduced presumptions, which must be rebutted by the plaintiff.

15.1.1 Limitations

A defendant may sometimes plead that a cause of action is time barred under the relevant *Limitations of Action* legislation. Time begins to run in negligence when the third element of harm to the plaintiff is satisfied. Bear in mind that the harm to the plaintiff may occur long after the negligent conduct and that a single event or set of facts can give rise to liability under more than one tort - and that time may begin to run at a different point for each cause of action.

Case example

In *Wilson v Horne* (1999), a case of child sexual abuse, liability arose both for battery as well as negligence. The liability for battery arose in the period 1973–1980 when the original physical contact between the defendant and the plaintiff occurred. By contrast, the liability for negligence arose much later in 1994, when the damage to the plaintiff occurred (as PTSD).

LEGISLATION ALERT!

Consult your study materials for any statutory provisions in your jurisdiction on limitations periods.

Note any differences between the time allowed for bringing actions 'in tort' and actions for personal injury.

Note the rules on extension of time.

Defences to negligence fall into three categories:

- Complete defences
  - Voluntary acceptance of risk (common law)
  - Inherent risks (statute)
  - Obvious risks (statute). See also any relevant statutory provisions on dangerous recreational activities.
  - Joint illegal enterprise (common law). See 'criminal conduct' below, which is a partial defence in most, but not all, jurisdictions.
- Partial defences
  - Criminal conduct (statute)
  - Contributory negligence/apportionment of liability (statute)

  Note that contributory negligence was formerly a complete defence, but under the apportionment legislation it is now a partial defence.
- Other statutory defences
  - Intoxication
  - Seat belts
  - Good Samaritans
  - Volunteers carrying out community work
  - Food donors and/or distributors
  - Licensed drug injection facilities (eg Kings Cross)
  - Recreational service providers

LEGISLATION ALERT!

Check your study materials to see whether any of the above or any other special defences are in the legislation in your jurisdiction.

Note any limits on the application of these statutory defences.

The history of the defences to negligence has seen many swings of the pendulum. In times past, the early common law judges were exceptionally harsh to plaintiffs and applied the defences in favour of defendants. This occurred most notably during the Industrial Revolution, in cases where an employee sought to sue an employer for a workplace injury.[1] During the 20th century, the rise of the welfare state saw the pendulum swing back in favour of plaintiffs as both legislators and judges acted to soften the harshness of earlier laws. More recently, legislators in the 21st century have forced the pendulum back towards a more defendant-friendly position as they responded to increasingly loud calls not only to protect deserving defendants like community volunteers, but also to punish some plaintiffs who were seen as undeserving of the law's protection. Under these new provisions, the principle of personal responsibility was used to justify a

1 See Luntz et al, *Torts: Cases and Commentary* (2017) at 358–9, on the 'unholy trinity': common employment, contributory negligence and voluntary assumption of risk.

posture of greater harshness towards plaintiffs who were injured while committing a criminal offence, while intoxicated, or because they had failed to take sufficient care for their own safety in the face of an obvious risk. The result is that the law on the defences is not only an extremely complicated mix of common law and statute but is also completely inconsistent across Australia.

15.1.2 Critique

The legislative changes which were enacted in response to the Ipp Report (2002) were criticised as harsh and draconian. The tone of that criticism was neatly summed up by Barbara McDonald, who concluded in 'The Impact of the Civil Liability Legislation on Fundamental Policies and Principles of the Common Law of Negligence' (2006) at 299:

> Given the many circumstances when the aim of this legislation seems to be to empower courts to allow a defendant to walk away from even the most serious wrongdoing, simply because the plaintiff is also at fault, it may be asked whether this Act is as much about 'no responsibility' as 'personal responsibility'.

Examples

- McDonald, B, 'The Impact of the Civil Liability Legislation on Fundamental Policies and Principles of the Common Law of Negligence' (2006).
- Dietrich, J, 'Duty of Care under the "Civil Liability Acts"' (2005).
- Luntz, H, 'Reform of the Law of Negligence: Wrong Questions – Wrong Answers' (2002).

One of the complications in negligence arises out of the fact that many issues tend to reoccur in different guises at different stages of a case. For example, it is not certain where the issues of illegality or obvious risks belong; they are sometimes raised in the elements of duty and breach but may also reappear as defences. You also need to remember that many of the cases in this area may include facts that are relevant to more than one of the defences; for example, the fact of intoxication may be relevant to voluntary assumption of risk, contributory negligence and illegality. The fact that the defences overlap not only with each other but also with some of the other issues canvassed under the elements of negligence adds to the complexity of the law.

Case examples

- In *Insurance Commissioner v Joyce* (1948), Latham CJ explained at 46 that the 'legal position of a person who allows himself to be driven in a motor car by an obviously drunken driver' can raise three separate issues, including no breach of duty, contributory negligence, and *volenti non fit injuria*.
- *Gala v Preston* (1991) concerned two parties who had jointly stolen a car after both had been drinking heavily. Some hours (and some hundreds of kilometres) later, the passenger was injured when the driver crashed the car. The trial judge entered judgment for the defendants on the grounds that it was not possible to determine the appropriate standard of care. The Full

Court of the Supreme Court of Queensland gave judgment for the plaintiff but reduced the damages by 60 per cent because of the plaintiff's contributory negligence. The judges in the High Court of Australia ('High Court') denied liability altogether, but for different reasons, including:

- there was no duty owed because the joint criminal activity meant that there was no requisite relationship of proximity and it was not possible to determine an appropriate standard of care in such circumstances (Mason CJ, Deane, Gaudron and McHugh JJ at 254–5);
- because the 'normative influence' of the criminal law would be destroyed (Brennan J at 271);
- because allowing one accomplice to succeed in recovering damages from another accomplice 'would be wholly repugnant to the accepted standards of the law' (Dawson J at 278); and
- to allow compensation between those who had jointly participated in a serious criminal act would offend against 'prevailing community standards' (Toohey J at 291).

- In *Miller v Miller* (2009) an intoxicated plaintiff was injured when a motor vehicle that she had helped to steal crashed while it was being driven by the defendant, who was also intoxicated. This case, as pleaded at first instance, raised issues of joint illegality, contributory negligence, intoxication, and voluntary acceptance of risk. The appeal against the Western Australian Court of Appeal's decision in *Miller v Miller* (2009) was heard in November 2010 and the High Court's decision in *Miller v Miller* (2011) provided some solutions to the difficulties that lawyers, judges and law students encounter in this complex area of the law, as you will see below.

15.2 Voluntary acceptance of risk (common law)

If a plaintiff has freely and knowingly accepted a risk of harm, it seems unjust that they should then complain about the consequences if that harm occurs. For this reason, the common law has long accepted the defence of voluntary assumption of risk. It is known by the Latin phrase *volenti non fit injuria* (to one who is willing, no wrong is done) and is often referred to simply as *volenti*. Wills J said in *Osbourne v London and North-Western Railway Co* (1888) at 223–4:

> If the defendants desire to succeed on the basis that the maxim 'volenti non fit injuria' is applicable they must obtain a finding 'that the plaintiff freely and voluntarily, with full knowledge of the risk he ran, impliedly agreed to incur it.'

Another helpful definition of the defence was given by Kirby J in *Woods v Multi-Sport Holdings Pty Ltd* (2002) at [125]:

> To satisfy the test of voluntary assumption of risk, it must be shown that the claimant fully comprehended the extent of the risk and *chose to accept or ignore it*. [Emphasis added and reference deleted.]

This defence is based on the autonomy principle and the common law's insistence that we must respect a person's choices about the way that they live their life and the risks that they choose to face. The principle of personal responsibility therefore justifies the refusal of the common law to allow a plaintiff to complain about suffering a harm that they have freely chosen to encounter – and this principle is seen as outweighing the neighbour principle, which provides that a defendant who has failed to take reasonable care to avoid causing harm to another should compensate that person for their losses.

Voluntary assumption of risk is related to the defence of consent that is used in the intentional torts, because both defences amount to a claim that the plaintiff should be disentitled from recovering any damages because of their prior agreement, either:

- to accept the *risk of harm* (in a negligence case); or
- to allow the *invasion of their protected interests* (in the intentional torts).

Consequently, while the two defences are different in their focus, both defences insist upon the requirements that the plaintiff's agreement was given freely and knowingly.

To succeed in the defence of voluntary assumption of risk, the defendant must prove the following three elements on the balance of probabilities:

1. *Knowledge:* The plaintiff knew of the facts constituting the risk of harm.
2. *Understanding:* The plaintiff fully appreciated the danger inherent in those factual circumstances.
3. *Voluntariness:* The plaintiff freely and willingly agreed to encounter the risk.

These ingredients are drawn from the following Australian authorities: *Roggenkamp v Bennett* (1950), McTiernan and Williams JJ at 300; *Scanlon v American Cigarette Co (Overseas) Pty Ltd (No 3)* (1987), Nicholson J at 291; and *Imbree v McNeilly* (2008), Gummow, Hayne and Kiefel JJ at [81], and are based on much older English cases. Note that the older cases tended to use the language of 'danger' whereas the more recent cases focus on the 'risk of harm', but the terms are often used interchangeably.

In *Roggenkamp v Bennett* (1950) McTiernan and Williams JJ noted at 300:

> The question whether the plaintiff's acceptance of the risk was voluntary is generally *a question of fact*, and the answer to it may be *inferred from his conduct* in the circumstances. [Emphasis added.]

However, while a plaintiff's acceptance of a risk may be inferred from their conduct, one of the landmark cases in the development of the law in this area, *Smith v Charles Baker & Sons* (1891), made it clear that mere knowledge of a risk is insufficient to satisfy the defence.

Case example

Smith v Charles Baker & Sons (1891) was a crucial case that marked one of the first swings of the pendulum away from the protection of defendants and towards the protection of plaintiffs. The plaintiff, who sued as a pauper, was employed by the defendant railway contractors to drill holes in the rock face of a railway cutting. He was aware that other workers were also employed to use a crane to carry heavy stones above him, and despite the fact that complaints about the danger had been made, he continued in this employment. Whenever he could see that heavy stones were being lifted above him, he would try to get out of the way, but one day a stone was dropped on him, causing injuries. At first instance, his employer was found to be negligent and he was awarded damages. The employers appealed, arguing that the plaintiff had known of the risk and had voluntarily incurred it by choosing to continue in his contract of employment. The Court of Appeal reversed the judgment of the court below and the employee appealed to the House of Lords.

By a 4:1 majority the House of Lords found for the employee on the grounds that, merely by continuing in his employment knowing that the job was subject to some danger, he was not to be taken to have consented to take upon himself all the legal risk that the defendant might be negligent. (The dissenting judge, Lord Bramwell maintained the traditional view, saying plainly at 339 that 'the plaintiff had no claim in law or morality'.)

The Lord Chancellor held that the *volenti* defence had no application, and explained at 338 that while it was true that 'consent may be inferred from a general course of conduct' (eg sailors who climb the rigging of a ship 'know and appreciate' the risks that they are encountering), nevertheless, to make out a claim of *volenti*, it was necessary:

> to affirm that he consented to the particular thing being done which would involve the risk and consented to take the risk upon himself.

Lord Watson at 355 formulated the question as 'whether he agreed that, if injury should befall him, the risk was to be his and not his masters' and said:

> When, as is commonly the case, his acceptance or non-acceptance of the risk is left to implication, the workman cannot reasonably be held to have undertaken it unless he knew of its existence and appreciated or had the means of appreciating its danger. But assuming that he did so, I am unable to accede to the suggestion that the mere fact of his continuing at his work, with such knowledge and appreciation, will in every case necessarily imply his acceptance.

Lord Herschell at 360 made it clear that the risk had to be 'properly defined' and pointed out at 361–2 that there is a difference between accepting a risk that is inherent in a dangerous undertaking and accepting the risk of an employer's negligence that creates extra danger or enhances that danger. Lord Morris agreed at 369 that the employee may have:

> voluntarily entered on a risky business; but he did not voluntarily undertake it plus the risk from defective machinery. There must be an assent to undertake the risk with the full appreciation of its extent.

Lord Morris therefore concluded at 370 that the employee was both *sciens* (Latin, knowing) and *volens* (willing or accepting) of 'all the danger except that arising from unfit machinery. Of that danger he was not aware.'

This case showed how the courts narrowed the scope of the defence by insisting that for the defence to succeed, the plaintiffs must have consented to take the legal risk of a 'properly defined' kind of negligence on the part of the defendants upon themselves. This defence is rarely successful, but if a plaintiff has clearly and deliberately engaged in a dangerous course of conduct, the defence can be made out.

Case example

The plaintiff in *ICI Ltd v Shatwell* (1965) was employed to test explosive charges in a quarry. He and a fellow employee decided to ignore a new statutory safety regulation and disobey their employer's rule forbidding the use of an outdated method of testing explosive charges. He suffered serious injuries as a result. Lord Reid explained at 672–3 why the plaintiff should not recover any damages:

> There is a world of difference between two fellow-servants collaborating carelessly so that the acts of both contribute to cause injury to one of them, and two fellow-servants combining to disobey an order deliberately though they know the risk involved. It seems reasonable that the injured man should recover some compensation in the former case but not in the latter. If the law treats both as merely cases of negligence it cannot draw a distinction. But in my view the law does and should draw a distinction. In the first case only the partial defence of contributory negligence is available. In the second *volenti non fit injuria* is a complete defence if the employer is not himself at fault and is only liable vicariously for the acts of the fellow-servant. If the plaintiff invited or freely aided and abetted his fellow-servant's disobedience, then he was volens in the fullest sense.

The defence appeared to be successfully raised in two later English cases where the defendants expressly drew a particular risk to the attention of the plaintiffs by way of a notice.

Case examples

- In *Bennett v Tugwell* (1971), a son who frequently drove his father's car, placed a sign in the car that was headed 'Warning' and read: 'Passengers travelling in this vehicle do so *at their own risk*.' He did this because he mistakenly thought that his father would not be covered if a passenger was injured while he was driving. His passenger (who had been in the car up to 30 times before) was aware of the notice, but he thought that if he were to be injured, that he would nevertheless be covered by the father's insurance policy. The passenger was injured in an accident caused by the son's negligent driving.

  The judge held at 273 that the test of whether a plaintiff has accepted a risk is an objective one, and maintained that even though both the driver and the injured passenger were mistaken about the true nature of the insurance coverage, the fact of the passenger's awareness of the wording on the notice meant that he was to be taken as having accepted the legal risk of any negligence on the part of the driver. So, even though the insurance company had been 'happily accepting premiums from the owner of the car' they were not obliged to indemnify him against the claim by the injured passenger (because there was 'nothing against which to indemnify').
- *Birch v Thomas* (1972) was another case where a young driver (who had been refused insurance because of his age) had placed a small notice in his car that read: 'Passengers ride at their own risk and on the condition that no claims shall be made against the driver or owner.'

After being sued by a passenger who was injured as a result of the driver's negligence, the driver gave evidence that on the day he had brought the notice to his passenger's attention, he warned him that he was not insured for passenger liability, and left it up to him whether to go with him under those conditions or, alternatively, to travel in another vehicle with some other friends. The trial judge expressed 'doubt whether the maxim of *volenti non fit injuria* was applicable to the type of case under consideration' but held that the notice was sufficient to exempt the defendant from liability. This decision was upheld on appeal. Lord Denning MR held at 298 that the conduct of the driver was equivalent to saying to the plaintiff, 'Mark, you ride at your own risk', and concluded at 299 that this was a case where it was 'reasonable for a party to stipulate for exemption from liability, and it is just for the court to give effect to the stipulation'.

It has been doubted, however, whether these 'exclusion by notice' cases are properly to be interpreted as *volenti* cases at all. In *Scanlon v American Cigarette Co (Overseas) Pty Ltd (No 3)* (1987), Nicholson J at 293 quoted (with approval) from the 1985 edition of Trindade and Cane, *The Law of Torts in Australia* at 433 (now at 613 in the 2012 edition by Barker et al), where the authors said:

> The defence of exclusion of liability differs from that of *volenti* in that it is objectively based and the knowledge and acceptance which it requires is not of the risk but of a stipulation that the defendant is not to be liable if a risk, whatever it might be, materialises.

Regardless of whether these two notice cases are true examples of the successful use of the *volenti* defence, recent Australian cases have emphasised that the test is subjective, not objective.

Case examples

- The plaintiff in *Paltidis v The State Council of the Young Men's Christian Association of Victoria Inc* (2006) was playing a social game of beach volleyball when he was injured after striking his chin on a tyre that was used to mark the boundaries of the court. Ashley JA (with whom the other judges agreed) explained at [37] that the issue of *volenti* is not to be resolved by reference to an objective test of what a reasonable person in the plaintiff's position would or ought to have known; rather, it needs to be proved that:

  > the plaintiff in fact was seised of full knowledge and appreciation of the risk of injury posed by the tyres before he began to play the game; and that by playing he impliedly agreed to incur that risk.

  The plaintiff was not held to have accepted the risk but was found to be contributorily negligent to the extent of 25 per cent.

- In *Carey v Lake Macquarie City Council* (2007), the plaintiff, who was riding his bicycle along a concrete pathway in a public park, fell off and was injured after striking a bollard in the middle of the path. McClellan CJ maintained at [75] that at common law 'the test of voluntary assumption of risk is a subjective one' and pointed out at [76]:

> A plaintiff is not presumed or deemed to have voluntarily accepted a risk merely because he or she knew about it and exposed themselves to it. However, *there will rarely, if ever, be direct evidence that the plaintiff voluntarily agreed to accept a risk*. Their agreement will usually have to be implied or inferred from their conduct. [Emphasis added.]

McClellan CJ also noted at [82]:

> Even if a plaintiff perceived and fully appreciated a risk, the inference of free and voluntary agreement cannot be made if the plaintiff had *a genuine belief that the risk would not materialise*. This is because a person cannot agree to accept something that they honestly believe will not happen. [Emphasis added.]

The Chief Justice concluded at [107]:

> The question is not simply whether the plaintiff freely and voluntarily decided to embark upon a course of conduct that involved a risk of which he or she was aware. There must also be some *conscious advertence* to the possibility that the known risk might eventuate, and *a decision to proceed with the conduct regardless*. [Emphasis added.]

- In *Leyden v Caboolture Shire Council* (2007), a 15-year-old BMX bike rider, who had been riding bicycles since he was four or five (and who had been riding BMX bikes since the age of 10) was injured in a crash while attempting to ride over a jump on a BMX track that was maintained by the defendants. The jump had been made more challenging (and dangerous) by unauthorised modifications carried out by other users of the track, and the plaintiff knew this. However, despite the plaintiff's young age, the trial judge and two of the judges in the Queensland Court of Appeal found that he had voluntarily accepted the risk of being injured. This was based on the plaintiff's long experience in riding BMX bikes, his experience of going over that particular jump, and his admitted knowledge of the specific risks that he faced: see [38]. Mackenzie J at [22] referred to the views of McClellan CJ in *Carey v Lake Macquarie City Council* (2007), noted above, and pointed out at [41] 'that while the defence of volenti may be a highly endangered species, it is not yet extinct'. Helman J concluded at [42] that the 'track upon which the appellant came to grief was certainly a dangerous allurement but the appellant was fully aware of the risk he ran and voluntarily incurred it'.

So, you need to understand that while the defence requires proof that the plaintiff subjectively accepted the risk of the harm (or subjectively chose to ignore it), it is nevertheless possible to infer from a person's conduct in all the circumstances that they must have either accepted the risk or consciously chosen to ignore it.

Case example

In *Morris v Murray* (1991), the plaintiff was injured in a light plane crash. The plaintiff and the pilot (who had consumed at least the equivalent of 17 whiskies and who died in the crash) were friends who had been drinking heavily in a pub for several hours one afternoon before deciding to go for a joy ride in the pilot's plane. The trial judge found for the plaintiff but reduced the damages by 20 per cent because of his contributory negligence. The English Court of Appeal upheld the appeal, deciding that notwithstanding the plaintiff's own state of intoxication, he must be taken to have accepted fully the risk of serious injury for the following reasons: he knew that he was going on a plane that was to be flown by the pilot in poor flying conditions; he knew that the pilot had been drinking heavily that afternoon; and he had actively participated in organising the flight. So, in the light of the obvious, glaring and intrinsically dangerous fact of the pilot's drunkenness, the plaintiff, by embarking upon the flight, 'had implicitly waived his rights in the event of injury consequent on Mr Murray's failure to fly with reasonable care': see Fox LJ at 16–17, Stocker LJ at 29 and Waller J at 31–2.

Morris v Murray (1991) illustrates the extra difficulties that arise in cases where a drunken plaintiff is rendered less capable (or incapable) of appreciating or accepting a specific risk, and many Australian cases reveal that judges have been more inclined in these situations to find contributory negligence by the plaintiff rather than to accept the defence of *volenti*, and to apportion liability between the plaintiff and the defendant according to their relative degrees of fault: see section 15.6 below. Because this defence completely absolves a negligent defendant of all liability and forces the plaintiff to shoulder the costs of their injury, it has been subject to strict limits, imposed not only by judges but also by parliaments.

Example

In some jurisdictions the defence is not available in cases of motor vehicle accidents or is excluded insofar as it relates to the voluntary assumption of a risk arising from the intoxication of another. (Check your study materials to see whether this is the case in your jurisdiction.)

The Ipp Review Panel (2002) noted at [8.23]:

> Since the introduction of the defence of contributory negligence, the defence of voluntary assumption of risk has become more or less defunct. This is because any conduct that could amount to voluntary assumption of risk would also amount to contributory negligence.

The Ipp Panel explained at [8.28] that there were three reasons why the defence was rarely used: the unwillingness of the courts 'to hold that the plaintiff actually *knew of the risk*', the unwillingness of the courts 'to hold that the plaintiff freely and voluntarily *accepted the risk*', and the tendency of the courts 'to define risks narrowly and at a relatively high level of detail'. The Panel made two recommendations designed to make it easier to establish the defence. The first, noted at [8.30], was 'to reverse the burden of proof on the issue of awareness of risk in relation to obvious risks' and the second, noted at [8.31], was to provide that 'the test of whether a person was aware of a risk is whether he or she was aware of a risk of the type or kind of risk and not of its precise nature, extent or manner of occurrence'. Many parliaments acted upon these recommendations, but the responses differed across jurisdictions and some parliaments went much further than the Ipp Panel's recommended changes. The law in this area is a patchwork, marked out by significant regional variations and combinations. The different approaches to illegality, obvious risks, inherent risks, intoxication, etc make it imperative for you to check your study materials and be aware of the specific legislative provisions in your jurisdiction.

LEGISLATION ALERT!

Consult your study materials for any statutory provisions in your jurisdiction on special rules relating to these defences.

15.3 Obvious risks (statutes)

One of the important changes brought about in the wake of the Ipp Review was the introduction of provisions in all states dealing with 'obvious risks'. (Note that there are also special provisions in some jurisdictions relating to the materialisation of 'inherent risks' and other special rules covering the liability of recreational service providers.)

Legislative example

Civil Liability Act 2002 **(NSW) ss 5F–5H**

5F Meaning of 'obvious risk'

(1) For the purposes of this Division, an 'obvious risk' to a person who suffers harm is a risk that, in the circumstances, would have been obvious to a reasonable person in the position of that person.

(2) Obvious risks include risks that are patent or a matter of common knowledge.

(3) A risk of something occurring can be an obvious risk even though it has a low probability of occurring.

(4) A risk can be an obvious risk even if the risk (or a condition or circumstance that gives rise to the risk) is not prominent, conspicuous or physically observable.

5G Injured persons presumed to be aware of obvious risks

(1) In determining liability for negligence, a person who suffers harm is presumed to have been aware of the risk of harm if it was an obvious risk, unless the person proves on the balance of probabilities that he or she was not aware of the risk.

(2) For the purposes of this section, a person is aware of a risk if the person is aware of the type or kind of risk, even if the person is not aware of the precise nature, extent or manner of occurrence of the risk.

5H No proactive duty to warn of obvious risk

(1) A person ('the defendant') does not owe a duty of care to another person ('the plaintiff') to warn of an obvious risk to the plaintiff.

(2) This section does not apply if—

(a) the plaintiff has requested advice or information about the risk from the defendant, or

(b) the defendant is required by a written law to warn the plaintiff of the risk, or

(c) the defendant is a professional and the risk is a risk of the death of or personal injury to the plaintiff from the provision of a professional service by the defendant.

(3) Subsection (2) does not give rise to a presumption of a duty to warn of a risk in the circumstances referred to in that subsection.

LEGISLATION ALERT!

Consult your study materials for the statutory provisions in your jurisdiction on obvious risk. Note the content and scope of these provisions.

Barbara McDonald, when discussing this provision in 'Legislative Intervention in the Law of Negligence: The Common Law, Statutory Interpretation and Tort Reform in Australia' (2005), concluded at 469:

> Clearly the presumption of awareness of obvious risks now makes the defence of voluntary assumption of risk easier for defendants to prove in cases of obvious risks: a person is presumed to have been aware of an obvious risk, unless he or she proves that he or she was not, whereas the common law placed the onus of proof on the defendant to prove the plaintiff's awareness and assumption of risk. However, the NSW CLA makes no further provision to render the plaintiff's awareness of a risk a defence to a claim so that this provision does not replace the common law defence. Nor, as mentioned above, does it make any provision about the need for proof that the risk was voluntarily assumed, which is one of the other key elements of the common law defence.

So, even though a person will be deemed to be aware of an obvious risk under these new provisions, you should note:

- It is nevertheless possible for a plaintiff to rebut that presumption by proving that they were not actually aware of the risk.
- The fact that a person is deemed to be aware of an obvious risk does not mean that they are deemed to have accepted the liability for that risk, as required by the third element of the *volenti* defence, and so this will have to be proved by the defendant.
- The statutes do not absolve a defendant from taking reasonable care to respond to a foreseeable risk to avoid causing a foreseeable risk of harm to another (even though the defendant may have been relieved of a duty to *warn* the plaintiff about such an obvious risk).

Case example

- In *Carey v Lake Macquarie City Council* (2007), noted above, the defendant council was not liable for *failing to warn* the plaintiff cyclist about the existence of the bollard because it was an obvious risk. However, the council was found liable for breaching its duty of care to the plaintiff by *placing the bollard in the centre of a pathway* where it had 'little if any practical utility', but posed a risk which was 'entirely disproportionate to any benefit, if it had any benefit at all' and in circumstances where council staff knew or ought to have known that bicycles would be ridden along the paths in the park and where the bollards 'created a real and significant hazard for cyclists, particularly during the night time': see McClellan CJ at [49] and [54], and McColl JA at [7]. On the issue of the obviousness of the risk, McClellan CJ noted at [34] that 'in the context of *breach of duty*, the statutory definition of an "obvious risk" in s 5F of the *Civil Liability Act* has no operation'.

- The obviousness of a risk is an important issue to be taken into account under the element of breach when assessing the extent to which a defendant must respond to a foreseeable risk, as discussed in section 15.2 above. See also Lunney, 'Personal Responsibility and the "New" Volenti' (2005) and Barker et al, *The Law of Torts in Australia* (2012) at 618, noting that it will in most cases be easier to argue that the defendant was not in breach of their duty rather than to argue that the plaintiff has accepted the risk of the injury. This is because at the breach stage the issue is assessed prospectively from the point of view of what a reasonable person in the defendant's position would do in the face of the obvious risk, whereas the defence of *volenti* requires proof that the particular plaintiff actually adverted to the risk and accepted it.
- The courts do take the plaintiff's personal characteristics into account when determining whether or not a risk would have been 'in the circumstances ... obvious to a reasonable person in the position of that person'. So, the fact that the plaintiff is a child will be taken into account, as will the plaintiff's lack of knowledge or experience of the relevant area or conditions.

Case examples

- The plaintiff in *Doubleday v Kelly* (2005) was seven years old when she went for a pre-Christmas sleepover at her friend's house. The two girls woke early, went outside unsupervised, and the plaintiff (who had never been on a trampoline before) was injured after attempting to roller-skate on a trampoline in the yard. Bryson JA (with whom the other members of the Court agreed) rejected the contention at [28] that 'the full force' of the New South Wales obvious risk provisions (extracted above) 'applies to children as though they were adults' and maintained at [29] that the legislation:

  > requires consideration of the position of the person who suffers harm and whatever else is relevant to establishing that position. The characteristics of being a child of seven with no previous experience in the use of trampolines or roller skates, who chose to get up early in the morning and play unsupervised, is part of that position.

- In *Queensland v Kelly* (2015), the plaintiff, a young Irish tourist, ran down a sand dune and fell into Lake Wabby on Fraser Island, sustaining serious injuries. He had passed two signs warning of the dangers associated with the lake and sand dunes. The Queensland Court of Appeal affirmed the decision of the judge at first instance, deciding at [31] that the risk that materialised was not obvious to the plaintiff, taking into account the fact that Kelly was 'relatively young, had no experience with sand dunes, and had not previously been to Lake Wabby'.

- In *Nikolich v Webb* (2020), the plaintiff suffered injuries to her shoulder after slipping on a wet bathroom floor in short-term accommodation. She sued the owners, alleging that they had been negligent for not placing warnings in the bathroom with respect to the floor or making the bathroom flooring permanently non-slip. The Western Australian Court of Appeal dismissed the plaintiff's appeal from the decision of the primary judge as (at [109]) 'it could not sensibly be suggested that the risk of slipping and falling on a wet bathroom floor was not an obvious risk'. The Court also noted at [91]:

  > In broad terms, an 'obvious risk', ... is one which is clearly apparent or easily recognised or understood. The risk must be obvious in the sense that, in the circumstances, it would have been obvious to a reasonable person in the position of the plaintiff. Thus the test of obviousness is objective and does not turn on the subjective knowledge or beliefs of the plaintiff (although taking into account personal characteristics of the plaintiff; for example, whether he or she was a child).

15.3.1 Obvious risks of dangerous recreational activities

Some states, including New South Wales, Queensland and Western Australia, have enacted statutory provisions relating to 'dangerous recreational activities'. The provisions are not consistent between the states; however, all provide a complete defence if the plaintiff suffers harm as a result of the materialisation of an 'obvious risk' when the plaintiff is engaged in a 'dangerous recreational activity'. See, for example, *Fallas v Mourlas* (2006), *Falvo v Australian Oztag Sports Association* (2006), *Goode v Angland* (2016), *Carter v Hastings River Greyhound Racing Club* (2020) and *Tapp v Australian Bushmen's Campdraft & Rodeo Association Ltd* (2022).

15.3.2 Inherent risk

Similarly, most states have statutory provisions that provide there can be no liability for inherent risks – that is, risks that cannot be avoided by the exercise of reasonable care and skill. An example is the *Civil Liability Act 2002* (WA) s 5P.

Case example

In *Marks v Skydive Holdings Pty Ltd* (2021), the plaintiff suffered spinal injuries as a result of landing heavily after a tandem skydive. The Court held that the heavy landing was the result of an unexpected, localised down-draft of wind – in other words, the manifestation of an inherent risk of skydiving, rather than due to any failure to exercise due care and skill on the part of the instructor.

15.3.3 Recreational service providers

Special provisions exist in New South Wales, South Australia, Victoria and Western Australia for cases where plaintiffs may seek to sue recreational service providers. When commenting on the *Civil Liability Act 2002* (NSW) s 5N, which allows a recreational service provider to exclude any liability 'that results from breach of an express or implied warranty that the services will be rendered with reasonable care and skill', Barbara McDonald said in 'Legislative Intervention in the Law of Negligence: The Common Law, Statutory Interpretation and Tort Reform in Australia' (2005) at 467:

> It seems offensive to the fundamental values of a modern civilised society to include this shedding of responsibility in a 'personal responsibility' program.

See *Insight Vacations Pty Ltd v Young* (2011) where the High Court considered the application of s 5N of the *Civil Liability Act 2002* (NSW).

15.4 Illegality and joint illegal enterprise (common law)

At common law, the defence of joint illegal enterprise is a complete defence, which, when satisfied, will absolve a negligent defendant of all liability. However, the High Court has made it clear that not all forms of illegality associated with the tort will attract the defence because 'there is no rule denying to a person who is doing an unlawful thing the protection of the general law imposing upon others duties of care for his safety': *Henwood v Municipal Tramways Trust (SA)* (1938), Dixon and McTiernan JJ at 462; *Gala v Preston* (1991), Mason CJ, Deane, Gaudron and McHugh JJ at 248; *Miller v Miller* (2011), the joint judgment of French CJ, Gummow, Hayne, Crennan, Kiefel and Bell JJ at [70]. See also Windeyer J in *Smith v Jenkins* (1970) who said at 416 that the proposition that a wrongdoer can have no remedy at law 'cannot possibly be sustained' and who emphasised very firmly at 414 that 'the maxim "*ex turpi causa non oritur actio*" should be confined to the law of contracts and conveyances'.

Case example

In *Henwood v Municipal Tramways Trust (SA)* (1938), a passenger on a tram became sick, left his seat, leaned out over a rail and vomited. He was killed when his head struck two steel standards fixed into the middle of the street. It was argued by his parents in a successful action for wrongful death that the MTT had been negligent in failing to construct the window in such a way as to prevent passengers from being able to lean out. On appeal, the High Court unanimously rejected the MTT's argument that the passenger had no case in negligence simply because at the time of the accident, he was in breach of a by-law forbidding passengers from projecting any part of their body out of the windows. Dixon and McTiernan JJ pointed out at 460:

> [I]n every case, the question must be whether it is part of the purpose of the law against which the plaintiff has offended to disentitle a person doing the prohibited act from complaining of the other party's neglect or default, without which his own act would not have resulted in injury.

To make out the defence it is not enough to prove that there is some illegality associated with the commission of the tort. Rather, the cases of *Smith v Jenkins* (1970), *Gala v Preston* (1991) and *Miller v Miller* (2011) suggest that the defence of joint illegal enterprise requires the defendant to prove on the balance of probabilities the following factors:

1. *joint illegality:* The plaintiff and the defendant were engaged in a 'joint illegal enterprise' together; and
2. *significant connection:* There is a significant relationship between the negligence complained of and the commission of the illegal act, which justifies denying liability when considered in the light of:
   - the totality of the relationship between the parties: *Miller v Miller* (2011) at [46];
   - the purpose of any relevant statutes: *Miller v Miller* (2011) at [56] and [74]; and
   - the coherence of the law: *Miller v Miller* (2011) at [15] and [74].

The second of these factors reflects the uncertainty associated with this defence and the difficulty of resolving the clash between the relevant principles and drawing a satisfactory line in the law. This defence exists in part to maintain the coherence of the law, as the High Court pointed out in *Miller v Miller* (2011) at [15] and [74]. So, if the community denounces certain conduct in the criminal law, it is said that the courts should not appear to condone that conduct by allowing a plaintiff (who has broken the criminal law) to be protected from the consequences of their own wrongdoing under the community's system of tort law. See, for example, the reasons given by High Court in the case of *Gala v Preston* (1991) on the need to maintain the normative influence of the criminal law and to avoid acting in a way that is repugnant to commonly accepted community standards. This general sentiment seems to have special influence in cases where one party to a criminal activity sues a fellow accomplice and, as Kitto J explained in *Smith v Jenkins* (1970) at 403, the defence ensures that such offenders 'have no legal rights' between themselves ('*inter se*') 'by reason of their respective participations in that act'.

On the other hand, this approach can have harsh results, and the judges in the English Court of Appeal maintained in *Revill v Newbery* (1996) at 577 and 579 that a plaintiff who is engaged in a criminal act should not thereby become 'an outlaw' who is 'debarred by the law from recovering compensation for any injury which he might sustain'. Objectively speaking, the rights of a wrongdoer are just as important – and just as worthy of vindication – as the rights of the innocent. From this point of view, there is no inconsistency in upholding both the criminal law (by insisting that the criminal courts punish criminals for their offences) and upholding the norms established by the law of torts (by insisting that tortfeasors must compensate others whose rights they have wrongfully invaded). If a criminal turns out to be a victim of a tort, there is no logical inconsistency in holding the tortfeasor liable, because once the two processes have been carried out, all the relevant wrongdoers will have been held accountable, the rights of each person will have been vindicated, and justice will have been done. Furthermore, if a criminal is engaging in a particularly dangerous criminal activity (like blowing up a bank vault or speeding away from a robbery) then the other defences (like contributory negligence or voluntary assumption of risk) can be applied to reduce or remove their entitlement to damages.

While Australian courts have drawn back from declaring that wrongdoers must always be taken to have placed themselves outside the law's protection, they have, at the same time, struggled to find an appropriate balance between the two positions on the issue: see *Gala v Preston* (1991), Mason CJ, Deane, Gaudron and McHugh JJ at 253. Until the case of *Miller v Miller* (2011) they also struggled to agree on whether the denial of liability is a matter of principle or a matter of 'public policy' and (equally importantly) on where, in a negligence case, it would be best to consider the fact that a plaintiff has engaged in an illegal activity. It is sometimes dealt with as a defence, but in some cases it is also a relevant issue in the elements of duty and breach as well.

Case examples

- In *Progress & Properties Ltd v Craft* (1976), the defence failed because the plaintiff's illegality consisted of riding in a goods hoist, which, under the relevant regulations, was authorised only for lifting goods, not people. Jacobs J (Stephen, Mason and Murphy JJ agreeing) said at 668:

  > A plea of illegality in answer to a claim of negligence is a denial that in the circumstances a duty of care was owed to the injured person. A duty of care arises out of the relationship of particular persons one to another. An illegal activity adds a factor to the relationship which may *either extinguish or modify the duty of care otherwise owed.* A joint illegal activity may absolve the one party from the duty towards the other to perform the activity with care for the safety of that other. [Emphasis added.]

- In *Gala v Preston* (1991), where the defence succeeded, Mason CJ, Deane, Gaudron and McHugh JJ at 249 (and Dawson J at 278) noted this difficulty, all citing Windeyer J in *Smith v Jenkins* (1970) at 422:

  > If two or more persons participate in the commission of a crime, each takes the risk of the negligence of the other or others in the actual performance of the criminal act. That formulation can be regarded as founded on the negation of duty, or on some extension of the rule *volenti non fit injuria*, or simply on the refusal of the courts to aid wrongdoers. How it be analysed and explained matters not.

  The joint judgment also went on to point out at 249–50 that 'it would be wrong' to accept:

  > the proposition that in all circumstances the participation of plaintiff and defendant in a joint illegal enterprise will negate the existence of a duty of care on the part of the defendant to the plaintiff, even when the alleged breach of duty arises in the execution of the criminal act.

The difficulty in interpreting the earlier cases had been increased by the fact that in *Gala v Preston* (1991) many members of the High Court used the concept of proximity to help to justify the decision. So, while all members of the High Court in *Gala v Preston* (1991) agreed in the outcome of that case (ie that the plaintiff could not recover damages from the driver because they were both engaged in a joint illegal enterprise), the reasons given in the four judgments differ (as noted above in section 15.1 above). This problem of interpreting *Gala v Preston* (1991) was resolved by the High Court in the later case of *Miller v Miller* (2011).

Case example

In *Miller v Miller* (2011) an intoxicated plaintiff, Danelle Miller, was injured when a motor vehicle that she had helped to steal was crashed while it was being driven by the defendant, who was also intoxicated. The 16-year-old plaintiff had been out drinking with her sister and her cousin and at the end of the night, when they had run out of money, they decided to steal a car to get home. Maurin Miller, a male relative aged 27, saw the girls and insisted that he drive the car, which he knew had been stolen. He was intoxicated and had no licence. The car was overloaded with nine people. During the trip the defendant began to speed and to drive through red lights. He refused the plaintiff's request to slow down. The plaintiff asked him to let her out of the car twice, but he did not comply. While driving the car at an excessive speed, he eventually crashed it into a metal pole, killing one of the passengers and injuring the plaintiff, who became a tetraplegic. He was convicted and sentenced to five years imprisonment for the crimes of dangerous driving causing death, dangerous driving causing grievous bodily harm, and driving under the influence of alcohol.

This case, as pleaded at first instance, raised issues of joint illegality, contributory negligence, intoxication, and voluntary acceptance of risk, but at trial the parties agreed that the only live issue in the proceeding was whether the defendant owed the plaintiff a duty of care. The trial judge, who followed the 'salient features' approach, allowed the claim, rejected the defence of joint illegal enterprise and held that the appellant owed the respondent the usual duty of care that a driver owes a passenger. The Western Australian Court of Appeal upheld an appeal against the decision on the grounds that the driver did not owe a duty of care to the plaintiff, but the decision was overturned on appeal to the High Court in a 6:1 decision (Heydon J dissenting).

The judges in the High Court agreed at [54] that 'it is not useful to speak of a court not being able to fix a relevant standard of care' and affirmed at [16] that the 'ultimate' question is 'would it be incongruous for the law to proscribe the plaintiff's conduct and yet allow recovery in negligence for damage suffered in the course, or as a result, of that unlawful conduct?' The joint judgment of French CJ, Gummow, Hayne, Crennan, Kiefel and Bell JJ (with whom Heydon J agreed at [108]) identified at [16] the issue as whether there is 'some relevant intersection between the law that made the plaintiff's conduct unlawful and the legal principles that determine whether the plaintiff should have a cause of action for negligence against the defendant' and maintained that in deciding whether to deny a duty to take reasonable care on the grounds of joint illegal conduct, it was imperative to take into account:

- the totality of the relationship between the parties (at [46]);
- the purpose of any relevant statute (at [56] and [74]); and
- the coherence of the law (at [15] and [74]).

The joint judgment stated at [56]:

> More fundamentally, it is the statute and its purposes which will reveal whether it would be incongruous to hold that a participant in a joint enterprise to contravene the statutory prohibition owed a duty of care to another participant in the enterprise.

The joint judgment also explained at [74] that this approach ensured that the law of negligence took the same path that has been taken in relation to illegality in contract and trusts, noting:

> Incongruity (whether described by that word or as 'contrariety' or 'lack of coherence') will not be demonstrated or denied by bare assertion of the answer. More analysis is required. If a statute has been contravened, careful attention must be paid to the purposes of that statute. It will be by reference to the relevant statute, and identification of its purposes, that any incongruity, contrariety or lack of coherence denying the existence of a duty of care will be found.

So, when applying the law to the facts of the case, the joint judgment first considered in detail the relevant provisions and purposes of the *Criminal Code* (WA) and concluded as follows:

- On the nature of the joint venture (at [92]):

  > The venture between the parties may be described as a venture to use the vehicle illegally.

- On the resulting incongruity (at [93]):

  > If, as a result of the dangerous driving, the complicit passenger were injured, it would evidently be incongruous to decide that the offender who drove the vehicle owed that passenger a duty to drive with reasonable care.

- On the issue of duty (at [101]):

  > The refusal to find a duty of care between those complicit in the offence follows from the more precise identification of the way in which the statutory proscription of illegal use of a vehicle seeks to promote road safety. The offence of illegally taking and using a vehicle is dealt with as it is because of its association with reckless and dangerous driving. The statutory purpose of a law proscribing dangerous or reckless driving is not consistent with one offender owing a co-offender a duty to take reasonable care. And in a case where two or more are complicit in the offence of illegally using a vehicle, the statutory purpose of the law proscribing illegal use (here, s 371A) is not consistent with one offender owing a co-offender a duty to take reasonable care. The inconsistency or incongruity arises regardless of whether reckless or dangerous driving eventuates. It arises from the recognition that the purpose of the statute is to deter and punish using a vehicle in circumstances that often lead to reckless and dangerous driving.

The joint judgment noted the relevance of the plaintiff Danelle's request to be let out of the speeding car, applied the law to the facts and concluded at [106]:

> Because Danelle had withdrawn from, and was no longer participating in, the crime of illegally using the car when the accident happened, it could no longer be said that that Maurin owed her no duty of care. That he owed her no duty

> earlier in the journey is not to the point. When he ran off the road, he owed a passenger who was not then complicit in the crime which he was then committing a duty to take reasonable care. It arises from the recognition that the purpose of the statute is to deter and punish using a vehicle in circumstances that often lead to reckless and dangerous driving.

See also *Bevan v Coolahan* (2019).

15.5 Criminal conduct (statute)

While the decision in *Miller v Miller* (2011) has clarified the common law, it has not created uniformity in the law. This is because there are now significant differences in the statutory regimes across Australia that deal with the implications of criminal conduct by a plaintiff. After the Ipp Review, many jurisdictions introduced statutes that either limited or disentitled a plaintiff who had been engaged in serious forms of criminal conduct from recovering damages through the tort system. Most jurisdictions adopt the civil standard of proof, but in South Australia the *Civil Liability Act 1936* (SA) s 43(1) prescribes that the higher criminal standard be adopted for deciding whether 'the accidents occurred while a person was engaged in conduct constituting an indictable offence'. Many, but not all, of these statutes allow the courts a discretion to award damages in exceptional cases if the new rules would operate 'harshly or unjustly'.

LEGISLATION ALERT!

Consult your study materials for the statutory criminal conduct rules in your jurisdiction. Note the content and scope of these provisions and any limitations or exceptions.

15.6 Contributory negligence (statute)

This is one of the most important defences and its history reflects the swings in the negligence pendulum described in section 15.1 above. It began as a complete defence that was applied harshly against plaintiffs; it was then abolished by statute and reincarnated as a partial defence; and most recently the changes brought about by the civil liability legislation in some jurisdictions have allowed contributory negligence on the part of the plaintiff to reduce their damages by 100 per cent, thus bringing back the possibility that it can operate once more as a complete defence. Contributory negligence was defined by McHugh J in *Joslyn v Berryman* (2003) at [16]:

> At common law, a plaintiff is guilty of contributory negligence when the plaintiff exposes himself or herself to a risk of injury which might reasonably have been foreseen and avoided and suffers an injury within the class of risk to which the plaintiff was exposed.

Originally it seemed that any contributory negligence by the plaintiff, however small, was treated as a complete defence that completely negated the claim.

Case example

In *Butterfield v Forrester* (1809), the defendant placed a pole across his part of the road so that he could repair his house. At around 8 o'clock at night, while there was still enough light to see the pole, the plaintiff, who was drunk and riding his horse 'violently', crashed into the pole and injured himself. The jury found that the plaintiff had not used reasonable and ordinary care to avoid the obstruction and found for the defendant. Lord Ellenborough CJ upheld the decision on appeal and said at 927:

> One person being in fault will not dispense with another's using ordinary care for himself. Two things must concur to support this action, an obstruction in the road by the fault of the defendant, and no want of ordinary care to avoid it on the part of the plaintiff.

However, as the High Court pointed out in its survey of this 'unhappily confused field' in *Alford v Magee* (1952) at 45, the law on contributory negligence was by no means so simple. As the discussion in *March v Stramare* (1991) showed, this rule operated very harshly because it led to an 'all or nothing' result, even in cases where both parties shared the blame for the consequences of their wrongful conduct. So, in some cases this result was circumvented by the common law judges, who manipulated the notion of causation by resorting to the 'last clear opportunity' rule to assist deserving claimants. Eventually the unfairness of the rule was dealt with around the middle of the 20th century by parliaments throughout the common law world, who passed legislation modelled on the maritime law rules that allowed for the apportionment of liability between the parties according to their relative degrees of fault.

Legislative example

Law Reform Act 1995 (Qld) s 10(1)

10 Apportionment of liability in case of contributory negligence

(1) If a person (the claimant) suffers damage partly because of the claimant's failure to take reasonable care (contributory negligence) and partly because of the wrong of someone else –

(a) a claim in relation to the damage is not defeated because of the claimant's contributory negligence; and

(b) the damages recoverable for the wrong are to be reduced to the extent the court considers just and equitable having regard to the claimant's share in the responsibility for the damage.

Mason CJ explained in *March v Stramare* (1991) at 514 that 'the end result of the apportionment legislation was to abolish not only the defence of contributory negligence but also the last opportunity rule'. Some statutes also provide a definition of the term and others provide for limits on the scope of the legislation and for presumptions of contributory negligence in certain situations, including intoxication on the part of either the plaintiff or the defendant, the failure by the plaintiff to wear a seatbelt, etc. Other statutes specify that the reduction of a plaintiff's damages may amount to 100 per cent. Some examples of these statutory provisions are noted below.

Legislative examples

- The *Civil Liability Act 1936* (SA) s 3 defines the term:

  '[C]ontributory negligence' means a failure by a person who suffers harm to exercise reasonable care and skill for his or her own protection or for the protection of his or her own interests.

- The *Wrongs Act 1954* (Tas) s 2 defines the term:

  '[W]rongful act' means an act or omission that –

  (a) gives rise to a liability in tort or would, if it caused damage to another person, give rise to a liability in tort; or

  (b) amounts to a breach of a contractual duty of care that is concurrent and co-extensive with a duty of care in tort; or

  (c) amounts to a breach of a statutory duty –

  and includes an act or omission on the part of a person suffering damage that causes or contributes to the damage and that constitutes a failure on the part of that person to take reasonable care for the protection of his or her person or property.

LEGISLATION ALERT!

This is *not* an exhaustive list of the statutory provisions, so consult your study materials and download a copy of the relevant provisions of the statute in your jurisdiction, making note of any additional provisions (eg a failure to wear seatbelts, or intoxication).

Note any definitions in the statute and any limits on its scope.

This defence can be seen to mirror the fault principle that animates the breach element of negligence laid down by Lord Atkin in *Donoghue v Stevenson* (1932) and the 'golden rule' that you should treat others in the same way that you would like to be treated yourself. Given that liability in negligence is imposed on the defendant on the basis that they should have responded to a foreseeable risk of harm by taking reasonable precautions to avoid causing such harm to others, it is only just that the same principle should be applied to the plaintiff. In other words, if the wrongful conduct of both parties has combined to cause the harm being complained of by the plaintiff, both should rightly share the cost. More recently, the principle of personal responsibility has also been used to justify imposing the more pro-defendant aspects of these rules.

To succeed in a claim based on contributory negligence, the defendant must normally prove the following three elements on the balance of probabilities:

1. *Fault:* The plaintiff failed to take reasonable care for their own safety and protection.
2. *Causation of damage:* The damage suffered by the plaintiff was partly a result of their own conduct.
3. *Scope of liability:* The damage suffered by the plaintiff was within the class of risk to which the plaintiff was exposed.

These elements have been adapted from the passage quoted above by McHugh J at [16] in *Joslyn v Berryman* (2003), who cited the following cases in support: *Nance v British Columbia Electric Railway Co Ltd* (1951) at 611; *Jones v Livox Quarries Ltd* (1952) at 615; and *Froom v Butcher* (1976) at 291.

You can see how closely these elements mirror the elements of negligence – with the obvious exception of the element of 'duty', which is *not* a part of the defence, as Lord Denning pointed out in *Froom v Butcher* (1976) at 291. When you are working your way through the elements of this defence you should remember:

- Contributory negligence and apportionment of liability are questions of fact: *McLean v Tedman* (1984), Mason, Wilson, Brennan and Dawson JJ at 315; *Joslyn v Berryman* (2003), Kirby J at [100] and Hayne J at [158].
- The test is objective, and the law makes an allowance for the position of children, as McHugh J pointed out in *Joslyn v Berryman* (2003) at [32]:

  > The test of contributory negligence is an objective one. Contributory negligence, like negligence, 'eliminates the personal equation and is independent of the idiosyncrasies of the particular person whose conduct is in question.' One exception to that rule is that, in considering whether a child is guilty of contributory negligence, the standard of care is tailored to the age of the child. [References omitted.]

  In this respect, the defence operates in the same way as the law of negligence in the element of breach, as we saw in *McHale v Watson* (1966). In *Town of Port Hedland v Hodder (No 2)* (2012), the majority of the Western Australian Court of Appeal held that the test for contributory negligence should remain entirely objective even when a plaintiff had severe disabilities. This case is notable for the Chief Justice's vigorous dissent, in which his Honour considered physical disability to be a relevant factor that should alter the otherwise objective test.
- The 'agony of the moment' rule, laid down by Lord James in the case known as *The Bywell Castle* (1879) at 223, allows the courts to take into account the fact that a plaintiff may have been placed into a 'moment of extreme peril and difficulty' by the defendant's wrongdoing, and that 'perfect presence of mind, accurate judgment, and promptitude' under such circumstances are 'not to be expected'. See also the South Australian case of *Shelley v Szelley* (1971). This is consistent with the approach taken in the defence of necessity in the intentional torts: see *Proudman v Allen* (1954).
- In *Podrebersek v Australian Iron & Steel Pty Ltd* (1985), the High Court at 532–3 quoted *British Fame (Owners) v Macgregor (Owners)* (1943) at 201:

> A finding on a question of apportionment is a finding upon a 'question, not of principle or of positive findings of fact or law, but of proportion, of balance and relative emphasis, and of weighing different considerations.'

The judges in *Podrebersek* then went on to cite the earlier High Court case of *Pennington v Norris* (1956) and other earlier authorities to explain at 201:

> The making of an apportionment as between a plaintiff and a defendant of their respective shares in the responsibility for the damage involves a comparison both of *culpability, i.e. of the degree of departure from the standard of care of the reasonable man* and of the *relative importance* of the acts of the parties in causing the damage ... It is the whole conduct of each negligent party in relation to the circumstances of the accident which must be subjected to comparative examination. [Emphasis added.]

- In the earlier case of *Pennington v Norris* (1956) the High Court discussed at 16 the process of arriving at a 'just and equitable' apportionment as required under the Tasmanian statute:

> What has to be done is to arrive at a 'just and equitable' apportionment as between the plaintiff and the defendant of the 'responsibility' for the damage. It seems clear that this must of necessity involve a comparison of culpability. By 'culpability' *we do not mean moral blameworthiness but degree of departure from the standard of care of the reasonable man.* To institute a comparison in respect of blameworthiness in such a case as the present seems more or less impracticable, because, while the defendant's negligence is a breach of duty owed to other persons and therefore blameworthy, the plaintiff's 'contributory' negligence is not a breach of any duty at all, and it is difficult to impute 'moral' blame to one who is careless merely of his own safety. [Emphasis added.]

See also *T & X Co Pty Ltd v Chivas* (2014) and *Boral Bricks Pty Ltd v Cosmidis (No 2)* (2014).

- Apportionment of liability where contributory negligence is in issue will generally turn on the facts of each case. As a result, higher courts are normally reluctant to interfere with a lower court's decision; however, this reluctance can be overcome.

Case examples

- In *Pennington v Norris* (1956), the High Court reduced the trial judge's apportionment of liability from 50 per cent to the plaintiff down to a figure of 20 per cent.
- By contrast, in *Zanner v Zanner* (2010) the New South Wales Court of Appeal increased the apportionment of liability to the plaintiff from 50 per cent up to 80 per cent in a case where a mother was injured after she allowed her 11-year-old son to park her car in the family carport and stood in front of the car while he was making the attempt.

The courts distinguish between 'mere inattention' on the one hand and legal 'negligence' on the other.

Case example

In the case of *McLean v Tedman* (1984), an employer was held liable for failing to provide a safe system of work to an employee, a garbage collector who was hit by a car when crossing the road without paying proper attention as they were carrying a loaded rubbish bin. On the issue of contributory negligence by the employee, Mason, Wilson, Brennan and Dawson JJ at 315 said:

> The question is whether that failure should be characterized as *mere inattention or inadvertence* or whether it amounts to negligence, there being *a well recognized distinction between the two.* It is accepted that in considering whether there was contributory negligence by an employee in a case in which the employer has failed to provide a safe system of work, the circumstances and conditions in which he had to do his work must be taken into account. [Emphasis added.]

The Chair of the Ipp Review Panel criticised the decision in *McLean v Tedman* (1984) in 2007 as 'the high point of the nursemaid theory',[2] and the Ipp Report (2002) at [8.10] recommended that there should be no difference in the standard that is applied by the law of negligence to defendants and the standard to be applied to plaintiffs in the defence of contributory negligence. Drawing on 'widely held' community expectations and the 'principle of personal responsibility', the Panel recommended that 'the standard of care for both negligence and contributory negligence should be the same'. This recommendation was followed in five states: New South Wales, Queensland, Tasmania, Victoria and Western Australia.

Despite the fact that the High Court had decided in *Wynbergen v Hoyts Corporation Pty Ltd* (1997) that at common law a reduction of 100 per cent was not permissible, the Ipp Panel (2002) also noted at [8.24] that 'there may be cases in which the plaintiff's relative responsibility for the injuries suffered is so great that it seems fair to deny the plaintiff any damages at all' and concluded:

> It is important to remember that apportionment of damages is concerned with the issue of appropriate remedy, not with liability. It does not follow from a decision that the plaintiff should be denied any damages at all that the defendant was not at fault. Such a decision only means that as between the two parties at fault, the plaintiff should bear full legal responsibility for the harm suffered.

Statutes in New South Wales, Queensland, Victoria and the Australian Capital Territory now make provision for a full 100 per cent apportionment.

Intoxication is a factor that commonly complicates not only the defence of contributory negligence but other defences as well.

2 Ipp, 'Themes in the Law of Torts' (2007) at 610.

Case examples

- In *Joslyn v Berryman* (2003), P and D had both been drinking heavily at a party that began on a Saturday night and continued through until after 4.00 am on the Sunday morning. After a sleep of roughly three hours, the two decided to drive to a nearby town for breakfast. On the way back, the female passenger, Joslyn (D), noticed that the male driver Berryman (P), who was affected by alcohol, was dozing off at the wheel. D insisted on taking over the driving and P allowed her to do so, despite the fact that she was also affected by alcohol, had lost her licence and had not driven a car for three years. She lost control of the car while driving round a sharp curve and P was badly injured. He sued the driver for negligent driving and the local council for negligently failing to put up a sign warning of the danger.

  The trial judge found for P, apportioned the liability 10 per cent to the council and 90 per cent to D, and reduced the damages by 25 per cent on account of the P's contributory negligence. The New South Wales Court of Appeal allowed P's appeal and held that he was not contributorily negligent at the time that he allowed D to take over the wheel, because there was no evidence showing that she was affected by intoxication at that time. On further appeal, the High Court decided that the Court of Appeal had taken too narrow a view of the relevant time and should have taken into account the extended period of interaction between the parties (ie the preceding 36-hour period).

  McHugh J noted at [27] that 'since the introduction of the apportionment legislation, contributory negligence has been the preferred characterisation of the conduct of the plaintiff who accepts a lift from a driver known to be intoxicated', and emphasised at [38] that when assessing contributory negligence the courts must use an objective, and not a subjective, test:

  > The issue is not whether a reasonable person in the intoxicated passenger's condition – if there could be such a person – would realise the risk of injury in accepting the lift. *It is whether an ordinary reasonable person – a sober person – would have foreseen that accepting a lift from the intoxicated driver was exposing him or her to a risk of injury by reason of the driver's intoxication.* If a reasonable person would know that he or she was exposed to a risk of injury in accepting a lift from an intoxicated driver, an intoxicated passenger who is sober enough to enter the car voluntarily is guilty of contributory negligence. The relevant conduct is accepting a lift from a person whose driving capacity is known, or could reasonably be found, to be impaired by reason of intoxication. [Emphasis added.]

- In *Allen v Chadwick* (2015), the pregnant 21-year-old plaintiff (P) was a passenger in a car driven by her partner, the defendant (D). Since D had been drinking heavily during the day, P took responsibility for driving the car. However later that night, on the outskirts of town, she left the car to take a toilet break. When she returned to the car, D was in the driver's seat and insisting he drive. Despite telling him she did not want him to drive, she eventually relented and got into the passenger seat. D commenced driving and soon after, the car struck a tree and P, who was not wearing a seatbelt, was seriously injured. The High Court held that P, a young, pregnant woman on a dark and unfamiliar country road, was not contributorily negligent for choosing to travel in the car with her intoxicated partner. She was, however, assessed as being 25 per cent contributorily negligent for failing to wear a seatbelt.

Many statutes have now introduced the requirement that courts take into account not only the fact of a plaintiff's intoxication but also the fact that a plaintiff may have relied on a person known to be intoxicated. Most introduce a rebuttable presumption of contributory negligence; however, these statutory rules differ markedly throughout Australia and you must read the legislation in your jurisdiction very carefully to identify its precise effect and scope.

LEGISLATION ALERT!

Consult your study materials for the statutory intoxication rules in your jurisdiction.

Note the content and scope of these provisions and any limitations or exceptions.

15.7 The concept of reasonableness

Negligence law seeks to balance the rights of plaintiffs to be protected from unreasonably caused harm against the rights of defendants to a reasonable degree of freedom of action. This balancing process is dominated by the concept of reasonableness - and it is seen not only in the rules and principles governing the defences, but also in the elements of the tort itself. In the first stage of a negligence case, the elements of negligence are designed to answer the essential question about whether, in all the circumstances, the defendant has behaved reasonably towards others. At the second stage of the case, the question is whether it is reasonable as between the parties to insist that the defendant should pay for their unreasonable conduct by compensating the plaintiff for the harm that they have caused. The defences to this tort are designed to ensure that justice is done by applying the standard of reasonableness to judge the conduct of the plaintiff in the same way that the elements of the tort apply the standard of reasonableness to judge the conduct of the defendant. In this way the law aims to secure an acceptable balance between our competing rights to liberty and to be safe from harm, just as it does in the intentional torts.[3] The problem is that not all reasonable persons necessarily agree on where the balance should be set. This question of marking out the boundaries of the tort of negligence and imposing - and justifying - fair limits on the conduct that the law should condemn was discussed in Chapter 14, where we covered the more difficult topics in the tort of negligence.

15.8 The limits of negligence

Negligence can be complicated and confusing. It often deals with intricate fact patterns that can be analysed only in the light of the particular circumstances of each case. One

3 Note, however, that the goal of the trespass torts is to protect our *dignitary* rights - and so the rules found in the elements of the torts are clear 'bright line' rules and the issue of reasonableness features most often in the defences to these torts. Negligence, as the paradigm action on the case focused on the causing of harm, has to resort to using the fuzzy concept of reasonableness all the way through the case and it appears both in the elements and in the defences. See section 7.9 of Chapter 7 on the role of reasonableness in the intentional torts.

of the difficulties lies in the fact that there is no universally accepted moral or social justification for its existence that can help us to unravel those complications or provide us with a clear source of limits. It is further complicated not just because it contains a very wide concept of harm, but also because it requires us to identify and judge the defendant's failure to live up to a standard of reasonable care that caused the harm. So, unlike the trespass torts, the tort of negligence focuses not only on what the defendant *did do*, but also on what the defendant *did not do* – but *should have done*. It is easy when we are discussing the trespass torts to say what the defendant should have done. It is so obvious that it goes without saying: the defendant should simply not have performed the positive physical act that caused the forbidden interference with the plaintiff's recognised rights. But in a case of negligence we have to do much more than refer to a right and prove that the defendant has invaded that right. This is because negligence has a primary focus on indirectly caused harm caused by a breach of the standard of reasonable care. Negligence is therefore the law of human shortcomings, the law of not doing enough, the law of failure and falling short. Negligence requires us to imagine the world as essentially different from what it has turned out to be; negligence lawyers have to convince judges and juries not only *how* the world could have been different if the defendant had done the right thing, but also to persuade them *why* they should act to remedy the harm that has resulted from that defendant's failure to reach a proper standard of care.

Negligence is both a mystery and a challenge. It directly faces the fundamental – but imprecise and essentially contested – concepts of harm and wrongdoing. As Lord Atkin reminded us in *Donoghue v Stevenson* (1932), negligence asks the judges in our courts to base their decisions on a 'general public sentiment of moral wrongdoing for which the offender must pay'. Lord Atkin told us that those 'acts or omissions which any moral code would censure cannot in a practical world be treated so as to give a right to every person injured by them to demand relief'. This means negligence lawyers must assist the courts to draw the lines as best they can between acceptable harm-doing and wrongful harm-doing, and this cannot be done without resorting to the concept of reasonableness and building that concept into the fuzzy rules of negligence.

Our rights to the physical integrity of our bodies, land and goods and to be free from confinement are so fundamental that they give rise to straightforward, 'bright line' rules in the elements of the trespass torts that are relatively easy to apply. It is only when we look at the defences to the trespass torts that we see the now familiar concept of reasonableness enter the discussion, because it is only at the point where our rights collide that we must try to reach some reasonable accommodation between them. But the tort of negligence began where the trespass torts ended; it starts at the place where our rights collide. So, because it has to tackle the fundamental moral concepts of harm and wrongdoing where there are no obvious answers, and because it allows for indirectly caused harm where there are no clear limits, negligence forces judges to resort to the idea of reasonableness right from the beginning, and as we have seen in Chapters 11–14, this concept dominates every element of the tort.

Negligence is the law of reasonableness, but even reasonableness is not enough to assist us when we move beyond the recognised negligence categories. Once we leave behind the cases that allow liability for unreasonable conduct that indirectly causes an invasion of the primary rights and we move into the 'novel' categories that impose liability for conduct that has caused harms that do not seem to merit full rights-based protection (which was the traditional attitude towards pure psychiatric injury and pure economic loss) we are faced with a new challenge. In the hard cases of negligence where the primary rights have already run out, we must resort to other community values and goals to supplement the harm-based neighbour principle of reasonable foreseeability. But these principles do not dictate – they only indicate. They push us in directions that may conflict and this means that judges have to try to find a reasonable balance between them. So, negligence is the law of balance as well as the law of reasonableness; it seeks to balance the competing rights and duties of the parties and to weigh the principles of autonomy, vulnerability, certainty and coherence together to decide where the boundaries of negligence should be drawn.

Negligence is the law of gaps. It was crafted in 1932 to fill the spaces left open when the other causes of action had reached their limits, but it has never found its own limits. So, when judges hold that the defendant's harmful conduct does offend against the public conscience but find that there is no other source of a remedy, they face a dilemma. It is very similar to the one faced by the judges in *Donoghue v Stevenson* in 1932. In Australia, judges have moved on beyond the safety zone of the primary rights and, for the most part, they have rejected policy-based reasoning as well. They have been willing to construct duties that provide partial protection for plaintiffs in exceptional cases. They have recognised new harms and constructed new legal rights to compensation. The justifications for these new duties have not pleased everyone, and many have found them wanting. But is the move to construct these new limited secondary rights illegitimate? The full justification may not be clear – but it generally becomes clearer over time. As the centenary of *Donoghue v Stevenson* (1932) approaches and passes, we should draw some inspiration from the history of the justification for that decision.

The decision and its stated justification did not please everyone, but it seems to have become stronger as the years have passed. It took the judges a long time to explore the reasoning behind that seminal decision, and it may take more time before the deeper justification for steps taken by the High Court can be found. The principles of autonomy, vulnerability, certainty and coherence emerged slowly from long, hard decisions that were time consuming both to construct and to deconstruct. But although not all those principles were overtly written about in the case that gave us the neighbour principle, when we return to read *Donoghue v Stevenson* (1932) again it is striking to see how these new principles help us to see more clearly the sense contained in that first case. We can see more in *Donoghue v Stevenson* (1932) now than at any time since it was first written. The questions raised by the *Wagon Mound* cases in the 1960s took judges nearly 40 years to resolve. So, there are reasons for optimism and for looking forward to the next High Court case, because every new case helps us to read the older cases better – eventually. In a way, the inherent incompleteness and ever-evolving nature of the tort of negligence is both its greatest weakness and greatest strength.

Negligence may be doomed by its own nature to remain in a messy state – but its ambitions are still worthy. It is messy, but it is not necessarily 'a mess'. The High Court has developed the Australian methodology of negligence over many decades and as you read cases like *Sullivan v Moody* (2001) you notice that their search for a deeper source of principled limits has led them back many times to the origins of the tort and the seminal cases of *Heaven v Pender* (1883) and *Donoghue v Stevenson* (1932). However, while Australian judges appear to agree with Lord Macmillan that 'the categories of negligence are never closed', they are also clearly conscious of the warnings given by the minority judges in *Donoghue v Stevenson* (1932) about the 'logical impossibility' of imposing proper limits on the tort. The challenge posed by the tort of negligence means that this legal journey may never be completed, and that the answers given by judges as they re-tread the paths of negligence will not please everybody. Perhaps it is only fitting that the law of negligence – as the law of human shortcomings – itself falls short of its promise of coherence and clarity, as judges strive for justice and better outcomes in difficult cases where wrongful losses would otherwise be left unchallenged.

15.9 Problem-solving tips

Before you go through the problem-solving tips for a basic negligence case, it is important to revisit the 'six-point plan' in Figure 3.2 in Chapter 3, which assists you to analyse a problem question by asking and answering four important questions.

Example

- *Who* is upset with *whom*? This usually identifies the parties: the plaintiff and the defendant.
- *Why* are they upset? This directs you to the *conduct* and its *effects*.
- *What* do they want? This directs you to the *remedy* for those harmful effects.
- *How* can they get it? This directs you to the *tort* that may provide the remedy.

The answers to these questions may appear to be very simple (even superfluous at times) when you are practising an intentional torts problem but they are critically important in a negligence problem. In fact, answering these questions correctly is a vital step in a negligence case, and doing so will ensure that you will be able handle the analysis of each one of the elements and defences successfully.

Examples

You need to identify the *parties* very carefully

The fact patterns in negligence can be very complicated and so it is vitally important to make sure that you work out who the proper parties are. If you do not identify the parties correctly at the beginning, you will go horribly wrong in your analysis and you will not be able to apply the law in the elements or in the defences correctly.

The key to identifying the *plaintiff* is to identify any persons who have been harmed. Then you need to trace back to find any wrongdoers who might be blamed, remembering that in negligence there may be more than one potential *defendant* and that the harm can be caused indirectly as a result of the conduct of many different people, some of whom may have acted negligently and some of whom may have been perfectly innocent agents of the harm. Remember that you are looking for the person who either *caused the harm* by a positive act (either directly or indirectly) or who *should have prevented the harm* from occurring by doing the right thing and acting properly. The following are examples:

- A doctor who carelessly ruptures a patient's spleen during a routine endoscopy procedure may be liable for *causing harm* by a positive act.
- A doctor who carelessly neglected to follow up on a screening test for bowel cancer may be liable for *failing to prevent harm* if the undiagnosed cancer led to the patient's death and early treatment would have prevented it.

You need to note the nature of the relationship between the parties

Negligence treats certain relationship categories differently. If your case falls into one of the 'recognised duty' categories discussed in section 11.2.1 of Chapter 11, your task at the duty element is made much easier, but there may nevertheless be special rules that apply at the element of breach. The following is an example:

- There are special rules governing breach for professionals and their clients or for doctors and their patients.

You need to note the nature of the defendant

Negligence treats certain kinds of defendants differently. The following are examples:

- There are special categories of immunity that apply to certain categories of defendants, like barristers, police officers, etc, as noted in section 11.2.2 of Chapter 11.
- Child defendants are treated differently from adults in the element of breach, as noted in section 12.2.1 of Chapter 12.
- There is a special set of rules altogether for statutory authorities, and for those who are subject to a 'non-delegable duty', as discussed in section 14.2 of Chapter 14, and section 16.2 of Chapter 16.
- If the defendant was an employee acting in the course of their employment, then the doctrine of vicarious liability may operate to impose liability for the tort on the employer, as discussed in Chapter 16.
- Legislation in many Australian jurisdictions has imposed special rules if the defendant is a 'good Samaritan' or a volunteer working for a charitable organisation, etc as noted in section 11.2.2 of Chapter 11 and section 15.1 of Chapter 15.

You need to note the nature of the harm

This is because the tort of negligence treats different kinds of harm differently: it rules out some kinds of harm altogether, as noted in section 13.1.2 of Chapter 13, and it applies different sets of rules to different categories of harm, like pure economic loss or pure psychiatric injury, as discussed in Chapter 14.

You need to note the nature of the *conduct*

The tort of negligence treats different kinds of conduct differently. The following are examples:

- Positive acts of 'misfeasance' are treated differently from omissions or failures to act (which are known as 'nonfeasance'), as discussed in Chapter 14. Omissions are also harder to describe than positive acts, so you need to practise doing this as you read the relevant cases.
- There are special rules for harm that has been caused by 'mere words' that lead to 'pure economic loss', as discussed in sections 14.4 and 14.5 in Chapter 14.
- Special rules apply if the defendant has been sued over a failure to prevent animals from straying on the highway. Check your study materials!

The above set of examples is enough to illustrate the importance of learning how to identify the conduct, the effects and the parties before you launch into an analysis of a negligence question, and it is easy to see how a combination of more than one of these special factors can lead to a very complicated exercise indeed. You should try to write a 'six-point plan' for every case that you study so that you can learn how to identify these critical facts and master these basic steps in diagnosing a problem question. You should also add an extra step into the 'six-point plan' when you are working on the tort of negligence, by clearly identifying the *nature of the relationship between the parties* and the *basic content of the duty of care* before you lead into your discussion of the elements of the case (Figure 15.1). (To see why, reread section 11.1.3 of Chapter 11 for the advice given by the High Court on this issue.) Remember that the duty of care is a more general formulation, whereas the breach of the duty must be more specific. Figure 15.1 provides a template that you can use for practice when you are reading the negligence cases in your study materials and that you can adapt when you are introducing your answer to a problem question. Note that it explicitly includes the 'conduct and effect pair', which covers the *breach*, as well as the general identification of the nature and content of the *duty of care*.

Figure 15.1 Modification of the 'six-point plan' for negligence

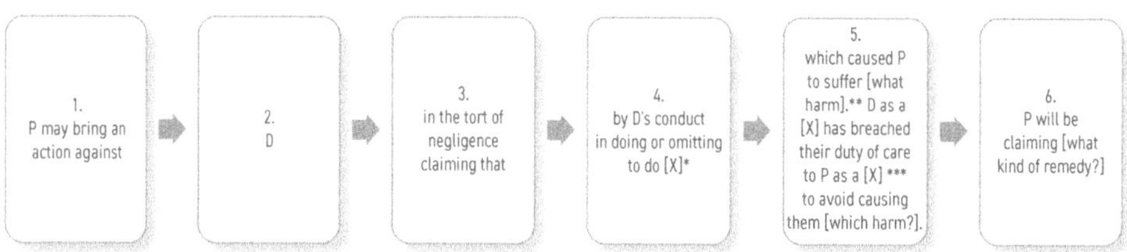

*Note the specific factual conduct by D, ie the breach.
**Note the specific harmful effects on P.
***Note the known person or class of persons and the relationship between P and D.

Example

Jane (P) may try to sue *Charles* (D) in the tort of *negligence*, claiming that by his *conduct* in failing to check the instructions on the bottle properly before injecting her with an overdose of 'Trufasix', which caused her to suffer the permanent *effect* of paralysis in her hand, Charles, *as a doctor* failed in the duty of care that he owed to her *as a patient* to avoid causing her physical injury.

She will be claiming compensatory *damages* to cover her pain, suffering and consequent loss of earning capacity due to her disability, as well as damages for loss of enjoyment of life as she can no longer dig in her garden or pursue her hobby of needlepoint.

Test your understanding

Write a modified 'six-point plan'.

Use this modified version to write a 'six-point plan' that introduces the facts and issues in *Donoghue v Stevenson* (1932), *Chapman v Hearse* (1961) and *March v Stramare* (1991).

Now you are ready to prepare for a problem-solving exercise.

Develop your skills

Preparing for problem solving

1. Before you begin the problem, download a copy of the *civil liability legislation* in your jurisdiction and familiarise yourself with its contents.
2. Make a *summary* of the relevant law to use in diagnosing a problem question. (It is a good idea to make this summary each week as you study each of the topics covered in sections 15.9.1 to 15.9.4 below.) Modify the lists in section 15.9.4.3 below to reflect the law in your jurisdiction.
3. When you are making your summary, make sure that you incorporate the steps noted in each of the relevant summary points features.

Putting it all together: with defences now considered, we are ready to examine how the essential elements of negligence combine with defences to establish liability.

15.9.1 Duty of care

You need to be aware of the neighbour principle from *Donoghue v Stevenson* (1932) and the test taken from *Chapman v Hearse* (1961). Make sure that you:

- note the established duty categories;
- note the categories of immunity; and
- are aware of the special duty categories.

When you are working your way through the element of duty, make sure that you note the items from the duty of care summary points (section 11.3.11 of Chapter 11).

15.9.2 Breach

You need to have ready access to the relevant legislation in your jurisdiction and know the rules and principles from the cases that were used to illustrate its operation. When you are working your way through the element of breach, make sure that you note the items from the breach summary points (see Chapter 12), including:

- Who is the 'reasonable person' in this case?
- How would a reasonable person have responded in this case?

Remember that in your discussion of the element of breach, you must not only identify from the facts of the problem question what the defendant did or did not do (ie the act or omission *constituting the breach*), but you must also identify in factual terms *what precautions* the defendant, as a reasonable person, *should have taken* in the light of the facts of the case. If you do not do this, you will not be able to answer this part properly. Remember that there may well be an issue between the parties here: the plaintiff may be arguing for one set of precautions that would favour their case, while the defendant may counterargue, suggesting a less onerous set.

15.9.3 Causation

You need to have ready access to the relevant legislation in your jurisdiction and know the rules and principles from the cases that were used to illustrate its operation. When you are working your way through the third element of causation, make sure that you note the items from the causation summary points (section 13.1.2 of Chapter 13) and the scope of liability summary points (section 13.3.6 of Chapter 13):

1. The harm must be of a kind that is recognised by law as damage.
2. The defendant must have factually caused the harm in the sense that their wrongful conduct was either:
   - a necessary condition (or 'but for' cause) of harm suffered by the plaintiff; or
   - (in exceptional cases), the defendant's wrongful conduct has materially increased the plaintiff's risk of suffering the harm.
3. The harm must fall within the appropriate scope of liability and must not be too remote.

15.9.4 Defences to negligence

You need to have a summary of the ingredients of the relevant common law defences as modified by the legislation in your jurisdiction:

- voluntary acceptance of risk (*volenti*) – and obvious risks (statute);
- joint illegal enterprise – and any criminal conduct provisions (statute);
- contributory negligence – and any modification (statute); and
- any other statutory provisions.

15.9.4.1 Diagnosing the problem question

When you are *diagnosing* the problem question, keep the lists in section 15.9.4.3 below handy, so that you know what to look for. Begin the diagnosis, as always, by looking for *harm* – and then note *who* suffered it, what *kind* of harm it was and *how extensive* it was. This will identify the plaintiff and the remedy. Remember that certain kinds of harm are dealt with by special rules, so check to see whether it is covered by the topics in Chapter 14 – for example:

- pure psychiatric injury;
- pure economic loss.

The next step is to work out whose *conduct* led to the harm because this will help you to identify:

- the defendant;
- the relationship between the defendant and the plaintiff; and
- the conduct amounting to the breach.

How to identify the *defendant:* Remember that you are looking for the person who either *caused the harm* by a positive act (either directly or indirectly) or who *should have prevented the harm* from occurring by doing the right thing and acting properly. So, make sure that you note whether it was a positive act, or an omission. Next note the *relationship* between the defendant and the plaintiff, because that will help you to work out the relevant duty category.

Make sure that you describe the defendant's *conduct* carefully in terms of the facts because this is relevant to the element of breach. If the conduct is 'mere words', or if it was an omission, it will be covered by the special topics in Chapter 14 – for example:

- omissions;
- statements.

Once you have identified the *defendant* and noted the *nature of their conduct,* check to see if they fit into any of the special categories of defendants covered in Chapters 11, 14 or 16:

- immune defendants, covered in section 11.2.2 of Chapter 11;
- public authorities, covered in section 14.2 of Chapter 14;
- medical professionals, covered in section 14.6 of Chapter 14;
- employers and employees, covered in Chapter 16 of Chapter 16;
- non-delegable duty, covered in section 16.2 of Chapter 16.

Once you have worked out who the parties are and whether any of the special rules on duty or breach apply, you need to conduct a further analysis. At this point you are looking for any issues that may relate to the third element of *causation.* So, check:

- Was the harm of a recognised kind?
- Were there any others whose conduct also contributed to cause the initial harm?
- Did the plaintiff's own conduct also contribute to causing the initial harm?
- Did the plaintiff have an extra susceptibility to suffering harm?
- Did any subsequent event occur after the initial harm crystallised, which caused any extra harm to the plaintiff?

Finally, make a quick check to see whether there are any factors that may give rise to a *defence*:

- Voluntary acceptance of risk: Was the plaintiff knowingly engaging in a risky or obviously dangerous activity?

- Joint illegality: Were the plaintiff and the defendant engaging in a joint illegal enterprise?
- Criminal conduct: Was the plaintiff committing a crime at the time they were injured?
- Contributory negligence: Was the plaintiff careless of their own safety?
- Other statutory defences: Was the plaintiff a 'good Samaritan', or providing a recreational service, etc?

15.9.4.2 Plan out your answer and start writing

Introduce the answer using the modified 'six-point plan'.

Body: Take each cause of action (or suit) in time order and work though the three elements of negligence using HIRAC (section 3.3.2 of Chapter 3) where matters may be in doubt, making sure that you demonstrate your knowledge of the cases to add depth to your answer.

Use your summary and checklists to make sure that you have dealt with all of the relevant rules and principles.

Once you have dealt with the elements, consider whether any defence can be made out.

Briefly consider the remedies and come to a conclusion.

Then move on to the next suit, and repeat the process.

Conclusion: Come to a conclusion and identify any further facts that you might need to ascertain in order to come to a definite conclusion.

Remember: you can cross-reference within an answer, so do not write out all of the law twice if you have two suits to argue out.

15.9.4.3 Look up: Negligence

Stage One

Identify all possible **defendants** and work though the **elements**. (The plaintiff must prove every element.)

DUTY OF CARE: The plaintiff must be a person, or a member of a class of persons, whom the defendant can **reasonably foresee** could be injured if the defendant does not take reasonable care, *and* the circumstances *either*:

- fit into an established duty category – for example:
  - manufacturer;
  - driver/road user;
  - employer;
  - school authority;
  - doctor, solicitor, other professional;
  - occupier of premises;
- *or* exhibit 'salient' features (see Chapter 11) – for example:
  - a relationship of proximity; or
  - the plaintiff is vulnerable to the defendant and cannot otherwise protect themself, because salient features may exist, including:

        - reliance by the plaintiff and assumption of responsibility by the defendant;
        - special control or knowledge by the defendant.
- *But no duty* will arise if the circumstances:
    - are within a category of immunity; or
    - would create:
        - undue interference with autonomy/freedom;
        - disrespect for personal responsibility;
        - indeterminate liability, uncertainty or difficulty in defining and complying with the duty, or measuring the damages; or
        - incoherency or inconsistency in the law.

BREACH: The defendant must take the **precautions** that:

- a **reasonable person** in the defendant's position would have taken at the time in response to a **reasonably foreseeable** and **not insignificant risk** of harm,
    - taking into account the:
        - probability that the harm would occur if care was not taken;
        - likely seriousness of the harm which may result;
        - burden of taking the precautions to avoid the risk of harm; and
        - social utility (usefulness) of the risk-creating activity;
    - and any other relevant factors, including:
        - professional or customary standards;
        - statutory standards;
        - anticipated carelessness by the plaintiff;
        - expectation that the plaintiff knows of obvious risks;
        - intoxication.

CAUSATION: The defendant will be liable for all the harm:

- that is of a **kind recognised by law** as damage,
- *and which* **the defendant has factually caused** in the sense that their wrongful conduct was either:
    - a necessary condition (or 'but for' cause) of the occurrence of the harm to the plaintiff; or
    - (in exceptional cases), where the defendant's wrongful conduct materially increased the plaintiff's risk of suffering the harm,
- *and which* **is within the proper scope of liability** in the sense that it is not too remote – that is, it is:
    - harm of a *kind* that is reasonably foreseeable as a result of the breach,
    - even if the *extent* of the harm was not reasonably foreseeable (see the eggshell skull principle, based on the plaintiff special vulnerability because of their psychological physical, cultural or social characteristics),
- *but not* if the harm is caused by:
    - the plaintiff's subsequent unreasonable conduct; or
    - a subsequent independent negligent or consciously chosen wrongful act of a third party (but note the special rules on negligent medical treatment).

Stage Two

Look for any **defences.** (The onus is on the defendant to prove any defence.)

1. **Voluntary acceptance of risk**
   Three elements to be proven by the defendant on the balance of probabilities:
   - *Knowledge:* The plaintiff knew of the facts constituting the risk of harm.
   - *Understanding:* The plaintiff fully appreciated the danger inherent in those factual circumstances.
   - *Voluntariness:* The plaintiff freely and willingly agreed to encounter the risk (a subjective test).
2. **Obvious risks**
   Check your study materials for relevant statutory provisions in your jurisdiction.
3. **Contributory fault/negligence**
   Three elements to be proven by the defendant on the balance of probabilities:
   - *Fault:* The plaintiff failed to take reasonable care for their own safety and protection (an objective test).
   - *Causation of damage:* The damage suffered by the plaintiff was partly a result of their own conduct.
   - *Scope of liability:* The damage suffered by the plaintiff was within the class of risk to which the plaintiff was exposed.
4. **Joint illegal enterprise**
   Two elements to be proven by the defendant on the balance of probabilities:
   - *Joint illegality:* The plaintiff and the defendant were engaged in a 'joint illegal enterprise' together.
   - *Significant connection:* There is a significant relationship between the negligence complained of and the commission of the criminal act, which justifies denying liability.
5. **Criminal conduct**
   Check your study materials for relevant statutory provisions in your jurisdiction.
6. **Other relevant statutory provisions**
   - Intoxication
   - Other provisions

Stage Three

Note any **remedies.** (The onus is on the plaintiff to prove entitlement.)

See Chapter 17.

Test your understanding

Tash and Hosni, both aged 16, were best friends. They were mad about sport and outdoor activities and always spent the school holidays each year in the bush, where they went walking, abseiling and swimming. Hosni was a brilliant student – an all-rounder who excelled at both sport and his studies. Tash, who hated school, dreamed of representing Australia in soccer and playing with the Matildas in a victorious World Cup team. Earlier this year they attended the annual soccer development camp that was organised by their school's soccer coach, Mr Martinez. The camp was designed to develop fitness and team spirit among the students in the school's elite soccer squad. Each morning they went for a long run and practised soccer drills; each afternoon they participated in team-building challenges and discussion groups. In the evenings they relaxed and played games in the main hall of the school's camping facility.

One of the favourite games was a variation on the children's party game of musical chairs. It was known as 'Blocks in the Dark' and the procedure was as follows. A set of small wooden blocks was placed in the centre of the hall – one less than the number of students present. Half of the main lights in the hall would be turned off and the squad would begin to jog around the hall. When one of Mr Martinez's assistant coaches turned off the rest of the lights, this was the signal for the students to rush at full speed into the centre of the hall and each try to grab a block. There was always a lot of scuffling and wrestling during the rush for the blocks as students would try to kick the blocks off to the side of the hall and then fight to retrieve them. The student who failed to grab a block would be eliminated and the next round would then be played with one less block in the centre. The hall was not in pitch darkness when the main lights were turned off, because there was a set of emergency lights on a different circuit. These lights were always kept on and gave enough light to see by. The students usually ended up with a few bruises, but nothing had ever gone seriously wrong.

On the second last day of the camp, Hosni and Tash were involved in a heated 'debate' with one of the other students during the final encounter group. This occurred after Mr Martinez had listed the topic of 'courage' for discussion and had encouraged the students to challenge each other about their weaknesses. Hosni told the others that he had always been afraid of being locked up in small spaces ever since he was a small child when his parents had brought him to Australia on a boat as a refugee. He and all the other children on the boat were hidden in the cupboard of a small, cramped and leaky cabin when pirates had boarded the boat and Hosni had been afraid that they would all be killed. Although he and his family survived the ordeal, Hosni has suffered from panic attacks since that time. One of the older students, Henry (an 18-year-old final-year student), challenged Hosni and called him a 'chicken' for still being afraid of small spaces. Mr Martinez, who believed in 'facing your fears', encouraged the other students to interrogate Hosni about his fear of confined spaces and the session quickly descended into chaos, with Tash attempting to defend her friend and some of the other students looking on and laughing as Hosni became more and more distressed. For the rest of the camp, some of the other students teased Hosni about his fear. They called him names and mocked him by pretending to cry whenever he walked past. Mr Martinez noticed but did nothing to stop them, hoping that this treatment might help to 'toughen Hosni up'.

On the final night, the students asked Mr Martinez if they could play 'Blocks in the Dark' for one last time. Unbeknown to Mr Martinez, however, the students had all snuck off after the last group discussion session that afternoon and most of them had shared a couple of bottles of vodka and rum that Henry had smuggled into the camp. Despite the fact that the school had a strict 'no alcohol' policy, it had become a well-known tradition among the senior students to bring alcohol to the development camps for a 'team bonding' drinking game that always occurred on the last afternoon of the camp. Although Hosni declined, Tash decided to participate by drinking shots along with the other students who were also drinking.

When the game got underway, it appeared to be played with a lot more boisterousness than usual and the wrestling and scuffling for the blocks during the first two rounds took on a new intensity. The assistant coach suggested that the game be abandoned, but Mr Martinez decided to keep on with the game and began blowing his whistle to try to reimpose order whenever things looked like heating up. Henry, who was the ringleader of the group that had teased Hosni, decided to play a practical joke that would 'cure' Hosni of his fear. He organised for another student to turn off the emergency lighting switch straight after the end of the fifth round of the game. When the next round of the game began, Henry and the other student kept close to Hosni during the run around the hall. Once the signal was given to dive for the blocks and the hall had been plunged into total darkness after the assistant coach had turned off the main lights, the two conspirators grabbed Hosni and bundled him into the cupboard that stored the hall's sporting equipment. No one heard Hosni's screams for help because of the excited noises coming from the other students who were making the most of the total darkness to fight over the remaining blocks. During the scuffles for the last two blocks, Tash (who was feeling a little dizzy after the shot drinking game) heard a block sliding past her after it had been kicked to the side of the hall by another player. She ran in the direction that she thought the block had been going and tripped in the darkness over a heavy wooden bench that had been left near the wall. She lost her balance, fell awkwardly, and crashed.

When the lights were finally turned on, the sounds of screaming led the teachers to find Hosni locked in the cupboard in an extremely distressed state and Tash writhing in agony next to the wall with her leg obviously badly broken (forming a right angle at the knee). They called for an ambulance to take Tash to the local area hospital and managed to calm Hosni down before calling his parents to come to take him home. On the way to the hospital, the driver of the ambulance was forced to swerve violently to avoid being hit by a large block of concrete that had been thrown from an overpass by a group of young people who regularly terrorised the neighbourhood. The ambulance side-swiped a concrete pillar and Tash, who had not been tightly strapped into the ambulance bed, was thrown to the floor, landing heavily on her shoulder. It was established that the ambulance attendant (who was on duty for the first time that night), had loosened Tash's bed straps because he did not want to put too much pressure on Tash's obviously injured body. Once she was admitted to the hospital, Tash was X-rayed and it was revealed that she had broken her leg in two places, dislocated her knee and broken her collarbone. It was known that her leg had been badly damaged before Tash had been placed into the ambulance, but the X-ray could not establish the cause of the broken collarbone.

Hosni suffered a nervous breakdown and was subsequently diagnosed with PTSD. His condition was treated successfully, but, having lost his trust in his schoolmates, Hosni decided to drop out of school early and became an apprentice bricklayer. Hosni's mother, who had worked many long hours to pay for Hosni's school fees, and who had always dreamed of the day when her son would become a doctor, reacted badly when he dropped out of school. Her work suffered and she was eventually sacked from her job and became a recluse.

Tash's leg injuries did not heal well and while she was eventually able to walk without pain, the injuries prevented her from playing soccer again. Her shoulder was permanently weakened and she had to give up her hobby of abseiling.

Advise Tash's parents, who consult you about her injuries.

Advise Hosni's father, who is worried about his wife and his son.

Conclusion

In this chapter, we explored the key defences to negligence, such as voluntary assumption of risk (*volenti*), the statutory defence provisions that exist in various jurisdictions, and contributory negligence. By examining the legal principles and important cases behind these defences, you've seen how the courts try to navigate the balance between holding individuals and organisations accountable and recognising how the conduct of the plaintiff can and will shape the outcome of the matter. These defences – like negligence itself – continue to evolve in accordance with shifting notions of reasonableness, new types of hazards, and evolving benchmarks for reasonable behaviour.

REFERENCES

CASES

Alford v Magee (1952) 85 CLR 437
Allen v Chadwick (2015) 256 CLR 148
Bennett v Tugwell [1971] 2 QB 267
Bevan v Coolahan (2019) 101 NSWLR 86
Birch v Thomas [1972] 1 WLR 294
Boral Bricks Pty Ltd v Cosmidis (No 2) (2014) 86 NSWLR 393
British Fame (Owners) v Macgregor (Owners) (1943) AC 197
Butterfield v Forrester (1809) 11 East 60; 103 ER 926
Carey v Lake Macquarie City Council [2007] NSWCA 4
Carter v Hastings River Greyhound Racing Club (2020) 102 NSWLR 69
Chapman v Hearse (1961) 106 CLR 112
Donoghue v Stevenson [1932] AC 562
Doubleday v Kelly [2005] NSWCA 151
Fallas v Mourlas (2006) 65 NSWLR 418
Falvo v Australian Oztag Sports Association (2006) Aust Torts Reports 81-831
Froom v Butcher [1976] QB 286
Gala v Preston (1991) 172 CLR 243
Goode v Angland (2016) NSWSC 1014
Heaven v Pender (1883) 11 QBD 503
Henwood v Municipal Tramways Trust (SA) (1938) 60 CLR 438
ICI Ltd v Shatwell [1965] AC 656
Imbree v McNeilly (2008) 236 CLR 567

Insight Vacations Pty Ltd v Young (2011) 243 CLR 149; 276 ALR 497
Insurance Commissioner v Joyce (1948) 77 CLR 39
Jones v Livox Quarries Ltd [1952] 2 QB 608
Joslyn v Berryman (2003) 214 CLR 552
Leyden v Caboolture Shire Council [2007] QCA 134
March v Stramare (1991) 171 CLR 506
Marks v Skydive Holdings Pty Ltd [2021] VSC 21
McHale v Watson (1966) 115 CLR 199
McLean v Tedman (1984) 155 CLR 306
Miller v Miller [2009] WASCA 199
Miller v Miller (2011) 242 CLR 446
Morris v Murray [1991] 2 QB 6
Nance v British Columbia Electric Railway Co Ltd [1951] AC 601
Nikolich v Webb [2020] WASCA 169
Osbourne v London and North-Western Railway Co (1888) 21 QBD 220
Paltidis v The State Council of the Young Men's Christian Association of Victoria Inc [2006] VSCA 122
Pennington v Norris (1956) 96 CLR 10
Podrebersek v Australian Iron & Steel Pty Ltd (1985) 59 ALR 529
Progress & Properties Ltd v Craft (1976) 135 CLR 651
Proudman v Allen [1954] SASR 336
Queensland v Kelly [2015] 1 Qd R 577
Revill v Newbery [1996] 2 WLR 239; [1996] 1 All ER 291
Roggenkamp v Bennett (1950) 80 CLR 292
Scanlon v American Cigarette Co (Overseas) Pty Ltd (No 3) [1987] VR 289
Shelley v Szelley [1971] SASR 430
Smith v Charles Baker & Sons [1891] AC 325
Smith v Jenkins (1970) 119 CLR 397
Sullivan v Moody (2001) 207 CLR 562
T & X Co Pty Ltd v Chivas (2014) 67 MVR 297
Tapp v Australian Bushmen's Campdraft & Rodeo Association Ltd (2022) 273 CLR 454; 399 ALR 535
The Bywell Castle (1879) LR 4 PD 219
Town of Port Hedland v Hodder (No 2) (2012) 43 WAR 383
Wilson v Horne (1999) 8 Tas R 363
Woods v Multi-Sport Holdings Pty Ltd (2002) 208 CLR 460
Wynbergen v Hoyts Corporation Pty Ltd [1997] HCA 52; (1997) 149 ALR 25
Zanner v Zanner [2010] NSWCA 343

ARTICLES, BOOKS AND REPORT

Barker, K, Cane, P, Lunney, M & Trindade, F, *The Law of Torts in Australia*, 5th ed (2012) Oxford University Press, Melbourne.
Dietrich, J, 'Duty of Care under the "Civil Liability Acts"' (2005) 13 *Torts Law Journal* 17.
Ipp, D, 'Themes in the Law of Torts' (2007) 81 *Australian Law Journal* 609.

Ipp, D, Cane, P, Sheldon, D & Macintosh, I, *Review of the Law of Negligence: Final Report* (2002) <https://treasury.gov.au/review/review-of-the-law-of-negligence>.

Lunney, M, 'Personal Responsibility and the "New" Volenti' (2005) 13 *Tort Law Review* 76.

Luntz, H, 'Reform of the Law of Negligence: Wrong Questions – Wrong Answers' (2002) 81 *University of New South Wales Law Journal* 836.

Luntz, H, Hambly, D, Burns, K, Dietrich, J, Foster, N, Grant, G & Harder, S, *Torts: Cases and Commentary*, 8th ed (2017) LexisNexis Butterworths, Sydney.

McDonald, B, 'Legislative Intervention in the Law of Negligence: The Common Law, Statutory Interpretation and Tort Reform in Australia' (2005) 27 *Sydney Law Review* 443.

McDonald, B, 'The Impact of the Civil Liability Legislation on Fundamental Policies and Principles of the Common Law of Negligence' (2006) 14 *Torts Law Journal* 268.

Trindade, F & Cane, P, *The Law of Torts in Australia* (1985) Oxford University Press, Melbourne.

16 VICARIOUS LIABILITY AND NON-DELEGABLE DUTY

Introduction

Chapters 11, 12 and 13 explained how a plaintiff who is injured by another person may bring an action in negligence. Those chapters dealt mainly with simple cases where one defendant's negligence harms a plaintiff and where no other parties are involved, as illustrated in Figure 16.1. However, because the tort of negligence allows liability for indirectly caused harm, it frequently gives rise to very complicated multiparty fact patterns, as the sections in Chapter 14 covering pure psychiatric injury and pure economic loss demonstrate. This chapter deals with two somewhat difficult – and unfortunately, still rather unclear – legal doctrines, both of which can add extra complications into a problem-solving exercise. These doctrines – known as 'vicarious liability' and 'non-delegable duty' – were developed because people often ask other people to do something for them that they do not want to do themselves. A problem may arise if the person who has accepted the 'mission' happens to commit a tort while they are carrying out their task. If the primary tortfeasor has no assets and no insurance, then the plaintiff might otherwise be left without a meaningful remedy. However, the law sometimes allows the injured plaintiff to sue the person who originally gave the task to the primary tortfeasor. Two common ways to achieve this outcome are vicarious liability and non-delegable duty.

Case examples

- *Vicarious liability:* In *Hollis v Vabu Pty Ltd* (2001) the plaintiff was injured in an accident caused by a bicycle courier (D1). The courier was never identified because he rode off before the plaintiff could get any of his details, but the courier was wearing the distinctive uniform provided to him by his employer (D2). The plaintiff successfully sued the employer who was held by the

High Court of Australia ('High Court') to be vicariously liable for the tort committed by their employee.

- *Non-delegable duty:* In *Kondis v State Transport Authority* (1984) the plaintiff Kondis was an employee who worked for STA (D2) at its railway yards. He was injured at work through the carelessness of the primary tortfeasor, a crane operator named Clissold (D1). The crane operator was not an employee of STA but was an independent contractor who was on site operating a crane at STA's request. The plaintiff successfully sued STA. Four judges in the High Court held that the plaintiff's employer, STA, owed him a personal, non-delegable duty to adopt a safe system of work that could not be discharged simply by contracting with another person to carry out the work.

These doctrines apply where three or more parties are involved and where there are two possible defendants, the two possible defendants being the person who caused the harm and the person or entity who might ultimately be held responsible. Table 16.1 (in section 16.1.3.3 below) summarises the distinguishing features of these two doctrines, and you can see that one of the key cross-over points between the two doctrines occurs in the context of employment. The interwoven and concurrent relationships that can exist between a group of defendants and plaintiffs often give rise to very complex factual scenarios that will test both your problem-solving skills and your understanding of the relevant law. We have seen multiperson factual scenarios in previous chapters: *Donoghue v Stevenson* (1932) itself involved multiple actors, as did many of the cases in the sections in Chapter 14 on pure psychiatric injury and pure economic loss. But in all those cases, the unsuccessful defendants were held liable for their own wrongful conduct. The interesting legal conundrum raised by these two doctrines is the fact that the ultimate defendant (D2) is held liable to compensate the plaintiff for harm that has been caused by the conduct of another person (D1). From an ethical or philosophical point of view, they might be seen as controversial doctrines because they appear to cast blame on a person who has done nothing wrong; this is one of the reasons courts have generally not been inclined to expand their scope. From a practical point of view they are difficult doctrines to apply because the law in both of these areas is so unclear, with the majority in *Bird v DP (A Pseudonym)* (2024) describing the history of vicarious liability in Australia and in other jurisdictions as '*tortured*' (at 48).

The doctrines of vicarious liability and non-delegable duty both have the effect of giving a plaintiff who has been the victim of a tort committed by a primary wrongdoer an extra claim against another defendant. But although both doctrines increase a plaintiff's chances of obtaining a remedy, each doctrine takes the plaintiff on a different route to that remedy and each doctrine focuses on a different kind of special relationship to justify imposing liability.

Examples

- **Vicarious liability** is a form of strict liability that is imposed because of the special relationship that exists between the primary tortfeasor (D1) and the secondary defendant (D2), which operates to make D2 liable to compensate the plaintiff for the tort committed by D1. Some of these special relationships include:

- employment relationships where D1 is employed by D2; and
- agency relationships where D1 is D2's agent.

In such cases D2 can be liable to the plaintiff even though D2 themselves may have done nothing wrong. This doctrine applies to all torts, including the intentional torts.

- **Non-delegable duty** is imposed on the basis of the special relationship that exists directly between the secondary defendant (D2) and the plaintiff (P). Some of these special relationships that justify holding D2 liable include:
  - the relationship between an employer (D2) and an employee (P);
  - the relationship between a hospital (D2) and a patient (P);
  - the relationship between a school (D2) and a pupil (P);
  - the relationship between an occupier (D2) and a neighbour (P), where D2 is conducting an especially hazardous activity on their premises.

These special relationships justify allowing the plaintiff to recover compensation directly from D2 because D2 has failed to conform with a special personal duty owed directly to the plaintiff, even though the actual damage was caused by the conduct of another person, D1. The scope of this doctrine includes negligent conduct on the part of D1, but it does not extend to cover any intentional act of wrongdoing.

Vicarious liability is a form of strict liability that operates to make one person legally liable to compensate a plaintiff for a *tort* that has been committed by another person. The doctrine of non-delegable duty is slightly different, because it does not impose liability for the *tort* committed by another person, but rather it imposes liability directly on the ultimate defendant (D2) for their *own tort* (which is constituted by a combination of the harm-causing *conduct* of another tortfeasor (D1) and D2's own *failure to comply* with a personal duty owed directly to the plaintiff). So, while the two doctrines are similar in that they both focus on the harmful conduct of one person (D1) that is ultimately paid for by another person (D2), vicarious liability imposes liability on D2 for the *wrongdoing of another,* whereas the doctrine of non-delegable duty imposes liability on D2 for *their own wrongdoing.*

16.1 Vicarious liability

16.1.1 The nature of vicarious liability

Vicarious liability is a form of strict liability that operates to make one person (or entity) legally liable to compensate a plaintiff for a tort that has been committed by another. It is a derivative rather than a direct form of liability and it is based not on fault but on the special relationship that exists between the primary tortfeasor (D1) and the second defendant (D2). The doctrine of vicarious liability requires a two-step process that links two different kinds of legal relationships together.

The two-step process and some examples

- **Step 1 links P to D1:** The first legal relationship is between the plaintiff (P) and the primary tortfeasor (D1), due to the fact that D1 has committed a tort against P. P must establish to the requisite standard the elements of the tort that D1 has committed against them.
- **Step 2 links D1 to D2:** The second legal relationship is between D1 and D2. Some of the relationships that give rise to vicarious liability are:
  - employer (D2) and employee (D1), provided D1 was acting in the course of employment;
  - principal (D2) and agent (D1), provided D1 was acting within the scope or ostensible scope of their authority;
  - partner (D2) and fellow partner (D1) ('joint and several' liability);
  - car owner (D2) and person driving with their consent (D1): *Soblusky v Egan* (1960).

  Note: vicarious liability is not applicable to situations concerning planes (*Scott v Davis* (2000)) or boats (*Frost v Warner* (2002)).

Liability will be imposed on D2 upon proof that the tort was committed by D1, provided, for example, that the employee committed the tort in the course of their employment, or the agent was acting within the scope of their authority given by their principal.

The first step links P to D1 through the tracks of the harm-causing tort; the second step links D1 to D2 by following the tracks of the relationship between D1 and D2. The result of this process is that D2 will become responsible for compensating the plaintiff for the tort committed by D1, provided that D1 was acting within the scope of their employment or agency agreement. The liability is described as 'vicarious' because D2 has not done anything wrong but becomes linked to the tort committed by D1 solely due to the special relationship that exists between them. One of the most commonly occurring legal relationships that gives rise to vicarious liability is the employment relationship where D2 is the employer and D1 is their employee. The analysis in this section on vicarious liability is confined to the cases where the defendant is linked to the primary tortfeasor through an employment relationship and will not consider the other legal areas such as agency or partnership.

Figure 16.1 Vicarious liability – standard two-party factual scenario

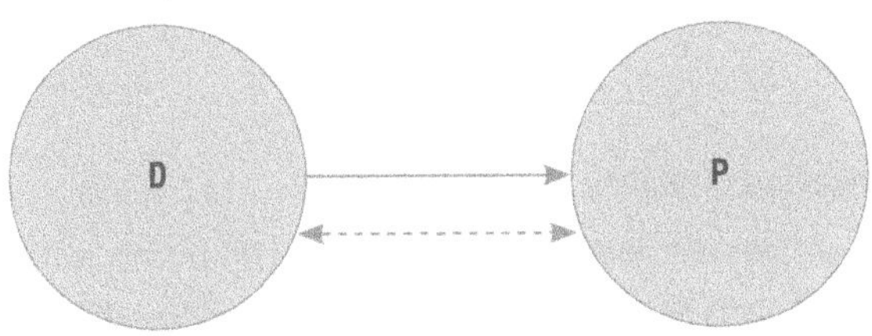

D causes P to suffer a recognised form of harm. The solid line shows the tracks of harm from D to P. The dotted line shows the legal relationship between D and P.

Figure 16.2 Vicarious liability – multiparty vicarious liability scenario

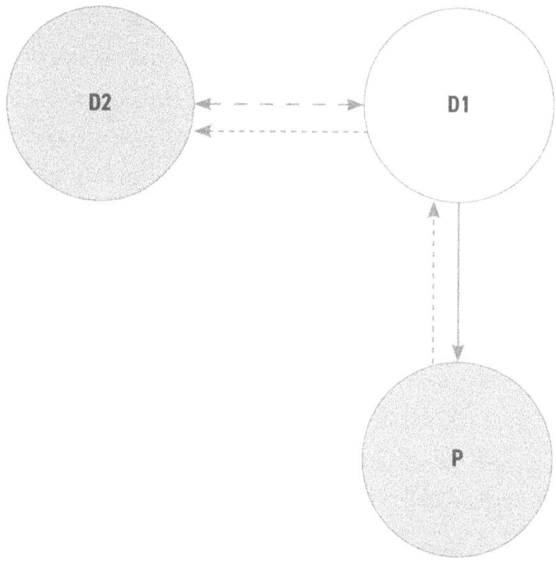

In Figure 26.2, the dashed line shows the relationship between D1 and D2. The solid line shows the tracks of harm from D1 to P. The single broken line and the two dotted lines show the two-step process that links P first to D1 and then follows the relationship through to D2.

16.1.2 Justifications for vicarious liability

The cases invariably begin by noting that 'a fully satisfactory rationale for the imposition of vicarious liability in the employment relationship has been slow to appear' – these words appear in the joint judgment in *Hollis v Vabu Pty Ltd* (2001) at [35]. The doctrine originated in Roman times to impose liability on a master for a slave's wrongs and re-emerged in feudal times to attach liability to a medieval head of a household for the torts committed by his wife or servants: see *Scott v Davis* (2000), Gummow J at [230]; *Sweeney v Boylan Nominees Pty Ltd* (2006), joint judgment at [20]. These origins, combined with the lack of a clearly agreed goal, make it difficult to apply and adapt the doctrine in modern times. Gummow and Hayne JJ summarised some of the possible justifications in *New South Wales v Lepore; Samin v Queensland; Rich v Queensland* (2003) *('New South Wales v Lepore')* at [196]–[202] and [221] – these are listed below.

Examples

Justifications for vicarious liability

- **The 'deep pocket' or 'loss-distribution' justification** (at [197]): This justification suggests that the real reason for imposing liability on an employer is based on a simple desire to find a source of compensation for an injured plaintiff. See also Kirby J at [306].
- **The 'enterprise risk' justification** (at [197], [221]): This justification suggests that if an employer sets up an enterprise in the community that creates a risk to others so that they can receive the benefits of that enterprise, then fairness requires that they should also bear the

burdens of their enterprise, if that risk materialises and causes harm to the plaintiff. See also Kirby J at [303].

- **The 'deterrence' justification** (at [198]–[202]): This justification, derived from Frederick Pollock's 1882 book *Essays in Jurisprudence and Ethics*, suggests that one good reason for making an employer liable for the harmful conduct of their employees is that it will encourage employers to be more careful in the conduct of their business and will deter them from allowing any harmful practices to become established. This is particularly important if the employer had 'for his own convenience brought about or maintained some state of things which in the ordinary course of nature may work mischief to his neighbours'. See also Kirby J at [305].

Another justification was noted in the joint judgment of Gleeson CJ, Gummow, Hayne, Heydon and Crennan JJ at [12] in *Sweeney v Boylan Nominees Pty Ltd* (2006).

Example

Justification for vicarious liability

The 'promised indemnity' justification derives from Jason Neyers in 'A Theory of Vicarious Liability' (2005) at 301, who suggests that liability is fairly imposed on the grounds that the employer has promised in the contract of employment to indemnify the employee for any legal liability incurred by the employee in the conduct of the employer's business.

Despite the fact that no one can agree on *why* the doctrine of vicarious liability exists, all courts do nevertheless agree that it *does* exist as part of Australian law. Before vicarious liability can be imposed on a defendant in the context of employment, the plaintiff must prove that:

1. the employee (D1) committed a tort against the plaintiff;
2. the primary tortfeasor (D1) was an employee of the defendant (D2); and
3. the tort was committed in the course of their employment.

The first element needs no extensive discussion, but the other two have caused two practical – as opposed to theoretical – legal problems for the High Court, in large part because there is no single test that can identify whether a person is an employee. Furthermore, historically there has been confusion over the appropriate test that should be used to decide whether an employee has committed a tort 'in the course of their employment'.

16.1.3 Key cases: Vicarious liability of an employer

16.1.3.1 Has D1 committed a tort?

The plaintiff must first establish that a tort has been committed by the primary tortfeasor (D1), by proving the usual elements of the tort in the usual way. This doctrine applies to all torts, including negligence and the intentional torts. However, when the tort is an intentional tort, the analysis becomes very difficult in circumstances where the courts must decide whether the tort was committed in the course of D1's employment, as discussed below.

16.1.3.2 Is D1 an employee of D2?

Once the plaintiff has established that the primary tortfeasor (D1) did in fact commit a tort by proving all the relevant elements, the next step is to make the link between D1 and the second defendant (D2), by proving that the tortfeasor was actually an employee of D2. One of the important distinctions that applies in this area of the law is the difference between an *employee* who is linked to an *employer*, and an *independent contractor* who is linked to a *principal*. In the context of modern business, employment and taxation law, where the relationships between different participants have become very complex, it is not always easy to tell whether a person is working for another person as their employee under a contract of employment (or 'contract of service') or whether they are working for themselves as an independent contractor who conducts their own business by offering themselves out to others under a contract to provide them with a service ('contract for services'). This 'deeply rooted' and longstanding distinction is critical because the rule is that an employer will be vicariously liable only for the torts committed by an employee – but that a principal will *not* be vicariously liable for a tort committed by an independent contractor, as the joint judgment in the case of *Sweeney v Boylan Nominees Pty Ltd* (2006) pointed out at [12] and [33]; see also *Leighton Contractors Pty Ltd v Fox* (2009), French CJ, Gummow, Hayne, Heydon and Bell JJ at [21].

In the past, the courts tended to use a single test to decide the matter, but since *Stevens v Brodribb Sawmilling Co Pty Ltd* (1986), the High Court has abandoned the attempt to construct a 'bright line' rule that uses only one indicator and has adopted a more flexible test that focuses on a number of different indicators that may be relevant, depending on the circumstances. However, the High Court subsequently made it clear in *Construction, Forestry, Maritime, Mining and Energy Union v Personnel Contracting Pty Ltd* (2022) and *ZG Operations Australia Pty Ltd v Jamsek* (2022) that where a detailed contract clearly defines the terms of the relationship, the multifactor test is not the appropriate way to resolve the question of whether a relationship is one of employment, unless the contract is a sham or an inaccurate reflection of the relationship.

Case examples

- In *Zuijs v Wirth Brothers Pty Ltd* (1955), the plaintiff, Zuijs, was a trapeze artist who was injured when his partner (D1) dropped him during their circus act. He sued the circus (D2) and claimed workers' compensation, and the High Court had to determine whether the two trapeze artists were employees of the circus (D2) or independent contractors working for themselves. The trial judge who had decided that they were independent contractors based the decision on the fact that they had a 'special skill or knowledge' but this was rejected as the sole test by the joint majority judgment at 571, where it was noted that the key point was whether there 'is lawful authority to command so far as there is scope for it'. Given that the men were under the control of the circus, it was held that they were both employees.

- *Stevens v Brodribb Sawmilling Co Pty Ltd* (1986) concerned a plaintiff, Stevens, who worked as trucker carting logs from a logging area to a sawmill run by Brodribb Pty Ltd (D2). He was injured when a log fell on him due to the carelessness of Gray (D1), who was moving logs to a landing to load them onto the plaintiff's truck. The issue before the High Court was whether the two men were employees or independent contractors. The Court decided that the men were not employees. This meant that the company (D2) was not vicariously liable to the plaintiff for the negligence of Gray (D1) and it was not personally liable to the plaintiff for any breach of duty it owed him as an employer. However, the Court did hold that D2 owed a general common law duty to the plaintiff, but found that on the facts it had not breached the standard of care.

  Mason J said at 24 that a 'prominent factor' in past decisions had been the right of the employer to exercise control over their employee but added:

  > [T]he existence of control, whilst significant, is not the sole criterion by which to gauge whether a relationship is one of employment, [and] the approach of this Court has been to regard it as merely one of a number of indicia which must be considered ... Other relevant matters include, but are not limited to, the mode of remuneration, the provision and maintenance of equipment, the obligation to work, the hours of work and provision for holidays, the deduction of income tax and the delegation of work by the putative employee.

  Mason J said at 29 that 'the totality of the relationship between the parties' must be considered. Wilson and Dawson JJ also emphasised at 36 the importance of the right to control as 'the surest guide' but noted that it was not a 'sufficient' or even an 'appropriate test ... in all cases'. Their Honours also noted at 36 that other indicators ('indicia') of an employment relationship were:

  - 'the right to have a particular person do the work';
  - 'the right to suspend or dismiss the person engaged';
  - 'the right to the exclusive services of the person engaged'; and
  - 'the right to dictate the place of work, hours of work and the like'.

  Indicators of an independent contractor were noted at 37:

  - 'work involving a profession, trade or distinct calling on the part of the person engaged';
  - 'the provision by him of his own place of work or of his own equipment';
  - 'the creation by him of goodwill or saleable assets in the course of his work';
  - 'the payment by him from his remuneration of business expenses of any significant proportion'; and
  - 'the payment to him of remuneration without deduction for income tax'.

  Their Honours concluded, at 37:

  > [T]he ultimate question will always be whether a person is acting as the servant of another or on his own behalf and the answer to that question may be indicated in ways which are not always the same and which do not always have the same significance.

  On the facts of the case, the critical features indicating that P and D1 were independent contractors were the fact that they regarded themselves as independent contractors, they provided and maintained their own vehicles and machinery, they set their own hours of work, they were paid by volume of timber, they did not have income tax deducted from their pay, they were not guaranteed work and they were free to do other work if they chose. No control was exercised by the mill over the manner in which they conducted their tasks, and furthermore D2 employed his own son as an employee and delegated work to him.

- In *Hollis v Vabu Pty Ltd* (2001), the plaintiff, Hollis, was injured in an accident caused by a bicycle courier (D1). D1 was never identified because he rode off before the plaintiff could get any of his details, but D1 was wearing a distinctive uniform labelled 'Crisis Couriers' provided to him by Vabu Pty Ltd (D2). The couriers had to provide their own bicycles and were able to deal with D2 either as sole traders, as members of a partnership or by means of their own companies. The High Court held by majority that D1 was an employee of D2 and held D2 to be vicariously liable for his tort. The joint judgment of Gleeson CJ, Gaudron, Gummow, Kirby and Hayne JJ endorsed the approach taken by Mason J in the earlier case of *Stevens v Brodribb Sawmilling Co Pty Ltd* (1986) and stated at [42]:

  > In general, under contemporary Australian conditions, the conduct by the defendant of an enterprise in which persons are identified as representing that enterprise should carry an obligation to third persons to bear the cost of injury or damage to them which may fairly be said to be characteristic of the conduct of that enterprise.

  The joint majority judgment noted, at [58], that the terms used by the parties to a contract 'are not of themselves determinative' and explained at [48]–[58] that the relevant factors indicating that the courier was an employee were as follows:

  - The couriers were not providing skilled labour or labour which required special qualifications, nor were they running their own enterprise: at [48].
  - The couriers had little control over the manner of performing their work and were not able to refuse work once they had arrived at work: at [49], [57].
  - Couriers were presented to the public and to those using the courier service as emanations of Vabu. They were to wear uniforms bearing Vabu's logo and were subject to rules dictating their dress and appearance: at [50].
  - Vabu superintended the couriers' finances, the couriers could not bargain for the rate of their pay and Vabu deducted money from the couriers' pay for any failure to return Vabu's equipment, including the uniforms: at [54].
  - The couriers had to apply for leave: at [55].
  - Couriers were required to bear the cost of replacing or repairing any equipment of Vabu that was lost or damaged, including radios and uniforms: at [56].
- In *Construction, Forestry, Maritime, Mining and Energy Union v Personnel Contracting Pty Ltd* (2022) ('*CFMMEU*') the High Court considered whether a construction worker (Mr McCourt) was an independent contractor or an employee under his agreement with Personnel Contracting Pty Ltd. The contract the worker signed with Personnel Contracting, a labour hire company, described him as a 'self-employed contractor'. The Court held that the true nature of the relationship was determined by the rights and obligations outlined in the agreement. Noting at 57 that in neither *Stevens* nor *Hollis* had the terms of the work relationship been committed 'comprehensively to a written agreement', Kiefel CJ, Keane and Edelman JJ went on to state at 59:

> Where the parties have comprehensively committed the terms of their relationship to a written contract the validity of which is not in dispute, the characterisation of their relationship as one of employment or otherwise proceeds by reference to the rights and obligations of the parties under that contract. Where no party seeks to challenge the efficacy of the contract as the charter of the parties' rights and duties, on the basis that it is either a sham or otherwise ineffective under the general law or statute, there is no occasion to seek to determine the character of the parties' relationship by a wide-ranging review of the entire history of the parties' dealings.

In this case, the Court determined that the provisions of the contract aligned more closely with an employment relationship and highlighted that simply labelling Mr McCourt as 'contractor' in the agreement could not alter the fundamental characteristics of the relationship, which were defined by Personnel Contracting's significant amount of control over the worker.

- *ZG Operations Australia Pty Ltd v Jamsek* (2022), which was heard together with *CFMMEU*, involved two truck drivers. Both drivers had initially been employees of ZG Operations but 40 years prior, each of the drivers had set up a separate legal entity, purchased their own vehicles and entered into a comprehensive written agreement with the company to provide delivery services. The High Court found that both drivers were independent contractors. It ruled that when the terms of a relationship are thoroughly documented in a written contract, the nature of the relationship should be assessed based on the terms of the contract itself and that there was no need for a detailed analysis of how the parties behaved after the agreement was formed.

From time to time the courts have entertained the possibility that vicarious liability could or should be extended beyond the traditionally recognised relationships. For example, in *Sweeney v Boylan Nominees Pty Ltd* (2006), McHugh J argued at [72]–[74] that the law should move on from the medieval 'dichotomy' between employees and independent contractors and allow vicarious liability to be imposed when the primary tortfeasor's 'conduct occurs while the agent is carrying out a task for the benefit of the principal as his or her representative'.

This last suggestion by McHugh J was firmly rejected in the joint majority judgment of Gleeson CJ, Gummow, Hayne, Heydon and Crennan JJ in *Sweeney v Boylan Nominees Pty Ltd* (2006) at [29]. Similarly, the plaintiff in *Scott v Davis* (2000) was unsuccessful in seeking to hold the defendant vicariously liable for the tort of a pilot who had accepted an invitation to fly the defendant's plane – they were neither an employee nor an agent and were only an 'agent' in a 'non-technical' sense. Most recently, in *Bird v DP (A Pseudonym)* (2024) the Court held:

> [A] relationship of employment has always been a necessary precursor in this country to a finding of vicarious liability and it has always been necessary that the wrongful acts must be committed in the course or scope of the employment. There is no solid foundation for expansion of the doctrine or for its bounds to be redrawn.

Case examples

- In *Sweeney v Boylan Nominees Pty Ltd* (2006), the plaintiff, Sweeney, was injured when she was shopping at a service station and a refrigerator door fell off and hit her head. Boylan Nominees (D2) had earlier organised for a mechanic (D1) to service the refrigerator. The plaintiff sued D2, arguing that the company was vicariously liable for the negligence of D1. D1 was not D2's employee but worked for himself as an independent contractor. It was argued in the High Court (at 162–3) that vicarious liability should nevertheless be imposed on the much broader basis that D2 had asked D1 to repair the refrigerator, the work was being carried out for D2's benefit, and D1 was therefore a 'representative' of D2 or was an 'agent' in a 'non-technical or loose sense'.

  The joint majority judges held that the mechanic (D1) was not an employee and decided that the proposed extension of the basis for imposing vicarious liability to cover an independent contractor should be rejected, saying at [27] that the bounds of vicarious liability should not be redrawn.
- *Bird v DP (A Pseudonym)* (2024) concerned the Roman Catholic Diocese of Ballarat (D2) and whether it could be held vicariously liable for historical sexual assaults committed against the plaintiff, Bird, by one of its Assistant Priests, Father Bryan Coffey (D1). The relationship between D2 and D1 was governed by canon law, which established mechanisms for control and oversight; however, this did not equate to a relationship of employer and employee, and neither could it be said that D2 was acting as a 'true agent' of D1 (at 35]). Notwithstanding that there was no employer and employee relationship, the judge at first instance and the Court of Appeal of the Supreme Court of Victoria nevertheless found D2 vicariously liable, on the basis that the work of D1 was the public manifestation of D2 and that D1 was 'in a real and relevant sense ... the servant of the Diocese'. While the High Court recognised that '[t]he relationship between the Diocese and Coffey ... exhibited certain features that resembled that of a relationship of employer and employee' (at 64), the majority was unequivocal in response to the question as to whether (at 47):

  > the Court should now expand the boundaries of vicarious liability beyond a relationship of employment to one that is 'akin to employment'. Contrary to the decisions of the courts below and the submissions of DP, the answer is no.

  As noted by Gleeson J in her minority judgment, this position contrasts with jurisdictions such as the United Kingdom and Canada, which have expanded the doctrine to encompass relationships that fall outside formal employment relationships in comparable cases. Gleeson J described the case (at 79) as 'a missed opportunity for the Australian common law to develop in accordance with changed social conditions'. This recent decision has, however, made very clear the boundaries of vicarious liability in Australia, where it remains tied to a more traditional definition of employer–employee relationships.

Vicarious liability is ruled out if the primary tortfeasor (D1) is an independent contractor. In that case, the plaintiff is limited to suing D1 and will not have an action against the principal (D2) unless they can establish either that the D2 owed them a personal common law duty of care under one of the recognised categories (as was argued in *Stevens v Brodribb Sawmilling Co Pty Ltd* (1986) – see above) or that the D2 owed them a special non-delegable duty.

Labour hire organisations are an increasingly common feature of the modern workforce. In these arrangements, a labour hire firm (the general employer) will provide outsourced workers to another organisation (the particular employer) for a certain period of time. In most circumstances, it is the general employer who will remain vicariously liable for the workers. While it is possible for the particular employer to assume legal responsibility for the worker, as Lord Simon noted in *Mersey Docks & Harbour Board v Coggins & Griffith (Liverpool) Ltd* (1947) at 10, the burden of proof is on the general employer to show that responsibility had shifted to the particular employer and this was a 'heavy burden, which could only be discharged in quite exceptional circumstances'.

Although courts in the United Kingdom have accepted since *Viasystems (Tyneside) Ltd v Thermal Transfer (Northern) Ltd* (2006) that dual vicarious liability can exist between the general employer and particular employer, Australian courts have consistently declined to do so. For example, McLure P noted in *Kelly v Bluestone Global Ltd (in liq)* (2016) at [63] that it was 'preferable to leave the determination of this important legal issue to another day'. See also *Day v Ocean Beach Hotel Shellharbour Pty Ltd* (2013), in which Leeming JA stated at 33 that in his opinion it was 'not possible for any court other than the High Court to adopt the submission ... that Australian law admits of a theory of dual vicarious liability where two different persons had control over a tortfeasor'.

16.1.3.3 Was the tort committed by D1 'in the course of their employment'?

One of the most difficult aspects of the law in this area concerns the final issue: establishing that the primary tortfeasor (D1) was acting 'in the course of their employment' when they committed the tort. Ever since *Lloyd v Grace, Smith & Co* (1912), where the House of Lords held a law firm vicariously liable for the intentional wrongdoing of their managing clerk, who took advantage of the opportunity that his position offered him to defraud a client, the courts have struggled to agree on an appropriate test. The problem is particularly acute in cases where employees have committed outrageous criminal acts of a kind that that they were obviously never employed to do. However, it has been the increase in litigation brought by plaintiffs seeking compensation for sexual abuse, committed by teachers, clergy and others in positions of trust relative to the plaintiff, which has challenged the courts around the common law world to find a satisfactory test to use in these circumstances.

Case example

In *Lloyd v Grace, Smith & Co* (1912), the plaintiff was a widow who owned two cottages. She was unhappy with the income that she was earning from the cottages so she consulted a firm of solicitors (D2) and saw their managing clerk (D1), who conducted the conveyancing business of the firm without supervision. Acting as the representative of the firm, D1 induced the plaintiff to give him instructions to sell the cottages. He asked her to give him her deeds and to sign two documents. The documents were in fact a conveyance to him of the cottages and a transfer to him of the mortgage. He then dishonestly disposed of the property for his own benefit. The trial judge applied the old rule that a dishonest act committed by a servant for his own benefit was by definition beyond the scope of his employment, but the House of Lords held that D2 was vicariously liable to the plaintiff for the wrongful conduct of their agent, D1.

It was held that while D2 clearly did not authorise *the act* of inducing the plaintiff to sign the cottages over D1, they had nevertheless placed D1 into the position to do that *class of acts*, by putting him in charge of doing their conveyancing and asking him to advise their client as their agent. This led to the conclusion that D1 was acting as D2's representative and acting within the scope of his authority when he committed the fraud, because, as Lord Shaw said at 740, 'the apparent authority is, as is well settled, equivalent to the real authority and binds the principal'. Lord Macnaghten stated at 733, citing an earlier case:

> In all these cases it may be said, as it was said here, that the master had not authorised the act. It is true he has not authorized the particular act, but he has put the agent in *his place to do that class of acts*, and he must be answerable for the manner in which that agent has conducted himself in doing the business which it was the act of his master to place him in. (Emphasis added.)

The firm in *Lloyd v Grace, Smith & Co* (1912) was vicariously liable for the wrongdoing of their clerk, but the first High Court case to consider the matter, *Deatons Pty Ltd v Flew* (1949), was decided differently.

Case example

In *Deatons Pty Ltd v Flew* (1949) the plaintiff, Flew, went to a bar owned by Deatons (D2) and became involved in an altercation with their employee, a barmaid named Opal Ruby Pearl Barlow (D1). The plaintiff claimed that he had asked the barmaid a polite question, and that she had thrown a glass of beer into his face, causing him to lose the sight in one eye. D1 claimed that P had been rude and abusive and had hit her, and that the glass had slipped when she was retaliating by throwing the beer into his face. A jury found for the plaintiff against D1 and D2, but on appeal the High Court held that D1 had not been acting in the course of her employment and that therefore D2 was not vicariously liable for her tort.

It had been argued that the barmaid (D1) had thrown the beer, either in the course of responding to an inquiry, or in the course of acting to deal with an unruly customer with the aim of restoring order in the bar, and that therefore she could be seen to be acting badly but still in the course of her employment. However, Dixon J, distinguished the case from *Lloyd v Grace, Smith & Co* (1912) and said at 381–2:

> It is not a case of a negligent or improper act, due to error or ill judgment, but done in the supposed furtherance of the master's interests. Nor is it one of those wrongful acts done for the servant's own benefit for which the master is liable when they are acts to which the ostensible performance of his master's work gives occasion or which are committed under cover of the authority the servant is held out as possessing or of the position in which he is placed as a representative of his master ... The

> truth is that it was an act of passion and resentment done neither in furtherance of the master's interests nor under his express or implied authority nor as an incident to or in consequence of anything the barmaid was employed to do.

In this case, the barmaid (D1) was not carrying out an act that she was authorised to do – but it would have been different if she had been doing an authorised act but had done it badly or negligently. So, if she had been authorised to control the crowd in the bar and had done so in a rage and carelessly injured a patron, that would have been a tort committed in the course of her employment for which the employers (D2) would have been liable. Or, if D2 had given her the authority to take any large items from the patrons and store them for safekeeping, and she had, under cover of that authority, removed an item from one of those packages for herself, that too would have been enough to justify liability, as the next case shows.

Case example

Morris v CW Martin & Sons Ltd (1966) concerned a plaintiff, Morris, who sent her mink fur to be stored. Before it was stored, it was sent to the cleaners CW Martin & Sons Ltd (D2). An employee at the cleaners named Morrissey (D1) stole the mink. The plaintiff sued D2, arguing that the company was vicariously liable for the tort of conversion that had been committed by D1. The trial judge held that the act by D1 had not been done in the course of his employment. It was held by the Court of Appeal that D2 was liable, but not all judges agreed on the basis for the decision.

Lord Denning explained at 723:

> During the 19th century it was accepted law that a master was liable for the dishonesty or fraud of his servant if it was done in the course of his employment and for his master's benefit. Dishonesty or fraud by the servant for his own benefit took the case out of the course of his employment. The judges took this simple view: No servant who turns thief and steals is acting in the course of his employment. He is acting outside it altogether.

Lord Denning then reviewed the more recent cases like *Lloyd v Grace* (1912) (see above), which had taken a different approach and said at 723:

> [W]e may deduce the general proposition that when a principal has in his charge the goods or belongings of another in such circumstances that he is under a duty to take all reasonable precautions to protect them from theft or depredation, then if he entrusts that duty to a servant or agent, he is answerable for the manner in which that servant or agent carries out his duty. If the servant or agent is careless so that they are stolen by a stranger, the master is liable. So also if the servant or agent himself steals them or makes away with them.

Lord Diplock pointed out at 733 that 'two distinct lines of authority: that of the frolicsome coachman and that of the dishonest servant' had been confused in the case law. In older cases it had been said that if an employee, like a coachman, had been off on a 'frolic of his own' – for example, by 'borrowing' his master's coach to go off racing with other coachmen – then if any harm occurred, the employer would not be liable for the tort. The 'frolic doctrine' had then become confused with the 'dishonest servant cases' such as *Lloyd v Grace, Smith & Co* (1912), but Lord Diplock explained at 737 that it was possible to resolve this case on the basis that 'the fur was stolen by the very servant whom the defendants as bailees for reward had employed to take care of it and clean it'.

So, the mere fact that an employee has committed a criminal act is not enough on its own to prove that they were acting outside the course of their employment. The usefulness of the underlying reasoning in these cases has been doubted, and Gummow and Hayne JJ suggested in *New South Wales v Lepore* (2003) at [238] that the decisions in some of the English cases could be accounted for in other ways. However, the two propositions for which the early cases stand have not been overturned. They were summarised by Gummow and Hayne JJ in *New South Wales v Lepore* (2003) at [239] where they note that vicarious liability may be imposed in two circumstances:

- where the conduct was done in the *intended* pursuit of the employer's interests or in the intended performance of the contract of employment; or
- where the conduct was done in the *ostensible* pursuit of the employer's business or the apparent execution of the authority which the employer held out the employee as having.

These two propositions have caused some difficulty, but as time went by the law became even less clear. The next case concerned a case of negligence rather than an intentional tort and the difficulty occurred because the employee in this case had acted in defiance of an express written order given by his employer.

Case example

In *Rose v Plenty* (1976) a milkman, Plenty (D1), was employed by Co-operative Retail Services Ltd (D2) to deliver milk. Disregarding an express written prohibition issued to all milkmen forbidding them from employing children to assist them to deliver the milk in any circumstances, Plenty did employ a boy, Rose (the plaintiff), to help deliver the milk. He injured the plaintiff by his careless driving, and the plaintiff sued D2, arguing that the company was vicariously liable for the negligence of D1. The trial judge held that while D1 was liable for his own tort, D2 was not liable because D1 was acting outside the scope of his employment and because the plaintiff was a trespasser on the milk float. The Court of Appeal decided in a 2:1 majority that the negligence did occur during the course of employment because D1 was employed to deliver milk and the plaintiff was there on the float in order to assist D1 to do that job.

Lord Denning said at 144 that when considering whether a prohibited act was within the course of the employment:

> it depends very much on the purpose for which it is done. If it is done for his employers' business, it is usually done in the course of his employment, even though it is a prohibited act ... But if it is done for some purpose other than his masters' business,

as, for instance, giving a lift to a hitchhiker, such an act, if prohibited, may not be within the course of his employment.

So, in this case, even though the act of employing a child was expressly forbidden, the fact that the child was employed to help deliver the milk, meant, as Scarman LJ said at 148, that it could nevertheless be interpreted as 'a matter of common sense' as 'a mode, albeit a prohibited mode, of doing the job with which he was entrusted'.

This last phrase was derived from the classic formulation of the law given by one of the great legal authorities, judge and legal academic Sir John Salmond, whose classic statement of the law in the first edition of *Law of Torts* in 1907 at 83 provided the courts with three tests that, if satisfied, showed that an employee (or servant) could be seen to have been acting in the course of their employment. The tests focus on whether the employee was engaged in:

- 'a wrongful act authorised by the master';
- 'a wrongful and unauthorised mode of doing some act authorised by the master'; or
- an unauthorised act that is 'so connected with acts which [the employer] has authorised that they may rightly be regarded as modes – although improper modes – of doing them'.

Many cases since 1907 have used this approach to assist in deciding whether an intentional act of wrongdoing was committed in the course of a person's employment. The 'close connection' test that is derived from Salmond's third category has been given support in the cases brought by former pupils who have made claims against school authorities for acts of abuse committed by teachers, but as *New South Wales v Lepore* (2003) demonstrates, the judges are far from agreeing on the best way to give some substance to the 'close connection' test. The courts in Canada have adopted a formulation of the 'close connection' test that imposes vicarious liability if there is such a 'significant connection between the creation or enhancement of a risk' by the allocation of a task or role to the employee by the employer and the subsequent act of wrongdoing by the employee that occurs when the employee is carrying out that role. So, under the Canadian test, liability is justified if 'the employer's enterprise and empowerment of the employee' has 'significantly created' or 'materially increased the risk of the sexual assault and hence the harm' occurring: see *Bazley v Curry* (1999), McLachlin J for the Supreme Court of Canada at [39]–[42].

Case example

The defendant in *Bazley v Curry* (1999) was a foundation (D2) that operated two residential care facilities for the treatment of emotionally troubled children. They employed Curry (D1), a paedophile, as one of their employees who was given the task of doing everything that a parent would do, from general supervision to intimate duties like bathing and tucking in at bedtime. D1 committed many acts of criminal sexual abuse against the children in his care. The Supreme

Court of Canada held D2 had materially increased the risk of the abuse occurring by giving D1 such an intimate role.

McLachlin J for the Supreme Court of Canada reviewed the cases that discussed and applied the 'Salmond test', formulated the 'material increase of risk' approach as noted in the text above, and suggested at [41] that in the context of the intentional torts, the relevant factors may include, but are not limited to:

> (a) the opportunity that the enterprise afforded the employee to abuse his or her power; (b) the extent to which the wrongful act may have furthered the employer's aims (and hence be more likely to have been committed by the employee); (c) the extent to which the wrongful act was related to friction, confrontation or intimacy inherent in the employer's enterprise; (d) the extent of power conferred on the employee in relation to the victim; and (e) the vulnerability of potential victims to the wrongful exercise of the employee's power.

The House of Lords considered the Canadian case of *Bazley v Curry* (1999) and the later case of *Jacobi v Griffiths* (1999) in *Lister v Hesley Hall Ltd* (2002), another case about vicarious liability for sexual abuse committed by an employee. The Lords endorsed the 'close connection' test and the reasoning in the earlier case of *Morris v CW Martin & Sons Ltd* (1966).

Case example

The plaintiffs in *Lister v Hesley Hall Ltd* (2002) claimed damages against Hesley Hall Ltd (D2) for the harm done to them by the warden (D1) of their boarding house, who had systematically abused the boys while they were living in the home under in his care. The House of Lords applied the 'close connection' test and concluded on the facts that D1 had committed the abuse in the course of his employment in D2's commercial enterprise.

Lord Steyn reviewed the Canadian decisions and stated at [24] that the 'better approach is to concentrate on the relative closeness of the connection between the nature of the employment and the particular tort'.

Lord Millett discussed the Salmond approach and said at [68] that it would be 'stretching language to breaking-point to describe the series of deliberate sexual assaults ... as merely a wrongful and unauthorised mode' of performing the warden's duty to 'to look after the boys in his care and secure their welfare'. Consequently, his Lordship suggested at [69] that a better version of the Salmond test might be:

> where the unauthorised acts of the employee are so connected with acts which the employer has authorised that they may properly be regarded as being within the scope of his employment.

All of these earlier cases were considered in Australia in 2003, when three cases were heard together by a full bench of seven judges in the High Court in *New South Wales v Lepore; Samin v Queensland; Rich v Queensland* (2003) ('*New South Wales v Lepore*').

The reasoning in these cases is significant, not because the High Court resolved the issues of vicarious liability that the cases raised, but because the cases illustrate the difficulty of the legal questions raised when an employer is sued for the harm caused by the intentional wrongful conduct of an employee who has used the opportunity given to them by their employment to commit the wrong. Judges in all jurisdictions agree that the mere fact that the primary tortfeasor's employment by the defendants gave them the opportunity to commit the tort does not suffice to impose vicarious liability (see, eg, *Morris v CW Martin & Sons Ltd* (1966), Diplock LJ at 737; *Bazley v Curry* (1999) at [49]; and *New South Wales v Lepore* (2003), Gleeson CJ at [74], Gummow and Hayne JJ at [227]). But the next step towards imposing liability is not as clear, and the judges in *New South Wales v Lepore* (2003) were unable to reach any agreement, beyond deciding that there does have to be 'something more' and that the Canadian approach that focuses on the 'increased risk' does not of itself provide that 'something more'. One of the most frustrating aspects of this decision arose from the fact that it also raised the twin issue of non-delegable duty, and that one of the judges, McHugh J, who decided the issues on the basis of the non-delegable duty, chose not to address the issue of vicarious liability. This left the other six judges, who were united in rejecting any claim based on non-delegable duty in cases where the conduct is an intentional act of wrongdoing, to remain locked in disagreement over how the test for the 'course of employment' was to be resolved and what the proper basis for imposing vicarious liability actually is.

Case example

New South Wales v Lepore (2003)

Gleeson CJ emphasised at [65] and [74] the need to examine the nature and scope of the employee's duties when deciding upon the 'sufficiency of the connection' and commented:

> In practice, in most cases, the considerations that would justify a conclusion as to whether an enterprise materially increases the risk of an employee's offending would also bear upon an examination of the nature of the employee's responsibilities, which are regarded as central in Australia. [65]
>
> If there is sufficient connection between what a particular teacher is employed to do, and sexual misconduct ... it must be because the nature of the teacher's responsibilities, and of the relationship with pupils created by those responsibilities, justifies that conclusion ... However, where the teacher-student relationship is invested with a high degree of power and intimacy, the use of that power and intimacy to commit sexual abuse may provide a sufficient connection ... The degree of power and intimacy in a teacher-student relationship must be assessed by reference to factors such as the age of students, their particular vulnerability if any, the tasks allocated to teachers, and the number of adults concurrently responsible for the care of students. [74]

Gaudron J, who based her decision on estoppel at [130], discussed the 'sufficient connection' test and the 'increase in risk' test and concluded at [126]:

> The fact that a person has materially increased the risk of criminal conduct on the part of an employee ... does not provide a clear basis for determining whether a person should be held vicariously liable for the deliberate criminal acts of an employee.
>
> The only principled basis upon which vicarious liability can be imposed for the deliberate criminal acts of another, in my view, is that the person against whom liability is asserted is estopped from asserting that the person whose acts are in question was not acting as his or her servant, agent or representative when the acts occurred. [130]

Gummow and Hayne JJ concluded, at [222]–[223], that the Canadian 'risk' test was too 'radical' a departure from the established approach because 'the risks to be considered are not confined to those risks which attend the furtherance of the venture but include the risks of conduct that is directly antithetical to those aims' and this carries the danger of reducing the question to a simple 'but for' analysis of causation. Their Honours concluded at [239] that vicarious liability should be imposed only if the conduct was done:

- in the intended pursuit of the employer's interests or in the intended performance of the contract of employment; or
- in the ostensible pursuit of the employer's business or the apparent execution of the authority which the employer held out the employee as having.

Kirby J noted at [316] the importance under the Salmond test of 'an examination of the connection between the enterprise and the acts alleged to constitute wrongdoing'. While generally agreeing that the Canadian 'increased risk' test does include some relevant considerations, his Honour concluded at [320] and [324] that the 'significant connection' test is not 'a rigid formula' and 'cannot be subject to mechanical rules and technicalities, posing as objective criteria'.

Callinan J at [345] refused to adopt the English 'close connection' test 'or any like test', saying that 'deliberate criminal conduct is not properly to be regarded as connected with an employee's employment' because 'it is the antithesis of a proper performance of the duties of an employee'.

So, while the Australian High Court did not adopt the Canadian test, and the majority generally agreed on the need for a 'close connection' between the employment and the wrongful act, it was unable to provide any more guidance on the issue. When reading these decisions that apply the 'connection test', one is reminded of the High Court's criticism of the usefulness of proximity as a test for the existence of a duty of care in negligence: it seems to be nothing more than a statement of conclusion rather than a process of reasoning.

In *Prince Alfred College Inc v ADC* (2016), the issue of vicarious liability for sexual abuse of students arose once again and provided the opportunity to further define the appropriate legal framework. In this case, the plaintiff had been sexually assaulted when he was a boarder at the college by a boarding housemaster, Bain. He commenced civil proceedings against Bain in 1997 but chose not to sue the school at that point, instead accepting an arrangement for payment of medical and legal expenses as well his son's school fees. In 2008, he commenced legal action against Prince Alfred College, contending that the school should be held vicariously liable for Bain's actions. Because the limitation period had expired, the plaintiff required an extension under the limitation statute in South Australia. At first instance, the judge refused the extension and found that, in any event, the school was not vicariously liable. On appeal, the Full Court of the Supreme Court of South Australia granted the extension of time, holding the school vicariously liable. Prince Alfred College then appealed to the High Court.

The High Court allowed the appeal, deciding that the extension of time should not have been granted as the lengthy delay (11 years from the apparent resolution of the matter in 1997 to 2008, when proceedings against the school were eventually brought) and the loss of some evidence meant that 'a fair trial on the merits was no longer possible' (at [8]). The plurality (French CJ, Kiefel, Bell, Keane and Nettle JJ) noted at [10] that although it would be inappropriate to make a ruling on the vicarious liability issue, since the principles were related to the granting of an extension of time and since there had been differing views expressed in *New South Wales v Lepore* (2003), it was appropriate for the Court to consider the issue and to provide some general guidance.

After reviewing authorities from Australia and other common law jurisdictions, the plurality determined at [81] that:

> in cases of this kind, the relevant approach is to consider any special role that the employer has assigned to the employee and the position in which the employee is thereby placed vis-à-vis the victim. In determining whether the apparent performance of such a role may be said to give the 'occasion' for the wrongful act, particular features may be taken into account. They include authority, power, trust, control and the ability to achieve intimacy with the victim. The latter feature may be especially important. Where, in such circumstances, the employee takes advantage of his or her position with respect to the victim, that may suffice to determine that the wrongful act should be regarded as committed in the course or scope of employment and as such render the employer vicariously liable.

In *CCIG Investments Pty Ltd v Schokman* (2023), the plaintiff and his co-worker, Hewett, both employed as hospitality workers by the defendant company on Daydream Island, were required to reside in shared accommodation. Late one night, the plaintiff's co-worker returned to their accommodation in a state of intoxication. The plaintiff was asleep but was woken up by his co-worker urinating on his face. As a result of this incident, the plaintiff suffered from an exacerbation of his pre-existing conditions of cataplexy and narcolepsy. The plaintiff sued his employer, arguing that requiring him to share accommodation with his co-worker put him in a position of vulnerability (and thereby seeking to draw an analogy with the facts in *Prince Alfred College*). The High Court rejected this suggestion, noting at [36]–[37]:

> In the passage from [*Prince Alfred College*] on which the argument relies, it was said that the appropriate enquiry concerning the sexual abuser was whether his role as a housemaster placed him in such a position of power and intimacy that the performance of his role could be said to give the occasion for his wrongful

> acts such that they could be said to have been committed in the course or scope of the employment. No such enquiry is presented by the circumstances of this case. Mr Hewett was not assigned any special role concerning Mr Schokman and no part of what Mr Hewett was employed to do was required to be done in the accommodation.

The most that could be said to arise from the circumstance of shared accommodation was that it created physical proximity between the two men. It therefore provided the opportunity for Mr Hewett's drunken actions to affect Mr Schokman. But, as has been seen, the cases hold that mere opportunity provides an insufficiently strong connection with the employment to establish vicarious liability.

In *Bird v DP (A Pseudonym)* (2024) Gleeson J was in the minority in her acceptance of an extension of the doctrine of vicarious liability to relationships 'akin to employment' (at [79]). However, she did agree that the appeal ought to be allowed, finding that the abuse was not committed in the course of any duties arising from the relationship between the Assistant Priest and the Diocese and that the position of trust created by the provision of pastoral duties was not enough to bring the acts within the course of the Assistant Priest's employment. Furthermore, Gleeson J at [182] stated:

> [Father Brian] Coffey's role gave him neither authority nor power to insist on being alone with DP, nor any capacity to control DP's parents in relation to decisions about allowing DP to be in Coffey's sole care. There is no evidence to think that Coffey's role in providing pastoral care to DP's family enabled him to achieve intimacy with DP beyond the incidents in which DP was assaulted. That role did not involve, for example, providing religious instruction to DP alone or securing DP's participation with Coffey in religious activities alone together, such as preparation for masses in which DP might have been Coffey's altar boy. Accordingly, Coffey's role gave him the opportunity to harm DP, but it was not the occasion for that harm in the sense explained in *Prince Alfred College*.

The recent cases make it clear that, in assessing whether the secondary defendant (D2) should be held vicariously liable for the tortious acts of the primary tortfeasor (D1), consideration should go beyond the classic formulation of the law as stated by Salmond (see above) – namely, whether the employee was engaged in:

- 'a wrongful act authorised by the master';
- 'a wrongful and unauthorised mode of doing some act authorised by the master'; or
- an unauthorised act that is 'so connected with acts which [the employer] has authorised that they may rightly be regarded as modes – although improper modes – of doing them'.

In addition to this classic formulation, the principles established in *Prince Alfred College*, *Schokman* and *Bird v DP* should now also be applied. This involves considering whether D1's role encompassed authority, power, trust, control, and the potential for intimacy with the victim, thereby making the wrongful act part of the course or scope of employment – referred to in the above quote from Gleeson J as 'the occasion'. Furthermore, it is essential to determine whether the wrongful act genuinely fell within the performance of D1's role or if the role merely provided the opportunity for the misconduct, with the latter insufficient to establish vicarious liability.

LEGISLATION ALERT!

Consult your study materials and note any relevant statutory provisions in your jurisdiction that deal with: (1) the application of the civil liability legislation to the intentional torts; (2) an employer's entitlement to claim an indemnity from an employee for any acts of wrongdoing committed during the course of their employment; and (3) claims arising as a result of the Royal Commission into Institutional Responses to Child Sexual Abuse.

Develop your skills

Exercise 1: Active learning – prepare for problem solving

- Make your own summary of the law on vicarious liability, using the cases discussed in section 16.1.3 as your source.
- Work out a modification to the 'six-point plan' that you can use to introduce a problem question in this area and include it in your problem-solving summary. There is a problem-solving exercise at the end of the chapter (Exercise 4).

Exercise 2: Case analysis and oral presentation

- Write a case note on the case of *CCIG Investments Pty Ltd v Schokman* (2023).
- Read the cases of *Bazley v Curry* (1999) and *Lister v Hesley Hall Ltd* (2002). Prepare a 10-minute oral presentation explaining:
  - the key issues that arise in cases where plaintiffs bring an action to recover damages from an employer of a person who has committed acts of sexual or physical abuse against them; and
  - the differences between the approach taken to the issue in Canada and England compared with Australia.

Exercise 3: Essay writing

- Write a 2000-word essay explaining the legal difficulties that plaintiffs who bring actions for childhood sexual abuse against the state and the church have faced and continue to face.
- Read the case of *Trustees of the Roman Catholic Church v Ellis* (2007) and consider the steps that state legislatures have taken since to close the legal loophole of the 'Ellis defence'.

Table 16.1 Non-delegable duties and vicarious liability

	Non-delegable duty	**Vicarious liability**
Relevant relationship	The focus is on the relationship between the defendant and the plaintiff, eg: • employer (D2) and employee (P); • hospital (D2) and patient (P); • school (D2) and pupil (P); • occupier (D2) and neighbour (P) (in hazardous activities cases).	The focus is on the relationship between the two defendants, eg: • employment – D1 is employed by D2; • agency – D1 is D2's agent; • partnerships – D1 is D2's partner; • motor vehicles – D2 allows D1 to drive D2's car.
Fault	The defendant (D2) is seen as personally liable for breaching a duty owed directly to the plaintiff to ensure that reasonable care is taken for P's safety.	The defendant (D2) is not seen as being personally at fault but is held to be strictly liable for the wrongdoing of the related wrongdoer, or primary tortfeasor (D1).
Scope	The non-delegable duty does apply to negligent conduct by the primary tortfeasor (D1), but it does not extend to cover any intentional act of wrongdoing: *New South Wales v Lepore* (2003).	Vicarious liability may cover any tort committed by the primary defendant (D1), including any intentional torts, provided D1 is acting within the scope of their agency or employment.

Problem-solving tips

These tips may be used generally when answering a question on liability for others and will be of particular use in answering the question at the end of the chapter.

If D1 is an employee

- If D1 is an employee who negligently injures another employee (P), then P may seek to hold the employer (D2) liable under both doctrines, claiming that D2 is both:
  - vicariously liable for D1's torts; and
  - personally liable for D2's own breach of a non-delegable duty owed directly to P.
- If D1 is an employee who has negligently injured P, then the employer (D2) may be liable under the doctrine of vicarious liability, but only if D1 was acting in the course of their employment. D2 may also be liable under the non-delegable duty doctrine if P fits into one of the recognised categories.
- If D1 is an employee who commits an intentional tort against P, then the employer (D2) can be liable only under the doctrine of vicarious liability because the doctrine of non-delegable duties does not apply to intentional torts, so if D1 was not acting in the course of their employment, D2 will not be liable.

If D1 is an independent contractor

- If D1 is an independent contractor (and not an employee), D2 will not usually be vicariously liable for any of D1's torts at all, unless D1 is acting as D2's agent.
- If D1 is an independent contractor who has committed the tort of negligence, then the only route to D2 is to use the non-delegable duty doctrine.
- If D1 is an independent contractor who has committed an intentional tort against P, D2 will not be liable at all because:
    - non-delegable duty does not apply to the intentional torts; and
    - vicarious liability does not apply to an independent contractor.

16.2 Non-delegable duty

The concept of a non-delegable duty, which is illustrated in Figure 16.3, bears some similarity to the doctrine of vicarious liability, in that it provides a plaintiff with an extra defendant to pursue in certain categories of case where one person has delegated a task to another person, and where that delegate has in turn committed a tort against the plaintiff. However, as noted above, the non-delegable duty does not impose liability for a tort committed by another person, but rather it imposes liability directly on the ultimate defendant (D2) *for their own tort*. One of the reasons why the doctrine is invoked by plaintiffs lies in the fact that it offers them a way around the rule that a principal is not vicariously liable for the torts of an independent contractor. It has the same practical effect as the doctrine of vicarious liability, but it is imposed on different grounds. So in cases where it is not clear that the relationship between the immediate tortfeasor (D1) and the alternative defendant (D2) is an employment relationship, the doctrine of non-delegable duty becomes an important, though controversial, option.

16.2.1 The nature of a non-delegable duty

A non-delegable duty is a special duty that attaches to certain special relationships between a defendant and a plaintiff that are characterised by vulnerability, special danger and an assumption of responsibility. The legal significance of classifying a duty as non-delegable is that it adds an extra character to the duty, which means that it cannot be discharged by giving the responsibility to another person – even if all reasonable care has been taken in choosing that person and in instructing them in how to carry out their task. It is important to understand that the fact that a defendant owes a plaintiff a special non-delegable duty does not mean that they are forbidden from actually delegating a particular task to another person. Rather, it means that if they do delegate the performance of a task to another person, then that fact alone will not be enough to satisfy their own personal duty owed to the plaintiff. This is because a non-delegable duty imposes on the holder of that duty a more 'stringent' requirement that obliges them to take positive steps to ensure that the delegates themselves take reasonable care to avoid foreseeable risks when they undertake the task that has been given to them: see, for example, the classic statement of the non-delegable duty by Mason J in *Kondis v State Transport Authority* (1984) at 679–81, and the summary provided by Gaudron J in *New South Wales v Lepore* (2003) at [99]–[105], noted below. In other words, an ordinary duty of care requires a defendant to take reasonable care and skill, while a non-delegable duty requires the defendant to 'ensure' that reasonable care is taken.

Example

If a defendant employer (D2) has given an independent contractor (D1) the task of designing the operating procedures for demolishing a building on a site owned by the employer, it will be no defence for the employer to claim that they took all reasonable care when choosing the contractor, if that contractor designs inadequate procedures and causes one of the employer's own employees to be injured during the demolition.

A non-delegable duty is not dissolved by the act of delegation. Rather, the delegation has the effect of duplicating the duty. As Figure 16.4 shows, the act of delegation leads to the creation of two concurrent duties owed by two different defendants to the plaintiff. It is not unusual for two different defendants to owe duties to a single plaintiff, but the intriguing feature of a non-delegable duty is that when the claim is made against the delegator (D2) for a breach of their own personal duty owed to the plaintiff, the conduct of the original tortfeasor (D1) is the immediate cause of the harm that the plaintiff has suffered. So, in Figure 16.4, the non-delegable duty placed on D2 requires D2 to ensure that when D1 carries out the task, D1 takes reasonable care to respond to reasonably foreseeable risks of harm to the plaintiff (P). This special kind of non-delegable duty is not always imposed on a person who entrusts another person to undertake a task for them. It is imposed only when a special relationship exists between P and D2, which 'is marked by special dependence or vulnerability' as Mason CJ, Deane, Dawson, Toohey and Gaudron JJ pointed out in *Burnie Port Authority v General Jones Pty Ltd* (1994) at 551. When it is imposed, the non-delegable duty gives an injured plaintiff two possible routes to a remedy:

- The first option is to sue D1 in a regular negligence action, arguing that D1 has breached their personal duty to take reasonable care.
- The second option is to sue D2, arguing that they are in breach of their personal, non-delegable duty owed directly to P because P and D2 are in one of the special relationship categories.

Figure 16.3 Non-delegable duty – standard two-party factual scenario involving one case

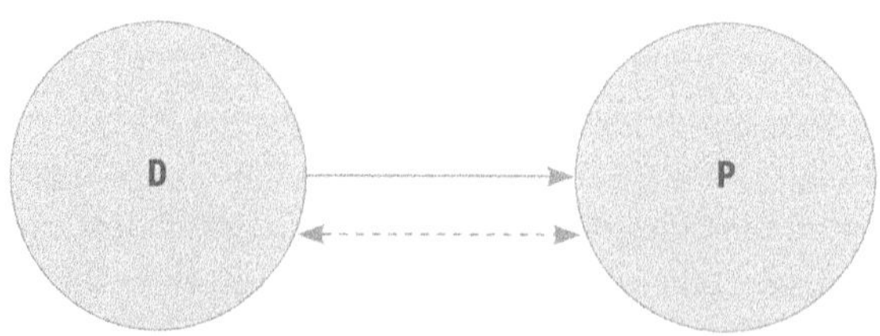

In Figure 16.3, the defendant (D) causes the plaintiff (P) to suffer a recognised form of harm. The solid line shows the tracks of harm from D to P. The dotted line shows the legal relationship between P and D.

In Figure 16.4, the dashed line shows D2 delegating a task to D1. The solid line shows the tracks of harm from D1 to P. The dotted lines are the concurrent duties owed to P by both defendants: D1 (ordinary) and D2 (more stringent).

Figure 16.4 Non-delegable scenario involving two cases

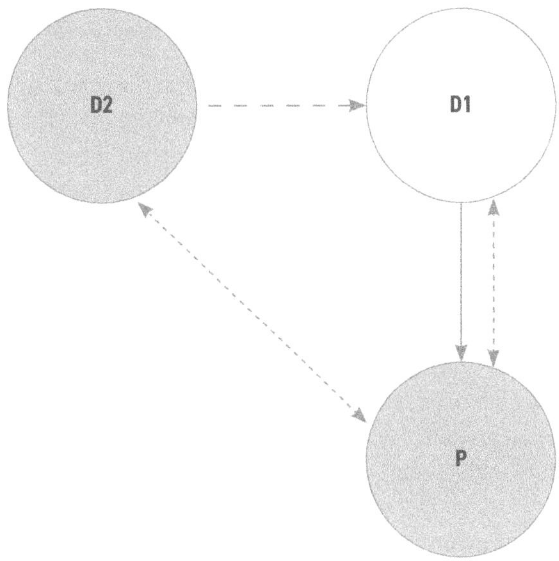

Because the non-delegable duty is conceptualised as a personal duty owed by D2 to P, it allows P to sue D2 directly (and so the fact that the harm was caused indirectly through the conduct of another is not relevant). This means it offers a different and direct route to the remedy that does not involve first tracking back through the tort to D1 and then following the link provided by the relationship between D1 and D2. However, some commentators and judges have argued that the idea of a 'direct personal duty' is nothing more than an unwarranted exception to the rule of vicarious liability that refuses to hold a principal liable for the torts of an independent contractor and is merely a fiction designed to get around the effects of this rule. One of the issues that has not yet been resolved by the High Court is whether non-delegable duty is truly a separate doctrine or is merely a label for a set of special exceptions to the doctrine of vicarious liability.

Mason J encapsulated the difference between an ordinary duty of care and a non-delegable duty in *Kondis v State Transport Authority* (1984) at 681, saying that the concept of a personal, non-delegable duty imposes a 'more stringent obligation than that imposed by the general duty to exercise reasonable care and skill' by requiring the duty holder to 'ensure that reasonable care and skill is exercised in relevant respects' by the person to whom the task has been delegated. Gleeson CJ said in *New South Wales v Lepore* (2003) at [26] 'it is clear that Mason J intended to make no distinction between a duty to ensure that reasonable care is taken and a duty to see that reasonable care is taken' and added:

> It also seems clear that the increased stringency to which he was referring lay, not in the extent of the responsibility undertaken (reasonable care for the safety of the pupils), but in the inability to discharge that responsibility by delegating the task of providing care to a third party or third parties.

Gaudron J also elaborated upon the non-delegable duty in *New South Wales v Lepore* (2003) at [100]–[105] and made several helpful explanations of the special duty:

- *Underlying justification:* 'The relationships which give rise to a non-delegable or personal duty of care have been described as involving a person being so placed in relation to another as 'to assume a particular responsibility for [that other person's] safety' because of the latter's "special dependence or vulnerability"': at [100].
- *Not absolute liability:* 'Liability is not established simply by proof of injury; there must first be a duty of care on the part of the person against whom liability is asserted. And, obviously, there must also have been a breach of that duty and resulting injury': at [101].
- *Content of duty to 'ensure safety':* 'There is a tendency to speak, in the case of an employer, of a duty to provide a safe system of work or, in the case of an education authority, a duty to provide a safe school environment, without acknowledging either that, in that context, "safe" means "free of a foreseeable risk of harm" or that the duty is a duty to take reasonable care': at [103].
- *Positive nature of duty:* '[T]he relevant duty can be expressed positively and not merely in terms of a duty to refrain from doing something that involves a foreseeable risk of injury. Thus, the relevant duty of adjoining owners can be expressed as a duty to take reasonable care to provide support; that of an employer, to take reasonable care to provide a safe system of work; that of a hospital, to take reasonable care to provide proper nursing and medical care; that of a school authority, to take reasonable care to provide a safe school environment' at [104].

If a non-delegable duty does apply, then it imposes a special duty to take positive action. If it is not applicable on the facts, then the plaintiff is restricted only to the first option of suing the primary tortfeasor (unless the primary tortfeasor is an employee, in which case the employer may be liable for the tort of their employee, provided the tort was committed in the course of their employment). An argument based on non-delegable duty is most often raised when a plaintiff has been injured by an impecunious or uninsured independent contractor and is looking for another person with 'deep pockets' who can provide them with a remedy. So, in a case where the employment status of the primary tortfeasor is unclear, it is important to argue in the alternative, and consider first whether D1 is an employee, and then, if it turns out that D1 is an independent contractor, to consider whether D2 may have owed a non-delegable duty to the plaintiff.

16.2.1.1 Scope of the doctrine

As noted in section 16.1 above, the doctrine of vicarious liability applies to any tort, not just to the tort of negligence. However, the precise scope of the doctrine of non-delegable duty is not entirely clear. We do know that it does apply in some special cases of negligence, and, since *New South Wales v Lepore* (2003), we know that it does not apply in cases where the primary tortfeasor has committed an intentional act of wrongdoing, but whether it is to be treated only as a special category of negligence is not clear. In the case of *Leichhardt Municipal Council v Montgomery* (2007), Kirby J explored two contrasting suggestions put forward by academic commentators. Kirby J disagreed with Christian Witting (2006) who argues that the non-delegable duty is a 'separate and independent tort' distinct from negligence and with its own elements, whereas his Honour did agree with John Murphy (2007) who suggests that 'they exist as "sub-species" within particular torts': see [71]–[73].

16.2.1.2 Categories of non-delegable duty

Despite the fact that the law on non-delegable duties is not entirely clear in Australia, it is generally accepted that there are five main categories where the relationship between a defendant and a plaintiff will justify imposing a special non-delegable duty that offers the plaintiff extra protection and an extra option when seeking a remedy in negligence.

Main categories of non-delegable duty

- **Employer and employee:** An employer has a duty to provide:
  - safe tools and equipment;
  - a safe workplace;
  - safe systems of work; and
  - properly qualified fellow employees and supervisors.

  See *Kondis v State Transport Authority* (1984); *Stevens v Brodribb Sawmilling Co Pty Ltd* (1986).
- **Hospital and patient:** A hospital has a duty to:
  - use reasonable care in treatment and proper nursing and medical care; and
  - provide a safe physical environment.

  See *Gold v Essex County Council* (1942); *Cassidy v Ministry of Health* (1951); *Albrighton v Royal Prince Alfred Hospital* (1980); *Ellis v Wallsend District Hospital* (1989).
- **School and pupil:** A school has a duty to provide:
  - a safe school environment; and
  - proper care and supervision.

  See *Commonwealth v Introvigne* (1982); *New South Wales v Lepore* (2003).
- **Occupier and neighbour:** An occupier has a duty to take reasonable care in the conduct of ultra-hazardous activities.

  See *Burnie Port Authority v General Jones Pty Ltd* (1994).
- **Prison authority and detainee:** A prison authority has a duty to provide proper care.

  See *Price v New South Wales* (2011); *AS v Minister for Immigration and Border Protection* (2017).

- **Other relationships:** The categories are not closed, but they *do not* include:
  - landlord and tenant: *Northern Sandblasting Pty Ltd v Harris* (1997);
  - road authority and pedestrian: *Leichhardt Municipal Council v Montgomery* (2007).

The categories of non-delegable duty, like the categories of negligence, are not closed and a new category may be recognised, or meritorious cases may be successful if the circumstances justify imposing the special duty. However, given the uncertainty over the underlying justification for the doctrine, new categories will not be developed without the exercise of 'considerable caution': Gummow and Hayne JJ in *New South Wales v Lepore* (2003) at [246]. For example, the High Court refused to allow that a principal contractor could owe the same kind of a non-delegable duty to a subcontractor working on their site that they owe to an employee in *Leighton Contractors Pty Ltd v Fox* (2009) at [20].

16.2.2 The problem of non-delegable duty

In *Leichhardt Municipal Council v Montgomery* (2007), Gleeson CJ noted at [6] that the non-delegable duty enables a plaintiff to 'outflank the general principle that a defendant is not vicariously responsible for the negligence of an independent contractor' and said at [23]: 'One of the things that is special about this duty is that it is a duty to do the impossible.' The general thrust of the criticism was summed up by Kirby J in *Leichhardt Municipal Council v Montgomery* (2007) at [31]–[32]:

> The law governing non-delegable duties of care has been described as a 'mess', comprising 'a random group of cases' giving rise to a basis of liability that is 'remarkably under-theorised'. The instances in which a non-delegable duty has been upheld have been variously labelled 'an inexplicable rag-bag of cases' comprising an erroneous feature of the 'über tort of negligence' and an 'embarrassing coda' to judicial and scholarly writings on the scope of vicarious liability for wrongs done by others.
>
> Judges have been taken to task for their reluctance, or incapacity, to express a clear theory to account for the nature and ambit of non-delegable duties of care. The whole field has been assailed as one involving serious defects, containing numerous 'aberrations' that have plunged this area of the law of tort into 'juridical darkness' and 'conceptual uncertainty'. [References omitted.]

Discussion about the non-delegable duty generally begins by noting that it may have been developed simply as a response to the inadequacies of the doctrine of vicarious liability or 'to avoid the doctrine of common employment' and is motivated only by a desire to obtain compensation for an 'innocent' plaintiff, as Gummow and Hayne JJ explain in *New South Wales v Lepore* (2003) at [250]–[269] and Kirby J noted in *Leichhardt Municipal Council v Montgomery* (2007) at [111]–[112]. Gleeson CJ explained the implications of deciding that the doctrine of non-delegable duty is either an exception to the doctrine of vicarious liability or is a special species of vicarious liability, in *Leichhardt Municipal Council v Montgomery* (2007) at [24]:

> If the law were frankly to acknowledge that what is involved is not a breach by the defendant of a special kind of duty, but an imposition upon a defendant of a special kind of vicarious responsibility, a different problem would have to be faced. It would be necessary to identify and justify the exceptions to the general rule that a defendant is not vicariously responsible for the negligence of an independent contractor, and to provide a means by which other exceptions may be identified when they arise. That, in turn, would require an explanation of the general rule so as to account for the circumstances in which it yields to exceptions. It may be difficult to justify those circumstances in terms of fixed categories. Within those categories there may be individual cases some of which may be thought to merit making them an exception and others of which may not.

Furthermore, if there is 'no conceptual unity to the recognised instances of non-delegable duties', as Kirby J said in the same case at [36], then treating non-delegable duty as a special category of vicarious liability, which also has a highly problematic and elusive rationale, is courting even further incoherence.

Another source of critique is based on the fault principle. Given that liability is normally justified by fault, 'holding one person liable for wrongs done by another' requires 'something exceptional': see, for example, Kirby J in *Leichhardt Municipal Council v Montgomery* (2007) at [38]. The difficulty, once more, is that no one seems to agree on what that 'something exceptional' might be. In one sense, the problem facing judges seeking to solve the non-delegable duty problem is very similar to the problem facing the judges in *Donoghue v Stevenson* (1932), as you can see if you compare Figure 16.3 with Figure 10.1. In both cases, judges have been faced with the existence of a set of strictly limited special categories where a special kind of duty was imposed that seemed to run counter to a normally accepted rule and with a challenge of trying to find some uniting element that is common to all categories, so that the individual categories could be seen as belonging together.

Case examples

- In *Donoghue v Stevenson* (1932), the judges had to find a new basis for imposing a duty of care (eg in circumstances where the doctrine of privity of contract appeared to deny a remedy). The solution was the 'neighbour principle', which recognised and imposed new legal obligations on the basis of the closeness and directness of the relationship between the two parties and the reasonable foreseeability of harm.
- In the cases of non-delegable duty, courts have been asked to find a new basis for imposing an extra 'stringent' duty to ensure that reasonable care is taken for a plaintiff's safety in circumstances where (most often) it is the doctrine of vicarious liability that appears to deny a remedy. As the judges often point out, a satisfying solution has not been found, although the judges have begun the search by suggesting that the special vulnerability of the plaintiffs and their inability to take any steps to protect themselves, combined with an assumption of responsibility by the defendant in those circumstances, will be a critical factor: see, for example, *Burnie Port*

Authority v General Jones Pty Ltd (1994), Mason CJ, Deane, Dawson, Toohey and Gaudron JJ at 551; *New South Wales v Lepore* (2003), Gaudron J at [100]; and *Leichhardt Municipal Council v Montgomery* (2007), Kirby J at [117]–[121].

The next subsection will explore the High Court's search for a principle justifying non-delegable duty.

16.2.3 Key cases: The search for a uniting principle

The search for a principled Australian approach to non-delegable duty was led by Mason J. It began at the same time that Deane J was leading the High Court's search for a new principle of proximity that would supplement Lord Atkin's neighbour principle and help to justify the imposition of a duty in the 'novel' categories of negligence. Proximity theory has faded and been replaced by the concept of vulnerability, which, as you will see below, has also proved to be one of the key principles said to justify the imposition of a non-delegable duty. The modern history of the non-delegable duty in Australia began in *Commonwealth v Introvigne* (1982) but reached its true theoretical starting point in the leading case of *Kondis v State Transport Authority* (1984).

Case examples

In *Commonwealth v Introvigne* (1982) the plaintiff, a pupil at a school established by the Commonwealth (D2) but administered by the State of New South Wales (D1), was injured one morning before school while playing on a flagpole. Most of the teachers were at an early staff meeting, leaving only one to supervise the students in the grounds. The pupil claimed damages from the Commonwealth (and the architects and builders of the flagpole). In the High Court it was held that by establishing the school, the Commonwealth was under a personal, non-delegable duty to provide adequate supervision of the students and to ensure that the school premises were safe by ensuring that the flagpole's halyard was locked to the pole. Mason J explained at 269:

> The liability of a school authority in negligence for injury suffered by a pupil attending the school is not a purely vicarious liability. A school authority owes to its pupil a duty to ensure that reasonable care is taken of them whilst they are on the school premises during hours when the school is open for attendance.

His Honour noted, at 271, that the 'immaturity and inexperience of the pupils and their propensity for mischief suggest that there should be a special responsibility on a school authority to care for their safety'; maintained at 270 that when the liability 'is for breach of a 'personal' duty ... then the distinction between servant and independent contractor is immaterial'; and concluded at 271–2:

> [T]he fact that the Commonwealth delegated the teaching function to the State, including the selection and control of teachers, does not affect its liability for breach of duty. Neither the duty, nor its performance, is capable of delegation.

Murphy J also held at 274–5 that the Commonwealth 'became fixed with certain non-delegable duties' that included:

> 1. To take all reasonable care to provide suitable and safe premises. The standard of care must take into account the well-known mischievous propensities of children, especially in relation to attractions and lures with obvious or latent hazards.
> 2. To take all reasonable care to provide an adequate system to ensure that no child is exposed to any unnecessary risk of injury; and to take all reasonable care to see that the system is carried out.

Kondis v State Transport Authority (1984) arose out of a complicated fact pattern. The plaintiff, Kondis, was an employee who worked for the State Transport Authority (STA) (D2) at its railway yards. He was injured at work through the carelessness of the primary tortfeasor, a crane operator named Clissold (D1), who dropped a part of the crane onto him while extending the crane's jib. The crane operator was not an employee of the STA but was himself an employee of an independent contractor who was on site operating a crane at STA's request. One of the plaintiff's fellow employees, his supervisor, had failed to instruct him to stand away from the crane during the jib operation. The plaintiff brought action against the STA. Four judges in the High Court held that the STA, as employer, owed the plaintiff a personal, non-delegable duty to adopt a safe system of work that could not be discharged simply by contracting with another person to carry out the work. Four judges also held that STA was liable for the negligence of its employee, the foreman.

Mason J wrote the leading judgment and noted at 686:

> The principal objection to the concept of personal duty is that it departs from the basic principles of liability in negligence by substituting for the duty to take reasonable care a more stringent duty, a duty to ensure that reasonable care is taken.

His Honour analysed several of the categories where such a duty had been imposed and explained the reason why in each case the extra duty was justified:

- *Employer:* 'The concept of the employer's personal duty ... amounts to a duty to see that care is taken, e.g., in the provision of safe premises and of a safe system of work. Although in this respect it imposes on the employer a more stringent obligation than that imposed by the general duty to exercise reasonable care and skill, Lord Wright characterized it as a particular exemplification of the general duty in its application to an employer with respect to the safety of his employees': at [681].
- *Hospital:* 'The liability of a hospital arises out of its undertaking an obligation to treat its patient, an obligation which carries with it a duty to use reasonable care in treatment, so that the hospital is liable, if a person engaged to perform the obligation on its behalf acts without due care': at [686].
- *School authority:* 'It is under a duty to ensure that reasonable care is taken of pupils attending the school. It is the immaturity and inexperience of the children and their propensity for mischief that lie at the basis of the special responsibility which the law imposes on a school authority to take care for their safety': at [686].

- *Occupier of premises:* 'If the invitor's duty is non-delegable it is because the invitor's invitation to the invitee to enter his premises imposes upon the invitor a duty to see that reasonable care and skill is exercised in making the premises safe': at [686].

When searching for the uniting feature of these cases Mason J referred to the special needs of the plaintiff, the special undertakings of the defendants, and the consequent reasonable expectations of the plaintiffs, saying at 687:

> The element in the relationship between the parties which generates a special responsibility or duty to see that care is taken may be found in one or more of several circumstances. The hospital undertakes the care, supervision and control of patients who are in special need of care. The school authority undertakes like special responsibilities in relation to the children whom it accepts into its care. If the invitor be subject to a special duty, it is because he assumes a particular responsibility in relation to the safety of his premises and the safety of his invitee by inviting him to enter them. And in *Meyers v Easton* the undertaking of the landlord to renew the roof of the house was seen as impliedly carrying with it an undertaking to exercise reasonable care to prevent damage to the tenant's property. In these situations the special duty arises because the person on whom it is imposed has undertaken the care, supervision or control of the person or property of another or is so placed in relation to that person or his property as to assume a particular responsibility for his or its safety, in circumstances where the person affected might reasonably expect that due care will be exercised.

When discussing the special non-delegable duty owed by an employer to an employee at 687–8, Mason J highlighted the powerlessness of the employee because:

> the exclusive responsibility for the safety of the appliances, the premises and the system of work to which he subjects his employee and the employee has no choice but to accept and rely on the employer's provision and judgment in relation to these matters.

The analysis in the leading judgement in *Kondis v State Transport Authority* (1984) became the starting point for all of the subsequent cases in this area. Mason J's focus on the assumption of responsibility and the relative powerlessness of the plaintiffs that creates a special relationship of vulnerability suggests that the doctrine of non-delegable duty is seen by the High Court, if not as a special, more stringent part of the tort of negligence, then at least as something parallel to or analogous to that tort. The next case saw the High Court use the theory of proximity to change the common law by bringing the old rule in *Rylands v Fletcher* (1868) under the umbrella of negligence and extending the doctrine of non-delegable duty.

Case example

In *Burnie Port Authority v General Jones Pty Ltd* (1994) the plaintiff, General Jones, suffered fire damage to its frozen goods which were stored in a building owned by the Burnie Port Authority (D2). The fire had been caused when D2 delegated some building work to an independent contractor (D1). The work involved welding activities in close proximity to cardboard cartons containing Isolite, an insulating material which burned fiercely if brought into sustained contact with flame. Due to D1's negligence, sparks or molten metal fell on the containers and caused the Isolite to burn. It was held by a 5:2 majority that the Burnie Port Authority (D2) as owner of the building owed the plaintiff a non-delegable duty of care which extended to ensuring that its independent contractor (D1) took reasonable care to prevent the Isolite being set alight as a result of the welding activities.

On the issue of non-delegable duty, Mason CJ, Deane, Dawson, Toohey and Gaudron JJ quoted the points made by Mason J in the earlier cases of *Kondis v State Transport Authority* (1984) and *Commonwealth v Introvigne* (1982) noted above, and concluded at 551 that the key elements uniting the categories of non-delegable duty were the 'central element of control' and the 'special dependence or vulnerability' of the plaintiff:

> Commonly, he or she will have neither the right nor the opportunity to exercise control over, or even to have foreknowledge of, what is done or allowed by the other party within the premises. Conversely, the person who introduces (or allows another to introduce) the dangerous substance or undertakes (or allows another to undertake) the dangerous activity on premises which he or she controls is 'so placed in relation to [the other] person or his property as to assume a particular responsibility for his or its safety'.

The decision in *Burnie Port Authority v General Jones Pty Ltd* (1994) extended the focus of the non-delegable duty by allowing liability for causing damage to the property of the plaintiff rather than limiting it to cases of bodily injury, and clarified the nature and underlying justification of one of the four current categories of non-delegable duty. It appeared to unite it with the tort of negligence by using the principle of proximity and the associated indicators of vulnerability in the special legal sense. The next case saw the High Court refuse to add another category to the list, and illustrated why plaintiffs who are injured by independent contractors (rather than employees) may have difficulty in sheeting liability home to a principal.

Case example

In *Northern Sandblasting Pty Ltd v Harris* (1997), the plaintiff, Nicole Harris, was a child who lived with her parents as tenants of the landlords, Northern Sandblasting Pty Ltd (D2). D2 had arranged for an independent contractor, an electrician named Briggs (D1), to repair a faulty electric stove on the property, but through his negligence, he allowed a live current to be wired to an outside tap. Later, when the plaintiff turned the tap off, she was electrocuted and was reduced to a vegetative state. In the High Court liability was imposed on D2 by a 4:3 majority decision. The judges were not in agreement over the basis for the decision, however; while two judges, Toohey J and McHugh J, in separate decisions invoked the non-delegable duty as a justification for imposing liability, none of the other judges were willing to add to the existing categories of non-delegable duty.

Toohey J focused on the aspect of control exercised by a landlord and the special dependence or vulnerability on the part of the plaintiff that gave rise to an assumption of responsibility by the landlord, and emphasised that the imposition of a non-delegable duty would not create any indeterminate liability: at 349–55. McHugh J focused on the specific undertaking to have the stove repaired and the risk of 'death or serious bodily injury': at 368–9.

The other judges did not agree and some of the relevant features of the relationship and the circumstances that pointed away from recognising a new category of non-delegable duty included:

- the fact that there was no inherent danger in the activity of repairing a stove: Brennan CJ at 333;
- there were no hazardous activities being undertaken by the landlord: Dawson J at 347;
- the anomaly that would be created by imposing a more stringent duty on the landlord than on the occupier: Dawson J at 347, Kirby J at 401;
- the fact that the law only imposes a duty to take steps that a reasonable person would take – and it was impossible to say that a landlord should have taken any greater precautions in the face of the risk than engaging a qualified electrician, combined with the fact that the repair was a task that involved a special skill: Gaudron J at 362;
- the fact that the supply of electricity to a domestic dwelling does not ordinarily involve an element of extraordinary danger such as to attract the non-delegable duty: Kirby J at 401; and
- it would have been more than an 'incremental step': Kirby J at 400.

The next major development occurred when the three cases of *New South Wales v Lepore*; *Samin v Queensland*; *Rich v Queensland* (2003) ('*New South Wales v Lepore*') were heard together by a full bench of seven judges in the High Court. Unlike their decision on vicarious liability, discussed in section 16.1.3 above, the decision of the judges on the applicability of the doctrine of non-delegable duty to an intentional act of wrongdoing by an employee was clear. A majority of the judges decided that the scope of the non-delegable duty owed by a school authority to a pupil does not include a duty to prevent any intentional criminal conduct committed by an employee against the pupil: see Gleeson CJ at [31]–[38], Gummow and Hayne JJ at [265], and Callinan J at [339]–[340]. This means that a plaintiff who has been abused by an employee of a school authority will be able to recover damages only through the doctrine of vicarious liability – and that the alternative, direct route to a remedy has been closed. Each of the judgments contains useful discussion of the doctrine that explores the nature and content of a non-delegable duty.

Case examples

- *Gleeson CJ* pointed out at [31] that 'intentional wrongdoing, especially intentional criminality, introduces a factor of legal relevance beyond a mere failure to take care' and concluded at [31]–[34] that the issue must therefore be determined only by the application of the doctrine on non-delegable duty, saying at [34]:

> The proposition that, because a school authority's duty of care to a pupil is non-delegable, the authority is liable for any injury, accidental or intentional, inflicted

> at school upon a pupil by a teacher, is too broad, and the responsibility with which it fixes school authorities is too demanding.

- *Gaudron J* noted at [99]–[105] that the issue was not whether an educational authority owes a non-delegable duty to a pupil, but whether the nature of that duty should encompass intentional acts of wrongdoing by an employee. After reviewing the doctrine (see section 16.2.1 above) her Honour noted that the non-delegable duty may impose a strict liability of a stringent kind but added at [103]:

> If the duty of an education authority to provide a safe school environment were not confined by considerations of foreseeability and reasonable care, it would result in strict liability in the sense that the authority would be liable upon proof of injury being sustained on school premises during school hours.

- *Gummow and Hayne JJ* began by expressing the view at [247] that any extension of the doctrine warranted 'considerable caution'. After discussing the ambit of a non-delegable duty to take reasonable care, their Honours concluded at [265] that the duty did not require a defendant to ensure that there is an 'absence of harm' and that it should not be 'extended to include responsibility for intentional defaults by delegates'. There were three main reasons supporting this conclusion, noted at [266]–[269]:
  1. It 'would remove the duty altogether from any connection with the law of negligence' and would 'introduce a new and wider form of strict liability to prevent harm, a step sharply at odds' with the trend of recent decisions by the High Court by making the employer 'an insurer': at [266].
  2. It 'would remove any need to consider whether the party concerned could or should have done something to avoid the harm': at [267].
  3. Any extension of the non-delegable duty 'would give no room for any operation of orthodox doctrines of vicarious liability' and would 'distort the proper development of that aspect of the law' at [269].
- *McHugh J*, in the minority on this issue, held that a school authority does owe a non-delegable duty in such circumstances, stating at [136]:

> In my opinion a State education authority owes a duty to a pupil to take reasonable care to prevent harm to the pupil. The duty cannot be delegated. If, as is invariably the case, the State delegates the performance of the duty to a teacher, the State is liable if the teacher fails to take reasonable care to prevent harm to the pupil. The State is liable even if the teacher intentionally harms the pupil. The State cannot avoid liability by establishing that the teacher intentionally caused the harm even if the conduct of the teacher constitutes a criminal offence. It is the State's duty to protect the pupil, and the conduct of the teacher constitutes a breach of the State's own duty. In a non-delegable duty case, however, the liability is direct – not vicarious. The wrongful act is a breach of the duty owed by the person who cannot delegate the duty.

The decision in *New South Wales v Lepore* (2003) showed that the High Court was not inclined to allow the doctrine of non-delegable duty to expand beyond its narrow categories – or to be used as an alternative direct route to a remedy when the indirect route via vicarious liability was blocked. Given the insecure theoretical foundations of the doctrine and its ability to 'outflank' not only the doctrine of vicarious liability, but also, on a deeper level, the foundational fault principle on which negligence law is based, it seemed unlikely that the trend towards narrowing the scope of the doctrine would be reversed. The next two cases confirmed this trend.

Case examples

- *Leichhardt Municipal Council v Montgomery* (2007) concerned a pedestrian, Montgomery (the plaintiff), who was injured one evening when he fell into a pit that had a broken cover. The pit had been concealed by a piece of carpet placed on the footpath by employees of an independent contractor, Roan Constructions Pty Ltd (D1), who had been engaged by the Leichhardt Council (D2) to work on its road. The High Court refused to allow that D2 owed the plaintiff a non-delegable duty in these circumstances.

  Gleeson CJ expressed concern at [6] and [9] about the fact that the non-delegable duty doctrine has the practical effect of allowing a plaintiff to 'outflank' the doctrine of vicarious liability. His Honour also expressed concern at [23] about the impossibility of satisfying a duty that requires a defendant to ensure that an independent contractor takes reasonable care, asking:

  > How can a hospital ensure that a surgeon is never careless? If the answer is that it cannot, what does the law mean when it speaks of a duty to ensure that care is taken? It may mean something different. It may mean that there should be an exception to the general rule that a defendant is not vicariously responsible for the negligence of an independent contractor.

  The views of the Chief Justice and Kirby J on the further problems associated with the doctrine have already been noted in section 16.2.2 above. Hayne J echoed many of those concerns and concluded at [156]:

  > It may readily be accepted that vicarious liability is itself a doctrine, or series of doctrines, lacking any single unifying and principled explanation. But whatever deficiencies there are in the law relating to vicarious liability, the identification of certain duties (said to be duties of care) as 'non-delegable duties' serves only to add to those difficulties. That should not be done where there is no sound doctrinal basis for the notion, and there is no pressing practical reason for doing so.

- The fact pattern in *Leighton Contractors Pty Ltd v Fox* (2009) was extremely complicated, because it involved a chain of contracting and subcontracting leading from the primary contractor Leighton Pty Ltd, through a series of subcontractors to the eventual subcontractors who employed several men to pump concrete onto Leighton's building project. When the men, some of whom were working as independent subcontractors, were cleaning the pump, the plaintiff, who was also one of those independent subcontractors, was injured as a result of their carelessness. He brought proceedings for negligence against the principal contractor Leighton Pty Ltd, the head subcontractor, Downview Pty Ltd, and the company which employed another of the men. In the High Court the plaintiff argued that Leighton owed him a non-delegable duty to ensure his safety. The High Court unanimously refused to open up another category of non-delegable duty by allowing that a principal owed a special personal duty to ensure that one independent subcontractor took reasonable care for the safety of another independent subcontractor. The Court analysed the relationship between the parties and the content of the asserted duty (which was to provide training) at [48] and [51] and concluded that there was 'no justification' for recognising a duty to train.

> The relationship between principal and independent contractor is not one which, of itself, gives rise to a common law duty of care, much less to the special duty resting on employers to ensure that care is taken. [48]
>
> If Leighton owed a duty to Mr Fox and Mr Stewart to provide induction training to them in the safe method of line cleaning, it owed a duty to provide training in the safe method of carrying on every trade and conducting every specialised activity carried out on the site to every worker on the site. There is no reason in principle to impose a duty having this scope on a principal contractor. The latter is unlikely to possess detailed knowledge of safe work methods across the spectrum of trades involved in construction work. And a duty to provide training in the safe method of carrying out the contractor's specialised task is inconsistent with maintenance of the distinction that the common law draws between the obligations of employers to their employees and of principals to independent contractors. [51]

The current High Court has not been sympathetic to any expansion of the doctrine of non-delegable duty, and recent decisions have suggested that any attempt to bypass the effects of the established rules and principles underlying the doctrine of vicarious liability will be unsuccessful. The difficulties in keeping these doctrines within secure bounds and reserving to each one a distinct and coherent role will not be solved easily because the underlying justification for these two doctrines remains unclear and the proper relationship between the two doctrines cannot be settled until the primary issue is first resolved. This means that the law is likely to remain unclear for some time. The fact that these two doctrines have the same practical effect (but have a different, but unclear underlying justification), led the Ipp Panel to suggest in Recommendation 43 in the *Review of Negligence* (2002) as follows:

> Liability for breach of a non-delegable duty shall be treated as equivalent in all respects to vicarious liability for the negligence of the person to whom the doing of the relevant work was entrusted by the person held liable for breach of the non-delegable duty.

LEGISLATION ALERT!

Consult your study materials and note any relevant statutory provisions in your jurisdiction that affect the law on non-delegable duty and its application to the civil liability legislation.

Develop your skills

Exercise 1: Essay writing

Write a 2000-word essay critically assessing the Australian High Court's approach to the issue of non-delegable duty.

Exercise 2: Active learning – prepare for problem solving

- Make your own summary of the law on non-delegable duty, using the cases discussed in section 16.2 above as your source.
- Work out a modification to the 'six-point plan' that you can use to introduce a problem question in this area and include it in your problem-solving summary.

Exercise 3: Case analysis

- Read the facts in the High Court case of *Leighton Contractors Pty Ltd v Fox* (2009).
- Draw a diagram that identifies all of the actors in the factual scenario and then work out all of the relationships between them, noting whether there are any possible issues of vicarious liability and non-delegable duty that could potentially arise within those relationships.

Exercise 4: Problem solving

Judy O'Khair was employed by DVD Enterprises Ltd. She applied for promotion to an executive position and was required to undergo a psychological evaluation and provide a urine sample for drug testing. DVD Enterprises engaged a local firm, Julie Noted Recruiting (JNR), to assess Judy's suitability for the position and to provide them with a full report. Unfortunately, Alex Quinn, who worked at DVD Enterprises on an irregular basis as a bicycle courier and who was responsible for taking the samples over to JNR, managed to mix up Judy's urine sample with the sample of one of Judy's main rivals for the position, Jim Breaux, who happened to have a heavy drug habit. The mix-up occurred when Alex stopped off at the zoo halfway through their ride to JNR's drug lab to visit their partner, Michael 'Ranga' Tang, who worked in the primate department. Alex and Michael were watching the orang-utans play when one of the larger males grabbed Alex's backpack and emptied the contents onto the ground. Alex shoved the containers back into the bag and stuck the labels back on without ever realising they had put them onto the incorrect bottles. The final lab report noted that Judy O'Khair's results indicated that her apparent drug use was so high that she was not suitable for any position that involved advanced cognitive activity.

The head psychologist who normally conducted the evaluations for JNR was on recreation leave at the time that Judy's response form came in to be assessed, so JNR sent it to one of the city's leading psychologists, Annie Luck, who carried out the assessment for JNR. By coincidence, Annie had become engaged to Jim on the weekend before Judy's forms were delivered and the two went away for the weekend to celebrate. On the journey Jim told Annie all about his plans for promotion and mentioned that Judy was the only person standing in his way. Jim introduced Annie to a new party drug called OMG! while they were enjoying themselves in the country and Annie suffered a long-lasting adverse reaction that robbed her of her normal mental acuity for the entirety of the following week. During her drug 'hangover' Annie assessed Judy's forms, but she misread the labels on each end of the scaled answers and instead of reporting that Judy's answer placed her in the top 10 per cent of suitable applicants, Annie wrote a report for JNR concluding that Judy was in the bottom 10 per cent of applicants. JNR passed the report on to DVD Enterprises, along with all the other reports (which had been carried out earlier by their usual psychologist). Judy not only failed in her application for promotion but was sacked by DVD Enterprises after its human resources manager read the two reports. Jim is now enjoying his new job.

Discuss the legal issues arising from these facts, identifying any extra information that you would need to discover in order to advise Judy fully.

You will find some problem-solving tips in the section below Table 16.1.

Conclusion

In this chapter, you've seen how the doctrines of vicarious liability and non-delegable duties can go some way towards ensuring that those in positions of control can bear responsibility for harm caused by others. Vicarious liability essentially focuses on whether the wrongful act in question is closely connected to the relationship in question, while non-delegable duties emphasise the obligation to safeguard against harm, regardless of delegation to another. The doctrines of vicarious liability and non-delegable duties are certainly complex; however, they remain important mechanisms in tort law for extending responsibility and accountability beyond tortfeasors.

REFERENCES

CASES

Albrighton v Royal Prince Alfred Hospital [1980] 2 NSWLR 542

AS v Minister for Immigration and Border Protection [2017] VSC 137

Bazley v Curry [1999] 2 SCR 534; (1999) 174 DLR (4th) 45

Bird v DP (A Pseudonym) (2024) 419 ALR 552; (2024) 98 ALJR 1349; (2024) 334 IR 404

Burnie Port Authority v General Jones Pty Ltd (1994) 179 CLR 520

Cassidy v Ministry of Health [1951] 2 KB 343

CCIG Investments Pty Ltd v Schokman (2023) 278 CLR 165

Construction, Forestry, Maritime, Mining and Energy Union v Personnel Contracting Pty Ltd (2022) 275 CLR 165

Commonwealth v Introvigne (1982) 150 CLR 258

Day v Ocean Beach Hotel Shellharbour Pty Ltd (2013) 85 NSWLR 335

Deatons Pty Ltd v Flew (1949) 79 CLR 370

Donoghue v Stevenson [1932] AC 562

Ellis v Wallsend District Hospital (1989) 17 NSWLR 553

Frost v Warner (2002) 209 CLR 509

Gold v Essex County Council [1942] 2 KB 293
Hollis v Vabu Pty Ltd (2001) 207 CLR 21
Jacobi v Griffiths (1999) 174 DLR (4th) 71
Kelly v Bluestone Global Ltd (in liq) [2016] WASCA 90
Kondis v State Transport Authority (1984) 154 CLR 672
Leichhardt Municipal Council v Montgomery (2007) 230 CLR 22
Leighton Contractors Pty Ltd v Fox (2009) 240 CLR 1
Lister v Hesley Hall Ltd [2002] 1 AC 215
Lloyd v Grace, Smith & Co [1912] AC 716
Mersey Docks & Harbour Board v Coggins & Griffith (Liverpool) Ltd [1947] AC 1
Morris v CW Martin & Sons Ltd [1966] 1 QB 716
New South Wales v Lepore; Samin v Queensland; Rich v Queensland (2003) 212 CLR 511
Northern Sandblasting Pty Ltd v Harris (1997) 188 CLR 313
Price v New South Wales [2011] NSWCA 341
Prince Alfred College Inc v ADC (2016) 258 CLR 134; 335 ALR 1
Rose v Plenty [1976] 1 WLR 529
Rylands v Fletcher (1868) LR 3 HL 330
Scott v Davis (2000) 204 CLR 333
Soblusky v Egan (1960) 103 CLR 215
Stevens v Brodribb Sawmilling Co Pty Ltd (1986) 160 CLR 16
Sweeney v Boylan Nominees Pty Ltd (2006) 226 CLR 161
Trustees of the Roman Catholic Church v Ellis [2007] NSWCA 117
Viasystems (Tyneside) Ltd v Thermal Transfer (Northern) Ltd [2006] QB 510
ZG Operations Australia Pty Ltd v Jamsek (2022) 275 CLR 254
Zuijs v Wirth Brothers Pty Ltd (1955) 93 CLR 561

ARTICLES, BOOKS AND REPORT

Ipp, D, Cane, P, Sheldon, D & Macintosh, I, *Review of the Law of Negligence Final Report* (2002) <https://treasury.gov.au/review/review-of-the-law-of-negligence>.

Murphy, J, 'The Liability Bases of Common Law Non-Delegable Duties – A Reply to Christian Witting' (2007) 30 *University of New South Wales Law Journal* 86.

Neyers, J, 'A Theory of Vicarious Liability' (2005) 43 *Alberta Law Review* 287.

Pollock, F, *Essays in Jurisprudence and Ethics* (2008) Kessinger Publishing.

Salmond, J W, *Law of Torts* (1907) Stevens and Haynes, London.

Witting, C, 'Breach of the Non-Delegable Duty: Defending Limited Strict Liability in Tort' (2006) 29 *University of New South Wales Law Journal* 33.

DOING JUSTICE: PRINCIPLES OF DAMAGES

17

Introduction

In 2002, a man named Liam Magill sued his former wife in the tort of deceit, after he discovered that he was not the father of two of the three children who had been born during the course of their marriage. After DNA testing confirmed that his wife had deceived him and that another man was the biological father of the two children, Mr Magill sued his wife, claiming damages and seeking justice. Although he succeeded at first instance in the County Court of Victoria, Mr Magill's case then went all the way to the High Court of Australia ('High Court') on appeal, where, in a unanimous decision, it was held that he could not recover damages for the conduct of his wife: see *Magill v Magill* (2006). Mr Magill had sought compensatory damages for personal injury (consisting of anxiety and depression), lost earnings that flowed from his injury (lost income) and other financial losses related to the time and costs associated with the upkeep of the children. He also claimed exemplary damages that were aimed at condemning his former wife's conduct and punishing her for her deceit. As reported in *The Age* newspaper on 23 November 2002 at 3, Mr Magill's new partner, Cheryl, said after their first successful case:

> It's the mere fact that we've been able to get a judgment in favour. Money does not come into the equation—it's the fact that we have been able to set a precedent. We wanted this woman to be held accountable for her actions. So far as setting a precedent, we have achieved what we set out to achieve.

Mr Magill went to the civil law system seeking justice and he based his claim on the tort of deceit. He wanted to stand up for his rights as a husband and as a father and hoped to set a precedent so that no one would have to suffer in the same way that he had suffered. He sought recognition for the wrong that had been done to him, and he wanted his wife to be held accountable for what she had done. In our civil justice system, the courts generally hold a tortfeasor to account by making an order for the payment of damages, and so in the County Court, when Mr Magill won his first case, the price that the judge placed on Mrs Magill's wrongdoing was $70 000. In our civil justice system, every wrong has its price and cash is the currency of justice.

Chapter 1 defined a tort as an act of civil wrongdoing that has the capacity to harm another person, which attracts a legal remedy that is seen as doing justice between the parties, and which does not fit better into any other civil law category. Justice is one of the essential dimensions of every tort. Without an enforceable remedy, the law's pronouncements carry no power and deliver no promises to the victims of wrongdoing. For our civil justice system, rule without a remedy is not a rule at all; it is just a piece of advice. So, responding to wrongdoing is an indispensable part of doing justice. When the judges decide a case and give a judgment for the plaintiff, they include an order specifying what must be done by the defendant to put matters right between the parties. But not every community responds in the same way. As you saw in Chapter 1, the law of torts reflects the community that it serves - and different communities not only have different rules, but they may also impose different legal responses when their rules are broken. If the facts of Mr Magill's case had occurred 1400 years earlier in Anglo-Saxon England, the response of the courts would have been different. Under the laws of one of the earliest English Kings, King Ethelbert, which were issued in the year 602–3, justice took a different form: see Griffiths, *An Introduction to Early English Law* (1995) at 36:

> If one freeman lies with another freeman's wife, he shall render the wergeld [damages] and procure with his own money a second wife for the man and bring her to his house.

The law of torts is dominated by an ideal vision of corrective justice, as Chapter 2 explained. It requires a person who has wronged another to make amends by correcting the harmful consequences that have flowed from their conduct. So, in this sense, our system of tort law is infused with exactly the same sense of justice as the laws of King Ethelbert, because they are both built on the desire for corrective justice. In both legal systems, any breach of the duty imposed by the law is seen as creating an imbalance, which is then corrected by imposing a corresponding duty on the wrongdoer to remedy their breach and do something to put the world back to rights. The difference between our laws and King Ethelbert's laws is their content - and that is because King Ethelbert's laws reflected the community that existed in 602 when women were seen as a special kind of property, and when men were their owners. In those times, if one man took another man's property of any kind, corrective justice required him to replace it. In our times, corrective justice typically requires a tortfeasor to pay for their wrongdoing by a payment of money, although as Chapter 6 explained, it is sometimes possible for a court to order the return of goods of special personal value - and, fortunately, human beings, whether men or women, are no longer included in that definition.

Chapter 1 explained that the law of torts is made up of a set of rules and principles that, when taken together, tell us how to live a life that is respectful of others, and how to treat them properly - according to the community's standards. It also contains a set of rules and principles that tell judges what to do once a plaintiff has proved their case and becomes entitled to an award of damages. There are four key principles of justice that dominate the law of damages. They are:

- the compensation principle;
- the finality principle;
- the certainty principle; and
- the fault principle revisited: mitigation of loss.

The first two principles are new, but the second two are already familiar from the earlier chapters on negligence. This chapter will explore these four principles of justice and conclude by considering the role that lawyers play in advancing the cause of doing justice.

17.1 Corrective justice and the compensation principle

In the case of *Todorovic v Waller* (1981), Gibbs CJ and Wilson J at 412 laid down four famous rules of compensation:

> Certain fundamental principles are so well established that it is unnecessary to cite authorities in support of them. In the first place, a plaintiff who has been injured by the negligence of the defendant should be awarded such a sum of money as will, as nearly as possible, put him in the same position as if he had not sustained the injuries. Secondly, damages for one cause of action must be recovered once and forever, and (in the absence of any statutory exception) must be awarded as a lump sum; the court cannot order a defendant to make periodic payments to the plaintiff. Thirdly, the court has no concern with the manner in which the plaintiff uses the sum awarded to him; the plaintiff is free to do what he likes with it. Fourthly, the burden lies on the plaintiff to prove the injury or loss for which he seeks damages.

17.1.1 The compensation principle

As you can see from the first rule noted in *Todorovic v Waller* (1981), corrective justice requires a wrongdoer to make amends for their wrong and so a tortfeasor is required to pay a sum of money that is calculated to put the plaintiff into the same position that they would have been in if the tort had not occurred. This is also known as '*restitutio in integrum*' - or restoration of wholeness by putting the plaintiff back into their original position. This ideal vision of justice is in most cases unattainable. If we consider Mr Magill's case, for example, it is hard to see how any payment of money could have put him into the same position as if his wife's conduct had not occurred. Similarly, a person whose leg has been amputated as a result of wrongdoing cannot be put back into their original position. Nevertheless, the judges do attempt the impossible and it is instructive to read a few cases to see how the sum of money is calculated. Gibbs CJ and Wilson J explained at 412–13 in *Todorovic v Waller* (1981):

> Although the aim of the court in awarding damages is to make good to the plaintiff, so far as money can do, the loss which he has suffered, it is obvious that it is impossible to assess damages for pain and suffering and loss of amenities of life by any process of arithmetical calculation. It may be less obvious, but is no less certain, that the assessment of damages for future pecuniary loss resulting from personal injuries can never be a mere matter of mathematics. In many cases this means that the court has to engage in 'a double exercise in the art of prophesying': *Paul v Rendell* ... Ultimately the process must always be one of judgment rather than calculation.
>
> The difficulty inherent in the assessment of damages provides no reason for the courts to shirk the task of arriving at the estimate most likely to provide fair and reasonable compensation. But it may provide a reason for approaching with some caution a proposal to overturn an established method of assessment, in an attempt to achieve an accuracy which it is not humanly possible to attain. [References omitted.]

17.1.1.1 Critique of the compensation principle

Despite the fact that our system of tort law is broadly based on the goal of corrective justice, its results are not always satisfactory. There are three main streams of criticism that ask whether our community is well served by a system of corrective justice. Those in the first stream use a fault-based perspective to criticise the harm-based focus of tort law. They focus on the fact that there is often a disproportion between the damages that a defendant may have to pay and their actual degree of fault. This happens quite often in the tort of negligence – for example, where a moment's inattention behind the wheel of a car can lead to massive amounts of damage.

Example

It is sometimes said that liability in the law of torts can be disproportionate to the fault of the defendant. This is sometimes used as a reason to deny liability altogether by refusing to impose a duty (see, eg, McHugh J in *Woolcock Street Investments Pty Ltd v CDG Pty Ltd* (2004) at [88]–[104]). The authors of successive versions of *Atiyah's Accidents, Compensation and the Law* (Patrick Atiyah, who wrote the original version and Peter Cane, who wrote the most recent version in 2018), both argue that when viewed from a wider 'legal and social landscape' (at xv), it is clear that the tort of negligence, which relies on an incoherent and flawed account of fault, should be replaced by a fairer compensation scheme. They criticise the fault principle chiefly on the grounds that the compensation payable by a defendant often bears no relation to their degree of fault.

A different manifestation of the same problem arises out of difficult cases such as those involving 'wrongful life' claims (discussed in Chapters 10, 11 and 14). If you reflect back on the respective (and very diverging!) reasonings of Crennan and Kirby JJ in *Harriton v Stephens* (2006), there are complex harm situations in which the compensation principle can cause wrongdoing to be left without a remedy.

These critics use the concept of retributive justice to point out that our system of tort law, with its focus on corrective justice, can sometimes give rise to a perceived injustice. (Retributive justice takes into account both the degree of fault as well as the degree of harm done, when deciding on criminal punishment.) Other critics use the concept of distributive justice to criticise tort law. Distributive justice is based on the goal of achieving a fair distribution of benefits and burdens throughout a community or group, and the classic rule of distributive justice requires us to treat like cases alike and different cases differently.

Cane and Atiyah also make the point that a fault-based system of tort law is distributively unfair and discriminatory because it does not treat like cases alike. Some victims of misfortune, who have a tortfeasor to sue, receive full compensation, whereas others who suffer the same injury may receive nothing, either because they cannot identify their tortfeasor, or because there is no one else to blame at all. These accident victims who suffer the same injuries as tort victims must bear the cost of their losses themselves.

For Cane and Atiyah, there is no relevant difference between the victims of innocent accidents and the victims wronged by a tort. There is a perceived injustice, because while both groups are suffering in the same way, some receive an award of damages and others miss out because they have no one to blame. These critics also invoke the idea of efficiency to back up their claims of injustice.

Examples

- In *The Damages Lottery* (1997), Atiyah suggests that a no-fault road accident scheme combined with new, more widespread forms of personal first-party insurance would offer a better solution than our current system of tort law. Atiyah's central claim is that public resources would be better spent by diverting them out of the cumbersome, sometimes irrational and unfair system of tort law and devoting them to a less wasteful, more modest and more certain system that can deliver better outcomes to more victims of misfortune.
- An illuminating critique of the effectiveness of the civil law system in compensating tort victims in Australia can be found in chapter 1 of Harold Luntz et al's classic case book *Torts: Cases and Commentary* (2017).
- Stephen D Sugarman argues in 'Doing Away with Tort Law' (1985) that tort law is a 'bizarre system' of compensation. This article was published in a special edition of the *California Law Review*, which also contains many other articles from the Symposium on Alternative Compensation Schemes and Tort Theory.
- In New Zealand, the Accident Compensation Corporation is a comprehensive no-fault compensation scheme for victims of accidents. The scheme has a rich history, starting back in 1974, and today it covers all forms of accidents (at work, on the street, in the medical context, etc), thereby

removing Cane and Atiyah's concern around the differential treatment between the victims of innocent accidents and the victims wronged by a tort

- See also Robert Abel's article 'A Critique of Torts' (1994), which argues that our method of awarding damages in negligence serves only to reproduce inequality, commodify our experience and encourage inefficient safety levels.

These critics argue that the system of tort law – at least insofar as it relates to negligently caused injuries – should be replaced by a fairer, more efficient and more certain system of dealing with the injured, and in fact many jurisdictions in Australia have developed alternative means of compensation. For example, it is worth noting that most state and territories now have compensation schemes in place for accidents occurring at work, and for fatal accidents.

LEGISLATION ALERT!

Consult your study materials and note any relevant statutory provisions in your jurisdiction on alternative compensation schemes.

17.1.2 Types of damages

There are several different categories of damages that may be awarded, as Table 17.1 shows. In the trespass torts, which are actionable per se – that is, without proof of actual damage – an award of nominal damages can be made to mark the fact that the defendant has done the wrong thing and to vindicate the rights of the plaintiff. If any actual damage has also been caused by the invasion of the plaintiff's rights, an award of compensatory damages will also be made. Compensatory damages are the most commonly awarded form of damages in the law of torts.

17.1.2.1 Aggravated versus exemplary damages

Two other types of damages may also be claimed in torts cases: aggravated damages, which compensate the plaintiff for any extra distress, insult or humiliation that they have suffered because of the way that the tort was committed; and exemplary (or punitive) damages, which are awarded to punish the defendant and to deter others from any similar kinds of wrongdoing. In a sense, both kinds of damages are made in response to the moral character of the defendant's conduct, but the aggravated damages recognise and compensate for the extra emotional impact on the plaintiff because of the way that the harm was inflicted, whereas the exemplary damages focus directly on the defendant's degree of moral blameworthiness. The joint judgment of Gleeson CJ, Gummow, Kirby, Heydon and Crennan JJ in *New South Wales v Ibbett* (2006) explained at [31] that aggravated damages 'are a form of general damages, given by way of compensation for injury to the plaintiff, which may be intangible, resulting from the circumstances and manner of the wrongdoing'. So, aggravated damages are seen as consistent with the principle of corrective justice, but punitive damages are an anomaly, best justified by the idea of

Table 17.1 Types of damages

Type	Definition
Nominal damages	Recognise the fact that the plaintiff's rights have been invaded. These damages are awarded even if no actual damage has been caused.
Compensatory damages	Are based on different tests, depending on the tort: • In the intentional torts the plaintiff is compensated for all the harmful consequences *directly* caused by the defendant's conduct. • In the torts of negligence and nuisance the plaintiff is compensated only for the *reasonably foreseeable* consequences that are not too 'remote' a result of the defendant's conduct.
Aggravated damages	May be awarded to compensate for any extra distress, insult or humiliation suffered by the plaintiff when the harm done by a wrongful act was aggravated by the manner in which the act was done.
Contemptuous damages	A trifling amount may be awarded when a jury wants to mark the fact that they believe the plaintiff's case was worthless or decides to mark their disapproval of the plaintiff's own conduct. These damages are rarely awarded in modern times.
Exemplary or punitive damages	Are awarded to punish the defendant in cases where there has been a 'contumelious and flagrant disregard' of the plaintiff's rights. These damages go to the plaintiff, not to the state, and there are limits on the torts where this remedy is available. Once liability is found, a plaintiff is entitled to damages 'as of right' but if the defendant does not have the means to pay, a plaintiff may have a hollow victory.

retributive justice. The difference between the two kinds of damages was summed up by Gleeson CJ, McHugh, Gummow and Hayne JJ in *Gray v Motor Accident Commission* (1998) at [6], citing Windeyer J in *Uren v John Fairfax & Sons Pty Ltd* (1996):

> The distinction between aggravated and exemplary damages is often drawn. In *Uren v John Fairfax & Sons Pty Ltd,* Windeyer J noted that it is a distinction that is 'not easy to make in defamation, either historically or analytically and in practice it is hard to preserve'. Nevertheless, in the present context, it is a distinction which it is as well to bear in mind, if only to attempt to ensure greater accuracy of expression. In *Uren,* Windeyer J described the difference as being:
>
> > 'that aggravated damages are given to compensate the plaintiff when the harm done to him by a wrongful act was aggravated by the manner in which the act was done: exemplary damages, on the other hand, are intended to punish the defendant, and presumably to serve one or more of the objects of punishment—moral retribution or deterrence.' [References omitted.]

The joint judgment went on at [15]–[16] to explain that exemplary damages are 'a windfall' to the plaintiff because they are not compensatory in nature and to note that this kind of damages therefore gives rise to 'an appearance of tension between using civil proceedings to compensate a party who is wronged and using the same proceedings to punish the wrongdoer':

> In considering whether to award exemplary damages, the first, if not the principal, focus of the inquiry is upon the wrongdoer, not upon the party who was wronged. (The reaction of the party who is wronged to high-handed or deliberate conduct may well be a reason for awarding aggravated damages in further compensation for the wrong done. But it is not ordinarily relevant to whether exemplary damages should be allowed.) The party wronged is entitled to whatever compensatory damages the law allows (including, if appropriate, aggravated damages). By hypothesis then, the party wronged will receive just compensation for the wrong that is suffered. If exemplary damages are awarded, they will be paid in addition to compensatory damages and, in that sense, will be a windfall in the hands of the party who was wronged. Nevertheless, they are awarded at the suit of that party and, although awarded to punish the wrongdoer and deter others from like conduct, they are not exacted by the State or paid to it.

Because these damages are designed to punish the wrongdoer, they are awarded only exceptionally and will not be awarded in cases of mere inadvertence or negligence, as the joint judgment explained at [20]–[21]:

> If, as we have earlier suggested, the remedy is exceptional in the sense that it arises (chiefly, if not exclusively) in cases of conscious wrongdoing in contumelious disregard of the plaintiff's rights, at least two further questions arise: are exemplary damages available where the plaintiff's claim is for damages for negligence rather than some intentional wrong, and is the award of exemplary damages a matter of right or does it depend on the exercise of a discretion informed by some identifiable criteria? [20]
>
> No question arises here of an intentional wrong being committed by inadvertence. For present purposes it is enough to note two things. First, exemplary damages could not properly be awarded in a case of alleged negligence in which there was no conscious wrongdoing by the defendant. Ordinarily, then, questions of exemplary damages will not arise in most negligence cases be they motor accident or other kinds of case. But there can be cases, framed in negligence, in which the defendant can be shown to have acted consciously in contumelious disregard of the rights of the plaintiff or persons in the position of the plaintiff. Cases of an employer's failure to provide a safe system of work for employees in which it is demonstrated that the employer, well knowing of an extreme danger thus created, persisted in employing the unsafe system might, perhaps, be of that latter kind. [21]

The joint judgment concluded at [40] by making a rule that in cases where a tortfeasor has already been punished by the criminal law for the same conduct that is under scrutiny in the tortious claim, then 'exemplary damages may not be awarded'. There were two reasons for this rule noted at [42]–[43]. One of the reasons was to avoid double punishment; the other was because:

> the purposes for the awarding of exemplary damages have been wholly met if substantial punishment is exacted by the criminal law. The offender is punished; others are deterred. There is, then, no occasion for their award.

One of the most common reasons for awarding punitive damages was given in *New South Wales v Ibbett* (2006) at [38]–[39] where the joint judgment explained that it is one of the methods where 'the State is called to account by the common law for the misconduct of those acting under or with the authority of the Executive Government'. This is because:

> an award of exemplary damages may serve 'a valuable purpose in restraining the arbitrary and outrageous use of executive power' and 'oppressive, arbitrary or unconstitutional action by the servants of the government'. [References omitted.]

These damages, which are used to punish the wrongdoer, to deter the particular wrongdoer – and any other potential wrongdoers – and to mark the court's disapproval of the conduct, have been criticised not only by academics, but also by the Ipp Panel's *Review of the Law of Negligence: Final Report* (2002). The Final Report listed the advantages of using this retributive measure within the civil justice system at [13.163]:

> **a)** It is a legitimate function of the civil law to penalise reprehensible conduct; exemplary damages fulfil this function.
> **b)** Exemplary damages provide a way of punishing defendants where criminal, regulatory and administrative sanctions are inadequate.

The disadvantages were noted at [13.164]:

> **a)** Exemplary damages confuse the punishment function of the criminal law with the compensation function of the civil law.
> **b)** Exemplary damages constitute an undeserved windfall for the plaintiff.
> **c)** Awards of exemplary damages are unpredictable especially in jury trials.
> **d)** Awards for exemplary damages are often too high.

The Panel recommended in the Final Report that both aggravated and exemplary damages be abolished (Recommendation 60).

LEGISLATION ALERT!

Consult your study materials and note any statutory provisions in your jurisdiction covering exemplary and aggravated damages awards.

17.1.2.2 Compensatory damages

As noted above, compensatory damages are the most commonly awarded form of damages in personal injury cases. These damages are typically divided into different 'heads' or categories, as Windeyer J explained in *Teubner v Humble* (1963) at 505–6:

> Broadly speaking there are, it seems to me, three ways in which a personal injury can give rise to damage: First, it may destroy or diminish, permanently or for a time, an existing capacity, mental or physical: Secondly, it may create needs that would not otherwise exist: Thirdly, it may produce physical pain and suffering.

His Honour explained, however, that the ultimate goal is to arrive at 'a single amount that is appropriate in the circumstances of the case, and that it is not the sum of rigidly separate and independent items' at 505:

> So-called principles of assessment of damages for personal injuries can be made the subject of almost endless discussion. The consequences of such injuries are not all susceptible of evaluation in money, and seeming logic can be pushed too far ... The conventional headings, economic loss, deprivation of amenities, and pain and suffering, provide a convenient reminder of matters that ought not to be forgotten. But it is not always appropriate, I think, to consider them as if they were distinct items in a balance sheet; for one may overlap and impinge upon another.

So, as Windeyer J explained at 506, a person's 'labour and skill have a market value' but a person cannot sell their 'capacity for enjoyment' and so this means that these two heads of damages cannot be 'compensated on the same principles':

> Pain and suffering fall into another category. What is usually contemplated by the description is actual physical pain. Of all forms of damage this is perhaps the one that is least susceptible of monetary assessment. But in so far as the possession of money can in a particular case give pleasure or provide comfort, money can properly be said to compensate for pain and suffering.

These passages have been quoted and requoted many times in the cases dealing with the difficulty of calculating an award of damages. They show that the task is often symbolic and suggest that in an imperfect world, human beings can only aim to do justice as best they can – and they affirm that perfect justice is unattainable.

17.1.3 The language of loss

There are other ways of describing the different kinds of damages that a plaintiff may claim – see Table 17.2. While Table 17.1 covers damages from the perspective of a defendant – that is, the types of damages that a defendant may be liable for – Table 17.2 covers loss from the perspective of the plaintiff.

In *CSR Ltd v Eddy* (2005), McHugh J went back to the case of *Paff v Speed* (1961) to explain the difference between 'general damages' and 'special damages' at [89]:

> 'Special damages' are awarded in such cases in respect of monetary loss actually suffered and expenditure actually incurred. Their two characteristics are (1) that they are assessed only up to the date of verdict, and (2) that they are capable of precise arithmetical calculation or at least of being estimated with a close approximation to accuracy. The familiar examples are medical and

Table 17.2 The language of loss

Type of loss or damages	Definition
Pecuniary loss	Covers the loss of earning capacity and other calculable expenses.
Non-pecuniary losses	Are less easily measured losses that arise because of pain, suffering and the loss of enjoyment or amenities of life.
Special damages	Are awarded to compensate for monetary loss actually suffered and expenditure actually incurred. They are characterised by a) the fact that they are assessed only up to the date of verdict and b) the fact that they can be measured with close accuracy.
General damages	Cover losses that are of their very nature incapable of mathematical calculation. They are said to be 'at large' and they include a) pain and suffering and b) loss of amenities or enjoyment of life. They also include c) future pecuniary or economic losses that may be suffered after the date of judgment.

> surgical fees paid or payable, ambulance and hospital expenses, and loss of income. Where the plaintiff has been employed at a fixed wage or salary, his loss of income can commonly be calculated with exactness. Where the plaintiff has not been employed, but is, for example, a professional man, his monetary loss can be estimated without difficulty by reference to his past earnings. In a high proportion of cases the amount of the 'special damages' is agreed between counsel for the plaintiff and counsel for the defendant.
>
> 'General damages' on the other hand, are, of their very nature, incapable of mathematical calculation, and (although the expression is apt to be misleading) commonly very much 'at large'. They are at large in the sense that a jury has, in serious cases, a wide discretion in assessing them. Also general damages may be assessed not with reference to any limited period, but with reference to an indefinite future. Damages may be awarded for 'pain and suffering', and such damages are assessable for past, present and future pain and suffering. But here calculation is obviously impossible, and damages for pain and suffering should clearly be regarded as 'general' and not 'special' damages. In fact, the question of general damages is generally, I think, put to a jury under three heads—(1) economic loss, (2) loss of 'amenities' or 'enjoyment of life', and (3) pain and suffering.

In the same case, Gleeson CJ, Gummow and Heydon JJ went further to explain the other terminology used in the personal injury cases and noted that a plaintiff who has been injured is traditionally seen as able to recover three types of loss, saying at [29]–[31]:

> The first covers non-pecuniary losses such as pain and suffering, disfigurement, loss of limbs or organs, loss of the senses—sight, taste, hearing, smell and touch; and loss of the capacity to engage in hobbies, sport, work, marriage

> and child-bearing. Damages can be recovered in relation to these losses even if no actual financial loss is caused and even if the damage caused by them cannot be measured in money.
>
> The second type of loss is loss of earning capacity both before the trial and after it. Although the damages recoverable in relation to reduced future income are damages for loss of earning capacity, not damages for loss of earnings simpliciter, those damages are awardable only to the extent that the loss has been or may be productive of financial loss. Hence 'the valuation of the loss of earning capacity involves the consideration of what moneys could have been produced by the exercise of the [plaintiff's] former earning capacity'.
>
> The third type of recoverable loss is actual financial loss, for example, ambulance charges; charges for medical, hospital and professional nursing services; travel and accommodation expenses incurred in obtaining those services; the costs of rehabilitation needs, special clothing and special equipment; the costs of modifying houses; the costs of funds management; and the costs of professionally supplied home maintenance services. It is not necessary for the costs actually to have been incurred by the time of the trial, but it is necessary that they will be incurred.

Non-pecuniary loss, as described by Gleeson CJ, Gummow and Heydon JJ, is a particularly complex form of damage. On one hand, it allows courts to tailor their response to the individual plaintiff's specific circumstances. For example, in the case of *Trevorrow v South Australia (No 5)* (2007), the Supreme Court of South Australia recognised the plaintiff Bruce Trevorrow's loss of cultural identity resulting from him being taken away from his family as an infant pursuant to South Australia's policies governing removals of Aboriginal children in the 1950s. On the other hand, compensation for non-pecuniary loss can be inadequate and disproportionately inferior to that which plaintiffs are able to attain for pecuniary losses. This is due to a fear of overcompensation for types of harm that are definitionally difficult to quantify in monetary terms. However, it entails a differential application of the compensation principle, the goal of which is in theory to put the plaintiff back in the position they were before the harm occurred.

17.1.4 Parliamentary justice

The Ipp Panel's Review of the Law of Negligence was also asked to consider the need to impose thresholds and caps on damages awards. In chapter 13 of the Final Report the Panel members emphasised the need for national consistency in this area, but their warnings were not heeded and now any hope of uniformity has been lost.

LEGISLATION ALERT!

Consult your study materials and note any relevant statutory provisions in your jurisdiction that impose either a threshold or a cap on liability.

17.1.5 Other kinds of damages

There are two other species of damages awards, not shown in Tables 17.1 or 17.2, that have been very controversial, and they are named after the cases where they were first recognised. They are '*Griffiths v Kerkemeyer*' (1977) damages and '*Sullivan v Gordon*' (1999) damages. The first category remains available at common law, but damages of the second kind, which were once recognised in some states, are no longer available at common law after the High Court refused to recognise them in *CSR Ltd v Eddy* (2005). These different kinds of damages focus on the issues that are raised when a plaintiff claims compensation for services that are provided gratuitously *to* the plaintiff because of their incapacity or for services that were once performed *by* a plaintiff, who has lost the capacity to carry out those services because of their injuries.

Case examples

- The case of *Griffiths v Kerkemeyer* (1977) allowed a plaintiff to recover an amount equivalent to the commercial cost of nursing and domestic services that had been provided in the past and would be provided in the future by the family or friends of the plaintiff. McHugh J noted in *CSR Ltd v Eddy* (2005) at [101] that Australian courts had extended the *Griffiths v Kerkemeyer* damages to gratuitous services that previously would not have been the subject of compensation, namely:
    - to care provided by a plaintiff-mother to her children;
    - to cleaning work performed by a plaintiff-wife in her husband's hairdressing salon; and
    - to the cost of care for a plaintiff-mother's children for the period after her injury caused her death until they no longer required such care.

  McHugh explains at [113] why these damages should no longer be awarded:

  > *Griffiths v Kerkemeyer* damages arise as a direct result of the creation of a need in the plaintiff of the provision of the particular services. It is therefore inherently limited. By contrast, no inherent limit exists to the [types of damages listed above].

- In *Van Gervan v Fenton* (1992), Mason CJ, Brennan, Toohey, Gaudron and McHugh JJ explained at 332–3, 340 and 347 that the true basis of the claim was the need of the plaintiff for the services and noted that the plaintiff did not have to show that the need was or might be productive of financial loss. They were to be determined by reference to the cost of providing those services generally in the market.
- In *Sullivan v Gordon* (1999) the New South Wales Court of Appeal awarded damages to compensate plaintiffs in situations where they could no longer provide gratuitous services to other people due to their incapacity arising from the injury. This form of damages was overruled by the High Court in *CSR Ltd v Eddy* (2005).

Some states have modified the rule in *Griffiths v Kerkemeyer* (1977), and other states have considered the usefulness of the *Sullivan v Gordon* (1999) awards as well.

LEGISLATION ALERT!

Consult your study materials and note any statutory provisions in your jurisdiction covering gratuitous services.

Test your understanding and develop your skills

Matching concepts with results

Read the case of *CSR Ltd v Eddy* (2005) and create a table that sets out:

- the different types of damages available;
- a practical rationale supporting each type of damage; and
- the underlying principle justifying each type of damage.

17.2 Justice and the finality principle

17.2.1 The 'once and for all' rule

The successful plaintiff is awarded damages for all of the consequences of the defendant's wrongdoing in one lump sum. As the passage quoted at the beginning of section 17.1 from *Todorovic v Waller* (1981) made clear at 412:

> [D]amages for one cause of action must be recovered once and forever, and (in the absence of any statutory exception) must be awarded as a lump sum; the court cannot order a defendant to make periodic payments to the plaintiff.

This rule, which is justified by the principle of finality, means that the plaintiffs get one chance to prove all of their actual losses leading up to the trial as well as all of their probable losses that may occur after the trial. This rule, providing that plaintiffs cannot reopen their case, was laid down in *Fitter v Veal* (1701) at 1506:

> If after recovering damages in an action of assault, battery and wounding, the plaintiff is put to great expense, in consequence of the injury he received, yet he cannot bring a second action to recover further compensation for the consequential damage he sustains; for it shall be intended that the jury considered all possible consequences on the trial of the first action.

This effect of this rule was explained by McHugh J in *Nominal Defendant v Gardikiotis* (1996), with His Honour pointing out at [24]:

> [A]t common law, compensation is given on a one off basis; there are no periodic payments of compensation. The court awards a single sum and enters judgment. Its role is then finished. To the inadequate extent that monetary

> compensation can compensate for the effects of personal injury, a court has done its duty when it makes its award of damages.

The finality principle aims to put an end to the matter and allow the parties, who were tied together by the doing and the suffering of the wrong, to be freed from one another and to move on with their lives. It is linked to the doctrine of *res judicata* (a thing decided), which provides that once a case has been decided by a court, it cannot be reopened. It provides a defence to the defendant if the plaintiff tries to argue the matter again. So, justice is done when the tort has been undone – at least in theory. Of course, all that the court actually does is to make the order for the payment of damages; the victory may be a hollow one if the defendant is without any means and has no insurance. From the perspective of injured parties, a further issue can arise where the wrongdoing is widespread enough as to warrant a class action. Finality requires that once the class action settles, or the court awards damages, only injured parties that joined the class will be able to obtain compensation. There is always a risk that individual victims who would otherwise have a legitimate cause of action may miss out on the award and become unable to bring an action independently.

17.2.2 The discount rule

The lump sum rule creates certain difficulties, particularly when the plaintiff must prove a future loss, as section 17.2.3 below explains. However, it can also lead to a windfall for the plaintiff who receives a large cash sum in the present to cover losses that have not actually occurred at the time of payment, and which may not occur for many years. The notion that the plaintiffs will in fact be overcompensated if they invest that money and multiply its value before they actually incur the need for any expenditure appears to run counter to the compensation principle. On the other hand, the assumption that the money will increase in value if invested can be undercut by the effects of inflation. These concerns led the courts to apply the 'discount' rule, which reduces the total award by a prescribed amount to maintain fairness between the parties. In *Todorovic v Waller* (1981), the High Court published a special statement at the beginning of the judgment at 409:

> In an action for damages for personal injuries, evidence as to the likely course of inflation, or of possible future changes in rates of wages or of prices, is inadmissible. Where there has been a loss of earning capacity which is likely to lead to financial loss in the future, or where the plaintiff's injuries will make it necessary to expend in the future money to provide medical or other services, or goods necessary for the plaintiff's health or comfort, the present value of the future loss ought to be quantified by adopting a discount rate of 3 per cent in all cases, subject, of course, to any relevant statutory provisions. This rate is intended to make the appropriate allowance for inflation, for future changes in rates of wages generally or of prices, and for tax (either actual or notional) upon income from investment of the sum awarded. No further allowance should be made for these matters.

Todorovic v Waller (1981) set the discount rate at three per cent, but many jurisdictions have since legislated to alter that figure.

LEGISLATION ALERT!

Consult your study materials and note any statutory provisions in your jurisdiction covering discount rates.

The nature of this 'discount rate' was explained by McHugh J at 61 in *Nominal Defendant v Gardikiotis* (1996):

> Use is made of a discount rate to assess the present value of future economic loss and expense because it is perceived to be the conceptual tool best suited to determine what is fair and reasonable compensation for that loss or expense. The discounting exercise is a hypothetical construct and does not attempt to reflect, anticipate or govern the future actions or intentions of the plaintiff. It simply attempts to determine what sum represents the present value of the anticipated losses or expenses of the plaintiff. When that sum is determined, then, subject to any allowance for the contingencies of life, the law will equate it with fair compensation for those losses or expenses, irrespective of what the plaintiff intends to do with that sum.

The courts also make further discounts that take into account future contingencies or the 'vicissitudes of life' like premature death, injury, sickness or unemployment (see, eg, *Wynn v Insurance Ministerial Corporation* (1995) and *De Sales v Ingrilli* (2002)).

17.2.3 Statutory exceptions to the lump sum rule

As a result of dissatisfaction with the lump sum rule, parliaments in some jurisdictions have introduced measures known as 'structured settlements' that allow for periodic payments rather than the full common law 'lump sum' payment. The Ipp Review Panel recommended that more use be made of this method of structuring payments. They were seen as being 'good for society generally' and as offering greater security to plaintiffs, because as the Panel's Final Report noted at 13.124: 'the amount awarded often runs out before the end of the period, even if it is well and wisely invested'.

LEGISLATION ALERT!

Consult your study materials and note any statutory provisions in your jurisdiction that allow for structured settlements.

More generally, the lump sum rule has been subject to criticisms in so far as lump sums tend to run out faster than expected. This can put injured parties in particularly difficult positions, as there exist rules precluding individuals who are awarded damages through litigation from accessing social security benefits. While the rationale of avoiding 'double dipping' may be sound in the abstract, it can create significant injustices in practice, as discussed by authors such as Prue Vines and Genevieve Grant – see, for example, their article 'When Lump Sum Compensation Runs Out: Personal Responsibility or Legal System Failure?' (2017).

17.3 Justice and the certainty principle

17.3.1 Dealing with uncertainty

The fourth rule laid down in *Todorovic v Waller* (1981) at 412 provided that 'the burden lies on the plaintiff to prove the injury or loss for which he seeks damages'. The civil standard of proof is on the balance of probabilities, so a plaintiff must prove that it is more likely than not that they have suffered, or will suffer, loss. Proving pecuniary losses suffered up to the date of trial is relatively easy, but given that damages are normally awarded 'once and for all', the problem lies in proving the future losses. In *Sellars v Adelaide Petroleum NL* (1994), the joint judgment of Mason CJ, Dawson, Toohey and Gaudron JJ at 349–55 explained the difference in the courts' approach to these two questions. The most famous passage appears at 351:

> Damages in tort have also been assessed by reference to the probabilities or possibilities of what will happen or what would have happened. That approach has been frequently adopted in the assessment of damages for personal injuries where a court has been called upon to assess future possibilities and past hypothetical situations. In *Malec v JC Hutton Pty Ltd* (1990) 169 CLR 638, this Court drew a distinction between, on the one hand, proof of historical facts—what has happened—and, on the other hand, proof of future possibilities and past hypothetical situations. The civil standard of proof applies to the first category but not to the second, particularly when it is necessary to determine future possibilities and past hypothetical situations for the purpose of assessing damages (at 639–640 per Brennan and Dawson JJ, 642–643 per Deane, Gaudron and McHugh JJ).

In the earlier case of *Malec v JC Hutton Pty Ltd* (1990), cited by the judgment in *Sellars v Adelaide Petroleum NL* (1994) above, Deane, Gaudron and McHugh JJ at 643 explained the way the courts deal with the matter of past losses:

> When liability has been established and a common law court has to assess damages, its approach to events that allegedly would have occurred, but cannot now occur, or that allegedly might occur, is different from its approach to events which allegedly have occurred. A common law court determines on the balance of probabilities whether an event has occurred. If the probability of the event having occurred is greater than it not having occurred, the occurrence of the event is treated as certain; if the probability of it having occurred is less than it not having occurred, it is treated as not having occurred. Hence, in respect of events which have or have not occurred, damages are assessed on an all or nothing approach.

The judgment in *Sellars v Adelaide Petroleum NL* (1994) then went on at 643 to explain how the court deals with a possible future loss by taking a different approach:

> If the law is to take account of future or hypothetical events in assessing damages, it can only do so in terms of the degree of probability of those events occurring.

> But unless the chance is so low as to be regarded as speculative—say less than 1 per cent—or so high as to be practically certain—say over 99 per cent—the court will take that chance into account in assessing the damages. Where proof is necessarily unattainable, it would be unfair to treat as certain a prediction which has a 51 per cent probability of occurring, but to ignore altogether a prediction which has a 49 per cent probability of occurring. Thus, the court assesses the degree of probability that an event would have occurred, or might occur, and adjusts its award of damages to reflect the degree of probability.

In the same case, Brennan and Dawson JJ noted at 639–40:

> Hypothetical situations of the past are analogous to future possibilities: in one case the court must form an estimate of the likelihood that the hypothetical situation would have occurred, in the other the court must form an estimate of the likelihood that the possibility will occur. Both are to be distinguished from events which are alleged to have actually occurred in the past. ...
>
> The role of the court in making an assessment of damages which depends upon its view as to what will be and what would have been is to be contrasted with its ordinary function in civil actions of determining what was. In determining what did happen in the past a court decides on the balance of probabilities. Anything that is more probable than not it treats as certain. But in assessing damages which depend upon its view as to what will happen in the future or would have happened in the future if something had not happened in the past, the court must make an estimate as to what are the chances that a particular thing will or would have happened and reflect those chances, whether they are more or less than even, in the amount of damages which it awards.

So, when assessing damages for past events or losses, the court must be persuaded on the balance of probability (ie to at least 51 per cent) that the event or loss actually did occur. But in the case of possible future losses, the court takes the total amount of the loss and reduces it in proportion to the percentage chance that the event or loss will actually occur. So if there is a 50 per cent chance that a loss of $100 000 may occur in the future, the court awards the plaintiff $50 000. This means of course that the plaintiff will either gain a windfall if the loss does not materialise, and will be left short if the loss does occur. These passages illustrate once again the impossibility of doing complete justice and so, although the courts strive for certainty, they accept that true justice is not possible in an imperfect world where rules must be made that are incapable of measuring out exact and complete compensation.

17.3.2 Date of assessment

Damages are normally assessed as at the date the cause of action arose. So, the date in a battery action will be the date on which the forbidden physical contact occurred; and in a negligence action, the date is the date on which the damage occurred. In *Johnson v Perez* (1988) Mason CJ said at 355–6:

> Damages are usually assessed by reference to the date on which the cause of action arose, but the court has a discretion to fix its own date in order to provide

> fair compensation. The guiding principle in the assessment of damages is compensatory. The object is to award the plaintiff an amount of money that will, as nearly as money can, put him in the same position as if he had not been injured by the defendant. ... However, the time as at which damages are assessed can significantly affect the amount actually awarded. This aspect of the assessment of compensation is particularly noticeable in the present era of inflation, with its fluctuating economic values. This is because in times of inflation the amount awarded is likely to be larger if it is assessed at a later rather than an earlier date.

Mason CJ explained that while the 'practice of awarding fixed sums of money worked well when money values and prices were stable', it could cause problems in times of 'inflation and changing economic values':

> If an early date is used for assessment (the date of the injury for example) in an inflationary economy or where goods of the kind injured are appreciating, it is the plaintiff's position which is eroded. If a later date such as the date of judgment is used, it is the defendant who is exposed.

Given that the aim of an award of damages is to do justice to the plaintiff, Mason CJ decided that it would be possible to 'depart from the general rule whenever it is necessary to do so in the interests of justice' and indicated that there would be times when the date of judgment would be a more appropriate date. This flexibility is allowed in cases where the goal of the 'full compensation' principle would be jeopardised – for example, in cases where many years may have passed between the date that the cause of action accrued and the date of trial and judgment.

17.4 The fault principle revisited: Mitigation of loss

The plaintiff must take reasonable care to reduce the damage flowing from the tort. This is the familiar fault principle that dominates all torts, particularly the tort of negligence, as the earlier chapters explain. The burden is on the defendant to show that the plaintiff has not acted reasonably in mitigation. If they have not acted reasonably, the amount of damages payable may be reduced; however, the courts do take into account the fact that the plaintiff has been put into a difficult position by the defendant's tort, and emphasise that the defendant must 'take their victims as they find them'. Mason CJ explained in *Johnson v Perez* (1988) at 357 that the 'requirement of mitigation can in turn be explained in part by notions of fairness to the party at fault'. In *Watts v Rake* (1960) Dixon CJ said at 159:

> Only in one respect is the burden of proof upon the defendant and this is when he sets up matter in mitigation of damages. If it appears satisfactorily that damage in a particular form or to a particular degree has been suffered by the plaintiff as a result of the wrong but the defendant maintains that the plaintiff might have avoided or mitigated that consequence by adopting some course which it was reasonable for him to take, it seems clear enough that the law places upon the defendant the burden of proof upon the question whether by

> the course suggested the damage could have so been mitigated and upon the reasonableness of pursuing that course. Probably in claims for damages for personal injuries a question of the burden of proof in mitigation of damages is unlikely to arise often in any serious form. But it may do so; for example if the plaintiff declines to submit himself to some surgical procedure or medical treatment.

In the same case, Menzies J pointed out at 163 that 'a negligent defendant must take his victim as he finds him and pay damages accordingly' and noted:

> The fact that the person injured was peculiarly susceptible to ensuing complications that would not in a normal person have followed from the injuries received, or that the person injured already had a disability which made the injury the more disabling—e.g., the loss of an only eye—does not mean that damages are not to be assessed according to the circumstances of the particular case.

If the defendant knows that a plaintiff is taking extraordinary measures in response to a particular loss and says nothing at the time, they will be taken to have agreed to those measures: *Gardner v The Queen* (1993). In *Medlin v State Government Insurance Commission* (1995), the High Court maintained that reasonableness at this point of a case is evaluated by looking at what is reasonable as between the plaintiff and the defendant and assessing their relative degree of fault for the circumstances that they find themselves in. Deane, Dawson, Toohey and Gaudron JJ said at 11, when discussing whether a plaintiff's decision to retire early in response to the effects of the injuries he had sustained as a result of the defendant's negligence amounted to a failure to mitigate:

> In these circumstances, the relevant question was not whether the plaintiff 'should' have continued in his University post or whether his decision to retire was not 'reasonable' but whether, in the context of what was reasonable between the plaintiff and the defendant in determining the defendant's liability in damages, the premature termination of the plaintiff's employment was the product of the plaintiff's loss of earning capacity notwithstanding that it was brought about by his own decision to accept voluntary retirement.

The issues raised in the negligence cases where a defendant argues that a plaintiff has acted unreasonably in failing to mitigate their losses are very similar to those raised at the earlier stages of a negligence action – for example, issues of causation, 'remoteness' of damage or 'scope of liability'. Particularly complex cases involve plaintiffs acting unreasonably as a result of the harm initially suffered – for example, an injured party self-medicating with alcohol, or refusing to seek counselling, thereby not only failing to mitigate loss, but aggravating their initial injury. The questions of fairness and reasonableness arise because a tort deals not only with factual 'but for' questions but also with normative or moral questions, which must be evaluated in terms of reasonableness and fairness. So, the fact that these themes emerge at the final stages of a negligence action in particular should not be surprising.

Test your understanding and develop your skills

Essay writing

Write a 1500-word essay analysing the similarities and differences between the issues of causation, remoteness or 'scope of liability', contributory negligence and failure to mitigate in the case of *Kavanagh v Akhtar* (1998) 45 NSWLR 588.

Conclusion

While tort law strives to do justice in the face of wrongdoing, it cannot fully succeed in its aim because perfect justice is impossible in an imperfect world. But this does not mean that the lawyers and the judges working every day in our courts on torts cases are wasting their time following an impossible dream that in the end can only result in disappointment. This chapter has shown that the goal of perfect compensation is impossible, but justice in responding to wrongdoing is not the only form of justice that is found in the law of torts. There is arguably a deeper sense of justice encapsulated in the rules and principles of tort law that *is* attainable, because that body of law prescribes standards for everyday conduct that are attainable.

The body of rules and principles that constitute the substantive law of torts paints a picture of a particular ideal-type of a just community: a community where each person respects the socially prevalent understanding of dignity, bodily inviolability and liberty of their fellows, where each person's rights to autonomy and privacy are respected and where those who assume responsibilities to the vulnerable act with all reasonable care to protect them from foreseeable risks of harm. This specific picture of justice is potentially attainable every day of our lives, and it is this vision of doing justice to others that lies at the heart of the law of torts.

Tort law is a mirror of the community that creates it. It reflects our own image back to us. Tort law's faults are our own faults. The fact that we are yet to envisage ways to account for the compounding harm of climate change, or the arguably arbitrary distinction between the loss of a chance of a better medical outcome vs the loss of a chance of a better financial outcome, or the fact that we continue to leave certain individuals at the margins of the law (think of those born to a life of disability who have no remedy against a doctor who negligently advised their pregnant mother) are all stark reminders of the imperfections of our regime of civil liability. On the other hand (and in law there is always 'on the other hand'), tort law's glories are also our glories. While we cannot expect the law to be any more perfect than we are, we can take comfort from this huge community project that is the law of torts, and take the law's aspirations as our own. The law aspires to improve and to do better, one case at a time. We will have played our part as lawyers and legal educators if we make sure that we leave the law in a better state than we found it and that we do justice to our clients and students each time we deal with them. If you treat your clients with the same respect that the law of torts asks each one of us to use when we deal with one another, then you will have done your part properly, whether you win or lose. The same goes for educators with their students.

If you do your best to make the law work better when you go out into the legal profession, you will be a good lawyer. If you treat your own clients with the respect and care that they deserve, you will be doing justice every day in your working life. You may not win every case and you may never get to the High Court and change the law, but if you can treat others around you with all reasonable care, if you respect their autonomy and their dignity as human beings and act with respect for their rights to be heard, then you will be living up to your calling. You will be doing justice, imperfect as it may be.

REFERENCES

CASES

CSR Ltd v Eddy (2005) 226 CLR 1
De Sales v Ingrilli (2002) 212 CLR 338
Fitter v Veal (1701) 12 Mod 542; 88 ER 1506
Gardner v The Queen [1993] NZLR 730
Gray v Motor Accident Commission (1998) 196 CLR 1
Griffiths v Kerkemeyer (1977) 139 CLR 161
Harriton v Stephens (2006) 226 CLR 52
Johnson v Perez (1988) 166 CLR 351
Kavanagh v Akhtar (1998) 45 NSWLR 588
Magill v Magill (2006) 226 CLR 551
Malec v JC Hutton Pty Ltd (1990) 169 CLR 638
Medlin v State Government Insurance Commission (1995) 182 CLR 1
New South Wales v Ibbett (2006) 229 CLR 638
Nominal Defendant v Gardikiotis (1996) 186 CLR 49
Paff v Speed (1961) 105 CLR 549
Paul v Rendell (1981) 55 ALJR 372; 34 ALR 571
Sellars v Adelaide Petroleum NL (1994) 179 CLR 351
Sullivan v Gordon (1999) 47 NSWLR 319
Teubner v Humble (1963) 108 CLR 491
Todorovic v Waller (1981) 150 CLR 402
Trevorrow v South Australia (No 5) (2007) 98 SASR 136
Uren v John Fairfax & Sons Pty Ltd (1996) 117 CLR 118
Van Gervan v Fenton (1992) 175 CLR 327
Watts v Rake (1960) 108 CLR 158
Woolcock Street Investments Pty Ltd v CDG Pty Ltd (2004) 216 CLR 515
Wynn v Insurance Ministerial Corporation (1995) 184 CLR 485

ARTICLES, BOOKS AND REPORT

Abel, R, 'A Critique of Torts' (1994) 2 *Tort Law Review* 99.
Atiyah, P, *The Damages Lottery* (1997) Hart Publishing, Oxford.
Cane, P, *Atiyah's Accidents, Compensation and the Law*, 9th ed (2018) Cambridge University Press, Cambridge.

Griffiths, B, *An Introduction to Early English Law* (1995) Anglo-Saxon Books, Norfolk.

Ipp, D, Cane, P, Sheldon, D & Macintosh, I, *Review of the Law of Negligence: Final Report* (2002) <https://treasury.gov.au/review/review-of-the-law-of-negligence>.

Luntz, H, Hambly, D, Burns, K, Dietrich, J, Foster, N, Grant, G & Harder, S, *Torts: Cases and Commentary*, 8th ed (2017) LexisNexis Butterworths, Sydney.

Sugarman, S D, 'Doing Away with Tort Law' (1985) 73 *California Law Review* 555.

Vines, P, Butt, M & Grant, G, 'When Lump Sum Compensation Runs Out: Personal Responsibility or Legal System Failure?' (2017) 39 *Sydney Law Review* 365.

TABLE OF CASES

Zaghloul v Bayly [2021] WASCA 125, 555
Zanker v Vartzokas (1988) 34 A Crim R 11, 134, 136, 138, 140
Zanner v Zanner [2010] NSWCA 343, 438, 674
Zaravinos v New South Wales (2004) 62 NSWLR 58, 141
Zbyszko v New York American Inc, 239 NYS 411 (1930), 290
Zecevic v Director of Public Prosecutions (Vic) (1987) 162 CLR 645, 218
Zey v New South Wales (No 2) [2024] NSWDC 289, 137
ZG Operations Australia Pty Ltd v Jamsek (2022) 275 CLR 254, 700, 703
Ziaee v Rubino [2023] ACTA 7, 485
Zuijs v Wirth Brothers Pty Ltd (1955) 93 CLR 561, 700

TABLE OF STATUTES

AUSTRALIA

Commonwealth

Australian Capital Territory

New South Wales

Northern Territory

Queensland

South Australia

Tasmania

Victoria

Western Australia

UNITED KINGDOM

INTERNATIONAL INSTRUMENTS

INDEX

www.ingramcontent.com/pod-product-compliance
Ingram Content Group UK Ltd.
Pitfield, Milton Keynes, MK11 3LW, UK
UKHW062038180726
473428UK00012B/562
* 9 7 8 1 0 0 9 5 9 3 2 6 7 *